S0-BTA-562

TEACHER'S EDITION

PRENTICE HALL LITERATURE

Timeless Voices, Timeless Themes

COPPER LEVEL

Upper Saddle River, New Jersey
Needham, Massachusetts

ISBN 0-13-180438-3
3 4 5 6 7 8 9 10 07 06 05

Get results with Prentice

The nation's leading language arts program

Prentice Hall Literature:

- Features a powerful combination of great literature and superior instruction.
- Ensures student success with a proven, research-based reading approach.
- Provides meaningful, logical, and systematic language skills instruction.
- Helps you monitor student progress with a rich array of assessment tools.
- Allows you to share the same great literature with all your students.

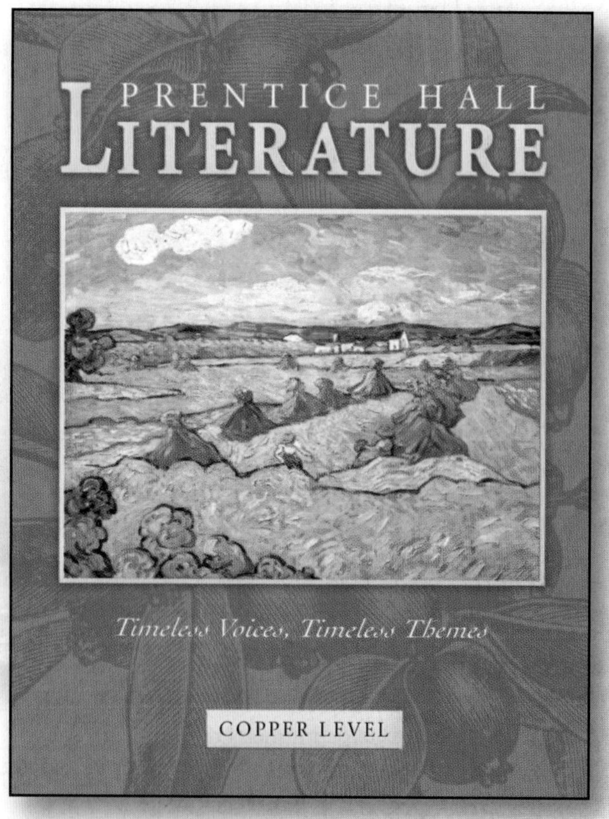

Hall Literature.

What educators think about Prentice Hall Literature

Increases student achievement

"Our teachers are extremely pleased with the series and feel it has contributed to improved student performance."
—*Dr. Karen Gibson, Program Leader, Appleton School District, Appleton, WI*

"I stay in touch with quite a number of teachers in the district who report that scores have increased on high-stakes performance tests for students using the *Prentice Hall Literature* program."
—*Audrey Hawkins, Language Arts Supervisor, Washington, D.C.*

Connects to students' lives

"The pre-reading activities are extremely helpful. The importance of making connections with literature is immeasurable—it makes education 'real' for students."
—*Matthew Scanlon, Language Arts Teacher, Chester, NJ*

"The entire program is 'student-friendly' and yet does not 'talk down' to them with simplistic comments. The layout is easy to read and the selections inviting!"
—*Niki Locklear, Language Arts Teacher, Independence, KY*

"All around the buildings, you see students reading the literature book on their own time. You hear about them discussing the literature with other kids or asking their teachers about it. There's just a lot of talk about the book."
—*Patty Foster, Curriculum Consultant, Edmond Public School District, Edmond, OK*

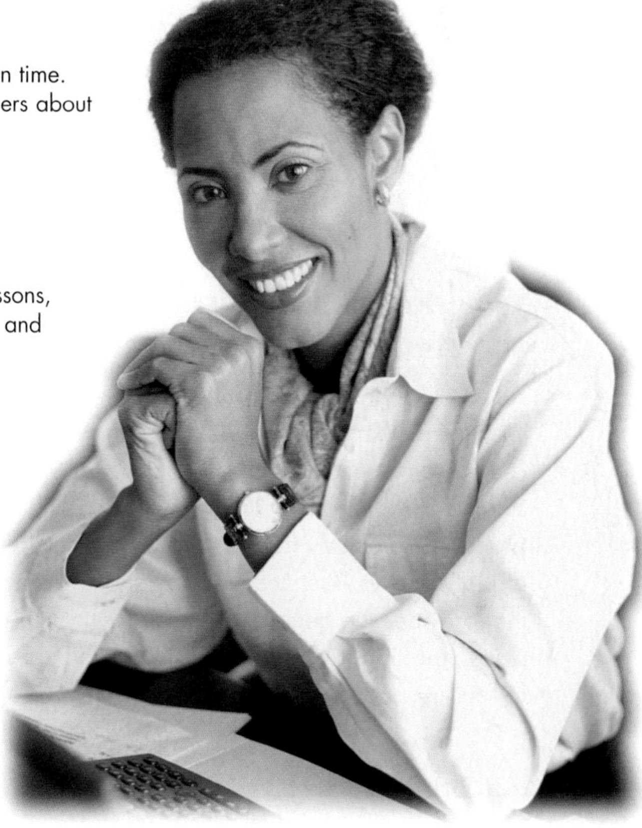

Delivers the most comprehensive support

"The best features of the program are the vocabulary instruction and supporting lessons, literary analysis and connecting elements, use of Bloom's taxonomy in the Review and Assess sections, and the quality of literary selections."
—*Gail Hacker, Language Arts Teacher, North Charleston, SC*

"I like having the Literary Analysis feature to help explain theme, plot, characterization, etc.—many textbooks do not have this."
—*Sheila Colson, Language Arts Teacher, Philadelphia, PA*

"My teachers have enthusiastically praised the *Reader's Companions*. These tools allow everyone in the class to participate in the discussion so that no one, especially the struggling reader, feels left out."
—*Paulette Kirkwood, Communication Arts Supervisor, St. Louis, MO*

"Overall, I give the *Prentice Hall Literature* program a grade of 'A'!"
—*Kathy Litherland, Language Arts Teacher, Lincoln, IL*

Put reading first.

The truth about the single-column format

It's about reading.

The ability to read and understand text is the most vital and crucial lifelong skill students will possess. Teachers recognize that, through a variety of systematic instructional features and nondistracting point-of-use reading tools in the Student Edition, *Prentice Hall Literature* offers students more reading support in the Student Edition than any other program—thanks to the single-column format.

How is the single-column format more reader-friendly than the dual-column format?

While there are many reasons why the single column can be regarded as more readable than the dual-column format, its greatest virtue is the way the single-column format allows for embedded, nondistracting reading support. This support appears in the form of point-of-use annotations with comprehension checks, vocabulary support, literary analysis, and critical thinking and reading strategies throughout each selection, acting as a kind of "personal reading tutor."

Why don't all publishers use the single-column format?

Actually, all educational publishers use the single-column format in one way or another, usually in texts in other reading-intensive content areas such as social studies or science. Some publishers even use the single-column format in the ancillary reading support of their literature programs, precisely for the unique benefits that the single-column format conveys. *Prentice Hall Literature*, however, is the only program that provides the benefits of the single-column format consistently for every selection throughout the student text, providing a greater degree of reading support than any other reading program.

For more information, ask your representative for the brochure, *It's About Reading: Why* Prentice Hall Literature *Is the Nation's Leading Literature Program.*

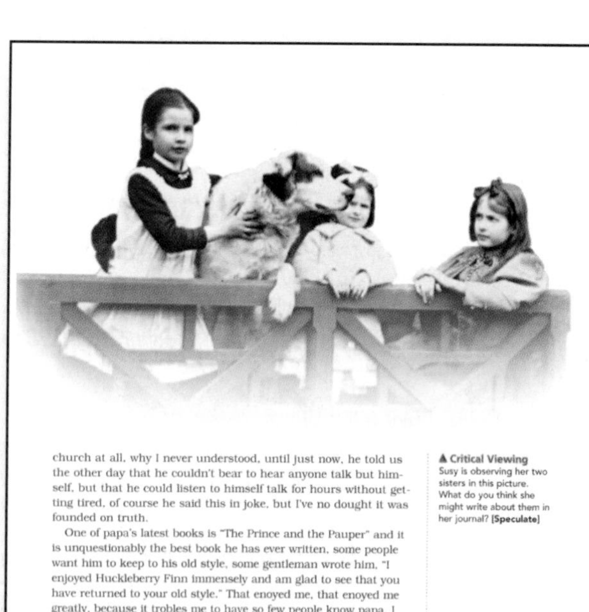

church at all, why I never understood, until just now, he told us the other day that he couldn't bear to hear anyone talk but himself, but that he could listen to himself talk for hours without getting tired, of course he said this in joke, but I've no dought it was founded on truth.

One of papa's latest books is "The Prince and the Pauper" and it is unquestionably the best book he has ever written, some people want him to keep to his old style, some gentleman wrote him, "I enjoyed Huckleberry Finn immensely and am glad to see that you have returned to your old style." That enoyed me, that enoyed me greatly, because it trobles me to have so few people know papa, I mean realy know him, they think of Mark Twain as a humorist joking at everything; "And with a mop of reddish brown hair which sorely needs the barbar brush, a roman nose, short stubby mustache, a sad care-worn face, with maney crows' feet" etc. That is the way people picture papa. I have wanted papa to write a book that would reveal something of his kind sympathetic nature, and "The Prince and the Pauper" partly does it. The book is full of lovely charming ideas, and oh the language! It is perfect. I think that one of the most touching scenes in it is where the pauper is riding on horseback with his nobles in the "recognition procession" and he

▲ Critical Viewing
Susy is observing her two sisters in this picture. What do you think she might write about them in her journal? **[Speculate]**

Literary Analysis
Biography and Autobiography
What details on this page show how the writer's role of daughter helps her as a biographer?

556 ◆ *Nonfiction*

Research-based reading instruction supports students BEFORE, DURING, and AFTER every lesson

PROGRAM OVERVIEW

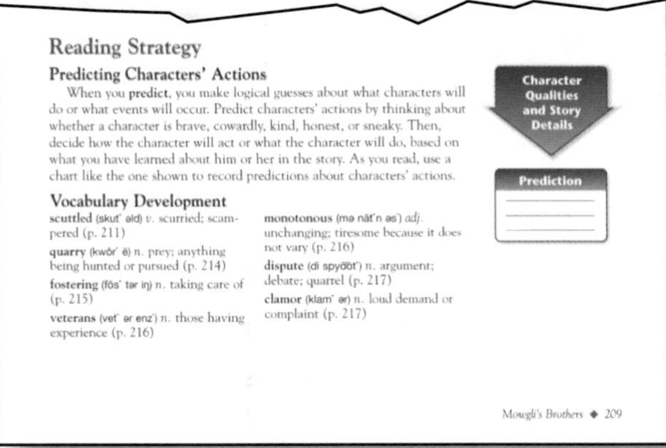

Reading Strategy

Predicting Characters' Actions

When you **predict**, you make logical guesses about what characters will do or what events will occur. Predict characters' actions by thinking about whether a character is brave, cowardly, kind, honest, or sneaky. Then, decide how the character will act or what the character will do, based on what you have learned about him or her in the story. As you read, use a chart like the one shown to record predictions about characters' actions.

Vocabulary Development

scuttled (skut' əld) *v.* scurried; scampered (p. 211)

quarry (kwôr' ē) *n.* prey; anything being hunted or pursued (p. 214)

fostering (fôs' tər iŋ) *n.* taking care of (p. 215)

veterans (vet' ər ənz') *n.* those having experience (p. 216)

monotonous (mə nät'n əs') *adj.* unchanging; tiresome because it does not vary (p. 216)

dispute (di spyo͞ot') *n.* argument; debate; quarrel (p. 217)

clamor (klam' ər) *n.* loud demand or complaint (p. 217)

Mowgli's Brothers ◆ 209

Before

Prepare to Read

A successful reading experience depends on the adequate preteaching of skills. *Prentice Hall Literature* consistently provides direct instruction and modeling of reading skills and strategies before each selection.

Reading Strategy
Predicting What do you predict will happen to the man's cub?

Apply the Skills

Prentice Hall Literature provides consistent reinforcement of reading strategies during each selection at point-of-use in the student text. To help students monitor their understanding, quick Reading Checks are provided at the bottom of every right-hand page.

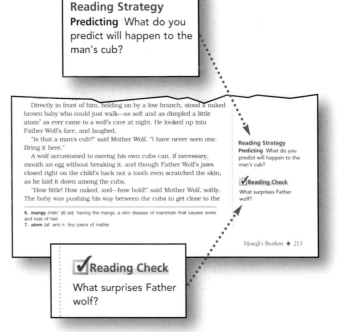

Directly in front of him, holding on by a low branch, stood a naked brown baby who could just walk—as soft and as dimpled a little atom[7] as ever came to a wolf's cave at night. He looked up into Father Wolf's face, and laughed.

"Is that a man's cub?" said Mother Wolf. "I have never seen one. Bring it here."

A wolf accustomed to moving his own cubs can, if necessary, mouth an egg without breaking it, and though Father Wolf's jaws closed right on the child's back not a tooth even scratched the skin, as he laid it down among the cubs.

"How little! How naked, and—how bold!" said Mother Wolf, softly. The baby was pushing his way between the cubs to get close to the

Reading Strategy
Predicting What do you predict will happen to the man's cub?

Reading Check
What surprises Father wolf?

6. **mangy** (mān' jē) *adj.* having the mange, a skin disease of mammals that causes sores and loss of hair.
7. **atom** (at' əm) *n.* tiny piece of matter.

Mowgli's Brothers ◆ 213

Reading Check

What surprises Father wolf?

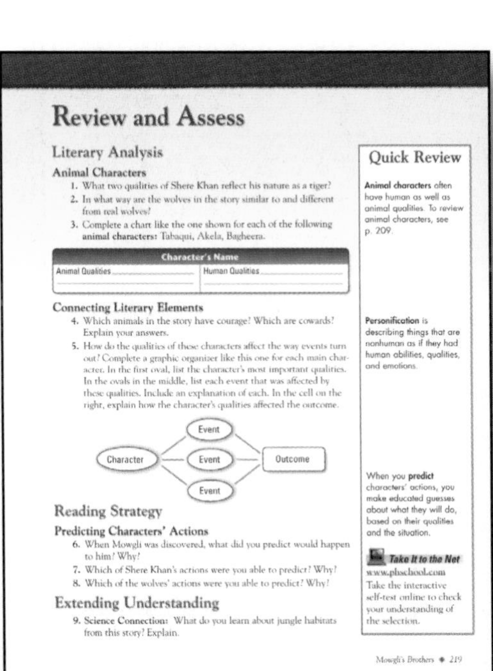

Review and Assess

Literary Analysis

Animal Characters

1. What two qualities of Shere Khan reflect his nature as a tiger?
2. In what way are the wolves in the story similar to and different from real wolves?
3. Complete a chart like the one shown for each of the following **animal characters:** Tabaqui, Akela, Bagheera.

Character's Name	
Animal Qualities	Human Qualities

Connecting Literary Elements

4. Which animals in the story have courage? Which are cowards? Explain your answers.
5. How do the qualities of these characters affect the way events turn out? Complete a graphic organizer like this one for each main character. In the first oval, list the character's most important qualities. In the ovals in the middle, list each event that was affected by these qualities. Include an explanation of each. In the cell on the right, explain how the character's qualities affected the outcome.

Reading Strategy

Predicting Characters' Actions

6. When Mowgli was discovered, what did you predict would happen to him? Why?
7. Which of Shere Khan's actions were you able to predict? Why?
8. Which of the wolves' actions were you able to predict? Why?

Extending Understanding

9. **Science Connection:** What do you learn about jungle habitats from this story? Explain.

Quick Review

Animal characters often have human as well as animal qualities. To review animal characters, see p. 209.

Personification is describing things that are nonhuman as if they had human abilities, qualities, and emotions.

When you **predict** characters' actions, you make educated guesses about what they will do, based on their qualities and the situation.

Take It to the Net
www.phschool.com
Take the interactive self-test online to check your understanding of the selection.

Mowgli's Brothers ◆ 219

After

Review and Assess

In order to become lifelong, independent readers, students must learn to apply reading comprehension strategies automatically. In the Review and Assess pages after every selection, students practice using the targeted reading strategies to sharpen their understanding of the text and to help them transfer these skills to other texts.

Share the same selection

Prentice Hall's Reader's Companions

Unique, appropriately leveled reading support that meets the needs of all your students.

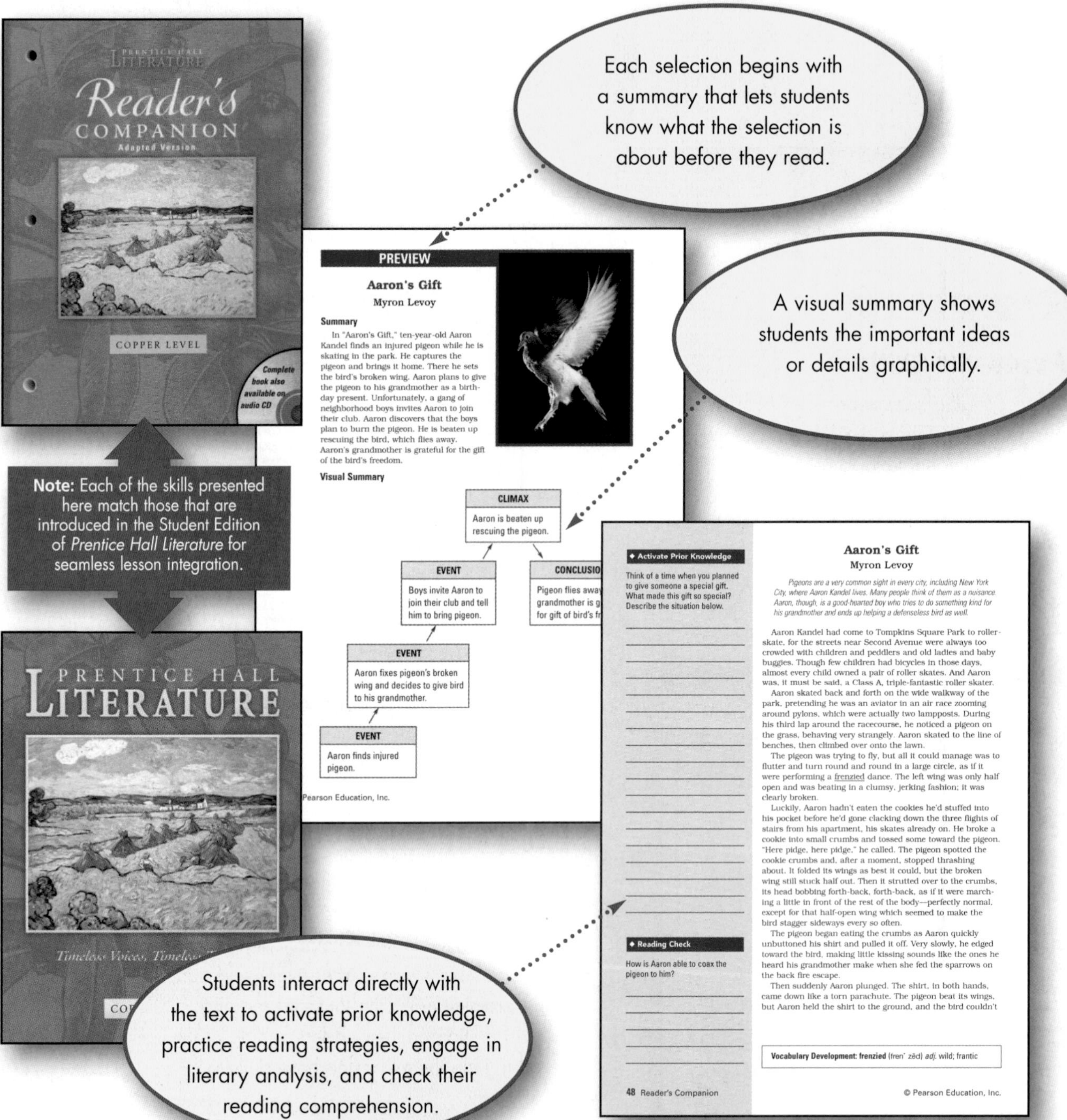

with all your students!

Choose the version that's right for your students

Reader's Companion

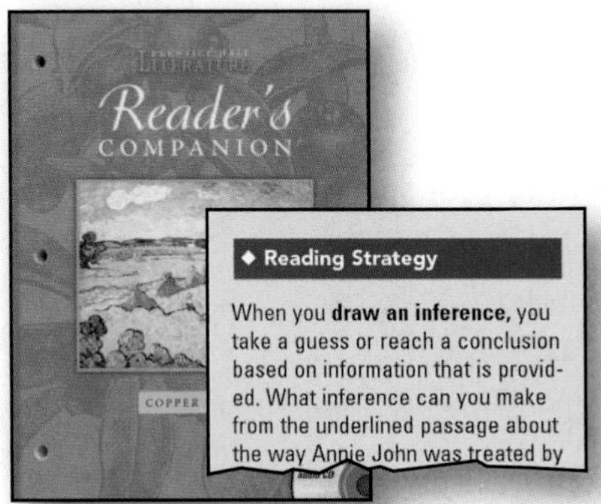

PRENTICE HALL LITERATURE
Reader's
COMPANION
COPPER
◆ Reading Strategy
When you **draw an inference,** you take a guess or reach a conclusion based on information that is provid-ed. What inference can you make from the underlined passage about the way Annie John was treated by

Basic reading support

- Full-length selections with interactive reading support
- Critical thinking questions
- Vocabulary and pronunciation guides

Adapted Version

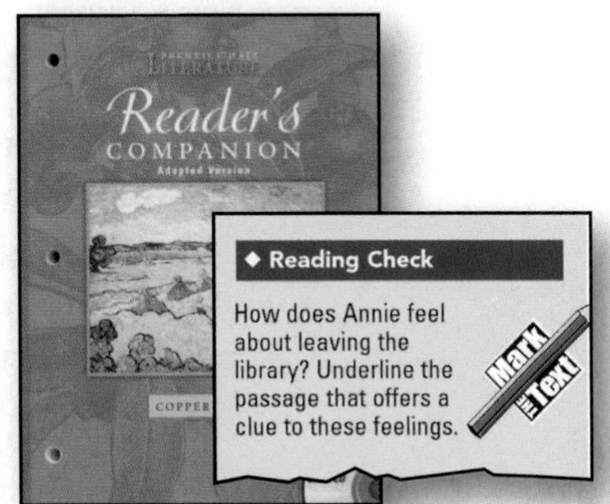

PRENTICE HALL LITERATURE
Reader's
COMPANION
Adapted Version
◆ Reading Check
How does Annie feel about leaving the library? Underline the passage that offers a clue to these feelings.
Mark the Text

Enhanced reading support

- Selection adaptations and authentic text
- Enhanced design for easier readability
- Frequent Reading Checks and customized comprehension strategies

English Learner's Version

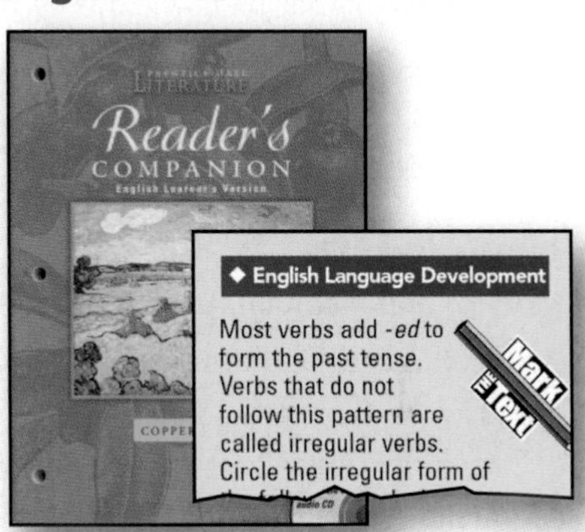

PRENTICE HALL LITERATURE
Reader's
COMPANION
English Learner's Version
◆ English Language Development
Most verbs add *-ed* to form the past tense. Verbs that do not follow this pattern are called irregular verbs. Circle the irregular form of
Mark the Text

English learner's support

- Enhanced reading support
- Specialized vocabulary and pronunciation support
- Focus on idioms, colloquialisms, and cultural information

Need more reading support?

The Prentice Hall Reading Achievement System has the answer!

Reading Diagnostic Test and Improvement Plan

- Diagnostic tests determine what reading skills remediation is needed
- Individualized improvement plans guide teachers to specific skills lessons

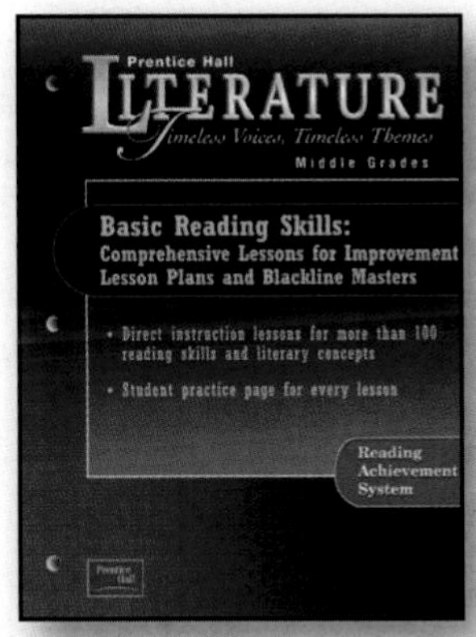

Basic Reading Skills: Comprehensive Lessons for Improvement

- Lesson plans for direct instruction
- Teaching transparencies for lesson modeling
- Blackline masters for student application and practice

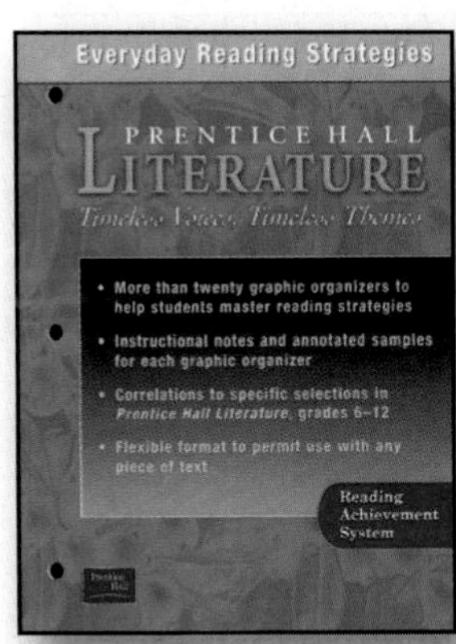

Everyday Reading Strategies

- More than 20 graphic organizers to help students master lifelong reading strategies
- Correlated to specific selections in *Prentice Hall Literature*

Prentice Hall Literature meets all your needs

Reading

Customize comprehensive reading instruction to ensure No Child Is Left Behind.

- Everyday Reading Strategies
- Teacher's Guidebook for Universal Access
- Reading Diagnostic and Improvement Plan
- Basic Reading Skills: Comprehensive Lessons for Improvement
- Basic Reading Skills: Teaching Transparencies
- Reader's Companion
- Reader's Companion, Adapted Version
- Reader's Companion, English Learner's Version

Assessment

Monitor and maintain Adequate Yearly Progress.

- Standardized Test Preparation: Diagnostic Tests
- Formal Assessment
- Open Book Tests
- Portfolio Assessment and Performance Management
- Review and Remediation Skillbook
- Skills Practice: Answers and Explanations Transparencies

Student Workbooks

Provide ample opportunities for skills practice and success on standardized tests.

- Selection Support: Skills Development Workbook
- Vocabulary and Spelling Practice Book
- Standardized Test Preparation Workbook
- Literary Analysis for Enrichment

Language Skills

Guarantee student success through consistent, systematic instruction in all language arts skills.

- Writing and Grammar Handbook Edition
- Integrated Lesson Planning Assistant
- Daily Language Practice Transparencies
- Vocabulary and Spelling Practice
- Writing Models and Graphic Organizers on Transparencies
- Fine Art Transparencies
- Extension Activities

Spanish Support

Meet the evolving needs of your Spanish speakers.

- *Literatura* Spanish Anthology (grades 6–8)
- *Literatura en español* Interactive Reader
- Spanish Readings Audio Program
- Spanish/English Summaries Audio Program

Technology

Plan, teach, and assess with a comprehensive, multimedia program for every grade level.

- Interactive Textbook Student Edition Online and on CD-ROM
- Standardized Test Preparation CD-ROM
- Reader's Companions Audio Program
- Listening to Literature Audio Program
- Listening to Music Audio Program
- Interest Grabber Video Program
- Got It! Assessment Video Program
- Literature in Performance Video Library

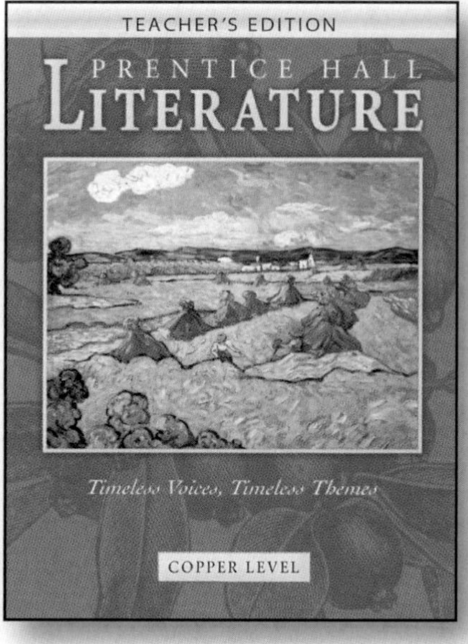

Prentice Hall Literature has the only Teacher's Edition that:

- **provides a Time and Resource Manager for EVERY selection.**
- **encourages extensive planning support via direct instruction while helping set pace and priorities.**
- **gives all learners access to literature through ample customization notes.**

ACADEMIC ACHIEVEMENT HANDBOOK

Research, Standards, and Planning Tools

Prentice Hall Literature Is Research-Based and Proven to Work

The stakes for language arts educators are high. The plain fact is, you are expected to raise student achievement. Prentice Hall understands your dedicated efforts and gives you the confidence to meet this challenge. In developing Prentice Hall programs, the use of research studies is a central, guiding construct. Research on *Prentice Hall Literature* indicated that the key elements of a literature program that ensure student success are considerate text, consistent skills instruction, and an ongoing assessment strand. This research was conducted in three phases:

Phase 1: Exploratory Needs Assessment

Phase 2: Formative Research, Prototype Development and Field Testing

Phase 3: Summative Research, Validation Research

1 EXPLORATORY NEEDS ASSESSMENT

In conjunction with Prentice Hall authors, research was done to explore educational research about reading. This research was incorporated into our instructional strategy and pedagogy to create a more effective literature program.

Along with periodic surveys concerning curriculum issues and challenges, we conducted specific product development research, which included discussions with teachers and advisory panels, focus groups, and quantitative surveys. We explored the specific needs of teachers, students, and other educators regarding each book we developed in *Prentice Hall Literature.*

2 FORMATIVE RESEARCH, PROTOTYPE DEVELOPMENT AND FIELD TESTING

During this phase of research, we developed prototype materials for each feature in *Prentice Hall Literature*. Then we tested the materials, including field testing with students and teachers qualitative and quantitative evaluations. We received solid feedback in our early prototype testing. Results were channeled back into the program development for improvement. For example, teachers commented positively on the easy navigation of instructional pages.

3 SUMMATIVE RESEARCH, VALIDATION RESEARCH

Finally, we conducted and continue to conduct long-term research under actual classroom conditions. This research identifies what works and what can be improved in the next revision of *Prentice Hall Literature*. We also continue to monitor the program in the marketplace. We talk to our users about what works, and then we begin the cycle over again. Highlights of this research follow in the next section.

Prentice Hall Research Timeline

Exploratory needs assessment
(Quantitative & qualitative)

- Reading research
- Teacher interviews
- Classroom observations
- Mail surveys
- Conference participation

Formative research
(Quantitative & qualitative)

- Field testing of prototypes
- Classroom observations
- Teacher reviews
- Supervisor reviews
- Educator advisory panels
- Prentice Hall sales force input

Summative research
(Experimental and quasi-experimental study designs & qualitative research)

- Prepublication learner verification research
- Postpublication validation studies
- Classroom observations
- Evaluation of in-market results on standardized tests

Prentice Hall Literature

Research-Based and Classroom-Tested for Proven Results

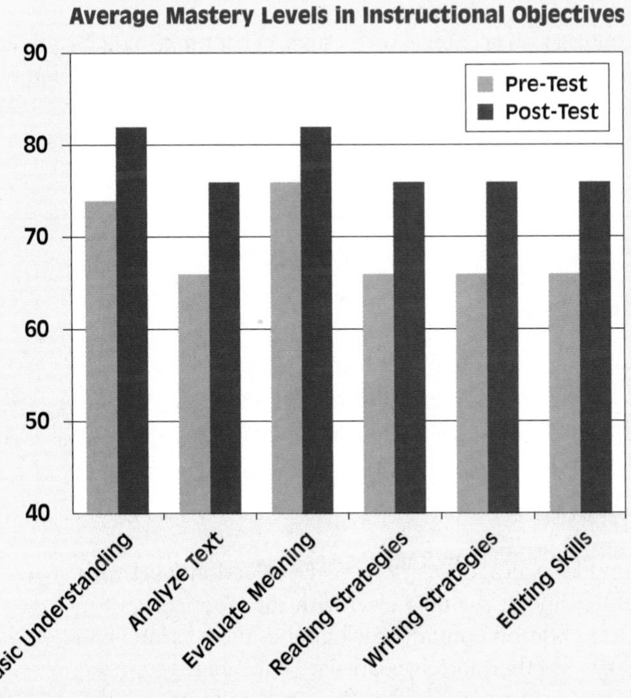

† Scores between 0 and 49 are regarded as the nonmastery level. Scores between 50 and 74 are regarded as indications of partial mastery. Scores of 75 and above are regarded as the mastery level.

All tests were scored by CTB/McGraw Hill, the publisher of TerraNova™. Statistical analyses and conclusions were performed by an independent firm, Pulse Analytics, Inc., Ridgewood, New Jersey.

In a yearlong learner verification study, students using the *Prentice Hall Literature: Timeless Voices, Timeless Themes* program increased their mastery levels in several diagnostic skill areas for reading/language arts.

All students were tested at the start of the year with a nationally normed standardized test, the TerraNova™ Complete Battery Plus exam. At the end of the treatment period, students were retested with the same standardized test. Only students who completed both the pre- and post-tests were included in this analysis. All tests were scored by CTB/McGraw Hill, publisher of the TerraNova™.

In the study, students progressed from the partial mastery level to the mastery level (as defined by CTB/McGraw Hill)† in identifying reading strategies, analyzing text, writing strategies, and editing skills. In the other two reading objectives, Basic Understanding and Evaluate/Extend Meaning, the treatment group maintained mastery from the pre-test to the post-test.

PUTTING RESEARCH INTO PRACTICE

What Research Indicates

To aid comprehension, critical vocabulary words should be explained with meanings and background information before students read selections. To further improve reading fluency and comprehension, common prefixes and suffixes should be systematically introduced and explained (Carnine).

Studies indicate the efficacy of direct instruction of vocabulary, as well as programs that emphasize context. For a comprehensive approach, researchers advocate teaching decoding skills, introducing sight words, emphasizing context clues to determine if constructed meanings make sense, teaching vocabulary meanings explicitly, and extensively using comprehension strategies and modeling (Pressley, "What Should").

Integrate Language Skills

Vocabulary Development Lesson

Word Analysis: Latin Prefix *pre-*

The Latin prefix *pre-*, as found in *precluded*, means "before" or "in advance." Identify the word from the list below that best fits each definition.

preview precaution prejudice

1. To see in advance
2. Judgment without sufficient facts
3. Care taken in advance

Spelling Strategy

When you add an ending that begins with a vowel to a word that ends in a silent *e*, the *e* is usually dropped. For example, when adding *-ing* to the word *subside*, drop the silent *e* to form *subsiding*. Write the word formed

Concept Development: Antonyms

Identify the antonym, or opposite, of the first word.

1. precluded: (a) prevented, (b) aided, (c) started
2. retribution: (a) reward, (b) disaster, (c) assignment
3. accosted: (a) sought, (b) retreated, (c) discovered
4. subsided: (a) increased, (b) created, (c) challenged
5. afflicted: (a) weary, (b) skeptical, (c) blessed
6. explicit: (a) unnecessary, (b) vague, (c) impatient

Prentice Hall's Response

Vocabulary instruction in *Prentice Hall Literature* utilizes a combination of direct instruction and context-based approaches. Vocabulary words and their definitions are introduced before the selection, then again at point-of-use in the minor column of the selection. Reading strategies model the use of context-based approaches before the selection, then students are encouraged to use these approaches to answer questions after the selection. Also, students are given opportunities to assimilate new vocabulary words by applying them in exercises that follow the selection.

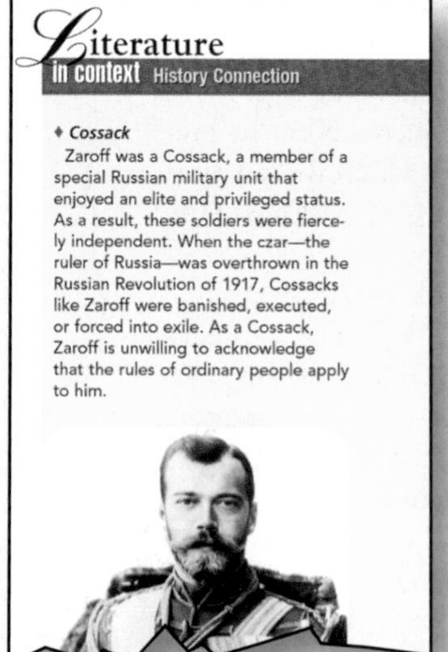

Literature in context History Connection

♦ *Cossack*

Zaroff was a Cossack, a member of a special Russian military unit that enjoyed an elite and privileged status. As a result, these soldiers were fiercely independent. When the czar—the ruler of Russia—was overthrown in the Russian Revolution of 1917, Cossacks like Zaroff were banished, executed, or forced into exile. As a Cossack, Zaroff is unwilling to acknowledge that the rules of ordinary people apply to him.

What Research Indicates

Schools that "beat the odds" in teaching middle- and high-school students to read and write well use materials that make overt connections among knowledge, skills, and ideas across lessons, classes, and grades, and across in-school and out-of-school applications (Langer).

Prentice Hall's Response

Prentice Hall Literature provides overt connections at the selection level with the Literature in Context features and at the unit level with the Connection to Literature features. The Teacher's Edition contains background information about each selection, author, and genre. Furthermore, students are encouraged to make connections between the literature selections and the fine art that illustrates the textbook. Extension Activities at the end of each selection and Reading Instructional Materials selections foster connections between students' reading and the world outside the classroom.

What Research Indicates

To enhance reading comprehension and retention, students must master reading strategies such as scanning, predicting, using background knowledge, summarizing main ideas, and asking questions (Every Child Reading).

Teaching a combination of reading comprehension techniques is the most effective way to increase students' understanding. When students use them appropriately, these techniques assist in recall, question answering, question generation, and summarization of texts. When used in combination, these techniques can improve results in standardized comprehension tests (National Reading Panel).

Reading Strategy

Predicting

Predicting, or making guesses about what will happen before a story ends, can often help you check your understanding of a story.

- To make a prediction, start by looking for small but unusual details. These details might be minor events that catch your attention but that the characters in the story seem to ignore.
- Ask yourself what would happen if the detail were to become more important. In "The Birds," for example, think about what would happen if a disturbing detail were multiplied many times.
- Note your predictions, but be prepared to revise your guesses as the story develops.

Use a chart to help you record your predictions. The chart shown here presents a small but unusual detail from "The Birds."

Unusual Detail
Nat enjoys working alone.

Magnified Detail
When trouble comes, Nat will have to stand against it alone.

Prediction

Prentice Hall's Response

Prentice Hall Literature provides extensive instruction in reading strategies with introduction, development, and conclusion of each reading skill. Reading strategies include predicting, questioning, rereading, scanning, drawing inferences, determining word meaning from context, using prior knowledge, identifying the main idea, and summarizing. Each reading skill is introduced in the Prepare to Read section of each selection. The skill is then practiced throughout the selection. Assessment of the skill occurs in the postselection material. Additionally, the Teacher's Edition provides direct instruction for the skills being taught at point-of-use in the selection.

What Research Indicates

In order to be effective, comprehension skills should be taught using a consistent format and sequence, with examples, practice, and review (Carnine).

Prentice Hall's Response

Comprehension skills are taught before the selection on the Prepare to Read page, along with appropriate examples. Students apply these skills by answering questions within the selection and directly afterward. In Reading Informational Material selections, reading skills are introduced before the selection, then tested immediately after.

STEP-BY-STEP TEACHING GUIDE	PACING GUIDE
PRETEACH	
Motivate Students and Provide Background	
Use the Motivation activity (ATE p. 4)	5 min.
Read and discuss the Preview material and Background information (SE/ATE p. 4) A	5 min.
Introduce the Concepts	
Introduce the Literary Analysis and Reading Strategy (SE/ATE p. 5) A	15 min.
Pronounce the vocabulary words and read their definitions (SE p. 5)	5 min.
TEACH	
Monitor Comprehension	
Informally monitor comprehension by circulating while students read independently or in groups A	30 min.
Monitor students' comprehension with the Reading Check notes (SE/ATE pp. 7, 9, 11)	as students read
Develop vocabulary with Vocabulary notes (SE pp. 7, 9, 10, 11; ATE p. 7)	as students read
Develop Understanding	
Develop students' understanding of mood with the Literary Analysis annotations (SE p. 8; ATE pp. 7, 8, 9, 11) A	10 min.
Develop students' ability to break down confusing sentences with the Reading Strategy annotations (SE p. 10; ATE pp. 8,10)	10 min.
ASSESS	
Assess Mastery	
Assess students' mastery of the Reading Strategy and Literary Analysis by having them answer the Review and Assess questions (SE/ATE p. 13)	20 min.
Use one or more of the print and media Assessment Resources (ATE p. 15) A	up to 45 min.
EXTEND	
Apply Understanding	
Have students complete the Vocabulary Development Lesson and the Grammar Lesson (SE p. 14) A	20 min.
Apply students' ability to select precise details using the Writing Lesson (SE/ATE p. 15) A	45 min.
Apply students' understanding using one or more of the Extension Activities (SE p. 15)	20–90 min.

A ACCELERATED INSTRUCTION: Use the strategies and activities identified with an A.

UNIVERSAL ACCESS
● = Below Level Students
▲ = On-Level Students
■ = Above Level Students

RESEARCH OVERVIEW

What Research Indicates

Text structure is vital to both comprehension and retention of information. "Signaling," through the use of headings, different typefaces, and pointer words, can aid significantly in comprehension. When text structure is "considerate," i.e. consistent and logically ordered, students are more likely to remember information (Armbruster).

Readers use structural cues to construct meaning from written texts. Headings, linguistic cues, and parallel structure aid comprehension and assist with key skills such as identifying the main idea in a passage (Goldman).

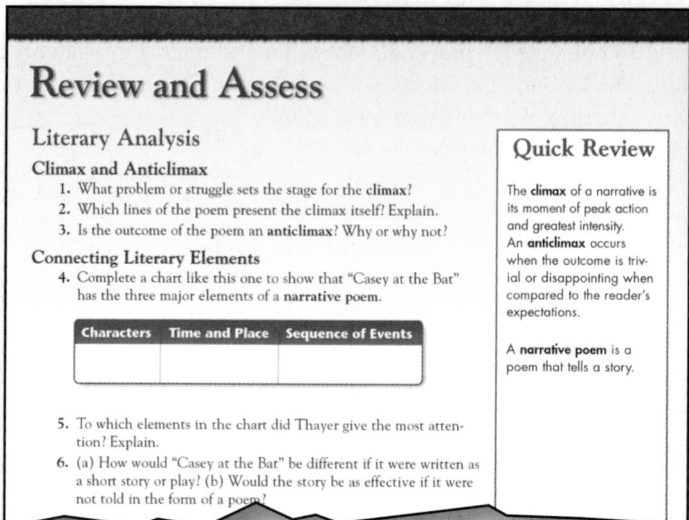

Review and Assess

Literary Analysis

Climax and Anticlimax

1. What problem or struggle sets the stage for the **climax**?
2. Which lines of the poem present the climax itself? Explain.
3. Is the outcome of the poem an **anticlimax**? Why or why not?

Connecting Literary Elements

4. Complete a chart like this one to show that "Casey at the Bat" has the three major elements of a **narrative poem**.

Characters	Time and Place	Sequence of Events

5. To which elements in the chart did Thayer give the most attention? Explain.
6. (a) How would "Casey at the Bat" be different if it were written as a short story or play? (b) Would the story be as effective if it were not told in the form of a poem?

Quick Review

The **climax** of a narrative is its moment of peak action and greatest intensity.
An **anticlimax** occurs when the outcome is trivial or disappointing when compared to the reader's expectations.

A **narrative poem** is a poem that tells a story.

Prentice Hall's Response

The design of *Prentice Hall Literature* uses headings to identify particular skills or strategies, and uses graphic organizers to demonstrate skills such as identifying the main idea or making inferences. The structure and order of these various components is consistent throughout the program to maximize retention of information. Additionally, Reading Informational Materials selections explicitly identify the structure of informational materials such as brochures, contracts, and feature articles so that students will be familiar with the common features of these materials.

What Research Indicates

Because most real-world reading is nonfiction, students must gain fluency in reading informational texts. Necessary skills for reading nonfiction include activating prior knowledge, noting important headings and subheadings, skimming, determining a purpose for reading, finding main ideas and supporting details, using graphics and illustrations, and analyzing text structure (Harvey).

Prentice Hall's Response

In addition to the Nonfiction unit in each grade level of *Prentice Hall Literature*, every unit in each book includes at least one Reading Informational Materials selection. These selections consist of real-world nonfiction materials such as newspaper articles, product warranties, operating instructions, business letters, meeting agendas, and brochures. Skills taught with these informational materials include analyzing information, evaluating a text, using information to make a decision, questioning, recognizing different types of appeals, following steps in sequence, and following technical directions.

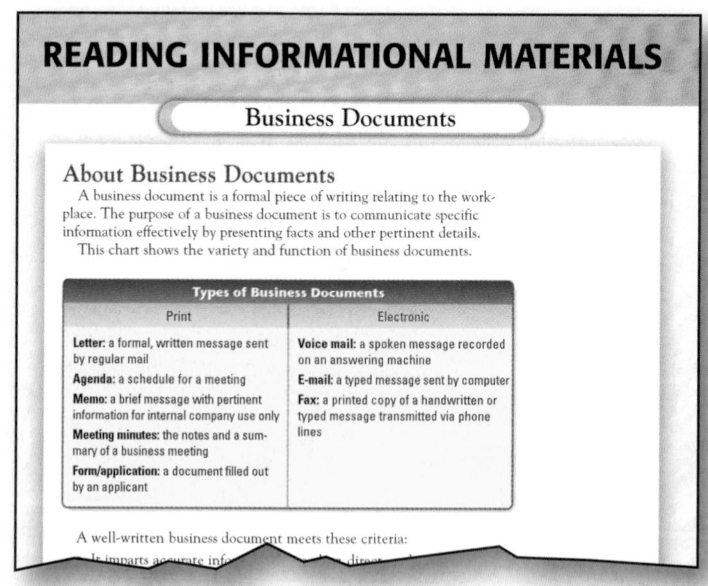

READING INFORMATIONAL MATERIALS

Business Documents

About Business Documents

A business document is a formal piece of writing relating to the workplace. The purpose of a business document is to communicate specific information effectively by presenting facts and other pertinent details.

This chart shows the variety and function of business documents.

Types of Business Documents

Print	Electronic
Letter: a formal, written message sent by regular mail **Agenda:** a schedule for a meeting **Memo:** a brief message with pertinent information for internal company use only **Meeting minutes:** the notes and a summary of a business meeting **Form/application:** a document filled out by an applicant	**Voice mail:** a spoken message recorded on an answering machine **E-mail:** a typed message sent by computer **Fax:** a printed copy of a handwritten or typed message transmitted via phone lines

A well-written business document meets these criteria:

What Research Indicates

Research shows that engaged readers have higher achievement scores. Instructional techniques that can positively affect motivation include using reading strategies, linking to prior knowledge, introducing real-world interactions and related activities, promoting student choice in reading matter, having students ask their own questions, promoting collaboration between students, using scaffolding, assigning a variety of informational and literary texts, linking reading, writing, and knowledge through coherent instruction, and having students conduct self-evaluations of their work (Guthrie).

Prentice Hall's Response

Prentice Hall Literature incorporates multiple strategies to engage and motivate readers. Each selection is introduced with a section that connects to students' prior knowledge and demonstrates the reading strategy for the selection. These strategies motivate students to ask questions of the text and are specially designed to help foster reader autonomy. At each grade level, the literature selections include a diverse mixture of different genres, classic and contemporary works, and informational texts. The postselection section includes both response questions and scaffolded analytical questions that utilize the skills taught before the selection. Extension activities such as role plays and readers' panels promote collaboration among students. Writing Workshops and Listening and Speaking Workshops include rubrics and criteria charts that allow students to evaluate their work and that of their peers.

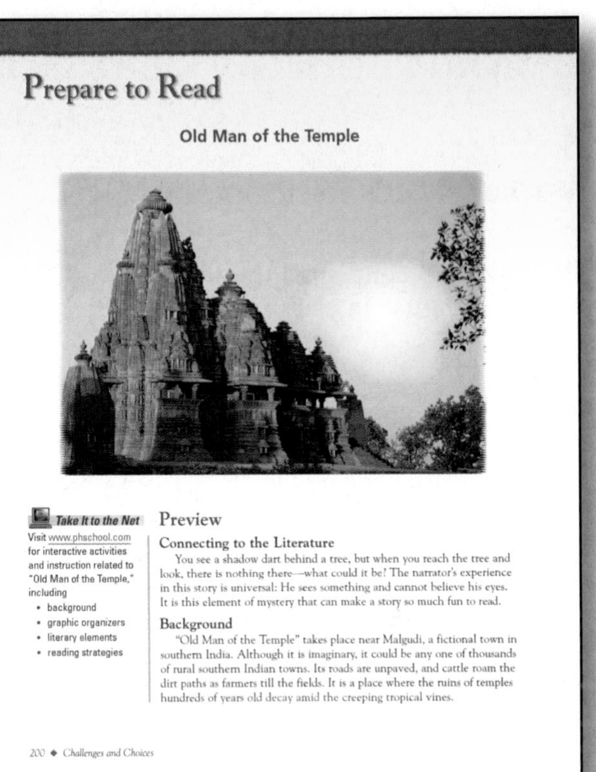

Prepare to Read

Old Man of the Temple

Take It to the Net
Visit www.phschool.com for interactive activities and instruction related to "Old Man of the Temple," including
- background
- graphic organizers
- literary elements
- reading strategies

Preview

Connecting to the Literature

You see a shadow dart behind a tree, but when you reach the tree and look, there is nothing there—what could it be? The narrator's experience in this story is universal: He sees something and cannot believe his eyes. It is this element of mystery that can make a story so much fun to read.

Background

"Old Man of the Temple" takes place near Malgudi, a fictional town in southern India. Although it is imaginary, it could be any one of thousands of rural southern Indian towns. Its roads are unpaved, and cattle roam the dirt paths as farmers till the fields. It is a place where the ruins of temples hundreds of years old decay amid the creeping tropical vines.

200 ◆ *Challenges and Choices*

What Research Indicates

Schools that "beat the odds" in teaching middle- and high-school students to read and write well use test preparation that is integrated into ongoing goals, curriculum, and regular lessons (Langer).

Prentice Hall's Response

Prentice Hall Literature provides test preparation as a separate activity with Assessment Workshops at the end of each unit and with a Test Preparation workbook. The Test Preparation workbook is selection specific, allowing for integration of the assessment into regular lessons.

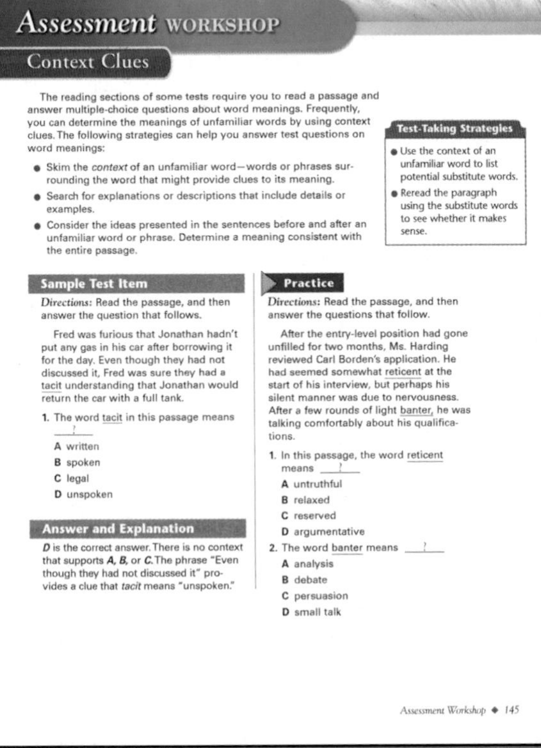

Assessment WORKSHOP

Context Clues

The reading sections of some tests require you to read a passage and answer multiple-choice questions about word meanings. Frequently, you can determine the meanings of unfamiliar words by using context clues. The following strategies can help you answer test questions on word meanings:

- Skim the *context* of an unfamiliar word—words or phrases surrounding the word that might provide clues to its meaning.
- Search for explanations or descriptions that include details or examples.
- Consider the ideas presented in the sentences before and after an unfamiliar word or phrase. Determine a meaning consistent with the entire passage.

Test-Taking Strategies
- Use the context of an unfamiliar word to list potential substitute words.
- Reread the paragraph using the substitute words to see whether it makes sense.

Sample Test Item

Directions: Read the passage, and then answer the question that follows.

Fred was furious that Jonathan hadn't put any gas in his car after borrowing it for the day. Even though they had not discussed it, Fred was sure they had a tacit understanding that Jonathan would return the car with a full tank.

1. The word tacit in this passage means __?__
   A written
   B spoken
   C legal
   D unspoken

Answer and Explanation

D is the correct answer. There is no context that supports *A, B,* or *C*. The phrase "Even though they had not discussed it" provides a clue that *tacit* means "unspoken."

Practice

Directions: Read the passage, and then answer the questions that follow.

After the entry-level position had gone unfilled for two months, Ms. Harding reviewed Carl Borden's application. He had seemed somewhat reticent at the start of his interview, but perhaps his silent manner was due to nervousness. After a few rounds of light banter, he was talking comfortably about his qualifications.

1. In this passage, the word reticent means __?__
   A untruthful
   B relaxed
   C reserved
   D argumentative
2. The word banter means __?__
   A analysis
   B debate
   C persuasion
   D small talk

Assessment Workshop ◆ 145

Incorporating Classroom Teacher Input

Market Needs Assessment

Prentice Hall conducted the following research to measure teacher responses to the literature textbooks in use in classrooms in 1999:

- **User Survey, September 9, 1999** Prentice Hall interviewed, by phone, 30 high-school teachers who used the previous edition of *Prentice Hall Literature*.
- **Focus Testing of Existing Programs, September 1999** Six focus groups of Grades 6–12 Language Arts teachers were conducted in three different cities. Participants reviewed then-current editions of *Prentice Hall Literature* and other literature programs.
- **Interviews with Department of Education Officials** Interviews were conducted in various key states in September and October 1999 and were ongoing through product development, December 2000.

Key Findings:

- The main reasons the program was adopted were:
  - Close fit with the curriculum
  - Selections offered
  - Amount and variety of the supplementary materials
  - Skill support
  - Thematic connections
  - Block scheduling resources
  - Test support
- Teachers liked the use of fine art.
- Teachers liked cross-curricular and real-world connections they perceived as solid and meaningful.
- Teachers preferred a streamlined design that was easy to work with; they considered the two-column design with call-out instructional boxes busy.
- Teachers wanted depth of information and instruction in Writing Workshops.
- Compared with other Language Arts textbooks, Prentice Hall was consistently cited by teachers as having strong instructional strategies.
- Commissioners and state and federal Department of Education officials asked that textbooks address the following elements:
  - Program pedagogy must include direct instruction in the Student Edition and Teacher's Edition.
  - Product must be research-based.
  - Reading skills such as decoding and phonics must be included.
  - Diagnostic testing and interventions need to be ongoing.
  - Program must be standards-based.

End Result:

In the new edition of *Prentice Hall Literature*, we've:

- retained the features that teachers love.
- developed a design that maintains a strong instructional focus through cleaner presentation. Selections appear in a single-column format, allowing instruction to be presented in a minor column.
- increased the length of Writing Workshops from two to four pages and included a full student model, a rubric, and more strategies for each stage of the writing process.
- developed the Student Edition and Teacher's Edition following the rules of direct instruction, defining terms at point-of-use and providing clear direction for students and teachers.
- consulted program authors and current research to confirm the direction and pedagogy of the series.
- developed Monitor Progress and Reteach notes in the Teacher's Edition for ongoing intervention opportunities.
- reviewed academic standards while instruction was developed.

One Saturday in 1965 I happened to be walking past the National Archives building in Washington. Across the interim years I had thought of Grandma's old stories—otherwise I can't think what diverted me up the Archives' steps. And when a main reading room desk attendant asked if he could help me, I wouldn't have dreamed of admitting to him some curiosity hanging on from boyhood about my slave forebears. I kind of bumbled that I was interested in census records of Alamance County, North Carolina, just after the Civil War.

The microfilm rolls were delivered, and I turned them through the machine with a building sense of intrigue, viewing in different census takers' penmanship an endless parade of names. After about a dozen microfilmed rolls, I was beginning to tire, when in utter astonishment I looked upon the names of Grandma's parents: Tom Murray, Irene Murray . . . older sisters of Grandma's as well—every one of them a name that I'd heard countless times on her front porch.

It wasn't that I hadn't believed Grandma. You just *didn't* not believe my Grandma. It was simply so uncanny actually seeing those names in print and in official U.S. Government records.

During the next several months I was back in Washington whenever possible, in the Archives, the Library of Congress, the Daughters of the American Revolution Library. (Whenever black attendants understood the idea of my search, documents I requested reached me with miraculous speed.) In one source or another during 1966 I was able to document at least the highlights of the cherished family story. I would have given anything to have told Grandma, but, sadly, in 1949 she had gone. So I went and told the only survivor of those Henning front-porch storytellers: Cousin Georgia Anderson, now in her 80's in Kansas City, Kan. Wrinkled, bent, not well herself, she was so overjoyed, repeating to me the old stories and sounds; they were like Henning echoes: "Yeah, boy, that African say his name was '*Kin-tay*'; he say the banjo was '*ko*,' an' the river '*Kamby Bolong*,' an' he was off choppin' some wood to make his drum when they grabbed 'im!" Cousin Georgia grew so excited we had to stop her, calm her down. "You go 'head, boy! Your grandma an' all of 'em—they up there watching what you do!"

That week I flew to London on a magazine assignment. Since by now I was steeped in the old, in the past, scarcely a tour guide missed me—I was awed at so many historical places and treasures I'd heard of and read of. I came upon the Rosetta stone in the British Museum, marveling anew at how Jean Champollion, the French archaeologist, had miraculously deciphered its ancient demotic and hieroglyphic texts[1] . . .

Literary Analysis
Personal Essay What details in the first two paragraphs show that this is a personal essay?

intrigue (in' trēg) *n.* curiosity and interest

uncanny (un kan' ē) *adj.* strange; eerie

cherished (cher' isht) *adj.* beloved; valued

Reading Strategy
Breaking Down Long Sentences Identify the subject of the sentence beginning "since by now..." What does the sentence tell you?

❹ Reading Check
What does Haley find in the microfilm?

1. **demotic and hieroglyphic texts** (dē mät' ik and hī' ər ō glif' ik) *adj.* ancient Egyptian writing, using symbols and pictures to represent words

My Furthest-Back Person ◆ 47

❷ Literary Analysis

Personal Essay

- Read the bracketed passage with students. Ask them if the opening of the essay grabs their interest. Have students who find it engaging explain why.
- Then, have students answer the Literary Analysis question on p. 47: What details in the first two paragraphs show that this is a personal essay?
Answer: The use of the pronoun *I*, Haley's conversational style, the way he refers to his grandmother as "Grandma," and the personal feelings he shares are all signs that this is a personal essay.

Monitor Progress Invite students to write a first sentence for a personal essay of their own. Ask volunteers to share their sentences.
Answer: Students' sentences should feature first-person pronouns, have a conversational tone, and focus on an event of personal importance.

❸ Reading Strategy

Breaking Down Long Sentences

- Read aloud the second bracketed passage. Then, read the Reading Strategy question on p. 47 aloud.
- Allow time for students to examine the sentence and think about the question. Have each student write his or her response on a piece of paper and fold it.
- Collect the papers, read the responses, and tally common and unique responses on the board. Discuss the correct answers.
Answer: The subject is "tour guide." The sentence tells you that Haley spent a lot of time as a tourist visiting historical places and seeing treasures from the past.

❹ Reading Check

Answer: He finds the names of family members in the microfilm.

CUSTOMIZE INSTRUCTION FOR UNIVERSAL ACCESS

For Less Proficient Readers	For Advanced Readers
If students are having difficulty following the events of this story, have them take turns reading aloud. Each time there is a change in readers, pause to allow students the opportunity to ask questions. Encourage students to answer one another's questions. Since many names are mentioned in the story, suggest that students keep a running list of characters and a separate list of relatives that Haley learns about.	Although some students may be familiar with Alex Haley's *Roots*, they may not know how much time, money, and effort Haley spent in tracing his heritage. Have students summarize the steps Haley has followed in his quest so far. Then, ask students to write a response to the following question: What might motivate you to begin a new and difficult project such as tracing your roots?

47

Formative Research

Prentice Hall conducted the following research to prototype and test new features, elements, and designs with teachers:

- **Prototype Testing: Focus Groups, December 1999** Focus groups were conducted among Grades 6–12 Language Arts teachers in New Jersey, Indiana, and California. Teachers reviewed several prototype versions of one literature selection.
- **Design Confirmation, February 2000, Quantitative Research** Using one-on-one interviews, Prentice Hall solicited reactions to prototype pages.
- **Design Confirmation, February 2000, Qualitative Research** Prentice Hall conducted two focus groups in New York for reactions to prototype pages.
- **Design Confirmation, April 2000** Prentice Hall conducted four focus groups in New Jersey and Oklahoma.

Ongoing Informal Research:

- In-school interviews
- Teacher advisory boards
- Adoption committee members

Key Findings:

- Most teachers agreed that the Student Edition should cover fewer elements in a more meaningful way.
- Teachers wanted vocabulary definitions to appear before selections; vocabulary words should be underlined at point-of-use within selections.
- Teachers wanted a visually engaging design that appealed to students.
- Teachers needed ancillary support for lower-level students.
- Teachers preferred Prentice Hall's ancillary package to that of the competitors, especially the following products:
  - Literature audiocassettes
  - Materials for high-level readers
  - Reader's Companions
- Teachers wanted a program that focused on the student by providing ways to engage and methods to teach important skills, and by offering accessibility for all ability levels. They also wanted a program that focused on the teacher by functioning as an aid or resource, rather than a way to train or "manage" teachers.

End Result:

In the new edition of *Prentice Hall Literature,* we've:

- developed the program according to the tenets of *considerate text.* These include:
  - a clear, consistent system of headings
  - chunked text to avoid paragraphs that are too dense
  - bulleted text when appropriate
  - boldfaced terms defined at point-of-use
- developed the Reading Achievement System to support lower-level students. Components include:
  - three levels of *Reader's Companions* to support struggling readers
  - *Basic Reading Skills: Comprehensive Lessons for Improvement*
  - *Teaching Guidebook for Universal Access*
- included panoramic images and large visuals to engage student interest.

Summary of Key Needs

Based on the collected research and classroom teacher input, Prentice Hall developed a literature program that meets these needs.

Strong skills instruction for successful test performance:

- Improved students' reading skills
- Strong instruction in communication skills
- Standardized test preparation

Strong teaching support and materials:

- Easy-to-follow materials for both students and teachers
- Instructional pathways to help all student populations—core, English-language learners, struggling readers, advanced students
- Companion Web site offering additional student activities, teacher resources, and professional development links

Standards-driven program with specific support/instruction for teachers:

- Strong skills activities and instruction with depth-based and standards-based outcomes
- Simple, direct lesson plans that clearly satisfy specific standards, including:
  - Daily lesson plans for special-education instruction
  - Daily lesson plans for English learners
  - Direct instruction in teaching reading and phonics

Bibliography of Research Articles

Alexander, Patricia A., and Tamara Jetton. "Learning from Text: A Multidimensional and Developmental Perspective." In *Handbook of Reading Research*, vol. 3, ed. M. L. Kamil, P. B. Mosenthal, P. D. Pearson, and R. Barr, 285–310. Mahwah, N.J.: Lawrence Erlbaum Associates, 2000.

Armbruster, Bonnie, and Thomas H. Anderson. "On Selecting 'Considerate' Content Area Textbooks." *Remedial and Special Education* 9 (1): 47–52.

Blachowicz, Camille, and Peter Fisher. *Teaching Vocabulary in All Classrooms*. Upper Saddle River, N.J.: Prentice Hall, 1996.

Carnine, Douglas, Jerry Silbert, and Edward J. Kameenui. *Direct Instruction Reading. 3rd ed.* Upper Saddle River, N.J.: Prentice Hall, 1997.

Goldman, Susan R., and John A. Rakestraw, Jr. "Structural Aspects of Constructing Meaning From Text." In *Handbook of Reading Research*, vol. 3, ed. M. L. Kamil, P. B. Mosenthal, P. D. Pearson, and R. Barr, 311–335. Mahwah, N.J.: Lawrence Erlbaum Associates, 2000.

Guthrie, John T. and Allan Wigfield. "Engagement and Motivation in Reading." In *Handbook of Reading Research*, vol. 3, ed. M. L. Kamil, P. B. Mosenthal, P. D. Pearson, and R. Barr, 403–422. Mahwah, N.J.: Lawrence Erlbaum Associates, 2000.

Harvey, Stephanie, and Anne Goudvis. "Determining Importance in Text: The Nonfiction Connection." In *Strategies That Work: Teaching Comprehension to Enhance Understanding*. Portland, Me.: Stenhouse Publishers, 2000.

Langer, Judith. "Beating the Odds: Teaching Middle and High School Students to Read and Write Well," 1999. Center on English Learning and Achievement. May 2003. <http://cela.albany.edu/eie2/main.html>

Learning First Alliance. *Every Child Reading: An Action Plan*. Washington, D.C.: Learning First Alliance, 1998.

Morrow, Lesley Mandel. "Story Retelling: A Discussion Strategy to Develop and Assess Comprehension." In *Lively Discussions! Fostering Engaged Reading*, ed. Linda B. Gambrell and Janice F. Almasi, 265–285. Newark, Del.: International Reading Association, 1996.

National Reading Panel. *Teaching Children to Read: An Evidence-Based Assessment of the Scientific Research on Reading and Its Implications for Reading Instruction*. NIH Publication 00-4769. Bethesda, Md.: U.S. Department of Health and Human Services, 2000.

Pressley, Michael. "What Should Comprehension Instruction Be the Instruction Of?" In *Handbook of Reading Research*, vol. 3, ed. M. L. Kamil, P. B. Mosenthal, P. D. Pearson, and R. Barr, 545–562. Mahwah, N.J.: Lawrence Erlbaum Associates, 2000.

Pressley, Michael, Vera Woloshyn, et al. *Cognitive Strategy Instruction That REALLY Improves Children's Academic Performance*. Cambridge, Mass.: Brookline Books, 1995.

POWERFUL RESEARCH-BASED SOLUTIONS TO GUARANTEE TEACHER AND STUDENT SUCCESS!

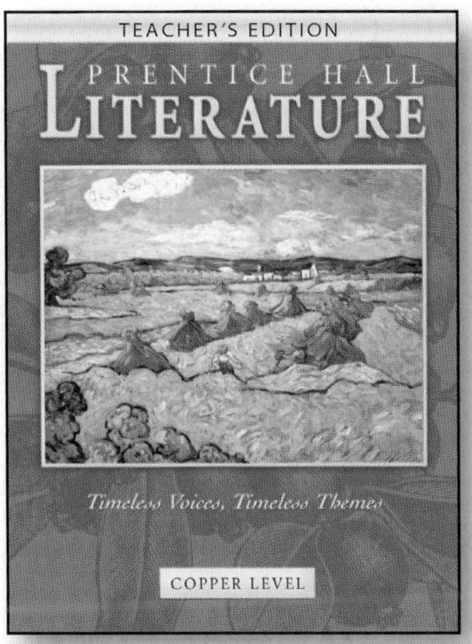

The Resource Teachers Use Most

The strategic instructional approach to teaching reading, grounded in reading research, is at the core of *Prentice Hall Literature*. This research is translated into direct program instruction to help teachers close the achievement gap in literacy.

Not only are teachers supported through research-based teaching techniques, but direct instruction within the Teacher's Edition offers customization ideas to reach students of all ability levels *before*, *during*, and *after* literary selections.

PROFESSIONAL DEVELOPMENT

Anytime, Anywhere Professional Development

To enhance the powerful teacher support in *Prentice Hall Literature*, Prentice Hall offers the Online Literacy Series, powered by LessonLab. The *Prentice Hall Literature* authors lend their expertise to guide users of the Online Literacy Series toward exemplary practices and instructional methods. Five courses have been designed specifically to help teachers become even more proficient with their classroom materials, while mastering the skills they need to deliver the research-based strategy instruction.

Online Courses:

- Foundations of Coaching and Mentoring
- Active Learning: Structures to Engage All Students
- Vocabulary Development
- Comprehension of Literary and Informational Materials
- Literary Response and Analysis

The Online Literacy Series empowers administrators and teachers with the ability to:

- Observe a standards-based lesson
- Access resources, lesson plans, and student work
- Engage in ongoing dialogue with colleagues
- Apply best practices in your classroom
- Increase your content knowledge while building proficiency with your instructional materials

For more information, visit PHSchool.com/professional_development

NCTE/IRA Standards Correlation

The National Council of Teachers of English (NCTE) and the International Reading Association (IRA), two professional organizations dedicated to improving the teaching and learning of English, have drafted a set of twelve comprehensive standards for the Language Arts. These standards are meant to provide a general framework for programs that encourage the development of language skills. The following pages show how *Prentice Hall Literature* meets these standards.

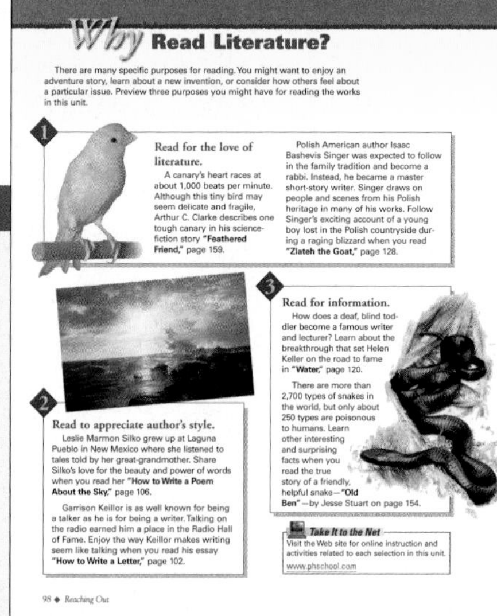

Why Read Literature?

There are many specific purposes for reading. You might want to enjoy an adventure story, learn about a new invention, or consider how others feel about a particular issue. Preview three purposes you might have for reading the works in this unit.

1 Read for the love of literature.

A canary's heart races at about 1,000 beats per minute. Although this tiny bird may seem delicate and fragile, Arthur C. Clarke describes one tough canary in his science-fiction story **"Feathered Friend,"** page 159.

Polish American author Isaac Bashevis Singer was expected to follow in the family tradition and become a rabbi. Instead, he became a master short-story writer. Singer draws on people and scenes from his Polish heritage in many of his works. Follow Singer's exciting account of a young boy lost in the Polish countryside during a raging blizzard when you read **"Zlateh the Goat,"** page 128.

2 Read to appreciate author's style.

Leslie Marmon Silko grew up at Laguna Pueblo in New Mexico where she listened to tales told by her great-grandmother. Share Silko's love for the beauty and power of words when you read her **"How to Write a Poem About the Sky,"** page 106.

Garrison Keillor is as well known for being a talker as he is for being a writer. Talking on the radio earned him a place in the Radio Hall of Fame. Enjoy the way Keillor makes writing seem like talking when you read his essay **"How to Write a Letter,"** page 102.

3 Read for information.

How does a deaf, blind toddler become a famous writer and lecturer? Learn about the breakthrough that set Helen Keller on the road to fame in **"Water,"** page 120.

There are more than 2,700 types of snakes in the world, but only about 250 types are poisonous to humans. Learn other interesting and surprising facts when you read the true story of a friendly, helpful snake—**"Old Ben"**—by Jesse Stuart on page 154.

Take It to the Net
Visit the Web site for online instruction and activities related to each selection in this unit.
www.phschool.com

98 ◆ *Reaching Out*

NCTE/IRA STANDARD	PRENTICE HALL LITERATURE
1. Students read a wide range of print and nonprint texts to build an understanding of texts, of themselves, and of the cultures of the United States and the world; to acquire new information; to respond to the needs and demands of society and the workplace; and for personal fulfillment. Among these texts are fiction and nonfiction, both classic and contemporary works.	• *Prentice Hall Literature* brings together the finest quality literature from around the world in a carefully balanced mix of classic and contemporary selections. • The Reading Informational Materials selections in each unit introduce students to real-world nonfiction texts and give them the tools to analyze informational materials, including editorials, warranties, business documents, critical reviews, and Web sites. • The Why Read Literature? page in each unit presents a variety of purposes for reading, each one connected to at least one selection in the unit.
2. Students read a wide range of literature from many periods in many genres to build an understanding of the many dimensions (e.g., philosophical, ethical, aesthetic) of human experience.	Following is a representative sampling of selections that support this standard: • **Short Stories** "Overdoing It," Anton Chekhov; "Becky and the Wheels-and-Brake Boys," James Berry • **Poetry** "How to Write a Poem About the Sky," Leslie Marmon Silko; "The Fairies' Lullaby," William Shakespeare • **Nonfiction** "Jackie Robinson: Justice at Last," Geoffrey C. Ward and Ken Burns; "Letter to Scottie," F. Scott Fitzgerald • **Drama** *The Phantom Tollbooth,* Susan Nanus; *Grandpa and the Statue,* Arthur Miller • **The Oral Tradition** "The Ant and the Dove," Leo Tolstoy; "Why Monkeys Live in Trees," Julius Lester; "A Crippled Boy," My-Van Tran
3. Students apply a wide range of strategies to comprehend, interpret, evaluate, and appreciate texts. They draw on their prior experience, their interactions with other readers and writers, their knowledge of word meaning and of other texts, their word identification strategies, and their understanding of textual features (e.g., sound-letter correspondence, sentence structure, context, graphics).	• Reading skills and strategies are taught before, during, and after each selection. • The *Selection Support Skills Development Workbook* includes practice pages that reinforce the skills taught with every selection in the Student Edition, including vocabulary, grammar, reading strategies, and literary analysis.

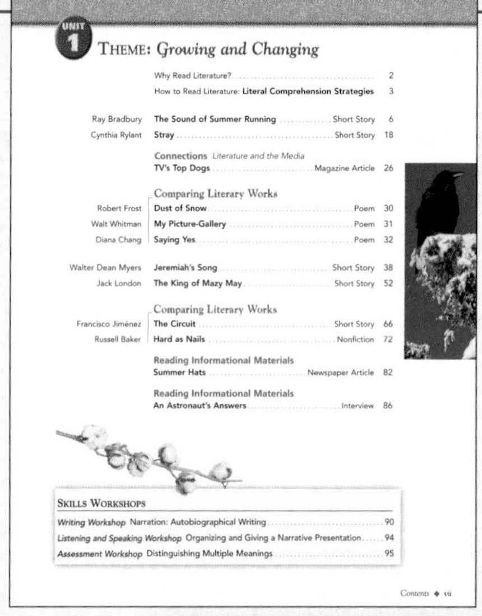

UNIT 1 THEME: *Growing and Changing*

Contents ◆ vii

Literary Analysis

Conflict with Nature

Stories develop around a conflict, a struggle between opposing forces. In a **conflict with nature,** a character or characters struggle against a natural element. In "Zlateh the Goat," two characters battle a blizzard.

> Aaron did not want to admit the danger, but he knew just the same that if they did not find shelter they would freeze to death. This was no ordinary storm. It was a mighty blizzard.

How the conflict will turn out is a question of life and death.

Connecting Literary Elements

A story's **setting** is the time and place of the action. In many stories, especially stories about a conflict with nature, the setting contributes to the conflict. In "Zlateh the Goat," the time is winter in the days before cars. The place is rural Eastern Europe in an area where houses and villages are far apart. Think about these focus questions as you read.

1. What natural elements are a result of the time of the setting?
2. What details of the place add to Aaron's problems?

Reading Strategy

Summarizing

You can better understand what is going on in a story if you pause occasionally to **summarize**—to review what has happened so far. Summarize using the following steps:

1. Identify the main events.
2. Organize them in the order in which they happen.
3. Note when one event causes another event.

As you read "Zlateh the Goat," pause at the events indicated on the timeline. Summarize what has happened up to that point by noting main events on a timeline of your own.

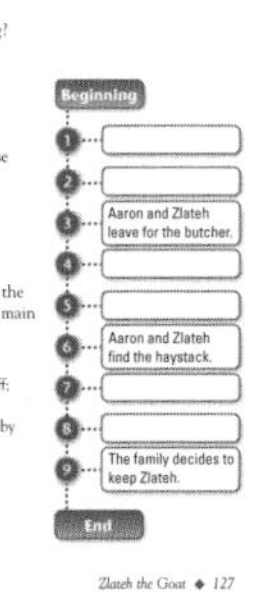

Beginning
1
2
3 Aaron and Zlateh leave for the butcher.
4
5
6 Aaron and Zlateh find the haystack.
7
8
9 The family decides to keep Zlateh.
End

Vocabulary Development

bound (bound) *v.* tied (p. 129)
conclusion (kən klōō′ zhən) *n.* belief or decision reached by reasoning (p. 129)
rapidly (rap′ id lē) *adv.* quickly (p. 129)
exuded (eg zyōōd′ əd) *v.* gave off; oozed; radiated (p. 131)
trace (trās) *n.* mark left behind by something (p. 133)

Zlateh the Goat ◆ 127

NCTE/IRA STANDARD	PRENTICE HALL LITERATURE
4. Students adjust their use of spoken, written, and visual language (e.g., conventions, style, vocabulary) to communicate effectively with a variety of audiences and for different purposes.	• Vocabulary skills and strategies are taught before, during, and after each selection. • Writing lessons offered at both the selection level and the unit level provide instruction in the writing process. Each Writing Lesson contains links to *Prentice Hall Writing and Grammar* to further strengthen the program's support. • Listening and Speaking activities are among the Extension Activities that follow each selection. In addition, each unit ends with a Listening and Speaking Workshop.
5. Students employ a wide range of strategies as they write and use different writing process elements appropriately to communicate with different audiences for a variety of purposes.	• In the selection-level Writing Lessons, students are given consistent instruction in prewriting, drafting, and revising, as well as in developing the appropriate voice and tone for a specific audience. • Unit-level Writing Workshops provide in-depth instruction on prewriting strategies, such as note taking, outlining, and collecting source material; drafting strategies, such as point-by-point organization and pacing; and revising strategies, such as adding vivid language, adjusting tone, and varying sentence structure.
6. Students apply knowledge of language structure, language conventions (e.g., spelling and punctuation), media techniques, figurative language, and genre to create, critique, and discuss print and nonprint texts.	• Language arts skills development is thoroughly integrated in *Prentice Hall Literature.* Each selection includes applied grammar, usage, mechanics, writing, and word-study activities related to the reading. • Grammar is presented sequentially so that students are able to cover and master the basic concepts before moving on to more complex structures. Grammar is taken from the context of the story so that authentic application comes naturally. • Listening and speaking instruction ranges from Extension Activities, such as evaluating advertisements and analyzing media messages, to Listening and Speaking Workshops.

Extension Activities

Listening and Speaking In a group, present a **dramatic reading** of the scene in which the youngest son approaches the cave.

1. Act out the parts of the boy and the dragon using exact words from the text.
2. Vary volume and tone of voice to show different levels of feeling, such as "annoyed" and "blistering mad."
3. For each reading, have other group members determine which feelings are being shown. Revise the reading to incorporate group feedback.

Research and Technology Make a **compare-and-contrast chart** about dragons in world literature. Using the word *dragon*, perform key word searches in online databases to find information about dragons in many cultures. In your chart, explore some of the following characteristics: physical features, potential for good and evil, and the types of tales in which they typically appear.

Take It to the Net www.phschool.com

Go online for an additional research activity using the Internet.

Dragon, Dragon ◆ 445

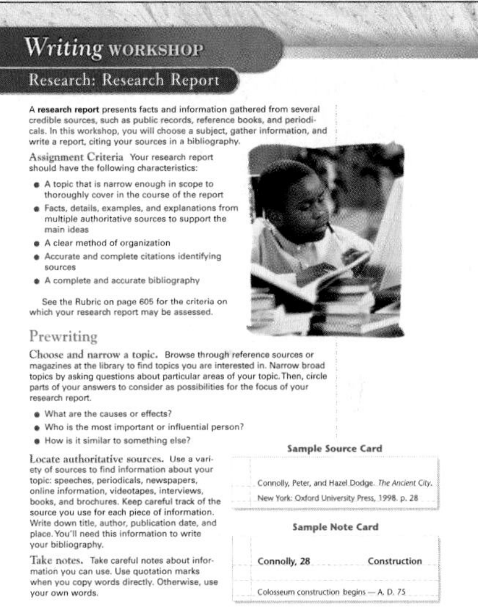
Writing WORKSHOP
Research: Research Report

A **research report** presents facts and information gathered from several credible sources, such as public records, reference books, and periodicals. In this workshop, you will choose a subject, gather information, and write a report, citing your sources in a bibliography.

Assignment Criteria Your research report should have the following characteristics:

- A topic that is narrow enough in scope to thoroughly cover in the course of the report
- Facts, details, examples, and explanations from multiple authoritative sources to support the main ideas
- A clear method of organization
- Accurate and complete citations identifying sources
- A complete and accurate bibliography

See the Rubric on page 605 for the criteria on which your research report may be assessed.

Prewriting

Choose and narrow a topic. Browse through reference sources or magazines at the library to find topics you are interested in. Narrow broad topics by asking questions about particular areas of your topic. Then, circle parts of your answers to consider as possibilities for the focus of your research report.

- What are the causes or effects?
- Who is the most important or influential person?
- How is it similar to something else?

Locate authoritative sources. Use a variety of sources to find information about your topic: speeches, periodicals, newspapers, online information, videotapes, interviews, books, and brochures. Keep careful track of the source you use for each piece of information. Write down title, author, publication date, and place. You'll need this information to write your bibliography.

Take notes. Take careful notes about information you can use. Use quotation marks when you copy words directly. Otherwise, use your own words.

Sample Source Card

Connolly, Peter, and Hazel Dodge. *The Ancient City.* New York: Oxford University Press, 1998. p. 28

Sample Note Card

Connolly, 28 — Construction

Colosseum construction begins — A. D. 75

600 ◆ *Nonfiction*

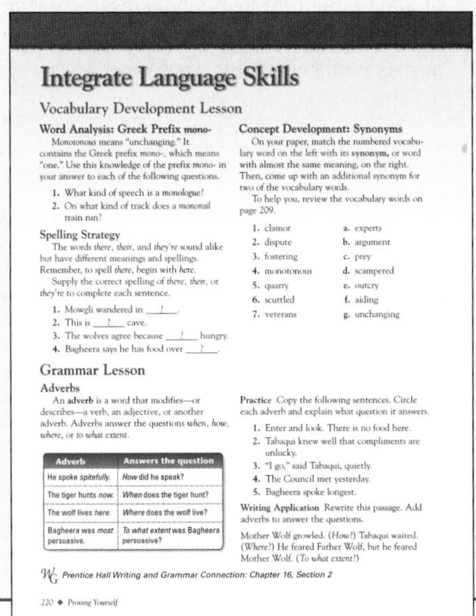
Integrate Language Skills

Vocabulary Development Lesson

Word Analysis: Greek Prefix *mono-*

Monotonous means "unchanging." It contains the Greek prefix *mono-*, which means "one." Use this knowledge of the prefix *mono-* in your answer to each of the following questions.

1. What kind of speech is a *monologue?*
2. On what kind of track does a *monorail* train run?

Spelling Strategy

The words *there*, *their*, and *they're* sound alike but have different meanings and spellings. Remember, to spell *there*, begin with *here*.

Supply the correct spelling of *there*, *their*, or *they're* to complete each sentence.

1. Mowgli wandered in __?__.
2. This is __?__ cave.
3. The wolves agree because __?__ hungry.
4. Bagheera says he has food over __?__.

Concept Development: Synonyms

On your paper, match the numbered vocabulary word on the left with its **synonym,** or word with almost the same meaning, on the right. Then, come up with an additional synonym for two of the vocabulary words.

To help you, review the vocabulary words on page 209.

1. clamor — a. experts
2. dispute — b. argument
3. fostering — c. prey
4. monotonous — d. scampered
5. quarry — e. outcry
6. scuttled — f. aiding
7. veterans — g. unchanging

Grammar Lesson

Adverbs

An **adverb** is a word that modifies—or describes—a verb, an adjective, or another adverb. Adverbs answer the questions *when*, *how*, *where*, or *to what extent*.

Adverb	Answers the question
He spoke *spitefully.*	*How* did he speak?
The tiger hunts *now.*	*When* does the tiger hunt?
The wolf lives *here.*	*Where* does the wolf live?
Bagheera was *most* persuasive.	*To what extent* was Bagheera persuasive?

Practice Copy the following sentences. Circle each adverb and explain what question it answers.

1. Enter and look. There is no food here.
2. Tabaqui knew well that compliments are unlucky.
3. "I go," said Tabaqui, quietly.
4. The Council met yesterday.
5. Bagheera spoke longest.

Writing Application Rewrite this passage. Add adverbs to answer the questions.

Mother Wolf growled. (*How?*) Tabaqui waited. (*Where?*) He feared Father Wolf, but he feared Mother Wolf. (*To what extent?*)

Prentice Hall Writing and Grammar Connection: Chapter 16, Section 2

220 ◆ *Proving Yourself*

NCTE/IRA STANDARD	PRENTICE HALL LITERATURE
7. Students conduct research on issues and interests by generating ideas and questions, as well as by posing problems. They gather, evaluate, and synthesize data from a variety of sources (e.g., print and nonprint texts, artifacts, people) to communicate their discoveries in ways that suit their purpose and audience.	• Extension Activities encourage students to explore additional dimensions of the selections through collaborative research, panel presentations, and discussions. • Each grade level includes unit-level workshops on writing and delivering a research paper. • Students practice research skills, such as asking questions and evaluating data, at the selection level and in the Reading Informational Materials features.
8. Students use a variety of technological and information resources (e.g., libraries, databases, computer networks, video) to gather and synthesize information and to create and communicate knowledge.	• Students practice research skills, such as searching the Internet and summarizing primary research articles, at the selection level in the Research and Technology Extension Activities and in the Reading Informational Materials features.
9. Students develop an understanding of and respect for diversity in language use, patterns, and dialects across cultures, ethnic groups, geographic regions, and social roles.	Following is a representative sampling of selections that support this standard: "Jeremiah's Song," Walter Dean Myers; "Dust of Snow," Robert Frost; "The Circuit," Francisco Jiménez; "How to Write a Letter," Garrison Keillor; "Thunder Butte," Virginia Driving Hawk Sneve; "Lob's Girl," Joan Aiken; "Becky and the Wheels-and-Brake Boys," James Berry; "Eleven," Sandra Cisneros. • The Connections feature includes literary works from around the world, which are connected to individual selections in the Student Edition.

Listening and Speaking WORKSHOP

Delivering a Research Presentation

Delivering an effective **research presentation** has many of the same characteristics as preparing a research report. (To review the characteristics of a successful research report, see the Writing Workshop, pp. 600–605.) For hints on preparing and delivering a research report, use some of the strategies suggested here.

Effective Preparation

Before giving a research presentation, take time to go over your material and organize your notes and any visual aids you plan to use. Have on hand a list of reliable sources, including Web site addresses that you used.

Draw from multiple sources. Make the audience aware that your information is drawn from a number of reliable sources, such as expert interviews, books, newspapers, videotapes, periodicals, and online sites. Keep in mind that some sources, such as government Web sites, are more reliable than others.

Support your topic. Develop your topic so that you introduce your main ideas and then support them with interesting facts, details, and explanations from a variety of sources. Providing examples will further enhance your presentation.

Use visual aids. As often as possible, present photographs, charts, and diagrams. Use slides and videotapes when appropriate. These aids will give your presentation variety.

Using Visual Aids

- **Maps** Use **maps** when presenting a report on a country or region.
- **Charts and Graphs** Use **charts and graphs** to show statistics or changes in amount.
- **Diagrams** Use **diagrams** with explanations of parts or processes.

Effective Delivery

Before giving a research presentation, take time to rehearse, practicing ways to use your voice for emphasis. Be sure that your topic is not so broad that you cannot adequately cover it in the allotted time.

Pose relevant questions. It's a good idea to begin your presentation with a few good questions, sufficiently narrow in scope to be completely and thoroughly answered in your presentation. This technique will let your audience know exactly what you will cover.

Slow down; take your time. Sometimes, presenters speak too quickly because they are nervous. Pause for a moment before you begin and take a deep breath.

Activity: Presentation Choose a subject related to a current event in the news. Research the background, as well as the importance of the event, using newspapers, magazines, and Web sites. Prepare and deliver a research presentation on your topic.

606 ◆ *Nonfiction*

READING INFORMATIONAL MATERIALS

Web Sites and Web Pages

About Web Sites

Web sites are specific locations on the Internet. If you think of the Internet as a giant library, Web sites are individual books within that library. As you explore a Web site on a computer, what you see on the screen is a part of the site called a Web page. A Web site can have many Web pages, just as a book has many pages. You can move from one Web page to another easily (or from one part of a long Web page to another) by using the mouse to click on a picture, a "button," or a highlighted or underlined word or phrase, called a *link*.

Reading Strategy

Using Structural Features of Web Sites

Use the special features of Web sites to move quickly around the site and find the information you need. Web sites and Web pages have some of the same structural features as textbooks and magazines, such as headings and graphics, but they have some special features unique to electronic texts as well. Learn to navigate, or find your way from place to place, in a Web site by using these special features. The features will make your searches for information more efficient by getting you to the right place in the shortest amount of time.

The chart shows some of the special features of Web sites and Web pages.

Web Site Features	
Link	A connection to another spot on the same Web page or to a different Web page or Web site. A link can be underlined or highlighted text, or an image or photograph. Links are what make the Web a "web."
Icon	An image or small drawing that may appear by itself or with accompanying text. Icons are often links as well.
Graphics	Pictures, maps, tables, and other graphic sources are often featured on a Web site. These graphics are often sources of information in themselves, but they may also be links to other Web pages.

Use bookmarks to "save" useful Web sites so that you can quickly return to them when you need to verify or find additional information. Most Web browsers—the software that allows you to get to the material on the Web—have a "bookmark" or "favorites" feature that creates an easy-to-access list of your favorite sites.

374 ◆ *Mysterious Worlds*

CONNECTIONS

Literature and Science

Environmental Emergencies

In "Turkeys," Bailey White gives a personal account of her experience with efforts to save populations of wild turkeys. At the turn of the twentieth century, wild turkeys had disappeared from 18 of the 39 states they had inhabited. In 1937, the Federal Aid in Wildlife Restoration Act began funding the acquisition of wildlife habitats. In the early 1950s, wildlife biologists in South Carolina trapped healthy wild turkeys and released them in habitats where there were few wild turkeys. When the National Wild Turkey Federation was founded in 1973, the restoration of wild turkeys was underway in many states. Today, more than five million wild turkeys roam the fields and forests of North America.

This article discusses another wildlife "emergency." Saving the many species of migrating birds and fish from the increasingly polluted Salton Sea is a challenge facing engineers and scientists. The Salton Sea is a landlocked lake in Southern California's Imperial Valley. This popular, 360-mile-square saltwater lake has become polluted by agricultural runoff, including chemicals and silt. Lacking a steady supply of fresh water, it is becoming more salty and polluted every day and increasingly dangerous for wildlife.

588 ◆ *Nonfiction*

NCTE/IRA STANDARD	PRENTICE HALL LITERATURE
10. Students whose first language is not English make use of their first language to develop competency in the English language arts and to develop understanding of content across the curriculum.	• *Literatura* is a Spanish-literature anthology that combines authentic Spanish literature with translations of selections from the Student Edition. Instruction in Spanish parallels the instruction in the English-language Student Edition. • *Literatura en español* provides authentic Spanish-language literature and Spanish translations of selections from the text. Each grade-level book includes thirty works of literature, accompanied by questions and activities. • The *Spanish/English Summaries Audio CDs* include summaries of every selection in both English and Spanish. These summaries provide help for struggling readers, special-education students, and English learners prior to having them read. • The *Spanish Readings on Audio CDs* contain Spanish-language recordings of every selection in *Literatura en español.* • The *Teaching Guidebook for Universal Access* gives proven strategies for adapting instruction for English-language learners. In addition, the *Reader's Companion English Learner's Version* provides language support for students who are ready to work in English.
11. Students participate as knowledgeable, reflective, creative, and critical members of a variety of literacy communities.	• After each selection, the Extend Understanding question on the Review and Assess page and the Extension Activities invite students to go beyond the text to explore many connected areas. • The Writing Workshop in each unit includes several publishing and presenting opportunities that allow students to share their writing with classmates or with a larger audience. • Three levels of interactive readers—*Reader's Companion, Reader's Companion Adapted Version,* and *Reader's Companion English Learner's Version*—enable students at all ability levels to enjoy the same work of literature. 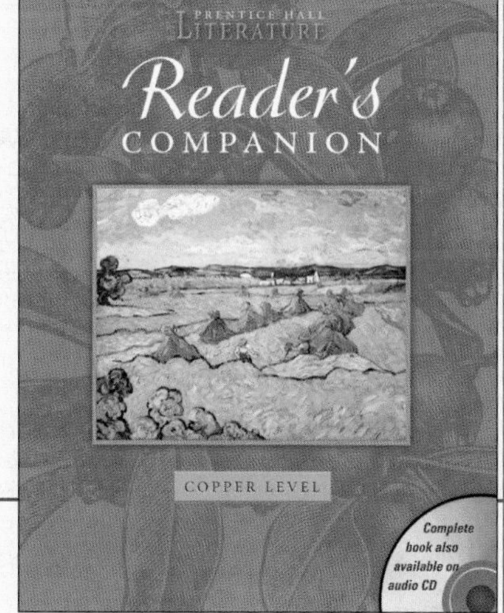
12. Students use spoken, written, and visual language to accomplish their own purposes (e.g., for learning, enjoyment, persuasion, and the exchange of information).	• Establishing a Purpose for Reading is one of the many Reading Strategies that are taught at each grade level. • Students learn to read for information in the Reading Informational Materials selections. The instruction that accompanies these selections teaches students to understand and utilize a vast array of real-world nonfiction texts. • Extension Activities at the selection level and Writing Lessons at the unit level often encourage students to choose their own topics for exploration.

READING INFORMATIONAL MATERIALS

xxiv ◆ Contents

NCTE/IRA STANDARDS

Program Planner

Selection	Reading	Literary Analysis	Vocabulary	Grammar
"The Sound of Summer Running," Ray Bradbury, SE p. 6 Reading Level: Average	• Reading Fluently, SE p. 5; TR Selection Support, p. 4; TR Literary Analysis and Reading Transparencies, p. 1	• Characters' Motives, SE p. 5; TR Selection Support, p. 5; TR Literary Analysis and Reading Transparencies, p. 2	• Vocabulary Development, SE p. 5: seized, suspended, loam, barometer, alien, limber, revelation • Greek Root *-meter-*, SE p. 14; TR Selection Support, p. 1	• Nouns, SE p. 14; TR Selection Support, p. 3; WG Writing and Grammar, p. 294
"Stray," Cynthia Rylant, SE p. 18 Reading Level: Easy	• Distinguish Shades of Meaning, SE p. 17; TR Selection Support, p. 9; TR Literary Analysis and Reading Transparencies, p. 3	• Surprise Ending, SE p. 17; TR Selection Support, p. 10; TR Literary Analysis and Reading Transparencies, p. 4	• Vocabulary Development, SE p. 17: timidly, trudged, grudgingly, ignore, exhausted • Suffix *-ly*, SE p. 24; TR Selection Support, p. 6	• Compound Nouns, SE p. 24; TR Selection Support, p. 8; WG Writing and Grammar, p. 296
"Dust of Snow," Robert Frost, SE p. 30; **"My Picture-Gallery,"** Walt Whitman, SE p. 31; **"Saying Yes,"** Diana Chang, SE p. 32 Reading Levels: Average, Average, Easy	• Rereading to Clarify, SE p. 29; TR Selection Support, p. 14; TR Literary Analysis and Reading Transparencies, p. 5	• Images in Poetry, SE p. 29; TR Selection Support, p. 15; TR Literary Analysis and Reading Transparencies, p. 6	• Vocabulary Development, SE p. 29; rued, suspended, tableaus • Homophones, SE p. 34; TR Selection Support, p. 11	• Common and Proper Nouns, SE p. 34; TR Selection Support, p. 13; WG Writing and Grammar, p. 297
"Jeremiah's Song," Walter Dean Myers, SE p. 38 Reading Level: Average	• Using Context to Determine Meaning, SE p. 37; TR Selection Support, p. 19; TR Literary Analysis and Reading Transparencies, p. 7	• First-Person Point of View, SE p. 37; TR Selection Support, p. 20; TR Literary Analysis and Reading Transparencies, p. 8	• Vocabulary Development, SE p. 37: diagnosis, disinfect • Latin Prefix *dis-*, SE p. 48; TR Selection Support, p. 16	• Pronouns, SE p. 48; TR Selection Support, p. 18; WG Writing and Grammar, p. 506
"The King of Mazy May," Jack London, SE p. 52 Reading Level: Challenging	• Recognizing Signal Words, SE p. 51; TR Selection Support, p. 24; TR Literary Analysis and Reading Transparencies, p. 9	• Conflict Between Characters, SE p. 51; TR Selection Support, p. 25; TR Literary Analysis and Reading Transparencies, p. 10	• Vocabulary Development, SE p. 51: toil, endured, prospectors, liable, poising, declined, summit • Latin Suffix *-or*, SE p. 62; TR Selection Support, p. 21	• Pronouns and Antecedents, SE p. 62; TR Selection Support, p. 23; WG Writing and Grammar, p. 300
"The Circuit," Francisco Jiménez, SE p. 66; **"Hard as Nails,"** Russell Baker, SE p. 72 Reading Levels: Average, Average	• Reading With Expression, SE p. 65; TR Selection Support, p. 29; TR Literary Analysis and Reading Transparencies, p. 11	• Theme, SE p. 65; TR Selection Support, p. 30; TR Literary Analysis and Reading Transparencies, p. 12	• Vocabulary Development, SE p. 65: drone, instinctively, savoring, embedded, exhaust, sublime, immense • Compound Nouns, SE p. 80; TR Selection Support, p. 26	• Pronoun-Antecedent Agreement, SE p. 80; TR Selection Support, p. 28; WG Writing and Grammar, p. 528

Key to Program References: SE: Student Edition **TR:** Teaching Resources **WG:** Writing and Grammar

Unit 1 *Growing and Changing*

Writing	Extension Activities	Assessment	Technology
• Writing Lesson: Sneaker Advertisement, SE p. 15; WG Writing and Grammar, p. 100	• Listening and Speaking: Read Aloud, SE p. 15 • Research and Technology: Shoe Research, SE p. 15 • TR Extension Activities, p. 1	• Selection Test, TR Formal Assessment, pp. 1–3 • TR Open Book Test, pp. 1–3 • Writing rubric and Listening and Speaking rubric, TR Performance Assess. and Portfolio Mgmt., pp. 9, 23	• Interest Grabber Videotapes, Tape 1 • Listening to Literature, Audiocassettes, Side 1; Audio CDs, CD 1 • Got It! Assessment Videotapes, Tape 1 • WG Writing and Grammar iText CD-ROM
• Writing Lesson: News Report, SE p. 25; WG Writing and Grammar, p. 182	• Listening and Speaking: Oral Presentation, SE p. 25 • Research and Technology: Pet Care Chart, SE p. 25 • TR Extension Activities, p. 2	• Selection Test, TR Formal Assessment, pp. 4–6 • TR Open Book Test, pp. 4–6 • Writing rubric, TR Performance Assess. and Portfolio Mgmt., p. 18	• Interest Grabber Videotapes, Tape 1 • Listening to Literature, Audiocassettes, Side 1; Audio CDs, CD 1 • Got It! Assessment Videotapes, Tape 1 • WG Writing and Grammar iText CD-ROM
• Writing Lesson: Description of a Scene, SE p. 35; WG Writing and Grammar, p. 100	• Listening and Speaking: Brief Drama, SE p. 35 • Research and Technology: Mind Map, SE p. 35 • TR Extension Activities, p. 3	• Selection Test, TR Formal Assessment, pp. 7–9 • TR Open Book Test, pp. 7–9 • Writing rubric and Listening and Speaking rubric, TR Performance Assess. and Portfolio Mgmt., pp. 9, 23	• Interest Grabber Videotapes, Tape 1 • Listening to Literature, Audiocassettes, Side 1; Audio CDs, CD 1 • Got It! Assessment Videotapes, Tape 1 • WG Writing and Grammar iText CD-ROM
• Writing Lesson: Character Description, SE p. 49; WG Writing and Grammar, p. 102	• Listening and Speaking: Role-Play, SE p. 49 • Research and Technology: Talent Timeline, SE p. 49 • TR Extension Activities, p. 4	• Selection Test, TR Formal Assessment, pp. 10–12 • TR Open Book Test, pp. 10–12 • Writing rubric and Listening and Speaking rubric, TR Performance Assess. and Portfolio Mgmt., pp. 9, 23	• Interest Grabber Videotapes, Tape 1 • Listening to Literature, Audiocassettes, Side 2; Audio CDs, CD 1 • Got It! Assessment Videotapes, Tape 1 • WG Writing and Grammar iText CD-ROM
• Writing Lesson: Personal Narrative, SE p. 63; WG Writing and Grammar, p. 84	• Listening and Speaking: Acceptance Speech, SE p. 63 • Research and Technology: Visual Presentation, SE p. 63 • TR Extension Activities, p. 5	• Selection Test, TR Formal Assessment, pp. 13–15 • TR Open Book Test, pp. 13–15 • Writing rubric, TR Performance Assess. and Portfolio Mgmt., p. 13	• Interest Grabber Videotapes, Tape 1 • Listening to Literature, Audiocassettes, Side 2; Audio CDs, CD 1 • Got It! Assessment Videotapes, Tape 1 • WG Writing and Grammar iText CD-ROM
• Writing Lesson: Letter to a Character, SE p. 81; WG Writing and Grammar, p. 256	• Listening and Speaking: Interview, SE p. 81 • Research and Technology: Profile of a Reporter, SE p. 81 • TR Extension Activities, p. 6	• Selection Test, TR Formal Assessment, pp. 16–18 • TR Open Book Test, pp. 16–18 • Writing rubric and Listening and Speaking rubric, TR Performance Assess. and Portfolio Mgmt., pp. 8, 25	• Interest Grabber Videotapes, Tape 1 • Listening to Literature, Audiocassettes, Side 3; Audio CDs, CD 2 • Got It! Assessment Videotapes, Tape 1 • WG Writing and Grammar iText CD-ROM

Program Planner

Selection	Reading	Literary Analysis	Vocabulary	Grammar
"How to Write a Letter," Garrison Keillor, SE p. 102; **"How to Write a Poem About the Sky,"** Leslie Marmon Silko, SE p. 106 Reading Levels: Average, Easy	• Reading Aloud With Expression, SE p. 101; TR Selection Support, p. 34; TR Literary Analysis and Reading Transparencies, p. 13	• Informal Essay, SE p. 101; TR Selection Support, p. 35; TR Literary Analysis and Reading Transparencies, p. 14	• Vocabulary Development, SE p. 101: confidence, anonymity, obligatory, episode, sibling, dense, membranes • Latin Suffix *-ory,* SE p. 108; TR Selection Support, p. 31	• Verbs, SE p. 108; TR Selection Support, p. 33; WG Writing and Grammar, p. 314
"Aaron's Gift," Myron Levoy, SE p. 112; **"Water,"** Helen Keller, SE p. 120 Reading Levels: Challenging, Average	• Using Context to Clarify Meaning, SE p. 111; TR Selection Support, p. 39; TR Literary Analysis and Reading Transparencies, p. 15	• Climax, SE p. 111; TR Selection Support, p. 40; TR Literary Analysis and Reading Transparencies, p. 16	• Vocabulary Development, SE p. 111: frenzied, mascot, coaxed, consoled • Using forms of *console,* SE p. 124; TR Selection Support, p. 36	• Verb Phrases, SE p. 124; TR Selection Support, p. 38; WG Writing and Grammar, p. 320
"Zlateh the Goat," Isaac Bashevis Singer, SE p. 128 Reading Level: Average	• Summarizing, SE p. 127; TR Selection Support, p. 44; TR Literary Analysis and Reading Transparencies, p. 17	• Conflict with Nature, SE p. 127; TR Selection Support, p. 45; TR Literary Analysis and Reading Transparencies, p. 18	• Vocabulary Development, SE p. 127: bound, conclusion, rapidly, exuded, trace • Latin Prefix *ex-,* SE p. 136; TR Selection Support, p. 41	• Principle Parts of Verbs, SE p. 136; TR Selection Support, p. 43; WG Writing and Grammar, p. 480
"Door Number Four," Charlotte Pomerantz, SE p. 140; **"Count That Day Lost,"** George Eliot, SE p. 141; **"The World Is Not a Pleasant Place to Be,"** Nikki Giovanni, SE p. 142 Reading Levels: Challenging, Average, Average	• Paraphrasing, SE p. 139; TR Selection Support, p. 49; TR Literary Analysis and Reading Transparencies, p. 19	• Speaker, SE p. 139; TR Selection Support, p. 50; TR Literary Analysis and Reading Transparencies, p. 20	• Vocabulary Development, SE p. 139: eased • Analogies, SE p. 144; TR Selection Support, p. 46	• Verb Tenses, SE p. 144; TR Selection Support, p. 48; WG Writing and Grammar, p. 488
"Old Ben," Jesse Stuart, SE p. 154; **"Feathered Friend,"** Arthur C. Clarke, SE p. 159 Reading Levels: Easy, Challenging	• Using Context Clues, SE p. 153; TR Selection Support, p. 54; TR Literary Analysis and Reading Transparencies, p. 21	• Narratives, SE p. 153; TR Selection Support, p. 55; TR Literary Analysis and Reading Transparencies, p. 22	• Vocabulary Development, SE p. 153: scarce, regulation, fusing, ceased • Forms of *regulate,* SE p. 164; TR Selection Support, p. 51	• Perfect Verb Tense, SE p. 164; TR Selection Support, p. 53; WG Writing and Grammar, p. 490

Key to Program References: SE: Student Edition **TR:** Teaching Resources **WG:** Writing and Grammar

Unit 2 *Reaching Out*

Writing	Extension Activities	Assessment	Technology
• Writing Lesson: Letter, SE p. 109; WG Writing and Grammar, p. 58	• Listening and Speaking: Speech, SE p. 109 • Research and Technology: Internet Research, SE p. 109 • TR Extension Activities, p. 7	• Selection Test, TR Formal Assessment, pp. 27–29 • TR Open Book Test, pp. 19–21 • Writing rubric and Listening and Speaking rubric, TR Performance Assess. and Portfolio Mgmt., p. 8	• Interest Grabber Videotapes, Tape 1 • Listening to Literature, Audio-cassettes, Side 4; Audio CDs, CD 2 • Got It! Assessment Videotapes, Tape 1 • WG Writing and Grammar iText CD-ROM
• Writing Lesson: Interview, SE p. 125; WG Writing and Grammar, p. 108	• Listening and Speaking: Oral Presentation, SE p. 125 • Research and Technology: Visual Presentation, SE p. 125 • TR Extension Activities, p. 8	• Selection Test, TR Formal Assessment, pp. 30–32 • TR Open Book Test, pp. 22–24 • Writing rubric and Listening and Speaking rubric, TR Performance Assess. and Portfolio Mgmt., pp. 12, 29	• Interest Grabber Videotapes, Tape 1 • Listening to Literature, Audio-cassettes, Side 5; Audio CDs, CDs 2, 3 • Got It! Assessment Videotapes, Tape 1 • WG Writing and Grammar iText CD-ROM
• Writing Lesson: Persuasive Speech, SE p. 137; WG Writing and Grammar, p. 132	• Listening and Speaking: Monologue, SE p. 137 • Research and Technology: Presentation, SE p. 137 • TR Extension Activities, p. 9	• Selection Test, TR Formal Assessment, pp. 33–35 • TR Open Book Test, pp. 25–27 • Writing rubric and Listening and Speaking rubric, TR Performance Assess. and Portfolio Mgmt., pp. 27, 51	• Interest Grabber Videotapes, Tape 1 • Listening to Literature, Audio-cassettes, Side 6; Audio CDs, CD 3 • Got It! Assessment Videotapes, Tape 1 • WG Writing and Grammar iText CD-ROM
• Writing Lesson: Friendly Letter, SE p. 145; WG Writing and Grammar, p. 16	• Listening and Speaking: Poetry Reading, SE p. 145 • Research and Technology: Friendship Dictionary, SE p. 145 • TR Extension Activities, p. 10	• Selection Test, TR Formal Assessment, pp. 36–38 • TR Open Book Test, pp. 28–30 • Writing rubric and Listening and Speaking rubric, TR Performance Assess. and Portfolio Mgmt., pp. 9, 29	• Interest Grabber Videotapes, Tape 1 • Listening to Literature, Audio-cassettes, Side 6; Audio CDs, CD 3 • Got It! Assessment Videotapes, Tape 1 • WG Writing and Grammar iText CD-ROM
• Writing Lesson: Feature Story, SE p. 165; WG Writing and Grammar, p. 134	• Listening and Speaking: Multimedia Presentation, SE p. 165 • Research and Technology: Pet Care Fair, SE p. 165 • TR Extension Activities, p. 11	• Selection Test, TR Formal Assessment, pp. 39–41 • TR Open Book Test, pp. 31–33 • Writing rubric and Listening and Speaking rubric, TR Performance Assess. and Portfolio Mgmt., pp. 12, 24	• Interest Grabber Videotapes, Tape 1 • Listening to Literature, Audio-cassettes, Sides 6–7; Audio CDs, CD 3 • Got It! Assessment Videotapes, Tape 1 • WG Writing and Grammar iText CD-ROM

Program Planner

Selection	Reading	Literary Analysis	Vocabulary	Grammar
from **The Pigman & Me,** Paul Zindel, SE p. 182 Reading Level: Average	• Recognize Word Origins, SE p. 181; TR Selection Support, p. 59; TR Literary Analysis and Reading Transparencies, p. 23	• Internal Conflict, SE p. 181; TR Selection Support, p. 60; TR Literary Analysis and Reading Transparencies, p. 24	• Vocabulary Development, SE p. 181: exact, tactics, undulating, goading, distorted, condemnation, groveled • Latin suffix *-tion,* SE p. 190; TR Selection Support, p. 56	• Adjectives, SE p. 190; TR Selection Support, p. 58; WG Writing and Grammar, p. 330
"Thunder Butte," Virginia Driving Hawk Sneve, SE p. 194 Reading Level: Average	• Understanding Shades of Meaning in Related Words, SE p. 193; TR Selection Support, p. 64; TR Literary Analysis and Reading Transparencies, p. 25	• Atmosphere, SE p. 193; TR Selection Support, p. 65; TR Literary Analysis and Reading Transparencies, p. 26	• Vocabulary Development, SE p. 193: meanderings, diminutive, variegated, heathen, adamant • Forms of *vary,* SE p. 206; TR Selection Support, p. 61	• Adjectives, SE p. 206; TR Selection Support, p. 63; WG Writing and Grammar, p. 330
"Mowgli's Brothers," Rudyard Kipling, SE p. 210 Reading Level: Challenging	• Predicting Characters' Actions, SE p. 209; TR Selection Support, p. 69; TR Literary Analysis and Reading Transparencies, p. 27	• Animal Characters, SE p. 209; TR Selection Support, p. 70; TR Literary Analysis and Reading Transparencies, p. 28	• Vocabulary Development, SE p. 209: scuttled, quarry, fostering, veterans, monotonous, dispute, clamor • Greek Prefix *mono-,* SE p. 220; TR Selection Support, p. 66	• Adverbs, SE p. 220; TR Selection Support, p. 68; WG Writing and Grammar, p. 340
"Names/Nombres," Julia Alvarez, SE p. 224; **"The Southpaw,"** Judith Viorst, SE p. 229; **"Alone in the Nets,"** Arnold Adoff, SE p. 232 Reading Levels: Average, Easy, Easy	• Set a Purpose for Reading, SE p. 223; TR Selection Support, p. 74; TR Literary Analysis and Reading Transparencies, p. 29	• Narrator's Perspective, SE p. 223; TR Selection Support, p. 75; TR Literary Analysis and Reading Transparencies, p. 30	• Vocabulary Development, SE p. 223: transport, initial, inevitably, chaotic, inscribed, opposition, evaporate • Latin Prefix *trans-,* SE p. 236; TR Selection Support, p. 71	• Modifying Adverbs, SE p. 236; TR Selection Support, p. 73; WG Writing and Grammar, p. 340
"Adventures of Isabel," Ogden Nash, SE p. 246; **"I'll Stay,"** Gwendolyn Brooks, SE p. 247; **"Wilbur Wright and Orville Wright,"** Rosemary and Stephen Vincent Benét, SE p. 248; **"Dream Dust,"** Langston Hughes, SE p. 250 Reading Levels: Average, Easy, Average, Challenging	• Use Context to Clarify Meaning, SE p. 245; TR Selection Support, p. 79; TR Literary Analysis and Reading Transparencies, p. 31	• Stanzas, SE p. 245; TR Selection Support, p. 80; TR Literary Analysis and Reading Transparencies, p. 32	• Vocabulary Development, SE p. 245: ravenous, cavernous, rancor, grant • Latin suffix *-ous,* SE p. 252; TR Selection Support, p. 76	• Adjective or Adverb?, SE p. 252; TR Selection Support, p. 78; WG Writing and Grammar, p. 342

Key to Program References: SE: Student Edition **TR:** Teaching Resources **WG:** Writing and Grammar

Unit 3 *Proving Yourself*

Writing	Extension Activities	Assessment	Technology
• Writing Lesson: School Rules, SE p. 191; WG Writing and Grammar, p. 226	• Listening and Speaking: Media Communications, SE p. 191 • Research and Technology: Identify Emotional Appeals, SE p. 191 • Writing: Essay, SE p. 191 • TR Extension Activities, p. 12	• Selection Test, TR Formal Assessment, pp. 50–52 • TR Open Book Test, pp. 34–36 • Writing rubric and Listening and Speaking rubric, TR Performance Assess. and Portfolio Mgmt., p. 22	• Interest Grabber Videotapes, Tape 2 • Listening to Literature, Audiocassettes, Side 8; Audio CDs, CD 3 • Got It! Assessment Videotapes, Tape 2 • WG Writing and Grammar iText CD-ROM
• Writing Lesson: Opinion Paper, SE p. 207; WG Writing and Grammar, p. 132	• Listening and Speaking: Oral Presentation, SE p. 207 • Research and Technology: Sioux Customs, SE p. 207 • Writing: Essay, SE p. 207 • TR Extension Activities, p. 13	• Selection Test, TR Formal Assessment, pp. 53–55 • TR Open Book Test, pp. 37–39 • Writing rubric and Listening and Speaking rubric, TR Performance Assess. and Portfolio Mgmt., p. 11, 29	• Interest Grabber Videotapes, Tape 2 • Listening to Literature, Audiocassettes, Side 9; Audio CDs, CD 4 • Got It! Assessment Videotapes, Tape 2 • WG Writing and Grammar iText CD-ROM
• Writing Lesson: Comparison and Contrast of Characters, SE p. 221; WG Writing and Grammar, p. 154	• Listening and Speaking: Role-Play, SE p. 221 • Research and Technology: Wolf Research, SE p. 221 • TR Extension Activities, p. 14	• Selection Test, TR Formal Assessment, pp. 56–58 • TR Open Book Test, pp. 40–42 • Writing rubric and Listening and Speaking rubric, TR Performance Assess. and Portfolio Mgmt., p. 16	• Interest Grabber Videotapes, Tape 2 • Listening to Literature, Audiocassettes, Side 10; Audio CDs, CD 4 • Got It! Assessment Videotapes, Tape 2 • WG Writing and Grammar iText CD-ROM
• Writing Lesson: Sports Scene, SE p. 237; WG Writing and Grammar, p. 230	• Listening and Speaking: Restate Directions, SE p. 237 • Research and Technology: Presentation, SE p. 237 • Writing: Essay, SE p. 237 • TR Extension Activities, p. 15	• Selection Test, TR Formal Assessment, pp. 59–61 • TR Open Book Test, pp. 43–45 • Writing rubric and Listening and Speaking rubric, TR Performance Assess. and Portfolio Mgmt., p. 21	• Interest Grabber Videotapes, Tape 2 • Listening to Literature, Audiocassettes, Sides 10–11; Audio CDs, CD 4 • Got It! Assessment Videotapes, Tape 2 • WG Writing and Grammar iText CD-ROM
• Writing Lesson: Response to a Poem, SE p. 253; WG Writing and Grammar, p. 250	• Listening and Speaking: Interview, SE p. 253 • Research and Technology: Timeline, SE p. 253 • TR Extension Activities, p. 16	• Selection Test, TR Formal Assessment, pp. 62–64 • TR Open Book Test, pp. 46–48 • Writing rubric and Listening and Speaking rubric, TR Performance Assess. and Portfolio Mgmt., pp. 15, 29	• Interest Grabber Videotapes, Tape 2 • Listening to Literature, Audiocassettes, Side 11; Audio CDs, CD 4 • Got It! Assessment Videotapes, Tape 2 • WG Writing and Grammar iText CD-ROM

Program Planner

Selection	Reading	Literary Analysis	Vocabulary	Grammar
"Lob's Girl," Joan Aiken, SE p. 270; **"The Tiger Who Would Be King,"** James Thurber, SE p. 282; **"The Lion and the Bulls,"** Aesop, SE p. 284 Reading Levels: Average, Average, Easy	• Compare and Contrasting Characters, SE p. 269; TR Selection Support, p. 84; TR Literary Analysis and Reading Transparencies, p. 33	• Foreshadowing, SE p. 269; TR Selection Support, p. 85; TR Literary Analysis and Reading Transparencies, p. 34	• Vocabulary Development, SE p. 269: decisively, atone, resolutions, melancholy, intimated, aggrieved, prowled, repulse, slanderous • Forms of *decide,* SE p. 286; TR Selection Support, p. 81	• Prepositional Phrases, SE p. 286; TR Selection Support, p. 83; WG Writing and Grammar, p. 354
"Greyling," Jane Yolen, SE p. 290 Reading Level: Easy	• Predicting, SE p. 289; TR Selection Support, p. 89; TR Literary Analysis and Reading Transparencies, p. 35	• Conflict and Resolution, SE p. 289; TR Selection Support, p. 90; TR Literary Analysis and Reading Transparencies, p. 36	• Vocabulary Development, SE p. 289: grief, sheared, slough, wallowed • Forms of *grief,* SE p. 296; TR Selection Support, p. 86	• Interjections, SE p. 296; TR Selection Support, p. 88; WG Writing and Grammar, p. 370
"Abuelito Who," Sandra Cisneros, SE p. 300; **"The Open Road,"** Walt Whitman, SE p. 302; **"Life Doesn't Frighten Me,"** Maya Angelou, SE p. 304; **"who knows if the moon's,"** E. E. Cummings, SE p. 306 Reading Levels: Average, Challenging, Average, Easy	• Drawing Inferences, SE p. 299; TR Selection Support, p. 94; TR Literary Analysis and Reading Transparencies, p. 37	• Free Verse, SE p. 299; TR Selection Support, p. 95; TR Literary Analysis and Reading Transparencies, p. 38	• Vocabulary Development, SE p. 299: henceforth, whimper, querulous • Compound Transition Words, SE p. 308; TR Selection Support, p. 91	• Conjunctions, SE p. 308; TR Selection Support, p. 93; WG Writing and Grammar, p. 364
"A Backwoods Boy," Russell Freedman, SE p. 316; **"Jackie Robinson: Justice at Last,"** Geoffrey C. Ward and Ken Burns, SE p. 325 Reading Levels: Challenging, Average	• Determining Main Ideas, SE p. 315; TR Selection Support, p. 99; TR Literary Analysis and Reading Transparencies, p. 39	• Historical Account, SE p. 315; TR Selection Support, p. 100; TR Literary Analysis and Reading Transparencies, p. 40	• Vocabulary Development, SE p. 315: aptitude, intrigued, treacherous, integrate, retaliated • Latin Prefix *re-,* SE p. 330; TR Selection Support, p. 96	• Conjunctions, SE p. 330; TR Selection Support, p. 98; WG Writing and Grammar, p. 364

Key to Program References: SE: Student Edition **TR:** Teaching Resources **WG:** Writing and Grammar

Unit 4 *Seeing It Through*

Writing	Extension Activities	Assessment	Technology
• Writing Lesson: Fable, SE p. 287; WG Writing and Grammar, p. 78	• Listening and Speaking: TV News Program, SE p. 287 • Research and Technology: Annotated List, SE p. 287 • TR Extension Activities, p. 17	• Selection Test, TR Formal Assessment, pp. 73–75 • TR Open Book Test, pp. 49–51 • Writing rubric and Listening and Speaking rubric, TR Performance Assess. and Portfolio Mgmt., pp. 13, 24	• Interest Grabber Videotapes, Tape 2 • Listening to Literature, Audiocassettes, Sides 11–12; Audio CDs, CD 5 • Got It! Assessment Videotapes, Tape 2 • WG Writing and Grammar iText CD-ROM
• Writing Lesson: Letter, SE p. 297; WG Writing and Grammar, p. 134	• Listening and Speaking: Role-Play, SE p. 297 • Research and Technology: Report, SE p. 297 • TR Extension Activities, p. 18	• Selection Test, TR Formal Assessment, pp. 76–78 • TR Open Book Test, pp. 52–54 • Writing rubric and Listening and Speaking rubric, TR Performance Assess. and Portfolio Mgmt., p. 12	• Interest Grabber Videotapes, Tape 2 • Listening to Literature, Audiocassettes, Side 12; Audio CDs, CD 5 • Got It! Assessment Videotapes, Tape 2 • WG Writing and Grammar iText CD-ROM
• Writing Lesson: Portrait, SE p. 309; WG Writing and Grammar, p. 102	• Listening and Speaking: Advertisement Review, SE p. 309 • Research and Technology: Moon Booklet, SE p. 309 • TR Extension Activities, p. 19	• Selection Test, TR Formal Assessment, pp. 79–81 • TR Open Book Test, pp. 55–57 • Writing rubric and Listening and Speaking rubric, TR Performance Assess. and Portfolio Mgmt., pp. 9, 22	• Interest Grabber Videotapes, Tape 2 • Listening to Literature, Audiocassettes, Side 12; Audio CDs, CD 5 • Got It! Assessment Videotapes, Tape 2 • WG Writing and Grammar iText CD-ROM
• Writing Lesson: Writer's Choice, SE p. 331; WG Writing and Grammar, p. 226	• Listening and Speaking: Role-Play, SE p. 331 • Research and Technology: Timeline, SE p. 331 • TR Extension Activities, p. 20	• Selection Test, TR Formal Assessment, pp. 82–84 • TR Open Book Test, pp. 58–60 • Writing rubric and Listening and Speaking rubric, TR Performance Assess. and Portfolio Mgmt., pp. 9, 23	• Interest Grabber Videotapes, Tape 2 • Listening to Literature, Audiocassettes, Sides 12–13; Audio CDs, CD 6 • Got It! Assessment Videotapes, Tape 2 • WG Writing and Grammar iText CD-ROM

Program Planner

Selection	Reading	Literary Analysis	Vocabulary	Grammar
"The Fun They Had," Isaac Asimov, SE p. 352, Reading Level: Easy	• Evaluating the Author's Message, SE p. 351; TR Selection Support, p. 104; TR Literary Analysis and Reading Transparencies, p. 41	• Science Fiction, SE p. 351; TR Selection Support, p. 105; TR Literary Analysis and Reading Transparencies, p. 42	• Vocabulary Development, SE p. 351: calculated, loftily, dispute, nonchalantly • Latin Prefix *non-,* SE p. 358; TR Selection Support, p. 101	• Simple Subjects and Predicates, SE p. 358; TR Selection Support, p. 103; WG Writing and Grammar, p. 380
"A Dream Within a Dream," Edgar Allan Poe, SE p. 366; **"The Spring and the Fall,"** Edna St. Vincent Millay, SE p. 368; **"Ankylosaurus,"** Jack Prelutsky, SE p. 370 Reading Levels: Challenging, Average, Easy	• Drawing Inferences, SE p. 365; TR Selection Support, p. 109; TR Literary Analysis and Reading Transparencies, p. 43	• Rhyme, SE p. 365; TR Selection Support, p. 110; TR Literary Analysis and Reading Transparencies, p. 44	• Vocabulary Development, SE p. 365: deem, bough, raucous, inedible, cudgel • Latin Prefix *in-,* SE p. 372; TR Selection Support, p. 106	• Complete Sentences, SE p. 372; TR Selection Support, p. 108; WG Writing and Grammar, p. 454
from **"Exploring the *Titanic,*"** Robert Ballard, SE p. 380 Reading Level: Average	• Distinguishing Between Fact and Opinion, SE p. 379; TR Selection Support, p. 114; TR Literary Analysis and Reading Transparencies, p. 45	• Suspense, SE p. 379; TR Selection Support, p. 115; TR Literary Analysis and Reading Transparencies, p. 46	• Vocabulary Development, SE p. 379: majestically, collision, novelty, watertight • Compound Adjectives, SE p. 388; TR Selection Support, p. 111	• Types of Sentences, SE p. 388; TR Selection Support, p. 113; WG Writing and Grammar, p. 438
"Breaker's Bridge," Laurence Yep, SE p. 392, Reading Level: Average	• Determining Cause and Effect, SE p. 391; TR Selection Support, p. 119; TR Literary Analysis and Reading Transparencies, p. 47	• Character Traits, SE p. 391; TR Selection Support, p. 120; TR Literary Analysis and Reading Transparencies, p. 48	• Vocabulary Development, SE p. 391: obstacle, writhing, piers, executioner, immortals • Forms of *execute,* SE p. 402; TR Selection Support, p. 116	• Direct and Indirect Objects, SE p. 402; TR Selection Support, p. 118; WG Writing and Grammar, p. 398
"The Loch Ness Monster," George Laycock, SE p. 406; **"Why the Tortoise's Shell Is Not Smooth,"** Chinua Achebe, SE p. 411 Reading Levels: Challenging, Average	• Evaluating Logic and Reasoning, SE p. 405; TR Selection Support, p. 124; TR Literary Analysis and Reading Transparencies, p. 49	• Oral Tradition, SE p. 405; TR Selection Support, p. 125; TR Literary Analysis and Reading Transparencies, p. 50	• Vocabulary Development, SE p. 405: elusive, abundant, famine, orator, eloquent • Forms of *orate,* SE p. 416; TR Selection Support, p. 121	• Subject Complements, SE p. 416; TR Selection Support, p. 123; WG Writing and Grammar, p. 398

Key to Program References: SE: Student Edition **TR:** Teaching Resources **WG:** Writing and Grammar

Unit 5 *Mysterious Worlds*

Writing	Extension Activities	Assessment	Technology
• Writing Lesson: Comparison of School Then and Now, SE p. 359; WG Writing and Grammar, p. 154	• Listening and Speaking: Pros and Cons of Technical Advances, SE p. 359 • Research and Technology: Multimedia Display, SE p. 359 • Writing: Journal Entry, SE p. 359 • TR Extension Activities, p. 21	• Selection Test, TR Formal Assessment, pp. 93–95 • TR Open Book Test, pp. 61–63 • Writing rubric and Listening and Speaking rubric, TR Performance Assess. and Portfolio Mgmt., pp. 16, 29	• Interest Grabber Videotapes, Tape 3 • Listening to Literature, Audiocassettes, Side 13; Audio CDs, CD 6 • Got It! Assessment Videotapes, Tape 3 • WG Writing and Grammar iText CD-ROM
• Writing Lesson: Dinosaur Description, SE p. 373; WG Writing and Grammar, p. 21	• Listening and Speaking: Listening to a Poetry Reading, SE p. 373 • Research and Technology: Research Summary, SE p. 373 • Writing: Interpretation, SE p. 373 • TR Extension Activities, p. 22	• Selection Test, TR Formal Assessment, pp. 96–98 • TR Open Book Test, pp. 64–66 • Writing rubric and Listening and Speaking rubric, TR Performance Assess. and Portfolio Mgmt., p. 9	• Interest Grabber Videotapes, Tape 3 • Listening to Literature, Audiocassettes, Side 13; Audio CDs, CD 6 • Got It! Assessment Videotapes, Tape 3 • WG Writing and Grammar iText CD-ROM
• Writing Lesson: Investigative Report, SE p. 389; WG Writing and Grammar, p. 226	• Listening and Speaking: Identify False and Misleading Information, SE p. 389 • Research and Technology: Create a Timeline, SE p. 389 • TR Extension Activities, p. 23	• Selection Test, TR Formal Assessment, pp. 99–101 • TR Open Book Test, pp. 67–69 • Writing rubric and Listening and Speaking rubric, TR Performance Assess. and Portfolio Mgmt., pp. 14, 22	• Interest Grabber Videotapes, Tape 3 • Listening to Literature, Audiocassettes, Side 14; Audio CDs, CD 6 • Got It! Assessment Videotapes, Tape 3 • WG Writing and Grammar iText CD-ROM
• Writing Lesson: Proposal for Research, SE p. 403; WG Writing and Grammar, p. 226	• Listening and Speaking: Dramatization, SE p. 403 • Research and Technology: Essay, SE p. 403 • Writing: Letter, SE p. 403 • TR Extension Activities, p. 24	• Selection Test, TR Formal Assessment, pp. 102–104 • TR Open Book Test, pp. 70–72 • Writing rubric and Listening and Speaking rubric, TR Performance Assess. and Portfolio Mgmt., pp. 14, 24	• Interest Grabber Videotapes, Tape 3 • Listening to Literature, Audiocassettes, Side 14; Audio CDs, CD 7 • Got It! Assessment Videotapes, Tape 3 • WG Writing and Grammar iText CD-ROM
• Writing Lesson: Invitation to a Feast, SE p. 417; WG Writing and Grammar, p. 102	• Listening and Speaking: Presentation on Nessie, SE p. 417 • Research and Technology: Loch Ness Theory Update Summary, SE p. 417 • TR Extension Activities, p. 25	• Selection Test, TR Formal Assessment, pp. 105–107 • TR Open Book Test, pp. 73–75 • Writing rubric and Listening and Speaking rubric, TR Performance Assess. and Portfolio Mgmt., p. 28	• Interest Grabber Videotapes, Tape 3 • Listening to Literature, Audiocassettes, Side 15; Audio CDs, CD 7 • Got It! Assessment Videotapes, Tape 3 • WG Writing and Grammar iText CD-ROM

Program Planner

Selection	Reading	Literary Analysis	Vocabulary	Grammar
"Dragon, Dragon," John Gardner, SE p. 434 Reading Level: Average	• Comparing and Contrast, SE p. 433; TR Selection Support, p. 129; TR Literary Analysis and Reading Transparencies, p. 51	• Plot, SE p. 433; TR Selection Support, p. 130; TR Literary Analysis and Reading Transparencies, p. 52	• Vocabulary Development, SE p. 433: plagued, ravaged, tyrant, reflecting, craned • Forms of *tyrant,* SE p. 444; TR Selection Support, p. 126	• Clauses, SE p. 444; TR Selection Support, p. 128; WG Writing and Grammar, p. 424
"Becky and the Wheels-and-Brake Boys," James Berry, SE p. 448 Reading Level: Easy	• Predicting, SE p. 447; TR Selection Support, p. 134; TR Literary Analysis and Reading Transparencies, p. 53	• Conflict, SE p. 447; TR Selection Support, p. 135; TR Literary Analysis and Reading Transparencies, p. 54	• Vocabulary Development, SE p. 447: veranda, menace, reckless • Regional Synonyms, SE p. 456; TR Selection Support, p. 131	• Independent Clauses, SE p. 456; TR Selection Support, p. 133; WG Writing and Grammar, p. 424
"Overdoing It," Anton Chekhov, SE p. 60; **"Eleven,"** Sandra Cisneros, SE p. 465 Reading Levels: Challenging, Easy	• Recognizing Word Origins, SE p. 459; TR Selection Support, p. 139; TR Literary Analysis and Reading Transparencies, p. 55	• Characterization, SE p. 459; TR Selection Support, p. 140; TR Literary Analysis and Reading Transparencies, p. 56	• Vocabulary Development, SE p. 459: prolonged, emaciated, wry, foresee, emerged, mediated • Recognizing Commonly Used Foreign Words, SE p. 470; TR Selection Support, p. 136	• Subordinate Clauses, SE p. 470; TR Selection Support, p. 138; WG Writing and Grammar, p. 425
"The Lawyer and the Ghost," Charles Dickens, SE p. 478; **"The Wounded Wolf,"** Jean Craighead George, SE p. 482 Reading Levels: Challenging, Average	• Picturing the Setting, SE p. 477; TR Selection Support, p. 144; TR Literary Analysis and Reading Transparencies, p. 57	• Setting, SE p. 477; TR Selection Support, p. 145; TR Literary Analysis and Reading Transparencies, p. 58	• Vocabulary Development, SE p. 477: sufficient, expend, inconsistent, massive, stoic, gnashes • Latin Prefix *-in,* SE p. 488; TR Selection Support, p. 141	• Simple and Compound Sentences, SE p. 488; TR Selection Support, p. 143; WG Writing and Grammar, p. 426
"The All-American Slurp," Lensey Namioka, SE p. 496; **"The Stone,"** Lloyd Alexander, SE p. 505 Reading Levels: Average, Average	• Drawing Inferences, SE p. 495; TR Selection Support, p. 149; TR Literary Analysis and Reading Transparencies, p. 59	• Theme, SE p. 495; TR Selection Support, p. 150; TR Literary Analysis and Reading Transparencies, p. 60	• Vocabulary Development, SE p. 495: emigrated, etiquette, consumption, plight, jubilation, rue, fallow • Forms of *migrate,* SE p. 514; TR Selection Support, p. 146	• Compound and Complex Sentences, SE p. 514; TR Selection Support, p. 148; WG Writing and Grammar, pp. 427–428

Key to Program References: SE: Student Edition **TR:** Teaching Resources **WG:** Writing and Grammar

Unit 6 *Short Stories*

Writing	Extension Activities	Assessment	Technology
• Writing Lesson: Help-Wanted Ad, SE p. 445; WG Writing and Grammar, p. 132	• Listening and Speaking: Dramatic Reading, SE p. 445 • Research and Technology: Dragons in Literature, SE p. 445 • TR Extension Activities, p. 26	• Selection Test, TR Formal Assessment, pp. 116–118 • TR Open Book Test, pp. 76–78 • Writing rubric and Listening and Speaking rubric, TR Performance Assess. and Portfolio Mgmt., p. 9	• Interest Grabber Videotapes, Tape 3 • Listening to Literature, Audiocassettes, Side 16; Audio CDs, CD 8 • Got It! Assessment Videotapes, Tape 3 • WG Writing and Grammar iText CD-ROM
• Writing Lesson: Journal Entry, SE p. 457; WG Writing and Grammar, p. 84	• Listening and Speaking: Give Directions, SE p. 457 • Research and Technology: Research Bikes for Sale, SE p. 457 • TR Extension Activities, p. 27	• Selection Test, TR Formal Assessment, pp. 119–121 • TR Open Book Test, pp. 79–81 • Writing rubric and Listening and Speaking rubric, TR Performance Assess. and Portfolio Mgmt., pp. 13, 14	• Interest Grabber Videotapes, Tape 3 • Listening to Literature, Audiocassettes, Side 16; Audio CDs, CD 8 • Got It! Assessment Videotapes, Tape 3 • WG Writing and Grammar iText CD-ROM
• Writing Lesson: Character Description, SE p. 471; WG Writing and Grammar, p. 106	• Listening and Speaking: Group Discussion, SE p. 471 • Research and Technology: Chart, SE p. 471 • TR Extension Activities, p. 28	• Selection Test, TR Formal Assessment, pp. 122–124 • TR Open Book Test, pp. 82–84 • Writing rubric and Listening and Speaking rubric, TR Performance Assess. and Portfolio Mgmt., pp. 9, 29	• Interest Grabber Videotapes, Tape 3 • Listening to Literature, Audiocassettes, Side 17; Audio CDs, CD 8 • Got It! Assessment Videotapes, Tape 3 • WG Writing and Grammar iText CD-ROM
• Writing Lesson: Annotated Bibliography, SE p. 489; WG Writing and Grammar, p. 226	• Listening and Speaking: Presentation on Wolves, SE p. 489 • Research and Technology: Historical Setting, SE p. 489 • TR Extension Activities, p. 29	• Selection Test, TR Formal Assessment, pp. 125–127 • TR Open Book Test, pp. 85–87 • Writing rubric and Listening and Speaking rubric, TR Performance Assess. and Portfolio Mgmt., p. 27	• Interest Grabber Videotapes, Tape 3 • Listening to Literature, Audiocassettes, Side 17; Audio CDs, CD 8 • Got It! Assessment Videotapes, Tape 3 • WG Writing and Grammar iText CD-ROM
• Writing Lesson: Story Plot, SE p. 515; WG Writing and Grammar, p. 78	• Listening and Speaking: Oral Response, SE p. 515 • Research and Technology: Human Growth Report, SE p. 515 • TR Extension Activities, p. 30	• Selection Test, TR Formal Assessment, pp. 128–130 • TR Open Book Test, pp. 88–90 • Writing rubric and Listening and Speaking rubric, TR Performance Assess. and Portfolio Mgmt., pp. 13, 29	• Interest Grabber Videotapes, Tape 3 • Listening to Literature, Audiocassettes, Side 18; Audio CDs, CD 9 • Got It! Assessment Videotapes, Tape 3 • WG Writing and Grammar iText CD-ROM

Program Planner

Selection	Reading	Literary Analysis	Vocabulary	Grammar
"The Shutout," Patricia C. McKissack and Frederick McKissack, Jr., SE p. 532 Reading Level: Average	• Clarifying the Author's Meaning, SE p. 531; TR Selection Support, p. 154; TR Literary Analysis and Reading Transparencies, p. 61	• Historical Essay, SE p. 531; TR Selection Support, p. 155; TR Literary Analysis and Reading Transparencies, p. 62	• Vocabulary Development, SE p. 531: anecdotes, evolved, diverse, composed, irrational • Latin Prefix *ir-,* SE p. 538; TR Selection Support, p. 151	• Compound and Complex Sentences, SE p. 538; TR Selection Support, p. 153; WG Writing and Grammar, pp. 427–428
"Letter to Scottie," F. Scott Fitzgerald, SE p. 542; **"Olympic Diary,"** Amanda Borden, SE p. 545 Reading Levels: Easy, Average	• Understanding the Author's Purpose, SE p. 541; TR Selection Support, p. 159; TR Literary Analysis and Reading Transparencies, p. 63	• Letters and Journals, SE p. 541; TR Selection Support, p. 160; TR Literary Analysis and Reading Transparencies, p. 64	• Vocabulary Development, SE p. 541: documentation, intrigued, compulsory • Forms of *document,* SE p. 550; TR Selection Support, p. 156	• Subject and Object Pronouns, SE p. 550; TR Selection Support, p. 158; WG Writing and Grammar, pp. 508–509
"My Papa, Mark Twain," Susy Clemens, SE p. 554; **"The Drive-In Movies,"** Gary Soto, SE p. 558; **"Space Shuttle *Challenger,*"** William Harwood, SE p. 562 Reading Levels: Easy, Average, Challenging	• Author's Evidence, SE p. 553; TR Selection Support, p. 164; TR Literary Analysis and Reading Transparencies, p. 65	• Biography and Autobiography, SE p. 553; TR Selection Support, p. 165; TR Literary Analysis and Reading Transparencies, p. 66	• Vocabulary Development, SE p. 553: incessantly, consequently, monitoring, accumulations, moot, peripheral, catastrophic • Latin Root *-sequi-,* SE p. 568; TR Selection Support, p. 161	• Writing Proper Nouns, SE p. 568; TR Selection Support, p. 163; WG Writing and Grammar, p. 600
"Restoring the Circle," Joseph Bruchac, SE p. 572; **"How the Internet Works,"** Kerry Cochrane, SE p. 576; **"Turkeys,"** Bailey White, SE p. 580 Reading Levels: Challenging, Average, Easy	• Using Context to Determine Meaning, SE p. 571; TR Selection Support, p. 169; TR Literary Analysis and Reading Transparencies, p. 67	• Types of Essays, SE p. 571; TR Selection Support, p. 170; TR Literary Analysis and Reading Transparencies, p. 68	• Vocabulary Development, SE p. 571: tolerance, detrimental, dilution, vigilance • Forms of *tolerate,* SE p. 586; TR Selection Support, p. 166	• Punctuation and Capitalization in Dialogue, SE p. 586; TR Selection Support, p. 168; WG Writing and Grammar, p. 89

Key to Program References: SE: Student Edition **TR:** Teaching Resources **WG:** Writing and Grammar

Unit 7 *Nonfiction*

Writing	Extension Activities	Assessment	Technology
• Writing Lesson: Researched Response, SE p. 539; WG Writing and Grammar, p. 226	• Listening and Speaking: Presentation, SE p. 539 • Research and Technology: Timeline, SE p. 539 • Writing: Summary, SE p. 539 • TR Extension Activities, p. 31	• Selection Test, TR Formal Assessment, pp. 139–141 • TR Open Book Test, pp. 91–93 • Writing rubric and Listening and Speaking rubric, TR Performance Assess. and Portfolio Mgmt., pp. 14, 29	• Interest Grabber Videotapes, Tape 4 • Listening to Literature, Audiocassettes, Side 19; Audio CDs, CD 9 • Got It! Assessment Videotapes, Tape 4 • WG Writing and Grammar iText CD-ROM
• Writing Lesson: Letter to an Author, SE p. 551; WG Writing and Grammar, p. 250	• Listening and Speaking: Oral Presentation, SE p. 551 • Research and Technology: Olympic Presentation, SE p. 551 • Writing: Journal Entry, SE p. 551 • TR Extension Activities, p. 32	• Selection Test, TR Formal Assessment, pp. 142–144 • TR Open Book Test, pp. 94–96 • Writing rubric and Listening and Speaking rubric, TR Performance Assess. and Portfolio Mgmt., pp. 15, 27	• Interest Grabber Videotapes, Tape 4 • Listening to Literature, Audiocassettes, Side 19; Audio CDs, CD 9 • Got It! Assessment Videotapes, Tape 4 • WG Writing and Grammar iText CD-ROM
• Writing Lesson: Autobiographical Narrative, SE p. 569; WG Writing and Grammar, p. 82	• Listening and Speaking: Watch a Newscast, SE p. 569 • Research and Technology: Character Poster, SE p. 569 • Writing: Response, SE p. 569 • TR Extension Activities, p. 33	• Selection Test, TR Formal Assessment, pp. 145–147 • TR Open Book Test, pp. 97–99 • Writing rubric, TR Performance Assess. and Portfolio Mgmt., p. 8	• Interest Grabber Videotapes, Tape 4 • Listening to Literature, Audiocassettes, Sides 19–20; Audio CDs, CDs 9–10 • Got It! Assessment Videotapes, Tape 4 • WG Writing and Grammar iText CD-ROM
• Writing Lesson: Compare and Contrast Composition, SE p. 587; WG Writing and Grammar, p. 158	• Listening and Speaking: Directions for Using a Computer, SE p. 587 • Research and Technology: Research Native American Authors, SE p. 587 • Writing: Letter, SE p. 587 • TR Extension Activities, p. 34	• Selection Test, TR Formal Assessment, pp. 148–150 • TR Open Book Test, pp. 100–102 • Writing rubric and Listening and Speaking rubric, TR Performance Assess. and Portfolio Mgmt., pp. 16, 21	• Interest Grabber Videotapes, Tape 4 • Listening to Literature, Audiocassettes, Side 20; Audio CDs, CD 10 • Got It! Assessment Videotapes, Tape 4 • WG Writing and Grammar iText CD-ROM

Program Planner

Selection	Reading	Literary Analysis	Vocabulary	Grammar
"The Phantom Tollbooth, Act I," Susan Nanus, SE p. 614 Reading Level: Average	• Summarizing, SE p. 613; TR Selection Support, p. 174; TR Literary Analysis and Reading Transparencies, p. 69	• Elements of Drama, SE p. 613; TR Selection Support, p. 175; TR Literary Analysis and Reading Transparencies, p. 70	• Vocabulary Development, SE p. 613: ignorance, precautionary, misapprehension • Latin Prefix *pre-,* SE p. 635; TR Selection Support, p. 171	• Subject and Verb Agreement, SE p. 635; TR Selection Support, p. 173; WG Writing and Grammar, p. 520
"The Phantom Tollbooth, Act II," Susan Nanus, SE p. 637 Reading Level: Average	• Recognizing Word-Play, SE p. 636; TR Selection Support, p. 179; TR Literary Analysis and Reading Transparencies, p. 71	• Theme, SE p. 636; TR Selection Support, p. 180; TR Literary Analysis and Reading Transparencies, p. 72	• Vocabulary Development, SE p. 636: dissonance, admonishing, iridescent, malicious • Latin Root *-son-*, SE p. 662; TR Selection Support, p. 176	• Indefinite Pronouns, SE p. 662; TR Selection Support, p. 178; WG Writing and Grammar, p. 524
"Grandpa and the Statue," Arthur Miller, SE p. 666 Reading Level: Average	• Distinguishing Fact and Fantasy, SE p. 665; TR Selection Support, p. 184; TR Literary Analysis and Reading Transparencies, p. 73	• Dialogue, SE p. 665; TR Selection Support, p. 185; TR Literary Analysis and Reading Transparencies, p. 74	• Vocabulary Development, SE p. 665: subscribed, peeved, uncomprehending, tempest • Latin Root *-scrib-,* SE p. 682; TR Selection Support, p. 181	• Pronoun and Antecedent Agreement, SE p. 682; TR Selection Support, p. 183; WG Writing and Grammar, p. 528

Key to Program References: SE: Student Edition **TR:** Teaching Resources **WG:** Writing and Grammar

Unit 8 *Drama*

Writing	Extension Activities	Assessment	Technology
• Writing Lesson: Letter from Milo, SE p. 635; WG Writing and Grammar, p. 520	• Listening and Speaking: Speech, SE p. 635 • TR Extension Activities, p. 35	• Selection Test, TR Formal Assessment, pp. 159–161 • TR Open Book Test, pp. 103–105 • Listening and Speaking rubric, TR Performance Assess. and Portfolio Mgmt., p. 25	• Interest Grabber Videotapes, Tape 4 • Listening to Literature, Audiocassettes, Sides 21–22; Audio CDs, CD 11 • Got It! Assessment Videotapes, Tape 41 • WG Writing and Grammar iText CD-ROM
• Writing Lesson: Drama Review, SE p. 663; WG Writing and Grammar, p. 250	• Listening and Speaking: Debate, SE p. 663 • Research and Technology: Big Numbers, SE p. 663 • Writing: Summary, SE p. 663 • TR Extension Activities, p. 36	• Selection Test, TR Formal Assessment, pp. 162–164 • TR Open Book Test, pp. 106–108 • Writing rubric and Listening and Speaking rubric, TR Performance Assess. and Portfolio Mgmt., pp. 15, 22	• Interest Grabber Videotapes, Tape 4 • Listening to Literature, Audiocassettes, Sides 23–24; Audio CDs, CD 12 • Got It! Assessment Videotapes, Tape 4 • WG Writing and Grammar iText CD-ROM
• Writing Lesson: Position Paper, SE p. 683; WG Writing and Grammar, p. 132	• Listening and Speaking: Reader's Theater, SE p. 683 • Research and Technology: Liberty Island Fair, SE p. 683 • Writing: Explanation, SE p. 683 • TR Extension Activities, p. 37	• Selection Test, TR Formal Assessment, pp. 165–167 • TR Open Book Test, pp. 106–108 • Writing rubric and Listening and Speaking rubric, TR Performance Assess. and Portfolio Mgmt., pp. 11, 23	• Interest Grabber Videotapes, Tape 4 • Listening to Literature, Audiocassettes, Side 25; Audio CDs, CD 13 • Got It! Assessment Videotapes, Tape 4 • WG Writing and Grammar iText CD-ROM

Program Planner

Selection	Reading	Literary Analysis	Vocabulary	Grammar
"The Geese," Richard Peck, SE p. 706; **"Jimmy Jet and His TV Set,"** Shel Silverstein, SE p. 707; **"The Walrus and the Carpenter,"** Lewis Carroll, SE p. 708 Reading Levels: Average, Average, Average	• Identifying the Speaker, SE p. 705; TR Selection Support, p. 189; TR Literary Analysis and Reading Transparencies, p. 75	• Narrative and Lyric Poetry, SE p. 705; TR Selection Support, p. 190; TR Literary Analysis and Reading Transparencies, p. 76	• Vocabulary Development, SE p. 705: lean, antennae, beseech • Using Multiple Meanings, SE p. 714; TR Selection Support, p. 186	• Comparisons With Adjectives and Adverbs, SE p. 714; TR Selection Support, p. 188; WG Writing and Grammar, p. 538
"The Sidewalk Racer," Lillian Morrison, SE p. 718; **"Haiku,"** Bashō, SE p. 720; **"Limerick,"** Anonymous, SE p. 720 Reading Levels: Easy, Easy, Easy	• Using Your Senses, SE p. 717; TR Selection Support, p. 194; TR Literary Analysis and Reading Transparencies, p. 77	• Special Forms of Poetry, SE p. 717; TR Selection Support, p. 195; TR Literary Analysis and Reading Transparencies, p. 78	• Vocabulary Development, SE p. 717: skimming, flue, flee, flaw • Homophones, SE p. 722; TR Selection Support, p. 191	• Irregular Comparisons, SE p. 722; TR Selection Support, p. 193; WG Writing and Grammar, p. 538
"Wind and water and stone," Octavio Paz, SE p. 726; **"February Twilight,"** Sara Teasdale, SE p. 727; **"The Fairies' Lullaby,"** William Shakespeare, SE p. 728; **"Cynthia in the Snow,"** Gwendolyn Brooks, SE p. 729; **"Parade,"** Rachel Field, SE p. 730 Reading Levels: Average, Average, Challenging, Average, Average	• Reading According to Punctuation, SE p. 725; TR Selection Support, p. 199; TR Literary Analysis and Reading Transparencies, p. 79	• Sound Devices, SE p. 725; TR Selection Support, p. 200; TR Literary Analysis and Reading Transparencies, p. 80	• Vocabulary Development, SE p. 725: nigh, offense, hence, gilded, leisurely • Suffix *-ly*, SE p. 732; TR Selection Support, p. 196	• Commas and Semicolons, SE p. 732; TR Selection Support, p. 198; WG Writing and Grammar, pp. 564, 574
"Simile: Willow and Ginkgo," Eve Merriam, SE p. 740; **"Fame Is a Bee,"** Emily Dickinson, SE p. 741; **"April Rain Song,"** Langston Hughes, SE p. 742 Reading Levels: Average, Average, Average	• Paraphrasing, SE p. 739; TR Selection Support, p. 204; TR Literary Analysis and Reading Transparencies, p. 81	• Figurative Language, SE p. 739; TR Selection Support, p. 205; TR Literary Analysis and Reading Transparencies, p. 82	• Vocabulary Development, SE p. 739: soprano, chorus • Musical words, SE p. 744; TR Selection Support, p. 201	• Colons, SE p. 744; TR Selection Support, p. 203; WG Writing and Grammar, p. 574

Key to Program References: SE: Student Edition **TR:** Teaching Resources **WG:** Writing and Grammar

Unit 9 *Poetry*

Writing	Extension Activities	Assessment	Technology
• Writing Lesson: Story With Dialogue, SE p. 715; WG Writing and Grammar, p. 85	• Listening and Speaking: Persuasive Presentation, SE p. 715 • Research and Technology: Invention of the Television, SE p. 715 • Writing: Literary Response, SE p. 715 • TR Extension Activities, p. 38	• Selection Test, TR Formal Assessment, pp. 176–178 • TR Open Book Test, pp. 112–114 • Writing rubric and Listening and Speaking rubric, TR Performance Assess. and Portfolio Mgmt., pp. 13, 27	• Interest Grabber Videotapes, Tape 5 • Listening to Literature, Audiocassettes, Side 25; Audio CDs, CD 13 • Got It! Assessment Videotapes, Tape 5 • WG Writing and Grammar iText CD-ROM
• Writing Lesson: Limerick, SE p. 723; WG Writing and Grammar, p. 78	• Listening and Speaking: Oral Response, SE p. 723 • Research and Technology: Create a Poem, SE p. 723 • TR Extension Activities, p. 39	• Selection Test, TR Formal Assessment, pp. 179–181 • TR Open Book Test, pp. 115–117 • Writing rubric and Listening and Speaking rubric, TR Performance Assess. and Portfolio Mgmt., p. 28	• Interest Grabber Videotapes, Tape 5 • Listening to Literature, Audiocassettes, Sides 25–26; Audio CDs, CD 13 • Got It! Assessment Videotapes, Tape 5 • WG Writing and Grammar iText CD-ROM
• Writing Lesson: Response to a Poem, SE p. 733; WG Writing and Grammar, p. 257	• Listening and Speaking: Listen and Analyze, SE p. 733 • Research and Technology: Résumé, SE p. 733 • TR Extension Activities, p. 40	• Selection Test, TR Formal Assessment, pp. 182–184 • TR Open Book Test, pp. 118–120 • Writing rubric and Listening and Speaking rubric, TR Performance Assess. and Portfolio Mgmt., p. 15	• Interest Grabber Videotapes, Tape 5 • Listening to Literature, Audiocassettes, Side 26; Audio CDs, CD 13 • Got It! Assessment Videotapes, Tape 5 • WG Writing and Grammar iText CD-ROM
• Writing Lesson: Description, SE p. 745; WG Writing and Grammar, p. 102	• Listening and Speaking: Explanations, SE p. 745 • Research and Technology: Multimedia Report on Trees, SE p. 745 • Writing: Poem, SE p. 745 • TR Extension Activities, p. 41	• Selection Test, TR Formal Assessment, pp. 185–187 • TR Open Book Test, pp. 121–123 • Writing rubric and Listening and Speaking rubric, TR Performance Assess. and Portfolio Mgmt., p. 29	• Interest Grabber Videotapes, Tape 5 • Listening to Literature, Audiocassettes, Side 26; Audio CDs, CD 13 • Got It! Assessment Videotapes, Tape 5 • WG Writing and Grammar iText CD-ROM

Program Planner

Selection	Reading	Literary Analysis	Vocabulary	Grammar
"The Ant and the Dove," Leo Tolstoy, SE p. 764; **"He Lion, Bruh Bear, and Bruh Rabbit,"** Virginia Hamilton, SE p. 765; **"Señor Coyote and the Tricked Trickster,"** I. G. Edmonds, SE p. 770 Reading Levels: Easy, Average, Average	• Recognize the Storyteller's Purpose, SE p. 763; TR Selection Support, p. 209; TR Literary Analysis and Reading Transparencies, p. 83	• Folk Tales, SE p. 763; TR Selection Support, p. 210; TR Literary Analysis and Reading Transparencies, p. 84	• Vocabulary Development, SE p. 763: startled, lair, cordial, ungrateful, reproachfully, indignantly • Forms of *dignity,* SE p. 776; TR Selection Support, p. 206	• Using Capitals for Titles of People, SE p. 776; TR Selection Support, p. 208; WG Writing and Grammar p. 600
"Why Monkeys Live in Trees," Julius Lester, SE p. 780; **"Arachne,"** Olivia E. Coolidge, SE p. 784; **"The Three Wishes,"** Ricardo E. Alegria, SE p. 789; **"A Crippled Boy,"** My-Van Tran, SE p. 791 Reading Levels: Easy, Challenging, Average, Average	• Making Predictions, SE p. 779; TR Selection Support, p. 214; TR Literary Analysis and Reading Transparencies, p. 85	• Oral Tradition, SE p. 779; TR Selection Support, p. 215; TR Literary Analysis and Reading Transparencies, p. 86	• Vocabulary Development, SE p. 779: obscure, mortal, obstinacy, embraced, covetousness • Latin Root *-mort-,* SE p. 802; TR Selection Support, p. 211	• Variety in Sentence Structure and Style, SE p. 794; TR Selection Support, p. 213; WG Writing and Grammar p. 424

Key to Program References: SE: Student Edition **TR:** Teaching Resources **WG:** Writing and Grammar

Unit 10 *The Oral Tradition*

Writing	Extension Activities	Assessment	Technology
• Writing Lesson: Folk Tale, SE p. 777; WG Writing and Grammar, pp. 74–97	• Listening and Speaking: Oral Presentation, SE p. 777 • Research and Technology: Research and Presentation on Folk Art, SE p. 777 • Writing: Explanation, SE p. 777 • TR Extension Activities, p. 42	• Selection Test, TR Formal Assessment, pp. 196–198 • TR Open Book Test, pp. 124–126 • Writing rubric and Listening and Speaking rubric, TR Performance Assess. and Portfolio Mgmt., pp. 13, 29	• Interest Grabber Videotapes, Tape 5 • Listening to Literature, Audiocassettes, Side 27; Audio CDs, CD 13 • Got It! Assessment Videotapes, Tape 5 • WG Writing and Grammar iText CD-ROM
• Writing Lesson: Ancient Theme in a Modern Setting, SE p. 795; WG Writing and Grammar, pp. 74–97	• Listening and Speaking: Oral Presentation, SE p. 795 • Research and Technology: Tales in the Oral Tradition, SE p. 795 • TR Extension Activities, p. 43	• Selection Test, TR Formal Assessment, pp. 199–201 • TR Open Book Test, pp. 127–129 • Writing rubric and Listening and Speaking rubric, TR Performance Assess. and Portfolio Mgmt., pp. 13, 29	• Interest Grabber Videotapes, Tape 5 • Listening to Literature, Audiocassettes, Sides 27–28; Audio CDs, CD 14 • Got It! Assessment Videotapes, Tape 5 • WG Writing and Grammar iText CD-ROM

Unit Features

Unit	How to Read Literature	Reading Informational Materials	Writing Workshop	Listening and Speaking Workshop	Assessment Workshop
1 Growing and Changing	Literal Comprehension Strategies, p. 3	Newspaper Articles, p. 82; Interviews, p. 86	Narration: Autobiographical Writing, p. 90	Organizing and Giving a Narrative Presentation, p. 94	Distinguishing Multiple Meanings, p. 95
2 Reaching Out	Literal Comprehension Strategies, p. 99	Interviews, p. 149; Reviews, p. 166	Description: Descriptive Essay, p. 170	Evaluating Persuasive Messages, p. 174	Identifying and Supporting Main Ideas, p. 175
3 Proving Yourself	Interactive Reading Strategies, p. 179	Applications, p. 239; Cause-and-Effect Articles, p. 254	Expository Writing: Problem-Solution Essay, p. 258	Presenting a Problem-Solution Proposal, p. 262	Identifying Main Idea, p. 263
4 Seeing It Through	Strategies to Construct Meaning, p. 267	Magazine Articles, p. 332; Persuasive Speeches, p. 336	Persuasion: Persuasive Composition, p. 340	Delivering a Persuasive Speech, p. 344	Identifying Cause and Effect, p. 345
5 Mysterious Worlds	Strategies to Read Critically, p. 349	Web Sites and Web Pages, p. 374; Social Studies Texts, p. 418	Expository Writing: Cause-and-Effect Essay, p. 422	Following Oral Directions, p. 426	Draw Conclusions, p. 427
6 Short Stories	Strategies for Reading Fiction, p. 431	Magazine Articles, p. 490; Book Reviews, p. 516	Narration: Short Story, p. 520	Identifying Tone, Mood, and Emotion, p. 524	Describing Plot, Setting, Character, and Mood, p. 525
7 Nonfiction	Strategies for Reading Nonfiction, p. 529	Textbooks, p. 592; Research Report, p. 596	Research: Research Report, p. 600	Delivering a Research Presentation, p. 606	Distinguishing Fact and Opinion, p. 607
8 Drama	Strategies for Reading Drama, p. 611	Newspaper Feature Articles, p. 686; How-to Essay, p. 690	Response to Literature, p. 694	Delivering an Oral Response to Literature, p. 698	Sentence Construction, p. 699
9 Poetry	Strategies for Reading Poetry, p. 703	Literary Backgrounds, p. 734; Comparison-and-Contrast Articles, p. 748	Exposition: Comparison-and-Contrast Essay, p. 752	Engaging Listeners, p. 756	Identifying Appropriate Usage, p. 757
10 The Oral Tradition	Strategies for Reading Folk Literature, p. 761	Comparison-and-Contrast Articles, p. 798; Web Sites, p. 803	Research: Multimedia Report, p. 806	Using Visual Aids, p. 810	Spelling, Capitalization, Punctuation, p. 811

From the Classroom: Strategies for Success

How do we teach the literature we love and still prepare students for high-stakes standardized tests?

The recent emphasis on state and national standards has increased the demands on teachers. Language arts instructors face a daunting balancing act in the classroom. We asked teachers who use *Prentice Hall Literature* for practical advice on confronting this challenge. Here are some of their responses.

Using the Student Edition

Make Cross-Curricular Connections Since I teach both world geography and world literature, my challenge is to open students' minds and hearts to diverse global viewpoints *while* preparing them to perform well on high-stakes standardized tests. In my classroom, I often pair Prentice Hall social studies texts with *Prentice Hall Literature.* The former points out how cultures are shaped by their geography; the latter provides thought-provoking excerpts from diverse classic works. What's more, Prentice Hall's well-rounded package of humanities enrichment materials adds depth and breadth to students' understanding of other cultures.

We must help students "read to understand" to succeed on standardized tests and to succeed in an integrated global society. Thanks to Prentice Hall, one does not have to be sacrificed for the other.

John Ludy
Fremont High School
Fremont, IN

Develop Themes I divide state standards into categories of concepts and themes. I then develop units around these themes. Prentice Hall textbooks provide me with ideas and literature selections to include in each unit. I simply choose the one main concept I want to focus on and center the unit on that particular work. This process connects literary works to specific state standards, while also making these works relevant to students' lives.

Agathaniki (Niki) Locklear
Simon Kenton High School
Independence, KY

Extend Learning I often use the Extension Activities in *Prentice Hall Literature* as resources for research and writing activities that connect with post-scholastic, "real world" problems. The challenge is to find an appropriate degree of difficulty for my students. I view the assignment in the Student Edition as a framework that I adjust to meet the identified objectives.

John Scott
Middlesex High School
Saluda, VA

Maximize Resources Prentice Hall has developed a cohesive program of reading selections, connections to extend meaning, skills lessons, vocabulary study, and grammatical and literary studies that provide the teacher with everything needed to promote learning and ensure students' success on standardized tests.

Martha L. Wildman
Lynn Middle School
Las Cruces, NM

Make Connections Prentice Hall's literary selections come complete with sidebars on reading strategies, literary analysis, critical viewing, vocabulary, and literature in context. I use these prompts as motivational hooks, mini-lessons, or assignment prompts. Such features help my students make meaningful connections in an effort to raise their test scores as well as their awareness of the world of ideas, language, and literature.

Charles E. Youngs
Bethel Park High School
Bethel Park, PA

Use Poetry for Practice Here's an idea to try with students who need help with handling poetry on a standardized test. Put a poem on the overhead for the students to see. As a class, read the poem twice, and then give students 7 to 10 minutes to write about the poem's structure and the ideas it conveys. When students have finished writing, comment quickly on structural and thematic issues, asking students to jot down any important points that they did not include in their own responses. As the year goes on, ask students to write longer responses. All *Prentice Hall Literature* textbooks have dozens of useful poems for this literature/high-stakes testing exercise.

Helen Mundy Hudson
Crawfordsville High School
Crawfordsville, IN

Using the Ancillaries

☑ **Monitor Progress** As a former language arts teacher, I have learned that familiarity doth breed . . . success! By using the Selection Tests in the *Formal Assessment* booklet, students become more comfortable with the accepted standardized test format—multiple choice. This workbook helps students not only learn to recognize the language of multiple-choice testing, but also to use the language to guide them in the process of elimination. Class time should be devoted to reviewing the test items and focusing on the specific language of the discriminators. This will increase students' comfort level and better prepare them for a variety of testing experiences.

In addition, the Literary Terms Handbook in the back of the Student Edition is a valuable resource that few make adequate use of.

Helen Spaith
Franklin Heights High School
Columbus, OH

☑ **Use Labels** An aspect of the Prentice Hall materials that I find very helpful is the labeling that accompanies the Thinking About the Selection questions in the Student Edition. These labels help students gain a better understanding of the language of standardized testing as it pertains to recalling, inferring, analyzing, evaluating, and extending information. Prentice Hall also provides materials for less proficient readers, allowing them to increase their level of understanding rather than struggling and becoming frustrated. Finally, Prentice Hall makes materials available on the Internet, allowing students to perform self-assessments and explore information without the time constraints of the classroom.

Holly Carr
Central Crossing High School
Grove City, OH

☑ **Review and Assess** Once students have read a selection in *Prentice Hall Literature* and we have reviewed the skills in focus, I assign the corresponding workbook pages in the *Selection Support: Skills Development Workbook.* Most of the time I allow students to work in pairs or groups. After students have completed the pages, we review and make any necessary corrections. Later these pages become study sheets for test preparation, as the pages can be easily removed from the workbook. Using the Resource Pro, I then design student tests. One of the best features of this portion of the CD-ROM is that the test questions include questions on the vocabulary, grammar, and literary analysis covered in the selection and practiced in the workbook.

Gail Hacker
North Charleston High School
North Charleston, SC

Using the Critical Viewing Questions

☑ **Practice Paragraph Development** One way that I help students prepare for standardized testing is to work on paragraph development. I use artwork in the Student Edition to give the students something to work from. The Critical Viewing question provides the writing prompt, and I show students on the overhead or the chalkboard how to turn the prompt into the topic sentence for a paragraph that answers the question. Then, I ask that students help me develop a paragraph that provides three pieces of evidence to support the topic sentence. This exercise can lead to stronger essays of the kind often asked for with free-responses or reading comprehension on state assessments.

Steve Thalheimer
Laurenceburg High School
Laurenceburg, IN

☑ **Use Picture Prompts** Although I have used *Prentice Hall Literature* consistently as a reading resource and teaching tool, I have found it useful in another invaluable way. The photographs and fine art in the Student Edition can be used as picture prompts, providing students with writing practice for standardized tests.

Linda Fund
Ezra L. Nolan Middle School
Jersey City, NJ

☑ **Analyze Art** Initially, one of the most challenging language arts standards for me to teach was viewing and representing. However, the fine art and Critical Viewing questions in *Prentice Hall Literature* have made this standard much more attainable. I select paintings from each unit in *Prentice Hall Literature* for my students to analyze critically. For example, my students view *Washington Crossing the Delaware* by Emanuel Gottlieb Leutze and answer questions about the setting, mood, and conflict. They then draw conclusions and make inferences about the action in the painting. This task covers an array of learning expectations and helps to prepare students for standardized tests. The questions for these assignments can be objective like most standardized tests or subjective to help students develop writing skills. Perhaps the best outcome is that my students now love "reading" art!

Cathy Robbs
Chattanooga Central High School
Harrison, TN

PRENTICE HALL LITERATURE

Timeless Voices, Timeless Themes

COPPER LEVEL

Upper Saddle River, New Jersey
Needham, Massachusetts

ISBN 0-13-180430-8

2 3 4 5 6 7 8 9 10 08 07 06 05 04

Cover: *The Haystacks,* oil on canvas, Vincent van Gogh/Nationalmuseum, Stockholm, Sweden/Bridgeman Art Library, London/New York

ACKNOWLEDGMENTS

Grateful acknowledgment is made to the following for permission to reprint copyrighted material:

Airmont Publishing Company, Inc. "Water" from *The Story of My Life* by Helen Keller. Copyright © 1965 by Airmont Publishing Company, Inc. Reprinted by permission of Airmont Publishing Company, Inc.

Ricardo E. Alegría "The Three Wishes" from *The Three Wishes: A Collection of Puerto Rican Folktales,* selected and adapted by Ricardo E. Alegría, translated by Elizabeth Culbert. Reprinted by permission of the author.

Archaeological Institute of America (Newsbrief) "Human Footprints at Chauvet Cave" by Spencer P. M. Harrington, *Archaeology,* Volume 52, Number 5, 1999. Reprinted with the permission of *Archaeology* Magazine, Vol. 52, No. 5 (Copyright the Archaeological Institute of America, 1999).

A. H. Belo Corp., The Dallas Morning News From "Chinese immigrants remember detention at Angel Island" by Esther Wu, from *The Dallas Morning News,* May 19, 2000. Used by permission.

Susan Bergholz Literary Services From "Something to Declare to My Readers" by Julia Alvarez. Copyright © 1982, 1998 by Julia Alvarez. Published in *Something to Declare,* Algonquin Books of Chapel Hill, 1998. "Eleven" from *Woman Hollering Creek,* by Sandra Cisneros. Copyright © 1991 by Sandra Cisneros. Published by Vintage Books, a division of Random House, Inc., New York and originally in hardcover by Random House, Inc. New York. "Names/Nombres," by Julia Alvarez. Copyright © 1985 by Julia Alvarez. First published in *Nuestro.* March, 1985. Reprinted by permission of Susan Bergholz Literary Services, New York. All rights reserved.

Georges Borchardt, Inc., for the Estate of John Gardner "Dragon, Dragon" from *Dragon, Dragon and Other Tales* by John Gardner. Copyright © 1975 by Boskydell Artists Ltd. Reprinted by permission of Georges Borchardt, Inc., for the Estate of John Gardner.

Amanda Borden and ESPN Internet Group "Olympic Diary " by Amanda Borden, from ESPNET *Sportzone/1996 Olympic Diaries/Gymnastics.* Copyright © 1996, 1997 ESPN, Inc. Used by permission.

Brandt & Hochman Literary Agents, Inc. "Lob's Girl," from *A Whisper in the Night* by Joan Aiken, copyright © 1984 by Joan Aiken Enterprises, Ltd. "Wilbur Wright and Orville Wright" by Rosemary Benét and Stephen Vincent Benét, from *A Book of Americans* by Rosemary and Stephen Vincent Benét (Holt, Rinehart & Winston, Inc.). Copyright © 1933 by Rosemary and Stephen Vincent Benét. Copyright renewed © 1961 by Rosemary Benét. Reprinted by permission.

Candlewick Press From "Obie's Gift" by Martin Waddell, from *Little Obie and the Flood.* Text © 1991 by Martin Waddell. Reproduced by permission of the publisher Candlewick Press Inc., Cambridge, MA, on behalf of Walker Books Ltd., London.

Diana Chang "Saying Yes" by Diana Chang, copyright by Diana Chang. Reprinted by permission of the author.

Clarion Books, a division of Houghton Mifflin Company "A Backwoods Boy" from *Lincoln: A Photobiography.* Copyright © 1987 by Russell Freedman. Reprinted by permission of Clarion Books/Houghton Mifflin Company. All rights reserved.

(Acknowledgments continue on page R56, which constitutes an extension of this copyright page.)

PRENTICE HALL LITERATURE

Timeless Voices, Timeless Themes

COPPER

BRONZE

SILVER

GOLD

PLATINUM

THE AMERICAN EXPERIENCE

THE BRITISH TRADITION

CONTRIBUTING AUTHORS

The contributing authors guided the direction and philosophy of *Prentice Hall Literature: Timeless Voices, Timeless Themes*. Working with the development team, they helped to build the pedagogical integrity of the program and to ensure its relevance for today's teachers and students.

Kate Kinsella

Kate Kinsella, Ed.D., is a faculty member in the Department of Secondary Education at San Francisco State University. A specialist in second-language acquisition and adolescent reading and writing, she teaches coursework addressing language and literacy development across the secondary curricula. She has taught high-school ESL and directed SFSU's *Intensive English Program* for first-generation bilingual college students. She maintains secondary classroom involvement by teaching an academic literacy class for second-language learners through the University's *Step to College* partnership program. A former Fulbright lecturer and perennial institute leader for TESOL, the California Reading Association, and the California League of Middle Schools, Dr. Kinsella provides professional development nationally on topics ranging from learning-style enhancement to second-language reading. Her scholarship has been published in journals such as the *TESOL Journal,* the *CATESOL Journal,* and the *Social Studies Review.* Dr. Kinsella earned her M.A. in TESOL from San Francisco State University and her Ed.D. in Second Language Acquisition from the University of San Francisco.

Kevin Feldman

Kevin Feldman, Ed.D., is the Director of Reading and Early Intervention with the Sonoma County Office of Education (SCOE). His career in education spans thirty-one years. As the Director of Reading and Early Intervention for SCOE, he develops, organizes, and monitors programs related to K–12 literacy and prevention of reading difficulties. He also serves as a Leadership Team Consultant to the California Reading and Literature Project and assists in the development and implementation of K–12 programs throughout California. Dr. Feldman earned his undergraduate degree in Psychology from Washington State University and has a Master's degree in Special Education, Learning Disabilities, and Instructional Design from U.C. Riverside. He earned his Ed.D. in Curriculum and Instruction from the University of San Francisco.

Colleen Shea Stump

Colleen Shea Stump, Ph.D., is a Special Education supervisor in the area of Resource and Inclusion for Seattle Public Schools. She served as a professor and chairperson for the Department of Special Education at San Francisco State University. She continues as a lead consultant in the area of collaboration for the California State Improvement Grant and travels the state of California providing professional development training in the areas of collaboration, content literacy instruction, and inclusive instruction. Dr. Stump earned her doctorate at the University of Washington, her M.A. in Special Education from the University of New Mexico, and her B.S. in Elementary Education from the University of Wisconsin–Eau Claire.

Joyce Armstrong Carroll

In her forty-year career, Joyce Armstrong Carroll, Ed. D., has taught on every grade level from primary to graduate school. In the past twenty years, she has trained teachers in the teaching of writing. A nationally known consultant, she has served as president of TCTE and on NCTE's Commission on Composition. More than fifty of her articles have appeared in journals such as *Curriculum Review, English Journal, Media & Methods, Southwest Philosophical Studies, English in Texas,* and the *Florida English Journal.* With Edward E. Wilson, Dr. Carroll co-authored *Acts of Teaching: How to Teach Writing* and co-edited *Poetry After Lunch: Poetry to Read Aloud.* She co-directs the New Jersey Writing Project in Texas.

Edward E. Wilson

A former editor of *English in Texas,* Edward E. Wilson has served as a high-school English teacher and a writing consultant in school districts nationwide. Wilson has served on both the Texas Teacher Professional Practices Commission and NCTE's Commission on Composition. Wilson's poetry appears in Paul Janeczko's anthology *The Music of What Happens.* With Dr. Carroll, he co-wrote *Acts of Teaching: How to Teach Writing* and co-edited *Poetry After Lunch: Poetry to Read Aloud.* Wilson co-directs the New Jersey Writing Project in Texas.

Comparing Literary Works

Writing Workshops

Listening and Speaking Workshops

Assessment Workshops

Reading Informational Materials

Connections

How To Read Literature

Objectives

1. To identify the purposes and characteristics of the major literary genres
2. To apply an in-depth understanding of genre as an aid to reading comprehension

How to Use Learn About Literature

"Learn About Literature" pages help students become better readers by acquainting them with the conventions of the major literary genres. Each page contains definitions, sample passages, and comprehension questions about the major genres. These elements will help students build an in-depth understanding of genre that will improve their reading comprehension skills.

Literary Genres

Novel and Novella, Short Story, and Nonfiction

- Have students read the excerpt from the novel *Tuck Everlasting* on this page and answer the question.
  Answer: The excerpt reveals that the story is set in a village at dawn on a day in the first week of August. It also tells of a character named Mae Tuck, who knows how to ride a horse.
- Ask students to read the information about the genre of the short story. Then, discuss the answer to the question.
  Answer: The problem is how to get rid of an unwanted dragon.
- After students read the definition of nonfiction, ask them to identify the key difference between the genres of nonfiction and short story.
  Possible answer: Nonfiction deals with real people and events, and short stories tell about fictional events and characters.
- Ask students to read the nonfiction passage and answer the question.
  Answer: The subject of the passage is the launch of a space craft.

Learn About Literature

Forms of Literature

Novel and Novella • Short Story • Nonfiction • Poetry • Drama • The Oral Tradition

Each form of literature, called a genre (zhän′ rə)**, has its own characteristics. In this introduction, you can learn about the genres of literature.**

- **Prose** is organized in sentences and paragraphs and does not have a regular rhythm. **Fiction** is prose writing that tells about imaginary characters and events. **Nonfiction** is prose writing that presents and explains ideas or that tells about real people, places, or events.
- **Poetry,** whose sentences appear in lines that do not always extend across the page, often has a regular beat or rhythm.

Novel and Novella

Novels and novellas are long works of fiction. They have a plot or a sequence of events that explores characters facing a problem in a specific time and place. These long works of fiction may introduce subplots or minor stories within the larger one. Novels and novellas address a theme or insight into life.

What does the opening of this novel reveal about the setting?

> The first week of August hangs at the very top of summer . . . At dawn, Mae Tuck set out on her horse for the wood at the edge of the village. . .
>
> FROM *TUCK EVERLASTING*, NATALIE BABBITT, PRENTICE HALL LITERATURE LIBRARY

Short Story

A **short story** is a brief form of prose fiction with characters, a setting, and a plot. It resembles longer forms of fiction in exploring an insight into life.

What problem do you think will be solved in the course of this story?

> There was once a king whose kingdom was plagued by a dragon. The king did not know which way to turn. . . .
>
> FROM "DRAGON, DRAGON," JOHN GARDNER, PAGE 434

Nonfiction

Nonfiction is literature that deals with the real world. It tells the story of actual events or people and addresses the world of ideas.

What is the subject of this nonfiction account?

> I witnessed the launch from the Kennedy Space Center press site just 4.2 miles from pad 39B. . . .
>
> FROM "SPACE SHUTTLE *CHALLENGER*," WILLIAM HARWOOD, PAGE 562

ENRICHMENT: Further Reading

To extend students' understanding of different genres, use the titles in the **Prentice Hall Literature Library**. This collection includes novels and special literature anthologies, each with its own study guide.

Novels

The Adventures of Ulysses
Bridge to Terabithia
Ghosts I Have Been
Going Home
Hatchet
The House of Dies Drear
Journey Home
The Master Puppeteer
The Mouse Rap
The Moves Make the Man
The Road to Memphis
Roll of Thunder, Hear My Cry
The Second Mrs. Giaconda
Shark Beneath the Reef
Sing Down the Moon
Sounder
The Trojan War
The True Confessions of Charlotte Doyle
Tuck Everlasting
A Wrinkle in Time

Special Anthologies

Authors In Depth, Copper Level
Appreciating Poetry
Biography and Autobiography

"Just remember that reading is an art. . . . So please keep at it."

—Martin Amis

Poetry

Poetry is literature written in verse. Because the form uses comparatively few words, poets choose highly concise and emotionally packed language to convey their ideas. In addition, poetry includes rhythm and rhyme to make the writing musical.

Which characteristics identify the passage at right as poetry?

My father was the first to hear
The passage of the geese each
fall,
Passing above the house so near
He'd hear within his heart
their call. . . .

FROM "THE GEESE," RICHARD PECK, PAGE 706

Drama

Drama tells a story through the words and actions of actors who impersonate the characters on stage. In the text of a drama, the characters' words are called the dialogue.

In addition to dialogue, a drama includes stage directions telling actors how to move and speak. Because a drama is usually written to be performed, you should imagine actors speaking the dialogue as you read it.

How does the text of this drama differ from the text of a short story?

[LIGHTS UP *on the clock, a huge alarm clock. The clock reads 4:00. The lighting should make it appear that the clock is suspended in mid-air (if possible). The clock ticks for 30 seconds.*]

CLOCK. See that! Half a minute gone by. Seems like a long time when you're waiting for something to happen. . . .

FROM *THE PHANTOM TOLLBOOTH*, SUSAN NANUS, PAGE 614

The Oral Tradition

Most literary works travel from the author's imagination to a page. Forms of fiction in the **oral tradition** make a different journey. They travel from the mouths of many tellers to the ears of many listeners. Such works include myths and folk tales that generations of storytellers shape for hundreds of years before people finally write them down. Telling and retelling tales ensures that they express the values of the culture from which they come.

In which part of the world was this tale told before it was written down?

One day long ago in Mexico's land of sand and giant cactus *Señor Coyote* and *Señor Mouse* had a quarrel. . . .

FROM "SEÑOR COYOTE AND THE TRICKED TRICKSTER," RETOLD BY I. G. EDMONDS, PAGE 770

Discuss the Quotation

- Students may be interested to know that Martin Amis is a British novelist and former journalist whose father, Kingsley Amis, was also a well-known writer. Martin Amis's novels offer satirical commentary on modern society.
- Have students read Amis's quotation. Then, ask them what Amis means when he says that reading is an art.
  Possible response: By calling reading a form of art, Amis suggests that it is more than a skill; it is a talent that must be developed.

Literary Genres

Poetry, Drama, and The Oral Tradition

- Have students read the definition of poetry. Then, ask them to discuss their experiences of reading poems. Do they enjoy reading poetry? Do they have a favorite form of poetry or a favorite poet?
  Possible responses: Some students may say that they do not care for poetry because it is not as easy to read as stories. Others may say that they enjoy the rhythm and rhyme of poetry and that it reminds them of their favorite songs. Students may name specific forms of poetry or mention specific poets they enjoy.
- Next, ask students to read the excerpt from Richard Peck's poem "The Geese" and to answer the question about it.
  Answer: The passage has line breaks, words that rhyme, and a distinct rhythm.
- Read aloud the instruction about drama and the excerpt from *The Phantom Tollbooth*. Then, ask students to respond to the question.
  Answer: The text is made up of dialogue and stage directions; there is no narration.
- Finally, ask a volunteer to read aloud the instruction about oral tradition and the excerpt. Then, ask students to answer the question.
  Answer: The tale was told in Mexico before it was written down.

CUSTOMIZE INSTRUCTION FOR UNIVERSAL ACCESS

For Less Proficient Readers	For English Learners	For Advanced Readers
Students may remember the information about the six genres if they record it in a chart. Work with students to create a six-column chart, labeling each column with a genre. Next, have students fill in the columns with key words or phrases that describe the various genres. Challenge students to think of at least one title for each genre.	Organize students in small groups. Ask each group to list at least one title for each genre they have learned about. Talk with students about which genres are most popular in students' original cultures. Allow time for interested students to talk about which genres they enjoy most and why.	Challenge students to think of at least two examples of each of the genres discussed here. Make a master list of the titles on the board, and then talk about how the literary works are (or are not) good models of the genres. Make sure that students defend their choices by referring to the definitions provided on pp. xxvi–IN1.

Short Stories

- Read aloud the introduction to the instruction about short stories.
- Instruct each student to draw a four-column chart, labeling the columns *Plot, Character, Setting,* and *Theme.* Tell students to record notes in their charts on the elements of short stories as they read pp. IN2–IN3.

Elements of a Short Story

Plot and Conflict

- After students read the information about plot, explain that a plot can be imagined as a series of events on a timeline. Then, have students examine the plot diagram. Explain that a plot diagram is like a timeline that has been bent almost like a coat hanger in order to show the emotional development in a plot.
- Have students read the excerpt from "Becky and the Wheels-and-Brake Boys" and answer the question about it.
  Answer: The neighborhood boys will not spend time with the speaker because she is a girl.

Elements of a Short Story

Character

- Before students read the definition of character, ask them to name some of their favorite characters from books, stories, movies, or television. Briefly discuss the key qualities of one or two of the characters mentioned.
- Have a volunteer read aloud the instruction about character and another volunteer read aloud the excerpt from "Eleven."
- Tell students that the words characters use often reveal a great deal about their personalities. Then, ask students to respond to the question.
  Possible response: The narrator's words reveal that he or she is a thoughtful young person who understands that people do not always feel the way they expect to on their birthdays; the tone of her words reveals that she is disappointed.

Short Stories

Plot and Conflict • Character • Setting • Theme

The short stories in this book will take you to fictional worlds as far away as Russia and as close as the family next door. No two of these tales are exactly alike. However, they all share common characteristics. This introduction will help you understand these characteristics as you peek into some of the fictional worlds you will be exploring later.

Plot and Conflict

The **plot** of a story is a sequence of events linked by cause and effect—earlier events advance the plot by bringing about later ones. A typical plot, diagramed below, focuses on a **conflict** or problem between opposing forces. As the problem or conflict becomes worse, the story builds to the point of greatest tension, the climax. Then, there is a resolution, or solving, of the problem and the story ends.

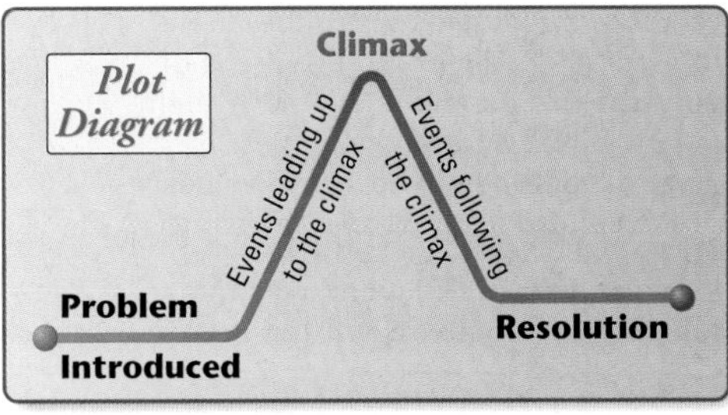

What problem does the person telling this story face?

> . . . I only want to be with Nat, Aldo, Jimmy, and Ben. It's no fair reason they don't want to be with me. . . . A girl can not, not, let boys get away with it all the time. . . .
>
> FROM "BECKY AND THE WHEELS-AND-BRAKE BOYS," JAMES BERRY, PAGE 448

Character

The **characters** in a story are the people or animals who take part in the action. Authors use characterization to bring characters to life. For example, authors can tell you directly about characters' qualities, such as courage or cowardice. Authors may also reveal these qualities indirectly, through characters' words and actions. In either case, the qualities that characters display influence the plot and the resolution of its problem or conflict.

What quality or qualities of the narrator do her opening words reveal? Explain.

> What they don't understand about birthdays and what they never tell you is that when you're eleven, you're also ten, and nine, and eight, and seven, and six, and five, and four, and three, and two, and one. And when you wake up on your eleventh birthday you expect to feel eleven, but you don't. You open your eyes and everything's just like yesterday, only it's today. And you don't feel eleven at all. You feel like you're still ten. And you are—underneath the year that makes you eleven. . . .
>
> FROM "ELEVEN," SANDRA CISNEROS, PAGE 465

"A short story is like a stripped-down racer; there's no room for anything extra in there."
—*Robert Asprin*

Setting

The plot and characters, which are the *what* and *who* of a story, must also have a *where* and *when*. That is why every story has a **setting**—the imaginary place and time of the action. In addition to details of time and place setting also includes information that shows a group's customs and beliefs.

- In a contemporary story, the made-up world of the setting usually includes details that are true to life.
- Historical fiction, which is partly based on events from history, may include a mixture of fact and fantasy.

In all types of stories, the setting can influence the plot and the resolution of the central problem.

"The Lawyer and the Ghost" is set in nineteenth-century London. What details of setting does the author provide in the opening of the story?

I knew a man—let me see—it's forty years ago now—who took an old, damp, rotten set of chambers, in one of the most ancient Inns, that had been shut up and empty for years and years before. There were lots of old women's stories about the place, and it certainly was very far from being a cheerful one; but he was poor, and the rooms were cheap, and that would have been quite a sufficient reason for him, if they had been ten times worse than they really were. . . .

FROM "THE LAWYER AND THE GHOST,"
CHARLES DICKENS, PAGE **478**

Theme

In short stories, authors use literary elements like character, plot, conflict, and setting to convey and explore a **theme,** an insight into life.

Authors sometimes state a theme directly at the beginning or end of a short story. More often, however, they imply or suggest the theme through what happens to the characters. To figure out an implied theme, think about how a character changes or solves a problem. Then, consider how this change or growth hints at a general idea about life.

In this story, which contrasting customs may suggest an insight into life?

"As any respectable Chinese knows, the correct way to eat your soup is to slurp."

The first time our family was invited out to dinner in America, we disgraced ourselves while eating celery. We had emigrated to this country from China, and during our early days here we had a hard time with American table manners. . . ."

FROM "THE ALL-AMERICAN SLURP,"
LENSEY NAMIOKA, PAGE **496**

Discuss the Quotation

- Explain to students that Robert Asprin is an American author of more than fifty popular fantasy z / and science fiction novels and story collections.
- Ask a volunteer to read aloud the quotation. Then, ask students to use what they already know about plot and character to comment on Asprin's idea that a short story should contain only essential elements or information.
  Answer: Students may say that because stories are generally short, they do not have room for more than one plot or more than a few characters.

Elements of a Short Story
Setting

- After students have read the definition of setting, ask them to identify the setting (time and place) of a favorite story.
- Talk with students about how the setting limits and supports the action in a story.
- Then, have students read the excerpt and answer the question about its setting.
  Answer: The setting is a set of cheap rooms in an old inn. The rooms are damp, rotten, and cheerless, after having been left empty for years.

Elements of a Short Story
Theme

- After students have read the instruction about theme, explain that a story's theme is usually the most difficult element to identify. A theme usually reveals itself slowly. Identifying the theme can be almost like solving a mystery. Like a detective, the reader must consider all the signs.
- Next, have students read the excerpt from "The All-American Slurp" and answer the question about theme.
  Answer: The contrast between American and Chinese ways of eating may lead to an insight about how people from different cultures act and view one another's actions.

CUSTOMIZE INSTRUCTION FOR UNIVERSAL ACCESS

For Special Needs Students	For Less Proficient Readers	For Gifted/Talented Students
Students may need help understanding how the plot diagram on p. IN2 relates to the movement of events in a story. Draw the diagram on the board, and ask students to think about the movement of events in a simple story, such as "Cinderella." Work with students to identify the problem, the climax, and the conclusion of the story.	Students may find it helpful to know that the events of a story can be tracked using a Series of Events Chain, like the one on p. 69 of **Writing Models and Graphic Organizers on Transparencies.** Take time to demonstrate how the diagram works, using a story that is already familiar to students.	Challenge students to work in groups to invent a short story that demonstrates the dynamic shown in the plot diagram. Students should make sure that their stories include well-developed characters and well-described settings. Invite students to retell their stories to the class.

Nonfiction

- Read aloud the introduction to the instruction about nonfiction. Then, ask students to identify the three types of nonfiction described in the passage and their purposes.
  Answer: Practical writing informs, expository writing explains, and persuasive writing convinces readers to take action or change their beliefs.
- Before students begin reading about the characteristics of nonfiction, ask them to think of examples of practical, expository, and persuasive writing that they have read or seen.
  Possible response: Students may say that they have encountered practical writing in instruction manuals, expository writing in textbooks, and persuasive writing on the editorial pages of newspapers.

Elements of Nonfiction

Historical Essay

- Read aloud the definition of a historical essay. Then, ask students to read the excerpt from "The Shutout" and answer the question about its subject.
  Answer: African American baseball players are the subject of the essay.
- Ask students to identify the details that point to the event or time in history that is under discussion.
  Answer: The mention of the Civil War and Union soldiers in conjunction with baseball are details that make it clear that the essay is about the history of African Americans in baseball, which started in the mid-nineteenth century.

Elements of Nonfiction

Biography and Autobiography

- After students have read the definitions of biography and autobiography, ask them to review the main difference between the two forms.
  Answer: An autobiography is written by the person who actually lived through the events. A biography is written about a person by someone else.

continued

Nonfiction

Historical Essay • Biography and Autobiography • Letters and Journals • Types of Essays • Informational Text

If fiction takes you on imaginative flights of fancy, nonfiction brings you back down to Earth. Nonfiction includes true stories about real people, places, experiences, and ideas. It also includes practical writing that informs, expository writing that explains, and persuasive writing meant to convince you to take action or change your beliefs. The terms defined on these pages will help you discover the characteristics of nonfiction.

Historical Essay

A **historical essay** is a short piece of nonfiction that gives you facts and ideas about an event or series of events in history. Historical essays often help you understand what life was like at a specific time in the past or help provide insight into why certain conditions existed.

The subject for such an essay might include anything from pyramid-building in ancient Egypt to Jackie Robinson and the integration of major league baseball.

What seems to be the subject of this historical essay?

> Baseball's development was slow during the Civil War years but teams continued to compete, and military records show that, sometimes between battles, Union soldiers chose up teams and played baseball games. It was during this time that records began mentioning African-American players. . . ."
>
> FROM "THE SHUTOUT," PATRICIA C. MCKISSACK AND FREDRICK MCKISSACK, JR., PAGE 532

Biography and Autobiography

In a **biography**, an author tells the story of someone else's life. A biography is therefore a third-person narration. This means that the narrator or speaker refers to the subject by name or as "he" or "she." Usually, the subject of a biography is a person whose life has special meaning or value.

By contrast, an **autobiography** is the story of part or all of a person's life, written by that person. An autobiography is therefore a first-person narration. This means that the narrator or speaker is at the center of the action and refers to herself or himself as "I." The author's purpose may be to teach lessons in life, to tell how he or she developed, to entertain, or any combination of these.

Is this the beginning of a biography or an autobiography? Why?

> We are a very happy family. We consist of Papa, Mamma, Jean, Clara, and me. It is papa I am writing about, and I shall have no trouble in not knowing what to say about him, as he is a *very* striking character.
>
> FROM "MY PAPA, MARK TWAIN," SUSY CLEMENS, PAGE 554

Answers continued

- Have a volunteer read aloud the excerpt from "My Papa, Mark Twain." Then, discuss students' responses to the question.
  Answer: The excerpt is the beginning of a biography. The subject is not the writer herself, but the writer's father.

> "Essays come in all shapes and sizes. . . ."
>
> —John Gross

Letters and Journals

A **letter** is a written communication from one person to another, sharing information, thoughts, and feelings. A **journal** is a regular account of events and the writer's thoughts and feelings about them.

What events does this journal describe?

> July 21, 1996
> What a whirlwind I've been on since the Olympic trials! We arrived in Atlanta at 1:30 P.M. and had processing, which took seven hours. . . .
>
> FROM *OLYMPIC DIARY*, AMANDA BORDEN, PAGE 545

Types of Essays

Essays share one common characteristic: They are brief prose works that are based on fact. However, essays can have different purposes, as follows.

- **Persuasive essays** try to convince you to think or act in a certain way.
- **Informational essays** convey and explain facts.
- **Narrative essays** tell a true story.

From which type of essay do you think this passage comes? Why?

> Something about my mother attracts ornithologists. It all started years ago when a couple of them discovered she had a rare species of woodpecker coming to her bird feeder. They came in the house and sat around the window, exclaiming and taking pictures with big fancy cameras. . . .
>
> FROM "TURKEYS," BAILEY WHITE, PAGE 580

Informational Text

Informational texts are the written documents that help you manage your life in today's world. From bank applications and instructions for using a calculator to campaign speeches and magazine articles, informational texts can help you discover what is happening in the world, learn a subject, or master a sport.

In what type of publication would you expect to find an article like the one from which this passage is taken?

> Like dozens of other volunteers, I felt compelled to help when a cargo ship spilled 5,000 gallons of fuel oil in the Humboldt Bay, near my home on California's north coast. When we released rehabilitated birds, we all felt great. Later, I learned that what we had done was controversial. Many biologists believe that rescuing oiled birds serves more to soothe human feelings than to help wildlife and some studies show that many cleaned birds survive for only a few days. But there are a number of encouraging success stories. . . .
>
> FROM "CAN OILED SEABIRDS BE RESCUED, OR ARE WE JUST FOOLING OURSELVES?" SHARON LEVY, PAGE 490

CUSTOMIZE INSTRUCTION FOR UNIVERSAL ACCESS

For Special Needs Students	For Less Proficient Readers	For English Learners
Organize students in groups. Supply each group with at least four different types of nonfiction writing. Ask groups to identify the types of nonfiction and to explain their answers in a short journal entry. Allow groups to meet to share their findings.	Work with students to make a list of familiar writings that illustrate each type of nonfiction mentioned on pp. IN4–IN5. Take a moment to talk about how each example contains the elements discussed on these pages. Record the examples in a five-column chart on the board.	Students may have trouble with the vocabulary used to describe each type of nonfiction. Allow students to work with partners to look up the definitions of unfamiliar terms and to write a short journal entry explaining the differences between the types of essays.

Discuss the Quotation

- Writer John Gross is probably best known for the works he has edited, which include *The New Oxford Book of English Prose, The Oxford Book of Essays,* and *The Oxford Book of Comic Verse,* an anthology of humorous poetry.
- Ask students to comment on what the quotation suggests about the essay form.
  Possible response: The essay form is a flexible or versatile type of writing.

Elements of Nonfiction

Letters and Journals

- Ask students to read the information about letters and journals and to answer the question about the journal entry.
  Answer: The journal describes arriving in Atlanta for the Olympics.
- Ask students to identify the key difference between a journal entry and a letter.
  Answer: A letter is written to another person. A journal is a private account of events in a person's life.

Elements of Nonfiction

Types of Essays

- Read aloud the information about types of essays and the passage from "Turkeys," and ask students to answer the question.
  Answer: This passage probably comes from a narrative essay. The writer is describing a real-life experience.
- Tell students to use the following question to help them distinguish between narrative, persuasive, and informative essays: Is the purpose of the essay to tell an interesting story, to argue an opinion, or to share information?

Elements of Nonfiction

Informational Text

- Read aloud the instruction about informational text.
- Have a volunteer read aloud the excerpt from the essay. Ask students to answer the question.
  Possible response: The article might appear in a wildlife magazine.

Drama

- Read aloud the introduction to the instruction about drama. Then, invite students to talk about their experiences of seeing or acting in plays. Finally, ask them to discuss how reading a play might be different from reading other forms of literature.
  Possible response: Some students may suggest that a drama tells a story, just as short stories and narrative nonfiction do, so it should not be so different from other kinds of reading. Others may be aware that the format for a drama is unlike any other kind of writing.

Elements of Drama

- Before students read about the elements of drama, draw a cluster diagram on the board. In the center bubble, write the word *Drama*. Surround that bubble with five other bubbles labeled *Acts, Dialogue, Stage Directions, Set,* and *Props*. As students read, have them tell you how to fill in additional bubbles that explain each new term.
- Have several volunteers read the descriptions of the main elements of drama. Challenge students to explain each element in their own words.
- Next, ask students to read the excerpt from *The Phantom Tollbooth* and to answer the question about it.
  Answer: The set should include a car for Milo to drive and a backdrop that shows a road going through an unfamiliar place. Props might include a sign and a cutout of a car.

Drama

Elements of Drama • Dialogue • Theme

When you read a drama, you are likely to get completely swept up in the experience. This is because reading a play gives your imagination a full workout. You, the reader, have to picture the setting, the lighting, and the actors' movements. In addition, all the action unfolds through conversation and you have to imagine each character's thoughts and feelings. The terms defined on these pages will help you discover the characteristics of drama.

Elements of Drama

Like fiction, drama has literary elements such as characters, setting, and plot. However, fiction is meant to be read, while drama is meant to be performed.

At a performance, an audience sees the story coming to life as actors move across a stage and speak the words of the characters. The following elements make such a performance possible, whether it is on a real stage or in your imagination:

- **acts,** the units of the action in a drama. Acts are often divided into parts called scenes.
- **dialogue,** the words of the characters, which appear next to their names in scripts
- **stage directions,** bracketed information that tells what the set looks like and how the characters should move and speak
- **set,** a construction on the stage that suggests the time and place of the action
- **props,** movable items, like a book, a pencil, or a flashlight that the actors use to make their actions look realistic

What would you expect the stage and scenery to be for the scene shown here?

ACT I, SCENE II The Road to Dictionopolis

[ENTER MILO *in his car.*]

MILO. This is weird! I don't recognize any of this scenery at all. [A SIGN *is held up before* MILO, *startling him.*] Huh? . . .

FROM *THE PHANTOM TOLLBOOTH*, SUSAN NANUS, PAGE 614

"There is no joy so great as that of reporting that a good play has come to town." —*Brooks Atkinson*

Dialogue

Dialogue—what characters say—is written next to their names in the text of a drama. Sometimes stage directions, written in brackets, tell actors how to speak their words, gesture, and move. By paying attention to what characters say and to what others say about them, you can figure out their qualities and predict their actions.

How do you think Monaghan's grandfather will react when he is asked to contribute to a fund for the Statue of Liberty? Why?

> MONAGHAN. Well. My grandfather was the stingiest man in Brooklyn. "Mercyless" Monaghan, they used to call him. He even used to save umbrella handles.
>
> AUGUST. What for?
>
> MONAGHAN. Just couldn't stand seeing anything go to waste. After a big windstorm there'd be a lot of broken umbrellas laying around in the streets.
>
> AUGUST. Yeh?
>
> MONAGHAN. He'd go around picking them up. . . .
>
> FROM *GRANDPA AND THE STATUE*, ARTHUR MILLER, PAGE 666

Theme

Like a work of fiction, a play has a **theme**—an insight, idea, or a question about life—that it explores. Often the theme relates to the way in which the main character solves a problem or changes.

If you see a performance of a play, you can discuss its theme with others in the audience. If you read a play, you can test the theme against your own experience. You can also discuss the theme with classmates who have read the play.

Does the problem that the main character faces in this play seem easy to solve? Why or why not?

> HUMBUG. Well, all that he would have to do is cross the dangerous, unknown countryside between here and Digitopolis, where he would have to persuade the Mathemagician to release the Princesses, which we know to be impossible because the Mathemagician will never agree with Azaz about anything. . . .
>
> FROM *THE PHANTOM TOLLBOOTH*, SUSAN NANUS, PAGE 614

CUSTOMIZE INSTRUCTION FOR UNIVERSAL ACCESS

For Less Proficient Readers	For English Learners	For Gifted/Talented Students
Students may struggle with the format of written dialogue. Organize students in small groups, and have them read an excerpt from one of the plays in this book. After students have become comfortable doing simple readings, encourage them to incorporate relevant stage directions into their readings.	Play a small excerpt from a recorded version of a play for students, and ask them to transcribe the dialogue. Review the format for written dialogue with students before they begin. Allow students to listen to the recording as many times as they need. Have students work with partners fluent in English to clarify words they find difficult.	Invite students to work in groups of three to write one-act plays. The plays should contain the dramatic elements discussed on pp. IN6–IN7, including theme and stage directions. Invite students to use items available in the classroom as props. Allow students time to perform their plays. Ask the audience to identify the elements of drama in each production.

Discuss the Quotation

- Explain that Brooks Atkinson was an influential drama critic who wrote for *The New York Times* for nearly thirty-five years.
- Ask students to think of words that describe Atkinson's attitude toward good drama.
Possible responses: Students may suggest *joyful* or *enthusiastic.*

Elements of Drama
Dialogue

- Before students read the discussion of dialogue, explain that because plays are to be spoken and performed rather than read, good dialogue is essential to a successful drama.
- Ask a volunteer to read aloud the instruction and the question about dialogue. Have two other volunteers read the excerpt from *Grandpa and the Statue* in a dramatic fashion.
- Explain that in the story that this excerpt is from, Monaghan's grandfather is asked to donate money to support the construction of the Statue of Liberty. Then, ask students to answer the question.
Possible response: Monaghan's grandfather is extremely careful with money, so he probably will not contribute to the fund.

Elements of Drama
Theme

- After students have read the instruction about theme, remind them that, just as in short stories, the theme is not always immediately clear. Remind students to consider how the characters act, what they say, and how they change, when trying to identify a drama's theme.
- Ask students to read the excerpt from *The Phantom Tollbooth* and to answer the question.
Answer: The problem seems difficult to solve. The problem will require the main character to attempt dangerous and impossible tasks.
- Challenge students to speculate about how the excerpt might relate to the theme of the play.
Possible response: Students may suggest that the play will be about meeting challenges or overcoming obstacles.

Learn About Literature
continued

Poetry

- Read aloud the introduction to the instruction about poetry. Then, discuss students' ideas about or associations with poetry. Students may think that poetry is only about love. Explain that poetry can be about anything.
- Before students read about the different forms of poetry, make a list of the types on the board. As students read, ask them to provide information about the forms, and add their responses to the appropriate lists.

Elements of Poetry
Narrative and Lyric Poetry

- Ask volunteers to read aloud the descriptions of narrative and lyric poems. Before students read the lines from "Jimmy Jet and His TV Set" and answer the question, ask them to identify the differences and similarities between the two forms of poetry.
  Answer: A narrative poem tells a story using the same elements used in a short story. A lyric poem is about feelings or emotions, like a song. Both poems may use rhyme and rhythm.
- Have students answer the question.
  Answer: The difference is that the poem has a distinct rhythm and rhyme scheme.

Elements of Poetry
Special Forms of Poetry

- Read aloud the instruction about special forms of poetry. Ask students whether they are familiar with any of the forms described in the instruction.
- Have students read the poem and answer the question about its form.
  Answer: The poem is a limerick.
- Ask students to identify the characteristics of a limerick that appear in the poem.
  Answer: The poem is short and funny. The first, second, and fifth lines rhyme and have the same rhythm, as do the third and fourth lines.

Poetry

Narrative and Lyric Poetry • Special Forms of Poetry • Sound Devices • Figurative Language

In poetry, each word rings with meaning. In some poems, repetition and rhyme create musical rhythms. In other poems, fresh new language can help you see the world in a whole new way. The terms defined on these pages will help you discover the characteristics of poetry.

Narrative and Lyric Poetry

A **narrative poem** tells a story using plot, characters, dialogue, setting, and theme. However, a narrative poem tells a story more musically than prose fiction does. The poem uses sounds and regular rhythms to make the story memorable.

A **lyric poem** expresses the thoughts and feelings of the poem's speaker, the one who says its words. Once, lyric poems were actually sung to the accompaniment of a string instrument called a lyre. Today, these poems rely on their own music created through rhythm and sound.

What makes the beginning of this narrative poem different from a prose narrative?

I'll tell you the story of Jimmy Jet—
And you know what I tell you is true.
He loved to watch his TV set
Almost as much as you. . . .

FROM "JIMMY JET AND HIS TV SET," SHEL SILVERSTEIN, PAGE 707

Special Forms of Poetry

A **poetic form** is a special way of arranging the lines and stanzas of a poem. Form includes not only the appearance of a poem on the page, but also the sound of its rhymes and rhythms. These are three examples of poetic forms:

- **Limerick** — a short, funny poem of five lines; the first, second, and fifth lines rhyme and have the same rhythm, and the third and fourth lines rhyme and have the same rhythm.
- **Haiku** — a Japanese verse form with three lines of five, seven, and five syllables each
- **Concrete poem** — a poem whose words take the shape of the poem's subject

What is the form of this poem?

A flea and a fly in a flue
Were caught, so what could they do?
　　Said the fly, "Let us flee."
　　"Let us fly," said the flea.
So they flew through a flaw in the flue.

FROM "A FLEA AND A FLY IN A FLUE," ANONYMOUS, PAGE 720

"The crown of literature is poetry."

—Somerset Maugham

Sound Devices

Sound devices are ways of adding music to poetry. Following are some common types of sound devices:

- **Rhyme** — the similarity of final sounds in accented syllables, as in *roar* and *before*
- **Onomatopoeia** (än′ ō mat′ ō pē′ ə) — the use of words like *hush* and *buzz* that sound like what they mean
- **Alliteration** — the repetition of consonant or vowel sounds in beginning or accented syllables of nearby words, as in "*wh*iteness,/ And *wh*itely *wh*irs away" (p. 729)

Which sound devices are in these lines?

> . . . Till leisurely and last of all
> Camels and elephants will pass
> Beneath our elms, along our grass.
>
> FROM "PARADE," RACHEL FIELD, PAGE 730

Tone

The **tone** is the author's attitude or feeling about the subject of the poem and the audience. An author's tone can be amused, angry, or superior, among many other possibilities.

Would you describe the tone of this stanza as serious or amused? Why?

> "The time has come," the Walrus said,
> "To talk of many things:
> Of shoes—and ships—and sealing wax—
> Of cabbages—and kings—
>
> FROM "THE WALRUS AND THE CARPENTER," LEWIS CARROLL, PAGE 708

Figurative Language

Poems use **figurative language,** words not meant in their exact dictionary sense, to take you by surprise. Each type of figurative language is based on a comparison of apparently unlike items. However, when you think about the comparison, you will usually see that the items really are similar.

Type	Description	Example
Simile (sim′ ə lē)	Uses *like* or *as* to compare two apparently unlike items	"The will is like an etching, . . ."
Metaphor (met′ ə fər′)	Describes one thing as if it were another, apparently unlike thing	"Fame is a bee, . . ."
Personification (pər sän′ i fi kā′ shən)	Gives human qualities to something nonhuman	"Let the rain kiss you."

What type of figurative language does this passage contain?

> The rain makes running pools
> in the gutter.
> The rain plays a little sleep-song on
> our roof at night . . .
>
> FROM "APRIL RAIN SONG," LANGSTON HUGHES, PAGE 742

CUSTOMIZE INSTRUCTION FOR UNIVERSAL ACCESS

For Special Needs Students	For English Learners	For Gifted/Talented Students
Supply each student with several pairs of seemingly unrelated nouns such as *cat* and *bike,* or *water* and *love,* on slips of paper. Ask students to write a simile using each pair of nouns. Remind students to think about how the nouns look, sound, smell, feel, or taste, as well as how they are used, when they write their similes.	Writing and explaining similes and metaphors is one way of expanding vocabulary. Offer students pairs of nouns, one of which may be new to students. Then, ask each student to write a simile or metaphor, using the pair of words, as well as a statement that explains the comparison. Allow students to use the dictionary.	Invite students to make a list of at least ten completely unrelated objects. Then, challenge students to write a short poem that includes similes and metaphors that connect at least three pairs of words from their lists. Invite volunteers to read their poems to the class.

Discuss the Quotation

- Explain to students that Somerset Maugham was a celebrated British playwright, novelist, essayist, and story writer. Among his most famous novels are *Of Human Bondage, Cakes and Ale,* and *The Razor's Edge.*
- Ask students to read Maugham's quotation and speculate about why he valued poetry so highly. Possible responses: Students may suggest that Maugham valued poetry because it expresses feelings that capture the essence of human nature or because it is difficult to write.

Elements of Poetry
Sound Devices

- Read and discuss the sound devices explained here. Invite students to think of additional examples of each device.
- Next, have a volunteer read the lines from the poem and the question about it. Have students answer the question. Answer: The repetition of the sound of the letter *l* in the words *leisurely, last, elephants,* and *elms* creates alliteration. The words *pass* and *grass* rhyme.

Elements of Poetry
Tone

- After students have read the description of tone, explain that tone is often difficult to recognize. Explain that tone is related to sound and that, often, reading poetry aloud helps listeners hear the tone.
- Read aloud the lines from "The Walrus and the Carpenter," using your voice to convey a tone of amusement. Then, have students answer the question about tone. Answer: The stanza has an amused tone.

Elements of Poetry
Figurative Language

- Allow students to look at the chart on p. IN9 before they read the discussion of figurative language.
- Read aloud the instruction, and review the definitions and examples in the chart. Then, have a volunteer read the lines from the poem. Ask students to answer the question. Answer: This passage contains personification.

Learn About Literature
continued

Folk Literature

- Ask a volunteer to read aloud the introduction to the instruction about folk literature. Then, point out that such tales were often told and retold for many years, changing a little bit with each retelling, before they were eventually written down.
- Ask students why they think the same tales were told again and again.
  Possible response: Some students may suggest that the same stories might be told over and over again because they are always entertaining. Others may point out that many tales are told in order to teach listeners a lesson; as long as the lesson holds true, the tales are told.

Elements of Folk Literature
Folk Tales

- Read the definition of folk tales to the class. Then, ask students to review the three possible purposes for folk tales.
  Answer: Folk tales may entertain, teach a lesson, or explain something.
- Next, ask a volunteer to read aloud the excerpt from the folk tale. Have students answer the question.
  Answer: The folk tale features a talking animal.

Elements of Folk Literature
Characters in Folk Literature

- Ask a volunteer to read aloud the instruction about characters in folk literature.
- Guide students to understand that listeners or readers may find it easier to recognize character flaws or frailties when they are acted out by animals rather than human characters. Also, remind students that certain qualities or characteristics are associated with certain animals. For example, owls are associated with wisdom.
- Finally, ask a volunteer to read aloud the passage from "The Ant and the Dove." Discuss students' responses to the question.
  Possible response: The dove may represent generosity or kindness.

Folk Literature

Folk Tales • Characters in Folk Literature • The Oral Tradition • Themes in Folk Literature

Imagine that instead of reading literature, you heard it told to you by storytellers around a campfire or a fireplace. Telling and listening to made-up stories, rather than writing them down, is part of the oral tradition. Individual tales in this tradition were usually told in different ways by storytellers entertaining different audiences. Eventually, versions of these tales were written down. As a result, you can join in the campfire circle and appreciate stories of animals, humans, and gods. These pages will teach you about the characteristics of works in the oral tradition.

Folk Tales

Folk tales are stories passed on by word of mouth among a group of people, the "folk." This type of literature often features talking animals or exaggerated situations to make a point. Their purpose may be not only to entertain, but also to teach a lesson or to explain something in nature. As you read the folk tales of a variety of cultures, you may see similarities in the lessons or values they teach.

What characteristic of folk tales does this passage demonstrate?

> Say that he Lion would get up each and every mornin. Stretch and walk around. He'd roar, ME AND MYSELF, ME AND MYSELF, like that. Scare all the little animals so they were afraid to come outside in the sunshine. . . .
>
> FROM "HE LION, BRUH BEAR, AND BRUH RABBIT," RETOLD BY VIRGINIA HAMILTON, PAGE 766

Characters in Folk Literature

Characters in folk literature usually do not have the same individuality as characters in stories and novels do. Whether they are people or animals, folk characters usually symbolize, or stand for, general qualities like cleverness, laziness, or courage. By focusing on what happens to these symbolic characters, listeners and readers can determine the message of the tale.

What quality do you think the dove in this story might represent?

> A thirsty ant went to the stream to drink. Suddenly it got caught in a whirlpool and was almost carried away.
>
> At that moment a dove was passing by with a twig in its beak. The dove dropped the twig for the tiny insect to grab hold of. So it was that the ant was saved. . . .
>
> FROM "THE ANT AND THE DOVE," RETOLD BY LEO TOLSTOY, PAGE 764

"Folk tales travel wherever people travel."

—Rudolfo Anaya

The Oral Tradition

Stories passed down by word of mouth in the **oral tradition** reflect the beliefs, customs, and values of the culture that created them. In addition to folk tales, the oral tradition also includes myths, tales of gods, goddesses, and heroes that explain something in nature.

Judging by the beginning of this myth, what did the ancient Greeks value?

Arachne [ä räk′ nē] was a maiden who became famous throughout Greece, though she was neither wellborn nor beautiful and came from no great city. She lived in an obscure little village, and her father was a humble dyer of wool. In this he was very skillful, producing many varied shades, while above all he was famous for the clear, bright scarlet which is made from shellfish, and this was the most glorious of all the colors used in ancient Greece. Even more skillful than her father was Arachne. It was her task to spin the fleecy wool into a fine, soft thread and to weave it into cloth on the high, standing loom within the cottage. . . . So soft and even was her thread, so fine her cloth, so gorgeous her embroidery, that soon her products were known all over Greece. . . .

FROM "ARACHNE," RETOLD BY OLIVIA E. COOLIDGE, PAGE 784

Themes in Folk Literature

Like most other forms of literature, tales in the oral tradition also explore an idea about life called a **theme**. Usually the theme addresses the values or behaviors of a culture. These values may provide guidelines for living justly or honorably.

Sometimes the theme is stated directly at the end of the tale. Other times, you must use the characters' actions and the images, or word pictures, to figure out the theme.

What idea related to riches do you think this folk tale will explore? Why?

Many years ago, there lived a woodsman and his wife. They were very poor but very happy in their little house in the forest. Poor as they were, they were always ready to share what little they had with anyone who came to their door. They loved each other very much and were quite content with their life together. Each evening, before eating, they gave thanks to God for their happiness. . . .

FROM "THE THREE WISHES," RETOLD BY RICARDO E. ALEGRÍA, PAGE 789

Discuss the Quotation

- Tell students that Rudolfo Anaya is a Mexican American writer and teacher whose best-known work, *Bless Me, Ultima,* is a novel about a Hispanic boy who grew up in New Mexico in the 1940s.
- Ask students to explain the quotation from Anaya. How is it that folk tales travel with people?
  Possible response: People tell stories no matter where they are; when people move, immigrate, or travel, they take their stories with them.

Elements of Folk Literature

Oral Tradition

- After students have read the description of oral tradition, talk as a class about the kinds of beliefs, customs, and values that might show up in a folk tale or myth. Challenge students to think of a folk tale or myth that reveals something about the culture from which it comes.
- Read aloud the excerpt from "Arachne" and then pose the question about ancient Greek values.
  Answer: Being born rich and beautiful and living in a great city were important to the ancient Greeks, but so was the ability to use one's skills to create something of lasting beauty.

Elements of Folk Literature

Themes in Folk Literature

- Before students read about themes in folk literature, review what they have already learned about themes in short stories and drama. Students should recall that themes may be stated directly by the writer, or they may be revealed indirectly by the actions and words of the characters.
- Invite volunteers to read aloud the instruction about theme as well as the passage from "The Three Wishes." Then, pose the question about theme.
  Possible response: The folk tale probably will explore the idea that wealth does not equal happiness; the poor couple seems very happy.

CUSTOMIZE INSTRUCTION FOR UNIVERSAL ACCESS

For Less Proficient Readers

To help students see beyond the literal events in folk tales, ask them to read a folk tale or myth of your choosing and to answer the following questions.

- What happens in the tale or myth?
- Who is the hero? Does he or she have an enemy?
- Do any of the characters "stand" for a particular quality?
- What lesson can readers learn from this tale or myth?

For Advanced Readers

Invite students to read a folk tale or myth that they have not read before, and ask them to compare it to a familiar tale or myth. Ask students to write a brief report that compares and contrasts the two stories. Challenge students to find folk tales or myths that are from different cultures and to address the cultural differences and similarities in their reports.

Unit Objectives

1. To read selections in different genres that develop the theme of "Growing and Changing"
2. To apply a variety of reading strategies, particularly literal comprehension strategies, appropriate for reading these selections
3. To analyze literary elements
4. To use a variety of strategies to build vocabulary
5. To learn elements of grammar, usage, and style
6. To use recursive writing processes to write in a variety of forms
7. To develop listening and speaking skills
8. To express and support responses to various types of texts
9. To prepare, organize, and present literary interpretations

Meeting the Objectives

With each selection, you will find instructional materials through which students can meet these objectives. Further, you will find additional practice pages for reading strategies, literary analysis, vocabulary, and grammar in the **Selection Support: Skills Development Workbook** in your **Teaching Resources.**

Background

Art

In the Garden by Joseph Raphael

Joseph Raphael spent most of his adult life in Europe but returned to the United States before World War II. He is known as one of California's best impressionistic painters. Connect the painting to the theme of Growing and Changing by asking this question:

What role do you think the elders in this painting will play in the growth and change of these children?
Possible response: The painting shows adults who are keeping an eye on the children; one adult seems to be teaching a child something; another child is being cared for; all of these factors will help in the development of these children.

UNIT 1 Growing and Changing

In the Garden, Joseph Raphael, The Redfern Gallery

UNIT FEATURES

Connections	Reading Informational Material
Every unit contains a feature that connects literature to a related topic, such as art, science, or history. In this unit, the Literature and the Media feature on p. 26 links a fictional story about a stray dog with the real-life glamour of dogs who star in television shows and movies. Use the information and questions on the Connections page to enrich students' understanding of the selections presented within the unit.	These selections will help students learn to analyze and evaluate informational texts, such as workplace documents, technical directions, and consumer materials. They will expose students to the organization and features unique to nonnarrative texts. In this unit, students will learn strategies for finding information in newspaper articles and for understanding interviews.

Exploring the Theme

All around you, the world changes in large and small ways. The tree outside has more branches than it did last year. A new store opens on the next block. All growth involves change—especially in people. The literature in this unit will introduce you to people who grow and change through life's experiences. For example, in "Jeremiah's Song," music helps a young boy learn to listen to the cherished stories of his Grandpa. Poets such as Diana Chang and Walt Whitman express their experiences in verse.

◀ **Critical Viewing** In what ways does this picture suggest growing and changing? **[Connect]**

ASSESSMENT RESOURCES

- Selection Support: Skills Development Workbook
- Formal Assessment
- Open Book Tests
- Performance Assess. and Portfolio Mgmt.
- Extension Activities

Assessing Student Progress

Listed below are the tools that are available to measure the degree to which students meet the unit objectives.

Informal Assessment

The questions in the Review and Assess sections are a first level of response to the concepts and skills presented within the selections. Students' responses are a brief, informal measure of their grasp of the material. These responses can indicate where further instruction and practice are needed. Follow up with the practice pages in the **Selection Support: Skills Development Workbook.**

Formal Assessment

The **Formal Assessment** booklet contains the Selection Tests and Unit Tests.

- Selection Tests measure comprehension and skills acquisition for each selection or group of selections.
- Each Unit Test provides students with thirty multiple-choice questions and five essay questions designed to assess students' knowledge of the literature and skills taught in the unit.

The **Open-Book Tests** ask students to demonstrate their ability to synthesize and communicate information from selections or groups of selections.

To assess student writing, you will find rubrics and scoring models in the **Performance Assessment and Portfolio Management** booklet. In this booklet, you will also find scoring rubrics for listening and speaking activities.

Alternative Assessment

The **Extension Activities** booklet contains writing activities, listening and speaking activities, and research and technology activities that are appropriate for students with different ability levels. You may also use these activities as an alternative measurement of students' growth.

▶Critical Viewing

Possible responses: The young children will change as they grow up; different ages are shown; the foliage in the background appears springlike, and spring is a season of growth and change.

Why Read Literature?

The "Why Read Literature?" page in each unit presents a list of possible purposes for reading. Each purpose for reading is connected to one or more of the selections in the unit. Good readers set a purpose before reading in order to help them read actively and focus on meaningful details.

Unit 1 introduces three purposes for reading. "Read for the Love of Literature" encourages students to enjoy a tale of adventure in the Klondike region of Canada and a poem about a winter day. "Read to Consider Another Viewpoint" introduces a fictional account of a boy who talks his way into getting a coveted pair of shoes as well as a true-life story of a young newsboy. "Read for Information" gives students practical tips for finding and enjoying summer jobs.

How to Use This Page

- Tell students that before reading each selection in this unit, they should set a purpose for reading. This will help them read in an active and focused manner.
- Explain that reading a poet's description of a crow on a snow-covered branch or an account of a young man with a sense of justice will increase their love of literature.
- Predict that students will be enlightened by tales of two boys from different eras. Tennis shoes are the focus of "The Sound of Summer Running," and Russell Baker's first venture into the news business is described in "Hard as Nails."
- Point out that information about jobs can be useful all year. The Reading Informational Material feature in this unit will give useful advice to students who are interested in making the most of their summer vacations.

Why Read Literature?

You will find that, whenever you read, you have a purpose, or reason, for reading. Your purpose will vary depending on the content, style, and form of the work you will read. Preview three of the purposes you might see before reading the works in this unit.

Read for the love of literature.

Robert Frost is known as a "New England" poet, but he was born and raised in California! Read **"Dust of Snow,"** page 30, for a quick look at one of Frost's New England scenes.

Sometimes a life of high adventure leads an author to write action-packed fiction. Jack London is such a writer. At age seventeen, he went to sea to hunt seals. Several years later, feeling restless, he headed to the Klondike in search of gold. London wrote stories based on his adventures. Read London's **"The King of Mazy May,"** page 52, for the story of a boy's wild ride on a dog sled while being pursued by robbers.

Read to consider another viewpoint.

Russell Baker was a newspaper man when he was still a boy! Read **"Hard as Nails"** on page 72 to learn about his first job.

Science-fiction writer Ray Bradbury has a crater on the moon named after one of his books. When you read **"The Sound of Summer Running,"** page 6, you may be surprised to discover that Bradbury's character has both feet planted firmly on Earth.

3 Read for information.

For tips and guidance on how to find and choose a summer job, read **"Summer Hats,"** page 83.

Find out why John Glenn, the first American to orbit the Earth, returned to space at the age of seventy-seven. Read **"An Astronaut's Answers,"** page 86.

Take It to the Net

Visit the Web site for online instruction and activities related to each selection in this unit.

www.phschool.com

ENRICHMENT: Further Reading

Have students choose one or more of the works below to extend one or more of the works below to extend the unit theme "Growing and Changing" or to read more by the unit authors.

Voyages: Poems by Walt Whitman selected by Lee Bennett Hopkins

This illustrated volume contains 53 of Whitman's poems; Whitman's life and work are discussed in the introduction.

And Now Miguel by Joseph Krumgold

Miguel grows up suddenly when his wish to go to the mountains comes true in this Newbery Award book.

From the Mixed-Up Files of Mrs. Basil E. Frankweiler by E. L. Konigsburg

Claudia runs away to a museum and tries to solve a mystery with her brother.

Bridge to Terabithia by Katherine Paterson

Two friends make their own magical kingdom and rule it in this **Prentice Hall Literature Library** selection.

How to Read Literature

Literal Comprehension Strategies

When you build a house, you first construct a foundation on which the other levels are built. In reading, too, you construct a foundation. This foundation is the literal meaning—the basic facts and details. The following strategies will help you understand a writer's words on a literal level.

1. Read fluently.

To read fluently means to read groups of words rather than one word at a time. Reading fluently helps you understand what you are reading. Improve your fluency in the following ways:

- Read aloud.
- Preview what you will read to check for unfamiliar words.
- Practice reading groups of words rather than individual words.

2. Use context to determine meaning.

Use the context, or the surroundings, of an unfamiliar word to find its meaning. In the following passage, words with similar meanings help you figure out that *timidly* means "showing shyness."

> The puppy stopped in the road, wagging its tail *timidly*, trembling with *shyness* and cold.

3. Recognize signal words.

Use signal words—*next* and *most important*, for example— to identify relationships, such as time or importance among ideas. The notepad shows commonly used signal words and what they indicate.

Signal Words

That Show Time
while
then
next
before

That Show Contrast
however
although
but

That Show Cause and Effect
because
consequently
as a result

4. Reread to clarify.

If a word or phrase is unclear, reread the text in which it appears. The poem "My Picture-Gallery" seems to be describing a house. You may be confused about how a house could fit everything the poet says is in it. On rereading, however, you will discover the house is round and not fixed in place. These clues show that the house stands for something else.

5. Read accurately.

To read accurately, find the main parts of the sentence by breaking it down into meaningful sections. Note whom or what the sentence is about and what happens.

As you read the selections in this unit, review the reading strategies and look at the notes in the side columns. Use the suggestions to apply the strategies for literal comprehension.

How to Read Literature

The "How to Read Literature" page in each unit presents a set of strategies to help readers understand authors' words and ideas. Each reading strategy is taught in conjunction with one or more of the selections within the unit. Good readers develop a bank of strategies from which they can draw as needed.

Unit 1 introduces five strategies for literal comprehension. To understand a selection fully, students must interact with the text to understand the basic facts and details. The strategies on this page help readers find and interpret the meaning of reading material.

How to Use This Page

Introduce the strategies for literal comprehension, presenting each as a tool for reading the selections in this unit.

- As they read "The Sound of Summer Running" (p. 6), students will learn to read fluently in order to improve their understanding.
- As they read "The Circuit" (p. 66) and "Hard as Nails" (p. 72), readers will learn to read fluently with expression.
- As they read "Jeremiah's Song" (p. 38), students will learn to use context clues surrounding words to determine their meaning.
- As they read "The King of Mazy May" (p. 52), students will identify relationships between elements of sentences by using signal words.
- As they read "Dust of Snow" (p. 30), "My Picture-Gallery" (p. 31), and "Saying Yes" (p. 32), students will gain the skill of rereading to clarify ideas presented in poetry.

MODEL A READING STRATEGY: Recognize Signal Words

Good readers use signal words to understand the relationships among ideas. Demonstrate how to use signal words to relate the ideas about Walt Masters's past in "The King of Mazy May," by modeling your thinking with this passage:

> *After* his mother died, his father and he came up on the river . . . *till now* they are settled down on the Mazy May Creek. . . . *Last year* they and several others had spent much toil and time on the Mazy May . . .

Tell students:

After is a signal word showing that things are being reported in time order. *Till now* indicates that the story has caught up with the present. *Last year* lets the reader know that the narrator is looking back in time. All of these words together tell me that the narrator is giving information to outline what has happened in the past and will set the stage for the action in the story.

The Sound of Summer Running

Lesson Objectives

1. **To analyze and respond to literary elements**
   - Literary Analysis: Character's Motives
   - Connecting Literary Elements: Character's Qualities
2. **To read, comprehend, analyze, and critique a short story**
   - Reading Strategy: Read Fluently
   - Reading Check Questions
   - Review and Assess Questions
   - Assessment Practice (ATE)
3. **To develop word analysis skills, fluency, and systematic vocabulary**
   - Vocabulary Development Lesson: Word Analysis: Greek Root *-meter-*
4. **To understand and apply written and oral language conventions**
   - Spelling Strategy
   - Grammar Lesson: Nouns
5. **To understand and apply appropriate writing and research strategies**
   - Writing Lesson: Sneaker Advertisement
   - Extension Activity: Shoe Research
6. **To understand and apply listening and speaking strategies**
   - Extension Activity: Dramatic Reading

STEP-BY-STEP TEACHING GUIDE	PACING GUIDE
PRETEACH	
Motivate Students and Provide Background	
Use the Motivation activity (ATE p. 4)	5 min.
Read and discuss the Preview material and Background information (SE/ATE p. 4) [A]	10 min.
Introduce the Concepts	
Introduce the Literary Analysis and Reading Strategy (SE/ATE p. 5) [A]	25 min.
Pronounce the vocabulary words and read their definitions (SE p. 5)	5 min.
TEACH	
Monitor Comprehension	
Informally monitor comprehension by circulating while students read independently or in groups [A]	20–25 min.
Monitor students' comprehension with the Reading Check notes (SE/ATE pp. 7, 9, 11)	as students read
Develop vocabulary with Vocabulary notes (SE pp. 7, 8, 10, 11)	as students read
Develop Understanding	
Develop students' understanding of character's motives with the Literary Analysis annotations (SE pp. 5, 7, 8, 9, 10; ATE pp. 7, 8, 9, 10) [A]	5 min.
Develop students' ability to read fluently with the Reading Strategy annotations (SE pp. 8, 10; ATE pp. 8, 10)	5 min.
ASSESS	
Assess Mastery	
Assess students' mastery of the Reading Strategy and Literary Analysis by having them answer the Review and Assess questions (SE/ATE p. 13)	25 min.
Use one or more of the print and media Assessment Resources (ATE p. 15) [A]	up to 45 min.
EXTEND	
Apply Understanding	
Have students complete the Vocabulary Development Lesson and the Grammar Lesson (SE p. 14) [A]	20 min.
Apply students' ability to write a sneaker advertisement using the Writing Lesson (SE/ATE p. 15) [A]	45 min.
Apply students' understanding using one or more of the Extension Activities (SE p. 15)	25–90 min.

ACCELERATED INSTRUCTION:
Use the strategies and activities identified with an [A].

UNIVERSAL ACCESS
● = Below Level Students
▲ = On-Level Students
■ = Above Level Students

Time and Resource Manager

Reading Level: Average
Average Number of Instructional Days: 4

RESOURCES		
PRINT	**TRANSPARENCIES**	**TECHNOLOGY**
• **Beyond Literature,** Workplace Skills: Persuasiveness, p. 1 ▲ ■		• **Interest Grabber Videotapes,** Tape 1 ● ▲ ■
• **Selection Support Workbook:** ● ▲ ■ Literary Analysis, p. 5 Reading Strategy, p. 4 Build Vocabulary, p. 1	• **Literary Analysis and Reading Transparencies,** pp. 1 and 2 ● ▲ ■	
• **Adapted Reader's Companion** ● • **Reader's Companion** ●		• **Listening to Literature** ● ▲ ■ Audiocassettes, Side 1 Audio CDs, CD 1
• **English Learner's Companion** ● ▲ • **Literatura en español** ● ▲ • **Literary Analysis for Enrichment** ■	• **Fine Art Transparencies, Volume 1,** Transparency 2 ● ▲ ■	
• **Formal Assessment:** Selection Test, pp. 1–3 ● ▲ ■ • **Open Book Test,** pp. 1–3 ● ▲ ■ • **Performance Assessment and Portfolio Management,** pp. 9, 23 ● ▲ ■ • PRENTICE HALL ASSESSMENT SYSTEM ● ▲ ■	• PRENTICE HALL ASSESSMENT SYSTEM ● ▲ ■ Skills Practice Answers and Explanations on Transparencies	• **Test Bank Software** ● ▲ ■ • **Got It! Assessment Videotapes,** Tape 1 ● ▲
• **Selection Support Workbook:** ● ▲ ■ Build Spelling Skills, p. 2 Build Grammar Skills, p. 3 • **Writing and Grammar,** Copper Level ● ▲ ■ • **Extension Activities,** p. 1 ● ▲ ■	• **Daily Language Practice Transparencies** ● ▲ • **Writing Models and Graphic Organizers on Transparencies** ● ▲ ■	• **Writing and Grammar iText CD-ROM** ● ▲ ■ ***Take It to the Net*** www.phschool.com

BLOCK SCHEDULING: Use one 90-minute class period to preteach the selection and have students read it. Use a second 90-minute class period to assess students' mastery of skills and have them complete one of the Extension Activities.

❸ Writing Lesson

Sneaker Advertisement

Douglas uses vivid, precise words such as *packed snow* and *coiled springs* to create powerful impressions. Advertisers use words to create appealing impressions of a product. Write an advertisement for the sneakers Douglas longs for in the story.

Prewriting Fold a sheet of paper into three panels as shown below. On the first panel, list the qualities of the sneakers. On the second panel, name something else that has that quality. On the third panel, list additional vivid words that describe or name qualities of the sneakers.

Model: Trifold to Identify Precise Language

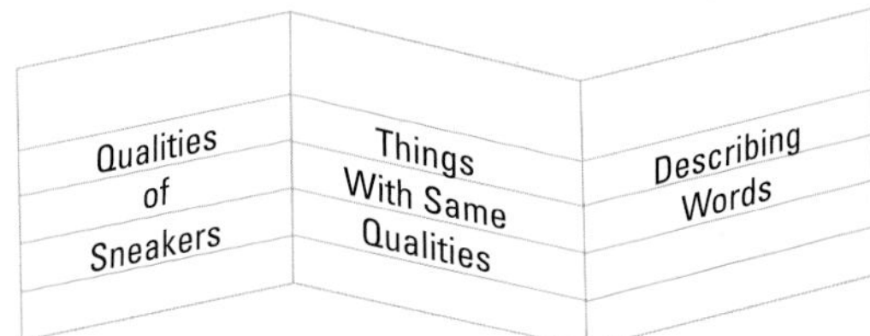

Drafting Review the words you have listed. Use the ones you think are most appealing in a headline. Follow your headline with one or more paragraphs consisting of short sentences with words that capture how the sneakers look and feel.

Revising Ask a peer to circle words in your draft that do not create a strong impression. Replace these words with more vivid, precise words.

WG *Prentice Hall Writing and Grammar Connection: Chapter 6, Section 1*

❹ Extension Activities

Listening and Speaking With a partner, perform a **dramatic reading** of the conversation between Douglas and Mr. Sanderson. Use your voice to help communicate meaning.

1. Pause before introducing an important point.
2. Speak quickly to show excitement, impatience, or eagerness. Speak slowly to show thoughtfulness or curiosity.
3. Speak clearly so that all your points are heard.

Research and Technology When Bradbury wrote this story, there were not many varieties of running shoes. Research different types of running shoes: their uses, purposes, durability, and benefits for feet. Use an electronic source such as a library database. Present your results in a graph or chart, using a computer, if possible, to create a **display of the information.**

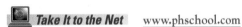

www.phschool.com

Go online for an additional research activity using the Internet.

ASSESSMENT RESOURCES

The following resources can be used to assess students' knowledge and skills.

Selection Assessment

- **Formal Assessment,** pp. 1–3
- **Open Book Test,** pp. 1–3
- **Got It! Assessment Videotapes,** Tape 1
- **Test Bank Software**

Writing Rubric

- **Performance Assess. and Portfolio Mgmt.,** p. 9

Listening and Speaking Rubric

- **Performance Assess. and Portfolio Mgmt.,** p. 23

PRENTICE HALL ASSESSMENT SYSTEM

- **Workbook**
- **Skill Book**
- **Transparencies**
- **CD-ROM**

❸ Writing Lesson

- Point out to students that advertisements are among the most persuasive types of communication in the media. Ads are often successful because of their descriptions.
- Tell students that finding useful and descriptive words sometimes is hard work. Bring to class copies of various advertisements so students can see examples of effective descriptive language.
- Use the writing lesson to guide students in one technique for generating descriptive lists and for drafting a sneaker advertisement.
- Use the Description rubric, p. 9 in **Performance Assessment and Portfolio Management** to evaluate students' advertisements.

❹ Listening and Speaking

- Have students select partners and choose a part to play. Have each pair discuss the conversation between Douglas and Mr. Sanderson.
- Then, have each pair write a script for the exchange between Douglas and Mr. Sanderson.
- Have each pair practice reading their scripts and present their work to the class.
- Have students use the Understanding Tone, Mood, or Emotion rubric, p. 23 in **Performance Assessment and Portfolio Management.**

CUSTOMIZE INSTRUCTION For Universal Access

To address different learning styles, use the activities suggested in the **Extension Activities** booklet, p. 1.

- For Verbal/Linguistic and Bodily/Kinesthetic Learners, use Activity 5.
- For Musical/Rhythmic Learners, use Activity 6.
- For Interpersonal/Mathematical Learners, use Activity 7.

Stray

Lesson Objectives

1. **To analyze and respond to literary elements**
   - Literary Analysis: Surprise Ending
   - Connecting Literary Elements: Plot
2. **To read, comprehend, analyze, and critique a short story**
   - Reading Strategy: Distinguishing Shades of Meaning
   - Reading Check Questions
   - Review and Assess Questions
   - Assessment Practice (ATE)
3. **To develop word analysis skills, fluency, and systematic vocabulary**
   - Vocabulary Development Lesson: Word Analysis: Using the Suffix *-ly*
4. **To understand and apply written and oral language conventions**
   - Spelling Strategy
   - Grammar Lesson: Compound Nouns
5. **To understand and apply appropriate writing and research strategies**
   - Writing Lesson: News Report
   - Extension Activity: Pet Care Chart
6. **To understand and apply listening and speaking strategies**
   - Extension Activity: Oral Presentation

STEP-BY-STEP TEACHING GUIDE	PACING GUIDE
PRETEACH	
Motivate Students and Provide Background	
Use the Motivation activity (ATE p 16)	5 min.
Read and discuss the Preview material and Background information (SE/ATE p. 16) [A]	5 min.
Introduce the Concepts	
Introduce the Literary Analysis and Reading Strategy (SE/ATE p. 17) [A]	15 min.
Pronounce the vocabulary words and read their definitions (SE p. 17)	5 min.
TEACH	
Monitor Comprehension	
Informally monitor comprehension by circulating while students read independently or in groups [A]	10–15 min.
Monitor students' comprehension with the Reading Check notes (SE/ATE pp. 19, 21)	as students read
Develop vocabulary with Vocabulary notes (SE pp. 19, 20, 21)	as students read
Develop Understanding	
Develop students' understanding of surprise endings with the Literary Analysis annotations (SE pp. 20, 21; ATE pp. 20, 21) [A]	5 min.
Develop students' ability to distinguish shades of meaning with the Reading Strategy annotations (SE p. 18; ATE pp. 18, 19)	5 min.
ASSESS	
Assess Mastery	
Assess students' mastery of the Reading Strategy and Literary Analysis by having them answer the Review and Assess questions (SE/ATE p. 23)	15 min.
Use one or more of the print and media Assessment Resources (ATE p. 25) [A]	up to 45 min.
EXTEND	
Apply Understanding	
Have students complete the Vocabulary Development Lesson and the Grammar Lesson (SE p. 24) [A]	20 min.
Apply students' ability to write news reports using the Writing Lesson (SE/ATE p. 25) [A]	30–45 min.
Apply students' understanding of the selection using one or more of the Extension Activities (SE p. 25)	20–90 min.

ACCELERATED INSTRUCTION:
Use the strategies and activities identified with an [A].

UNIVERSAL ACCESS
● = Below Level Students
▲ = On-Level Students
■ = Above Level Students

Time and Resource Manager

Reading Level: Easy
Average Number of Instructional Days: 3

RESOURCES		
PRINT	**TRANSPARENCIES**	**TECHNOLOGY**
• **Beyond Literature,** Workplace Skills: Acting Responsibly, p. 2 ▲ ■		• **Interest Grabber Videotapes,** Tape 1 ● ▲ ■
• **Selection Support Workbook:** ● ▲ ■ Literary Analysis, p. 10 Reading Strategy, p. 9 Build Vocabulary, p. 6	• **Literary Analysis and Reading Transparencies,** pp. 3 and 4 ● ▲ ■	
		• **Listening to Literature** ● ▲ ■ Audiocassettes, Side 1 Audio CDs, CD 1
• **Literary Analysis for Enrichment** ■		
• **Formal Assessment:** Selection Test, pp. 4–6 ● ▲ ■ • **Open Book Test,** pp. 4–6 ● ▲ ■ • **Performance Assessment and Portfolio Management,** p. 18 ● ▲ ■ • PRENTICE HALL ASSESSMENT SYSTEM ● ▲ ■	• PRENTICE HALL ASSESSMENT SYSTEM ● ▲ ■ Skills Practice Answers and Explanations on Transparencies	• **Test Bank Software** ● ▲ ■ • **Got It! Assessment Videotapes,** Tape 1 ● ▲
• **Selection Support Workbook:** ● ▲ ■ Build Spelling Skills, p. 7 Build Grammar Skills, p. 8 • **Writing and Grammar,** Copper Level ● ▲ ■ • **Extension Activities,** p. 2 ● ▲ ■	• **Daily Language Practice Transparencies** ● ▲ • **Writing Models and Graphic Organizers on Transparencies** ● ▲ ■	• **Writing and Grammar iText CD-ROM** ● ▲ ■ *Take It to the Net* www.phschool.com

BLOCK SCHEDULING: Use one 90-minute class period to preteach the selection and have students read it. Use a second 90-minute class period to assess students' mastery of skills and have them complete one of the Extension Activities.

PRETEACH

Step-by-Step Teaching Guide for pp. 16–17

Motivation

Ask students to imagine watching a puppy through a window as it walks outside on a cold day. Then, have partners role-play a scene in which a child tries to convince an adult to take in the lost puppy and adopt it. Ask the partner playing the adult to suggest other options. Next, ask volunteers to share actual experiences they have had while owning a pet. Tell students that this is a story about a girl who wants to keep a stray dog she finds on a cold, snowy day.

Interest Grabber Video

As an alternative, play "Dog Training" on Tape 1 to engage student interest.

❶ Background

Social Studies

It is thought that dogs were the first animals to be domesticated, or to become part of human households. Evidence suggests that dogs were a part of prehistoric civilizations. They have rescued people from danger, carried messages during wars, guarded cattle, and assisted police officers. Dogs are also very useful companions to humans; they guide blind people and signal deaf people that doorbells or telephones are ringing. In addition to being useful, dogs are known as faithful companions to their owners.

Prepare to Read

❶ Stray

Take It to the Net

Visit www.phschool.com for interactive activities and instruction related to "Stray," including

- background
- graphic organizers
- literary elements
- reading strategies

Preview

Connecting to the Literature

Sometimes, you cannot have what you want because there is not enough time, not enough space, or not enough money. The main character in this story knows her family cannot afford a pet. Words will not change the facts, so she keeps her feelings quiet.

Background

Animal shelters take in stray animals as well as pets that people can no longer keep. Although good animal shelters have the best interests of the animals at heart, many shelters at first appear frightening or depressing because of the noises, smells, and rows of cages.

TEACHING RESOURCES

The following resources can be used to enrich or extend the instruction for pp. 16–17.

Motivation

Interest Grabber Video, Tape 1

Background

Beyond Literature, p. 2

Take It to the Net

Visit www.phschool.com for Background and hotlinks for "Stray."

Literary Analysis

Literary Analysis and Reading Transparencies, Surprise Ending, p. 4

Reading

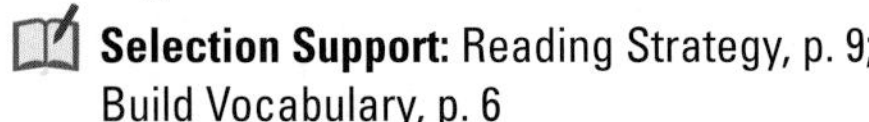

Selection Support: Reading Strategy, p. 9; Build Vocabulary, p. 6

Literary Analysis and Reading Transparencies, Distinguishing Shades of Meaning, p. 3

BLOCK SCHEDULING: Resources marked with this symbol provide varied instruction during 90-minute blocks.

❷ Literary Analysis

Surprise Ending

When you read a story, the details lead you to expect a certain kind of ending. Sometimes, a story has a **surprise ending**— it ends differently from what you expected. Use a graphic like the one here to track details that lead you to expect "Stray" to end one way and details that lead to the actual ending.

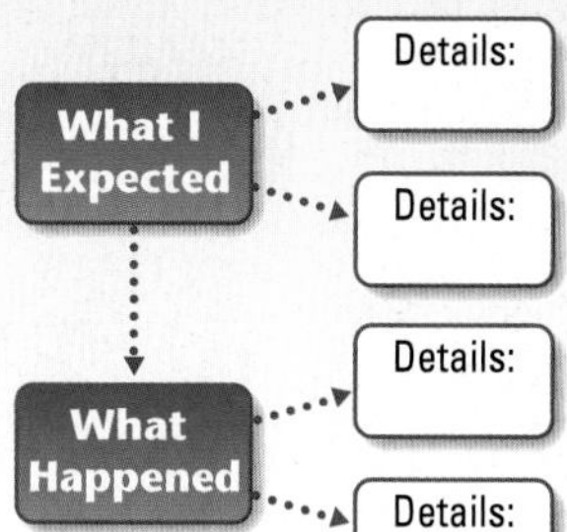

Connecting Literary Elements

When you are surprised by the ending of a story, it is because the **plot,** or sequence of related events, did not turn out the way you expected. In most short stories, plot events are related to a single problem or situation. The events lead up to the moment when the problem is solved or the situation turns out one way or another.

Use these focus questions to help you think about the plot of "Stray."

1. What problem does Doris face in "Stray"?
2. What seems to be the most likely outcome of the situation?

❸ Reading Strategy

Distinguishing Shades of Meaning

Many words have similar meanings. For example, *softly* and *quietly* have about the same meaning. However, each word conveys a shade of meaning, a slight difference, that makes it the best choice for a particular situation. To understand the effect of shades of meaning, notice how the following sentences would change if the italicized words were exchanged.

It always wagged its tail, eyes all *sleepy*, when she found it there.

Lying there, like stone, still *exhausted*, she wondered if she would ever in her life have anything.

When you come across a word that describes how a character thinks or feels, pause for a moment to identify the precise meaning of that word.

Vocabulary Development

timidly (tim′ id lē) *adv.* in a way that shows fear or shyness (p. 18)

trudged (trujd) *v.* walked as if tired or with effort (p. 18)

grudgingly (gruj′ iŋ lē) *adv.* in an unenthusiastic or resentful way (p. 19)

ignore (ig nôr′) *v.* pay no attention to (p. 20)

exhausted (eg zôs′ tid) *adj.* tired out (p. 21)

❷ Literary Analysis

Surprise Ending

- Call students' attention to the puppy shown on p. 16. Ask them to describe the puppy's personality, based on the picture.
- Tell students that details in a story also lead readers to have expectations about the ending. When a story ends in an unexpected way, it is called a "surprise ending."
- Read the instruction about surprise endings together as a class. Call students' attention to the graphic organizer.
- Use the instruction for Connecting Literary Elements to connect the story's plot to its outcome. Encourage students to remember the focus questions as they read.
- Use the Surprise Ending transparency on p. 4 in **Literary Analysis and Reading Transparencies** to explain how some details may support one ending but other details will support another ending.

❸ Reading Strategy

Distinguishing Shades of Meaning

- Remind students that many words have meanings that are close to the meanings of other words, such as *cool* and *chilly*.
- Then, tell students that a reader's job is to understand the small differences between word meanings. Together, read the instruction about shades of meaning.
- Instruct students to reflect on shades of meanings as they read.

Vocabulary Development

- Pronounce each vocabulary word for students, and read the definitions as a class. Have students identify any words with which they are already familiar.

CUSTOMIZE INSTRUCTION FOR UNIVERSAL ACCESS

For Less Proficient Readers	For English Learners	For Advanced Readers
Have students select partners. Partners should take turns acting out the vocabulary words on p. 17. After students have acted out the words, instruct them to list an opposite word for each vocabulary word (for example, *boldly, skipped, gladly, notice,* and *energetic*). Then have students act out the list of opposites.	Have students make a list of verbs. Tell students that *-ed* is a suffix that is added to most verbs to show something that happened in the past, as *trudge* changes to *trudged.* Have students use a grammar book to review the rules for adding *-ed* to verbs.	Have students check a thesaurus to find synonyms for each of the Vocabulary Development words on p. 17. Then, have them create a chart that shows synonyms of greater, lesser, or equal intensity. Discuss with students how the effects of the sentences would be changed by using the synonyms.

E-Teach

Visit E-Teach at www.phschool.com for teachers' essays on how to teach, with questions and answers.

TEACH

Step-by-Step Teaching Guide for pp. 18–22

CUSTOMIZE INSTRUCTION For Verbal/Linguistic Learners

Have small groups of students take turns reading aloud parts of the story. Then, have them discuss the difference between reading stories silently and hearing them read.

1 About the Selection

Mr. and Mrs. Lacey and their daughter Doris are stranded at home following a severe winter storm. Doris notices an abandoned puppy on the snowy road and brings it indoors. She knows and is reminded by her parents that the family cannot afford a pet. They tell her that she can keep the puppy only until the roads clear enough for Mr. Lacey to drive it to the pound. Doris forms a bond with the puppy and is heartbroken when the time comes for her father to take it away. The events that follow illustrate the individual ways in which the Laceys find a voice to express their feelings.

2 Reading Strategy

Distinguishing Shades of Meaning

- Ask a volunteer to read aloud the bracketed passages.
- Call attention to the word *shivering* and the word *trembling.*
- Ask students the Reading Strategy question on p. 18: How is the meaning of *shivering* similar to and different from that of *trembling*?
  Answer: The words are similar because they both mean moving just a little bit. They are different because *shivering* usually happens because of the cold but *trembling* happens because of fear.

1 # Stray

Cynthia Rylant

In January, a puppy wandered onto the property of Mr. Amos Lacey and his wife, Mamie, and their daughter, Doris. Icicles hung three feet or more from the eaves of houses, snowdrifts swallowed up automobiles and the birds were so fluffed up they looked comic.

The puppy had been abandoned, and it made its way down the road toward the Laceys' small house, its ears tucked, its tail between its legs, shivering.

2 Doris, whose school had been called off because of the snow, was out shoveling the cinderblock front steps when she spotted the pup on the road. She set down the shovel.

"Hey! Come on!" she called.

The puppy stopped in the road, wagging its tail timidly, trembling with shyness and cold.

Doris trudged through the yard, went up the shoveled drive and met the dog.

"Come on, Pooch."

Reading Strategy
Distinguish Shades of Meaning How is the meaning of *shivering* similar to and different from that of *trembling*?

timidly (tim´ id lē) *adv.* in a way that shows fear or shyness

trudged (trujd) *v.* walked as if tired or with effort

TEACHING RESOURCES

The following resources can be used to enrich or extend the instruction for pp. 18–22.

Literary Analysis
- **Selection Support:** Literary Analysis, p. 10
- **Literary Analysis for Enrichment**

Reading
- **Listening to Literature Audiocassettes,** Side 1
- **Listening to Literature Audio CDs,** CD 1

BLOCK SCHEDULING: Resources marked with this symbol provide varied instruction during 90-minute blocks.

"Where did *that* come from?" Mrs. Lacey asked as soon as Doris put the dog down in the kitchen.

Mr. Lacey was at the table, cleaning his fingernails with his pocketknife. The snow was keeping him home from his job at the warehouse.

"I don't know where it came from," he said mildly, "but I know for sure where it's going."

Doris hugged the puppy hard against her. She said nothing.

Because the roads would be too bad for travel for many days, Mr. Lacey couldn't get out to take the puppy to the pound[1] in the city right away. He agreed to let it sleep in the basement while Mrs. Lacey grudgingly let Doris feed it table scraps. The woman was sensitive about throwing out food.

By the looks of it, Doris figured the puppy was about six months old, and on its way to being a big dog. She thought it might have some shepherd in it.

3 **grudgingly** (gruj′ iŋ lē) *adv.* in an unenthusiastic or resentful way

4 **Reading Check**

What does Mr. Lacey plan to do with the puppy?

1. **pound** animal shelter.

3 Reading Strategy

Distinguishing Shades of Meaning

- Tell students to consult a dictionary when they have difficulty distinguishing shades of meaning between words.
- Call students' attention to the word *grudgingly*, and ask them how its meaning is similar to and different from that of *reluctantly*.
  Answer: The word *grudgingly* implies a stronger sense of reluctance to give up or release the puppy than does the word *reluctance*. To be *reluctant* is merely to be *unwilling*.

Monitor Progress Have students discuss similarities and differences between *figured* and *thought* in the paragraph beginning "By the looks of it . . . ."
Answer: Both words describe what Doris was thinking. *Figured* makes it sound like math or another logical skill was used to arrive at a conclusion, but *thought* can describe an opinion that is not based on facts.

Reteach If students have difficulty answering the questions, suggest that they reread the sentences to find context clues. They could also consult a dictionary or a thesaurus for specific meanings of the words in question.

4 Reading Check

Answer: He plans to take it to the pound.

CUSTOMIZE INSTRUCTION FOR UNIVERSAL ACCESS

For Special Needs Students	For English Learners	For Gifted/Talented Students
Have students imagine looking out the window on a cold, icy day when they see a shivering puppy outside. Have them discuss how it would feel to be outside the window looking in and then inside looking out. Encourage students to use this and other images in the story to help them understand the characters' thoughts and feelings.	To help students understand the phrases that describe the setting, read the first paragraph of the selection chorally. Use a yardstick to show how long a three-foot icicle (define *icicle* if necessary) would be. Put desks together to simulate the size of a car. Have students figure out how much snow would "swallow" a car.	Have students work in small groups to plan a speech that Doris might make to convince her parents to let her keep the dog. Students may wish to include reasons that show how she would benefit from keeping the dog. They should also prepare arguments she might use to counter her parents' possible objections.

5 Literary Analysis

Surprise Ending

- Read the bracketed passage aloud. Then, have students name the details in the passage. Record student contributions on the board.
  Possible responses: Doris didn't name the dog; she knew her parents wouldn't let her keep it; the family couldn't afford pets; the pup would definitely go to the pound.
- Ask students the Literary Analysis question on p. 20: What outcome do these details lead you to expect?
  Answer: Doris will not be allowed to keep the dog.

6 Critical Thinking

Draw Conclusions

- Read aloud the bracketed passage. Ask students why Doris is pointing out positive things about the puppy.
  Answer: She is trying to change her parents' minds.
- Ask students what Mrs. Lacey's reaction to Doris's comments means.
  Answer: Mrs. Lacey's feelings about keeping the dog will not change.

Four days passed and the puppy did not complain. It never cried in the night or howled at the wind. It didn't tear up everything in the basement. It wouldn't even follow Doris up the basement steps unless it was invited.

It was a good dog.

Several times Doris had opened the door in the kitchen that led to the basement and the puppy had been there, all stretched out, on the top step. Doris knew it had wanted some company and that it had lain against the door, listening to the talk in the kitchen, smelling the food, being a part of things. It always wagged its tail, eyes all sleepy, when she found it there.

5 Even after a week had gone by, Doris didn't name the dog. She knew her parents wouldn't let her keep it, that her father made so little money any pets were out of the question, and that the pup would definitely go to the pound when the weather cleared.

Still, she tried talking to them about the dog at dinner one night.

6 "She's a good dog, isn't she?" Doris said, hoping one of them would agree with her.

Her parents glanced at each other and went on eating.

"She's not much trouble," Doris added. "I like her." She smiled at them, but they continued to ignore her.

"I figure she's real smart," Doris said to her mother. "I could teach her things."

Mrs. Lacey just shook her head and stuffed a forkful of sweet potato in her mouth. Doris fell silent, praying the weather would never clear.

But on Saturday, nine days after the dog had arrived, the sun was shining and the roads were plowed. Mr. Lacey opened up the trunk of his car and came into the house.

Doris was sitting alone in the living room, hugging a pillow and rocking back and forth on the edge of a chair. She was trying not to cry but she was not strong enough. Her face was wet and red, her eyes full of distress.

Mrs. Lacey looked into the room from the doorway.

"Mama," Doris said in a small voice. "Please."

Mrs. Lacey shook her head.

"You know we can't afford a dog, Doris. You try to act more grown-up about this."

Doris pressed her face into the pillow.

Outside, she heard the trunk of the car slam shut, one of the doors open and close, the old engine cough and choke and finally start up.

"Daddy," she whispered. "Please."

She heard the car travel down the road, and, though it was early afternoon, she could do nothing but go to her bed. She

Literary Analysis
Surprise Ending What outcome do these details lead you to expect?

ignore (ig nôr′) *v.* pay no attention to

ENRICHMENT: Math Connection

How Many Dogs?

Animal shelters are overcrowded with stray animals because the number of stray animals grows exponentially. That is, the numbers multiply in increasing proportions. Suppose one pair of stray dogs has six puppies in a year, and each of those puppies grows up to have six puppies, and so on. To find out how many puppies result in six years from that first group, multiply $6 \times 6 \times 6 \times 6 \times 6 \times 6$.

cried herself to sleep, and her dreams were full of searching and searching for things lost.

7 It was nearly night when she finally woke up. Lying there, like stone, still exhausted, she wondered if she would ever in her life have anything. She stared at the wall for a while.

But she started feeling hungry, and she knew she'd have to make herself get out of bed and eat some dinner. She wanted not to go into the kitchen, past the basement door. She wanted not to face her parents.

But she rose up heavily.

Her parents were sitting at the table, dinner over, drinking coffee. They looked at her when she came in, but she kept her head down. No one spoke.

exhausted (eg zôs′ tid) *adj.* tired out

8 **Reading Check**

What does Doris do when Mr. Lacey takes the dog?

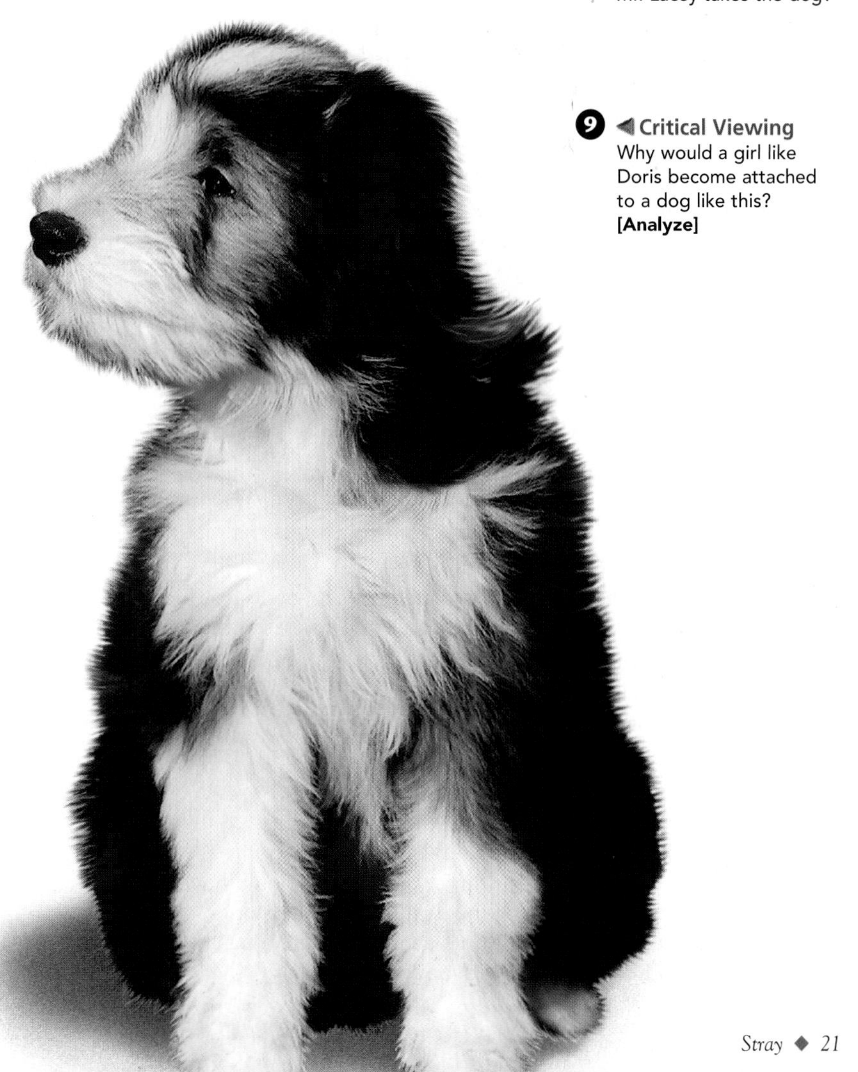

9 ◄ **Critical Viewing** Why would a girl like Doris become attached to a dog like this? **[Analyze]**

7 Literary Analysis

Surprise Ending

- Call on a volunteer to read the bracketed passage.
- Then, ask the question: Considering Mr. Lacey's actions, what do you expect to happen now?
  Answer: Doris will find out that the dog is gone for certain.
- Ask students to explain how the character's words and actions led them to predict as they did.
  Possible answer: Since Mr. Lacey hasn't shown any sign that he wants to keep the dog, he probably took it to the pound the first chance he had.

8 Reading Check

Answer: Doris goes to bed and cries when her father takes the dog.

9 ►Critical Viewing

Possible responses: Doris might like all dogs; the puppy is cute; the puppy might like to cuddle and play.

CUSTOMIZE INSTRUCTION FOR UNIVERSAL ACCESS

For Less Proficient Readers	For Advanced Readers
Because many of the characters' thoughts and actions are implied rather than directly stated, students may benefit from listening to the story on audiocassette in small groups. They can then stop the tape from time to time to discuss what is happening. As they listen and discuss, take notes on the Surprise Ending transparency, p. 4 of **Literary Analysis and Reading Transparencies.**	Encourage students to consider their opinions of the characters. Have students list character traits as they read, adding more traits when they finish reading and have a better idea of the characters. Students can make charts or webs that describe character traits at the beginning and at the end of the story. Have each student select a character and describe how and why his or her opinion of that character changed by the end of the story.

ASSESS

Answers for p. 22

Review and Assess

1. Students should support their opinions with evidence from the story.
2. **(a)** The Laceys wait because the weather is bad. **(b)** The dog is easy to keep. **(c)** The waiting makes it harder to give up the dog because Doris becomes attached to him.
3. **(a)** Doris says nothing but hugs the puppy. **(b)** She wants to keep the puppy but understands her parents' reasoning.
4. **(a)** Possible response: The pound is a smelly, noisy place. **(b)** He doesn't want to leave the dog at the pound because of the conditions there.
5. **(a)** Possible response: He might like the dog and feel bad about hurting Doris's feelings. **(b)** Doris shows love in the way she cares about the dog and respects her parents. Mr. Lacey shows love by bringing the dog home. Mrs. Lacey shows love when she smiles at the end. Mr. and Mrs. Lacey show common sense when they talk about the reasons not to keep the dog. Doris shows common sense when she tries to accept the reasons that she won't be allowed to keep the dog.
6. **(a)** Possible response: Yes, because she might have convinced her parents. **(b)** Possible response: Doris can take responsibility for the dog, including feeding and training it.

Doris made herself a glass of powdered milk and drank it all down. Then she picked up a cold biscuit and started out of the room.

"You'd better feed that mutt before it dies of starvation," Mr. Lacey said.

Doris turned around.

"What?"

"I said, you'd better feed your dog. I figure it's looking for you."

Doris put her hand to her mouth.

"You didn't take her?" she asked.

"Oh, I took her all right," her father answered. "Worst looking place I've ever seen. Ten dogs to a cage. Smell was enough to knock you down. And they give an animal six days to live. Then they kill it with some kind of a shot."

Doris stared at her father.

"I wouldn't leave an *ant* in that place," he said. "So I brought the dog back."

Mrs. Lacey was smiling at him and shaking her head as if she would never, ever, understand him.

Mr. Lacey sipped his coffee.

"Well," he said, "are you going to feed it or not?"

Cynthia Rylant

(b. 1954)

As a child, Cynthia Rylant didn't think she would be a writer.

"I always felt my life was too limited," she says. "Nothing to write about." At the age of twenty-four, however, she discovered that her life did in fact contain the seeds of many stories.

Her first book, *When I Was Young in the Mountains*, describes her childhood in the hills of West Virginia. Cynthia lived with her grandparents for four years in a tiny house without plumbing. This experience of hardship may be reflected in "Stray." Rylant has a special attachment to her young characters who, she feels, have more "possibilities": "They can get away with more love, more anger, more fear than adult characters . . ."

Review and Assess

Thinking About the Selection

1. **Respond:** Do you think the Laceys care about Doris's feelings? Why or why not?
2. **(a) Recall:** Why do the Laceys wait before taking the dog to the pound? **(b) Evaluate:** How difficult is keeping the dog during this time? **(c) Analyze:** In what way does the waiting make giving the dog away more difficult for Doris?
3. **(a) Recall:** What does Doris do when her father tells her she can't keep the dog? **(b) Analyze:** Explain why Doris reacts this way.
4. **(a) Recall:** In your own words, restate Mr. Lacey's description of the pound. **(b) Analyze Cause and Effect:** Why does Mr. Lacey change his mind about keeping the dog?
5. **(a) Draw Conclusions:** For what reasons, other than the condition of the pound, might Mr. Lacey have brought the dog home? **(b) Interpret:** Which character(s) show love? Which character(s) show common sense? Explain.
6. **(a) Take a Position:** Do you feel like Doris should have made a stronger case for keeping the dog? Why or why not? **(b) Speculate:** What can Doris do in the future to make her father feel like he made the right decision?

ASSESSMENT PRACTICE: Reading Comprehension

Using Context Clues (For more practice, see Test Preparation Workbook, p. 2)

Many tests require students to use context clues to determine word meanings. Use the following sample item to show students how they can infer the meaning of an unfamiliar word from the surrounding text.

The puppy stopped in the road, wagging its tail timidly, trembling with shyness and cold.

In this passage, the word timidly most nearly means ______ .

A boldy
B shyly
C angrily
D carelessly

The puppy is described as "trembling with shyness," so it probably is not bold, angry, or careless. Thus, *A*, *C*, and *D* are incorrect. A shy puppy shaking from the cold probably is also afraid. *B* is the correct answer.

Review and Assess

Literary Analysis

Surprise Ending

1. Identify two facts about the family that make it unlikely they will keep the dog.
2. What details make you believe that the dog is gone forever?
3. How does Doris's father let her know that he kept the dog? Explain how this action makes the ending a surprise.

Connecting Literary Elements

4. What problem does Doris face in "Stray"?
5. What seems to be the most likely outcome of the situation?
6. On a diagram like the one below, identify **plot** events that lead up to the moment when the final decision seems to be made.
7. Identify the plot event that shows how the situation turns out.

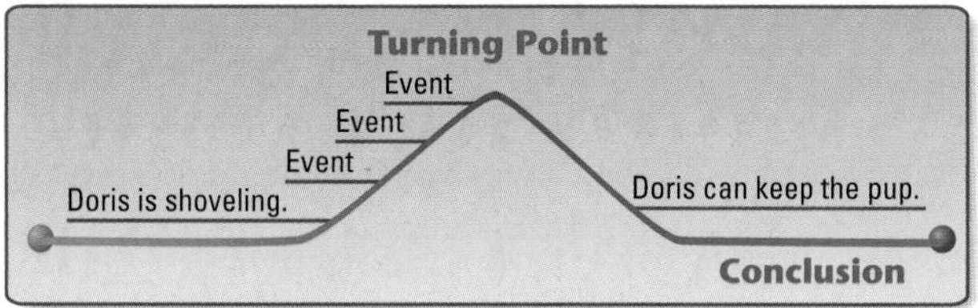

Reading Strategy

Distinguishing Shades of Meaning

8. Explain the different **shades of meaning** for the words in italics.
   It never *cried* in the night or *howled* at the wind.
9. Complete the following chart by supplying words that convey shades of meaning related to the word at the top of each column. Explain how each word you provide is different from the original word.

timid	trembling	hungry

Extending Understanding

10. **Make a Judgment:** Why might one person choose to have a pet and another choose not to?

Quick Review

A **surprise ending** occurs when the events of the story lead you to expect a different ending. To review surprise ending, see page 17.

Plot is the sequence of events that unfolds in the story. To review plot, see page 17.

Shades of meaning are the slight differences between words that have similar meanings.

Take It to the Net

www.phschool.com

Take the interactive self-test online to check your understanding of the selection.

ENRICHMENT: Further Reading

Other Works by Cynthia Rylant

Missing May

A Fine White Dust

But I'll Be Back Again

Take It to the Net

Visit www.phschool.com for more information on Cynthia Rylant.

Answers for p. 23

Review and Assess

1. The parents seem certain about not keeping the dog; the family doesn't have enough money to keep a pet.
2. Doris hears her father open the car trunk and then slam it closed; then she hears him get in the car and drive away.
3. Mr. Lacey's casually telling Doris to feed her dog, which she thought was gone, helps make the ending a surprise.
4. She wants to keep a dog, but her parents say that she can't.
5. The dog will probably go to the pound.
6.

Turning Point

Event Doris finds dog.

Event Parents say she can't keep dog.

Event Dad brings dog dog to pound.

Event Dad takes dog back home.

Event Dad tells Doris to feed the dog.

Conclusion

7. Dad tells Doris to feed the dog.
8. Crying is softer and sadder than howling. Howling is unpleasant and loud.
9. Timid: shy, scared. To be timid is to hang back; to be shy is to be unwilling to call attention to yourself; to be scared is to be afraid of something. Trembling: shaking, shivering. To tremble is to shake because of fear; to shake is to move for any number of reasons; to shiver is to shake because of cold. Hungry: famished, ravenous. To be hungry is to feel a need for food; to be famished is to be very hungry; to be ravenous is to be almost mad with hunger.
10. A person might choose to have a pet for protection or for companionship. Another person might decide not to have a pet because it is expensive and bothersome.

EXTEND

Answers for p. 24

❶ Vocabulary Development

Word Analysis

1. beautifully; in a very pretty way
2. sadly; in a way that shows sorrow
3. immediately; in a very prompt way, doing something right now

Spelling Strategy

1. trudge
2. large; huge
3. courage
4. garage

Concept Development: Connotations

1. timidly
2. grudgingly
3. trudged
4. exhausted
5. ignore

❷ Grammar

1. Doris shoveled the driveway.
2. Doris does a lot of work for an eleven-year-old.
3. She had a sweet potato, meatloaf, and a milkshake for dinner.
4. Mr. Lacey's sister is Mrs. Lacey's sister-in-law.
5. Snowdrifts covered the treetops.

Writing Application

Students' paragraphs should be about their favorite pet or other animal and should include three compound words.

Integrate Language Skills

❶ Vocabulary Development Lesson

Word Analysis: Suffix *-ly*

Words that end in the suffix *-ly* usually answer the question *how* or *in what way*. In "Stray," the puppy wags its tail *timidly*—in a shy and fearful way. Add the suffix *-ly* to each word below. Define each new word.

1. beautiful 2. sad 3. immediate

Spelling Strategy

English words that end in the *j* sound, such as *grudge*, are spelled with a *ge* or *dge* at the end. Practice this unexpected consonant spelling. For each of the following phrases, write a synonym that spells the *j* sound with one of those letter combinations.

1. walk slowly
2. very big
3. bravery
4. building for parked cars

Concept Development: Connotations

Besides dictionary meanings, words have **connotations**—associations that they call to mind. The word *cheap*, for example, has a similar meaning to the word *inexpensive*. However, the word *cheap* may call to mind something that is shoddy.

Choose the word from this list that is similar in meaning to the italicized word. Then, explain the different connotations of the two words.

exhausted grudgingly ignore
trudged timidly

1. Darren was relieved that the strange dog approached him *shyly*.
2. When Dad told Ryan to share the ball, he handed it to me *unenthusiastically*.
3. Dreading the test, Maya *walked* up the hill.
4. Taylor was *tired* after doing extra chores.
5. Ms. Wolfson said to *disregard* the questions.

❷ Grammar Lesson

Compound Nouns

Nouns—words that name people, places, or things—sometimes contain two or more words. Nouns made up of more than one word are called **compound nouns**. Compound nouns can be written as one word, as separate words, or as words linked by a hyphen.

Written as one word:
thunderstorm sunlight
Written with a hyphen between words:
ten-year-old mother-in-law
Written as separate words:
ice cream pen pal

Practice Copy the following sentences and underline each compound noun.

1. Doris shoveled the driveway.
2. Doris does a lot of work for an eleven-year-old.
3. She had a sweet potato, meatloaf, and a milkshake for dinner.
4. Mr. Lacey's sister is Mrs. Lacey's sister-in-law.
5. Snowdrifts covered the treetops.

Writing Application Write a short paragraph about a favorite animal or pet. Include three compound nouns in your paragraph.

WG *Prentice Hall Writing and Grammar Connection: Chapter 14, Section 1*

24 ◆ *Growing and Changing*

TEACHING RESOURCES

The following resources can be used to enrich or extend the instruction for pp. 24–25.

Vocabulary

- **Selection Support:** Build Spelling Skills, p. 7
- **Vocabulary and Spelling Practice Book** (Use this booklet for skills enrichment) ■

Grammar

- **Selection Support:** Build Grammar Skills, p. 8
- **Writing and Grammar,** Copper Level, p. 296
- **Daily Language Practice Transparencies** ■

Writing

- **Writing and Grammar,** Copper Level, p. 182 ■
- **Writing Models and Graphic Organizers on Transparencies,** KWL Organizer, p. 61
- **Writing and Grammar iText CD-ROM**

■ **BLOCK SCHEDULING:** Resources marked with this symbol provide varied instruction during 90-minute blocks.

❸ Writing Lesson

News Report

Doris's father has strong words to say about the local animal shelter. News reporters often respond to people's negative reactions by investigating. Write your own investigative news report about the problems facing animal shelters and the ways these problems are being addressed.

Prewriting Use library resources or call animal shelters to gather details. Use the five W's—who, what, where, when, and why—to guide you.

Drafting Begin with a lead sentence that contains a statistic, quotation, or other detail to capture readers' attention. Follow it with one or more short, clear sentences that sum up the basic facts. Continue with examples and details that illustrate your overall point.

Model: Beginning With an Effective Lead

"I wouldn't leave an ant in that place," said Amos Lacey. Mr. Lacey is speaking about the animal shelter in his town, where animals are kept in overcrowded, unhealthy conditions. Other shelters, however, do fine work.

Mr. Lacey's words make readers wonder why he wouldn't leave a dog there. This statement grabs readers' interest and leads them to read further.

Revising Identify the question raised by your lead. If no question is raised, consider rewriting to build curiosity in your readers.

WG Prentice Hall Writing and Grammar Connection: Chapter 9, Section 3

❹ Extension Activities

Listening and Speaking With a small group of students, organize a **presentation** about stray animals. Include a speaker from the local animal shelter. Group members may choose from the following tasks:

1. Call local shelters to find a speaker.
2. Prepare questions to ask the speaker.
3. Prepare an introduction to the speaker.
4. Lead a discussion of the problems facing shelters and possible solutions.

Research and Technology Create a **chart** showing the cost and time involved in owning a dog. Use prices from pet supply stores and do an Internet search for dog care information based on the type and size of dog. If possible, use a word processing or graphics program to create your chart.

Take It to the Net www.phschool.com

Go online for an additional research activity using the Internet.

ASSESSMENT RESOURCES

The following resources can be used to assess students' knowledge and skills.

Selection Assessment

Formal Assessment, pp. 4–6

Open Book Test, pp. 4–6

Got It! Assessment Videotapes, Tape 1

Test Bank Software

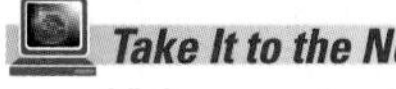

Take It to the Net

Visit www.phschool.com for self-tests and additional questions on "Stray."

Writing Rubric

Performance Assess. and Portfolio Mgmt., p. 18

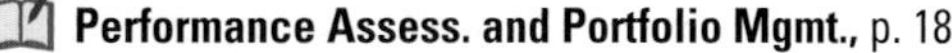

Workbook

Transparencies

Skill Book

CD-ROM

Lesson Support for p. 25

❸ Writing Lesson

- Read students short newspaper stories to show how reporters include necessary information in their articles.
- Use the writing lesson to guide students in developing a news story about animal shelters.
- Use the Exposition rubric on p. 18 in **Performance Assessment and Portfolio Management** to evaluate students' news reports.

❹ Research and Technology

- Divide the class into groups. Assign each group a research activity related to the topic, such as vaccinations, exercise needs, or food needs.
- Show some students how to use a search engine to find prices for pet supplies. Other students may consult local newspapers or pet stores to get similar information.
- Other groups can research dog breeds and sizes on the Internet or at the library.
- Have students use appropriate software to compile the information.
- Have students make the chart available to prospective pet owners.

CUSTOMIZE INSTRUCTION For Universal Access

To address different learning styles, use the activities suggested on p. 2 in the **Extension Activities** booklet.

- For Logical/Mathematical Learners, use Activity 5.
- For Verbal/Linguistic and Interpersonal Learners, use Activities 6 and 7.

Lesson Objectives

1. To understand the connection between dogs described in literature and dogs who appear in television shows and movies
2. To understand the lifestyle of dogs that appear in the media

Connections

Just as the puppy in "Stray" found its way into the hearts of the Lacey family, the dogs described in this article from *TV Guide* entertain and find their way into the hearts of millions of television viewers and movie patrons. Ask students to speculate on the differences between the treatment of the puppy in "Stray" and of celebrity animals.

Animal Characters

- Discuss with students their favorite animal stars. List the names of the animals on the board.
- If possible, show short video clips of animal stars in action.
- Explain to students that the dogs that they see on television and in movies are considered actors. These dogs have agents and other representatives, just as people who star in movies and on television shows do.
- Point out to students that the dogs in "TV's Top Dogs" were found in dog pounds or given up by their owners. Although they have had special coaching and training, they are not very different from the pets that some of the students may have at home.
- Connect this article to the short story "Stray" by discussing the qualities that set some dogs apart, such as their intelligence or personality. Use examples of patience and intelligence from the article and from "Stray."

CONNECTIONS

Literature and the Media

Animal Characters

More than one of the dogs you will read about in this article from *TV Guide* once lived in a pound as a stray—just like the puppy in "Stray." These dogs were lucky that humans saw something special in them—something that made each dog a star.

TV's Top Dogs

Deborah Starr Seibel

The star's handlers were clearly worried. Their anxiety had been filtering through phone and fax lines for more than a week over a request for an important photo session—known in the business as a "cover try." They were interested, but would their star be on the cover? No guarantee. Would their client have to share the spotlight with other celebrities? Maybe. Publicists conferred with other handlers, including studio executives in charge of the star's next big project. Suddenly, negotiations stalled.

Elizabeth Taylor? Julia Roberts? The women of "Melrose Place"? No, that little photo-shoot nightmare involved getting Lassie— Lassie!—to pose.

It epitomizes, however, the new pecking order among TV's top dogs, suddenly superbig, superhot. Superdogs. New power pooches—including Comet and Barkley from "Full House," Eddie from "Frasier," and Murray from "Mad About You"[1]—are forcing Lassie to make room as they paw their way into the ranks of Hollywood's power players.

How powerful? Well, their newfound clout[2] is propelling the canine craze into daytime. Vinnie, a lovable one-eared mutt, has the run of ABC's new daytime talk show "Mike & Maty." The dog often sits on Maty's lap during interviews. Another talk show is going even further by giving its bowwow top billing: On "Pet Department," on the fX channel, Jack the Dog is—hang onto your leash—the *co-host.* "The other host, Steve Walker, is human," explains the show's publicist.

It's a Cinderella story for many of these dogs. Vinnie was rescued from the pound.

---

1. **"Full House," . . . "Frasier," . . . "Mad About You"** television shows popular in the 1990s.
2. **clout** (klout) n. power; influence.

ENRICHMENT: Science Connection

A World of Working Dogs

The partnership between humans and dogs dates back about 10,000 years. Like TV's top dogs in America, dogs throughout history have had jobs reflecting the times and cultures in which they lived.

In the prehistoric hunting society in what is now Algiers, rock art shows dogs helping a hunter corner a wild ox. In ancient Egypt, faithful dogs appear in wall paintings of royal tombs, sitting under their masters' chairs or assisting in a hunt.

In modern times, breeds of dogs from long ago still work. In the 1600s, the Saint Bernard was bred in Switzerland to rescue people stranded in the snowy Alps. In Japan, large and powerful akitas were owned only by royalty and were bred to hunt large animals. Today, they are used as effective guard dogs. As long ago as 1000 B.C., the Siberian husky was bred as a sled dog to transport people across the tundra. In the pastures of Scotland, collies were bred to help herd and protect sheep.

Eddie was given up by his owners because he was too much to handle. Seeing a certain something—energy, intelligence, or an unusual personality—Hollywood animal trainers adopt these dogs, refine their skills, and take them to casting calls. If they make the cut and the show is a hit, the transformation from house dog to superdog is complete.

Two-hundred-fifty dollars a day is the standard superdog rate (roughly $31 an hour, if you're doing the math). And then there are the extras. When Lassie makes out-of-town appearances, for example, she (he, really—all eight Lassies have been males) flies first class in a reserved seat. He also has his own traveling companion, a Jack Russell[3] named Mel Gibson. At their hotel, Lassie often drinks bottled water and indulges in gourmet biscuits.

Barkley, the sometimes ferocious-looking Jack Russell terrier with a two-picture deal at MGM, also flies first class, has his own director's chair, and demands ground transport worthy of a visiting dignitary.

Eddie, another scrappy Jack Russell, who regularly unnerves—and upstages—Dr. Frasier Crane with his persistent stare, sports Holiday cologne for dogs and eats "high-quality cooked chicken, hot dogs, and stew beef," according to his trainer, Mathilde deCagny. How good is the chow? "I eat it myself when I get hungry," she says, looking guilty.

It's a glam life. But these are special animals. At the *TV Guide* photo shoot, Barkley puts Murray and Eddie—and every other canine you've ever met—to shame. He's like a little old lady, full of dignity, never making noise or changing position until asked. The setup calls for the three dogs to ape the luxe life[4] in a convertible roadster. "Can you put his hands on the steering wheel?" asks the photographer, who, like the rest of us, has quickly mistaken this animal for a human being. "He doesn't have hands," says his trainer, laughing. So she poses his paws and he stays there—forever. When Murray gets out of position, when Eddie prematurely jumps out of the car for more food... Barkley drives on.

"That dog is incredible," says the photographer, staring at Barkley. "Easier than most of the people I work with."

3. **Jack Russell** small and energetic breed of dog.
4. **ape the luxe life** mimic (ape) the life of luxury.

Deborah Starr Seibel

Writer/ producer Deborah Starr Seibel has written extensively for *TV Guide* magazine. She has reviewed many television shows, including *Star Trek, the Next Generation*, and interviewed the stars of *Dr. Quinn, Medicine Woman* and *The Wonder Years*. She was also a co-producer of the 1998–1999 United Paramount Network science-fiction series, *Mercy Point*.

Connecting Literature and the Media

1. What appealing qualities does the puppy in "Stray" share with the dogs in this article?
2. Why do you think people enjoy television programs with animal actors in them?
3. Do you think the puppy in "Stray" could be trained to become one of "TV's Top Dogs"? Why or why not?

Background

Lassie

Lassie, one of the dogs referred to in this selection, was the name of a collie in a book by Eric Knight. *Lassie Come Home,* a movie based on the book, was made in 1943. Elizabeth Taylor played one of the children in the movie, which was set in the British Isles. Lassie was known for her loyalty to her owners and would travel great distances to return to them. The popularity of the original movie and book spawned several sequels and a television series set in the United States. The television series received the Outstanding Children's Program Emmy™ Award in both 1954 and 1955.

Answers

Connecting Literature and the Media

1. The puppy in "Stray" is well behaved and does not cause problems for the people in the house. Dogs who are selected to perform on TV shows must be likable, well behaved, and well trained.
2. Possible response: People probably like to see animals on television because animals are cute and funny, and they may remind people of their own pets.
3. Possible response: Students may say that the puppy in "Stray" learns to be quiet and that Doris thought the puppy was smart, so the dog might be able to be trained for acting jobs.

CUSTOMIZE INSTRUCTION FOR UNIVERSAL ACCESS

For Less Proficient Readers	For English Learners	For Advanced Readers
Preview the selection with students, and clarify any unfamiliar technical terms or jargon, such as *handlers, canine,* and *gourmet biscuits.* Then, have students read the article aloud, pausing to discuss sentences or ideas that are confusing. Help students break sentences into meaningful sections as they read.	Call students' attention to the phrase *Cinderella story* in the last paragraph on p. 26. Explain the origin of the phrase by telling the story's plot. Explain that the phrase is now used to describe a sudden and unexpected rise to fame or prominence. Have students explain why this is an appropriate phrase to introduce this paragraph.	Point out that much is expected of TV dogs but that the dogs also get a lot in return. Suggest that students make and fill in a chart showing the different ways average dogs and TV dogs are cared for and the behavior expected of each. Have students discuss their charts with classmates.

Dust of Snow ✦ My Picture-Gallery ✦ Saying Yes

Lesson Objectives

1. **To analyze and respond to literary elements**
   - Literary Analysis: Images in Poetry
   - Comparing Literary Works
2. **To read, comprehend, analyze, and critique three poems**
   - Reading Strategy: Rereading to Clarify
   - Reading Check Questions
   - Review and Assess Questions
   - Assessment Practice (ATE)
3. **To develop word analysis skills, fluency, and systematic vocabulary**
   - Vocabulary Development Lesson: Concept Development: Homophones
4. **To understand and apply written and oral language conventions**
   - Spelling Strategy
   - Grammar Lesson: Common and Proper Nouns
5. **To understand and apply appropriate writing and research strategies**
   - Writing Lesson: Description of a Scene
   - Extension Activity: Mind Map
6. **To understand and apply listening and speaking strategies**
   - Extension Activity: Dramatic Presentation

STEP-BY-STEP TEACHING GUIDE	PACING GUIDE
PRETEACH	
Motivate Students and Provide Background	
Use the Motivation activity (ATE p. 28)	5 min.
Read and discuss the Preview material and Background information (SE/ATE p. 28) [A]	10 min.
Introduce the Concepts	
Introduce the Literary Analysis and Reading Strategy (SE/ATE p. 29) [A]	15 min.
Pronounce the vocabulary words and read their definitions (SE p. 29)	5 min.
TEACH	
Monitor Comprehension	
Informally monitor comprehension by circulating while students read independently or in groups [A]	5–10 min.
Develop vocabulary with Vocabulary notes (SE pp. 30, 31)	as students read
Develop Understanding	
Develop students' understanding of images in poetry with the Literary Analysis annotations (ATE p. 30) [A]	5 min.
Develop students' ability to reread for clarification with the Reading Strategy annotations (ATE p. 31)	5 min.
ASSESS	
Assess Mastery	
Assess students' mastery of the Reading Strategy and Literary Analysis by having them answer the Review and Assess questions (SE/ATE p. 33)	15 min.
Use one or more of the print and media Assessment Resources (ATE p. 35) [A]	up to 45 min.
EXTEND	
Apply Understanding	
Have students complete the Vocabulary Development Lesson and the Grammar Lesson (SE p. 34) [A]	20 min.
Apply students' ability to describe a scene using the Writing Lesson (SE/ATE p. 35) [A]	30–45 min.
Apply students' understanding of the selections using one or more of the Extension Activities (SE p. 35)	20–90 min.

ACCELERATED INSTRUCTION:
Use the strategies and activities identified with an [A].

UNIVERSAL ACCESS
● = Below Level Students
▲ = On-Level Students
■ = Above Level Students

Time and Resource Manager

Reading Level: Average, Average, Easy
Average Number of Instructional Days: 3

RESOURCES		
PRINT	**TRANSPARENCIES**	**TECHNOLOGY**
• **Beyond Literature,** Cross-Curricular Connection: Science, p. 3 ▲ ■		• **Interest Grabber Videotapes,** Tape 1 ● ▲ ■
• **Selection Support Workbook:** ● ▲ ■ Literary Analysis, p. 15 Reading Strategy, p. 14 Build Vocabulary, p. 11	• **Literary Analysis and Reading Transparencies,** pp. 5 and 6 ● ▲ ■	
		• **Listening to Literature** ● ▲ ■ Audiocassettes, Side 1 Audio CDs, CD 1
• **Literary Analysis for Enrichment** ■		
• **Formal Assessment:** Selection Test, pp. 7–9 ● ▲ ■ • **Open Book Test,** pp. 7–9 ● ▲ ■ • **Performance Assessment and Portfolio Management,** pp. 9, 23 ● ▲ ■ • PRENTICE HALL ASSESSMENT SYSTEM ● ▲ ■	• PRENTICE HALL ASSESSMENT SYSTEM ● ▲ ■ Skills Practice Answers and Explanations on Transparencies	• **Test Bank Software** ● ▲ ■ • **Got It! Assessment Videotapes,** Tape 1 ● ▲
• **Selection Support Workbook:** ● ▲ ■ Build Spelling Skills, p. 12 Build Grammar Skills, p. 13 • **Writing and Grammar,** Copper Level ● ▲ ■ • **Extension Activities,** p. 3 ● ▲ ■	• **Daily Language Practice Transparencies** ● ▲ • **Writing Models and Graphic Organizers on Transparencies** ● ▲ ■	• **Writing and Grammar iText CD-ROM** ● ▲ ■ ***Take It to the Net*** www.phschool.com

BLOCK SCHEDULING: Use one 90-minute class period to preteach the selection and have students read it. Use a second 90-minute class period to assess students' mastery of skills and have them complete one of the Extension Activities.

PRETEACH

Step-by-Step Teaching Guide for pp. 28–29

Motivation

Give students a few moments to think about ways they can describe themselves. Then write this sentence on the board: "I am both ______ and ______." Ask students to distill their descriptions down to two words and fill in the blanks of the sentence. Discuss with them whether they think this type of brief description is accurate and complete. Tell students that the poems that they will read use brief descriptions.

Interest Grabber Video

As an alternative, play "Reading and Student Response" on Tape 1 to engage student interest.

1 Background

Social Studies

In some ways, the poems in this grouping are like riddles. A riddle is a word puzzle that requires the listener to make an analogy between a statement and real life in order to find the answer. Riddles are part of our ancient literary heritage. They are found in African oral tradition. They also appear in the Koran, the Bible, and mythological stories. Many folk songs are based on riddles.

Prepare to Read

1 Dust of Snow ◆ My Picture-Gallery ◆ Saying Yes

Take It to the Net

Visit www.phschool.com for interactive activities and instruction related to these selections, including

- background
- graphic organizers
- literary elements
- reading strategies

Preview

Connecting to the Literature

The poets in this group—Diana Chang, Walt Whitman, and Robert Frost—show how people look at the same things in different ways. Recall times when you and a friend have looked at the same thing in two ways. As you read these poems, you will see that things are not always what they at first seem to be.

Background

Reading poetry is sometimes like solving a riddle: The answer is not always obvious. Diana Chang's poem "Saying Yes" is a series of questions and answers about her Chinese American heritage. In Walt Whitman's poem "My Picture-Gallery," the speaker describes an art gallery, but this gallery is not what you might expect. In Robert Frost's poem "Dust of Snow," a seemingly unimportant event in nature turns the speaker's day completely around.

TEACHING RESOURCES

The following resources can be used to enrich or extend the instruction for pp. 28–29.

Motivation

Interest Grabber Video, Tape 1

Background

Beyond Literature, p. 3

Take It to the Net

Visit www.phschool.com for Background and hotlinks for the selections.

Literary Analysis

Literary Analysis and Reading Transparencies, Images in Poetry, p. 6

Reading

Selection Support: Reading Strategy, p. 14; Build Vocabulary, p. 11

Literary Analysis and Reading Transparencies, Rereading to Clarify, p. 5

BLOCK SCHEDULING: Resources marked with this symbol provide varied instruction during 90-minute blocks.

❷ Literary Analysis

Images in Poetry

In general, poems tend to be more brief than works of prose. As a result, every word takes on increased importance. For this reason, poets make generous use of **images**—word pictures that appeal to the senses. A single image such as the "dust of snow" falling from a hemlock tree can make a memorable impression and stir up memories and associations in a reader's mind.

Comparing Literary Works

"My Picture-Gallery" and "Dust of Snow" are both built around a single, thought-provoking image. "Saying Yes," in contrast, conveys a meaningful message through **dialogue**—conversations among characters.

As you read, use these focus questions to examine the similarities and differences among the poems.

1. What do you picture in your mind as you read each poem?
2. Which poem creates the strongest impression and how does the poet create the impression?

❸ Reading Strategy

Rereading to Clarify

At times, you may need to **reread to clarify,** or make clear, the meaning of expressions used in unusual ways or words with more than one meaning. In the following example, you may be confused by the word *fix'd*. Because *fix'd* can mean "repaired" or "stays in one place," you must clarify which is meant in this line.

In a little house keep I pictures suspended, it is not a *fix'd* house,

Rereading helps you clarify that here, *fix'd* refers to a house that does not stay in one place. This detail, in turn, helps you clarify that Whitman is not talking about a real house.

As you read these poems, use a chart like the one shown to jot down words or phrases you do not understand on the first reading. Reread and write what you were able to clarify.

Passage with Unclear words

Clarification on Second Reading

Vocabulary Development

rued (ro͞od) *v.* regretted (something) (p. 30)

suspended (sə spend′ id) *adj.* hung with a support from above (p. 31)

tableaus (ta blōz′) *n.* dramatic scenes or pictures (p. 31)

❷ Literary Analysis

Images in Poetry

- Tell students that as they read the selections they will need to interpret images created by poets.
- Read the instruction for Images in Poetry to the class. Call attention to the "dust of snow" image. Invite students to share what they associate with the image of a dust of snow falling from a hemlock tree.
- Use the instruction for Comparing Literary Works to analyze images in the poems and to compare and contrast the various aspects of the poems.
- Use the Images in Poetry transparency on p. 6 in **Literary Analysis and Reading Transparencies** to assist students.

❸ Reading Strategy

Rereading to Clarify

- Tell students that images in poetry often can be very complicated.
- Ask students whether they have ever had to listen to the lyrics of a song several times before realizing what those lyrics meant. Encourage students to share examples. Then, tell students that they may need to read a poem several times to find the poet's message.
- Review the Rereading to Clarify transparency on p. 5 in **Literary Analysis and Reading Transparencies.**
- Instruct students to make similar charts to show their increasing understanding of the poems.

Vocabulary Development

- Pronounce each vocabulary word for students, and read the definitions as a class. Have students identify any words with which they are already familiar.

CUSTOMIZE INSTRUCTION FOR UNIVERSAL ACCESS

For Less Proficient Readers	For English Learners	For Advanced Readers
Students may have trouble understanding the image in "My Picture-Gallery." In this poem, the speaker describes his memories as pictures in an art gallery. Lead a discussion in which students suggest other images that could describe memories (for example, snapshots or television episodes). List students' ideas on the board.	Help students focus on the images in these poems by having them visually create some of the images. Allow students to choose one of the poems. Then ask them to pick an image in the poem that brings a vivid picture to their minds. Encourage students to recreate that picture in a drawing or collage.	The title "Dust of Snow" comes from an image that describes a winter scene. Have students think of images that describe a season and to use one of them as the basis for a poem. Have students share their poems with the class, then discuss which images created the strongest impression and why.

E-Teach

Visit E-Teach at www.phschool.com for teachers' essays on how to teach, with questions and answers.

TEACH

Step-by-Step Teaching Guide for pp. 30–32

CUSTOMIZE INSTRUCTION
For Musical/Rhythmic Learners

Play the audiocassette of "Dust of Snow," encouraging students to notice the rhyme scheme and rhythm. Have students evaluate whether the poem sounds natural or forced.

❶ About the Selections

In "Dust of Snow," Robert Frost describes a small incident in nature. In "My Picture-Gallery" (p. 31), the speaker's mind is compared to an art gallery in which "pictures," or memories, of the speaker's life are displayed. "Saying Yes" (p. 32) is about the speaker's struggle to express herself as a Chinese American.

❷ Literary Analysis

Images in Poetry

- Remind students that poems contain words that appeal to the reader's senses.
- Have students identify words and phrases in the first four lines of the poem that appeal to the senses.
  Answer: *crow, Shook, dust of snow,* and *hemlock tree* appeal to the senses.

Monitor Progress Invite students to suggest sensory words that they might use to describe a snowy scene in nature.
Possible responses: Sparkling, clean, bright, cold, frost.

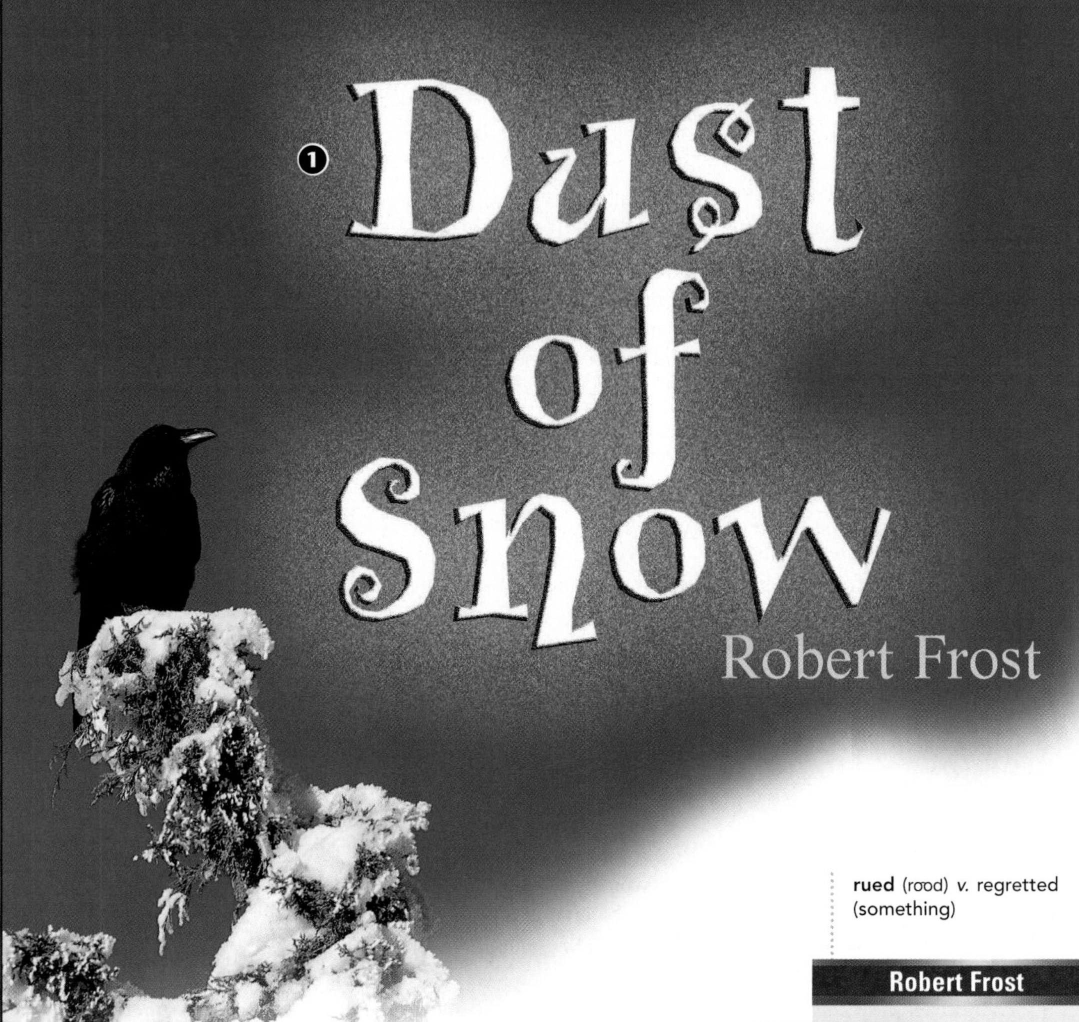

❶ Dust of Snow

Robert Frost

❷ The way a crow
Shook down on me
The dust of snow
From a hemlock tree

Has given my heart
A change of mood
And saved some part
Of a day I had rued.

rued (ro͞od) *v.* regretted (something)

Robert Frost

(1874–1963)

Robert Frost began writing poetry as a high school student in New England. However, he wasn't recognized as a major poet until his book of poetry, *North of Boston*, became a bestseller. Before becoming a poet, Frost was a farmer.

TEACHING RESOURCES

The following resources can be used to enrich or extend the instruction for pp. 30–32.

Literary Analysis
- **Selection Support:** Literary Analysis, p. 15 ■
- **Literary Analysis for Enrichment**

Reading
- **Listening to Literature Audiocassettes,** Side 1 ■
- **Listening to Literature Audio CDs,** CD 1 ■

■ **BLOCK SCHEDULING:** Resources marked with this symbol provide varied instruction during 90-minute blocks.

My Picture-Gallery ①

Walt Whitman

In a little house keep I pictures suspended, it is not a
fix'd house,
It is round, it is only a few inches from one side to the other;
Yet behold, it has room for all the shows of the world,
all memories! ③
Here the tableaus of life, and here the groupings of death;
Here, do you know this? this is cicerone[1] himself,
With finger rais'd he points to the prodigal[2] pictures.

suspended (sə spend´ id) *adj.* hung with a support from above

tableaus (ta blōz´) *n.* dramatic scenes or pictures

1. **cicerone** (sis´ ə rō´ nē) *n.* guide who explains the history and important features of a place to sightseers.
2. **prodigal** (präd´ i gəl) *adj.* very plentiful.

Review and Assess

Thinking About the Selection

1. **Respond:** In "Dust of Snow," Frost describes how he was changed by an event in nature. What other events in nature could change a person in some way?
2. (a) **Recall:** What action changes how the speaker feels? (b) **Classify:** Would you describe this action as deliberate or as occurring by chance? Explain.
3. (a) **Recall:** What effect does the crow's action have on the speaker? (b) **Draw Conclusions:** Why do you think the crow's action has the effect on the speaker that it does?
4. (a) **Recall:** How does the speaker feel before and after the crow's action? (b) **Generalize:** What lesson do you think the speaker learned from this experience?
5. (a) **Support:** What details in "My Picture-Gallery" reveal that the picture-gallery to which Whitman is referring is his own mind? (b) **Evaluate:** Do you think that a "picture-gallery" is a strong choice for an image to describe a person's mind? Why or why not? (c) **Extend:** If you were to choose an image to capture your own memories, what would it be? Why?

Walt Whitman

(1819–1892)

Walt Whitman changed American poetry. Before his famous book *Leaves of Grass* came out in 1855, American poets had been imitating British poets. With his unrhymed verse and irregular rhythms, Whitman burst on the scene with a new and sometimes shocking voice. He held many different jobs and proudly declared in one of his poems that he was "an American, one of the roughs . . . "

③ Reading Strategy

Rereading to Clarify

- Have students skim "My Picture-Gallery" quickly, noting any questions they have.
- Ask students to read the poem a second time, seeing how many of their own questions they can answer as they read.

Answers for p. 31

Review and Assess

1. Possible answers: A person could change because of a flood, a hurricane, or an earthquake. Other people might change because seasonal changes affect them.
2. **(a)** A crow shakes snow on the speaker. **(b)** It happens by chance; it is a coincidence that the speaker and the crow are in the same place at the same time.
3. **(a)** The crow's action makes the speaker feel better. **(b)** Perhaps the action reminds the speaker of the beauty of nature and other good things.
4. **(a)** Before the action, the speaker was having a bad day; after the action, the speaker felt happier. **(b)** Possible responses: Small pleasures can help ease a bad day; attitudes can change unexpectedly.
5. **(a)** It is small, portable, and round; it contains memories. **(b)** Possible response: Yes, both the mind's gallery and an art gallery contain images. **(c)** Students may say that they would use the image of a picture book or a photo album to capture their own memories.

CUSTOMIZE INSTRUCTION FOR UNIVERSAL ACCESS

For Special Needs Students	For Gifted/Talented Students	For Advanced Readers
Students may not understand which of the poems are literal and which are figurative. Point out that the incident described in "Dust of Snow" is based on a real experience. However, the "picture-gallery" in Whitman's poem is imagined.	Ask students to identify which of the two poems they like best and to explain their preference. Then, have students take turns giving dramatic readings of poems of their choice.	"Dust of Snow" and "My Picture-Gallery" seem to respond to an experience or conversation that inspired the poets. Have students explore each poem's inspiration. Students can use the Open Mind organizer on p. 93 in **Writing Models and Graphic Organizers on Transparencies** to record their ideas.

ASSESS

Step-by-Step Teaching Guide for p. 32

Review and Assess

1. Students may have been confronted with similar questions by people who were curious about their looks or last names.
2. **(a)** Someone is asking whether the speaker is really Chinese and really American. **(b)** The questions make the poet uneasy because people don't understand why the speaker answers "yes" to both.
3. **(a)** The poet wants to say "yes" twice to show that he or she is both American and Chinese. **(b)** The poet feels proud about saying it. **(c)** The poet is happy to be both Chinese and American. **(d)** Possible response: Yes, by being proud of both parts of his or her heritage, the speaker maintains a positive sense of identity.

Critical Viewing

Possible response: She seems to like what she sees because she has a slight smile on her face.

Saying Yes

Diana Chang

"Are you Chinese?"
"Yes."

"American?"
"Yes."

"*Really* Chinese?"
"No . . . not quite."

"*Really* American?"
"Well, actually, you see . . ."

But I would rather say
yes.
Not neither-nor,
not maybe,
but both, and not only

The homes I've had,
the ways I am

I'd rather say it
twice,
yes.

▲ **Critical Viewing** Do you think the poet (pictured here) likes what she sees in the mirror? Explain. **[Infer]**

Diana Chang

(b. 1934)

Diana Chang admits that she is "preoccupied" with identity. Although she sometimes thinks of her Chinese American identity as confusing and lopsided, she also celebrates it by exploring it in her novels and poems. Chang's self-expression doesn't stop with writing. She also paints and has exhibited her paintings in art galleries.

Review and Assess

Thinking About the Selection

1. **Respond:** Have you ever asked or answered questions like the ones in "Saying Yes"? Explain.
2. **(a) Recall:** What questions is someone asking the speaker in "Saying Yes"? **(b) Infer:** Why do these questions make the poet feel uneasy?
3. **(a) Recall:** What would the poet rather say twice? **(b) Infer:** How does the poet feel about saying it? **(c) Extend:** What do the poet's responses reveal about her outlook on her own identity? **(d) Evaluate:** Do you feel that this is a good outlook? Why or why not?

ASSESSMENT PRACTICE: Reading Comprehension

Using Context Clues (For more practice, see Test Preparation Workbook, p. 3.)

Many tests require students to use context clues to determine the meaning of a word. Write the following sentences on the board.

In Walt Whitman's poem, the speaker's head is described as a gallery where all of his or her memories are displayed like pictures.

In this sentence, a gallery is most like a ______.

A theater
B library
C workshop
D museum

The sentences state that *all* of the speaker's memories are displayed like pictures. Ask students what type of place displays pictures. They should recognize that *C* is incorrect because pictures are generally not hung in workshops. Explain that although *A* and *B* are places where pictures might appear, they would display fewer than a museum would. *D* is the correct answer.

Review and Assess

Literary Analysis

Images in Poetry

1. What are the key details of the **image** in "My Picture-Gallery"?
2. A **metaphor** is an implied comparison between two strikingly dissimilar things. Explain how Whitman uses the central image in "My Picture-Gallery" as part of a metaphor.
3. Although Robert Frost's poem contains only a single image, the image appeals to several senses. In a chart like the one below, write *yes* or *no* to indicate the senses to which Frost appeals. Provide an explanation for each answer.

Sight	Hearing	Smell	Taste	Touch

Comparing Literary Works

4. What do you picture in your mind as you read each poem?
5. Both "My Picture-Gallery" and "Dust of Snow" are built around a single image. What is different about the way the two poets present the images to readers?
6. All three poems present a vivid impression of the **speaker,** the voice behind the words in a poem. Explain how each speaker reveals information about herself or himself.

Reading Strategy

Rereading to Clarify

7. Which poem creates the strongest impression and how does the poet create the impression?
8. **(a)** What are two possible meanings of the word *dust*? **(b)** What does it mean in Frost's poem "Dust of Snow"?
9. **(a)** What does *suspended* mean in "My Picture-Gallery"? **(b)** How does this meaning help you clarify Whitman's description of his imagination and memory?

Extending Understanding

10. **Art Connection:** Compare and contrast the ways artists and poets capture images.

Quick Review

An **image** is a word picture that appeals to one or more of the senses. To review images in poetry, see page 29.

When you **reread to clarify,** you read a second time to better understand the meaning of words and phrases.

Take It to the Net

www.phschool.com

Take the interactive self-test online to check your understanding of these selections.

ENRICHMENT: Further Reading

Other Works by the Poets

Works by Robert Frost

Selected Poems

You Come, Too

Works by Walt Whitman

Leaves of Grass

Works by Diana Chang

Earth Water Light

Answers for p. 33

Review and Assess

1. It is movable, round, a few inches wide, and contains pictures.
2. A gallery is compared to the mind.
3.

Sight	Yes; snow shakes down like dust; Frost describes a crow and a tree.
Hearing	Yes; you can hear the falling snow.
Smell	Yes; you get the feeling of the smell of clean air on a clear day.
Taste	No.
Touch	Yes; you can feel the cold wetness of the snow.

4. Possible responses: "Dust of Snow": students may picture a snowy path in a forest; "My Picture-Gallery": students may picture either a head or a traditional gallery; "Saying Yes": students may picture two students talking in a schoolyard.
5. The main image in "Dust of Snow" is the crow in the tree and is outside of the author; the main image of "My Picture-Gallery" is inside the speaker's head.
6. "My Picture-Gallery"—speaker: an older person who has led an interesting life; impression created by: language and details. "Dust of Snow"— speaker: a nature lover who can be too serious; impression created by: speaker's positive response to the dust of snow. "Saying Yes"—speaker: a thoughtful person who doesn't like to be put into categories; impression created by: what the speaker wants to say to the people who ask the questions.
7. Possible response: "Dust of Snow" because the poet uses vivid images.
8. **(a)** *Dust* is "fine particles of matter" (n) or the action "to make free of dust" (vt). **(b)** The dust is a small scattering of snow.

continued

Answers continued

9. **(a)** *Suspended* means "hung with a support from above." **(b)** The word implies mobility, which clarifies how "all the shows of the world" can fit inside the speaker's memory.
10. Both artists and poets try to show their views of the world. Artists capture images with paints or markers on a range of surfaces; poets create images with words on paper.

Harmonizing, 1979, Robert Gwathmey, Courtesy Terry Dintenfass Gallery, © Estate of Robert Gwathmey, Licensed by VAGA, New York, NY

13 ◀ Critical Viewing
What story characters might be represented in this picture?

Grandpa wasn't getting no better, but he wasn't getting no worse, either.

12 "You liking Macon now?" I asked Ellie when we got to the middle of July. She was dishing out a plate of smothered chops for him and I hadn't even heard him ask for anything to eat.

"Macon's funny," Ellie said, not answering my question. "He's in there listening to all of those old stories like he's really interested in them. It's almost as if he and Grandpa Jeremiah are talking about something more than the stories, a secret language."

I didn't think I was supposed to say anything about that to Macon, but once, when Ellie, Sister Todd, and Macon were out on the porch shelling butter beans after Grandpa got tired and was resting, I went into his room and told him what Ellie had said.

"She said that?" Grandpa Jeremiah's face was skinny and old looking but his eyes looked like a baby's, they was so bright.

"Right there in the kitchen is where she said it," I said. "And I don't know what it mean but I was wondering about it."

14 ✓Reading Check
What does the narrator tell Macon?

12 Critical Thinking

Speculate

- Read aloud the bracketed passage on p. 43. Ask: What do Ellie's actions show about her feelings for Macon?
  Answer: She is beginning to like him because she is giving him food before he asks for it.
- Invite students to think about the relationship between Ellie, the narrator, and Macon. Ask: What has brought about the friendships between the narrator and Macon and between Ellie and Macon?
  Answer: Because Macon has been visiting so often, they have all spent time together; the narrator looks up to Macon and feels safe with him. Ellie probably appreciates how Macon is helping with the farm and Grandpa.

13 ▶Critical Viewing

Answer: The man playing the guitar could be Macon, and the listener could be Grandpa Jeremiah.

14 ✓Reading Check

Answer: The narrator tells Macon that Grandpa's stories aren't as scary when Macon is with the narrator.

CUSTOMIZE INSTRUCTION FOR UNIVERSAL ACCESS

For Less Proficient Readers	For Gifted/Talented Students
To help students understand the progression of events in the story, have them make a timeline. They should begin with Ellie's return from college and record the events of that summer. Ellie's return to college in the fall also belongs in the timeline, as well as events that happen during the school year. Ellie returns again in summer; have students note what happens during the second summer, too.	Invite students to illustrate scenes from the story. Allow students to select the setting and characters they wish to portray. Have students use drawing materials to make a poster or use a cardboard box to make a model of part of the narrator's home, such as the porch or Grandpa's room. Where details are not included in the text, have students research typical furnishings of a southern farm. Have students display their work in the classroom.

15 Reading Strategy

Using Context Clues to Determine Meaning

- Invite a volunteer to read aloud the bracketed passage on p. 44.
- Ask the Reading Strategy question on p.44: What context clues might help you figure out the meaning of *break* as it is used here? **Answer:** You can tell that it has to do with how people react to difficult situations. *Breaking* is worse than being bent, or twisted or falling.

16 Background

Art

Springtime Rain, by Ogden M. Pleissner

Pleissner's love of the outdoors led him to paint landscapes. He is noted for his ability to re-create the mood of specific seasons or times of the day by varying the light in his paintings. Use these questions for discussion of the painting:

1. The title of this painting is *Springtime Rain.* What details show that the season is spring? **Answer:** Spring is indicated by the people enjoying the outdoors in light clothing, the buds on the tree, and the rain that usually falls in spring.
2. Do you think this painting represents the setting of the story? **Answer:** It looks like the setting of the story because it shows a small house with a porch, like the house in the story.

17 ▶Critical Viewing

Answer: The figures in the painting could be Macon or the narrator, Dr. Crawford, and Ellie.

"I didn't think she had any feeling for them stories," Grandpa Jeremiah said. "If she think we talking secrets, maybe she don't."

"I think she getting a feeling for Macon," I said.

"That's okay, too," Grandpa Jeremiah said. "They both young."

"Yeah, but them stories you be telling, Grandpa, they about old people who lived a long time ago," I said.

"Well, those the folks you got to know about," Grandpa Jeremiah said. "You think on what those folks been through, and what they was feeling, and you add it up with what you been through and what you been feeling, then you got you something."

"What you got Grandpa?"

15 "You got you a bridge," Grandpa said. "And a meaning. Then when things get so hard you about to break, you can sneak across that bridge and see some folks who went before you and see how they didn't break. Some got bent and some got twisted and a few fell along the way, but they didn't break."

"Am I going to break, Grandpa?"

Reading Strategy
Using Context to Determine Meaning What context clues might help you figure out the meaning of *break* as it is used here?

16

Springtime Rain, 1975, Ogden M. Pleissner, Ogden M. Pleissner Estate Marion G. Pleissner Trust, Bankers Trust Company

17 ▲ **Critical Viewing** Which characters from the story could be represented in this painting? **[Connect]**

"You? As strong as you is?" Grandpa Jeremiah pushed himself up on his elbow and give me a look. "No way you going to break, boy. You gonna be strong as they come. One day you gonna tell all them stories I told you to your young'uns and they'll be as strong as you."

"Suppose I ain't got no stories, can I make some up?"

"Sure you can, boy. You make 'em up and twist 'em around. Don't make no mind. Long as you got 'em."

"Is that what Macon is doing?" I asked. "Making up stories to play on his guitar?"

"He'll do with 'em what he see fit, I suppose," Grandpa Jeremiah said. "Can't ask more than that from a man."

18 It rained the first three days of August. It wasn't a hard rain but it rained anyway. The mailman said it was good for the crops over East but I didn't care about that so I didn't pay him no mind. What I did mind was when it rain like that the field mice come in and get in things like the flour bin and I always got the blame for leaving it open.When the rain stopped I was pretty glad. Macon come over and sat with Grandpa and had something to eat with us. Sister Todd come over, too.

"How Grandpa doing?" Sister Todd asked. "They been asking about him in the church."

"He's doing all right," Ellie said.

"He's kind of quiet today," Macon said. "He was just talking about how the hogs needed breeding."

19 "He must have run out of stories to tell," Sister Todd said. "He'll be repeating on himself like my father used to do. That's the way I *hear* old folks get."

Everybody laughed at that because Sister Todd was pretty old, too. Maybe we was all happy because the sun was out after so much rain. When Sister Todd went in to take Grandpa Jeremiah a plate of potato salad with no mayonnaise like he liked it, she told him about how people was asking for him and he told her to tell them he was doing okay and to remember him in their prayers.

Sister Todd came over the next afternoon, too, with some rhubarb pie with cheese on it, which is my favorite pie. When she took a piece into Grandpa Jeremiah's room she come right out again and told Ellie to go fetch the Bible.

It was a hot day when they had the funeral. Mostly everybody was there. The church was hot as anything, even though they had the window open. Some yellowjacks flew in and buzzed around Sister Todd's niece and then around Deacon Turner's wife and settled right on her hat and stayed there until we all stood and sang "Soon-a Will Be Done." 20

At the graveyard Macon played "Precious Lord" and I cried hard

Literary Analysis
First-Person and Third-Person Point of View
How does the first-person point of view make this narration personal?

20 **Reading Check**
What does Grandpa explain about his stories?

18 Literary Analysis

First-Person and Third-Person Point of View

- Remind students that the narrator's point of view determines how much the reader knows about the characters and what they think. In first-person point of view narration, the narrator only tells readers only what he or she thinks and feels. A third-person point of view narrator tells readers what other characters think and feel.
- Read aloud the bracketed passage on p. 45. Then discuss and answer the Literary Analysis question on p. 45.
  Answer: It helps the reader understand the story from the narrator's perspective.

Monitor Progress Direct students to look at how the narrator uses the personal pronoun *I*, and how he describes his own thoughts about the rain.

Reteach If students have difficulty answering the question, have them reread the Literary Analysis instruction on p. 37. Then instruct them to reread the bracketed paragraph. Ask: Which part of the reading could be in the third person? Why?
Answer: The first two sentences could be in the third person because they tell something everybody knows.

19 Critical Thinking

Predict

- Tell students that predicting is saying what will happen in the future.
- Read the bracketed passage on p. 45. Ask students what they can predict when the story says Grandpa has run out of stories.
  Answer: Grandpa will die soon. Invite students to read further to check their predictions.

20 Reading Check

Answer: Grandpa explains that knowing stories will make the narrator stronger because the stories tell how other people have overcome difficulties.

CUSTOMIZE INSTRUCTION FOR UNIVERSAL ACCESS

For Gifted/Talented Students	For Advanced Readers
Have students dramatize the actions of this story's major characters, using an actor for each character, including the narrator. Students should be given some time to read over their part and decide what kind of tone they want to use. Encourage students to use body language and facial expressions as they read the narration and dialogue. Discuss with students what they learn about characters through dramatization.	Tell students that a eulogy is a speech given at a funeral. A eulogy tells about the life and character of the person who died. It also includes information about the people and things that the deceased person cared about. Have students write a eulogy for Grandpa Jeremiah, basing their work on information in the story. When students are finished, ask volunteers to read their eulogies to the class.

ASSESS

Answers for p. 46

Review and Assess

1. Possible response: I would tell the narrator that his grandfather loved him and that his grandfather's stories will comfort him in the future.
2. **(a)** Ellie and the narrator are cousins. **(b)** The narrator likes Ellie but is sad that she has changed while at college.
3. **(a)** Possible response: She liked the songs because they were entertaining and she liked to be close to Grandpa. **(b)** Ellie thinks that these stories will keep them living in the past instead of progressing with modern times.
4. **(a)** Ellie doesn't want Macon around because she thinks he is tiring Grandpa. **(b)** The narrator enjoys Macon's company.
5. **(a)** Macon respects and appreciates Grandpa. **(b)** Macon helps Grandpa by listening to the stories, playing the guitar, and keeping him company.
6. Possible responses: The narrator behaves most appropriately because he lets him know that he will remember the stories. OR Macon behaves most appropriately because he plays music and listens to Grandpa. OR Ellie behaves most appropriately because she cares about Grandpa's health.
7. Possible response: The songs will bind them together in their memories of Grandpa Jeremiah.
8. Students may say that stories from the past are important because they help people connect with and preserve their heritage.

even though I told myself that I wasn't going to cry the way Ellie and Sister Todd was, but it was such a sad thing when we left and Grandpa Jeremiah was still out to the grave that I couldn't help it.

During the funeral and all, Macon kind of told everybody where to go and where to sit and which of the three cars to ride in. After it was over he come by the house and sat on the front porch and played on his guitar. Ellie was standing leaning against the rail and she was crying but it wasn't a hard crying. It was a soft crying, the kind that last inside of you for a long time.

Macon was playing a tune I hadn't heard before. I thought it might have been what he was working at when Grandpa Jeremiah was telling him those stories and I watched his fingers but I couldn't tell if it was or not. It wasn't nothing special, that tune Macon was playing, maybe halfway between them Delta blues he would do when Sister Todd wasn't around and something you would play at church. It was something different and something the same at the same time. I watched his fingers go over that guitar and figured I could learn that tune one day if I had a mind to.

Walter Dean Myers

(b. 1937)

You would expect a preschooler to prefer picture books over other kinds of reading materials. Young Walter Dean Myers didn't. He was reading at age four. By age five, he was reading a newspaper every day. In spite of this impressive start with words, Myers didn't think that writing would be his career. Then, in his twenties, he won a writing contest. He hasn't stopped writing since—mostly about his heritage and his experiences growing up in Harlem, a part of New York City. Like the child in this story, Myers understands loss: He was three years old when his mother died.

Review and Assess

Thinking About the Selection

1. **Respond:** What would you say to the narrator to comfort him after his grandfather's death?
2. (a) **Recall:** What is the relationship of Ellie to the narrator? (b) **Interpret:** Describe the narrator's feelings about Ellie.
3. (a) **Recall:** Why did Ellie like to hear Grandpa Jeremiah's songs? (b) **Speculate:** Why is Ellie's attitude different when she returns from college?
4. (a) **Recall:** Why doesn't Ellie want Macon around? (b) **Draw Conclusions:** Why does the narrator like Macon?
5. (a) **Recall:** How does Macon feel about Grandpa? (b) **Infer:** In what ways does Macon help Grandpa Jeremiah?
6. **Evaluate:** The narrator, Ellie, and Macon each behave differently toward Grandpa. Who do you think behaves most appropriately and why?
7. **Speculate:** Macon seems to understand Grandpa Jeremiah's "song." What role do you think these songs will play in the lives of Ellie, Macon, and the narrator?
8. **Take a Position:** How important do you think it is for traditional stories and songs like those of Grandpa Jeremiah to live on for future generations?

ASSESSMENT PRACTICE: Reading Comprehension

Using Context Clues (For more practice, see Test Preparation Workbook, p. 4.)

Many tests require students to use context clues to determine the meanings of unfamiliar words. Use the following exercise to help students understand that the surrounding passage can help readers infer definitions of words with multiple meanings.

> . . . She didn't have no use for Macon even when things was going right, and when Grandpa Jeremiah was fixing to die I just knowed she wasn't gonna be liking him hanging around . . .

In this passage, the word fixing means ______.

A repairing
C putting together
B mending
D getting ready

A, *B*, and *C* do not make sense in the context of the passage. Judging from the context of the sentence, Grandpa Jeremiah was getting ready to die, so *D* is the best answer.

Review and Assess

Literary Analysis

First-Person Point of View

1. Who is the narrator of "Jeremiah's Song"?
2. How does the **first-person** narration make this story more personal?
3. Describe the narrator's thoughts or feelings about two of the other characters. Use a chart like the following.

Character's name	What the narrator says	What the narrator thinks	What the narrator does

Connecting Literary Elements

4. Identify at least two details that only the narrator could tell you—that Macon or Ellie could not.
5. Explain how you think the story might be different if it had been told from a **third-person** point of view.
6. Do you think the story would have been more or less effective if it had been told from a third-person point of view? Why?

Reading Strategy

Using Context to Determine Meaning

7. Compare the meanings of the two italicized words in the following sentences.
   (a) Grandpa and Ellie used to be real *close* before Ellie went away.
   (b) Grandpa asked Macon to *close* the door.
8. Identify the clues in the sentences above that help you determine which way to say the italicized word and to know what it means.
9. Using the chart you created as you read, list at least three unfamiliar words you encountered in this story, and explain how context clues can be used to determine their meanings.

Extending Understanding

10. **Social Studies Connection:** What story do you know that preserves something from the past?
11. **Evaluate:** Are stories and songs a good way to pass culture along from generation to generation? Why or why not?

Quick Review

In **first-person point of view,** the narrator takes part in the action and tells the story from his or her perspective. To review first-person point of view, see page 37.

In **third-person point of view,** the narrator does not participate in the action.

The **context** of a word is the situation in which it is used—the words, sentences, and paragraphs around the word.

Take It to the Net

www.phschool.com

Take the interactive self-test online to check your understanding of the selection.

ENRICHMENT: Further Reading

Other Works by Walter Dean Myers

The Glory Field

Somewhere in the Darkness

Scorpions

Take It to the Net

Visit www.phschool.com for more information on Walter Dean Myers.

Answers for p. 47

Review and Assess

1. The narrator is Ellie's cousin, Jeremiah's grandchild.
2. The first-person narration makes the story more personal because the narrator describes his hopes and fears.
3. **Macon** *Narrator* Says: Likes Macon, Thinks: Macon makes him feel safe, Does: Sits with Macon; **Ellie** *Narrator* Says: Ellie questions the doctor, Thinks: Ellie has changed, Does: Notices Ellie crying after funeral; **Grandpa** *Narrator* Says: Asks why stories are important, Thinks: Worries whether he will "break" or not, Does: Talks with Grandpa
4. Possible response: The narrator loves Grandpa the most; the stories frighten the narrator.
5. Possible response: A third-person point of view would include the thoughts of all of the characters, thereby explaining each character's actions.
6. Some may say that the story would be less effective because the narrator keeps the story moving well. Others may say that it would be more effective because we would know why Ellie behaves as she does.
7. **(a)** *Close* means "good friends." **(b)** *Close* means "to shut."
8. **(a)** This sentence uses "real" and "before Ellie went away" as clues. **(b)** "Door" is the best clue.
9. *Powder* is called "dusting powder" and is used to fight heat, so it is a cosmetic. *Mess* means "play" because it is done with a musical instrument. *Make it* means "live" because the doctor is discussing Grandpa's condition.
10. Students may tell family stories or stories from history.
11. Students may say that stories are a good way to pass culture along because they give information about people from past generations and tell about the things that were important to those people.

EXTEND

Answers for p. 48

❶ Vocabulary Development

Word Analysis

1. disagree
2. place
3. disrespectful
4. service

Spelling Strategy

1. distrust
2. disconnect
3. disobey
4. disinterested

Concept Development

1. You might be relieved that your illness isn't serious.
2. A doctor should disinfect his or her hands in order to not spread germs.
3. Both of the diagnoses give information, but the doctor diagnoses a person's health and a mechanic diagnoses a car.
4. Disinfecting a counter will kill germs; wiping it down will not.

❷ Grammar

1. she: personal
2. him: personal
3. Who: interrogative
4. Some: indefinite; others: indefinite
5. whom: interrogative

Writing Application

The narrator is sometimes frightened by Grandpa's stories, but he isn't scared when Macon listens, too. He and Macon enjoy Grandpa's stories. Ellie used to enjoy the stories, but since she went to college, she doesn't listen anymore.

Integrate Language Skills

❶ Vocabulary Development Lesson

Word Analysis: Latin Prefix *dis-*

The Latin prefix *dis-* changes the meaning of a word to its opposite meaning. On your paper, write the opposite of each word by adding or removing *dis-* from it.

1. agree, __?__
2. displace, __?__
3. respectful, __?__
4. disservice, __?__

Spelling Strategy

A prefix never changes the spelling of the original word—even when the word begins with a vowel. For example, when you add *dis-* to *infect*, you write *disinfect*, not *dissinfect*.

On your paper, add *dis-* to the following words:

1. trust
2. connect
3. obey
4. interested

Concept Development: Word Choice

On your paper, respond to each of the following questions containing vocabulary words from the story. Explain each response.

1. What might you do when you are given a *diagnosis*?
2. Why should a doctor *disinfect* his or her hands?
3. What are the similarities and differences between a *diagnosis* provided by a doctor and one given by an auto mechanic?
4. Why is it better to clean and *disinfect* a counter than to simply wipe it down with a cloth?

❷ Grammar Lesson

Pronouns

A **pronoun** is a word that takes the place of a noun or another pronoun. Writers use pronouns to avoid the awkwardness of repeating the same noun over and over.

Personal pronouns refer to specific nouns that are named elsewhere in the sentence or paragraph. **Interrogative pronouns** are used in questions. **Indefinite pronouns** can be plural or singular, depending on how they are used.

Personal Pronouns	Interrogative pronouns	Indefinite pronouns
he, she, him, her, they, them, it	who, whom	some, other, none

Practice Copy the following sentences on your paper. Underline the pronoun(s). Identify the type of each pronoun.

1. After Ellie went to college, she didn't go to church much.
2. Grandpa was sick, so Macon visited him.
3. Who will learn the stories?
4. Some like to listen, others do not.
5. To whom did Grandpa tell the story?

Writing Application Revise the following paragraph by replacing nouns with pronouns.

The narrator is sometimes frightened by Grandpa's stories, but the narrator isn't scared when Macon listens, too. The narrator and Macon enjoy Grandpa's stories. Ellie used to enjoy the stories, but since Ellie went to college, Ellie doesn't listen anymore.

WG Prentice Hall Writing and Grammar Connection: Chapter 23

TEACHING RESOURCES

The following resources can be used to enrich or extend the instruction for pp. 48–49.

Vocabulary

- **Selection Support:** Build Vocabulary, p. 16; Build Spelling Skills, p. 17
- **Vocabulary and Spelling Practice Book** (Use this booklet for skills enrichment)

Grammar

- **Selection Support:** Build Grammar Skills, p. 18
- **Writing and Grammar,** Copper Level, p. 506

- **Daily Language Practice Transparencies** ■

Writing

- **Writing and Grammar,** Copper Level, p. 102 ■
- **Writing Models and Graphic Organizers on Transparencies,** p. 85
- **Writing and Grammar iText CD-ROM**

■ **BLOCK SCHEDULING:** Resources marked with this symbol provide varied instruction during 90-minute blocks.

❸ Writing Lesson

Character Description

In "Jeremiah's Song," the young grandson describes all the characters. Choose a character and write a brief description based on what you read in the story.

Prewriting Use a cluster diagram like the one shown to list details that describe the character—the character's appearance, actions, and personality.

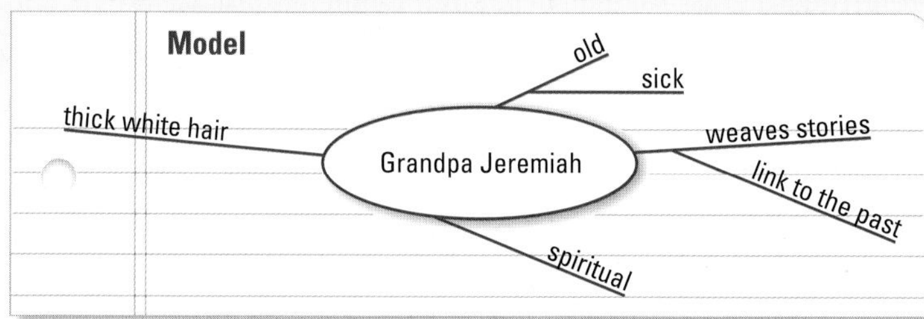

Drafting Start with a paragraph that introduces the character and sums up your overall impression. Follow with paragraphs that support your impression. Focus on using precise language to create a strong image. For example, "Grandpa looks bad" is not precise. "Grandpa's skin hung loosely from his body" paints an image that helps your reader see Grandpa.

Revising Look through your draft for vague words like *good* and *nice*. Replace them with words or phrases that describe the character more precisely.

WG *Prentice Hall Writing and Grammar Connection: Chapter 6, Section 2*

❹ Extension Activities

Listening and Speaking With two others, **role-play** a conversation among Ellie, the narrator, and Macon. Have each character tell how he or she feels about Grandpa's stories.

- Find details in the story that indicate how your character feels about the stories.
- Come up with a rough idea of how to get the conversation started.
- Role-play the conversation. Use facial expressions and gestures for emphasis.
- After the role-play, explain to one another what you thought each character was feeling.

Research and Technology Research the music of the "blues." Use print and media resources to find information about the people who made the "blues" famous. Then create a **timeline** including dates, names, and places for this music form. Include significant events such as

- birth years of musicians
- years musicians recorded
- other significant world events for context.

Take It to the Net www.phschool.com

Go online for an additional research activity using the Internet.

Lesson Support for p. 49

❸ Writing Lesson

- Model a character description of Grandpa Jeremiah by reading paragraph 7 on p. 39.
- Draw the cluster diagram from p. 49 on the board. Explain to students that such diagrams help organize thoughts before writing.
- Use the Writing Lesson to guide students in describing one of the characters.
- Use the Description rubric on p. 9 in **Performance Assessment and Portfolio Management** to evaluate students' descriptions.

❹ Listening and Speaking

- Divide the class into groups. Have each group discuss the relationships between Ellie, Macon, and the narrator.
- Have students assign roles within their group. Suggest that each group construct an outline of what should be covered in the conversation.
- Urge students to consider using actions to show emotions and ideas.
- Have each group practice the conversation and present it to the class.
- Have students use the Understanding, Tone, Mood, and Emotion rubric on p. 23 in **Performance Assessment and Portfolio Management.**

CUSTOMIZE INSTRUCTION For Universal Access

To address different learning styles, use the activities suggested in the **Extension Activities** booklet p. 4.

ASSESSMENT RESOURCES

The following resources can be used to assess students' knowledge and skills.

Selection Assessment
- **Formal Assessment,** pp. 10–12
- **Open Book Test,** pp. 10–12
- **Got It! Assessment Videotapes,** Tape 1
- **Test Bank Software**

Visit www.phschool.com for self-tests and additional questions on "Jeremiah's Song."

Writing Rubric
- **Performance Assess. and Portfolio Mgmt.,** p. 9

Listening and Speaking Rubric
- **Performance Assess. and Portfolio Mgmt.,** p. 23

- **Workbook**
- **Skill Book**
- **Transparencies**
- **CD-ROM**

The King of Mazy May

Lesson Objectives

1. **To analyze and respond to literary elements**
   - Literary Analysis: Conflict Between Characters
   - Connecting Literary Elements: Resolution of Conflict
2. **To read, comprehend, analyze, and critique a short story**
   - Reading Strategy: Recognizing Signal Words
   - Reading Check Questions
   - Review and Assess Questions
   - Assessment Practice (ATE)
3. **To develop word analysis skills, fluency, and systematic vocabulary**
   - Vocabulary Development Lesson: Word Analysis: Latin Suffix *-or*
4. **To understand and apply written and oral language conventions**
   - Spelling Strategy
   - Grammar Lesson: Pronouns and Antecedents
5. **To understand and apply appropriate writing and research strategies**
   - Writing Lesson: Personal Narrative
   - Extension Activity: Visual Presentation
6. **To understand and apply listening and speaking strategies**
   - Extension Activity: Acceptance Speech

STEP-BY-STEP TEACHING GUIDE	PACING GUIDE
PRETEACH	
Motivate Students and Provide Background	
Use the Motivation activity (ATE p. 50)	5 min.
Read and discuss the Preview material and Background information (SE/ATE p. 50) [A]	5 min.
Introduce the Concepts	
Introduce the Literary Analysis and Reading Strategy (SE/ATE p. 51) [A]	25 min.
Pronounce the vocabulary words and read their definitions (SE p. 51)	5 min.
TEACH	
Monitor Comprehension	
Informally monitor comprehension by circulating while students read independently or in groups [A]	20–25 min.
Monitor students' comprehension with the Reading Check notes (SE/ATE pp. 53, 55, 57, 59)	as students read
Develop vocabulary with Vocabulary notes (SE pp. 53, 54, 56, 57, 59; ATE p. 53)	as students read
Develop Understanding	
Develop students' understanding of conflict with the Literary Analysis annotations (SE pp. 54, 57, 59; ATE pp. 54, 57, 59) [A]	5 min.
Develop students' ability to recognize signal words with the Reading Strategy annotations (SE pp. 56, 58; ATE pp. 53, 56, 58)	5 min.
ASSESS	
Assess Mastery	
Assess students' mastery of the Reading Strategy and Literary Analysis by having them answer the Review and Assess questions (SE/ATE p. 61)	15 min.
Use one or more of the print and media Assessment Resources (ATE p. 63) [A]	up to 45 min.
EXTEND	
Apply Understanding	
Have students complete the Vocabulary Development Lesson and the Grammar Lesson (SE p. 62) [A]	20 min.
Apply students' ability to write a personal narrative using the Writing Lesson (SE/ATE p. 63) [A]	20–45 min.
Apply students' understanding using one or more of the Extension Activities (SE p. 63)	10–90 min.

ACCELERATED INSTRUCTION:
Use the strategies and activities identified with an [A].

UNIVERSAL ACCESS
● = Below Level Students
▲ = On-Level Students
■ = Above Level Students

Time and Resource Manager

Reading Level: Challenging
Average Number of Instructional Days: 4

	RESOURCES		
	PRINT	**TRANSPARENCIES**	**TECHNOLOGY**
	• **Beyond Literature,** Cross-Curricular Connection: Physical Education, p. 5 ▲ ■		• **Interest Grabber Videotapes,** Tape 1 ● ▲ ■
	• **Selection Support Workbook:** ● ▲ ■ Literary Analysis, p. 25 Reading Strategy, p. 24 Build Vocabulary, p. 21	• **Literary Analysis and Reading Transparencies,** pp. 9 and 10 ● ▲ ■	
	• **Adapted Reader's Companion** ● • **Reader's Companion** ●		• **Listening to Literature** ● ▲ ■ Audiocassettes, Side 2 Audio CDs, CD 1
	• **English Learner's Companion** ● ▲ • **Literary Analysis for Enrichment** ■		
	• **Formal Assessment:** Selection Test, pp. 13–15 ● ▲ ■ • **Open Book Test,** pp. 13–15 ● ▲ ■ • **Performance Assessment and Portfolio Management,** p. 13 ● ▲ ■ • PRENTICE HALL ASSESSMENT SYSTEM ● ▲ ■	• PRENTICE HALL ASSESSMENT SYSTEM ● ▲ ■ Skills Practice Answers and Explanations on Transparencies	• **Test Bank Software** ● ▲ ■ • **Got It! Assessment Videotapes,** Tape 1 ● ▲
	• **Selection Support Workbook:** ● ▲ ■ Build Spelling Skills, p. 22 Build Grammar Skills, p. 23 • **Writing and Grammar,** Copper Level ● ▲ ■ • **Extension Activities,** p. 5 ● ▲ ■	• **Daily Language Practice Transparencies** ● ▲ • **Writing Models and Graphic Organizers on Transparencies** ● ▲ ■	• **Writing and Grammar iText CD-ROM** ● ▲ ■ *Take It to the Net* www.phschool.com

BLOCK SCHEDULING: Use one 90-minute class period to preteach the selection and have students read it. Use a second 90-minute class period to assess students' mastery of skills and have them complete one of the Extension Activities.

PRETEACH

Step-by-Step Teaching Guide for pp. 50–51

Motivation

Show a video of a chase scene from a current action film. Ask students to suggest why chase scenes are included.
Possible response: Chase scenes add to the suspense, excitement, and interest of a movie.

Tell students that, like an action movie, the story they are about to read contains a chase scene. As they read, they can look for ways that the chase is similar to and different from one in a movie. Start them off with a Venn diagram like this one:

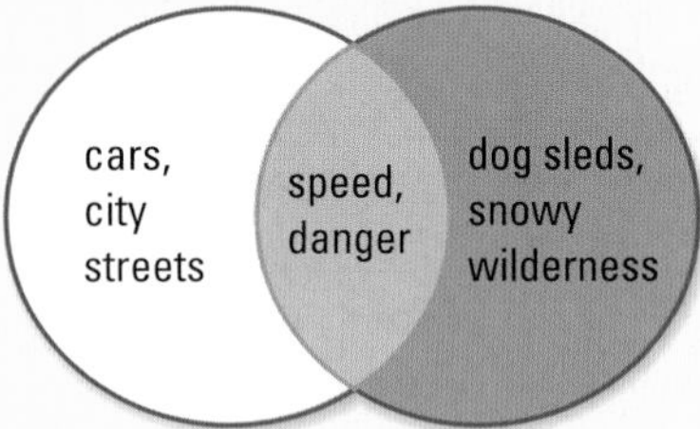

Interest Grabber Video

As an alternative, play "Sled Dogs" on Tape 1 to engage student interest.

❶ Background

Social Studies

For many years, people living in the far north have relied on dog sleds to carry people and cargo over ice- and snow-covered terrain. Sleds and dogs also provide transportation for winter hunting. Sled dog racing is a popular and exciting sport today.

Early sleds were made by attaching hollow wooden runners to crosspieces with strips of sealskin. Harnesses made of sealskin were tied around the dogs' shoulders and then attached to the reins. The sleds were sturdy enough to be used for long-distance transportation.

Prepare to Read

❶ The King of Mazy May

Take It to the Net

Visit www.phschool.com for interactive activities and instruction related to "The King of Mazy May," including

- background
- graphic organizers
- literary elements
- reading strategies

Preview

Connecting to the Literature

At times, you have probably stood up for a friend or defended someone who was being treated unfairly. In "The King of Mazy May" by Jack London, a young boy in the wilderness protects the property of a friend from thieves.

Background

In 1896, George Carmack found gold in the Klondike region of northwestern Canada. His find began with a quarter ounce of the precious metal—equal in value to what an average worker could earn in a week! Carmack was followed by thousands of others. Most found hardship, but no gold. In Jack London's short story, dangerous outlaws prey on gold-seekers in the Klondike.

TEACHING RESOURCES

The following resources can be used to enrich or extend the instruction for pp. 50–51.

Motivation

Interest Grabber Video, Tape 1

Background

Beyond Literature, p. 5

Take It to the Net

Visit www.phschool.com for Background and hotlinks for "The King of Mazy May."

Literary Analysis

Literary Analysis and Reading Transparencies, Conflict Between Characters, p. 10

Reading

Selection Support: Reading Strategy, p. 24; Build Vocabulary, p. 21

Literary Analysis and Reading Transparencies, Recognizing Signal Words, p. 9

BLOCK SCHEDULING: Resources marked with this symbol provide varied instruction during 90-minute blocks.

❷ Literary Analysis

Conflict Between Characters

A conflict is a struggle between opposing forces. A **conflict between characters** occurs when characters with different goals battle each other to achieve their goals.

In "The King of Mazy May," men who are desperate for gold battle a boy who is intent on justice. While reading "The King of Mazy May," identify the conflict by asking yourself the following focus questions:

1. How do different goals cause the strangers and Walt to clash?
2. What are two possible outcomes of the conflict?

Connecting Literary Elements

The **resolution** is the way the conflict turns out. In a story involving a conflict among characters, the resolution involves which character "wins." As you read "The King of Mazy May," try to predict how the conflict will be resolved. Use a chart like this one to track details that lead you to expect a specific resolution.

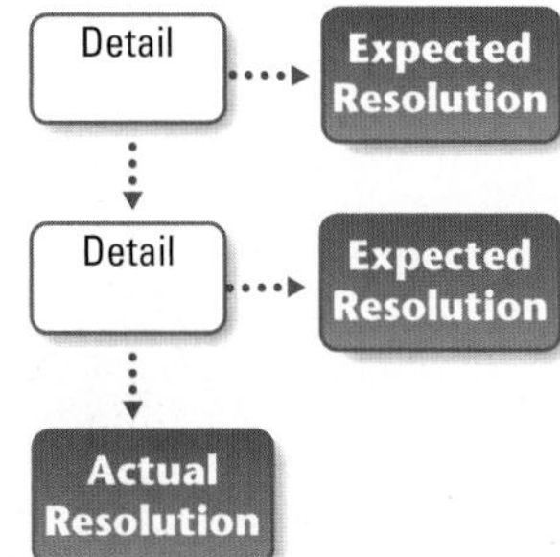

❸ Reading Strategy

Recognizing Signal Words

Signal words indicate order of events and relationships among ideas and details. For example, the word *but* signals that the next idea differs from what you've just read. The word *next* indicates sequence of events.

- **Signal Words Indicating Time Use**
  first then after before
- **Signal Words Indicating Cause and Effect**
  because as a result
- **Signal Words Indicating Spatial Relationships**
  above below on top

As you read, pay close attention to signal words and note what they indicate about the relationships among details.

Vocabulary Development

toil (toil) *n.* hard work (p. 53)

endured (en doord´) *v.* suffered through (p. 53)

prospectors (prä´ spekt´ erz) *n.* people who make their living searching for valuable ores, such as gold (p. 53)

liable (lī´ ə bəl) *adj.* likely (to do something or have something happen to one) (p. 54)

poising (poiz´ iŋ) *adj.* balancing (p. 56)

declined (di klīnd´) *v.* refused (p. 57)

summit (sum´ it) *n.* highest part (p. 59)

CUSTOMIZE INSTRUCTION FOR UNIVERSAL ACCESS

For Special Needs Students	For Less Proficient Readers	For English Learners
Have students read the adapted version of "The King of Mazy May" in the **Adapted Reader's Companion.** This version provides basic-level instruction in an interactive format with questions and write-on lines. Completing the adapted version will prepare students to read the selection in the Student Edition.	Have students read "The King of Mazy May" in the **Reader's Companion.** This version provides basic-level instruction in an interactive format with questions and write-on lines. After students finish the selection in the Reader's Companion, have them complete the questions and activities in the Student Edition.	Have students read the adapted version of "The King of Mazy May" in the **English Learner's Companion.** This version provides basic-level instruction in an interactive format with questions and write-on lines. Completing the adapted version will prepare students to read the selection in the Student Edition.

❷ Literary Analysis

Conflict Between Characters

- Tell students that the plot of "The King of Mazy May" centers on conflict, or disagreement, between characters.
- Explain to students that conflict can also occur between characters and nature, such as a tornado threatening to destroy a town.
- Invite students to share examples of conflict from stories they have read or movies they have seen.
- Use the instruction for Connecting Literary Elements to help students understand that the resolution in a story ends the conflict. Invite students to describe the resolutions in the stories or movies mentioned earlier.
- Use the Conflict Between Characters transparency on p. 10 in **Literary Analysis and Reading Transparencies** to show how to define the sides in a conflict.

❸ Reading Strategy

Recognizing Signal Words

- Read the instruction about signal words together as a class.
- Write the following sentence on the board, leaving a blank where a signal word is needed: Jack London died at the young age of forty, _____ he wrote more than 50 books. Ask students to identify the missing word and to explain its purpose.
  Answer: The missing word is *but*. It indicates contrast between the two sentence parts.
- To assist students with signal words, use the Recognizing Signal Words transparency on p. 9 in **Literary Analysis and Reading Transparencies.**

Vocabulary Development

- Pronounce each vocabulary word for students, and read the definitions as a class. Have students identify any words with which they are already familiar.

E-Teach

Visit E-Teach at www.phschool.com for teachers' essays on how to teach, with questions and answers.

Step-by-Step Teaching Guide for pp. 52–60

CUSTOMIZE INSTRUCTION
For Visual/Spatial Learners

Explain that the story takes place on Mazy May Creek. Have students look at the photograph on p. 52. Ask them to use the expression on the men's faces and their clothing, as well as the rugged terrain pictured in the photograph, to make inferences about life on the Mazy May.

❶ About the Selection

Fourteen-year-old Walt Masters has lived all his life in the lonely Yukon wilderness, where he and his father have staked and recorded a prospecting claim. While Walt's father is away on a short trip, Walt comes across men plotting to steal the claim of his neighbor, Loren Hall. To foil their plan, Walt takes one of their sleds and dog teams, hoping to beat the claim jumpers to Dawson. When the men realize what Walt has done, they try to stop him in a thrill-packed chase scene.

❷ ▶Critical Viewing

Possible response: It is difficult to tell because honest stakeholders and claim jumpers could look alike and have the same equipment. They would be engaged in the same activities, and the rough life in the Yukon could give both honest and dishonest men a dangerous look.

❶ The King of Mazy May

Jack London

Walt Masters is not a very large boy, but there is manliness in his make-up, and he himself, although he does not know a great deal that most boys know, knows much that other boys do not know. He has never seen a train of cars nor an elevator in his life, and for that matter he has never once looked upon a cornfield, a plow, a cow, or even a chicken. He has never had a pair of shoes on his feet, nor gone to a picnic or a party, nor talked to a girl. But he has seen the sun at midnight, watched the ice jams on one of the mightiest of rivers, and

❷ ▼**Critical Viewing** Why is it difficult to tell if these men are honest stakeholders or if they are claim jumpers? **[Generalize]**

TEACHING RESOURCES

The following resources can be used to enrich or extend the instruction for pp. 52–60.

Literary Analysis

- **Selection Support:** Literary Analysis, p. 25
- **Literary Analysis for Enrichment**

Reading

- **Adapted Reader's Companion**
- **Reader's Companion**
- **English Learner's Companion**

- **Listening to Literature Audiocassettes,** Side 2 
- **Listening to Literature Audio CDs,** CD 1

BLOCK SCHEDULING: Resources marked with this symbol provide varied instruction during 90-minute blocks.

played beneath the northern lights,[1] the one white child in thousands of square miles of frozen wilderness.

Walt has walked all the fourteen years of his life in suntanned, moose-hide moccasins, and he can go to the Indian camps and "talk big" with the men, and trade calico and beads with them for their precious furs. He can make bread without baking powder, yeast, or hops, shoot a moose at three hundred yards, and drive the wild wolf dogs fifty miles a day on the packed trail.

Last of all, he has a good heart, and is not afraid of the darkness and loneliness, of man or beast or thing. His father is a good man, strong and brave, and Walt is growing up like him.

Walt was born a thousand miles or so down the Yukon,[2] in a trading post below the Ramparts. After his mother died, his father and he came up on the river, step by step, from camp to camp, till now they are settled down on the Mazy May Creek in the Klondike[3] country. Last year they and several others had spent much toil and time on the Mazy May, and endured great hardships; the creek, in turn, was just beginning to show up its richness and to reward them for their heavy labor. But with the news of their discoveries, strange men began to come and go through the short days and long nights, and many unjust things they did to the men who had worked so long upon the creek.

toil (toil) *n.* hard work

endured (en doord′) *v.* suffered through

Si Hartman had gone away on a moose hunt, to return and find new stakes driven and his claim jumped.[4] George Lukens and his brother had lost their claims in a like manner, having delayed too long on the way to Dawson to record them. In short, it was the old
3 story, and quite a number of the earnest, industrious prospectors had suffered similar losses.

prospectors (prä′ spekt′ erz) *n.* people who make their living searching for valuable ores, such as gold

But Walt Masters's father had recorded his claim at the start, so Walt had nothing to fear now that his father had gone on a short trip up the White River prospecting for quartz. Walt was well able to stay by himself in the cabin, cook his three meals a day, and look after things. Not only did he look after his father's claim, but he had agreed to keep an eye on the adjoining one of Loren Hall, who had started for Dawson to record it.

4 Loren Hall was an old man, and he had no dogs, so he had to travel very slowly. After he had been gone some time, word came up the river that he had broken through the ice at Rosebud Creek and frozen his feet so badly that he would not be able to travel for a

5 
Reading Check

Why did Walt stay behind?

1. **northern lights** glowing bands or streamers of light, sometimes appearing in the night sky of the Northern Hemisphere.
2. **Yukon** (yoo′ kän′) river flowing through the Yukon Territory of northwest Canada.
3. **Klondike** (klän′ dīk′) gold-mining region along a tributary of the Yukon River.
4. **claim jumped** a claim is a piece of land staked out by a miner (stakes are markers driven into the ground to show where the borders of the claim are). A claim that is jumped is stolen by someone else.

3 Vocabulary Development

Latin Suffixes: *-or*

- Call students' attention to the word *prospector* and its definition.
- Tell students that the suffix *-or* means "a person or thing that does something." A *prospector* is one who prospects, or looks, for gold.
- Have students suggest other words that end in *-or* and list them on the board.
  Possible responses: Students may suggest *actor, inventor, sailor,* and *orator.*

4 Reading Strategy

Recognizing Signal Words

- Call students' attention to the first sentence of the sixth full paragraph on p. 53. Then ask: In this sentence, what two ideas are connected by the word so?
  Answer: Loren was an old man and had no dogs; he had to travel slowly.
- Remind students that *so* signals that the next idea will be a result of the previous idea in the sentence. Ask students how they could rewrite the bracketed sentence as two sentences, using the phrase "as a result" instead of *so.*
  Answer: Loren Hall was an old man, and he had no dogs. As a result, he had to travel very slowly.
- Direct the students to keep track of the signal words they see in this story. Provide each student with a photocopy of the Recognize Signal Words transparency, p. 9 in **Literary Analysis and Reading Transparencies,** to record how various signal words are used.

5 Reading Check

Answer: Walt stayed behind to look after his father's claim and the claim of a neighbor.

CUSTOMIZE INSTRUCTION FOR UNIVERSAL ACCESS

For Special Needs Students	For English Learners	For Advanced Readers
Have students preview the photographs, vocabulary words, and footnotes. Tell students to reread the footnotes and vocabulary words on pp. 52–53, then write an extended caption for the photograph on p. 52, using as many of the new words as possible *(toil, endured, prospectors, northern lights, Yukon, Klondike, claim jumped).*	Have students work in pairs to paraphrase the sentences on this page that contain vocabulary words. They may use a dictionary, a thesaurus, and strategies such as context clues. They may also choose to illustrate some of the concepts.	Invite students to make a map of the United States, indicating the cities and states that were founded because of gold rushes. Suggest that students begin their research by using an encyclopedia. They may do further research using the Internet or other materials. Suggest that they begin by creating a map legend.

6 Literary Analysis

Conflict Between Characters

- Ask students to recall how Walt has been described.
  Answer: He is young, experienced in taking care of himself, honest, and strong.
- After reading the first bracketed passage, invite students to share their responses to the Literary Analysis question on p. 54.
  Answer: The conflict will probably be that Walt will try to defend claims against the claim jumpers.

Monitor Progress Have a volunteer read the second bracketed passage. Ask students: What conflict has developed among the claim jumpers?
Answer: They cannot decide whether to travel at night or wait until morning to go to Dawson.

Reteach If students have difficulty answering the questions about conflict, explain that conflict can be shown in many ways. Point out that in the first passage, conflict is shown through Walt's internal thoughts; in the second passage, it is shown through the dialogue of two arguing characters. Reread the bracketed passages, pausing after each one to ask students to name the two opposing forces that are in conflict.

couple of weeks. Then Walt Masters received the news that old Loren was nearly all right again, and about to move on afoot for Dawson as fast as a weakened man could.

6 Walt was worried, however; the claim was liable to be jumped at any moment because of this delay, and a fresh stampede had started in on the Mazy May. He did not like the looks of the newcomers, and one day, when five of them came by with crack dog teams and the lightest of camping outfits, he could see that they were prepared to make speed, and resolved to keep an eye on them. So he locked up the cabin and followed them, being at the same time careful to remain hidden.

He had not watched them long before he was sure that they were professional stampeders, bent on jumping all the claims in sight. Walt crept along the snow at the rim of the creek and saw them change many stakes, destroy old ones, and set up new ones.

In the afternoon, with Walt always trailing on their heels, they came back down the creek, unharnessed their dogs, and went into camp within two claims of his cabin. When he saw them make preparations to cook, he hurried home to get something to eat himself, and then hurried back. He crept so close that he could hear them talking quite plainly, and by pushing the underbrush aside he could catch occasional glimpses of them. They had finished eating and were smoking around the fire.

6 "The creek is all right, boys," a large, black-bearded man, evidently the leader, said, "and I think the best thing we can do is to pull out tonight. The dogs can follow the trail; besides, it's going to be moonlight. What say you?"

"But it's going to be beastly cold," objected one of the party. "It's forty below zero now."

"An' sure, can't ye keep warm by jumpin' off the sleds an' runnin' after the dogs?" cried an Irishman. "An' who wouldn't? The creek's as rich as a United States mint! Faith, it's an ilegant chanst to be gettin' a run fer yer money! An' if ye don't run, it's mebbe you'll not get the money at all, at all."

"That's it," said the leader. "If we can get to Dawson and record, we're rich men; and there's no telling who's been sneaking along in our tracks, watching us, and perhaps now off to give the alarm. The thing for us to do is to rest the dogs a bit, and then hit the trail as hard as we can. What do you say?"

Evidently the men had agreed with their leader, for Walt Masters could hear nothing but the rattle of the tin dishes which were being washed. Peering out cautiously, he could see the leader studying a piece of paper. Walt knew what it was at a glance—a list of all the unrecorded claims on Mazy May. Any man could get these lists by applying to the gold commissioner at Dawson.

liable (lī´ ə bəl) *adj.* likely (to do something or have something happen to one)

Literary Analysis
Conflict Between Characters From what you know about Walt's character, what conflict might develop between him and these men?

CUSTOMIZE INSTRUCTION FOR UNIVERSAL ACCESS

For Gifted/Talented Students

Have students role-play an interview between Walt and a reporter for the *Klondike News.* Tell students that the reporter should ask questions beginning with *who, what, where, why, when,* and *how* to get information about events in the story so far. Walt should supply facts for the reporter. Tell students that they can present the interview in any style of their choice, such as a dramatic breaking news story or a comic event. Allow students to make up details that are not specifically mentioned in the story to make their skits more interesting. Invite students to use objects from around the classroom as props. Encourage students to present their work to the class.

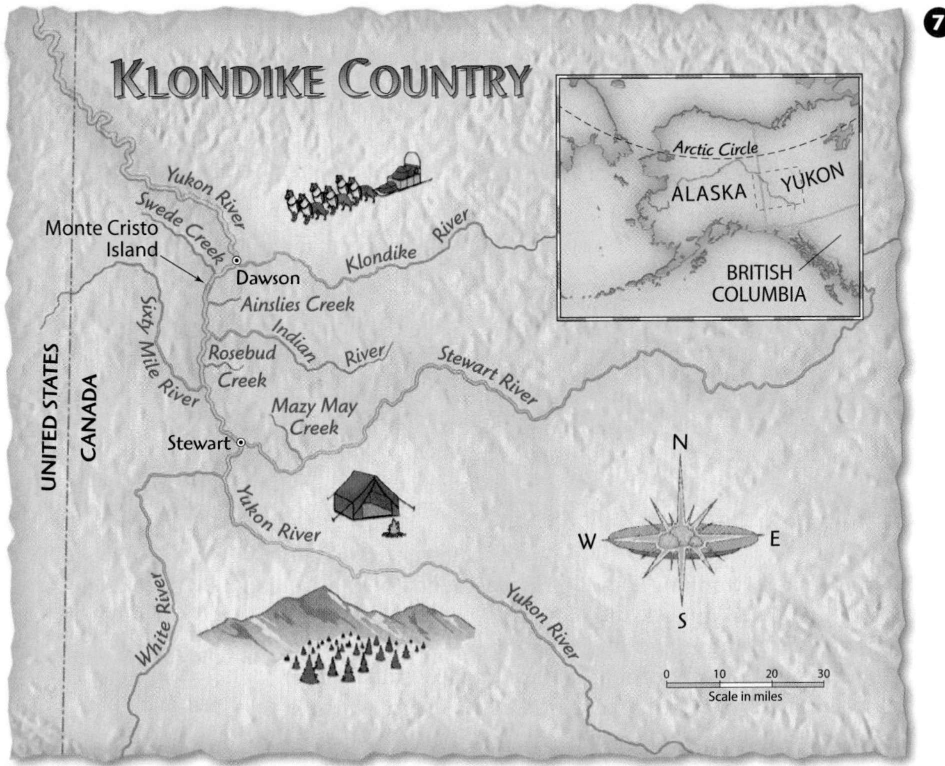

❼

"Thirty-two," the leader said, lifting his face to the men. "Thirty-two isn't recorded, and this is thirty-three. Come on; let's take a look at it. I saw somebody had been working on it when we came up this morning."

Three of the men went with him, leaving one to remain in camp. Walt crept carefully after them till they came to Loren Hall's shaft. One of the men went down and built a fire on the bottom to thaw out the frozen gravel, while the others built another fire on the dump and melted water in a couple of gold pans. This they poured into a piece of canvas stretched between two logs, used by Loren Hall in which to wash his gold.

In a short time a couple of buckets of dirt were sent up by the man in the shaft, and Walt could see the others grouped anxiously about their leader as he proceeded to wash it. When this was finished, they stared at the broad streak of black sand and yellow gold grains on the bottom of the pan, and one of them called excitedly for the man who had remained in camp to come. Loren Hall had struck it rich and his claim was not yet recorded. It was plain that they were going to jump it.

❽ ▲ **Critical Viewing**
Based on what you have read, why do you think so few towns are settled in this area? **[Connect]**

❾ **✓Reading Check**
What was Walt's reason for following the men?

❼ Background

Social Studies

The Yukon Territory is located in northwestern Canada, bordering on the Arctic Ocean. Today, most of the Yukon's 31,000 citizens live in the capital, Whitehorse, which has a population just under 23,000. The next largest city, Dawson, has a population of about 2,000.

Because the Yukon is in the subarctic climate zone, temperatures are generally quite cold. Individual temperatures range widely, however, from as low as –80 degrees Fahrenheit (the lowest temperature ever recorded in North America) in winter to a record high of 95 degrees in summer.

❽ ▶Critical Viewing

Possible response: It is a very cold place, where it would be hard to make a living if it were not for the discovery of gold. There are no large cities nearby and no jobs to draw people to live there. There probably are not good roads, making transportation difficult, so very few towns have been established.

❾ ✓Reading Check

Answer: Walt followed the men because he suspected that they were claim jumpers. Since Walt is guarding his father's and Loren's claims, he wanted to see what the men would do next.

CUSTOMIZE INSTRUCTION FOR UNIVERSAL ACCESS

For Less Proficient Readers	For Advanced Readers
Use the map on p. 55 to help students visualize Walt's route to Dawson. First, have students reread the route Walt took, noting the names that are on the map and in the story. Then have students locate Mazy May Creek on the map and use their fingers to trace the route that Walt took to Dawson. Ask students to comment on how the map aids their understanding of the story.	The root of the conflict in this story is the system for establishing claims. Have students use information from the story and additional research to understand the system that was in place at the time this story was written, approximately 1900. Then have students write a letter to the *Klondike News* proposing and defending a better method of establishing claims.

3 Yes, it was that time of year. When I opened the front door to the shack, I stopped. Everything we owned was neatly packed in cardboard boxes. Suddenly I felt even more the weight of hours, days, weeks, and months of work. I sat down on a box. The thought of having to move to Fresno[4] and knowing what was in store for me there brought tears to my eyes.

That night I could not sleep. I lay in bed thinking about how much I hated this move.

A little before five o'clock in the morning, Papá woke everyone up. A few minutes later, the yelling and screaming of my little brothers and sisters, for whom the move was a great adventure, broke the silence of dawn. Shortly, the barking of the dogs accompanied them.

While we packed the breakfast dishes, Papá went outside to start the "Carcanchita."[5] That was the name Papá gave his old '38 black Plymouth. He bought it in a used-car lot in Santa Rosa in the winter of 1949. Papá was very proud of his little jalopy. He had a right to be proud of it. He spent a lot of time looking at other cars before buying this one. When he finally chose the "Carcanchita," he checked it thoroughly before driving it out of the car lot. He examined every inch of the car. He listened to the motor, tilting his head from side to side like a parrot, trying to detect any noises that spelled car trouble. 4 After being satisfied with the looks and sounds of the car, Papá then insisted on knowing who the original owner was. He never did find out from the car salesman, but he bought the car anyway. Papá figured the original owner must have been an important man because behind the rear seat of the car he found a blue necktie.

Papá parked the car out in front and left the motor running. "*Listo*,"[6] he yelled. Without saying a word, Roberto and I began to carry the boxes out to the car. Roberto carried the two big boxes and I carried the two smaller ones. Papá then threw the mattress on top of the car roof and tied it with ropes to the front and rear bumpers.

Everything was packed except Mamá's pot. It was an old large galvanized[7] pot she had picked up at an army surplus store in Santa María the year I was born. The pot had many dents and nicks, and the more dents and nicks it acquired the more Mamá liked it. "*Mi olla*,"[8] she used to say proudly.

I held the front door open as Mamá carefully carried out her pot by both handles, making sure not to spill the cooked beans. When she got to the car, Papá reached out to help her with it. Roberto opened the rear car door and Papá gently placed it on the floor behind the

Literary Analysis
Theme In what way do this event and the narrator's actions give you a clue about the theme?

Reading Strategy
Reading With Expression What is being said about Papá in the sentence beginning "After being"? How would you read this sentence aloud?

5 **✔Reading Check**
How does the family feel about moving again?

---

4. **Fresno** (frezʹ nō) *n.* city in central California.
5. **Carcanchita** (kär kän chēʹ tä) affectionate name for the car.
6. ***Listo*** (lēs to) Spanish for "Ready."
7. **galvanized** (galʹ və nīzdʹ) *adj.* coated with zinc to prevent rusting.
8. ***Mi olla*** (mē ōʹ yä) Spanish for "My pot."

3 Literary Analysis

Theme

- Remind students that sometimes a theme is not stated directly by the author.
- Have a volunteer read the bracketed passage. Ask the Literary Analysis question on p. 66: In what way do this event and the narrator's actions give you a clue about the theme?
  Answer: The theme will be about a child's unhappiness with change or moving.
- Then, ask students which words or phrases in the passage led them to their conclusion about the theme.
  Answer: "packed in cardboard boxes," "having to move," "tears to my eyes."
- Invite students to check their predictions of the theme as the story progresses.

4 Reading Strategy

Reading With Expression

- Read aloud the bracketed sentence on p. 67.
- Then ask the Reading Strategy question.
  Answer: Papá was thoroughly investigating the car before he bought it. Emphasis should be placed on *insisted*.

5 ✔Reading Check

Answer: The family feels weary and sad about moving again. The younger children are excited.

CUSTOMIZE INSTRUCTION FOR UNIVERSAL ACCESS

For Less Proficient Readers	For English Learners	For Advanced Readers
Before students begin reading the selection, explain the meanings of the title to them. Tell them that a circuit refers to a closed, circular line that goes around an object or area. Then explain that the expression "hard as nails" refers to someone who is very tough. Have them speculate what the selections are about based on these titles.	Make a three-column chart (Spanish, English, Other). Have students scan the selection for Spanish terms and list them in the proper column. Interpret the terms in English together, and list the interpretations under "English." Ask students who speak other languages to suggest phrases for the same idea. List those under "Other."	Have students take notes about Panchito's character as they read. They can use the notes to write a character analysis of Panchito. Tell them that the analyses should explore the relationship between Panchito's feelings and his behavior.

6 Reading Strategy

Reading With Expression

- Tell students that it is possible to learn a lot about Panchito's family from the information given in only one sentence.
- Call on a volunteer to read the bracketed passage.
- Then, ask the Reading Strategy question on p. 68: Who is the subject of the sentence beginning "That night"? What else does the sentence tell you?
  Answer: The subject is "we," meaning Panchito's family. His family unpacked and cleaned their home, working by the light of a kerosene lamp. The sentence reveals that there is no electricity in the garage and that the family works very hard.

7 Reading Strategy

Reading With Expression

- Tell students that when reading aloud we emphasize the most important part of the sentence.
- Then, ask students the Reading Strategy question.
  Answer: The emphasis is on "one hundred degrees."
- Call on a volunteer to read the bracketed passage.

front seat. All of us then climbed in. Papá sighed, wiped the sweat off his forehead with his sleeve, and said wearily: "*Es todo.*"[9]

As we drove away, I felt a lump in my throat. I turned around and looked at our little shack for the last time.

At sunset we drove into a labor camp near Fresno. Since Papá did not speak English, Mamá asked the camp foreman if he needed any more workers. "We don't need no more," said the foreman, scratching his head. "Check with Sullivan down the road. Can't miss him. He lives in a big white house with a fence around it."

When we got there, Mamá walked up to the house. She went through a white gate, past a row of rose bushes, up the stairs to the front door. She rang the doorbell. The porch light went on and a tall husky man came out. They exchanged a few words. After the man went in, Mamá clasped her hands and hurried back to the car. "We have work! Mr. Sullivan said we can stay there the whole season," she said, gasping and pointing to an old garage near the stables.

The garage was worn out by the years. It had no windows. The walls, eaten by termites, strained to support the roof full of holes. The dirt floor, populated by earthworms, looked like a gray road map.

6 That night, by the light of a kerosene lamp, we unpacked and cleaned our new home. Roberto swept away the loose dirt, leaving the hard ground. Papá plugged the holes in the walls with old newspapers and tin can tops. Mamá fed my little brothers and sisters. Papá and Roberto then brought in the mattress and placed it on the far corner of the garage. "Mamá, you and the little ones sleep on the mattress. Roberto, Panchito, and I will sleep outside under the trees," Papá said.

Reading Strategy
Reading With Expression
Who is the subject of the sentence beginning "That night"? What else does the sentence tell you?

Early next morning Mr. Sullivan showed us where his crop was, and after breakfast, Papá, Roberto, and I headed for the vineyard to pick.

7 Around nine o'clock the temperature had risen to almost one hundred degrees. I was completely soaked in sweat and my mouth felt as if I had been chewing on a handkerchief. I walked over to the end of the row, picked up the jug of water we had brought, and began drinking. "Don't drink too much; you'll get sick," Roberto shouted. No sooner had he said that than I felt sick to my stomach. I dropped to my knees and let the jug roll off my hands. I remained motionless with my eyes glued on the hot sandy ground. All I could hear was the drone of insects. Slowly I began to recover. I poured water over my face and neck and watched the dirty water run down my arms to the ground.

Reading Strategy
Reading With Expression
Which part of the first sentence in this paragraph would you emphasize when reading it aloud?

drone (drōn) *n.* continuous humming sound

I still felt a little dizzy when we took a break to eat lunch. It was

9. ***Es todo*** (es tō´ thō) Spanish for "That's everything."

ENRICHMENT: Social Studies Connection

Child Labor Laws

As a result of the Industrial Revolution, many children worked long hours in dangerous and dirty conditions. Even though the first laws regulating child labor were passed in England in 1802, they were rarely enforced.

Today, laws in most industrialized countries prevent children under the age of fifteen from working except in businesses owned by their families. In the United States, the Fair Labor Standards Act of 1938 and the laws of individual states prohibit children under the age of sixteen from working during school hours. Laws also regulate the amount and kind of work done by people ages sixteen to eighteen, even outside of school hours.

Ask students to find out more about the labor laws of the state in which they live and in another state. Encourage students to discuss reasons that the laws differ, and to evaluate which laws they think are most reasonable and useful.

past two o'clock and we sat underneath a large walnut tree that was on the side of the road. While we ate, Papá jotted down the number of boxes we had picked. Roberto drew designs on the ground with a stick. Suddenly I noticed Papá's face turn pale as he looked down the road. "Here comes the school bus," he whispered loudly in alarm. Instinctively, Roberto and I ran and hid in the vineyards. We did not want to get in trouble for not going to school. The neatly dressed boys about my age got off. They carried books under their arms. After they crossed the street, the bus drove away. Roberto and I came out from hiding and joined Papá. "*Tienen que tener cuidado*,"[10] he warned us.

After lunch we went back to work. The sun kept beating down. The buzzing insects, the wet sweat, and the hot dry dust made the afternoon seem to last forever. Finally the mountains around the valley reached out and swallowed the sun. Within an hour it was too dark to continue picking. The vines blanketed the grapes, making it difficult to see the bunches. "*Vámonos*,"[11] said Papá, signaling to us that it was time to quit work. Papá then took out a pencil and began to figure out how much we had earned our first day. He wrote down numbers, crossed some out, wrote down some more. "*Quince*,"[12] he murmured.

When we arrived home, we took a cold shower underneath a waterhose. We then sat down to eat dinner around some wooden crates that served as a table. Mamá had cooked a special meal for us. We had rice and tortillas with "*carne con chile*,"[13] my favorite dish.

The next morning I could hardly move. My body ached all over. I felt little control over my arms and legs. This feeling went on every morning for days until my muscles finally got used to the work.

It was Monday, the first week of November. The grape season was over and I could now go to school. I woke up early that morn-
9 ing and lay in bed, looking at the stars and savoring the thought of not going to work and of starting sixth grade for the first time that year. Since I could not sleep, I decided to get up and join

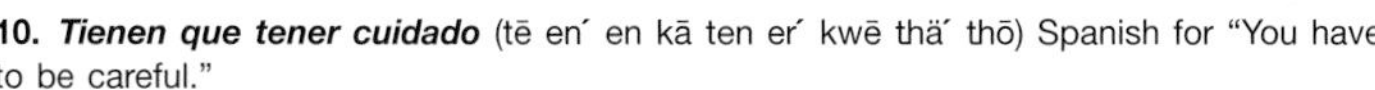

10. ***Tienen que tener cuidado*** (tē en´ en kā ten er´ kwē thä´ thō) Spanish for "You have to be careful."
11. ***Vámonos*** (vä´ mō nōs) Spanish for "Let's go."
12. ***Quince*** (kēn´ sā) Spanish for "fifteen."
13. ***carne con chile*** (kär´ nē kən chil´ ē) dish of ground meat, hot peppers, beans, and tomatoes.

Literature in context Geography Connection

8 ***Agricultural Seasons***

With sunny weather and a favorable climate, California produces more crops than any other state. At every point in the year, there is a different crop ready to be harvested in some part of the state. Migrant workers, such as Panchito's family, migrate from place to place to harvest the available crop. Grapes are picked in the summer and fall in the lush valleys of central and northern California, peak strawberry season hits the southern coastal regions in spring, and cotton is harvested in the dry valleys of central and southern California during the winter.

instinctively (in stiŋk´ tiv lē) *adv.* done by instinct, without thinking

savoring (sā´ vər iŋ) *v.* enjoying with appreciation; tasting; relishing

10 Reading Check

When and why is Panchito finally able to go to school?

8 Background

Agriculture

For over 50 years, California has been the largest producer of food and agricultural products in the United States. About 350 different commodities and crops are grown in California. A few of these crops—almonds, figs, olives, raisins, and walnuts—are grown almost solely in California.

9 Critical Thinking

Analyze

- Ask a volunteer to read the bracketed passage on p. 69.
- Point out to students Panchito's enthusiasm for starting sixth grade "for the first time that year." Ask students what Panchito's comment reveals about his experiences and expectations of school.
  Answer: Panchito expects to start school several times that year because his family is always moving.

10 Reading Check

Answer: Panchito starts school in early November. He can go then because the grape season is over.

CUSTOMIZE INSTRUCTION FOR UNIVERSAL ACCESS

For Less Proficient Readers	For Special Needs Students	For Advanced Readers
Students may benefit from an awareness of the settings in the story. Have them make a two-column chart, with one column labeled Setting and the other labeled Panchito's Feelings About It. As they read, students should use the chart to record how Panchito's feelings change throughout the story.	Students may benefit from hearing the story as well as reading it. Have students use the **Listening to Literature Audiocassettes,** Sides 5 and 6, or **Listening to Literature Audio CDs,** CD 2 to hear the selections read.	Have students analyze the breakfast scene on pp. 69–70. Ask students to describe the feelings that dampen Panchito's excitement as he prepares to begin his first day of sixth grade. Also have them describe the reasons he feels a sense of relief when his brother and father leave for the fields.

11 Literary Analysis

Theme

- Have a volunteer read the bracketed sentence on p. 70.
- Ask the Literary Analysis question. Answer: The sentence shows that Roberto can go to school only when he is not needed to pick crops because his family's work follows the cycles of nature and crop harvests. This relates to the theme that the family cannot improve their lot because the children cannot get a good education since they must work.

12 Reading Strategy

Reading With Expression

- Have students read the bracketed passage. Then have students pause to discuss and answer the Reading Strategy question on p. 70. Answer: The sentence is about how hard it was for Panchito to find the English words to explain what he wanted.

Monitor Progress Ask a volunteer to read aloud the bracketed passage and be sure to use expression as if he or she were the author.

Reteach If students have difficulty answering the question, have them reread the Reading Strategy instruction on p. 65. You also may want to use the Reading With Expression transparency on p. 11 in **Literary Analysis and Reading Transparencies.**

Papá and Roberto at breakfast. I sat at the table across from Roberto, but I kept my head down. I did not want to look up and face him. I knew he was sad. He was not going to school today. He
was not going tomorrow, or next week, or next month. He would
11 not go until the cotton season was over, and that was sometime in
February. I rubbed my hands together and watched the dry, acid stained skin fall to the floor in little rolls.

When Papá and Roberto left for work, I felt relief. I walked to the top of a small grade next to the shack and watched the "Carcanchita" disappear in the distance in a cloud of dust.

Two hours later, around eight o'clock, I stood by the side of the road waiting for school bus number twenty. When it arrived I climbed in. Everyone was busy either talking or yelling. I sat in an empty seat in the back.

When the bus stopped in front of the school, I felt very nervous. I looked out the bus window and saw boys and girls carrying books under their arms. I put my hands in my pant pockets and walked to the principal's office. When I entered I heard a woman's voice say: "May I help you?" I was startled. I had not heard English for months. For a few seconds I remained speechless. I looked at the lady who waited for my answer. My first instinct was to answer her in Spanish,
but I held back. Finally, after struggling for English words, I man-
12 aged to tell her that I wanted to enroll in the sixth grade. After
answering many questions, I was led to the classroom.

Mr. Lema, the sixth-grade teacher, greeted me and assigned me a desk. He then introduced me to the class. I was so nervous and scared at that moment when everyone's eyes were on me that I wished I were with Papá and Roberto picking cotton. After taking roll, Mr. Lema gave the class the assignment for the first hour. "The first thing we have to do this morning is finish reading the story we began yesterday," he said enthusiastically. He walked up to me, handed me an English book, and asked me to read. "We are on page 125," he said politely. When I heard this, I felt my blood rush to my head; I felt dizzy. "Would you like to read?" he asked hesitantly. I opened the book to page 125. My mouth was dry. My eyes began to water. I could not begin. "You can read later," Mr. Lema said understandingly.

For the rest of the reading period I kept getting angrier and angrier at myself. I should have read, I thought to myself.

During recess I went into the restroom and opened my English book to page 125. I began to read in a low voice, pretending I was in class. There were many words I did not know. I closed the book and headed back to the classroom.

Mr. Lema was sitting at his desk correcting papers. When I entered he looked up at me and smiled. I felt better. I walked up to him and asked if he could help me with the new words. "Gladly," he said.

Literary Analysis

Theme How does the sentence that begins "He would not go" convey the idea that the family's life follows a cycle? How might this relate to the story's theme?

Reading Strategy

Reading With Expression Read aloud the sentence beginning *Finally,* and pause for punctuation. What is the sentence about?

ENRICHMENT: Social Studies Connection

Migrant Workers

Migrant workers continually move to find jobs picking fruit, harvesting crops, or doing manual labor. These jobs are often boring and physically demanding. Migrant workers are often paid minimum wage, and they work long, hard hours. They receive no health care benefits or vacation. Many migrant workers cannot find higher paying or permanent jobs because they lack education and sometimes do not speak English well.

Like Panchito in "The Circuit," many migrant children have difficulty attending school because they move frequently and must often work during the school day.

Ask students to brainstorm questions for research on migrant families. Possible topics include where they work, how long they stay in one place, their living conditions, and their average wages. After students have used the Internet, encyclopedias, and nonfiction books to find the answers, have them present their findings to the class.

The rest of the month I spent my lunch hours working on English with Mr. Lema, my best friend at school.

One Friday during lunch hour Mr. Lema asked me to take a walk with him to the music room. "Do you like music?" he asked me as we entered the building.

"Yes, I like *corridos*,"[14] I answered. He then picked up a trumpet, blew on it and handed it to me. The sound gave me goose bumps. I knew that sound. I had heard it in many *corridos*. "How would you like to learn how to play it?" he asked. He must have read my face because before I could answer, he added: "I'll teach you how to play it during our lunch hours."

That day I could hardly wait to get home to tell Papá and Mamá the great news. As I got off the bus, my little brothers and sisters ran up to meet me. They were yelling and screaming. I thought they were happy to see me, but when I opened the door to our shack, I saw that everything we owned was neatly packed in cardboard boxes.

14. ***corridos*** (kō rē´ thōs) *n.* ballads.

Review and Assess

Thinking About the Selection

1. **Respond:** What do you admire about Panchito? Why?
2. **(a) Recall:** What brings tears to Panchito's eyes at the beginning of "The Circuit"? **(b) Draw Conclusions:** Why does he react this way?
3. **(a) Recall:** What does Panchito do on his school lunch hours? **(b) Infer:** Why do you think Panchito calls Mr. Lema his "best friend at school"? **(c) Synthesize:** Based on what you learn in the story, how would you describe Panchito's personality?
4. **(a) Infer:** What is the best thing that happens on the last day of school? **(b) Infer:** What is the worst thing? **(c) Analyze:** What clues indicate that Panchito has been through this before?
5. **(a) Analyze:** In what way does the final paragraph bring Panchito back to where he was at the beginning? **(b) Interpret:** Explain how this return to the beginning is connected to the title.
6. **Generalize:** What are the main difficulties of constantly moving and attending new schools?
7. **Extend:** What might other students do to make Panchito feel more comfortable?
8. **Extend:** What, if anything, might be done to ease the hardships faced by families like Panchito's? Support your answer.

Francisco Jiménez

(b. 1943)

Born in Mexico, Francisco Jiménez (hē mä´ nez) came with his family to the United States when he was four. The Jiménez family settled in California, becoming migrant workers. Like the young man in "The Circuit," Jiménez couldn't go to school before the harvest ended.

In high school, Jiménez supported himself by working as a janitor. His excellent grades won him three college scholarships. He went on to become an outstanding teacher and college official. He has also won awards as a writer.

CUSTOMIZE INSTRUCTION FOR UNIVERSAL ACCESS

For Less Proficient Readers	For Gifted/Talented Students	For Advanced Readers
Students may have trouble discovering the implied theme in this story. Use the Theme transparency on p.12 in **Literary Focus and Reading Transparencies** to record the title and major events in the story. Discuss this information with students, and assist them in discerning the theme.	Invite students to make up skits based on scenes from the story. Possible scenes include picking grapes with Panchito's father and Roberto, the family packing the car, and Panchito with Mr. Lema in the music room. Have students write scripts and enact them for the class.	Some students may wonder whether anything can be done for migrant families to break the cycle of poverty. Students may use the Internet and other library resources to discover social and government agencies that help workers and families caught in the poverty cycle. Have students report their findings to the class.

Answers for p. 71

Review and Assess

1. Students may admire his determination and hard work. These qualities show that he wants to improve his life.
2. **(a)** The thought of having to move to Fresno brings tears to his eyes. **(b)** He knows that he will have to work hard, and that makes him sad. Also, he doesn't like to keep moving.
3. **(a)** He studies English with Mr. Lema. **(b)** Panchito calls Mr. Lema his "best friend at school" because Mr. Lema helps him study and offers to teach him to play the trumpet. **(c)** He is shy, hard-working, thoughtful, and ambitious.
4. **(a)** Mr. Lema offers to teach Panchito to play the trumpet. **(b)** Panchito sees that his family will move again. **(c)** He knows that the boxes signal a move.
5. **(a)** The story began with his family moving. **(b)** *Circuit* means a circle or a track; Panchito's family must keep moving in order to find new jobs and support themselves.
6. It is difficult for a person to fit in and make new friends. It is also hard to learn while attending school irregularly.
7. Possible response: The other students could be friendly and invite the new student to join them on the playground or at lunch and help the new student learn about the schedule and how things are done.
8. Possible response: Families like Panchito's could be helped by agencies and organizations that give them things they need or help them become educated. Government agencies could enforce laws for better working and living conditions.

13 About the Selection

This essay describes Russell Baker's first job—delivering newspapers in Baltimore. Hired on his twelfth birthday by Mr. Deems, a man whose supervision isn't entirely honest, Baker is very proud to be a newsboy and deliver the day's news to the doorsteps of America. His essay describes his nervousness about attending a banquet for "honor carriers" and his awe when he visits the newsroom of the *News-Post.* Baker concludes by expressing his hope that he learned his first lessons about the newspaper business from the real thing—a person as hard as nails.

14 ▶ Critical Viewing

Answer: Some students may say that they would enjoy working with a group of people. Others may feel they would concentrate better in a quieter or more solitary environment.

13 Hard as Nails

Russell Baker

My mother started me in newspaper work in 1937 right after my twelfth birthday. She would have started me younger, but there was a law against working before age twelve. She thought it was a silly law, and said so to Deems.

Deems was boss of a group of boys who worked home delivery routes for the *Baltimore News-Post.* She found out about him a few weeks after we got to Baltimore. She just went out on the street, stopped a paperboy, and asked how he'd got his job.

"There's this man Deems . . ."

Deems was short and plump and had curly brown hair. He owned a car and a light gray suit and always wore a necktie and white shirt. A real businessman, I thought the first time I saw him. My mother was talking to him on the sidewalk in front of the Union Square Methodist Church and I was standing as tall as I could, just out of earshot.

14 ▼ **Critical Viewing** Would you enjoy working in a group like this one? Why or why not? **[Support]**

ENRICHMENT: Science Connection

Typewriters

Point out that the newspaper reporters shown on p. 72 are using typewriters. A typewriter is a small but complex machine that neatly prints letters and numbers directly on a sheet of paper. A typewriter keyboard looks like a computer keyboard. Unlike a computer keyboard, however, the keys on a typewriter are each attached to a lever bar with a metal letter or number template on the end of the bar. As the typist pushes the keys, the lever moves forward, striking first an inked ribbon and then the paper, leaving the inked impression of the key on the paper. If the typist makes a mistake, it is necessary to erase the mistake, back up, and type the correct letter.

A newspaper reporter using a typewriter could expect to hand the editor an actual typed copy of the story with all of the mistakes painstakingly corrected. Today, mistakes can easily be corrected online, and computers can store hundreds of documents in electronic memory. Stories can be recalled at any time, edited, and printed, or stored for use in the future.

"Now, Buddy, when we get down there keep your shoulders back and stand up real straight," she had cautioned me after making sure my necktie was all right and my shirt clean.

Watching the two of them in conversation, with Deems glancing at me now and then, I kept my shoulders drawn back in the painful military style I'd seen in movies, trying to look a foot taller than I really was.

"Come over here, Russ, and meet Mister Deems," she finally said, and I did, managing to answer his greeting by saying, "The pleasure's all mine," which I'd heard people say in the movies. I probably blushed while saying it, because meeting strangers was painfully embarrassing to me.

"If that's the rule, it's the rule," my mother was telling Deems, "and we'll just have to put up with it, but it still doesn't make any sense to me."

As we walked back to the house she said I couldn't have a paper route until I was twelve. And all because of some foolish rule they had down here in Baltimore. You'd think if a boy wanted to work they would encourage him instead of making him stay idle so long that laziness got embedded in his bones.

15 That was April. We had barely finished the birthday cake in August before Deems came by the apartment and gave me the tools of the newspaper trade: an account book for keeping track of the customers' bills and a long, brown web belt. Slung around one shoulder and across the chest, the belt made it easy to balance fifteen or twenty pounds of papers against the hip. I had to buy my own wire cutters for opening the newspaper bundles the trucks dropped at Wisengoff's store on the corner of Stricker and West Lombard streets.

16 In February my mother had moved us down from New Jersey, where we had been living with her brother Allen ever since my father died in 1930. This move of hers to Baltimore was a step toward fulfilling a dream. More than almost anything else in the world, she wanted "a home of our own." I'd heard her talk of that "home of our own" all through those endless Depression years when we lived as poor relatives dependent on Uncle Allen's goodness. "A home of our own. One of these days, Buddy, we'll have a home of our own."

That winter she had finally saved just enough to make her move, and she came to Baltimore. There were several reasons for Baltimore. For one, there were people she knew in Baltimore, people she could go to if things got desperate. And desperation was possible, because the moving would exhaust her savings, and the apartment rent was twenty-four dollars a month. She would have to find a job quickly. My sister Doris was only nine, but I was old enough for an after-school job that could bring home a few dollars a week. So as soon as it was legal I went into newspaper work.

embedded (em bed′ əd) *adj.* firmly fixed in a surrounding material

Literary Analysis
Theme What do these events tell you about the theme of this essay?

exhaust (ig zôst′) v. use up

17 **✓Reading Check**
Why does Russ want a paper route?

15 Literary Analysis

Theme

- Read the bracketed passage aloud. Then have students suggest details that relate to the theme. Write the suggestions on the board.
  Possible responses: His mother is angry that Russ cannot get a job yet; Deems shows up on Russ's birthday; the account book and the belt are supplied, but Russ must supply his own wire cutters.
- Ask students the Literary Analysis question on p. 73: What do these events tell you about the theme of this essay?
  Answer: Russ will get a job as soon as he can, will work hard, and will get little support from Deems.

16 Background

Social Studies

A financial depression is an extended slump in business activity that causes people to have lower incomes and lose jobs. The Great Depression lasted from 1929 through most of the 1930s. At its worst, in 1933, one out of every four workers in the United States was unemployed. Russell Baker's father died in 1930, leaving his family living with relatives.

17 ✓Reading Check

Answer: Russ wants a paper route to earn money to help his family.

CUSTOMIZE INSTRUCTION FOR UNIVERSAL ACCESS

For Less Proficient Readers	For English Learners	For Advanced Readers
Students may benefit from previewing the text before reading it. Invite them to look at the title, photographs, vocabulary words, and questions. Ask them what they expect to read in the story, and have them record any questions they may have about it. As they read, instruct students to cross off questions as they are answered.	Students may benefit from further sentence analysis. Invite them to write down any sentences that they find difficult to understand. Suggest that the students divide the sentences into phrases, using punctuation and other word clues. Ask them to label the subject and verb. Check their work and correct errors, if necessary.	Advanced readers may benefit from further study of the Depression. Encourage them to find photographs and first-person accounts in the library and on the Internet. Students may want to draw parallels between the situations of Russ's and Panchito's families. They may also benefit from finding differences between the families' situations.

18 Reading Strategy

Reading With Expression

- Tell students to think about when they should pause and use expression as they read the story silently.
- Then, direct their attention to the bracketed passage.
- Read the Reading Strategy question on p. 74.
  Answer: The subject is *I*, meaning Russ, and he hides the newspapers and loses money on them.

19 Literary Analysis

Theme

- Tell students that themes usually weave throughout a story and are not necessarily stated clearly.
- Ask a volunteer to read the bracketed text.
- Ask the Literary Analysis question on p. 74: Why do you think Deems comes up with schemes to get newsboys to sell more papers? How might his schemes relate to the theme?
  Answer: Deems probably comes up with these ideas because he makes more money if the boys sell more papers. Russ learns to be aware of others' actions and motives, and this experience helps him grow.

18 The romance of it was almost unbearable on my first day as I trudged west along Lombard Street, then south along Gilmor, and east down Pratt Street with the bundle of newspapers strapped to my hip. I imagined people pausing to admire me as I performed this important work, spreading the news of the world, the city, and the racetracks onto doorsteps, through mail slots, and under door jambs. I had often gazed with envy at paperboys; to be one of them at last was happiness sublime.

Very soon, though, I discovered drawbacks. The worst of these was Deems. Though I had only forty customers, Deems sent papers for forty-five. Since I was billed for every paper left on Wisengoff's corner, I had to pay for the five extra copies out of income or try to hustle them on the street. I hated standing at streetcar stops yelling, "Paper! Paper!" at people getting off trolleys.[1] Usually, if my mother wasn't around to catch me, I stuck the extras in a dark closet and took the loss.

Deems was constantly baiting new traps to dump more papers on me. When I solved the problem of the five extras by getting five new subscribers for home delivery, Deems announced a competition with mouth-watering prizes for the newsboys who got the most new subscribers. Too innocent to cope with this sly master of private enterprise,[2] I took the bait.

"Look at these prizes I can get for signing up new customers," I told my mother. "A balloon-tire bicycle. A free pass to the movies for a whole year."

The temptation was too much. I reported my five new subscribers to help me in the competition.

Whereupon Deems promptly raised my order from forty-five to fifty papers, leaving me again with the choice of hustling to unload the five extras or losing money.

I won a free pass to the movies, though. It was good for a whole year. And to the magnificent Loew's Century located downtown on Lexington Street. The passes were good only for nights in the middle of the week when I usually had too much homework to allow for movies. Still, in the summer with school out, it was thrilling to go all the way downtown at night to sit in the Century's damask[3] and velvet splendor and see MGM's glamorous stars in their latest movies.

To collect my prize I had to go to a banquet the paper gave for its "honor carriers" at the Emerson Hotel. There were fifty of us, and I was sure the other forty-nine would all turn out to be slicksters

Reading Strategy
Reading With Expression Determine the subject of the first sentence and what he does. Read the sentence aloud with expression.

sublime (sə blīm′) *adj.* majestic; causing awe

Literary Analysis
Theme Why do you think Deems comes up with schemes to get newsboys to sell more papers? How might his schemes relate to the theme?

---

1. **trolleys** (träl′ ēz) *n.* electric passenger trains, also called streetcars, running on rails in the city streets; discontinued in many American cities after the mid-1900s.
2. **private enterprise** business run for profit.
3. **damask** (dam′ əsk) *adj.* decorated with the shiny cloth called damask.

ENRICHMENT: Social Studies Connection

Photographs as Research Documents

Point out that the photographs on pp. 72 and 75 show newspaper offices in the 1920s. People who conduct research often use old photographs to learn more about how people lived in earlier times.

Ask students to describe how the offices in the photographs are different from offices today. Have them suggest specific ways working in the offices illustrated in the selection would be easier or more difficult.

Provide students with magazines or catalogs that show contemporary offices. Have students work in small groups or pairs to illustrate a modern office and glue their "office" to the top of a sheet of paper. At the bottom of the paper, have them list differences they can see between the offices on their paper and the newspaper offices illustrated in their books.

 wised up to the ways of the world, who would laugh at my doltish ignorance of how to eat at a great hotel banquet. My fear of looking foolish at the banquet made me lie awake nights dreading it and imagining all the humiliating mistakes I could make.

I had seen banquets in movies. Every plate was surrounded by a baffling array of knives, forks, and spoons. I knew it would be the same at the Emerson Hotel. The Emerson was one of the swankiest hotels in Baltimore. It was not likely to hold down on the silverware. I talked to my mother.

"How will I know what to eat what with?"

The question did not interest her.

"Just watch what everybody else does, and enjoy yourself," she said.

I came back to the problem again and again.

"Do you use the same spoon for your coffee as you do for dessert?"

"Don't worry about it. Everybody isn't going to be staring at you."

"Is it all right to butter your bread with the same knife you use to cut the meat?"

"Just go and have a good time."

Close to panic, I showed up at the Emerson, found my way to the banquet, and was horrified to find that I had to sit beside Deems throughout the meal. We probably talked about something, but I was so busy sweating with terror and rolling my eyeballs sidewise to see what silverware Deems was using to eat with that I didn't hear a word all night. The following week, Deems started sending me another five extras.

21 ▲ **Critical Viewing**
Why might it be difficult to concentrate in a room like this one? **[Infer]**

 **Reading Check**
What was Russ's challenge as a paperboy?

20 Critical Thinking

Analyze

- Ask a volunteer to read the bracketed passage beginning on p. 74 and ending on p. 75.
- Discuss with students how Russell's job provides opportunities for him to learn about a variety of things. Ask what Russell may have learned from overcoming his fear of making a mistake at the banquet. **Possible response:** Russell may have learned that the things we fear are often not as bad as we expect. Russell is also learning to face life and be "tough as nails."

21 ▶Critical Viewing

Answer: The newsroom is congested, with a lot of people, noise, and activity, which would make it hard to concentrate.

22 Reading Check

Answer: Russell's challenge was to sell the extra papers that Deems sent him.

CUSTOMIZE INSTRUCTION FOR UNIVERSAL ACCESS

For Less Proficient Readers	For Gifted/Talented Students	For Advanced Readers
Some students may not understand particular phrases such as "took the loss," "swankiest," and "hold down on the silverware." Students may benefit from recording the words and phrases on cards, writing a meaning based on the context, and checking the meaning in a dictionary. Students may need to use a dictionary of slang or idioms.	Invite students to make a comic strip based on one of the incidents in the selection. Possible subjects include meeting Deems, hiding papers in a closet, going to the banquet, and visiting the newsroom. Students can draw their cartoons in the style of an editorial cartoonist or a comic strip writer.	Have students write a news story about the banquet, answering the traditional questions: *who, what, why, where, when,* and *how.* They may want to make up information that is not available in the story, such as the date and the banquet menu. They should include quotations from guests, including Russell and Deems.

23 Reading Strategy

Reading With Expression

- Have students try to imagine the story from young Russ's perspective—his hopes and dreams.
- Read aloud the bracketed sentence to the students.
- Then ask the Reading Strategy question on p. 76: What is the main idea of the sentence beginning "To see such a place"? **Answer:** Russell is thrilled to be in a place where news reporters work.

Monitor Progress Have students look in the same paragraph to find examples of Russ's dreams about working in a newsroom.
Answer: Students should find the following examples: he also provided a treat; to see the newsroom of a great metropolitan newspaper; They were glamorous places full of exciting people; in the city room of a great newspaper . . . that was a thrilling prospect.

Reteach For students who are having difficulty finding the main idea of the sentence, have them softly read aloud the sentence to themselves. Then, ask them where and why they placed emphasis.

24 Literary Analysis

Theme

- Read the bracketed paragraph aloud. Ask students to summarize the appearance of the newsroom. **Answer:** It is dirty, messy, crowded, and poorly furnished.
- Ask the Literary Analysis question on p. 76: How do the realities of the newsroom conflict with Baker's previous ideas? Why might this contrast be a clue to the theme? **Answer:** He thought the newsroom would be glamorous and busy, but it was ugly and boring. This is a clue to the theme that Russell was learning and changing because of his job.

---

23 Now and then he also provided a treat. One day in 1938 he asked if I would like to join a small group of boys he was taking to visit the *News-Post* newsroom. My mother, in spite of believing that nothing came before homework at night, wasn't cold-hearted enough to deny me a chance to see the city room[4] of a great metropolitan newspaper. I had seen plenty of city rooms in the movies. They were glamorous places full of exciting people like Lee Tracey, Edmund Lowe, and Adolphe Menjou[5] trading wisecracks and making mayors and cops look like saps. To see such a place, to stand, actually stand, in the city room of a great newspaper and look at reporters who were in touch every day with killers and professional baseball players—that was a thrilling prospect.

Because the *News-Post* was an afternoon paper, almost everybody had left for the day when we got there that night. The building, located downtown near the harbor, was disappointing. It looked like a factory, and not a very big factory either. Inside there was a smell compounded of ink, pulp, chemicals, paste, oil, gasoline, greasy rags, and hot metal. We took an elevator up and came into a long room filled with dilapidated[6] desks, battered telephones, and big blocky typewriters. Almost nobody there, just two or three men in shirt-sleeves. It was the first time I'd ever seen Deems look awed.

"Boys, this is the nerve center of the newspaper," he said, his voice heavy and solemn like the voice of Westbrook Van Voorhis, the *March of Time*[7] man, when he said, "Time marches on."

24 I was confused. I had expected the newsroom to have glamour, but this place had nothing but squalor. The walls hadn't been painted for years. The windows were filthy. Desks were heaped with mounds of crumpled paper, torn sheets of newspaper, overturned paste pots, dog-eared telephone directories. The floor was ankle deep in newsprint, carbon paper, and crushed cigarette packages. Waist-high cans overflowed with trash. Ashtrays were buried under cigarette ashes and butts. Ugly old wooden chairs looked ready for the junk shop.

It looked to me like a place that probably had more cockroaches than we had back home on Lombard Street, but Deems was seeing it through rose-colored glasses.[8] As we stood looking

Reading Strategy
Reading With Expression What is the main idea of the sentence beginning "To see such a place"?

Literary Analysis
Theme How do the realities of the newsroom conflict with Baker's previous ideas? Why might this contrast be a clue to the theme?

4. **city room** the office at a newspaper used by those who report on city events.
5. **Lee Tracey, Edmund Lowe, and Adolphe Menjou** actors in movies of the period.
6. **dilapidated** (də lap´ ə dāt´ əd) *adj.* run-down; in bad condition.
7. **the *March of Time*** the *March of Time* was a newsreel series that ran from 1935 to 1951, showing current news events along with interviews and dramatizations. Newsreels were shown between feature films at movie theaters.
8. **seeing it through rose-colored glasses** ignoring its unappealing features or drawbacks.

ENRICHMENT: Language/Writing Connection

A Class Newspaper

Invite students to organize, write, duplicate, and distribute a class newspaper. Have students use the information from Literature in Context on p. 77 to organize themselves into newspaper staff roles. Make up a production schedule and assign articles for the paper. Suggest that students write about school news and issues, sports, and drama. Students might interview other students, faculty, or staff. Students might draw cartoons while others could create an advice column. Find out whether students may use school copying facilities. Students may need to sell the paper, or it could be distributed to students at no charge.

around at the ruins, he started telling us how lucky we were to be newsboys. Lucky to have a foot on the upward ladder so early in life. If we worked hard and kept expanding our paper routes we could make the men who ran this paper sit up and notice us. And when men like that noticed you, great things could happen, because they were important men, the most important of all being the man who owned our paper: Mr. Hearst Himself, William Randolph Hearst, founder of the greatest newspaper organization in America. A great man, Mr. Hearst, but not so great that he didn't appreciate his newsboys, who were the backbone of the business. Many of whom would someday grow up and work at big jobs on this paper. Did we realize that any of us, maybe all of us, could end up one of these days sitting right here in this vitally important room, the newsroom, the nerve center of the newspaper?

Yes, Deems was right. Riding home on the streetcar that night, I realized I was a lucky boy to be getting such an early start up the ladder of journalism. It was childish to feel let down because the city room looked like such a dump instead of like city rooms in the movies. Deems might be a slave driver, but he was doing it for my own good, and I ought to be grateful. In *News Selling*, the four-page special paper Mr. Hearst published just for his newsboys, they'd run a piece that put it almost as beautifully as Deems had.

YOU'RE A MEMBER OF THE FOURTH ESTATE was the headline on it. I was so impressed that I put the paper away in a safe place and often took it out to read when I needed inspiration. It told how "a great English orator" named Edmund Burke "started a new name for a new profession—the Fourth Estate . . . the press . . . NEWSPAPER MEN."[9]

And it went on to say:

"The Fourth Estate was then . . . and IS now . . . a great estate for HE-men . . . workers . . . those who are proud of the business they're in!"

(Mr. Hearst always liked plenty of exclamation marks, dots, and capital letters.)

"Get that kick of pride that comes from knowing you are a newspaper man. That means something!

9. **Edmund Burke . . . Fourth Estate** Edmund Burke (1729–1797) was an English political figure famous for his speeches and essays. He called the press the "Fourth Estate."

in context Humanities Connection

25 ***Journalism***

Journalism is an important profession, responsible for informing people about local and world events. Journalists gather, write, and edit material for news stories. They work for newspapers, news services, magazines, radio, or television. In democracies such as the United States, journalists are free to report news without government interference. Reporters are responsible for accuracy and telling all sides of a news story. Editorial writers, meanwhile, express a news organization's views on issues.

26 ✓ **Reading Check**

What did Russ learn about a newsroom during his visit?

25 Background

Journalism

It takes highly skilled journalists to produce a quality newspaper day after day. Explain that people with a variety of talents make this happen:

- The publisher is responsible for the overall business of the newspaper.
- Editors supervise the writing of the news and other editorial features, correct mistakes, and sometimes write opinion columns.
- Reporters gather facts and write about the news.
- Advertising people sell, write, and design advertisements that help pay for the newspaper.
- Photographers, cartoonists, and layout designers give the paper its visual appeal.

26 ✓ Reading Check

Answer: Russ learned that the newsroom was not as wonderful as he thought it would be.

CUSTOMIZE INSTRUCTION FOR UNIVERSAL ACCESS

For Special Needs Students	For Less Proficient Readers	For Advanced Readers
Have students identify the compound nouns in the last full paragraph on p. 76—the paragraph that begins "I was confused." Students should find the compound words *newsroom, newspapers, overturned, newsprint, overflowed,* and *ashtrays.*	Less proficient readers may have difficulty with the punctuation and capitalization in the copy from the newsboys' paper. Model reading the copy, showing students where to pause and where capital letters and exclamation points indicate emphasis. Encourage students to practice reading the copy with expression.	Ask students to evaluate the contrasting tone of the two selections. They should consider how the subject matter, details, and word choice emphasize the writers' messages. Have them write an essay about the contrasts between the two selections.

ASSESS

Answers for p. 78

Review and Assess

1. Some students may want to work for Mr. Deems because he would teach them a lot; others would not want to work for someone who is so dishonest.
2. **(a)** She wants him to get a job and help support the family. **(b)** Russ's mother dreams of Russ being a success and not being lazy. Russell dreams about newspaper work because it is a noble profession.
3. **(a)** He thought that being a newsboy was important and that people would admire him for being a newsboy. **(b)** The conflict is shown when Deems cheats Russell by making him take extra papers and when Russell sees how awful the newsroom looks.
4. **(a)** Deems gives Russ five extra papers. **(b)** Deems could be teaching Russ that he should always try to do better or that people in power can take advantage of those under them. **(c)** He wants Deems to fit the image of a hard newspaperman. **(d)** Yes, because it taught him discipline and about sales, as well as started him in a newspaper career.
5. Deems treats the newsboys fairly because he's trying to toughen them up for working at the newspaper, which is hard work. OR Deems treats the newsboys unfairly because he continues to supply them with more papers than they actually are selling.

"A newspaper man never ducks a dare. YOU are a newspaper man. A salesman of newspapers . . . the final cog[10] in the immense machine of newspaper production—a SERVICE for any man to be proud of.

"So throw back the chest. Hit the route hard each day. Deliver fast and properly. Sell every day. Add to your route because you add to the NEWSPAPER field when you do. And YOU MAKE MONEY DOING IT. It is a great life—a grand opportunity. Don't boot it—build it up. Leave it better than when you came into it."

"It is a great life." I kept coming back to that sentence as I read and reread the thing. No matter how awful it got, and it sometimes got terrible, I never quit believing it was a great life. I kept at it until I was almost sixteen, chest thrown back, delivering fast and properly, selling every day and adding to my route. At the end I'd doubled its size and was making as much as four dollars a week from it.

A few months after he took us down to see the city room, Deems quit. My mother said he'd found a better job. Later, when I thought about him, I wondered if maybe it wasn't because he hated himself for having to make life hell for boys. I hoped that wasn't the reason because he was the first newspaperman I ever knew, and I wanted him to be the real thing. Hard as nails.

immense (i mens') *adj.* huge

10. **cog** (cäg) *n.* gear.

Russell Baker

(b. 1925)

Russell Baker grew up in Virginia, New Jersey, and Maryland. When he was in the seventh grade, he decided to become a writer. He thought that "making up stories must surely be almost as fun as reading them." As it turned out, Baker became a reporter. He won a Pulitzer Prize for his newspaper column in *The New York Times*. In "Hard as Nails," he describes his very first boss in the news business.

Review and Assess

Thinking About the Selection

1. **Respond:** Would you like to work for Deems? Why or why not?
2. **(a) Recall:** What does Russ's mother want her son to do? **(b) Compare and Contrast:** How are Russ's dreams for himself similar to and different from his mother's dreams for him?
3. **(a) Recall:** What did Russ think about newspaper work when he first started in the business? **(b) Support:** Find two examples that show the conflict between the realities of newspaper work and Baker's first ideas about it.
4. **(a) Recall:** What does Deems do when Russ sells all his papers? **(b) Infer:** What lesson do you think Deems is teaching Russ? **(c) Draw Conclusions:** At the end of "Hard as Nails," why does Russ want to believe that Deems really was "hard as nails"? **(d) Speculate:** Do you think this experience might help Baker in the future? Why or why not?
5. **Evaluate:** Do you think Deems treats the news boys fairly or unfairly? Why?

ASSESSMENT PRACTICE: Reading Comprehension

Using Context Clues **(For more practice, see Test Preparation Workbook, p. 8.)**

Many tests ask students to use context clues to determine the meanings of unfamiliar words. Write the following text on the board:

> . . . Slung around one shoulder and across the chest, the belt made it easy to balance fifteen or twenty pounds of papers against the hip. . . .

In this passage, the word slung means—

A beaten
B hidden
C bandaged
D thrown

The passage explains that the belt was placed "around one shoulder and across the chest" to help carry the newspapers, so the correct answer is *D*. *A, B,* and *C* do not fit the context of the passage.

Review and Assess

Literary Analysis

Theme

1. In what two ways does the word "circuit" apply to Panchito's life?
2. What circumstances prevent Panchito from getting out?
3. What **theme**, or message, is Jiménez communicating through the title and the events in the story? To whom does the message apply? Explain.
4. Which people in "Hard as Nails" could be described by the words "hard as nails"?
5. What lessons does Baker learn and how might these lessons be applied to other people's lives?

Comparing Literary Works

6. Use a Venn diagram to compare and contrast Panchito and young Baker. Consider their circumstances, their experiences, their reactions to their experiences, and the personality traits they exhibit.

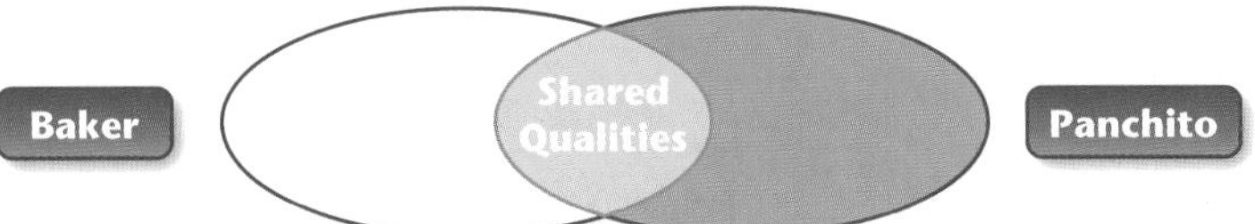

Reading Strategy

Reading with Expression

For sentences 7 and 8, record the subject of each sentence and the key event on a chart like the one shown. Then read each sentence aloud with expression.

Subject	What happens	Additional details

7. I walked to the top of a small grade next to the shack and watched the "Carcanchita" disappear in the distance in a cloud of dust.
8. Because the *News-Post* was an afternoon paper, almost everybody had left for the day when we got there that night.

Extending Understanding

9. **Career Connection:** What qualities did young Russ learn that could be used in many jobs other than the newspaper business?

Quick Review

The **theme** is the central idea or thought about life that is expressed in a work of literature. To review theme, see page 65.

Reading with expression means using your voice to communicate, or express, the meaning of the words.

www.phschool.com

Take the interactive self-test online to check your understanding of these selections.

ENRICHMENT: Further Reading

Other Works by the Authors

Works by Francisco Jiménez

The Circuit: Stories from the Life of a Migrant Child

Works by Russell Baker

Growing Up

Take It to the Net

Visit www.phschool.com for more information on the authors.

Answers for p. 79

Review and Assess

1. Panchito's life is like a circuit because his family travels a circuit of farms looking for work and he is caught in a cycle of poverty since he cannot go to school to be educated and get a better job.
2. He cannot get out because he cannot spend enough time in school.
3. Jiménez is saying that migrant workers need a chance to break out of the cycle of poverty and ignorance. The message applies to the migrant workers to help them see the need to do better and also to the rest of the world to give the migrant workers a chance to change.
4. Russ, Russ's mother, and Deems could all be called "hard as nails."
5. Baker learns to work hard, face things he is afraid of, overcome shyness, and find his way in the world. All of these lessons would help anyone succeed.
6.

Russ: lives in Baltimore; has hopes of newspaper work; regularly goes to school; speaks English well

Shared Qualities: parents get them jobs; from poor families

Panchito: lives in California; seldom goes to school; has few hopes; struggles with English

7. Subject: I

   What happens: walked to a small hill and watched car go away

   Additional details: hill next to the shack; car disappears in cloud of dust
8. Subject: almost everybody

   What happens: had left

   Additional details: an afternoon paper; they got there at night
9. Russ learned to be determined, that life isn't as glamorous as it appears in the movies, to work hard, and to watch out for tricky people.

EXTEND

Answers for p. 80

❶ Vocabulary Development

Word Analysis

1. streetcar: a car that travels on the street
2. sidewalk: a place to walk on the side of the street
3. newsroom: a room where news is gathered and written

Spelling Strategy

1. streetcar
   street—"ee" makes one sound
2. sidewalk
   side—"e" is silent
3. newsroom
   room—"oo" makes one sound

Concept Development

1. c
2. e
3. f
4. g
5. b
6. d
7. a

❷ Grammar

1. they
2. he
3. their
4. their
5. his or her

Writing Application

Mr. Lema and Panchito always spent their lunchtime together. Neither Mr. Lema nor Panchito felt he was missing out on lunch with the others. Panchito asked Mr. Lema questions, which he always answered. The two became friends who enjoyed spending their time together.

Integrate Language Skills

❶ Vocabulary Development Lesson

Word Analysis: Compound Nouns

A **compound noun** is a noun made up of two or more smaller words. Most compound nouns take their meaning from the two words in the compound. Explain how the words in each compound noun below contribute to its meaning.

1. streetcar 2. sidewalk 3. newsroom

Spelling Strategy

Copy each compound word above. Then, write each smaller word separately. Which word contains a silent letter? Which contain two vowels combining to make one sound?

Concept Development: Synonyms

Synonyms are words that have similar meanings, such as *journalist* and *reporter*. On your paper, write the letter for the word or phrase that is closest in meaning to each first word.

1. drone	a. very large
2. instinctively	b. drain
3. savoring	c. hum
4. embedded	d. majestic
5. exhaust	e. naturally
6. sublime	f. enjoying
7. immense	g. fixed in

❷ Grammar Lesson

Pronoun-Antecedent Agreement

Pronouns must agree with their antecedents (the words to which they refer).

Use a singular pronoun with a singular antecedent.
Example: *Tom* will lend Melissa *his* suitcase.

Use a plural pronoun with a plural antecedent.
Example: The *boys* have all brought *their* boots.

Use a singular pronoun with two or more singular antecedents joined by *or* or *nor*. Use a plural pronoun with two or more antecedents joined by *and*.
Example: Either *Andrew* or *Keith* will give *his* report.
Joyce and *Bill* showed *their* father the drawing.

Use a singular pronoun to refer to a singular indefinite pronoun. Use a plural pronoun to refer to a plural indefinite pronoun.
Example: *One* of the boys will print *his* documents.
Example: *All* of the boys will print *their* documents.

Practice Copy the following sentences. Use pronouns that agree with their antecedents.

1. Panchito and Roberto worked in the fields, but __?__ would have preferred to go to school.
2. Neither boy knows what __?__ will say about the Yukon.
3. Fred and Tony are preparing __?__ presentation.
4. Some of the reporters completed __?__ stories on time.
5. One of the journalists rewrote __?__ story.

Writing Application Write a brief explanation of how Mr. Lema influenced Panchito. Use each of the pronoun-antecedent agreement rules shown at the left.

WG *Prentice Hall Writing and Grammar Connection: Chapter 24, Section 2*

TEACHING RESOURCES

The following resources can be used to enrich or extend the instruction for pp. 80–81.

Vocabulary
- **Selection Support:** Building Spelling Skills p. 27
- **Vocabulary and Spelling Practice Book** (Use this booklet for skills enrichment)

Grammar
- **Selection Support:** Build Grammar Skills, p. 28 
- **Writing and Grammar,** Copper Level, p. 528
- **Daily Language Practice Transparencies**

Writing
- **Writing and Grammar,** Copper Level, p. 256
- **Writing Models and Graphic Organizers on Transparencies,** p. 3
- **Writing and Grammar iText CD-ROM**

Take It to the Net
Visit www.phschool.com for self-tests and additional questions on the selections.

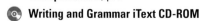

BLOCK SCHEDULING: Resources marked with this symbol provide varied instruction during 90-minute blocks.

❸ Writing Lesson

Letter to a Character

Assume the role of Russell Baker and write a letter to Deems expressing your feelings about him and telling him what you learned from him.

Prewriting Start by reviewing "Hard as Nails." Use a cluster diagram like the one below to note key experiences involving Baker and Deems, Baker's feelings about Deems, and what he learned from him.

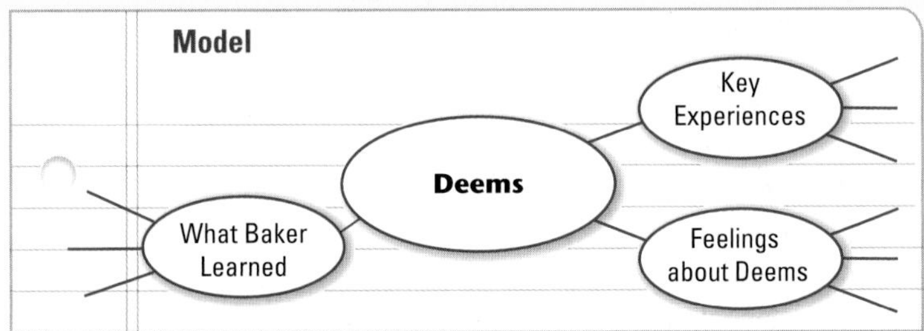

Drafting Using the details in your diagram, draft your letter. Begin with a paragraph reintroducing yourself. Then, follow with two or more paragraphs sharing your feelings and telling what you learned. Cite experiences involving Deems to back each point you make.

Revising Review your draft to ensure that all of the content of your letter focuses on your feelings about Deems and what you learned from him. Each paragraph should focus on a single idea and contain details that support it.

WG Prentice Hall Writing and Grammar Connection: Chapter 12, Section 3

❹ Extension Activities

Listening and Speaking Russ was interested in the newspaper field, especially journalism. Take some time to **interview** an adult who works in a field that interests you. Prepare a list of questions about how to achieve success in that work.

- Be polite and speak clearly.
- Maintain eye contact with the person you are interviewing.
- Ask additional questions if something is unclear.

Tell the class about the results of your interview.

Research and Technology In a small group, research interesting jobs. Do a keyword search using a career or field such as *journalism*. Use Internet resources such as online news groups, newspapers, encyclopedias, and Web sites to gather statistics about each job, including education, skills, and salary ranges. Prepare a **report** to share your findings with the class.

www.phschool.com

Go online for an additional research activity using the Internet.

ASSESSMENT RESOURCES

The following resources can be used to assess students' knowledge and skills.

Selection Assessment
- **Formal Assessment,** pp. 16–18
- **Open Book Test,** pp. 16–18
- **Got It! Assessment Videotapes,** Tape 1
- **Test Bank Software**

Writing Rubric
- **Performance Assess. and Portfolio Mgmt.,** p. 8

Listening and Speaking Rubric
- **Performance Assess. and Portfolio Mgmt.,** p. 25

PRENTICE HALL ASSESSMENT SYSTEM
- **Workbook**
- **Transparencies**
- **Skill Book**
- **CD-ROM**

Lesson Support for p. 81

❸ Writing Lesson

- Tell students that they will often have to write letters to friends and business associates.
- Suggest to students that, like any other kind of writing, letters need to be well organized.
- Use the writing lesson to guide students through the process of writing a letter.
- Use the Autobiographical Narrative rubric on p. 8 in **Performance Assessment and Portfolio Management** to evaluate student letters.

❹ Listening and Speaking

- Guide students in selecting fields that interest them and in finding people to interview.
- Have students research their chosen fields in the library or on the Internet in preparation for the interview. Students should prepare a list of questions for the interview.
- Have students take notes at the interview and prepare a presentation about what they have learned.
- Have students write thank-you notes to their subjects as a follow-up to the interview.
- Use the Narrative Account rubric on p. 25 in **Performance Assessment and Portfolio Management** to evaluate student work.

CUSTOMIZE INSTRUCTION For Universal Access

To address different learning styles, use the activities suggested in the **Extension Activities** booklet on p. 6.

- For Verbal/Linguistic and Interpersonal Learners, use Activity 5.
- For Musical/Rhythmic Learners, use Activity 6.
- For Visual/Spatial Learners, use Activity 7.

Lesson Objectives

1. To learn how to use newspapers to find information
2. To learn how the different sections of the newspaper are organized

About Newspaper Articles

- Invite a student volunteer to read "About Newspaper Articles" aloud. Clarify the differences between a large-city daily and a local weekly newspaper.
- Discuss the daily and weekly newspapers that cover the community your school is in. If possible, bring in several issues of the papers, and have students make generalizations about the number and types of articles in them.
- Discuss why different types of newspapers are published and whom they serve.
  Possible response: Large-city daily newspapers serve a large audience and must carry stories that will appeal to many interests. Smaller, weekly papers cover a smaller area and probably contain articles that appeal to a more limited audience.

Reading Strategy

Using Newspapers to Find Information

- Have students read about using newspapers to find information.
- Review the *Feature and Function* table. Explain that newspapers are divided into sections that contain articles about the particular topics. Using a newspaper or the article on pp. 83–84, point out features listed in the table.
- Point out that newspapers are organized so that readers can easily find articles. Ask students how this organization benefits them when they are looking for articles.
  Possible response: Newspaper organization makes it easier to find favorite sections of the paper, such as the comics or the entertainment section.
- Review a newspaper table of contents. Point out that some newspapers have a brief table of contents on the front page and a more extensive table on an inside page.

READING INFORMATIONAL MATERIALS

Newspaper Articles

About Newspaper Articles

Newspapers are one kind of print medium. Most large-city newspapers are published daily. Newspapers keep people informed about local, national, and world events. Local or regional events, such as a fire or an election, make up most of a local paper, while daily papers published in cities include more national and world news. In addition, different sections of the paper cover specific subjects—for example, sports, business, the arts, and lifestyles. Usually, one or two pages are dedicated to editorial columns, with letters and essays written by people with opinions on current events.

Reading Strategy

Using Newspapers to Find Information

Few people read a newspaper from beginning to end. Instead, most people locate specific sections or articles and read only those that are of interest to them. Most large newspapers are divided into sections. Each section covers a particular category. The numbering of newspaper pages is usually a letter indicating the section followed by a numeral. This chart shows some of the structural features that can help you find information in a newspaper.

Feature	Function
Section heads, such as *Local News*, *Editorials*, or *Home*	Tell the focus of the articles within the section
Article titles are set on their own line in larger, heavier type than the article text.	Indicate topic of article
Run-in heads are printed in heavier type than the article but are not set on a separate line	Call out the key points in the article. The text that follows a run-in head gives more detail.
Pull-quotes	Highlight an important or interesting statement made by someone in the article
Photos and captions	Add visual information to be used with the text
Table of contents usually appears on the first page of the first section	Shows how the newspaper is broken into sections. Tells readers what page to turn to for regular features.

The article title hints at the topic and grabs readers' interest.

Summer Hats

By Amy Lindgren

The pull-quote calls attention to the main idea of the article.

If you're looking for work, different work, or more work, summertime is a great time to try a variety of jobs.

Summer's back! And our worker shortage prevails. These look like good conditions for a little experimenting with new jobs.

Of course, if you are a parent with school-age children, you may feel your summer "job" already has been chosen for you. Just arranging the kids' schedules for three months gives you training to be a high-level events planner.

Some of those kids are probably the right age for summer employment. Other people who might benefit from a short-term job include retirees; students; "winter workers," such as teachers and snowplow drivers; and, of course, the unemployed.

Summer employment is also a good option for the underemployed and dissatisfied workers who wonder what else they could do for a living. And, if you are struggling with a debt load, you might find relief by working to pay off a specific bill.

Some common summer jobs— for adults or kids—include farm work, lawn care, tourism work, anything in retail or food service, day-care/camp work, construction and some kinds of food production. Positions are available at all levels in most of these fields, although the short-term jobs tend to be at the entry level.

Be careful. As many of my readers have reminded me, it's possible to choose poorly. Indeed, bad summer jobs are almost a rite of passage in this country. To increase your chances of success, take these two simple steps:

Summer Hats

- Newspapers often carry articles that are of interest to young people. This article contains information about summer jobs.
- Point out to students that newspapers often contain photographs and other art that illustrates articles. Ask students how the photograph in "Summer Hats" helps them understand the article.
  Answer: The photograph helps clarify the topic of the article.
- Have students read the article and the notes that accompany it.
- Then, ask students whether they think the headline is useful.
  Possible responses: Some students may find that the headline is not clear enough for readers to know the topic of the article. Others may think that it is useful because it catches the reader's eye and arouses curiosity.
- Have students describe the intended audience for this article.
  Answer: The audience appears to be adults because the author addresses parents, teachers, unemployed people, and students. Younger people might find the article useful because of the information about jobs that they might like.

CUSTOMIZE INSTRUCTION FOR UNIVERSAL ACCESS

For Special Needs Students	For Less Proficient Readers	For Advanced Readers
Make available to students copies of the Main Idea and Supporting Details organizer on p. 73 in **Writing Models and Graphic Organizers on Transparencies.** Have students determine the main idea of the article and write it in the proper section. Then, have students add supporting details in the appropriate spaces.	Point out to students that the run-in heads of most news articles give clues about the article's main points. Ask students to read the run-in heads for this article. Discuss whether the run-in heads reveal the main point of the article. Challenge students to write a summary of the article, using the run-in heads.	Challenge students to find articles in the newspaper index in your local or school library. Have students choose a specific event, such as a particular space mission, and work with a librarian in the school or local library to find newspaper articles about that event. Students may need assistance with microfilm machines.

continued from p. 83

- Have students finish reading the article.
- Direct students' attention to the run-in heads. Ask students to note the relationship between the run-in heads and the paragraphs that the heads introduce.
  Answer: The run-in heads tell what the paragraph is about. They summarize the information in the paragraph.
- Then, ask students to evaluate the advice given in the article. Does any of it surprise them? Is all of it useful?
  Possible responses: Some students may be surprised by "Don't overwork," because they may think that people are supposed to work very hard. Most students will note that the advice is useful and full of common sense.
- Call attention to the concluding paragraph of the article. Explain to students what a résumé is. Ask them which statements show that the writer considers a summer job a steppingstone to future jobs.
  Answer: The advice about putting experience on a résumé shows that the author encourages people to use their experiences in summer jobs for future employment.

First, define success. If you are taking a job purely for the money, figure out how much money you want to clear and establish a savings plan to safeguard the funds. If you are trying something new just for fun, how many hours a week can you spare? Perhaps you are trying to get experience in a new field so you can impress an employer later in your career; what kind of work would fit that bill?

Second, choose a job that meets the criteria you just established. You may have to approach employers instead of waiting for ads in the paper, but you'll be glad you took the initiative.

For example, if you would like to work at a garden center because you love plants and want to learn more about them (maybe you just want the discount!), don't hesitate to ask the manager of the center nearest you if the store needs help for the summer. If you can only work certain days, stick as close to that plan as possible. Otherwise, what started out to be fun will become a strain on your schedule.

Whatever your reasons for choosing a summer job, use these tips to make the experience a good one for you and your employer:

• **Take it seriously.** This may be just a summer fling for you, but it means everything to the employer. Your boss is counting on you to be dependable and to help keep the operation running.

• **Learn a new skill.** From corn detasseling to computer tutoring, every job has something to teach you. Perhaps you'll pick up some supervisory skills, or learn how to teach somebody else how to do what you're doing.

• **Learn about the business.** So you're delivering phone books? Why not ask a few questions about how the routes are created. Someday you may use that knowledge when you're setting up your own business as a product distributor. Working at an amusement park? How do they create promotions to attract visitors to the slow days? Ask questions and keep learning. If nothing else, it makes the time pass faster.

• **Get along with your co-workers and customers.** Whatever you do, make this a priority. After all, this is just a summer job. If you can't deal with difficult people for a few months, how will you ever manage it over the long haul?

Run-in heads call out key points in the article.

• **Don't overwork.** Keep a balance between time off and your job so you don't collapse in September.

• **Leave on a good note.** There are several steps to take when leaving a short-term job. First, give plenty of notice. Ask for letters of recommendation and select a few samples of your work for your portfolio. For example, photos of you helping kids onto a carnival ride can work well later to demonstrate patience and responsibility. Give your contact information to anyone who might be able to connect you to more work later, and take down their names and numbers as well. Finally, thank your boss for the opportunity. Even if you hated the job, it's a classy touch.

The writer presents direct statements that offer practical advice for readers.

Of course, don't forget to put your experiences on your resume. If you already have a career, you might include this job as a single line in an "Other" category. Workers just starting out will want to give this job higher billing and include more detail.

Have a good summer!

Check Your Comprehension

1. Who might be most interested in short-term jobs?
2. What might make summer employment advantageous?
3. List a few ways to ensure successful summer employment.
4. Why are summer jobs important to employers?

Applying the Reading Strategy

Using Text Features to Find Information

Use the text features in the chart on page 82 to find the information to answer these questions:

5. What is the topic of the article? Where did you find that information?
6. What are three key points about choosing a summer job that are called out by run-in heads?
7. In which section of the newspaper is this article most likely to be found? Why? **(a)** World News, **(b)** Living, **(c)** Entertainment

Activity

Use the text features of a newspaper to choose an article to read.

1. Begin by looking at the section heads. Choose one section that appeals to you.
2. Look over the article titles in that section. Choose three articles.
3. Read the run-in heads and the picture captions for each of the three articles. Choose and read the article that appears most interesting to you.
4. Explain why you made each choice. What information did you learn from section heads, article titles, run-in heads, and picture captions that guided you toward your final choice?

Comparing Informational Materials

Complete a chart like the one shown here to compare the structural features of a local newspaper and a national newspaper. Use newspapers that are printed on the same day.

	What are the sections?	What is the biggest section?	What is the first article on the first page?
Local			
National			

Answers continued

Comparing Informational Materials

Possible response:

	Sections?	Biggest section?	First article?
Local	News/sports/ads	News	Police Get Pay Hike
National	News/business/sports/entertainment/features	News	President Travels to Mexico

Answers for p. 85

Check Your Comprehension

1. Students and teachers might be most interested in short-term jobs.
2. People who are busy during the school year have their summers free for summer jobs, and people who like to be outdoors will be able to find jobs that keep them outdoors.
3. Ways to be successful at a summer job include taking it seriously, learning a new skill, learning about the business, getting along with others, not overworking, and leaving on a good note.
4. Summer jobs are important to employers because they may be short-staffed during the summer and need dependable employees to keep their businesses running.

Apply the Reading Strategy

5. The topic of the article is working a summer job. The pull-quote reveals the article's topic.
6. Three key points about choosing summer jobs include being careful, defining what you want to get out of the job, and choosing a job that meets your personal criteria. Three key points in run-in heads include taking the job seriously, learning a new skill, and learning about the business.
7. This article most likely would be in the Living section (b.) of the paper because it is neither entertainment nor news; it is about an everyday topic.

Activity

Students should be able to explain their choice of articles and tell from which section of the paper it came. They also should be able to tell what sort of information was available through the different text features, including the various heads, picture captions, and titles. You might want to have students turn in a copy of the article they selected, with written answers to question 4.

continued

Lesson Objectives

1. To use prior knowledge to understand interviews
2. To learn about the format of interviews
3. To find information in interviews

About Interviews

- Invite a volunteer to read aloud the About Interviews instruction. Ask students: What is the purpose of an interview?
  Answer: The purpose of an interview is to gather a person's thoughts, feelings, and knowledge.
- Discuss the types of publications that contain interviews that students might read for entertainment or information. Point out that interviews are most likely to be found in newspapers and magazines, although some books may contain them.
- Ask students to explain the main difference between a biography of a person and an interview with that same person.
  Answer: A biography would be based mostly on the facts of the person's life, but an interview would concentrate on the person's thoughts and ideas.

Reading Strategy

Using Prior Knowledge

- Have students read the material about using prior knowledge.
- Review the concept of prior knowledge. Point out that whenever students read, they make connections between what they already know and what they are learning. To illustrate this, copy the top of the Prior Knowledge chart onto the board. Have students tell what they already know about astronauts, John Glenn, and space travel; write their contributions on the board.
- Instruct students to make their own charts to organize their prior knowledge and what they learn from the interview.

READING INFORMATIONAL MATERIALS

Interviews

About Interviews

An interview is an informational meeting that consists of questions asked by an interviewer and answers supplied by the person being interviewed. Interviews are a good way to gather people's opinions and knowledge of a subject or event.

To identify the kinds of information you will find in an interview, read the questions. (Questions are usually set off in a separate color or font.) "An Astronaut's Answers" is an interview with John Glenn on his memories of being the first American to orbit the Earth. The questions show that the interview contains the following information:

- Details about Glenn's first space mission
- Glenn's reasons for becoming an astronaut
- Glenn's reflections on space exploration

Reading Strategy

Using Prior Knowledge

To help you understand and connect to the main ideas or topic of an interview, draw on your prior knowledge. Your prior knowledge is the information, experiences, and thoughts you already have before you read any kind of written material. For example, you might already know that John Glenn was the first American to orbit the Earth. Use this prior knowledge to help you appreciate and understand Glenn's responses.

As you read the interview with John Glenn, use a graphic organizer like the one shown to think about what prior knowledge you have about astronauts and space travel. Then, when you have finished reading, write down what you learned from reading the interview.

My Prior Knowledge
astronauts:
John Glenn:
space travel:
What I Learned
astronauts:
John Glenn:
space travel:
Other:

An Astronaut's Answers

John Glenn

This interview was conducted shortly before Glenn returned to space at the age of seventy-seven on board the shuttle *Discovery.*

Questions are set off in red to distinguish them from Glenn's words.

The first time you went into space, how did it feel to be all alone except for communication through radio?

In 1962, I looked down from an orbit high above our planet and saw our beautiful Earth and its curved horizon against the vastness of space. I have never forgotten that sight nor the sense of wonder it engendered. Although I was alone in *Friendship 7*, I did not feel alone in space. I knew that I was supported by my family, my six fellow astronauts, thousands of NASA engineers and employees, and millions of people around the world.

These questions show that this section contains more opinions than facts.

Why did you want to be an astronaut? How did you fly around the Earth three times? Was it hard?

I served as a fighter pilot in World War II and the Korean conflict. After Korea, I graduated from the Naval Test Pilot School and worked as a fighter test pilot. I applied for the astronaut program because I thought it was a logical career step, a challenging opportunity and one in which I could help start a new area of research that would be very valuable to everyone here on Earth. I have always considered myself very fortunate to be selected in the first group of seven astronauts.

An Atlas rocket boosted me into space and I orbited the Earth in my space capsule, the *Friendship 7.* It certainly was a challenge but one for which I was well prepared. The National Aeronautics and Space Administration (NASA)

An Astronaut's Answers

- Newspapers and magazines often carry interviews with famous people and people who are experts in their fields. These articles provide information that students may find useful or personal opinions that students might find insightful or entertaining.
- Point out the photograph on p. 87. Ask: Why would a photograph be included with an interview? **Possible responses:** Photographs might be included to show what the subject of the interview looks like, to show another image that is related to the interview, or to catch the eye of people who are looking through the publication in which the interview appears.
- Before students read the portion of the interview on p. 87 and the notes that accompany it, point out the red interview questions. Ask students: Why would interview questions be set off like this? **Answer:** Questions are set off so that readers can easily tell the difference between the questions and the answers.
- Point out the information in the callout box next to the second question. Ask students: How can you tell that this section will contain more opinion than facts? **Answer:** Two of the three questions ask for opinions.
- Have students read the part of the article that appears on p. 87. Allow time for them to record information about what they are learning in their charts before they read further.

CUSTOMIZE INSTRUCTION FOR UNIVERSAL ACCESS

For Less Proficient Readers	For English Learners	For Advanced Readers
Some students may benefit from looking at the organization of the article. Point out the questions in boldface red type and the answers in regular type. To help students understand that interviews are dialogues, have students reread the article aloud in pairs, with one reader as the interviewer and the other as John Glenn.	Students may not understand words associated with the space program, such as *orbit, NASA, capsule,* and *retrorocket.* Have illustrated library books or charts available to help students understand the concepts behind the terms. Point out that many of these terms are new to everyone.	Have students locate information about John Glenn's 1998 journey aboard the space shuttle *Discovery.* Have interested students research the experiments Glenn performed in space and find out the results. Instruct each student to organize his or her findings in a poster and to prepare a summary to share with the class.

continued from p. 87

- Have students read the first question and answer it silently.
- Ask a volunteer to read aloud the second question and answer it aloud. Ask students what sort of prior knowledge helps them understand Glenn's answer. **Answer:** To understand the answer, a reader has to know the kinds of foods that Glenn is talking about, what baby food is like, and how toothpaste tubes operate. Readers also need to know that because everything is weightless in space, the food needs to be packaged a special way.
- After students read the last question and answer, point out that Glenn made these remarks before his return to space in 1998. Ask: How does knowing the timing of these remarks increase understanding of his thoughts? **Possible responses:** Students may note that this prior knowledge explains why Glenn does not refer to specific achievements or examples of his *Discovery* flight.
- Allow time for students to record additional notes in their charts when they have finished reading the selection.

wanted people who were test pilots and accustomed to working under very unusual conditions, including emergencies. During my first orbit I experienced some troubles with the automatic control system and so I had to take control of the capsule's movements by hand for the rest of the trip. Another problem developed when the signals showed that the heat shield was loose. To keep it secured during re-entry, I kept the retrorocket pack in place to steady the shield. When the *Friendship 7* entered the atmosphere, the retrorocket pack burned off and flew by my window, but the heat shield stayed in place. These were problems we could not have foreseen prior to the flight.

How long was your trip around the Earth?

My trip around the Earth lasted 4 hours and 55 minutes, and I flew about 81,000 miles.

What did you eat while you were in outer space?

I took along a number of different kinds of food, such as applesauce and a mixture of meat and vegetables, all emulsified like baby food. It was packaged in containers much like toothpaste tubes so I could squeeze food into my mouth. I had no trouble eating any of it, and it tasted fine.

Prior knowledge about weightlessness in a space vehicle helps you understand why the food is packaged as it is.

Why do astronauts go to the moon?

As adventurers of earlier eras crossed oceans and scaled mountains, astronauts in our time have flown to the moon and explored the heavens. The crucial hands-on experience of my flight in the Mercury program helped make the Gemini flights possible. The Gemini flights then helped make the Apollo missions to the moon a reality. Apollo gave us valuable information for the Shuttle missions, and the Shuttle/Mir program prepares us for the International Space Station. This is the nature of progress. Each of these missions has built on the knowledge gained from previous flights.

Use your knowledge that Glenn makes these comments before his return to space to increase your understanding of his thoughts.

We are curious, questing people and our research in this new laboratory of space represents an opportunity to benefit people right here on Earth and to increase our understanding of the universe. the potential scientific, medical, and economic benefits from space are beyond our wildest dreams. That's why astronauts went to the moon, and that's why we continue to pursue our dreams of space exploration.

CUSTOMIZE INSTRUCTION FOR UNIVERSAL ACCESS

For Gifted/Talented Students

Have students work in pairs to choose a person whom they would like to interview. The person may be a well-known sports, entertainment, or political figure; or he or she may be someone who is known locally. Have students prepare a list of questions to ask, making sure that the questions elicit extended responses. In addition, make sure students have enough information about the interviewee so that they can answer questions as if they were that person. Have students choose who will take the roles of interviewer and interviewee. After a rehearsal, conduct the interview in front of the class. You may wish to tape the interview and play it for another class.

Check Your Comprehension

1. How did John Glenn feel being alone in space?
2. How did John Glenn become an astronaut?
3. What kinds of problems did John Glenn face when he was orbiting the Earth?
4. What does John Glenn believe to be the reasons for astronauts going to the moon?
5. What did John Glenn eat while he was in space?

Applying the Reading Strategy

Using Prior Knowledge

6. What do you think is important to know before reading this interview?
7. What prior knowledge do you think the interviewer had before interviewing John Glenn?

Activity

Interview Questions

John Glenn is not only the first person to travel around the Earth; he is also the oldest person ever to travel in space. In 1998, John Glenn returned to space aboard the shuttle *Discovery*. Locate information about Glenn's journey aboard the shuttle *Discovery*. Create an article similar to "An Astronaut's Answers" by writing five interview questions. Answer the questions as John Glenn might by using the information you found in your research. Keep track of questions you want to find the answers to and the information you find while doing your research.

Interview Questions	Information Found
1.	
2.	
3.	
4.	
5.	

Contrasting Informational Materials

Interviews and News Articles

Find a news article that describes the launching of the shuttle *Discovery*. How does the reporting of the event differ from John Glenn's personal account? Which do you think gives more information? Which one is more appealing to readers? Write a brief comparison of the two different accounts.

Answers for p. 89

Check Your Comprehension

1. Being alone in space did not upset John Glenn because he felt that his family, the people in the space program, and millions of people on Earth were supporting his flight.
2. He had been a fighter pilot and a test pilot, and then he applied for and was accepted into the space program.
3. In his first space flight, he had trouble with the automatic control system and with the heat shield.
4. He thinks that astronauts go to the moon for adventures, to gain knowledge to advance the space program, and to help improve life on Earth.
5. John Glenn ate special food that was packaged in tubes when he was in space.

Apply the Reading Strategy

6. Before reading this interview, readers should have knowledge of the space program, understanding of terms used about space, and knowledge of space flight and weightlessness in space.
7. Possible response: The interviewer knew that Glenn had only radio communication on his first flight and that he flew around Earth three times.

Activity

Assist students with finding resources, if necessary. Students should write relevant, interesting questions and appropriate answers for them. Students should use highlighters or colored markers or, if they have access to word processors, use different fonts or colors to distinguish questions from answers. You may wish to have students work with partners to combine their questions and present the interviews orally to the class.

continued

Answers continued

Contrasting Informational Materials

The news article is more fact-oriented and describes the *Discovery* launch from the perspective of a viewer. Glenn's personal account includes impressions and opinions, and fewer facts. Glenn's view would probably be more appealing to readers, who may be curious about the feelings he had while in space.

Lesson Objectives

1. To write an autobiographical narrative
2. To use writing strategies to generate ideas, plan, organize, evaluate, and revise the composition

Model From Literature

In "Hard as Nails" (p. 72), Russell Baker tells about his introduction to the news business.

Prewriting

- Model the quicklist technique for students by using a real or fictitious event from your own past. Make certain that students understand they are to use an event as the base of their narratives, not simply a description of a person or place.
- As students narrow their topics, suggest that they share their ideas with a partner to determine whether they have chosen an event that will interest readers. Partners should confirm that the writing will tell how the narrator solved a problem or overcame an obstacle.
- Tell students to use a timeline as they draft and add or delete items as they determine what is most important to the story. Advanced students may want to begin in the present and use flashbacks, but most students will probably begin with an event before the conflict and move forward to the present.
- Tell students to be discriminating as they add details, making sure that details enhance the effect they desire, and to delete extraneous information.
- Before students draft their essays, have them review the Rubric for Self-Assessment (p. 93), so they know what is expected.

Writing WORKSHOP

Narration: Autobiographical Writing

Narrative writing is writing that tells a story. An **autobiographical narrative** tells the story of an event, a period, or a person in the writer's life. This workshop will give you the opportunity to write about an interesting experience in your life.

Assignment Criteria. Your autobiographical narrative should have the following characteristics:

- you, the writer, as a character in the story
- an interest-grabbing first sentence or opening paragraph
- a central problem or conflict that you or someone else resolves
- true events presented in logical order
- descriptive details about people, setting, and actions

To preview the criteria on which your autobiographical narrative will be assessed, see the Rubric on page 93.

Prewriting

Choose a topic. Use a **quicklist** to come up with a topic idea. Fold a piece of paper into three columns. In the first, list important people, places, and events. In the second, list words that describe those people, places, and events. In the third, jot down an action or event that illustrates the quality you have named. Choose one of the events in the last column as the topic for your narrative.

People, Places, and Events	Description	Example

Narrow your topic. Once you have chosen your topic, narrow it to focus on the most interesting part. Identify the problem or the obstacle that you as the narrator (the person telling the story) will overcome.

Make a timeline. Use a timeline to plot events in your narrative. Note the most important things that happened and put them in chronological (time) order.

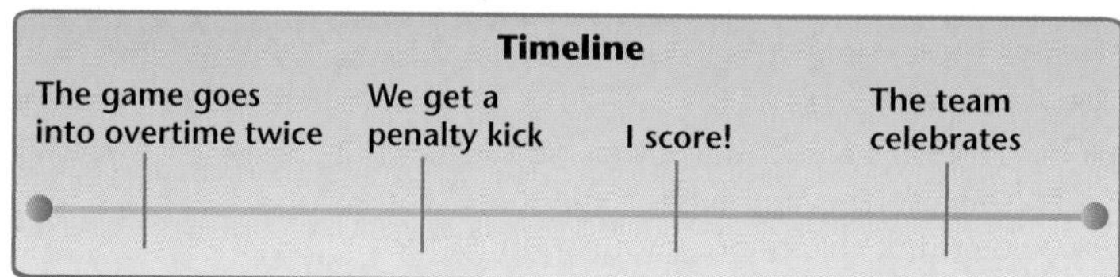

Timeline
The game goes into overtime twice
We get a penalty kick
I score!
The team celebrates

Add details about your thoughts and feelings. Review your timeline and add your reactions to events at different points in the narrative. Tell whether you were surprised, angry, joyous, or worried. If your reactions changed, tell how they changed in the narrative.

TEACHING RESOURCES

The following resources can be used to enrich or extend the instruction for pp. 90–93.

- **Writing and Grammar,** Copper Level, Chapter 4, pp. 48–67
- **Performance Assessment and Portfolio Management,** p. 8
- **Writing Models and Graphic Organizers on Transparencies,** p. 15

Writing and Grammar iText CD-ROM
Students can use the following tools as they complete their autobiographical narratives:

- Descriptive Word Bins
- Topic Bank
- Timeline

Student Model

Before you begin drafting your autobiographical narrative, read this student model and review the characteristics of a successful autobiographical narrative.

Christa Maikisch
Palos Verdes, CA

She Shoots! She Scores!

My heart was pounding in my ears, and sweat was running down my face. I was so nervous I couldn't feel my legs. Over and over in my imagination I sent the soccer ball flying over the net, completely missing the goal. I had just been through two overtimes and because of the heat, I didn't think I could last much longer. Sitting on the grass, waiting for my turn to make the penalty kick, I wandered back in my memory to my first years of soccer.

I started soccer when I was five. For my first two years, my mom was my coach. I played youth league for five years and club soccer for two. All those years had led up to this moment–when the whole team was depending on me. If I made this kick, we won. If I missed, we had to keep playing–and we were too hot and exhausted to play our best.

"Christa, you're up," said the coach.

"Uh, uh, OK . . ." I said.

"Relax, Christa, just relax," said the coach.

I took a deep breath and walked onto the field. "I can do this, I can do this" I told myself as I approached the referee. The ref checked the goalie, then nodded to me. The distance from the ball to the goal looked like an endless stretch of green. The goalie didn't look as tired as I felt. All these negative thoughts were not helping me! I shook my head to clear away the nerves. Then, I took five steps back . . . one more deep breath . . . I ran forward . . . kicked . . . and . . . it went in! The kick was good! Relief filled my heart because I knew I hadn't let my team down.

Suddenly, I saw my teammates rushing toward me. Just as I realized they were coming, I was mobbed. Everyone was screaming and laughing because we had won the game. Now, almost a year later, I look back on that day with pride and a smile on my face.

The writer grabs readers' interest by starting with details that create curiosity about why the writer is so nervous.

Because the writer is a character in the story, she can share her memories of what led up to this moment.

The conflict is the struggle between the writer's wish to make the goal and the possibility that she might miss.

These descriptive details help readers share the experience.

CUSTOMIZE INSTRUCTION FOR UNIVERSAL ACCESS

For Less Proficient Readers	For English Learners	For Advanced Readers
To help students generate details in the prewriting stage, suggest that they freewrite words and phrases that relate to their topics. They should start with a clean sheet of paper and write without thought to organization or grammar. After five minutes, have students stop writing and sift through the details and circle those that fit their message best.	Students may need help finding descriptive words for their quicklist. Have students work in partnership with students proficient in English to find descriptive words that suit their topics. Suggest that partners use the **Writing and Grammar iText CD-ROM** descriptive word bins or a thesaurus for ideas.	Invite students to generate ideas for their topics by using the Cluster diagram on p. 85 in **Writing Models and Graphic Organizers on Transparencies.** Have students record their topics in the center area and sensory details associated with the topic in the outer circles. Instruct students to use these details as they draft.

Student Model

- Explain that the Student Model is a sample, and that essays may be longer.
- Ask students to list details that grab their interest as they read the first paragraph.
  Possible responses: Students may suggest the following details: pounding heart, sweat, nervousness, and imagining a missed soccer shot.
- Discuss how Christa uses a flashback technique to show what has led her to this point in her soccer career.
- Point out how Christa presents the rest of the story as it chronologically happens. Ask students why Christa chose to do this.
  Answer: After the reader understands what has led up to Christa's anxious moment, the reader wants to find out what happens next. It makes sense to continue forward with the story and tell it in order.
- Make sure students understand that the conflict is between the writer's desire to make the goal and the possibility that she might miss. Ask students to identify a detail that heightens the conflict.
  Answer: The fact that the writer's team members are too hot and exhausted to play their best heightens the conflict.
- Finally, ask students how Christa keeps the reader's interest at the end of the narrative.
  Answer: Christa uses descriptive details to keep the reader interested in her kick and its aftermath.

Real-World Connection

Autobiographical writing in the real world: Point out to students that there will be many times when they can use personal narratives. Friendly letters often contain personal narratives, and college and employment applications often require personal essays.

Drafting

- Explain to students that because they are writing personal narratives, the narrator should be *I*.
- Point out to students that chronological order, or time order, will probably be the most logical order for their narratives.
- Discuss what makes a story suspenseful. Encourage students to experiment with descriptive details and pacing their narratives in order to create suspense.
- Suggest that students copy the graphic organizer on p. 92. Remind them to fill in all of the boxes. This information will help ensure that they include all of the essential details in their narratives.
- Use the examples of writing with and without dialogue to show how dialogue enhances a personal narrative.

Revising

- Have students check to be certain that events are in the most logical order.
- Read aloud the instruction about leads. Draw students' attention to the example revision based on the student model.
- Instruct students to trade papers with a partner to determine whether the lead grabs a reader's interest. Have students make constructive suggestions to each other about revising their leads.

(continued on page 93)

Drafting

Present the events in order. Present events in the order in which they happened. Tell enough about each event to give a clear picture. Stick to first-person point of view (use *I* to show that you are the narrator).

Create suspense. Build suspense in your narrative by focusing on the problem or conflict. If your story has little conflict, focus on what you learned or how the experience you are describing changed you. At the high point of your story, include details that tell how the conflict was resolved.

Use detail and dialogue. Include details from your timeline as you write. If it fits your narrative, add dialogue to show what people are thinking and feeling.

No dialogue: Ismail said that he wanted more cake.

With dialogue: "Oh please, please, puh-leez," begged Ismail, "I must have more triple-chocolate cake!"

Focus on the Conflict

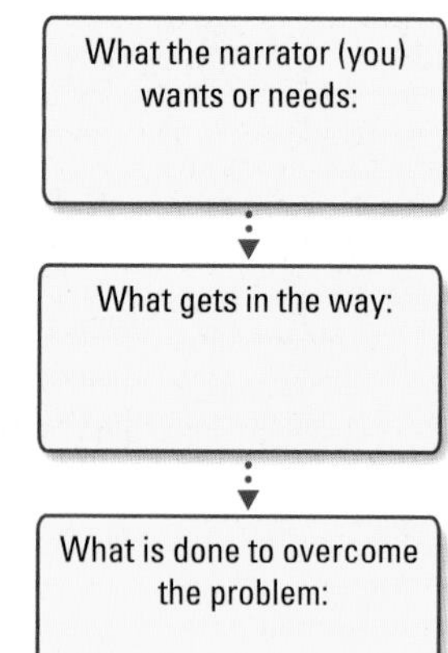

Revising

Connect your paragraphs. Draw an arrow from each paragraph to the next. Label each arrow, telling the relationship between the paragraphs it links.

- Do events in one paragraph cause those in the next?
- Does a paragraph give more information about the previous one?
- Does a paragraph create curiosity about what will happen next?

If a paragraph is not related to the ones before and after it, you might rewrite that paragraph, move it, or delete it.

Strengthen your lead. The start of a narrative—its **lead**—should make readers curious. Try these ideas:

- an exciting action
- a hint about a potential problem
- thought-provoking dialogue or a person's thoughts

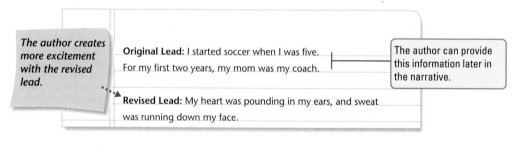

The author creates more excitement with the revised lead.

Original Lead: I started soccer when I was five. For my first two years, my mom was my coach.

The author can provide this information later in the narrative.

Revised Lead: My heart was pounding in my ears, and sweat was running down my face.

USING TECHNOLOGY IN WRITING

If students are using a word processing program, they might want to experiment with decorative typefaces for the title of their narratives. Point out to students that decorative typefaces have certain connotations, or additional meanings, just as words have certain connotations. Show students how to display various typefaces, and encourage them to use one that suits their topic. Students may also use clip-art.

Suggest that students also use the sentence length revision tool on the **Writing and Grammar iText CD-ROM** to make their writing more appealing.

Revise for word choice. Highlight the nouns in your draft. Evaluate each one, asking whether it might leave readers wondering *What kind?* Replace vague or general nouns with **precise nouns.**

Example: Eliza fed her *pet.*
Eliza fed her *hamster.*

Compare the model and the nonmodel. Why is the model more effective than the nonmodel?

Nonmodel	Model
Over and over in my head I completely missed the goal. I had just been through a long game and because of the heat, I didn't think I could last much longer. Sitting on the ground, I waited for my turn to make the penalty kick.	Over and over in my imagination I sent the soccer ball flying over the net, completely missing the goal. I had just been through two overtimes and because of the heat, I didn't think I could last much longer. Sitting on the grass, I waited for my turn to make the penalty kick.

Publishing and Presenting

Choose one of the following ways to share your writing with classmates or a wider audience.

Deliver a speech. Use your autobiographical narrative as the basis for a presentation.

Build an anthology. Use a word-processing program to create a neat final copy of your narrative. Gather narratives written by classmates, and compile them in an autobiographical anthology. Add art or photos to enhance each narrative.

WG *Prentice Hall Writing and Grammar Connection: Chapter 4*

Speaking Connection
To learn more about presenting an autobiographical narrative in a speech, see the **Listening and Speaking Workshop: Organizing and Giving a Narrative Presentation,** p. 94.

Rubric for Self-Assessment

Evaluate your autobiographical narrative, using the following criteria and rating scale:

Criteria	Rating Scale: Not very				Very
How consistently does the writer narrate events as someone who participates in the action?	1	2	3	4	5
How effective is the lead in grabbing your interest?	1	2	3	4	5
How clearly is the problem or conflict identified?	1	2	3	4	5
How clear is the order of events?	1	2	3	4	5
How detailed are the descriptions of the people, setting, and actions?	1	2	3	4	5

Revising (continued)

- Supply highlighters and have students follow the directions for revising for word choice.
- Have students examine the model and the nonmodel. Ask students to identify ways the model has changed and the effect of the changes.
  Possible response: "Sent the soccer ball flying over the net" is more descriptive than "completely missed the goal;" "sitting on the grass" is a clearer image than "sitting on the ground." The model is more descriptive and has clearer images than the nonmodel; this allows the reader to have a more vivid picture of the setting and the narrator's thoughts.

Publishing and Presenting

- Ask students to consider the target audience for their narratives.
- Discuss the most effective way of presenting the narratives to an audience. Allow students the option of working together in groups to modify their essays and present them as speeches. Encourage students to submit their essays for inclusion in a school literary magazine or essay contest. Organize a class anthology to publish student essays; send the anthology home for overnight sharing with students' families.

Assessment

- Take time to further explain each category in the rubric. For example, for the category about leads, you might score the original lead and revised lead on the bottom of p. 92 to give students a model to work from.
- The rubric on this page, and another rubric in an alternative format, can be found on pp. 8 and 34 of **Performance Assessment and Portfolio Management.**

TEST-TAKING TIP

When taking a test that includes a narrative writing prompt, students should be sensitive to the impact of their opening sentences. The opening is important, because it is the reader's introduction to the writer's presentation and sets expectations for the rest of the essay. Encourage students to set aside time to develop and polish their openings. Suggest that they reread their opening in the draft stage and revise it before they revise the rest of the essay. Ask students to double-check the rest of their compositions for powerful descriptions that will catch a reader's imagination.

Lesson Objectives

1. To prepare and deliver a narrative presentation
2. To develop a plot for the presentation
3. To correlate delivery techniques with content
4. To polish the presentation through rehearsing

Organize and Rehearse

- Have students use the Series of Events Chain on p. 70 in **Writing Models and Graphic Organizers on Transparencies** to organize their work.
- Provide note cards. Model writing one event from the organizer on each card.
- Have students revisit their cards to elaborate.
- Review the delivery techniques with students, modeling the techniques to clarify how they affect an oral presentation.
- Provide highlighters or color pencils. Suggest that students use different colors to underline or highlight words that deserve different types of treatment. For example, yellow could be used for slow speech, green for quick.
- Ask students to suggest gestures and voice pitches that would be appropriate for tense, joyful, or other moods in a speech.
- Remind students that their goal is to talk to the audience. They should strive to know their presentation well enough that they do not need note cards when they present it.
- Encourage students who feel that they need notes to write key words on a single note card. Point out that this will prompt their memory but will also give them an opportunity to look at their audience and use gestures without losing their place on note cards.
- As students prepare their presentations for the Activity, remind them that their feedback to student speakers should be *constructive* criticism.

Listening and Speaking WORKSHOP

Organizing and Giving a Narrative Presentation

A **narrative presentation** is simply a story told aloud. The story may be real or made up. It may be about you or about someone else. In this workshop, you will organize and develop a narrative presentation. (To review the characteristics of autobiographical narratives, see the writing workshop, pp. 90–93. To preview the characteristics of a fictional narrative, see p. 520.) To deliver an effective account, organize and rehearse it first. The following strategies will help you give an effective presentation.

Organize and Rehearse

Like a written autobiographical narrative, an oral narrative account tells what happens in the story in chronological order, focusing on the central conflict, or struggle, in the story. Use the following guidelines to plan your spoken narrative.

Develop your plot. Use note cards to help you develop your plot. Write one narrative event on each card. Then, add dialogue that helps reveal your characters' personalities. Add concrete and sensory details about the people, setting, and actions.

Plan your delivery. Consider using some of the following techniques to add pep to your presentation. On each card, note the ones you might use.

- Change the pace. Slow down or speed up to emphasize the action in the narrative.
- Use gestures and movements that fit the story. You need only a few.
- Vary the pitch, raising or lowering your voice.

Delivery Techniques
Pacing
Speak slowly to build suspense: "Slowly, slowly, the footsteps grew louder. Angela and I waited. Who, who was coming up the stairs?"
Gestures
Wave, make a fist, clap, snap fingers, cover face with hands, shade eyes, beckon, put hands on hips, point
Pitch
• Try a high, squeaky voice to show excitement.
• Try a low, rumbling voice to show anger.
• Let your voice go up to end a question. Lower it slightly at the end of a statement.

Rehearse. Practice your narrative in front of a mirror. Use your note cards to jog your memory, but put them aside when you no longer need them. Experiment with pace, pitch, and gestures.

Activity: **Presentation and Feedback** Prepare and deliver a narrative presentation about a goal you have accomplished recently. Present your narrative to a partner and ask for constructive suggestions. Write down what they are. After your presentation, ask for audience feedback. Check the areas in which you improved your presentation.

CUSTOMIZE INSTRUCTION FOR UNIVERSAL ACCESS

For Special Needs Students	For Less Proficient Readers	For English Learners
Have students work with partners and take turns checking the content of each others speeches. Student listeners should take notes on parts they find confusing or identify questions left unanswered. The speakers should then revise their presentations to fill these gaps. Students should switch roles and repeat the process.	After students have rehearsed their presentations by themselves, have them record their presentations on tape recorders. Students should listen to their recordings and evaluate their tone and pacing. After students have decided which areas of the speech require adjustments, have them tape and listen to their speeches again.	Have students make a list of new words that appear in their presentations. To assist students with rehearsing new words correctly, show students how to use the pronunciation key in the dictionary. As students are mastering the words, check to be certain that they are interpreting the pronunciation key correctly.

Assessment WORKSHOP

Distinguishing Multiple Meanings

Some test questions ask you to choose the meaning of a word in a passage when the word has multiple meanings. The following methods will help you answer these types of questions.

- Read the passage to get the general meaning of the text.
- Locate the word that is set off in italics, boldface, or with an underscore.
- Ask yourself what the word must mean in order for the passage to make sense.
- Use the text surrounding the word to identify clues to the correct meaning.

Test-Taking Strategies

- Read the word in context before answering the question.
- Plug each word choice into the passage and cross out answers that do not make sense.

Sample Test Item

Directions: Read the following passage, and then choose the letter of the best answer to the question.

Sean's mother had asked him to clean out the garage, and he was happy to do it. As he put tools away, he thought about how hard his mother worked at the electronics **plant** to support the family.

1. The word **plant** in this passage means—

 A factory
 B leaf
 C hotel
 D flower

Answers and Explanations

The correct answer is ***A***. If you place **B, C,** or **D** in the sentence, you realize that each one does not make sense within the context of the sentence.

Practice

Directions: Answer these test questions based on the following passage.

Garrison Keillor reaches out to more than two million public radio listeners who **tune** in every week to hear his variety show, *A Prairie Home Companion.* Through songs, comedy, **sketches**, and stories, Keillor nudges listeners into thinking about the really important things in life—along with the really funny ones.

1. The word **tune** in this passage means—

 A melody
 B air
 C listen
 D prepare

2. In this passage, the word **sketches** means—

 A cartoons
 B designs
 C funny drawings
 D short plays

Lesson Objective

To determine which sense of a multiple-meaning word is being used in a test situation

Applying Reading Strategies

Point out to students that many words have more than one meaning. The context, such as the words and phrases surrounding a multiple-meaning word, helps readers tell which meaning of the word is correct.

Test-Taking Skills

- Have students read the sample item. Then, ask them to reread the sentence containing the word in boldface type.
- Then, ask them what the test item is asking for.
 Answer: The test item is asking for a word that means the same as *plant* in this passage.
- With students, evaluate the answers by substituting each answer choice in the sentence and using context clues to determine the word's meaning.

Answer

1. The correct answer is C. None of the other choices make sense when inserted into the sentence.
2. The correct answer is C. Answers *A, B,* and *D* do not make sense because they are not to be heard, but to be looked at.

TEACHING RESOURCES

The following resources can be used to enrich or extend the instruction for p. 95.

PRENTICE HALL ASSESSMENT SYSTEM

- Workbook
- Skill Book
- Transparencies
- CD-ROM

Unit Objectives

1. To read selections in different genres that develop the theme "Reaching Out"
2. To apply a variety of reading strategies, particularly literal comprehension strategies, appropriate for reading these selections
3. To analyze literary elements
4. To use a variety of strategies to build vocabulary
5. To learn elements of grammar, usage, and style
6. To use recursive writing processes to write in a variety of forms
7. To develop listening and speaking skills
8. To express and support responses to various types of texts
9. To prepare, organize, and present literary interpretations

Meeting the Objectives

With each selection, you will find instructional materials through which students can meet these objectives. Further, you will find additional practice pages for reading strategies, literary analysis, vocabulary, and grammar in the **Selection Support: Skills Development Workbook** in your **Teaching Resources.**

Background

Art

First Steps
by Vincent van Gogh

Vincent van Gogh (1853–1890) was a Dutch painter and one of the greatest of the Post-Impressionists. His style, characterized by heavy brush strokes, exaggerated color, and contoured forms, influenced Expressionism.

The title of this painting is *First Steps.* What do you think the title means?
Answer: Students should realize that the man has his arms outstretched toward the toddler who is learning to walk and probably taking his or her first steps.

UNIT 2 Reaching Out

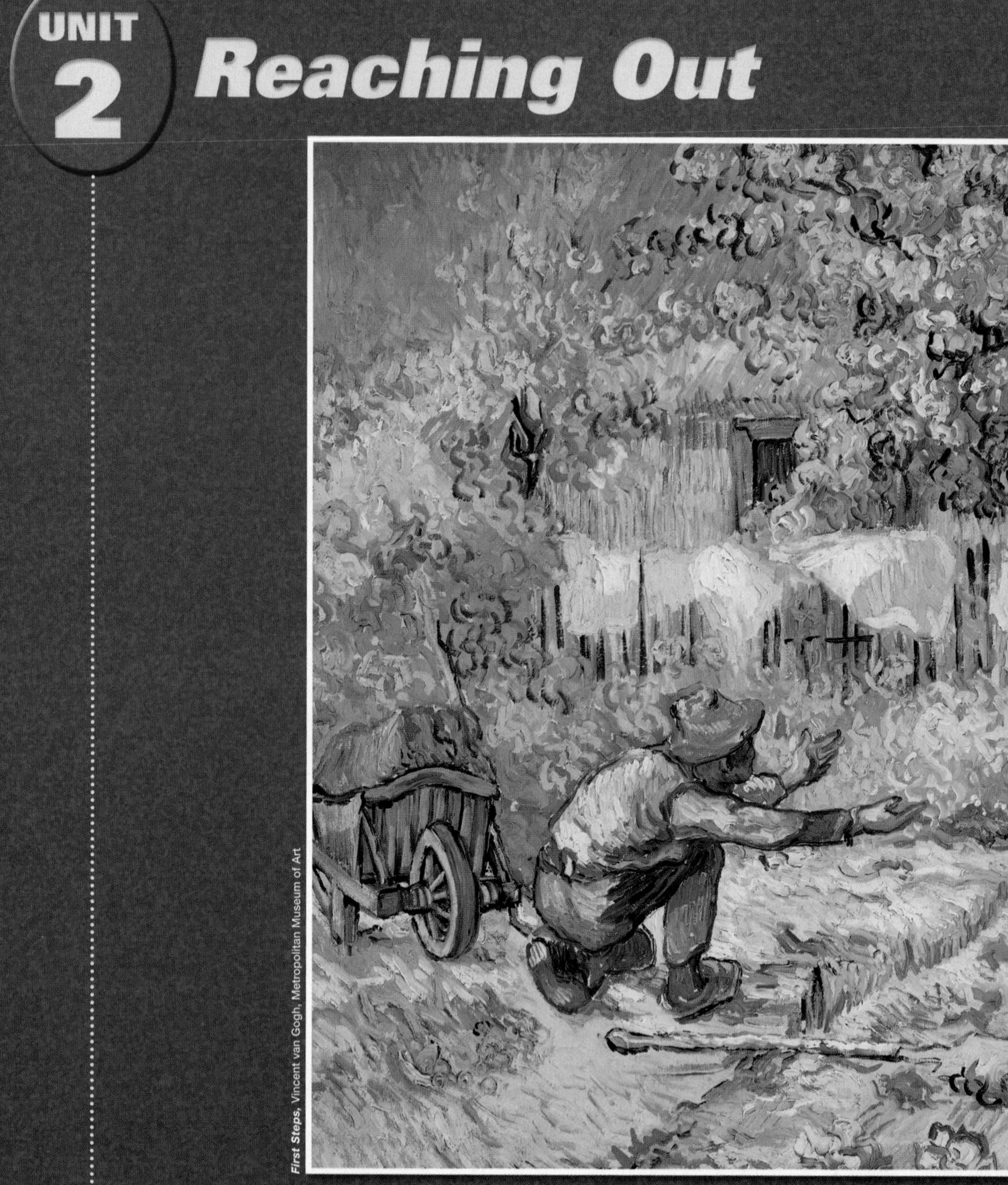

First Steps, Vincent van Gogh, Metropolitan Museum of Art

UNIT FEATURES	
Connections	**Reading Informational Material**
Every unit contains a feature that connects literature to a related topic, such as art, science, or history. In this unit, the selection "Stargirl" by Jerry Spinelli is connected thematically to the poems on pp. 140–142, particularly to George Eliot's "Count That Day Lost." Use the information and questions on the Connections page to enrich students' understanding of the selections presented within the unit.	These selections will help students learn to analyze and evaluate informational texts, such as workplace documents, technical directions, and consumer materials. They will expose students to the organization and features unique to nonnarrative texts. In this unit, students learn to connect information from a written interview to what they already know and to prepare their own interview questions. They will also analyze a music review.

Exploring the Theme

The man in this picture reaches out to encourage the toddler to walk. In the same way, the stories, poems, and essays in this unit encourage you to move forward—to open new doors and discover new friends. By sharing the experiences of literary characters and considering the ideas expressed by the authors, you will recognize the many different ways people can reach out.

As you read, think about the ways in which writers and characters reach out in difficult situations and take steps toward understanding the world and the people in it.

◀ **Critical Viewing** What feelings do the actions of the characters in this painting express? **[Assess]**

ASSESSMENT RESOURCES

- **Selection Support: Skills Development Workbook**
- **Formal Assessment**
- **Open Book Tests**
- **Performance Assessment and Portfolio Management**
- **Extension Activities**

Assessing Student Progress

Listed below are the tools that are available to measure the degree to which students meet the unit objectives.

Informal Assessment

The questions in the Review and Assess sections are a first level of response to the concepts and skills presented within the selections. Students' responses are a brief, informal measure of their grasp of the material. These responses can indicate where further instruction and practice are needed. Follow up with the practice pages in the **Selection Support: Skills Development Workbook.**

Formal Assessment

The **Formal Assessment** booklet contains Selection Tests and Unit Tests.

- Selection Tests measure comprehension and skills acquisition for each selection or group of selections.
- Each Unit Test provides students with thirty multiple-choice questions and five essay questions designed to assess students' knowledge of the literature and skills taught in the unit.

The **Open Book Tests** ask students to demonstrate their ability to synthesize and communicate information from selections or groups of selections.

To assess student writing, you will find rubrics and scoring models in the **Performance Assessment and Portfolio Management** booklet. In this booklet you will also find scoring rubrics for listening and speaking activities.

Alternative Assessment

The **Extension Activities** booklet contains writing activities, listening and speaking activities, and research and technology activities that are appropriate for students with different ability levels. You may also use these activities as an alternative measurement of students' growth.

▶Critical Viewing

Possible responses: Students may suggest feelings such as love, pride, and encouragement.

Why Read Literature?

The "Why Read Literature?" page in each unit presents a list of possible purposes for reading. Each purpose for reading is connected to one or more of the selections in the unit. Good readers set a purpose before reading in order to help them read actively and focus on meaningful details.

Unit 2 introduces three purposes for reading. "Read for the Love of Literature" encourages students to read two stories by famous authors. "Read to Appreciate Author's Style" suggests that students will be challenged and amazed by the ways that three writers use the English language. Finally, "Read for Information" reminds students to read to learn facts and details about unfamiliar topics.

How to Use This Page

- Tell students that before reading each selection in this unit, they should set a purpose for reading. This will help them read in an active and focused manner.
- Explain that reading works by acclaimed writers Isaac Bashevis Singer and Arthur C. Clarke will increase their love of literature.
- To appreciate an author's style, readers must let the writer lead them through a beautiful landscape or a humorous situation through their use of words. In "How to Write a Poem About the Sky," students will imagine a beautiful arctic sky as the writer sees it.
- A third purpose for reading is to obtain information. Explain that when setting a purpose, students should specify the type of information they want to learn. For example, when reading "Water," they may want to learn about how a person who was both blind and deaf learned to communicate.

Why Read Literature?

There are many specific purposes for reading. You might want to enjoy an adventure story, learn about a new invention, or consider how others feel about a particular issue. Preview three purposes you might have for reading the works in this unit.

1

Read for the love of literature.

A canary's heart races at about 1,000 beats per minute. Although this tiny bird may seem delicate and fragile, Arthur C. Clarke describes one tough canary in his science-fiction story **"Feathered Friend,"** page 159.

Polish American author Isaac Bashevis Singer was expected to follow in the family tradition and become a rabbi. Instead, he became a master short-story writer. Singer draws on people and scenes from his Polish heritage in many of his works. Follow Singer's exciting account of a young boy lost in the Polish countryside during a raging blizzard when you read **"Zlateh the Goat,"** page 128.

2

Read to appreciate author's style.

Leslie Marmon Silko grew up at Laguna Pueblo in New Mexico where she listened to tales told by her great-grandmother. Share Silko's love for the beauty and power of words when you read her **"How to Write a Poem About the Sky,"** page 106.

Garrison Keillor is as well known for being a talker as he is for being a writer. Talking on the radio earned him a place in the Radio Hall of Fame. Enjoy the way Keillor makes writing seem like talking when you read his essay **"How to Write a Letter,"** page 102.

3

Read for information.

How does a deaf, blind toddler become a famous writer and lecturer? Learn about the breakthrough that set Helen Keller on the road to fame in **"Water,"** page 120.

There are more than 2,700 types of snakes in the world, but only about 250 types are poisonous to humans. Learn other interesting and surprising facts when you read the true story of a friendly, helpful snake—**"Old Ben"**—by Jesse Stuart on page 154.

Take It to the Net

Visit the Web site for online instruction and activities related to each selection in this unit.
www.phschool.com

ENRICHMENT: Further Reading

Have students choose one or more of the works below to extend the unit theme "Reaching Out" or to read more by the unit authors.

The Talking Earth by Jean Craighead George

This novel follows the young Seminole Indian girl Billie Wind and her animal friends as she travels alone by raft through the Florida Everglades.

Tuck Everlasting by Natalie Babbitt

This whimsical fantasy novel is the story of a family who becomes immortal after drinking from a magic spring and the young girl who discovers the secret.

The Secret Garden by Frances Hodgson Burnett

This classic novel tells how life changes for the orphaned Mary Lennox when she moves to an old house filled with secrets and meets a magical boy who talks to animals.

The Story of My Life by Helen Keller

This autobiography is Helen Keller's classic retelling of her life.

How to Read Literature

Use Literal Comprehension Strategies

The first step in understanding a work of literature is to grasp its literal meaning—the basic facts and details the author is communicating. These strategies will help you understand a writer's words on a literal level:

1. Read words in groups.

When you read aloud, read words in groups. To do this, look ahead at the punctuation, which signals when to pause or stop and when to raise or lower your voice. Use expression to reflect the meaning of the words.

2. Use context to clarify meanings.

Use the context—or the surrounding words, sentences, and paragraphs—to find clues to the meaning of a familiar word that is used in a new or unusual way.

The surrounding words may include words that have similar or related meanings.

> . . . we had little trouble concealing our guest when VIP's from Earth came visiting. A space station has more hiding places than you can count; . . . —"Feathered Friend"

The word *concealing* may be unfamiliar to you, but the words *hiding places* are clues that *concealing* means "putting out of sight; hiding."

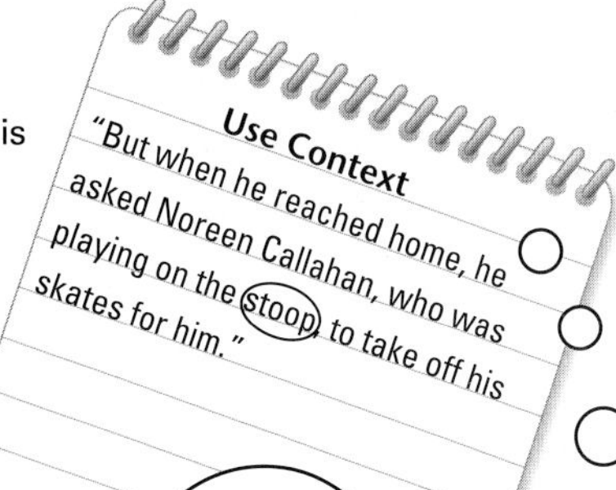

Use Context
"But when he reached home, he asked Noreen Callahan, who was playing on the stoop to take off his skates for him."

Noreen is playing on the stoop at home, so *stoop* cannot mean "to bend forward"; she is playing in front of Aaron's apartment house, so stoop must be part of the building. It's probably that little porch or set of steps in front of the building.

3. Summarize.

As you read, pause occasionally to think about and sum up the main points or events that have happened so far. Review the events in your mind, and then organize them in the sequence in which they occurred.

4. Paraphrase.

Restate a sentence or idea in your own words to make sure you understand it.

Longfellow's Words	Between the dark and the daylight, When the night is beginning to lower
Paraphrase	At twilight

As you read the selections in this unit, review the reading strategies and look at the notes in the side columns. Use the suggestions to apply the strategies for literal comprehension.

How to Read Literature

The "How to Read Literature" page in each unit presents a set of strategies to help readers understand authors' words and ideas. Each reading strategy is taught in conjunction with one or more of the selections within the unit. Good readers develop a bank of strategies from which they can draw as needed.

Unit 2 introduces four strategies for literal comprehension. To understand a selection fully, students must make sense of the words on the page as well as the author's ideas. The strategies on this page help readers comprehend what they read and make the ideas their own.

How to Use This Page

Introduce the strategies for literal comprehension, presenting each as a tool for developing understanding when reading the selections in this unit.

- As students read "How to Write a Letter" (p. 102) and "How to Write a Poem About the Sky" (p. 106), they will think about how to read aloud groups of words in a meaningful way.
- As students read "Aaron's Gift" (p. 112), "Water" (p.120), "Old Ben" (p. 154), and "Feathered Friend" (p. 159), they will figure out the meanings of unfamiliar words by looking for context clues.
- As students read "Zlateh the Goat" (p. 128), they will occasionally stop and summarize the events in the story in order to understand what is happening.
- As students read the poems "Door Number Four" (p. 140),"Count That Day Lost" (p. 141), and "The World Is Not a Pleasant Place to Be" (p. 142), they will paraphrase writers' ideas in order to comprehend them.

MODEL A READING STRATEGY: Paraphrase

Tell students that when they read poetry and the meaning is not clear, they can paraphrase the lines or stanzas, or put them into their own words, for better understanding.

Show students how to put a stanza from a poem into their own words by modeling a paraphrase of the first three stanzas from "The World Is Not a Pleasant Place to Be" (p. 142):

"The world would not be a very nice place if you did not have a friend or somebody to love and love you back. Rivers would stop flowing if they had only a stream to flow into, and the ocean would be less happy if the clouds were not there to rain."

Point out to students that there is no one way to paraphrase a stanza. Students should also notice that the beauty of the original language is lost in the paraphrase.

How to Write a Letter ✦ How to Write a Poem About the Sky

Lesson Objectives

1. **To analyze and respond to literary elements**
   - Literary Analysis: Informal Essay
   - Comparing Literary Works
2. **To read, comprehend, analyze, and critique an essay and a poem**
   - Reading Strategy: Reading Aloud with Expression
   - Reading Check Questions
   - Review and Assess Questions
   - Assessment Practice (ATE)
3. **To develop word analysis skills, fluency, and systematic vocabulary**
   - Vocabulary Development Lesson: Word Analysis: Latin Suffix *-ory*
4. **To understand and apply written and oral language conventions**
   - Spelling Strategy
   - Grammar Lesson: Verbs
5. **To understand and apply appropriate writing and research strategies**
   - Writing Lesson: Letter
   - Extension Activity: History of Mail Timeline
6. **To understand and apply listening and speaking strategies**
   - Extension Activity: Speech

STEP-BY-STEP TEACHING GUIDE	PACING GUIDE
PRETEACH	
Motivate Students and Provide Background	
Use the Motivation activity (ATE p. 100)	5 min.
Read and discuss the Preview material and Background information (SE/ATE p. 100) [A]	10 min.
Introduce the Concepts	
Introduce the Literary Analysis and Reading Strategy (SE/ATE p. 101) [A]	25 min.
Pronounce the vocabulary words and read their definitions (SE p. 101)	5 min.
TEACH	
Monitor Comprehension	
Informally monitor comprehension by circulating while students read independently or in groups [A]	25 min.
Monitor students' comprehension with the Reading Check notes (SE/ATE p. 103)	as students read
Develop vocabulary with Vocabulary notes (SE pp. 103, 104, 105, 106; ATE p. 103)	as students read
Develop Understanding	
Develop students' understanding of informal essays with the Literary Analysis annotations (SE p. 102; ATE p. 102) [A]	5 min.
Develop students' ability to read aloud with expression with the Reading Strategy annotations (SE p. 103; ATE pp. 103, 104)	5 min.
ASSESS	
Assess Mastery	
Assess students' mastery of the Reading Strategy and Literary Analysis by having them answer the Review and Assess questions (SE/ATE p. 105)	25 min.
Use one or more of the print and media Assessment Resources (ATE p. 109) [A]	up to 45 min.
EXTEND	
Apply Understanding	
Have students complete the Vocabulary Development Lesson and the Grammar Lesson (SE p. 108) [A]	20 min.
Apply students' ability to write letters using the Writing Lesson (SE/ATE p. 109) [A]	45 min.
Apply students' understanding of the selection using one or more of the Extension Activities (SE p. 109)	20–90 min.

ACCELERATED INSTRUCTION:
Use the strategies and activities identified with an [A].

UNIVERSAL ACCESS
● = Below Level Students
▲ = On-Level Students
■ = Above Level Students

Time and Resource Manager

Reading Level: Average, Easy
Average Number of Instructional Days: 4

RESOURCES			
	PRINT	**TRANSPARENCIES**	**TECHNOLOGY**
	• **Beyond Literature,** Workplace Skills: Writing a Business Letter, p. 7 ▲ ■		• **Interest Grabber Videotapes,** Tape 1 ● ▲ ■
	• **Selection Support Workbook:** ● ▲ ■ Literary Analysis, p. 35 Reading Strategy, p. 34 Build Vocabulary, p. 31	• **Literary Analysis and Reading Transparencies,** pp. 13 and 14 ● ▲ ■	
	• **Adapted Reader's Companion** ● • **Reader's Companion** ●		• **Listening to Literature** ● ▲ ■ Audiocassettes, Side 4 Audio CDs, CD 2
	• **English Learner's Companion** ● ▲ • **Literatura en español** ● ▲ • **Literary Analysis for Enrichment** ■		
	• **Formal Assessment:** Selection Test, pp. 27–29 ● ▲ ■ • **Open Book Test,** pp. 19–21 ● ▲ ■ • **Performance Assessment and Portfolio Management,** p. 8 ● ▲ ■ • PRENTICE HALL ASSESSMENT SYSTEM ● ▲ ■	• PRENTICE HALL ASSESSMENT SYSTEM ● ▲ ■ Skills Practice Answers and Explanations on Transparencies	• **Test Bank Software** ● ▲ ■ • **Got It! Assessment Videotapes,** Tape 1 ● ▲
	• **Selection Support Workbook:** ● ▲ ■ Build Spelling Skills, p. 32 Build Grammar Skills, p. 33 • **Writing and Grammar,** Copper Level ● ▲ ■ • **Extension Activities,** p. 7 ● ▲ ■	• **Daily Language Practice Transparencies** ● ▲ • **Writing Models and Graphic Organizers on Transparencies** ● ▲ ■	• **Writing and Grammar iText CD-ROM** ● ▲ ■ *Take It to the Net* www.phschool.com

BLOCK SCHEDULING: Use one 90-minute class period to preteach the selection and have students read it. Use a second 90-minute class period to assess students' mastery of skills and have them complete one of the Extension Activities.

PRETEACH

Step-by-Step Teaching Guide for pp. 100–101

Motivation

Hold up a recipe book and a "how-to" manual. Ask students what the books have in common. Lead them to see that both books take the reader step by step through a process that results in a product. Explain that although the essay and poem students are about to read are titled "How to . . ." they are somewhat different from a cookbook and a manual. In addition to telling how to write a letter, the essay also is entertaining and offers an opinion. The poem describes a natural scene.

Interest Grabber Video

As an alternative, play "Writing a Friendly Letter" on Tape 1 to engage student interest.

1 Background

Science

The poem "How to Write a Poem About the Sky," on page 106, describes the beauty of the sky, which most people don't take the time to appreciate. Another natural wonder that most people will never get to see is the aurora borealis. The aurora borealis, or northern lights, are amazing shows of natural lights that appear in the night skies above the Arctic Circle. The interaction of solar wind, light, and Earth's magnetic forces generate a vivid tableau of swirling green, pink, yellow, and red light. For reasons scientists have yet to explain, the light shows are most impressive in March and September.

Prepare to Read

1 How to Write a Letter ◆ How to Write a Poem About the Sky

The Calm After the Storm, Edward Moran, Private Collection

Take It to the Net

Visit www.phschool.com for interactive activities and instruction related to these selections, including

- background
- graphic organizers
- literary elements
- reading strategies

Preview

Connecting to the Literature

In "How to Write a Letter" and "How to Write a Poem About the Sky," Garrison Keillor and Leslie Marmon Silko demonstrate how to create a beautiful gift out of an ordinary moment. How? Put the moment in writing. Before reading these selections, recall a moment or experience that you would like to share with someone else.

Background

Leslie Marmon Silko wrote "How to Write a Poem About the Sky" while teaching creative writing to schoolchildren in Alaska. Her poem captures the vast, uninhabited beauty of the landscape there.

TEACHING RESOURCES

The following resources can be used to enrich or extend the instruction for pp. 100–101.

Motivation

Interest Grabber Video, Tape 1

Background

Beyond Literature, p. 7

Take It to the Net

Visit www.phschool.com for Background and hotlinks for the selections.

Literary Analysis

Literary Analysis and Reading Transparencies, Informal Essay, p. 14

Reading

Selection Support: Reading Strategy, p. 34; Build Vocabulary, p. 31

Literary Analysis and Reading Transparencies, Reading Aloud with Expression, p. 13

 **BLOCK SCHEDULING:** Resources marked with this symbol provide varied instruction during 90-minute blocks.

❷ Literary Analysis

Informal Essay

The titles of these two works suggest that they will be instructional essays—directions for writing. In fact, "How to Write a Letter" is an **informal essay**—a brief, nonfiction discussion of a topic, written in conversational language. It may contain humorous remarks. Although "How to Write a Poem About the Sky" is a poem, not an essay, it shares the informal conversational feeling of Keillor's essay. In this example, Keillor creates the feeling of conversation by using contractions and short sentences.

> Don't worry about form. It's not a term paper. When you come to the end of one episode, just start a new paragraph.

Comparing Literary Works

Although these two works are different genres (an essay and a poem), they share some common elements. Use a chart like the one here to compare and contrast the two works.

Use the chart to help you answer the following focus questions:

1. How are the topics of these works similar?
2. What is each writer's main point about writing?

How to Write a Letter		How to Write a Poem
Essay	Genre	Poem
	Topic	
	Language Style	
	Main point	

❸ Reading Strategy

Reading Aloud with Expression

When you read aloud with expression, you use your voice to reflect the meaning of the words. As you read these works, practice reading sections with expression. Adjust your reading in the following ways:

1. **Pacing:** Pacing is the speed and rhythm of your reading. Read at a normal speed as the text builds to a point. Slow down for a key point. Pause before a fact or short sentence.
2. **Intonation:** Intonation is the volume, tone, and pitch of your voice. These vocal qualities can be used to express emotion or add emphasis. Depending on the feeling you want to communicate, make your voice higher, lower, louder, softer, firmer, or gentler.

Vocabulary Development

confidence (kän′ fi dəns′) *n.* belief in one's own abilities (p. 103)

anonymity (an′ ə nim′ ə tē) *adj.* the condition of being unknown (p. 103)

obligatory (əb lig′ ə tor′ ē) *adj.* required (p. 103)

episode (ep′ ə sōd′) *n.* one in a series of related events (p. 104)

sibling (sib′ liŋ) *n.* brother or sister (p. 104)

dense (dens) *adj.* tightly packed; difficult to see through (p. 106)

membranes (mem′ brānz) *n.* thin, flexible layers of tissue (p. 106)

❷ Literary Analysis

Informal Essay

- To draw a parallel between formal and informal essays, have students think about how they might behave differently at a dinner party compared to a picnic with friends.
  Answer: Students will probably say that they would watch their manners at the dinner party but would be relaxed at the picnic. Suggest that students keep the picnic in mind as they read the informal essay and the poem.
- Read the instruction about informal essay to the class as students follow along. Take a moment to consider the purpose of the graphic organizer for Comparing Literary Works on p. 101. Stop students at points during their reading to remind them to fill in the organizer.
- Ask students to use the Informal Essay transparency in **Literary Analysis and Reading Transparencies**, p. 14, to keep track of informal and conversational language in the essay and the poem.

❸ Reading Strategy

Reading Aloud With Expression

- Illustrate the two strategies by reading aloud a short poem or limerick that students know.
- Read the piece two times, each time emphasizing one of the strategies—pacing or intonation. After each reading, ask students for their reactions.

Vocabulary Development

- Pronounce each vocabulary word for students, and read the definitions as a class. Have students identify any words with which they are already familiar.

CUSTOMIZE INSTRUCTION FOR UNIVERSAL ACCESS

For Special Needs Students	For Less Proficient Readers	For English Learners
Have students read the adapted version of "How to Write a Letter" in the **Adapted Reader's Companion.** This version provides basic-level instruction in an interactive format with questions and write-on lines. Completing the adapted version will prepare students to read the selection in the Student Edition.	Have students read "How to Write a Letter" in the **Reader's Companion.** This version provides basic-level instruction in an interactive format with questions and write-on lines. After students finish the selection in the Reader's Companion, have them complete the questions and activities in the Student Edition.	Have students read the adapted version of "How to Write a Letter" in the **English Learner's Companion.** This version provides basic-level instruction in an interactive format with questions and write-on lines. Completing the adapted version will prepare students to read the selection in the Student Edition.

 ***E-Teach***

Visit E-Teach at www.phschool.com for teachers' essays on how to teach, with questions and answers.

TEACH

Step-by-Step Teaching Guide for pp. 102–106

CUSTOMIZE INSTRUCTION
For Intrapersonal Learners

Invite students to reflect on a recent moment that they could have stretched into an hour—almost as if time had stopped. Have students consider whether this moment might best be suited for a letter or for a poem, and then ask them to write down a few phrases that capture the moment. Encourage students to put aside these phrases and then add to or rework them after finishing the selection.

❶ About the Selections

In "How to Write a Letter," Garrison Keillor uses humor to describe the value of letter writing. He believes that letters are gifts to those who receive them. He explains that a letter reaches out not only to the recipient but also to anyone who might read the letter in the future.

In "How to Write a Poem About the Sky" (p. 106), Leslie Marmon Silko creates word pictures for the reader, describing the sky and its relationship to the earth during cold, wintry conditions. Finally, she describes how bits of blue sky emerge as winter storm clouds subside. By ending with the single line, the poet opens a door for the reader to imagine how the sky might next be described.

❷ Literary Analysis

Informal Essay

- Ask students to locate details in the first paragraph that suggest the essay is informal.
  Possible responses: Students should point out contractions, slang, and casual style.
- Ask students the Literary Analysis question on p. 102.
  Answer: The writer speaks of himself ("I") and uses slang ("What's shakin', babes?") and informal spelling ("shakin'"). He seems to speak directly to the reader.

❶ How to Write a Letter

Garrison Keillor

❷ We shy persons need to write a letter now and then, or else we'll dry up and blow away. It's true. And I speak as one who loves to reach for the phone, dial the number, and talk. I say, "Big Bopper here—what's shakin', babes?" The telephone is to shyness what Hawaii is to February, it's a way out of the woods, and yet: a letter is better.

Such a sweet gift—a piece of handmade writing, in an envelope that is not a bill, sitting in our friend's path when she trudges home from a long day spent among wahoos and savages, a day our

Literary Analysis
Informal Essay How is this paragraph of the essay like a friendly letter?

TEACHING RESOURCES

The following resources can be used to enrich or extend the instruction for pp. 102–106.

Literary Analysis
- **Literary Analysis for Enrichment**
- **Writing Models and Graphic Organizer Transparencies,** p. 3
- **Selection Support:** Literary Analysis, p. 35

Reading
- **Adapted Reader's Companion**
- **Reader's Companion**

- **English Learner's Companion**
- **Literatura en español,** p. 57
- **Listening to Literature Audiocassettes,** Side 4 ■
- **Listening to Literature Audio CDs,** CD 2 ■

■ **BLOCK SCHEDULING:** Resources marked with this symbol provide varied instruction during 90-minute blocks.

words will help repair. They don't need to be immortal, just sincere. She can read them twice and again tomorrow: *You're someone I care about, Corinne, and think of often and every time I do you make me smile.*

We need to write, otherwise nobody will know who we are. They will have only a vague impression of us as A Nice Person, because, frankly, we don't shine at conversation, we lack the confidence to thrust our faces forward and say, "Hi, I'm Heather Hooten; let me tell you about my week." Mostly we say "Uh-huh" and "Oh, really." People smile and look over our shoulder, looking for someone else to meet.

confidence (kän′ fi dəns′) *n.* belief in one's own abilities

So a shy person sits down and writes a letter. To be known by another person—to meet and talk freely on the page—to be close despite distance. To escape from anonymity and be our own sweet selves and express the music of our souls.

anonymity (an′ ə nim′ ə tē) *n.* the condition of being unknown

Same thing that moves a giant rock star to sing his heart out in front of 123,000 people moves us to take ballpoint in hand and write a few lines to our dear Aunt Eleanor. *We want to be known.* We want her to know that we have fallen in love, that we quit our job, that we're moving to New York, and we want to say a few things that might not get said in casual conversation: *Thank you for what you've meant to me, I am very happy right now.*

3 The first step in writing letters is to get over the guilt of *not* writing. You don't "owe" anybody a letter. Letters are a gift. The burning shame you feel when you see unanswered mail makes it harder to pick up a pen and makes for a cheerless letter when you finally do. *I feel bad about not writing, but I've been so busy,* etc. Skip this. Few
4 letters are obligatory, and they are *Thanks for the wonderful gift and I am terribly sorry to hear about George's death and Yes, you're welcome to stay with us next month,* and not many more than that. Write those promptly if you want to keep your friends. Don't worry about the others, except love letters, of course. When your true love writes, *Dear Light of My Life, Joy of My Heart, O Lovely Pulsating Core of My Sensate*[1] *Life,* some response is called for.

Reading Strategy
Reading Aloud with Expression How would you adjust your intonation for the words *not* and "owe"?

obligatory (əb lig′ ə tor′ ē) *adj.* required

Some of the best letters are tossed off in a burst of inspiration, so keep your writing stuff in one place where you can sit down for a few minutes and (*Dear Roy, I am in the middle of a book entitled We Are Still Married but thought I'd drop you a line. Hi to your sweetie, too*) dash off a note to a pal. Envelopes, stamps, address book, everything in a drawer so you can write fast when the pen is hot.

A blank white eight-by-eleven sheet can look as big as Montana if the pen's not so hot—try a smaller page and write boldly. Or use a note card with a piece of fine art on the front; if your letter ain't 5

✓Reading Check

What is the first step in writing a letter?

1. **sensate** (sen′ sāt) *adj.* having the power of sensory perception.

3 Reading Strategy

Reading Aloud With Expression

- Have volunteers take turns reading aloud the first five sentences of the bracketed paragraph on this page.
- Ask students whether the sentences were easy or difficult to read aloud.
- Possible response: The sentences were easy to read because they sounded like a person speaking in conversation.
- Ask the Reading Strategy question. Answer: The words *not* and *"owe"* should both be stressed.
- Have a volunteer reread the sentence paying close attention to the words *not* and *"owe."*

Monitor Progress Ask students to identify and define, in their own words, the three strategies for reading aloud with expression. Answer: Students should know that pacing is the speed at which one reads, intonation is the way one raises or lowers the voice, and expression is speaking loudly or softly or with hesitation.

4 Vocabulary Development

Word Analysis: Latin Suffix *-ory*

- Point out the use of the word *obligatory,* and remind students that the suffix *-ory* means "having the quality or nature of." Explain that in this case, *-ory* turns a noun into an adjective.
- Invite students to identify other adjectives that have the same suffix. Possibilities include *mandatory, exploratory* and *sensory.*
- Next, ask students to guess at the meanings of the words they identify. Then, have them confirm their guesses by looking up the words in a dictionary.

5 ✓Reading Check

Answer: First, one should stop feeling guilty about not having written sooner.

CUSTOMIZE INSTRUCTION FOR UNIVERSAL ACCESS

For Special Needs Students	For Less Proficient Readers	For English Learners
Students may still have trouble because of the informal language. Place students in pairs, and have them do an echo reading. First, one student reads aloud a paragraph or section; then, the partner reads the same part aloud. Have students help one another identify the words or places that need to be read with expression.	Point out that the reason for reading an essay that explains how to do something is to translate the prose style into step-by-step directions. Have students summarize or list the steps in the paragraph that begins "A blank white." Challenge students to repeat the activity with another appropriate paragraph.	Students may feel more comfortable reading the essay aloud if they have a chance to hear it beforehand. Allow students to listen to the selection on the **Listening to Literature Audiocassettes,** Sides 7, 8, or the **Listening to Literature Audio CDs,** CDs 2, 3.

6 Reading Strategy

Reading Aloud With Expression

- Explain to students that the sentences in italic type are a visual clue—they are supposed to sound like a person speaking.

Monitor Progress Ask students which of the three strategies—pacing, intonation, or expression—is most important when reading the phrases that appear in italic.
Answer: Students may suggest expression, because the sentences in italic should convey more feeling.

Reteach If students still struggle with the reading strategy, try reading aloud a short passage from the text without any expression or intonation. Then, ask students to fine-tune your performance. Read it again, this time using their suggestions. Make sure that students understand when to use each of the strategies.

7 Critical Thinking

Make a Judgment

- Ask students to identify which kinds of letters are the easiest and which are the most difficult to write, according to the author.
Answers: A letter to a friend is the easiest to write. A letter intended to impress someone is the most difficult one to write.
- Next, ask students whether they agree or disagree with the author's opinion and why.
Possible response: Students will probably agree that writing a letter to a friend is easy because it is fun to write and allows them to be silly or serious, whereas writing to impress requires one to write carefully and correctly.

8 Critical Viewing

Answer: The man is probably reading a letter from someone special he cares about. He is so eager to read the letter that he opens it right at the mailbox. The letter might be from the girl who appears in the photograph on p. 102. She might be his grandchild or his friend.

good, at least they get the Matisse.[2] Get a pen that makes a sensuous[3] line, get a comfortable typewriter, a friendly word processor—whichever feels easy to the hand.

Sit for a few minutes with the blank sheet in front of you, and meditate on the person you will write to, let your friend come to mind until you can almost see her or him in the room with you. Remember the last time you saw each other and how your friend looked and what you said and what perhaps was unsaid between you, and when your friend becomes real to you, start to write.

Write the salutation—*Dear You*—and take a deep breath and plunge in. A simple declarative sentence will do, followed by another and another and another. Tell us what you're doing and tell it like you were talking to us. Don't think about grammar, don't think about lit'ry style, don't try to write dramatically, just give us your news. Where did you go, who did you see, what did they say, what do you think?

6 If you don't know where to begin, start with the present moment: *I'm sitting at the kitchen table on a rainy Saturday morning. Everyone is gone and the house is quiet.* Let your simple description of the present moment lead to something else, let the letter drift gently along.

7 The toughest letter to crank out is one that is meant to impress, as we all know from writing job applications; if it's hard work to slip off a letter to a friend, maybe you're trying too hard to be terrific. A letter is only a report to someone who already likes you for reasons other than your brilliance. Take it easy.

Don't worry about form. It's not a term paper. When you come to the end of one episode, just start a new paragraph. You can go from a few lines about the sad state of pro football to the fight with your mother to your fond memories of Mexico to your cat's urinary-tract infection to a few thoughts on personal indebtedness and on to the kitchen sink and what's in it. The more you write, the easier it gets, and when you have a True True Friend to write

8 ▲ **Critical Viewing** Judging from the expression on his face, who has written the letter this man is reading? **[Speculate]**

episode (ep′ ə sōd′) *n.* one in a series of related events

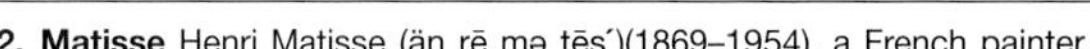

2. **Matisse** Henri Matisse (än rē mə tēs′)(1869–1954), a French painter.
3. **sensuous** (sen′ shoo͞ əs) *adj.* readily grasped by the senses.

CUSTOMIZE INSTRUCTION FOR UNIVERSAL ACCESS

For Gifted/Talented Students

Students may enjoy performing Keillor's essay as a theater production. Put students into small groups to prepare a script. Remind them not to change any of the author's words, but to write down in their scripts how to read them. In preparation, students should consider how to present the different "voices." Students may take time to rehearse their material, practicing the strategies for reading aloud effectively. When performing, students should stand or sit facing the audience. Students who are speaking should step forward or stand and maintain good eye contact with the audience. After the production, ask students to talk about what they learned from the experience.

to, a compadre,[4] a soul sibling, then it's like driving a car down a country road, you just get behind the keyboard and press on the gas.

Don't tear up the page and start over when you write a bad line—try to write your way out of it. Make mistakes and plunge on. Let the letter cook along and let yourself be bold. Outrage, confusion, love—whatever is in your mind, let it find a way to the page. Writing is a means of discovery, always, and when you come to the end and write *Yours ever* or *Hugs and kisses*, you'll know something you didn't when you wrote *Dear Pal*.

Probably your friend will put your letter away, and it'll be read again a few years from now—and it will improve with age. And forty years from now, your friend's grandkids will dig it out of the attic and read it, a sweet and precious relic of the ancient eighties that gives them a sudden clear glimpse of you and her and the world we old-timers knew. You will then have created an object of art. Your simple lines about where you went, who you saw, what they said, will speak to those children and they will feel in their hearts the humanity of our times.

You can't pick up a phone and call the future and tell them about our times. You have to pick up a piece of paper.

sibling (sib′ liŋ) *n.* brother or sister

4. **compadre** (kəm päd′ rā) *n.* Spanish for buddy; close friend.

Review and Assess

Thinking About the Selection

1. **Respond:** Do you like writing letters? Why or why not?
2. (a) **Recall:** According to Keillor, why do people need to write letters? (b) **Analyze:** What can a writer accomplish in a letter that he or she cannot accomplish in everyday conversation? (c) **Distinguish:** Identify two situations for which a letter is the better form of communication and two situations for which a conversation is better.
3. (a) **Recall:** What does Keillor say is the first step in writing a letter? (b) **Analyze Cause and Effect:** How might following this suggestion result in a better letter?
4. (a) **Recall:** What are two kinds of letters you are obligated to write? (b) **Contrast:** How are these letters different from letters to close friends? (c) **Deduce:** How can you tell that Keillor has written many letters to friends?
5. (a) **Draw Conclusions:** In what ways is a letter more than just a good way to communicate? (b) **Evaluate:** Do you think letter writing is important in today's society? Explain.

Garrison Keillor

(b. 1942)

Over the years, Garrison Keillor's name has become a synonym for his public radio program called *A Prairie Home Companion*. In this award-winning variety show, Keillor uses songs, comedy sketches, and stories to nudge listeners into thinking about the really important things in life—along with the really funny ones. The highlight of the show is "News from Lake Wobegon," Keillor's monologue about doings in an imaginary midwestern town. Keillor is also the author of several books of humor and a member of the Radio Hall of Fame.

Answers for p. 105

Review and Assess

1. Possible responses: Some students may say that they enjoy writing letters because they are able to say things that they might not be able to say in conversation. Others may prefer communicating face-to-face or by phone.
2. **(a)** People need to write letters in order to let others know who they really are. **(b)** A writer can reveal his or her feelings about life or about the recipient. **(c)** A letter is better if people want to communicate deeper thoughts and feelings or if the writer is shy. A conversation is better if the information needs to be shared immediately or if one wants eye contact, such as with a very important discussion.
3. **(a)** The first step in writing a letter is to let go of any guilt about not writing. **(b)** By letting go of guilty feelings, the letter will be cheerful rather than cheerless.
4. **(a)** The letters that are obligatory are thank-you letters, condolence letters, and letters responding to requests. **(b)** These letters are slightly more formal than letters to close friends. **(c)** In the essay, Keillor uses examples from letters that he has written. From the ease and humor of this essay, Keillor also gives the impression that he has written many letters.
5. **(a)** Letters are more than just a way to communicate in that they record moments in life. They will become part of history as well as a testament to the time when they were written. **(b)** Students may suggest that with the development of e-mail, traditional letters are no longer important. Some students may consider e-mail to be a form of letter writing and therefore important.

CUSTOMIZE INSTRUCTION FOR UNIVERSAL ACCESS

For Less Proficient Readers	For Advanced Readers
Have students work in pairs to share their own letter-writing experiences or techniques. Ask them to discuss which of Keillor's steps they have followed. Then, have pairs work together to write a letter in which they use all the steps that Keillor mentions. Ask volunteers to read their letters to the class.	Keillor is very familiar with the process of writing a letter. That fact probably helped him write his informal essay. Have students write an informal essay on a topic with which they are comfortable. Encourage students to use some of Keillor's techniques for creating an informal tone. Have volunteers share their essays with the class.

ASSESS

Answers for p. 106

Review and Assess

1. Students may find the first stanza the most real because it is the easiest to visualize.
2. **(a)** The sky is white. **(b)** The sky is like the frozen river because it is solid white and the birds are able to walk on it. **(c)** The speaker is unable to see the horizon because the white sky blends with the white snow on the ground.
3. **(a)** When the wind shifts, sun and blue sky appear. **(b)** Possible response: The poet compares the sky to skin and membranes because, just as the skin hides the amazing workings of the body, the clouds in the sky hide the wonder of the blue sky. **(c)** Students may say that the sky is indescribable and that Silko captures it nicely. Others may say that Silko is not effective because they have trouble picturing what she describes.

How to Write a Poem About the Sky

Leslie Marmon Silko

You see the sky now
colder than the frozen river
so dense and white
little birds
walk across it.

You see the sky now
but the earth
is lost in it
and there are no horizons.
It is all
a single breath.

You see the sky
but the earth is called
by the same name
                    the moment
                    the wind shifts
sun splits it open
and bluish membranes
push through slits of skin.

You see the sky

dense (dens) *adj.* tightly packed; difficult to see through

membranes (mem´ brānz) *n.* thin, flexible layers of tissue

Leslie Marmon Silko

(b. 1948)

In addition to writing two well-received novels about Native American life (*Ceremony* and *Almanac of the Dead*), Leslie Marmon Silko has always been a poet and a lover of poetry.

Her work embraces her experiences growing up on a Laguna Pueblo reservation in New Mexico, as well as her love of landscape—such as the cold, barren region of Alaska, described in "How to Write a Poem About the Sky."

Review and Assess

Thinking About the Selection

1. **Respond:** Which verse in the poem seems most real to you?
2. **(a) Recall:** What color is the sky? **(b) Interpret:** In what way is the sky like the frozen river? **(c) Draw Conclusions:** Why is the speaker unable to see the horizon?
3. **(a) Synthesize:** In your own words, describe the change in the sky's appearance after the wind shifts. **(b) Interpret:** Why does the poet compare the sky to skin and membranes? **(c) Evaluate:** How effective is Silko in capturing true images of the sky?

ASSESSMENT PRACTICE: Reading Comprehension

Recognize Facts and Details (For more practice, see Test Preparation Workbook, p. 9.)

Many tests require students to recognize details. Help students practice this skill by using the following example:

[The thing that] . . . moves us to take ballpoint in hand and write a few lines to our dear Aunt Eleanor . . . We want her to know that we have fallen in love, that we quit our job, that we're moving to New York, and we want to say a few things that might not get said in casual conversation. . . .

According to the passage, why do people write letters?

A To complain to someone
B To express their love
C To be known to another person
D To avoid doing other chores

The correct answer is *C*. The details show that writing letters allows people to share their experiences and feelings with others.

Review and Assess

Literary Analysis

Informal Essay

1. Explain why "How to Write a Letter" can be categorized as an **informal essay.**
2. Explain which characteristics "How to Write a Poem About the Sky" shares with an informal essay.

Comparing Literary Works

3. Identify the topics, the points discussed, and the use of informal language in each work on a chart like the one shown below.

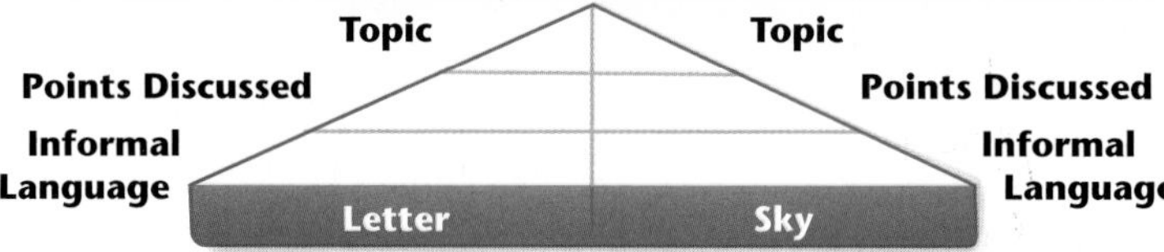

4. How much of each work focuses on how to do the writing?
5. How much does each work focus on the reason for writing or the writer's feelings about writing?
6. Which of these works most closely fits your image of "how to"?

Reading Strategy

Reading Aloud with Expression

7. Choose a paragraph from the essay and a verse from the poem to read aloud. On a chart like the one shown, identify specific words, phrases, or sentences for which you adjusted your pacing and intonation. Explain why you made adjustments.

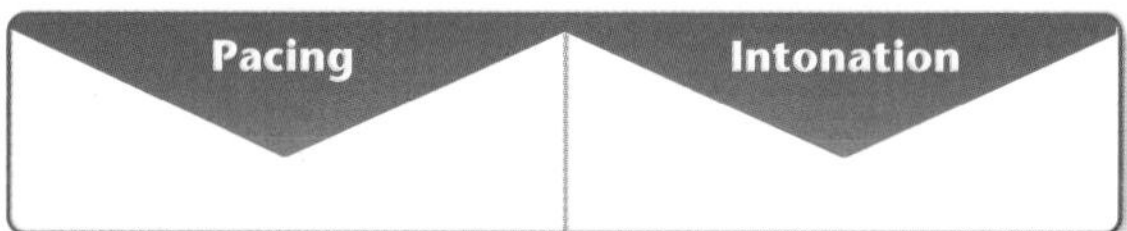

Extending Understanding

8. **Career Connection:** How might Keillor's advice be different if he were explaining how to write a business letter?

Quick Review

An **essay** is a brief, nonfiction discussion of a topic.

An **informal essay** is an essay that uses casual, conversational language.

To review informal essay, see page 101.

Pacing is the use of pauses and varied reading speeds.

Intonation is the use of a higher or lower voice.

To review reading with expression, see page 101.

Take It to the Net

www.phschool.com

Take the interactive self-test online to check your understanding of these selections.

ENRICHMENT: Further Reading

Other Works by the Authors

Works by Garrison Keillor

Lake Wobegon Days

Leaving Home

Works by Leslie Marmon Silko

"Storyteller"

Take It to the Net

Visit www.phschool.com for more information on the authors.

Answers for p. 107

Review and Assess

1. It can be categorized as an informal essay because it uses conversational language and has a humorous tone.
2. Both an essay and the poem share the writer's thoughts, and both address the reader.
3. **Topics:**

Letter: How to write a letter
Sky: The winter sky

Points discussed:

Letter: letters cheer up recipients, reveal something about writers, steps to writing a letter, letters are important
Sky: the sky is white, the sky and the earth appear to be the same, the sky is like skin

Informal language:

Letter: "what's shakin', babes?" "wahoos," "ain't," "lit'ry," "*compadre*"
Sky: "you"

4. The essay focuses mostly on how to write a letter. The poem, on the other hand, does not tell how to write a poem, but is an example to the reader of what a poem about the sky might contain.
5. The essay writer's main focus is the reason for writing letters. It can be seen from his tone that it is something very important to him. The poet does not address reasons for writing or feelings about writing, yet she conveys deep feelings for her subject, the sky.
6. Most students will suggest that the essay conveys more "how to" information than the poem.
7. Students should note that they changed their pace when encountering punctuation, as well as for words and phrases that are particularly meaningful, such as, "Thank you for what you meant to me." Intonation should have changed to indicate the writer's excitement and enthusiasm. Students should have adjusted their expressions to match the emotions of the words.
8. Possible response: Keillor would not have advised ignoring mistakes and grammar.

EXTEND

Answers for p. 108

❶ Vocabulary Development

Word Analysis

1. senses
2. regulate
3. accusation

Spelling Strategy

1. difference
2. independence
3. presence

Fluency: Using Words in Context

Possible responses:

1. Yes.
2. I would feel loved.
3. Yes; a scene is part of a series of events.
4. People drop trays every day.
5. Getting good grades increases my confidence.
6. Failing a test makes me lose confidence.
7. Water.
8. No, people should wear what they want.
9. When I want to keep my identity a secret I would wish for anonymity.
10. Anonymity protects the person from unjust punishment.

❷ Grammar

1. brightens
2. Take; plunge
3. seems
4. becomes
5. is

Writing Application

1. does, want; He wants you to write a letter.
2. are; I am twelve years old.
3. do, talk; I talk on the phone twice a day.
4. did, eat; I ate a sandwich.
5. is, want; I want to go to the park.

Integrate Language Skills

❶ Vocabulary Development Lesson

Word Analysis: Latin Suffix *-ory*

The Latin suffix *-ory* indicates "the quality or nature of." For example, *obligations* are *obligatory*. Copy the following items on your paper. Fill in the missing words.

1. Things related to the __?__ are sensory.
2. Systems that __?__ are regulatory.
3. You might use an accusatory tone when making an __?__.

Spelling Strategy

The *ens* sound at the end of words like *confidence* is often spelled *ence*. You may need to memorize the spelling of words that end in *-ence*.

On your paper, write the ending for each word by adding *-ence*.

1. differ__?__
2. independ__?__
3. pres__?__

Fluency: Using Words in Context

On separate paper, answer these questions. Explain each answer.

1. Could someone call you a *sibling*?
2. How would you feel if someone called you a *sibling*?
3. Is one scene in a play an *episode*? Explain.
4. What is a common *episode* in the lunchroom at your school?
5. What increases your *confidence*?
6. When have you lost *confidence*?
7. Name one thing that is *obligatory* for staying alive.
8. Do you think a dress code should be *obligatory* at your school?
9. When would you wish for *anonymity*?
10. Why is *anonymity* important for a person who is accused of a crime but not yet tried?

❷ Grammar Lesson

Verbs

A **verb** is a word that shows an action or state of being in a sentence. *Send, think,* and *run* are verbs that show action. *Was, am, became,* and *seem* are verbs that show state of being.

Practice Copy the following sentences on paper. Circle the verbs. (There may be more than one.)

1. A letter brightens a friend's day.
2. Take a deep breath and plunge in.
3. A blank piece of paper seems scary.
4. The letter becomes a precious relic.
5. It is not a report.

Writing Application Copy the following questions. Answer each with a complete sentence. Circle the verb or verbs in each question and each answer.

1. What does Keillor want you to do?
2. How old are you?
3. How often do you talk on the phone?
4. What did you eat for lunch yesterday?
5. What is something you want to do tomorrow?

WG Prentice Hall Writing and Grammar Connection: Chapter 15, Section 1

TEACHING RESOURCES

The following resources can be used to enrich or extend the instruction for pp. 108–109.

Vocabulary

- **Selection Support:** Build Vocabulary, p. 31; Build Spelling Skills, p. 32
- **Vocabulary and Spelling Practice Book** (Use this booklet for skills enrichment)

Grammar

- **Selection Support:** Build Grammar Skills, p. 33
- **Writing and Grammar,** Copper Level, p. 314
- **Daily Language Practice Transparencies** ■

Writing

- **Writing and Grammar,** Copper Level, p. 58 ■
- **Writing and Grammar iText CD-ROM**

■ **BLOCK SCHEDULING:** Resources marked with this symbol provide varied instruction during 90-minute blocks.

❸ Writing Lesson

Letter

Use Keillor's suggestions in "How to Write a Letter" to write a letter to a friend.

Prewriting Think about a recent activity that you want to write about. Jot down what the activity was, whom you were with, and how you enjoyed it.

Drafting Open your letter with a friendly greeting and a sentence that tells your friend about the activity. The body of your letter should expand on the activity and how you felt about it. Include specific details that make it personal and informal, such as "The roller coaster has more loops than any other I've been on." The last paragraph of your letter should sum up your thoughts and feelings.

Revising Review your writing and add personal details that connect to your reader. Look for places where you can make your language more informal.

Model: Revising To Add Details

Dear Kaitlin,

It's very hot here. *It's even hotter than the last day of school!* We don't mind because we swim in the ocean all day anyway! The waves are huge!

The writer uses contractions because a friendly letter is informal. She adds a personal detail here that the reader will appreciate.

WG *Prentice Hall Writing and Grammar Connection: Chapter 4, Section 4*

❹ Extension Activities

Research and Technology Make an illustrated **timeline** that shows the history of mail. Use the Internet and other sources to get information about the milestones leading to the postal services we have today. To gather information, use a key word search on a search engine to find the Internet address for the U.S. Postal Service. Illustrate some of these milestones by including pictures on your timeline.

Listening and Speaking Choose a portion of Keillor's essay and present it as a **speech**. Practice delivering the speech. Slow down to emphasize the main points for your listeners. Give examples to emphasize the main points for your listeners. Deliver your speech to your class.

Take It to the Net www.phschool.com

Go online for an additional research activity using the Internet.

ASSESSMENT RESOURCES

The following resources can be used to assess students' knowledge and skills.

Selection Assessment

- **Formal Assessment,** pp. 27–29
- **Open Book Test,** pp. 19–21
- **Got It! Assessment Videotapes,** Tape 1
- **Test Bank Software**

Take It to the Net

Visit www.phschool.com for self-tests and additional questions on the selections.

Writing Rubric

- **Performance Assess. and Portfolio Mgmt.,** p. 8

- **Workbook**
- **Skill Book**
- **Transparencies**
- **CD-ROM**

❸ Writing Lesson

- Ask students to bring in letters they have received in the mail, or to compose sample letters and share them with the class.
- As a class, generate a list of some common features of letters.
- Remind students that if they cannot think of a recent activity, they can invent one.
- Use the Narration rubric in **Performance Assessment and Portfolio Management,** p. 8, to evaluate students' letters.

❹ Research and Technology

- You may wish to search the Internet yourself in order to locate acceptable Web sites for students to use. Make a list of the sites, or bookmark them and limit students' searches to these Web pages.
- Before students begin searching, work as a class to identify some key words they might use.
- Remind students that although the Internet is a public resource, it is important that they give credit to the sources of the information they collect. Offer students a simple form of documentation, such as noting the Internet address and the day on which it was accessed.

CUSTOMIZE INSTRUCTION For Universal Access

To address different learning styles, use the activities suggested in the **Extension Activities** booklet, p. 7.

- For Visual/Spatial Learners, use Activity 5.
- For Logical/Mathematical Learners, use Activity 6.
- For Verbal/Linguistic and Bodily/Kinesthetic Learners, use Activity 7.

Aaron's Gift ✦ Water

Lesson Objectives

1. **To analyze and respond to literary elements**
   - Literary Analysis: Climax
   - Comparing Literary Works
2. **To read, comprehend, analyze, and critique a short story and an autobiography**
   - Reading Strategy: Using Context to Clarify Meaning
   - Reading Check Questions
   - Review and Assess Questions
   - Assessment Practice (ATE)
3. **To develop word analysis skills, fluency, and systematic vocabulary**
   - Vocabulary Development Lesson: Word Analysis: Forms of *console*
4. **To understand and apply written and oral language conventions**
   - Spelling Strategy
   - Grammar Lesson: Verb Phrases
5. **To understand and apply appropriate writing and research strategies**
   - Writing Lesson: Interview
   - Extension Activity: Visual Presentation
6. **To understand and apply listening and speaking strategies**
   - Extension Activity: Oral Presentation

STEP-BY-STEP TEACHING GUIDE	PACING GUIDE
PRETEACH	
Motivate Students and Provide Background	
Use the Motivation activity (ATE p. 110)	5 min.
Read and discuss the Preview material and Background information (SE/ATE p. 110) [A]	10 min.
Introduce the Concepts	
Introduce the Literary Analysis and Reading Strategy (SE/ATE p. 111) [A]	25 min.
Pronounce the vocabulary words and read their definitions (SE p. 111)	5 min.
TEACH	
Monitor Comprehension	
Informally monitor comprehension by circulating while students read independently or in groups [A]	20–25 min.
Monitor students' comprehension with the Reading Check notes (SE/ATE pp. 113, 115, 117, 121)	as students read
Develop vocabulary with Vocabulary notes (SE pp. 112, 115, 116; ATE p. 116)	as students read
Develop Understanding	
Develop students' understanding of climax with the Literary Analysis annotations (SE pp. 113, 117, 118, 121; ATE pp. 113, 114, 117, 118, 121) [A]	5 min.
Develop students' ability to use context to clarify meaning with the Reading Strategy annotations (SE pp. 113, 115, 118; ATE pp. 113, 115, 118)	5 min.
ASSESS	
Assess Mastery	
Assess students' mastery of the Reading Strategy and Literary Analysis by having them answer the Review and Assess questions (SE/ATE p. 123)	25 min.
Use one or more of the print and media Assessment Resources (ATE p. 125) [A]	up to 45 min.
EXTEND	
Apply Understanding	
Have students complete the Vocabulary Development Lesson and the Grammar Lesson (SE p. 124) [A]	20 min.
Apply students' knowledge of interviews using the Writing Lesson (SE/ATE p. 125) [A]	45 min.
Apply students' understanding of the selection using one or more of the Extension Activities (SE p. 125)	20–90 min.

ACCELERATED INSTRUCTION:
Use the strategies and activities identified with an [A].

UNIVERSAL ACCESS
● = Below Level Students
▲ = On-Level Students
■ = Above Level Students

Time and Resource Manager

Reading Level: Challenging, Average
Average Number of Instructional Days: 4

RESOURCES		
PRINT	**TRANSPARENCIES**	**TECHNOLOGY**
• **Beyond Literature,** Career Connections: Veterinarian, p. 8 ▲ ■		• **Interest Grabber Videotapes,** Tape 1 ● ▲ ■
• **Selection Support Workbook:** ● ▲ ■ Literary Analysis, p. 40 Reading Strategy, p. 39 Build Vocabulary, p. 36	• **Literary Analysis and Reading Transparencies,** pp. 15 and 16 ● ▲ ■	
• **Adapted Reader's Companion** ● • **Reader's Companion** ●		• **Listening to Literature** ● ▲ ■ Audiocassettes, Side 5 Audio CDs, CDs 2, 3
• **English Learner's Companion** ● ▲ • **Literatura en español** ● ▲ • **Literary Analysis for Enrichment** ■		
• **Formal Assessment:** Selection Test, pp. 30–32 ● ▲ ■ • **Open Book Test,** pp. 22–24 ● ▲ ■ • **Performance Assessment and Portfolio Management,** pp. 12, 29 ● ▲ ■ • PRENTICE HALL ASSESSMENT SYSTEM ● ▲ ■	• PRENTICE HALL ASSESSMENT SYSTEM ● ▲ ■ Skills Practice Answers and Explanations on Transparencies	• **Test Bank Software** ● ▲ ■ • **Got It! Assessment Videotapes,** Tape 1 ● ▲
• **Selection Support Workbook:** ● ▲ ■ Build Spelling Skills, p. 37 Build Grammar Skills, p. 38 • **Writing and Grammar,** Copper Level ● ▲ ■ • **Extension Activities,** p. 8 ● ▲ ■	• **Daily Language Practice Transparencies** ● ▲ • **Writing Models and Graphic Organizers on Transparencies** ● ▲ ■	• **Writing and Grammar iText CD-ROM** ● ▲ ■ *Take It to the Net* www.phschool.com

BLOCK SCHEDULING: Use one 90-minute class period to preteach the selection and have students read it. Use a second 90-minute class period to assess students' mastery of skills and have them complete one of the Extension Activities.

PRETEACH

Step-by-Step Teaching Guide for pp. 110–111

Motivation

Bring to class gift-wrapped boxes of varying sizes. Ask students to speculate what kinds of gifts might fit in each box, starting with the largest box and working to the smallest. Then, ask students to consider gifts that need no wrapping, such as a thoughtful gesture or a kind word. Ask them to provide examples of such gifts from their own experiences.

Interest Grabber Video

As an alternative, play "Helen Keller Meets President Kennedy" on Tape 1 to engage students' interest.

❶ Background

Communication

American Sign Language (ASL), the system of communicating nonverbally with hand signals, had been established in the United States for seventy years when Annie Sullivan met Helen Keller. The system of signs had been developed by Abbé Charles-Michel de L'Epée, a French educator of deaf children in the late 1700s. ASL generally uses signs for words and concepts; spelling out names—as Sullivan did with Keller—is reserved for words that have no sign, such as proper names or specialized terms.

Prepare to Read

❶ Aaron's Gift ◆ Water

Take It to the Net

Visit www.phschool.com for interactive activities and instruction related to these selections, including

- background
- graphic organizers
- literary elements
- reading strategies

Preview

Connecting to the Literature

The main characters in "Aaron's Gift" and "Water" find solutions to problems by explaining new approaches and new ways of looking at things. Connect your experience to the experiences of the characters by recalling a time when you have found a new approach or viewpoint that helped you solve a problem.

Background

The author of "Water," Helen Keller, became blind and deaf before she was two years old. When her teacher Annie Sullivan entered her life, Helen did not even know what "words" were. She had no idea that the people and things she felt with her hands had names.

TEACHING RESOURCES

The following resources can be used to enrich or extend the instruction for pp. 110–111.

Motivation

Interest Grabber Video, Tape 1

Background

Beyond Literature, p. 8

Take It to the Net

Visit www.phschool.com for Background and hotlinks for the selections.

Literary Analysis

Literary Analysis and Reading Transparencies, Climax, p. 16

Reading

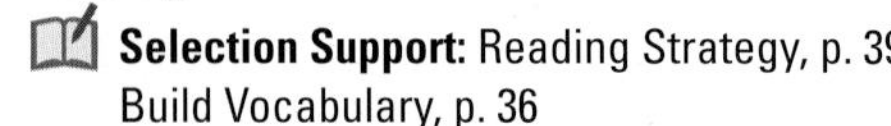

Selection Support: Reading Strategy, p. 39; Build Vocabulary, p. 36

Literary Analysis and Reading Transparencies, Using Context to Clarify Meaning, p. 15

BLOCK SCHEDULING: Resources marked with this symbol provide varied instruction during 90-minute blocks.

❷ Literary Analysis

Climax

A narrative starts with a problem or conflict. Each event in the narrative moves readers toward the moment when the outcome is decided. That moment is the **climax**, or turning point of the story. It is the high point of interest or suspense. As you read "Aaron's Gift," use a diagram like the one shown to record the events leading to the climax. Keep the following points in mind:

- All of the events before the climax help build tension in the story.
- All of the events following the climax lead to the resolution or final outcome.

Comparing Literary Works

Compare and contrast the types of problems or conflicts that Aaron and Helen Keller face. As you read both selections, use these focus questions to guide you:

1. Which character faces a problem with other characters?
2. Which character faces a problem within himself or herself?

❸ Reading Strategy

Using Context to Clarify Meaning

Sometimes you may read a word you recognize, but the word is used in a way that is different from what you expected. Some words have more than one meaning. Clarify the meaning of such words by looking at the **context,** the situation in which the word is used. The word *dashed* commonly means "ran quickly." Here, the word has a different meaning.

> I became impatient at her repeated attempts and, seizing the new doll, I *dashed* it upon the floor. I was keenly delighted when I felt the fragments of the broken doll at my feet.

The writer's impatience, and the fact that the doll is broken, are clues that *dashed* probably means "threw down with force and anger."

Vocabulary Development

frenzied (fren′ zēd) *adj.* wild; frantic (p. 112)

mascot (mas′ kät) *n.* any person, animal, or thing adopted by a group; meant to bring good luck (p. 115)

coaxed (kōkst) *v.* tried to persuade (p. 115)

consoled (kän sōld′) *v.* comforted (p. 116)

CUSTOMIZE INSTRUCTION FOR UNIVERSAL ACCESS

For Special Needs Students	For Less Proficient Readers	For English Learners
Have students read the adapted versions of the selections in the **Adapted Reader's Companion.** These versions provide basic-level instruction in an interactive format with questions and write-on lines. Completing the adapted versions will prepare students to read the selections in the Student Edition.	Have students read the selections in the **Reader's Companion.** These versions provide basic-level instruction in an interactive format with questions and write-on lines. After students finish the selections in the Reader's Companion, have them complete the questions and activities in the Student Edition.	Have students read the adapted versions of the selections in the **English Learner's Companion.** These versions provide basic-level instruction in an interactive format with questions and write-on lines. Completing the adapted versions will prepare students to read the selections in the Student Edition.

❷ Literary Analysis

Climax

- Explain to students that the climax is the high point of interest in a story or narrative.
- After students have read the instruction about climax, draw their attention to the diagram. Suggest that students think of the diagram as a roller coaster. Ask students to describe such a ride.
- Then, explain to the students how a roller coaster ride can be compared to the climax of a story.
- As students read the selections, tell them to refer back to the Comparing Literary Works questions.
- Use the Climax transparency in **Literary Analysis and Reading Transparencies** on p. 18 to demonstrate how students can track the climaxes in the selections.

❸ Reading Strategy

Using Context to Clarify Meaning

- After reading the instruction on p. 111, explain to the students that the context clue can appear either in the same sentence or before or after it.
- Take time to tell students about another type of context clue—restatement. *Restatement* provides the clue right in the same sentence. Example: "Helen dashed, or ran quickly, out of the house."
- Suggest that students keep a log of unfamiliar words as they read the selections. Students should write their own definitions for the words using the context clues.

Vocabulary Development

- Pronounce each vocabulary word for students, and read the definitions as a class. Have students identify any words with which they are already familiar.

 ***E-Teach***

Visit E-Teach at www.phschool.com for teachers' essays on how to teach, with questions and answers.

TEACH

Step-by-Step Teaching Guide for pp. 112–122

CUSTOMIZE INSTRUCTION For Musical/Rhythmic Learners

Students may recognize the way that music is used in movies and television programs to indicate significant events that lead to the climax. Play portions of typical "movie music" used to signify danger. Encourage students to identify places in the selections where this music might be used.

❶ About the Selection

While skating in a park, ten-year-old Aaron Kandel finds a wounded pigeon. At home, he sets the bird's broken wing and plans to give the bird to his grandmother for her birthday. He hopes that the bird will make up for a pet she lost as a girl in the Ukraine when her family home was destroyed by Cossack soldiers. When a gang of boys invites Aaron to join them and to bring his bird to a meeting, Aaron goes, not suspecting that the boys mean to harm the bird. Aaron fights to protect the bird from the boys, and the bird flies away. Next, Aaron must face his grandmother and learn an important lesson about the gift of freedom.

❷ ▶Critical Viewing

Answer: Students may suggest that the bird pictured here is getting ready to fly away—the bird that Aaron finds has a broken wing and cannot fly.

❶

Aaron's Gift

Myron Levoy

Aaron Kandel had come to Tompkins Square Park to roller-skate, for the streets near Second Avenue were always too crowded with children and peddlers and old ladies and baby buggies. Though few children had bicycles in those days, almost every child owned a pair of roller skates. And Aaron was, it must be said, a Class A, triple-fantastic roller skater.

Aaron skated back and forth on the wide walkway of the park, pretending he was an aviator in an air race zooming around pylons, which were actually two lampposts. During his third lap around the racecourse, he noticed a pigeon on the grass, behaving very strangely. Aaron skated to the line of benches, then climbed over onto the lawn.

The pigeon was trying to fly, but all it could manage was to flutter and turn round and round in a large circle, as if it were performing a frenzied dance. The left wing was only half open and was beating in a clumsy, jerking fashion; it was clearly broken.

❷ ▲ **Critical Viewing** How would you compare this bird to Aaron's bird? **[Compare and Contrast]**

frenzied (fren′ zēd) *adj.* wild; frantic

TEACHING RESOURCES

The following resources can be used to enrich or extend the instruction for pp. 112–122.

Literary Analysis
- **Literary Analysis for Enrichment**
- **Selection Support:** Literary Analysis, p. 40

Reading
- **Adapted Reader's Companion**
- **Reader's Companion**
- **English Learner's Companion**

- **Literatura en español**
- **Listening to Literature Audiocassettes,** Side 5 ■
- **Listening to Literature Audio CDs,** CDs 2, 3 ■
- **Writing Models and Graphic Organizers on Transparencies,** pp. 69, 89

■ **BLOCK SCHEDULING:** Resources marked with this symbol provide varied instruction during 90-minute blocks.

3 Luckily, Aaron hadn't eaten the cookies he'd stuffed into his pocket before he'd gone clacking down the three flights of stairs from his apartment, his skates already on. He broke a cookie into small crumbs and tossed some toward the pigeon. "Here pidge, here pidge," he called. The pigeon spotted the cookie crumbs and, after a moment, stopped thrashing about. It folded its wings as best it could, but the broken wing still stuck half out. Then it strutted over to the crumbs, its head bobbing forth-back, forth-back, as if it were marching a little in front of the rest of the body—perfectly normal, except for that half-open wing which seemed to make the bird stagger sideways every so often.

The pigeon began eating the crumbs as Aaron quickly unbuttoned his shirt and pulled it off. Very slowly, he edged toward the bird, making little kissing sounds like the ones he heard his grandmother make when she fed the sparrows on the back fire escape.

4 Then suddenly Aaron plunged. The shirt, in both hands, came down like a torn parachute. The pigeon beat its wings, but Aaron held the shirt to the ground, and the bird couldn't escape. Aaron felt under the shirt, gently, and gently took hold of the wounded pigeon.

"Yes, yes, pidge," he said, very softly. "There's a good boy. Good pigeon, good."

The pigeon struggled in his hands, but little by little Aaron managed to soothe it. "Good boy, pidge. That's your new name. Pidge. I'm gonna take you home, Pidge. Yes, yes, *ssh*. Good boy. I'm gonna fix you up. Easy, Pidge, easy does it. Easy, boy."

5 Aaron squeezed through an opening between the row of benches and skated slowly out of the park, while holding the pigeon carefully with both hands as if it were one of his mother's rare, precious cups from the old country. How fast the pigeon's heart was beating! Was he afraid? Or did all pigeons' hearts beat fast?

It was fortunate that Aaron was an excellent skater, for he had to skate six blocks to his apartment, over broken pavement and sudden gratings and curbs and cobblestones. But when he reached home, he asked Noreen Callahan, who was playing on the stoop, to take off his skates for him. He would not chance going up three flights on roller skates this time.

"Is he sick?" asked Noreen.

"Broken wing," said Aaron. "I'm gonna fix him up and make him into a carrier pigeon or something."

"Can I watch?" asked Noreen.

"Watch what?"

"The operation. I'm gonna be a nurse when I grow up."

"OK," said Aaron. "You can even help. You can help hold him while I fix him up."

Literary Analysis
Climax What detail about the pigeon begins to build interest in the situation?

Reading Strategy
Using Context How does the word *escape* help you understand what *beat* means in this situation?

6 ✓ **Reading Check**
What is Aaron doing for the pigeon? Why?

CUSTOMIZE INSTRUCTION FOR UNIVERSAL ACCESS

For Special Needs Students	For English Learners
For their first reading of the story, have students listen to side 5 of the **Listening to Literature Audiocassettes** or CDs 2, 3 of the **Listening to Literature Audio CDs.** Challenge students to write down unfamiliar words and listen carefully to their contexts during a second reading of the selection.	Have students identify unfamiliar vocabulary words on pp. 112–113. Suggest that students make a list of new words as they read through the selection. Then, allow them time to look for context clues that hint at the meanings of the words. Encourage students to guess at the words' meanings before they consult a dictionary.

3 Literary Analysis
Climax
- Before posing the Literary Analysis question on p. 113, ask students to summarize what they know about the pigeon at this point.
  Answer: It appears to have a broken, or "half-open," wing. It cannot fly.
- Then ask the Literary Analysis question.
  Answer: The details about the pigeon that create an interest in the situation are its wing that won't fold, its staggering when it walks, and the fact that it is walking toward Aaron.

4 Reading Strategy
Using Context
- Remind students that one reason readers need context clues is that words often have multiple meanings.
- Ask students to think of at least two meanings for the word *beat*.
  Possible responses: The word *beat* means "to hit something hard" or, in cooking, "to stir up very quickly." Birds beat or flap their wings quickly when they fly.
- Pose the Reading Strategy question on p. 113.
  Answer: The word *escape* helps the reader understand that the bird is flapping its wings very hard in an attempt to fly away.

5 Critical Thinking
Infer
- Ask students what they can tell about Aaron so far.
  Answer: Aaron is a young boy who is good at roller-skating; he is caring and compassionate.
- Then, ask how Aaron's character might affect the outcome of the story.
  Answer: He will probably help the bird become well.

6 ✓ Reading Check
Aaron is taking the pigeon home because it has a broken wing.

7 Background

Art

Pigeons, by John Sloan

John Sloan (1871–1951) is best known for his paintings of daily life in New York City.

Help students connect the artwork to the selection by asking questions such as these:

1. Why might the man in the painting be waving a flag?
   Possible responses: He is trying to get someone's attention; he might be signaling to the pigeons if they are homing pigeons; he is trying to scare the pigeons away.
2. Would Aaron enjoy being a part of this scene?
   Answer: Students may suggest that Aaron would enjoy watching the birds, sharing companionship, and spending time outdoors.

8 ▶Critical Viewing

Answer: Details that suggest freedom include the birds flying about and the boy sitting in a carefree fashion on the top of the building. Being on top of the building allows the humans to enjoy an unobstructed view of the city.

9 Literary Analysis

Climax

- Ask students to consider how this event may help lead to the climax.
  Answer: Students will probably recognize that the pigeon's injury will affect the way the events turn out at the climax.

▶ **Monitor Progress** Ask students to identify the correct order of the following terms: *climax, conclusion, events,* and *rising action.*
Answer: Events are part of the rising action. The rising action leads to the climax, which is followed by the conclusion.

Aaron wasn't quite certain what his mother would say about his new-found pet, but he was pretty sure he knew what his grandmother would think. His grandmother had lived with them ever since his grandfather had died three years ago. And she fed the sparrows and jays and crows and robins on the back fire escape with every spare crumb she could find. In fact, Aaron noticed that she sometimes created crumbs where they didn't exist, by squeezing and tearing pieces of her breakfast roll when his mother wasn't looking.

7

Pigeons, John Sloan, The Hayden Collection, Courtesy, Museum of Fine Arts, Boston, Massachusetts

Aaron didn't really understand his grandmother, for he often saw her by the window having long conversations with the birds, telling them about her days as a little girl in the Ukraine.[1] And once he saw her take her mirror from her handbag and hold it out toward the birds. She told Aaron that she wanted them to see how beautiful they were. Very strange. But Aaron did know that she would love Pidge, because she loved everything.

To his surprise, his mother said he could keep the pigeon, temporarily, because it was sick, and we were all strangers in the land of Egypt,[2] and it might not be bad for Aaron to have a pet. *Temporarily.*

8 ▲ **Critical Viewing** What details in this painting suggest freedom? **[Interpret]**

9 The wing was surprisingly easy to fix, for the break showed clearly and Pidge was remarkably patient and still, as if he knew he was being helped. Or perhaps he was just exhausted from all the thrashing about he had done. Two Popsicle sticks served as splints, and strips from an old undershirt were used to tie them in place. Another strip held the wing to the bird's body.

Aaron's father arrived home and stared at the pigeon. Aaron waited for the expected storm. But instead, Mr. Kandel asked, "Who *did* this?"

"Me," said Aaron. "And Noreen Callahan."

"Sophie!" he called to his wife. "Did you see this! Ten years old and it's better than Dr. Belasco could do. He's a genius!"

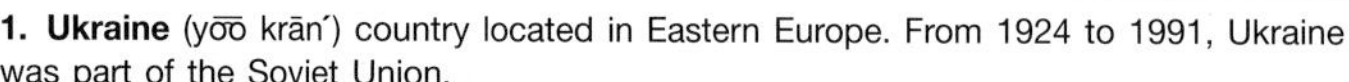

1. **Ukraine** (yōō krān′) country located in Eastern Europe. From 1924 to 1991, Ukraine was part of the Soviet Union.
2. **we were all . . . land of Egypt** a reference to the biblical story of the enslavement of the Hebrew people in Egypt. Around 1300 B.C., the Hebrews were led out of Egypt by Moses.

CUSTOMIZE INSTRUCTION FOR UNIVERSAL ACCESS

For Less Proficient Readers

Aaron's problems are at the center of the story, so it may help students to track them and their solutions. Help students by making a two-column chart on the board. Label one column *Problem* and one *Solution.* Then, invite students to identify Aaron's problems as they surface in the story. Have students look for both large and small problems and their solutions. If you wish, add a third column marked *Possible Solutions* in which students offer predictions about how the problems will be resolved. Remind students that the moment at which the problems are resolved or solved is the story's climax. When students finish the story and the chart, ask them if all of the problems were solved.

As the days passed, Aaron began training Pidge to be a carrier pigeon. He tied a little cardboard tube to Pidge's left leg and stuck tiny rolled-up sheets of paper with secret messages into it: THE ENEMY IS ATTACKING AT DAWN. Or: THE GUNS ARE HIDDEN IN THE TRUNK OF THE CAR. Or: VINCENT DEMARCO IS A BRITISH SPY. Then Aaron would set Pidge down at one end of the living room and put some popcorn at the other end. And Pidge would waddle slowly across the room, cooing softly, while the ends of his bandages trailed along the floor. 10

At the other end of the room, one of Aaron's friends would take out the message, stick a new one in, turn Pidge around, and aim him at the popcorn that Aaron put down on his side of the room.

And Pidge grew fat and contented on all the popcorn and crumbs and corn and crackers and Aaron's grandmother's breakfast rolls.

Aaron had told all the children about Pidge, but he only let his very best friends come up and play carrier-pigeon with him. But telling everyone had been a mistake. A group of older boys from down the block had a club—Aaron's mother called it a gang—and Aaron had longed to join as he had never longed for anything else. To be with them and share their secrets, the secrets of older boys. To be able to enter their clubhouse shack on the empty lot on the next street. To know the password and swear the secret oath. To belong.

Reading Strategy
11 **Using Context** The most common meaning of "long" is to describe length. How do you know that *longed* is not related to length? What does it mean?

About a month after Aaron had brought the pigeon home, Carl, the gang leader, walked over to Aaron in the street and told him he could be a member if he'd bring the pigeon down to be the club mascot. Aaron couldn't believe it; he immediately raced home to get Pidge. But his mother told Aaron to stay away from those boys, or else. And Aaron, miserable, argued with his mother and pleaded and cried and coaxed. It was no use. Not with those boys. No.

mascot (mas´ kät) *n.* a person or animal, adopted by a group for luck

coaxed (kōkst) *v.* tried to persuade

Aaron's mother tried to change the subject. She told him that it would soon be his grandmother's sixtieth birthday, a very special birthday indeed, and all the family from Brooklyn and the East Side would be coming to their apartment for a dinner and celebration. Would Aaron try to build something or make something for Grandma? A present made with his own hands would be nice. A decorated box for her hairpins or a crayon picture for her room or anything he liked.

In a flash Aaron knew what to give her: Pidge! Pidge would be her present! Pidge with his wing healed, who might be able to carry messages for her to the doctor or his Aunt Rachel or other people his grandmother seemed to go to a lot. It would be a surprise for everyone. And Pidge would make up for what had happened to Grandma 12

✓ Reading Check
What group does Aaron want to join?

10 Critical Thinking

Deduce

- You may wish to explain that carrier pigeons are birds that are trained to carry messages over distances and then return to their "home base."
- Ask students why Aaron writes messages such as these for the pigeon to carry.
  Answer: He and his friends play war games and pretend that the pigeon is carrying important secret messages.

11 Reading Strategy

Using Context

- Before asking the Reading Strategy question on p. 115, explain to students that the context clue to the word *longed* is a subtle one. Instead of looking for specific words, suggest that students consider the feelings that Aaron shows at the end of the paragraph.
- Pose the Reading Strategy question on p. 115 to students.
  Answer: The experiences that Aaron wants from membership in the gang suggest that he really wants to join. It is clear that *longed* means "desired greatly."

12 ✓ Reading Check

Answer: Aaron wants to join a club formed by older boys who live in his neighborhood.

CUSTOMIZE INSTRUCTION FOR UNIVERSAL ACCESS

For Special Needs Students	For Gifted/Talented Students
Students may become distracted by the details of the story and lose track of what is happening. After they have read p. 115, ask them to sum up what has happened so far. If they continue to get caught up in small details, guide them toward focusing on only main or key events. Offer students the Series of Events Chain transparency in the **Writing Models and Graphic Organizers on Transparencies,** p. 69.	Students probably have encountered many animal stories, whether in books, in movies, or on television. Challenge students to make a list of all the animal stories they have read or watched. Then, ask them to generate a list of typical plots. (For example, in some stories the animal dies at the end and the characters learn from the death.) Invite students to work in groups to act out the plots for the class.

⓭ Background

Social Studies

Pogrom is a Russian word meaning "a destructive riot." Pogroms were violent, government-sanctioned attacks against Jewish people. They first occurred in Russia in 1881, the year that Alexander III became czar, and lasted until the end of the Russian Revolution and Civil War, in 1921. Many of the worst assaults took place in what is now the country of Ukraine. More than 600,000 people were killed in pogroms. Fear of pogroms caused waves of Russian Jews to immigrate to the United States. Many settled in New York City, the setting of "Aaron's Gift."

⓮ Vocabulary Development

Word Analysis: Using Forms of *Console*

- Explain to students that knowing that the word *consoled* means "comforted" will help them understand the meaning of other forms of the word.
- Give students time to explore the origin and definition of the word *console* in a dictionary. Then, challenge them to think of other forms of the word.
  Possible responses: consolation; inconsolable; consolable; consolatory

when she'd been a little girl in the Ukraine, wherever that was.

Often, in the evening, Aaron's grandmother would talk about the old days long ago in the Ukraine, in the same way that she talked to the birds on the back fire escape. She had lived in a village near a place called Kishinev with hundreds of other poor peasant families like her own. Things hadn't been too bad under someone called Czar Alexander the Second,[3] whom Aaron always pictured as a tall handsome man in a gold uniform. But Alexander the Second was assassinated, and Alexander the Third, whom Aaron pictured as an ugly man in a black cape, became the Czar. And the Jewish people of the Ukraine had no peace anymore.

⓭ One day, a thundering of horses was heard coming toward the village from the direction of Kishinev. *The Cossacks!* ◆ *The Cossacks!* someone had shouted. The Czar's horsemen! Quickly, quickly, everyone in Aaron's grandmother's family had climbed down to the cellar through a little trapdoor hidden under a mat in the big central room of their shack. But his grandmother's pet goat, whom she'd loved as much as Aaron loved Pidge and more, had to be left above, because if it had made a sound in the cellar, they would never have lived to see the next morning. They all hid under the wood in the woodbin and waited, hardly breathing.

Suddenly, from above, they heard shouts and calls and screams at a distance. And then the noise was in their house. Boots pounding on the floor, and everything breaking and crashing overhead. The smell of smoke and the shouts of a dozen men.

The terror went on for an hour and then the sound of horses' hooves faded into the distance. They waited another hour to make sure, and then the father went up out of the cellar and the rest of the family followed. The door to the house had been torn from its hinges and every piece of furniture was broken. Every window, every dish, every stitch of clothing was totally destroyed, and one wall had been completely bashed in. And on the floor was the goat, lying quietly. Aaron's grandmother, who was just a little
⓮ girl of eight at the time, had wept over the goat all day and all night and could not be consoled.

But they had been lucky. For other houses had been burned to the ground. And everywhere, not goats alone, nor sheep, but men and women and children lay quietly on the ground. The word for this sort

Literature in context — History Connection

◆ ***Cossacks***
Aaron's grandmother has a memory of Cossacks destroying her village. Cossacks were soldiers on horseback. At the time when Aaron's grandmother lived in the Ukraine, Cossacks held a special and privileged status. The Russian army used these soldiers to put down revolutionary activities. Sometimes, the Cossacks took the law into their own hands and attacked innocent people.

consoled (kän sōld′) *v.* comforted

3. **Czar Alexander the Second** leader of Russia from 1855 to 1881.

of massacre, Aaron had learned, was *pogrom.* It had been a pogrom. And the men on the horses were Cossacks. Hated word. Cossacks.

And so Pidge would replace that goat of long ago. A pigeon on Second Avenue where no one needed trapdoors or secret escape passages or woodpiles to hide under. A pigeon for his grandmother's sixtieth birthday. *Oh wing, heal quickly so my grandmother can send you flying to everywhere she wants!*

But a few days later, Aaron met Carl in the street again. And Carl told Aaron that there was going to be a meeting that afternoon in which a map was going to be drawn up to show where a secret treasure lay buried on the empty lot. "Bring the pigeon and you can come into the shack. We got a badge for you. A new kinda membership badge with a secret code on the back."

Aaron ran home, his heart pounding almost as fast as the pigeon's. He took Pidge in his hands and carried him out the door while his mother was busy in the kitchen making stuffed cabbage, his father's favorite dish. And by the time he reached the street, Aaron had decided to take the bandages off. Pidge would look like a real pigeon again, and none of the older boys would laugh or call
15 him a bundle of rags.

Gently, gently he removed the bandages and the splints and put them in his pocket in case he should need them again. But Pidge seemed to hold his wing properly in place.

When he reached the empty lot, Aaron walked up to the shack, then hesitated. Four bigger boys were there. After a moment, Carl came out and commanded Aaron to hand Pidge over.

"Be careful," said Aaron. "I just took the bandages off."

"Oh sure, don't worry," said Carl. By now Pidge was used to people holding him, and he remained calm in Carl's hands.

"OK," said Carl. "Give him the badge." And one of the older boys handed Aaron his badge with the code on the back. "Now light the fire," said Carl.

"What . . . what fire?" asked Aaron.

"The fire. You'll see," Carl answered.

"You didn't say nothing about a fire," said Aaron. "You didn't say nothing to—"

"Hey!" said Carl. "I'm the leader here. And you don't talk unless I tell you that you have p'mission. Light the fire, Al."

The boy named Al went out to the side of the shack, where some wood and cardboard and old newspapers had been piled into a
16 huge mound. He struck a match and held it to the newspapers.

"OK," said Carl. "Let's get 'er good and hot. Blow on it. Everybody blow."

Aaron's eyes stung from the smoke, but he blew alongside the others, going from side to side as the smoke shifted toward them and away.

Literary Analysis
Climax How does this event help to increase the tension and move the story toward a climax?

Literary Analysis
Climax Why does the fire increase the tension?

17 
Reading Check
What happened to Aaron's grandmother's goat in the Ukraine?

15 Literary Analysis

Climax

- Before asking the first Literary Analysis question on p. 117, ask students to review the events that have led up to the climax, including this one.
  Answer: Aaron found a pigeon, fixed the pigeon's broken wing, decided to give the pigeon to his grandmother, was asked by the boys to bring the pigeon to the club, and is now sneaking the pigeon out of the house.
- Read aloud the Literary Analysis question and ask volunteers for their answers.
  Answer: Aaron has been told to avoid the boys because they are bad, but Aaron trusts them enough to take the pigeon to their meeting. This turn of events could have bad or good results, which causes tension for the reader.

16 Literary Analysis

Climax

Have students read the bottom of p. 117 before asking the second Literary Analysis question: "Why does the fire increase the tension?"
Answer: The fire increases the tension because it suggests a danger to Pidge or Aaron.

- Finally, ask students to make some predictions about what will happen next.

17 Reading Check

Answer: The goat was killed by the Cossacks.

CUSTOMIZE INSTRUCTION FOR UNIVERSAL ACCESS

For Special Needs Students	For Advanced Readers
Students may be confused by the story of Aaron's grandmother, which is told within Aaron's own story. Point out how at the beginning of the first full paragraph on p. 116, the story shifts into his grandmother's past and stays there until the top of p. 117. Remind students that the grandmother's story took place many years before Aaron's story. Guide students to put the details of the grandmother's story at the beginning of the Series of Events Chain on p. 69 in **Writing Models and Graphic Organizers on Transparencies.**	Students may be familiar with the concept of stories within stories or flashbacks. Ask students to compile a list of examples from books, stories, comic books, or movies. Challenge students to explain the purposes of these stories and to write about why writers do not tell the events in chronological order. Students may suggest that writers develop stories within stories or flashbacks to increase suspense.

18 Reading Strategy

Using Contex to Clarify Meaning

- Remind students that a word may have more than one meaning, as well as be pronounced differently.
- Say aloud the two different pronunciations of the word *wound* before asking students the Reading Strategy question on p. 118.
  Answer: The word sounds like the word *bound* in this context and is the past tense of the word *wind.*
- Ask students to identify the context clues that helped them understand the meaning of the word.
  Answer: "cord,""around the pigeon," "tight against its body."

19 Literary Analysis

Conflict and Climax

- Help students identify the climax of the story in this paragraph and the events building to the showdown. Ask students how they know the story has reached a turning point.
  Answer: When Pidge flies away, the reader knows he will be safe from the boys.
- Ask students the Literary Analysis question on p. 118.
  Answer: The conflict is solved by Pidge flying away. The tension is released because the boys can no longer hurt the pigeon.
- Help students recognize that readers' questions might change after the climax. Instead of asking "What happens next?" they tend to ask "How will this change things for the characters?"

Reteach Students may gain greater understanding of a story's climax by noticing how the events in the story affect the main character. Have students complete a chart with three columns, labeled as follows: *Aaron at the beginning of the story, Events that cause change,* and *Aaron at the end of the story.* Guide students to see how Aaron reaches his discoveries.

"Let's fan it," said Al.

In a few minutes, the fire was crackling and glowing with a bright yellow-orange flame.

"Get me the rope," said Carl.

18 One of the boys brought Carl some cord and Carl, without a word, wound it twice around the pigeon, so that its wings were tight against its body.

"What . . . what are you *doing!*" shouted Aaron. "You're hurting his wing!"

"Don't worry about his wing," said Carl. "We're gonna throw him into the fire. And when we do, we're gonna swear an oath of loyalty to—"

"No! *No!*" shouted Aaron, moving toward Carl.

"Grab him!" called Carl. "Don't let him get the pigeon!"

But Aaron had leaped right across the fire at Carl, taking him completely by surprise. He threw Carl back against the shack and hit out at his face with both fists. Carl slid down to the ground and the pigeon rolled out of his hands. Aaron scooped up the pigeon and ran, pretending he was on roller skates so that he would go faster and faster. And as he ran across the lot he pulled the cord off Pidge and tried to find a place, *any* place, to hide him. But the boys were on top of him, and the pigeon slipped from Aaron's hands.

"Get him!" shouted Carl.

19 Aaron thought of the worst, the most horrible thing he could shout at the boys. "Cossacks!" he screamed. "You're all Cossacks!"

Two boys held Aaron back while the others tried to catch the pigeon. Pidge fluttered along the ground just out of reach, skittering one way and then the other. Then the boys came at him from two directions. But suddenly Pidge beat his wings in rhythm, and rose up, up over the roof of the nearest tenement, up over Second Avenue toward the park.

With the pigeon gone, the boys turned toward Aaron and tackled him to the ground and punched him and tore his clothes and punched him some more. Aaron twisted and turned and kicked and punched back, shouting "Cossacks! Cossacks!" And somehow the word gave him the strength to tear away from them.

When Aaron reached home, he tried to go past the kitchen quickly so his mother wouldn't see his bloody face and torn clothing. But it was no use; his father was home from work early that night and was seated in the living room. In a moment Aaron was surrounded by his mother, father, and grandmother, and in another moment he had told them everything that had happened, the words tumbling out between his broken sobs. Told them of the present he had planned, of the pigeon for a goat, of the gang, of the badge with the secret code on the back, of the shack, and the fire, and the pigeon's flight over the tenement roof.

And Aaron's grandmother kissed him and thanked him for his

Reading Strategy
Using Context The word *wound* can be pronounced and used in more than one way. What is its pronunciation and meaning in this context?

Literary Analysis
Climax In what way is the conflict solved and the tension released?

CUSTOMIZE INSTRUCTION FOR UNIVERSAL ACCESS

For English Learners

Building background through visual images will help students understand the selection. Using magazines, history books, and other reference sources, locate as many of these images as possible: a child roller skating, early twentieth-century immigrant apartments and neighborhoods in New York City, a bird with a bandaged wing, Cossacks on horseback, Eastern European peasant dwellings from the late nineteenth century, domestic goats. Also provide a map showing both Ukraine and the United States. As students read the selection aloud, use the images to illustrate the setting, characters, or events.

present which was even better than the pigeon.

"What present?" asked Aaron, trying to stop the series of sobs.

And his grandmother opened her pocketbook and handed Aaron her mirror and asked him to look. But all Aaron saw was his dirty, bruised face and his torn shirt.

Aaron thought he understood and then, again, he thought he didn't. How could she be so happy when there really was no present? And why pretend that there was?

Later that night, just before he fell asleep, Aaron tried to imagine what his grandmother might have done with the pigeon. She would have fed it, and she certainly would have talked to it, as she did to all the birds, and . . . and then she would have let it go free. Yes, of course. Pidge's flight to freedom must have been the gift that had made his grandmother so happy. Her goat has escaped from the Cossacks at last, Aaron thought, half dreaming. And he fell asleep with a smile.

Review and Assess

Thinking About the Selection

1. **Respond:** What would you have done if Carl had asked you to join his club? Explain.
2. **(a) Recall:** How does Aaron find Pidge? **(b) Speculate:** Why does Aaron try to help Pidge? **(c) Infer:** What do Aaron's actions reveal about his personality?
3. **(a) Recall:** What is the reference to "strangers in the land of Egypt"? **(b)Interpret:** What does Aaron's mother mean when she says they are "all strangers in the land of Egypt"? **(c) Analyze Cause and Effect:** What does this saying have to do with her decision to allow Aaron to keep the injured bird until it recovers?
4. **(a) Recall:** What happened to Aaron's grandmother as a child? **(b) Analyze Cause and Effect:** How does the grandmother's childhood experience help Aaron decide what to give her for her birthday?
5. **(a) Recall:** What does Carl want to do with Pidge? **(b) Compare and Contrast:** How are Carl and the boys like the Cossacks?
6. **(a) Draw Conclusions:** Why is Aaron's grandmother happy that Pidge is set free? **(b) Evaluate:** Which is the better gift: the pigeon or the pigeon's freedom? Explain. **(c) Apply:** What are two other "gifts" that are not physical things that one person can give to another?

Myron Levoy

(b. 1930)

Myron Levoy has loved reading ever since he was a boy growing up in New York City. He studied to be a chemical engineer but soon turned to writing as a career. Most of his stories and novels focus on the teen or child who is somehow an outsider or a loner. These characters feel separation from what they think is the normal teen experience. Levoy's most well-known work, a novel called *Alan and Naomi*, has been made into a film. Levoy has also written works for adults.

Answers for p. 119

Review and Assess

1. Some students may say that they would join because they would like to belong. Others may say that they would not join, especially if a parent or teacher warned them not to do it.
2. **(a)** While skating in the park, Aaron finds Pidge with a broken wing. **(b)** Aaron may feel sorry for the bird or may want a pet. **(c)** Aaron's actions show that he is a sensitive and thoughtful person who is quick-thinking.
3. **(a)** The reference recalls Moses leading the Hebrews out of Egypt around 1300 B.C. **(b)** Aaron's family might be new to the area and not know a lot of people, or they might be the only Jewish family in the neighborhood. **(c)** Aaron's mother might see the bird as a lost creature who needs friends just as she and her family do.
4. **(a)** His grandmother's village was attacked by Cossack soldiers, and her house and her pet goat were destroyed. **(b)** Aaron hopes Pidge might replace the goat his grandmother lost when she was a child.
5. **(a)** Carl wants to throw Pidge into the fire. **(b)** Carl and the boys are like the Cossacks because they both are cruel and try to hurt innocent people or animals.
6. **(a)** Aaron's grandmother knows how important freedom is, and she wants other creatures to enjoy freedom. **(b)** Students will probably suggest that the pigeon's freedom is more important because the bird can live as it is meant to and still make the grandmother happy. **(c)** Two possible gifts include love and friendship.

CUSTOMIZE INSTRUCTION FOR UNIVERSAL ACCESS

For Gifted/Talented Students	For Advanced Learners
Ask students to further characterize Aaron and his grandmother. First, they should list all details from the story. Then, they should make inferences and develop a complete physical description of the characters. Have students consider Aaron's and his grandmother's expressions, including his grandmother when she was a child during the pogrom. Students should consider how the characters speak, how they characteristically move, and so on.	As students read, have them note details about the story's setting. Point out that even though the setting is not stated directly, students can make inferences from details included in the story. Once they make those inferences, have them discuss what impact setting has on the story. Ask students to consider how a change in the setting, such as a different season or a different location, would affect the story.

20 About the Selection

In "Water," Helen Keller describes her first experiences with Miss Sullivan, her new teacher. Although Keller learns to hand-spell certain words, she does not understand what the words mean. Keller's frustration and impatience cause her to act destructively. Finally, after many attempts, Keller grasps the idea that a word Sullivan is spelling—*water*—corresponds to the water flowing over Keller's hand. This communication insight leads Keller to make connections that open doors of knowledge and opportunity previously closed to her.

21 ▶Critical Viewing

Answer: The woman's wide eyes and open mouth indicate anticipation of what she hopes the girl is about to discover. The girl's intense expression shows her focus on the process of discovery.

20 Water

HELEN KELLER

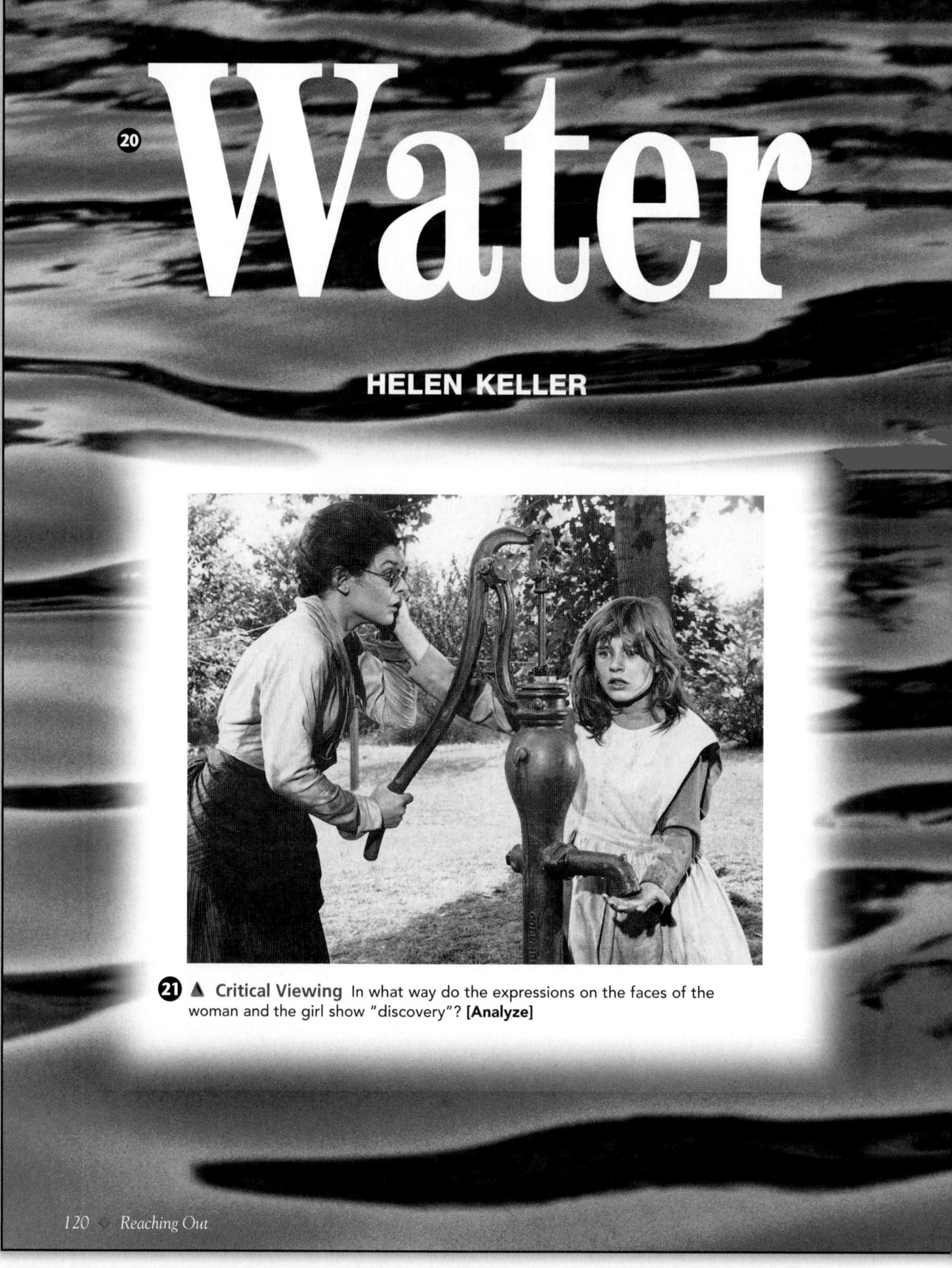

21 ▲ **Critical Viewing** In what way do the expressions on the faces of the woman and the girl show "discovery"? **[Analyze]**

CUSTOMIZE INSTRUCTION FOR UNIVERSAL ACCESS

For Gifted/Talented Students

Remind students that a mural is a large artwork that is displayed or created directly on a building wall. Discuss the types of images that might appear on a mural honoring someone: pictures of the person, places he or she has lived, and objects or events important to the person. Invite students to research Helen Keller's life, using encyclopedia articles and her autobiography, or by viewing Internet Web sites. Have students brainstorm what to include on a mural, writing or sketching their ideas. Tape long strips of butcher paper to the walls. Referring to their written plans or sketches as they work, students can use colored markers, crayons, tempera paints, or magazine cutouts to create their murals. Display the completed murals for the class, and have students explain why they included certain images. Murals should show variety in design and accuracy of information.

The morning after my teacher came she led me into her room and gave me a doll. The little blind children at the Perkins Institution had sent it and Laura Bridgman had dressed it; but I did not know this until afterward. When I had played with it a little while, Miss Sullivan slowly spelled into my hand the word "d-o-l-l." I was at once interested in this finger play and tried to imitate it. When I finally succeeded in making the letters correctly I was flushed with childish pleasure and pride. Running downstairs to my mother I held up my hand and made the letters for doll. I did not know that I was spelling a word or even that words existed; I was simply making my fingers go in monkey-like imitation. In the days that followed I learned to spell in this uncomprehending way a great many words, among them
22 *pin, hat, cup* and a few verbs like *sit, stand* and *walk*. But my teacher had been with me several weeks before I understood that everything has a name.

One day, while I was playing with my new doll, Miss Sullivan put my big rag doll into my lap also, spelled "d-o-l-l" and tried to make me understand that "d-o-l-l" applied to both. Earlier in the day we had had a tussle over the words "m-u-g" and "w-a-t-e-r." Miss Sullivan had tried to impress it upon me that "m-u-g" is *mug* and that "w-a-t-e-r" is *water*, but I persisted in confounding the two. In despair she had dropped the subject for the time, only to renew it at the first opportunity. I became impatient at her repeated attempts and, seizing the new doll, I dashed it upon the floor. I was keenly delighted when I felt the fragments of the broken doll at my feet. Neither sorrow nor regret followed my passionate outburst. I had not loved the doll. In the still, dark world in which I lived there was no strong sentiment or tenderness. I felt my teacher sweep the fragments to one side of the hearth,[1] and I had a sense of satisfaction that the cause of my discomfort was removed. She brought me my hat, and I knew I was going out into the warm sunshine. This thought, if a wordless sensation may be called a thought, made me hop and skip with pleasure.

We walked down the path to the well-house, attracted by the fra-
23 grance of the honeysuckle with which it was covered. Some one was drawing water and my teacher placed my hand under the spout. As the cool stream gushed over one hand she spelled into the other the

Literary Analysis
Climax In what way does this statement start building interest?

Reading Strategy
Using Context to Clarify Meaning How do you know that in this context, *drawing water* means making water come from the pump?

24 **✓Reading Check**
What is Miss Sullivan trying to teach Helen?

1. **hearth** (härth) *n.* stone or brick floor of a fireplace, sometimes stretching out into the room.

22 Literary Analysis
Climax

- Tell students that there are some clues in the first paragraph that foreshadow Keller's later success. Challenge students to find them.
  Answer: Keller says that she did not know things "until afterward," and then she says "in the days that followed" she would learn how to spell many names.
- Next, read aloud the Literary Analysis question on p. 121: In what way does this statement start building interest?
  Answer: Students may wonder how Keller could learn to spell words without understanding what they meant.

23 Reading Strategy
Using Context to Clarify Meaning

- Have a volunteer read aloud the bracketed passage.
- Then, ask students the Reading Strategy question: How do you know that in this context, *drawing water* means making water come from the pump?
  Answer: Students should answer that the meaning is clarified by "placed my hand under the spout." People place their hands or a bucket under the spout from a well when they draw water.

24 ✓Reading Check

Answer: Miss Sullivan is trying to teach Helen to understand the connection between a thing and its name. She is also trying to teach Helen how to spell and, therefore, to communicate.

CUSTOMIZE INSTRUCTION FOR UNIVERSAL ACCESS

For Less Proficient Readers	For English Learners	For Advanced Readers
To help students better understand Helen Keller's view of the world, have them use the Sensory Language chart on p. 81 of **Writing Models and Graphic Organizers on Transparencies** to describe a simple, everyday object, such as an apple. After they complete the chart, have students cross out the Sight and Sound sections.	Students may have a special understanding of Helen Keller's impatience and frustration with language. Invite them to write a brief journal entry in which they describe their own experiences with a new language and its barriers to their communication.	To help students understand Helen Keller's world, challenge them to describe objects they cannot see. Assign students to work in pairs. Ask one student to wear a blindfold and provide that student with an object to describe by touch, smell, or taste. Ask students to handle the objects and describe what the objects feel like.

ASSESS

Answers for p. 122

Review and Assess

1. Students may suggest that Helen should be excused because she did not understand what she was doing.
2. **(a)** Helen breaks the doll. **(b)** She breaks the doll because she is angry and frustrated.
3. **(a)** Feeling the water as Annie Sullivan spells the word into her hand helps Helen make the connection between water and its name. **(b)** The water from the pump is different from the water in the mug because it is not being contained, it is on its own. **(c)** Helen has learned the word *water* before, but she couldn't differentiate it from the mug it was in.
4. **(a)** Helen also learns the words *mother, father, sister,* and *teacher.* **(b)** She probably remembers them because they are important words that have deep emotional meanings attached to them.
5. **(a)** Helen is happy and eager to learn. **(b)** She is happy because now she knows that there is much to learn about the world. **(c)** Students may suggest that the most valuable part of being able to communicate is sharing ideas and feelings with loved ones.

word *water,* first slowly, then rapidly. I stood still, my whole attention fixed upon the motions of her fingers. Suddenly I felt a misty consciousness as of something forgotten—a thrill of returning thought; and somehow the mystery of language was revealed to me. I knew then that "w-a-t-e-r" meant the wonderful cool something that was flowing over my hand. That living word awakened my soul, gave it light, hope, joy, set it free! There were barriers still, it is true, but barriers that could in time be swept away.

I left the well-house eager to learn. Everything had a name, and each name gave birth to a new thought. As we returned to the house every object which I touched seemed to quiver with life. That was because I saw everything with the strange, new sight that had come to me. On entering the door I remembered the doll I had broken. I felt my way to the hearth and picked up the pieces. I tried vainly to put them together. Then my eyes filled with tears; for I realized what I had done, and for the first time I felt repentance and sorrow.

I learned a great many new words that day. I do not remember what they all were; but I do know that *mother, father, sister, teacher* were among them—words that were to make the world blossom for me, "like Aaron's rod, with flowers." It would have been difficult to find a happier child than I was as I lay in my crib at the close of that eventful day and lived over the joys it had brought me, and for the first time longed for a new day to come.

Review and Assess

Thinking About the Selection

1. **Respond:** Do you think Helen should be excused for her behavior before she learned to communicate? Explain.
2. (a) **Recall:** What does Helen do to the doll? (b) **Infer:** Why does she do it?
3. (a) **Recall:** What event helps Helen recognize the meaning of "water"? (b) **Compare and Contrast:** How is the water from the pump different from the water in the mug? (c) **Draw Conclusions:** How does the difference between the water from the pump and the water in the mug make it possible for her finally to understand?
4. (a) **Recall:** What are two other words Helen remembers learning that day? (b) **Infer:** Why are those the words she remembers?
5. (a) **Recall:** How does Helen feel when she goes to bed that night? (b) **Infer:** Why does she feel that way? (c) **Evaluate:** What is the most valuable part of being able to communicate?

Helen Keller

(1880–1968)

Helen Keller was cut off from the world by an illness that left her deaf and blind at the age of one and one-half years.

In 1887, Helen was rescued from her darkness by a gifted teacher, Annie Sullivan, who came to live with her. Annie taught Helen the manual alphabet. Helen learned to communicate using this finger spelling. Eventually, Helen learned to speak by feeling the vibrations in Sullivan's throat with her hands and copying them. In "Water," from her autobiography, Helen describes the moment she learned to communicate.

ASSESSMENT PRACTICE: Reading Comprehension

Recognize Facts and Details (For more practice, see Test Preparation Workbook, p. 10.)

In many tests, students will have to demonstrate reading comprehension by identifying details. Use this example to help students practice the skill.

Aaron skated back and forth on the wide walkway of the park. . . . During his third lap around the racecourse he noticed a pigeon on the grass behaving very strangely. Aaron skated to the line of benches, then climbed over onto the lawn.

Which detail in the passage gives a clue to why Aaron stops skating?

A The race is over.
B He needs a rest.
C The walkway is too crowded.
D He wants to see a pigeon.

The details in the passage do not support *A, B,* or *C.* Choice *D* is correct. Aaron saw a pigeon behaving strangely, and he went to investigate.

Review and Assess

Literary Analysis

Climax

1. What event is the **climax**, or turning point, in "Aaron's Gift"?
2. What is the climax in "Water"?
3. Fill out a graphic organizer like the one shown here for "Water" to explore two possible outcomes for the climax of "Aaron's Gift." Circle the actual outcome.

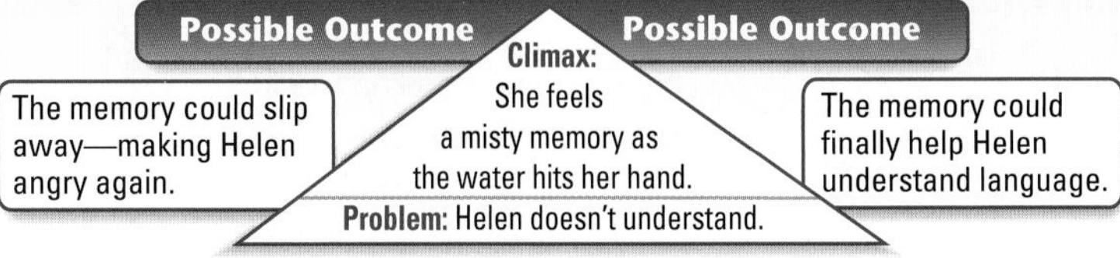

Possible Outcome
Possible Outcome
Climax: She feels a misty memory as the water hits her hand.
The memory could slip away—making Helen angry again.
The memory could finally help Helen understand language.
Problem: Helen doesn't understand.

Comparing Literary Works

4. How is Aaron's problem different from Helen's?
5. In what way does each character solve his or her problem by reaching out?

Reading Strategy

Using Context to Clarify Meaning

Copy the numbered sentence. Then, copy the lettered sentence that uses the italicized word in the same way. Explain how **context** helps you make your choice.

6. The runners finished their last *lap*.
   (a) Miss Sullivan put my big rag doll into my *lap*.
   (b) During his third *lap* around the racecourse, he noticed a pigeon on the grass.
7. Miss Sullivan had tried to *impress* it upon me that m-u-g is mug.
   (a) Miss Sullivan wanted to *impress* me with her knowledge.
   (b) Miss Sullivan wanted to *impress* upon me the importance of language.

Extending Understanding

8. **Career Connection:** Based on what you know about Aaron's interests, actions, and personality, what careers do you think he should consider?

Quick Review

The **climax** of a story is the turning point at which the outcome of the conflict becomes clear. To review climax, see page 111.

Context is the situation in which a word is used: the surrounding words, sentences, and paragraphs.

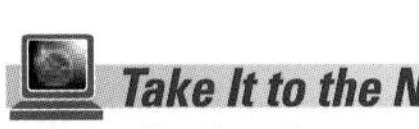

www.phschool.com

Take the interactive self-test online to check your understanding of these selections.

Answers for p. 123

Review and Assess

1. The climax in "Aaron's Gift" occurs when the pigeon flies away.
2. The climax in "Water" occurs when Helen Keller understands the meaning of the word *water*.
3. Problem: Aaron wants to give his grandmother a pigeon and join a gang.
   Climax: When the boys try to hurt the pigeon, it flies away.
   Possible Outcome: Pidge could have been killed, and the boys might have hurt Aaron.
   Possible Outcome: The pigeon could have escaped, and Aaron might have learned the meaning of the gift of freedom.
4. Aaron wants to be accepted in the world and make people happy. Helen does not understand that there is a large world to learn about and know.
5. Both Aaron and Helen learn that happiness can be caused by a thoughtful gesture or a simple connection to another person.
6. **(b)** During his third *lap* around the racecourse, he noticed a pigeon on the grass.
7. **(b)** Miss Sullivan wanted to impress upon me the importance of language.
8. Aaron would probably make a good veterinarian.

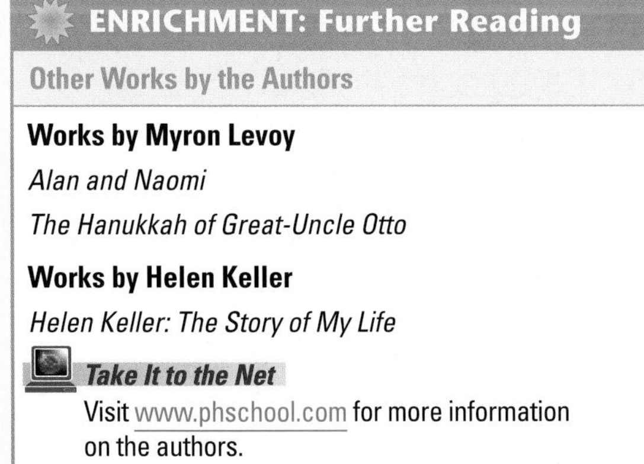

ENRICHMENT: Further Reading

Other Works by the Authors

Works by Myron Levoy

Alan and Naomi

The Hanukkah of Great-Uncle Otto

Works by Helen Keller

Helen Keller: The Story of My Life

Take It to the Net

Visit www.phschool.com for more information on the authors.

EXTEND

Answers for p. 124

❶ Vocabulary Development

Word Analysis

1. c
2. a
3. b

Spelling Strategy

1. merriment
2. cried
3. replied
4. journeying

Fluency: Sentence Completions

1. coaxed
2. frenzied
3. mascot
4. coaxing
5. consoled
6. frenzied
7. consoled

❷ Grammar

1. The pigeon's heart was beating fast.
2. The boys were waiting for Aaron.
3. You should have seen Helen's face.
4. He should not join.
5. She will remember.

Writing Application
Possible responses:

1. Aaron must have worried when he saw the fire.
2. Only Annie Sullivan could help Helen learn to spell.
3. Aaron should have listened to his mother.

Integrate Language Skills

❶ Vocabulary Development Lesson

Word Analysis: Forms of *console*

Console means "to comfort." On a piece of paper, match each form of *console* with its definition.

1. consolation
2. console
3. inconsolable

a. give comfort
b. unable to be comforted
c. comfort

Spelling Strategy

When adding an ending to a word that ends in *y*, usually follow these rules: If a consonant comes before the final *y*, change the *y* to *i* unless the ending begins with *i*, as in cry + *-ing* = crying. If a vowel comes before the final *y*, just add the ending, as in play + *-ed* = played.

Write the correct spelling for the following.

1. merry + *-ment*
2. cry + *-ed*
3. reply + *-ed*
4. journey + *-ing*

Fluency: Sentence Completions

On your paper, write the vocabulary word that belongs in each numbered sentence. Some words are used more than once.

1. Aaron __?__ the pigeon to eat the crumbs.
2. Pidge's __?__ movements showed the bird's fear.
3. They said a pigeon would be a good __?__.
4. The smoke from the fire was __?__ tears from Aaron's eyes.
5. If Pidge had died, could anyone have __?__ Aaron?
6. Aaron slipped into a __?__ anger when the boys attacked him.
7. In some ways, Aaron's grandmother __?__ him on the loss of the pigeon.

❷ Grammar Lesson

Verb Phrases

A **verb phrase** is a group of words made up of a main verb and one or more helping verbs. Verbs that can act as helping verbs include *do*, *will*, *should*, and the forms of *be*. The helping verb helps indicate the tense of the verb. In the example, the helping verb is underlined once. The main verb is underlined twice.

Helen *was playing* with a new doll.

The word *not* sometimes appears between a main verb and a helping verb.

She *did* not *know*.

Practice Copy these sentences. Underline each helping verb once and each main verb twice.

1. The pigeon's heart was beating fast.
2. The boys were waiting for Aaron.
3. You should have seen Helen's face.
4. He should not join.
5. She will remember.

Writing Application On separate paper, write three sentences about Aaron or Helen. Use each of the following verb phrases at least once. You may use the word *not* between parts of the verb phrase.

1. must have worried
2. could help
3. should have listened

WG *Prentice Hall Writing and Grammar Connection: Chapter 15, Section 2*

TEACHING RESOURCES

The following resources can be used to enrich or extend the instruction for pp. 124–125.

Vocabulary

Selection Support: Build Vocabulary, p. 36; Build Spelling Skills, p. 37

Vocabulary and Spelling Practice Book (Use this booklet for skills enrichment)

Grammar

Selection Support: Build Grammar Skills, p. 38

Writing and Grammar, Copper Level, p. 320

Daily Language Practice Transparencies

Writing

Writing and Grammar, Copper Level, p. 108

Writing Models and Graphic Organizers on Transparencies, p. 61

Writing and Grammar iText CD-ROM

BLOCK SCHEDULING: Resources marked with this symbol provide varied instruction during 90-minute blocks.

❸ Writing Lesson

Interview

Aaron learned about his grandmother's past by talking to her. Interview an older person you know. An interview is a formal conversation in which one person asks questions, and the other person answers them. Write a record of your interview, including your comments.

Prewriting Organize your questions in categories. Conduct the interview, taking careful notes. You might use a tape recorder as well.

Model: Organizing Questions by Category

People	Activities	School	Events
Who was the most popular celebrity?	What did you like to do on weekends?	What subjects did you study?	What is your most vivid memory?

Use some of these sample categories and questions, but add your own as well. For examples of interview questions, see the interview with Jerry Spinelli, p. 150.

Drafting Begin by introducing the subject of your interview. Then, write questions and answers from each category. Include your comments, such as why you asked a question. Use formatting or labels to distinguish between your words and the subject's.

Revising When you revise, strengthen your organization by making sure information is presented in categories.

WG Prentice Hall Writing and Grammar Connection: Chapter 6, Section 4

❹ Extension Activities

Listening and Speaking Annie Sullivan taught Helen Keller how to communicate with sign language. In small teams, conduct research on American Sign Language. Then, **present a program** on American Sign Language using these guidelines.

1. Select a focus for each team; for example, explain the development of sign language, demonstrate its use, and show diagrams.
2. Plan the organization of the presentation: what to include and in what order.
3. Adjust volume and pacing for your audience.

Practice the oral delivery before presenting.

Research and Technology As an adult, Helen Keller attended college and wrote her autobiography. Research the devices Keller used to read and write. Then, find out what devices are used by deaf and blind people today. Make a **chart** of some technological advances that have been made in tools for people with physical disabilities since Keller's time.

 ***Take It to the Net*** www.phschool.com

Go online for an additional research activity using the Internet.

Lesson Support for p. 125

❸ Writing Lesson

- Remind students that the best way to approach an interview is to ask: Who?, What?, Where? Why?, When?, and How?.
- Suggest that students make a six-column chart, placing a question at the top of each column.
- Next, have students brainstorm possible questions. Then, have them place the questions in the categories for the graphic organizer on p. 125.
- Use the Exposition rubric on p. 12 in **Performance Assessment and Portfolio Management** to evaluate students' interview questions.

❹ Listening and Speaking

- Assign students to small groups. You may wish to assign topics for their presentations in order to save time.
- Consider asking the school librarian or an expert on American Sign Language to speak to students in order to give them direction for their research and their presentations.
- Have students use the Speaking rubric on p. 29 in **Performance Assessment and Portfolio Management.**

CUSTOMIZE INSTRUCTION For Universal Access

To address different learning styles, use the activities in the **Extension Activities** booklet, p. 8.

- For Visual/Spatial Learners, use Activity 5.
- For Bodily/Kinesthetic and Interpersonal Learners, use Activity 6.
- For Intrapersonal and Verbal/Linguistic Learners, use Activity 7.

ASSESSMENT RESOURCES

The following resources can be used to assess students' knowledge and skills.

Selection Assessment

- **Formal Assessment,** pp. 30–32
- **Open Book Test,** pp. 22–24
- **Got It! Assessment Videotapes,** Tape 1
- **Test Bank Software**

Take It to the Net

Visit www.phschool.com for self-tests and additional questions on the selections.

Writing Rubric

- **Performance Assess. and Portfolio Mgmt.,** p. 12

Listening and Speaking Rubric

- **Performance Assess. and Portfolio Mgmt.,** p. 29

PRENTICE HALL ASSESSMENT SYSTEM

- **Workbook**
- **Skill Book**
- **Transparencies**
- **CD-ROM**

Zlateh the Goat

Lesson Objectives

1. **To analyze and respond to literary elements**
   - Literary Analysis: Conflict With Nature
   - Connecting Literary Elements: Setting
2. **To read, comprehend, analyze, and critique a short story**
   - Reading Strategy: Summarizing
   - Reading Check Questions
   - Review and Assess Questions
   - Assessment Practice (ATE)
3. **To develop word analysis skills, fluency, and systematic vocabulary**
   - Vocabulary Development Lesson: Word Analysis: Latin Prefix *ex-*
4. **To understand and apply written and oral language conventions**
   - Spelling Strategy
   - Grammar Lesson: Principle Parts of Verbs
5. **To understand and apply appropriate writing and research strategies**
   - Writing Lesson: Persuasive Speech
   - Extension Activity: Presentation
6. **To understand and apply listening and speaking strategies**
   - Extension Activity: Monologue

STEP-BY-STEP TEACHING GUIDE	PACING GUIDE
PRETEACH	
Motivate Students and Provide Background	
Use the Motivation activity (ATE p. 126)	5 min.
Read and discuss the Preview material and Background information (SE/ATE p. 126) [A]	5 min.
Introduce the Concepts	
Introduce the Literary Analysis and Reading Strategy (SE/ATE p. 127) [A]	15 min.
Pronounce the vocabulary words and read their definitions (SE p. 127)	5 min.
TEACH	
Monitor Comprehension	
Informally monitor comprehension by circulating while students read independently or in groups [A]	15–20 min.
Monitor students' comprehension with the Reading Check notes (SE/ATE pp. 129, 131, 133)	as students read
Develop vocabulary with Vocabulary notes (SE pp. 129, 131, 133; ATE p. 131)	as students read
Develop Understanding	
Develop students' understanding of conflict with nature with the Literary Analysis annotations (SE pp. 129, 132; ATE pp. 129, 132) [A]	5 min.
Develop students' ability to summarize with the Reading Strategy annotations (SE pp. 131, 133; ATE pp. 131, 133)	5 min.
ASSESS	
Assess Mastery	
Assess students' mastery of the Reading Strategy and Literary Analysis by having them answer the Review and Assess questions (SE/ATE p. 134)	15 min.
Use one or more of the print and media Assessment Resources (ATE p. 137) [A]	up to 45 min.
EXTEND	
Apply Understanding	
Have students complete the Vocabulary Development Lesson and the Grammar Lesson (SE p. 136) [A]	20 min.
Apply students' ability to write a persuasive speech using the Writing Lesson (SE/ATE p. 137) [A]	30–45 min.
Apply students' understanding using one or more of the Extension Activities (SE p. 137)	20–90 min.

[A] **ACCELERATED INSTRUCTION:**
Use the strategies and activities identified with an [A].

UNIVERSAL ACCESS
● = Below Level Students
▲ = On-Level Students
■ = Above Level Students

Time and Resource Manager

Reading Level: Average
Average Number of Instructional Days: 3

RESOURCES		
PRINT	**TRANSPARENCIES**	**TECHNOLOGY**
• **Beyond Literature,** Study Skills: Map Reading, p. 9 ▲ ■		• **Interest Grabber Videotapes,** Tape 1 ● ▲ ■
• **Selection Support Workbook:** ● ▲ ■ Literary Analysis, p. 45 Reading Strategy, p. 44 Build Vocabulary, p. 41	• **Literary Analysis and Reading Transparencies,** pp. 17 and 18 ● ▲ ■	
• **Adapted Reader's Companion** ● • **Reader's Companion** ● • **Authors In Depth,** Copper Level, p. 24 ■		• **Listening to Literature** ● ▲ ■ Audiocassettes, Side 6 Audio CDs, CD 3
• **English Learner's Companion** ● ▲ • **Literatura en español** ● ▲ • **Literary Analysis for Enrichment** ■		
• **Formal Assessment:** Selection Test, pp. 33–35 ● ▲ ■ • **Open Book Test,** pp. 25–27 ● ▲ ■ • **Performance Assessment and Portfolio Management,** pp. 27, 51 ● ▲ ■ • PRENTICE HALL ASSESSMENT SYSTEM ● ▲ ■	• PRENTICE HALL ASSESSMENT SYSTEM ● ▲ ■ Skills Practice Answers and Explanations on Transparencies	• **Test Bank Software** ● ▲ ■ • **Got It! Assessment Videotapes,** Tape 1 ● ▲
• **Selection Support Workbook:** ● ▲ ■ Build Spelling Skills, p. 42 Build Grammar Skills, p. 43 • **Writing and Grammar,** Copper Level ● ▲ ■ • **Extension Activities,** p. 9 ● ▲ ■	• **Daily Language Practice Transparencies** ● ▲ • **Writing Models and Graphic Organizers on Transparencies** ● ▲ ■	• **Writing and Grammar iText CD-ROM** ● ▲ ■ ***Take It to the Net*** www.phschool.com

BLOCK SCHEDULING: Use one 90-minute class period to preteach the selection and have students read it. Use a second 90-minute class period to assess students' mastery of skills and have them complete one of the Extension Activities.

PRETEACH

Step-by-Step Teaching Guide for pp. 126–127

Motivation

Display a photograph of a wintry scene in which everything is covered by a blanket of snow and ice. Ask students to describe how they would feel if they were lost in such a setting and were unable to find shelter. Write their ideas on the board. Then, tell students that the characters in the story face such a challenge. Encourage students, as they read, to compare their ideas with the thoughts and actions of the characters.

Interest Grabber Video

As an alternative, play "Survival in the Wild" on Tape 1 to engage student interest.

❶ Background

Health

In "Zlateh the Goat," Aaron faces the danger of getting frostbite when he is lost in a terrible snow storm. Frostbite can occur when skin is exposed to extremely cold temperatures. It is a condition in which the water in the skin, blood, and muscles begins to freeze. Just as water turns to ice, ice crystals form in the skin and muscles and prevent blood from circulating in that area of the body. Without blood to warm and nourish those cells, they break down and die.

Prepare to Read

❶ Zlateh the Goat

Take It to the Net

Visit www.phschool.com for interactive activities and instruction related to "Zlateh the Goat," including

- background
- graphic organizers
- literary elements
- reading strategies

Preview

Connecting to the Literature

In "Zlateh the Goat," snow becomes a deadly enemy for a boy and a goat, who must help each other survive a snowstorm. Think about times when weather has created problems or dangerous situations for you or someone you know.

Background

Aaron in "Zlateh the Goat" is lost outdoors in a winter storm. He runs the risk of frostbite and hypothermia. When hypothermia occurs, the body temperature drops below normal and breathing slows. If the victim is not warmed, he or she becomes unconscious.

TEACHING RESOURCES

The following resources can be used to enrich or extend the instruction for pp. 126–127.

Motivation

Interest Grabber Video, Tape 1

Background

Beyond Literature, p. 9

Take It to the Net

Visit www.phschool.com for Background and hotlinks for "Zlateh the Goat."

Literary Analysis

Literary Analysis and Reading Transparencies, Conflict With Nature, p. 18

Reading

Selection Support Workbook: Reading Strategy, p. 44; Build Vocabulary, p. 41

Literary Analysis and Reading Transparencies, Summarizing, p. 17

BLOCK SCHEDULING: Resources marked with this symbol provide varied instruction during 90-minute blocks.

❷ Literary Analysis

Conflict with Nature

Stories develop around a conflict, a struggle between opposing forces. In a **conflict with nature,** a character or characters struggle against a natural element. In "Zlateh the Goat," two characters battle a blizzard.

> Aaron did not want to admit the danger, but he knew just the same that if they did not find shelter they would freeze to death. This was no ordinary storm. It was a mighty blizzard.

How the conflict will turn out is a question of life and death.

Connecting Literary Elements

A story's **setting** is the time and place of the action. In many stories, especially stories about a conflict with nature, the setting contributes to the conflict. In "Zlateh the Goat," the time is winter in the days before cars. The place is rural Eastern Europe in an area where houses and villages are far apart. Think about these focus questions as you read.

1. What natural elements are a result of the time of the setting?
2. What details of the place add to Aaron's problems?

❸ Reading Strategy

Summarizing

You can better understand what is going on in a story if you pause occasionally to **summarize**—to review what has happened so far. Summarize using the following steps:

1. Identify the main events.
2. Organize them in the order in which they happen.
3. Note when one event causes another event.

As you read "Zlateh the Goat," pause at the events indicated on the timeline. Summarize what has happened up to that point by noting main events on a timeline of your own.

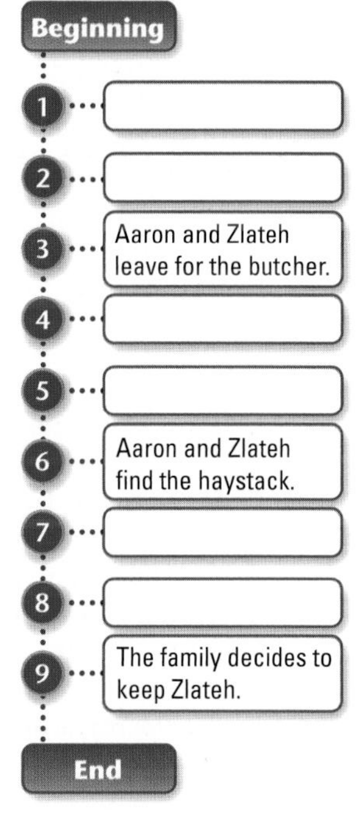

Beginning
1
2
3 Aaron and Zlateh leave for the butcher.
4
5
6 Aaron and Zlateh find the haystack.
7
8
9 The family decides to keep Zlateh.
End

Vocabulary Development

bound (bound) *v.* tied (p. 129)

conclusion (kən klo͞o′ zhən) *n.* belief or decision reached by reasoning (p. 129)

rapidly (rap′ id lē) *adv.* quickly (p. 129)

exuded (eg zyo͞od′ əd) *v.* gave off; oozed; radiated (p. 131)

trace (trās) *n.* mark left behind by something (p. 133)

CUSTOMIZE INSTRUCTION FOR UNIVERSAL ACCESS

For Special Needs Students	For Less Proficient Readers	For English Learners
Have students read the adapted version of "Zlateh the Goat" in the **Adapted Reader's Companion.** This version provides basic-level instruction in an interactive format with questions and write-on lines. Completing the adapted version will prepare students to read the selection in the Student Edition.	Have students read "Zlateh the Goat" in the **Reader's Companion.** This version provides basic-level instruction in an interactive format with questions and write-on lines. After students finish the selection in the Reader's Companion, have them complete the questions and activities in the Student Edition.	Have students read the adapted version of "Zlateh the Goat" in the **English Learner's Companion.** This version provides basic-level instruction in an interactive format with questions and write-on lines. Completing the adapted version will prepare students to read the selection in the Student Edition.

❷ Literary Analysis

Conflict With Nature

- Tell students that as they read "Zlateh the Goat," they will focus on conflict with nature.
- Before students read the Literary Analysis instruction on p. 127, ask them to describe their favorite season. If answers focus on the positive sides of each season, guide students toward the destructive and unpredictable sides of nature.
- Then, have students read the instruction silently. Before they read Connecting Literary Elements, ask them to recall what they know about setting.
- Finally, show students the Conflict with Nature transparency on p. 18 in **Literary Analysis and Reading Transparencies.** Explain the first entry. Tell students that they will fill in the organizer after they finish the story.

❸ Reading Strategy

Summarizing

- Ask students to think of times when it is necessary to give a summary. Students may suggest describing a movie, a book, or a poem to someone.
- Have students read the Reading Strategy instruction on p. 127 before showing them the Summarize transparency on p. 17 of **Literary Analysis and Reading Transparencies.** Point out that students will need to identify other key events of the story.
- Then, demonstrate the skill by summarizing the contents of an article or a daily event in one or two sentences. Point out how you reduced details to one main idea.

Vocabulary Development

- Pronounce each vocabulary word for students, and read the definitions as a class. Have students identify any words with which they are already familiar.

E-Teach

Visit E-Teach at www.phschool.com for teachers' essays on how to teach, with questions and answers.

TEACH

Step-by-Step Teaching Guide for pp. 128–134

CUSTOMIZE INSTRUCTION
For Interpersonal Learners

Have groups of students discuss and give examples of the ways animals express themselves. For example, cats purr when they are content and hiss when they are frightened. Encourage students to debate whether animals can actually communicate their thoughts and feelings.

1 About the Selection

The mild winter has been bad for Aaron's father's fur business. Hanukkah is approaching, but the family does not have enough money to buy the things they need for the celebration. Aaron is told to take Zlateh, the family's goat, and sell her to the butcher. As Aaron sadly leads her off to town, the weather begins to change. Before long, a blizzard and blowing snow cause Aaron to lose his way. Aaron and Zlateh become lost in the terrible snowstorm and take shelter in a snow-covered haystack. For three days, Zlateh eats hay, and Aaron drinks Zlateh's milk. When the weather clears, Aaron takes Zlateh home, where they are both welcomed.

2 ▶Critical Viewing

Answer: Students might suggest that the goat would say "I wonder where we are going now," or "I like being with Aaron."

1 

Isaac Bashevis Singer

At Hanukkah[1] time the road from the village to the town is usually covered with snow, but this year the winter had been a mild one. Hanukkah had almost come, yet little snow had fallen. The sun shone most of the time. The peasants complained that because of the dry weather there would be a poor harvest of winter grain. New grass sprouted, and the peasants sent their cattle out to pasture.

2 ▲ **Critical Viewing** What do you think the goat would say if she could speak? **[Speculate]**

1. **Hanukkah** (khä′ noo kä) Jewish festival celebrated for eight days in early winter. Hanukkah is also called the "festival of lights" because a new candle is lit on each night of Hanukkah—one candle on the first night, two on the second night, and so on.

TEACHING RESOURCES

The following resources can be used to enrich or extend the instruction for pp. 128–134.

Literary Analysis
- **Literary Analysis for Enrichment**
- **Selection Support:** Literary Analysis, p. 45

Reading
- **Reader's Companion**
- **Adapted Reader's Companion**
- **English Learner's Companion**
- **Literatura en español**

- **Listening to Literature Audiocassettes,** Side 6 ■
- **Listening to Literature Audio CDs,** CD 3 ■

Extension
- **Authors In Depth,** Copper Level, p. 24 (This collection includes three additional selections by Isaac Bashevis Singer for extended reading.)

■ **BLOCK SCHEDULING:** Resources marked with this symbol provide varied instruction during 90-minute blocks.

For Reuven the furrier it was a bad year, and after long hesitation he decided to sell Zlateh the goat. She was old and gave little milk. Feivel the town butcher had offered eight gulden[2] for her. Such a sum would buy Hanukkah candles, potatoes and oil for pancakes, gifts for the children, and other holiday necessaries for the house. Reuven told his oldest boy Aaron to take the goat to town.

Aaron understood what taking the goat to Feivel meant, but had to obey his father. Leah, his mother, wiped the tears from her eyes when she heard the news. Aaron's younger sisters, Anna and Miriam, cried loudly. Aaron put on his quilted jacket and a cap with earmuffs, bound a rope around Zlateh's neck, and took along two slices of bread with cheese to eat on the road. Aaron was supposed to deliver the goat by evening, spend the night at the butcher's, and return the next day with the money.

bound (bound) *v.* tied

While the family said goodbye to the goat, and Aaron placed the rope around her neck, Zlateh stood as patiently and good-naturedly as ever. She licked Reuven's hand. She shook her small white beard. Zlateh trusted human beings. She knew that they always fed her and never did her any harm.

3 When Aaron brought her out on the road to town, she seemed somewhat astonished. She'd never been led in that direction before. She looked back at him questioningly, as if to say, "Where are you taking me?" But after a while she seemed to come to the conclusion that a goat shouldn't ask questions. Still, the road was different. They passed new fields, pastures, and huts with thatched roofs. Here and there a dog barked and came running after them, but Aaron chased it away with his stick.

conclusion (kən klo͞o′ zhən) *n.* belief or decision reached by reasoning

4 The sun was shining when Aaron left the village. Suddenly the weather changed. A large black cloud with a bluish center appeared in the east and spread itself rapidly over the sky. A cold wind blew in with it. The crows flew low, croaking. At first it looked as if it would rain, but instead it began to hail as in summer. It was early in the day, but it became dark as dusk. After a while the hail turned to snow.

rapidly (rap′ id lē) *adv.* quickly

In his twelve years Aaron had seen all kinds of weather, but he had never experienced a snow like this one. It was so dense it shut out the light of the day. In a short time their path was completely covered. The wind became as cold as ice. The road to town was narrow and winding. Aaron no longer knew where he was. He could not see through the snow. The cold soon penetrated his quilted jacket.

Literary Analysis
Conflict with Nature
In what two ways are the snow and wind in conflict with Aaron?

5 ✓ **Reading Check**
Why is Aaron taking the goat to Feivel?

2. **gulden** (go͝ol′ dən) *n.* unit of money.

3 Critical Thinking

Interpret

- Ask students what the details in these paragraphs reveal about Zlateh.
  Answer: Zlateh feels safe and secure with the family and has no reason to think that anything bad will happen to her.
- Have students compare their answers to responses they gave to the Critical Viewing question on p. 128. How have their responses changed?
  Possible response: Students may say that Zlateh fears that something bad may happen to her during the snowstorm.

4 Literary Analysis

Conflict With Nature

- Ask students to explain the ways the weather changes in the first paragraph.
  Answer: First, the sun shines; then, a black cloud appears; next, it threatens to rain but hails instead. The sky then turns as dark as dusk, and snow begins to fall.
- Ask students the Literary Analysis question on p. 129: In what two ways are the snow and wind in conflict with Aaron?
  Answer: The wind blows the snow over the road, which causes Aaron to lose his way. The snow does not allow Aaron to see anything in front of him, and the wind causes him to become very cold.

Monitor Progress Ask students to explain why the weather's action is a conflict for Aaron.
Answer: Weather prevents Aaron from going to town and completing the task his father has given him.

5 ✓ Reading Check

Answer: Feivel will pay money for Zlateh. The butcher will turn Zlateh into meat for food.

CUSTOMIZE INSTRUCTION FOR UNIVERSAL ACCESS

For Special Needs Readers	For English Learners	For Advanced Readers
Provide students with Side 8 of **Listening to Literature Audiocassettes.** Tell students first to listen to the story for pleasure. Afterward, ask students to read the story to identify the events in the order they happened. Offer students the Timeline transparency, p. 77 in **Writing Models and Graphic Organizers on Transparencies.**	Display pictures of haystacks, an old-fashioned butcher shop, a snowstorm, a farmer milking a goat or a cow, and a family engaged in a Hanukkah celebration. Assign students to groups, and ask them to read the story aloud. Have one student point to and name pictures that help illustrate what is happening.	Ask students to think about why summaries are useful. Explain that a summary compresses a story by focusing on only its key events and ideas. Challenge students to summarize a story, a book, or a movie and to share their summaries with the class. Have the class try to compress the story even further.

6 Critical Thinking

Interpret

- Point out that the narrator explains that both Zlateh and Aaron are twelve years old. Ask students what significance this has for the relationship between Aaron and Zlateh.
  Possible response: Students may describe the deep attachment that has developed between Aaron and Zlateh.
- Then, encourage students to use their own experiences or details in the story to help them understand how Aaron feels as he takes Zlateh to the butcher.

7 Background

Art; Social Studies

Writer and illustrator Maurice Sendak, who was born in 1928 in Brooklyn, New York, loved books from an early age. He began working as a book illustrator in high school and published his first book at age nineteen. He is best known for his Caldecott Medal-winning book *Where the Wild Things Are.*

Tell students that both Sendak and writer Isaac Bashevis Singer had many relatives in Poland who were killed in the Holocaust during World War II. Explain that the Holocaust essentially wiped out the Jewish populations in the villages.

1. Discuss how this shared experience might have led the two artists to work together on a book that describes Jewish life in small Eastern European villages.
   Answer: They might have wanted to honor their relatives who died.
2. How does the fact that the way of life described in "Zlateh the Goat" no longer exists affect the importance of the writer's and artist's collaboration?
   Answer: It makes their effort even more meaningful because it documents a way of life that has been lost.

8 ▶ Critical Viewing

Possible answers: Zlateh feels stubborn about going and wants to stop. She feels cold and tired and wants to find shelter.

6 At first Zlateh didn't seem to mind the change in weather. She, too, was twelve years old and knew what winter meant. But when her legs sank deeper and deeper into the snow, she began to turn her head and look at Aaron in wonderment. Her mild eyes seemed to ask, "Why are we out in such a storm?" Aaron hoped that a peasant would come along with his cart, but no one passed by.

7

Illustrations copyright © 1966 by Maurice Sendak, copyright renewed 1994 by Maurice Sendak. Printed with permission from HarperCollins Publishers.

The snow grew thicker, falling to the ground in large, whirling flakes. Beneath it Aaron's boots touched the softness of a plowed field. He realized that he was no longer on the road. He had gone astray. He could no longer figure out which was east or west, which way was the village, the town. The wind whistled, howled, whirled the snow about in eddies.[3] It looked as if white imps were playing tag on the fields. A white dust rose above the ground. Zlateh stopped. She could walk no longer. Stubbornly she anchored her cleft hooves in the earth and bleated as if pleading to be taken home. Icicles hung from her white beard, and her horns were glazed with frost.

Aaron did not want to admit the danger, but he knew just the same that if they did not find shelter they would freeze to death. This was no ordinary storm. It was a mighty blizzard. The snow had reached his knees. His hands were numb, and he could no longer feel his toes. He choked when he breathed. His nose felt like wood, and he rubbed it with snow. Zlateh's bleating began to sound like crying. Those humans in whom she had so much confidence had dragged her

8 ▲ **Critical Viewing** What does Zlateh's posture seem to indicate about her feelings? **[Infer]**

3. **eddies** (ed′ ēz) *n.* currents of air moving in circular motions; little whirlwinds.

ENRICHMENT: Social Studies Connection

Hanukkah: The Festival of Lights

Known as the Festival of Lights, the Jewish holiday Hanukkah (also spelled Chanukah) is celebrated for eight days during the Hebrew month of Kislev, which falls during November or December. The word *hanukkah* means "dedication," and the holiday celebrates the rededication of the Temple in Jerusalem after the city was reclaimed from the Syrian Greeks by the Jews in about 165 B.C. To reconsecrate the Temple, the Temple lamp, which was to burn continually, was relit, but there was only enough oil to keep it burning for one day. It would take eight days for priests to prepare more of the special oil. Amazingly, the one-day supply of oil burned steadily until the new oil was ready.

into a trap. Aaron began to pray to God for himself and for the innocent animal.

Suddenly he made out the shape of a hill. He wondered what it could be. Who had piled snow into such a huge heap? He moved toward it, dragging Zlateh after him. When he came near it, he realized that it was a large haystack which the snow had blanketed.

Aaron realized immediately that they were saved. With great effort he dug his way through the snow. He was a village boy and knew what to do. When he reached the hay, he hollowed out a nest for himself and the goat. No matter how cold it may be outside, in the hay it is always warm. And hay was food for Zlateh. The moment she smelled it she became contented and began to eat. Outside, the snow continued to fall. It quickly covered the passageway Aaron had dug. But a boy and an animal need to breathe, and there was hardly any air in their hideout. Aaron bored a kind of a window through the hay and snow and carefully kept the passage clear.

> **9 Reading Strategy**
> **Summarizing** Retell the two most important events since Aaron and Zlateh left home.

Zlateh, having eaten her fill, sat down on her hind legs and seemed to have regained her confidence in man. Aaron ate his two slices of bread and cheese, but after the difficult journey he was still hungry. He looked at Zlateh and noticed her udders were full. He lay down next to her, placing himself so that when he milked her he could squirt the milk into his mouth. It was rich and sweet. Zlateh was not accustomed to being milked that
10 way, but she did not resist. On the contrary, she seemed eager to reward Aaron for bringing her to a shelter whose very walls, floor, and ceiling were made of food.

Through the window Aaron could catch a glimpse of the chaos outside. The wind carried before it whole drifts of snow. It was completely dark, and he did not know whether night had already come or whether it was the darkness of the storm. Thank God that in the hay it was not cold. The dried hay, grass, and field flowers exuded the warmth of the summer sun. Zlateh ate frequently; she nibbled from above, below, from the left and right. Her body gave forth an animal warmth, and Aaron cuddled up to her. He had always loved Zlateh, but now she was like a sister. He was alone, cut off from his family, and wanted to talk. He began to talk to Zlateh. "Zlateh, what do you think about what has happened to us?" he asked.

> **exuded** (eg zyo͞od′ əd) *v.* gave off; oozed; radiated

"Maaaa," Zlateh answered.

"If we hadn't found this stack of hay, we would both be frozen stiff by now," Aaron said.

"Maaaa," was the goat's reply.

"If the snow keeps on falling like this, we may have to stay here for days," Aaron explained.

> **11**  **Reading Check**
> What food and shelter do Aaron and Zlateh have?

9 Reading Strategy

Summarizing

- Pause here to give students time to fill in their summarizing graphic organizers.
- Then, ask students the Reading Strategy question on p. 131: Retell the two most important events since Aaron and Zlateh left home.
  Answer: After Aaron and Zlateh set off for town, the weather changes, and it begins to snow. After losing their way in the deep snow, Aaron finds a haystack, and he and Zlateh climb inside and are saved.

10 Vocabulary Development

Word Analysis: Latin Prefix *ex-*

- Explain that the word *exude* is made up of the Latin prefix *ex-* and another Latin word, *sudare*, meaning "to sweat." In English the word might be used in a sentence like this: "The movie star exudes talent."
- Ask students in what other contexts they might use the word *exude*.
  Answer: The word might be used to describe a person sweating, or a hot sidewalk releasing heat.
- Challenge students to use the word *exude* or *exuded* in a sentence.

11 Reading Check

Answer: The haystack provides them with warmth and shelter from the wind and snow. Zlateh can eat the hay walls and floor of their shelter, and Aaron can drink Zlateh's milk after finishing his bread and cheese.

CUSTOMIZE INSTRUCTION FOR UNIVERSAL ACCESS

For English Learners	For Gifted/Talented Students
Point out that every language has its own way of making and writing animal sounds. Ask students to compile of list of sounds that animals, including a goat, make. Students should write the sounds in their native languages and in English. Invite students to comment on the differences and similarities between the sounds. Be sure students understand how the different sounds translate from their native languages to English.	Point out that, in the story, Aaron interprets Zlateh's bleatings in his own words. Invite students to rewrite the story from Zlateh's point of view. Students should be sure to describe the same events from another point of view. If you wish to save time, consider having students each select a scene to rewrite in Zlateh's "voice," and then ask students to read their scenes aloud to the class in order.

12 Literary Analysis

Conflict With Nature

- Point out that even though Aaron has found shelter, he must be watchful because the storm can still harm them.
- Ask students the Literary Analysis question on p. 132.
  Answer: The falling snow can suffocate Aaron and Zlateh by covering up their window. Also, the snow is so deep that Aaron might not be able to dig his way out of the haystack.

13 ▶Critical Viewing

Answer: Aaron is concerned that he and Zlateh will be stuck inside the haystack until the storm passes.

"Maaaa," Zlateh bleated.

"What does 'Maaaa' mean?" Aaron asked. "You'd better speak up clearly."

"Maaaa-Maaaa," Zlateh tried.

"Well, let it be 'Maaaa' then," Aaron said patiently. "You can't speak, but I know you understand. I need you and you need me. Isn't that right?"

"Maaaa."

Aaron became sleepy. He made a pillow out of some hay, leaned his head on it, and dozed off. Zlateh, too, fell asleep.

12 When Aaron opened his eyes, he didn't know whether it was morning or night. The snow had blocked up his window. He tried to clear it, but when he had bored through to the length of his arm, he still hadn't reached the outside. Luckily he had his stick with him and was able to break through to the open air. It was still dark outside. The snow continued to fall and the wind wailed, first with one voice and then with many. Sometimes it had the sound of devilish laughter. Zlateh, too, awoke, and when Aaron greeted her, she answered, "Maaaa." Yes, Zlateh's language consisted of only one word, but it meant many things. Now she was saying, "We must accept all that God gives us—heat, cold, hunger, satisfaction, light, and darkness."

Literary Analysis
Conflict with Nature In what way are Aaron and Zlateh still in danger from the storm?

▶Critical Viewing
Why does Aaron look downcast in this picture? **[Connect]**

CUSTOMIZE INSTRUCTION FOR UNIVERSAL ACCESS

For Advanced Readers

Suggest that students read additional works by Isaac Bashevis Singer. Provide students with the titles listed in the Enrichment box ATE p. 135. You may also wish to use **Authors In Depth,** Copper Level, which contains the following selections:

- from *Stories for Children*

"Shrewd Todie & Lyzer the Miser" (fiction p. 24)

"Utzel & His Daughter, Poverty" (fiction p. 29)

"The Parakeet Named Dreidel" (fiction p. 32)

After students have read these or other works by Singer, have them form discussion groups in which they compare and contrast the selections they have read. Suggest criteria for comparison, such as setting, conflict, and summarizing. To extend the activity, have volunteers present to the class brief oral reports on their favorite Singer selections.

12 Aaron had awakened hungry. He had eaten up his food, but Zlateh had plenty of milk.

For three days Aaron and Zlateh stayed in the haystack. Aaron had always loved Zlateh, but in these three days he loved her more and more. She fed him with her milk and helped him keep warm. She comforted him with her patience. He told her many stories, and she always cocked her ears and listened. When he patted her, she licked his hand and his face. Then she said, "Maaaa," and he knew it meant, I love you, too.

The snow fell for three days, though after the first day it was not as thick and the wind quieted down. Sometimes Aaron felt that there could never have been a summer, that the snow had always fallen, ever since he could remember. He, Aaron, never had a father or mother or sisters. He was a snow child, born of the snow, and so was Zlateh. It was so quiet in the hay that his ears rang in the stillness. Aaron and Zlateh slept all night and a good part of the day. As for Aaron's dreams, they were all about warm weather. He dreamed of green fields, trees covered with blossoms, clear brooks, and singing birds. By the third night the snow had stopped, but Aaron did not dare to find his way home in the darkness. The sky became clear and the moon shone, casting silvery nets on the snow. Aaron dug his way out and looked at the world. It was all white, quiet, dreaming dreams of heavenly splendor. The stars were large and close. The moon swam in the sky as in a sea.

On the morning of the fourth day Aaron heard the ringing of sleigh bells. The haystack was not far from the road. The peasant who drove the sleigh pointed out the way to him—not to the town and Feivel the butcher, but home to the village. Aaron had decided in the haystack that he would never part with Zlateh.

Aaron's family and their neighbors had searched for the boy and the goat but had found no trace of them during the storm. They feared they were lost. Aaron's mother and sisters cried for him; his father remained silent and gloomy. Suddenly one of the neighbors came running to their house with the news that Aaron and Zlateh were coming up the road.

There was great joy in the family. Aaron told them how he had found the stack of hay and how Zlateh had fed him with her milk. Aaron's sisters kissed and hugged Zlateh and gave her a special treat of chopped carrots and potato peels, which Zlateh gobbled up hungrily.

Nobody ever again thought of selling Zlateh, and now that the cold weather had finally set in, the villagers needed the services

14 **Reading Strategy**
Summarizing Review and summarize the events that have occurred so far.

trace (trās) *n.* mark left behind by something

15 **Reading Check**
How long does the blizzard last?

14 Reading Strategy

Summarizing

- At this point, students should have nearly filled up their timelines or summarizing organizers. Ask students to review their notes before posing the Reading Strategy question.
- Then, have them review and summarize the events that have occurred so far.
  Answer: Aaron and Zlateh were on their way to town when a snowstorm hit. They found their way to a haystack and dug into it for warmth. Zlateh ate hay, and Aaron drank her milk, kept the air hole open, slept, dreamed, and talked to Zlateh to pass the time. After three days, the snow stopped.

15 Reading Check

Answer: The blizzard lasts for three days.

CUSTOMIZE INSTRUCTION FOR UNIVERSAL ACCESS

For Special Needs Students	For Gifted/Talented Students	For Advanced Readers
Struggling readers may not understand the story's conflict because nature is less tangible than a villain. To help students understand nature's part, have them reread the story and chart on a time-line everything the weather "does." For each of the weather's actions, students should note a character's response or reaction.	Invite students to read the story aloud using inflections, varied pitch, and changing rates of speech to create drama. For example, when reading about the blizzard and how the snow is piling up, slow down. Challenge students to invent different voices for Aaron and Zlateh. After students read, discuss how they approached the story.	Students have probably read other stories or novels that center around a conflict with nature. For example, *Hatchet* by Gary Paulsen is a popular one. Have students summarize the plots of their favorite stories or books in which characters are in conflict with nature. Have students analyze the ways in which nature acts as an opposing force.

ASSESS

Answers for p. 134

16 Reading Strategy

Summarizing

Ask students the Reading Strategy question on p. 134: How would you summarize the end of the story to include Zlateh? Answer: Aaron arrives home with Zlateh. His family is so happy that Zlateh helped keep Aaron alive that they decide to keep Zlateh safely at home.

Review and Assess

1. Possible response: The most frightening part occurred when Aaron and Zlateh first became lost and were beginning to freeze.
2. **(a)** Reuven plans to sell Zlateh because business has been slow, and the family needs money for the Hanukkah celebration. **(b)** The decision is difficult because Zlateh is like the family's pet.
3. **(a)** Aaron is supposed to spend the night at the butcher's. **(b)** Aaron plans to stay because the round-trip walk to the butcher would be too long to do in one day.
4. **(a)** Aaron and Zlateh are lost in a blizzard and nearly freeze. Then, Aaron finds a haystack in which they take shelter. **(b)** They could die from the cold or from the lack of food and water. **(c)** The haystack keeps them warm and dry and provides food for Zlateh.
5. **(a)** After staying in the haystack with Zlateh, Aaron realizes that she is like family. **(b)** The message is that friends who trust and care for each other will weather any storm. **(c)** Possible response: Students may say that, when it comes to survival in extraordinary circumstances, the limit of what a person can ask of a friend is much different than it would be in normal circumstances.

of Reuven the furrier once more. When Hanukkah came, Aaron's mother was able to fry pancakes every evening, and Zlateh got her portion, too. Even though Zlateh had her own pen, she often came to the kitchen, knocking on the door with her horns to indicate that she was ready to visit, and she was always admitted. In the evening Aaron, Miriam, and Anna played dreidel.[4] Zlateh sat near the stove watching the children and the flickering of the Hanukkah candles.

Once in a while Aaron would ask her, "Zlateh, do you remember the three days we spent together?"

And Zlateh would scratch her neck with a horn, shake her white bearded head, and come out with the single sound which expressed all her thoughts, and all her love.

16 Reading Strategy
Summarizing How would you summarize the end of the story to include Zlateh?

---

4. **dreidel** (drā′ dəl) *n.* small top with Hebrew letters on each of four sides, spun in a game played by children.

Review and Assess

Thinking About the Selection

1. **Respond:** What do you think is the most frightening part of Aaron's experience?
2. (a) **Recall:** Why does Reuven decide to sell Zlateh? (b) **Infer:** Why is it a difficult decision for him?
3. (a) **Recall:** Where is Aaron supposed to spend the night after delivering the goat? (b) **Draw Conclusions:** Why doesn't Aaron plan to return from the butcher the same day?
4. (a) **Recall:** What happens to Aaron and Zlateh on the way to town? (b) **Deduce:** Why is their situation dangerous? (c) **Synthesize:** Explain how the haystack helps solve their problems.
5. (a) **Draw Conclusions:** Why does the stay in the haystack change Aaron's mind about what he must do with Zlateh? (b) **Apply:** What is this story's message about friendship and trust? (c) **Take a Position:** What is the limit on what one friend can ask of another?

Isaac Bashevis Singer

(1904–1991)

Isaac Bashevis Singer wrote many stories about Polish villages and neighborhoods like the ones he grew up in. Singer moved to the city of Warsaw when he left home. Faced with prejudice against Jews, Singer left Poland for New York City in 1935. Soon after, World War II devastated the Jews of Eastern Europe and their neighborhoods. Yet Singer kept writing stories about the places of his youth. "Zlateh the Goat" helps recapture this vanished world. Throughout his life, Singer wrote in Yiddish, translating his stories into English afterward.

ASSESSMENT PRACTICE: Reading Comprehension

Recognize Facts and Details (For more practice, see Test Preparation Workbook, p. 13.)

In many tests, students must demonstrate reading comprehension by identifying details in a variety of written texts. After students read the passage below, ask them the question that follows:

> Aaron realized . . . that they were saved. With great effort he dug his way through the snow. . . . When he reached the hay, he hollowed out a nest for himself and the goat. No matter how cold it may be outside, in the hay it is always warm.

Why did Aaron make a nest in the hay?

A He was hiding from a village boy.
B He was hiding from a goat.
C He was trying to stay warm.
D He was making a nest for the goat.

A and *B* are not supported by the text. While *D* is correct, it misses the clues that show the nest was for both the goat and the boy himself. *C* is correct.

Review and Assess

Literary Analysis

Conflict with Nature

1. What two problems do Aaron and Zlateh face in their **conflict with nature**?
2. Explain how the snowstorm both creates a problem and solves a problem.
3. Identify the conflicts with nature in the story using the chart shown. In the first column, record the conflict for Aaron. In the second column, write what nature does to create the conflict.

Aaron's Conflict	How Nature Creates Conflict

Connecting Literary Elements

4. How does the **setting** contribute to the dangerous and isolated position in which Aaron and Zlateh find themselves?
5. What details of the place add to Aaron's problems?
6. What influence does the setting have on the characters? In a diagram like the one shown, record the details that explain how the setting affects the characters' thoughts and actions.

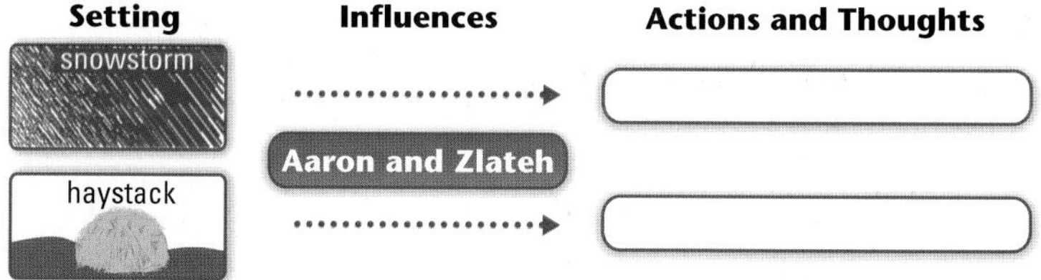

Reading Strategy

Summarizing

7. Identify two events that occurred before Aaron and Zlateh left for the butcher.
8. Tell three things that happened in the haystack.
9. Summarize the events that led to Zlateh's not being sold.

Extending Understanding

10. **Apply:** In what ways do weather, geography, and climate affect people's lives?

Quick Review

A **conflict with nature** is a struggle between a character and some forces of nature. To review conflict, see page 127.

The **setting** is the time and place in which the action of a story takes place. To review setting, see page 127.

When you **summarize**, you organize main events and ideas in order and identify the connections between them.

 ***Take It to the Net***

www.phschool.com

Take the interactive self-test online to check your understanding of the selection.

ENRICHMENT: Further Reading

Other Works by Isaac Bashevis Singer

When Schlemiel Went to Warsaw and Other Stories

The Fools of Chelm and Their History

Naftali the Storyteller and His Horse, Sus, and Other Stories

 ***Take It to the Net***

Visit www.phschool.com for more information on Isaac Bashevis Singer.

Answers for p. 135

Review and Assess

1. Nature causes Aaron and Zlateh to get lost and nearly freeze. Nature nearly suffocates and starves them.
2. The snowstorm sends Aaron and Zlateh off course and into a haystack. It solves a problem by creating snow, which causes business to improve so that Aaron can keep Zlateh.
3.

Aaron's Conflict	How Nature Creates Conflict
family needs supplies	dry weather hurts business
Aaron takes goat to butcher	dry weather means family has no money; must sell Zlateh
Aaron loses way	fierce snowstorm erupts
Aaron nearly suffocates	heavy snow covers air hole
Aaron is hungry	snowstorm keeps Aaron in haystack

4. Snow results from a winter setting.
5. The setting adds to Aaron's problems. He must walk far; when he gets lost, no one can help him.
6. The snowstorm forces Aaron to think practically: he uses the haystack for shelter.

   The haystack calms Zlateh; she eats and produces milk.
7. The father decided to sell Zlateh, the family said goodbye, and the goat licked the father's hand.
8. Zlateh eats hay, Aaron eats bread and cheese; Aaron drinks Zlateh's milk; both sleep; Aaron makes a window.
9. Aaron realizes how much Zlateh means; the family was grateful that Zlateh helped Aaron; the blizzard helped business, so Zlateh was not sold.
10. Weather and geography affect people's work, food, and houses.

EXTEND

Answers for p. 136

❶ Vocabulary Development

Word Analysis

1. put forth
2. tired out
3. to make known

Fluency: Sentence Completions

1. bound
2. exuded
3. conclusion
4. rapidly
5. trace

Spelling Strategy

1. rice
2. mice
3. place

❷ Grammar

1. I *am looking* for shelter.
2. We *have been* down this road before.
3. The snow *changed* the hay's shape.
4. I think that hill *has moved.*
5. We *are starting* to get cold.

Writing Application

Possible answers:

It had not snowed, so Aaron wore only a light jacket. As he walked, it began to snow. It kept snowing for days. It snowed until the haystack was covered.

Integrate Language Skills

❶ Vocabulary Development Lesson

Word Analysis: Latin Prefix *ex-*

The Latin prefix *ex-* means "out" or "away from." Knowing the meaning of *ex-* can help you figure out the meaning of the italicized word in the following sentence.

The haystack *exuded* the warmth of the summer sun.

Use the meanings of *ex-* to define the italicized word in the following sentences. Write your answers on your paper. You may use a dictionary to check your responses.

1. Aaron and Zlateh *exerted* a great effort to trudge through the snow.
2. Aaron was *exhausted* when they reached the haystack.
3. Zlateh made one sound that *expressed* all her thoughts.

Fluency: Sentence Completions

On your paper, complete each sentence with one of these words:

bound conclusion rapidly exuded trace

1. The packages were __?__ with string.
2. The goat __?__ a strong smell.
3. What __?__ have you reached?
4. The news spread __?__ through town.
5. They found no __?__ of the path.

Spelling Strategy

Sometimes you spell the *s* sound at the end of a word with *ce*, as in *trace*. On your paper, unscramble each word to match the definition.

1. ceir (a grainlike food)
2. icme (small furry animals)
3. pacle (a spot or location)

❷ Grammar Lesson

Principal Parts of Verbs

Every verb has four main forms, or **principal parts**. These parts are used to form verb tenses that show time. The chart here shows the four principal parts. Notice that regular verbs form their past tense and past participles by adding *-ed* or *-d*. Irregular verbs, such as *be*, form their past tense and/or past participles in different ways.

Base (present)	Present Participle	Past	Past Participle
howl	(*am, are,* or *is*) howling	howled	(*have* or *has*) howled
be	(*am, are,* or *is*) being	been	(*have* or *has*) been
eat	(*am, are,* or *is*) eating	ate	(*have* or *has*) eaten

WG Prentice Hall Writing and Grammar Connection: Chapter 22, Section 1

Practice Rewrite each sentence, replacing the italicized verb with the principal part indicated in parentheses.

1. I *look* for shelter. (present participle)
2. We *be* down this road before. (past participle)
3. The snow *change* the hay's shape. (past)
4. I think that hill *move*. (past participle)
5. We *start* to get cold. (present participle)

Writing Application Write four sentences about the story. In each sentence, use a different principal part of *snow*.

TEACHING RESOURCES

The following resources can be used to enrich or extend the instruction for pp. 135–136.

Vocabulary

Selection Support: Build Vocabulary, p. 41; Build Spelling Skills, p. 42

Vocabulary and Spelling Practice Book (Use this booklet for skills enrichment)

Grammar

Selection Support: Build Grammar Skills, p. 43

Writing and Grammar, Copper Level, p. 480

Daily Language Practice Transparencies ■

Writing

Writing and Grammar, Copper Level, p. 132 ■

Writing Models and Graphic Organizers on Transparencies, p. 65

Writing and Grammar iText CD-ROM

■ **BLOCK SCHEDULING:** Resources marked with this symbol provide varied instruction during 90-minute blocks.

❸ Writing Lesson

Persuasive Speech

Write a short persuasive speech that Aaron might give to his father, with the purpose of changing Reuven's mind.

Prewriting List the reasons for keeping the goat. Focus on reasons that will appeal to Reuven, because your purpose is to affect his decision. For example, Reuven would not be influenced by the fact that Zlateh is cute. He would be influenced by the fact that Zlateh saved Aaron.

Drafting State your position clearly in the first paragraph and make your purpose known. Organize the reasons for your position.

Model: Establish a Clear Purpose

This goat has shown us great friendship. Reconsider your decision to sell her. No matter how much we need the money, *you must not sell her . . .*

The first paragraph includes a clear statement of the writer's position: You must not sell her.

Revising Revise your speech to remove details that will not influence Reuven.

WG *Prentice Hall Writing and Grammar Connection: Chapter 7, Section 3*

❹ Extension Activities

Research and Technology With a small group, find out about *shtetls*, Jewish villages of Eastern Europe. Use the word *shtetl* as a key word to begin a search on the Internet. Prepare **charts** and make **dioramas** to show a setting similar to Aaron's home.

Find out about Aaron's day-to-day life by answering the following questions.

1. What are the homes like?
2. What responsibilities would a twelve-year-old boy have?
3. How do most people make a living?

Listening and Speaking Deliver a humorous **monologue,** a funny speech given by one person, in which you, as Zlateh, say what you think about the humans' behavior.

1. Use exaggerated facial expressions to reflect the meaning of your words.
2. Occasionally change your position on the stage or in the room.
3. Change the tone and volume of your voice to show happiness, fear, or annoyance.

 ***Take It to the Net*** www.phschool.com

Go online for an additional research activity using the Internet.

ASSESSMENT RESOURCES

The following resources can be used to assess students' knowledge and skills.

Selection Assessment

- **Formal Assessment,** pp. 33–35
- **Open Book Test,** pp. 25–27
- **Got It! Assessment Videotapes,** Tape 1
- **Test Bank Software**

Take It to the Net
Visit www.phschool.com for self-tests and additional questions on "Zlateh the Goat."

Writing Rubric

- **Performance Assess. and Portfolio Mgmt.,** p. 51

Listening and Speaking Rubric

- **Performance Assess. and Portfolio Mgmt.,** p. 27

- **Workbook**
- **Skill Book**
- **Transparencies**
- **CD-ROM**

❸ Writing Lesson

- Explain that a persuasive speech tries to influence the listener to agree with the speaker.
- Point out the two ways to appeal to an audience—through emotion and through logic.
- Suggest that students draw a two-column chart and label the columns *emotion* and *logic*. As students think of reasons Aaron might give, they should place them in the proper column. Once they have at least three good reasons, students are ready to write.
- Use the Speaking rubric on p. 27 in **Performance Assessment and Portfolio Management,** to evaluate students' speeches.

❹ Research and Technology

- You may wish to do some research on the topic before assigning this activity to students in order to get a sense of the types of sources available. In fact, you may wish to limit students to a few Web sites.
- Offer the following checklist:
  - ✔ Is the site sponsored by a reliable source?
  - ✔ Is the site updated regularly?
  - ✔ Does the site list its sources?
- Explain that students should do more than copy and paste or print information. They need to evaluate their findings. Have students use the Research Scoring Model on p. 51 in **Performance Assessment and Portfolio Management.**
- Tell students that if they cannot answer "yes," to each question, they need to find another source.

CUSTOMIZE INSTRUCTION
For Universal Access

To address different learning styles, use the activities suggested in the **Extension Activities** booklet, p. 9.

- For Verbal/Linguistic and Interpersonal Learners, use Activity 5.
- For Musical/Rhythmic Learners, use Activity 6.
- For Visual/Spatial Learners, use Activity 7.

Door Number Four ✦ Count That Day Lost ✦ The World Is Not a Pleasant Place to Be

Lesson Objectives

1. **To analyze and respond to**
   - Literary Analysis: Speaker
   - Comparing Literary Works
2. **To read, comprehend, analyze, and critique three poems**
   - Reading Strategy: Paraphrasing
   - Reading Check Questions
   - Review and Assess Questions
   - Assessment Practice (ATE)
3. **To develop word analysis skills, fluency, and systematic vocabulary**
   - Vocabulary Development Lesson: Concept Development: Analogies
4. **To understand and apply written and oral language conventions**
   - Spelling Strategy
   - Grammar Lesson: Verb Tenses
5. **To understand and apply appropriate writing and research strategies**
   - Writing Lesson: Friendly Letter
   - Extension Activity: Word Origins
6. **To understand and apply listening and speaking strategies**
   - Extension Activity: Friendship Song Presentation

STEP-BY-STEP TEACHING GUIDE	PACING GUIDE
PRETEACH	
Motivate Students and Provide Background	
Use the Motivation activity (ATE p. 138)	5 min.
Read and discuss the Preview material and Background information (SE/ATE p. 138) [A]	10 min.
Introduce the Concepts	
Introduce the Literary Analysis and Reading Strategy (SE/ATE p. 139) [A]	15 min.
Pronounce the vocabulary words and read their definitions (SE p. 139)	5 min.
TEACH	
Monitor Comprehension	
Informally monitor comprehension by circulating while students read independently or in groups [A]	5–10 min.
Develop vocabulary with Vocabulary notes (SE p. 141)	as students read
Develop Understanding	
Develop students' understanding of speakers with the Literary Analysis annotations (ATE p. 140) [A]	5 min.
ASSESS	
Assess Mastery	
Assess students' mastery of the Reading Strategy and Literary Analysis by having them answer the Review and Assess questions (SE/ATE p. 143)	15 min.
Use one or more of the print and media Assessment Resources (ATE p. 145) [A]	up to 45 min.
EXTEND	
Apply Understanding	
Have students complete the Vocabulary Development Lesson and the Grammar Lesson (SE p. 144) [A]	20 min.
Apply students' ability to write a friendly letter using the Writing Lesson (SE/ATE p. 145) [A]	30–45 min.
Apply students' understanding of the selection using one or more of the Extension Activities (SE p. 145)	20–90 min.

ACCELERATED INSTRUCTION:
Use the strategies and activities identified with an [A].

UNIVERSAL ACCESS
● = Below Level Students
▲ = On-Level Students
■ = Above Level Students

Time and Resource Manager

Reading Level: Easy, Challenging, Average
Average Number of Instructional Days: 3

RESOURCES		
PRINT	**TRANSPARENCIES**	**TECHNOLOGY**
• **Beyond Literature,** Workplace Skills: Getting Along With Others, p. 10 ▲ ■		
• **Selection Support Workbook:** ● ▲ ■ Literary Analysis, p. 50 Reading Strategy, p. 49 Build Vocabulary, p. 46	• **Literary Analysis and Reading Transparencies,** pp. 19 and 20 ● ▲ ■	
		• **Listening to Literature** ● ▲ ■ Audiocassettes, Side 6 Audio CDs, CD 3
• **Literary Analysis for Enrichment** ■		
• **Formal Assessment:** Selection Test, pp. 36–38 ● ▲ ■ • **Open Book Test,** pp. 28–30 ● ▲ ■ • **Performance Assessment and Portfolio Management,** pp. 9, 29 ● ▲ ■ • PRENTICE HALL ASSESSMENT SYSTEM ● ▲ ■	• PRENTICE HALL ASSESSMENT SYSTEM ● ▲ ■ Skills Practice Answers and Explanations on Transparencies	• **Test Bank Software** ● ▲ ■ • **Got It! Assessment Videotapes,** Tape 1 ● ▲
• **Selection Support Workbook:** ● ▲ ■ Build Spelling Skills, p. 47 Build Grammar Skills, p. 48 • **Writing and Grammar,** Copper Level ● ▲ ■ • **Extension Activities,** p. 10 ● ▲ ■	• **Daily Language Practice Transparencies** ● ▲ • **Writing Models and Graphic Organizers on Transparencies** ● ▲ ■	• **Writing and Grammar iText CD-ROM** ● ▲ ■ *Take It to the Net* www.phschool.com

BLOCK SCHEDULING: Use one 90-minute class period to preteach the selection and have students read it. Use a second 90-minute class period to assess students' mastery of skills and have them complete one of the Extension Activities.

PREVIEW

Step-by-Step Teaching Guide for pp. 138–139

Motivation

Hold up a piece of chalk and ask students to imagine that the chalk can talk to them. Discuss how the chalk might describe a typical day at school. Next, have students imagine that the piece of chalk is a poet. Ask them what it might say in a poem. Have students consider, as they read the poems in this grouping, how recognizing the speaker's identity helps them understand each poem.

❶ Background

Social Studies

Charlotte Pomerantz, the author of "Door Number Four," uses both English and Indonesian words in her poems. Indonesia is a chain of more than 13,000 islands located between the Indian and Pacific Oceans. Because Indonesia is located between China and Australia, it has a widely diverse population. Despite their varied ethnic origins, most Indonesians can speak the language of Bahasa, Indonesia, which is the language taught in their schools.

Prepare to Read

❶ Door Number Four ◆ Count That Day Lost The World Is Not a Pleasant Place to Be

Take It to the Net

Visit www.phschool.com for interactive activities and instruction related to these selections, including

- background
- graphic organizers
- literary elements
- reading strategies

Preview

Connecting to the Literature

These three poems explore the importance of caring about others and having others who care about you. Connect to these poems by thinking about the important people in your life and the different ways you show one another you care.

Background

Friendship depends more on actions than on words. Language, therefore, should not be a barrier to friendship. Charlotte Pomerantz illustrates this point by using Indonesian words for *door, number, four,* and *friend* in her poem of friendship, "Door Number Four."

TEACHING RESOURCES

The following resources can be used to enrich or extend the instruction for pp. 138–139.

Background

Beyond Literature, p. 10

Take It to the Net

Visit www.phschool.com for Background and hotlinks for the selections.

Literary Analysis

Literary Analysis and Reading Transparencies, Speaker, p. 20

Reading

Selection Support: Reading Strategy, p. 49; Build Vocabulary, p. 46

Literary Analysis and Reading Transparencies, Paraphrasing, p. 19

BLOCK SCHEDULING: Resources marked with this symbol provide varied instruction during 90-minute blocks.

❷ Literary Analysis

Speaker

The **speaker** is the imaginary voice a poet uses to "tell" a poem. The speaker may be the poet or a character the poet invents. The personality and age of the speaker are partly indicated through the way the speaker uses language. A young speaker would use simple language. Non-English words may be used to establish the culture of the speaker. In "Door Number Four," the Indonesian word *teman* is used for "friend." In a poem with a speaker from a Spanish-speaking culture, the speaker might use the word *amigo*.

Look for other kinds of details in each of the poems that give you clues about the speakers.

Comparing Literary Works

Each of these works communicates a message about the way people interact. However, the messages are conveyed in different ways. Compare the three poems by focusing on the following questions as you read:

1. How is the speaker of each poem similar to and different from the speakers of the other poems?
2. How is the message of each poem similar to and different from the messages of the other poems?

❸ Reading Strategy

Paraphrasing

When you **paraphrase**, you put an author's sentences or ideas into your own words. By "saying back" what you have read (even if it is in your head), you make sure you understand what you read.

Use a chart like the one shown to help you paraphrase difficult or confusing lines from the poems. Write the words from the poem in one column. In the other column, use your own words to explain what is meant.

Lines From Poem	My Paraphrase
If you sit down at set of sun	If you sit down at the end of the day
That eased the heart of him who heard	That made someone feel better

Vocabulary Development

eased (ēzd) *v.* comforted; freed from pain or worry (p. 141)

CUSTOMIZE INSTRUCTION FOR UNIVERSAL ACCESS

For Less Proficient Readers	For English Learners	For Advanced Readers
Students may benefit from listening to the audiocassette of the poems prior to reading. Then, have small groups of students read the poems aloud, stopping to paraphrase each sentence or meaningful phrase.	Point out that students already paraphrase when they translate from one language to another. Have students translate one of the poems into their native language. Challenge students by having them translate orally, as a partner reads the poem aloud.	Challenge students to write a description of how one of the poems would differ if the speaker were different. For example, they might describe "Door Number Four" with the uncle as the speaker or "The World Is Not a Pleasant Place to Be" with the point of view of the river.

❷ Literary Analysis

Speaker

- As a class, read the explanation of what a speaker is, and make sure that students understand that the speaker is not always the poet. Explain to students that a poem may be told from either the first-person or the third-person point of view as well as be spoken directly to the reader. These facts may also help the reader find clues about the speaker.
- Provide students with the Speaker transparency on p. 19 in **Literary Analysis and Reading Transparencies.** This transparency provides some key questions that students may ask to determine the identity of a poem's speaker.
- Finally, provide students with three copies of the Open Mind organizer on p. 93 of **Writing Models and Graphic Organizers on Transparencies.** They may use the copies of the organizer to jot down the thoughts of each poem's speaker. Students' notes here will help them answer the Comparing Literary Works questions, which will appear again on page 143.

❸ Reading Strategy

Paraphrasing

- Explain that paraphrasing is different from summarizing, a skill with which students may already be familiar.
- Tell students that a paraphrase is a retelling of a sentence or story in one's own words. Generally, paraphrasing uses simpler or more colloquial language. Paraphrasing is used to check your understanding as you read.
- Demonstrate how to paraphrase by paraphrasing a sentence from the textbook. Then, challenge volunteers to paraphrase a different sentence.

Vocabulary Development

- Pronounce the vocabulary word for students, and read the definitions as a class.

 **E-Teach**

Visit E-Teach at www.phschool.com for teachers' essays on how to teach, with questions and answers.

TEACH

Step-by-Step Teaching Guide for pp. 140–142

CUSTOMIZE INSTRUCTION
For Interpersonal Learners

Invite groups of students to plan, practice, and perform readings of one or more of the poems. Encourage groups to be creative in the method of presentation. For example, group members might take turns reading lines or verses, or they might read the poems in unison.

❶ About the Selection

The speaker in "Door Number Four" provides directions in both English and Indonesian that tell a friend how to find him or her.

❷ ▶ Critical Viewing

Possible answers: You're not always sure what you will find on the other side of a door or in a new friendship.

❸ Literary Analysis

Speaker

- Ask students to locate clues as to the speaker's identity.
  Answer: The language is simple and childlike, mentioning the uncle's grocery store, and telling the reader to be quiet.
- Then, ask students to identify the speaker of the poem.
  Answer: The speaker might be a child.

▶ **Monitor Progress** Ask students to list what they know about the speaker of this poem.
Possible response: The speaker sounds young, is Indonesian, is quiet, and wants a friend to come visit.

One Child Between Doors, **(Seorang Anak de Antara Pintu Ruang)** 1984, Dede Eri Supria, Courtesy of Joseph Fischer

❷ ◀ **Critical Viewing** How is starting a friendship like opening a door? **[Relate]**

❶ Door Number Four

CHARLOTTE POMERANTZ

Above my uncle's grocery store
is a pintu,
is a door.
On the pintu
is a number,
nomer empat,
number four.
In the door
there is a key.
❸ Turn it,
enter quietly.
Hush hush, diam-diam,
quietly.
There, in lamplight,
you will see
a friend,
teman,
a friend
who's me.

Charlotte Pomerantz

(b. 1930)

Charlotte Pomerantz has been making friends with young readers for years. She won the Jane Addams Children's Book Award for *The Princess and the Admiral*. You can see her fascination with language in her books, especially *If I Had a Paka*, which is the source of "Door Number Four."

TEACHING RESOURCES

The following resources can be used to enrich or extend the instruction for pp. 140–142.

Literary Analysis
- **Selection Support:** Literary Analysis, p. 50
- **Literary Analysis for Enrichment**

Reading
- **Literatura en español**
- **Listening to Literature Audiocassettes,** Side 6 ■
- **Listening to Literature Audio CDs,** CD 3 ■

■ **BLOCK SCHEDULING:** Resources marked with this symbol provide varied instruction during 90-minute blocks.

❹ COUNT THAT DAY LOST

George Eliot

If you sit down at set of sun
And count the acts that you have done,
And, counting, find
One self-denying[1] deed, one word
That eased the heart of him who heard,
One glance most kind
That fell like sunshine where it went—
Then you may count that day well spent.

But if, through all the livelong day,
You've cheered no heart, by yea or nay—
If, through it all
You've nothing done that you can trace
That brought the sunshine to one face—
No act most small
That helped some soul and nothing cost—
Then count that day as worse than lost.

eased (ēzd) *v.* comforted; freed from pain or worry

1. **self-denying** *adj.* opposite of selfish; done without concern for one's own interests.

Review and Assess

Thinking About the Selections

1. **Respond:** Which of these poems would you give to your best friend? Why?
2. (a) **Recall:** In "Door Number Four," where is the speaker? (b) **Infer:** At what time of day do you think "Door Number Four" takes place? (c) **Speculate:** Why do you think the speaker wants someone to visit?
3. (a) **Recall:** What does the speaker of "Count That Day Lost" say one needs to do in order to have a day well spent? (b) **Interpret:** Why does the speaker say that a day is lost if you haven't helped someone? (c) **Apply:** Give an example of a "self-denying deed" and words that might ease someone's heart.
4. **Make a Judgment:** Identify three qualities you value in a friend. Explain why each quality is important to you. Give examples.

George Eliot

(1819–1880)

The writer George Eliot (her real name was Mary Ann Evans) grew up in the English countryside. She describes the life there vividly in her very successful novels. Eliot was a friend of many important thinkers of her time, and she thought and wrote much about the ties between people.

❹ About the Selections

In "Count That Day Lost," the speaker explains that a day in which one has done no good deeds is not a day to be proud of.

The speaker in Nikki Giovanni's "The World Is Not a Pleasant Place to Be," p. 142, personifies a river and the ocean to express the idea that the world is only pleasant when it is shared with friends.

Answers for p. 141

Review and Assess

1. Students should support answers with reasons.
2. **(a)** The speaker is behind the door. **(b)** It takes place in the evening because a lamp is lit. **(c)** **Possible response:** The speaker wants someone to play with.
3. **(a)** One needs to do a good deed in order to have a day well spent. **(b)** **Possible response:** Every day is an opportunity to help someone. If a day passes without doing good, then the opportunity is lost forever. **(c)** An example might be giving your lunch to a hungry person or telling someone who is sad that things will get better.
4. **Possible responses:** Loyalty, a sense of humor, and kindness are valuable qualities. Loyalty is important because it means that one can rely on and confide in that friend. Humor lightens things up. Kindness is a valuable quality because people can expect their friends to help them and look out for them.

CUSTOMIZE INSTRUCTION FOR UNIVERSAL ACCESS

For Special Needs Students	For English Learners	For Gifted/Talented Students
Have students who have difficulty paraphrasing unfamiliar material practice on familiar material. Read aloud a well-known fable such as "The Fox and the Hare." Ask a volunteer to paraphrase the story. Then, build up to the poems in the text by paraphrasing a short but unfamiliar poem.	As you read the poems aloud with students, use body language and pantomime to illustrate actions and feelings. For example, you might hold your index finger up to your lips as you read "Hush hush, diam-diam, quietly"; show a counting motion with your fingers in the first sentence of "Count That Day Lost"; and so forth.	Have students write a poem with sentiments that match those of George Eliot in "Count That Day Lost." In this new poem, however, students should write from the viewpoint of a person who has had something nice done for them. The poem might begin with the kind act being performed.

ASSESS

Answers for p. 142

Review and Assess

1. Students may say that it is more effective because it does not lecture as "Count That Day Lost" does, and it captures the feeling of friendship by mentioning kissing and laughing.
2. **(a)** The images are of a river emptying into a stream and an ocean without clouds. **(b)** Possible response: She uses good images. Just as a river needs an ocean to flow into, friends need each other to feel complete. **(c)** Another possible image of companionship is the sun shining down and warming the earth just as a friend's smile might cheer someone up.
3. **(a)** The words are almost exactly the same in the two stanzas. The last stanza is missing the words "to hold and be held by." Also, the lines are broken differently. **(b)** The poet ends the poem with only one word to emphasize the loneliness of not having "someone."

The World Is Not a Pleasant Place to Be

NIKKI GIOVANNI

the world is not a pleasant place
to be without
someone to hold and be held by

a river would stop
its flow if only
a stream were there
to receive it

an ocean would never laugh
if clouds weren't there
to kiss her tears

the world is not
a pleasant place to be without
someone

Review and Assess

Thinking About the Selections

1. **Respond:** Do you think this poem is more or less effective than the other two at capturing the importance of caring? Explain.
2. **(a) Recall:** What two images does Nikki Giovanni use to show companionship in "The World Is Not a Pleasant Place to Be"? **(b) Support:** Explain why you do or do not think Giovanni uses good images for friendship. **(c) Extend:** Think of another image that could be used to describe companionship.
3. **(a) Compare and Contrast:** How are the last lines of the first and last stanzas (groups of lines) similar and different? **(b) Analyze:** What effect does the difference have on the way you read each stanza?

Nikki Giovanni

(b. 1943)

In her poems, Nikki Giovanni shares her thoughts and experiences. Born in Knoxville, Tennessee, and raised both there and in Cincinnati, Ohio, she has become one of America's most popular poets.

ASSESSMENT PRACTICE: Reading Comprehension

Recognize Facts and Details (For more practice, see Test Preparation Workbook, p. 14.)

Many tests require students to identify facts and details. Use this passage from "The World Is Not a Pleasant Place to Be" to help students with this skill.

an ocean would never laugh
if clouds weren't there
to kiss her tears

What words in this stanza indicate that the poet is *personifying* the ocean, or giving it human characteristics?

A ocean, never, clouds, kiss
B laugh, kiss, her, tears
C never, laugh, clouds, kiss
D would, laugh, her, kiss

While each of the answer choices contain some words that indicate personification, only *B* lists all of the details about personification in this stanza.

Review and Assess

Literary Analysis

Speaker

1. Describe the speaker of "Door Number Four." Provide details in each of the following categories:
   - age
   - language(s) spoken
   - where he or she lives
   - what matters to him or her
2. (a) How would "Door Number Four" be different if the speaker were from a country where Spanish, French, Chinese or another language was spoken? (b) What are some commonly used words for *friend*, or related to friendship, that come from other languages?
3. What do you think is the age of the speaker in "Count That Day Lost"? Explain.
4. What two clues does "The World Is Not a Pleasant Place to Be" give you about the feelings of the speaker?

Comparing Literary Works

5. Fill out a chart like the one shown here with quotations from the poems that show the speaker's personality, the mood or feeling of the poem, and the poem's message.

Poem	Personality	Mood	Message
"Door Number Four"			
"Count That Day Lost"			
"The World Is Not a Pleasant Place to Be"			

6. How is the speaker of each poem similar to and different from the speakers of the other poems?
7. How is the message of each poem similar to and different from the messages of the other poems?

Reading Strategy

Paraphrasing

8. Paraphrase lines 8–11 of "Door Number Four."
9. Paraphrase lines 11–16 of "Count That Day Lost."

Extending Understanding

10. **Social Studies Connection:** In what ways could the messages of these poems be applied to relationships between countries?

Quick Review

The **speaker** is the imaginary voice a poet uses when writing a poem. To review speaker, see page 139.

Paraphrasing is restating an author's ideas in your own words.

Take It to the Net

www.phschool.com

Take the interactive self-test online to check your understanding of these selections.

ENRICHMENT: Further Reading

Other Works by the Poets

Works by Charlotte Pomerantz

You're Not My Best Friend Anymore

Works by Nikki Giovanni

Vacation Time

Take It to the Net

Visit www.phschool.com for more information on the poets.

8. Possible response: Use the key to open the door and then come in.

9. Possible response: If you do not make someone happy by a good deed, you have done worse than just wasting a day.

10. Countries can reach out in friendship.

Answers for p. 143

Review and Assess

1. **Age:** young child; **Languages Spoken:** English and Indonesian; **Where lives:** above uncle's grocery store, behind door number 4; **What matters:** friendship.
2. **(a)** Words such as *pintu, nomer empat,* and *diam-diam* would be in that language.
   (b) Other words for friend include *amigo, compadre,* and any other related words that students may share from their native languages.
3. The language and wisdom of "Count That Day Lost" suggest an older adult. The speaker seems to have an adult's wisdom.
4. **Clue 1:** The poem begins and ends with a statement about loneliness. **Clue 2:** The images of nature embracing and kissing suggest that the speaker is lonely or fears loneliness.
5. **"Door Number Four" Personality:** "you will see a friend, / teman, / a friend who's me." **Mood:** "Hush hush, diam-diam, /quietly. / There, in lamplight, **Message:** "you will see a friend" **"Count That Day Lost" Personality:** "But if, through all the livelong day, / You've cheered no heart, by yea or nay—" **Mood:** "If you sit down at set of sun" **Message:** "Then count that day as worse than lost." **"The World Is Not . . ." Personality:** "the world is not a pleasant place / to be without / someone to hold and be held by" **Mood:** "an ocean would never laugh / if clouds weren't there / to kiss her tears" **Message:** "the world is not / a pleasant place to be without / someone"
6. The speakers acknowledge the need for friendship. The speakers of "Count That Day Lost" and "The World Is Not a Pleasant Place to Be" seem wiser and more experienced than the speaker of "Door Number Four."
7. The messages of "Door Number Four" and "The World Is Not a Pleasant Place to Be" are that we need friends. The message of "Count That Day Lost" is that we should be kind.

EXTEND

Answers for p. 144

❶ Vocabulary Development

Word Analysis

1. eased
2. pause
3. pleasant

Spelling Strategy

1. pleasant
2. gazed
3. pause
4. surprised
5. confused

❷ Grammar

1. He was. He is. He will be.
2. You sat. You sit. You will sit.
3. You eased. You ease. You will ease.
4. It was. It is. It will be.
5. We helped. We help. We will help.

Writing Application

Possible answers:

Past: I went to school yesterday.

Present: I enjoy social studies.

Future: I will take French in high school.

Integrate Language Skills

❶ Vocabulary Development Lesson

Concept Development: Analogies

An **analogy** makes a comparison between two or more things that are otherwise unalike. Analogies can be made between ideas, situations, or even single words. The relationship between the words in each pair will be similar. Look at the following example:

helped : aided :: glance : look

The relationship between *helped* and *aided* is similar to the relationship between the words *glance* and *look:* Both pairs are synonyms. The chart shows two types of word relationships.

Word Relationships

Synonyms		Antonyms	
helped →	← aided	← cheerful	sullen →
happy →	← joyful	← sunny	rainy →

Word Analysis: Word Pairs

On your paper, complete each word pair analogy with a word from the list.

pause pleasant eased

1. angered : enraged :: comforted : ___?___
2. laugh : cry :: continue : ___?___
3. high : low :: nasty : ___?___

Spelling Strategy

Sometimes, you spell the *z* sound with the letter *s*, as in *eased*. Sometimes you spell it with a *z*, as in *prize*. On your paper, write the correct spelling of the word that contains the *z* sound.

1. Try to be (pleazant/pleasant) each day.
2. She (gazed/gased) at them kindly.
3. When angry, (pauze/pause) before you speak.
4. She was (surprized/surprised) at the party.
5. Don't be (confuzed/confused).

❷ Grammar Lesson

Verb Tenses

A **verb** is a word that expresses an action or a state of being. A **verb tense** shows the time of the action or state of being that is expressed by the verb.

Form the past tense of regular verbs with *-ed* or *-d*. Memorize the past tense of irregular verbs. All future tenses use the helping verb *will*.

Tenses	Regular verb: cheer	Irregular verb: sit	Irregular verb: be
Present	I cheer.	I sit.	I am.
Past	I cheered.	I sat.	I was.
Future	I will cheer.	I will sit.	I will be.

Practice On your paper, write each of the following sentences in the past, present, and future tense.

1. He (be).
2. You (sit).
3. You (ease).
4. It (be).
5. We (help).

Writing Application Write three sentences about school. Write one sentence in the past tense, one in the present tense, and one in the future tense. Check your writing for correct capitalization.

WG Prentice Hall Writing and Grammar Connection: Chapter 22, Section 2

TEACHING RESOURCES

The following resources can be used to enrich or extend the instruction for pp. 144–145.

Vocabulary

Selection Support: Build Vocabulary, p. 46
Build Spelling Skills, p. 47

Vocabulary and Spelling Practice Book
(Use this booklet for skills enrichment)

Grammar

Selection Support: Build Grammar Skills, p. 48

Writing and Grammar, Copper Level, p. 488

Daily Language Practice Transparencies ■

Writing

Writing and Grammar, Copper Level, p. 16 ■

Writing Models and Graphic Organizers on Transparencies, pp. 3, 97

Writing and Grammar iText CD-ROM

■ **BLOCK SCHEDULING:** Resources marked with this symbol provide varied instruction during 90-minute blocks.

❸ Writing Lesson

Friendly Letter

Write a letter to tell a friend, family member, or other special person why he or she is special to you.

Prewriting Make a list of special people. Write one word to describe each of those people. Then, write an example of how that person shows the quality you have identified. Choose a person from the list as the subject of your letter.

Drafting Organize the paragraphs of your letter by category. For example, list three or four qualities. Then, focus on a single quality.

Model: Organize by Category

Aunt Edna's Qualities	How Aunt Edna Shows Generosity
Generous	to family
Funny	to friends
Good	to others

No matter what categories you use to organize your letter, be sure to give examples that support your statements.

Revising Revise your letter by moving any details that belong in a different category. Check your use of capital letters.

Prentice Hall Writing and Grammar Connection: Chapter 2, Section 1

❹ Extension Activities

Research and Technology Some words are almost as familiar in other languages as they are in English. For instance, the Spanish *amigo* is widely recognized to mean "friend," even by people who do not speak Spanish.

1. Use a dictionary to find the languages from which these other two friendship words come: *confidante, comrade.*
2. Collect other words from other languages related to friends and friendship.
3. Use the words to make a **friendship dictionary** in which you categorize and define these words.

Listening and Speaking With a group, prepare and present a poetry reading and discussion. For each poem, have one group member do the following.

1. Read the poem aloud.
2. Explain its message.
3. Point out how the poet uses repeated words and phrases to emphasize the message.

Take It to the Net www.phschool.com

Go online for an additional research activity using the Internet.

ASSESSMENT RESOURCES

The following resources can be used to assess students' knowledge and skills.

Selection Assessment
- **Formal Assessment,** pp. 36–38
- **Open Book Test,** pp. 28–30
- **Got It! Assessment Videotapes,** Tape 1
- **Test Bank Software**

Take It to the Net
Visit www.phschool.com for self-tests and additional questions on the selections.

Writing Rubric
- **Performance Assess. and Portfolio Mgmt.,** p. 9

Listening and Speaking Rubric
- **Performance Assess. and Portfolio Mgmt.,** p. 29

PRENTICE HALL ASSESSMENT SYSTEM
- **Workbook**
- **Transparencies**
- **Skill Book**
- **CD-ROM**

Lesson Support for p. 145

❸ Writing Lesson

- Review the format of a personal letter with the Personal Letter transparency on p. 3 in **Writing Models and Graphic Organizers on Transparencies**. Point out the parts of the letter.
- If students need help in generating qualities to write about, offer them the Sunburst transparency on p. 97 in the **Writing Models and Graphic Organizers on Transparencies.** Tell students to put the person's name in the circle and fill in the surrounding rectangles with words or phrases that describe the person. Suggest that students think about important or enjoyable moments.
- As students prepare to write, remind them that they may use conversational language, such as contractions and slang.
- Finally, use the Description rubric on p. 9 in **Performance Assessment and Portfolio Management** to evaluate students' letters.

❹ Listening and Speaking

- Have students work in small groups.
- Students should keep in mind what they have learned about speaker, mood, and message in this lesson as they look at the poems they select.
- Have students fill out the Speaking rubric on p. 29 in **Performance Assessment and Portfolio Management.**

CUSTOMIZE INSTRUCTION For Universal Access

To address different learning styles, use the activities suggested in the **Extension Activities** booklet, p. 10.

- For Musical/Rhythmic Learners, use Activity 5.
- For Interpersonal and Logical/Mathematical Learners, use Activity 6.
- For Intrapersonal and Verbal/Linguistic Learners, use Activity 7.

Lesson Objectives

1. To understand the connection between past and present depictions of caring and giving
2. To understand the value of different ideas between friends

Connections

The main character in the excerpt from Spinelli's *Stargirl* lives life to the fullest by observing the world around her and sharing kindness wherever she can. In this way, she seems to live by the message of George Eliot's "Count That Day Lost." Have students review the poems on pp. 140–142. What similarities and differences do students see between the characters in *Stargirl* and the messages in the poems?

Themes of Giving and Caring

- Tell students that this excerpt reveals the special gifts Stargirl has given the narrator.
- Have students read the excerpt. Then, ask them to make a list of the gifts the narrator mentions. Students should think about the similarities and differences between the excerpt and the poems.
- With the help of the cluster diagram on p. 85 of **Writing Models and Graphic Organizers on Transparencies,** have students list all the ways that giving and caring are either mentioned or revealed in the selections.
- Finally, challenge students to use their notes to form a generalization about caring and giving.

CONNECTIONS

Literature Past and Present

Themes of Giving and Caring

The importance of giving and the many ways people can give to one another are common themes in literature. In "Door Number Four," Charlotte Pomerantz shows that people from different backgrounds can share a friendship. Writing a century ago, poet and novelist George Eliot expressed the view that a day in which you do not do at least one kind deed is a lost day. In her poem "The World Is Not a Pleasant Place to Be," Nikki Giovanni captures the loneliness of being without at least one friend you can count on.

The related themes of these poems are also explored in other types of literature. In his novel *Stargirl,* contemporary author Jerry Spinelli tells the story of an unusual girl who gives to others for the joy of giving. The story is told from the viewpoint of a high-school boy who is at first frightened by the difference between this girl and the other students. Although he comes to appreciate her unique personality, he has trouble understanding the reasons she acts as she does. In this excerpt from *Stargirl,* the narrator and Stargirl have a conversation in which they discuss their very different ideas about doing nice things for other people.

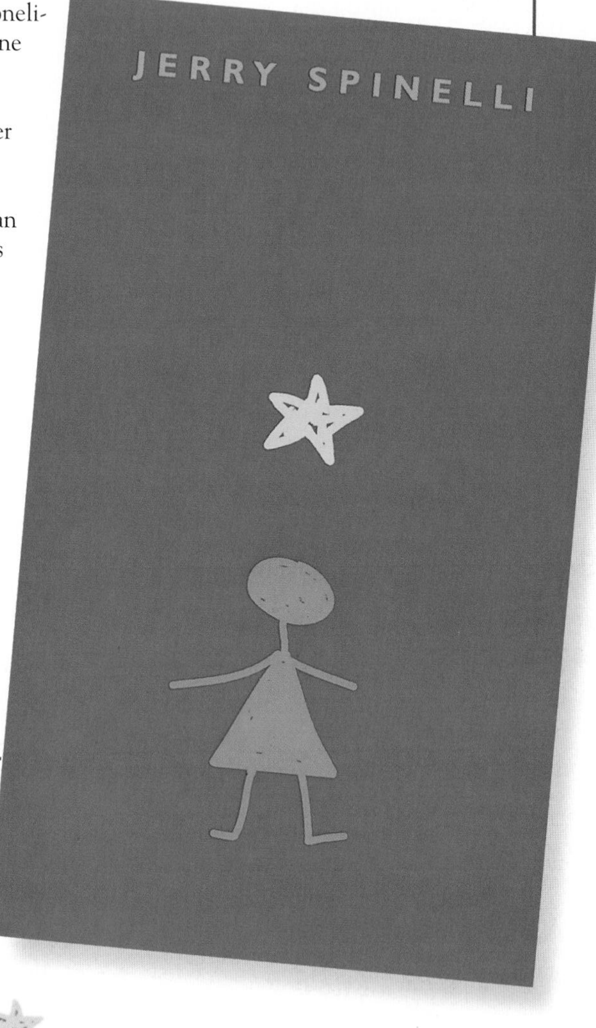

ENRICHMENT: Social Studies Connection

The Red Cross

The idea of caring for others is an important theme in literature and in everyday life. Many organizations exist today to help people in need. One such organization, the Red Cross, was established by Jean Henri Dunant of Switzerland in 1863. It was one of the first worldwide voluntary relief organizations. The goal of the Red Cross has been to provide shelter and resources, as well as legal and health services, to people who are forced from their homes by a disaster, such as a war or an earthquake. The American branch of the Red Cross was founded in 1881 by Civil War nurse Clara Barton. That organization always has been run by volunteers and funded by private donations. The Red Cross helps care for people who are unable to care for themselves.

Stargirl

Jerry Spinelli

I told her I wanted to be a TV director. She said she wanted to be a silver-lunch-truck driver.

"Huh?" I said.

"You know," she said, "people work all morning and then it's twelve o'clock. The secretaries in the offices walk out the door, the construction workers put down their hard hats and hammers, and everybody's hungry, and they look up and there I am! No matter where they are, no matter where they work, I'm there. I have a whole fleet of silver lunch trucks. They go everywhere. 'Let Lunch Come to You!' That's my slogan. Just seeing my silver lunch truck makes them happy." She described how she would roll up the side panels and everyone would practically faint at the cloud of wonderful smells. Hot food, cold food, Chinese, Italian, you name it. Even a salad bar. "They can't believe how much food I fit into my truck. No matter where you are—out in the desert, the mountains, even down in the mines—if you want my silver lunch service, I get it to you. I find a way."

I tagged along on missions. One day she bought a small plant, an African violet in a plastic pot on sale for ninety-nine cents at a drugstore.

"Who's it for?" I asked her.

"I'm not exactly sure," she said. "I just know that someone at an address on Marion Drive is in the hospital for surgery, so I thought whoever's back home could use a little cheering up."

"How do you know this stuff?" I said.

She gave me a mischievous grin. "I have my ways."

We went to the house on Marion Drive. She reached into the saddle pack behind her bicycle seat. She pulled out a handful of ribbons. She chose a pale violet one that matched the color of the tiny blossoms and stuffed the remaining ribbons back into the seat pack. She tied the violet ribbon around the pot. I held her bike while she set the plant by the front door.

Riding away, I said, "Why don't you leave a card or something with your name on it?"

Thematic Connection
What poem from the previous grouping do Stargirl's actions bring to mind?

Reading Check
What is special about Stargirl?

Thematic Connection

Answer: Stargirl's actions should remind students of "Count the Day Lost," which is about the need to do good deeds for other people, including total strangers.

Reading Check

Possible answer: Stargirl sees meaning and wonder in ordinary things that most people overlook. She also has a deep compassion for others and is wondrously curious about the world.

CUSTOMIZE INSTRUCTION FOR UNIVERSAL ACCESS

For Less Proficient Readers	For English Learners	For Advanced Readers
To help students think more about Stargirl's actions, ask them what occupations they consider to be generous and why. For example, some people consider the work of a nurse to be very generous because nurses help sick people feel better. Then, ask students if they consider Stargirl's job in her silver lunch truck to be a generous and thoughtful job.	Stargirl's description of the silver lunch truck might be confusing to English learners. To make sure that students understand the kind of service her truck would provide, describe how she would "roll up the side panels" to serve food. Then, ask students how they picture the truck to make sure they understand her description.	Have students compare the narrator's perceptions of his surroundings on pp. 147–148 of *Stargirl* with the narrator's perceptions in "The World Is Not a Pleasant Place to Be." Be sure that students note how they think the narrator of *Stargirl* changes his perceptions after meeting Stargirl.

Answers

Connecting Literature Past and Present

1. The message in the excerpt is similar to that of Eliot's poem—it is important to do kind things for people, even people you do not know.
2. The narrator thinks that it is acceptable and pleasurable to receive credit for kind gestures. Stargirl does not agree. She seems to do kind things simply for the joy of making others happy.
3. Possible responses: The speaker in George Eliot's "Count That Day Lost" would most appreciate Stargirl because she makes sure that no day is lost—she fills her days by doing nice things for people.
4. Stargirl would probably like "Door Number Four" best because it is about finding a friend in a surprising way. She might find the tone of "Count That Day Lost" too stern, although she would appreciate the poem's message.
5. The narrator might prefer "Count That Day Lost" because it clearly shows the cause-and-effect relationship between doing good and having a fulfilling day.
6. Students' answers should reflect their understanding of the themes of giving and caring.
7. Students should support their answers with details from the literary work they choose.

The question surprised her. "Why should I?"

Her question surprised me. "Well, I don't know, it's just the way people do things. They expect it. They get a gift, they expect to know where it came from."

"Is that important?"

"Yeah, I guess—"

I never finished that thought. My tires shuddered as I slammed my bike to a halt. She stopped ahead of me. She backed up. She stared.

"Leo, what is it?"

I wagged my head. I grinned. I pointed to her. "It was you."

"Me what?"

"Two years ago. My birthday. I found a package on my front step. A porcupine necktie. I never found out who gave it to me."

She walked her bike alongside mine. She grinned. "A mystery."

"Where did you find it?" I said.

"I didn't. I had my mother make it."

She didn't seem to want to dwell on the subject. She started pedaling and we continued on our way.

"Where were we?" she said.

"Getting credit," I said.

"What about it?"

"Well, it's nice to get credit."

The spokes of her rear wheel spun behind the curtain of her long skirt. She looked like a photograph from a hundred years ago. She turned her wide eyes on me. "Is it?" she said.

Jerry Spinelli

(b. 1941)

Jerry Spinelli, the father of six children and grandfather of eleven, has written more than fifteen books for young readers. He has won many honors, among them the Newbery Medal.

A popular writer with young adults, Spinelli is best known for his fiction about the ups and downs of teenage life. Although most of his work is fiction, the characters are realistic and experience "real-life" situations to which readers can relate. Spinelli advises young writers to "write what you really care about."

Connecting Literature Past and Present

1. How does the message in the excerpt from *Stargirl* compare with the message in George Eliot's poem "Count That Day Lost"?
2. Compare and contrast the narrator's and Stargirl's ideas about doing nice things for other people.
3. Which speaker in the three poems do you think would most appreciate Stargirl? Explain.
4. Which poem do you think Stargirl would like best? Explain.
5. Which poem do you think the narrator would like best? Explain.
6. What is another work you have read that addresses the themes of giving and caring? Explain how that work is similar to and different from *Stargirl* and the poems. Include in your answer the genre or form of the work, the message itself, and the time period and culture from which the work comes.
7. Which work do you think has the most useful or relevant message for people today? Explain.

READING INFORMATIONAL MATERIALS

Interviews

About Interviews

An interview is a formal conversation in which one person (the interviewer) asks questions, and another person (the subject of the interview, or interviewee) answers them. Interviews with writers, actors, sports figures, and other celebrities are often featured in newspapers and magazines. Initials, formatting, or other design elements are used to distinguish between the words of the interviewer and those of the interviewee. An interview usually has a limited scope—that is, the questions focus on a particular area or time period of the subject's life.

Reading Strategy

Connecting and Clarifying Main Ideas

An interview gives you a firsthand look at the subject's opinions and ideas. The types of questions and the answers the subject gives can help you identify a few main ideas about the subject. The interview itself, however, is not the whole picture. As an active reader, you will clarify these ideas by connecting them to what you already know about the subject from other sources. In addition, you can clarify main ideas by making connections to related topics. The chart shows other sources and topics related to different kinds of celebrities whose interviews you might read. Explore these sources and topics to clarify ideas you read in interviews.

	Actors	Writers	Athletes
Other Sources	Other interviews	Other interviews	Other interviews
	His or her performances	Themes in his or her written works	The athlete's performance in the sport
	Talk show appearances	Reviews of his or her works	Articles about the athlete
	Comments from other actors or directors	Biography or autobiography of the writer	Comments from coaches and teammates
Related Topics	Style of acting	Other writers' treatment of similar themes	The athlete's particular sport
	Topics related to specific references in interview	Topics related to specific comments in the interview	Topics related to specific comments in the interview

Lesson Objectives

1. To connect and clarify main ideas in an interview
2. To recognize the format and limited scope of a written interview

About Interviews

- Before students read "About Interviews," ask them what they already know from having seen interviews on television or from having read them in magazines. **Possible responses:** Students should point out that an interviewer, usually a journalist, asks an interviewee, often a celebrity or expert, questions about his or her life and work.
- Ask students to identify a few typical interview questions. **Possible answers:** Students might suggest the following questions: "Where were you born?" "Why are people interested in you?" "What are you doing now?"
- Next, have students read "About Interviews." Discuss why interviews usually have only a limited time frame. Guide students toward understanding that an interview is like a quick conversation—it is an opportunity to ask only a few questions.

Reading Strategy

Connecting and Clarifying Main Ideas

- Have students discuss the concept of main idea in an interview. Help students understand that each answer to an interview question will probably have its own main idea. Suggest that each answer is like a separate paragraph that connects to the main idea of the essay.
- Have students look at the information in the chart. Tell students that their understanding of the questions and answers in interviews will be more meaningful if readers have some previous knowledge about the interviewee. Discuss with students how part of the appeal of reading an interview is getting the opportunity to learn more about the interviewee.

Interview with Jerry Spinelli

- Before students read the interview, point out written elements of the layout, such as the use of initials to identify the speakers, the introductory paragraph, and the two-column format. Ask students to guess what kind of publication *The Borzoi Young Reader* is.
  Possible response: Students may suggest that *The Borzoi Young Reader* is a magazine or annual volume that is devoted to articles about young-adult books and their authors.
- Next, read the introductory note on p. 150. Make sure that students understand that the book *Knots in My Yo-yo String* is Spinelli's autobiography.
- Have students read the interview. As they read, have them make a list of the topics that are covered by the interviewer.
- After students read, ask them to identify any repeated theme in the questions.
  Answer: The questions all seem to be asking about Spinelli's life and how it relates to his books.
- Finally, ask students to sum up what they learned from the interview with Jerry Spinelli.

Interview with Jerry Spinelli

from The Borzoi Young Reader 1998

The text of an interview begins with the identification of the interviewer (in this case, Borzoi Young Reader, or **BYR**) and the subject (in this case, the author **JS**).

Interview questions are usually specific and focused. Here, Jerry Spinelli answers the specific question of how he compares himself today to young Jerry in *Knots in My Yo-yo String*.

Jerry Spinelli gives us a glimpse of the artist as a (very) young man in *Knots in My Yo-yo String*.

Borzoi Young Reader: You have an incredible memory of your early childhood. Has this always been the case—or did you do a lot of research and conduct interviews to fill in the gaps?

JS: Memories of childhood seem to come naturally to me. Until I started writing books for kids, I thought that was the case with everybody. I did consult my mother and brother at length, and the family scrapbooks. Others I spoke with are listed in the "Acknowledgments."

BYR: Readers who know your books can find many seeds and details from your novels in your own childhood. Is there a character in one of your novels who's the most like you as a boy?

JS: No one character in any book is all me. I guess the one who comes closest is Jason in *Space Station Seventh Grade.* Others include Maniac Magee and Eddie Mott in the School Daze series.

BYR: We learn from your memoir that you weren't much of a reader (of books) all through your childhood. When did this change?

JS: I finally became a willing, enthusiastic reader during my year in graduate school at the Writing Seminars, Johns Hopkins University. Because I regret that it took me so long, I put a book in Maniac Magee's hand everywhere he goes.

BYR: What are you reading right now?

JS: A book about tuning into your life called *Callings* by Gregg Lavoy and a murder mystery, *Nocturne,* by Ed McBain.

BYR: How similar are you to the young Jerry in *Knots in My Yo-yo String?* Do movies, baseball, yo-yos, and fanatical neatness still have a place in your life?

JS: The game I play now is tennis rather than baseball; I haven't spun a yo-yo in years; and no father of six kids is fanatically neat. But I recently watched a bunch of Flash Gordon episodes on the AMC channel, and I still hate war and love cowboys and sports, and I still feel bad for not visiting Garfield Shainline, and I still swoon when I look at the night sky and try to imagine eternity. I finally learned to swim (a little) and eat hot peppers (a little), but I still can't blast an earsplitting, two-fingered whistle.

CUSTOMIZE INSTRUCTION FOR UNIVERSAL ACCESS

For Special Needs Students	For Less Proficient Readers
Students may need help navigating the unusual format of the interview. To help special needs students, ask a pair of proficient readers to perform the interview while reading it. Invite the readers to sit at the front of the class in chairs facing one another, as if in an interview setting. Have the students read the interview in natural voices. Allow special needs students to watch the interview before they read it. Once they understand who is asking and who is answering questions, students should be able to follow the written interview.	Before students read, show them a videotaped excerpt of an interview from a television news or talk show. As students watch, point out how the journalist asks the question, listens to the answer, and then responds to the answer with another question. Also, make sure that students notice that the subject of the interview does most of the talking because he or she is the point of interest. Help students see the connection between the elements of the television interview and those of the printed interview on p. 150.

Check Your Comprehension

1. Whom did Jerry Spinelli consult about his childhood when he wrote his autobiography *Knots in My Yo-yo String*?
2. Which character from one of his novels does Spinelli think is most like himself as a young boy?

Applying the Reading Strategy

Connecting and Clarifying Main Ideas

3. Identify two main ideas from the interview.
4. What information in the author biography on page 148 helps you clarify information in this interview?
5. What else could you read to clarify the main ideas you have identified?

Activity

Interview Questions

Interviewers prepare for an interview by doing preliminary research about the interview subject. The researched information helps interviewers pose relevant questions—questions that are meaningful to the interviewee and questions that will interest the reader.

Choose a famous person of interest to you and about whom you know something. Write five questions you would ask this person in an interview. Use a graphic organizer like the one shown here to show the relationship between what you know about the subject and the questions you ask. The first row contains an example from the Spinelli interview.

What you know	What you want to know	Why you want to know
Jerry Spinelli's stories are often based on his life.	Which characters are most similar to him as a boy?	It will give insight into what he was like as a kid.

Comparing Informational Materials

Interviews and Biographical Writing

Reread the biographical information about Jerry Spinelli on page 148.

6. In what way does an interview look different from biographical writing?
7. What can you learn by reading a biography that you might not learn from an interview?

Answers for p. 151

Check Your Comprehension

1. Spinelli consulted his brother, mother, family scrapbooks, and others listed in the "Acknowledgments."
2. The character who is most like Spinelli is Jason from *Space Station Seventh Grade.*

Apply the Reading Strategy

3. One main idea is that Spinelli's fiction is not based entirely on his own life. Another main idea is that Spinelli has many memories of his childhood.
4. The biography clarifies that Spinelli writes books about teenagers, has written fifteen books for young readers, and has six children of his own.
5. Students could read Spinelli's books or the author biography on one of his books. They might also read other interviews with Spinelli.

Activity

If you want the whole class to work together on this, ask students to vote and decide on one person to interview. Then, divide the class into smaller groups to work on filling in the graphic organizer. Bring students together to share their results after they have completed the organizer. Invite students to share their questions. Even if they have written questions for different interview topics, challenge students to find some common ideas among all their questions.

Comparing Informational Materials

6. The interview is set in columns, and the names of the interviewer and the interviewee are shown as initials. Also, each question is a new paragraph.
7. In a biography, you can learn about the person's entire life. Interviews cover a limited period of time.

Old Ben ✦ Feathered Friend

Lesson Objectives

1. **To analyze and respond to literary elements**
   - Literary Analysis: Narratives
   - Comparing Literary Works
2. **To read, comprehend, analyze, and critique nonfiction and a short story**
   - Reading Strategy: Using Context Clues
   - Reading Check Questions
   - Review and Assess Questions
   - Assessment Practice (ATE)
3. **To develop word analysis skills, fluency, and systematic vocabulary**
   - Vocabulary Development Lesson: Word Analysis: Forms of *regulate*
4. **To understand and apply written and oral language conventions**
   - Spelling Strategy
   - Grammar Lesson: Perfect Verb Tenses
5. **To understand and apply appropriate writing and research strategies**
   - Writing Lesson: Feature Story
   - Extension Activity: Pet Care Fair
6. **To understand and apply listening and speaking strategies**
   - Extension Activity: Multimedia Presentation

STEP-BY-STEP TEACHING GUIDE	PACING GUIDE
PRETEACH	
Motivate Students and Provide Background	
Use the Motivation activity (ATE p. 152)	5 min.
Read and discuss the Preview material and Background information (SE/ATE p. 152) [A]	10 min.
Introduce the Concepts	
Introduce the Literary Analysis and Reading Strategy (SE/ATE p. 153) [A]	25 min.
Pronounce the vocabulary words and read their definitions (SE p. 153)	5 min.
TEACH	
Monitor Comprehension	
Informally monitor comprehension by circulating while students read independently or in groups [A]	20–25 min.
Monitor students' comprehension with the Reading Check notes (SE/ATE pp. 155, 157, 159, 161)	as students read
Develop vocabulary with Vocabulary notes (SE pp. 157, 159, 160; ATE p. 159)	as students read
Develop Understanding	
Develop students' understanding of narratives with the Literary Analysis annotations (SE pp. 154, 157, 160; ATE pp. 154, 156, 157, 160) [A]	5 min.
Develop students' ability of context clues with the Reading Strategy annotations (SE/ATE pp. 155, 156, 160)	5 min.
ASSESS	
Assess Mastery	
Assess students' mastery of the Reading Strategy and Literary Analysis by having them answer the Review and Assess questions (SE/ATE p. 163)	25 min.
Use one or more of the print and media Assessment Resources (ATE p. 165) [A]	up to 45 min.
EXTEND	
Apply Understanding	
Have students complete the Vocabulary Development Lesson and the Grammar Lesson (SE p. 164) [A]	20 min.
Apply students' ability to write a feature story using the Writing Lesson (SE/ATE p. 165) [A]	45 min.
Apply students' understanding using one or more of the Extension Activities (SE p. 165)	20–90 min.

ACCELERATED INSTRUCTION:
Use the strategies and activities identified with an [A].

UNIVERSAL ACCESS
● = Below Level Students
▲ = On-Level Students
■ = Above Level Students

Time and Resource Manager

Reading Level: Easy, Challenging
Average Number of Instructional Days: 4

	RESOURCES		
	PRINT	**TRANSPARENCIES**	**TECHNOLOGY**
	• **Beyond Literature,** Humanities Connection: Friendship, p. 11 ▲ ■		• **Interest Grabber Videotapes,** Tape 1 ● ▲ ■
	• **Selection Support Workbook:** ● ▲ ■ Literary Analysis, p. 55 Reading Strategy, p. 54 Build Vocabulary, p. 51	• **Literary Analysis and Reading Transparencies,** pp. 21 and 22 ● ▲ ■	
			• **Listening to Literature** ● ▲ ■ Audiocassettes, Sides 6, 7 Audio CDs, CD 3
	• **Literary Analysis for Enrichment** ■		
	• **Formal Assessment:** Selection Test, pp. 39–41 ● ▲ ■ • **Open Book Test,** pp. 31–33 ● ▲ ■ • **Performance Assessment and Portfolio Management,** pp. 12, 24 ● ▲ ■ • PRENTICE HALL ASSESSMENT SYSTEM ● ▲ ■	• PRENTICE HALL ASSESSMENT SYSTEM ● ▲ ■ Skills Practice Answers and Explanations on Transparencies	• **Test Bank Software** ● ▲ ■ • **Got It! Assessment Videotapes,** Tape 1 ● ▲
	• **Selection Support Workbook:** ● ▲ ■ Build Spelling Skills, p. 52 Build Grammar Skills, p. 53 • **Writing and Grammar,** Copper Level ● ▲ ■ • **Extension Activities,** p. 11 ● ▲ ■	• **Daily Language Practice Transparencies** ● ▲ • **Writing Models and Graphic Organizers on Transparencies** ● ▲ ■	• **Writing and Grammar iText CD-ROM** ● ▲ ■ ***Take It to the Net*** www.phschool.com

BLOCK SCHEDULING: Use one 90-minute class period to preteach the selection and have students read it. Use a second 90-minute class period to assess students' mastery of skills and have them complete one of the Extension Activities.

PRETEACH

Step-by-Step Teaching Guide for pp. 152–153

Motivation

Bring to class and display one or two stuffed animals, such as a teddy bear and a soft puppy. Ask students whether they can recall children's books in which a friendship develops between a child and such a toy. Students may suggest "The Velveteen Rabbit" or the Winnie-the-Pooh books. Explain that bonds of friendship can develop, not just between two people, but also between people and animals. Tell students that as they read the following narratives, they will discover the details of some unusual and surprising friendships.

Interest Grabber Video

As an alternative, play "Facts About Reptiles" on Tape 1 to engage student interest.

1 Background

Science

"Feathered Friend" is the story of a canary that travels in space. Many animals have traveled in space. In fact, animals traveled in space before humans did. Scientists wanted to study how space travel would affect living beings before sending humans to space. Animal space travelers include fruit flies, mice, cats, dogs, bullfrogs, monkeys, and chimpanzees. The first creature to orbit the Earth was Laika, a dog from the former Soviet Union.

Prepare to Read

1 Old Ben ◆ Feathered Friend

 ***Take It to the Net***

Visit www.phschool.com for interactive activities and instruction related to these selections, including

- background
- graphic organizers
- literary elements
- reading strategies

Preview

Connecting to the Literature

The joys and sorrows of animal companions are the subject of Jesse Stuart's "Old Ben" and Arthur C. Clarke's "Feathered Friend." Connect to the selections by thinking about animals you have known or animal characters in movies, television, and literature.

Background

In "Feathered Friend," a canary travels into space. Historically, canaries have traveled down, rather than up. Miners used to bring these birds into mines to detect odorless but deadly fumes that sometimes accumulated. Because it is small, a canary would pass out long before the miners were affected. The early warning allowed miners to address the danger before there were tragic results.

TEACHING RESOURCES

The following resources can be used to enrich or extend the instruction for pp. 152–153.

Motivation

Interest Grabber Videotapes, Tape 1

Background

Beyond Literature, p. 11

 ***Take It to the Net***

Visit www.phschool.com for Background and hotlinks for the selections.

Literary Analysis

Literary Analysis and Reading Transparencies, Narratives, p. 22

Reading

Selection Support: Reading Strategy, p. 54; Build Vocabulary, p. 51

Literary Analysis and Reading Transparencies, Using Context Clues, p. 21

BLOCK SCHEDULING: Resources marked with this symbol provide varied instruction during 90-minute blocks.

❷ Literary Analysis

Narratives

Each of these works is a **narrative**, that is, each work tells a series of events that make a story. Narratives can be fiction (made up) like "Feathered Friend" or nonfiction (true) like "Old Ben."

- **Fictional narratives:** short stories, novels, novellas
- **Nonfiction narratives:** Autobiography, biography, historical accounts

Use a chart like the one shown to track the events in each narrative.

Old Ben
Boy finds friendly snake.
↓
↓
↓

Comparing Literary Works

Although both of these works are narratives, they belong to different genres, or types, of literature.

"Old Ben" is **nonfiction**. The narrator is a real person telling a true story.

"Feathered Friend" is **fiction**, a made-up story about events and people that the writer creates.

As you compare the two works, think about the following focus questions:

1. In what ways do both selections seem as if they could be true stories?
2. In what ways do both selections seem as if they could be made-up stories?

❸ Reading Strategy

Using Context Clues

When you come across an unknown word, or a word used in an unusual way, you can figure out the meaning by using **context clues**, information provided in the words, phrases, and sentences around the unfamiliar word. You can use context clues in all kinds of reading—short stories, nonfiction narratives, textbooks, and other materials. In the following example, you can use context clues to figure out the meaning of *garbs:*

> It was a skilled and difficult job, for a space suit is not the most convenient of *garbs* in which to work.

Since a space suit is a type of *garb*, you can figure out that *garbs* are things you wear.

Vocabulary Development

scarce (skers) *adj.* few in number or infrequent; not common (p. 157)

regulation (reg´ yə lā´ shən) *n.* rule (p. 159)

fusing (fyo͞o´ ziŋ) *adj.* joining permanently (p. 159)

ceased (sēsd) *v.* stopped (p. 160)

CUSTOMIZE INSTRUCTION FOR UNIVERSAL ACCESS

For Less Proficient Readers	For English Learners	For Advanced Readers
Ask students why people have pets, and invite them to name common and uncommon pets. Guide students to see that even people with very different pets can still have some things in common. Use the Venn Diagram on p. 89 of **Writing Models and Graphic Organizers on Transparencies.**	Expand students' vocabulary by talking about pets. Draw the beginnings of a cluster diagram on the board. Then, ask students to list common types of pets, and write them in the central circles of the diagram. Challenge students to fill in other circles with words that describe the pets. Make sure to mention birds and snakes.	Have students write short, fictional dialogues between pet owners and their pets. The dialogues should focus on what people and their pets like about and need from one another. Ask students to imagine what pets think about. Tell students that their dialogues can be humorous and that the pets can be ordinary or unusual.

❷ Literary Analysis

Narratives

- Before students read the instruction, explain that a narrative describes a series of events.
- Demonstrate the concept by telling something that happened to you recently. Use a chart like the one on the student page to map out your retelling.
- Then, have students read aloud the instruction about narratives on p. 153.
- After students read the selections and complete their series of events organizers, remind them to return to the Comparing Literary Works questions. Students may benefit from using the Venn Diagram organizer on p. 89 of **Writing Models and Graphic Organizers on Transparencies** to make their comparisons.

❸ Reading Strategy

Using Context Clues

- Explain that texts often provide clues to the meanings of unfamiliar words.
- Ask students to read the last sentence of the Reading Strategy section on p. 153 before you read the instructions aloud.
- Demonstrate the process of searching for context clues by reading the example aloud and then asking questions and making comments such as the following: "What are garbs? From the sentence I can tell that the word *garbs* is a noun because you work in them. If you work in them, then garbs must be something that you wear. What do people in space wear? Space suits."
- Next, allow students to finish reading the page.

Vocabulary Development

- Pronounce each vocabulary word for students, and read the definitions as a class. Have students identify any words with which they are already familiar.

 ***E-Teach***

Visit E-Teach at www.phschool.com for teachers' essays on how to teach, with questions and answers.

TEACH

Step-by-Step Teaching Guide for pp. 154–162

CUSTOMIZE INSTRUCTION
For Bodily/Kinesthetic Learners

Have groups of students work together to pantomime the events in one of the selections. Encourage them to use facial expressions and body language to show what is happening. Challenge students who are watching to call out an impromptu narration as they watch.

1 About the Selection

In "Old Ben," a boy comes across a large, friendly blacksnake in a field, and names it Old Ben. He takes the snake home and places it in the corncrib so it will eat the mice that routinely steal corn. After some time, the snake becomes a pet and, indeed, mice are no longer a problem. During the following spring and summer, Old Ben ventures from the corncrib into other parts of the barnyard, looking for mice, and eventually meets his death after crawling into the hog pen. The family mourns the loss of Old Ben, who showed them that a snake could be a friend indeed.

2 Literary Analysis

Narratives

- Before students begin reading, explain that "Old Ben" is a straightforward narrative—the events move forward from beginning to end. Tell them that they may wish to stop after every paragraph or two to jot down notes about what has taken place.
- Next, pose the Literary Analysis question on p. 154.
  Answer: The boy picks up a snake and names it Old Ben.

1

Old Ben

Jesse Stuart

One morning in July when I was walking across a clover field to a sweet-apple tree, I almost stepped on him. There he lay coiled like heavy strands of black rope. He was a big bull blacksnake. We looked at each other a minute, and then I stuck the toe of my shoe up to his mouth. He drew his head back in a friendly way. He didn't want trouble. Had he shown the least fight, I would have soon finished him. My father had always told me there was only one good snake—a dead one.

2 When the big fellow didn't show any fight, I reached down and picked him up by the neck. When I lifted him he was as long as I was tall. That was six feet. I started calling him Old Ben as I held him by the neck and rubbed his back. He enjoyed having his back rubbed and his head stroked. Then I lifted him into my arms. He was the first snake I'd ever been friendly with. I was afraid at first to let Old Ben wrap himself around me. I thought he might wrap himself around my neck and choke me.

Literary Analysis
Narratives What two important events occur in this paragraph?

TEACHING RESOURCES

The following resources can be used to enrich or extend the instruction for pp. 154–162.

Literary Analysis
- **Selection Support:** Literary Analysis, p. 55
- **Literary Analysis for Enrichment**
- **Writing Models and Graphic Organizers on Transparencies,** p. 89

Reading
- **Literatura en español**
- **Listening to Literature Audiocassettes,** Sides 6, 7
- **Listening to Literature Audio CDs,** CD 3

BLOCK SCHEDULING: Resources marked with this symbol provide varied instruction during 90-minute blocks.

The more I petted him, the more affectionate he became. He was so friendly I decided to trust him. I wrapped him around my neck a couple of times and let him loose. He crawled down one arm and went back to my neck, around and down the other arm and back again. He struck out his forked tongue to the sound of my voice as I talked to him.

"I wouldn't kill you at all," I said. "You're a friendly snake. I'm taking you home with me."

I headed home with Old Ben wrapped around my neck and shoulders. When I started over the hill by the pine grove, I met my cousin Wayne Holbrook coming up the hill. He stopped suddenly when he saw me. He started backing down the hill.

"He's a pet, Wayne," I said. "Don't be afraid of Old Ben."

It was a minute before Wayne could tell me what he wanted. He had come to borrow a plow. He kept a safe distance as we walked on together.

Before we reached the barn, Wayne got brave enough to touch Old Ben's long body.

"What are you going to do with him?" Wayne asked. "Uncle Mick won't let you keep him!"

"Put him in the corncrib," I said. "He'll have plenty of delicate food in there. The cats we keep at this barn have grown fat and lazy on the milk we feed 'em."

3 I opened the corncrib door and took Old Ben from around my neck because he was beginning to get warm and a little heavy.

"This will be your home," I said. "You'd better hide under the corn."

4 Besides my father, I knew Old Ben would have another enemy at our home. He was our hunting dog, Blackie, who would trail a snake, same as a possum or mink. He had treed blacksnakes, and my father had shot them from the trees. I knew Blackie would find Old Ben, because he followed us to the barn each morning.

The first morning after I'd put Old Ben in the corncrib, Blackie followed us. He started toward the corncrib holding his head high, sniffing. He stuck his nose up to a crack in the crib and began to bark. Then he tried to tear a plank off.

"Stop it, Blackie," Pa scolded him. "What's the matter with you? Have you taken to barking at mice?"

"Blackie is not barking at a mouse," I said. "I put a blacksnake in there yesterday!"

"A blacksnake?" Pa asked, looking unbelievingly. "A blacksnake?"

"Yes, a pet blacksnake," I said.

"Have you gone crazy?" he said. "I'll move a thousand bushels of corn to get that snake!"

"You won't mind this one," I said. "You and Mom will love him."

My father said a few unprintable words before we started back

Reading Strategy
Using Context Clues
What clues in these two sentences help tell you the meaning of *corncrib*?

5 
Reading Check
How do people react to Old Ben?

3 Reading Strategy

Using Context Clues

- Point out that context clues are not always in the same sentence as the unfamiliar word. Sometimes students must look back or read further.
- Now pose the Reading Strategy question on p. 155: What clues in these two sentences help tell you the meaning of *corncrib*?
  Answer: The corncrib has a door, and it is full of corn.

4 Critical Thinking

Speculate

- Ask students to identify Old Ben's potential enemies.
  Answer: The boy's father and Blackie the dog.
- Then, invite students to make predictions about what role the enemies will have in Old Ben's future.
  Possible response: The boys' father may try to get rid of Old Ben. The dog, because it is a hunter, may try to hunt and kill Old Ben.

5 Reading Check

Answer: People are afraid of Old Ben when they first meet him.

CUSTOMIZE INSTRUCTION FOR UNIVERSAL ACCESS

For Special Needs Students	For Less Proficient Readers
Students may have trouble identifying events in the selection. Have students work in pairs to read the selection aloud. One student should read a paragraph or two at a time before stopping. When the reader stops, the other student should ask, "What happened?" Students will be able to answer the question only if an event has taken place. The student who is not reading should write down his or her answers and then switch roles to become the reader.	Invite students to work in pairs or small groups to think of characteristics or qualities they look for in a friend. Have them write these characteristics in the first column of a two-column chart. As students read "Old Ben," they should be able to identify the qualities that the narrator values, too. Have students write "Jesse" at the top of the second column. Tell them that as they read, they should take notes about the kinds of qualities the narrator values in his friendships with humans or with animals.

6 Reading Strategy

Using Context Clues

- Before asking students to answer the Reading Strategy question, lead students to understand that the word *shelled* in this context is a verb.
- Then, ask the Reading Strategy question on p. 156.
  Answer: The clue "for her geese and chickens" helps readers know that shelling corn means "removing the kernels from the cob," which would make it easier for the birds to eat.

7 Literary Analysis

Narratives

- Explain that narratives include details that reveal the characters' thoughts and feelings.
- Then, ask students what the details in this paragraph reveal about Pa.
  Answer: He has changed his mind about Old Ben and now likes the snake and worries about its well-being.

Monitor Progress Mix up the order of the following narrative events: boy finds friendly snake; boy names snake Old Ben; boy brings snake home and puts it in the corncrib; boy's father is afraid the snake will harm the birds; Old Ben gets rid of the mice in the corncrib; boy's father begins to like the snake. Ask students to arrange the events in the order they occurred in the narrative.

Reteach If students have trouble understanding what a narrative is, offer them a narrative puzzle. Type a retelling of a fairy tale or other story that is not familiar to students. Then, cut the story into sections and mix the sections up. Next, arrange students into groups of two or three and give them the scrambled sections of the fairy tale. Challenge students to put the sections in the correct sequence. Call on groups to read their assembled narratives. Ask students how they knew the order of events.

to the house. After breakfast, when Pa and Mom came to the barn, I was already there. I had opened the crib door and there was Old Ben. He'd crawled up front and was coiled on a sack. I put my hand down and he crawled up my arm to my neck and over my shoulder. When Mom and Pa reached the crib, I thought Pa was going to faint.

"He has a pet snake," Mom said.

"Won't be a bird or a young chicken left on this place," Pa said. "Every time I pick up an ear of corn in the crib, I'll be jumping."

"Pa, he won't hurt you," I said, patting the snake's head. "He's a natural pet, or somebody has tamed him. And he's not going to bother birds and young chickens when there are so many mice in this crib."

"Mick, let him keep the snake," Mom said. "I won't be afraid of it."

This was the beginning of a long friendship.

6 Mom went to the corncrib morning after morning and shelled corn for her geese and chickens. Often Old Ben would be lying in front on his burlap sack. Mom watched him at first from the corner of her eye. Later she didn't bother to watch him any more than she did a cat that came up for his milk.

Reading Strategy
Using Context Clues
Name two context clues that help you figure out what *shelled* means in this sentence.

Later it occurred to us that Old Ben might like milk, too. We started leaving milk for him. We never saw him drink it, but his pan was always empty when we returned. We know the mice didn't drink it, because he took care of them.

"One thing is certain," Mom said one morning when she went to shell corn. "We don't find any more corn chewed up by the mice and left on the floor."

July passed and August came. My father got used to Old Ben, but not until he had proved his worth. Ben had done something our nine cats couldn't. He had cleaned the corncrib of mice.

7 Then my father began to worry about Old Ben's going after water, and Blackie's finding his track. So he put water in the crib.

September came and went. We began wondering where our pet would go when days grew colder. One morning in early October we left milk for Old Ben, and it was there when we went back that afternoon. But Old Ben wasn't there.

"Old Ben's a good pet for the warm months," Pa said. "But in the winter months, my cats will have to do the work. Maybe Blackie got him!"

"He might have holed up for the winter in the hayloft,"[1] I told Pa after we had removed all the corn and didn't find him. "I'm worried about him. I've had a lot of pets—groundhogs, crows and hawks—but Old Ben's the best yet."

1. **hayloft** (hā´ lôft´) *n.* upper story in a barn or stable used for storing hay.

ENRICHMENT: Social Studies Connection

The Changing of America's Farms

Until recently in our country's history, a large percentage of the population lived and worked on family farms. Following the industrial revolution of the late nineteenth century, people began moving into cities to work. Companies bought many of these small farms and combined them to create large agricultural businesses. Throughout the country, small farms still exist, and these farmers often provide fresh produce, meat, eggs, and cheese at local stores or farmers' markets.

If there are any independent farmers in your area, invite interested students to locate and interview them. Encourage students to ask questions such as these: What kinds of crops do you grow? Do you raise animals? What do you like best about farming? What is your routine on an average day? How are small farms different from those run by large businesses? Have students share the results of their interviews with the class.

8 November, December, January, February, and March came and went. Of course we never expected to see Old Ben in one of those months. We doubted if we ever would see him again.

One day early in April I went to the corncrib, and Old Ben lay stretched across the floor. He looked taller than I was now. His skin was rough and his long body had a flabby appearance. I knew Old Ben needed mice and milk. I picked him up, petted him, and told him so. But the chill of early April was still with him. He got his tongue out slower to answer the kind words I was saying to him. He tried to crawl up my arm but he couldn't make it.

That spring and summer mice got scarce in the corncrib and Old Ben got daring. He went over to the barn and crawled up into the hayloft, where he had many feasts. But he made one mistake.

He crawled from the hayloft down into Fred's feed box, where it was cool. Old Fred was our horse.

There he lay coiled when the horse came in and put his nose down on top of Old Ben. Fred let out a big snort and started kicking. He kicked down a partition,[2] and then turned his heels on his feed box and kicked it down. Lucky for Old Ben that he got out in one piece. But he got back to his crib.

Old Ben became a part of our barnyard family, a pet and darling of all. When children came to play with my brother and sisters, they always went to the crib and got Old Ben. He enjoyed the children, who were afraid of him at first but later learned to pet this kind old reptile.

9 Summer passed and the late days of September were very humid. Old Ben failed one morning to drink his milk. We knew it wasn't time for him to hole up for the winter.

We knew something had happened.

Pa and I moved the corn searching for him. Mom made a couple of trips to the barn lot to see if we had found him. But all we found was the rough skin he had shed last spring.

"Fred's never been very sociable with Old Ben since he got in his box that time," Pa said. "I wonder if he could have stomped Old Ben to death. Old Ben could've been crawling over the barn lot, and Fred saw his chance to get even!"

"We'll see," I said.

Pa and I left the crib and walked to the barn lot. He went one way and I went the other, each searching the ground.

Literary Analysis
Narratives How do these details strengthen the impression that this is a nonfiction narrative?

scarce (skers) *adj.* few in number or infrequent; not common

10 **Reading Check**
Why does the family search for Old Ben?

2. **partition** (pär tish´ ən) *n.* something that separates or divides, such as an interior wall that separates one room from another.

8 Literary Analysis

Narratives

- Remind students that fiction is imaginary, or made up, and nonfiction is based on real life. A narrative may be either fiction or nonfiction.
- With these definitions in mind, ask students the Literary Analysis question on p. 157: How do these details strengthen the impression that this is a nonfiction narrative?
  Answer: The mundane passing of the months gives the impression that the selection is nonfiction and that the writer actually lived through those months; in fiction, the writer might have used more vivid language such as, "It was not until spring burst into bloom again that we saw Old Ben."

9 Critical Thinking

Compare and Contrast

- Ask students to compare Old Ben's disappearance this time with his disappearance earlier in the selection.
  Answer: Earlier, it made sense that Old Ben went into hibernation for winter. This time, it is still warm when Old Ben disappears.
- Now, ask students how the family knows for certain that something bad has happened to the snake. Again, they should compare his behavior now with his behavior earlier in the story.
  Answer: At the same time the previous year, Old Ben was eating mice and drinking milk. This time, he has not touched his milk.

10 Reading Check

Answer: The family misses Old Ben and is worried that something has happened to him.

CUSTOMIZE INSTRUCTION FOR UNIVERSAL ACCESS

For English Learners	For Advanced Readers
Have students make a list of words that relate to friendship. Challenge small groups of students to brainstorm at least ten English words, both formal and informal, that describe friendship or identify a kind of friendly relationship. Then, have students look up the words in the dictionary. If slang words are not in the dictionary, students should provide their own definitions. Have groups compare lists and notice differences in the selected words and their definitions. Ask a volunteer to create a master list with definitions to post in class.	Challenge students to turn the selection into a script. Remind them that a script is different from a written text because it relies on dialogue, or the character's spoken words, to reveal information. Have students choose at least four key scenes from the selection and turn them into a script with stage directions. Or, you may wish to assign scenes to students and have them read their scripts aloud.

Answers for p. 158

Review and Assess

1. Some students may say they are now less afraid of and more interested in snakes. Others may say their attitudes have not changed toward snakes.
2. **(a)** The narrator's father once told his son that the only good snake was a dead snake. **(b)** Pa's feelings change because Old Ben does not disturb the birds and is so effective at killing mice. **(c)** It is clear that his feelings have changed when he worries about the snake.
3. **(a)** **Possible responses:** He liked being petted; he returned after the winter; he enjoyed the children. **(b)** Old Ben trusts that Fred will treat him as kindly as the people do, but Fred does not.
4. **(a)** Ben has not touched his milk, and it is still too early and warm for him to go into hiding. **(b)** He sees how Ben's tracks lead to an opening in the hog pen.
5. **(a)** The narrator almost steps on Ben in a field. **(b)** Most people would not expect a family who lives on a farm to make friends with a snake. **(c)** **Possible response:** The story shows that it is important to have high expectations and to avoid making judgments. The narrator never questions that Ben would make a fine pet, and Ben does a great job.

Mom came through the gate and walked over where my father was looking. She started looking around, too.

"We think Fred might've got him," Pa said. "We're sure Fred's got it in for him over Old Ben getting in his feed box last summer."

"You're accusing Fred wrong," Mom said. "Here's Old Ben's track in the sand."

I ran over to where Mom had found the track. Pa went over to look, too.

"It's no use now," Pa said, softly. "Wouldn't have taken anything for that snake. I'll miss him on that burlap sack every morning when I come to feed the horses. Always looked up at me as if he understood."

The last trace Old Ben had left was in the corner of the lot near the hogpen. His track went straight to the woven wire fence and stopped.

"They've got him," Pa said. "Old Ben trusted everything and everybody. He went for a visit to the wrong place. He didn't last long among sixteen hogs. They go wild over a snake. Even a biting copperhead can't stop a hog. There won't be a trace of Old Ben left."

We stood silently for a minute looking at the broad, smooth track Old Ben had left in the sand.

Review and Assess

Thinking About the Selection

1. **Respond:** Have your feelings about snakes changed as a result of reading "Old Ben"? Explain why or why not.
2. (a) **Recall:** What kind of snake does the narrator's father say is the only good kind? (b) **Analyze Causes and Effects:** Why do Pa's feelings change? (c) **Draw Conclusions:** How do you know Pa's feelings have changed?
3. (a) **Recall:** List three examples of Old Ben's trusting, friendly nature. (b) **Deduce:** How does Ben's trusting nature get him into trouble with Fred?
4. (a) **Recall:** How does the family know something has happened to Ben? (b) **Infer:** How does Pa know that Ben went to the hog pen?
5. (a) **Recall:** How do the narrator and Old Ben meet? (b) **Support:** Explain how "Old Ben" illustrates the idea that friends can be found in the most unexpected places. (c) **Extend:** Explain another lesson this story teaches about expectations and making judgments.

Jesse Stuart

(1906–1984)

A writer for the *Chicago Tribune* once said that Jesse Stuart's stories "all have a heart." Stuart's narrative about an unusual pet—"Old Ben"—is no exception. The Kentucky-born novelist, poet, and short-story writer received a number of awards for his writing.

⓫ Feathered Friend

ARTHUR C. CLARKE

⓬ To the best of my knowledge, there's never been a regulation that forbids one to keep pets in a space station. No one ever thought it was necessary—and even had such a rule existed, I am quite certain that Sven Olsen would have ignored it.

regulation (reg´ yə lā´ shən) *n.* rule

With a name like that, you will picture Sven at once as a six-foot-six Nordic giant, built like a bull and with a voice to match. Had this been so, his chances of getting a job in space would have been very slim. Actually he was a wiry little fellow, like most of the early spacers, and managed to qualify easily for the 150-pound bonus[1] that kept so many of us on a reducing diet.

Sven was one of our best construction men, and excelled at the tricky and specialized work of collecting assorted girders[2] as they floated around in free fall, making them do the slow-motion, three-dimensional ballet that would get them into their right positions, and fusing the pieces together when they were precisely dovetailed into the intended pattern: it was a skilled and difficult job, for a space suit is not the most convenient of garbs in which to work. However, Sven's team had one great advantage over the construction gangs you see putting up skyscrapers down on Earth. They could step back and admire their handiwork without being abruptly parted from it by gravity. . . .

fusing (fyo͞o´ ziŋ) *adj.* joining permanently

⓭ ✓ **Reading Check**

Where does Sven do his construction work?

1. **150-pound bonus** extra money for being lightweight.
2. **girders** (gur´ dərz) *n.* long, thick pieces of metal.

⓫ About the Selection

In "Feathered Friend," Sven, a construction worker, smuggles a canary named Claribel on the space station where he works and lives. One morning, after everyone awakes out of sorts, Claribel is nowhere to be found. When Sven finds the bird, she appears to be dead. Someone suggests giving the bird oxygen, and she responds right away. The narrator recalls that miners used canaries to warn them of changes in air quality; if the canary became ill or died, the miners knew to leave the mine immediately. He urges the engineer to check the air quality in the space station. They learn that a backup system had failed and that, in fact, they were in danger. The problem was quickly fixed, and Claribel proved to be a friend indeed.

⓬ Vocabulary Development

Word Analysis: Forms of *regulate*

- Call students' attention to the word *regulation.* Explain that the word root *-reg-* comes from the Latin word for "rule." The word *regulation* means a "ruling."
- Have students make a list of other words that contain the word root *-reg-* , and list them on the board. Possibilities include *regular, regulator, regiment,* and *regulatory.*
- Have students look up the meanings of these words in the dictionary.

⓭ ✓ Reading Check

Answer: Sven works on a space station.

CUSTOMIZE INSTRUCTION FOR UNIVERSAL ACCESS

For Gifted/Talented Students

Tell students that a dialogue is a conversation between two or more characters in a narrative. Explain that writers use dialogue in a narrative to share characters' inner thoughts and feelings. Arrange students in pairs, and have them decide which animal, Old Ben or Claribel, they will role-play. (You may wish to broaden this activity by pairing advanced readers with less proficient readers or with English learners.) Then, have the pair brainstorm things each animal might say about its owner. For example, Old Ben might say, "It was really great of my family to let me live in the corncrib. I never go hungry." Encourage students to discuss similarities between the pet owners. Have pairs rehearse and perform their dialogues for the class. Encourage students in the audience to listen for a variety of ideas in the conversations. Finally, after students present, ask them to tell what they liked or disliked about their dialogues.

14 Literary Analysis

Narratives

- Ask students what clues appear on this page that finally let the reader know that the story is fiction.
  Answer: The first clue is the statement that Sven had taken a ferry to the space station. Another clue is that VIPs, or Very Important Persons, were coming to visit. Presently, there are no regular ferries to space stations, and people of importance do not regularly visit space.
- Read aloud the Literary Analysis question on p. 160.
  Answer: When the speaker bangs his head in surprise at seeing Claribel, the story begins to focus on events that are currently happening. All the paragraphs before this are descriptive and do not move the story forward.

15 Reading Strategy

Using Context Clues

- Pose the Reading Strategy question on p. 160: Name two context clues that help you figure out what *bulkheads* means in this sentence.
  Answer: It is clear that the bulkheads are hollow (because Claribel sits inside them and sings) and are used for storage.
- Confirm or correct students' guesses by explaining that a *bulkhead* is a boxlike container or opening over a staircase.

Don't ask me why Sven wanted a pet, or why he chose the one he did. I'm not a psychologist, but I must admit that his selection was very sensible. Claribel weighed practically nothing, her food requirements were tiny—and she was not worried, as most animals would have been, by the absence of gravity.

14 I first became aware that Claribel was aboard when I was sitting in the little cubbyhole laughingly called my office, checking through my lists of technical stores to decide what items we'd be running out of next. When I heard the musical whistle beside my ear, I assumed that it had come over the station intercom, and waited for an announcement to follow. It didn't; instead, there was a long and involved pattern of melody that made me look up with such a start that I forgot all about the angle beam just behind my head. When the stars had ceased to explode before my eyes, I had my first view of Claribel.

Literary Analysis
Narratives How does this event move the story forward?

ceased (sēsd) *v.* stopped

She was a small yellow canary, hanging in the air as motionless as a hummingbird—and with much less effort, for her wings were quietly folded along her sides. We stared at each other for a minute; then, before I had quite recovered my wits, she did a curious kind of backward loop I'm sure no earthbound canary had ever managed, and departed with a few leisurely flicks. It was quite obvious that she'd already learned how to operate in the absence of gravity, and did not believe in doing unnecessary work.

Sven didn't confess to her ownership for several days, and by that time it no longer mattered, because Claribel was a general pet. He had smuggled her up on the last ferry from Earth, when he came back from leave—partly, he claimed, out of sheer scientific curiosity. He wanted to see just how a bird would operate when it had no weight but could still use its wings.

Claribel thrived and grew fat. On the whole, we had little trouble concealing our guest when VIP's from Earth came visiting. A space station has more hiding places than you can count; the only problem was that Claribel got rather noisy 15 when she was upset, and we sometimes had to think fast to explain the curious peeps and whistles that came from ventilating shafts and storage bulkheads. There were a couple of narrow escapes—but then who would dream of looking for a canary in a space station?

Reading Strategy
Using Context Clues
Name two context clues that help you figure out what *bulkheads* means in this sentence.

We were now on twelve-hour watches, which was not as bad as it sounds, since you need little sleep in space. Though of course there is no "day" and "night" when you are floating in permanent sunlight, it was still convenient to stick to the terms. Certainly 16 when I woke that "morning" it felt like 6:00 A.M. on Earth. I had a nagging headache, and vague memories of fitful, disturbed

CUSTOMIZE INSTRUCTION FOR UNIVERSAL ACCESS

For Special Needs Students	For English Learners
Students may not realize that the story is fiction. Allow them time to find information about life in space by searching the Internet or skimming youth science magazines. Challenge students to write brief statements based on their research about what life in outer space is like for astronauts.	Allow students time to expand their knowledge of vocabulary words that deal with outer space and space technology. Bring in an article about space travel or life in a space station, or allow students to use the Internet to find articles and information on their own. Ask students to compile a list of words and their definitions.

dreams. It took me ages to undo my bunk straps, and I was still only half awake when I joined the remainder of the duty crew in the mess. Breakfast was unusually quiet, and there was one seat vacant.

"Where's Sven?" I asked, not very much caring.

"He's looking for Claribel," someone answered. "Says he can't find her anywhere. She usually wakes him up."

Before I could retort that she usually woke me up, too, Sven came in through the doorway, and we could see at once that something was wrong. He slowly opened his hand, and there lay a tiny bundle of yellow feathers, with two clenched claws sticking pathetically up into the air.

"What happened?" we asked, all equally distressed.

"I don't know," said Sven mournfully. "I just found her like this."

"Let's have a look at her," said Jock Duncan, our cook-doctor-dietitian. We all waited in hushed silence while he held Claribel against his ear in an attempt to detect any heartbeat.

Presently he shook his head. "I can't hear anything, but that doesn't prove she's dead. I've never listened to a canary's heart," he added rather apologetically.

"Give her a shot of oxygen," suggested somebody, pointing to the green-banded emergency cylinder in its recess beside the door. Everyone agreed that this was an excellent idea, and Claribel was tucked snugly into a face mask that was large enough to serve as a complete oxygen tent for her.

To our delighted surprise, she revived at once. Beaming broadly, Sven removed the mask, and she hopped onto his finger. She gave her series of "Come to the cookhouse, boys" trills—then promptly keeled over again.

"I don't get it," lamented Sven. "What's wrong with her? She's never done this before."

For the last few minutes, something had been tugging at my memory. My mind seemed to be very sluggish that morning, as if I was still unable to cast off the burden of sleep. I felt that I could do with some of that oxygen—but before I could reach the mask, understanding exploded in my brain. I whirled on the duty engineer and said urgently:

17 ▲ **Critical Viewing**
Do you think these crew members get along with one another? Explain. **[Infer]**

18 ✔ **Reading Check**
What did the crew members do to wake up Claribel?

16 Critical Thinking

Infer

- Ask students why it would be convenient to stick to the terms "night," "day," and "morning."
  Answer: It would help people keep schedules that felt natural.
- Invite students who have experienced jet lag to explain how travel across time zones leaves travelers confused. Ask them to draw connections between their own experiences and those of the astronauts in the story.

17 ▶ Critical Viewing

Answer: The astronauts are all smiling, so they probably get along well, even though they are in close quarters.

18 ✔ Reading Check

Answer: The crew members placed Claribel under the mouthpiece of an oxygen tank and let her breathe the oxygen.

CUSTOMIZE INSTRUCTION FOR UNIVERSAL ACCESS

For Less Proficient Readers	For Advanced Readers
Work with students to find moments in the story in which events might have gone in a different direction. Then, challenge students to think of alternate plot developments, based on those changes. Ask students to devise a flowchart that shows both the sequence of the events as they happened and the alternative events. Finally, ask students which version they prefer and why.	Students who read science fiction may notice that there is a distinct lack of emphasis on technology in this story. Ask students to discuss the author's decision. Students may suggest that the story really is about people's reliance on animals—even in space. After all, the computers failed, but Claribel saved the crew members' lives. Then, challenge students to rewrite the story to include more technology. After students write, ask them to comment on how the change also affected the message of the story.

ASSESS

Answers for p. 162

Review and Assess

1. Students may say it was a good idea to bring Claribel because she made people happy, and she ended up saving them. Other students may say it was a bad idea to bring a pet without first getting permission.
2. **(a)** It takes place on a space station. **(b)** There is no gravity; it is always daytime.
3. **(a)** The crew hides Claribel from the visitors. **(b)** They enjoy having her aboard. **(c)** A pet makes people happy and, in Claribel's case, warns them when the air begins to go bad.
4. **(a)** The narrator wakes late and feels groggy; Claribel is found unconscious; Claribel revives after breathing oxygen but collapses again. **(b)** Both the narrator and Claribel are responsible. The narrator would not have figured out the problem without Claribel's help.
5. **(a)** One of the alarm circuits was not connected and the other circuit failed to go off. Possible responses: **(b)** A canary is a living thing that could get sick or die due to reasons other than bad air quality. **(c)** An electronic alarm is more reliable because, if maintained properly, it will work more efficiently and last longer than a canary.

"Jim!" There's something wrong with the air! That's why Claribel's passed out. I've just remembered that miners used to carry canaries down to warn them of gas."

"Nonsense!" said Jim. "The alarms would have gone off. We've got duplicate circuits, operating independently."

"Er—the second alarm circuit isn't connected up yet," his assistant reminded him. That shook Jim; he left without a word, while we stood arguing and passing the oxygen bottle around like a pipe of peace.

He came back ten minutes later with a sheepish expression. It was one of those accidents that couldn't possibly happen; we'd had one of our rare eclipses by Earth's shadow that night; part of the air purifier had frozen up, and the single alarm in the circuit had failed to go off. Half a million dollars' worth of chemical and electronic engineering had let us down completely. Without Claribel, we should soon have been slightly dead.

So now, if you visit any space station, don't be surprised if you hear an inexplicable snatch of birdsong. There's no need to be alarmed; on the contrary, in fact. It will mean that you're being doubly safeguarded, at practically no extra expense.

Arthur C. Clarke

(b. 1917)

When he first got his television set, noted science-fiction writer Arthur C. Clarke became the only television owner on Sri Lanka, the island off India where he lives.

Clarke holds another, more important television "first." He was the first to think of sending television and radio signals around the world by bouncing them off satellites. If not for his own idea, his television set would have no signals to pick up! Though "Feathered Friend" is science fiction, some of Clarke's dreams about the future have become "science fact."

Review and Assess

Thinking About the Selection

1. **Respond:** Do you think it was a good idea for Sven to bring Claribel into space? Why or why not?
2. (a) **Recall:** Where does the story take place? (b) **Compare and Contrast:** Name two features of life in the story that differ from life on Earth.
3. (a) **Recall:** What do the crew members do with Claribel when VIPs visit the space station? (b) **Infer:** How do the crew members feel about Claribel? (c) **Apply:** What is the benefit of having a pet in the space station?
4. (a) **Synthesize:** Explain at least three events or factors that help the narrator figure out that something is wrong with the air. (b) **Make a Judgment:** Who is responsible for saving the crew's lives: Claribel or the narrator?
5. (a) **Analyze Causes and Effects:** Explain reasons that the alarm did not warn the crew about the problem.
(b) **Speculate:** What are some potential problems with using a canary instead of an electric alarm? (c) **Evaluate:** Which do you think is the better alarm? Why?

ASSESSMENT PRACTICE: Reading Comprehension

Recognize Facts and Details **(For more practice, see Test Preparation Workbook, p. 15)**

Many tests require students to identify facts and details found in the text. It is also important to separate fact, a statement that can be proved, from opinion, a person's feelings or beliefs. Write this text on the chalkboard:

> One morning in July when I was walking across a clover field . . . , I almost stepped on him. . . . He was a big bull blacksnake. . . . He drew his head back in a friendly way. He didn't want trouble. Had he shown the least fight, I would soon have finished him. . . .

Which of these details is not a fact?

A He didn't want trouble.
B He was a big bull blacksnake.
C I almost stepped on him.
D He drew his head back.

B, C, and *D* are statements that can be proved. Since *A* is the narrator's feeling or belief, it is an opinion and the correct answer.

Review and Assess

Literary Analysis

Narratives

1. Tell the sequence of events in "Old Ben."
2. Tell the sequence of events in "Feathered Friend."
3. Who tells the story in each narrative?

Comparing Literary Works

4. In what ways do both selections seem as if they could be true stories?
5. In what ways do both selections seem as if they could be made-up stories?
6. Complete an organizer like the one shown here to compare and contrast the works.

	Characters	Plot	Ending
"Old Ben"	Boy my age, friendly snake		
"Feathered Friend"		Bird is pet on spaceship. Astronauts don't know what's wrong.	

7. Which story did you prefer? Explain, using details from the chart.

Reading Strategy

Using Context Clues

8. Find each of the following words in the story. Use a graphic organizer like the one shown to list the context clues that help you figure out the meaning of each word.
   a. *stroked*, p. 154 **b.** *coiled*, p. 154 **c.** *corncrib*, p. 155

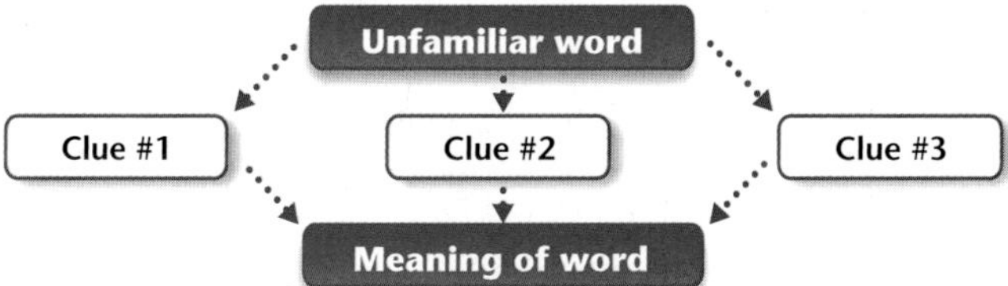

9. Use context clues to explain the meaning of *eclipses* below.
   We'd had one of our rare *eclipses* by Earth's shadow that night.

Extend Understanding

10. **Science Connection:** Name three reasons that space travelers might take plants and animals into space.

> ## Quick Review
>
> A **narrative** is a story. A **fictional narrative** is a made-up story from the writer's imagination. A **nonfictional narrative** is a true story about events that actually happened.
> To review narratives, see page 153.
>
> **Context clues** are words and phrases around an unfamiliar word that help you figure out its meaning.
> To review context clues, see page 153.
>
>  ***Take It to the Net***
> www.phschool.com
> Take the interactive self-test online to check your understanding of these selections.

Answers for p. 163

Review and Assess

1. The narrator finds a blacksnake, names it Old Ben, and puts it in the corncrib in the barn. Eventually Old Ben becomes a good pet. The snake disappears for the winter but returns in the spring. The snake disappears again and the family concludes that he has been killed.
2. Sven brings a bird called Claribel onto a space station. Later, the narrator wakes up groggy. Claribel seems dead but revives after breathing oxygen and then passes out again. The narrator remembers that birds used to warn miners about bad air. Engineers check the air system and find it has failed. Everyone realizes that Claribel saved the crew.
3. In "Old Ben," the narrator is the boy who finds the snake. In "Feathered Friend," the narrator is a space station crew member.
4. Both selections tell events that seem realistic in the order they happen.
5. The narrator's acceptance of Old Ben may seem unusual. The narrator's description of life on the space station is futuristic.
6. **"Old Ben" Plot:** Boy finds a friendly snake and keeps it as a pet. **Ending:** The snake is killed by hogs. **"Feathered Friend" Characters:** Sven; Claribel the canary; the narrator; the crew members. **Ending:** The narrator figures out what is wrong with Claribel and the air system and saves the crew.
7. Students should support their answers with details from the chart.
8. **(a) Clue 1:** The narrator rubs the snake's neck. **Clue 2:** He rubs the snake's back. **Clue 3:** The snake likes the feeling. **Meaning:** a repeated enjoyable movement **(b) Clue 1:** The snake looks like a rope. **Clue 2:** The snake looks like strings. **Clue 3:** The narrator is afraid the snake will wrap around him and choke him. **Meaning:** curled or wound around something **(c) Clue 1:** There will be delicate food in there. **Clue 2:** The corncrib has a door. **Clue 3:** The snake can hide under the corn. **Meaning:** a structure used to hold corn
9. When Earth causes a shadow, it is between the sun and the spacecraft, blocking the sun. An *eclipse* occurs when something blocks out sunlight.
10. Plants and animals might make space seem more like Earth; animals could provide friendship and food; plants could provide oxygen and food.

> **ENRICHMENT: Further Reading**
>
> **Other Works by the Authors**
>
> **Works by Jesse Stuart**
> *Daughter of the Legend*
>
> **Works by Arthur C. Clarke**
> *Expedition to Earth*
>
>  ***Take It to the Net***
> Visit www.phschool.com for more information on the authors.

EXTEND

Answers for p. 164

❶ Vocabulary Development

Word Analysis

regulator, regulation, regulatory, regulate

Concept Development: Definition

1. c
2. d
3. b
4. a

Spelling Strategy

1. precisely
2. ventilating
3. peaceful
4. faker

❷ Grammar

1. had told/past perfect
2. has noticed/present perfect
3. had liked/past perfect
4. have seen/present perfect
5. will have grown/future perfect

Writing Application

Possible answers:

1. Old Ben has slithered into the barn. (present perfect)
2. He had slithered into the hayloft. (past perfect)
3. Soon, he will have slithered all over the farm. (future perfect)

Integrate Language Skills

❶ Vocabulary Development Lesson

Word Analysis: Forms of *regulate*

You can form many new words by adding endings to certain verbs, or action words. For example, the verb *regulate* means "to govern according to a rule." When you add the ending *-tion* to *regulate* (after dropping the final *e*), you form the word *regulation*, meaning "rule." On your paper, use a form of *regulate* to fill in each blank.

regulate regulation regulator regulatory

Taisha was the __?__ for quality control at a catcher's mitt factory. She knew every __?__ in the book. One day, she received a memo from a __?__ agency. Taisha now had to __?__ the way workers checked gloves for holes.

Concept Development: Definition

On your paper, match each numbered word with its definition.

1. scarce
2. fusing
3. regulation
4. ceased

a. stopped
b. rule
c. infrequent
d. joining

Spelling Strategy

When a word ends in silent *e*, drop the *e* when adding a suffix, or ending, beginning with a vowel. Do not drop the *e* when adding a suffix beginning with a consonant. Add the suffix to each word.

1. precise + *-ly*
2. ventilate + *-ing*
3. peace + *-ful*
4. fake + *-er*

❷ Grammar Lesson

Perfect Verb Tenses

The **perfect verb tenses** of verbs combine a form of *have* with the past participle.

- The **present perfect tense** shows an action that began in the past and continues into the present.
- The **past perfect tense** shows a past action or condition that ended before another past action began.
- The **future perfect tense** shows a future action or condition that will have ended before another begins.

Present Perfect	Past Perfect	Future Perfect
have, has + past participle	*had* + past participle	*will have* + past participle
There *has been* no rule against pets in space.	Sven *had smuggled* his pet on the last ferry.	Before long, others *will have brought* pets, too.

Practice Identify the verbs and their tenses.

1. Pa had told me not to play with snakes.
2. He has noticed snakes before.
3. He had liked no snakes until now.
4. I have not seen a snake like that before.
5. By next year, it will have grown.

Writing Application Write three sentences about Old Ben. Use a different perfect tense in each. To review the principal parts of verbs, see page 136.

WG Prentice Hall Writing and Grammar Connection: Chapter 22, Section 2

TEACHING RESOURCES

The following resources can be used to enrich or extend the instruction for pp. 164–165.

Vocabulary

- **Selection Support:** Build Vocabulary, p. 51; Build Spelling Skills, p. 52
- **Vocabulary and Spelling Practice Book** (Use this booklet for skills enrichment)

Grammar

- **Selection Support:** Build Grammar Skills, p. 53
- **Writing and Grammar,** Copper Level, p. 490

- **Daily Language Practice Transparencies** ■

Writing

- **Writing and Grammar,** Copper Level, p. 134 ■
- **Writing Models and Graphic Organizers on Transparencies,** p. 23
- **Writing and Grammar iText CD-ROM**

■ **BLOCK SCHEDULING:** Resources marked with this symbol provide varied instruction during 90-minute blocks.

❸ Writing Lesson

Feature Story

Write a brief feature story—a newspaper article about something that is not actually news but is interesting or unusual—about Claribel or Ben.

Prewriting Think of the questions your readers will have, such as what makes this animal different from other animals of its kind? Gather details to answer those questions.

Drafting Describe the interesting features, activities, or abilities of the animal. Organize each paragraph around a main idea. Then, supply examples, explanations, and details.

Revising Revise your paragraph to improve the organization. Highlight the main idea in each paragraph. Delete any sentences in the paragraph that do not support, explain, or give details about that main idea.

Model: Deleting Unrelated Details

You might expect a bird to be timid or at least cautious. Although Claribel is tiny, she is not afraid of anything. ~~She can hide in the smallest space.~~ Whatever the crew is working on, no matter how noisy, Claribel wants to be part of the action.

The detail about Claribel's ability to hide is deleted because it does not contribute to the main idea that she is not afraid.

WG *Prentice Hall Writing and Grammar Connection: Chapter 7, Section 4*

❹ Extension Activities

Listening and Speaking Create a **multimedia presentation** about your own or someone else's experience with a pet. Identify the people involved and the events. Include details to make your story come alive, and use photos, recordings, charts, or other visuals. To tell your story,

- include your own thoughts and actions.
- tell listeners how you or the subject of the story feels about the pet.

After you make your presentation to your class, ask your classmates to share their experiences with a similiar pet.

Research and Technology With a small group, choose a type of pet to research for a pet fair. Go online to get photos and gather information about the pet's habits, pet care (including training and feeding), and costs involved in having pets. Create **fact sheets** and hand them out at the fair. **[Group Activity]**

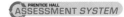

Take It to the Net www.phschool.com

Go online for an additional research activity using the Internet.

ASSESSMENT RESOURCES

The following resources can be used to assess students' knowledge and skills.

Selection Assessment

- **Formal Assessment,** pp. 39–41
- **Open Book Test,** pp. 31–33
- **Got It! Assessment Videotapes,** Tape 1
- **Test Bank Software**

Take It to the Net
Visit www.phschool.com for self-tests and additional questions on the selections

Writing Rubric

- **Performance Assess. and Portfolio Mgmt.,** p. 12

Listening and Speaking Rubric

- **Performance Assess. and Portfolio Mgmt.,** p. 24

PRENTICE HALL ASSESSMENT SYSTEM

- **Workbook**
- **Skill Book**
- **Transparencies**
- **CD-ROM**

Lesson Support for p. 165

❸ Writing Lesson

- Remind students, as they generate questions to answer, that in a narrative the most important question is "What happened?"
- Before students write, work with them to generate a list of words that indicate the passage of time or transition. Examples include: *first, second, next, then, later, soon,* and *finally.* Encourage students to use these words in their writing.
- You may also wish to provide students with some examples of feature writing from the local or school newspaper. Point out how the articles arrange the events they describe in the order that they happened.
- Use the Exposition rubric on p. 12 in **Performance Assessment and Portfolio Management** to evaluate students' feature stories.

❹ Listening and Speaking

- Before students begin, remind them that even though they are using technology in their presentations, they must still practice good speaking skills.
- Generate a list of good speaking skills on the board. Students may suggest the following skills: facing the audience at all times and maintaining good eye contact, speaking in a clear and confident voice, and using appropriate language.
- Suggest that students work in pairs to write and revise their stories.
- Have students use the Engaging Listeners rubric on p. 24 of **Performance Assessment and Portfolio Management.**

CUSTOMIZE INSTRUCTION
For Universal Access

To address different learning styles, use the activities in the **Extension Activities** booklet, p. 11.

- For Visual/Spatial Learners, use Activity 5.
- For Interpersonal and Verbal/Linguistic Learners, use Activity 6.
- For Logical/Mathematical Learners, use Activity 7.

Lesson Objectives

1. To read a review accurately
2. To understand the purposes of reviews
3. To develop a strategy for recognizing and defining unfamiliar terms or specialized vocabulary

About Reviews

- Before students read "About Reviews," ask them whether they have ever read a review and what their purpose was for reading it. Possible response: Students may say that they have read movie reviews in order to determine whether a movie was worth seeing.
- Then, have students read "About Reviews."
- Explain the format of a typical review. First, the reviewer introduces the subject of the review. Then, in the body of the review, the reviewer evaluates the subject. Tell students that reviewers have a list of criteria, or standards, that the subject may or may not meet. For example, a restaurant reviewer would want a restaurant to be clean, employ friendly wait staff, and serve good food. If the restaurant failed to meet these criteria, or exceeded them, the reviewer would say so in the review. Finally, a reviewer gives a final judgment, positive or negative.

Reading Strategy

Reading Accurately

- Before students read the Reading Strategy, ask them how they deal with unfamiliar vocabulary words when they read. Do they skip the words? Do they stop and look them up in a dictionary? Do they try to determine the meaning from other words in the sentence? Explain that the reading strategy suggests that students preview a selection for unfamiliar words and then look up their definitions and pronunciations before reading the selection.
- Have students read the Reading Strategy, and then show them the chart on p. 166. If necessary, walk through the process of identifying and defining an unfamiliar term.

READING INFORMATIONAL MATERIALS

Reviews

About Reviews

A **review** describes and evaluates a product or performance. Reviews are one source of information you can use to find out about the following topics.

- a book
- a movie or television program
- a stage performance
- a music disc, collection, or performance
- a restaurant

By describing a product or performance, the reviewer gives the reader information that can be used to make a decision. If a reviewer likes something, he or she will rave about it and thereby influence readers positively. On the other hand, a negative review can discourage people from buying, visiting, reading, or viewing.

The following selection, "As Close As We Can Get," is a music review about the *Smithsonian Folkways' Anthology of American Folk Music*. As you read, think about whether you would or would not purchase the collection, based on the review.

Reading Strategy

Reading Accurately

To **read accurately** means to read each word correctly and to understand the meaning of each word. When you are reading informational texts, you are likely to encounter specialized vocabulary that is unfamiliar. To ensure that you read accurately, scan a text—run your eyes quickly over the words—before you read it closely.

- Identify unfamiliar words and terms.
- Look them up in a dictionary or other resource.
- Learn their pronunciations.

Each of these steps will help you read and comprehend more accurately during reading. Before you read the review, scan the text.

Use a chart like the one shown to write down any unfamiliar words you notice. Then, look up their pronunciations as well as their meanings and record them in the space provided. After reading, review new words so you will read them accurately when you see them again.

Unfamiliar Word	Meaning	Pronunciation
self-conscious	awkward or embarrassed in the presence of others; ill at ease	self′ känshəs

As Close As We Can Get

Carl Zebrowski

The Banjo Lesson, 1893, Henry Ossawa Tanner, Hampton University Museum, Hampton, Virginia

Scan the text to find the words *anthology, medium, pretensions, bowing, virtuosity,* and *era.* Look up each word in a dictionary, decide which definition fits in this situation, and make sure you can pronounce each word.

Listening to the recordings in *Smithsonian Folkways' Anthology of American Folk Music* is like looking at a photo of a Civil War soldier dressed in a crumpled uniform. Beneath the medium's time-worn surface you can sense the presence of a vibrant living person.

Music Review, *Civil War Times*, October 1999

As Close As We Can Get

- Before students read "As Close As We Can Get," have them look for the words suggested in the marginal boxes. If students are not familiar with these words, have them look up the words in a dictionary.
- Tell students to look for other words that are unfamiliar to them in addition to the ones listed in the marginal boxes.
- Have students list each word and the word's meaning and pronunciation in a chart like the one on p. 166.
- Ask students to name the subject of the review. Then, ask them where they found this information. **Answer:** The subject of the review is the recording *Smithsonian Folkways' Anthology of American Folk Music.* The reviewer mentions the subject of the review in the first sentence.
- Point out to students that the reviewer gives some hints about his feelings for the musical recording—the image of the recording looking like a Civil War–era photograph is a compliment.

continued

CUSTOMIZE INSTRUCTION FOR UNIVERSAL ACCESS

For Special Needs Students	For English Learners
Students may find that the review here is very subtle. The reviewer does not explicitly state "I loved this recording." Explain that the language in the review, however, provides clues to the reviewer's feelings. It may help students to watch excerpts from a television movie-review program. Videotape a segment or two and allow students to watch with you in class. Point out how the reviewer introduces the movies and then gives his or her reasons for the final evaluation. Ask students to look for the same elements in the review on pp. 167–168.	The reviewer of the American folk music recording does not plainly state that he loved the recording. In fact, he relies on readers' understandings of words and phrase connotations to convey his idea. For example, students may not understand that the comparison of the recording to a nineteenth-century photograph is complimentary. Work with students to find and define words and phrases that are not only unfamiliar but have unusual connotations or associations. Examples include *plain folk, other-worldly,* and *historical gold dust.*

continued from p. 16

- Challenge students to look for specific words that indicate the reviewer's feelings about the recording.
  Answers: Students may point to the following words and phrases as indicative of the reviewer's feelings: "vibrant," "earthy yet at the same time other-worldly," "timeless," "made the music come alive," and "gold dust shows up on these recordings."
- Ask students to sum up the reviewer's feelings about the recording.
  Answer: The reviewer liked it, imperfections and all.
- Ask students how the review made them feel about the recording.
  Possible response: Students may say they are interested in listening to the recording after reading the review.
- Have students compare their charts of unfamiliar words with other students' charts. Discuss the similarities and differences between students' charts.

What cuts through the mild surface noise of the anthology's 70-year-old recordings is people in all their joy and sorrow. These are plain folk, mostly from south of the Mason-Dixon Line. They have no pretensions. They are not self-conscious. Their music is earthy yet at the same time other-worldly.

There's plenty of sloppy string plucking and bowing here, and warbling voices, too, but surely that's what folk music sounded like in the 1860s (and often still does). It was a time when entertainment for a social gathering often meant a friend playing his banjo. He probably wasn't an accomplished musician by traditional standards, but his confident rhythm and enthusiasm made the music come alive in ways sheer virtuosity can't. This anthology is about as close as we can get to the music of that era.

The reviewer identifies the strengths and weaknesses of the collection.

Although the recordings here were, of course, not made during the war, the performances are timeless. The songs are even more so. Indeed, many of them have been around for hundreds of years. They were played in the 1860s and are still played today. As everything in history does, these simple tunes have picked up a little bit of all the generations they've passed through. That historical gold dust shows up on these recordings.

Music Review, *Civil War Times*, October 1999

CUSTOMIZE INSTRUCTION FOR UNIVERSAL ACCESS

For Advanced Readers

Students who are accomplished readers may enjoy reading reviews. Challenge them to find two reviews that cover the same subject, such as a book, restaurant, movie, video game, theater performance, or musical recording, and to compare and contrast the two reviews. Suggest that students look at the criteria the reviewers used as well as their reactions to the subject. In addition, have students make a list of any unfamiliar words they found in the reviews and then record them in a chart like the one on p. 166. Finally, ask students to write a two- or three-paragraph paper that compares and contrasts the two reviews. Have students conclude their papers by explaining which reviewer they agree with and why.

Check Your Comprehension

1. How old are the recordings on the anthology?
2. Where are most of the people who made the recordings from?
3. In the 1860s, what kind of entertainment would there have been at a social gathering?

Applying the Reading Strategy

Reading Accurately

4. What is the meaning and pronunciation of the word "anthology"?
5. Which words did you look up for definition or pronunciation? Read aloud the sentences in which the words appear.

Activity

Radio Review

Prepare a reading of "As Close As We Can Get" as if you were giving a review on a radio broadcast. Make sure you know the meaning of each word in the text as well as how to pronounce it. When you are confident of your ability, perform your radio review for your class.

Contrasting Informational Materials

Music Reviews and Advertisements

Reviewers have the ability to influence readers positively or negatively, which may then sway readers to go out and buy, watch, visit, or read whatever is being reviewed. Although reviewers may influence people's decisions to buy something, the reviewer does not benefit from the reader's decision one way or another.

Like music reviews, advertisements use descriptive language and persuasion to influence their audience. However, the purpose of an advertisement is to persuade readers or listeners to buy the product.

In a newspaper or magazine, find a review of a movie, CD, or performance. Then, find an advertisement for the same movie, CD, or performance. (It does not have to appear in the same magazine or newspaper.) Then, using a chart like the one provided, compare the advertisement to the review.

	Advertisement	Music Review
Purpose		
Kinds of words used to persuade		
Biased or unbiased? How do you know?		
Would you buy the product? Why?		

Answers for p. 169

Check Your Comprehension

1. They are 70 years old.
2. Most of the people are from the southern United States.
3. The entertainment would have been musical, with local people playing instruments and singing.

Apply the Reading Strategy

4. An anthology (an thäl'ə jē) is a collection of pieces of music or literature that is chosen by an editor or collector. In this case, it is a collection of songs.
5. Students' answers will vary. Ask them to identify and define the words.

Activity

To prepare students, play a recording of a review from a radio program, and ask students what they notice. They should notice the confidence with which the reviewer speaks as well as his or her pace of speaking and use of clear pronunciation. Challenge students, as they prepare their readings, to pay attention to pace, enunciation, and the flow of sentences. If there is time, have students practice reading aloud in front of peers or into tape recorders. Students should ask for positive feedback from classmates, or listen carefully to their own recordings.

continued

Answers continued

Contrasting Informational Materials

Music Reviews and Advertisements: You may wish to prepare the review and advertisement materials in advance. Otherwise, give students time to find the materials. Consider allowing students to work in pairs so they can discuss the elements of the two forms of writing. You may want to talk with students briefly about the concepts of connotation and bias in writing. Ultimately, students should see that the product descriptions are persuasive and often biased and use language that suggests that the product is essential to good living. The purpose of the review is to inform as well as persuade. Also, a review may be positive yet still suggest that the product has flaws. As a class, discuss the power of advertisements and reviews to persuade people to buy or use a particular product.

Lesson Objectives

1. To write a descriptive essay
2. To use writing strategies to generate ideas, plan, organize, evaluate, and revise the composition

Model From Literature

Even though Helen Keller could not see or hear, her description of her early childhood in "Water" (p. 120) includes rich sensory details.

Prewriting

- Suggest that students use a cluster diagram to choose a topic. Have them write the general topic words suggested on p. 170 in the center of the diagram and then create additional circles and fill them in with ideas.
- Involve the whole class in the process of narrowing the topics. First, discuss the difference between a too-broad topic, a too-narrow topic, and a just-right topic. Then, ask volunteers to share their topics with the class. Let the class vote on whether the topic is too broad, too narrow, or just right. If the topic is too broad or too narrow, ask the class for positive suggestions on making adjustments.
- Remind students as they prepare their sensory detail charts that they should strive to include at least two details for each sense.
- Before students draft their essays, have them review the Rubric for Self-Assessment on p. 173 so they know what is expected.

Writing WORKSHOP

Description: Descriptive Essay

A **descriptive essay** creates a picture of a person, place, thing, or event. In this workshop, you will write a descriptive essay focused on a topic that interests you.

Assignment Criteria. Your descriptive essay should have the following characteristics:

- main impression to which each detail adds specific information
- rich sensory language that appeals to the five senses
- organizational pattern appropriate to the type of composition
- figurative language that creates vivid comparisons

See the Rubric on page 173 for the criteria on which your descriptive essay may be assessed.

Prewriting

Choose a topic. Use **trigger words** to help you think of a topic. Think of three general words, such as *vacation, family, memories.* Take a few minutes to list specific words that you associate with each general word. Then, review what you have written, circle descriptive words, and choose the most interesting topic from your list.

Narrow your topic. When you have chosen your topic, narrow it to focus on a part that is specific enough to be described in a single composition. For example, "the national park" is too broad. You could not give a clear picture of the whole park in one composition. However, "our campsite at the national park" and "the old pine next to our campsite" are narrowed topics that you could fully describe in one composition.

Use sensory details. Use a sensory details chart like the one shown to help you gather details about the sights, scents, textures, sounds, and tastes associated with a campsite.

Model: Gathering Sensory Details

Taste	Touch	Smell	Sight	Hearing
None	Rough tail	Hay	Star	Clopping

TEACHING RESOURCES

The following resources can be used to enrich or extend the instruction for pp. 170–173.

- **Writing and Grammar,** Copper Level, Chapter 6, pp. 98–117
- **Performance Assessment and Portfolio Management,** p. 9
- **Writing Models and Graphic Organizers on Transparencies,** p. 11

Writing and Grammar iText CD-ROM
Students can use the following tools as they complete their descriptive essays:

- Unity and Coherence
- Language Variety
- Troublesome Adjectives and Adverbs

Student Model

Before you begin drafting your descriptive essay, read this student model and review the characteristics of successful description.

Jessica Kile

Short and Sweet

The day looked too gray and foggy to bother going outside. I looked out the window once more, then turned back toward the kitchen. Suddenly I realized I had seen something strange. My father was walking up the driveway with—a dog? No. What was that thing? It was mostly black, with a shaggy black coat that contrasted with the white mane and tail. Mane and tail? I realized that I was describing a horse, but this animal clopping up the driveway was too small to be a horse. Or was it?

Outside, where my father introduced Lucky, the miniature horse, I examined our new pet. I began by examining Lucky's face. Like a full-sized horse, Lucky had a broad forehead with a wisp of mane tossed down between his ears. His eyes were deep brown and peaceful. The black coat was not shaggy here. The hair on Lucky's head was soft, but a little bumpy, like a terry cloth towel. The smoothest, softest part of any horse's head is his nose—and Lucky was no exception. The hair around his nose was so short and soft it felt like velour. I gave his neck a hug and breathed in the horsy smell that seemed like a mix of warm hay and wet leaves. When I hugged him, he nickered—a sound like a little chuckle that moves from his throat to his nose.

I ran my hands across his back, noticing how much tinier it was than a full-sized horse. Here, his coat was rough and shaggy. I checked his legs, which seemed to be healthy and straight. The hooves, too, seemed in good shape. They were smooth with a thick "shell" that had no cracks.

His tail was thick and the hair here was much coarser and rougher than any human hair. It was strange because from a distance the tail looked smooth and flowing. When you touched it though, it became a rough rope. Lucky became impatient with my "health inspection." He nudged me with his velvety nose to get me back to scratching his ears.

"What do you think?" asked Dad after I had examined Lucky from head to toe.

"Well," I said, "I've never seen a horse like this! I like him though. He may be short, but he's sweet!"

> The writer establishes a main impression of a horse—just a smaller horse than people expect.

> Beginning with Lucky's head, the author will describe the horse, in spatial order.

> The writer uses details that appeal to the senses. Here, smell and sound are described.

> Through figurative language, the writer establishes the feel of the horse's tail.

CUSTOMIZE INSTRUCTION FOR UNIVERSAL ACCESS

For Less Proficient Readers	For English Learners	For Advanced Readers
If students seem reluctant to choose a topic, guide them to choose a person, place, or thing that is memorable. If possible, have students revisit the scene or spend time with the person or object. Then, have students write observations and questions that they have about their topics.	If students have trouble with adjectives that accurately convey their ideas, work with them to create a word bank for different colors, smells, and sounds. Have students create a graphic organizer like the one on p. 170 to contain and organize the adjectives. Allow students to use a dictionary and thesaurus as they work.	Challenge students to describe an event in history or an imaginary event. This activity will help them rely less on their abilities to observe than on their abilities to generate sensory details. Encourage students to create a scene with characters and a setting that they must describe in full detail. Invite students to read their essays to the class.

Student Model

- Explain that the Student Model is a sample, and that essays may be longer.
- Ask students to read the title and to skim the contents of the model in order to identify the topic of the essay.
  Answer: The essay is about a miniature horse that the author's father has just brought home.
- Take a moment to talk about why the topic is neither too broad nor too narrow.
- As a class, make note of the sensory details included in the writing model. Draw a chart on the board, or use the Sensory Language transparency on p. 81 in **Writing Models and Graphic Organizers on Transparencies.**
- Ask students to draw conclusions from the list of sensory details and to think about why the writer emphasized some types of details over others.
- Finally, ask students whether they thought the writer's description was effective, and have them explain why.

Real-World Connection

Descriptive writing in the workplace: Descriptive writing is required in some challenging and creative careers. Journalists, for example, must have a keen eye and ear for sensory details in order to relay news events in an accurate and descriptive way. Radio journalists, in particular, must be able to use words to convey scenes to an audience that cannot see what is happening. Travel writers, too, must be able to re-create through their writing a breathtaking view or a marvelous meal in order to entice travelers to follow in their footsteps. Discuss in class other careers that might require descriptive writing, such as movie and art critics, fiction writers, and historians.

Drafting

- If possible, offer students models of writing that use the three organizational orders. Explain that chronological order works best when describing an event. Spatial order works best when describing a room or a scene. Order of importance works best when describing a person.
- For students who want to use the chronological order, offer them the Series of Events transparency on p. 69 of **Writing Models and Graphic Organizers on Transparencies.**
- Have students practice using spatial order with a partner to describe the classroom in different orders (near to far, left to right, top to bottom). Ask them to think about whether the order makes any difference in their descriptions.
- Explain that the order of importance may be the most difficult order to use because it requires students to decide which details are the most important. Tell students that they will want to leave the reader with a strong impression, so the most important detail should appear last. Have students use a pyramid-shaped graphic organizer to arrange their details. They should write the least important detail in the top of the pyramid and work their way down, writing the most important detail at the bottom.
- Discuss the figurative language examples in the directions, and tell students that figurative language conveys details and adds variety to the essay.

Revising

- Illustrate the importance of sentence length by reading to students from a children's story or from a book for young readers. Ask students what they notice about the sentences.
  Answers: Sentences are short and repetitious. Sentences begin mostly with nouns and verbs.
- Explain that using sentences of the same length and pattern is helpful for young readers but boring for more sophisticated readers.

(continued on page 173)

Drafting

Organize the details. Arrange the details in an order that will help the reader picture your subject. Use the organization chart to decide which organization is most appropriate for a descriptive essay. Then, write the draft of your essay using that organization.

Chronological Order
- Present events in the order in which they occur.
- Use for a remembrance or other description of an event.

Spatial Order
- Present details from left to right, top to bottom, or back to front.
- Use for descriptions of places or objects.

Order of Importance
- Present least important details at the beginning and the most important at the end.
- Use for descriptions that will be used to evaluate the thing being described or to show its significance.

Use figurative language. Figurative language is writing that is not meant to be taken literally. In your description, use figurative language such as metaphors and similes to emphasize qualities of your subject.

- **Simile:** A comparison expressed using the word *like* or *as.*
  "His tail was like a rough rope."
- **Metaphor:** A comparison expressed without the words *like* or *as.* One thing is referred to as if it were another.
  "His tail was a rough rope."
  "The rough rope of his tail . . ."

Create a main impression. Make connections between the details to create a single impression—an idea or a feeling—about your subject. Focus mainly on details that contribute to that main impression.

Revising

Revise to vary sentence length. Revise in places where you have several sentences containing long lists of descriptive words. Group some related details in lists. Emphasize unusual or unique details by breaking them into individual sentences. Use the model on page 172 as a guide.

Model: Revising Sentence Length

Outside, where my father introduced Lucky, the miniature horse, I examined our new pet.
Draft: ~~I went outside. My father introduced Lucky, the minature horse. Lucky, the miniature horse. I examined our new pet.~~ I began by examining Lucky's face. Like a full-sized horse, Lucky had a broad forehead *with* ~~He had~~ a wisp of mane tossed down between his ears.

Because several short sentences in a row gave a choppy sound to the writing, the writer combined some sentences to create variety with two long sentences around one short one.

USING TECHNOLOGY IN WRITING

Students may use the character function in a word-processing program to help them keep track of the details in their essays. Suggest that after students prepare a first draft, they set sentences with sensory details in a different color. Students may expand on this idea by placing details for each sense in a different color. For example, sentences that contain visual details might be blue; details about hearing might be red. Remind students that they also can use the organizing tools and revision checkers on **Writing and Grammar iText CD-ROM.**

Revise word choice. Check your adjectives—the words that describe nouns—to make sure they add specific details to your description. Vague words like *great, nice,* and *good* do not add details that readers can identify. Vague adjectives leave readers wondering in what way the thing you are describing is *great, nice,* or *good.* Use precise adjectives like *exciting, helpful,* and *spicy* to give readers specific information.

Compare the nonmodel and the model. Why is the model stronger than the nonmodel?

Nonmodel	Model
Lucky was a nice horse. His coat was soft—especially around his nose. His legs and hooves looked good, and his coat was great.	Lucky was a friendly and curious horse. His coat was like velvet—especially around his nose. His legs and hooves looked solid, and his coat was shiny.

Publishing and Presenting

Choose one of the following ways to share your writing with classmates or a wider audience.

Record it. Make an audio recording of your description. Play the tape for a group of classmates or family members.

Mail it. Send your descriptive essay to a friend or relative by e-mail.

Save it for future use. Descriptive writing is used in almost all other forms of writing, including narration and persuasion. Save your description. You can use part or all of it in a story, persuasive essay, or speech. Depending on the topic of your description and the new writing, you might incorporate the whole description or only specific details.

WG *Prentice Hall Writing and Grammar Connection: Chapter 5*

Listening Connection

To learn to evaluate and make judgments about descriptions in advertisements and other persuasive messages, see the **Listening and Speaking Workshop** on page 174.

Rubric for Self-Assessment

Evaluate your descriptive essay using the following criteria and rating scale:

Criteria	Rating Scale: Not very				Very
How clear is the main impression?	1	2	3	4	5
Do details contribute to the main impression?	1	2	3	4	5
Is the description logically organized?	1	2	3	4	5
How vivid and varied is the sensory language?	1	2	3	4	5
How effective is the figurative language?	1	2	3	4	5

TEST-TAKING TIP

Remind students that when taking a test that involves responding to a descriptive prompt, they should do what they learned in this workshop. The only difference is that they will have less time. Offer students this acronym for writing description: TIPS (Topic, Impression, organizational Pattern, and Sensory details.) After students read the test prompt, they should identify an appropriate topic, generate sensory details, think of the best order to arrange details, and state the overall impression. Remind them to use a cluster diagram or a chart like the one on p. 170.

Revising (continued)

- Point out that many long sentences with strings of adjectives are difficult to read. Explain that although students are writing descriptive essays, they should focus as much on active verbs as on descriptive adjectives. Encourage students to use active voice and to rely on vivid verbs and nouns to create a scene.
- Students may need help understanding the difference between a weak and a strong adjective. As a class, generate a list of weak adjectives, and write them on the board or overhead transparency. Then, challenge students to think of strong alternatives to the weak adjectives. Explain that strong adjectives help readers actually picture the scene in their minds as they read.

Publishing and Presenting

- The audience is probably the last thing on students' minds as they write. Remind students that one purpose for writing is to share their ideas and experiences with other people. Ask students what audience or type of people might be interested in their descriptive essays.
- Ask students to share their essays with members of an audience and to get feedback from them. Have students write a short journal entry about the audience members' reactions.

Assessment

- Review the assessment criteria in class.
- Have students practice assessment skills by comparing the Student Model on page 171 to the rubric here. Remind students to be objective in their evaluations.
- For further practice, have students evaluate a partner's paper.
- The rubric on this page, and another rubric in an alternative format, can be found on p. 9 of **Performance Assessment and Portfolio Management.**

Lesson Objectives

1. To evaluate a persuasive message by understanding the persuasive techniques incorporated within
2. To recognize the persuasive techniques of bandwagon and emotional appeal, testimonial, and loaded language
3. To recognize the point of persuasive messages by analyzing the factual content of the messages, as well as the techniques used in making them

Evaluate Information

- Display copies of advertisements, or show a videotape of commercials that demonstrate the techniques discussed on p. 174. After pointing out how each advertisement uses the techniques, challenge students to think of other advertisements that also use them.
- Remind students that persuasive techniques in themselves are not bad but providing false or misleading information is wrong.
- If possible, find advertisements or editorials that demonstrate bias, opinion, and propaganda. Point out that the purpose of this workshop is to make students aware that many messages are designed to change students' minds or encourage them to do something they had not originally planned.

Evaluate Delivery

- Challenge students to think of messages that make them feel a particular way. Explain that the emotional impact of such messages is powerful.
- Explain that the point of persuasive messages may not always be clear. Often, the message is hidden behind the feelings it generates or behind creative techniques.
- Complete the workshop as a class by preparing ahead of time a videotape of some commercials for students to evaluate, using the questions on p. 174.

Listening and Speaking WORKSHOP

Evaluating Persuasive Messages

A **persuasive message** encourages the audience to think or act in a certain way. Many persuasive messages—such as political presentations, debates, editorials, advertisements, infomercials, and others—are communicated on television. Learn to evaluate persuasive messages.

Evaluate Information

Identify false and misleading information. Do not believe that everything stated as a fact is accurate.

- **Consider the source.** Facts supplied by the person or group that is selling or persuading may be slanted to favor a particular point of view.
- **Distinguish between fact and opinion.** Opinions can be supported, but not proved. A fact can be proved true.
- **Recognize propaganda.** Propaganda is the spreading of distorted or misleading ideas to promote a special interest or to damage a person, group, or cause.

Evaluate Delivery

A persuasive message on television may include speech, music, and visual images that add appeal but do not add factual content.

Notice persuasive techniques. Be aware of the persuasive techniques shown here that are sometimes used in place of factual information.

Technique	Example
Bandwagon appeal	Every sixth-grader thinks this, so you should too.
Testimonial	Famous people use this product, so it must be good.
Loaded language (words meant to give a positive or negative slant to a statement)	My opponent is *wavering.* I am *considering the options . . .*

Recognize emotional appeals. An emotional appeal is a persuasive technique through which your choice is influenced with feelings rather than information. For example, an advertisement may be very entertaining but give very little information about the product. Images shown with the product can make it seem as if people who buy or use the product are more popular, happy, or successful. Always ask yourself if the associations made in an ad are valid—can the product really create a situation like the one shown in the ad?

Evaluate several television advertisements by asking these questions.

- How reliable and accurate is the information?
- What persuasive techniques are used?
- What associations are made? Are they valid?
- Is the advertisement entertaining or memorable?
- Are you persuaded? Why or why not?

Few persuasive messages are strictly factual. Evaluate each message, and use sound reasoning to make up your mind about the advertisement.

CUSTOMIZE INSTRUCTION FOR UNIVERSAL ACCESS

For Special Needs Students	For Less Proficient Readers
Have students name a few products with which they are familiar. Then, single out the products with which all students are familiar, and have them discuss the words and slogans used to market the product. As students discuss the words and slogans, write them on the board so students can read the impact that the slogans carry. Then, challenge students to question the slogans and words and the impact they make.	Have students write a short advertisement for a product they use or with which they are familiar. Tell students to write a couple of paragraphs describing the product in an ordinary and honest manner. Then, have students compare their own descriptions with how the actual advertisement describes the product. Challenge students to notice the persuasive language in the advertisement and whether or not the language is factual.

Assessment WORKSHOP

Identifying and Supporting Main Ideas

In the reading sections of some tests, you may be required to read a passage and answer multiple-choice questions about the main idea or supporting details in a passage. Use the strategies to help you answer test questions about details.

Read the question carefully to identify whether you are being asked for a main idea or a supporting detail. Then, read the answer choices to see if you can eliminate any answer that is not the kind of information being asked for.

Test-Taking Strategies

- Look over the questions before reading passages to help you focus on key points.
- Before choosing an answer, make sure you have identified whether the question asks for a main idea or a supporting detail.

Sample Test Item

A strong breeze made the leaves rustle. A twig snapped beneath his foot, and Martin jumped. He had never walked the woodsy path between his house and Andy's alone at night. An owl's hoot didn't exactly scare him, but it did make him nervous.

1. How does Martin feel about his walk?

A He feels uneasy.

B He is walking the path alone for the first time.

C It is dark.

D The owl's hoot doesn't frighten him.

Answer and Explanation

The question asks you to identify the main idea of how Martin feels about the walk. *B, C,* and *D* are incorrect because they are details that contribute to the main idea. The answer is ***A***.

Practice

Answer the questions based on this passage:

The world's tropical rain forests are filled with treasures more valuable than gold or jewels. Rain forests include many varieties of fruits, thousands of species of animals, and many plants with healing properties. The trees give off oxygen, which is necessary to humans. Rubber trees yield natural rubber, necessary for many products. The sap of one kind of tree is similar to diesel oil.

1. Treasures of the rain forests include

A oxygen, fruits, gold.

B fruits, rubber, oxygen.

C diesel fuel, animals, jewels.

D fruits, medicine, wheat.

2. Why are the rain forests important?

A They have fruit.

B The sap of one kind of tree is like diesel oil.

C Plants have healing properties.

D There are a wide variety of useful resources found only in the rain forest.

Lesson Objective

To determine a text's main ideas and how those ideas are supported by related details

Applying Reading Strategies

Explain to students that summarizing is a skill that can help them identify the main idea of a reading passage and its related details. Although students have used summarizing to keep track of the events that happen in a story, they also can use the skill to identify key details in a short reading passage. Then, students can trace the details back to the main idea.

Test-Taking Skills

- Ask students to read the sample test item. Before they try to answer the question, challenge students to summarize the reading passage by following the steps below.
- First, have students identify all the key details.
  Answer: Details include rustling leaves, a snapping twig, Martin alone on a woodsy path, a hoot owl, and Martin's nervousness.
- Next, have students use the details to figure out the main idea of the passage.
  Answer: It is an eerie experience for Martin to walk in the woods at night by himself.
- Finally, have students summarize the reading passage in a single sentence.
  Possible response: Rustling leaves, a snapped twig, and an owl's hoot make Martin's walk in the woods an eerie experience.

Answer

1. The correct answer is B. The passage misleads the reader by mentioning that the forest contains things that are more valuable than jewels or gold. It is the second sentence that contains the most important information—the forest contains animals, fruits, and plants that heal. *A* is incorrect because the passage does not say that the forests contains gold. *C* is incorrect because the passage does not say that the forests contain

continued

Answer continued

jewels. *D* is incorrect because wheat is not mentioned in the passage at all.

2. The correct answer is D. *A, B,* and *C* all mention treasures that are found in the rain forest but *D* provides a brief summary on why rain forests are important.

TEACHING RESOURCES

The following resources can be used to enrich or extend the instruction for p. 175.

PRENTICE HALL ASSESSMENT SYSTEM

- Workbook
- Skill Book
- Transparencies
- CD-ROM

Unit Objectives

1. To read selections in different genres that develop the theme of "Proving Yourself"
2. To apply a variety of reading strategies, particularly interactive reading strategies, appropriate for reading these selections
3. To analyze literary elements
4. To use a variety of strategies to build vocabulary
5. To learn elements of grammar, usage, and style
6. To use recursive writing processes to write in a variety of forms
7. To develop listening and speaking skills
8. To express and support responses to various types of texts
9. To prepare, organize, and present literary interpretations

Meeting the Objectives

With each selection, you will find instructional materials through which students can meet these objectives. Further, you will find additional practice pages for reading strategies, literary analysis, vocabulary, and grammar in the **Selection Support: Skills Development Workbook** in your **Teaching Resources.**

Background

Art

Maze at Sunset by Garry Nichols

Garry Nichols was born in Tasmania, Australia. He uses both symbols of nature and repetitive patterns in his colorful paintings.

1. What do you think the man on the ladder is trying to do? Answer: He is trying to see over the walls of the maze to view the sunset. He may also be looking for a way out of the maze.
2. How does this painting relate to the theme "Proving Yourself"? Possible responses: The man must prove himself by finding his way out of the maze; the man proves himself by choosing to view the sunset rather than worrying about getting out.

UNIT 3 Proving Yourself

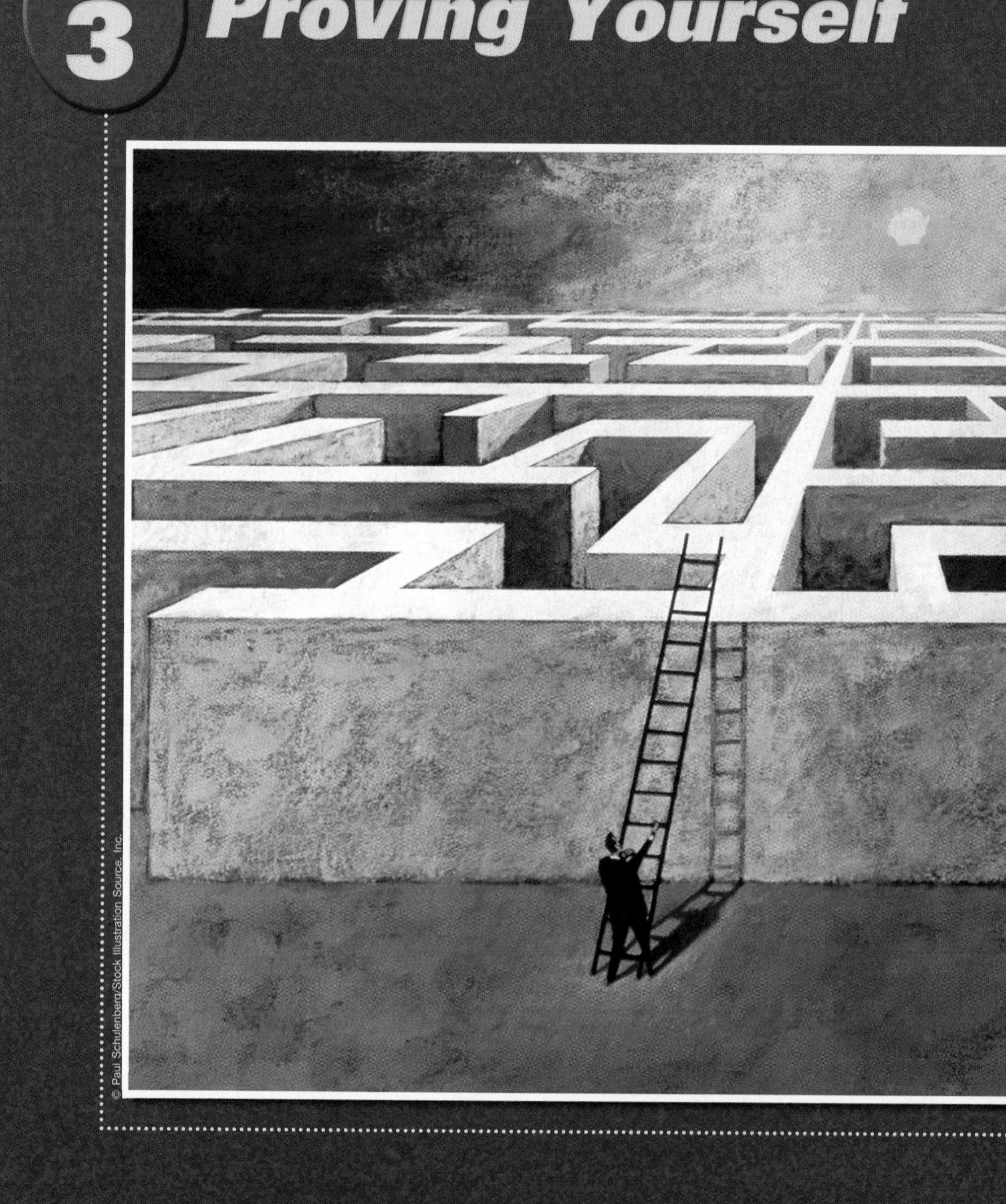

UNIT FEATURES

Connections	Reading Informational Material
Every unit contains a feature that connects literature to a related topic, such as art, science, or history. In this unit, the Women and Sports selection on p. 238 links real-world achievers with fictional selections about girl athletes. Use the information and questions on the Connections page to enrich students' understanding of the selections presented within the unit.	These selections will help students learn to analyze and evaluate informational texts, such as workplace documents, technical directions, and consumer materials. They will expose students to the organization and features unique to nonnarrative texts. In this unit, students will learn strategies for reading and completing applications, and will read about endangered animals.

Exploring the Theme

Life is full of twists and turns, choices and challenges. Each choice leads to a different path that gives you the chance to test your abilities and find new strengths. The literature in this unit introduces you to authors and characters who are put to the test at significant points in their lives. As you read about the experiences of others—real people and fictional characters—think about how they test their skills and prove their abilities in challenging situations.

Assessing Student Progress

Listed below are the tools that are available to measure the degree to which students meet the unit objectives.

Informal Assessment

The questions in the Review and Assess sections are a first level of response to the concepts and skills presented within the selections. Students' responses are a brief, informal measure of their grasp of the material. These responses can indicate where further instruction and practice are needed. Follow up with the practice pages in the **Selection Support: Skills Development Workbook.**

Formal Assessment

The **Formal Assessment** booklet contains the Selection Tests and Unit Tests.

- Selection tests measure comprehension and skills acquisition for each selection or group of selections.
- Each Unit Test provides students with thirty multiple-choice questions and five essay questions designed to assess students' knowledge of the literature and skills taught in the unit.

The **Open Book Tests** ask students to demonstrate their ability to synthesize and communicate information from selections or groups of selections.

To assess student writing, you will find rubrics and scoring models in the **Performance Assessment and Portfolio Management** booklet. In this booklet, you will also find scoring rubrics for listening and speaking activities.

Alternative Assessment

The **Extension Activities** booklet contains writing activities, listening and speaking activities, and research and technology activities that are appropriate for students with different ability levels. You may also use these activities as an alternative measurement of students' growth.

ASSESSMENT RESOURCES

- Selection Support: Skills Development Workbook
- Formal Assessment
- Open Book Tests
- Performance Assessment and Portfolio Management
- Extension Activities

Why Read Literature?

The "Why Read Literature?" page in each unit presents a list of possible purposes for reading. Each purpose for reading is connected to one or more of the selections in the unit. Good readers set a purpose before reading in order to help them read actively and focus on meaningful details.

Unit 3 introduces three purposes for reading. "Read for the Love of Literature" encourages students to enjoy a tale of how a baby came to be raised by wolves and a poem about a popular sport. "Read to Be Inspired" introduces a fictional account of a girl who writes her way onto a baseball team as well as true-life stories of women athletes. "Read for Information" gives students a peek at real-world reading tasks, such as reading and completing application forms.

How to Use This Page

- Tell students that before reading each selection in this unit, they should set a purpose for reading. This will help them read in an active and focused manner.
- Explain that reading about how jungle animals make decisions will increase their love of literature.
- Predict that students will be entertained by two feuding friends in "The Southpaw," intrigued by the challenges that an immigrant girl meets in "Names/Nombres" and that a boy meets in the excerpt from *The Pigman & Me*, and they will be encouraged in their own sports endeavors by "Women in Sports."
- Point out that information can come in many forms. Even a poem, such as "Wilbur Wright and Orville Wright," can supply facts for observant readers. Students will also learn about application forms in Reading Informational Material.

Why Read Literature?

There are a variety of reasons for reading literature. You might read to explore the theme in this unit—proving yourself—to see how others meet the challenge of adversity. You might read a poem aloud to enjoy the poet's rhythm and word choice. Preview three purposes you might have for reading the works in this unit.

Read for the love of literature.

In 1920, a missionary in Northern India raided a den of wolves and hauled out two children, aged three and five, who were being raised by wolves. Read Nobel Prize winner Rudyard Kipling's story **"Mowgli's Brothers,"** on page 210 for an imaginative fictional account of wolves raising a human child.

To see a line of poetry "bounce" in a poem about soccer, read **"Alone in the Nets,"** page 232.

Read to be inspired.

Growing up in the Dominican Republic, Julia Alvarez was a happy, lively child with lots of friends. Then, when she was 10, her family was forced to flee her native land. To learn what it was like to arrive as a new immigrant, at a new school, in a strange country, read **"Names/Nombres"** on page 224.

The first female Olympic champion was a Greek princess who rode to victory as a champion charioteer in the ancient Olympic Games in the fourth century B.C. In the modern Olympics Games, women began competing in 1900. Learn more about accomplished women athletes in **"Women in Sports,"** page 238.

It was not until 1974 that girls were allowed to play on Little League baseball and softball teams. Read a humorous fictional account of how one girl finds her place on a previously all-boy team in **"The Southpaw,"** page 229.

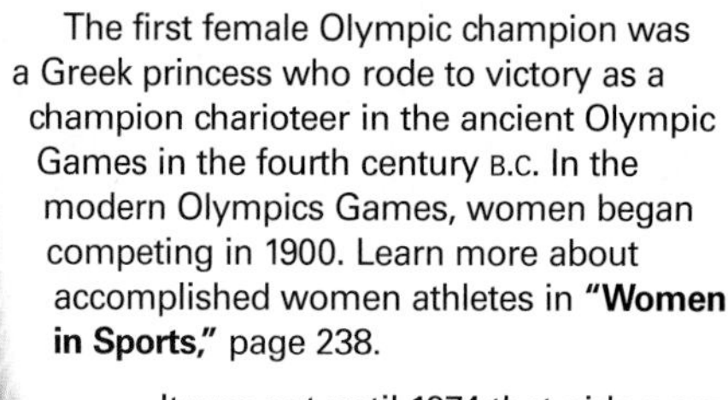

Read for information.

The inventors of the airplane worked as bicycle repairmen! Find out more about them when you read the poem **"Wilbur Wright and Orville Wright,"** p. 248.

Learn how to read and accurately fill out applications when you read the applications for a bank account, a library card, and a sports league, p. 239.

Take It to the Net

Visit the Web site for online instruction and activities related to each selection in this unit.

www.phschool.com

ENRICHMENT: Further Reading

Have students choose one or more of the works below to extend the unit theme "Proving Yourself "or to read more by the unit authors.

Hatchet by Gary Paulsen

This tale of a boy who spends the summer alone in the Canadian wilderness can be found in the Prentice Hall Literature Library.

A Wrinkle in Time by Madeleine L'Engle

This novel about a teen-age girl and her younger brother who go on a fantastic adventure to save their scientist father is part of the **Prentice Hall Literature Library.**

The Adventures of Ulysses by Charles Lamb

This classic tale of the adventures of a warrior returning from battle is retold for younger folks by the English writer Charles Lamb. It can be found in the **Prentice Hall Literature Library.**

Jumanji by Chris Van Allsburg

In this imaginative tale, a brother and sister begin to play a game that causes live jungle animals to appear in their apartment.

How to Read Literature

Interactive Reading Strategies

Books do not come with plugs or batteries. To make a book work, you have to plug yourself in by interacting with the words on the page. The following strategies will help you make the connection that lights up your imagination.

1. Understand shades of meaning.

To get the most meaning from a word, recognize and react to its particular shade of meaning. In the following example, notice how the sentence would have a slightly different meaning if *sleepy* were replaced with *exhausted, tired,* or *drowsy.*

> "You must get an early start if you are going to go to the west side of the butte and return by supper," John said to the sleepy boy—*from* "Thunder Butte"

In this unit, you will learn to recognize shades of meaning and analyze your reaction to them.

2. Predicting characters' actions.

Increase your involvement in a narrative, or story, by making predictions—educated guesses based on story facts and your experience. Predicting what characters will do next leads you to get to know them better. As you read the works in this unit, you will develop skill in recognizing details that help you make predictions.

Details

Janet is a good player.
+
Richard's team is losing.
+
Several players are injured.

Prediction

Richard will ask Janet to play.

3. Set a purpose for reading.

Before you begin, set a purpose for reading. The following example shows you how the purpose you set determines the details you focus on.

Reading for Enjoyment	Reading for Insight
Janet really wants to be on Richard's team—I want to find out if she can convince him to let her play.	I wonder what would happen if Richard wanted to play on Janet's all-girls team.

4. Interpret meaning.

If you listened to people speaking another language, you would hear what they say but you would need an interpreter—someone to explain the meaning—to understand it. Be your own interpreter when you read literature. In this unit, you will learn to find the meanings of words that can be used in more than one way and the meaning of figurative language—words and phrases that are not meant to be interpreted literally.

As you read the selections in this unit, review the reading strategies and look at the notes in the side column. Use the suggestions to apply the strategies for interactive reading.

How to Read Literature

The "How to Read Literature" page in each unit presents a set of strategies to help readers understand authors' words and ideas. Each reading strategy is taught in conjunction with one or more of the selections within the unit. Good readers develop a bank of strategies from which they can draw as needed.

Unit 3 introduces four interactive reading strategies. To understand a selection fully, students must interact with the text to discover its meaning. The strategies on this page help readers find and interpret the meaning of reading material.

How to Use This Page

Introduce the interactive reading strategies, presenting each as a tool for developing understanding when reading the selections in this unit.

- As they read "Thunder Butte" (p. 194), students will become sensitive to shades of meaning and how they affect a writer's message.
- As they read "Mowgli's Brothers" (p. 210), students will become involved with a story by making predictions based on their knowledge of the characters and personal experience.
- As they read "Names/Nombres" (p. 224), "The Southpaw" (p. 229), and "Alone in the Nets" (p. 232), students will learn that setting a purpose for reading will help them focus on important details within a selection.
- As students read "Adventures of Isabel" (p. 246), "I'll Stay" (p. 247), "Wilbur Wright and Orville Wright" (p. 248), and "Dream Dust" (p. 250), they will learn that some words and phrases are not meant to be taken literally. Instead, words and phrases sometimes have more than one meaning, and it is, therefore, important to interpret meaning.

MODEL A READING STRATEGY: Interpreting Meaning

As they read "Adventures of Isabel" (p. 246), "I'll Stay" (p. 247), "Wilbur Wright and Orville Wright" (p. 248), and "Dream Dust" (p. 250), students will gain the skill of interpreting figurative language and words with multiple meanings.

Tell students that they should be alert to words that have more than one meaning. Knowing the appropriate meaning, or meanings, for a word will help students understand the author's message.

Illustrate this strategy of interpreting meaning by using a passage from "I'll Stay":

Mother says, "You rise in the morning—You must be the Sun!"

Students should easily understand that the mother is comparing her child to the sun. The mother's comparison hinges on the word *rise.*

Model the following interpretation strategy for students: "I know that the sun rises, or comes up in the sky, in the morning. To rise is also to get out of bed. The mother must be having fun with the child by comparing her to the sun."

You may wish to suggest that students use dictionaries to help them find multiple meanings of key words.

from The Pigman & Me

Lesson Objectives

1. **To analyze and respond to literary elements**
   - Literary Analysis: Internal Conflict
   - Connecting Literary Elements: External Conflict
2. **To read, comprehend, analyze, and critique an autobiography**
   - Reading Strategy: Recognizing Word Origins
   - Reading Check Questions
   - Review and Assess Questions
   - Assessment Practice (ATE)
3. **To develop word analysis skills, fluency, and systematic vocabulary**
   - Vocabulary Development Lesson: Word Analysis: Latin Suffix *-tion*
4. **To understand and apply written and oral language conventions**
   - Spelling Strategy
   - Grammar Lesson: Adjectives
5. **To understand and apply appropriate writing and research strategies**
   - Writing Lesson: School Rules
   - Extension Activity: Emotional Appeals
6. **To understand and apply listening and speaking strategies**
   - Extension Activity: News Report
   - Extension Activity: Essay

STEP-BY-STEP TEACHING GUIDE	PACING GUIDE
PRETEACH	
Motivate Students and Provide Background	
Use the Motivation activity (ATE p. 180)	5 min.
Read and discuss the Preview material and Background information (SE/ATE p. 180) **A**	5 min.
Introduce the Concepts	
Introduce the Literary Analysis and Reading Strategy (SE/ATE p. 181) **A**	25 min.
Pronounce the vocabulary words and read their definitions (SE p. 181)	5 min.
TEACH	
Monitor Comprehension	
Informally monitor comprehension by circulating while students read independently or in groups **A**	25 min.
Monitor students' comprehension with the Reading Check notes (SE/ATE pp. 183, 185, 187)	as students read
Develop vocabulary with Vocabulary notes (SE pp. 183, 184, 187; ATE p. 187)	as students read
Develop Understanding	
Develop students' understanding of internal conflicts with the Literary Analysis annotations (SE p. 186; ATE pp. 184, 186) **A**	5 min.
Develop students' ability to recognize word origins with the Reading Strategy annotations (SE pp. 183, 184, 186; ATE pp. 183, 184, 186)	5 min.
ASSESS	
Assess Mastery	
Assess students' mastery of the Reading Strategy and Literary Analysis by having them answer the Review and Assess questions (SE/ATE p. 188)	15 min.
Use one or more of the print and media Assessment Resources (ATE p. 191) **A**	up to 45 min.
EXTEND	
Apply Understanding	
Have students complete the Vocabulary Development Lesson and the Grammar Lesson (SE p. 190) **A**	20 min.
Apply students' knowledge of school rules using the Writing Lesson (SE/ATE p. 191) **A**	45 min.
Apply students' understanding of the selection using one or more of the Extension Activities (SE p. 191)	20–90 min.

A **ACCELERATED INSTRUCTION:**
Use the strategies and activities identified with an .

UNIVERSAL ACCESS
● = Below Level Students
▲ = On-Level Students
■ = Above Level Students

Time and Resource Manager

Reading Level: Average
Average Number of Instructional Days: 4

RESOURCES		
PRINT	**TRANSPARENCIES**	**TECHNOLOGY**
• **Beyond Literature,** Workplace Skills: Conflict Resolution, p. 12 ▲ ■		• **Interest Grabber Videotapes,** Tape 2 ● ▲ ■
• **Selection Support Workbook:** ● ▲ ■ Literary Analysis, p. 60 Reading Strategy, p. 59 Build Vocabulary, p. 56	• **Literary Analysis and Reading Transparencies,** pp. 23 and 24 ● ▲ ■	
• **Adapted Reader's Companion** ● • **Reader's Companion** ●		• **Listening to Literature** ● ▲ ■ Audiocassettes, Side 8 Audio CDs, CD 3
• **English Learner's Companion** ● ▲ • **Literatura en español** ● ▲ • **Literary Analysis for Enrichment** ■		
• **Formal Assessment:** Selection Test, pp. 50–52 ● ▲ ■ • **Open Book Test,** pp. 34–36 ● ▲ ■ • **Performance Assessment and Portfolio Management,** p. 22 ● ▲ ■ • PRENTICE HALL ASSESSMENT SYSTEM ● ▲ ■	• PRENTICE HALL ASSESSMENT SYSTEM ● ▲ ■ Skills Practice Answers and Explanations on Transparencies	• **Test Bank Software** ● ▲ ■ • **Got It! Assessment Videotapes,** Tape 2 ● ▲
• **Selection Support Workbook:** ● ▲ ■ Build Spelling Skills, p. 57 Build Grammar Skills, p. 58 • **Writing and Grammar,** Copper Level ● ▲ ■ • **Extension Activities,** p. 12 ● ▲ ■	• **Daily Language Practice Transparencies** ● ▲ • **Writing Models and Graphic Organizers on Transparencies** ● ▲ ■	• **Writing and Grammar iText CD-ROM** ● ▲ ■ ***Take It to the Net*** www.phschool.com

BLOCK SCHEDULING: Use one 90-minute class period to preteach the selection and have students read it. Use a second 90-minute class period to assess students' mastery of skills and have them complete one of the Extension Activities.

PRETEACH

Step-by-Step Teaching Guide for pp. 180–181

Motivation

Bring to class examples of newspaper or magazine advice columns, and have small groups of students read and briefly discuss them. Ask each student to write a question to submit to an advice column from the point of view of a new student asking about school rules or making friends. Collect the questions, mix them up, and redistribute them. Have students write answers to the questions they are given. Then, ask volunteers to read aloud their questions and answers. Introduce the selection by explaining that the narrator of the story is a new student who does not know the school rules, which causes trouble.

Interest Grabber Video

As an alternative, play "Karate" on Tape 2 to engage student interest.

❶ Background

Social Studies

The subject of "rules" plays an important part in this story. Written rules and laws are used to keep order in society. Rules usually apply to specific groups of people or to activities such as sports. Laws are formalized rules that bind larger groups of people and are enforced by institutions such as the police and the court system. Laws may establish beneficial changes, such as equal rights, or may limit or prohibit actions that could harm people or property.

Prepare to Read

❶ *from* The Pigman & Me

Take It to the Net

Visit www.phschool.com for interactive activities and instruction related to *The Pigman & Me,* including

- background
- graphic organizers
- literary elements
- reading strategies

Preview

Connecting to the Literature

In this excerpt from *The Pigman & Me* by Paul Zindel, the author looks back with humor on one of his experiences as the new kid in school. Connect to the author's experience by recalling a blunder you have made in a new place or an unfamiliar situation.

Background

Different places have different rules. Usually rules are spelled out or written for everyone to read. Sometimes rules are unwritten and are just as important as the written ones. In the excerpt from *The Pigman & Me,* Paul Zindel recalls a time when, according to an unwritten rule, he was "not allowed" to back down from a fight.

TEACHING RESOURCES

The following resources can be used to enrich or extend the instruction for pp. 180–181.

Motivation

Interest Grabber Video, Tape 2 

Background

Beyond Literature, p. 12

Take It to the Net

Visit www.phschool.com for Background and hotlinks for *The Pigman and Me.*

Literary Analysis

Literary Analysis and Reading Transparencies, Internal Conflict, p. 24 

Selection Support: Literary Analysis, p. 60

Reading

Literary Analysis and Reading Transparencies, Recognizing Word Origins, p. 23

BLOCK SCHEDULING: Resources marked with this symbol provide varied instruction during 90-minute blocks.

❷ Literary Analysis

Internal Conflict

An **internal conflict** is a struggle within a person or character. The character struggles with two different feelings, needs, or choices.

In *The Pigman & Me,* Paul wants to avoid a fight, but he also wants to prove he is not afraid. These feelings produce an internal conflict.

Record other details of Paul's internal conflict in a chart like the one shown here.

	Internal Conflict	
1. Paul is ashamed to call off the fight. →		← 1. Paul is afraid to fight.
2. →		← 2.
3. →		← 3.

Connecting Literary Elements

Paul's internal conflict is connected to an **external conflict**—a conflict with a force outside himself. In this case, the outside force is another student.

As you read, use the following focus questions to explore Paul's internal and external conflicts:

1. What events lead to Paul's external conflict?
2. How is Paul's external conflict connected to his internal conflict?

❸ Reading Strategy

Recognizing Word Origins

Many words in English are borrowed from other languages. Some words have been used in English for so long that they are no longer considered to be a foreign language. Look at the examples below.

- pizza
- siesta
- cliché
- amigo

Other commonly used words from languages other than English appear in *The Pigman & Me.* Notice them as you read.

Vocabulary Development

exact (eg zakt′) *v.* take using force or authority (p. 183)

tactics (tak′ tiks) *n.* methods used for a particular purpose; tricks (p. 184)

undulating (un′ dyo͞o lā′ tiŋ) *adj.* moving in waves, like a snake (p. 187)

goading (gō′ diŋ) *v.* pushing a person into acting, especially by using pain or insults (p. 187)

distorted (di stôr′ tid) *adj.* twisted out of the normal shape (p. 187)

groveled (grä′ vəld) *v.* lay or crawled about before someone in hope of mercy (p. 187)

❷ Literary Analysis

Internal Conflict

- Define for students the two kinds of conflict: *internal conflict,* which is within a person, and *external conflict,* which is between a person and another force, such as another person or nature.
- Have students think either of books they have read or films they have seen where a character struggles with an internal conflict. Discuss how the conflicts were resolved.
- Use the Internal Conflict transparency on p. 24 in **Literary Analysis and Reading Transparencies** to show students how to record Paul's inner conflicts.

❸ Reading Strategy

Recognizing Word Origins

- Point out to students that English is a living language—it is continually growing and changing as it is used. As people speak about new ideas and inventions or share words from other cultures, they form new words that sometimes become part of the English language.
- Elicit from students some words that have been adopted from another language. For example, *hors d'oeuvre, ziti,* and *kimono.*
- Read the text as a class and note the bulleted words. Have students attempt to define the words without using a dictionary. Then, if necessary, have them use a dictionary to check the origins of the words.
- Encourage students who speak a language other than English to contribute words that are shared by English and their native language.

Vocabulary Development

- Pronounce each vocabulary word for students, and read the definitions as a class. Have students identify any words with which they are already familiar.

CUSTOMIZE INSTRUCTION FOR UNIVERSAL ACCESS

For Special Needs Students	For Less Proficient Readers	For English Learners
Have students read the adapted version of "The Pigman & Me" in the **Adapted Reader's Companion.** This version provides basic-level instruction in an interactive format with questions and write-on lines. Completing the adapted version will prepare students to read the selection in the Student Edition.	Have students read "The Pigman & Me" in the **Reader's Companion.** This version provides basic-level instruction in an interactive format with questions and write-on lines. After students finish the selection in the Reader's Companion, have them complete the questions and activities in the Student Edition.	Have students read the adapted version of "The Pigman & Me" in the **English Learner's Companion.** This version provides basic-level instruction in an interactive format with questions and write-on lines. Completing the adapted version will prepare students to read the selection in the Student Edition.

 ***E-Teach***

Visit E-Teach at www.phschool.com for teachers' essays on how to teach, with questions and answers.

TEACH

Step-by-Step Teaching Guide for pp. 182–188

CUSTOMIZE INSTRUCTION For Intrapersonal Learners

Ask students to think of a time when they had to react to something unexpected. How did they manage the situations? What might they have done differently if they had had time to prepare? Encourage students to suggest ways to prepare for or cope with unexpected events.

1 About the Selection

In this excerpt from Paul Zindel's memoir of his teenage years, Paul is near the end of his first week at a new school. Unaware of a time limit on using gym equipment, Paul refuses to give his paddle to John. Paul's mind is a jumble of fears about being the new kid. Without thinking, he hits John with the paddle. When John vows revenge after school on Monday, Paul is terrified to fight but unwilling to back out. He gets some helpful, if unusual, advice from Nonno Frankie, a grandfatherly friend. John and Paul have their showdown after school. Paul survives the fight, using Nonno Frankie's advice, his own wits, and the help of an unexpected savior.

2 ▶Critical Viewing

Possible responses: Students could argue about the rules of their playground games, behavior, and sports equipment.

from THE PIGMAN & ME

1

Paul Zindel

When trouble came to me, it didn't involve anybody I thought it would. It involved the nice, normal, smart boy by the name of John Quinn. Life does that to us a lot. Just when we think something awful's going to happen one way, it throws you a curve and the something awful happens another way. This happened on the first Friday, during gym period, when we were allowed to play games in the school yard. A boy by the name of Richard Cahill, who lived near an old linoleum factory, asked me if I'd like to play paddle ball with him, and I said, "Yes." Some of the kids played softball, some played warball, and there were a few other games where you could sign out equipment and do what you wanted. What I didn't know was that you were allowed to sign out the paddles for only fifteen minutes per period so more kids could get a chance to use them. I just didn't happen to know that little rule, and Richard Cahill didn't think to tell me about it. Richard was getting a drink from the water fountain when John Quinn came up to me and told me I had to give him my paddle.

"No," I said, being a little paranoid about being the new kid and thinking everyone was going to try to take advantage of me.

"Look, you *have* to give it to me," John Quinn insisted.

That was when I did something berserk. I was so wound up and frightened that I didn't think, and I struck out at him with my right fist. I had forgotten I was holding the paddle, and it smacked into

2 ▲Critical Viewing What are some conflicts between students that might occur in a scene like this one? **[Analyze]**

TEACHING RESOURCES

The following resources can be used to enrich or extend the instruction for pp. 182–188.

Literary Analysis

- **Literary Analysis for Enrichment**
- **Literary Analysis and Reading Transparencies,** p. 24

Reading

- **Selection Support:** Reading Strategy, p. 59; Build Vocabulary, p. 56
- **Adapted Reader's Companion**
- **Reader's Companion**
- **English Learner's Companion**
- **Literatura en español**
- **Listening to Literature Audiocassettes,** Side 8
- **Listening to Literature Audio CDs,** CD 3

BLOCK SCHEDULING: Resources marked with this symbol provide varied instruction during 90-minute blocks.

3 his face, giving him an instant black eye. John was shocked. I was shocked. Richard Cahill came running back and he was shocked.

"What's going on here?" Mr. Trellis, the gym teacher, growled.

"He hit me with the paddle," John moaned, holding his eye. He was red as a beet, as Little Frankfurter, Conehead, Moose, and lots of the others gathered around.

"He tried to take the paddle away from me!" I complained.

"His time was up," John said.

Mr. Trellis set me wise to the rules as he took John over to a supply locker and pulled out a first-aid kit.

"I'm sorry," I said, over and over again.

Then the bell rang, and all John Quinn whispered to me was that he was going to get even. He didn't say it like a nasty rotten kid, just more like an all-American boy who knew he'd have to regain his dignity about having to walk around school with a black eye. Before the end of school, Jennifer came running up to me in the halls and told me John Quinn had announced to everyone he was going to exact revenge on me after school on Monday. That was the note of disaster my first week at school ended on, and I was terrified because I didn't know how to fight. I had never even been in a fight. What had happened was all an accident. It really was.

exact (eg zakt′) *v.* take using force or authority

4 When Nonno Frankie arrived on Saturday morning, he found me sitting in the apple tree alone. Mom had told him it was O.K. to walk around the whole yard now, as long as he didn't do any diggings or mutilations other than weed-pulling on her side. I was expecting him to notice right off the bat that I was white with fear, but instead he stood looking at the carvings Jennifer and I had made in the trunk of the tree. I thought he was just intensely curious about what "ESCAPE! PAUL & JENNIFER!" meant. Of course, the twins, being such copycats, had already added their names so the full carving away of the bark now read, "ESCAPE! PAUL & JENNIFER! & NICKY & JOEY!" And the letters circled halfway around the tree.

Reading Strategy
Recognizing Word Origins *Nonno* is the Italian word for "grandfather." *Nonna* is "grandmother." What English word for "grandmother" sounds similar to *Nonna*?

"You're killing it," Nonno Frankie said sadly.

"What?" I jumped down to his side.

"The tree will die if you cut any more."

I thought he was kidding, because all we had done was carve off the outer pieces of bark. We hadn't carved deep into the tree, not into the *heart* of the tree. The tree was too important to us. It was the most crucial place to me and Jennifer, and the last thing we'd want to do was hurt it.

"The heart of a tree isn't deep inside of it. Its heart and blood are on the *outside*, just under the bark," Nonno Frankie explained. "That's the living part of a tree. If you carve in a circle all around the 5 trunk, it's like slitting its throat. The water and juices and life of the

Reading Check
Why is Paul afraid?

3 Critical Thinking

Infer

- Remind students that readers sometimes must draw conclusions about why a character feels a certain way. Drawing these conclusions is called *inferring*.
- Invite students to make an inference about Paul. Ask: Why is Paul shocked?
  Answer: He has just lost control of himself and hit John in the face with the paddle without really meaning to.

4 Reading Strategy

Recognizing Word Origins

- Point out to students that many of the words that are borrowed from other languages are words that identify family members.
- Ask the Reading Strategy question on p. 183: *Nonno* is the Italian word for "grandfather." *Nonna* is "grandmother." What English word for "grandmother" sounds similar to *Nonna*?
  Answer: *Nana* is sometimes used to mean "grandmother."
- Brainstorm with students for a list of foreign words that identify family members.
  Possible responses: The words *oma* and *opa* are used for "grandmother" and "grandfather," *tia* is a common word for "aunt," and *bubbe* is a well-known Yiddish name for "grandmother."

5 Reading Check

Answer: Paul is afraid because he knows John wants to fight him, and Paul does not know how to fight.

CUSTOMIZE INSTRUCTION FOR UNIVERSAL ACCESS

For Special Needs Students	For Gifted/Talented Students	For Advanced Readers
Tell students that Paul's anxiety about the fight on Monday helps build suspense, which pulls readers into the story. Because the conversation with Nonno Frankie can be confusing, urge students to pause briefly as they read and jot down any questions they have. As they read, they can cross out questions that get answered.	Challenge students to consider how the details of the story would be different if the narrator were John, the gym teacher, or another student in the class. Suggest that students select a character other than the narrator, and have them write a brief summary of the story from that character's point of view.	Challenge students to check up on some of Nonno Frankie's lessons. Ask some students to find out if Alexander the Great really ordered his army to shave or if Genghis Khan really killed two million enemies. Ask others to write a brief history of the yo-yo. Encourage students to share their information with the class.

6 Reading Strategy

Recognizing Word Origins

- Remind students that names for food are often borrowed from other languages.
- Read the bracketed passage and ask the Reading Strategy question on p. 184.
  Answer: The origin of the word *pizza* is Italian.

7 Literary Analysis

Internal and External Conflict

- Remind students that Paul has conflicts within himself and with another student.
- Ask students to explain how Paul's confusion led to an external and an internal conflict.
  Answer: Paul's confusion led him to hurt John, creating a conflict between John and Paul. Because of this external conflict, Paul is upset with himself; this feeling leads to his internal conflict.

Monitor Progress If students have difficulty answering the question, ask them to describe the difference between internal and external conflicts.
Answer: Internal conflicts occur within a person; external conflicts occur between a person and another force, such as another person or nature.

Reteach If students are still struggling with this concept, point out that the prefix *in-* shows something *within* a person. The prefix *ex-* means *outside* of a person. You may also wish to review the information on p. 181 in the Literary Analysis section.

tree can't move up from the roots!" I knew about the living layer of a tree, but I didn't know exposing it would kill the whole tree. I just never thought about it, or I figured trees patched themselves up.

"Now it can feed itself from only half its trunk," Nonno Frankie explained. "You must not cut any more."

"I won't," I promised. Then I felt worse than ever. Not only was I scheduled to get beat up by John Quinn after school on Monday, I was also a near tree-killer. Nonno Frankie finally looked closely at me.

"Your first week at school wasn't all juicy meatballs?" he asked.

That was all he had to say, and I spilled out each and every horrifying detail. Nonno Frankie let me babble on and on. He looked as if he understood exactly how I felt and wasn't going to call me stupid or demented or a big yellow coward. When I didn't have another word left in me, I just shut up and stared down at the ground.

"Stab nail at ill Italian bats!" Nonno Frankie finally said.

"What?"

He repeated the weird sentence and asked me what was special about it. I guessed, "It reads the same backward as forward?"

6 "Right! Ho! Ho! Ho! See, you learn! You remember things I teach you. So today I will teach you how to fight, and you will smack this John Quinn around like floured pizza dough."

"But I can't fight."

"I'll show you Sicilian combat tactics."

"Like what?"

"Everything about Italian fighting. It has to do with your mind and body. Things you have to know so you don't have to be afraid of bullies. Street smarts my father taught me. Like 'Never miss a good chance to shut up!'"

VAROOOOOOOOOOM!

A plane took off over our heads. We walked out beyond the yard to the great field overlooking the airport.

Nonno Frankie suddenly let out a yell. "*Aaeeeeeyaaaayeeeeeh!*" It was so blood-curdlingly weird, I decided to wait until he felt like explaining it.

"*Aaeeeeeyaaaayeeeeeh!*" he bellowed again. "It's good to be able to yell like Tarzan!" he said. "This confuses your enemy, and you can also yell it if you have to retreat. You run away roaring and everyone thinks you at least have guts! It confuses everybody!"

"Is that all I need to know?" I asked, now more afraid than ever of facing John Quinn in front of all the kids.

"No. Tonight I will cut your hair."

"Cut it?"

"Yes. It's too long!"

"It is?"

Reading Strategy
Recognizing Word Origins What word in this paragraph has its origin in Italian?

tactics (tak´ tiks) *n.* methods used for a particular purpose; tricks

ENRICHMENT: Science Connection

Trees

After Nonno Frankie explains the damage that carving can cause to a tree, Paul feels bad for harming the apple tree.

The trunk and branches of a tree have four layers of plant tissue: cork, phloem, cambium, and xylem. The cork is the outer bark that protects the tree from injury. The phloem, or inner bark, carries food made by the leaves to other parts of the tree. The cambium makes the trunk, branches, and roots grow thicker. The xylem is the woody central part of the trunk. It carries water from the roots of the tree to the leaves.

Encourage interested students to conduct research to learn more about trees. Suggest that students focus on topics such as tree conservation, how leaves make plant food, how trunks grow thicker, how the rings on trees can help identify the age of a tree, and what market value trees have. Have students share their findings with the class in a written report.

"Ah," Nonno Frankie said, "you'd be surprised how many kids lose fights because of their hair. Alexander the Great always ordered his entire army to shave their heads. Long hair makes it easy for an enemy to grab it and cut off your head." 8

"John Quinn just wants to beat me up!"

"You can never be too sure. This boy might have the spirit of Genghis Khan!"

"Who was Genghis Khan?"

"Who? He once killed two million enemies in one hour. Some of them he killed with yo-yos."

"Yo-yos?"

"See, these are the things you need to know. The yo-yo was first invented as a weapon. Of course, they were as heavy as steel pipes and had long rope cords, but they were still yo-yos!"

"I didn't know that," I admitted.

"That's why I'm telling you. You should always ask about the rules when you go to a new place."

"I didn't think there'd be a time limit on hand-
7 ball paddles."

"That's why you must ask."

"I can't ask everything," I complained.

"Then you *read*. You need to know all the rules wherever you go. Did you know it's illegal to hunt camels in Arizona?"

"No."

"See? These are little facts you pick up from books and teachers and parents as you grow older. Some facts and rules come in handy, some don't. You've got to be observant. Did you know that Mickey Mouse has only *four* fingers on each hand?"

"No."

"All you have to do is look. And rules change! You've got to remember that. In ancient Rome, my ancestors worshipped a god who ruled over mildew. Nobody does anymore, but it's an interesting thing to know. You have to be connected to the past and present and future. At NBC, when they put in a new cookie-cutting machine, I had to have an open mind. I had to prepare and draw upon everything I knew so that I didn't get hurt."

Nonno Frankie must have seen my mouth was open so wide a baseball could have flown into my throat and choked me to death. He stopped at the highest point in the rise of land above the airport. 10

"I can see you want some meat and potatoes. You want to know exactly how to beat this vicious John Quinn."

"He's not vicious."

Elephant Tree, © 1996, Robert Vickrey/Licensed by VAGA, New York, NY

9 ▲ **Critical Viewing** What details express the way Paul feels during the first school week? **[Interpret]**

Reading Check

What does Nonno Frankie teach the narrator to do?

8 Background

Art

Elephant Tree, by Robert Vickrey

The solitary figure and washed-out colors in this painting call to mind feelings of isolation. Have a volunteer describe how this painting relates to *The Pigman and Me.* Then, use the following questions for discussion:

Why do you think the artist entitled the painting Elephant Tree?
Possible responses: The tree's size is like an elephant; its branches are like outstretched elephant trunks; its texture resembles wrinkled elephant skin.

9 ▶Critical Viewing

Emphasize to students that Paul's feelings during his first week at school are not unusual.
Suggested response: Students may mention that Paul's fear, sadness, and loneliness are shown in details such as the boy sitting alone in the tree and the threatening shadows on the tree.

10 Reading Check

Answer: Nonno Frankie teaches Paul to ask about rules in a new place, to be observant, and to have an open mind.

CUSTOMIZE INSTRUCTION FOR UNIVERSAL ACCESS

For Special Needs Students	For English Learners
Students may never have been "the new kid" or been challenged to a fight, but they likely have felt scared, nervous, or confused about rules. Have students relate their own experiences to Paul's by recording details in a T-chart. Then have students think about Paul's actions and compare them with how they themselves might have acted in a similar situation.	To help students understand the events of the story, have them role-play various scenes. For example, have two students act out the scene between Nonno Frankie and Paul in which Nonno gives advice about fighting. Or, have students act out the fight scene between Paul and John at the end of the story. Have students use dialogue to enhance the role-play. Suggest that volunteers perform their role-plays for the class.

11 Reading Strategy

Recognizing Word Origins

- Remind students to look for context clues to find the meaning of a word.
- Before students read the bracketed passage, ask them if they have ever heard of the words *sombrero* or *espresso.* If students are unable to recognize the words, elicit the meanings from them by giving examples of situations when they are used.
- After students have read the bracketed passage, ask the Reading Strategy question on p. 186.
  Answer: *Espresso* means "pressed out" and is a type of strong Italian coffee. A *sombrero* is a large Mexican hat.

12 Literary Analysis

Internal Conflict

- Discuss with students how other people can help with a difficult situation. Point out that Nonno Frankie tries to help resolve Paul's internal conflict. Does it work?
  Answer: No, because Paul is still numb with fear on Monday.
- Point out that Jennifer, too, wants to help Paul. Have a volunteer read the passage that begins with "Jennifer had offered . . ." Ask the Literary Analysis question on p. 186: Would Jennifer's offer solve Paul's problem?
  Possible responses: No, because Paul needs to settle the problem with John himself. Yes, because Jennifer's brothers or the teacher could keep John from hurting Paul.

"Make believe he is. It'll give you more energy for the fight. When he comes at you, don't underestimate the power of negative thinking! You must have only positive thoughts in your heart that you're going to cripple this monster. Stick a piece of garlic in your pocket for good luck. A woman my mother knew in Palermo did this, and she was able to fight off a dozen three-foot-tall muscular Greeks who landed and tried to eat her. You think this is not true, but half her town saw it. The Greeks all had rough skin and wore backpacks and one-piece clothes. You have to go with what you feel in your heart. One of my teachers in Sicily believed the Portuguese man-of-war jellyfish originally came from England. He felt that in his heart, and he eventually proved it. He later went on to be awarded a government grant to study tourist swooning sickness in Florence."

"But how do I hold my hands to fight? How do I hold my fists?" I wanted to know.

"Like *this!*" Nonno Frankie demonstrated, taking a boxing stance with his left foot and fist forward.

"And then I just swing my right fist forward as hard as I can?"

"No. First you curse him."

"*Curse* him?"

11 "Yes, you curse this John Quinn. You tell him, 'May your left ear wither and fall into your right pocket!' And you tell him he looks like a fugitive from a brain gang! And tell him he has a face like a mattress! And that an espresso coffee cup would fit on his head like a sombrero. And then you just give him the big Sicilian surprise!"

"What?"

"You *kick* him in the shins!"

By the time Monday morning came, I was a nervous wreck. Nonno Frankie had gone back to New York the night before, but had left me a special bowl of pasta and steamed octopus that he said I should eat for breakfast so I'd have "gusto" for combat. I had asked him not to discuss my upcoming bout with my mother or sister, and Betty didn't say anything so I assumed she hadn't heard about it.

12 Jennifer had offered to get one of her older brothers to protect me, and, if I wanted, she was willing to tell Miss Haines so she could stop anything from happening. I told her, "No." I thought there was a chance John Quinn would have even forgotten the whole incident and wouldn't make good on his revenge threat. Nevertheless, my mind was numb with fear all day at school. In every class I went to, it seemed there were a dozen different kids coming over to me and telling me they heard John Quinn was going to beat me up after school.

At 3 P.M. sharp, the bell rang.

All the kids started to leave school.

I dawdled.

Reading Strategy
Recognizing Word Origins What are the meanings of the Italian word *espresso* and the Spanish word *sombrero*?

Literary Analysis
Internal Conflict Would Jennifer's offer solve Paul's problem?

CUSTOMIZE INSTRUCTION FOR UNIVERSAL ACCESS

For Less Proficient Readers

Explain to students that asking themselves questions as they read will enhance their understanding of a passage. As they read, they can look for answers to their questions. Write the passage from p. 184 on the board:

"Nonno Frankie suddenly let out a yell, 'Aaeeeeeyaaaayeeeeeh!' "

Demonstrate how to ask questions as you read by modeling your thinking for students.

As I read this description from the story, I asked myself:

- Who is Nonno Frankie?
- Why does Nonno Frankie yell?
- Why does he yell that particular sound?
- Was the narrator scared?

You may want to point out to students that some of their questions may not be answered and that they must continue reading further.

13 I cleaned my desk and took time packing up my books. Jennifer was at my side as we left the main exit of the building. There, across the street in a field behind Ronkewitz's Candy Store, was a crowd of about 300 kids standing around like a big, undulating horseshoe, with John Quinn standing at the center bend glaring at me.

"You could *run*," Jennifer suggested, tossing her hair all to the left side of her face. She looked much more than pretty now. She looked loyal to the bone.

13 "No," I said. I just walked forward toward my fate, with the blood in my temples pounding so hard I thought I was going to pass out. Moose and Leon and Mike and Conehead and Little Frankfurter were sprinkled out in front of me, goading me forward. I didn't even hear what they said. I saw only their faces distorted in ecstasy and expectation. They looked like the mob I had seen in a sixteenth-century etching where folks in London had bought tickets to watch bulldogs attacking water buffalo.

John stood with his black eye, and his fists up.

I stopped a few feet from him and put my fists up. A lot of kids in the crowd started to shout, "Kill him, Johnny!" but I may have imagined that part.

John came closer. He started to dance on his feet like all father-trained fighters do. I danced, too, as best I could. The crowd began to scream for blood. Jennifer kept shouting, "Hey, there's no need to fight! You don't have to fight, guys!"

But John came in for the kill. He was close enough now so any punch he threw could hit me. All I thought of was Nonno Frankie, but I couldn't remember half of what he told me and I didn't think any of it would work anyway.

"Aaeeeeeyaaaayeeeeeh!" I suddenly screamed at John. He stopped in his tracks and the crowd froze in amazed silence. Instantly, I brought back my right foot, and shot it forward to kick

14 John in his left shin. The crowd was shocked, and booed me with mass condemnation for my Sicilian fighting technique. I missed John's shin, and kicked vainly again. He threw a punch at me. It barely touched me, but I was so busy kicking, I tripped myself and fell down. The crowd cheered. I realized everyone including John thought his punch had floored me. I decided to go along with it. I groveled in the dirt for a few moments, and then stood up slowly holding my head as though I'd received a death blow. John put his fists down. He was satisfied justice had been done and his black eye had been avenged. He turned to leave, but Moose wasn't happy.

"Hey, ya didn't punch him enough," Moose complained to John.

"It's over," John said, like the decent kid he was.

"No, it's not," Moose yelled, and the crowd began to call for more blood. Now it was Moose coming toward me, and I figured I was dead

undulating (un′ dyo͞o lā′ tiŋ) *adj.* moving in waves, like a snake

goading (gō′ diŋ) *v.* pushing a person into acting, especially by using pain or insults

distorted (di stôr′ tid) *adj.* twisted out of the normal shape

groveled (grä′ vəld) *v.* lay or crawled about before someone in hope of mercy

15 **Reading Check**

What happens to the narrator during the fight?

13 Critical Thinking

Infer

- Have students consider the behavior of the students in the story who are waiting in the field by asking the following question: What can you infer about the people who are waiting for Paul after school?
  Possible response: They want to see the fight.
- Read the second bracketed passage on p. 187, this time asking students to pay attention to the names of the characters. Ask students whose side Moose, Conehead, and Little Frankfurter are on.
  Answer: The boys are on John's side because they are insulting Paul and are anxious for the fight to begin.

14 Vocabulary Development

Latin Suffix *-tion*

- Point out the word *condemnation*, and tell students that it means "a disapproving judgment." Ask: What is the root word of *condemnation?*
  Answer: The root word is *condemn*.
- Lead students to understand the relationship between the verb *condemn* and its noun form *condemnation*.
- With students, brainstorm for a list of other words ending in *-tion*. Possible choices include *action*, *demonstration*, and *convention*. List the root words and their *-tion* forms on the board. Note that adding the suffix sometimes changes the spelling.

15 Reading Check

Answer: During the fight, Paul trips himself and falls when he tries to kick John.

CUSTOMIZE INSTRUCTION FOR UNIVERSAL ACCESS

For Gifted/Talented Readers	For Advanced Readers
Have groups of students write news reports about Paul's fight. Students should describe the events leading up to the fight, including Paul's encounter with John on the playground. Have students write scripts for the anchors and reporters as well as for the participants, practice the reports, and then present them to the class. Tell students that the news anchors summarize important details, the reporters need to be certain that their facts are correct, and both anchors and reporters should speak clearly.	Tell students that many unwritten rules concern social etiquette—how to behave in social situations. Have students look for an unwritten rule in the paragraph that begins with "'Aaeeeeeyaaaayeeeeeh!'" on p. 187. Tell them that the rule governs why the crowd condemns Paul. When students find the rule that Sicilian fighting techniques such as kicking are considered taboo, have them each write a paragraph about why they think fighting—something that is often dictated by emotion and irrationality—is governed by rules.

ASSESS

Answers for p. 188

Review and Assess

1. **Possible responses:** Yes, fighting is wrong, and Paul could have been hurt. No, Paul would have looked like a coward.
2. **(a)** Paul does not want his mother or his sister to know. **(b) Possible responses:** He does not want them to worry or to interfere; he is embarrassed. **(c)** They would have asked him not to fight.
3. **(a) Possible responses:** Nonno Frankie tells Paul to yell like Tarzan; he tells him to pretend his opponent is vicious. **(b)** Most of the advice applies to fighting; some applies to life.
4. **(a)** Paul acts as if he were hurt. **(b)** He wants the fight to be over. **(c) Possible response:** Paul's strategy is good because it works.
5. **(a)** John wants the fight to end, and the other students want it to continue. **(b)** The only reason John wanted to fight was to regain his dignity, so when Paul falls, he has regained his dignity and has no desire to do any more harm to Paul. The rest of the kids find it exciting, so they want the fight to continue. **(c)** Both John and Paul want the fight to end, so the cheers of the other kids make it difficult for them to stop fighting. **(d) Possible responses:** If Paul had won the fight with Moose, other students would have either been afraid of him or wanted to be his friend.
6. **(a)** The fight is important because Paul is the new kid at school. **(b)** Paul learns the rules, how to fight, and that his sister and Jennifer are loyal.
7. Students should support their opinions.

meat. He came closer and closer. Jennifer shouted for him to stop and threatened to pull his eyeballs out, but he kept coming. And that was when something amazing happened. I was aware of a figure taller than me, running, charging. The figure had long blond hair, and it struck Moose from behind. I could see it was a girl and she had her hands right around Moose's neck, choking him. When she let him go, she threw him about ten feet, accidentally tearing off a religious medal from around his neck. Everyone stopped dead in their tracks, and I could see my savior was my sister.

"If any of you tries to hurt my brother again, I'll rip your guts out," she announced.

Moose was not happy. Conehead and Little Frankfurter were not happy. But the crowd broke up fast and everyone headed home. I guess that was the first day everybody learned that if nothing else, the Zindel kids stick together. As for Nonno Frankie's Sicilian fighting technique, I came to realize he was ahead of his time. In fact, these days it's called karate.

Review and Assess

Thinking About the Selection

1. **Respond:** Do you think Paul should have backed out of the fight? Why or why not?
2. **(a) Recall:** Whom does Paul not want to know about his planned fight? **(b) Infer:** Why do you think Paul asks Nonno Frankie not to tell them? **(c) Speculate:** How do you think they would have reacted?
3. **(a) Recall:** Identify two pieces of advice that Nonno Frankie gives Paul. **(b) Analyze:** Does the advice apply more to the fight or to life?
4. **(a) Recall:** What does Paul do after he falls down during the fight? **(b) Infer:** Why does he do this? **(c) Evaluate:** Is his strategy a good one? Explain.
5. **(a) Contrast:** Describe the difference in John's attitude and the attitude of the other students after Paul falls down. **(b) Analyze:** Why do they each react as they do? **(c) Apply:** What problems does the attitude of the other students create for John and for Paul? **(d) Speculate:** If Paul had fought Moose and won the fight, how do you think the other students would have reacted? Explain.
6. **(a) Deduce:** Why is the fight important to Paul? **(b) Synthesize:** What lesson does Paul learn?
7. **Take a Position:** Is it ever okay to resort to fighting? Explain.

Paul Zindel

(b. 1936)

When he was growing up in Staten Island, New York, Paul Zindel met Nonno Frankie Vivona. Frankie gave him much advice, some of it unusual. Zindel describes Frankie in loving detail in the memoir, *The Pigman & Me*.

Frankie also inspired a character in Zindel's first novel, *The Pigman*, which draws on Zindel's confusing, lonely teenage days.

Before he wrote *The Pigman*, Zindel taught high-school science for ten years. After the success of this book and a play, he started writing full time. As one of his English teachers had predicted, Zindel had become a writer!

ASSESSMENT PRACTICE: Reading Comprehension

Identify the Main Idea (For more practice, see Test Preparation Workbook, p. 16.)

Use the sample to help students identify the main idea.

. . . Before the end of school, Jennifer came running up to me . . . and told me John Quinn had announced to everyone he was going to exact revenge on me. . . . That was the note of disaster my first week at school ended on, and I was terrified . . . I had never been in a fight. What had happened was all an accident. It really was.

What is the main idea of this passage?

A The speaker has been in a fight.
B John Quinn dislikes the speaker for no reason.
C The speaker doesn't know Quinn.
D The speaker is afraid of fighting with John Quinn.

Answer choices *A* and *C* are not supported by the text. Choice *B* is incorrect because the speaker must have done something to make Quinn want revenge. *D* is the correct answer.

Review and Assess

Literary Analysis

Internal Conflict

1. Explain the **internal conflict** that Paul experiences. Use a graphic organizer like this one to help you develop your answer.

2. Is Paul's internal conflict settled at the end of the story? Support your answer with at least two details from the story.
3. What internal conflict might John have?

Connecting Literary Elements

4. What **external conflict** does Paul experience and what events lead to it?
5. How does Paul's external conflict lead to his internal conflict?

Reading Strategy

Recognizing Word Origins

6. Use your own knowledge and a dictionary to complete a chart like the one shown. In the last column, write a sentence that gives clues to the meaning of the word.

Word	Origin	Meaning	Sentence
pizza			
espresso			
cliché			The corny speech was full of clichés.
siesta	Spanish	rest	
adios			
bon voyage		"Have a good trip."	

7. Why can some words from languages other than English be understood and used by English speakers?

Extending Understanding

8. **Apply:** Explain why you think children fight and how fights can be avoided.

Quick Review

An **internal conflict** is a struggle that takes place within the mind of a person or character. To review internal conflict, see page 181.

An **external conflict** is a struggle that takes place between a character and an outside force. To review external conflict, see page 181.

Word origins are the original languages or uses of words. To review word origins, see page 181.

Take It to the Net

www.phschool.com

Take the interactive self-test online to check your understanding of the selection.

Answers for p. 189

Review and Assess

1. Paul is afraid of fighting, but he is also afraid of calling off the fight.
2. Possible response: Paul's internal conflict is settled because he faces John, even though he loses the fight. Also, Paul is assured that the other students probably will not pick fights with him because they see that his sister will come to his aid.
3. John may not want to fight, but he does not want to lose his dignity either.
4. Paul's external conflict comes from accidentally hurting John and from John's declaration that he will get even.
5. Paul's external conflict of not wanting but needing to fight John causes Paul's internal conflict of fear from not knowing how to fight.
6.

Word	Meanings
pizza (origin: Italian)	a food made of dough spread with toppings
The children enjoyed pizza for lunch.	
espresso (origin: Italian)	very strong coffee
Espresso is served in very small cups because it is so strong.	
cliché (origin: French)	overused term
The corny speech was full of clichés.	
siesta (origin: Spanish)	rest
I would like to take a siesta today.	
adios (origin: Spanish)	goodbye
Mother said "Adios" as we left for school.	
bon voyage (origin: French)	"Have a good trip"
She came to wish us bon voyage as we left on our trip.	

continued

Continued from right column

7. Words from other languages can be understood because the foreign words have been used by English speakers for a long time.
8. Possible response: Some children fight to prove that they are tough or cool. Fights could be avoided if people could accept each other as they are or find another way to resolve their conflicts.

ENRICHMENT: Further Reading

Other Works by Paul Zindel

A Begonia for Miss Applebaum

Loch

The Pigman's Legacy

Take It to the Net

Visit www.phschool.com for more information on Paul Zindel.

EXTEND

Answers for p. 190

❶ Vocabulary Development

Word Analysis

1. the act of or result of aggravating
2. the act of hesitating
3. the act of or result of reducing

Spelling Strategy

1. subscription
2. intention
3. application
4. reaction

Concept Development

1. negative—If something looks distorted, it does not look typical or normal.
2. neutral—A tactic is a strategy, and it is not good or bad.
3. neutral—To undulate is to move in waves, which is not good or bad.
4. negative—To grovel is to debase oneself, which is humiliating.
5. negative—Goading someone is like pushing someone, which can seem forceful.
6. positive—To be exact is to be precise or accurate, which is helpful.

❷ Grammar

1. Nonno Frankie took (a) <u>boxing</u> stance.
2. I stopped (a) <u>few</u> feet from him.
3. Everyone stopped dead in their tracks.
4. They looked like (the) mob I had seen in (a) <u>sixteenth-century</u> etching.
5. (The) crowd froze in <u>amazed</u> silence.

Writing Application

Possible responses:

1. My <u>best</u> friend lives near me.
2. The <u>large</u> crowd left peacefully.
3. His <u>underhanded</u> tactics caused trouble.
4. There is no such thing as a <u>friendly</u> foe.
5. His <u>damaged</u> pride collapsed when he lost the chess match.

Integrate Language Skills

❶ Vocabulary Development Lesson

Word Analysis: Latin Suffix *-tion*

The Latin suffix *-tion* means "the act, condition, or result of." For example, to *condemn* is to judge someone as deserving punishment. *Condemnation* is the act of condemning. Define each of the following on your paper.

1. aggravation 2. hesitation 3. reduction

Spelling Strategy

Words that contain the *shun* sound are frequently misspelled because the *shun* sound can be spelled *-tion*, *-ssion*, or *-sion*. Learn words that spell the *shun* sound *-tion*. Unscramble the letters to write a word that ends in *-tion*.

1. snoibirscupt
2. netnotini
3. paplicnatio
4. treaconi

Concept Development: Connotations

The **connotation** of a word is the set of ideas associated with it in addition to its literal meaning. Some words, like *confident*, have positive connotations. Others, like *aggressive*, can have negative connotations. Some words are neutral—they have neither positive nor negative connotations or associations.

On your paper, write whether each of the following words has a positive, negative, or neutral connotation. Write a sentence explaining each of your answers.

1. distorted
2. tactics
3. undulating
4. groveled
5. goading
6. exact

❷ Grammar Lesson

Adjectives

An **adjective** is a word that describes a person, place, or thing. An adjective answers one of the following questions: *What kind? Which one? How many? How much?*

Adjective	Answers the question . . .
a *black* eye	*What kind of eye?* A *black* one.
my *right* fist	*Which one?* The *right* one.
about *300* kids	*How many? 300.*
some meat and potatoes	*How much? Some.*

A special category of adjectives, called **articles,** includes *a, an,* and *the.*

Practice Write these sentences. Then, underline the adjectives and circle the articles.

1. Nonno Frankie took a boxing stance.
2. I stopped a few feet from him.
3. Everyone stopped dead in their tracks.
4. They looked like the mob I had seen in a sixteenth-century etching.
5. The crowd froze in amazed silence.

Writing Application For each noun below, write a sentence in which the noun is modified by an adjective. Underline the adjective.

Example: crowd: The <u>angry</u> crowd roared.

1. friend
2. crowd
3. tactics
4. foe
5. pride

WG Prentice Hall Writing and Grammar Connection: Chapter 16, Section 1

TEACHING RESOURCES

The following resources can be used to enrich or extend the instruction for pp. 190–191.

Vocabulary

- **Selection Support:** Build Vocabulary, p. 56; Build Spelling Skills, p. 57
- **Vocabulary and Spelling Practice Book** (Use this booklet for skills enrichment)

Grammar

- **Selection Support:** Build Grammar Skills, p. 58
- **Writing and Grammar,** Copper Level, p. 330

- **Daily Language Practice Transparencies** ■

Writing

- **Writing and Grammar,** Copper Level, p. 42 ■
- **Writing Models and Graphic Organizers on Transparencies,** p. 97
- **Writing and Grammar iText CD-ROM**

■ **BLOCK SCHEDULING:** Resources marked with this symbol provide varied instruction during 90-minute blocks.

❸ Writing Lesson

School Rules

Having a list of rules, including those for gym, might have helped Paul avoid a fight. Write the twenty most important rules that new students in your school need to know.

Prewriting Write as many of your school's rules as you can think of. Then, choose the twenty most important.

Drafting Write in imperative sentences—sentences that give an order. Use the positive rather than the negative. For instance, write "Put trash in trash barrels" instead of "Don't litter." Organize rules in order of importance, from most to least.

Model: Drafting Imperative Sentences

BAKER SCHOOL RULES

1. Be in your homeroom at *8 a.m.*
2. Call in absences. (*Absences must be reported by 8:30.*)
3. Pay attention to dress code. (**NO** cutoffs!)
4. Use the library for studying. (*Talk Quietly!*)
5. Keep the halls clean—use the wastebaskets.

Revising Format your list of rules by using different sizes and types of letters, underlining, and arrangement of the text on the page. If possible, use a word-processing program to format your rules electronically. Find and use the commands for tabs, **boldface,** underscore, and *italics*.

WG Prentice Hall Writing and Grammar Connection: Chapter 11, Section 2

❹ Extension Activities

Research and Technology Television often tries to "hook" consumers by suggesting that a product will make them happier, better looking, stronger, or more popular. **Identify emotional appeals** used in at least five television advertisements.

- Present an oral explanation of each ad.
- Tell which character—Paul, Nonno Frankie, Moose, or Jennifer—would be most influenced and why.

After presenting your findings to your class, ask them if they agree or disagree with you.

Listening and Speaking With others, present a **news report** on Paul's fight. Two students might act as anchors, while another gives a live report. [Group Activity]

Writing Write a brief **essay** in which you explain why children fight and how fights can be avoided. Use examples drawn from experience.

Take It to the Net www.phschool.com

Go online for an additional research activity using the Internet.

❸ Writing Lesson

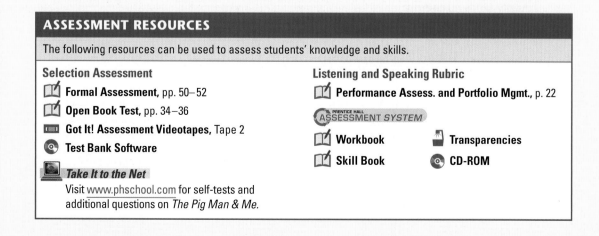

- Display the Sunburst Organizer transparency on p. 97 in **Writing Models and Graphic Organizers on Transparencies,** and write "school rules" in the center.
- Point out to students that each school rule they propose should have a clear purpose. Ask students for examples of rules they think are useful, and include them in the sunburst.
- Allow students to use this strategy to prepare their list of the school's rules.

❹ Research and Technology

- If possible, prepare a videotape of commercials with strong emotional appeal.
- Show the videotape to the students several times. The first time, students should be looking for the main idea. During subsequent viewings, have students evaluate the appeals used by the advertisers.
- Have groups of students present their evaluations of appeals in the commercials.
- Have students evaluate their classmates' presentations with the Listening rubric on p. 22 in **Performance Assessment and Portfolio Management.**

CUSTOMIZE INSTRUCTION
For Universal Access

To address different learning styles, use the activities suggested in the **Extension Activities** booklet, p. 12.

- For Verbal/Linguistic and Interpersonal Learners, use Activities 5 and 7.
- For Visual/Spatial Learners, use Activity 6.

ASSESSMENT RESOURCES

The following resources can be used to assess students' knowledge and skills.

Selection Assessment

- **Formal Assessment,** pp. 50–52
- **Open Book Test,** pp. 34–36
- **Got It! Assessment Videotapes,** Tape 2
- **Test Bank Software**

Take It to the Net

Visit www.phschool.com for self-tests and additional questions on *The Pig Man & Me.*

Listening and Speaking Rubric

- **Performance Assess. and Portfolio Mgmt.,** p. 22

PRENTICE HALL ASSESSMENT SYSTEM

- **Workbook**
- **Transparencies**
- **Skill Book**
- **CD-ROM**

Thunder Butte

Lesson Objectives

1. **To analyze and respond to literary elements**
   - Literary Analysis: Atmosphere
   - Connecting Literary Elements: Setting
2. **To read, comprehend, analyze, and critique a short story**
   - Reading Strategy: Understanding Shades of Meaning in Related Words
   - Reading Check Questions
   - Review and Assess Questions
   - Assessment Practice (ATE)
3. **To develop word analysis skills, fluency, and systematic vocabulary**
   - Vocabulary Development Lesson: Word Analysis: Forms of *vary*
4. **To understand and apply written and oral language conventions**
   - Spelling Strategy
   - Grammar Lesson: Possessive Adjectives
5. **To understand and apply appropriate writing and research strategies**
   - Writing Lesson: Opinion Paper
   - Extension Activity: Sioux Customs
   - Extension Activity: Essay
6. **To understand and apply listening and speaking strategies**
   - Extension Activity: Informative Presentation

STEP-BY-STEP TEACHING GUIDE	PACING GUIDE
PRETEACH	
Motivate Students and Provide Background	
Use the Motivation activity (ATE p. 192)	5 min.
Read and discuss the Preview material and Background information (SE/ATE p. 192) [A]	5 min.
Introduce the Concepts	
Introduce the Literary Analysis and Reading Strategy (SE/ATE p. 193) [A]	20 min.
Pronounce the vocabulary words and read their definitions (SE p. 193)	5 min.
TEACH	
Monitor Comprehension	
Informally monitor comprehension by circulating while students read independently or in groups [A]	35–40 min.
Monitor students' comprehension with the Reading Check notes (SE/ATE pp. 195, 197, 199, 201, 203)	as students read
Develop vocabulary with Vocabulary notes (SE pp. 194, 197, 198, 202)	as students read
Develop Understanding	
Develop students' understanding of atmosphere with the Literary Analysis annotations (SE pp. 196, 198, 199, 203; ATE pp. 196, 198, 199, 203) [A]	5 min.
Develop students' understanding of shades of meaning in related words with the Reading Strategy annotations (SE pp. 195, 197, 199, 201; ATE pp. 195, 197, 199, 202)	5 min.
ASSESS	
Assess Mastery	
Assess students' mastery of the Reading Strategy and Literary Analysis by having them answer the Review and Assess questions (SE/ATE p. 205)	25 min.
Use one or more of the print and media Assessment Resources (ATE p. 207) [A]	up to 45 min.
EXTEND	
Apply Understanding	
Have students complete the Vocabulary Development Lesson and the Grammar Lesson (SE p. 206) [A]	20 min.
Apply students' ability to write an opinion paper using the Writing Lesson (SE/ATE p. 207) [A]	45 min.
Apply students' understanding using one or more of the Extension Activities (SE p. 207)	20–90 min.

ACCELERATED INSTRUCTION:
Use the strategies and activities identified with an [A].

UNIVERSAL ACCESS
● = Below Level Students
▲ = On-Level Students
■ = Above Level Students

Time and Resource Manager

Reading Level: Average
Average Number of Instructional Days: 4

RESOURCES		
PRINT	**TRANSPARENCIES**	**TECHNOLOGY**
• **Beyond Literature,** Community Connection: Learning from Elders, p. 13 ▲ ■		• **Interest Grabber Videotapes,** Tape 2 ● ▲ ■
• **Selection Support Workbook:** ● ▲ ■ Literary Analysis, p. 65 Reading Strategy, p. 64 Build Vocabulary, p. 61	• **Literary Analysis and Reading Transparencies,** pp. 25 and 26 ● ▲ ■	
• **Adapted Reader's Companion** ● • **Reader's Companion** ●		• **Listening to Literature** ● ▲ ■ Audiocassettes, Side 9 Audio CDs, CD 4
• **English Learner's Companion** ● ▲ • **Literary Analysis for Enrichment** ■	• **Fine Art Transparencies, Volume 1,** Transparency 5 ● ▲ ■	
• **Formal Assessment:** Selection Test, pp. 53–55 ● ▲ ■ • **Open Book Test,** pp. 37–39 ● ▲ ■ • **Performance Assessment and Portfolio Management,** pp. 11, 29 ● ▲ ■ • PRENTICE HALL ASSESSMENT SYSTEM ● ▲ ■	• PRENTICE HALL ASSESSMENT SYSTEM ● ▲ ■ Skills Practice Answers and Explanations on Transparencies	• **Test Bank Software** ● ▲ ■ • **Got It! Assessment Videotapes,** Tape 2 ● ▲
• **Selection Support Workbook:** ● ▲ ■ Build Spelling Skills, p. 62 Build Grammar Skills, p. 63 • **Writing and Grammar,** Copper Level ● ▲ ■ • **Extension Activities,** p. 13 ● ▲ ■	• **Daily Language Practice Transparencies** ● ▲ • **Writing Models and Graphic Organizers on Transparencies** ● ▲ ■	• **Writing and Grammar iText CD-ROM** ● ▲ ■ *Take It to the Net* www.phschool.com

BLOCK SCHEDULING: Use one 90-minute class period to preteach the selection and have students read it. Use a second 90-minute class period to assess students' mastery of skills and have them complete one of the Extension Activities.

PRETEACH

Step-by-Step Teaching Guide for pp. 192–193

Motivation

Write the headings "Old Ways" and "New Ways" on the chalkboard. Ask students to think of ideas, traditions, or procedures that have been replaced or changed by newer ones. Have a volunteer pantomime an action that represents an old way of doing something. Invite students to guess what is being pantomimed. For example, a student might pantomime using a typewriter. List a description under the "Old Ways" heading. Then, have students suggest a corresponding new way of performing the action and record its description in the "New Ways" column. Students might suggest using a computer instead of a typewriter. Repeat the activity as time allows. Introduce the selection by explaining that the main character must cope with a conflict between old and new in his own family.

Interest Grabber Video

As an alternative, play "Native American Tradition" on Tape 2 to engage student interest.

❶ Background

Social Studies

This story brings the old ways of the Sioux into conflict with the new ways. Today, some Sioux Indians remain on reservations on the northern plains; others live throughout the United States. The *coup* (ko͞o) stick in this story is a symbol of Sioux bravery and fighting skill, and it calls to mind the ancient traditions of the Sioux.

Prepare to Read

❶ Thunder Butte

Take It to the Net

Visit www.phschool.com for interactive activities and instruction related to "Thunder Butte," including
- background
- graphic organizers
- literary elements
- reading strategies

Preview

Connecting to the Literature

You probably have privileges now that you did not have last year. However, you may also have had to let go of some old habits. The main character in "Thunder Butte" must find a way to balance new ideas with traditions from his Native American past.

Background

The Sioux are one of the many Native American peoples who once lived throughout the Midwest. In the plains of the Dakotas and Nebraska, steep, flat-topped hills appear suddenly, rising as if out of nowhere. These land formations are called *buttes* (byo͞ots) or *mesas* (mā′ səs). In the past, Native Americans climbed these buttes to scan the plains for miles around for enemies, animals, or other activity.

TEACHING RESOURCES

The following resources can be used to enrich or extend the instruction for pp. 192–193.

Motivation

Interest Grabber Video, Tape 2 

Background

Beyond Literature, p. 13

Take It to the Net

Visit www.phschool.com for Background and hotlinks for "Thunder Butte."

Literary Analysis

Literary Analysis and Reading Transparencies, Atmosphere, p. 26

Reading

Selection Support: Reading Strategy, p. 64

Literary Analysis and Reading Transparencies, Understanding Shades of Meaning in Related Words, p. 25

BLOCK SCHEDULING: Resources marked with this symbol provide varied instruction during 90-minute blocks.

❷ Literary Analysis

Atmosphere

Atmosphere is the feeling or mood of a work. Just as the atmosphere of the Earth can produce weather such as rain, wind, or snow, the atmosphere of a story can create emotional weather—fear, sadness, joy, or silliness. In "Thunder Butte," descriptive details produce a dark, threatening atmosphere.

> . . . the hill *looming* high above . . . was capped with *dark, low-hanging clouds*.

As you read, identify the story's atmosphere and the details that contribute to it.

Connecting Literary Elements

One element that shapes a story's atmosphere is **setting**—the time and place of the action. In "Thunder Butte," details of the setting—such as the stormy weather and the deserted butte—contribute to an atmosphere of tension and pressure. Use these focus questions to help you consider the setting and its impact on the story's atmosphere:

1. What details of the setting are dark and threatening?
2. How do these details influence your feelings about the story?

❸ Reading Strategy

Understanding Shades of Meaning in Related Words

Although many words have similar definitions, most have different **shades of meaning**—variations in the intensity of the word or associations with the word.

Examples: old ⟶ ancient
clean ⟶ immaculate

Look at this chart showing the use of the word *old* in the story and providing closely related words with similar shades of meaning. As you read, pay close attention to the writer's use of descriptive words. Think about other words that could have been used, and how using these other words would have changed the shade of meaning.

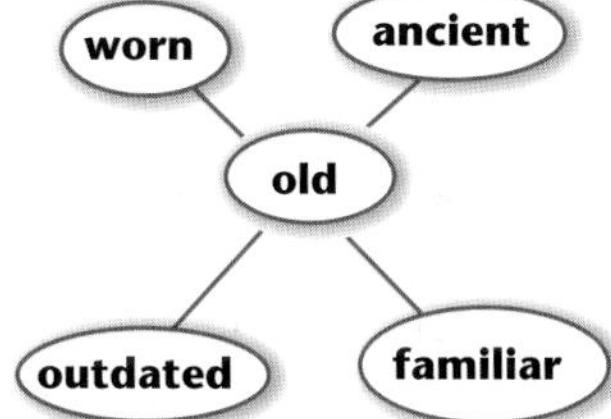

Vocabulary Development

meanderings (mē an′ dər iŋz) *n.* aimless wanderings (p. 194)

diminutive (də min′ yo͞o tiv) *adj.* very small (p. 197)

variegated (ver′ ē ə gāt′ id) *adj.* streaked with different colors (p. 198)

heathen (hē′ *th*ən) *adj.* uncivilized (p. 202)

adamant (ad′ ə mənt′) *adj.* not flexible; not willing to give in (p. 202)

CUSTOMIZE INSTRUCTION FOR UNIVERSAL ACCESS

For Special Needs Students	For Less Proficient Readers	For English Learners
Have students read the adapted version of "Thunder Butte" in the **Adapted Reader's Companion.** This version provides basic-level instruction in an interactive format with questions and write-on lines. Completing the adapted version will prepare students to read the selection in the Student Edition.	Have students read "Thunder Butte" in the **Reader's Companion.** This version provides basic-level instruction in an interactive format with questions and write-on lines. After students finish the selection in the Reader's Companion, have them complete the questions and activities in the Student Edition.	Have students read the adapted version of "Thunder Butte" in the **English Learner's Companion.** This version provides basic-level instruction in an interactive format with questions and write-on lines. Completing the adapted version will prepare students to read the selection in the Student Edition.

❷ Literary Analysis

Atmosphere

- Invite students to describe the atmosphere in one of their favorite places. Explain that the atmosphere is not only the physical description of the place, it also includes the way the place makes them feel. List the adjectives they use on the board.
- Connect the idea of atmosphere described in the text with the adjectives written on the board.
- Use the Atmosphere transparency on p. 26 in **Literary Analysis and Reading Transparencies** to show students how details contribute to atmosphere.

❸ Reading Strategy

Understanding Shades of Meaning in Related Words

- Obtain a color wheel or a model of a light spectrum. Direct students' attention to how the colors blend from one shade into another. Point out to students that words have shades of meaning, just as colors have variations.
- After reading the Reading Strategy text, write the word *jubilant* on the board. Ask students for the definition. Then, write the word *happy* on the board. Discuss with students the different shades of meaning of each word. Then, brainstorm for a list of other words that have different shades of meanings for the word *happy.*
- Using the Understanding Shades of Meaning in Related Words transparency on p. 25 in **Literary Analysis and Reading Transparencies,** model making an organizer that shows shades of meaning.
- Encourage students to make organizers with any remaining phrases.

Vocabulary Development

- Pronounce each vocabulary word for students, and read the definitions as a class. Have students identify any words with which they are already familiar.

E-Teach

Visit E-Teach at www.phschool.com for teachers' essays on how to teach, with questions and answers.

TEACH

Step-by-Step Teaching Guide for pp. 194–204

CUSTOMIZE INSTRUCTION
For Visual/Spatial Learners

Call students' attention to the photograph on p. 194. Invite students to discuss what it might be like to hike across the land and climb one of the buttes shown in the picture. Ask students to speculate on whether they would enjoy such a hike and what dangers they might face.

1 About the Selection

In "Thunder Butte," a story about the conflict between old and new beliefs, Norman's grandfather has an important dream. As a result of the dream, he sends Norman to climb Thunder Butte. Norman manages the difficult climb and successfully reaches the top. On his way down, he finds a leather-covered stick. When he returns to his grandfather and shows him the stick, his grandfather recognizes it as a *coup* stick used long ago by a Sioux warrior. Grandfather tells Norman that the stick can help him understand the values of "the old ones." When Norman takes the stick home, however, his mother calls it a symbol of "heathen ways." Norman's father argues that the stick is an important part of history. At the end of the day, Norman realizes that the triumph of meeting his grandfather's challenge has been overshadowed by disagreement over old and new values.

1 Thunder Butte

Virginia Driving Hawk Sneve

The sun was just beginning to rise when John woke Norman the next morning.

"You must get an early start if you are going to go to the west side of the butte and return by supper," John said to the sleepy boy. "If you are not home by the time I get back from work, I'll come looking for you."

Norman reluctantly rose. Last night he had accepted his grandfather's command to go to the Thunder Butte without too many doubts. Yet now in the morning's chill light the boy wondered if his grandfather's dreams were the meaningless meanderings of an old mind, or if his grandfather was really worthy of the tribe's respect as one of the few remaining wise elders who understood the ancient ways.

meanderings (mē an′ dər iŋz) *n.* aimless wanderings

Norman dressed in his oldest clothes and pulled on worn and scuffed boots to protect his feet from the rocks and snakes of the butte. He heard his parents talking in the other room and knew his father was telling his mother where Norman was going.

As the boy entered the room, which was kitchen and living room as well as his parents' bedroom, he heard his mother say, "What if there is a rock slide and Norman is hurt or buried on the butte? We won't know anything until you get home from work, John. I don't want Norman to go."

TEACHING RESOURCES

The following resources can be used to enrich or extend the instruction for pp. 194–204.

Literary Analysis
- **Selection Support:** Literary Analysis, p. 65
- **Literary Analysis for Enrichment**
- **Writing Models and Graphic Organizers on Transparencies,** p. 89

Reading
- **Adapted Reader's Companion**
- **Reader's Companion**
- **English Learner's Companion**
- **Listening to Literature Audiocassettes,** Side 9 ■
- **Listening to Literature Audio CDs,** CD 4 ■

Extension
- **Fine Art Transparencies, Volume 1,** Transparency 5. (Lead a discussion about how the landscape depicted in this painting resembles the butte described in the story.) ■

■ **BLOCK SCHEDULING:** Resources marked with this symbol provide varied instruction during 90-minute blocks.

"The boy is old enough to have learned to be careful on the butte. He'll be all right," John answered as he tried to reassure Sarah. "Besides," he added, "my father dreamed of this happening."

Sarah grunted scornfully, "No one believes in dreams or in any of those old superstitious ways anymore."

"I'll be okay, Mom," Norman said as he sat down at the table. "I should be able to find lots of agates[1] on the west side where there is all that loose rock. Maybe I can talk the trader into giving
2 me money for them after all." He spoke bravely despite his own inner misgivings about going to the butte.

Sarah protested no more. Norman looked at her, but she lowered her head as she set a plate of pancakes in front of him. He knew she was hiding the worry she felt for him.

John put on his hat and went to the door. "Don't forget to take the willow branch with you," he said to Norman, "and be careful."

Norman nodded and ate his breakfast. When he was finished he stood up. "Guess I'll go," he said to his mother, who was pouring hot water from the tea kettle into her dish pan. When she didn't speak Norman took the willow cane from where he had propped it by the door and his hat from the nail above it.

"Wait," Sarah called and handed him a paper bag.

1. **agates** (ag´ its) *n.* hard, semiprecious stones with striped or clouded coloring.

Reading Strategy
Understanding Shades of Meaning What words are related in meaning to *misgivings?*

3 

Why is Norman going to the west side of the butte?

2 Reading Strategy

Understanding Shades of Meaning

- Read the bracketed sentence aloud. Ask students to use context clues to define the word *misgivings.*
  Answer: If Norman speaks "bravely despite his own inner misgivings," *misgivings* probably means that he is having *doubts.*
- Next, ask students the Reading Strategy question.
  Possible responses: *Worries, second thoughts,* or *concerns* are close in meaning.
- Have students complete a diagram that is similar to the one found on p. 193.
- Challenge students to offer words that are similar in meaning to the word *bravely.*
  Answer: Students may suggest *fierce*ly, *fearlessly,* or *courageously.*

3 Reading Check

Answer: Norman is going to the west side of the butte because his grandfather tells him to go there. He is also going to pick up agates that he may sell.

CUSTOMIZE INSTRUCTION FOR UNIVERSAL ACCESS

For Less Proficient Readers	For English Learners	For Advanced Readers
Have students read the story with partners or in small groups, with each student taking a turn reading aloud a passage. Instruct students to stop after each passage to discuss and clarify what is happening in the story. Encourage students to help one another with unfamiliar words and concepts.	Help students keep track of events in the story by having them listen to the recording of "Thunder Butte" in segments. Then, have students work with a partner who is proficient in English to review the story and complete a graphic organizer such as the Series of Events Chain on p. 69, in **Writing and Language Transparencies.**	Have students make notes on the changing thoughts and feelings Norman experiences on the day he climbs the butte. Suggest that students use the Open Mind organizer on p. 93 in **Writing and Language Transparencies** to record what Norman is thinking and feeling at important moments in the story.

❹ Literary Analysis

Atmosphere

- Remind students that the setting of a story helps create a convincing atmosphere. Have students find details that contribute to the atmosphere in the bracketed paragraph.
  Answer: Details include whistling like meadowlarks, "early morning air," "bushy sage," and the sun warming his neck.
- Ask the Literary Analysis question on p. 196: What atmosphere is created by the details of whistling meadowlarks and Norman swiping at the sage and spearing the pear cactus?
  Answer: The atmosphere is cheerful and energetic.

❺ Critical Thinking

Connect

- Tell students that authors use action to show how characters feel about one another. Have students read the passage that begins "Then Norman smiled." Students should try to determine what Norman's smile says about his relationship with his grandfather.
  Answer: Norman likes his grandfather.
- Further explore the relationship between the family members. Ask: Why does Norman choose to take the more difficult route up the mountain?
  Answer: He respects his grandfather and wants to please him.

❻ ▶Critical Viewing

Answer: Students may respond that the atmosphere seems majestic, lonely, scary, or sad.

"Here is a lunch for you. You'll need something to eat since you'll be gone all day." She gave him an affectionate shove. "Oh, go on. I know you'll be all right. Like your dad said, you're old enough to be careful."

Norman smiled at his mother. "Thanks," he said as he tucked the lunch into his shirt. He checked his back pocket to see if he'd remembered the salt bag to put the agates in.

❹ He walked briskly across the open prairie and turned to wave at his mother, who had come outside to watch him leave. She waved back and Norman quickened his pace. He whistled, trying to echo the meadowlarks who were greeting the day with their happy song. He swiped the willow cane at the bushy sage and practiced spearing the pear cactus that dotted his path. The early morning air was cool, but the sun soon warmed the back of his neck and he knew it would be a hot day.

He crossed the creek south of where Matt Two Bull's tent was pitched and then he was climbing the gentle beginning slope of the butte. He stopped and studied the way before him and wondered if it wouldn't be easier to reach the west side by walking around the base of the butte even though it would be longer. ❺ Then Norman smiled as he remembered his grandfather's command to climb the south trail that wound to the top. He decided to do what the old man wanted.

Literary Analysis
Atmosphere What atmosphere is created by the details of whistling meadowlarks and Norman swiping at the sage and spearing the pear cactus?

❻ ▼ **Critical Viewing** What is the atmosphere of this photo? **[Analyze]**

ENRICHMENT: Science Connection

Rattlesnakes

The rattlesnake that Norman sees on the butte is common in the northern United States, west of the Mississippi Valley. Classified as a pit viper, the rattlesnake is a poisonous snake named for the rattle on the tip of its tail. Rattlesnakes release their poison through two long fangs in the upper jaw. The fangs fold up into the roof of the mouth when not in use.

There are several types of rattlesnakes. Diamondback rattlesnakes can grow up to seven feet in length. These snakes are very dangerous and should be carefully avoided.

Have students work in groups using classroom or library resources to answer questions such as these:

> What is a rattlesnake's rattle made of and how is it used? Where are rattlesnakes found? What do rattlesnakes eat? What first-aid treatment should be given for a rattlesnake bite?

The ascent sharply steepened and the sun rose with him as Norman climbed. What looked like a smooth path from the prairie floor was rough rocky terrain. The trail spiraled up a sharp incline and Norman had to detour around fallen rocks. He paused to rest about half way up and then saw how sharply the overhanging ledge of the butte protruded. Getting to the top of it was going to be a difficult struggle. He climbed on. His foot slipped and his ankle twisted painfully. Small pebbles bounced down the slope
7 and he saw a rattlesnake slither out of the way. He tightly clutched the willow branch and leaned panting against the butte. He sighed with relief as the snake crawled out of sight. He wiggled his foot until the pain left his ankle. Then he started to trudge up the incline again.

At last only the ledge of the butte loomed over him. There appeared to be no way up. Disgusted that his laborious climb seemed dead-ended he stubbornly tried to reach the top. Remembering the courage of the ancient young men who had struggled in this same place to gain the summit and seek their visions, he was determined not to go back. His fingers found tiny cracks to hold on to. The cane was cumbersome and in the way. He was tempted to drop it, but he thought of the snake he'd seen and struggled on with it awkwardly under his arm.

Finally Norman spied a narrow opening in the ledge which tapered down to only a few feet from where he clung. He inched his way up until he reached the base of the opening and then he
8 found a use for the cane. He jammed the stout branch high into the boulders above him. Cautiously he pulled to see if it would hold his weight. It held. Using the cane as a lever he pulled himself to the top.

This final exertion winded the boy and he lay exhausted on the summit, boots hanging over the edge. Cautiously he pulled his feet under him, stood and looked around.

He gazed at a new world. The sun bathed the eastern valley in pale yellow which was spotted with dark clumps of sage. The creek was a green and silver serpent winding its way to the southeast. His grandfather's tent was a white shoe box in its clearing, and beside it stood a diminutive form waving a red flag. It was Matt Two Bull signaling with his shirt, and Norman knew that his grandfather had been watching him climb. He waved his hat in reply and then walked to the outer edge of the butte.

The summit was not as smoothly flat as it looked from below. Norman stepped warily over the many cracks and holes that pitted the surface. He was elated that he had successfully made the difficult ascent, but now as he surveyed the butte top he had a sense of discomfort.

Reading Strategy
Understanding Shades of Meaning Look at the words *slither* and *crawled*, which describe the rattlesnake's actions. What are the different shades of meaning each word conveys?

diminutive (də min′ yo͞o tiv) *adj.* very small

9 **Reading Check**

How does Norman get to the top of the butte?

7 Reading Strategy

Understanding Shades of Meaning

- Tell students that verbs, or action words, also have shades of meaning. To show this, write *walk*, *saunter*, and *shuffle* on the board. Ask students to describe the shades of meaning for these words. Answer: *To shuffle* is to walk slowly, dragging one's feet. *To saunter* is to walk proudly and boastfully.
- Have a student volunteer read the description of the rattlesnake. Ask students to respond to the Reading Strategy instruction on p. 197: Look at the words *slither* and *crawled*, which describe the rattlesnake's actions. What are the different shades of meaning each word conveys?
  Answer: *Slither* means "move on one's stomach" and is usually used to describe the movement of animals. *Crawl* means "move low to the ground on hands and feet" and can describe the movement of people or animals.

8 Critical Thinking

Infer

- Remind students to pay attention to details in the story in order to make inferences, or judgments, about the characters.
- Ask students what they can infer about Norman's physical and mental abilities from this description.
  Answer: Norman must be in good physical condition. Norman also seems mentally determined, because he keeps finding ways to get to the top of the butte.

9 Reading Check

Answer: Norman pulls himself to the top of the butte by using his cane.

CUSTOMIZE INSTRUCTION FOR UNIVERSAL ACCESS

For Special Needs Students	For Less Proficient Readers	For Advanced Readers
Some students may benefit from additional opportunities to visualize the scenery in this selection. Use travel books or on-line resources to find additional pictures of this part of the United States. Then show the pictures to students. Encourage students to write descriptions of the pictures.	The descriptions of scenery in this selection may cause problems for some readers. Invite students to find the passages containing descriptions, look up definitions of problem words in a dictionary, and rewrite the descriptions using their own words.	Advanced readers may be interested in analyzing how Norman interacts with the scenery and what that interaction tells readers about Norman's character. Have students note the hazards and barriers he meets while he hikes. Then, have students write or explain orally what his reaction to these difficulties reveals about his personality.

10 Literary Analysis

Atmosphere and Setting

- Ask students to recall the atmosphere of the story when Norman set out on his journey.
  Answer: It was bright, happy, and energetic.
- Remind students that as settings change, atmosphere also changes. Have a volunteer read aloud the bracketed passage.
- Ask students for details from the passage that tell about the atmosphere.
  Answer: There are no flowers or birds and no music. The summit is rough and has burn marks. Norman knows that it is a sacred place and feels uneasy.
- Ask students the Literary Analysis question on p. 198: In what ways has the atmosphere changed?
  Answer: The atmosphere is scarier and more threatening than before.

Monitor Progress Have students relate which setting they preferred and why.
Answer: Some students may prefer the earlier setting because it felt happier and safer. Others may prefer the later setting because they enjoy heights and suspense.

Reteach If students have difficulty understanding the difference between the settings, have them list the qualities of each setting on a sheet of paper. Ask them to compare the lists. Help students understand that details in a setting contribute to atmosphere.

11 Critical Thinking

Speculate

- Explain to students that *hewn*, in the second paragraph, means "cut or formed with heavy blows, such as with an ax."
- Have students suggest reasons that rock steps have been cut into the opening.
  Answer: They were cut there because this is a sacred place, and at one time a trail probably went to the top of the butte. Steps would have made it easier to climb to the summit.

10 There were burn scars on the rough summit, and Norman wondered if these spots were where the lightning had struck, or were they evidence of ancient man-made fires? He remembered that this was a sacred place to the old ones and his uneasiness increased. He longed to be back on the secure level of the plains.

On the west edge he saw that the butte cast a sharp shadow below because the rim protruded as sharply as it had on the slope he'd climbed. 11 Two flat rocks jutted up on either side of a narrow opening, and Norman saw shallow steps hewn into the space between. This must be the trail of which his grandfather had spoken.

Norman stepped down and then quickly turned to hug the butte face as the steps ended abruptly in space. The rest of the rocky staircase lay broken and crumbled below. The only way down was to jump.

He cautiously let go of the willow branch and watched how it landed and bounced against the rocks. He took a deep breath as if to draw courage from the air. He lowered himself so that he was hanging by his fingertips to the last rough step, closed his eyes and dropped.

The impact of his landing stung the soles of his feet. He stumbled and felt the cut of the sharp rocks against one knee as he struggled to retain his balance. He did not fall and finally stood upright breathing deeply until the wild pounding of his heart slowed. "Wow," he said softly as he looked back up at the ledge, "that must have been at least a twenty foot drop."

He picked up the willow branch and started walking slowly down the steep slope. The trail Matt Two Bull had told him about had been obliterated by years of falling rock. Loose shale and gravel shifted under Norman's feet, and he probed cautiously ahead with the cane to test the firmness of each step.

He soon found stones which he thought were agates. He identified them by spitting on each rock and rubbing the wet spot with his finger. The dull rock seemed to come alive! Variegated hues of brown and gray glowed as if polished. They were agates all right. Quickly he had his salt bag half full.

It was almost noon and his stomach growled. He stopped to rest against a large boulder and pulled out his lunch from his shirt. But his mouth was too dry to chew the cheese sandwich. He couldn't swallow without water.

Thirsty and hungry, Norman decided to go straight down the butte and head for home.

Walking more confidently as the slope leveled out he thrust the pointed cane carelessly into the ground. He suddenly fell as the cane went deep into the soft shale.

Literary Analysis
Atmosphere and Setting In what ways has the atmosphere changed?

variegated (ver′ ē ə gāt′ id) *adj.* marked with different colors in spots or streaks

ENRICHMENT: Cultural Connection

Traditions of the Past

Norman does not seem to fully appreciate or even know very much about his grandfather's values and the traditions of the "old ones." Discuss whether Norman's attitude is unusual among young people. Point out that in any cultural group, the lives of present generations can be enriched by learning about the values and traditions of earlier generations.

In solemn ceremonies that continue today, Sioux people learn valuable lessons about how to live their lives. Many stories and legends about their beliefs are told by older adults.

Ask students to consider ways that Norman can benefit from being more attentive to his grandfather's wisdom about the old ways. Then, suggest that they write a letter to Norman, in which they give reasons for and try to persuade him to respect his heritage and to be more sympathetic to those in his cultural group who live by that heritage.

Norman slid several feet. Loose rocks rolled around him as he came to rest against a boulder. He lay still for a long time fearing that his tumble might cause a rock fall. But no thundering slide came, so he cautiously climbed back to where the tip of the willow branch protruded from the ground.

⓬ He was afraid that the cane may have plunged into a rattlesnake den. Carefully he pulled at the stout branch, wiggling it this way and that with one hand while he dug with the other. It came loose, sending a shower of rocks down the hill, and Norman saw that something else was sticking up in the hole he had uncovered.

Curious, and seeing no sign of snakes, he kept digging and soon found the tip of a leather-covered stick. Bits of leather and wood fell off in his hand as he gently pulled. The stick, almost as long as he was tall and curved on one end, emerged as he tugged. Holding it before him, his heart pounding with excitement, he realized that he had found a thing that once belonged to the old ones.

Norman shivered at the thought that he may have disturbed a grave, which was *tehinda* [tā khin´ dä], forbidden. He cleared more dirt away but saw no bones nor other sign that this was a burial place. Quickly he picked up the stick and his willow cane and hurried down the hill. When he reached the bottom he discovered that in his fall the salt bag of agates had pulled loose from his belt. But he did not return to search for it. It would take most of the afternoon to travel around the base of the butte to the east side.

⓭ The creek was in the deep shade of the butte when he reached it and thirstily flopped down and drank. He crossed the shallow stream and walked to his grandfather's tent.

"You have been gone a long time," Matt Two Bull greeted as Norman walked into the clearing where the old man was seated.

"I have come from the west side of the butte, Grandpa," Norman said wearily. He sat down on the ground and examined a tear in his jeans and the bruise on his knee.

"Was it difficult?" the old man asked.

"Yes," Norman nodded. He told of the rough climb up the south slope, the jump down and finally of his fall which led him to discover the long leather-covered stick. He held the stick out to his grandfather who took it and examined it carefully.

"Are you sure there was no body in the place where you found this?"

Norman shook his head. "No, I found nothing else but the stick. Do you know what it is, Grandpa?"

"You have found a *coup* [ko͞o] stick which belonged to the old ones."

"I know that it is old because the wood is brittle and the leather is peeling, but what is—was a *coup* stick?" Norman asked.

Literary Analysis
Atmosphere What details contribute to the atmosphere of suspense in this paragraph?

Reading Strategy
Shades of Meaning
What shade of meaning is communicated by *flopped* that would not be communicated by *sank*?

⓮ 
Reading Check
What does Norman find in the hole?

⓬ Literary Analysis
Atmosphere

- Have students recall the change in atmosphere between the opening of the story and when Norman reached the top of the butte. Ask them to describe the change.
  Answer: The atmosphere changes from pleasant to ominous.
- After students have read the bracketed text, ask them to describe the atmosphere in the paragraph.
  Answer: It is suspenseful.
- Reread the paragraph. Ask students to listen for details that create the suspenseful atmosphere. Ask the Literary Analysis question on p. 199.
  Answer: The details that create suspense include Norman's fear, the idea of a rattlesnake, carefully pulling on the branch, digging with his hands, the shower of rocks, and something sticking out of the hole.

⓭ Reading Strategy
Shades of Meaning

- Remind students that an author's choice of action words helps show meaning. Ask a volunteer to read aloud the bracketed text.
- Have students describe what *flopped* means in this context.
  Answer: *Flopped* means "fell down quickly."
- Ask the Reading Strategy question on p. 199: What shade of meaning is communicated by *flopped* that would not be communicated by *sank*?
  Answer: *Sank* describes a slow, quiet action, but *flopped* describes a quick and noisy motion.

⓮  Reading Check

Answer: Norman finds an ancient, leather-covered stick.

CUSTOMIZE INSTRUCTION FOR UNIVERSAL ACCESS

For Gifted/Talented Students	For Advanced Readers
Have three volunteers give a dramatic reading of the conversation between Norman and his grandfather on these pages. The third student can read the part of the narrator. Encourage students to use vocal tone, facial expressions, and body language to convey the emotions of the characters. Lead a discussion of how the reading enhanced understanding of an important moment in the story.	Have students create a web diagram for each character. For each web, a central circle should contain the character's name. In other circles, students should record descriptive terms from the story as well as their inferences about the characters. Have students analyze the finished webs to discover why each character is unique.

15 Critical Thinking

Compare and Contrast

- Tell students that they can use a diagram to compare and contrast elements of the text. Draw a Venn diagram on the board or use the Venn Diagram Transparency on p. 89 in **Writing Models and Graphic Organizers on Transparencies.**
- After students have read the bracketed passage, ask them to supply words that describe the stick in old times, at present, and always. Write these words on the board.
  Possible answer: Old times: new; decorated with leather, feathers, and fur; painted; used by a warrior. Present: old; has remnants of leather decorations and painting; hidden in the earth. Always: curved, sacred.
- Model for students how to fill in the graphic organizer. In the left circle, place words that describe the stick when it was new. In the right circle, place descriptions of the stick as Norman found it. In the overlapping area, place descriptions of the stick at both times.

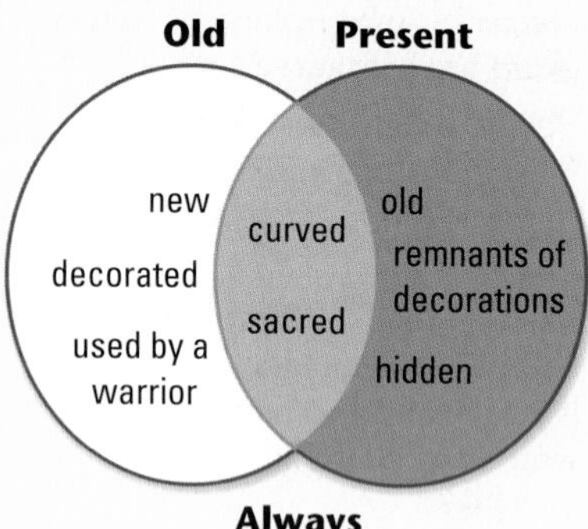

- Have students write a paragraph comparing and contrasting the stick over time. Ask: What qualities make the stick valuable to Matt Two Bull?

"In the days when the old ones roamed all of the plains," the old man swept his hand in a circle, "a courageous act of valor was thought to be more important than killing an enemy. When a warrior rode or ran up to his enemy, close enough to touch the man with a stick, without killing or being killed, the action was called *coup*.♦"

"The French, the first white men in this part of the land, named this brave deed *coup*. In their language the word meant 'hit' or 'strike.' The special stick which was used to strike with came to be known as a *coup* stick.

"Some sticks were long like this one," Matt Two Bull held the stick upright. "Some were straight, and others had a curve on the end like the sheep herder's crook," he pointed to the curving end of the stick.

"The sticks were decorated with fur or painted leather strips. A warrior kept count of his coups by tying an eagle feather to the crook for each brave deed.
15 See," he pointed to the staff end, "here is a remnant of a tie thong which must have once held a feather."

The old man and boy closely examined the *coup* stick. Matt Two Bull traced with his finger the faint zig zag design painted on the stick. "See," he said, "it is the thunderbolt."

"What does that mean?" Norman asked.

"The Thunders favored a certain few of the young men who sought their vision on the butte. The thunderbolt may have been part of a sacred dream sent as a token of the Thunders' favor. If this was so, the young man could use the thunderbolt symbol on his possessions."

"How do you suppose the stick came to be on the butte?" Norman asked.

His grandfather shook his head. "No one can say. Usually such a thing was buried with a dead warrior as were his weapons and other prized belongings."

"Is the *coup* stick what you dreamed about, Grandpa?"

"No. In my dream I only knew that you were to find a *Wakan*, [wä kän] a holy thing. But I did not know what it would be."

Norman laughed nervously. "What do you mean, *Wakan*? Is this stick haunted?"

Matt Two Bull smiled, "No, not like you mean in a fearful way. But in a sacred manner because it once had great meaning to the old ones."

"But why should I have been the one to find it?" Norman questioned.

His grandfather shrugged, "Perhaps to help you understand the ways—the values of the old ones."

Literature in context: Cultural Connection 

♦ *Coup*

The word *coup* is a French word that is also used in English. In French, *coup* means "blow, hit, or strike." In English, *coup* has several meanings, including

- a brilliant or clever move that is often unexpected
- a sudden overthrow of a government (also called a *coup d'état*)
- among certain Native Americans, an act of bravery performed in battle, such as touching an enemy with a stick and then escaping unharmed

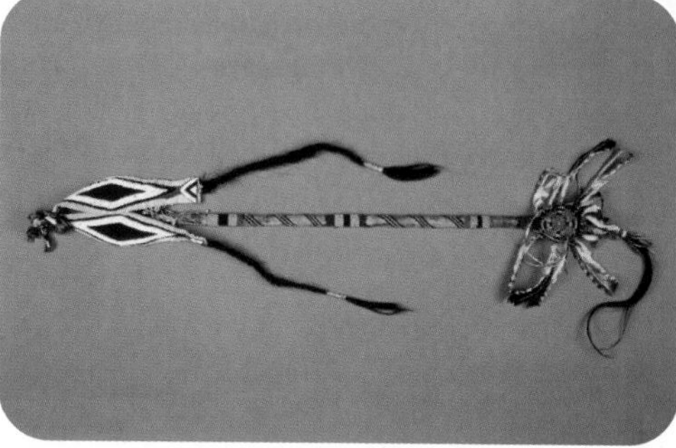

A *coup* stick

CUSTOMIZE INSTRUCTION FOR UNIVERSAL ACCESS

Less Proficient Readers

Some students may need additional practice with the questioning strategy. Write the following question words on the board: Who, What, Where, Why, When, and How. Then, read aloud the first two paragraphs of the story. Model the following strategy for students:

I know that Norman is a boy and that he is going on an all-day journey, but there are some things I don't know. Here are my questions:

Who is John? What is a butte? Where is Norman going? Why is Norman going there? When is he leaving? How is he traveling?

Advise students to record their questions in list form. They may cross off questions as they learn the answers and add new questions as they occur. At the end of the story, invite students to share any unanswered questions with a peer tutor who will help answer them.

"But nobody believes in that kind of thing anymore," Norman scoffed. "And even if people did, I couldn't run out and hit my enemy with the stick and get away with it." He smiled thinking of Mr. Brannon. "No one would think I was brave. I'd probably just get thrown in jail."

Suddenly Norman felt compelled to stop talking. In the distance he heard a gentle rumble which seemed to come from the butte. He glanced up at the hill looming high above and saw that it was capped with dark, low-hanging clouds.

Matt Two Bull looked too and smiled. "The Thunders are displeased with your thoughts," he said to Norman. "Listen to their message."

17 A sharp streak of lightning split the clouds and the thunder cracked and echoed over the plains.

Norman was frightened but he answered with bravado, "The message I get is that a storm is coming," but his voice betrayed him by quavering. "Maybe you'd better come home with me, Grandpa. Your tent will get soaked through if it rains hard."

"No," murmured Matt Two Bull, "no rain will come. It is just the Thunders speaking." There was another spark of lightning, and an explosive reverberation sounded as if in agreement with the old man.

Norman jumped to his feet. "Well, I'm going home. Mom will be worried because I'm late now." He turned to leave.

"Wait!" Matt Two Bull commanded. "Take the *coup* stick with you."

Norman backed away, "No, I don't want it. You can have it."

The old man rose swiftly despite the stiffness of his years and sternly held out the stick to the boy. "You found it. It belongs to you. Take it!"

Norman slowly reached out his hands and took the stick.

"Even if you think the old ways are only superstition and the stick no longer has meaning, it is all that remains of an old life and must be treated with respect." Matt Two Bull smiled at the boy. "Take it," he repeated gently, "and hang it in the house where it will not be handled."

Norman hurried home as fast as he could carrying the long stick
18 in one hand and the willow cane in the other. He felt vaguely uneasy and somehow a little frightened. It was only when he reached the security of his home that he realized the thunder had stopped and there had been no storm.

"Mom," he called as he went into the house, "I'm home."

His mother was standing at the stove. "Oh, Norman," she greeted him smiling. "I'm glad you're back. I was beginning to worry." Her welcoming smile turned to a frown as she saw the *coup* stick in Norman's hand. "What is that?"

Reading Strategy
Understanding Shades of Meaning How does the use of the words *sharp* and *cracked* create a vivid picture of the lightning?

19 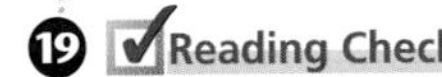

Reading Check

Why does Matt Two Bull say the *coup* stick is important?

16 Background

Culture

As Norman's grandfather explains, the Sioux believed that touching or striking an enemy at close range, rather than killing him, was an act of very great bravery. The action, known as "counting *coup*," needed to be witnessed by another brave. A Sioux warrior used a three- or four-foot stick, such as the one Norman found, or even an open hand to count *coup*. For each *coup* that a brave counted, he earned the right to wear a feather or decorate a *coup* stick with a feather.

17 Reading Strategy

Shades of Meaning

- Call students' attention to the description of the thunder and lightning. Then ask the Reading Strategy question: How does the use of the words *sharp* and *cracked* create a vivid picture?
  Answer: These words convey a loud and flashing, frightening storm.

Reteach If students have trouble answering the Reading Strategy question, have a volunteer read the sentence, omitting the words *sharp* and *cracked*. Help students understand that the storm now seems much less threatening.

18 Reading Strategy

Understanding Shades of Meaning

- Tell students that sometimes an understated word is the most appropriate description for an emotion.
- Ask a student volunteer to read aloud the bracketed sentence. Ask: What is one word that communicates a more intense feeling than *uneasy*?
  Possible response: Students may suggest *nervous* or *afraid*.

19 Reading Check

Answer: The *coup* stick is important because it is a reminder of the "old ways" and should be treated with respect.

CUSTOMIZE INSTRUCTION FOR UNIVERSAL ACCESS

For Special Needs Students	For Gifted/Talented Students
The author uses a great deal of dialogue to move the story forward. She represents the characters as individuals by altering the way each one speaks. Have students note the formal manner in which Norman's grandfather speaks. Ask students to find the differences between his speech and Norman's. Have them find examples of informal speech, such as contractions and shorter sentences, in Norman's dialogue. Ask students what these differences reveal about the characters.	Have students review the story for descriptions of the characters. Invite students to use their imaginations and the descriptions in the selection to create likenesses of the people. Permit them to choose from media that are readily available, such as papier-mâché, clay, yarn, sterilized feathers (available at craft stores), fabric, paint, or pen and ink. Display their work in a class gallery.

20 Critical Thinking

Analyze

- Ask students to reread the bracketed passage. Ask them to summarize Norman's mother's and grandfather's feelings about the *coup* stick.
  Answer: Norman's mother is suspicious of it and tells Norman to take it out of the house. His grandfather, however, believes that it is a sacred object and should be treated with respect.
- Ask: Is there a way that Norman can resolve this difference?
  Possible response: Probably not, because his relatives have very strong and opposing views of the *coup* stick.

"Grandpa says it's a *coup* stick. Here," Norman handed it to her, "take a look at it. It's interesting the way it is made and decor—"

"No," Sarah interrupted and backed away from him. "I won't touch that heathen thing no matter what it is! Get it out of the house!"

heathen (hē′ *th*ən) *adj.* uncivilized

"What?" Norman asked, surprised and puzzled. "There is nothing wrong with it. It's just an old stick I found up on the butte."

"I don't care," Sarah insisted. "I won't have such a thing in the house!"

"But, Mom," Norman protested, "it's not like we believe in those old ways the way Grandpa does."

But Sarah was adamant. "Take it out of the house!" she ordered, pointing to the door. "We'll talk about it when your dad gets home."

adamant (ad′ ə mənt′) *adj.* not flexible; not willing to give in

20 Reluctantly Norman took the *coup* stick outside and gently propped it against the house and sat on the steps to wait for his father. He was confused. First by his grandfather's reverent treatment of the *coup* stick as if it were a sacred object and then by Sarah's rejection of it as a heathen symbol.

He looked at the stick where it leaned against the wall and shook his head. So much fuss over a brittle, rotten length of wood. Even though he had gone through a lot of hard, even dangerous, effort to get it he was now tempted to heave it out on the trash pile.

Norman wearily leaned his head against the house. He suddenly felt tired and his knee ached. As he sat wearily rubbing the bruise John Two Bull rode the old mare into the yard. Norman got up and walked back to the shed to help unsaddle the horse.

John climbed stiffly out of the saddle. His faded blue work shirt and jeans were stained with perspiration and dirt. His boots were worn and scuffed.

"Hard day, Dad?" Norman asked.

"Yeah," John answered, slipping the bridle over the mare's head. "Rustlers got away with twenty steers last night. I spent the day counting head and mending fences. Whoever the thief was cut the fence, drove a truck right onto the range and loaded the cattle without being seen." He began rubbing the mare down as she munched the hay in her manger.

"How did your day on the butte go?" John asked.

"Rough," Norman answered. "I'm beat too. The climb up the butte was tough and coming down was bad too." He told his father all that had happened on the butte, winding up with the climax of his falling and finding the old *coup* stick.

ENRICHMENT: Science Connection

Thunder and Lightning

Thunder and lightning usually occur during rainstorms but can also happen during hailstorms, snowstorms, sandstorms, and even tornadoes. A single flash of lightning can carry up to one hundred million volts of electricity. A flash of lightning superheats the surrounding air to a temperature of 60,000°F, five times hotter than the temperature on the sun's surface. The sound that we identify as thunder is produced when the air around a lightning flash expands and vibrates. Because light travels faster than sound, we see lightning before we hear the thunder.

Have students find out more about lightning by finding answers to these questions:

1. How do electrical charges inside clouds produce lightning?
2. What are three types of lightning? What are the characteristics of each type?
3. In what regions of the United States does lightning most often strike?
4. What safety tips can protect people from the dangers of lightning?

John listened attentively and did not interrupt until Norman told of Matt Two Bull's reaction to the stick. "I think Grandpa's mind has gotten weak," Norman said. "He really believes that the *coup* stick has some sort of mysterious power and that the Thunders were talking."

"Don't make fun of your grandfather," John reprimanded, "or of the old ways he believes in."

"Okay, okay," Norman said quickly, not wanting another scolding. "But Mom is just the opposite from Grandpa," he went on. "She doesn't want the *coup* stick in the house. Says it's heathen."

He walked to the house and handed the stick to his father. John examined it and then carried it into the house.

"John!" Sarah exclaimed as she saw her husband bring the stick into the room. "I told Norman, and I tell you, that I won't have that heathenish thing in the house!"

But John ignored her and propped the stick against the door while he pulled his tool box out from under the washstand to look for a hammer and nails.

22 "John," Sarah persisted, "did you hear me?"

"I heard," John answered quietly, but Norman knew his father was angry. "And I don't want to hear anymore."

Norman was surprised to hear his father speak in such a fashion. John was slow to anger, usually spoke quietly and tried to avoid conflict of any kind, but now he went on.

"This," he said holding the *coup* stick upright, "is a relic of our people's past glory when it was a good thing to be an Indian. It is a symbol of something that shall never be again."

Sarah gasped and stepped in front of her husband as he started to climb a chair to pound the nails in the wall above the window. "But that's what I mean," she said. "Those old ways were just superstition. They don't mean anything now—they can't because such a way of life can't be anymore. We don't need to have those old symbols of heathen ways hanging in the house!" She grabbed at the *coup* stick, but John jerked it out of her reach.

21 ▲ **Critical Viewing** How would you describe the atmosphere of this picture? **[Analyze]**

Literary Analysis
Atmosphere What details increase the atmosphere of tension?

23 ✓ **Reading Check**
What is Sarah's reaction to the *coup* stick?

21 ▶ **Critical Viewing**

Answer: The bolt of lightning gives the picture an ominous or scary atmosphere.

22 Literary Analysis

Atmosphere

- Point out to students that sometimes an author uses characters to create atmosphere. Read aloud the bracketed passage. Ask students to listen for details that convey atmosphere. Read the passage again; this time read the dialogue with emphasis, in order to convey the emotion involved.
- Ask the Literary Analysis question on p. 203: What details increase the atmosphere of tension?
  Answer: The details that show tension include: John's father's quiet anger, his statement about the "past glory" of his people, his insistence on displaying the stick, and John's mother's persistence.

23 ✓ **Reading Check**

Answer: She does not like it and wants it out of the house. She is suspicious of it.

CUSTOMIZE INSTRUCTION FOR UNIVERSAL ACCESS

For Special Needs Students	For Less Proficient Readers	For Advanced Readers
After students have finished reading the story, revisit the Atmosphere transparency on p. 26 in **Literary Analysis and Reading Transparencies.** Invite students to fill in the cloud shapes in the transparency. Discuss how the details contribute to the story's overall atmosphere.	Some of the descriptions of the characters' actions may be unfamiliar to students. Have students who are familiar with the terms use facial expressions, voice tones, and gestures to demonstrate acting or speaking "with bravado," in a "quavering" voice, murmuring, commanding, and "sternly" handing someone an object.	Have students put themselves in the place of Norman or his grandfather. Suggest that students choose one character and reread the passage on pp. 199–202, examining the character's thoughts and feelings about the coup stick. Invite students to write a description of the thoughts and feelings of either Norman or his grandfather.

ASSESS

Answers for p. 204

Review and Assess

1. Possible response: Students who agree with Norman's mother may say that the past does not matter. Students who agree with Norman's father may see honor and dignity in remembering one's family's heritage.
2. **(a)** Norman's grandfather tells him to climb the butte. **(b)** He wants to please his grandfather. **(c)** His regret shows that he is unsure if it is a wise decision for him to climb the butte.
3. **(a)** Sioux warriors used the stick to show their bravery by touching their enemies with it. **(b)** The stick represents their people's past glory. **(c)** Norman's mother thinks the stick represents heathen beliefs.
4. **(a)** Norman's mother does not like the stick. His father wants to display it with honor.
   (b) Possible response: Norman's parents have opposing viewpoints, so he is confused.
5. **(a)** John becomes angry.
   (b) John reacts this way because he respects the "old ways."
6. **(a)** The past and present clash when John decides to hang the *coup* stick in the house against Sarah's wishes.
   (b) Possible response: Students may respond that tradition is more important because it helps us understand ourselves. Some may respond that progress is more important because it helps us improve ourselves.

"Don't touch it!" he shouted and Sarah fell back against the table in shocked surprise. Norman took a step forward as if to protect his mother. The boy had never seen his father so angry.

John shook his head as if to clear it. "Sarah, I'm sorry. I didn't mean to yell. It's just that the old ones would not permit a woman to touch such a thing as this." He handed Norman the stick to hold while he hammered the nails in the wall. Then he hung the stick above the window.

"Sarah," he said as he put the tools away, "think of the stick as an object that could be in a museum, a part of history. It's not like we were going to fall down on our knees and pray to it." His voice was light and teasing as he tried to make peace.

But Sarah stood stiffly at the stove preparing supper and would not answer. Norman felt sick. His appetite was gone. When his mother set a plate of food before him he excused himself saying, "I guess I'm too tired to eat," and went to his room.

But after he had undressed and crawled into bed he couldn't sleep. His mind whirled with the angry words his parents had spoken. They had never argued in such a way before. "I wish I had never brought that old stick home," he whispered and then pulled the pillow over his head to shut out the sound of the low rumble of thunder that came from the west.

Review and Assess

Thinking About the Selection

1. **Respond:** Do you agree with Norman's mother or his father? Why?
2. (a) **Recall:** Who tells Norman to climb the butte? (b) **Infer:** Why does Norman agree to climb the butte?
   (c) **Draw Conclusions:** What do his regrets about agreeing indicate about his feelings?
3. (a) **Recall:** What do Sioux warriors use a *coup* stick for?
   (b) **Analyze:** What does a *coup* stick represent to Norman's father and grandfather? (c) **Contrast:** What does the *coup* stick represent to Norman's mother?
4. (a) **Contrast:** In what way is Norman's mother's reaction to the *coup* stick different from his father's? (b) **Deduce:** Why is Norman unsure of his feelings about his heritage?
5. **Recall:** How does John react when Norman makes fun of his grandfather's beliefs? (b) **Infer:** Why does he react as he does?
6. (a) **Analyze:** In what ways do the past and present come into conflict at the end of "Thunder Butte"? (b) **Take a Position:** Which is more important: progress or tradition? Explain.

Virginia Driving Hawk Sneve

(b. 1933)

Virginia Driving Hawk Sneve was born on a Sioux Indian Reservation in South Dakota. As a teacher and a writer, she devotes herself to sharing Native American life as she has experienced it. She portrays Indians and their heritage from a Native American point of view. "Thunder Butte" (from the novel *When Thunders Spoke*) reflects conflicts that many Native Americans experience today. She works "to interpret history from the viewpoint of the American Indian" because she feels they have been misrepresented by historians who are not Native Americans.

ASSESSMENT PRACTICE: Reading Comprehension

Identify the Main Idea (For more practice, see Test Preparation Workbook, p. 17.)

Many tests require students to identify the main idea of a reading passage. In the passage below, students may infer the main focus of the passage.

> Norman reluctantly rose. Last night he had accepted his grandfather's command to go to the Thunder Butte without too many doubts. Yet now in the morning's chill light the boy wondered if his grandfather's dreams were the meaningless meanderings of an old mind. . . .

In this passage, the main idea is that Norman is:

A respectful of his grandfather's wishes
B enthusiastic about his climbing trip
C too cold to go to the Thunder Butte
D unsure his grandfather's dream is reliable

Answer choices *A* through *C* are not supported by the passage. Norman has mixed feelings about his grandfather and his trip to the Thunder Butte. *D* is the correct answer.

Review and Assess

Literary Analysis

Atmosphere

1. Identify three details at the beginning of "Thunder Butte" that create an **atmosphere** of danger. Record them on a chart like the one shown.

2. How would you describe the atmosphere as Norman climbs the butte? List three details to support your answer.
3. How does the atmosphere at breakfast differ from the atmosphere at dinner?

Connecting Literary Elements

4. How do the changes in the weather affect the atmosphere in the story?
5. What other details of the **setting** contribute to the atmosphere of "Thunder Butte"?
6. Use a chart like the one shown to list ways in which details of the setting affect events in the story.

	Details of Setting	Story Events
Time		
Place		

Reading Strategy

Understanding Shades of Meaning in Related Words

7. Reread pages in the opening of the story and use the surrounding words to explain the difference in **shades of meaning** between *doubts* on page 194 and *misgivings* on page 195.
8. What is the difference in meaning between being *reprimanded*, as Norman is by his father, and being *scolded*, as he is by his mother? Which would be preferable? Why?

Extend Understanding

9. **Cultural Connection:** In what way are artifacts valuable to understanding past cultures? Why might it be important for you to understand your own heritage?

Quick Review

Atmosphere is the mood or feeling of a work. To review atmosphere, see page 193.

Setting is the time and place of the action. To review setting, see page 193.

Shades of meaning are the slight differences in the meanings of related words. To review shades of meaning, see page 193.

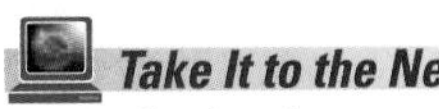

www.phschool.com

Take the interactive self-test online to check your understanding of the selection.

Answers for p. 205

Review and Assess

1. Possible response: Norman puts on boots to protect against snakes; his mother is worried; he has misgivings about going to the butte.
2. The atmosphere is ominous. A rattlesnake slithers away; Norman leans panting against the butte; he draws courage from "ancient young men."
3. The atmosphere at breakfast is anxious because Norman's mother is worried. At dinner it is tense because of the disagreement about the *coup* stick.
4. The weather is pleasant as the story opens; the atmosphere is pleasant. On the butte, heat creates discomfort. When Norman and his grandfather talk, thunder and lightning make the atmosphere scary. At the end, thunder reinforces the tension of the quarrel.
5. Flowers and birds at the beginning enhance the pleasant atmosphere. On the butte, the snake and scarred rock add to the ominous atmosphere.
6.

Details of Setting	Story Events
Time: morning; peaceful	beginning of trip
night; ominous	end of journey
Place: pleasant fields	beginning, reassurance from his father
atop the butte	seeing the snake, hearing thunder

7. *Doubts* seem milder than *misgivings:* Norman has few doubts when the trip is far off, but his misgivings mount as it nears.
8. **(a)** To *reprimand* is to correct formally. To *scold* is to find fault with anger. **(b)** A *reprimand* is a more deliberate action than a *scolding* and can have more drastic consequences. A *scolding* tends to be an off-the-cuff expression with fewer lasting consequences. Therefore, a *scolding* might be preferable to a *reprimand*.

continued

Answers continued

9. Artifacts show how previous cultures lived. Our heritage affects our thoughts, customs, and how we think about ourselves.

ENRICHMENT: Further Reading

Other Works by Virginia Driving Hawk Sneve

Dancing Teepees: Poems of American Indian Youth

The Seminoles

The Sioux

Take It to the Net

Visit www.phschool.com for more information on Virginia Driving Hawk Sneve.

EXTEND

Answers for p. 206

❶ Vocabulary Development

Word Analysis

1. variety
2. variable
3. varied
4. various

Fluency: Word Meanings

1. False; *Heathen* means uncivilized.
2. True; Something that is *variegated* has different colors.
3. False; People who are *adamant* are firm in their beliefs.
4. True; *Diminutive* means small.
5. False; *Meanderings* are paths in crooked lines.

Spelling Strategy

1. i
2. variety, variable
3. vari-

❷ Grammar

1. her → head
2. My → father
3. Norman's → father
4. its → secrets;
   his → eyes
5. stick's → meaning

Writing Application

1. Grandfather spoke of his past.
2. He wanted Norman to know their traditions.

Integrate Language Skills

❶ Vocabulary Development Lesson

Word Analysis: Forms of *vary*

The word *vary* means "to make different." Forms of *vary* include the idea of difference in their meaning. For example, in "Thunder Butte," Norman finds *variegated* stones, or stones of different colors.

Use a form of *vary* to complete each sentence below.

variety varied various variable

1. They offer a wide __?__ of flowers.
2. An experiment should have only one __?__.
3. He __?__ the music by playing some fast tunes and some slow ones.
4. You can choose from __?__ candies.

Fluency: Word Meanings

Explain why each statement is true or false.

1. Calling someone a *heathen* is a compliment.
2. A *variegated* leaf has a few different colors.
3. *Adamant* people are unsure of their beliefs.
4. A hut is a *diminutive* building.
5. *Meanderings* are paths in straight lines.

Spelling Strategy

Learn how spellings change when the form of a word changes. Write the words or word parts from the list at left that answer the following questions about forms of *vary*.

1. What letter is *y* changed to before an ending is added?
2. Which two forms have four syllables?
3. Which word part is the same in all forms?

❷ Grammar Lesson

Possessive Adjectives

Adjectives are words that modify nouns or pronouns by answering the questions *What kind? Which one? How many?* and *How much?*

Nouns that show possession, or ownership—such as *mother's* or *Norman's*—function as **possessive adjectives.** They answer the question *whose?*

Pronouns are words that stand for a noun or take the place of a noun. **Possessive pronouns**, such as *my, your, his, her, its, our, your,* and *their,* function as adjectives. They also answer the question *whose?*

Example: Last night he had accepted *his grandfather's* command . . .

Practice On your paper, circle the possessives that function as adjectives. Draw an arrow to the word each possessive modifies.

1. She lowered her head.
2. My father dreamed of this.
3. Norman's father spoke of the event.
4. The butte hid its secrets from his eyes.
5. The stick's meaning was not understood.

Writing Application Rewrite the following sentences so that they contain possessive adjectives.

1. Grandfather spoke of the past that belonged to him.
2. He wanted Norman to know the traditions that belonged to them.

WG *Prentice Hall Writing and Grammar Connection: Chapter 16, Section 1*

TEACHING RESOURCES

The following resources can be used to enrich or extend the instruction for pp. 206–207.

Vocabulary

- **Selection Support:** Build Vocabulary, p. 61; Build Spelling Skills, p. 62
- **Vocabulary and Spelling Practice Book** (Use this booklet for skills enrichment)

Grammar

- **Selection Support:** Build Grammar Skills, p. 63
- **Writing and Grammar,** Copper Level, p. 336

- **Daily Language Practice Transparencies** ■

Writing

- **Writing and Grammar,** Copper Level, p. 132 ■
- **Writing Models and Graphic Organizers on Transparencies,** p. 73
- **Writing and Grammar iText CD-ROM**

■ **BLOCK SCHEDULING:** Resources marked with this symbol provide varied instruction during 90-minute blocks.

❸ Writing Lesson

Opinion Paper

Each adult in Norman's family has an opinion about how the past and the future are related to the present. Do you think people benefit more from looking back or from looking forward? Write a few paragraphs to explain and support your ideas. Include examples from the story as well as from life to support your opinion.

Prewriting Use a graphic organizer such as the following to plan your writing. First, state your opinion. Then, list three main ideas on which you base your opinions. These ideas are the reasons you think as you do.

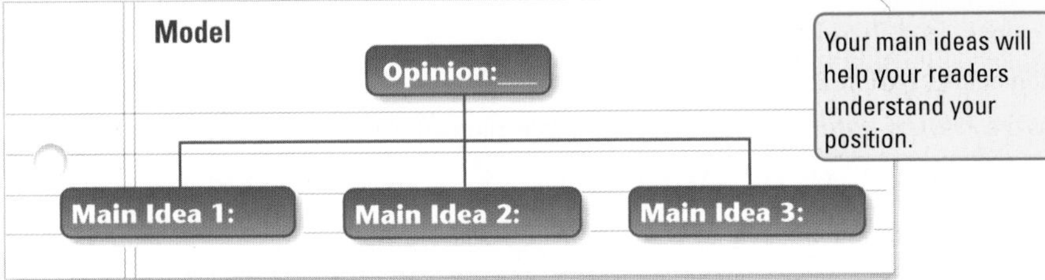

Drafting Begin by stating your position. Then, write a paragraph based on each of your main ideas. Include details and facts to support them. Conclude with a summary of your opinion and main ideas.

Revising Ask a classmate to read your paper and restate your opinion and three main ideas. If he or she cannot clearly restate any of these elements, revise the appropriate section.

WG Prentice Hall Writing and Grammar Connection: Chapter 7, Section 3

❹ Extension Activities

Speaking and Listening With a small group, prepare an **informative presentation** on how the Sioux's lifestyle has changed from the 1800s to the present day. To begin, identify questions based on what you read in the story. Possible questions include

- What were the responsibilities of boys in a Native American family of the 1800s?
- Is Matt Two Bull's tent a common dwelling today?
- To what is John referring when he speaks of "our people's past glory"?

Research and Technology Conduct research to find out more about Sioux customs. Choose one and **write an explanation** of how Norman, Norman's mother, and Norman's father would feel about the custom.

Writing Write an **essay** in which you explain how the past and present come into conflict in the story.

Take It to the Net www.phschool.com

Go online for an additional research activity using the Internet.

ASSESSMENT RESOURCES

The following resources can be used to assess students' knowledge and skills.

Selection Assessment

- **Formal Assessment,** pp. 53–55
- **Open Book Test,** pp. 37–39
- **Got It! Assessment Videotapes,** Tape 2
- **Test Bank Software**

Take It to the Net
Visit www.phschool.com for self-tests and additional questions on "Thunder Butte."

Writing Rubric

- **Performance Assess. and Portfolio Mgmt.,** p. 11

Listening and Speaking Rubric

- **Performance Assess. and Portfolio Mgmt.,** p. 29

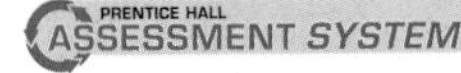

- **Workbook**
- **Skill Book**
- **Transparencies**
-  **CD-ROM**

❸ Writing Lesson

- Ask students to summarize the beliefs Norman's parents and grandfather hold about the past and their relationship with it.
- Have students decide which person's opinion is more similar to their own. Encourage them to write down phrases containing their reasons for their beliefs. Have students include examples from the story, as well as from life, to support their opinions.
- Model using the diagram on p. 207 or the Main Idea and Supporting Details transparency on p. 73 of **Writing Models and Graphic Organizers on Transparencies** to record ideas and details.
- Use the Writing Lesson to guide students in developing their paragraphs.
- Use the Persuasion rubric on p. 11 in **Performance Assessment and Portfolio Management** to evaluate student writing.

❹ Listening and Speaking

- Divide the class into groups. Have each group review the story and write research questions based on what the lives of the Sioux people must have been like.
- Direct students to research sources for finding the answers to their questions.
- Encourage students to create visual aids in their presentations.
- Have students present their questions and findings to the class.
- Use the Speaking rubric on p. 29 in **Performance Assessment and Portfolio Management** to assess student work.

CUSTOMIZE INSTRUCTION For Universal Access

To address different learning styles, use the activities suggested in the **Extension Activities** booklet, p. 13.

- For Visual/Spatial Learners, use Activity 5.
- For Bodily/Kinesthetic and Interpersonal Learners, use Activity 6.
- For Verbal/Linguistic and Intrapersonal Learners, use Activity 7.

Mowgli's Brothers

Lesson Objectives

1. **To analyze and respond to literary elements**
   - Literary Analysis: Animal Characters
   - Connecting Literary Elements: Personification
2. **To read, comprehend, analyze, and critique a short story**
   - Reading Strategy: Predicting Characters' Actions
   - Reading Check Questions
   - Review and Assess Questions
   - Assessment Practice (ATE)
3. **To develop word analysis skills, fluency, and systematic vocabulary**
   - Vocabulary Development Lesson: Word Analysis: Greek Prefix *mono-*
4. **To understand and apply written and oral language conventions**
   - Spelling Strategy
   - Grammar Lesson: Adverbs
5. **To understand and apply appropriate writing and research strategies**
   - Writing Lesson: Compare and Contrast Characters
   - Extension Activity: Wolf Research
6. **To understand and apply listening and speaking strategies**
   - Extension Activity: Role Play

STEP-BY-STEP TEACHING GUIDE	PACING GUIDE
PRETEACH	
Motivate Students and Provide Background	
Use the Motivation activity (ATE p. 208)	5 min.
Read and discuss the Preview material and Background information (SE/ATE p. 208) A	5 min.
Introduce the Concepts	
Introduce the Literary Analysis and Reading Strategy (SE/ATE p. 209) A	15 min.
Pronounce the vocabulary words and read their definitions (SE p. 209)	5 min.
TEACH	
Monitor Comprehension	
Informally monitor comprehension by circulating while students read independently or in groups A	25 min.
Monitor students' comprehension with the Reading Check notes (SE/ATE pp. 211, 213, 215, 217)	as students read
Develop vocabulary with Vocabulary notes (SE pp. 211, 214, 215, 216, 217; ATE p. 216)	as students read
Develop Understanding	
Develop students' understanding of animal characters with the Literary Analysis annotations (SE pp. 211, 213, 215, 217; ATE pp. 211, 213, 215, 217) A	5 min.
Develop students' ability to predict characters' actions with the Reading Strategy annotations (SE pp. 212, 213, 215; ATE pp. 212, 213, 215)	5 min.
ASSESS	
Assess Mastery	
Assess students' mastery of the Reading Strategy and Literary Analysis by having them answer the Review and Assess questions (SE/ATE p. 219)	15 min.
Use one or more of the print and media Assessment Resources (ATE p. 221) A	up to 45 min.
EXTEND	
Apply Understanding	
Have students complete the Vocabulary Development Lesson and the Grammar Lesson (SE p. 220) A	20 min.
Apply students' ability to compare and contrast characters using the Writing Lesson (SE/ATE p. 221) A	30–45 min.
Apply students' understanding using one or more of the Extension Activities (SE p. 221)	10–90 min.

ACCELERATED INSTRUCTION:
Use the strategies and activities identified with an A.

UNIVERSAL ACCESS
● = Below Level Students
▲ = On-Level Students
■ = Above Level Students

Time and Resource Manager

Reading Level: Challenging
Average Number of Instructional Days: 3

RESOURCES		
PRINT	**TRANSPARENCIES**	**TECHNOLOGY**
• **Beyond Literature,** Cross-Curricular Connection: Science, p. 14 ▲ ■		• **Interest Grabber Videotapes,** Tape 2 ● ▲ ■
• **Selection Support Workbook:** ● ▲ ■ Literary Analysis, p. 70 Reading Strategy, p. 69 Build Vocabulary, p. 66	• **Literary Analysis and Reading Transparencies,** pp. 27 and 28 ● ▲ ■	
• **Adapted Reader's Companion** ● • **Reader's Companion** ● • **Authors In Depth,** Copper Level, p. 40 ■		• **Listening to Literature** ● ▲ ■ Audiocassettes, Side 10 Audio CDs, CD 4
• **English Learner's Companion** ● ▲ • **Literatura en español** ● ▲ • **Literary Analysis for Enrichment** ■		
• **Formal Assessment:** Selection Test, pp. 56–58 ● ▲ ■ • **Open Book Test,** pp. 40–42 ● ▲ ■ • **Performance Assessment and Portfolio Management,** p. 16 ● ▲ ■ • PRENTICE HALL ASSESSMENT SYSTEM ● ▲ ■	• PRENTICE HALL ASSESSMENT SYSTEM ● ▲ ■ Skills Practice Answers and Explanations on Transparencies	• **Test Bank Software** ● ▲ ■ • **Got It! Assessment Videotapes,** Tape 2 ● ▲
• **Selection Support Workbook:** ● ▲ ■ Build Spelling Skills, p. 67 Build Grammar Skills, p. 68 • **Writing and Grammar,** Copper Level ● ▲ ■ • **Extension Activities,** p. 14 ● ▲ ■	• **Daily Language Practice Transparencies** ● ▲ • **Writing Models and Graphic Organizers on Transparencies** ● ▲ ■	• **Writing and Grammar iText CD-ROM** ● ▲ ■ ***Take It to the Net*** www.phschool.com

BLOCK SCHEDULING: Use one 90-minute class period to preteach the selection and have students read it. Use a second 90-minute class period to assess students' mastery of skills and have them complete one of the Extension Activities.

PRETEACH

Step-by-Step Teaching Guide for pp. 208–209

Motivation

Show a video of wolves caring for their young. Ask students to identify similarities and differences between the needs of young humans and those of young wolves.

Interest Grabber Video

As an alternative, play "Can We Save the Tigers?" on Tape 2 to engage student interest.

1 Background

Science

The wolves depicted in "Mowgli's Brothers" are probably gray wolves. Also known as timber wolves, gray wolves aren't always gray—their coloration may vary from black or brown to white, depending on where they live. The basic wolf pack consists of a male, a female, and their pups, but larger packs also assemble. In addition to howling, wolves communicate with one another by using sight and smell signals. They serve an important function in the food web, because they are valuable predators. In regions where the wolf population has diminished, overpopulation of other animals has resulted.

Prepare to Read

1 Mowgli's Brothers

Take It to the Net

Visit www.phschool.com for interactive activities and instruction related to "Mowgli's Brothers," including

- background
- graphic organizers
- literary elements
- reading strategies

Preview

Connecting to the Literature

In "Mowgli's Brothers" by Rudyard Kipling, a little boy faces a life-or-death choice—but others make it for him. Think about the choices you make for yourself and those that are made for you by others.

Background

The behavior of the animals in "Mowgli's Brothers" is based on the real habits of animals in the jungle. Wolves live in packs, have a social structure, and obey a pack leader. Although they do not have a "council" as described in the story, wolves are known for working as a group. Tigers, on the other hand, like Shere Khan in the story, are solitary hunters.

TEACHING RESOURCES

The following resources can be used to enrich or extend the instruction for pp. 208–209.

Motivation

Interest Grabber Video, Tape 2

Background

Beyond Literature, p. 14 

Take It to the Net

Visit www.phschool.com for Background and hotlinks for "Mowgli's Brothers."

Literary Analysis

Literary Analysis and Reading Transparencies, Animal Characters, p. 28

Selection Support: Literary Analysis, p. 70

Reading

Literary Analysis and Reading Transparencies, Predicting Characters' Actions, p. 27

BLOCK SCHEDULING: Resources marked with this symbol provide varied instruction during 90-minute blocks.

❷ Literary Analysis

Animal Characters

Characters in stories can be animals as well as humans. Most of the characters you will meet in "Mowgli's Brothers" are animals. **Animal characters** in fiction often behave according to their animal qualities, but they may also have human qualities, emotions, and abilities.

Connecting Literary Elements

Fictional animal characters are often brought to life through **personification.** Personification is the representation of an animal or an object as if it had a human personality, intelligence, or emotions.

In "Mowgli's Brothers," each animal shows at least one strong human quality. The human qualities of the animals affect the plot—the story's sequence of events. For example, Mother Wolf's compassion results in a boy being raised among wolves.

Use the following focus questions to help you analyze the story:

1. Which animals in the story have courage? Which are cowards?
2. What effect do the qualities of these characters have on story events and the way the story turns out?

❸ Reading Strategy

Predicting Characters' Actions

When you **predict**, you make logical guesses about what characters will do or what events will occur. Predict characters' actions by thinking about whether a character is brave, cowardly, kind, honest, or sneaky. Then, decide how the character will act or what the character will do, based on what you have learned about him or her in the story. As you read, use a chart like the one shown to record predictions about characters' actions.

Character Qualities and Story Details

Prediction

Vocabulary Development

scuttled (skut′ əld) *v.* scurried; scampered (p. 211)

quarry (kwôr′ ē) *n.* prey; anything being hunted or pursued (p. 214)

fostering (fôs′ tər iŋ) *n.* taking care of (p. 215)

veterans (vet′ ər enz′) *n.* those having experience (p. 216)

monotonous (mə nät′n əs′) *adj.* unchanging; tiresome because it does not vary (p. 216)

dispute (di spyo͞ot′) *n.* argument; debate; quarrel (p. 217)

clamor (klam′ ər) *n.* loud demand or complaint (p. 217)

❷ Literary Analysis

Animal Characters

- Ask students to recall favorite animal characters from childhood movies or stories that behaved more like people than animals.
- Have a volunteer read the Literary Analysis instruction. Discuss how students' favorite animal characters have some human qualities.
- Use the Animal Characters transparency on p. 28 in **Literary Analysis and Reading Transparencies** to list human and animal characteristics of favorite characters.
- Read the Connecting Literary Elements text. Remind students to keep the focus questions in mind as they read.

❸ Reading Strategy

Predicting Characters' Actions

- Ask students for the meaning of the word *predict*. Then, verify the definition by reading the Reading Strategy instruction.
- Have students practice predicting characters' actions by giving them an example situation, such as a kind person who sees a lost dog in the street. Ask students what they think will happen next. Explain to students that the description of the person helps them predict the person's actions.
- Use the Predicting Characters' Actions transparency on p. 27 in **Literary Analysis and Reading Transparencies** to show the relationship between characters, plot, and predictions.
- Suggest that students make charts to record their predictions as they read.

Vocabulary Development

- Pronounce each vocabulary word for students, and read the definitions as a class. Have students identify any words with which they are already familiar.

CUSTOMIZE INSTRUCTION FOR UNIVERSAL ACCESS

For Special Needs Students	For Less Proficient Readers	For English Learners
Have students read the adapted version of "Mowgli's Brothers" in the **Adapted Reader's Companion.** This version provides basic-level instruction in an interactive format with questions and write-on lines. Completing the adapted version will prepare students to read the selection in the Student Edition.	Have students read "Mowgli's Brothers" in the **Reader's Companion.** This version provides basic-level instruction in an interactive format with questions and write-on lines. After students finish the selection in the Reader's Companion, have them complete the questions and activities in the Student Edition.	Have students read the adapted version of "Mowgli's Brothers" in the **English Learner's Companion.** This version provides basic-level instruction in an interactive format with questions and write-on lines. Completing the adapted version will prepare students to read the selection in the Student Edition.

 ***E-Teach***

Visit E-Teach at www.phschool.com for teachers' essays on how to teach, with questions and answers.

TEACH

Step-by-Step Teaching Guide for pp. 210–218

CUSTOMIZE INSTRUCTION
For Musical/Rhythmic Learners

Have students explore the rhythm of Kipling's poem on p. 211. Ask one student to read the poem aloud, using his or her voice to emphasize the rhythm. Then have the student read the poem again, while other students clap, snap their fingers, or tap out the rhythm. Suggest that students clap twice after lines 2, 4, 6, and 8.

❶ About the Selection

One evening in the jungle, Father Wolf discovers a small child near his cave. The child had been pursued by Shere Khan, a tiger who was hunting near the wolves' home. Father Wolf brings the boy into the cave and gently places him among the wolf cubs. Mother Wolf is taken with the child and names him Mowgli. Before she can keep Mowgli as her own, though, the Pack Council, led by Akela, must give its approval. With the help of Baloo the Bear and Bagheera the Black Panther, the child is accepted into the pack and begins a new life among the animals of the jungle.

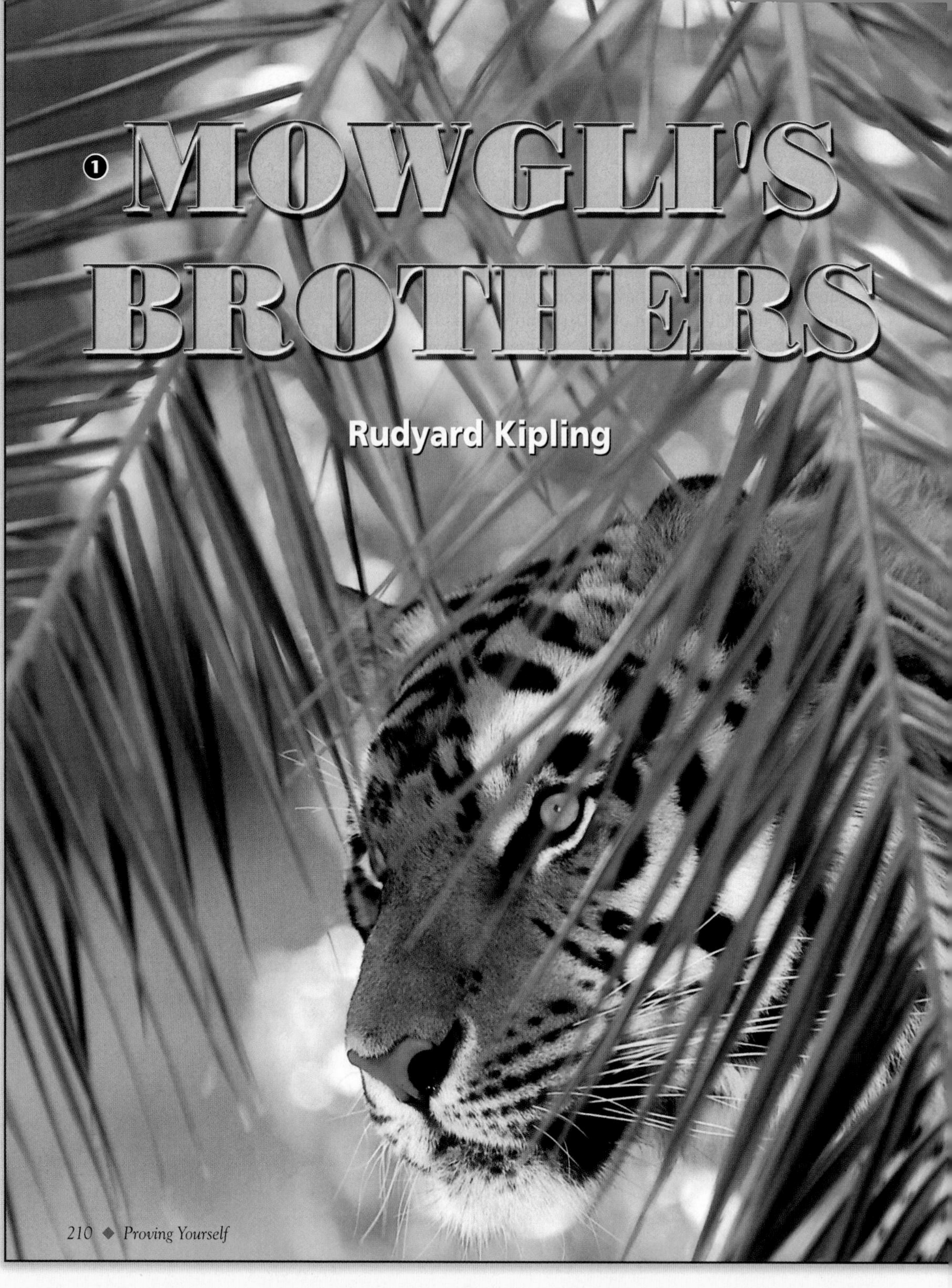

TEACHING RESOURCES

The following resources can be used to enrich or extend the instruction for pp. 210–218.

Literary Analysis
- **Literary Analysis for Enrichment**
- **Writing Models and Graphic Organizers on Transparencies,** p. 89 ■

Reading
- **Selection Support:** Reading Strategy, p. 69; Build Vocabulary, p. 66
- **Adapted Reader's Companion**
- **Reader's Companion**
- **English Learner's Companion**
- **Literatura en español**
- **Listening to Literature Audiocassettes,** Side 10 ■
- **Listening to Literature Audio CDs,** CD 4 ■

Extension
- **Authors In Depth,** Copper Level, p. 40 (The collection includes two additional selections by Rudyard Kipling for extended reading.) ■

■ **BLOCK SCHEDULING:** Resources marked with this symbol provide varied instruction during 90-minute blocks.

Now Chil the Kite[1] brings home the night
That Mang the Bat sets free—
The herds are shut in byre[2] and hut
For loosed till dawn are we.
This is the hour of pride and power,
Talon and tush[3] and claw.
Oh hear the call!—Good hunting all
That keep the Jungle Law!
Night-Song in the Jungle

It was seven o'clock of a very warm evening in the Seeonee hills[4] when Father Wolf woke up from his day's rest, scratched himself, yawned, and spread out his paws one after the other to get rid of the sleepy feeling in their tips. Mother Wolf lay with her big gray nose dropped across her four tumbling, squealing cubs, and the moon shone into the mouth of the cave where they all lived. "Augrh!" said Father Wolf, "it is time to hunt again"; and he was going to spring downhill when a little shadow with a bushy tail crossed the threshold and whined: "Good luck go with you, O Chief of the Wolves; and good luck and strong white teeth go with the noble children, that they may never forget the hungry in this world."

2 It was the jackal—Tabaqui the Dishlicker—and the wolves of India despise Tabaqui because he runs about making mischief, and telling tales, and eating rags and pieces of leather from the village rubbish-heaps. But they are afraid of him too, because Tabaqui, more than anyone else in the jungle, is apt to go mad, and then he forgets that he was ever afraid of anyone, and runs through the forest biting everything in his way. Even the tiger runs and hides when little Tabaqui goes mad, for madness is the most disgraceful thing that can overtake a wild creature. We call it hydrophobia, but they call it *dewanee*—the madness—and run. 3

"Enter, then, and look," said Father Wolf, stiffly; "but there is no food here."

"For a wolf, no," said Tabaqui; "but for so mean a person as myself a dry bone is a good feast. Who are we, the Gidur-log [the jackal-people], to pick and choose?" He scuttled to the back of the cave, where he found the bone of a buck with some meat on it, and sat cracking the end merrily. 5

Literary Analysis
Animal Characters
Which character has a trait that may lead to problems for other characters? What is the trait?

scuttled (skut′ əld) v. scurried; scampered

✓Reading Check
What is Mother Wolf doing?

4 ◀ **Critical Viewing** Do you think this tiger is friendly to humans? Why or why not? **[Speculate]**

1. **Kite** (kīt) *n.* bird of the hawk family.
2. **byre** (bīr) *n.* cow barn.
3. **tush** (tush) *n.* tusk.
4. **Seeonee** (sē ō′ nē) **hills** hills in central India.

2 Literary Analysis

Animal Characters

- Remind students that, throughout the story, they should be alert for animal characters with human qualities. Explain that these qualities can be positive or negative.
- After students have finished reading the first page, review with them the characters they have met so far: Father Wolf, Mother Wolf and their cubs, and Tabaqui the Dishlicker.
- Ask the Literary Analysis questions on p. 211: Which character has a trait that may lead to problems for other characters? What is the trait?
  Answer: The problem character is Tabaqui the Dishlicker, who is a jackal. Tabaqui makes mischief and is likely to go mad.

3 Background

Health

Hydrophobia is better known as rabies, a viral disease of animals that is spread by the bite or scratch of an infected animal. The disease affects the nervous system and is usually fatal. It produces mouth and throat spasms that are made worse by drinking water (*hydrophobia* means "fear of water"). Animals in the United States that most often carry rabies are the skunk, fox, bobcat, badger, bat, coyote, dog, raccoon, and cat. Antirabies vaccine can be used to prevent the disease from developing in animals and humans.

4 ▶Critical Viewing

Possible response: The tiger appears to be on the hunt and would be more likely to eat a human than to be friendly toward one.

5 ✓Reading Check

Answer: She is guarding her cubs and resting.

CUSTOMIZE INSTRUCTION FOR UNIVERSAL ACCESS

For Special Needs Students	For Less Proficient Readers	For Advanced Readers
Students may need help with the formal language and inverted sentence structures of some of the dialogue. For instance, point out to students that Tabaqui's words "How beautiful are the noble children" would usually be expressed "The noble children are beautiful."	Before students read the story, have them preview the text and call out any unusual names or words they see. Display the words and practice pronouncing them with students. Define those that need defining. Tackling these unusual words before reading will help students read the story more fluently.	Point out to students that Kipling is not the first to invent a story about a human baby brought up by wolves. Have students read the story of Romulus and Remus, the legendary founders of Rome, who were also raised by wolves. Tell students to make a Venn diagram to compare and contrast the Roman and Kipling stories.

6 Reading Strategy

Predicting

- Remind students that the combination of characters' traits and story details will help them predict what will happen in the story.
- Ask students what Tabaqui tells the wolves about Shere Khan.
Answer: He tells them that Shere Khan has changed his hunting grounds.
- Ask the Reading Strategy question on p. 212: What character traits and story details help you predict that there will be a problem between Shere Khan and the wolves?
Possible responses: The tiger seems to do whatever he pleases, including making trouble for other animals. The wolf is angry because the tiger is intruding on his hunting grounds.
- Have students predict what might happen further into the story.
Possible responses: Shere Khan might scare away all the animals; Father Wolf might fight with Shere Khan; villagers might burn down the jungle.

7 Critical Thinking

Infer

- Tell students that Kipling often has animals say things that are surprising. Students will need to infer, or make educated guesses, about how the animals know such things.
- Read the bracketed passage with Mother Wolf's comments. Ask: How does Mother Wolf know that Shere Khan is hunting Man instead of steers or bucks?
Answer: Perhaps Mother Wolf can tell by the sound of the tiger's whine that he is hunting Man.

"All thanks for this good meal," he said, licking his lips. "How beautiful are the noble children! How large are their eyes! And so young too! Indeed, indeed, I might have remembered that the children of Kings are men from the beginning."

Now, Tabaqui knew as well as anyone else that there is nothing so unlucky as to compliment children to their faces; and it pleases him to see Mother and Father Wolf look uncomfortable.

Tabaqui sat still, rejoicing in the mischief that he had made: then he said spitefully:

"Shere Khan, the Big One, has shifted his hunting-grounds. He will hunt among these hills for the next moon, so he has told me."

Shere Khan was the tiger who lived near the Waingunga River, twenty miles away.

"He has no right!" Father Wolf began angrily—"By the Law of the Jungle he has no right to change his quarters without due warning. He will frighten every head of game within ten miles, and I—I have to
6 kill for two, these days."

"His mother did not call him Lungri [the Lame One] for nothing," said Mother Wolf, quietly. "He has been lame in one foot from his birth. That is why he has only killed cattle. Now the villagers of the Waingunga are angry with him, and he has come here to make our villagers angry. They will scour the Jungle for him when he is far away, and we and our children must run when the grass is set alight. Indeed, we are very grateful to Shere Khan!"

Reading Strategy
Predicting What character traits and story details help you predict that there will be a problem between Shere Kahn and the wolves?

"Shall I tell him of your gratitude?" said Tabaqui.

"Out!" snapped Father Wolf. "Out and hunt with thy master. Thou hast done harm enough for one night."

"I go," said Tabaqui, quietly. "Ye can hear Shere Khan below in the thickets. I might have saved myself the message."

Father Wolf listened, and below in the valley that ran down to a little river, he heard the dry, angry, snarly, singsong whine of a tiger who has caught nothing and does not care if all the Jungle knows it.

"The fool!" said Father Wolf. "To begin a night's work with that noise! Does he think that our buck are like his fat Waingunga bullocks ?"[5]

"H'sh! It is neither bullock nor buck he hunts tonight," said Mother
7 Wolf. "It is Man." The whine had changed to a sort of humming purr that seemed to come from every quarter of the compass. It was the noise that bewilders woodcutters and gypsies sleeping in the open, and makes them run sometimes into the very mouth of the tiger.

"Man!" said Father Wolf, showing all his white teeth. "Faugh! Are there not enough beetles and frogs in the tanks that he must eat Man and on our ground too!"

5. **bullocks** (bool′ əks) *n.* steers.

ENRICHMENT: Social Studies Connection

Laws

The animals in "Mowgli's Brothers" live by the law of the jungle. The expression "law of the jungle" generally means the survival of the strongest. It refers to the jungle as a place where self-interest and brutality reign. In countries such as the United States, the law is the set of rules under which society is governed. The law establishes rules that define a person's rights and obligations. It also sets penalties for those who violate these rules and states how the government shall enforce the rules and penalties.

Discuss with students the importance of the law as a basic—and necessary—social institution. Have students work in groups to learn more about the legal system in the United States. Suggest that they focus their research on topics such as these: the two main branches of law, systems of law, how laws are developed, how laws are changed.

The Law of the Jungle, which never orders anything without a reason, forbids every beast to eat Man except when he is killing to show his children how to kill, and then he must hunt outside the hunting-grounds of his pack or tribe. The real reason for this is that man-killing means, sooner or later, the arrival of white men on elephants, with guns, and hundreds of brown men with gongs and rockets and torches. Then everybody in the jungle suffers. The reason the beasts give among themselves is that Man is the weakest and most defenseless of all living things, and it is unsportsmanlike to touch him. They say too—and it is true—that man-eaters become mangy,[6] and lose their teeth.

The purr grew louder, and ended in the full-throated "Aaarh!" of the tiger's charge.

Then there was a howl—an untigerish howl—from Shere Khan. "He has missed," said Mother Wolf. "What is it?"

8 Father Wolf ran out a few paces and heard Shere Khan muttering and mumbling savagely, as he tumbled about in the scrub.

"The fool has had no more sense than to jump at a woodcutter's campfire, and has burned his feet," said Father Wolf, with a grunt. "Tabaqui is with him."

9 "Something is coming up hill," said Mother Wolf, twitching one ear. "Get ready."

The bushes rustled a little in the thicket, and Father Wolf dropped with his haunches under him, ready for his leap. Then, if you had been watching, you would have seen the most wonderful thing in the world—the wolf checked in mid-spring. He made his bound before he saw what it was he was jumping at, and then he tried to stop himself. The result was that he shot up straight into the air for four or five feet, landing almost where he left ground.

"Man!" he snapped. "A man's cub. Look!"

Directly in front of him, holding on by a low branch, stood a naked brown baby who could just walk—as soft and as dimpled a little atom[7] as ever came to a wolf's cave at night. He looked up into Father Wolf's face, and laughed.

"Is that a man's cub?" said Mother Wolf. "I have never seen one. Bring it here."

10 A wolf accustomed to moving his own cubs can, if necessary, mouth an egg without breaking it, and though Father Wolf's jaws closed right on the child's back not a tooth even scratched the skin, as he laid it down among the cubs.

"How little! How naked, and—how bold!" said Mother Wolf, softly. The baby was pushing his way between the cubs to get close to the

6. **mangy** (mān′ jē) *adj.* having the mange, a skin disease of mammals that causes sores and loss of hair.
7. **atom** (at′ əm) *n.* tiny piece of matter.

Literary Analysis
Animal Characters and Personification What human quality does Shere Khan demonstrate?

Reading Strategy
Predicting What do you predict will happen to the man's cub?

11 ✓ **Reading Check**

What surprises Father wolf?

CUSTOMIZE INSTRUCTION FOR UNIVERSAL ACCESS

For Less Proficient Readers	For Gifted/Talented Students
Events in the story and dialogue between characters may be easier for students to follow if they listen to the recording of "Mowgli's Brothers." Have students follow along in their books as they listen to the audiocassette or CD version. Pause at regular intervals and have students summarize events in their own words.	Have students make animal masks representing the characters in the story. Suggest that they use paints, fur, fabric, and other items to embellish the masks. Then, have students wear the masks as they perform dramatic readings of segments of the story. Encourage students to use expressive voices and gestures to enhance the drama of their presentations.

8 Literary Analysis

Animal Characters and Personification

- Remind students that animal characters will sometimes have negative human traits.
- Invite a volunteer to read the bracketed passage. Ask the Literary Analysis question on p. 213: What human quality does Shere Khan demonstrate?
  Answer: Shere Khan demonstrates anger when he doesn't succeed.

9 Background

Science

Wolves have excellent hearing. They can easily tell from which direction a sound is coming by turning their ears from side to side, as Mother Wolf does when she hears something coming up the hill. Wolves twitch their ears to determine from which position the sound is loudest. By doing this, they can locate the direction of the sound.

10 Reading Strategy

Predicting

- Have students read the bracketed passages and the first two paragraphs on p. 214. Ask: What qualities does the man's cub show?
  Answer: The child is fearless and small.
- Invite the children to consider the qualities of the wolf parents. Ask: How do you think the wolves feel about the man's cub?
  Answer: The wolves seem to be amused by and curious about the little child.
- Challenge students to combine the story events with what they know about the wolves. Ask the Reading Strategy question on p. 213: What do you predict will happen to the man's cub?
  Possible response: He will probably become part of the wolf family.

11 ✓ Reading Check

Answer: The sudden appearance of a young child surprises Father Wolf.

⓬ Critical Thinking

Interpret

- Point out to students that Father Wolf's words to Shere Khan may be ironic, that is, say one thing and mean another. Ask: What do you think Father Wolf means by saying Shere Khan does them "honor"? Possible response: He is being sarcastic and actually means that the tiger is not welcome.
- Challenge students to find a detail in the passage that helps them interpret the wolf's remark. Answer: Father Wolf's eyes are angry.

⓭ ▶ Critical Viewing

Answer: Students may say that, like Mother Wolf, this animal is alert, is listening carefully, and seems ready to act if there is danger.

warm hide. "Ahai! He is taking his meal with the others. And so this is a man's cub. Now, was there ever a wolf that could boast of a man's cub among her children?"

"I have heard now and again of such a thing, but never in our Pack or in my time," said Father Wolf. "He is altogether without hair, and I could kill him with a touch of my foot. But see, he looks up and is not afraid."

The moonlight was blocked out of the mouth of the cave, for Shere Khan's great square head and shoulders were thrust into the entrance. Tabaqui, behind him, was squeaking: "My lord, my lord, it went in here!"

⓬ "Shere Khan does us great honor," said Father Wolf, but his eyes were very angry. "What does Shere Khan need?"

"My quarry. A man's cub went this way," said Shere Khan. "Its parents have run off. Give it to me."

quarry (kwôr′ ē) *n.* prey; anything being hunted or pursued

Shere Khan had jumped at a woodcutter's campfire, as Father Wolf had said, and was furious from the pain of his burned feet. But Father Wolf knew that the mouth of the cave was too narrow for a tiger to come in by. Even where he was, Shere Khan's shoulders and forepaws were cramped for want of room, as a man's would be if he tried to fight in a barrel.

"The Wolves are a free people," said Father Wolf. "They take orders from the Head of the Pack, and not from any striped cattle-killer. The man's cub is ours—to kill if we choose."

"Ye choose and ye do not choose! What talk is this of choosing? By the bull that I killed, am I to stand nosing into your dog's den for my fair dues? It is I, Shere Khan, who speak!"

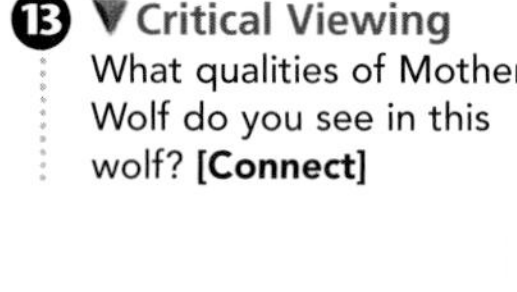

⓭ ▼ **Critical Viewing** What qualities of Mother Wolf do you see in this wolf? **[Connect]**

The tiger's roar filled the cave with thunder. Mother Wolf shook herself

CUSTOMIZE INSTRUCTION FOR UNIVERSAL ACCESS

For Advanced Readers

Suggest that students read additional works by Rudyard Kipling. Provide students with the titles listed in the Enrichment box, ATE p. 219. You may also wish to use **Authors In Depth,** Copper Level, which contains the following selections:

- from *Captains Courageous* (fiction, p. 40)
- "How Fear Came" (fiction, p. 45)

After students have read these or other works by Kipling, have them discuss the portrait Kipling paints of the British Empire. What qualities do the people in the stories value? What difficulties do they face? How do they solve their problems? Are their expectations of life different from the students' own expectations? To extend the activity, have students dramatize sections of their favorite Kipling selections.

clear of the cubs and sprang forward, her eyes, like two green moons in the darkness, facing the blazing eyes of Shere Khan.

"And it is I, Raksha [The Demon], who answer. The man's cub is mine, Lungri—mine to me! He shall not be killed. He shall live to run with the Pack and to hunt with the Pack; and in the end, look you, hunter of little naked cubs—frog-eater—fish-killer—he shall hunt *thee*! Now get hence, or by the Sambhur that I killed (I eat no starved cattle), back thou goest to thy mother, burned beast of the Jungle, lamer than ever thou camest into the world! Go!"

Father Wolf looked on amazed. He had almost forgotten the days when he won Mother Wolf in fair fight from five other wolves, when she ran in the Pack and was not called The Demon for compliment's sake. Shere Khan might have faced Father Wolf, but he could not stand up against Mother Wolf, for he knew that where he was she had all the advantage of the ground, and would fight to the death. So he backed out of the cave-mouth growling, and when he was clear he shouted:

"Each dog barks in his own yard! We will see what the Pack will say to this fostering of man-cubs. The cub is mine, and to my teeth he will come in the end, O bush-tailed thieves!"

Mother Wolf threw herself down panting among the cubs, and Father Wolf said to her gravely:

"Shere Khan speaks this much truth. The cub must be shown to the Pack. Wilt thou still keep him, Mother?"

14 "Keep him!" she gasped. "He came naked, by night, alone and very hungry; yet he was not afraid! Look, he has pushed one of my babies to one side already. And that lame butcher would have killed him and would have run off to the Waingunga while the villagers here hunted through all our lairs in revenge! Keep him? Assuredly I will keep him. Lie still, little frog. O thou Mowgli—for Mowgli the Frog I will call thee—the time will come when thou wilt hunt Shere Khan as he has hunted thee." 15

"But what will our Pack say?" said Father Wolf. The Law of the Jungle lays down very clearly that any wolf may, when he marries, withdraw from the Pack he belongs to; but as soon as his cubs are old enough to stand on their feet he must bring them to the Pack Council, which is generally held once a month at full moon, in order that the other wolves may identify them. After that inspection the 16 cubs are free to run where they please, and until they have killed their first buck no excuse is accepted if a grown wolf of the Pack kills one of them. The punishment is death where the murderer can be found; and if you think for a minute you will see that this must be so.

Father Wolf waited till his cubs could run a little, and then on the night of the Pack Meeting took them and Mowgli and Mother Wolf to the Council Rock—a hilltop covered with stones and boulders where a hundred wolves could hide. Akela, the great gray Lone Wolf, who

fostering (fôs´ tər iŋ) *n.* taking care of

Literary Analysis
Animal Characters How does the author portray Mother Wolf as similar to a human mother?

Reading Strategy
Predicting What do you think the pack will say about Mowgli?

17 ✔ **Reading Check**

How does Mother Wolf respond to Shere Khan's demands?

14 Literary Analysis

Animal Characters

- Ask students to list the qualities that make a good mother. Write student contributions on the board. Then, have students read the bracketed passage.
- Invite students to think about the qualities that Mother Wolf shows. Ask the Literary Analysis question on p. 215: How does the author portray Mother Wolf as similar to a human mother?
  Answer: Mother Wolf is tender with her cubs. She is also ready to fight anyone who might hurt her young.

15 Background

Language Arts

Rudyard Kipling writes in his notes in the original *Jungle Book* that he made up the name Mowgli. "It does not mean 'frog' in any language that I know of," says the author. The name may have been suggested by *Hooghly* (or *Hugli*), the name of a river in India.

16 Reading Strategy

Predicting

- Read the bracketed text aloud. Ask: Where must the wolves take Mowgli, and why?
  Answer: They must take him to the wolf Pack Council meeting, so that the other wolves will know he is a member of the pack.
- Ask students to use their knowledge about the wolves to answer the Reading Strategy question on p. 215.
  Answer: Some students may say that because Mother Wolf recognizes Mowgli's intelligence and fearlessness and is willing to accept Mowgli, the pack will also accept Mowgli. Others may say that, like Father Wolf, the pack members will have doubts about accepting a man's cub.

17 ✔ Reading Check

Answer: Mother Wolf becomes angry and threatens to fight with Shere Khan if he doesn't leave the den.

CUSTOMIZE INSTRUCTION FOR UNIVERSAL ACCESS

For Less Proficient Readers	For Advanced Readers
Invite students to work with the vocabulary in the selection. Have pairs of students work together to find the sentences containing the vocabulary words, practice pronouncing the words, learn the definitions, and use the words in new sentences. Invite students to take turns writing these sentences on the board.	Remind students that the story takes place in India. Tell them that India's ancient and diverse culture provides many opportunities for interesting research. Invite them to investigate an aspect of Indian culture: art, music, food, traditional clothing, religion, traditions, or festivals. They could also gather information on India's history, climate, and geography. Have students present their findings to the class in posters, photo essays, or oral reports.

⑱ Vocabulary Development

Greek Prefix *mono-*

- Have a student read the word *monotonous* and its definition aloud. Tell students that the Greek prefix *mono-* means "one." Point out that *monotonous* contains part of the word *tone.* Guide students to see how these parts explain the meaning of the word.
- Invite students to suggest other words that begin with this prefix. List the words on the board. **Possible response:** Students may suggest *monopoly, monotone, monosyllable,* and *monochrome.*
- Challenge students to define the words they suggest. Then, have them check their definitions against dictionary definitions.

led all the Pack by strength and cunning, lay out at full length on his rock, and below him sat forty or more wolves of every size and color, from badger-colored veterans who could handle a buck alone, to young black three-year-olds who thought they could. The Lone Wolf had led them for a year now. He had fallen twice into a wolf-trap in his youth, and once he had been beaten and left for dead; so he knew the manners and customs of men. There was very little talking at the Rock. The cubs tumbled over each other in the center of the circle where their mothers and fathers sat, and now and again a senior wolf would go quietly up to a cub, look at him carefully, and return to his place on noiseless feet. Sometimes a mother would push her cub far out into the moonlight, to be sure that he had not been overlooked. Akela from his rock would cry: "Ye know the Law—ye know the Law. Look well, O Wolves!" and the anxious mothers would take up the call: "Look—look well, O Wolves!"

veterans (vet´ ər enz´) *n.* those having experience

At last—and Mother Wolf's neck-bristles lifted as the time came—Father Wolf pushed "Mowgli the Frog," as they called him, into the center, where he sat laughing and playing with some pebbles that glistened in the moonlight.

⑱ Akela never raised his head from his paws, but went on with the monotonous cry: "Look well!" A muffled roar came up from behind the rocks—the voice of Shere Khan crying: "The cub is mine. Give him to me. What have the Free People to do with a man's cub?" Akela never even twitched his ears: all he said was: "Look well, O Wolves! What have the Free People to do with the orders of any save the Free People? Look well!"

monotonous (mə nät´n əs´) *adj.* tiresome because it does not vary

There was a chorus of deep growls, and a young wolf in his fourth year flung back Shere Khan's question to Akela: "What have the Free People to do with the man's cub?" Now the Law of the Jungle lays

ENRICHMENT: Science Connection

Tigers

The tiger is the largest of all cats. Like wolves, wild tigers prefer to avoid humans. Tigers that do attack people are usually sick or wounded animals, like Shere Khan, that are unable to hunt their natural prey. In the wild, tigers are found only in Asia. They can live in various types of climates. Adult tigers are usually solitary animals. They hunt large mammals such as deer, antelope, and wild pigs, as well as small animals such as frogs, peafowl, and monkeys. Tigers will also prey on domestic cattle and water buffalo in areas where hunters have reduced the number of wild animals.

Have students work in research groups to find answers to questions such as these:

- How do tigers and lions differ?
- What are the feeding habits of tigers?
- How do tigers communicate with one another?
- How do countries such as India protect tigers?

down that if there is any dispute as to the right of a cub to be accepted by the Pack, he must be spoken for by at least two members of the Pack who are not his father and mother.

"Who speaks for this cub?" said Akela. "Among the Free People who speaks?" There was no answer, and Mother Wolf got ready for what she knew would be her last fight, if things came to fighting.

Then the only other creature who is allowed at the Pack Council—Baloo, the sleepy brown bear who teaches the wolf cubs the Law of the Jungle: old Baloo, who can come and go where he pleases because he eats only nuts and roots and honey—rose up on his hind quarters and grunted.

"The man's cub—the man's cub?" he said. "I speak for the man's cub. There is no harm in a man's cub. I have no gift of words, but I speak the truth. Let him run with the Pack, and be entered with the others. I myself will teach him.""We need yet another," said Akela. "Baloo has spoken, and he is our teacher for the young cubs. Who speaks besides Baloo?"

19 A black shadow dropped down into the circle. It was Bagheera the Black Panther, inky black all over, but with the panther marking showing up in certain lights like the pattern of watered silk. Everybody knew Bagheera, and nobody cared to cross his path; for he was as cunning as Tabaqui, as bold as the wild buffalo, and as reckless as the wounded elephant. But he had a voice as soft as wild honey dripping from a tree, and a skin softer than down.

"O Akela, and ye the Free People," he purred, "I have no right in your assembly; but the Law of the Jungle says that if there is a doubt which is not a killing matter in regard to a new cub, the life of that cub may be bought at a price. And the Law does not say who may or may not pay that price. Am I right?"

"Good! good!" said the young wolves, who are always hungry. "Listen to Bagheera. The cub can be bought for a price. It is the Law."

"Knowing that I have no right to speak here, I ask your leave."

"Speak then," cried twenty voices.

"To kill a naked cub is shame. Besides, he may make better sport for you when he is grown. Baloo has spoken in his behalf. Now to Baloo's word I will add one bull, and a fat one, newly killed, not half a mile from here, if ye will accept the man's cub according to the Law. Is it difficult?"

There was a clamor of scores of voices, saying: "What matter? He will die in the winter rains. He will scorch in the sun. What harm can a naked frog do us? Let him run with the Pack. Where is the bull, Bagheera? Let him be accepted." And then came Akela's deep bay, crying: "Look well—look well, O Wolves !"

Mowgli was still deeply interested in the pebbles, and he did not notice when the wolves came and looked at him one by one. At last

dispute (di spyo͞ot′) *n.* argument; debate; quarrel

Literary Analysis
Animal Characters and Personification Find three details from this scene that are examples of personification.

clamor (klam′ ər) *n.* loud demand or complaint

20 **Reading Check**
Why doesn't Shere Kahn get to take Mowgli?

19 Literary Analysis

Animal Characters and Personification

- Point out to students that Kipling uses many details to reinforce the idea that the wolf pack is similar to a human society.
- Ask students to look for details about wolf society as they read the bracketed passage. Then, ask them to respond to the Literary Analysis instruction on p. 217: Find three details from this scene that are examples of personification. Possible responses: The wolves call themselves the Free People; the wolves have a teacher for their cubs; Baloo speaks for the man's cub and claims to speak the truth; the panther is described as cunning, bold, reckless, and soft-voiced; the panther asks for "leave" to speak at the meeting.

20 Reading Check

Answer: Shere Khan doesn't get to take Mowgli because the wolves accept the child into their pack.

CUSTOMIZE INSTRUCTION FOR UNIVERSAL ACCESS

For Special Needs Students	For Advanced Readers
Have students review the photographs of the wolves in the selection. Ask them to compare and contrast these wolves with the domestic dogs with which they are familiar. Suggest that students use the Venn diagram on p. 89 in **Writing Models and Graphic Organizers on Transparencies** to record similarities and differences between wolves and dogs. Allow students to work together in small groups to complete their diagrams if they wish.	Invite students to meet in small groups to critique Kipling's writing style. Suggest that they consider the following questions: Are Kipling's sentences easy to read? Why or why not? How does the prose in the story compare with the poetry that begins the story? What makes the dialogue unusual or unique? Have groups share their observations when they have finished.

ASSESS

Answers for p. 218

Review and Assess

1. Possible responses: Mowgli should stay in the pack because the panther offered to give the wolves food for accepting Mowgli. The boy should go because a human has never been a part of the pack and might bring trouble.
2. **(a)** She threatens to fight Shere Khan. **(b)** She wants to protect Mowgli. **(c)** Her nickname is "The Demon;" the name is appropriate because she shows how strongly she will protect Mowgli.
3. **(a)** Mowgli seems to be comfortable in the wild. **(b)** He differs from them in that he is human. **(c)** Mother Wolf's motherly instincts take over when she sees Mowgli, whereas Shere Khan is hungry and looks at the boy as food.
4. **(a)** Shere Khan says that the man's cub should be returned to him. **(b)** The wolves take orders only from other wolves. **(c)** The wolves agree because Baloo speaks for Mowgli and the panther offers them food.
5. **(a)** Bagheera pays for Mowgli's life. **(b)** Possible response: His reasons are helpful. **(c)** Possible response: Some students may say that Bagheera is helpful because he is settling a dispute and saving Mowgli's life.
6. Each member has a say in the decision, and it seems fair.

they all went down the hill for the dead bull, and only Akela, Bagheera, Baloo, and Mowgli's own wolves were left. Shere Khan roared still in the night, for he was very angry that Mowgli had not been handed over to him.

"Ay, roar well," said Bagheera, under his whiskers; "for the time comes when this naked thing will make thee roar to another tune, or I know nothing of man."

"It was well done," said Akela. "Men and their cubs are very wise. He may be a help in time."

"Truly, a help in time of need; for none can hope to lead the Pack forever," said Bagheera.

Akela said nothing. He was thinking of the time that comes to every leader of every pack when his strength goes from him and he gets feebler and feebler till at last he is killed by the wolves and a new leader comes up—to be killed in his turn.

"Take him away," he said to Father Wolf, "and train him as befits one of the Free People."

And that is how Mowgli was entered into the Seeonee wolf-pack at the price of a bull and on Baloo's good word.

Review and Assess

Thinking About the Selection

1. **Respond:** If you were a member of the Council, would you want Mowgli in the pack? Why or why not?
2. (a) **Recall:** What does Mother Wolf do when Shere Khan tries to take Mowgli from her? (b) **Infer:** Why does she react as she does? (c) **Interpret:** How do her actions show the meaning of her nickname?
3. (a) **Compare:** How is Mowgli similar to the wolf cubs? (b) **Contrast:** How is he different? (c) **Analyze:** Why do Mother Wolf and Shere Kahn have opposite reactions to the similarities and differences?
4. (a) **Recall:** At the council, what does Shere Khan say should be done with Mowgli? (b) **Infer:** Why doesn't Akela answer Shere Khan? (c) **Synthesize:** Why do the young wolves agree to let Mowgli join the pack?
5. (a) **Recall:** Who pays for Mowgli's life? (b) **Evaluate:** Are his reasons helpful or destructive? (c) **Support:** What examples from the story support your answer?
6. **Evaluate:** Describe the way the wolves in the pack make decisions. Is this a good way for a group to make a decision? Explain your answer.

Rudyard Kipling

(1865–1936)

Rudyard Kipling was born in India of British parents. When he was very little, his Indian nurses told him folk tales that featured talking animals. These stories provided inspiration for characters in Kipling's works, including *The Jungle Book*, in which "Mowgli's Brothers" appears. As a young boy, Kipling was sent to school in England. Not until 1882, at the age of seventeen, did he make his way back to India as a journalist. His work as a reporter, fiction writer, and poet earned him the 1907 Nobel Prize for Literature.

ASSESSMENT PRACTICE: Reading Comprehension

Identifying the Main Idea (For more practice, see Test Preparation Workbook, p. 16.)

Tell students that the main idea of a passage may be stated in a topic sentence, as in this example:

The Law of the Jungle, which never orders anything without a reason, forbids every beast to eat Man except when he is killing to show his children how to kill. . . . The real reason for this is that man-killing means . . . the arrival of white men. . . . Then everybody in the jungle suffers. The reason the beasts give among themselves is that Man is the weakest . . . of all living things. . . .

What is the main idea of this passage?

A The Law of the Jungle is logical and reasonable.
B The Law of the Jungle states that, in general, animals should not eat people.
C Humans are the weakest living things.
D Men kill animals if animals kill men.

B expresses the main idea. *A, C,* and *D* are details.

Review and Assess

Literary Analysis

Animal Characters

1. What two qualities of Shere Khan reflect his nature as a tiger?
2. In what way are the wolves in the story similar to and different from real wolves?
3. Complete a chart like the one shown for each of the following **animal characters:** Tabaqui, Akela, Bagheera.

Character's Name	
Animal Qualities ______	Human Qualities ______

Connecting Literary Elements

4. Which animals in the story have courage? Which are cowards? Explain your answers.
5. How do the qualities of these characters affect the way events turn out? Complete a graphic organizer like this one for each main character. In the first oval, list the character's most important qualities. In the ovals in the middle, list each event that was affected by these qualities. Include an explanation of each. In the cell on the right, explain how the character's qualities affected the outcome.

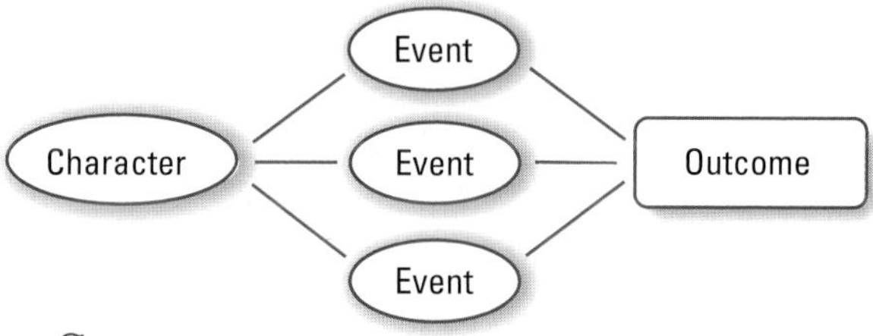

Reading Strategy

Predicting Characters' Actions

6. When Mowgli was discovered, what did you predict would happen to him? Why?
7. Which of Shere Khan's actions were you able to predict? Why?
8. Which of the wolves' actions were you able to predict? Why?

Extending Understanding

9. **Science Connection:** What do you learn about jungle habitats from this story? Explain.

Quick Review

Animal characters often have human as well as animal qualities. To review animal characters, see p. 209.

Personification is describing things that are nonhuman as if they had human abilities, qualities, and emotions.

When you **predict** characters' actions, you make educated guesses about what they will do, based on their qualities and the situation.

Take It to the Net

www.phschool.com

Take the interactive self-test online to check your understanding of the selection.

Answers for p. 219

Review and Assess

1. Shere Khan hunts alone and roars when he is angry.
2. They are similar to real wolves in that they live in packs, hunt for food, and care for and protect their young. They are different from real wolves in that they talk and have meetings.
3.

Tabaqui	
animal: hunts, gnaws bones, gets rabies	**human:** makes mischief, gossips
Akela	
animal: has been trapped, strong, leads wolves	**human:** runs meetings, contemplates his own death
Bagheera	
animal: other animals fear him, drops like a shadow into the circle	**human:** has a soft voice, bribes others, asks permission to speak

4. The wolf parents have courage because they are willing to fight for Mowgli. Akela has the courage to ignore Shere Khan. Baloo and Bagheera have the courage to speak for Mowgli. Shere Khan is a coward because he hunts the weakest animals. Tabaqui is a coward because he gossips and makes mischief.
5. Since Tabaqui gossips, Mother Wolf and Father Wolf are prepared for the coming of Shere Khan. Akela's strong leadership prevents Shere Khan from taking Mowgli. Bagheera's willingness to speak out leads to Mowgli's acceptance into the pack.
6. Possible response: I predicted he would be hurt or killed because he had no fear of the wolves.
7. Possible response: I predicted that Shere Khan would try to take Mowgli because Shere Khan is determined to get what he wants.
8. Students should identify specific actions and support their choices

continued

ENRICHMENT: Further Reading

Other Works by Rudyard Kipling

The Jungle Book

Just So Stories

Take It to the Net

Visit www.phschool.com for more information on Rudyard Kipling.

Answers continued

with characters' qualities and story details.

9. Possible response: Students may say they learned that jungle habitats are teeming with plant and animal life.

EXTEND

Answers for p. 220

❶ Vocabulary Development

Word Analysis

1. A monologue is a speech given by one person.
2. A monorail runs on one track.

Spelling Strategy

1. there
2. their
3. they're
4. there

Concept Development: Synonyms

1. e
2. b
3. f
4. g
5. c
6. d
7. a

Possible response: An additional synonym for *dispute* is *conflict,* and an additional synonym for *scuttled* is *scurried.*

❷ Grammar

1. here; Where is there no food?
2. well; To what extent did Tabaqui know that compliments are unlucky?
3. quietly; How did Tabaqui say "I go"?
4. yesterday; When did the Council meet?
5. longest; To what extent did Bagheera speak?

Writing Application

Possible responses: Mother Wolf growled *angrily.* Tabaqui waited *there.* He feared Father Wolf, but he feared Mother Wolf *more.*

Integrate Language Skills

❶ Vocabulary Development Lesson

Word Analysis: Greek Prefix *mono-*

Monotonous means "unchanging." It contains the Greek prefix *mono-*, which means "one." Use this knowledge of the prefix *mono-* in your answer to each of the following questions.

1. What kind of speech is a *monologue?*
2. On what kind of track does a *monorail* train run?

Spelling Strategy

The words *there, their,* and *they're* sound alike but have different meanings and spellings. Remember, to spell *there,* begin with *here.*

Supply the correct spelling of *there, their,* or *they're* to complete each sentence.

1. Mowgli wandered in __?__.
2. This is __?__ cave.
3. The wolves agree because __?__ hungry.
4. Bagheera says he has food over __?__.

Concept Development: Synonyms

On your paper, match the numbered vocabulary word on the left with its **synonym,** or word with almost the same meaning, on the right. Then, come up with an additional synonym for two of the vocabulary words.

To help you, review the vocabulary words on page 209.

1. clamor
2. dispute
3. fostering
4. monotonous
5. quarry
6. scuttled
7. veterans

a. experts
b. argument
c. prey
d. scampered
e. outcry
f. aiding
g. unchanging

❷ Grammar Lesson

Adverbs

An **adverb** is a word that modifies—or describes—a verb, an adjective, or another adverb. Adverbs answer the questions *when, how, where,* or *to what extent.*

Adverb	Answers the question
He spoke *spitefully.*	*How* did he speak?
The tiger hunts *now.*	*When* does the tiger hunt?
The wolf lives *here.*	*Where* does the wolf live?
Bagheera was *most* persuasive.	*To what extent* was Bagheera persuasive?

Practice Copy the following sentences. Circle each adverb and explain what question it answers.

1. Enter and look. There is no food here.
2. Tabaqui knew well that compliments are unlucky.
3. "I go," said Tabaqui, quietly.
4. The Council met yesterday.
5. Bagheera spoke longest.

Writing Application Rewrite this passage. Add adverbs to answer the questions.

Mother Wolf growled. (*How?*) Tabaqui waited. (*Where?*) He feared Father Wolf, but he feared Mother Wolf. (*To what extent?*)

WG Prentice Hall Writing and Grammar Connection: Chapter 16, Section 2

TEACHING RESOURCES

The following resources can be used to enrich or extend the instruction for pp. 220–221.

Vocabulary

Selection Support: Build Vocabulary, p. 66
Build Spelling Skills, p. 67 ■

Vocabulary and Spelling Practice Book
(Use this booklet for skills enrichment)

Grammar

Selection Support: Build Grammar Skills, p. 68

Writing and Grammar, Copper Level, p. 340

Daily Language Practice Transparencies ■

Writing

Writing and Grammar, Copper Level, p. 154 ■

Writing Models and Graphic Organizers on Transparencies, p. 89

Writing and Grammar iText CD-ROM ■

■ **BLOCK SCHEDULING:** Resources marked with this symbol provide varied instruction during 90-minute blocks.

❸ Writing Lesson

Comparison and Contrast of Characters

Write a brief composition in which you compare and contrast two animal characters in "Mowgli's Brothers."

Prewriting Choose two characters to compare and contrast. Make a list of details about each character. Circle all the details about appearance in blue. Underline all the details about personality in red.

Drafting Begin with an introductory paragraph that presents your general observations about the characters. For example, you might note that the characters have very similar personalities. Follow with body paragraphs, using one of the organizations shown below. End with a conclusion in which you restate your general observations.

Character by Character	Point by Point
Present all the details about one character first. Then, present all the details about the other.	Discuss each topic about each animal—for example, discuss the appearances of both animals, then go on to discuss the personalities of each animal.

Revising Highlight the details about each animal in a different color. Use this to check that you followed the organization you chose and that you have about the same number of details for each character.

WG *Prentice Hall Writing and Grammar Connection: Chapter 8, Section 2*

❹ Extension Activities

Listening and Speaking Role-play the conversation between Father Wolf and Shere Khan.

1. With a partner, read aloud sections of dialogue between the characters. Choose one of the dialogues as the starting point.
2. Begin where the written dialogue ends. Say the words that you think your character would say. Continue until each character has spoken at least five times.
3. Use postures, gestures, and facial expressions to indicate the emotions your character is feeling.

Research and Technology Prepare a short **presentation** on communication in a real wolf pack. Use the Internet, CD-ROM encyclopedias, and magazines and newspapers found in the library. Use visual aids such as charts, maps, or graphs to represent statistics. Identify the sources of your information.

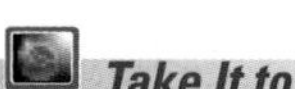

Take It to the Net www.phschool.com

Go online for an additional research activity using the Internet.

ASSESSMENT RESOURCES

The following resources can be used to assess students' knowledge and skills.

Selection Assessment

- **Formal Assessment,** pp. 56–58
- **Open Book Test,** pp. 40–42
- **Got It! Assessment Videotapes,** Tape 2
- **Test Bank Software**

Take It to the Net

Visit www.phschool.com for self-tests and additional questions on "Mowgli's Brothers."

Writing Rubric

- **Performance Assess. and Portfolio Mgmt.,** p. 16

- **Workbook**
- **Transparencies**
- **Skill Book**
- **CD-ROM**

❸ Writing Lesson

- Point out to students that *comparing* is finding similarities between two things and *contrasting* is finding differences.
- Model the use of the Venn Diagram on p. 89 in **Writing Models and Graphic Organizers on Transparencies** as an aide in organizing points.
- Review the different types of organization that students may use.
- To evaluate student compositions, use the Exposition: Comparison-and-Contrast Essay rubric on p. 16 in **Performance Assessment and Portfolio Management.**

❹ Research and Technology

- Divide the class into groups. Have students brainstorm for questions that they would like to answer as they research this topic.
- With your school or community librarian, make appropriate research resources available for student use.
- Encourage students to be creative in their presentations. Allow them to show video clips of wolves from documentaries or movies they have seen to capture their audience's interest.

CUSTOMIZE INSTRUCTION
For Universal Access

To address different learning styles, use the activities suggested in the **Extension Activities** booklet, p. 14.

- For Musical/Rhythmic Learners, use Activity 5.
- For Logical/Mathematical Learners, use Activity 6.
- For Bodily/Kinesthetic and Interpersonal Learners, use Activity 7.

Names/Nombres ✦ The Southpaw ✦ Alone in the Nets

Lesson Objectives

1. **To analyze and respond to literary elements**
   - Literary Analysis: Narrator and Speaker
   - Comparing Literary Works
2. **To read, comprehend, analyze, and critique an essay, a short story, and a poem**
   - Reading Strategy: Setting a Purpose for Reading
   - Reading Check Questions
   - Review and Assess Questions
   - Assessment Practice (ATE)
3. **To develop word analysis skills, fluency, and systematic vocabulary**
   - Vocabulary Development Lesson: Word Analysis: Latin Prefix *trans-*
4. **To understand and apply written and oral language conventions**
   - Spelling Strategy
   - Grammar Lesson: Adverbs Modifying Adjectives and Adverbs
5. **To understand and apply appropriate writing and research strategies**
   - Writing Lesson: Sports Scene
   - Extension Activity: Presentation
   - Extension Activity: Essay
6. **To understand and apply listening and speaking strategies**
   - Extension Activity: Directions and Demonstration

STEP-BY-STEP TEACHING GUIDE	PACING GUIDE
PRETEACH	
Motivate Students and Provide Background	
Use the Motivation activity (ATE p. 222)	5 min.
Read and discuss the Preview material and Background information (SE/ATE p. 222) [A]	10 min.
Introduce the Concepts	
Introduce the Literary Analysis and Reading Strategy (SE/ATE p. 223) [A]	25 min.
Pronounce the vocabulary words and read their definitions (SE p. 223)	5 min.
TEACH	
Monitor Comprehension	
Informally monitor comprehension by circulating while students read independently or in groups [A]	20–25 min.
Monitor students' comprehension with the Reading Check notes (SE/ATE pp. 225, 227, 229, 233)	as students read
Develop vocabulary with Vocabulary notes (SE pp. 226, 227, 228, 233, 234)	as students read
Develop Understanding	
Develop students' understanding of narrator and speaker with the Literary Analysis annotations (SE pp. 225, 227, 231; ATE pp. 225, 226, 227, 229, 231, 233) [A]	5 min.
Develop students' ability to set a purpose for reading with the Reading Strategy annotations (SE p. 225; ATE pp. 225, 233)	5 min.
ASSESS	
Assess Mastery	
Assess students' mastery of the Reading Strategy and Literary Analysis by having them answer the Review and Assess questions (SE/ATE p. 235)	25 min.
Use one or more of the print and media Assessment Resources (ATE p. 237) [A]	up to 45 min.
EXTEND	
Apply Understanding	
Have students complete the Vocabulary Development Lesson and the Grammar Lesson (SE p. 236) [A]	20 min.
Apply students' ability to write a sports scene using the Writing Lesson (SE/ATE p. 237) [A]	45 min.
Apply students' understanding using one or more of the Extension Activities (SE p. 237)	20–90 min.

ACCELERATED INSTRUCTION:
Use the strategies and activities identified with an [A].

UNIVERSAL ACCESS
● = Below Level Students
▲ = On-Level Students
■ = Above Level Students

Time and Resource Manager

Reading Level: Average, Easy, Easy
Average Number of Instructional Days: 4

RESOURCES		
PRINT	**TRANSPARENCIES**	**TECHNOLOGY**
• **Beyond Literature,** Media Connection: Film Adaptation, p. 15 ▲ ■		• **Interest Grabber Videotapes,** Tape 2 ● ▲ ■
• **Selection Support Workbook:** ● ▲ ■ Literary Analysis, p. 75 Reading Strategy, p. 74 Build Vocabulary, p. 71	• **Literary Analysis and Reading Transparencies,** pp. 29 and 30 ● ▲ ■	
• **Adapted Reader's Companion** ● • **Reader's Companion** ●		• **Listening to Literature** ● ▲ ■ Audiocassettes, Sides 10–11 Audio CDs, CD 4
• **English Learner's Companion** ● ▲ • **Literatura en español** ● ▲ • **Literary Analysis for Enrichment** ■	• **Fine Art Transparencies, Volume 1,** Transparency 16 ● ▲ ■	
• **Formal Assessment:** Selection Test, pp. 59–61 ● ▲ ■ • **Open Book Test,** pp. 43–45 ● ▲ ■ • **Performance Assessment and Portfolio Management,** p. 21 ● ▲ ■ • PRENTICE HALL ASSESSMENT SYSTEM ● ▲ ■	• PRENTICE HALL ASSESSMENT SYSTEM ● ▲ ■ Skills Practice Answers and Explanations on Transparencies	• **Test Bank Software** ● ▲ ■ • **Got It! Assessment Videotapes,** Tape 2 ● ▲
• **Selection Support Workbook:** ● ▲ ■ Build Spelling Skills, p. 72 Build Grammar Skills, p. 73 • **Writing and Grammar,** Copper Level ● ▲ ■ • **Extension Activities,** p. 15 ● ▲ ■	• **Daily Language Practice Transparencies** ● ▲ • **Writing Models and Graphic Organizers on Transparencies** ● ▲ ■	• **Writing and Grammar iText CD-ROM** ● ▲ ■ *Take It to the Net* www.phschool.com

BLOCK SCHEDULING: Use one 90-minute class period to preteach the selection and have students read it. Use a second 90-minute class period to assess students' mastery of skills and have them complete one of the Extension Activities.

PREVIEW

Step-by-Step Teaching Guide for pp. 222–223

Motivation

Write these statements on the board:

1. Immigrants to the United States should change their names so the names are more easily pronounced.
2. Two people from different cultures are unlikely to become friends.
3. Girls and boys should not play on the same sports teams.
4. Writing letters is a good way for two people to solve a disagreement.

Have students number a sheet of paper from 1 to 4. Then, ask them to read each statement and write "agree" or "disagree" next to the corresponding number on their paper. Encourage students to discuss their responses.

Interest Grabber Video

As an alternative, play "Julia Alvarez on Creative Writing" or "The History of Soccer" on Tape 2 to engage student interest.

❶ Background

Social Studies

Immigrants are people who settle in a country in which they were not born. Some move to find better opportunities for earning a living. Others move to escape political or religious persecution. From the 1820s to the 1920s, more than 30 million people came from other countries to live in the United States. Most were from Europe. In more recent times, large numbers of immigrants have come from Mexico, the Caribbean, Asia, India, and the Philippines. Julia Alvarez's family came to New York City from the Dominican Republic, an island nation in the Caribbean.

Prepare to Read

❶ Names/Nombres ◆ The Southpaw ◆ Alone in the Nets

Take It to the Net

Visit www.phschool.com for interactive activities and instruction related to these selections, including
- background
- graphic organizers
- literary elements
- reading strategies

Preview

Connecting to the Literature

The authors of "Names/Nombres," "The Southpaw," and "Alone in the Nets" write about group experiences. Connect to the selections by recalling your experiences as a member of groups such as family, friends, classes, clubs, and teams.

Background

In "Names/Nombres," Julia Alvarez tells how language differences make her feel like an outsider. In Spanish, the letter *j* is used for the sound English speakers associate with *h*. The letter *r* has a very different sound from its sound in English. Although many Spanish words have found their way into English, some of their pronunciations have changed over time, reflecting the influence of English speakers.

TEACHING RESOURCES

The following resources can be used to enrich or extend the instruction for pp. 222–223.

Motivation

Interest Grabber Video, Tape 2

Background

Beyond Literature, p. 15 

Take It to the Net

Visit www.phschool.com for Background and hotlinks for the selections.

Literary Analysis

Literary Analysis and Reading Transparencies, Narrator and Speaker, p. 30

Selection Support: Literary Analysis, p. 75 

Reading

Literary Analysis and Reading Transparencies, Setting a Purpose for Reading, p. 29

BLOCK SCHEDULING: Resources marked with this symbol provide varied instruction during 90-minute blocks.

❷ Literary Analysis

Narrator and Speaker

An author writes a story or a poem, but a **narrator** or **speaker** tells the story or "says" the poem. In works written in the first person, the narrator or speaker refers to himself or herself as *I*. The *I*, however, does not necessarily refer to the writer. Read the following example from "The Southpaw."

> If I'm not good enough to play on your team, I'm not good enough to be friends with.

Although the writer Judith Viorst uses the word *I*, she is referring to a character she invented to tell the story. (In fact, in "The Southpaw," two invented narrators tell the story.) As you read, use these focus questions to help you think about the narrator or speaker:

1. Who is telling the story?
2. How do his or her views shape how the story is told?

Comparing Literary Works

These three works are written in the first person, but the speakers and narrators have different qualities. In "Names/Nombres," the narrator is a real person—the author. Yet she shares some qualities with the made-up speaker of "Alone in the Nets." Use a Venn diagram like the one shown here to compare and contrast the qualities of the narrators or speakers. Use the overlapping portions of the circles for shared qualities. Include details for both narrators of "The Southpaw."

Names/Nombres

The Southpaw

Alone in the Nets

❸ Reading Strategy

Setting a Purpose for Reading

When you set a purpose, you give yourself a focus. Here are a few purposes a reader might have for reading "The Southpaw."

- to be entertained by a funny story about baseball
- to gain insight into disagreements
- to look at a situation from two different sides

Set a purpose before reading each of these works.

Vocabulary Development

transport (trans pôrt´) *v.* carry from one place to another (p. 226)

inevitably (in ev´ i tə blē) *adv.* unavoidably (p. 227)

chaotic (kā ät´ ik) *adj.* completely confused (p. 227)

inscribed (in skrībd´) *adj.* written on (p. 228)

opposition (äp´ ə zish´ ən) *n.* here, the other team (p. 233)

evaporate (i vap´ ə rāt´) *v.* disappear like vapor (p. 234)

CUSTOMIZE INSTRUCTION FOR UNIVERSAL ACCESS

For Special Needs Students	For Less Proficient Readers	For English Learners
Have students read the adapted version of "Names/Nombres" in the **Adapted Reader's Companion.** This version provides basic-level instruction in an interactive format with questions and write-on lines. Completing the adapted version will prepare students to read the selection in the Student Edition.	Have students read "Names/Nombres" in the **Reader's Companion.** This version provides basic-level instruction in an interactive format with questions and write-on lines. After students finish the selection in the Reader's Companion, have them complete the questions and activities in the Student Edition.	Have students read the adapted version of "Names/Nombres" in the **English Learner's Companion.** This version provides basic-level instruction in an interactive format with questions and write-on lines. Completing the adapted version will prepare students to read the selection in the Student Edition.

❷ Literary Analysis

Narrator and Speaker

- Elicit from students the meaning of the word *narrator.*
  Answer: A narrator is a person who tells a story.
- Point out to students that the narrator may not be the author. Explain to students that, usually in fictional writing, the author creates a character or "voice" to be the narrator. Usually in nonfictional works, if the narrator uses "I" when speaking, it can be assumed that the narrator is the author.
- Have a volunteer read aloud the instruction about narrators and speakers. Use the Narrator and Speaker transparency on p. 30 in **Literary Analysis and Reading Transparencies** to further clarify the difference between the writer and the author.

❸ Reading Strategy

Setting a Purpose for Reading

- Ask students why they watch television.
  Possible responses: To be entertained; to understand something; to get information.
- Point out to students that just as they watch television for various reasons, they also read for different reasons.
- Read the Reading Strategy text aloud. Before students read each selection, have them select and record a purpose for reading it. Lead students to understand that setting a purpose will give them a focus as they read.

Vocabulary Development

- Pronounce each vocabulary word for students, and read the definitions as a class. Have students identify any words with which they are already familiar.

E-Teach

Visit E-Teach at www.phschool.com for teachers' essays on how to teach, with questions and answers.

TEACH

Step-by-Step Teaching Guide for pp. 224–234

CUSTOMIZE INSTRUCTION
For Bodily/Kinesthetic Learners

Before reading "Alone in the Nets," invite students who play soccer to explain the rules of the game and roles of each player. If possible, have them use a soccer ball to demonstrate techniques to the class.

1 About the Selection

In "Names/Nombres," Julia Alvarez recalls her family's early years as immigrants to the United States from the Dominican Republic. She describes how the family adjusts to the continual mispronunciation of their names. Eager to fit in at school, Alvarez allows herself to be called various names—*Judy, Juliet,* even *Alcatraz.* Although proud of her rich heritage and beautiful native language, young Alvarez struggles to fit in and not appear different. During these years, Alvarez seems to straddle two cultures, while dreaming of becoming a writer and wondering which name she'll eventually use in her career.

Names/ 1 Nombres

Julia Alvarez

TEACHING RESOURCES

The following resources can be used to enrich or extend the instruction for pp. 224–234.

Literary Analysis
- **Literary Analysis for Enrichment**
- **Writing Models and Graphic Organizers on Transparencies,** pp. 77, 97 ■

Reading
- **Selection Support:** Reading Strategy, p. 74; Build Vocabulary, p. 71
- **Adapted Reader's Companion**
- **Reader's Companion**
- **English Learner's Companion**
- **Literatura en español**
- **Listening to Literature Audiocassettes,** Sides 10–11
- **Listening to Literature Audio CDs,** CD 4

Extension
- **Fine Art Transparencies, Volume 1,** Transparency 16 (Use the painting to generate discussion on the topic of baseball.) ■

■ **BLOCK SCHEDULING:** Resources marked with this symbol provide varied instruction during 90-minute blocks.

When we arrived in New York City, our names changed almost immediately. At Immigration,[1] the officer asked my father, *Mister Elbures,* if he had anything to declare. My father shook his head,
2 "No," and we were waved through. I was too afraid we wouldn't be let in if I corrected the man's pronunciation, but I said our name to myself, opening my mouth wide for the organ blast of the *a,* trilling my tongue for the drum-roll of the *r, All-vah-rrr-es!* How could anyone get *Elbures* out of that orchestra of sound?

At the hotel my mother was *Missus Alburest,* and I was little girl, as in, "Hey, *little girl,* stop riding the elevator up and down. It's *not* a toy."

When we moved into our new apartment building, the super[2] called my father *Mister Alberase,* and the neighbors who became mother's friends pronounced her name *Jew-lee-ah* instead of *Hoo-lee-ah.* I, her namesake, was known as *Hoo-lee-tah* at home. But at school, I was *Judy* or *Judith,* and once an English teacher mistook me for *Juliet.*

It took awhile to get used to my new names. I wondered if I shouldn't correct my teachers and new friends. But my mother argued that it didn't matter. "You know what your friend
3 Shakespeare said, *'A rose by any other name would smell as sweet.'* " My father had gotten into the habit of calling any famous author "my friend" because I had begun to write poems and stories in English class.

By the time I was in high school, I was a popular kid, and it showed in my name. Friends called me *Jules* or *Hey Jude,* and once a group of troublemaking friends my mother forbade me to hang out with called me *Alcatraz.* I was *Hoo-lee-tah* only to Mami and Papi and uncles and aunts who came over to eat *sancocho* on Sunday afternoons—old world folk whom I would just as soon go back to where they came from and leave me to pursue whatever mischief I wanted to in America. JUDY ALCATRAZ: the name on the Wanted Poster would read. Who would ever trace her to me?

My older sister had the hardest time getting an American name for herself because *Mauricia* did not translate into English. Ironically, although she had the most foreign-sounding name, she and I were the Americans in the family. We had been born in New York City when our parents had first tried immigration and then gone back "home,"

1. **Immigration** government agency that processes immigrants.
2. **super** superintendent; the person who manages an apartment building.

Reading Strategy
Setting a Purpose for Reading Based on the opening paragraph, what purpose will you set for reading?

Literary Analysis
Narrator and Speaker How does the detail about the author's life help you make the connection between the young Julia and the adult writer?

4 **Reading Check**
What does Julia experience when she arrives in New York City?

2 Reading Strategy
Setting a Purpose for Reading

- Remind students that they will be able to focus better if they have a purpose in mind as they read.
- Tell students that they will be reading about a family who immigrated to the United States from the Dominican Republic. Invite students to consider what they want to get out of the selection. Ask the Reading Strategy question on p. 225.
  Answer: Students may say their purpose for reading is to understand why names are important or to find out more about the immigrant experience of the author and her family. Students should support the purpose by noting parts of the story that relate to the purpose.

3 Literary Analysis
Narrator and Speaker

- Remind students that the author and speaker may not always be the same person. "Names/Nombres," however, is an autobiographical essay, so the author and speaker are the same person.
- To show how the author and speaker are the same in this selection, read the bracketed passage aloud. Have students point out words that show the identity of the narrator. Ask the Literary Analysis question on p. 225.
  Answer: The young Julia was already writing poems and stories.

4 Reading Check

Answer: When Julia arrives in New York City, she notices that people are mispronouncing her name and the names of her family members.

CUSTOMIZE INSTRUCTION FOR UNIVERSAL ACCESS

For Special Needs Students	For Less Proficient Readers	For Advanced Readers
You may wish to preview the Spanish terms in the story. When you have completed this preview, students will be better prepared to understand the cassette or CD version of the story. Explain that certain consonants have different pronunciations in English and Spanish; for example, a *j* in Spanish is usually pronounced as an *h* in English.	Help students follow the narrative by organizing the events in chronological order as they read. Suggest that they record events on a timeline like the one on p. 77 of **Writing Models and Graphic Organizers on Transparencies.** Give students a starting point: Julia's family arrives in New York City.	Explain that in paragraph 4 on p. 225, Julia's mother is paraphrasing a line from William Shakespeare's *Romeo and Juliet:* "That which we call a rose/By any other name would smell as sweet." Invite students to interpret the meaning of this line and to connect it to Julia's situation.

❺ Background

Art

Collage, by Juan Sanchez

Point out that the artist chose his own way to show relationships in this artwork. Have students describe the lines and colors the artist used. Then use the following questions for discussion:

1. How do the people in the artwork seem to feel about one another? Explain.
   Answer: Students may say that they love one another because they seem happy together.
2. What are some ways you might choose to communicate heritage in a work of art?
   Answer: Students may mention a collage of photographs or a drawing of themselves surrounded by relatives.

❻ Literary Analysis

Narrator and Speaker

- Ask students whether they like their names. Do they prefer names that are popular or unusual?
- Ask students to describe how the narrator's perspective in the bracketed passage on p. 226 affects the way she discusses her sister's name.
  Answer: The narrator feels that her sister's name is difficult for people in the United States to pronounce.
- Ask students to support their response.
  Possible response: Students should notice the mispronunciations and her statement that she pities her sister for having such an "awful" name.

❼ ▶Critical Viewing

Possible response: The people in the picture seem to be related, and the heart suggests a love of heritage.

too homesick to stay. My mother often told the story of how she had almost changed my sister's name in the hospital.

After the delivery, Mami and some other new mothers were cooing over their new baby sons and daughters and exchanging names and weights and delivery stories. My mother was embarrassed among the Sallys and Janes and Georges and Johns to reveal the rich, noisy name of *Mauricia*, so when her turn came to brag, she gave her baby's name as *Maureen*.

"Why'd ya give her an Irish name with so many pretty Spanish names to choose from?" one of the women asked.

My mother blushed and admitted her baby's real name to the group. Her mother-in-law had recently died, she apologized, and her husband had insisted that the first daughter be named after his mother, *Mauran*. My mother thought it the ugliest name she had ever heard, and she talked my father into what she believed was an improvement, a combination of *Mauran* and her own mother's name, *Felicia*.

"Her name is *Mao-ree-shee-ah*," my mother said to the group of women.

❻ "Why that's a beautiful name," the new mothers cried. "*Moor-ee-sha, Moor-ee-sha*," they cooed into the pink blanket. *Moor-ee-sha* it was when we returned to the States eleven years later. Sometimes, American tongues found even that mispronunciation tough to say and called her *Maria* or *Marsha* or *Maudy* from her nickname *Maury*. I pitied her. What an awful name to have to transport across borders!

My little sister, Ana, had the easiest time of all. She was plain *Anne*—that is, only her name was plain, for she turned out to be the pale, blond "American beauty" in the family. The only Hispanic thing about her was the affectionate nicknames her boyfriends sometimes gave her. *Anita*, or as one goofy guy used to sing to her to the tune of the banana advertisement, *Anita Banana*.[3]

Later, during her college years in the late '60s, there was a push to pronounce Third World names correctly. I remember calling her long distance at her group house and a roommate answering.

"Can I speak to Ana?" I asked, pronouncing her name the American way.

3. ***Anita Banana*** a play on the Chiquita Banana name.

❺ 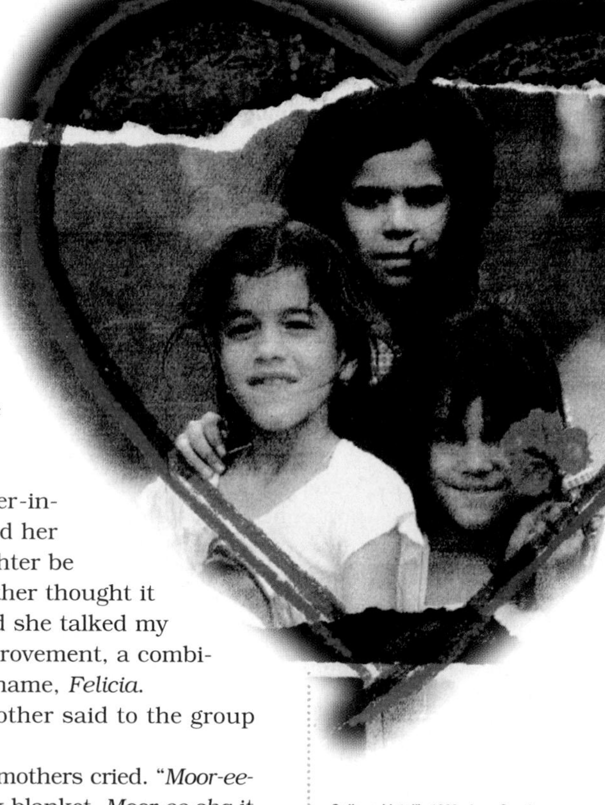

***Collage* (detail),** 1992, Juan Sanchez, Courtesy of Juan Sanchez and Guarighen, Inc. NYC

❼ **▼Critical Viewing** How does the artist of this picture communicate "heritage"? **[Analyze]**

transport (trans pôrt′) *v.* carry from one place to another

ENRICHMENT: Social Studies Connection

The Dominican Republic

The Alvarez family immigrated to the United States from the Dominican Republic, a mountainous country that occupies the eastern two thirds of the island of Hispaniola. (Haiti occupies the remaining third.) Soon after Christopher Columbus landed on the island in 1492, thousands of Spanish colonists settled Hispaniola. As a result, most of the 7 million inhabitants of the Dominican Republic speak Spanish and follow Spanish customs. The capital and largest city in the Dominican Republic is the bustling port of Santo Domingo.

Arrange students in groups and have each group conduct research to learn more about the history, government, economy, and daily life of the Dominican Republic. Invite students from each group to give a presentation of the group's findings.

"Ana?" The man's voice hesitated. "Oh! you must mean *Ah-nah*!"

Our first few years in the States, though, ethnicity was not yet "in." Those were the blond, blue-eyed, bobby sock years of junior high and high school before the '60s ushered in peasant blouses, hoop earrings, serapes.[4] My initial desire to be known by my correct Dominican name faded. I just wanted to be Judy and merge with the Sallys and Janes in my class. But inevitably, my accent and coloring gave me away. "So where are you from, Judy?"

inevitably (in ev′ i tə blē) *adv.* unavoidably

"New York," I told my classmates. After all, I had been born blocks away at Columbia Presbyterian Hospital.

"I mean, *originally*."

"From the Caribbean," I answered vaguely, for if I specified, no one was quite sure on what continent our island was located.

8 "Really? I've been to Bermuda. We went last April for spring vacation. I got the worst sunburn! So, are you from Portoriko?"

"No," I sighed. "From the Dominican Republic."

"Where's that?"

"South of Bermuda."

Literary Analysis
Narrator and Speaker
Why does the writer spell Puerto Rico this way? How does the spelling reveal the narrator's perspective?

They were just being curious, I knew, but I burned with shame whenever they singled me out as a "foreigner," a rare, exotic friend.

"Say your name in Spanish, oh please say it!" I had made mouths drop one day by rattling off my full name, which according to Dominican custom, included my middle names, Mother's and Father's surnames for four generations back.

"Julia Altagracia María Teresa Álvarez Tavares Perello Espaillat Julia Pérez Rochet González," I pronounced it slowly, a name as chaotic with sounds as a Middle Eastern bazaar[5] or market day in a South American village.

chaotic (kā ät′ ik) *adj.* completely confused

My Dominican heritage was never more apparent than when my extended family attended school occasions. For my graduation, they all came, the whole lot of aunts and uncles and the many little cousins who snuck in without tickets. They sat in the first row in order to better understand the Americans' fast-spoken English. But how could they listen when they were constantly speaking among themselves in florid-sounding phrases, rococo[6] consonants, rich, rhyming vowels?

Introducing them to my friends was a further trial to me. These relatives had such complicated names and there were so many of them, and their relationships to myself were so convoluted. There was my Tía Josefina, who was not really an aunt but a much older

9 **Reading Check**
Why does Julia try to hide her home country from her classmates?

4. **serapes** (sə rä′ pēz) *n.* colorful shawls worn in Latin America.
5. **bazaar** (bə zär′) *n.* marketplace; frequently, one held outdoors.
6. **rococo** (rə kō′ kō) fancy, ornate style of art of the early eighteenth century.

8 Literary Analysis

Narrator and Speaker

- Recall the narrator's use of different pronunciations of Mauricia to show how Americans "translated" her family's names. Point out that the narrator also uses spelling to show her perspective, or how she sees and hears events.
- Ask the Literary Analysis question on p. 227.
  Answer: The writer spells it this way to show that people are mispronouncing the word. Students may say this shows that the narrator thinks Americans don't appreciate the grace of the Spanish language.

9 Reading Check

Answer: She is embarrassed to be thought of as a foreigner.

CUSTOMIZE INSTRUCTION FOR UNIVERSAL ACCESS

For Less Proficient Readers	For English Learners	For Gifted/Talented Students
To help students visualize the Alvarez family's journeys, have students use a world map to locate the Dominican Republic and New York City. Recall with students that the Alvarez family moved to New York City twice from the Dominican Republic. Have students trace this route on the map.	Invite students proficient in Spanish to read aloud pp. 226–228 with a partner proficient in English, with each student taking a different role. Encourage students to emphasize the pronunciation of the words in italics.	Suggest that students create names similar to the full name of Julia Alvarez. They may want to make up long names, or they can include middle names and their parents' surnames from several generations back. Then, encourage students to write paragraphs in which they describe something about the person with that name.

Answers for p. 228

Review and Assess

1. Students may say that the name *Julia* best fits the author because it is her given name and because it shows pride in her heritage.
2. **(a)** Julia's family pronounces her name "Hoo–lee–tah." **(b)** In English, *Julia* is pronounced "Joo-lee-uh" or "Jool-yuh"; in Spanish, it is pronounced "Hoo-lee-uh." Also, in English, the spelling and pronunciation of *Julia* can be mistaken for *Judy, Julie, Judith,* or *Juliet.* **(c)** Students may say that they tell the person the correct way to pronounce it.
3. **(a)** Julia says she is from New York. **(b)** She doesn't want to appear foreign. **(c)** Students may say no, because they are proud of their heritage. Others may say yes, because they don't want to be seen as different.
4. **(a)** The title contains the English and Spanish words for *names,* and it reflects the author's dual identity as an immigrant. **(b)** She becomes proud of her heritage instead of trying to hide it. **(c)** Names reflect Alvarez's desire to fit in and allow her the choice of sharing different aspects of her identity.
5. Possible responses: Names are not important; as Julia's mother says, it is not your name, but who you are that is important. Or, names are important, as demonstrated by the amount of thought Julia's mother put into naming Mauricia.

cousin. And her daughter, Aida Margarita, who was adopted, *una hija de crianza.* My uncle of affection, Tío José, brought my *madrina* Tía Amelia and her *comadre* Tía Pilar. My friends rarely had more than a "Mom and Dad" to introduce.

After the commencement ceremony my family waited outside in the parking lot while my friends and I signed yearbooks with nicknames which recalled our high school good times: "Beans" and "Pepperoni" and "Alcatraz." We hugged and cried and promised to keep in touch.

Our goodbyes went on too long. I heard my father's voice calling out across the parking lot, "*Hoo-lee-tah! Vamonos!*"

Back home, my *tíos* and *tías* and *primas,* Mami and Papi, and *mis hermanas* had a party for me with *sancocho* and a store-bought *pudín,* inscribed with *Happy Graduation, Julie.* There were many gifts—that was a plus to a large family! I got several wallets and a suitcase with my initials and a graduation charm from my godmother and money from my uncles. The biggest gift was a portable typewriter from my parents for writing my stories and poems.

inscribed (in skrībd′) *adj.* written on

Someday, the family predicted, my name would be well-known throughout the United States. I laughed to myself, wondering which one I would go by.

Julia Alvarez

(b. 1950)

Like many immigrants, the Alvarez family came to the United States for political reasons. After working to overthrow the dictator of the Dominican Republic, Julia's father and his family fled the country. Julia was only ten years old when they arrived in the United States. Growing up here, Alvarez felt she had to "translate her experience in English." Sometimes, as she shows in "Names/Nombres," it was the Americans who did the "translating," blending the exotic-sounding syllables of her family's names into more familiar words.

Review and Assess

Thinking About the Selection

1. **Respond:** Which name do you think best fits the author? Why?
2. **(a) Recall:** How does Julia's family say her name? **(b) Analyze Cause and Effect:** Explain why some English speakers mispronounce her name. **(c) Connect:** What do you do or say when someone mispronounces your name?
3. **(a) Recall:** How does Julia respond when her classmates ask her where she's from? **(b) Draw Conclusions:** Why does she respond as she does? **(c) Evaluate:** Would you make the same decision in the same situation? Why or why not?
4. **(a) Interpret:** Explain how the title captures the focus of Alvarez's narrative. **(b) Analyze:** How do Alvarez's feelings about the topic change over time? **(c) Synthesize:** What do names represent for Alvarez and others?
5. **Assess:** How important are names in the way people view themselves and others? Support your answer with details from the selection.

CUSTOMIZE INSTRUCTION FOR UNIVERSAL ACCESS

For Less Proficient Readers	For Gifted/Talented Students
Have students make a list of the nicknames family or friends have given them. Tell students that nicknames can be ones they had when they were younger or ones they have now. Encourage each student to choose one of his or her nicknames and write a brief essay describing the origin of the nickname and how it felt to be called by that nickname. If some students do not have nicknames, have them use imaginary ones and explain why those would be appropriate.	Julia Alvarez's story revolves around her name and the distress it caused her. The fact that Alvarez shared the story indicates that her name is important to her. Have students write essays in which they explore their own feelings about their names—first, last, or both. They may wish to include stories about how people have pronounced or used their names. Invite volunteers to share their essays with the class.

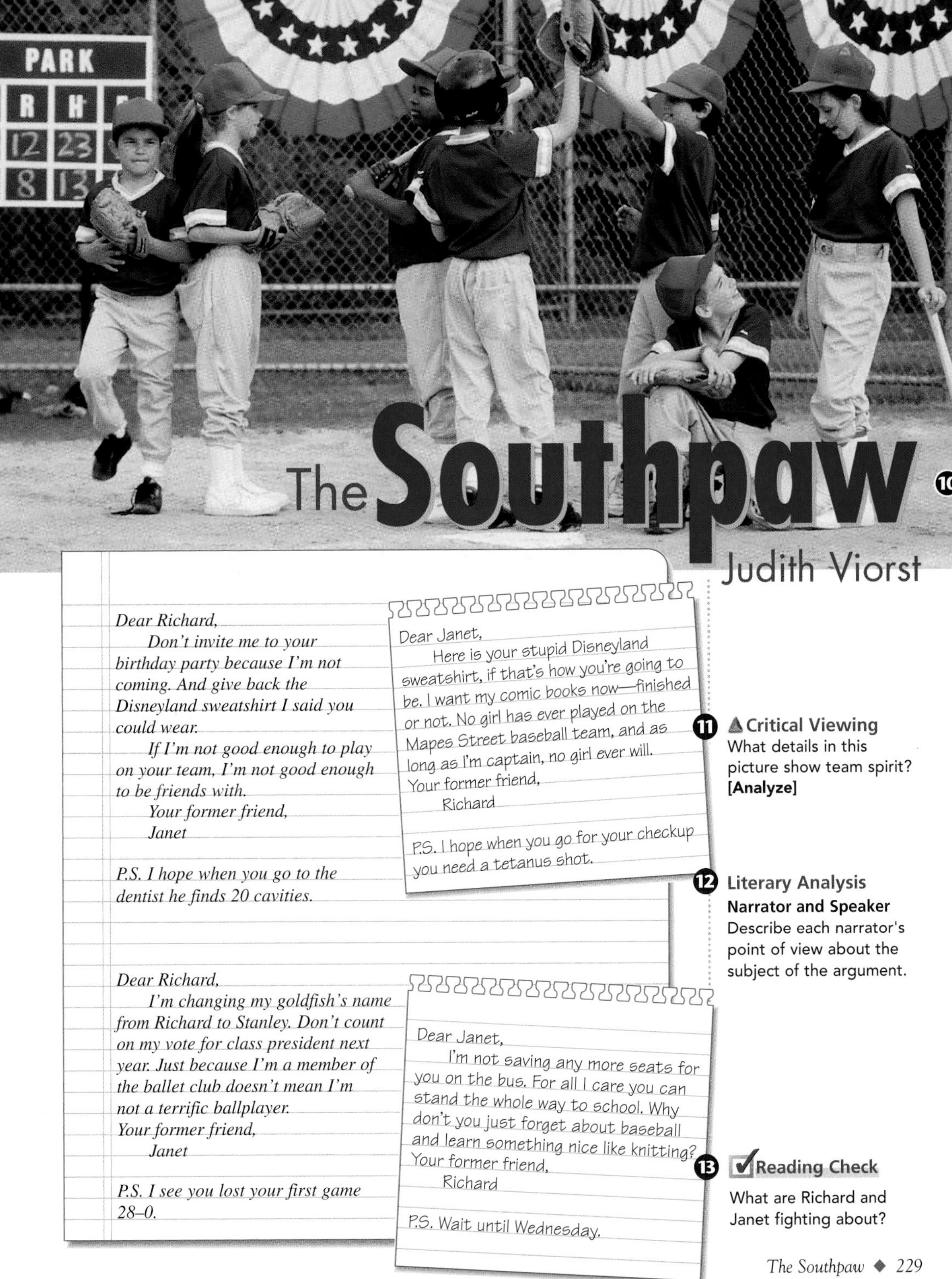

The Southpaw

Judith Viorst

Dear Richard,
Don't invite me to your birthday party because I'm not coming. And give back the Disneyland sweatshirt I said you could wear.
If I'm not good enough to play on your team, I'm not good enough to be friends with.
Your former friend,
Janet

P.S. I hope when you go to the dentist he finds 20 cavities.

Dear Janet,
Here is your stupid Disneyland sweatshirt, if that's how you're going to be. I want my comic books now—finished or not. No girl has ever played on the Mapes Street baseball team, and as long as I'm captain, no girl ever will.
Your former friend,
Richard

P.S. I hope when you go for your checkup you need a tetanus shot.

Dear Richard,
I'm changing my goldfish's name from Richard to Stanley. Don't count on my vote for class president next year. Just because I'm a member of the ballet club doesn't mean I'm not a terrific ballplayer.
Your former friend,
Janet

P.S. I see you lost your first game 28–0.

Dear Janet,
I'm not saving any more seats for you on the bus. For all I care you can stand the whole way to school. Why don't you just forget about baseball and learn something nice like knitting?
Your former friend,
Richard

P.S. Wait until Wednesday.

11 ▲Critical Viewing What details in this picture show team spirit? **[Analyze]**

12 Literary Analysis **Narrator and Speaker** Describe each narrator's point of view about the subject of the argument.

13 ✓Reading Check What are Richard and Janet fighting about?

10 About the Selection

The friendship between Janet and Richard is in trouble. As captain of a baseball team, Richard refuses to let Janet play because she is a girl. Janet responds with an angry letter to Richard, in which she vows not to come to his birthday party. Richard responds in kind, and a volley of angry letters and insults begins. Richard's resolve finally cracks as members of his team are injured, become ill, or are otherwise indisposed to play. He accepts a "package deal" from Janet that includes her as pitcher and three other girls on the team. By the last letter, the friendship is on the mend.

11 ▶Critical Viewing

Answer: The players in the center of the photograph are touching gloves, as in a "high five." All the team members seem friendly with one another. They seem eager to play.

12 Literary Analysis

Narrator and Speaker

- Point out to students that this story has two narrators. How does the author show which narrator is speaking?
  Answer: The speakers are identified as the authors of their respective letters.
- Read the Literary Analysis note on p. 229.
  Answer: Janet thinks she belongs on Richard's team because she is a good baseball player. Richard thinks she doesn't belong because she is a girl.

13 ✓Reading Check

Answer: Janet and Richard are fighting about whether she can play on his baseball team.

CUSTOMIZE INSTRUCTION FOR UNIVERSAL ACCESS

For Less Proficient Readers	For English Learners	For Advanced Readers
As students view the photograph on this page, have them create dialogue for the players. Ask them to cut pieces of paper in the shape of speech balloons. Have students write dialogue in each balloon. Then, have them arrange the balloons near each person in the photograph. Invite students to share their dialogues.	Assist students with interpreting the letter congratulating Richard on his losses. Explain that sarcasm is a literary device in which a writer says one thing and means the opposite. You may want to have proficient readers read this letter with a sarcastic tone and then with a normal tone to show the difference.	Explain to students that Janet and Richard are working out a conflict through letter writing. Invite students to put themselves in Richard's or Janet's place and write an explanation of how they would feel in either character's situation.

⓮ Critical Thinking

Interpret

- Invite a student to read aloud the bracketed letter. Have students put themselves in Richard's place. Ask them how they might feel after receiving this letter from Janet.
  Answer: Students may say that they would be especially angry, because Janet is rubbing in the fact of their game losses and turning Richard's earlier insult about knitting against him.
- Now invite another student to read the postscript in the following letter. Ask students what this statement reveals about Richard.
  Answer: Students may say that Richard shows he is upset by the losses and that his feelings are hurt by Janet's insults.

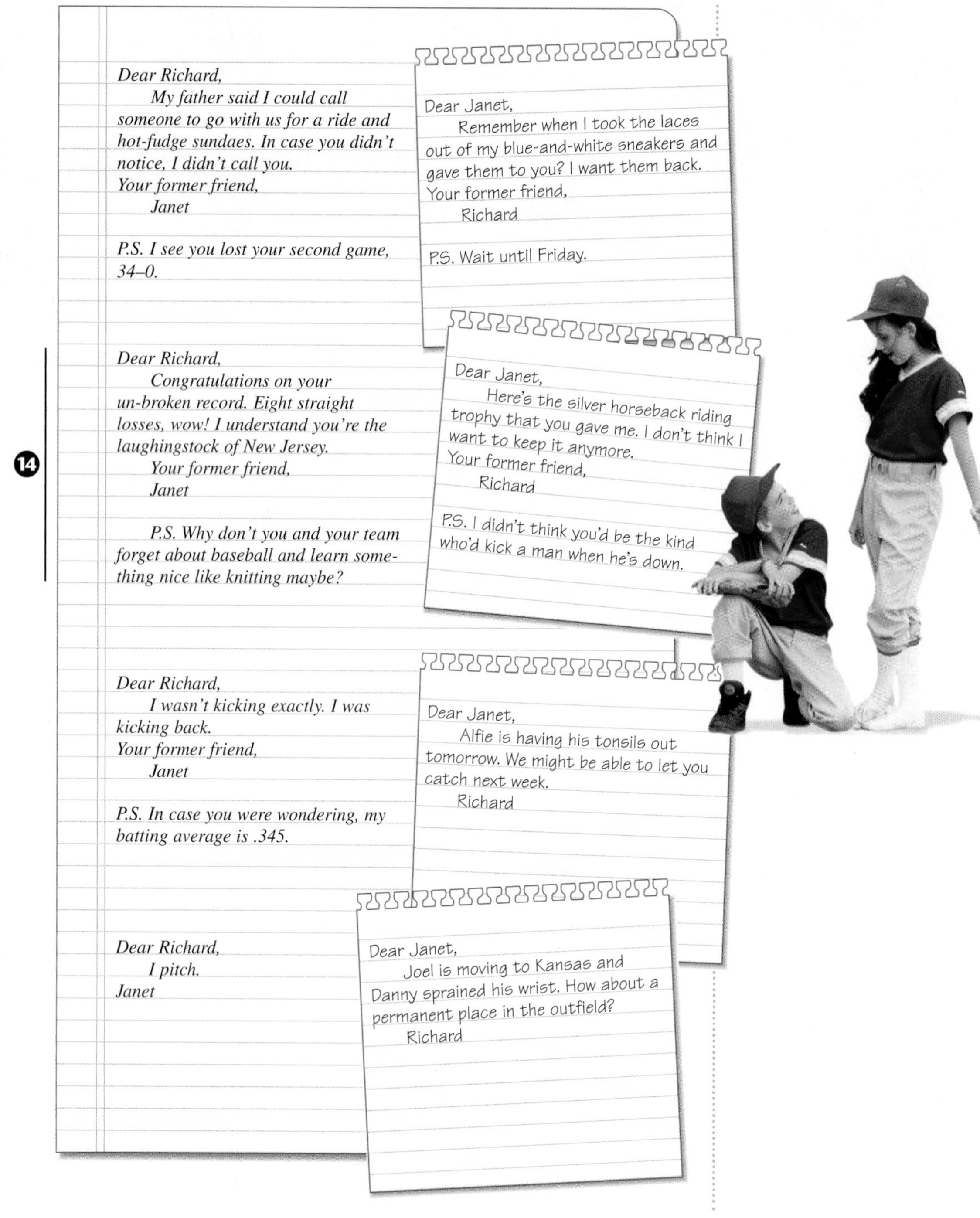

Dear Richard,
My father said I could call someone to go with us for a ride and hot-fudge sundaes. In case you didn't notice, I didn't call you.
Your former friend,
Janet

P.S. I see you lost your second game, 34–0.

Dear Janet,
Remember when I took the laces out of my blue-and-white sneakers and gave them to you? I want them back.
Your former friend,
Richard

P.S. Wait until Friday.

14 *Dear Richard,*
Congratulations on your un-broken record. Eight straight losses, wow! I understand you're the laughingstock of New Jersey.
Your former friend,
Janet

P.S. Why don't you and your team forget about baseball and learn something nice like knitting maybe?

Dear Janet,
Here's the silver horseback riding trophy that you gave me. I don't think I want to keep it anymore.
Your former friend,
Richard

P.S. I didn't think you'd be the kind who'd kick a man when he's down.

Dear Richard,
I wasn't kicking exactly. I was kicking back.
Your former friend,
Janet

P.S. In case you were wondering, my batting average is .345.

Dear Janet,
Alfie is having his tonsils out tomorrow. We might be able to let you catch next week.
Richard

Dear Richard,
I pitch.
Janet

Dear Janet,
Joel is moving to Kansas and Danny sprained his wrist. How about a permanent place in the outfield?
Richard

CUSTOMIZE INSTRUCTION FOR UNIVERSAL ACCESS

For Gifted/Talented Students

Math plays an important role in baseball and other sports. Team performances can be measured by comparing two teams' winning and losing averages. Batting averages and other statistics are used to compare players' performances. For example, Janet's batting average in "The Southpaw" is higher than that of most players. This indicates that she is an above-average player.

Direct students to sources of sports statistics. Have students research the types of statistics used in their favorite sports to report team and player performances. Then, have students show the class how these statistics are calculated and why they are useful indicators of a team's or player's proficiency. Suggest that students prepare posters or transparencies to show their calculations.

Students may also enjoy evaluating sports statistics that appear in daily newspapers. Invite them to compare team statistics over a period of time to determine whether the team is becoming stronger or weaker.

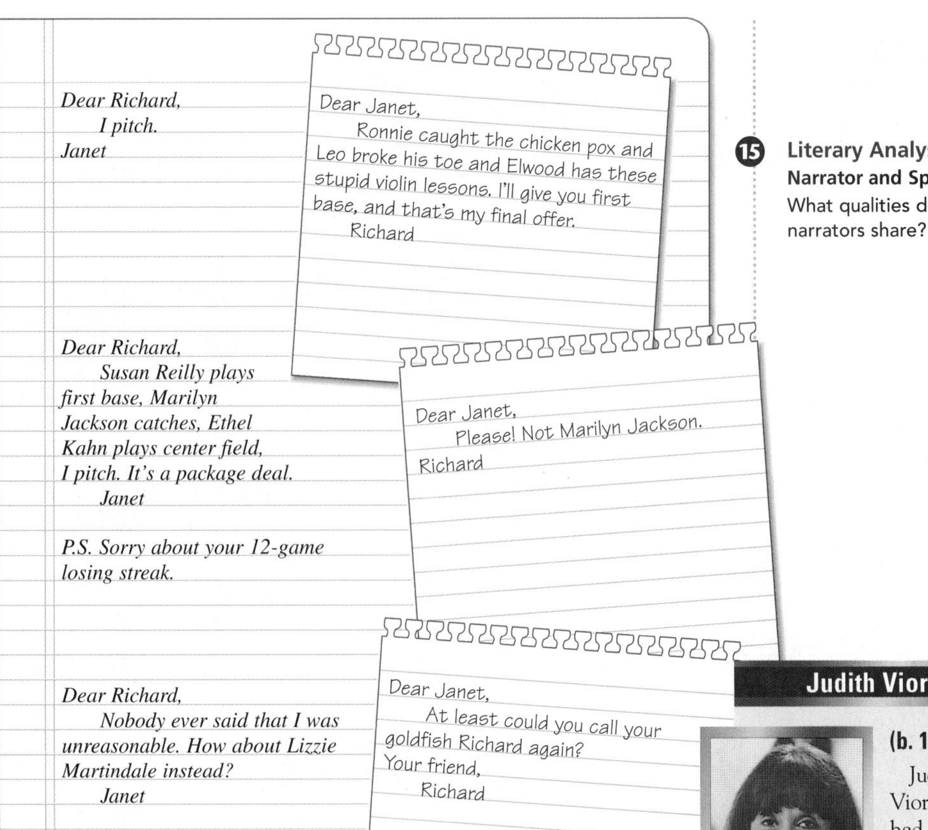

Dear Richard,
I pitch.
Janet

Dear Janet,
Ronnie caught the chicken pox and Leo broke his toe and Elwood has these stupid violin lessons. I'll give you first base, and that's my final offer.
Richard

Dear Richard,
Susan Reilly plays first base, Marilyn Jackson catches, Ethel Kahn plays center field, I pitch. It's a package deal.
Janet

P.S. Sorry about your 12-game losing streak.

Dear Janet,
Please! Not Marilyn Jackson.
Richard

Dear Richard,
Nobody ever said that I was unreasonable. How about Lizzie Martindale instead?
Janet

Dear Janet,
At least could you call your goldfish Richard again?
Your friend,
Richard

15 Literary Analysis
Narrator and Speaker
What qualities do the narrators share?

Judith Viorst

(b. 1931)

Judith Viorst has had some practice choosing her own way. Her first job was modeling in New York City. She always wanted to be a writer, though, and kept writing until she became a successful writer of stories and poetry for adults and children. Her three sons—Alexander, Nick, and Anthony—sometimes pop up as characters in her books. Choosing her own way, says Viorst, is an ongoing process. ". . . [You discover that] this is who you are and you trust that . . ."

Review and Assess

Thinking About the Selections

1. **(a) Recall:** In "The Southpaw," why is Janet angry at Richard? **(b) Analyze:** Using two examples, explain how each friend shows anger.
2. **(a) Recall:** What reason does Richard give for not including Janet on the team? **(b) Contrast:** How does his attitude change? **(c) Analyze:** Why does his attitude change?
3. **(a) Recall:** What position does Janet want to play? **(b) Infer:** What agreement do Janet and Richard reach about Janet's demands? **(c) Evaluate:** Explain why the arrrangement is fair to both sides or unfair to one side.

CUSTOMIZE INSTRUCTION FOR UNIVERSAL ACCESS

For Less Proficient Readers	For Advanced Readers
Point out that this story is written in letter format. Review the parts of a letter with students and have them determine whether these are business letters or friendly letters. Point out that letters using the friendly letter format can contain unfriendly messages. You may also want to comment on the use of postscripts as a way of adding messages to letters. Ask students to comment on the type of information Janet and Richard put into their postscripts. Have students write different postscripts that Janet and Richard could have used.	Both "Names/Nombres" and "The Southpaw" explore choosing your own way of becoming part of a group. In "Names/Nombres," Julia Alvarez is made to feel different because she is from another country. In "The Southpaw," Janet is excluded from a sport because she is a girl. Have students work as a group to compare and contrast Julia with Janet. Ask them to list ways that Julia and Janet try to fit in. Have students suggest additional ways in which the characters could fit in.

15 Literary Analysis

Narrator and Speaker

- Remind students that the two narrators are having a major disagreement. They are, however, good friends. Invite speculation on why they are such good friends.
  Answer: They have some interests in common, and they like each other.
- Ask the Literary Analysis question on p. 231: What qualities do the narrators share?
  Answer: They both enjoy baseball; they share clothes; they have other friends in common; they are both stubborn.

Monitor Progress Ask students to tell you the difference between the narrator and the author of a selection.
Answer: The narrator is the character in the story who is telling the story; the author, or writer, is the person who wrote the story.

Reteach If students cannot distinguish between the narrator and the author, review with them the selection opening on p. 223. Discuss the narrator/author difference in other selections they have read.

Review and Assess

1. **(a)** Janet is angry because Richard won't let her play baseball on his team. **(b)** Janet shows her anger with the words, "For all I care you can stand the whole way to school." Richard shows his anger when he says, "I hope when you go for your checkup you need a tetanus shot."
2. **(a)** Richard says that no girl has ever played on the team. **(b)** Richard shows an attitude change when he offers Janet a permanent place in the outfield. **(c)** His attitude changes because he needs players.
3. **(a)** Janet wants to pitch. **(b)** They come to a compromise. **(c)** It is fair because Richard lets Janet pitch, and Janet agrees not to choose Marilyn Jackson.

16 About the Selection

For the speaker in "Alone in the Nets," time seems to have frozen for a brief moment. The soccer goalie stands in place, watching the lead forward on the opposing team charge toward her, grinning. In the frozen moment, the goalie ruefully wonders why she put herself in this position. In the next instant, she sees that she can join the "moving world" to stop the forward from scoring. Carefully and fearlessly, the goalie prevents the goal and enjoys a brief moment of triumph before the game continues.

17 Background

Sports

Soccer, or "football" as it is called outside of the United States, is considered the most popular sport in the world. It is played in approximately 200 countries and has millions of fans. Soccer is played on a rectangular field, with two teams trying to kick the ball into the opponent's net, or goal. Only the player called the "goalie" is permitted to touch the ball with his or her hands; the other players may advance the ball with any part of their bodies except their hands.

16

Alone in the Nets

Arnold Adoff

17

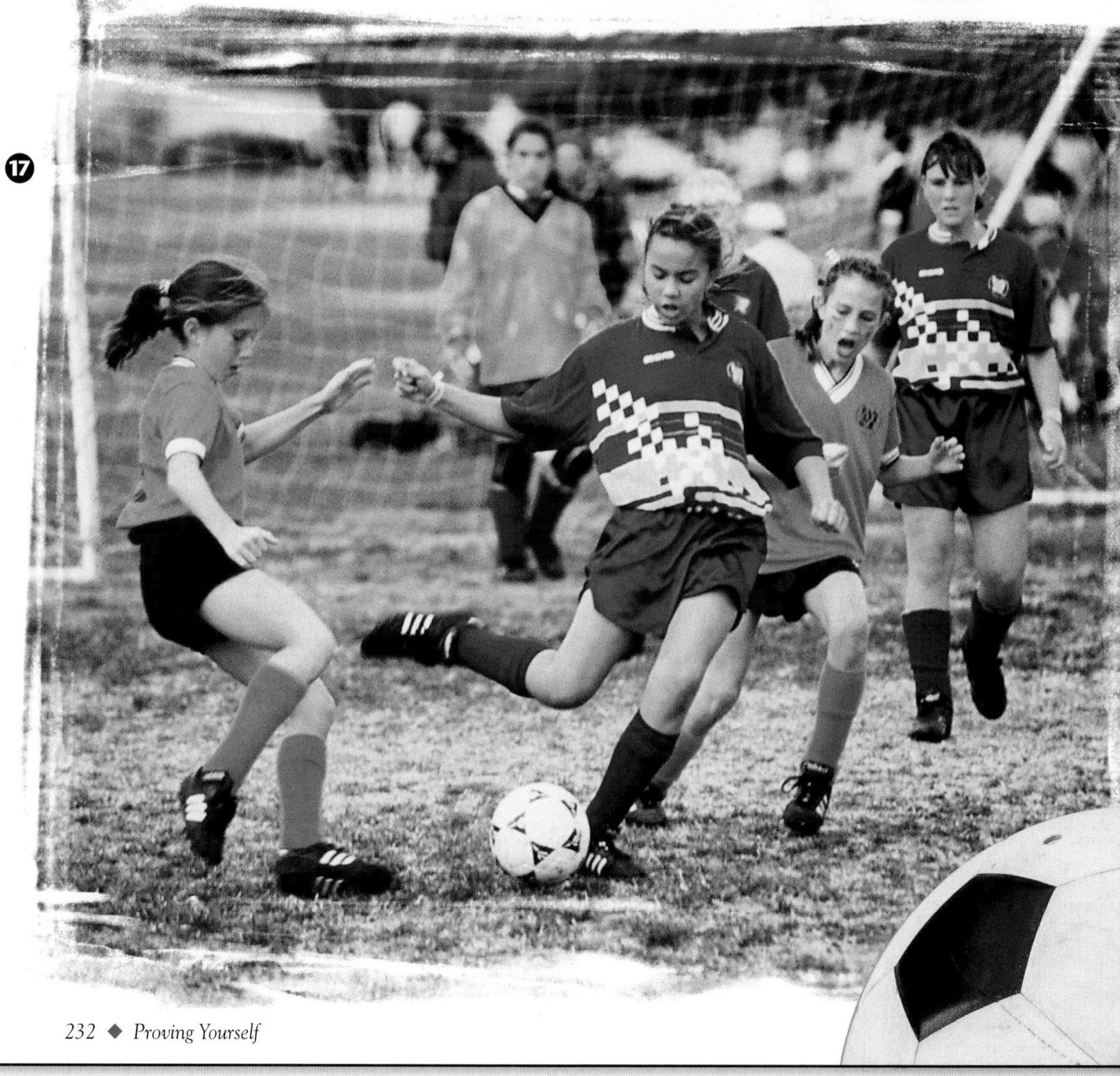

Alone in the Nets

I
am
alone of course,
in the nets, on this cold and raining afternoon,
and our best defending fullback
is lying on the wet ground out of position.
Half the opposition is pounding
down the field,
and their lead forward is gliding
so fast, she can just barely keep
the ball in front of her sliding
foot.
Her cleats are expensive.
and her hair b o u n c e s
neatly
like the after
girls in the shampoo commercials.
There is a big grin
on her face.
Now: In This Frozen Moment On This Moving World Through Space
is the right time to ask why am I here just standing
in my frozen place?
Why did I get up on time this morning?
Why did I get up at all?
Why did I listen to the coach and agree to play
this strange position in a r e a l game
in a strange town on this wet and moving world?
Why is it raining?
Why is it raining so h a r d?
Where
are all of our defenders?
Why do all of our players
do all of the falling
down?
Why am I here?
But Frozen Moments Can Unfreeze And I Can Stretch
and reach for the ball flying to the corner of
our
goal.

opposition (äp′ ə zish′ ən) *n.* here, the other team

20 **Reading Check**

What happens to the speaker when she sees the ball coming her way?

18 Reading Strategy

Setting a Purpose for Reading

- Ask students to read the title and look quickly at the selection. Ask: What kind of writing is this?
  Answer: This is a concrete poem about a sport.
- Ask: What might be a purpose for reading this selection?
  Answer: A purpose might be to read it for fun or to understand how a player feels about the sport.

19 Literary Analysis

Narrator and Speaker

- Ask a volunteer to read the poem all the way through. Give students a moment to note details that are clues about the narrator. Ask: Which details tell you something about the narrator?
  Answer: She is a girl who is the goalie on a soccer team. She notices her opponent's expensive shoes and bouncy hair. She has second thoughts about her skills, but she plays well.
- Ask: How is the narrator different from the writer of the poem?
  Answer: The poet is a man, and he probably doesn't play soccer with children.

20 Reading Check

Answer: The speaker reaches for the ball and makes the save for her team.

CUSTOMIZE INSTRUCTION FOR UNIVERSAL ACCESS

For Special Needs Students	For Less Proficient Readers	For Advanced Readers
You may wish to move to the playground or school gymnasium for this activity. Students may benefit from "walking" through the poem. Invite students to pantomime the speaker's part and those of other players. Encourage students to move as if they are playing, and permit props such as soccer balls, if feasible.	Have students read and discuss the poem with a partner. Then, have pairs work together to record the main idea and supporting details on a Sunburst organizer on p. 97 in **Writing Models and Graphic Organizers on Transparencies.** Encourage partners to share their organizers with other students.	Have students imagine that the poem was written to answer specific questions from the narrator's friend. As students read the selection, have them jot down questions that could have prompted the poem, such as "What do you think about when you are playing goalie?" Encourage students to share their questions with the class.

ASSESS

Answers for p. 234

Review and Assess

1. **Possible response:** I would tell the speaker to calm down and believe in herself because she is a good player.
2. **(a)** She is the goalie. **(b)** She is alone in the net and she is supposed to catch the ball.
3. **(a) Possible answers:** I think she is experienced because she knows to pace herself and is aware of how the other players are doing. Or, I think she is inexperienced because she doubts her abilities as a goalie. **(b) Possible answer:** She probably will, because most players are anxious during games.
4. **(a)** The poet captures the tension very well. **(b)** The lines that indicate her tension include when she is questioning herself, when the players are "pounding down the field," and when time is frozen.
5. **Possible response:** Advantages include a sense of pride and accomplishment, as shown at the end of the poem when the speaker catches the ball. Disadvantages include being nervous about how you perform, as shown when the speaker "freezes" as the ball comes toward her.

I can reach and jump
and dive into the s p a c e
between my out
stretched
hands
and the outside poles
of the nets.
My fears evaporate like my sweat in this chilling
breeze,
and I can move with this moving world
and pace my steps
like that old
movie
high
noon sheriff in his just
right
time.
That grinning forward gets her shot away too soon,
and I am there, on my own time, in the air,
to meet the ball,
and fall on it
for the save.
I wave my happy ending wave and get up.
The game goes on.

evaporate (i vap′ ə rāt′) *v.* disappear like vapor

Review and Assess

Thinking About the Selections

1. **Respond:** What advice would you give to the speaker of this poem?
2. **(a) Recall:** What position does the speaker play on the team? **(b) Support:** Which details indicate the position she plays?
3. **(a) Assess:** Do you think the speaker is an experienced player? Why or why not? **(b) Predict:** Will the speaker experience the same anxiety during every game? Explain.
4. **(a) Evaluate:** How well does the author of "Alone in the Nets" capture the tension of a goalie during a soccer game? **(b) Support:** What details indicate her tension?
5. **Evaluate:** What are some advantages and disadvantages to playing on an organized sports team? Use examples from the poem as well as from your own observations and experience.

Arnold Adoff

(b. 1935)

Poet, author, teacher, and lecturer, Arnold Adoff has been writing poetry since he was a boy! His own memories and his experiences as a teacher and a father help him understand the feelings and interests of young people. Adoff also benefits from the support of his wife, award-winning writer Virginia Hamilton.

ASSESSMENT PRACTICE: Reading Comprehension

Identifying the Main Idea (For more practice, see Test Preparation Workbook, p. 17.)

In many tests students will have to recognize the main idea of a passage. Encourage students to infer the main idea from the passage below:

> It took awhile to get used to my new names. I wondered if I shouldn't correct my teachers and new friends. But my mother argued that it didn't matter. "You know what your friend Shakespeare said, '*A rose by any other name would smell as sweet.*'"

What is the main idea of this passage?

A The speaker likes her new names.
B The speaker prefers her real name.
C The speaker can be herself no matter what she is called.
D The speaker must change her name because others cannot say her name.

A and *D* are not supported by the passage. *B* is a supporting detail. *C* is the correct answer.

Review and Assess

Literary Analysis

Narrator and Speaker

1. Which details indicate that the narrator of "Names/Nombres" is also the author?
2. Who are the narrators of "The Southpaw"?
3. Explain why "The Southpaw" would be more effective or less effective if it were told by just one of the two narrators or by a third-person narrator—one who does not participate in the story.
4. Who is the speaker of "Alone in the Nets"?
5. Explain how each of the narrators or speakers shapes your impression of the events in each selection.

Comparing Literary Works

6. Which two narrators or speakers are most similar? Explain.
7. Which two are most different? Explain.
8. What advice do you think Julia in "Names/Nombres" would have given to Janet in "The Southpaw"? Why?
9. What advice do you think Janet would have given to Julia? Why?

Reading Strategy

Setting a Purpose for Reading

10. On a chart like this one, record details from each selection that helped you achieve your purposes for reading.

Title	Purpose	Details
"Names/Nombres"		
"The Southpaw"		
"Alone in the Nets"		

11. Using details from the chart above, explain how setting a purpose increased your understanding of each selection.

Extending Understanding

12. **Media Connection:** Explain how a product's name can affect how people view that product.

Quick Review

The **narrator** or **speaker** is the one who tells the story or "says" the poem. To review narrator and speaker, see page 223.

Your **purpose for reading** is your reason.

Setting a purpose helps you focus your reading.

 ***Take It to the Net***

www.phschool.com

Take the interactive self-test online to check your understanding of these selections.

ENRICHMENT: Further Reading

Other Works by the Authors

Works by Julia Alvarez

Homecoming: New and Selected Poems

Works by Judith Viorst

The Alphabet from Z to A: With Much Confusion on the Way

If I Were in Charge of the World and Other Worries: Poems for Children and Their Parents

Works by Arnold Adoff

All the Colors of the Race

Sports Pages

 ***Take It to the Net***

Visit www.phschool.com for more information on the authors.

Answers for p. 235

Review and Assess

1. She wrote stories as a child, and she writes about how people mispronounced her name.
2. Richard and Janet are the narrators.
3. Possible response: It would be less effective because we would hear only one point of view.
4. The speaker is a goalie.
5. Possible responses: Since the speaker of "Names/Nombres" relates memories of her adolescence, students may relate to the events. Students may sympathize with both speakers in "Southpaw." The speaker of "Alone in the Nets" gives a first-person account of being a goalie.
6. Possible response: Janet and Richard enjoy baseball, are strong willed, and value friendship.
7. Possible response: Whereas Julia allows people to mispronounce her name, Janet confronts people when something bothers her.
8. Possible response: Julia avoids confrontation, so she might tell Janet to forget the baseball team.
9. Possible response: Janet is bold and would tell Julia to correct mispronunciations.
10. **"Names/Nombres" purpose:** to understand the immigrant experience; **details:** mispronunciations of names, classmates' reactions. **"The Southpaw" purpose:** to be entertained; **details:** Janet's threat to change her goldfish's name, Richard's suggestion that Janet take up knitting. **"Alone in the Nets" purpose:** to understand playing a demanding sport; **details:** rain, time standing still.
11. Possible response: In "Names/Nombres," the details about the narrator's life helped me understand an immigrant's life. In "The Southpaw," the friends' dispute was funny because of how they showed their anger. In "Alone in the Nets," the speaker's anxiety conveyed her pressure.
12. Possible response: A strange name can make consumers hesitant to buy.

EXTEND

Answers for p. 236

❶ Vocabulary Development

Word Analysis

1. move from one place to another
2. the sending of signals from one place to another
3. flights across the Atlantic Ocean

Spelling Strategy

You may not know it, but your name has a meaning. For example, if your name is Arthur, then your name means "great" or "noble." If your name is John, then you're "beloved." You're also sharing a name with Ian and Sean. These names are other versions of your name.

Fluency: Complete the Sentences

1. transport
2. inevitably
3. chaotic
4. inscribed
5. evaporate
6. opposition

❷ Grammar

1. Our names changed almost immediately.
2. Our goodbyes went on too long.
3. My heritage was never more apparent.
4. You don't think I'm good enough to play.
5. They settled their conflict, but not swiftly.

Writing Application

1. I was *extremely* afraid we were late.
2. They are *too* crowded.
3. Janet pitched *very* fast.

Integrate Language Skills

❶ Vocabulary Development Lesson

Word Analysis: Latin Prefix *trans-*

The Latin prefix *trans-* means "over, through, or across." Define the italicized words below.

1. Ships *transport* immigrants across the ocean.
2. The radio *transmission* was unclear.
3. *Transatlantic* flights are long.

Spelling Strategy

Your shows belonging, as in "*your* sweater." *You're* is the contraction for *you are*, as in "*You're* a good friend." Copy the following passage. Proofread for misspelled *you're* and *your*.

You may not know it, but your name has a meaning. For example, if you're name is Arthur, then your name means "great" or "noble." If you're name is John, then youre "beloved." Your also sharing a name with Ian and Sean. These names are other versions of you're name.

Fluency: Complete the Sentences

Write these sentences, filling in the blanks with the correct vocabulary words from the list on page 223.

1. The ship will __?__ passengers from island to island.
2. With an ace pitcher on the mound, the Sluggers __?__ won the championship.
3. The long lines made the lobby seem __?__.
4. The watch with my initials __?__ on the back is missing.
5. In this heat, the water will __?__ quickly.
6. We hoped to defeat the __?__.

❷ Grammar Lesson

Adverbs Modifying Adjectives and Adverbs

An **adverb** modifies—or describes—a verb, an adjective (a word that modifies a noun), or another adverb. *Almost, too, so, very, quite, rather, usually, much,* and *more* are some adverbs that modify adjectives and other adverbs.

Adverb	Modifies the word	Answers the question
The trip is *too* long.	*long* (adjective)	*To what extent?*
He walks *very* quickly.	*quickly* (adverb)	*How?*

Practice Write the following sentences. Underline each adverb and draw an arrow to the word it modifies.

1. Our names changed almost immediately.
2. Our goodbyes went on too long.
3. My heritage was never more apparent.
4. You don't think I'm good enough to play.
5. They settled their conflict, but not swiftly.

Writing Application To each sentence, add an adverb that answers the question in parentheses.

1. I was afraid we were late. (*How afraid?*)
2. They are crowded. (*To what extent?*)
3. Janet pitched fast. (*How fast?*)

WG *Prentice Hall Writing and Grammar Connection: Chapter 16, Section 2*

TEACHING RESOURCES

The following resources can be used to enrich or extend the instruction for pp. 236–237.

Vocabulary

Selection Support: Build Vocabulary, p. 71
Build Spelling Skills, p. 72 ■

Vocabulary and Spelling Practice Book
(Use this booklet for skills enrichment)

Grammar

Selection Support: Build Grammar Skills, p. 73

Writing and Grammar, Copper Level, p. 340 ■

Daily Language Practice Transparencies ■

Writing

Writing and Grammar, Copper Level, p. 230 ■

Writing Models and Graphic Organizers on Transparencies, p. 97

Writing and Grammar iText CD-ROM

■ **BLOCK SCHEDULING:** Resources marked with this symbol provide varied instruction during 90-minute blocks.

❸ Writing Lesson

Sports Scene

The form of writing you choose often depends as much on your purpose as on your topic. Because Arnold Adoff's purpose is to capture the goalie's thoughts, he writes a poem with the goalie as the speaker. Choose a different purpose. Then, write about the topic of the poem in a form that suits this different purpose.

Prewriting List possible purposes for writing. Choose one. Then, decide on the best form for achieving your purpose. Some common purposes and forms are suggested below.

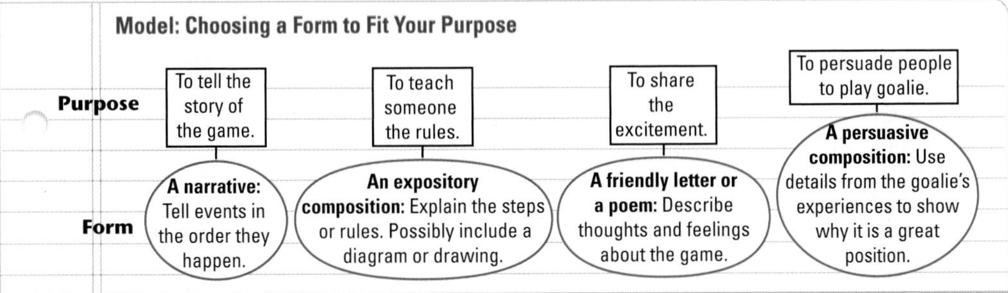

Model: Choosing a Form to Fit Your Purpose
Purpose
To tell the story of the game.
To teach someone the rules.
To share the excitement.
To persuade people to play goalie.
Form
A narrative: Tell events in the order they happen.
An expository composition: Explain the steps or rules. Possibly include a diagram or drawing.
A friendly letter or a poem: Describe thoughts and feelings about the game.
A persuasive composition: Use details from the goalie's experiences to show why it is a great position.

Drafting Consult the Writing Handbook on page R13 to learn more about the form of writing you have chosen. Then, as you write, focus on including details appropriate to your purpose and form.

Revising Delete details that do not help you achieve your writing purpose.

WG Prentice Hall Writing and Grammar Connection: Chapter 11, Section 3

❹ Extension Activities

Listening and Speaking Invite a coach to your class to explain how to swing a bat, kick a soccer ball, or make a free throw. After the coach speaks, work in small groups to prepare instructional presentations of your own. **Give directions and demonstrate** the skill.

1. Restate the directions.
2. Demonstrate each step.
3. Use and explain any key terms.
4. Finish by summarizing any tips the coach gave for effective practice or drill.

Research and Technology In a group, prepare a **presentation** on the political and economic factors that caused Julia's family to leave the Dominican Republic.

Writing Before 1974, girls were not allowed to play with boys on Little League teams. Write a short **essay** explaining whether or not you think this rule was a good one.

 ***Take It to the Net*** www.phschool.com

Go online for an additional research activity using the Internet.

ASSESSMENT RESOURCES

The following resources can be used to assess students' knowledge and skills.

Selection Assessment

- **Formal Assessment,** pp. 59–61
- **Open Book Test,** pp. 43–45
- **Got It! Assessment Videotapes,** Tape 2
- **Test Bank Software**

Visit www.phschool.com for self-tests and additional questions on the selections.

Listening and Speaking Rubric

- **Performance Assess. and Portfolio Mgmt.,** p. 21

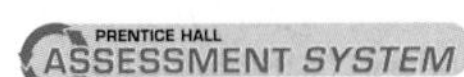

 **Workbook**
 **Transparencies**
 **Skill Book**
 **CD-ROM**

Lesson Support for p. 237

❸ Writing Lesson

- Explain to students that an author's purpose is as important as the topic in determining the form that the writing will take. To illustrate this, ask how "Alone in the Nets" would be different if it were a newspaper report about a soccer game.
- Tell students to consider their purpose as they choose forms for writing.
- Use the Writing Lesson to help students select a purpose and a form for their writing.

❹ Listening and Speaking

- Have a physical education teacher, coach, or local expert show students how to perform an athletic skill. You may wish to invite several such experts to provide a variety in presentations.
- Divide the class into small groups. Invite each group to choose a skill to demonstrate. Allow time for practice.
- Encourage students to include guidelines for warming up and cooling down exercises, if appropriate.
- As groups make their presentations, encourage listeners to take notes so they can try these skills later.
- As students learn the new skills, you may wish to have them use the Listening rubric on p. 21 in **Performance Assessment and Portfolio Management.**

CUSTOMIZE INSTRUCTION For Universal Access

To address different learning styles, use the activities suggested in the **Extension Activities** booklet, p. 15.

- For Visual/Spatial Learners, use Activity 5.
- For Logical/Mathmatical Learners, use Activity 6.
- For Interpersonal and Verbal/Linguistic Learners, use Activity 7.

Lesson Objectives

1. To understand the connection between past and present views of women in sports
2. To appreciate the contributions of early women athletes

Connections

We take many women's sporting events for granted. There was a time, however, when women's sports did not have the support that they have today. Have students reread "The Southpaw" (p. 229) and "Alone in the Nets" (p. 232) after they have read about women and sports. Have students compare the characters in those selections with the women described here.

Women in Sports

- If possible, show videotapes of women athletes or distribute magazine articles about women's achievements in sports. As students use these media, point out the training and conditioning necessary for anyone to achieve greatness in a sport.
- Invite students to read aloud the biographical information about the women achievers. Note that women athletes have proved themselves as both individual achievers and as team players. They also serve as models for young people who are interested in sports and fitness.

Answers

Connecting Literature and Culture

1. The speaker in "Alone in the Nets" would like to meet Tisha Venturini because they share an interest in soccer.
2. Janet would probably want to meet Nancy Lopez, because Lopez was an athlete at a young age, just as Janet is. She might also want to meet Rebecca Lobo or Tisha Venturini because they play team sports, just as Janet does.
3. Students should be able to support their choices with information from the text.
4. Possible responses: Students may suggest print resources, such as encylopedias, and Internet resources, such as sports Web sites.

CONNECTIONS

Literature and Culture

Women in Sports

Both "The Southpaw" and "Alone in the Nets" present girls in active athletic roles, which many people take for granted today. However, in the United States as recently as 1971, only one in twenty-seven girls participated in high-school varsity sports. Today, one out of every three girls participates. The following athletes are just a few of the women who have earned a place in sports history.

Babe Didrickson In the Olympics of 1932, Babe Didrickson entered three competitions, setting a world record and winning two gold medals. She then went on to become a golfing legend, winning seventeen tournaments in a row. She was one of the founders of the Ladies Professional Golf Association in 1949. The LPGA exists to this day.

Wilma Rudolph In 1960, Wilma Rudolph became the first African American female athlete to set a world record in the 200 meters during the Olympic trials. In the Olympics, she became the first American woman to win three gold medals in track.

Nancy Lopez Lopez grew up in New Mexico, where her father taught her to play golf when she was eight years old. She became a national celebrity in 1978 when she won the LPGA National Championship.

Rebecca Lobo Basketball player Rebecca Lobo was the youngest member of the 1996 Olympic women's basketball team. She went on to play professional basketball, and contributed to her team's success and the sport's popularity. With her mother, she has co-written an autobiography called *Home Team*.

Tisha Venturini Along with her teammates, including Mia Hamm, soccer player Tisha Venturini won a gold medal at the 1996 Olympics. She scored two of the goals that helped the team win the game. A California native, she has a degree in physical education.

Connecting Literature and Culture

1. Which athlete do you think the speaker in "Alone in the Nets" would want to meet? Why?
2. Which athlete do you think Janet in "The Southpaw" would want to meet? Why?
3. Which athlete would you like to meet? Why?
4. What resources could you use to find out more information about these athletes or their sports?

ENRICHMENT: Social Studies Connection

Women in the Olympics

The first woman to win an Olympic championship was Princess Kyniska of Sparta; she won the chariot race in 396 B.C.

When the modern Olympics were instituted in 1896, women were not permitted to participate. Although modern Olympic founder Pierre Coubertin believed that participating in sports helped develop important values in students, he opposed the participation of women in the games. Therefore, no women participated in the 1896 games.

Slowly, however, women gained a foothold in Olympic competition. In the 1900 games, women competed in golf and tennis. Twelve years later, women participated in swimming and diving. Women athletes were permitted in Olympic gymnastics in 1928, the same year that marked their entry into track and field competitions.

Today, women are well-represented in international competition: approximately half of the competing athletes are women.

READING INFORMATIONAL MATERIALS

Applications

About Applications

The purpose of an application is to provide specific information requested by a group or organization that will make a decision based on that information. At one time or another, you will probably fill out an application for one or more of the following reasons:

- to get a library card
- to get a job
- to be admitted to a school
- to open a savings account
- to join a club or sports league
- to get a driver's license

When preparing applications, read carefully to find out what information is needed, when and where the application should be turned in, and what, if any, other documents, payments, or paperwork should be included with the application.

Reading Strategy

Following Multiple-Step Directions

Applications often have **multiple-step directions**— instructions that have several steps or parts that must be done before the application is complete. On some applications, these directions are numbered and written in sentences. On other applications, the "directions" consist of brief labels that indicate what information is to be provided in each section.

To successfully complete multi-step directions on an application, preview and review the text and the form.

- **Preview** Before you begin following the directions to fill out the application, make sure you can answer the questions listed in the chart at the right.
- **Review** After you have filled out the application, review it. Check that you have completed all the necessary sections and that the information is legible, or readable.

Previewing an Application

1. What information is being asked for?
2. On which line or in which space is the information to be placed?
3. Does the information need to be typed, printed, or entered electronically?
4. Are there any places where I am not supposed to write?
5. What important dates do I need to know?
6. What do I need to include with the application?
7. What do I do with the completed application?

Lesson Objectives

1. To learn how to follow multiple-step directions
2. To analyze the purpose and features of applications

About Applications

- Invite a volunteer to read "About Applications" aloud. Then, discuss the types of situations that require applications. Ask students why applications are necessary. Possible response: Applications are necessary to commit to an activity or an organization that requires specific rules and procedures.
- Ask students why agencies, businesses, and organizations need information about their applicants. Possible response: Agencies, businesses, and organizations need information on applications to verify applicants' eligibility.

Reading Strategy

Following Multiple-Step Directions

- Have students read the information about following multiple-step directions.
- Discuss why some application forms are only part of the application process. Ask why additional materials may be needed. Possible responses: You might have to include money to pay for an activity, or you might need documents to prove your age or to fulfill another requirement.
- Review the "Previewing an Application" list. Explain that applications vary depending upon their purpose, so it is important to find out what every application requires.

Library Card Application

- Explain that students will need to fill out a library card application the first time they want to check out a book at their local library.
- Point out that it is important to review all application forms before filling them out. Becoming familiar with the application process will help students obtain these services with a minimum of difficulty.
- Have students read the application and the notes that accompany it.
- Ask students why an applicant should read the information at the top of the application form. **Answer:** Applicants should read the information at the top of the form to find out what else may be required when submitting the application.
- Point out to students that applications are kept on file in an agency (in this case, a library). Applications often have space for the agency's notes. Therefore, applicants should leave any blank spaces that contain phrases such as "Staff Use" or "Department Use" on an application.
- Discuss the need for references. Ask students why a library would ask for references. **Answer:** Libraries need references to determine that the applicant is trustworthy enough to borrow and return books.

VILLA PARK PUBLIC LIBRARY

Library Card Application

To obtain a Villa Park Public Library card, you will need to bring the following to the Library:

- Two forms of identification with your Villa Park address (one of which includes a photograph).
- An application form, which must be signed at the Library's circulation desk.
- If you are under the age of 18, you will also need a parent to sign the form at the Library's circulation desk.
- For Oakbrook Terrace residents, a certificate of residence from the City of Oakbrook Terrace (available at the City Clerk's office).
- Other non-residents must pay a fee for a library card.

These lines tell you what else you need to supply when you submit your application.

STAFF USE **Expiration**

Date: ______________ **Spec Designation** ______________
OBT—1/4ly—Family Fee

Name typed ______________________________
Last, First, MI

New - Renew - Ex Rew

Do not write in spaces marked "Office Use" or "Staff Use" or "Department Use."

REGISTRATION WORKSHEET

Today's Date ______________

Name ______________________________
Please Print First, Middle Initial, Last

Address ______________________________
Street City, State, Zip Code

Phone Number ______________ Social Security Number______________

Reference ______________ Phone Number ______________

Address ______________________________
Street City, State, Zip Code

Business Name ______________ Phone Number ______________

Business Address ______________________________
Street City, State, Zip Code

Date of Birth (if under 18) ______________

A *reference* is an adult who will give you a recommendation—a statement saying they think you are responsible enough to have your application approved. Ask for permission before using someone's name as a reference.

The lines below must be signed in person at the Library's circulation desk:

I agree to be responsible for all materials checked out on my library card and fines and fees accrued.

Signed______________________

If person signing this application is under 18, a parent's signature is needed.

I am responsible for all materials checked out on my child's library card and fines and fees accrued.

______________________ ______________________
Please Print Parent's Name Parent's Signature

Watch for specific directions that tell you when and where a step must be completed.

CUSTOMIZE INSTRUCTION FOR UNIVERSAL ACCESS

For Less Proficient Readers	For Gifted/Talented Students
Some students may benefit from visualizing the steps in the application process. Make a copy of the Series of Events Chain organizer on p. 69 in **Writing Models and Graphic Organizers on Transparencies.** Use the library card application on this page for this exercise. Have students write "preview the application" in the *Beginning Event* box, "fill in the application" in the second box, "review and submit the application" in the third box, and "receive the library card" in the *Final Outcome* box.	Ask students to prepare a dramatization about completing the application process. They can use one of the applications from this selection, obtain one from another organization, or make up one of their own. Have students enlarge the application form or project it so the audience can see it. Then, they should have a model applicant go through the application process. Other students can act as references and employees who process applications.

SAVINGS ACCOUNT APPLICATION

Simply complete this short form to start your application process.

1. What type of account would you like to open?

- ❑ Young Investors' Club
- ❑ Statement Savings
- ❑ Holiday Savings

2. Would you like Internet banking?

❑ Yes ❑ No

3. Provide the following information. (Please print.)

Name ______________________________

E-Mail ______________________________

Street Address ______________________________

Address (cont.) ______________________________

City ____________ State ____ Zip code ______

Work Phone ______________________________

Home Phone ______________________________

4. Today's Date [| | | | |] mm/dd/yy

5. Initial Deposit Amount ____________________

You must make an initial deposit as required by the type of savings account you are opening.

6. Date of Birth [| | | | |] mm/dd/yy

Social Security Number ____________________

Signature ______________________________

These lines require a choice to be made. If you do not understand the choices on an application, ask someone. Do not leave choices blank.

Here, specific directions are given for how information is to be entered.

If the application asks for information in a category that does not apply to you, such as a work phone number, write N/A. N/A stands for *not applicable.*

When boxes are provided, write one letter or numeral in each box. The label *mm/dd/yy* indicates that you should write the month, date, and year. Write the number of the month, not the letters. Use a 0 before any single digit numbers. Use the last two numerals of the year. For example, March 5, 2002 would be written as [0|3|0|5|0|2].

Savings Account Application

- Tell students that banks and other financial institutions need information about their customers. When students want to open accounts with banks, they will need to fill out application forms like this one.
- Have students read the application form and the notes that accompany it.
- Point out that the first item asks the applicant about the type of account desired. An applicant who is not certain what kinds of accounts these are should ask a bank employee before filling out this part of the application.
- Ask students whether they should leave any questions blank that do not apply to them.
  Answer: No, they should write *N/A,* which means "not applicable."
- Emphasize that students should write legibly, even in small spaces. Ask what might happen if a birth date or a social security number cannot be read.
  Possible responses: The application might be rejected; the bank would have incorrect information, which could make bank reports to the government incorrect.

Roller Hockey Registration Form

- Point out to students that sports teams often require registration forms. Registration forms are very much like application forms.
- Instruct students to read the registration form and the notes next to it.
- Call attention to the deadline for the application. Ask students why such deadlines are necessary for sports programs.
  Answer: Deadlines are necessary so that the teams can be organized and ready when the season begins.
- Next, discuss the equipment list. Ask: What does *mandatory* mean?
  Answer: *Mandatory* means "required."
- Then, ask why equipment is mandatory.
  Answer: Equipment is mandatory to protect participants and to be certain that everyone is ready to play.
- Ask students why the paragraph beginning "The player listed above . . ." is included in the form.
  Answer: A parent or guardian needs to sign the form and give consent for the child to play roller hockey. By signing, the parent or guardian also agrees that the team will not be responsible for any injuries to the child.

Deadlines indicate the date after which the application will not be accepted. Other important dates are also indicated here.

This list indicates what players will be expected to purchase if they are accepted to the program. The word *mandatory* means required.

These lines indicate that there is more than one acceptable way to submit your application.

In this section, the lines are labeled to indicate what information you should provide in each space. The abbreviation DOB stands for Date of Birth.

PASADENA YOUTH ROLLER HOCKEY REGISTRATION FORM

REGISTRATION DEADLINE APRIL 6, 2002
COST $75.00 ($65.00 IF YOU REGISTER BY APRIL 6, 2002)

Player Tryout & Draft: **Saturday, April 6, 2002**
League Starts: **Thursday, April 18, 2002**

EQUIPMENT NEEDED:
Skates—In-line or Regular Quad
Helmet—MANDATORY with full face mask or shield. No Goalie Helmet
Stick—Regulation hockey stick, preferred to be no higher than nose
Gloves—Regulation hockey gloves
Elbow Pads/Shin Guards—Recommended, but not Mandatory

ALL EQUIPMENT NEEDS ARE AVAILABLE AT THE PASADENA ROLLER RINK, USUALLY CHEAPER THAN OR EQUAL TO ATHLETIC STORE PRICES.

TO REGISTER—MAIL YOUR FORM(S) TO 4100 JANA LN, PASADENA, TX 77505 OR COME BY THE PASADENA ROLLER RINK AT 2602 CHERRYBROOK, PASADENA, TX.

PASADENA YOUTH ROLLER HOCKEY LEAGUE
Registration Form, 4100 Jana Ln, Pasadena, TX 77505
REGISTRATION DEADLINE APRIL 6, 2002

PLAYER'S NAME__________________ AGE ______ DOB _____

ADDRESS____________________ CITY __________ ZIP _____

PARENTS' NAME (Mom)______________(Dad)_______________

PHONE NUMBER (____)_____________ SHIRT SIZE ________

The player listed above has my permission to participate in this activity. I understand that the Pasadena Roller Rink and the Pasadena Youth Hockey League do not provide insurance and are not responsible for accident coverage.

PARENT'S SIGNATURE___________________ DATE __/__/__

Check Your Comprehension

1. What is a reference?
2. What does *mm/dd/yy* stand for?
3. Which of the following pieces of equipment are *required* to play roller hockey? (a) shin guards (b) helmets (c) gloves

Applying the Reading Strategy

Following Multiple-Step Directions

4. What documents do you need to submit with a library card application?
5. What questions would you ask before choosing the type of savings account you would like to open?
6. What do you do with your completed registration form for youth roller hockey?
7. Choose one of the applications and write the answers to the Preview the Application questions on p. 239.

Activity

Complete Applications

Obtain from local groups or organizations an application for at least two of the following:

- a volunteer organization
- a checking account
- a health club
- a job in a store

Fill out the applications. Make a list of the documents you will need to provide, fees you will need to pay, and deadlines you will need to meet.

Comparing and Contrasting Informational Materials

Types of Applications

Make a chart like the one shown. Complete each section to find the similarities and differences in the different applications. Add a column to include one of the applications from the activity.

	Library Card	Savings Account	Roller Hockey
Is identification required?			
Are references required?			
Does the application need to be signed by anyone other than the applicant?			
Can the application be mailed in?			
Is your birthday required?			
Is your address required?			
Is money required?			

Answers for p. 243

Check Your Comprehension

1. A reference is an adult who will recommend the applicant.
2. *Mm/dd/yy* stands for the date: *mm* stands for the two numbers that identify the month; *dd* stands for the day of the month; *yy* stands for the last two digits of the year.
3. Helmets are mandatory for roller hockey.

Applying the Reading Strategy

4. An applicant for a library card needs to submit two forms of identification (one with a picture) and an extra form if the applicant is a resident of Oakbrook Terrace.
5. Possible responses: "What are the differences between the types of accounts?"; "Which account pays a higher interest?"
6. The applicant can mail the completed form to a specific address or drop it off at the roller rink.
7. Be sure that students thoroughly answer every Previewing an Application question for whichever application they choose.

Activity

Depending upon the availability of application forms in your community, you may wish to obtain application forms and copy them, rather than having students get the forms. Have students work in groups to compare the requirements for at least two of the applications. After students have recorded similarities and questions, lead a class discussion about the differences, and answer student questions about the applications.

Comparing and Contrasting Informational Materials

	Card	Account	Hockey
identification?	yes	no	no
references?	yes	no	no
signed?	yes	no	yes
mailed?	no	no	yes
birthday?	yes	yes	yes
address?	yes	yes	yes
money?	no	yes	yes

Adventures of Isabel ✦ I'll Stay ✦ Dream Dust ✦ Wilbur Wright and Orville Wright

Lesson Objectives

1. **To analyze and respond to literary elements**
   - Literary Analysis: Stanzas
   - Comparing Literary Works
2. **To read, comprehend, analyze, and critique four poems**
   - Reading Strategy: Interpreting Meaning
   - Reading Check Questions
   - Review and Assess Questions
   - Assessment Practice (ATE)
3. **To develop word analysis skills, fluency, and systematic vocabulary**
   - Vocabulary Development Lesson: Word Analysis: Latin Suffix *-ous*
4. **To understand and apply written and oral language conventions**
   - Spelling Strategy
   - Grammar Lesson: Adjective or Adverb?
5. **To understand and apply appropriate writing and research strategies**
   - Writing Lesson: Response to a Poem
   - Extension Activity: Timeline
6. **To understand and apply listening and speaking strategies**
   - Extension Activity: Interview

STEP-BY-STEP TEACHING GUIDE	PACING GUIDE
PRETEACH	
Motivate Students and Provide Background	
Use the Motivation activity (ATE p. 244)	5 min.
Read and discuss the Preview material and Background information (SE/ATE p. 244) [A]	10 min.
Introduce the Concepts	
Introduce the Literary Analysis and Reading Strategy (SE/ATE p. 245) [A]	15 min.
Pronounce the vocabulary words and read their definitions (SE p. 245)	5 min.
TEACH	
Monitor Comprehension	
Informally monitor comprehension by circulating while students read independently or in groups [A]	5–10 min.
Monitor students' comprehension with the Reading Check notes (SE/ATE p. 249)	as students read
Develop vocabulary with Vocabulary notes (SE pp. 246, 248)	as students read
Develop Understanding	
Develop students' understanding of stanzas with the Literary Analysis annotations (SE p. 248; ATE p. 248) [A]	5 min.
Develop students' ability to use context to interpret meaning with the Reading Strategy annotations (SE p. 249; ATE pp. 247, 249)	5 min.
ASSESS	
Assess Mastery	
Assess students' mastery of the Reading Strategy and Literary Analysis by having them answer the Review and Assess questions (SE/ATE p. 251)	15 min.
Use one or more of the print and media Assessment Resources (ATE p. 253) [A]	up to 45 min.
EXTEND	
Apply Understanding	
Have students complete the Vocabulary Development Lesson and the Grammar Lesson (SE p. 252) [A]	20 min.
Apply students' ability to write a response to a poem using the Writing Lesson (SE/ATE p. 253) [A]	30–45 min.
Apply students' understanding using one or more of the Extension Activities (SE p. 253)	20–90 min.

ACCELERATED INSTRUCTION:
Use the strategies and activities identified with an [A].

UNIVERSAL ACCESS
● = Below Level Students
▲ = On-Level Students
■ = Above Level Students

Time and Resource Manager

Reading Level: Average, Easy, Challenging, Average
Average Number of Instructional Days: 3

RESOURCES		
PRINT	**TRANSPARENCIES**	**TECHNOLOGY**
• **Beyond Literature,** Workplace Skills: Keys to Success, p. 16 ▲ ■		• **Interest Grabber Videotapes,** Tape 2 ● ▲ ■
• **Selection Support Workbook:** ● ▲ ■ Literary Analysis, p. 80 Reading Strategy, p. 79 Build Vocabulary, p. 76	• **Literary Analysis and Reading Transparencies,** pp. 31 and 32 ● ▲ ■	
		• **Listening to Literature** ● ▲ ■ Audiocassettes, Side 11 Audio CDs, CD 4
• **Literatura en español** ● ▲ • **Literary Analysis for Enrichment** ■	• **Fine Art Transparencies, Volume 1,** Transparency 18 ● ▲ ■	
• **Formal Assessment:** Selection Test, pp. 62–64 ● ▲ ■ • **Open Book Test,** pp. 46–48 ● ▲ ■ • **Performance Assessment and Portfolio Management,** p. 15, 29 ● ▲ ■ • Prentice Hall Assessment System ● ▲ ■	• Prentice Hall Assessment System ● ▲ ■ Skills Practice Answers and Explanations on Transparencies	• **Test Bank Software** ● ▲ ■ • **Got It! Assessment Videotapes,** Tape 2 ● ▲
• **Selection Support Workbook:** ● ▲ ■ Build Spelling Skills, p. 77 Build Grammar Skills, p. 78 • **Writing and Grammar,** Copper Level ● ▲ ■ • **Extension Activities,** p. 16 ● ▲ ■	• **Daily Language Practice Transparencies** ● ▲ • **Writing Models and Graphic Organizers on Transparencies** ● ▲ ■	• **Writing and Grammar iText CD-ROM** ● ▲ ■ *Take It to the Net* www.phschool.com

BLOCK SCHEDULING: Use one 90-minute class period to preteach the selection and have students read it. Use a second 90-minute class period to assess students' mastery of skills and have them complete one of the Extension Activities.

PRETEACH

Step-by-Step Teaching Guide for pp. 244–245

Motivation

Ask students to imagine themselves doing something extraordinary now or later in their lives that requires confidence and determination. Have them write newspaper headlines that describe their extraordinary accomplishments. You may want to write headlines such as these on the board to spark students' imaginations:

- Sports phenomenon Jimmy Bynum swims across the Atlantic Ocean!
- Dr. Alicia Cantoe discovers cure for cancer!
- World-famous actor Timitra Briggs wins an Academy Award!

Tell students that these poems tell of confident people who pursue their dreams.

Interest Grabber Video

As an alternative, play "The History of Aviation" on Tape 2 to engage student interest.

❶ Background

Science

The third poem in this grouping is called "Wilbur Wright and Orville Wright." The Wright brothers were bicycle makers and printers who lived in Dayton, Ohio. When they were young, they were fascinated by machines, engineering, and mathematics. The Wrights invented the first successful self-propelled heavier-than-air plane. After winning a coin toss, Wilbur attempted the first flight, but he stalled. Orville took the next turn and flew.

Prepare to Read

❶ Adventures of Isabel ◆ I'll Stay
Wilbur Wright and Orville Wright ◆ Dream Dust

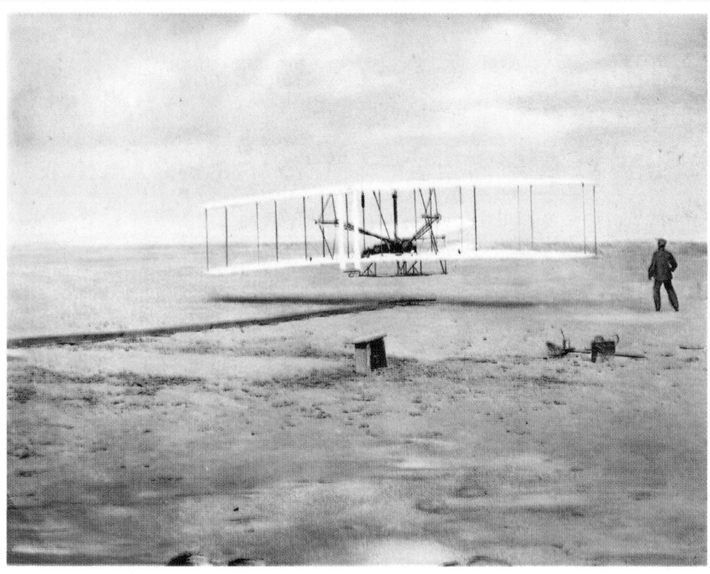

The Granger Collection, New York

Take It to the Net

Visit www.phschool.com for interactive activities and instruction related to these selections, including

- background
- graphic organizers
- literary elements
- reading strategies

Preview

Connecting to the Literature

The poems in this group describe success—real and imagined, small and large. Connect to the poems by considering how you feel on an "up" day—a day when you have achieved something or feel as if you could take on any challenge.

Background

"Wilbur Wright and Orville Wright," by Rosemary and Stephen Vincent Benét, tells the story of a success that affected the course of history. The Wright brothers, who spent years experimenting with gliders, flew the first power-driven, heavier-than-air machine on December 17, 1903, near Kitty Hawk, North Carolina. Their plane flew 120 feet and was in the air for twelve seconds.

TEACHING RESOURCES

The following resources can be used to enrich or extend the instruction for pp. 244–245.

Motivation

Interest Grabber Video, Tape 2

Background

Beyond Literature, p. 16

Take It to the Net

Visit www.phschool.com for Background and hotlinks for the selections.

Literary Analysis

Literary Analysis and Reading Transparencies, Stanzas, p. 32

Selection Support: Literary Analysis, p. 80

Reading

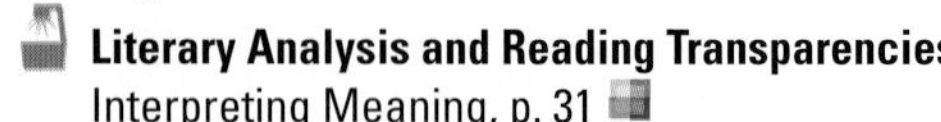

Literary Analysis and Reading Transparencies, Interpreting Meaning, p. 31

BLOCK SCHEDULING: Resources marked with this symbol provide varied instruction during 90-minute blocks.

❷ Literary Analysis

Stanzas

A **stanza** is a group of lines of poetry that are usually similar in length and pattern and are separated by spaces. A stanza is like a paragraph of poetry—it develops one main idea. Poets use stanzas to organize their ideas, and they sometimes break from a stanza-pattern to emphasize certain ideas.

Comparing Literary Works

Two of the poems you are about to read have regular stanzas. One has stanzas of irregular length; the other consists of single lines, not stanzas. As you read, use the following focus questions to help you compare and contrast the four poets' different uses—or lack of use—of stanzas.

1. Which two poems have the most regular stanzas?
2. What is the effect of not having regular stanzas?

❸ Reading Strategy

Interpreting Meaning

Interpreting the meaning of words is going beyond the pronunciation and expected meaning to figure out what is really meant. When you read these and other works, look for the following types of words that can cause confusion or misinterpretation:

- **Figurative language:** Words and phrases that are not meant to be read literally. For example, if a poet writes, "She was a rock," he or she is trying to convey that the person was strong.
- **Words with multiple meanings:** Words that can be used to mean different things in different situations. For example, the word *trying* often means "attempting." In the following lines, however, it means something else.

  "These birds are very trying.
  I'm sick of hearing them cheep-cheep . . ."

Because the speaker of the poem is sick of listening to the birds, you can figure out that trying means "annoying."

As you read, use a graphic organizer like this one to identify and interpret figurative language and words with multiple meanings.

Multiple Meaning → Clues → Meaning

Figurative Language → Clues → Meaning

Vocabulary Development

ravenous (rav´ ə nəs´) *adj.* greedily hungry (p. 246)

cavernous (kav´ ər nəs´) *adj.* deep and empty (p. 246)

rancor (raŋ´ kər) *n.* bitter hate (p. 246)

grant (grant) *v.* admit (p. 248)

❷ Literary Analysis

Stanzas

- Review basic units of prose compositions: words, phrases, sentences, and paragraphs.
- Point out that poetry uses words, phrases, and sentences, too. In place of paragraphs, however, poetry uses stanzas.
- Read the Literary Analysis instruction aloud to students. Call attention to the focus questions, and lead students to see that the Nash and Benét poems read more like rhymed narratives.
- Use the instruction for Comparing Literary Works to help explain the function of line length.
- To help students analyze the structure, use the Stanzas transparency on p. 32 in **Literary Analysis and Reading Transparencies.**

❸ Reading Strategy

Interpreting Meaning

- Remind students that words can have more than one meaning. In addition to *trying,* ask students for other words that have two distinct meanings. Students might suggest *round, leaves,* or *train.* Point out that poets like to use words in unusual or unexpected ways.
- Use the instruction for Interpreting Meaning to help students understand figurative language and words with multiple meanings.
- Use the Interpreting Meaning transparency on p. 31 in **Literary Analysis and Reading Transparencies** to help students acquire this skill.

Vocabulary Development

- Pronounce each vocabulary word for students, and read the definitions as a class. Have students identify any words with which they are already familiar.

CUSTOMIZE INSTRUCTION FOR UNIVERSAL ACCESS

For Less Proficient Readers	For English Learners	For Advanced Readers
Supply students with easy-to-read biographies of inventors. Invite students to find out what each person invented. Have students write paragraphs about the inventors and their inventions. Post the paragraphs on a bulletin board.	Ask your school librarian to recommend books that show the working parts of airplanes and other inventions. Invite students to familiarize themselves with the names of the various parts of the inventions. Encourage students to copy the drawings and label the parts.	Make resources about the Wright brothers available to students. Invite them to investigate the inventions the Wrights made in the process of inventing the airplane. For example, they had to invent the wind tunnel to test their designs. Have students report their findings to the class.

E-Teach

Visit E-Teach at www.phschool.com for teachers' essays on how to teach, with questions and answers.

TEACH

Step-by-Step Teaching Guide for pp. 246–250

CUSTOMIZE INSTRUCTION For Verbal/Linguistic Learners

Point out to students that certain poems are relatively easy to memorize and recite because the rhythm and rhyme give memory cues. Invite students to memorize selected lines from the poems. Encourage them to experiment with volume, tone, and speed in order to convey the poet's thoughts. Ask them to share their finished productions with classmates.

❶ About the Selection

Ogden Nash wastes no time introducing readers to the "Adventures of Isabel." First, Isabel meets an "enormous bear." Then, she encounters a "wicked old witch," and, after that, a "hideous giant." Finally—and unexpectedly—she meets a "troublesome doctor." Isabel calmly dispatches the bear, the witch, and the giant and cures the doctor. The humor of the poem lies in Nash's surprising rhymes and fantastic images of the unflappable Isabel defeating her foes.

❷ Critical Thinking

Analyze

- Remind students that stanzas, like paragraphs, are a major building block of poetry. Each stanza conveys an important idea and supports it.
- Read the first stanza aloud. Ask: What important trait do you learn about Isabel in the first stanza? **Answer:** She is brave.
- Ask students to examine the stanza again. Ask: What ideas in the stanza support your conclusion? **Answer:** She did not care; she prepared for a meal; she ate the bear quietly.

❶ ADVENTURES of ISABEL

OGDEN NASH

❷

Isabel met an enormous bear,
Isabel, Isabel, didn't care;
The bear was hungry, the bear was ravenous,
The bear's big mouth was cruel and cavernous.
The bear said, Isabel, glad to meet you,
How do, Isabel, now I'll eat you!
Isabel, Isabel, didn't worry,
Isabel didn't scream or scurry.
She washed her hands and she straightened her hair up,
Then Isabel quietly ate the bear up.

Once in a night as black as pitch
Isabel met a wicked old witch.
The witch's face was cross and wrinkled,
The witch's gums with teeth were sprinkled.
Ho ho, Isabel! the old witch crowed,
I'll turn you into an ugly toad!
Isabel, Isabel, didn't worry,
Isabel didn't scream or scurry,
She showed no rage and she showed no rancor,
But she turned the witch into milk and drank her.

Isabel met a hideous giant,
Isabel continued self-reliant.
The giant was hairy, the giant was horrid,
He had one eye in the middle of his forehead.
Good morning Isabel, the giant said,
I'll grind your bones to make my bread.
Isabel, Isabel, didn't worry,
Isabel didn't scream or scurry.
She nibbled the zwieback that she always fed off,
And when it was gone, she cut the giant's head off.

Isabel met a troublesome doctor,
He punched and he poked till he really shocked her.
The doctor's talk was of coughs and chills
And the doctor's satchel bulged with pills.
The doctor said unto Isabel,
Swallow this, it will make you well.
Isabel, Isabel, didn't worry,
Isabel didn't scream or scurry.
She took those pills from the pill concocter,
And Isabel calmly cured the doctor.

ravenous (rav′ ə nəs′) *adj.* greedily hungry

cavernous (kav′ ər nəs′) *adj.* deep and empty

rancor (raŋ′ kər) *n.* bitter hate or ill will

Ogden Nash

(1902–1971)

Ogden Nash threw away his first poetry attempt. Luckily, he pulled it out of the trash and sent it to a magazine—which published it immediately! Nash wrote light, humorous verse collected in titles such as *Parents Keep Out: Elderly Poems for Youngerly Readers*.

TEACHING RESOURCES

The following resources can be used to enrich or extend the instruction for pp. 246–250.

Literary Analysis

Literary Analysis and Reading Transparencies, p. 32

Reading

Selection Support: Reading Strategy, p. 79; Build Vocabulary, p. 76

Listening to Literature Audiocassettes, Side 11 ■

Listening to Literature Audio CDs, CD 4 ■

Extension

Fine Art Transparencies, Volume 1, Art Transparency 18 (Before reading "Adventures of Isabel," use the painting to discuss the concept of adventure with students.)

■ **BLOCK SCHEDULING:** Resources marked with this symbol provide varied instruction during 90-minute blocks.

❸

I'll Stay

GWENDOLYN BROOKS

I like the plates on the ledge
of the dining room wall (to the north)
standing on edge,
standing as if they thought they could stay.

❹ Confident things can stand and stay!

I am confident.
I always thought there was something to be
done about everything.
I'll stay.
I'll not go pouting and shouting out of the city.
I'll stay.
My name will be Up in Lights!
I believe it!
They will know me as Nora-the-Wonderful!
It will happen!
I'll stay.

Mother says "You rise in the morning—
You must be the Sun!
For wherever *you* are there is Light,
and those who are near you are warm,
feel Efficient."

I'll stay.

Gwendolyn Brooks

(1917–2000)

By age seven, Gwendolyn Brooks had convinced her parents that she would become a writer—a promise she fulfilled with many published poetry books and one novel. They probably didn't predict, however, that their daughter would become the first African American to win the Pulitzer Prize! Brooks also served as the Poet Laureate of Illinois.

Review and Assess

Thinking About the Selection

1. **(a) Recall:** What are three challenges Isabel faces? **(b) Infer:** What is Nash's purpose in describing such unbelievable adventures for Isabel? **(c) Evaluate:** How effectively does he achieve this purpose?
2. **(a) Support:** Describe Isabel's personality using details from the poem to support your answer. **(b) Assess:** Explain why Isabel is or is not someone you would want to have in your class.
3. **(a) Recall:** What does the speaker in "I'll Stay" like about the plates? **(b) Apply:** How does the description of the plates apply to the speaker herself?

❸ About the Selection

The speaker in "I'll Stay" notes similarities between the confidence of plates standing on edge on a shelf and her faith in herself. She announces that her name will be "Up In Lights!" The source of her confidence is her mother's words.

❹ Reading Strategy

Interpreting Meaning

- Remind students that poets use many meanings of words to convey an idea. Ask: What does *stay* mean in this poem?
  Answer: It means to remain or endure over long periods of time.
- Have students name other nonhuman objects that appear confident enough to "stand and stay."
  Possible responses: Buildings, rocks, trees, and bridges have staying power.

Answers for p. 247

Review and Assess

1. **(a)** She meets a bear, a witch, a giant, and a doctor. **(b)** Nash wants to entertain; he wants to remind readers to be resourceful. **(c)** He is effective because of his lively images.
2. **(a)** Isabel is calmly confident. She faces foes without fussing or straining. **(b) Possible response:** I'd like to have her in my class because she would get rid of bullies.
3. **(a)** The speaker likes that the plates stand on their edges. **(b)** The speaker is like the plates because she is confident and stays up despite difficulties.

CUSTOMIZE INSTRUCTION FOR UNIVERSAL ACCESS

For Special Needs Students	For English Learners	For Advanced Students
Have students listen to the recordings of the poems on the **Listening to Literature** audiocassettes or CDs before reading them. As students listen, encourage them to use their own knowledge and experiences to connect to the poems. Pause after each poem so that students can make notes on how their lives relate to the poem.	To help students understand the poems' meanings, have them observe as students proficient in English pantomime the action while another proficient student reads each poem aloud. Encourage the reader to use voice tone and facial expression to convey the meanings of words such as *enormous, wicked, confident,* and *praised.*	Have students use what they learn about the people in the poems to imagine other ways for these people to face challenges or solve problems. Ask students to choose one poem and rework it to show the person in a different situation. If students prefer, they may use prose. Invite students to read their work aloud.

5 About the Selections

In "Wilbur Wright and Orville Wright," Rosemary and Stephen Vincent Benét paint a gently humorous portrait of two confident and devoted brothers who are determined to find a way for humans to fly. In the poem's last stanza, the poets celebrate the Wright brothers' launch of the first airplane, a feat that will be remembered forever.

"Dream Dust," by Langston Hughes (p. 250), celebrates the ability to overcome—and even profit from—life's difficulties. The speaker in "Dream Dust" urges the reader to gather dreams from life's blessings as well as its troubles, and never give up these dreams.

6 Literary Analysis

Stanzas

- Ask students to recall the purpose of stanzas in poetry.
  Answer: Stanzas are like paragraphs; each one contains an important idea.

Monitor Progress Read the first stanza of the poem, and then ask the Literary Analysis question.
Answer: The brothers are determined to find a way for humans to fly.

Reteach If students have difficulty answering the question, continue to query them on the meaning of each stanza. Review the Literary Analysis instruction on p. 245, if necessary.

7 Background

Science

Before the Wrights made the first machine-powered aircraft, they designed and built gliders. In 1901, they built a wind tunnel to test models of various types of wings. Using information from the wind tunnel experiments, they designed a large glider, which they launched in 1902.

8 Critical Viewing

Possible response: This scene lacks the runways, buildings, and planes seen at a modern airport.

5 Wilbur Wright AND Orville Wright

ROSEMARY AND STEPHEN VINCENT BENÉT

6
Said Orville Wright to Wilbur Wright,
"These birds are very trying.
I'm sick of hearing them cheep-cheep
About the fun of flying.
A bird has feathers, it is true.
That much I freely grant.
But, must that stop us, W?"
Said Wilbur Wright, "It shan't."

7
And so they built a glider, first,
And then they built another.
—There never were two brothers more
Devoted to each other.
They ran a dusty little shop

Literary Analysis
Stanzas What does the first stanza say about the Wright brothers?

grant (grant) *v.* admit

8 **Critical Viewing** Compare this scene with a modern airport. **[Compare and Contrast]**

CUSTOMIZE INSTRUCTION FOR UNIVERSAL ACCESS

For Gifted/Talented Students

Have students discuss what Isabel, Nora, and the Wright brothers have in common. Encourage them to make lists of character traits shown in each poem and then compare the lists to find shared characteristics. Then, ask them to work with partners to imagine how the girls would interact with one another and with the Wright brothers. Allow interested students to work together to write a dialogue that takes place between the girls and the Wright brothers. Have students present their dialogues to the class.

For bicycle-repairing,
And bought each other soda-pop
and praised each other's daring.

They glided here, they glided there,
They sometimes skinned their noses.
—For learning how to rule the air
Was not a bed of roses—
But each would murmur, afterward,
While patching up his bro,
"Are we discouraged, W?"
"Of course we are not, O!"

And finally, at Kitty Hawk
In Nineteen-Three (let's cheer it!)
The first real airplane really flew
With Orville there to steer it!
—And kingdoms may forget their kings
And dogs forget their bites,
But, not till Man forgets his wings,
Will men forget the Wrights.

Reading Strategy
Interpreting Meaning
Explain the words "bed of roses." What is another way to convey the meaning?

Review and Assess

Thinking About the Selection

1. **Respond:** Would you have wanted to be the pilot in the Wright brothers' airplane? Why or why not?
2. **(a) Recall:** What kind of shop do the Wright brothers have? **(b) Infer:** What skills would they use in their work? **(c) Apply:** In what ways can the skills they use in their shop help them achieve their goal?
3. **(a) Recall:** In what year do the Wright brothers make their first successful airplane flight? **(b) Speculate:** What would their reaction be to airplanes and jets of today? **(c) Generalize:** What statement can you make about the Wright brothers' contribution to air travel?
4. **(a) Support:** What details in "Wilbur Wright and Orville Wright" reveal that the authors admire the Wright brothers? **(b) Evaluate:** Do you think the Wright brothers earned their fame? Why or why not?

Rosemary and Stephen Vincent Benét

Rosemary (1898–1962) and Stephen Vincent Benét (1898–1943)

This husband-and-wife team wrote a poetry collection, entitled *A Book of Americans*, from which "Wilbur Wright and Orville Wright" is taken. Rosemary Benét was a frequent contributor to many important magazines, including *The New Yorker*. Stephen Vincent Benét won the Pulitzer Prize for Poetry—twice!

9 Reading Strategy

Interpreting Meaning

- Recall with students the earlier discussion of figurative language. Read the bracketed passage aloud. Ask: Which phrases are figurative language? Ask students how they know.
  Answer: "Rule the air" and "bed of roses" are figurative language.
- Ask the Reading Strategy question: Explain the words "bed of roses." What is another way to convey the meaning?
  Answer: To say that something is not a "bed of roses" means that something is not easy. "Very difficult and dangerous" also conveys the idea.

Answers for p. 249

Review and Assess

1. Possible response: I would like to have been the pilot because I would have had a great adventure.
2. **(a)** The Wrights have a bicycle shop. **(b)** They would use metalworking and design skills in their work. **(c)** They would use design skills to plan the plane and metalworking skills to build it.
3. **(a)** Their first flight was in 1903. **(b)** They would probably be surprised at the size and speed of today's jets. **(c)** All air travel inventions since the Wrights' have depended on their contribution.
4. **(a)** The poets speak of the brothers' persistence (lines 7–8, 24–25), devotion to each other (lines 11–12, 15–16, 23), and the importance of their triumph (lines 31–34). **(b)** Possible response: Yes, the Wrights earned their fame because they succeeded where no one else had.

CUSTOMIZE INSTRUCTION FOR UNIVERSAL ACCESS

For Less Proficient Readers	For Gifted/Talented Students
Because the rhyme schemes and subject matter for "Wilbur Wright and Orville Wright" and "Dream Dust" make these poems accessible and enjoyable, students should be able to read them aloud with relative ease. Give students time to practice with a small, helpful audience before reading for a larger group. Model using inflection and changing speaking rate to show students how these techniques add to the effect of the poems.	Point out to students that poetry is not dependent upon length, but on strong images. Challenge students to compose a meaningful poem using fewer than twenty words. Emphasize that they will need to choose their words carefully to create successful images. Encourage them to use figurative language. They should make equally careful choices with regard to the structure of their poems.

Compare the model and the nonmodel. Why is the model more effective than the nonmodel?

Nonmodel	Model
The Florida Panther is one of our state's most interesting animals it is also one of the rarest. There are currently only about sixty panthers in Florida. Panther numbers don't grow because of decreasing panther habitat and increasing traffic in areas populated by panthers. To save the panther from extinction, we must make sure there is enough land set aside for panthers to live on they to have safe ways to move through the areas in which they live.	The Florida Panther is one of our state's most interesting animals, but, sadly, it is also one of the rarest. There are currently only about sixty panthers in Florida. Panther numbers don't grow because of decreasing panther habitat and increasing traffic in areas populated by panthers. To save the panther from extinction, we must make sure there is enough land set aside for panthers to live on and that they have safe ways to move through the areas in which they live.

Publishing and Presenting

Choose one of the following ways to share your writing with classmates or a wider audience.

Present a proposal. Use your problem-solution composition as the basis of a presentation.

Submit your paper for publication. Send a clean copy to your school paper or local newspaper. Enclose a cover letter.

WG *Prentice Hall Writing and Grammar Connection: Chapter 9 and Chapter 10*

Speaking Connection

To learn more about presenting a problem-solution speech, see the **Listening and Speaking Workshop: Present a Proposal**, p. 262.

Rubric for Self-Assessment

Evaluate your problem-solution composition, using the following criteria and rating scale:

Criteria	Rating Scale: Not very				Very
How clearly is the problem stated and explained?	1	2	3	4	5
How organized are the steps or parts of the solution?	1	2	3	4	5
How strong and convincing is the support?	1	2	3	4	5
How effectively are transitions used to connect ideas?	1	2	3	4	5
How consistently does the writer avoid run-on sentences?	1	2	3	4	5

TEST-TAKING TIP

When taking a test that includes a problem-solution writing prompt, students should keep their audiences in mind as they select the problem and outline the solution. It is important that readers understand the nature of the problem and solution, so students should take care to describe these fully. For example, a problem that occurs in a community, such as a construction hazard, may be an attractive topic to students. However, to score the essay fairly, students must describe the hazards fully and the solution clearly for readers who are unfamiliar with the community.

Revising (continued)

- Ask volunteers to read aloud the model and the nonmodel. Discuss why the model is more effective than the nonmodel.
  Answer: The run-on sentences have been corrected in the model; therefore, the text is easier to read and understand.
- Provide students with highlighters or colored pencils. Instruct them to highlight or circle run-on sentences in their essays. Then, have students use the instructions on p. 261 to correct any run-on sentences they find.

Publishing and Presenting

- Ask each student to list audiences that may be interested in his or her problem-solution essay.
- Discuss ways in which students can reach their audiences. Help students find the addresses of local newspapers or elected officials. They may also be interested in contacting community agencies that are concerned with the issue discussed in their essays. Be certain that their parents are aware that students are contacting any media or local organizations.

Assessment

- Review the assessment criteria in class.
- Before students assess their own work, have them score the Student Model in class, using one or more of the rubric categories. This will help them see how to apply the criteria.
- The rubric on this page, and another rubric in an alternative format, can be found on p. 10 of **Performance Assessment and Portfolio Management.**

Lesson Objectives

1. To prepare and present a problem-solution proposal
2. To evaluate a situation that is the basis of a problem
3. To organize and provide evidence for a solution or improvement for the problem
4. To effectively communicate the solution in an oral presentation

Prepare Your Proposal

- Invite students to identify a situation within your school or community that requires improvement. Point out that not all problems can be solved, but most situations can be at least partially improved.
- After students have identified a problem, suggest that they brainstorm ways of alleviating the problem. Encourage them to use graphic organizers or other devices to organize and prioritize their thoughts.
- Emphasize that students must show evidence that there is a problem and that their solution will work. Possible types of evidence include data from surveys and maps and interviews with affected people.
- Encourage students to provide visual aids, such as graphs, pictures, or videotapes, to illustrate their points.

Deliver Your Proposal

- Ask students what qualities make a speaker interesting to listen to. Possible response: Speakers are interesting when they use the proper tone of voice and volume and when they speak about an interesting topic.
- Discuss with students how a speaker's rate of speed and gestures enhance a presentation. Help them understand that even the best proposal can be disregarded if it is not presented clearly.

Listening and Speaking WORKSHOP

Presenting a Problem-Solution Proposal

A **problem-solution proposal** is a formal plan that suggests a course of action for solving a problem or improving a situation. A problem-solution proposal shares many of the characteristics of a problem-solution essay. (To review the guidelines for a problem-solution essay, see pp. 258–259.) The following strategies will help you present a spoken proposal persuasively and effectively.

Prepare Your Proposal

The following strategies will help you organize and prepare your presentation.

Problem: Accidents have increased each year.
Solution: Replace stop signs with a traffic light.

Organize your ideas. First, identify the problem and list the circumstances that you think cause the problem. Then, describe your proposed solution and list the reasons why you think it will work. Finally, add notes with statistics, examples, and other details that provide evidence for your points.

Establish connections and provide evidence. Use visual aids to show connections or provide evidence. A diagram can show the connection between the arrangement of streets and the need for a traffic light. A bar graph can show the connections between amounts. Look at the sample bar graph on this page. Notice how it captures the problem.

If you have access to a computer, use a presentation program to create your visual aids. As an alternative, you can draw them.

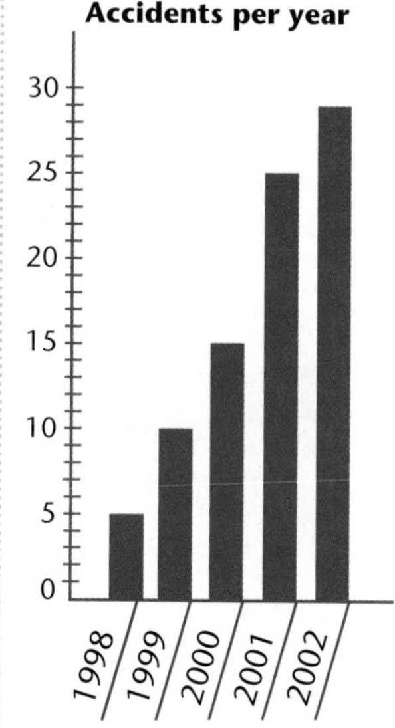

Deliver Your Proposal

Use delivery techniques to make your presentation more persuasive.

Adjust your speaking rate. Speak slowly enough that your audience will understand each word. Adjust your speaking rate by pausing after you make an important point. For example, pause for a few seconds after you state the problem to give the audience time to think about the problem. Pause more frequently as you present visuals. Your audience needs the time to "read" the visual as you speak.

Use gestures. Point to items on your visuals as you present the parts they are related to. When presenting a list of causes or steps, count them off on your fingers to focus your audience's attention on each item.

Activity: Proposal to Solve a Local Problem Prepare a proposal to solve a problem or improve a situation in your neighborhood or community. Present your proposal to a group of classmates. Use at least one visual aid.

CUSTOMIZE INSTRUCTION FOR UNIVERSAL ACCESS

For Special Needs Students

Point out to students that when they give oral presentations, they should use body language to help convey their messages. Show students a videotape of someone delivering a speech. Have them watch the nonverbal messages the person sends. Ask students questions such as the following:

- What kind of eye contact is the speaker using? Effective speakers make good eye contact with the audience. If a speaker looks interested in the audience, the audience will be interested in what the speaker has to say.
- What kind of speaking voice does the speaker have? An effective speech starts with a clear, strong, confident speaking voice.
- What kind of posture does the speaker have? Standing up straight sends the audience a message of confidence.

Encourage students to incorporate effective body movements into their presentations.

Assessment WORKSHOP

Identifying the Main Idea

The reading sections of some tests require you to read a passage and answer multiple-choice questions about main ideas. Use the following strategies to help you answer such questions:

- Look for a sentence that ties together or unifies the other sentences.
- Avoid making the assumption that the first sentence of a paragraph always contains the main idea.

Test-Taking Strategies

- Read the questions before reading the passage.
- If you are unsure of an answer, try to eliminate items you are sure are incorrect.

Sample Test Item

Identify the Stated Main Idea A main idea is often stated in a topic sentence that summarizes the passage. The topic sentence may be located anywhere in the passage. In a test question, the correct answer choice sometimes restates the topic sentence in different words. Look at the following passage and question:

Every year hundreds of powwows are held all over the United States and Canada. A powwow is a celebration of Native American heritage. With drummers setting the rhythm, dancers compete in various categories, including fancy dances, grass dances, and jingle dances. Between the contests, dances called intertribals are open to anyone.

1. What is the main idea of this passage?
   - A Dancers compete in different categories.
   - B A powwow celebrates Native American heritage.
   - C Every year hundreds of powwows are held.
   - D Intertribals are open to anyone.

Answers and Explanations

A and D are details. C is a general comment, not the main idea. ***B*** is the main idea.

Practice

Apply the Strategies Answer the questions based on this passage.

While Maria's neighbors were on vacation, she went to their apartment every morning to take care of the cats. First, she put out fresh food and water. Next, she cleaned the litter box. Then, Maria played with the cats. Taking care of cats was the best job she ever had.

Maria hoped to convince her parents to let her have a cat. "You would not have extra work," she argued. " I can take care of a cat by myself."

1. What is the main idea of the first paragraph?
   - A Maria went to her neighbor's apartment.
   - B She put out fresh food and water for the cats.
   - C Taking care of cats was her best job.
   - D Maria played with the cats.
2. What is the main idea of the second paragraph?
   - A Maria likes cats.
   - B Her parents would not let her have a cat.
   - C Cats make good pets.
   - D Maria believes she can take care of a cat.

Lesson Objective

To use topic sentences to identify main ideas in a test situation

Applying Reading Strategies

Tell students that setting a purpose for reading will help them find the main idea of a selection. Explain that this is because setting a purpose gives a reader something to focus on. As readers focus, they will find what is most important in a selection.

Test-Taking Skills

- Have students read the first sentence of the sample item. Then, ask them to determine a purpose for reading the item.
  Answer: A reason for reading would be to find out about powwows.
- Next, ask students to read the rest of the paragraph. Encourage them to read the passage several times, if necessary, to be certain that they understand it and then to try the sample question. After they check the answer to the sample question, show students the relationship between their purpose for reading and the main idea of the passage.

Answers

1. The correct answer is C. The paragraph is about how Maria liked taking care of the cats. Answers *A*, *B*, and *D* are incorrect because they are details about what she did when she took care of the cats.
2. The correct answer is D. Most of the paragraph is about Maria's arguments for getting a cat. Answers *A*, *B*, and *C* are not mentioned in the paragraph.

TEACHING RESOURCES

The following resources can be used to enrich or extend the instruction for p. 263.

PRENTICE HALL ASSESSMENT SYSTEM

- Workbook
- Skill Book
- Transparencies
- CD-ROM

Unit Objectives

1. To read selections in different genres that develop the theme of "Seeing It Through"
2. To apply a variety of reading strategies, particularly strategies for constructing meaning, appropriate for reading these selections
3. To analyze literary elements
4. To use a variety of strategies to build vocabulary
5. To learn elements of grammar, usage, and style
6. To use recursive writing processes to write in a variety of forms
7. To develop listening and speaking skills
8. To express and support responses to various types of texts
9. To prepare, organize, and present literary interpretations

Meeting the Objectives

With each selection, you will find instructional materials through which students can meet these objectives. Further, you will find additional practice pages for reading strategies, literary analysis, vocabulary, and grammar in the **Selection Support: Skills Development Workbook** in your **Teaching Resources**.

Background

Art

Emigrants Crossing the Plains, 1867, by Albert Bierstadt

Albert Bierstadt (1830–1902) was an American landscape painter, famous for his large canvases of romantic scenes of the Rocky Mountains and the Hudson River Valley. Use the following question for discussion.

How does this painting relate to the theme "Seeing It Through"? **Answer:** Most students will know that the settlers' trip was not an easy one, and showing the rough conditions of their camps hints at their determination.

UNIT 4 Seeing It Through

Emigrants Crossing the Plains, 1867, oil on canvas, 60 x 96 in. Albert Bierstadt, National Cowboy Hall of Fame Collection, Oklahoma City

UNIT FEATURES

Connections	Reading Informational Material
Every unit contains a feature that connects literature to a related topic, such as art, science, or history. In this unit, the selection *Bud, Not Buddy* by Christopher Paul Curtis is connected thematically to the poems by Walt Whitman and Maya Angelou on pp. 302–305. Use the information and questions on the Connections page to enrich students' understanding of the selections presented within the unit.	These selections will help students learn to analyze and evaluate informational texts, such as workplace documents, technical directions, and consumer materials. They will expose students to the organization and features unique to nonnarrative texts. In this unit, students learn to read a human-interest article in a magazine and contrast it with an autobiography. Students will also read a persuasive speech.

Exploring the Theme

The travelers in this painting are choosing a new road. It will take all their strength and determination to see their journey through to the end. The stories, poems, and essays in this unit deal with the struggles and triumphs that story characters and real people encounter when they choose a new path in life.

Reading about other persevering characters and real people who "see it through" to reach their goals and dreams may help you look at some of your own experiences in a new light.

◀ **Critical Viewing** What details of this picture indicate that the end of the journey will be worth the struggle of reaching it? **[Analyze]**

ASSESSMENT RESOURCES

- **Selection Support: Skills Development Workbook**
- **Formal Assessment**
- **Open Book Tests**
- **Performance Assessment and Portfolio Management**
- **Extension Activities**

Assessing Student Progress

Listed below are the tools that are available to measure the degree to which students meet the unit objectives.

Informal Assessment

The questions in the Review and Assess sections are a first level of response to the concepts and skills presented within the selections. Students' responses are a brief, informal measure of their grasp of the material. These responses can indicate where further instruction and practice are needed. Follow up with the practice pages in the **Selection Support: Skills Development Workbook.**

Formal Assessment

The **Formal Assessment** booklet contains Selection Tests and Unit Tests.

- Selection Tests measure comprehension and skills acquisition for each selection or group of selections.
- Each Unit Test provides students with thirty multiple-choice questions and five essay questions designed to assess students' knowledge of the literature and skills taught in the unit.

The **Open Book Tests** ask students to demonstrate their ability to synthesize and communicate information from selections or groups of selections.

To assess student writing, you will find rubrics and scoring models in the **Performance Assessment and Portfolio Management** booklet. In this booklet you will also find scoring rubrics for listening and speaking activities.

Alternative Assessment

The **Extension Activities** booklet contains writing activities, listening and speaking activities, and research and technology activities that are appropriate for students with different ability levels. You may also use these activities as an alternative measurement of students' growth.

▶Critical Viewing

Answer: The warm, golden hues of the sunset and the fact that the settlers are walking toward the light suggest that they will be successful.

Why Read Literature?

The "Why Read Literature?" page in each unit presents a list of possible purposes for reading. Each purpose for reading is connected to one or more of the selections in the unit. Good readers set a purpose before reading in order to help them read actively and focus on meaningful details.

Unit 4 introduces three purposes for reading. "Read for the Love of Literature" encourages students to read a poem that features words from the Spanish language. When students "Read for Information," they will learn about the lives of two major-league baseball players. Finally, "Read to Be Inspired" reminds students that they can learn from and wonder at the achievements of others.

How to Use This Page

- Tell students that before reading each selection in this unit, they should set a purpose for reading. This will help them read in an active and focused manner.
- Explain that reading works that include words from other languages, such as Sandra Cisneros's "Abuelito Who" (p. 300) will increase their appreciation of literature.
- When reading for information, students must read actively and take note of facts, statistics, and the writer's commentary. For example, as they read "Jackie Robinson: Justice at Last" (p. 325) students will learn what baseball was like before Robinson joined the Brooklyn Dodgers.
- Explain that another reason to read is to make a change or reach a goal. Students reading the story of Abraham Lincoln's youth, "A Backwoods Boy" (p. 316) and Maya Angelou's "Life Doesn't Frighten Me" (p. 304) will see that in order to realize their dreams, they will have to work hard and be determined.

Why Read Literature?

You will want to read the selections in this unit to learn how real people and story characters "see it through" difficult and challenging situations to reach their goals. Look ahead at some of the other purposes you will have for reading these selections.

1 Read for the love of literature.

After English, Spanish is the most commonly spoken language in the United States. Almost 20 million people in the U.S. claim Spanish as their native language. Experience the beauty of Spanish words in Sandra Cisneros's poem **"Abuelito Who,"** page 300.

Walt Whitman was turned down by every publisher he approached with *Leaves of Grass,* his now famous book of poetry. Read poetry from this book that changed the face of American poetry: **"The Open Road,"** page 302.

2 Read for information.

Jim Morris went from being a high-school science teacher and baseball coach to a major-league player, supported all the way by his hometown fans. Learn how Jim Morris realized his dream in **"Throw and Tell,"** page 333.

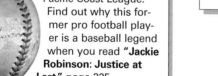

Jackie Robinson began his professional sports career as a football player before becoming a baseball player. In 1941, he played for the Los Angeles Bulldogs of the Pacific Coast League. Find out why this former pro football player is a baseball legend when you read **"Jackie Robinson: Justice at Last,"** page 325.

3 Read to be inspired.

As a boy, Abraham Lincoln attended school only when he could be spared from chores at home. His total days of formal schooling add up to approximately one year. Learn more about the early life of this inspiring president in **"A Backwoods Boy,"** page 316.

Maya Angelou toured Europe and Africa performing in the musical *Porgy and Bess.* She read her poetry at former president William Clinton's inauguration and has won a Grammy award. Read the brave words of this actress, poet, and songwriter in the poem **"Life Doesn't Frighten Me,"** page 304.

Take It to the Net

Visit the Web site for online instruction and activities related to each selection in this unit.

www.phschool.com

ENRICHMENT: Further Reading

Have students choose one or more of the works below to extend the unit theme "Seeing It Through" or to read more by the unit authors.

Kavik the Wolf Dog by Walt Morey

Walt Morey's classic tale describes the two-thousand-mile journey taken by a sled dog to be with a boy who was kind to him.

The Selkie Girl by Susan Cooper

Susan Cooper retells the Celtic legend of a young seal-woman who marries a human man and endures life on land.

Words Under the Words by Naomi Shihab Nye

The poems in this collection describe moments at home, on the road, and in the classroom.

Martha Graham: A Dancer's Life by Russell Freedman

Newbery Award winner Russell Freedman, author of "A Backwoods Boy," retells the life of one of the twentieth century's greatest dancers, choreographers, and teachers.

How to Read Literature

Strategies to Construct Meaning

Constructing is building. In this unit, you will learn to construct, or build, meaning from the pieces provided in the literature. You will learn to construct meaning using the following strategies.

1. Determine main ideas.

Main ideas are the building blocks of meaning. In this unit, you will learn how to clearly identify and restate main ideas and how to put them together to construct meaning.

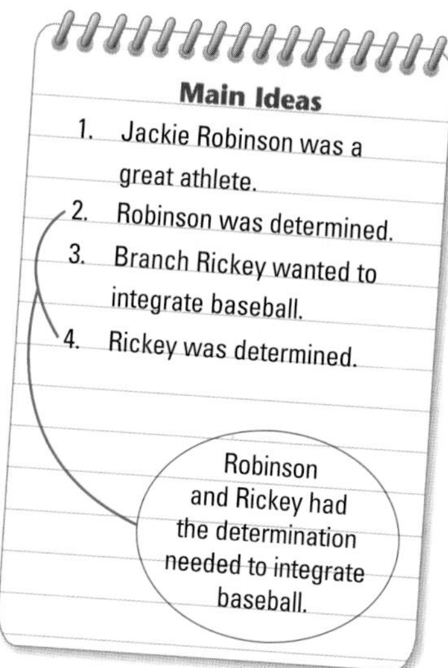

Main Ideas
1. Jackie Robinson was a great athlete.
2. Robinson was determined.
3. Branch Rickey wanted to integrate baseball.
4. Rickey was determined.
Robinson and Rickey had the determination needed to integrate baseball.

2. Compare and contrast characters.

A character's qualities will have more meaning when you compare and contrast one character with another. The similarities and differences will help you recognize the strengths and weaknesses in each. In this unit, you will meet a wide variety of characters that represent a range of good and bad qualities. As you notice what is alike and different about characters, consider why the author chose particular traits for individual characters and how these characters add to the story.

3. Predict.

To predict, you must make logical guesses about what will happen based on what you know. Predicting helps you construct meaning by focusing your attention on the significance of details and events.

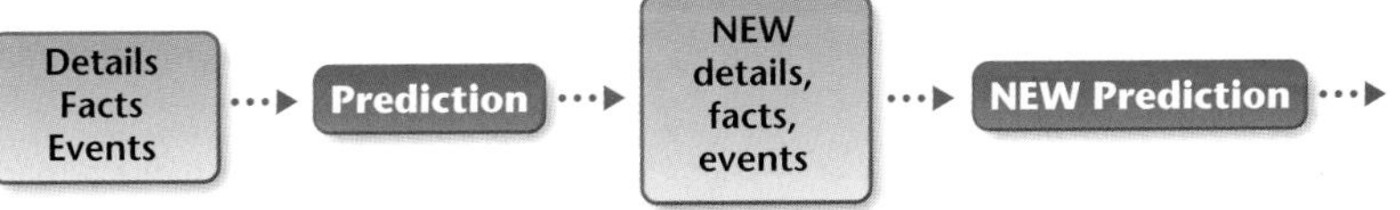

4. Draw inferences.

Drawing inferences is like "reading between the lines." When you draw inferences, you draw conclusions based on the details the author provides. To draw inferences,

- Consider the details about characters or events the author includes or does not include.
- Think about what this choice of details might mean.
- Read ahead to find out if your inference is supported.

As you read the selections in this unit, review the reading strategies and look at the notes in the side columns. Use the suggestions to apply the strategies for reading critically.

How to Read Literature

The "How to Read Literature" page in each unit presents a set of strategies to help readers understand authors' words and ideas. Each reading strategy is taught in conjunction with one or more of the selections within the unit. Good readers develop a bank of strategies from which they can draw as needed.

Unit 4 introduces four strategies for constructing meaning. To understand a selection fully, students must see the connections between ideas that are both stated and implied in the text. The strategies on this page help readers identify key ideas and make connections.

How to Use This Page

Introduce the strategies for constructing meaning, presenting each as a tool for developing understanding when reading the selections in this unit.

- As students read "A Backwoods Boy" (p. 316) and "Jackie Robinson: Justice at Last" (p. 325), they will determine main ideas from the details in each paragraph.
- As students read "Lob's Girl" (p. 270), "The Tiger Who Would Be King" (p. 282), and "The Lion and the Bulls" (p. 284), they will understand characters by comparing and contrasting their behaviors and personalities.
- As students read "Greyling" (p. 290), they will make predictions about the story's outcome and the characters' fates based on clues provided by the author.
- As students read the poems "Abuelito Who" (p. 300), "The Open Road" (p. 302), "Life Doesn't Frighten Me" (p. 304), and "who knows if the moon's" (p. 306), they will draw inferences from the details and poetic language.

MODEL A READING STRATEGY: Drawing Inferences

Explain to students that as they read, they must sometimes draw inferences in order to figure out what the author is trying to say. Model the thought process that is used in drawing inferences when reading the second stanza of Walt Whitman's "The Open Road" (p. 302):

> "In the second stanza, the speaker declares himself or herself to "be good fortune" and to "need nothing." The speaker is not going to listen to others complain, or sit around in libraries. At the end of the poem, the speaker describes himself or herself as "strong and content" as he or she heads out on the open road. The inference that I draw from these details and the tone of the speaker's voice is that the speaker has made a clear decision: he or she has chosen to rely only on himself or herself and to seek adventure."

Point out to students that inferences are based on clues in the text, such as word choice, but also on tone.

Lob's Girl ✦ The Tiger Who Would Be King ✦ The Lion and the Bulls

Lesson Objectives

1. **To analyze and respond to literary elements**
   - Literary Analysis: Foreshadowing
   - Comparing Literary Works
2. **To read, comprehend, analyze, and critique a short story and two fables**
   - Reading Strategy: Comparing and Contrasting Characters
   - Reading Check Questions
   - Review and Assess Questions
   - Assessment Practice (ATE)
3. **To develop word analysis skills, fluency, and systematic vocabulary**
   - Vocabulary Development Lesson: Word Analysis: Forms of *decide*
4. **To understand and apply written and oral language conventions**
   - Spelling Strategy
   - Grammar Lesson: Prepositional Phrases
5. **To understand and apply appropriate writing and research strategies**
   - Writing Lesson: Fable
   - Extension Activity: Electronic Resources Research
6. **To understand and apply listening and speaking strategies**
   - Extension Activity: TV News Feature

STEP-BY-STEP TEACHING GUIDE	PACING GUIDE
PRETEACH	
Motivate Students and Provide Background	
Use the Motivation activity (ATE p. 268)	5 min.
Read and discuss the Preview material and Background information (SE/ATE p. 268) [A]	10 min.
Introduce the Concepts	
Introduce the Literary Analysis and Reading Strategy (SE/ATE p. 269) [A]	25 min.
Pronounce the vocabulary words and read their definitions (SE p. 269)	5 min.
TEACH	
Monitor Comprehension	
Informally monitor comprehension by circulating while students read independently or in groups [A]	35–40 min.
Monitor students' comprehension with the Reading Check notes (SE/ATE pp. 271, 273, 275, 277, 279)	as students read
Develop vocabulary with Vocabulary notes (SE pp. 271, 273, 275, 278, 282, 283, 284; ATE p. 271)	as students read
Develop Understanding	
Develop students' understanding of foreshadowing with the Literary Analysis annotations (SE/ATE pp. 271, 273, 277, 279, 280, 282) [A]	5 min.
Develop students' ability to compare and contrast characters with the Reading Strategy annotations (SE pp. 274, 275, 278; ATE pp. 272, 274, 275, 278, 279)	5 min.
ASSESS	
Assess Mastery	
Assess students' mastery of the Reading Strategy and Literary Analysis by having them answer the Review and Assess questions (SE/ATE p. 285)	15 min.
Use one or more of the print and media Assessment Resources (ATE p. 287) [A]	up to 45 min.
EXTEND	
Apply Understanding	
Have students complete the Vocabulary Development Lesson and the Grammar Lesson (SE p. 286) [A]	20 min.
Apply students' ability to write a fable using the Writing Lesson (SE/ATE p. 287) [A]	45 min.
Apply students' understanding using one or more of the Extension Activities (SE p. 287)	20–90 min.

ACCELERATED INSTRUCTION:
Use the strategies and activities identified with an [A].

UNIVERSAL ACCESS
● = Below Level Students
▲ = On-Level Students
■ = Above Level Students

Time and Resource Manager

Reading Level: Average, Average, Easy
Average Number of Instructional Days: 4

RESOURCES		
PRINT	**TRANSPARENCIES**	**TECHNOLOGY**
• **Beyond Literature,** Study Skills: Devising a Strategy, p. 17 ▲ ■		• **Interest Grabber Videotapes,** Tape 2 ● ▲ ■
• **Selection Support Workbook:** ● ▲ ■ Literary Analysis, p. 85 Reading Strategy, p. 84 Build Vocabulary, p. 81	• **Literary Analysis and Reading Transparencies,** pp. 33 and 34 ● ▲ ■	
• **Adapted Reader's Companion** ● • **Reader's Companion** ●		• **Listening to Literature** ● ▲ ■ Audiocassettes, Sides 11, 12 Audio CDs, CD 5
• **English Learner's Companion** ● ▲ • **Literatura en español** ● ▲ • **Literary Analysis for Enrichment** ■	• **Fine Art Transparencies, Volume 1,** Transparency 17 ● ▲ ■	
• **Formal Assessment:** Selection Test, pp. 73–75 ● ▲ ■ • **Open Book Test,** pp. 49–51 ● ▲ ■ • **Performance Assessment and Portfolio Management,** pp. 13, 24 ● ▲ ■ • PRENTICE HALL ASSESSMENT SYSTEM ● ▲ ■	• PRENTICE HALL ASSESSMENT SYSTEM ● ▲ ■ Skills Practice Answers and Explanations on Transparencies	• **Test Bank Software** ● ▲ ■ • **Got It! Assessment Videotapes,** Tape 2 ● ▲
• **Selection Support Workbook:** ● ▲ ■ Build Spelling Skills, p. 82 Build Grammar Skills, p. 83 • **Writing and Grammar,** Copper Level ● ▲ ■ • **Extension Activities,** p. 17 ● ▲ ■	• **Daily Language Practice Transparencies** ● ▲ • **Writing Models and Graphic Organizers on Transparencies** ● ▲ ■	• **Writing and Grammar iText CD-ROM** ● ▲ ■ ***Take It to the Net*** www.phschool.com

BLOCK SCHEDULING: Use one 90-minute class period to preteach the selection and have students read it. Use a second 90-minute class period to assess students' mastery of skills and have them complete one of the Extension Activities.

PREACH

Step-by-Step Teaching Guide for pp. 268–269

Motivation

Draw on the chalkboard a diagram like this one:

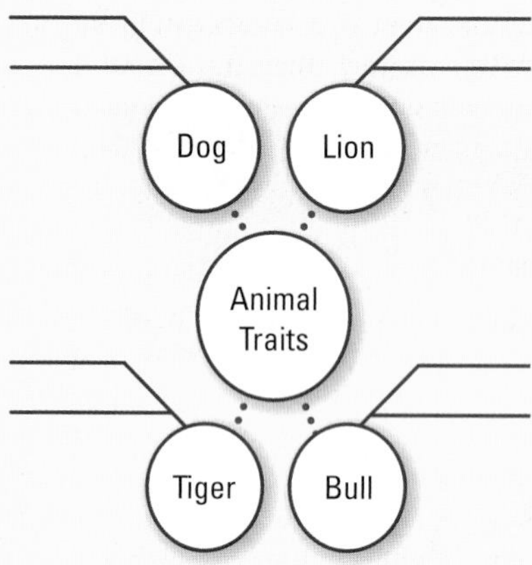

Have students brainstorm traits that they associate with each animal. Encourage them to include physical characteristics as well as traits associated with behavior, such as loyalty and cleverness. Add their responses to the web diagram.

Tell students that they will meet each of these animals as characters in the stories they are about to read. Explain that the struggles of the animal characters impart important lessons.

Interest Grabber Video

As an alternative, play "Native American Legend" on Tape 2 to engage student interest.

❶ Background

Social Studies

This story is set in a coastal town in England. England is the largest of the countries (England, Scotland, Wales, and Northern Ireland) that form the United Kingdom. The United Kingdom is bordered by the Atlantic Ocean, the North Sea, and the English Channel. These natural water barriers have saved the United Kingdom from invasion on several occasions during the last 500 years.

Prepare to Read

❶ Lob's Girl ◆ The Tiger Who Would Be King The Lion and the Bulls

Take It to the Net

Visit www.phschool.com for interactive activities and instruction related to these selections, including

- background
- graphic organizers
- literary elements
- reading strategies

Preview

Connecting to the Literature

Through their experiences, the characters in "Lob's Girl," "The Tiger Who Would Be King," and "The Lion and the Bulls" learn—sometimes too late—lessons about love, power, and working together. Think of experiences in your own life that have taught you lessons similar to those learned by the characters.

Background

In "Lob's Girl," a dog travels from Liverpool to Cornwall, England. Liverpool is a city in England. Cornwall is a seaside village in England. To get from one to the other, the dog must travel more than 400 miles.

TEACHING RESOURCES

The following resources can be used to enrich or extend the instruction for pp. 268–269.

Motivation

Interest Grabber Video, Tape 2

Background

Beyond Literature, p. 17

Take It to the Net

Visit www.phschool.com for Background and hotlinks for the selections.

Literary Analysis

Literary Analysis and Reading Transparencies, Foreshadowing, p. 34

Reading

Selection Support: Reading Strategy, p. 84; Build Vocabulary, p. 81

Literary Analysis and Reading Transparencies, Comparing and Contrasting Characters, p. 33

BLOCK SCHEDULING: Resources marked with this symbol provide varied instruction during 90-minute blocks.

❷ Literary Analysis

Foreshadowing

Foreshadowing is a word with two parts: *fore,* meaning "before," and *shadow,* meaning "image." **Foreshadowing** is a literary device in which the author gives clues to hint at what might happen later in a story. Authors give hints by including comments made by the narrator, experiences or feelings of characters, or events in the story. In "Lob's Girl," Joan Aiken includes this description to foreshadow that something bad is about to happen:

> The wind was howling through the shrouds of boats drawn up on the Hard.

As you read, look for hints and consider what they foreshadow.

Comparing Literary Works

Some examples of foreshadowing are more obvious than others. For example, by using the title "The Tiger Who Would Be King" rather than "The Tiger Who Is King," the author makes it obvious that the tiger probably will not succeed in becoming king. As you read, compare the different foreshadowing techniques and consider these focus questions:

1. Which story contains more examples of foreshadowing?
2. Which author uses more obvious examples of foreshadowing?

❸ Reading Strategy

Comparing and Contrasting Characters

Analyzing characters' behaviors or personalities can help you understand them. One way to examine characters is to **compare and contrast** them—identify similarities in behavior and personality. When you examine differences in behavior and personality, you contrast them. As you read, use a Venn diagram like this one to compare and contrast characters.

Character 1

Unique qualities or actions

Similar qualities or actions

Unique qualities or actions

Character 2

Vocabulary Development

decisively (di sī´ siv lē) *adv.* with determination (p. 271)

atone (a tōn´) *v.* make up for a wrong (p. 271)

resolutions (rez´ ə lo͞o´ shənz) *n.* intentions; things decided (p. 273)

melancholy (mel´ ən käl´ ē) *adj.* sad; gloomy (p. 273)

intimated (in´ tə māt´ id) *v.* hinted; made known (p. 275)

aggrieved (ə grēvd´) *adj.* offended; wronged (p. 278)

prowled (prould) *v.* crawled quietly and secretly (p. 282)

repulse (ri puls´) *v.* drive back; repel an attack (p. 283)

slanderous (slan´ der əs´) *adj.* untrue and damaging (p. 284)

❷ Literary Analysis

Foreshadowing

- Before they read the instruction on p. 269, tell students that they are already familiar with the concept of foreshadowing from watching television and movies.
- Ask students how they know something is going to happen in a movie or TV program.
  Possible Responses: Students may say that the music changes or the characters say something that alludes to a future event.
- Point out that the hints in the example are the words *shrouds,* which are coverings for the dead, and *howling,* which is the sound some animals make. Both words create a sense of eeriness in the story.
- Finally, use the Foreshadowing transparency on p. 34 in **Literary Analysis and Reading Transparencies** to demonstrate for students how writers provide clues to hint at a story's outcome.

❸ Reading Strategy

Comparing and Contrasting Characters

- Explain to students that writers will often include in a story characters that are similar to and different from each other.
- After students read the instruction on the bottom of p. 269, demonstrate or review how to use a Venn diagram. Use the diagram on p. 33 in **Literary Analysis and Reading Transparencies.** Challenge students to compare and contrast characters from a favorite film or television show.

Vocabulary Development

- Pronounce each vocabulary word for students, and read the definitions as a class. Have students identify any words with which they are already familiar.

CUSTOMIZE INSTRUCTION FOR UNIVERSAL ACCESS

For Special Needs Students	For Less Proficient Readers	For English Learners
Have students read the adapted version of "Lob's Girl" in the **Adapted Reader's Companion.** This version provides basic-level instruction in an interactive format with questions and write-on lines. Completing the adapted version will prepare students to read the selection in the Student Edition.	Have students read "Lob's Girl" in the **Reader's Companion.** This version provides basic-level instruction in an interactive format with questions and write-on lines. After students finish the selection in the Reader's Companion, have them complete the questions and activities in the Student Edition.	Have students read the adapted version of "Lob's Girl" in the **English Learner's Companion.** This version provides basic-level instruction in an interactive format with questions and write-on lines. Completing the adapted version will prepare students to read the selection in the Student Edition.

 ***E-Teach***

Visit E-Teach at www.phschool.com for teachers' essays on how to teach, with questions and answers.

TEACH

Step-by-Step Teaching Guide for pp. 270–284

CUSTOMIZE INSTRUCTION
For Logical/Mathematical Learners

Have students identify three cities that are about 400 miles from their school. Ask students how they might travel to one of these cities. Most students will suggest traveling by car, bus, or airplane. Remind students that Lob's journey is the equivalent of walking to one of those cities—but without food, water, or lodging.

❶ About the Selection

When Lob, a young German shepherd dog, travels over 400 miles on two different occasions to return to a girl named Sandy, his owner finally agrees to let him live with Sandy and her family. Sandy and Lob become best friends and grow up together.

Years later, while walking with Lob, Sandy is injured by a speeding truck. Sandy's grandmother sees Lob outside the hospital where Sandy is in a coma. The dog is allowed to go to Sandy's room where his presence wakes the girl from unconsciousness.

In a surprise ending, the reader learns that Lob had been killed by the truck that hit Sandy. The reader is left to decide what really happened.

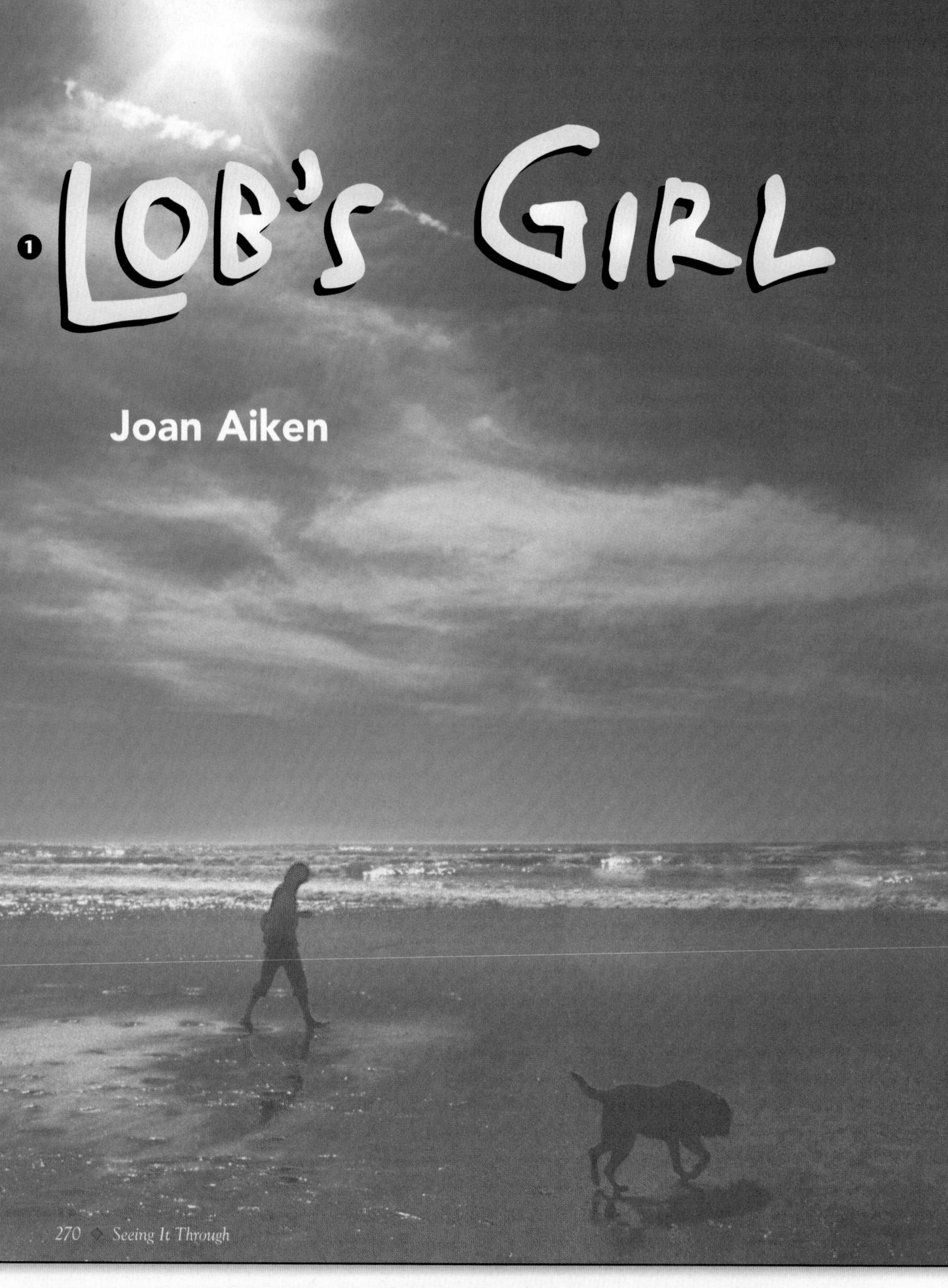

❶ Lob's Girl

Joan Aiken

TEACHING RESOURCES

The following resources can be used to enrich or extend the instruction for pp. 270–284.

Literary Analysis
- **Selection Support:** Literary Analysis, p. 85
- **Literary Analysis for Enrichment**
- **Writing Models and Graphic Organizers on Transparencies,** pp. 69, 77, 89 ▪

Reading
- **Reader's Companion**
- **Adapted Reader's Companion**
- **English Learner's Companion**

- **Literatura en español**
- **Listening to Literature Audiocassettes,** Sides 11, 12
- **Listening to Literature Audio CDs,** CD 5

Extension
- **Fine Art Transparencies, Volume 1,** Art Transparency 17 ▪ (Use the painting to generate a discussion of tigers, both in the wild and in captivity. Discuss other stories students know in which animals have human characteristics.)

▪ **BLOCK SCHEDULING:** Resources marked with this symbol provide varied instruction during 90-minute blocks.

2 **S**ome people choose their dogs, and some dogs choose their people. The Pengelly family had no say in the choosing of Lob; he came to them in the second way, and very decisively.

It began on the beach, the summer when Sandy was five, Don, her older brother, twelve, and the twins were three. Sandy was really Alexandra, because her grandmother had a beautiful picture of a queen in a diamond tiara and high collar of pearls. It hung by Granny Pearce's kitchen sink and was as familiar as the doormat. When Sandy was born everyone agreed that she was the living spit of the picture, and so she was called Alexandra and Sandy for short.

On this summer day she was lying peacefully reading a comic and not keeping an eye on the twins, who didn't need it because they were occupied in seeing which of them could wrap the most seaweed around the other one's legs. Father—Bert Pengelly—and Don were up on the Hard painting the bottom boards of the boat in which Father went fishing for pilchards. And Mother—Jean Pengelly—was getting ahead with making the Christmas puddings because she never felt easy in her mind if they weren't made and safely put away by the end of August. As usual, each member of the family was happily getting on with his or her own affairs. 3 Little did they guess how soon this state of things would be changed by the large new member who was going to erupt into their midst.

Sandy rolled onto her back to make sure that the twins were not climbing on slippery rocks or getting cut off by the tide. At the same moment a large body struck her forcibly in the midriff and she was covered by flying sand. Instinctively she shut her eyes and felt the sand being wiped off her face by something that seemed like a warm, rough, damp flannel. She opened her eyes and looked. It was a tongue. Its owner was a large and bouncy young Alsatian, or German shepherd, with topaz eyes, black-tipped prick ears, a thick, soft coat, and a bushy black-tipped tail.

"*Lob!*" shouted a man farther up the beach. "Lob, come here!"

But Lob, as if trying to atone for the surprise he had given her, went on licking the sand off Sandy's face, wagging his tail so hard while he kept on knocking up more clouds of sand. His owner, a gray-haired man with a limp, walked over as quickly as he could and seized him by the collar.

"I hope he didn't give you a fright?" the man said to Sandy. "He meant it in play—he's only young."

"Oh, no, I think he's *beautiful*," said Sandy truly. She picked up a bit of driftwood and threw it. Lob, whisking easily out of his master's grip, was after it like a sand-colored bullet. He came back with the

decisively (di sī′ siv lē) *adv.* with determination

Literary Analysis
Foreshadowing Based on this hint, what do you think is going to happen?

atone (a tōn′) *v.* make up for a wrong

4 **Reading Check**

How does Sandy meet Lob?

◀ **Critical Viewing** What clue does this picture give you about the identity of "Lob" in the title? **[Connect]**

2 Vocabulary Development

Word Analysis: Forms of *decide*

- Explain that the word *decisively* is a form of the word *decide.* A person who is decisive is one who is determined or sure of his or her actions.
- Point out that the ending *-ly* turns the adjective *decisive* into the adverb *decisively.* Remind students that adverbs modify verbs, adjectives, or other adverbs.
- Have students look for forms of the word *decide* in the selection and compare how the words are used in sentences.

3 Literary Analysis

Foreshadowing

- Point out to students the obvious verbal clue in this example of foreshadowing: "Little did they guess . . ."
- Explain that the clue lets readers know that something unexpected is going to happen.
- Finally, ask students the Literary Analysis question on p. 271: Based on this hint, what do you think is going to happen?
  Answer: The dog is going to enter unexpectedly and change their lives.
- Challenge students to make a list of phrases that indicate foreshadowing as they read.

4 Reading Check

Answer: Sandy meets Lob when he runs into her at the beach.

Critical Viewing

The dog walking with a person on the beach suggests that Lob might be a dog.

CUSTOMIZE INSTRUCTION FOR UNIVERSAL ACCESS

For Special Needs Students	For Less Proficient Readers
Students may not understand or remember aspects of the story, such as the characters' names, the places they go, or their activities. Suggest that students work in pairs and take turns reading one or two paragraphs on p. 271. After each student reads, pairs should discuss what has happened. The student who listens should jot down notes, including questions he or she could not answer. Then, the students should switch roles. Students should then meet in larger groups to discuss the story and answer any unresolved questions.	Invite students to participate in the unfolding of the story by predicting what will happen at different points. Have students work in pairs to read and make predictions. Tell students to pause at the end of each page and make predictions based on the foreshadowing in that part of the story. Have students turn their predictions into a flow chart like the Series of Events Chain on p. 69 in **Writing Models and Graphic Organizers on Transparencies.** After students complete the reading, ask them to circle the predictions that turn out to be true.

5 ▸ Critical Viewing

Possible responses: Students may say that the dog is a German shepherd like Lob. The dog appears to be young, smart, friendly, and alert—like Lob.

6 Background

Art

That's My Dog, by Jim Killen

Jim Killen, who grew up in Minnesota, is well known for his paintings and drawings of wildlife and domestic animals. As a conservationist, Killen captures in his artwork the serenity of nature and the interrelationship between animals and their environment. Killen has been selected by several states to create wildlife and waterfowl stamps. Use the following questions for discussion:

1. What does the title of the artwork tell you about its subject?
   Possible responses: Students may say that the title reveals that the artist knows and feels affection for the dog.
2. How would you describe the dog?
   Possible responses: The dog's eyes are bright and its ears are pointed forward as if it were alert. Its fur looks thick and soft.
3. How would you feel if a dog like this one knocked you down and licked your face?
   Possible responses: Some students may say that such an event would frighten them. Others may say that they would enjoy meeting a friendly dog.

7 Reading Strategy

Comparing and Contrasting Characters

- Have students compare the two parents' reactions to the noise in the kitchen.
  Answer: The mother reacts by worrying about her puddings. The father reacts by making a joke.
- Then, ask students what the parents' different reactions reveal about their two characters.
  Answer: The mother takes her role as cook seriously. The father has a sense of humor.

stick, beaming, and gave it to Sandy. At the same time he gave himself, though no one else was aware of this at the time. But with Sandy, too, it was love at first sight, and when, after a lot more stick-throwing, she and the twins joined Father and Don to go home for tea, they cast many a backward glance at Lob being led firmly away by his master.

"I wish we could play with him every day." Tess sighed.

"Why can't we?" said Tim.

Sandy explained. "Because Mr. Dodsworth, who owns him, is from Liverpool, and he is only staying at the Fisherman's Arms till Saturday."

"Is Liverpool a long way off?"

"Right at the other end of England from Cornwall, I'm afraid."

It was a Cornish fishing village where the Pengelly family lived, with rocks and cliffs and a strip of beach and a little round harbor, and palm trees growing in the gardens of the little whitewashed stone houses. The village was approached by a narrow, steep, twisting hill- road, and guarded by a notice that said LOW GEAR FOR $1\frac{1}{2}$ MILES, DANGEROUS TO CYCLISTS.

5 ▼ Critical Viewing What qualities of Lob do you see in this dog? **[Analyze]**

That's My Dog (German Shepherd) Jim Killen, Voyageur Art

6

The Pengelly children went home to scones with Cornish cream and jam, thinking they had seen the last of Lob. But they were much mistaken. The whole family was playing cards by the fire in the front room after supper when there was a loud thump and a crash of china in the kitchen.

7 "My Christmas puddings!" exclaimed Jean, and ran out.

"Did you put TNT in them, then?" her husband said.

But it was Lob, who, finding the front door shut, had gone around to the back and bounced in through the open kitchen window, where the puddings were cooling on the sill. Luckily only the smallest was knocked down and broken.

Lob stood on his hind legs and plastered Sandy's face with licks. Then he did the same for the twins, who shrieked with joy.

"Where does this friend of yours come from?" inquired Mr. Pengelly.

"He's staying at the Fisherman's Arms—I mean his owner is."

"Then he must go back there. Find a bit of string, Sandy, to tie to his collar."

ENRICHMENT: Science Connection

German Shepherds

Although Mr. Pengelly is worried about caring for a pedigreed, purebred dog, he does not need to worry about how Lob will fit into his family. German shepherd dogs are a very popular breed known for their adaptability, intelligence, and devotion to their owner.

The German shepherd breed evolved from sheepherding and farm dogs in Germany. Today, many German shepherds are used as working dogs: police and military work dogs, guide dogs for the blind, guardians or companions for elderly citizens, contraband detection dogs, and search and rescue dogs. However, like Lob, most German shepherds enjoy a position as a well-loved family member and are loyal and devoted pets.

Encourage students to find out more about a favorite kind or breed of dog (a specific breed or a type of mixed breed). A good source of information is the Web site of the American Kennel Club: <http://www.akc.org>. (We recommend that you preview the Web site before sending students there.)

8 "I wonder how he found his way here," Mrs. Pengelly said, when the reluctant Lob had been led whining away and Sandy had explained about their afternoon's game on the beach. "Fisherman's Arms is right around the other side of the harbor."

Lob's owner scolded him and thanked Mr. Pengelly for bringing him back. Jean Pengelly warned the children that they had better not encourage Lob any more if they met him on the beach, or it would only lead to more trouble. So they dutifully took no notice of him the next day until he spoiled their good resolutions by dashing up to them with joyful barks, wagging his tail so hard that he winded Tess and knocked Tim's legs from under him.

They had a happy day, playing on the sand.

The next day was Saturday. Sandy had found out that Mr. Dodsworth was to catch the half-past-nine train. She went out secretly, down to the station, nodded to Mr. Hoskins, the stationmaster, who wouldn't dream of charging any local for a platform ticket, and climbed up on the footbridge that led over the tracks. She didn't want to be seen, but she did want to see. She saw Mr. Dodsworth get on the train, accompanied by an unhappy-looking Lob with drooping ears and tail. Then she saw the train slide away out of sight around the next headland, with a melancholy wail that sounded like Lob's last good-bye.

9 Sandy wished she hadn't had the idea of coming to the station. She walked home miserably, with her shoulders hunched and her hands in her pockets. For the rest of the day she was so cross and unlike herself that Tess and Tim were quite surprised, and her mother gave her a dose of senna.

A week passed. Then, one evening, Mrs. Pengelly and the younger children were in the front room playing snakes and ladders. Mr. Pengelly and Don had gone fishing on the evening tide. If your father is a fisherman, he will never be home at the same time from one week to the next.

Suddenly, history repeating itself, there was a crash from the kitchen. Jean Pengelly leaped up, crying, "My blackberry jelly!" She and the children had spent the morning picking and the afternoon boiling fruit.

But Sandy was ahead of her mother. With flushed cheeks and eyes like stars she had darted into the kitchen, where she and Lob were hugging one another in a frenzy of joy. About a yard of his tongue was out, and he was licking every part of her that he could reach.

"Good heavens!" exclaimed Jean. "How in the world did *he* get here?"

"He must have walked," said Sandy. "Look at his feet."

They were worn, dusty, and tarry. One had a cut on the pad.

Literary Analysis
Foreshadowing What upcoming event might Mrs. Pengelly's questioning statement foreshadow?

resolutions (rez´ ə lo͞o´ shənz) n. intentions; things decided

melancholy (mel´ ən käl´ ē) *adj.* sad; gloomy

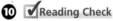

10 **Reading Check**
What happens the week after Sandy watched the train pull out of the town station?

8 Literary Analysis
Foreshadowing

- Remind students that the questions characters ask can foreshadow events. The answers to the questions may be found later in the story.
- Ask students the Literary Analysis question on p. 273: What upcoming event might Mrs. Pengelly's questioning statement foreshadow? Answer: Students may suggest that the question hints that Lob is easily able to find his way to places he wants to go, so perhaps he will come to the Pengelly's house again.

9 Critical Thinking
Infer

- Ask students why they think Sandy is "cross and unlike herself." Answer: Sandy is sad because she loves Lob, who has returned home to Liverpool with his owner.
- Have students write a brief journal entry describing what they do when they feel "cross and unlike themselves." Have them compare their solutions to the one Sandy's mother gives her (a dose of medicine).

10 Reading Check

Answer: The week after Sandy watches the train pull out, Lob comes crashing into the Pengelly's kitchen.

CUSTOMIZE INSTRUCTION FOR UNIVERSAL ACCESS

For Less Proficient Readers	For Advanced Readers
If students need help understanding the concept of comparing and contrasting characters, help them to complete a Venn diagram, like the one on p. 269, with information about characters in a story that students already know. You might select a simple folk or fairy tale. Remind students to think about several aspects of the characters, such as how they look, the things they say and think, and how they act. After this exercise, challenge students to compare and contrast any two characters from "Lob's Girl."	Challenge students to compare and contrast "Lob's Girl" with other stories, books, or movies that have animals as central characters. Have students use the Venn diagram on p. 89 in **Writing Models and Graphic Organizers on Transparencies** to show similarities and differences between the two stories. Students may focus on elements other than the characters, such as plot and style.

⓫ Reading Strategy

Comparing and Contrasting Characters

- Students may think it is difficult to compare and contrast characters that seem to have little connection in the story. Explain that comparison is simply a way of seeing if two characters have anything—ideas, actions, or thoughts—in common.
- Ask students the Reading Strategy question on p. 274.
  Answer: Sandy clearly adores the dog. Mr. Dodsworth likes him but is very frustrated with him. Both want Lob to have a good home and to be safe.

⓬ Critical Thinking

Deduce

- Read aloud this bracketed section and ask students to picture the scene in their minds as they listen.
- Then, ask students why the children get so excited when they hear their father ask if Lob is a big eater.
  Answer: The father's question suggests that he is considering taking the dog, even though the dog may be expensive.
- Finally, have students discuss how they figured out what was going on.
  Possible response: A likely clue is that Mr. Pengelly did not end the conversation by saying he could not afford the dog.

"They ought to be bathed," said Jean Pengelly. "Sandy, run a bowl of warm water while I get disinfectant."

"What'll we do about him, Mother?" said Sandy anxiously.

Mrs. Pengelly looked at her daughter's pleading eyes and sighed.

"He must go back to his owner, of course," she said, making her voice firm. "Your dad can get the address from the Fisherman's tomorrow, and phone him or send a telegram. In the meantime he'd better have a long drink and a good meal."

Lob was very grateful for the drink and the meal, and made no objection to having his feet washed. Then he flopped down on the hearthrug and slept in front of the fire they had lit because it was a cold, wet evening, with his head on Sandy's feet. He was a very tired dog. He had walked all the way from Liverpool to Cornwall, which is more than four hundred miles.

The next day Mr. Pengelly phoned Lob's owner, and the following morning Mr. Dodsworth arrived off the night train, decidedly put out, to take his pet home. That parting was worse than the first. Lob whined, Don walked out of the house, the twins burst out crying, and Sandy crept up to her bedroom afterward and lay with her face pressed into the quilt, feeling as if she were bruised all over.

Jean Pengelly took them all into Plymouth to see the circus on the next day and the twins cheered up a little, but even the hour's ride in the train each way and the Liberty horses and performing seals could not cure Sandy's sore heart.

⓫ She need not have bothered, though. In ten days' time Lob was back—limping this time, with a torn ear and a patch missing out of his furry coat, as if he had met and tangled with an enemy or two in the course of his four-hundred-mile walk.

Bert Pengelly rang up Liverpool again. Mr. Dodsworth, when he answered, sounded weary. He said, "That dog has already cost me two days that I can't spare away from my work—plus endless time in police stations and drafting newspaper advertisements. I'm too old for these ups and downs. I think we'd better face the fact, Mr. Pengelly, that it's your family he wants to stay with—that is, if you want to have him."

Bert Pengelly gulped. He was not a rich man; and Lob was a pedigreed dog. He said cautiously, "How much would you be asking for him?"

"Good heavens, man, I'm not suggesting I'd sell him to you. You must have him as a gift. Think of the train fares I'll be saving. You'll be doing me a good turn."

⓬ "Is he a big eater?" Bert asked doubtfully.

By this time the children, breathless in the background listening to one side of this conversation, had realized what was in the

Reading Strategy
Comparing and Contrasting Characters Compare and contrast Sandy's and Mr. Dodsworth's feelings about Lob.

ENRICHMENT: Culture Connection

Pets

People in almost all cultures have enjoyed keeping pets. Some provide companionship or protection; others are interesting to watch. The places people live influence the types of pets they choose. People on farms often have pets that are companions and that help with the work. For instance, horses and dogs are useful in herding; cats keep rodents out of the house and barns. An apartment dweller might choose a pet that does not need much space for exercise. Fish and other "container" pets are popular choices.

Most towns, villages, and cities have regulations about the kinds and number of pets a person can have. Many of these regulations are health measures; others are a way of making sure that animals are safely and humanely cared for. Ask students to explain the space requirements and the regulations governing a pet they have or would like to have. They may need to contact a local office to find out about licensing and other rules.

Time and Resource Manager

Reading Level: Easy
Average Number of Instructional Days: 3

	RESOURCES		
	PRINT	**TRANSPARENCIES**	**TECHNOLOGY**
	• **Beyond Literature,** Cross-Curricular Connection: Science, p. 18 ▲ ■		• **Interest Grabber Videotapes,** Tape 2 ● ▲ ■
	• **Selection Support Workbook:** ● ▲ ■ Literary Analysis, p. 90 Reading Strategy, p. 89 Build Vocabulary, p. 86	• **Literary Analysis and Reading Transparencies,** pp. 35 and 36 ● ▲ ■	
	• **Adapted Reader's Companion** ● • **Reader's Companion** ● • **Authors In Depth,** Copper Level, p. 62 ■		• **Listening to Literature** ● ▲ ■ Audiocassettes, Side 12 Audio CDs, CD 5
	• **English Learner's Companion** ● ▲ • **Literary Analysis for Enrichment** ■		
	• **Formal Assessment:** Selection Test, pp. 76–78 ● ▲ ■ • **Open Book Test,** pp. 52–54 ● ▲ ■ • **Performance Assessment and Portfolio Management,** p. 12 ● ▲ ■ • PRENTICE HALL ASSESSMENT SYSTEM ● ▲ ■	• PRENTICE HALL ASSESSMENT SYSTEM ● ▲ ■ Skills Practice Answers and Explanations on Transparencies	• **Test Bank Software** ● ▲ ■ • **Got It! Assessment Videotapes,** Tape 2 ● ▲
	• **Selection Support Workbook:** ● ▲ ■ Build Spelling Skills, p. 87 Build Grammar Skills, p. 88 • **Writing and Grammar,** Copper Level ● ▲ ■ • **Extension Activities,** p. 18 ● ▲ ■	• **Daily Language Practice Transparencies** ● ▲ • **Writing Models and Graphic Organizers on Transparencies** ● ▲ ■	• **Writing and Grammar iText CD-ROM** ● ▲ ■ *Take It to the Net* www.phschool.com

BLOCK SCHEDULING: Use one 90-minute class period to preteach the selection and have students read it. Use a second 90-minute class period to assess students' mastery of skills and have them complete one of the Extension Activities.

PRETEACH

Step-by-Step Teaching Guide for pp. 288–289

Motivation

If possible, bring to class a dog or cat carrier used to transport a pet, or invite a volunteer to describe a pet carrier that he or she has seen. Elicit that animals enjoy moving freely about and exploring their natural environment. Discuss reasons why pet owners, who love their pets very much, would confine their animals in an unnatural space like a carrier. Tell students that the story they are about to read revolves around a similar conflict.

Interest Grabber Video

As an alternative, play "Jane Yolen on Expressing Yourself Through Writing" on Tape 2 to engage student interest.

❶ Background

Science

Seals are mammals that live and hunt primarily in the water. There are at least eighteen species of true, or earless, seals. True seals live in waters all over the world—in both arctic and tropical climates and in both salt water and fresh water. Despite their differences, all seals maneuver better in water than on land because of the way that their rear flippers are formed. Just as our knees do not bend backward, their flippers do not move forward, and so the animals must drag their lower bodies along on land.

Prepare to Read

❶ Greyling

One, 1986, April Gornik, Edward Thorp Gallery

Take It to the Net

Visit www.phschool.com for interactive activities and instruction related to "Greyling," including

- background
- graphic organizers
- literary elements
- reading strategies

Preview

Connecting to the Literature

When you meet a challenge or overcome an obstacle, you usually discover new talents or strengths that you did not know you had. The main character in this story not only discovers a hidden talent—he discovers a hidden identity!

Background

"Greyling" is the story of a selchie. Selchies (or silkies) are common in the folk traditions of England, Ireland, Scotland, and Wales. There are many versions of selchie stories, but they all agree on one point: The selchie, who appears as a person on land, changes to a seal in the water.

TEACHING RESOURCES

The following resources can be used to enrich or extend the instruction for pp. 288–289.

Motivation

Interest Grabber Video, Tape 2

Background

Beyond Literature, p. 18 ■

Take It to the Net

Visit www.phschool.com for Background and hotlinks for "Greyling."

Literary Analysis

Literary Analysis and Reading Transparencies, Conflict and Resolution, p. 36

Reading

Selection Support: Reading Strategy, p. 89; Build Vocabulary, p. 86 ■

Literary Analysis and Reading Transparencies, Predicting, p. 35

■ **BLOCK SCHEDULING:** Resources marked with this symbol provide varied instruction during 90-minute blocks.

❷ Literary Analysis

Conflict and Resolution

A **conflict** is a struggle between two opposing forces. The events in the story all move toward the **resolution**—the way in which the conflict is settled. In "Greyling," the main conflict is the struggle between the two sides of Greyling's character: seal and human. This conflict is resolved when another conflict arises.

As you read, use the following focus questions to help you analyze the conflicts in the story and the resolutions:

1. What is the conflict inside Greyling?
2. What is the conflict between Greyling's father and the sea?

Connecting Literary Elements

In this story, Greyling's **character traits**, the qualities that make up his personality, contribute to the conflict. This excerpt from the story shows how his love for the sea that he came from creates an inner struggle.

> ". . . he often stood by the shore or high in the town on the great grey cliffs, looking and longing and grieving in his heart for what he did not really know . . ."

At the end of the story, notice Greyling's character traits that contribute to the resolution.

❸ Reading Strategy

Predicting

When you **predict,** you make logical guesses about upcoming events. To predict,

- think about what might happen based on a character's actions or words.
- pay attention to new information that might cause you to revise a prediction.
- keep track of your predictions and how accurate they were.

Use a graphic organizer like the one shown for each prediction you make.

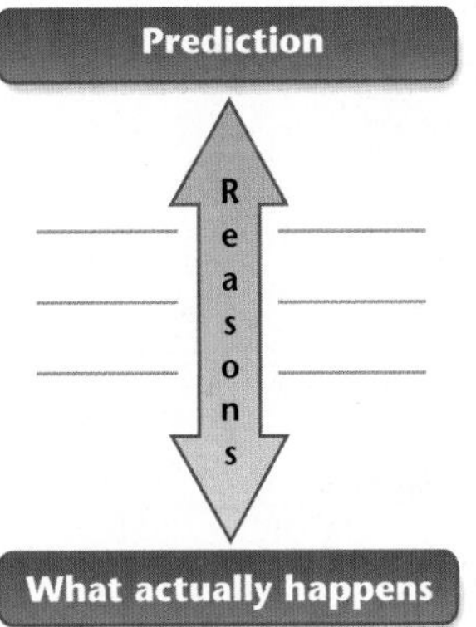

Vocabulary Development

grief (grēf) *n.* deep sadness (p. 291)

sheared (shird) *v.* cut off sharply (p. 291)

slough (sluf) *v.* be cast off (p. 293)

wallowed (wäl′ ōd) *v.* rolled and tilted (p. 293)

❷ Literary Analysis

Conflict and Resolution

- Tell students to take out a blank piece of paper. Then, tell them that they are going to write continuously for thirty seconds about a topic you will give them. First, say the word *conflict*, and when students have finished writing, say the word *resolution*. Explain to students that not all conflicts are physical or visible and that not all resolutions are peaceful or happy.
- Have volunteers share their writings with the class.
- Ask a volunteer to read aloud the instruction on p. 289. Make sure that students understand that the Connecting Literary Elements feature is giving a clue to understanding the story. Understanding characters' feelings will help students understand the story.

❸ Reading Strategy

Predicting

- Remind students that they make predictions all the time. For example, they make predictions about the weather when they look out the window and decide whether or not it may rain.
- Point out that predictions are not wild guesses but educated ones. Explain that, as readers, students will consider all the clues the writer has given them, as well as their own ideas and experiences, before they make a prediction.
- Use the Prediction transparency on p. 35 of **Literary Analysis and Reading Transparencies** to demonstrate how predictions are formed.

Vocabulary Development

- Pronounce each vocabulary word for students, and read the definitions as a class. Have students identify any words with which they are already familiar.

CUSTOMIZE INSTRUCTION FOR UNIVERSAL ACCESS

For Special Needs Students	For Less Proficient Readers	For English Learners
Have students read the adapted version of "Greyling" in the **Adapted Reader's Companion.** This version provides basic-level instruction in an interactive format with questions and write-on lines. Completing the adapted version will prepare students to read the selection in the Student Edition.	Have students read "Greyling" in the **Reader's Companion.** This version provides basic-level instruction in an interactive format with questions and write-on lines. After students finish the selection in the Reader's Companion, have them complete the questions and activities in the Student Edition.	Have students read the adapted version of "Greyling" in the **English Learner's Companion.** This version provides basic-level instruction in an interactive format with questions and write-on lines. Completing the adapted version will prepare students to read the selection in the Student Edition.

E-Teach

Visit E-Teach at www.phschool.com for teachers' essays on how to teach, with questions and answers.

TEACH

Step-by-Step Teaching Guide for pp. 290–294

CUSTOMIZE INSTRUCTION
For Bodily/Kinesthetic Learners

Challenge students to present a wordless performance of this simple story, using body language and facial expressions to describe the action. You may also suggest that a student or group of students learn the sign language necessary to narrate their presentation. Then, have students work together to state the story's theme.

❶ About the Selection

In "Greyling" the bountiful sea gives a fisherman and his wife everything they need, yet they are unhappy because they do not have a child. Then, one day the fisherman brings home a stranded seal pup that turns into a boy they name Greyling. Because the boy is a selchie—a seal in the water and a human on land—the fisherman and his wife never let him near the ocean. One day, the fisherman is drowning and the boy returns to the ocean to save him. He decides to remain in the ocean and never return to land.

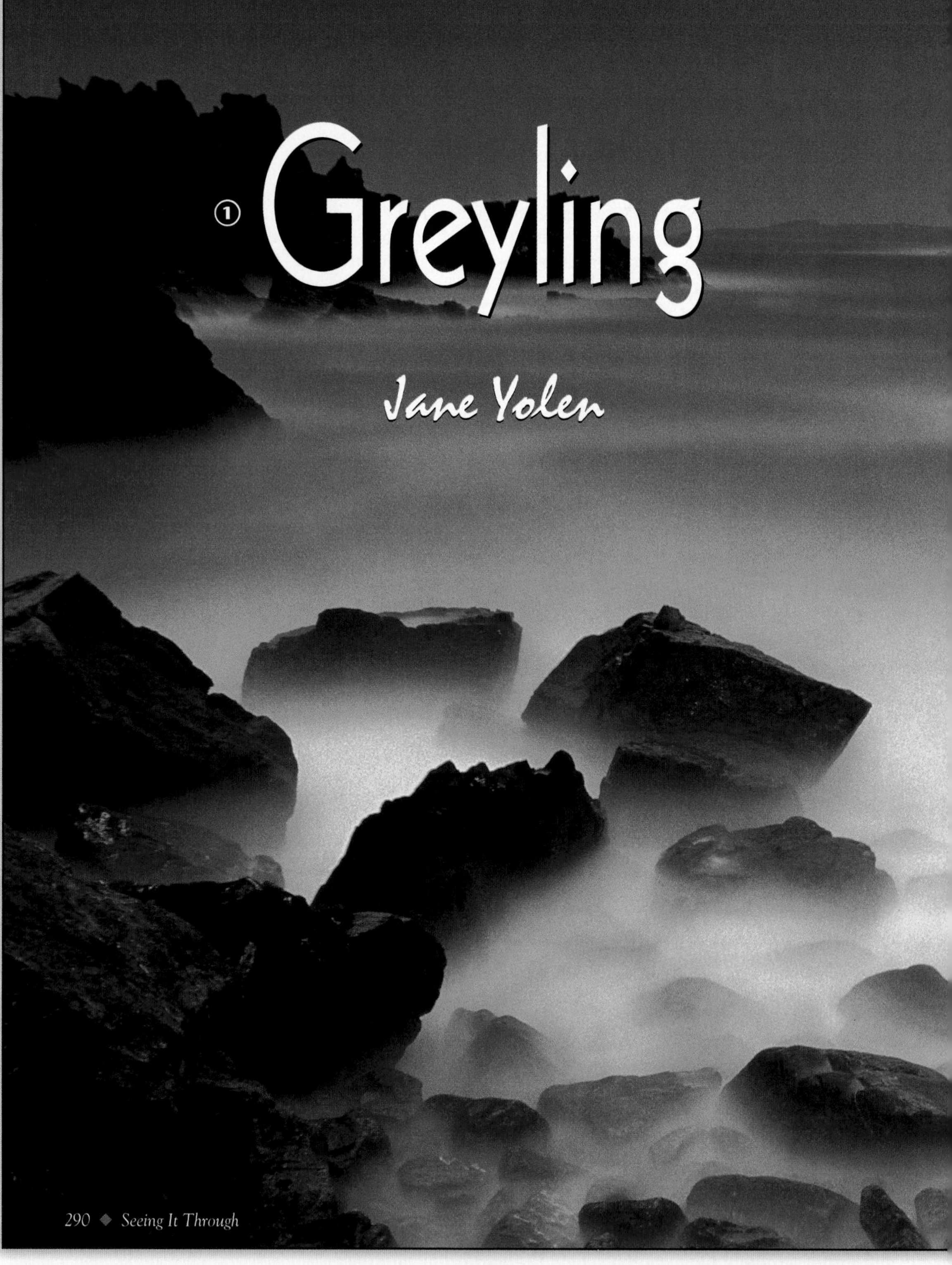

① Greyling

Jane Yolen

TEACHING RESOURCES

The following resources can be used to enrich or extend the instruction for pp. 290–294.

Literary Analysis
- **Selection Support:** Literary Analysis, p. 90
- **Literary Analysis for Enrichment**
- **Writing Models and Graphic Organizers on Transparencies,** p. 89

Reading
- **Reader's Companion**
- **Adapted Reader's Companion**
- **English Learner's Companion**
- **Literatura en español**
- **Listening to Literature Audiocassettes,** Side 16 ■
- **Listening to Literature Audio CDs,** CD 6 ■

Extension
- **Authors In Depth,** Copper Level (The collection includes four additional selections by Jane Yolen for extended reading.)

■ **BLOCK SCHEDULING:** Resources marked with this symbol provide varied instruction during 90-minute blocks.

Once on a time when wishes were aplenty, a fisherman and his wife lived by the side of the sea. All that they ate came out of the sea. Their hut was covered with the finest mosses that kept them cool in the summer and warm in the winter. And there was nothing they needed or wanted except a child.

Each morning, when the moon touched down behind the water and the sun rose up behind the plains, the wife would say to the fisherman, "You have your boat and your nets and your lines. But I have no baby to hold in my arms." And again, in the evening, it was the same. She would weep and wail and rock the cradle that stood by the hearth. But year in and year out the cradle stayed empty.

Now the fisherman was also sad that they had no child.
3 But he kept his sorrow to himself so that his wife would not know his grief and thus double her own. Indeed, he would leave the hut each morning with a breath of song and return each night with a whistle on his lips. His nets were full but his heart was empty, yet he never told his wife.

One sunny day, when the beach was a tan thread spun between sea and plain, the fisherman as usual went down to his boat. But this day he found a small grey seal stranded on the sandbar, crying for its own.

The fisherman looked up the beach and down. He looked in front of him and behind. And he looked to the town on the great grey cliffs that sheared off into the sea. But there were no other seals in sight.

So he shrugged his shoulders and took off his shirt. Then he dipped it into the water and wrapped the seal pup carefully in its folds.

4 "You have no father and you have no mother," he said. "And I have no child. So you shall come home with me."

And the fisherman did no fishing that day but brought the seal pup, wrapped in his shirt, straight home to his wife.

When she saw him coming home early with no shirt on, the fisherman's wife ran out of the hut, fear riding in her heart. Then she looked wonderingly at the bundle which he held in his arms.

"It's nothing," he said, "but a seal pup I found stranded in the shallows and longing for its own. I thought we could give it love and care until it is old enough to seek its kin."

The fisherman's wife nodded and took the bundle. Then she uncovered the wrapping and gave a loud cry. "Nothing!" she said. "You call this nothing?"

The fisherman looked. Instead of a seal lying in the folds, there

2 ▲ **Critical Viewing**
Why might people imagine human qualities or emotions in a seal? **[Connect]**

grief (grēf) *n.* deep sadness

sheared (shird) *v.* cut off sharply

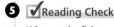

5 ✓ **Reading Check**
Why are the fisherman and his wife sad?

2 ▶ Critical Viewing

Answer: Students may say that the big eyes and playful, energetic nature of seals give them a childlike quality.

3 Vocabulary Development

Forms of *Grief*

- Point out that the words *grief, grieving,* and *grieves* all appear in the story. Ask student to look up the meanings of the three words.
- Then, have students replace the words with synonyms and discuss the impact each synonym has on the meaning of the sentence in which it is placed.

4 Reading Strategy

Predicting

- Discuss with students what they think will happen to the fisherman and his wife. Guide students to make predictions based on what they know so far.
- Ask students if they think the couple will find a child.
- Students will probably say yes.
- Ask students to predict what the wife will do when she sees the seal pup.
  Answer: Students will most likely predict that she will want to keep it.

5 ✓ Reading Check

Answer: They are sad because they have no children.

CUSTOMIZE INSTRUCTION FOR UNIVERSAL ACCESS

For Less Proficient Readers	For Advanced Readers
Understanding characters' emotions will help students understand the story's conflict and resolution. Have students prepare a three-column chart that has three rows. In the top row, students should write the names of each of the characters. In the second row, students should write down the characters' emotions at the beginning of the story. After students complete the story, they should fill in the remaining row with words that describe the characters at the end of the story.	Encourage students to draw connections between the conflicts they see in the story and those they have experienced in their own lives. At different points in the story, ask students to quickwrite a few sentences about the conflicts the characters experience and how the students do or do not identify with the conflict. After students have completed the story, ask each of them to write a paragraph about how Greyling's yearning for the sea and his love for his parents represent a conflict that is common among young people.

6 Reading Strategy

Predicting

- Ask students to predict what will happen in the story, basing their predictions on the wife's decision in this paragraph.
  Answer: Students may suggest that the child will return to the ocean. Maybe the child will drown or run away.
- Have students explain the basis of their predictions.
  Possible response: The wife wants to protect the child too much, and it seems impossible to keep him away from the water.

7 Literary Analysis

Conflict and Character

- Point out that, as a young man, Greyling does not understand his conflicting emotions.
- Then, pose the Literary Analysis question: What part of Greyling's character leads to the conflict he feels inside himself?
  Answer: The selchie part of him wishes to be in the ocean and to be free. That is why Greyling grieves at the sight of the open sea.

Monitor Progress Ask students to identify the conflicts that have been revealed thus far.
Answer: The fisherman and his wife want a child. In order to have a child, they keep a selchie from the sea, its home. Greyling yearns to be in the sea but does not know why.

Reteach If students have trouble identifying the conflict and resolution in the story, remind them that conflict causes problems. Similarly, the resolution of a story is like the solution to a problem. Ask students to return to the story to identify the characters' problems and how they are resolved at this point.

was a strange child with great grey eyes and silvery grey hair, smiling up at him.

The fisherman wrung his hands. "It is a selchie," he cried. "I have heard of them. They are men upon the land and seals in the sea. I thought it was but a tale."

6 "Then he shall remain a man upon the land," said the fisherman's wife, clasping the child in her arms, "for I shall never let him return to the sea."

"Never," agreed the fisherman, for he knew how his wife had wanted a child. And in his secret heart, he wanted one, too. Yet he felt, somehow, it was wrong.

"We shall call him Greyling," said the fisherman's wife, "for his eyes and hair are the color of a storm-coming sky. Greyling, though he has brought sunlight into our home."

7 And though they still lived by the side of the water in a hut covered with mosses that kept them warm in the winter and cool in the summer, the boy Greyling was never allowed into the sea.

He grew from a child to a lad. He grew from a lad to a young man. He gathered driftwood for his mother's hearth and searched the tide pools for shells for her mantel. He mended his father's nets and tended his father's boat. But though he often stood by the shore or high in the town on the great grey cliffs, looking and longing and grieving in his heart for what he did not really know, he never went into the sea.

Literary Analysis
Conflict and Character What part of Greyling's character leads to the conflict he feels inside himself?

Then one wind-wailing morning just fifteen years from the day that Greyling had been found, a great storm blew up suddenly in the North. It was such a storm as had never been seen before: the sky turned nearly black and even the fish had trouble swimming. The wind pushed huge waves onto the shore. The waters gobbled up the little hut on the beach. And Greyling and the fisherman's wife were forced to flee to the town high on the great grey cliffs. There they looked down at the roiling, boiling, sea. Far from shore they spied the fisherman's boat, its sails flapping like the wings of a wounded gull. And clinging to the broken mast was the fisherman himself, sinking deeper with every wave.

CUSTOMIZE INSTRUCTION FOR UNIVERSAL ACCESS

For Special Needs Students

Although the story is a simple one, students may still need help understanding what is happening. Offer students several cloze-type sentences that students can fill in as they read. Here are some sample sentences: "At the beginning of the story, a ______ and his wife are ______ because they do not have a ______. Then, one day the fisherman finds a ______." Students may work alone or in pairs. Ask students to read aloud their completed work. Explain that they have just completed an outline of the story.

For Less Proficient Readers

Have students use a reporter's formula to help them keep track of events in the story by writing a summary of the story that answers the following questions:

- Who is the subject of the story?
- What happens to the characters?
- When does the story take place?
- Where does the story take place?
- Why do the characters make the choices they make?
- How do the characters' choices affect the story?

The fisherman's wife gave a terrible cry. "Will no one save him?" she called to the people of the town who had gathered on the edge of the cliff. "Will no one save my own dear husband who is all of life to me?"

But the townsmen looked away. There was no man there who dared risk his life in that sea, even to save a drowning soul.

"Will no one at all save him?" she cried out again.

"Let the boy go," said one old man, pointing at Greyling with his stick. "He looks strong enough."

But the fisherman's wife clasped Greyling in her arms and held his ears with her hands. She did not want him to go into the sea. She was afraid he would never return.

"Will no one save my own dear heart?" cried the fisherman's wife for a third and last time.

But shaking their heads, the people of the town edged to their houses and shut their doors and locked their windows and set their backs to the ocean and their faces to the fires that glowed in every hearth.

8 "I will save him, Mother," cried Greyling, "or die as I try." And before she could tell him no, he broke from her grasp and dived from the top of the great cliffs, down, down, down into the tumbling sea.

Reading Strategy
Predicting What will happen when Greyling goes in the ocean?

"He will surely sink," whispered the women as they ran from their warm fires to watch.

"He will certainly drown," called the men as they took down their spyglasses from the shelves.

They gathered on the cliffs and watched the boy dive down into the sea.

9 As Greyling disappeared beneath the waves, little fingers of foam tore at his clothes. They snatched his shirt and his pants and his shoes and sent them bubbling away to the shore. And as Greyling went deeper beneath the waves, even his skin seemed to slough off till he swam, free at last, in the sleek grey coat of a great grey seal.

slough (sluf) *v.* be cast off; be gotten rid of

The selchie had returned to the sea.

But the people of the town did not see this. All they saw was the diving boy disappearing under the waves and then, farther out, a large seal swimming toward the boat that wallowed in the sea. The sleek grey seal, with no effort at all, eased the fisherman to the shore though the waves were wild and bright with foam. And then, with a final salute, it turned its back on the land and headed joyously out to sea.

wallowed (wäl′ ōd) *v.* rolled and tilted

The fisherman's wife hurried down to the sand. And behind her followed the people of the town. They searched up the beach and down, but they did not find the boy.

10 **Reading Check**

Why doesn't the fisherman's wife want Greyling to go in the sea?

8 Reading Strategy

Predicting

- Pause at this point, and have students summarize what has happened so far in the story. Ask them whether they think they know what is going to happen in the rest of story.
- Then, ask students to predict what may happen.
  Answer: Students may predict that Greyling will jump into the water. Some may also say that he will be able to save his father.
- Finally, pose the Reading Strategy question on p. 293.
  Answer: Students may say that he will probably become a seal.

9 Critical Thinking

Analyze

- Point out how the ocean foam has "fingers" that "snatch" Greyling's clothing and shoes. Explain to students that personification is the assignment of human attributes to nonhuman things.
- Ask students why the author may have used this example of personification.
  Answer: Students may say that it shows how the ocean welcomes Greyling back by helping him swim.

10 Reading Check

Answer: She knows that if Greyling goes into the water, he will not drown but will again become a seal.

CUSTOMIZE INSTRUCTION FOR UNIVERSAL ACCESS

For English Learners	For Gifted/Talented Students
Encourage students to think of folk tales about the sea from their native cultures. Help students compare the stories they find with "Greyling." Offer students a Venn diagram, like the one on p. 89 of **Writing Models and Graphic Organizers on Transparencies.** Students may compare the characters, plots, or settings of the two stories. Help students with any vocabulary that seems too challenging for them.	Point out to students that although the townspeople do not play an important role in the story, their actions help move the plot toward its resolution. Challenge students to think of other stories, books, or movies in which the inaction of others forces the main character to do something that will change his or her life—and possibly the lives of supporting characters. Ask students to draw comparisons between "Greyling" and the other examples.

ASSESS

Answers for p. 294

Review and Assess

1. Most students will agree that he belongs in the sea because he is unhappy on land.
2. **(a)** On the beach the fisherman finds a sealpup that turns into a boy. **(b)** Possible response: It is difficult to prevent the child from returning to the sea.
3. **(a)** She names the boy after the color of his eyes and hair. **(b)** The name reveals his animal nature because it is not a typical human name; it is a color that appears in nature. **(c)** The explanation of his name helps readers predict that a storm will have something to do with Greyling's future.
4. **(a)** He goes into the water to save his father. **(b)** Greyling probably does not know what will happen because he has not been in the sea since he was a baby.
5. **(a)** The fisherman and his wife are sad but accepting of Greyling's change. **(b)** The main idea is that parents have to let go of their children in order for them to be happy.
6. Students will probably agree that it was good that the fisherman and his wife did not keep Greyling from the sea. Keeping him on land would have prevented his happiness.

"A brave son," said the men when they found his shirt, for they thought he was certainly drowned.

"A very brave son," said the women when they found his shoes, for they thought him lost for sure.

"Has he really gone?" asked the fisherman's wife of her husband when at last they were alone.

"Yes, quite gone," the fisherman said to her. "Gone where his heart calls, gone to the great wide sea. And though my heart grieves at his leaving, it tells me this way is best."

The fisherman's wife sighed. And then she cried. But at last she agreed that, perhaps, it was best. "For he is both man and seal," she said. "And though we cared for him for a while, now he must care for himself." And she never cried again. So once more they lived alone by the side of the sea in a new little hut which was covered with mosses to keep them warm in the winter and cool in the summer.

Yet, once a year, a great grey seal is seen at night near the fisherman's home. And the people in town talk of it, and wonder. But seals do come to the shore and men do go to the sea; and so the townfolk do not dwell upon it very long.

But it is no ordinary seal. It is Greyling himself come home—come to tell his parents tales of the lands that lie far beyond the waters, and to sing them songs of the wonders that lie far beneath the sea.

Jane Yolen

(b. 1939)

Jane Yolen reads aloud every sentence she writes to hear how it sounds. When she completes a paragraph, she reads that out loud, too. That's a lot of reading because Jane Yolen has written more than two hundred books, most of them for children or young adults. Because she loves the timeless feelings and values in so many folk tales, fables, and fairy tales, Yolen often bases her stories on them. "Greyling" is a story from Yolen's imagination, but its main character, a selchie, comes from the folklore of Scotland and Ireland.

Review and Assess

Thinking About the Selection

1. **Respond:** Do you agree that Greyling belongs in the sea? Why or why not?
2. **(a) Recall:** How do the fisherman and his wife come to have a son? **(b) Speculate:** What problems does raising this child involve?
3. **(a) Recall:** Why does the fisherman's wife name the boy Greyling? **(b)** What does this name show about his animal nature? **(c) Connect:** How does this name help predict what happens to him?
4. **(a) Recall:** Why does Greyling finally go into the water? **(b) Support:** Does Greyling know what will happen when he dives into the sea? Support your answer.
5. **(a) Recall:** What response do the fisherman and his wife have to Greyling's change? **(b) Draw Conclusions:** What main idea about parents and children does this tale present?
6. **Make a Judgment:** Should the fisherman and his wife have kept Greyling from the sea? Why or why not?

ASSESSMENT PRACTICE: Reading Comprehension

Perceive Cause and Effect (For more practice, see Test Preparation Workbook, p. 27.)

In many tests students will have to identify cause and effect. Use the following sample to help students practice this skill.

> The fisherman wrung his hands. "It is a selchie," he cried. "I have heard of them. They are men upon the land and seals in the sea. I thought it was but a tale."
>
> "Then he shall remain a man upon the land," said the fisherman's wife, clasping the child in her arms, "for I shall never let him return to the sea."

Why does the wife keep the child from the sea?

A She is afraid he will drown.
B She is afraid he will not come home.
C She knows someone will take him.
D She knows he will turn into a seal.

A, B, and *C* are not supported by the text. The correct answer is *D*.

Review and Assess

Literary Analysis

Conflict and Resolution

1. What is the **conflict** inside Greyling?
2. What is the **conflict** between Greyling's father and the sea?
3. How are the resolutions of these conflicts related? Fill out a graphic organizer like the one shown here before you answer.

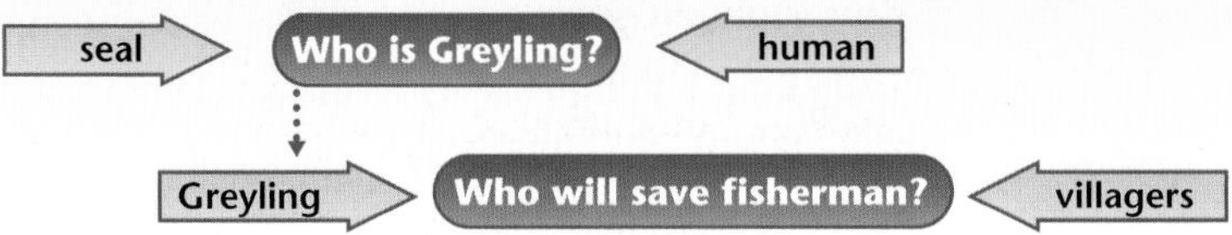

Connecting Literary Elements

4. Fill out a Venn diagram like the one shown here to explore Greyling's character traits as a seal and as a human. In the center section, write the qualities that apply to the seal and the human, such as love for the fisherman.

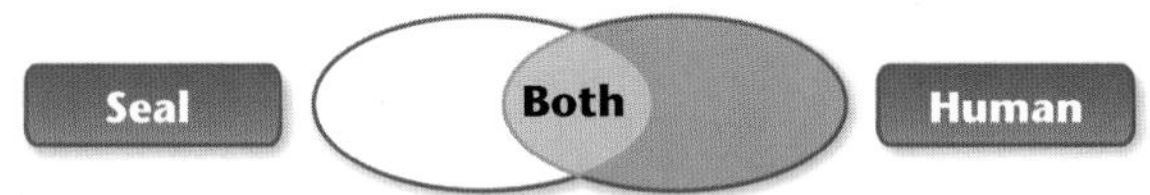

5. Which human traits lead Greyling to save the fisherman?
6. Which seal traits help Greyling save the fisherman?

Reading Strategy

Predict

7. When the man found the seal, what prediction did you make? Why?
8. When the seal became a baby, what prediction did you make? Why?
9. At which point, if any, in the story did you change your prediction? Why?

Extending Understanding

10. **Career Connection:** Explain how the lesson of this story could apply to the experiences of veterinarians (animal doctors) who work with wildlife.

Quick Review

The **conflict** is a struggle between two opposing forces.

The **resolution** is the way the conflict turns out.

To review conflict and resolution, see page 289.

Character traits are a character's qualities.

To review character traits, see page 289.

Predicting is making logical guesses about upcoming events by using information given in the story.

Take It to the Net

www.phschool.com

Take the interactive self-test online to check your understanding of the selection.

ENRICHMENT: Further Reading

Other Works by Jane Yolen

Here There Be Unicorns

Encounter

The Sea Man

Take It to the Net

Visit www.phschool.com for more information on Jane Yolen.

Answers for p. 295

Review and Assess

1. The conflict inside Greyling is his desire to be in the sea and his desire to obey and love his parents.
2. Greyling's father makes his living by the sea but wishes for a child. When the sea provides one for him, he knows that it is wrong to keep it. Later, the storm at sea threatens to drown the father.
3. The conflict within Greyling and the father's conflict with the sea are resolved when Greyling jumps into the sea to save his drowning father. Greyling discovers his true self. Both Greyling and his father understand that they belong to different worlds.
4.

seal	both	human
happy, wild, free, roaming	loving, devoted	longing, brave, grieving, obedient

5. Greyling's love, devotion, bravery, and obedience lead him to save the fisherman.
6. Greyling's swimming ability helped him save the fisherman.
7. Some students may have predicted that the couple would raise the seal in place of a child.
8. Students may have predicted that the child would turn back into a seal.
9. Most students will probably say that they thought all along that Greyling would turn back into a seal. Some students may say that they changed their prediction when Greyling's father was drowning.
10. The lesson of the story—that wild creatures need to be free—could remind veterinarians that although wild animals may sometimes need help from humans, they should remain free.

EXTEND

Answers for p. 296

❶ Vocabulary Development

Word Analysis

1. grieve
2. grief
3. grievous

Spelling Strategy

1. enough
2. tough
3. rough

Fluency: Complete the Sentences

1. wallowed
2. sheared
3. grief
4. slough
5. grief
6. wallowed
7. slough

❷ Grammar

1. (Please!) Won't someone help him?
2. (Well,) maybe the boy should go.
3. (No!) I won't believe it.
4. He swims fast. (Wow!)
5. (Oh no!) I can't see him!

Writing Application

Possible answers:

"Wow! He's such a good swimmer," said the fisherman's wife.

"Yes! He sure is," replied the fisherman. "Just look at him go."

"Well, I wish he didn't have to leave."

Integrate Language Skills

❶ Vocabulary Development Lesson

Word Analysis: Forms of *grief*

The fisherman in this story hides his *grief*—his deep sadness. In your notebook, write the form of grief next to its definition.

a. grief **b.** grievous **c.** grieve

1. feel deep sadness
2. deep sadness
3. bad enough to cause deep sadness

Spelling Strategy

Slough is one of the few words in English that spells the *uff* sound with *ough*. For each clue, write a word that rhymes with *slough* and is spelled with *ough*.

1. plenty **2.** very strong or sturdy **3.** not gentle

Fluency: Complete the Sentences

On your paper, write the vocabulary word that belongs in each numbered sentence. You will use some words twice.

1. The fisherman's little boat __?__ in the waves.
2. The mountains rose above Greyling, but the cliffs __?__ away.
3. At first, Greyling's mother felt __?__ when her son left.
4. Did Greyling __?__ off his old, human skin?
5. The fisherman's wife experienced __?__ more than once in this story.
6. The fish __?__ in the huge waves.
7. Was it Greyling's fate to __?__ off his human life?

❷ Grammar Lesson

Interjections

An **interjection** is a word or group of words that expresses emotion. A strong interjection is followed by an exclamation point, as in these examples from "Greyling."

Nothing! You call this nothing?

What! Do you expect me to believe that?

A comma follows a mild interjection.

Oh, you poor little thing.

Now, don't cry.

Practice Copy the sentences. Circle the interjection.

1. Please! Won't someone help him?
2. Well, maybe the boy should go.
3. No! I won't believe it.
4. He swims fast. Wow!
5. Oh no! I can't see him!

Writing Application Copy the following conversation. Add at least three interjections.

"He's such a good swimmer," said the fisherman's wife.

"He sure is," replied the fisherman. "Just look at him go."

"I wish he didn't have to leave."

WG Prentice Hall Writing and Grammar Connection: Chapter 18, Section 2

TEACHING RESOURCES

The following resources can be used to enrich or extend the instruction for pp. 296–297.

Vocabulary

- **Selection Support:** Build Vocabulary, p. 86; Build Spelling Skills, p. 87
- **Vocabulary and Spelling Practice Book** (Use this booklet for skills enrichment)

Grammar

- **Selection Support:** Build Grammar Skills, p. 88
- **Writing and Grammar,** Copper Level, p. 370
- **Daily Language Practice Transparencies** ■

Writing

- **Writing and Grammar,** Copper Level, p. 134 ■
- **Writing Models and Graphic Organizers on Transparencies,** p. 3
- **Writing and Grammar iText CD-ROM** ■

■ **BLOCK SCHEDULING:** Resources marked with this symbol provide varied instruction during 90-minute blocks.

❸ Writing Lesson

Letter

Write a letter from Greyling explaining why you returned to the sea after saving the fisherman. Use what you have learned about the mythical selchies to add details and reasons to your letter.

Prewriting Gather details from the story that indicate that Greyling is not completely happy on land. Jot these down to include as examples in your letter. Review the background on p. 288 for details about selchies that will help explain why you needed to return to the sea.

Drafting First, make clear that you have returned to the sea. Then, give an overall reason why, based on the details you will present. Finally, include the details and examples that support your reason.

Revising Look for places where you have included details that are not related to your reasons for returning to the sea. Eliminate these irrelevant details.

Model: Eliminate Unnecessary Details

You know I have always felt that I did not belong on land. When I jumped in the water~~, it was so cold.~~ I was amazed to discover how at home I felt.

The detail of the water temperature is deleted because it has nothing to do with why Greyling returned to the sea.

WG Prentice Hall Writing and Grammar Connection: Chapter 7, Section 4

Extension Activities

❹ **Research and Technology** Use a key word search to find possible explanations for selchie legends. Once you have found several sites, scroll or search text in documents to find the answers to the following questions.

1. Are there true stories of seals rescuing people?
2. What physical features of seals might appear human?

After answering the questions, prepare a **report** and share it with your class.

Listening and Speaking With other students, **role-play** the scene in which the villagers refuse to help. Use body language to show anger, fear, reluctance, or embarrassment. Communicate these emotions nonverbally—without words—through

- facial expressions.
- the way you stand.

As a group, discuss what each person's body language seemed to communicate. **[Group Activity]**

Take It to the Net www.phschool.com

Go online for an additional research activity using the Internet.

ASSESSMENT RESOURCES

The following resources can be used to assess students' knowledge and skills.

Selection Assessment

- **Formal Assessment,** pp. 76–78
- **Open Book Test,** pp. 52–54
- **Got It! Assessment Videotapes,** Tape 2
- **Test Bank Software**

Take It to the Net

Visit www.phschool.com for self-tests and additional questions on "Greyling."

Writing Rubric

- **Performance Assess. and Portfolio Mgmt.,** p. 12

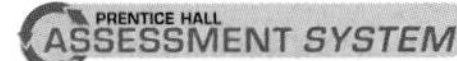
PRENTICE HALL ASSESSMENT SYSTEM

- **Workbook**
- **Transparencies**
- **Skill Book**
- **CD-ROM**

Lesson Support for p. 297

❸ Writing Lesson

- Before students read the instruction for the Writing Lesson, review the parts of a letter—date, greeting, body, closing, and signature. Remind students that a personal letter is informal in tone and language.
- Remind students that they are writing as if they were Greyling, so it is appropriate to write from the first-person point of view. The recipient of the letter is not specified; you may suggest that students write the letters to Greyling's parents.
- As students revise, ask them to read their letters to a partner. The language of the letters should sound natural and conversational.
- You may wish to adapt the Exposition rubric on p. 12 in **Performance Assessment and Portfolio Management** to assess the explanations provided in students' letters.

❹ Research and Technology

- Before students begin researching, tell them to compile a list of possible key words.
- Remind students not to accept the results of only one search. Explain that *selchie* is sometimes spelled as *selkie*, so students should try alternate spellings of *selchie* as well as several different search engines.
- Once students find appropriate Internet sites, they should bookmark, print out, or otherwise record the sites' names and Web addresses to use if they return to the site.

CUSTOMIZE INSTRUCTION
For Universal Access

To address different learning styles, use the activities suggested in the **Extension Activities** booklet, p. 18.

- For Musical/Rhythmic and Interpersonal Learners, use Activity 5.
- For Verbal/Linguistic Learners, use Activity 6.
- For Visual/Spatial and Verbal/Linguistic Learners, use Activity 7.

Abuelito Who ✦ The Open Road ✦ Life Doesn't Frighten Me ✦ who knows if the moon's

Lesson Objectives

1. **To analyze and respond to literary elements**
   - Literary Analysis: Free Verse
   - Comparing Literary Works
2. **To read, comprehend, analyze, and critique four poems**
   - Reading Strategy: Drawing Inferences
   - Reading Check Questions
   - Review and Assess Questions
   - Assessment Practice (ATE)
3. **To develop word analysis skills, fluency, and systematic vocabulary**
   - Vocabulary Development Lesson: Word Analysis: Compound Transition Words
4. **To understand and apply written and oral language conventions**
   - Spelling Strategy
   - Grammar Lesson: Coordinating and Subordinating Conjunctions
5. **To understand and apply appropriate writing and research strategies**
   - Writing Lesson: Portrait
   - Extension Activity: Booklet
6. **To understand and apply listening and speaking strategies**
   - Extension Activity: Advertisement Review

STEP-BY-STEP TEACHING GUIDE	PACING GUIDE
PRETEACH	
Motivate Students and Provide Background	
Use the Motivation activity (ATE p. 298)	5 min.
Read and discuss the Preview material and Background information (SE/ATE p. 298) A	10 min.
Introduce the Concepts	
Introduce the Literary Analysis and Reading Strategy (SE/ATE p. 299) A	15 min.
Pronounce the vocabulary words and read their definitions (SE p. 299)	5 min.
TEACH	
Monitor Comprehension	
Informally monitor comprehension by circulating while students read independently or in groups A	10 min.
Develop vocabulary with Vocabulary notes (SE p. 302)	as students read
Develop Understanding	
Develop students' understanding of free verse with the Literary Analysis annotations (ATE p. 302) A	5 min.
Develop students' ability to draw inferences with the Reading Strategy annotations (ATE p. 304)	5 min.
ASSESS	
Assess Mastery	
Assess students' mastery of the Reading Strategy and Literary Analysis by having them answer the Review and Assess questions (SE/ATE p. 307)	15 min.
Use one or more of the print and media Assessment Resources (ATE p. 309) A	up to 45 min.
EXTEND	
Apply Understanding	
Have students complete the Vocabulary Development Lesson and the Grammar Lesson (SE p. 308) A	20 min.
Apply students' knowledge of explanations using the Writing Lesson (SE/ATE p. 309) A	30–45 min.
Apply students' understanding of portraits using one or more of the Extension Activities (SE p. 309)	20–90 min.

ACCELERATED INSTRUCTION:
Use the strategies and activities identified with an A.

UNIVERSAL ACCESS
● = Below Level Students
▲ = On-Level Students
■ = Above Level Students

Time and Resource Manager

Reading Level: Average, Challenging, Average, Easy
Average Number of Instructional Days: 4

RESOURCES		
PRINT	**TRANSPARENCIES**	**TECHNOLOGY**
• **Beyond Literature,** Career Connection: Elder Care, p. 19 ▲ ■		• **Interest Grabber Videotapes,** Tape 2 ● ▲ ■
• **Selection Support Workbook:** ● ▲ ■ Literary Analysis, p. 95 Reading Strategy, p. 94 Build Vocabulary, p. 91	• **Literary Analysis and Reading Transparencies,** pp. 37 and 38 ● ▲ ■	
		• **Listening to Literature** ● ▲ ■ Audiocassettes, Side 12 Audio CDs, CD 5
• **Literary Analysis for Enrichment** ■	• **Fine Art Transparencies, Volume 1,** Transparency 13 ● ▲ ■	
• **Formal Assessment:** Selection Test, pp. 79–81 ● ▲ ■ • **Open Book Test,** pp. 55–57 ● ▲ ■ • **Performance Assessment and Portfolio Management,** pp. 9, 22 ● ▲ ■ • PRENTICE HALL ASSESSMENT SYSTEM ● ▲ ■	• PRENTICE HALL ASSESSMENT SYSTEM ● ▲ ■ Skills Practice Answers and Explanations on Transparencies	• **Test Bank Software** ● ▲ ■ • **Got It! Assessment Videotapes,** Tape 2 ● ▲
• **Selection Support Workbook:** ● ▲ ■ Build Spelling Skills, p. 92 Build Grammar Skills, p. 93 • **Writing and Grammar,** Copper Level ● ▲ ■ • **Extension Activities,** p. 19 ● ▲ ■	• **Daily Language Practice Transparencies** ● ▲ • **Writing Models and Graphic Organizers on Transparencies** ● ▲ ■	• **Writing and Grammar iText CD-ROM** ● ▲ ■ ***Take It to the Net*** www.phschool.com

BLOCK SCHEDULING: Use one 90-minute class period to preteach the selection and have students read it. Use a second 90-minute class period to assess students' mastery of skills and have them complete one of the Extension Activities.

PRETEACH

Step-by-Step Teaching Guide for pp. 298–299

Motivation

Bring to class examples of greeting cards—graduation cards, birthday cards, and "bon voyage" cards. Ask students why they enjoy receiving and sending such cards. Expand on the idea that these cards help people share experiences that come with important life transitions, or new roads. Tell students that the poets who wrote these poems touch on similar themes.

Interest Grabber Video

As an alternative, play "Walt Whitman" on Tape 2 to engage student interest.

1 Background

Literature

Maya Angelou, the author of "Life Doesn't Frighten Me," saw first-hand the upheaval in the American South during the Civil Rights movement in the 1950s and 1960s. Her autobiographical writings describe her life as a young black girl in the segregated South. Angelou grew up to become a renowned poet, playwright, and activist. In 1993, she read her poem "On the Pulse of Morning" at the inauguration of fellow Arkansan President Bill Clinton.

Prepare to Read

1 Abuelito Who ◆ The Open Road
Life Doesn't Frighten Me ◆ who knows if the moon's

Take It to the Net

Visit www.phschool.com for interactive activities and instruction related to these selections, including
- background
- graphic organizers
- literary elements
- reading strategies

Preview

Connecting to the Literature

The poets in this group—Sandra Cisneros, E. E. Cummings, Walt Whitman, and Maya Angelou—focus on change. Two of them—Cummings and Whitman—express the thrill and possibility of traveling new roads. What new roads do you look forward to traveling?

Background

E. E. Cummings created his own rules when writing poetry. By rarely using periods or capital letters, he let the rhythm of the words speak for itself. The lines "always/it's/Spring" would read more easily as one line—"it's always Spring"—but Cummings makes us slow down to appreciate the idea.

TEACHING RESOURCES

The following resources can be used to enrich or extend the instruction for pp. 298–299.

Motivation

Interest Grabber Video, Tape 2

Background

Beyond Literature, p. 19

Take It to the Net

Visit www.phschool.com for Background and hotlinks for the selections.

Literary Analysis

Literary Analysis and Reading Transparencies, Free Verse, p. 38

Reading

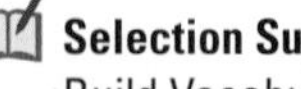

Selection Support: Reading Strategy, p. 94; Build Vocabulary, p. 91

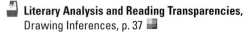

Literary Analysis and Reading Transparencies, Drawing Inferences, p. 37

BLOCK SCHEDULING: Resources marked with this symbol provide varied instruction during 90-minute blocks.

❷ Literary Analysis

Free Verse

A poem written in **free verse** does not reflect traditional structures or rules. Its lines do not necessarily rhyme at the end or contain a set number of syllables. Still, the poem works with the sound, sense, and rhythm of the words. For instance, the poet may repeat words or put rhyming words close to each other. In the following lines from "Abuelito Who," Sandra Cisneros creates rhythm by using repeated words:

who tells me in Spanish you are my diamond
who tells me in English you are my sky

Comparing Literary Works

The **tone** of a poem is the writer's attitude toward the subject and the audience. Tone can often be described in a single word, such as *formal, informal, serious*, or *humorous*. You can determine a poem's tone by examining the writer's word choice and the length and arrangement of lines. For example, in these lines from "Life Doesn't Frighten Me," the short, slang words and the singsong rhythm create an informal, almost childlike tone:

I go boo
Make them shoo

Compare the tones of these poems. Keep the following focus questions in mind as you read.

1. Which two poems have the most similar tones?
2. Which two poems have the most different tones?

❸ Reading Strategy

Drawing Inferences

When you **draw inferences,** you form ideas or come to conclusions based on the information you are given. The conclusion you form is usually not directly stated. For example, in "Abuelito Who" we learn that the grandfather calls his granddaughter a diamond. From this detail, we can infer that he loves his granddaughter. The chart shows another inference you can draw from details in "Abuelito Who."

Detail
Abuelito throws coins like rain.
Inference
Abuelito is generous.

Vocabulary Development

henceforth (hens fôrth′) *adv.* from now on (p. 302)

whimper (hwim′ pər) *v.* whine softly as in fear or pain (p. 302)

querulous (kwer′ yo͞o ləs) *adj.* inclined to find mistakes; complaining (p. 302)

CUSTOMIZE INSTRUCTION FOR UNIVERSAL ACCESS

For Less Proficient Readers	For English Learners	For Advanced Readers
Read aloud the poems before students look at them. Demonstrate the features of free verse by reading expressively and by reading each thought without stopping at line breaks. Allow students to listen to the poems on the **Listening to Literature Audiocassettes,** Sides 16, 17, or the **Listening to Literature CDs,** CD 6.	Because free verse often uses nontraditional punctuation, English learners may find it difficult to see where sentences begin and end. Allow students to listen to the poems to get a sense of the ideas expressed in them. Use the recordings on the **Listening to Literature Audiocassettes,** Sides 16, 17, or the **Listening to Literature CDs,** CD 6.	Invite students to identify their favorite poems and to explain why they enjoy them. Then, ask students to comment on the structure of those poems and to pinpoint those that use free verse. Have students note whether they prefer free verse or traditional verse. Ask them to write a brief journal entry on how verse structure affects enjoyment.

❷ Literary Analysis

Free Verse

- Write a short nursery rhyme or limerick on the board and ask students to read it aloud. Ask them to share their thoughts on the way poetry sounds or looks. Explain that they will be exploring a different kind of poetry on the following pages.
- Ask a volunteer to read aloud the instruction about free verse. Call attention to the example. Point out how free verse is different from the poem you wrote on the board.
- Use the Free Verse transparency on p. 38 of **Literary Analysis and Reading Transparencies** to show the criteria for identifying free verse.
- Before students read the Comparing Literary Works instruction, explain that students can hear tone as well as see it. Demonstrate tone by reading the excerpt from Angelou's poem in several different tones, such as sad, angry, happy, and indifferent.

❸ Reading Strategy

Drawing Inferences

- Explain that drawing inferences is a sophisticated way of thinking, requiring students to notice clues, sometimes subtle ones, and to draw connections between them.
- After students read the instruction and look at the chart, explain that another part of making inferences is drawing on one's own experience.
- Offer students the Drawing Inferences transparency on p. 37 of **Literary Analysis and Reading Transparencies** as a model.

Vocabulary Development

- Pronounce each vocabulary word for students, and read the definitions as a class. Have students identify any words with which they are already familiar.

 **E-Teach**

Visit E-Teach at www.phschool.com for teachers' essays on how to teach, with questions and answers.

TEACH

Step-by-Step Teaching Guide for pp. 300–306

CUSTOMIZE INSTRUCTION
For Verbal/Linguistic Learners

Once students are comfortable with the concept of free verse, invite them to write a free-verse poem responding to one of the poems in this lesson. Encourage them to follow E. E. Cummings's lead by inventing phrases, capitalizing important ideas, using punctuation creatively, or creating an image with the words of the poem.

1 About the Selection

In "Abuelito Who," the speaker weaves earlier, happier impressions of her grandfather with her impressions of him as a frail man who "sleeps in his little room all night and day."

2 Background

Art

Ezra Davenport, by Clarence Holbrook Carter

Although Carter, born in 1904, is not a well-known artist, his paintings are still sold and enjoyed today. Explain to students that, like the poem, this painting is a portrait of a person. Then, discuss the question below. How did the artist use posture and expression to show the man's feelings?

Answer: The man is slightly slumped in the chair, and he has a faraway look in his eyes, as if he is concerned.

3 ▶ Critical Viewing

Possible responses: The man could be a grandfather; he has short hair that might feel like fur; he looks sad, as if he might not feel well.

1 Abuelito Who

Sandra Cisneros

2

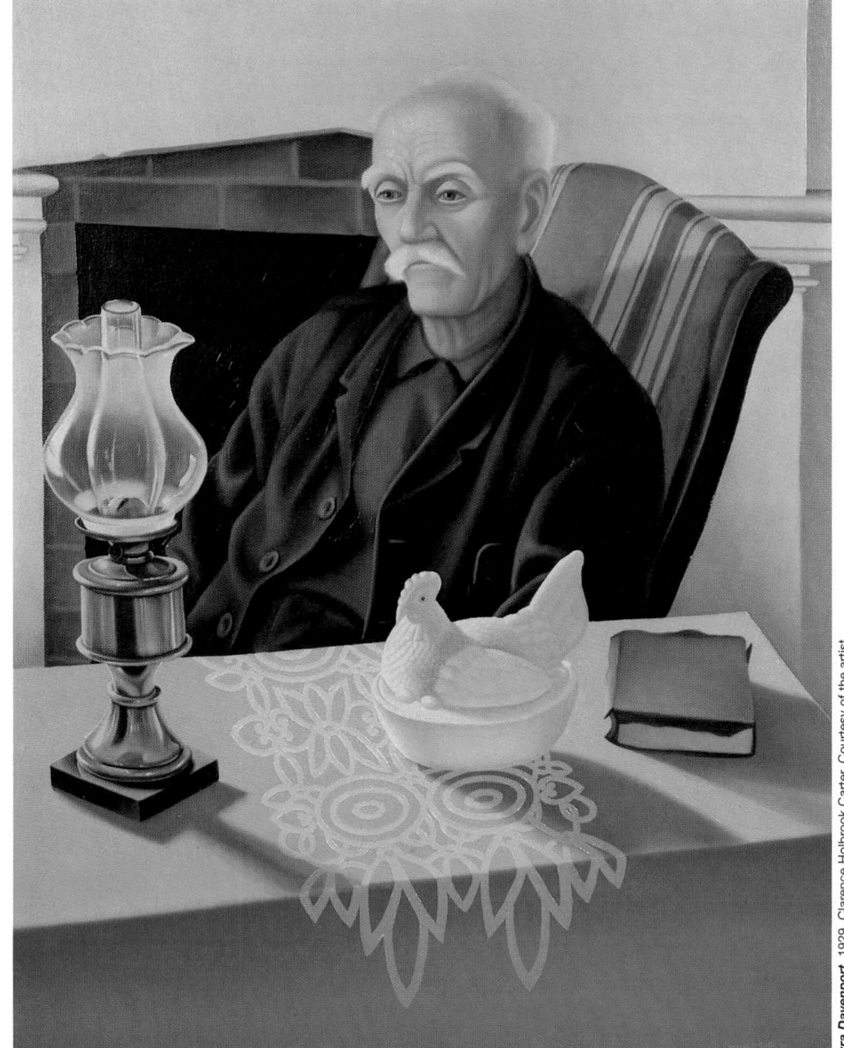

Ezra Davenport, 1929, Clarence Holbrook Carter, Courtesy of the artist

3 ▲ **Critical Viewing** Find two details in this painting that match the description of Abuelito. **[Connect]**

TEACHING RESOURCES

The following resources can be used to enrich or extend the instruction for pp. 300–306.

Literary Analysis

- **Selection Support:** Literary Analysis, p. 95
- **Literary Analysis for Enrichment**

Reading

- **Literatura en español**
- **Listening to Literature Audiocassettes,** Side 12 ■
- **Listening to Literature Audio CDs,** CD 5 ■

Extension

- **Fine Art Transparencies, Volume 1,** Art Transparency 13 (Use the painting to inspire students to write a free-verse poem about the moon. Encourage them to create images with words, as E. E. Cummings does in his poetry.)

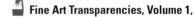

■ **BLOCK SCHEDULING:** Resources marked with this symbol provide varied instruction during 90-minute blocks.

Abuelito[1] who throws coins like rain
and asks who loves him
who is dough and feathers
who is a watch and glass of water
whose hair is made of fur
is too sad to come downstairs today
who tells me in Spanish you are my diamond
who tells me in English you are my sky
whose little eyes are string
can't come out to play
sleeps in his little room all night and day
who used to laugh like the letter k
is sick
is a doorknob tied to a sour stick
is tired shut the door
doesn't live here anymore
is hiding underneath the bed
who talks to me inside my head
is blankets and spoons and big brown shoes
who snores up and down up and down up and down again
is the rain on the roof that falls like coins
asking who loves him
who loves him who?

1. **Abuelito** (ä bwe lē´ tō) in Spanish, an affectionate term for a grandfather.

Review and Assess

Thinking About the Selection

1. **Respond:** Would you like to have Abuelito as a grandfather? Explain.
2. **(a) Analyze:** Who is Abuelito? **(b) Analyze Cause and Effect:** Why can't Abuelito come downstairs?
3. **(a) Recall:** Name two things Abuelito has done often in the past. **(b) Draw Conclusions:** What do these things show about Abuelito's personality?
4. **(a) Recall:** Describe Abuelito today. **(b) Interpret:** Why does the speaker feel as if Abuelito is "hiding underneath the bed"? **(c) Compare and Contrast:** How is Abuelito different today from how he was in the past?
5. **(a) Interpret:** Name three ways in which the speaker is reminded of Abuelito. **(b) Support:** Based on the descriptions of Abuelito, how does the speaker feel about him? **(c) Extend:** In what ways does this poem honor all grandparents?

Sandra Cisneros

(b. 1954)

Growing up in a poor neighborhood in Chicago, Illinois, made for difficult times. Sandra Cisneros kept her focus, though. Drawing on her Mexican heritage, she has written short stories, poetry, and the book *The House on Mango Street*.

Cisneros believes that writers must make connections between their own lives and those of others. In "Abuelito Who," she shares her feelings about her grandfather.

Answers for p. 301

Review and Assess

1. Some students may say that they would because he is affectionate and generous. Encourage students as they respond to tell how Abuelito is like their own grandfathers or like another older adult.
2. **(a)** Abuelito is the speaker's grandfather. **(b)** He can't come downstairs because he is sick.
3. **(a)** Possible response: He used to laugh and compliment the speaker. **(b)** These things show that Abuelito is a kind man who loves his grandchild.
4. **(a)** Possible responses: He is sad and tired; he snores; he is thin and frail and unable to get out of bed or laugh. **(b)** Students may say that the speaker feels as if Abuelito were not in the room at all. Others may say that because young children are often frightened by the space underneath a bed, these lines refer to the speaker's fear of death. **(c)** Where once Abuelito was full of life and joy, he is now frail and close to death.
5. **(a)** Possible response: The speaker remembers his laugh, his eyes like string, and his soft hair. **(b)** She cares for Abuelito and notices the changes in him. **(c)** The poem reflects the love that children often feel for their grandparents by describing a grandfather through a child's eyes.

CUSTOMIZE INSTRUCTION FOR UNIVERSAL ACCESS

For Less Proficient Readers	For Gifted/Talented Students
Explain that an inference is based not only on the poet's words, but also on the readers' experiences. Have each student draw a three-column chart with these headings: *What I know, What the poem says,* and *What I think the poem means.* Have students fill in the columns as they read. Students should fill in the first column with information they know about the subject of the poem, the second with details from the poem, and the third with their inferences, based on the other two columns.	Have students create portraits of older persons who have been positive influences in their lives. Explain to students that a portrait often contains a significant object, pose, or setting that contributes to a viewer's understanding of the subject of the portrait. Remind students to consider these elements as they design their portraits.

❹ About the Selection

In "The Open Road," the speaker expresses a feeling of freedom and confidence as he sets out on an open road.

❺ Literary Analysis

Free Verse

- Point out that free verse often contains repetition, as in a song.
- Ask volunteers to point out the words and phrases that are repeated in the poem.
  Answer: The words *before me, henceforth, good fortune,* and *no more* are each used twice in the poem.

Monitor Progress Invite students to read the poem aloud. Then, ask them what effect the repetition of words has.
Possible response: Students may say that the repetition highlights the important ideas. They may also point out that the repetition gives the poem a distinct rhythm.

Reteach To help students understand free verse, take a traditional poem with which students are not familiar, and write it on the board in a way that breaks up its lines and rhyme scheme. Next, ask students to read it aloud. Then, read the poem as it is actually written, and ask students to compare the two readings. Point out that free verse liberates the poem from having to rhyme and follow certain rhythmic patterns.

❹ The Open Road

Walt Whitman

Afoot and light-hearted, I take to the open road,
Healthy, free, the world before me,
The long brown path before me, leading wherever I choose.

❺ Henceforth I ask not good-fortune, I myself am good-fortune,
Henceforth I whimper no more, postpone no more,
    need nothing,
Done with indoor complaints, libraries, querulous criticisms,
Strong and content, I travel the open road.

henceforth (hens fôrth′) *adv.* from now on

whimper (hwim′ pər) *v.* whine softly as in fear or pain

querulous (kwer′ yo͞o ləs) *adj.* complaining

CUSTOMIZE INSTRUCTION FOR UNIVERSAL ACCESS

For Gifted/Talented Students

Suggest that students adapt one of the poems to a dramatic monologue. They will have to develop characters from the information in the poem. Suggest that students ask the following questions:

- What are some of the speaker's characteristics?
- What are some of the speaker's concerns?
- What happens in the poem?

Ask students to write short scripts, which they do not need to memorize, and perform them for the class. Remind students that the monologues should be true to the poems and may include actual lines from the poems.

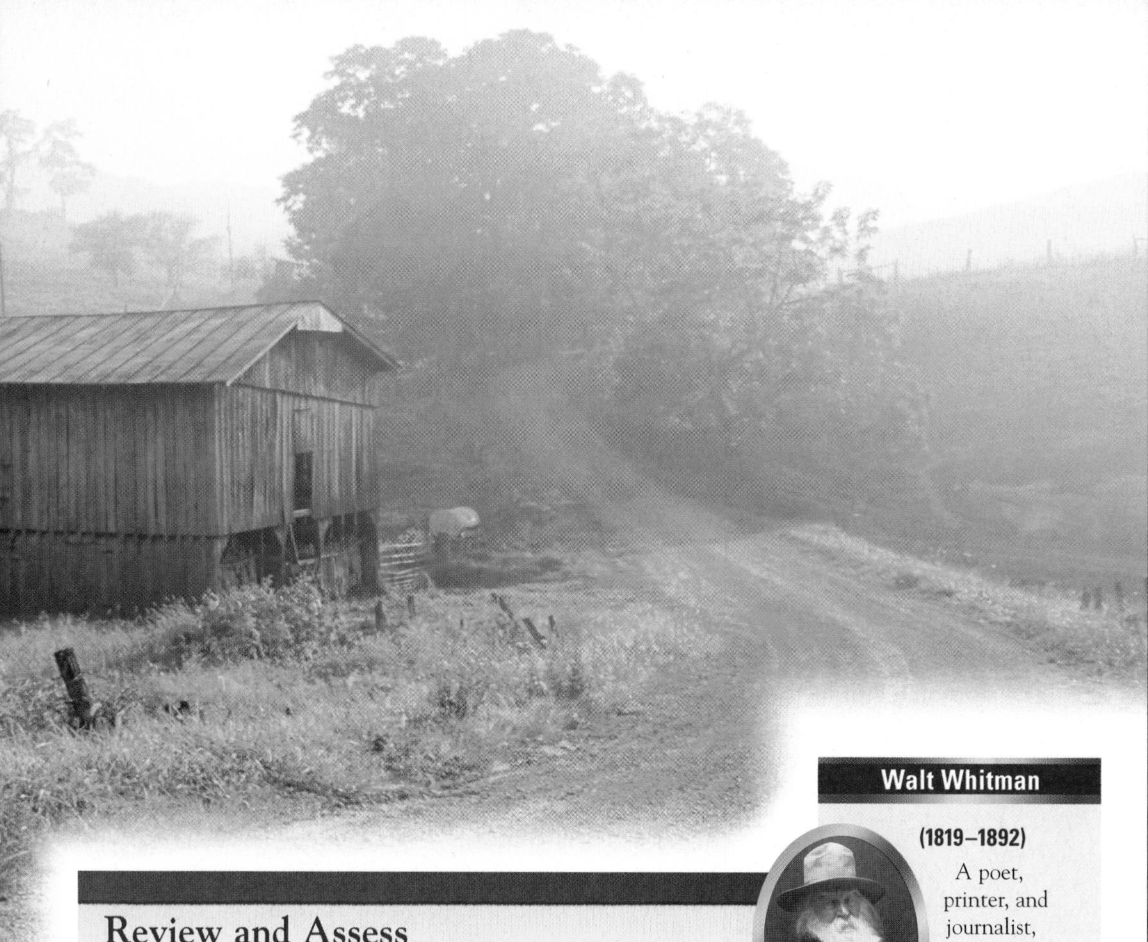

Walt Whitman

(1819–1892)

A poet, printer, and journalist, Walt Whitman considered himself first and foremost an American. In his book *Leaves of Grass*, he created a powerful vision of what democracy means. Around the time of the Civil War, when Whitman lived, writers in the United States thought they had much to learn from European writers. Whitman believed that they could find everything they needed to know in themselves and their fellow citizens.

Review and Assess

Thinking About the Selections

1. **Respond:** How did you feel reading this poem? Explain.
2. **(a) Recall:** At the beginning of "The Open Road," what is the speaker about to do? **(b) Analyze Cause and Effect:** Why does the speaker feel "light-hearted" at this moment?
3. **(a) Recall:** What decision does the speaker in "The Open Road" announce? **(b) Interpret:** Now that he "is" good fortune, how do you think the speaker will respond when things go wrong? **(c) Speculate:** Do you think this poem is about a road used for physical travel? What else might this "open road" be?
4. **(a) Recall:** What is the speaker done with? **(b) Interpret:** Give one example of each thing the speaker is done with. **(c) Deduce:** Why is the speaker done with these things?
5. **(a) Speculate:** What has led the speaker to this changed attitude? **(b) Evaluate:** Do you think that this is a good attitude for a person to have? Explain.

Answers for p. 303

Review and Assess

1. Students may say that they shared a similar emotion with the poet while reading the poem. Others might say that they didn't feel anything.
2. **(a)** The speaker is taking to the open road, or heading out on a trip. **(b)** The speaker feels as if the world with all its opportunities is open to him, and the speaker no longer feels dependent on others for happiness.
3. **(a)** The speaker has decided not to ask for good fortune, not to complain, not to postpone things, and not to listen to others' complaints. **(b)** The speaker will probably turn misfortune into opportunity. **(c)** The poem seems to be about actual, physical travel, but it may also be about spiritual or emotional journeys.
4. **(a)** The speaker is done with complaints associated with being cooped up indoors, quiet libraries, and other people's critical comments. **(b)** Possible response: The speaker is done with going to school, studying, and listening to people complain. **(c)** The speaker is done with these things because they cause unhappiness and a sense of being trapped.
5. **(a)** Possible response: The speaker may have felt trapped and has decided to change his or her life. **(b)** Possible response: Yes, because the speaker realizes the possibility of making choices that will lead to a more satisfying life.

CUSTOMIZE INSTRUCTION FOR UNIVERSAL ACCESS

For Special Needs Students	For English Learners
Students may have trouble identifying the tone of the poems. Remind them to use the visual clues in the poems and in their textbooks. Ask students to look at and think about the illustrations that accompany each poem. Give them a minute to make a short list of words that identify the feelings or associations they have when they look at the illustrations. Have students work with partners to narrow down the list to one word. Then, have students read each poem while keeping that one word in mind.	Students who are learning English may not recognize tone—either written or spoken. Help students by asking them to look in one of the poems for words that reveal the speaker's mood or feelings. After students compile a short list of words, work with them to name the predominant mood or feeling that they suggest. Then, ask a proficient English speaker to read aloud the poem in the tone that students have identified.

Time and Resource Manager

Reading Level: Challenging, Average
Average Number of Instructional Days: 4

RESOURCES		
PRINT	**TRANSPARENCIES**	**TECHNOLOGY**
• **Beyond Literature,** Workplace Connection: Personal Initiative, p. 20 ▲ ■		• **Interest Grabber Videotapes,** Tape 2 ● ▲ ■
• **Selection Support Workbook:** ● ▲ ■ Literary Analysis, p. 100 Reading Strategy, p. 99 Build Vocabulary, p. 96	• **Literary Analysis and Reading Transparencies,** pp. 39 and 40 ● ▲ ■	
• **Adapted Reader's Companion** ● • **Reader's Companion** ●		• **Listening to Literature** ● ▲ ■ Audiocassettes, Sides 12, 13 Audio CDs, CD 6
• **English Learner's Companion** ● ▲ • **Literatura en español** ● ▲ • **Literary Analysis for Enrichment** ■		
• **Formal Assessment:** Selection Test, pp. 82–84 ● ▲ ■ • **Open Book Test,** pp. 58–60 ● ▲ ■ • **Performance Assessment and Portfolio Management,** pp. 9, 23 ● ▲ ■ • PRENTICE HALL ASSESSMENT SYSTEM ● ▲ ■	• PRENTICE HALL ASSESSMENT SYSTEM ● ▲ ■ Skills Practice Answers and Explanations on Transparencies	• **Test Bank Software** ● ▲ ■ • **Got It! Assessment Videotapes,** Tape 2 ● ▲
• **Selection Support Workbook:** ● ▲ ■ Build Spelling Skills, p. 97 Build Grammar Skills, p. 98 • **Writing and Grammar,** Copper Level ● ▲ ■ • **Extension Activities,** p. 20 ● ▲ ■	• **Daily Language Practice Transparencies** ● ▲ • **Writing Models and Graphic Organizers on Transparencies** ● ▲ ■	• **Writing and Grammar iText CD-ROM** ● ▲ ■ *Take It to the Net* www.phschool.com

BLOCK SCHEDULING: Use one 90-minute class period to preteach the selection and have students read it. Use a second 90-minute class period to assess students' mastery of skills and have them complete one of the Extension Activities.

PREETEACH

Step-by-Step Teaching Guide for pp. 314–315

Motivation

Ask students what qualities they associate with leaders at school, in sports, and in their communities. On the board, create a word web of their responses. Tell students that the selections they are about to read tell about the lives of two men who followed new roads to become leaders in their fields.

Interest Grabber Video

As an alternative, play "Young Abraham Lincoln" on Tape 2 to engage students' interest.

1 Background

Physical Education

Although many people are familiar with baseball, not many know its history of excluding African American players from the major leagues. Jackie Robinson, about whom Geoffrey C. Ward and Ken Burns write in "Jackie Robinson: Justice at Last," was the first African American to play in the major leagues. In the 1950s and earlier, baseball was not what it is now. Baseball, which many consider to be the all-American sport, was adapted in the 1820s from the British games of rounders and cricket. By the 1860s, the game that came to be named baseball had established rules that players and spectators today would recognize. The first World Series game was played in 1903, and this championship game was to be canceled only twice in the next one hundred years, in 1904 and in 1994.

Prepare to Read

1 A Backwoods Boy ◆ Jackie Robinson: Justice at Last

Take It to the Net

Visit www.phschool.com for interactive activities and instruction related to these selections, including

- background
- graphic organizers
- literary elements
- reading strategies

Preview

Connecting to the Literature

Abraham Lincoln and Jackie Robinson were people who faced and overcame huge roadblocks on the road to success. What problems and roadblocks do you face as you try to achieve the things that mean the most to you?

Background

In the early 1900s, major league baseball clubs excluded African Americans. African American players formed their own teams, and in the 1920s, they organized the Negro leagues. Although they did not become as widely known as their white counterparts, some of the best players in baseball history played in the Negro leagues. Jackie Robinson began his professional baseball career on the Negro leagues' team, the Kansas City Monarchs.

TEACHING RESOURCES

The following resources can be used to enrich or extend the instruction for pp. 314–315.

Motivation

Interest Grabber Video, Tape 2

Background

Beyond Literature, p. 20

Take It to the Net

Visit www.phschool.com for Background and hotlinks for the selections.

Literary Analysis

Literary Analysis and Reading Transparencies, Historical Account, p. 40

Reading

Selection Support: Reading Strategy, p. 99; Build Vocabulary, p. 96

Literary Analysis and Reading Transparencies, Determining Main Idea, p. 39

BLOCK SCHEDULING: Resources marked with this symbol provide varied instruction during 90-minute blocks.

❷ Literary Analysis

Historical Account

A **historical account** tells about real people and events of the past. A historical account may tell a story, but it is not necessarily written in strict time order.

The details in the example below are drawn from various points in Lincoln's life to illustrate his lifelong love of reading.

> Mostly, he educated himself by borrowing books and newspapers. There are many stories about Lincoln's efforts to find enough books to satisfy him in that backwoods country. Those he liked he read again and again, losing himself in the adventures of *Robinson Crusoe* or the magical tales of *The Arabian Nights*.

Comparing Literary Works

These two historical accounts focus on important people in history whose actions changed the way people thought or acted. Compare and contrast the subjects of the accounts by thinking about the following focus questions.

1. In what way did each person affect history?
2. What qualities do you admire in each subject? Explain.

❸ Reading Strategy

Determining Main Ideas

The **main ideas** are the core of a piece of writing. To determine main ideas, you look at how the details work together to suggest or point to a big idea. The graphic organizer shows four details from which you can determine that Jackie Robinson was a good athlete.

Organize details in your mind to determine main ideas as you read these two works.

Rookie of the Year
hit .387
great bat control
great runner
He's a good athlete.

Vocabulary Development

aptitude (ap′ te tood′) *n.* natural ability (p. 322)

intrigued (in trēgd′) *v.* fascinated (p. 323)

treacherous (trech′ ər əs) *adj.* dangerous (p. 324)

integrate (in′ tə grāt′) *v.* remove barriers and allow access to all (p. 326)

retaliated (ri tal′ ē at′ id) *v.* harmed or did wrong to someone in return for an injury or wrong he or she has done (p. 328)

CUSTOMIZE INSTRUCTION FOR UNIVERSAL ACCESS

For Special Needs Students	For Less Proficient Readers	For English Learners
Have students read the adapted version of these selections in the **Adapted Reader's Companion.** This version provides basic-level instruction in an interactive format with questions and write-on lines. Completing the adapted version will prepare students to read the selection in the Student Edition.	Have students read these selections in the **Reader's Companion.** This version provides basic-level instruction in an interactive format with questions and write-on lines. After students finish the selection in the Reader's Companion, have them complete the questions and activities in the Student Edition.	Have students read the adapted version of these selections in the **English Learner's Companion.** This version provides basic-level instruction in an interactive format with questions and write-on lines. Completing the adapted version will prepare students to read the selection in the Student Edition.

❷ Literary Analysis

Historical Account

- Explain that the selections students will be reading are nonfiction, or factual, accounts of two men in history. Discuss with students the differences between fiction and nonfiction.
- Next, have students silently read the instruction on p. 315. Point out that the example is from one of the selections they will read.
- Have students think of books or films they have read or seen recently that are about a historical figure.
- After students read the Comparing Literary Works instruction, talk to them about the difference between objective and subjective writing. Explain that even in nonfiction accounts, the author will often include insights that are based on his or her perspective.
- Finally, use the Historical Account transparency on p. 40 in **Literary Analysis and Reading Transparencies** to help students identify the differences between factual information and a writer's ideas.

❸ Reading Strategy

Determining Main Ideas

- After students read the instruction on p. 315, discuss the difference between a main idea and a topic. Explain that a main idea is more than a topic; it expresses an idea about the topic.
- Offer students the following example: Jackie Robinson is the topic of the second reading selection, but "Jackie Robinson was a brave and noble athlete" is a main idea.

Vocabulary Development

- Pronounce each vocabulary word for students, and read the definitions as a class. Have students identify any words with which they are already familiar.

E-Teach

Visit E-Teach at www.phschool.com for teachers' essays on how to teach, with questions and answers.

TEACH

Step-by-Step Teaching Guide for pp. 316–328

CUSTOMIZE INSTRUCTION
For Musical/Rhythmic Learners

To help students "hear" how Lincoln may have sounded when he first began to give speeches in his community, have volunteers who are familiar with the sounds of various musical instruments find quotations from Lincoln's speeches to read in a "high, reedy" voice.

❶ About the Selection

"A Backwoods Boy" is a factual account of Abraham Lincoln's youth. It follows Lincoln's family as they move from home to home and describes the loss of his mother, Nancy, when he was nine years old. The account also tells how Lincoln loves to learn and charms people with his humorous tales. The selection ends with Lincoln's election to the Illinois House of Representatives, the beginning of his long and impressive journey down a new road.

❷ ▶Critical Viewing

Possible responses: Some students may find it surprising that a U.S. president could come from such humble beginnings. Other students may say that in the United States opportunities exist for people from all economic backgrounds.

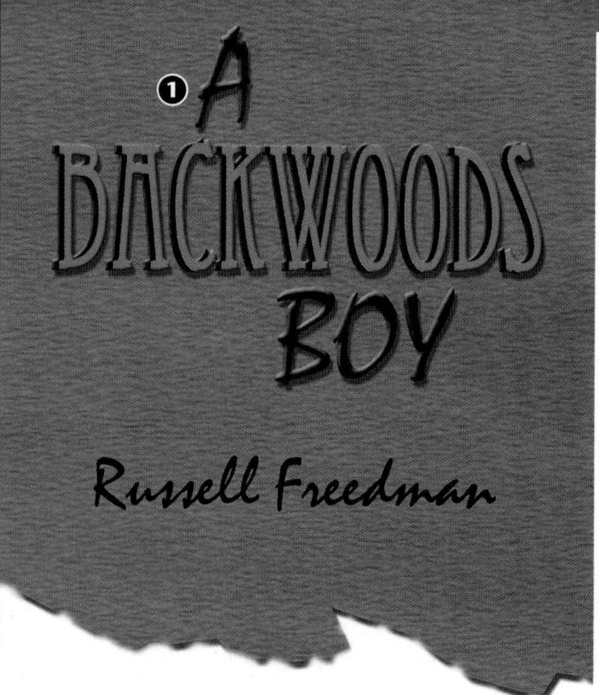

❶ A Backwoods Boy

Russell Freedman

❷ ▲ **Critical Viewing** Is it surprising that one of the presidents of the United States was born in a house like this one? **[Assess]**

"It is a great piece of folly to attempt to make anything out of my early life. It can all be condensed into a simple sentence, and that sentence you will find in Gray's Elegy[1]—'the short and simple annals[2] of the poor.' That's my life, and that's all you or anyone else can make out of it."[3]

Abraham Lincoln never liked to talk much about his early life. A poor backwoods farm boy, he grew up swinging an ax on frontier homesteads in Kentucky, Indiana, and Illinois.

❸ He was born near Hodgenville, Kentucky, on February 12, 1809, in a log cabin with one window, one door, a chimney, and a hardpacked dirt floor. His parents named him after his pioneer grandfather. The first Abraham Lincoln had been shot dead by hostile Indians

1. **elegy** (el´ ə jē) *n.* poem praising someone who has died.
2. **annals** (an´ əlz) *n.* historical records.
3. **"It is a great . . . out of it"** this is a quotation from Abraham Lincoln.

TEACHING RESOURCES

The following resources can be used to enrich or extend the instruction for pp. 316–328.

Literary Analysis
- **Selection Support:** Literary Analysis, p. 100
- **Literary Analysis for Enrichment**
- **Writing Models and Graphic Organizers,** pp. 69, 73, 77, 89, 93, 97

Reading
- **Reader's Companion**
- **Adapted Reader's Companion**
- **English Learner's Companion**
- **Literatura en español**
- **Listening to Literature Audiocassettes,** Sides 12, 13 ■
- **Listening to Literature Audio CDs,** CD 6 ■

■ **BLOCK SCHEDULING:** Resources marked with this symbol provide varied instruction during 90-minute blocks.

in 1786, while planting a field of corn in the Kentucky wilderness. ❸

Young Abraham was still a toddler when his family packed their belongings and moved to another log-cabin farm a few miles north, on Knob Creek. That was the first home he could remember, the place where he ran and played as a barefoot boy.

He remembered the bright waters of Knob Creek as it tumbled past the Lincoln cabin and disappeared into the Kentucky hills. Once he fell into the rushing creek and almost drowned before he was pulled out by a neighbor boy. Another time he caught a fish and gave it to a passing soldier.

Lincoln never forgot the names of his first teachers—Zachariah Riney followed by Caleb Hazel—who ran a windowless log schoolhouse two miles away. It was called a "blab school." Pupils of all ages sat on rough wooden benches and bawled out their lessons aloud. Abraham went there with his sister Sarah, who was two years older, when they could be spared from their chores at home. Holding hands, they would walk through scrub trees and across creek bottoms to the schoolhouse door. They learned their numbers from one to ten, and a smattering of reading, writing, and spelling. ❹

Reading Strategy
Determining Main Idea
What is the main idea about Lincoln's schooling?

Their parents couldn't read or write at all. Abraham's mother, Nancy, signed her name by making a shakily drawn mark. He would remember her as a thin, sad-eyed woman who labored beside her husband in the fields. She liked to gather the children around her in the evening to recite prayers and Bible stories she had memorized.

His father, Thomas, was a burly, barrel-chested farmer and carpenter who had worked hard at homesteading since marrying Nancy Hanks in 1806. A sociable fellow, his greatest pleasure was to crack jokes and swap stories with his chums. With painful

❺  **Reading Check**
What did Lincoln learn in school?

❸ Literary Analysis

Historical Account

- Have students identify sentences in this paragraph that state facts.
  Answer: All the sentences state facts.
- Review that facts that can be proved, like the date of Lincoln's birth or the number of windows and doors on his cabin.

❹ Reading Strategy

Determining Main Idea

- Explain to students that although they may be familiar with the process of finding the main ideas of a paragraph, identifying the main idea of a long selection requires piecing together the main ideas of each of the paragraphs.
- Then, ask the Reading Strategy question on p. 317: What is the main idea about Lincoln's schooling?
  Answer: The main idea is that Lincoln did not have much formal schooling when he was young.
- Tell students to keep a record of their answers to Reading Strategy questions that ask them to identify the main idea of a passage. They will use them again later.

❺ Reading Check

Answer: Lincoln learned to count from one to ten as well as how to read, write, and spell a little.

CUSTOMIZE INSTRUCTION FOR UNIVERSAL ACCESS

For Special Needs Students	For Less Proficient Readers
In order to help students recognize the main idea, offer them a graphic organizer like the Main Idea and Supporting Details organizer on p. 73 in **Writing Models and Graphic Organizers on Transparencies.** Then, select a single paragraph for students to analyze. Make sure that the paragraph has a clearly stated main idea. Next, help students identify details and evaluate sentences for a broader idea. If students feel confident, ask them to look at a paragraph whose main idea is only implied.	Review with students that the main idea of a paragraph may be in several different places within a paragraph. Tell students that the main idea may be the first or last sentence in the paragraph and that writers place their main ideas in those places so readers will recognize and remember them. Explain that main ideas may be implied or stated in the middle of the paragraph. Ask students to make up a checklist of locations for main ideas. Have students keep the list handy as they read, so they know where to check for a main idea.

6 Literary Analysis

Historical Account

- Remind students that the author's job is to present the facts and to help make sense of them. Have students look at the facts that appear in the first paragraph on p. 318.
- Ask students the Literary Analysis question at the top of p. 318. Answer: The author reminds the reader that it was not unusual to grow up without education in those days.

7 Critical Thinking

Connect

- Point out the use of the word *backwoods* here. Explain that it has two meanings: (1) a heavily wooded area and (2) a remote, thinly populated place.
- Ask students which definition the author refers to here. Answer: Students should understand that the first definition is implied here, as Lincoln and his family are described as hacking their way through underbrush.
- Point out that the author's use of the word *backwoods* in the title may reflect both the area in which Lincoln grew up and Lincoln's humble beginnings.

6 effort, Thomas Lincoln could scrawl his name. Like his wife, he had grown up without education, but that wasn't unusual in those days. He supported his family by living off his own land, and he watched for a chance to better himself.

In 1816, Thomas decided to pull up stakes again and move north to Indiana, which was about to join the Union as the nation's nineteenth state. Abraham was seven. He remembered the one-hundred-mile journey as the hardest experience of his life. The family set out on a cold morning in December, loading all their possessions on two horses. 7 They crossed the Ohio River on a makeshift ferry, traveled through towering forests, then hacked a path through tangled underbrush until they reached their new homesite near the backwoods community of Little Pigeon Creek.

Thomas put up a temporary winter shelter—a crude, three-sided lean-to of logs and branches. At the open end, he kept a fire burning to take the edge off the cold and scare off the wild animals. At night, wrapped in bearskins and huddled by the fire, Abraham and Sarah listened to wolves howl and panthers scream.

Abraham passed his eighth birthday in the lean-to. He was big for his age, "a tall spider of a boy," and old enough to handle an ax. He helped his father clear the land. They planted corn and pumpkin seeds between the tree stumps. And they built a new log cabin, the biggest one yet, where Abraham climbed a ladder and slept in a loft beneath the roof.

Soon after the cabin was finished, some of Nancy's kinfolk arrived. Her aunt and uncle with their adopted son Dennis had decided to follow the Lincolns to Indiana. Dennis Hanks became an extra hand to Thomas and a big brother to Abraham, someone to run and wrestle with.

A year later, Nancy's aunt and uncle lay dead, victims of the dreaded "milk sickness" (now known to be caused by a poisonous plant called white snake root). An epidemic of the disease swept through the Indiana woods in the summer of 1818. Nancy had nursed her relatives until the end, and then she too came down with the disease. Abraham watched his mother toss in bed with chills, fever, and pain for seven days before she died at the age of thirty-four. "She knew she was going to die," Dennis Hanks recalled. "She called up the children to her dying side and told them to be good and kind to their father, to one another, and to the world."

Thomas built a coffin from black cherry wood, and nine-year-old Abraham whittled the pegs that held the wooden planks together. They buried Nancy on a windswept hill, next to her aunt and uncle. Sarah, now eleven, took her mother's place, cooking, cleaning, and mending clothes for her father, brother, and cousin Dennis in the forlorn and lonely cabin.

Literary Analysis
Historical Account What comment does Freedman make on the facts he presents here?

ENRICHMENT: Social Studies Connection

Mrs. Lincoln, Pioneer Wife

When the new Mrs. Lincoln arrived in Pigeon Creek, Indiana, the Lincoln family cabin, which they had occupied since 1817, changed. Before she met Thomas Lincoln, Sarah Bush Johnston had been a widow. When she arrived at Pigeon Creek, she brought furniture, pewter dishes, pots and skillets, a flax wheel, feather pillows and mattresses, and a kettle for making soap. She asked Thomas to put down a wood floor and to install a real door, to keep out the dust. In addition, Abraham and her son John whitewashed the walls and ceilings to keep out insects.

Students may enjoy learning more about the cabins occupied by the pioneers of the early 1800s. Have them do research about the cabin that Abraham Lincoln lived in at Pigeon Creek and about other types of cabins used during that time. Some students may enjoy creating a drawing of the inside of Lincoln's cabin and explaining how some of the objects were used.

Thomas Lincoln waited for a year. Then he went back to Kentucky to find himself a new wife. He returned in a four-horse wagon with a widow named Sarah Bush Johnston, her three children, and all her household goods. Abraham and his sister were fortunate, for their stepmother was a warm and loving person. She took the motherless children to her heart and raised them as her own. She also spruced up the neglected Lincoln cabin, now shared by eight people who lived, ate, and slept in a single smoky room with a loft.

8 Abraham was growing fast, shooting up like a sunflower, a spindly youngster with big bony hands, unruly black hair, a dark complexion, and luminous gray eyes. He became an expert with the ax, working alongside his father, who also hired him out to work for others. For twenty-five cents a day, the boy dug wells, built pigpens, split fence rails, felled trees. "My how he could chop!" exclaimed a friend. "His ax would flash and bite into a sugar tree or a sycamore, and down it would come. If you heard him felling trees in a clearing, you would say there were three men at work, the way the trees fell."

Meanwhile, he went to school "by littles," a few weeks one winter, maybe a month the next. Lincoln said later that all his schooling together "did not amount to one year." Some fragments of his schoolwork still survive, including a verse that he wrote in his homemade arithmetic book: "Abraham Lincoln/his hand and pen/he will be good but/god knows When."

9 Mostly, he educated himself by borrowing books and newspapers. There are many stories about Lincoln's efforts to find enough books to satisfy him in that backwoods country. Those he liked he read again and again, losing himself in the adventures of *Robinson Crusoe* or the magical tales of *The Arabian Nights*. He was thrilled by a biography of George Washington, with its stirring account of the Revolutionary War. And he came to love the rhyme and rhythm of poetry, reciting passages from Shakespeare or the Scottish poet Robert Burns at the drop of a hat. He would carry a book out to the field with him, so he could read at the end of each plow furrow, while the horse was getting its breath. When noon came, he would sit under a tree and read while he ate. "I never saw Abe after he was twelve that he didn't have a book in his hand or in his pocket," Dennis Hanks remembered. "It didn't seem natural to see a feller read like that."

By the time he was sixteen, Abraham was six feet tall—"the gangliest awkwardest feller . . . he appeared to be all joints," said a neighbor. He may have looked awkward, but hard physical labor had given him a tough, lean body with muscular arms like steel cables. He could grab a woodsman's ax by the handle and hold it straight out at arm's length. And he was one of the best wrestlers and runners around.

Reading Strategy
Determining Main Idea
What is the main idea of this paragraph?

Literary Analysis
Historical Account
What interpretations of fact might Freedman be making here?

10 

How did Lincoln feel about reading?

8 Reading Strategy

Determining Main Idea

- Because the selection is covering events mostly in chronological order, students may not think that individual paragraphs have their own main idea.
- In addition, students may not understand that a main idea may be implied. Explain that a main idea, though not stated outright, may be indicated by the ideas in a paragraph.
- Refer to the bracketed text on p. 319, and pose the Reading Strategy question: What is the main idea of this paragraph?
  Answer: Students may say that the main idea of the paragraph is that Abraham Lincoln is able to help his family because he is an energetic worker who focuses on his task.
- Point out how all the details suggest that Abraham was a strong, hard-working, and willing worker.

9 Literary Analysis

Historical Account

- Ask students to list the facts in this paragraph.
  Answer: Students should mention the facts that Lincoln enjoyed certain books and that he would take books to work with him and read while eating.
- Then, ask the Literary Analysis question.
  Answer: Freedman suggests that Lincoln loved to read and to learn. His choice of facts backs up his idea.
- Discuss with students how the use of direct quotations from Lincoln's contemporaries really supports the author's ideas. Readers are likely to believe the words of a person who actually knew Lincoln.

10 Reading Check

Answer: Lincoln loved reading.

CUSTOMIZE INSTRUCTION FOR UNIVERSAL ACCESS

For Special Needs Students	For Advanced Readers
Have students work in pairs to read pp. 318–319. Ask students to take turns reading aloud two or three paragraphs of the selection. After each student reads, he or she should stop and think out loud about the information or ideas in the reading. The listening partner should take notes. Finally, students should review their notes and see what they learned. Ask each pair to write a summary or share their findings with the class.	As students read "A Backwoods Boy," ask them to keep a dialectical journal in which they make notes of interesting or difficult ideas or passages. For each idea or passage students record, they should also write a question or comment. Then, have students exchange journals with partners who will read the passage notes and respond in writing to the questions and comments. Encourage students to write thoughtful responses to their partners.

⓫ Critical Thinking

Connect

- Ask students if they have friends or relatives who are good storytellers. Ask students to describe what they believe are the qualities that make a good storyteller.
- Then, ask students what their experiences with these friends and family members reveal about what it would be like to be around Abe Lincoln.
  Possible response: Students may say that their story-telling friends and family enjoy being with others and that others enjoy being with them. The stories often include humorous details and vivid language. Lincoln may have had similar personality traits.

⓬ Critical Thinking

Infer

- Before posing the question below, ask students to review what they already know about Abraham Lincoln in his adult years. Make sure that students are aware that in 1863, Lincoln signed the Emancipation Proclamation, a document which began the long process of outlawing slavery in the United States.
- Then, ask students why they think the author mentions the African American slaves Lincoln saw in New Orleans as well as Lincoln's reaction.
  Answer: The author is showing that slavery made a bad impression on Lincoln, which would explain his decision years later to outlaw it.

⓭ ▶Critical Viewing

Answer: Students may say that the image of Thomas Lincoln is similar to the image of Abraham Lincoln in that they both seem determined and serious.

⓫ He also had a reputation as a comic and storyteller. Like his father, Abraham was fond of talking and listening to talk. About this time he had found a book called *Lessons in Elocution*, which offered advice on public speaking. He practiced before his friends, standing on a tree stump as he entertained them with fiery imitations of the roving preachers and politicians who often visited Little Pigeon Creek.

Folks liked young Lincoln. They regarded him as a good-humored, easy-going boy—a bookworm maybe, but smart and willing to oblige. Yet even then, people noticed that he could be moody and withdrawn. As a friend put it, he was "witty, sad, and reflective by turns."

At the age of seventeen, Abraham left home for a few months to work as a ferryman's helper on the Ohio River. He was eighteen when his sister Sarah died early in 1828, while giving birth to her first child.

That spring, Abraham had a chance to get away from the backwoods and see something of the world. A local merchant named James Gentry hired Lincoln to accompany his son Allen on a twelve-hundred-mile flatboat voyage to New Orleans. With their cargo of country produce, the two boys floated down the Ohio River and into the Mississippi, maneuvering with long poles to avoid snags and sandbars, and to navigate in the busy river traffic.

New Orleans was the first real city they had ever seen. Their eyes must have popped as the great harbor came into view, jammed with the masts of sailing ships from distant ports all over the world. ⓬ The city's cobblestone streets teemed with sailors, traders, and adventurers speaking strange languages. And there were gangs of slaves everywhere. Lincoln would never forget the sight of black men, women, and children being driven along in chains and auctioned off like cattle. In those days, New Orleans had more than two hundred slave dealers.

The boys sold their cargo and their flatboat and returned upriver by steamboat. Abraham earned twenty-four dollars—a good bit of money at the time—for the three-month trip. He handed the money over to his father, according to law and custom.

Thomas Lincoln was thinking about moving on again. Lately he had heard glowing reports about Illinois, where instead of forests there were endless prairies with plenty of rich black soil. Early in 1830, Thomas sold his Indiana farm. The Lincolns piled everything they owned into two ox-drawn wagons and set out over muddy roads, with Abraham, just turned twenty-one, driving one of the wagons himself. They traveled west to their new homesite in central Illinois, not far from Decatur. Once again, Abraham helped his father build a cabin and start a new farm.

⓭ **▼ Critical Viewing** How does this image of Thomas Lincoln compare with your image of Abraham Lincoln? **[Compare]**

ENRICHMENT: Literature Connection

Considering the Classics

Robinson Crusoe and *The Arabian Nights*, which Lincoln read devotedly, are considered classics in juvenile literature. *Robinson Crusoe* (1719) is a novel written by Daniel Defoe that describes the adventures of a man who is stranded on a desert island. *The Arabian Nights*, which is also called *The Thousand and One Nights*, is a collection of stories mostly of Arabian, Indian, or Persian origin. Three of the best-known stories, which were written between the fourteenth and sixteenth centuries, are "The History of Aladdin, or the Wonderful Lamp," "The History of Sinbad the Sailor," and "The History of Ali Baba and the Forty Thieves."

14 He stayed with his family through their first prairie winter, but he was getting restless. He had met an enterprising fellow named Denton Offutt, who wanted him to take another boatload of cargo down the river to New Orleans. Abraham agreed to make the trip with his stepbrother, John Johnston, and a cousin, John Hanks.

When he returned to Illinois three months later, he paid a quick farewell visit to his father and stepmother. Abraham was twenty-two now, of legal age, free to do what he wanted. His parents were settled and could get along without him. Denton Offutt was planning to open a general store in the flourishing village of New Salem, Illinois, and he had promised Lincoln a steady job.

15 Lincoln arrived in New Salem in July 1831 wearing a faded cotton shirt and blue jeans too short for his long legs—a "friendless, uneducated, penniless boy," as he later described himself. He tended the counter at Denton Offutt's store and slept in a room at the back.

The village stood in a wooded grove on a bluff above the Sangamon River. Founded just two years earlier, it had about one hundred people living in one- and two-room log houses. Cattle grazed behind split-rail fences, hogs snuffled along dusty lanes, and chickens and geese flapped about underfoot. New Salem was still a small place, but it was growing. The settlers expected it to become a frontier boom town.

With his gifts for swapping stories and making friends, Lincoln fit easily into the life of the village. He showed off his skill with an ax, competed in footraces, and got along with everyone from Mentor Graham, the schoolmaster, to Jack Armstrong, the leader of a rowdy gang called the Clary's Grove boys. Armstrong was the wrestling champion of New Salem. He quickly challenged Lincoln to a match.

On the appointed day, an excited crowd gathered down by the river, placing bets as the wrestlers stripped to the waist for combat. They circled each other, then came to grips, twisting and tugging until they crashed to the ground with Lincoln on top. As he pinned Armstrong's shoulders to the ground, the other Clary's Grove boys dived in to join the scuffle. Lincoln broke away, backed against a cliff, and defiantly offered to take them all on—one at a time. Impressed, Armstrong jumped to his feet and offered Lincoln his hand, declaring the match a draw. After that, they were fast friends.

Lincoln also found a place among the town's intellectuals. He joined the New Salem Debating Society, which met once a week in James Rutledge's tavern. The first time he debated, he seemed nervous. But as he began to speak in his high, reedy voice, he surprised everyone with the force and logic of his argument. "He was already a fine speaker," one debater recalled. "All he lacked was culture."

Lincoln was self-conscious about his meager education, and ambitious to improve himself. Mentor Graham, the schoolmaster and a

16 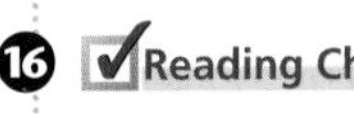

Reading Check

How does Denton Offutt change Lincoln's life?

14 Critical Thinking

Speculate

- Point out that Lincoln has taken his first trip outside of Indiana and, like many young adults, he feels restless being back home.
- Have students speculate about what event might logically follow. **Answer:** Students may say that Lincoln will probably leave home to start a life of his own.

15 Literary Analysis

Historical Account

- Point out that the author includes a quotation that Lincoln once used to describe himself as a young man.
- Then ask the following question: How does the use of this quotation make the reading selection more believable? **Possible response:** Students may say that a direct quotation from Lincoln is factual and aids the believability of the selection. The quotation shows Lincoln's self-conscious thoughts, which make Lincoln more multi-dimensional and therefore more real.

16 Reading Check

Answer: Mr. Offutt changes Lincoln's life by providing Lincoln with a job in a different town, which brings the opportunity to be on his own, meet new friends, have new interests, and new pursuits.

CUSTOMIZE INSTRUCTION FOR UNIVERSAL ACCESS

For Special Needs Students	For Gifted/Talented Students
If students have difficulty following the many changes in Lincoln's life as he grows into adulthood, suggest that they use the Series of Events Chain on p. 69 of **Writing Models and Graphic Organizers on Transparencies.** Explain that using the organizer will not only help them understand the historical account, but it will help them answer Review and Assess question 5 on p. 329.	Invite students to do research about what happened to Lincoln after the events described on pp. 319–321 and to chart their findings on an extended timeline. Students should include dates and key facts on their timelines and also provide some commentary about why each event was significant in Lincoln's life. Encourage students to include appropriate illustrations as well, as part of their timelines.

17 Reading Strategy

Determining Main Ideas

- Tell students that this paragraph focuses on a transition in Lincoln's life.
- Then, ask them the Reading Strategy question on p. 322. **Answer:** Lincoln's campaign was interrupted by war, but he gained a reputation as a leader.

18 Literary Analysis

Historical Account

- Ask students to think about how Lincoln's political defeat must have affected him.
- Then, ask: What information does Freedman include to make Lincoln's loss seem less significant? **Answer:** Freedman includes the information that Lincoln won nearly every vote in his home precinct.

fellow debater, took a liking to the young man, lent him books, and offered to coach him in the fine points of English grammar. Lincoln had plenty of time to study. There wasn't much business at Offutt's store, so he could spend long hours reading as he sat behind the counter.

When the store failed in 1832, Offutt moved on to other schemes. Lincoln had to find something else to do. At the age of twenty-three, he decided to run for the Illinois state legislature. Why not? He knew everyone in town, people liked him, and he was rapidly gaining confidence as a public speaker. His friends urged him to run, saying that a bright young man could go far in politics. So Lincoln announced his candidacy and his political platform. He was in favor of local improvements, like better roads and canals. He had made a study of the Sangamon River, and he proposed that it be dredged and cleared so steamboats could call at New Salem—insuring a glorious future for the town.

Reading Strategy
Determining Main Ideas
What is the main idea of this paragraph?

17 Before he could start his campaign, an Indian war flared up in northern Illinois. Chief Black Hawk of the Sauk and Fox tribes had crossed the Mississippi, intending, he said, to raise corn on land that had been taken from his people thirty years earlier. The white settlers were alarmed, and the governor called for volunteers to stop the invasion. Lincoln enlisted in a militia company made up of his friends and neighbors. He was surprised and pleased when the men elected him as their captain, with Jack Armstrong as first sergeant. His troops drilled and marched, but they never did sight any hostile Indians. Years later, Lincoln would joke about his three-month stint as a military man, telling how he survived "a good many bloody battles with mosquitoes."

18 By the time he returned to New Salem, election day was just two weeks off. He jumped into the campaign—pitching horseshoes with voters, speaking at barbecues, chatting with farmers in the fields, joking with customers at country stores. He lost, finishing eighth in a field of thirteen. But in his own precinct,[4] where folks knew him, he received 227 votes out of 300 cast.

Defeated as a politician, he decided to try his luck as a frontier merchant. With a fellow named William Berry as his partner, Lincoln operated a general store that sold everything from axes to beeswax. But the two men showed little aptitude for business, and their store finally "winked out," as Lincoln put it. Then Berry died, leaving Lincoln saddled with a $1,100 debt—a gigantic amount for someone who had never earned more than a few dollars a month. Lincoln called it "the National Debt," but he vowed to repay every cent. He spent the next fifteen years doing so.

aptitude (ap′ tə to͞od′) *n.* natural ability

4. **precinct** (prē′ siŋkt) *n.* election district.

ENRICHMENT: Social Studies Connection

Powered by Steam

Commercial travel by steamboat had been available for only a few years when Abraham Lincoln traveled by steamboat along the Mississippi River in 1828. The first steamboat on the Mississippi had been Robert Fulton's *New Orleans* in 1811. Then, the first commercial service began a few years later, in 1815, with the launch of the *Enterprise*. However, business grew quickly, and by 1830 nearly 200 steamboats operated on the river. Because the boats typically had flat bottoms and straight sides, they could easily be maneuvered in shallow waters. In fact, steamboat captains sometimes bragged that they could navigate their vessels on a "heavy dew." Discuss with students that, as an adult, Lincoln also traveled by train, another form of transportation powered by the steam engine.

To support himself, he worked at all sorts of odd jobs. He split fence rails, hired himself out as a farmhand, helped at the local gristmill.[5] With the help of friends, he was appointed postmaster of New Salem, a part-time job that paid about fifty dollars a year. Then he was offered a chance to become deputy to the local surveyor.[6] He knew nothing about surveying, so he bought a compass, a chain, and a couple of textbooks on the subject. Within six weeks, he had taught himself enough to start work—laying out roads and townsites, and marking off property boundaries.

As he traveled about the county, making surveys and delivering mail to faraway farms, people came to know him as an honest and dependable fellow. Lincoln could be counted on to witness a contract, settle a boundary dispute, or compose a letter for folks who couldn't write much themselves. For the first time, his neighbors began to call him "Abe."

19 In 1834, Lincoln ran for the state legislature again. This time he placed second in a field of thirteen candidates, and was one of four men elected to the Illinois House of Representatives from Sangamon County. In November, wearing a sixty-dollar tailor-made suit he had bought on credit, the first suit he had ever owned, the twenty-five-year-old legislator climbed into a stagecoach and set out for the state capital in Vandalia.

In those days, Illinois lawmakers were paid three dollars a day to cover their expenses, but only while the legislature was in session. Lincoln still had to earn a living. One of his fellow representatives, a rising young attorney named John Todd Stuart, urged Lincoln to take up the study of law. As Stuart pointed out, it was an ideal profession for anyone with political ambitions.

And in fact, Lincoln had been toying with the idea of becoming a lawyer. For years he had hung around frontier courthouses, watching country lawyers bluster and strut as they cross-examined witnesses and delivered impassioned speeches before juries. He had sat on juries himself, appeared as a witness, drawn up legal documents for his neighbors. He had even argued a few cases before the local justice of the peace.

Yes, the law intrigued him. It would give him a chance to rise in the world, to earn a respected place in the community, to live by his wits instead of by hard physical labor.

Yet Lincoln hesitated, unsure of himself because he had so little formal education. That was no great obstacle, his friend Stuart kept telling him. In the 1830's, few American lawyers had ever seen the inside of a law school. Instead, they "read law" in the office of a practicing attorney until they knew enough to pass their exams.

Literary Analysis
Historical Account What background is provided here to show the significance of Lincoln's election?

intrigued (in trēgd′) *v.* fascinated

20 **Reading Check**
Why does Lincoln buy his first suit?

5. **gristmill** (grist′ mil′) *n.* place where grain is ground into flour.
6. **surveyor** (sər vā′ ər) *n.* person who determines the boundaries of land.

19 Literary Analysis

Historical Account

- Before asking the Literary Analysis question on p. 323, invite students to think about a time they worked really hard to achieve something.
- Then, ask the following question: What background is provided here to show the significance of Lincoln's election?
  Answer: This time, Lincoln places second in a field of thirteen candidates and is one of four men sent to represent the county in the House of Representatives.

Monitor Progress Ask students to recount the main events in Lincoln's life, as related by the author. Then, ask students for one example of the author's commentary.
Possible response: Students may note that the author makes clear, at one point in the selection, that it was not unusual for intelligent people to be unable to read and write.

20 

Answer: Lincoln buys his first suit because he has been elected to the Illinois House of Representatives.

CUSTOMIZE INSTRUCTION FOR UNIVERSAL ACCESS

For Less Proficient Readers	For English Learners
To help students understand why Freedman wanted to write about Lincoln, ask them to complete an Open Mind diagram like the one on p. 93 of **Writing Models and Graphic Organizers on Transparencies.** Ask students to imagine that they are in the mind of the writer as he is learning about Lincoln. While filling out the diagram, students should answer the question "What thoughts might be going through the writer's mind?" Ask students to share their completed diagrams with the class.	If students are not familiar with Lincoln, ask them to identify some highly regarded and self-taught figures from their own cultures. Have students work alone or in pairs to fill in the Sunburst organizer on p. 97 in **Writing Models and Graphic Organizers on Transparencies.** Have students list the characteristics they admire in the person and the key events or actions for which this person is to be admired. Invite students to share their Sunburst organizers with the class.

Answers for p. 324

Review and Assess

1. Possible responses: Students may say that they were surprised to learn that Lincoln's parents could not read or write. Encourage students to think about what they learned about Lincoln's childhood.
2. **(a)** Possible responses: Students may recall that Lincoln moved many times, including to Little Pigeon Creek, before he turned eight; he helped his family build a log cabin. **(b)** Possible response: One possible generalization is that life was very hard in the backwoods.
3. **(a)** Possible response: Students may recall that Lincoln's mother died when Lincoln was nine and that his father soon remarried. Lincoln also started to go to school and read regularly.
(b) Possible response: Students might offer the words *strong, determined, dependable, awkward,* and *easy-going.*
4. **(a)** Lincoln moved to New Salem to work at Offutt's store. **(b)** In New Salem, Lincoln learned to speak in public debates and became involved in politics. He also enlisted in the militia. **(c)** In New Salem, Lincoln displayed the same courage, love of books, and ambition people often associate with him; however, he was also self-conscious, an inexperienced speaker, and he lost a political race.
5. **(a)** His first office was in the Illinois House of Representatives. **(b)** Lincoln went to law school, sat on juries, helped neighbors with legal problems, and eventually became a lawyer. **(c)** Possible response: Lincoln's patience and determination in pursuing those tasks helped him become a great leader.

Lincoln decided to study entirely on his own. He borrowed some law books from Stuart, bought others at an auction, and began to read and memorize legal codes[7] and precedents.[8] Back in New Salem, folks would see him walking down the road, reciting aloud from one of his law books, or lying under a tree as he read, his long legs stretched up the trunk. He studied for nearly three years before passing his exams and being admitted to practice on March 1, 1837.

By then, the state legislature was planning to move from Vandalia to Springfield, which had been named the new capital of Illinois. Lincoln had been elected to a second term in the legislature. And he had accepted a job as junior partner in John Todd Stuart's Springfield law office.

In April, he went back to New Salem for the last time to pack his belongings and say goodbye to his friends. The little village was declining now. Its hopes for growth and prosperity had vanished when the Sangamon River proved too treacherous for steamboat travel. Settlers were moving away, seeking brighter prospects elsewhere.

treacherous (trech´ ər əs) *adj.* dangerous

By 1840, New Salem was a ghost town. It would have been forgotten completely if Abraham Lincoln hadn't gone there to live when he was young, penniless, and ambitious.

---

7. **legal codes:** Body of law, as for a nation or a city, arranged systematically
8. **precedents** (pres´ ə dənts) *n.*: Legal cases that may serve as a reference

Review and Assess

Thinking About the Selection

1. **Respond:** What was the most interesting fact you learned about young Abraham Lincoln?
2. (a) **Analyze:** What are two facts you recall about Lincoln before the age of eight? (b) **Generalize:** What generalization could you make about Lincoln's early life?
3. (a) **Recall:** What are two facts from Lincoln's life between the ages of eight and twenty-one? (b) **Classify:** What words would you use to describe Lincoln at this time in his life?
4. (a) **Recall:** Why did Lincoln move to New Salem? (b) **Analyze:** In what ways did his life change there? (c) **Connect:** In what ways is the Lincoln of New Salem similar to or different from the Lincoln that most people know in American history?
5. (a) **Recall:** What was Lincoln's first political office? (b) **Interpret:** How did Lincoln continue to develop and change after he was elected to office? (c) **Speculate:** In what ways did these experiences help form the great leader he would become?

Russell Freedman

(b. 1929)

When Russell Freedman was growing up in San Francisco, California, his mother had a job in a bookstore and his father worked in publishing. It's not surprising, then, that Freedman eventually became a writer. After working as a reporter for the Associated Press, he went on to write more than thirty books for young readers. These include *Immigrant Kids*, *Children of the Wild West*, and *Cowboys of the Wild West*. "A Backwoods Boy" is from Freedman's award-winning book *Lincoln: A Photobiography*.

21 # Jackie Robinson: Justice at Last

Geoffrey C. Ward and Ken Burns

It was 1945, and World War II had ended. Americans of all races had died for their country. Yet black men were still not allowed in the major leagues. The national pastime was loved by all America, but the major leagues were for white men only.

22 ▲ **Critical Viewing** What details in this picture indicate that Jackie Robinson and his teammates shared team spirit? **[Analyze]**

21 ## About the Selection

"Jackie Robinson: Justice at Last" is the story of two brave men who changed the course of history in sports. Recognizing the importance of having players of all races on major league baseball teams, Branch Rickey, owner of the Brooklyn Dodgers, asks Jackie Robinson to become the first African American player on his team. In spite of warnings that this new road will be difficult, Robinson agrees. By accepting this challenge with dignity and strength, Robinson becomes a role model for future generations.

22 ▶**Critical Viewing**

Answer: Robinson and his teammate are shaking hands. The handshake seems genuine and respectful.

CUSTOMIZE INSTRUCTION FOR UNIVERSAL ACCESS

For Gifted/Talented Students

Explain to students that documentaries such as Ken Burns and Geoffrey C. Ward's *Civil War* and *Baseball* increase viewers' understanding of a subject by telling about real people and real events in history. Allow students time to watch the section of *Baseball* that deals with Jackie Robinson. Then, have students write a few paragraphs responding to the documentary and comparing the experience of reading the historical account with viewing the documentary. Write the following questions on the board for students to answer:

- How was Jackie Robinson similar to and different from what you expected, based on your reading of "Jackie Robinson: Justice at Last"?
- What did you learn about Robinson from the documentary that you did not learn from the reading?

Ask students to share their answers with the class.

23 ▶ Critical Viewing

Answer: The photograph shows Robinson's determination and physical strength.

24 Reinforcing Skills

Compare and Contrast

- Reinforce students' ability to identify the similarities and differences between two subjects.
- After students read this paragraph, ask them to think about what they learned in the previous selection about Abraham Lincoln.
- Then, ask students to compare Lincoln and Robinson based on these sentences.
  Answer: Both men are athletic and intelligent. They are also sensitive to others.
- Discuss how intelligence and sensitivity are qualities common to leaders.

Branch Rickey of the Brooklyn Dodgers thought that was wrong. He was the only team owner who believed blacks and whites should play together. Baseball, he felt, would become even more thrilling, and fans of all colors would swarm to his ballpark.

Rickey decided his team would be the first to integrate. There were plenty of brilliant Negro league players, but he knew the first black major leaguer would need much more than athletic ability.

integrate (inʹ tə grātʹ) *v.* remove barriers and allow access to all

Many fans and players were prejudiced—they didn't want the races to play together. Rickey knew the first black player would be cursed and booed. Pitchers would throw at him; runners

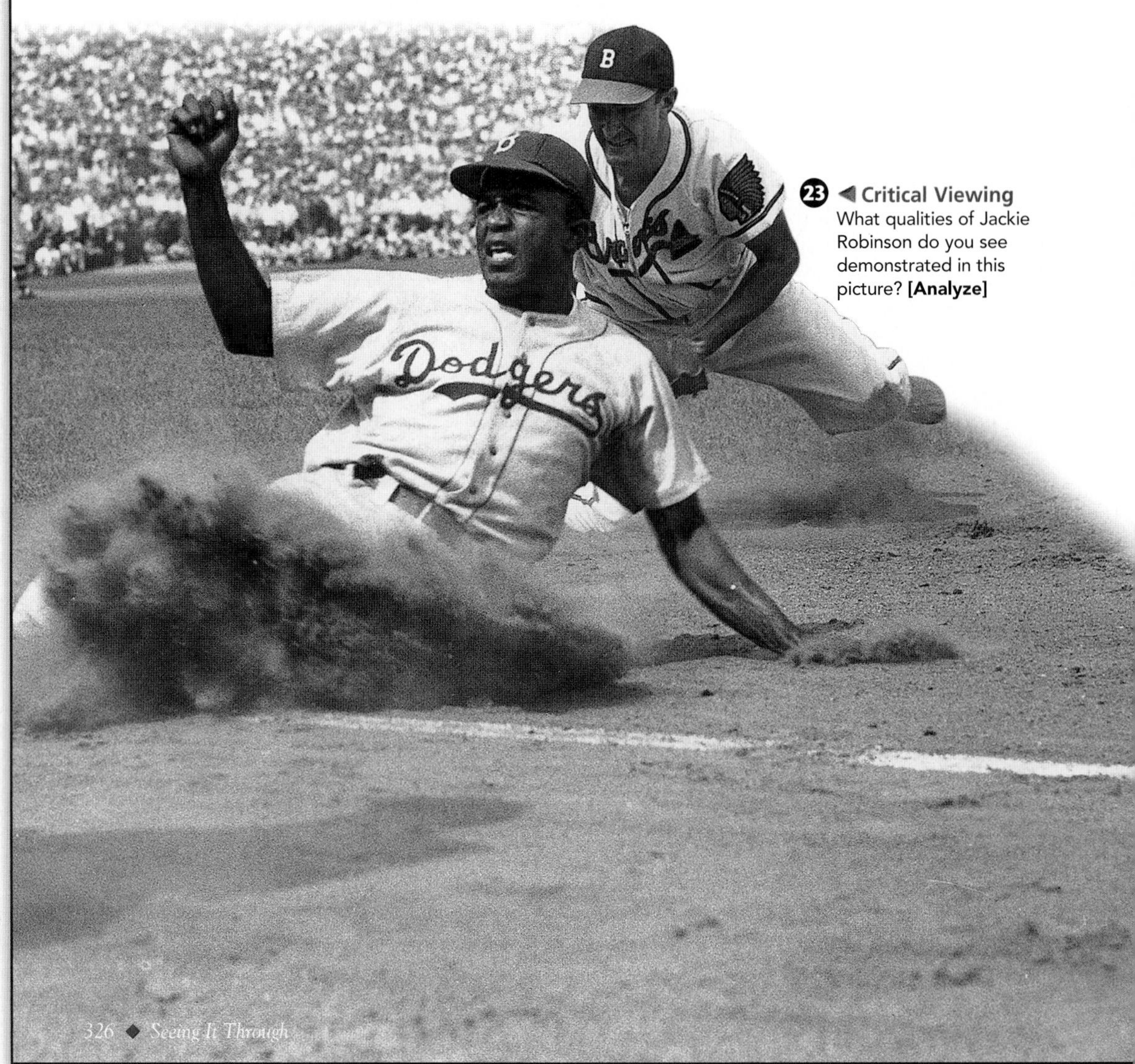

23 ◀ Critical Viewing What qualities of Jackie Robinson do you see demonstrated in this picture? **[Analyze]**

CUSTOMIZE INSTRUCTION FOR UNIVERSAL ACCESS

For Advanced Readers

Ask students to think of stories, books, films, or television programs that focus on sports or an athlete. Have students discuss why athletes, sports, and sports stories are compelling to read about or watch. What skills do athletes have that compel us to watch and read about them? Students should generate a list of at least five elements that make people want to read or watch sports stories. Challenge students to write a short fictional account of a sports figure in which all of the elements that make a successful sports story are reversed. Have students share their stories and ask the class what effect the changes have on them as readers or listeners.

would spike him. Even his own teammates might try to pick a fight.

But somehow this man had to rise above that. No matter what happened, he must never lose his temper. No matter what was said to him, he must never answer back. If he had even one fight, people might say integration wouldn't work.

24 When Rickey met Jackie Robinson, he thought he'd found the right man. Robinson was 28 years old, and a superb athlete. In his first season in the Negro leagues, he hit .387. But just as importantly, he had great intelligence and sensitivity. Robinson was college-educated, and knew what joining the majors would mean for blacks. The grandson of a slave, he was proud of his race and wanted others to feel the same.

In the past, Robinson had always stood up for his rights. But now Rickey told him he would have to stop. The Dodgers needed "a man that will take abuse."

25 At first Robinson thought Rickey wanted someone who was afraid to defend himself. But as they talked, he realized that in this case a truly brave man would have to avoid fighting. He thought for a while, then promised Rickey he would not fight back.

Reading Strategy
Determining Main Ideas
What is the main idea of this paragraph?

26 Robinson signed with the Dodgers and went to play in the minors in 1946. Rickey was right—fans insulted him, and so did players. But he performed brilliantly and avoided fights. Then, in 1947, he came to the majors.

Many Dodgers were angry. Some signed a petition demanding to be traded. But Robinson and Rickey were determined to make their experiment work.

On April 15—Opening Day—26,623 fans came out to Ebbets Field. More than half of them were black—Robinson was already their hero. Now he was making history just by being on the field.

The afternoon was cold and wet, but no one left the ballpark. The Dodgers beat the Boston Braves, 5–3. Robinson went hitless, but the hometown fans didn't seem to care—they cheered his every move.

27 **✓Reading Check**
What does Branch Rickey do to change baseball?

25 Reading Strategy
Determining Main Idea

- Point out that even a short paragraph, such as this one, will have a main idea.
- Then, ask the Reading Strategy question on p. 327: What is the main idea of this paragraph?
  Answer: Robinson understood that courage could be shown by refusing to fight.

26 Literary Analysis
Historical Account

- Remind students that writers often provide clues to their feelings or ideas about their subject.
- Challenge students to find the one word in this paragraph that hints at the writer's feelings about Robinson's performance.
  Answer: Students should identify the word *brilliantly.*
- Ask: What comments and interpretations are included here?
  Answer: The writer makes it clear that Robinson handled himself admirably, despite rude treatment by players and fans. The writer explains that Robinson played brilliantly.

Reteach To help students identify main ideas, have them create timelines of the lives of Abraham Lincoln and Jackie Robinson. Along each line, they should plot significant events from each man's life, assigning a number to each event. Ask students who are already filling in such timelines to add numbers. Then, students should write a sentence for each of these numbered events that describes the event's impact on the man's life.

27 ✓Reading Check

Answer: Rickey introduces an African American player to Major League Baseball.

CUSTOMIZE INSTRUCTION FOR UNIVERSAL ACCESS

For Special Needs Students	For English Learners
If students have trouble understanding how the figures in the two selections are connected, work with them to identify some qualities that political leaders and athletes have in common. Start by offering students a Venn diagram, like the one on p. 89 of **Writing Models and Graphic Organizers on Transparencies.** Label one circle "Political Leaders" and the other "Athletes." Challenge students to identify qualities the two groups have in common and qualities unique to each group.	Most cultures consider the worlds of sports and politics to be very different from each other. Ask students what qualities they associate with athletes and with politicians. Use the question to broaden students' vocabulary. Ask them to draw a two-column chart, with one column labeled "Qualities of Political Leaders" and the other labeled "Qualities of Athletes," and to fill in the columns with appropriate words. After students complete the chart, ask them to point out similarities and differences between the words and qualities.

ASSESS

Answers for p. 328

Review and Assess

1. Possible responses: Students who say that they would have accepted a place will probably emphasize the good they could accomplish; those who say they would not have accepted the place will probably emphasize the difficulties involved.
2. **(a)** He owned the Brooklyn Dodgers. **(b)** The writers give Rickey credit because he hired Robinson and because he thought that baseball should be open to players of all races.
3. **(a)** Robinson was a superb athlete and had great sensitivity and intelligence. **(b)** Rickey had to convince Robinson not to fight those who challenged him or were rude to him. **(c)** Rickey's advice was crucial to Robinson's success; had Robinson fought back, baseball might have lost the opportunity to become a game open to everyone.
4. **(a)** Fans insulted Robinson; players asked to be traded; another team threatened to strike if Robinson played. **(b)** Robinson played well and with dignity.
5. **(a)** They finally accepted him because they realized that he provided the inspiration for the team. **(b)** Everyone else finally realized that Robinson was an excellent player and that his skin color should never have mattered.

Robinson's first season was difficult. Fans threatened to kill him; players tried to hurt him. The St. Louis Cardinals said they would strike if he took the field. And because of laws separating the races in certain states, he often couldn't eat or sleep in the same places as his teammates.

Yet through it all, he kept his promise to Rickey. No matter who insulted him, he never retaliated.

retaliated (ri tal′ ē at′ id) *v.* harmed or did wrong to someone in return for an injury or wrong he or she has done

Robinson's dignity paid off. Thousands of fans jammed stadiums to see him play. The Dodgers set attendance records in a number of cities.

Slowly his teammates accepted him, realizing that he was the spark that made them a winning team. No one was more daring on the base paths or better with the glove. At the plate, he had great bat control—he could hit the ball anywhere. That season, he was named baseball's first Rookie of the Year.

Jackie Robinson went on to a glorious career. But he did more than play the game well—his bravery taught Americans a lesson. Branch Rickey opened a door, and Jackie Robinson stepped through it, making sure it could never be closed again. Something wonderful happened to baseball—and America—the day Jackie Robinson joined the Dodgers.

Geoffrey C. Ward Ken Burns

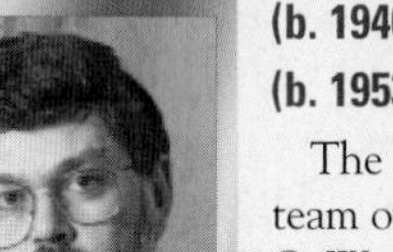

(b. 1940)
(b. 1953)

The creative team of Geoffrey C. Ward and Ken Burns is best known for documentaries, factual film presentations about real people and events. For example, Ward and Burns created an award-winning documentary on the United States Civil War. It told the story of that conflict using the words and photographs of those who lived it—from Abraham Lincoln to the soldier slogging through the mud. "Jackie Robinson: Justice at Last" is from a book based on their documentary *Baseball,* which presents the history of our national pastime.

Review and Assess

Thinking About the Selection

1. **Respond:** Would you have accepted a place on the team if you had been in Jackie Robinson's shoes? Why or why not?
2. **(a) Recall:** Who was Branch Rickey? **(b) Analyze:** Why do Ward and Burns give Rickey a great deal of credit in this article?
3. **(a) Recall:** Why did Jackie Robinson come to the attention of Branch Rickey? **(b) Analyze:** What did Rickey have to convince Robinson not to do? **(c) Connect:** How important was this advice?
4. **(a) Recall:** Name three difficult situations that Jackie Robinson and the Dodgers faced in Robinson's first season. **(b) Infer:** How did Robinson and the team overcome these difficulties?
5. **(a) Recall:** Why did Robinson's teammates eventually accept him? **(b) Speculate:** Why did everyone else eventually accept Robinson and integrate baseball?

ASSESSMENT PRACTICE: Reading Comprehension

Perceiving Cause and Effect (For more practice, see Test Preparation Workbook, p. 29.)

Many tests require students to identify cause and effect. Use the following passage to help students practice this skill:

> Lincoln was self-conscious about his meager education, and ambitious to improve himself . . . Lincoln had plenty of time to study. There wasn't much business at Offutt's store, so he could spend long hours reading as he sat behind the counter.

Why did Lincoln read so much when he worked at Offutt's store?

A He didn't like working at the store.
B Business was too fast at the store.
C Learning was important to Lincoln.
D He didn't know how to work at the counter.

Choices *A* and *D* are not supported by the passage. Choice *B* is incorrect because business was slow. *C* is the correct answer.

Review and Assess

Literary Analysis

Historical Account

1. What facts do you learn in this account about Lincoln's first home, first school, and parents? Add more facts to a chart like this one:

First Home	First School	Parents
in Kentucky wilderness	two miles away	father—farmer and carpenter

2. What do you learn about how Lincoln got involved in politics?
3. What do you learn about Robinson before Branch Rickey met him?
4. What facts do you learn about baseball during the days that Jackie Robinson played the game?

Comparing Literary Works

5. For each work, complete an organizer like the one shown. Record the most significant or important points.

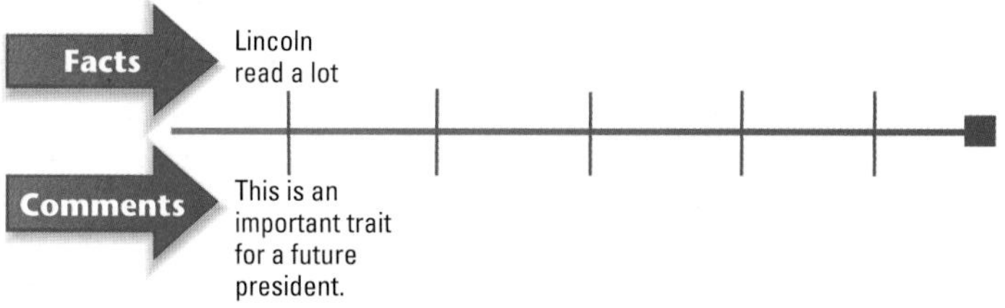

Facts
Lincoln read a lot
Comments
This is an important trait for a future president.

6. Which writer offers more opinions or comments on events?
7. Which writer provides more background information to show the significance of events?

Reading Strategy

Determining Main Ideas

8. List three main ideas about Abraham Lincoln that you identified while reading "A Backwoods Boy."
9. List two main ideas about the history of baseball that you identified while reading "Jackie Robinson: Justice at Last."

Extending Understanding

10. **History Connection:** What historical connection is there between Abraham Lincoln and Jackie Robinson?

Quick Review

A **historical account** tells about real people who lived in the past and real events that took place in the past. To review historical accounts, see page 315.

Main ideas are the most important points. To review main ideas, see page 315.

Take It to the Net

www.phschool.com

Take the interactive self-test online to check your understanding of these selections.

ENRICHMENT: Further Reading

Other Works by the Authors

Works by Russell Freedman

Buffalo Hunt

Eleanor Roosevelt: A Life of Discovery

Martha Graham: A Dancer's Life

Works by Geoffrey C. Ward and Ken Burns

The Civil War: An Illustrated History

Take It to the Net

Visit www.phschool.com for more information on the authors.

Answers for p. 329

Review and Assess

1. **First home:** log cabin, one window, one door, dirt floor

   First school: log school house, learned to count, read, and write

   Parents: uneducated; mother recited Bible stories and died when Lincoln was young
2. Lincoln got involved in debating clubs. People suggested he run for office. He lost his first race but later was elected.
3. Robinson was a fine athlete who excelled in the Negro leagues. He was college educated, sensitive, and proud.
4. When Robinson first started, there were two sets of leagues—the major leagues and the Negro leagues. Some white players and fans did not want African American players in their leagues. Robinson's presence on the Dodgers changed that.
5. Students will probably include the following events in Lincoln's life: his schooling, his move to Indiana, his mother's death, his discovery of reading, his trip to New Orleans, his move to New Salem, his first campaign, his first election, his law degree.

   Students may include the following events in Robinson's life: his success in the Negro leagues, his joining the Dodgers, his history-making Opening Day, his first season, his being named Rookie of the Year.
6. The writers of "Jackie Robinson: Justice at Last" offer more opinions or comments on events.
7. The author of "Backwoods Boy" provides more background information to show the events' significance. For example, Freedman gives Lincoln's ranks in political races.
8. Possible responses: Lincoln was hard-working, was known as a storyteller, and fit in well in New Salem.
9. Possible responses: Some fans and players were prejudiced when Robinson started; Robinson made history by playing on Opening Day.
10. Both overcame odds to become leaders.

EXTEND

Answers for p. 330

❶ Vocabulary Development

Word Analysis

1. a memory happens again
2. a design happens again
3. a direction goes back

Spelling Strategy

1. attitude 2. gratitude

Fluency: Using Words in Context

1. Yes; people enjoyed hearing him speak.
2. Yes; it interested him so much that he campaigned for the position twice.
3. Yes; navigation was dangerous.
4. Yes; players could no longer be banned because of their skin color.
5. Yes; he convinced Robinson not to return insults.
6. No; his natural skill made him one of the best players of all time.

❷ Grammar

1. and shows addition; but shows the contrast between ideas
2. so shows cause and effect

Writing Application

Rickey saw Robinson's talent, and he wanted Robinson on his team. Robinson agreed, but he was worried about people's reactions.

Integrate Language Skills

❶ Vocabulary Development Lesson

Word Analysis: Latin Prefix *re-*

The Latin prefix *re-* means "back," "again," or "against." You can see the meaning "back" in *retaliated,* which means "got revenge" or "paid back." Explain the meaning of each of these words.

1. remember 2. redesign 3. reverse

Spelling Strategy

Exaggerate your pronunciation before writing a word so that you don't leave syllables or letters out.

Example: ap–ti–tude

Pronounce each of the following words. Then choose the correct word for each sentence below.

at–ti–tude grat–i–tude

1. You show your ___?___ by how you act.
2. You show your ___?___ by saying thank you.

Fluency: Using Words in Context

Answer the following questions with *yes* or *no.* Then, explain your responses.

1. Did Abraham Lincoln have an *aptitude* for public speaking?
2. Did the job of state representative *intrigue* Lincoln?
3. Was the Sangamon River a *treacherous* place for steamboats?
4. Did Jackie Robinson help baseball become *integrated?*
5. Did Branch Rickey convince Robinson not to *retaliate* against prejudice?
6. Did Jackie Robinson lack *aptitude* for the game of baseball?

❷ Grammar Lesson

Conjunctions

A **conjunction** is a word that connects other words or groups of words. When conjunctions join sentences (complete thoughts), they show the relationship between the ideas in the complete thoughts that they join. The conjunction *and* shows addition. *But* and *yet* show a contrast between ideas. *For* and *so* show a cause-effect relationship between the sentences. When you join two complete thoughts with a conjunction, always use a comma before the conjunction.

Example: The Lincoln children were fortunate, *for* their stepmother was loving.

Practice Copy these sentences. Underline the conjunctions, and explain the connection between ideas.

1. The afternoon was cold and wet, but no one left the ballpark.
2. He carried a book around the field, so he could read at the end of each plow furrow.

Writing Application Rewrite the following passage. Use commas and conjunctions to combine sentences and to show relationships between ideas.

Rickey understood Robinson's talent. He wanted Robinson on his team. Robinson agreed. He was worried about people's reactions.

WG *Prentice Hall Writing and Grammar Connection: Chapter 18, Section 1*

TEACHING RESOURCES

The following resources can be used to enrich or extend the instruction for pp. 330–331.

Vocabulary

- **Selection Support:** Build Vocabulary, p. 96; Build Spelling Skills, p. 97
- **Vocabulary and Spelling Practice Book** (Use this booklet for skills enrichment)

Grammar

- **Selection Support:** Build Grammar Skills, p. 98
- **Writing and Grammar,** Copper Level, p. 364
- **Daily Language Practice Transparencies** ■

Writing

- **Writing and Grammar,** Copper Level, p. 226 ■
- **Writing Models and Graphic Organizers on Transparencies,** p. 69
- **Writing and Grammar iText CD-ROM**

■ **BLOCK SCHEDULING:** Resources marked with this symbol provide varied instruction during 90-minute blocks.

❸ Writing Lesson

Writer's Choice

The authors of these selections wrote historical accounts of people they admired. Use what you have learned in one of these accounts to write about the subject in another form.

Prewriting You might consider a poem, an essay, or a letter. The following chart shows some purposes and forms you might consider.

Model: Choose a Purpose and Form

Purpose	Possible Form
To imagine what you would like to tell the subject	Letter to the subject
To record feelings and impressions about the subject	Poem or journal entry
To persuade others to admire the subject	Persuasive speech, letter, or essay

Drafting Follow the format of your chosen form. Incorporate details you learned in the historical accounts.

Revising No matter what form of writing you choose, check that you have used correct spelling and have written legibly, or in a way that can be read.

WG *Prentice Hall Writing and Grammar Connection: Chapter 11, Section 2*

Extension Activities

❹ **Listening and Speaking** With a partner, **role-play** the first conversation between Jackie Robinson and Branch Rickey.

1. Begin by rereading the text for details you can incorporate in your role play.
2. Discuss with your partner the appropriate emotions each speaker should show.
3. Experiment with using gestures or louder or softer voices to indicate the emotions behind the words.
4. Present your role play to the class. Ask for feedback on how effectively you communicated the emotions behind the words.

Research and Technology In a group, prepare a **visual timeline** to tell the story of Abraham Lincoln's life. Find information by using the Internet, databases, and CD-ROMs. Download and print out various forms of visual information, such as photographs, drawings, and reproductions of letters and documents to include in the timeline. Be sure to label every visual clearly and accurately. **[Group Activity]**

www.phschool.com

Go online for an additional research activity using the Internet.

ASSESSMENT RESOURCES

The following resources can be used to assess students' knowledge and skills.

Selection Assessment

- **Formal Assessment,** pp. 82–84
- **Open Book Test,** pp. 58–60
- **Got It! Assessment Videotapes,** Tape 2
- **Test Bank Software**

Visit www.phschool.com for self-tests and additional questions on the selections.

Writing Rubric

- **Performance Assess. and Portfolio Mgmt.,** p. 9

Listening and Speaking Rubric

- **Performance Assess. and Portfolio Mgmt.,** p. 23

PRENTICE HALL ASSESSMENT SYSTEM

- **Workbook**
- **Skill Book**
- **Transparencies**
- **CD-ROM**

❸ Writing Lesson

- After students read the instruction on p. 331, discuss the characteristics of each of the possible forms.
- Remind students that historical accounts tend to present material in chronological order. Students may benefit from using the Series of Events transparency on p. 69 of **Writing Models and Graphic Organizers on Transparencies.**
- Challenge students to include at least five details in their historical accounts. Remind students that details may be facts, statistics, sensory details, or quotations.
- Use the Description rubric on p. 9 in **Performance Assessment and Portfolio Management** to assess students' comprehension.

❹ Listening and Speaking

- After students read the instruction on p. 331, arrange them into pairs.
- Tell them, as they begin to plan their roles, that they should not automatically decide which role they want to play but should explore each role first.
- Remind students that their role-playing is not scripted; rehearsing should help them remember the main ideas they want to include.
- As students perform, ask the class to comment on how each presentation was different from or similar to the one before it.
- Have students use the Understanding, Tone, Mood, and Emotion rubric on p. 23 in **Performance Assessment and Portfolio Management.**

CUSTOMIZE INSTRUCTION For Universal Access

- To address different learning styles, use the activities suggested in the **Extension Activities** booklet, p. 20.
- For Visual/Spatial Learners, use Activity 5.
- For Bodily/Kinesthetic and Interpersonal Learners, use Activity 6.
- For Verbal/Linguistic and Interpersonal Learners, use Activity 7.

Lesson Objectives

1. To analyze the purpose and features of magazine articles
2. To evaluate evidence for the author's conclusions presented in a magazine article

About Magazine Articles

- After students have read the instruction on p. 332, offer them copies of age-appropriate magazine articles for previewing. Allow students to work with partners to list features or characteristics that they notice about the articles, such as the inclusion of facts.
- Have students identify the kinds of articles they enjoy reading and the topics they prefer. Then, ask what appeals to them about these articles.
  Possible responses: Students may enjoy the articles because they are entertaining or because they provide information about a favorite subject, hobby, or activity.

Reading Strategy

Evaluating Evidence for an Author's Conclusions

- Have students read the Reading Strategy information.
- Talk with students about why it is important to evaluate a writer's evidence and conclusions.
- Review the three questions that will help students evaluate a writer's conclusion and evidence.
- Discuss the six different types of evidence shown in the graphic organizer on page 332. If time allows, work with students to generate at least one example of each type of evidence. Encourage students to find examples in the articles or magazines that you distributed earlier.
- Remind students that even an experienced, published writer may make claims that are not entirely accurate and that it is important for students to draw their own conclusions from the evidence and from their own experiences.

READING INFORMATIONAL MATERIALS

Magazine Articles

About Magazine Articles

Magazines may be published once a week, once a month, or every two months. Because they are published periodically, they are referred to as periodicals. One reference to use when looking for an article is the *Readers' Guide to Periodical Literature*. It is available electronically and in text form.

Magazine articles can be found on almost any subject you can name. Although each magazine article has unique characteristics, articles do share some common qualities.

- Articles give facts about a subject.
- Articles often include a comment by the writer on the subject.
- Articles are usually short enough to be read in one sitting.

One common type of article is a human-interest article. A human-interest article focuses on a single unique person, animal, or situation.

Reading Strategy

Evaluating Evidence for an Author's Conclusions

Authors of magazine articles can, and often do, draw conclusions based on the information they present. Do not let someone else do your thinking for you. Decide for yourself if you accept the author's conclusions. Evaluate the evidence. Then, evaluate whether the evidence actually supports the writer's claims.

1. What conclusion had the author drawn?
2. What reasons does the author give?
3. Does the evidence logically support the conclusion(s) the author has drawn?

Use an organizer like the one shown here to record and take notes on the information presented in this article. Put a star next to any facts or details you would like to check.

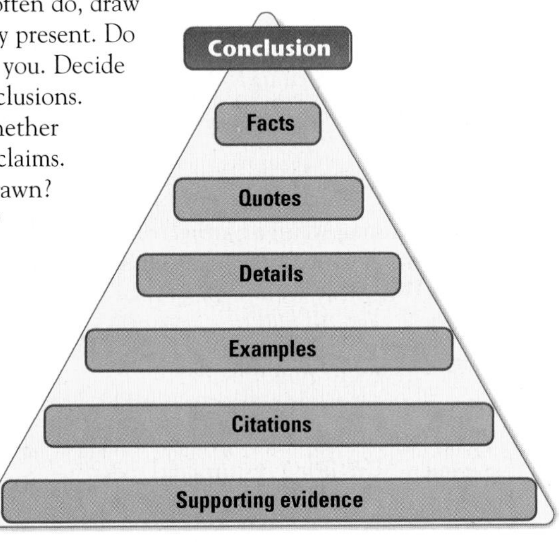

THROW AND TELL

The sentence in bold type is a summary of the article.

Gifted with a 98-mph fastball, teacher Jim Morris goes from a Texas classroom to baseball's big leagues.

The magazine title (italics) identifies the subject, and the date tells the reader when the article was published.

People Weekly, OCTOBER 1, 1999

"Throw and Tell"

- Introduce the article that appears on pp. 333–334 by explaining that it is a human-interest article about a high-school baseball coach and science teacher who joins the Major Leagues.
- Point out that the publishing date of a magazine is important. Explain that part of the appeal of magazine articles is their timeliness; people like to read about current events.
- Explain that the purpose of the summary sentence is both to attract readers and to help them decide whether they want to read the article. For example, a reader who is not interested in baseball might read the sentence and skip to the next article. A baseball fan would know that he or she would be interested in the article.
- Point out that quotations are excellent evidence because they give an article credibility. Here, the writer uses the words of the man described in the article. His own words directly reveal his experience. Challenge students to find other kinds of evidence in the article, including facts, details, and examples.

CUSTOMIZE INSTRUCTION FOR UNIVERSAL ACCESS

For Special Needs Students	For English Learners
Although the article is relatively short, it covers a time period of several months. Allow each student to work with a partner to complete a Series of Events Chain organizer like the one on p. 69 of **Writing Models and Graphic Organizers on Transparencies.** Once students understand the course of events, ask them to find key details about each event. Then, ask each student to write a two- or three-sentence summary of the article.	Students may not be familiar with some of the sports references in the article. Have students work with partners to read the article aloud, pausing to identify unfamiliar vocabulary words, such as *pitches, farm clubs,* and *playoffs.* If possible, ask a student who is proficient in English to work with students to define the terms or to locate the definitions in a dictionary.

- Ask students to comment on the photograph included with the article. They should understand that the photo is another form of evidence—it shows the subject of the article, Jim Morris, in the Tampa Bay team uniform pitching a ball.
- Challenge students to discuss the effect of including the photograph in the article.

The Reagan County High School baseball team had a beef. Not about their field in Big Lake, Texas—where dust from a nearby rodeo arena sometimes stops games—but about batting practice. According to the kids, coach Jim Morris, a former minor leaguer forced out of the game a decade earlier by arm problems, was making pitches that they just couldn't hit. "The team used to tell me I was throwing too hard," says Morris, 35, who also taught science. "I thought they were complaining because they didn't want to take batting practice." Finally, he proposed a deal: If the team made the state play-offs, he would try out for the major leagues.

The kids did their part, and in mid-June, Morris did his, dazzling scouts with his 98-mph fastball. Within a week Morris had signed with the Tampa Bay Devil Rays and, with the blessing of wife Lorri, was launched on one of the most improbable baseball adventures this side of Kevin Costner. After posting a 3-1 record at the Devil Rays' Durham, N.C., farm club, the big lefthander got his call to the majors last month. On Sept. 18, against the Texas Rangers, Morris entered the game in the eighth inning, becoming the oldest big league rookie in nearly three decades. As Lorri, a college admissions officer, and the couple's three children looked on, Morris struck out Royce Clayton on four pitches. "My 8-year-old is ecstatic—he took that ball to school," says Morris. "My 5-year-old just wants me to come home."

When an article is about a person's very recent experience, it often includes quotations from that person.

Unfortunately for little Jessica, Daddy still has work to do. He's headed to the Arizona Fall League, where teams send their most promising prospects. "It's been an unbelievable journey," says Morris. "It's strange to go from signing report cards to signing autographs almost overnight."

People Weekly, OCTOBER 1, 1999

CUSTOMIZE INSTRUCTION FOR UNIVERSAL ACCESS

For Less Proficient Readers	For Advanced Readers
Because the article is a profile, students may have trouble identifying the article's conclusion. Explain to students that the conclusion is implied by the evidence. All the evidence points to the idea that the subject, Jim Morris, has a promising career in baseball ahead of him. Remind students to use the graphic organizer that appears on p. 332 to keep track of the types of evidence the writer provides. Students should use the evidence in their organizers to answer questions 4 and 5 on p. 335.	Challenge students to write a follow-up article to "Throw and Tell." Have students research Jim Morris's baseball career since October 1999. You may need to have the school librarian help students use microfilm or other library material to find the most recent information. Tell students to develop their material into a two-column magazine article with an article title, a make-believe magazine title, and a date. Remind students to include quotations if possible.

Check Your Comprehension

1. Name three things you learned from the article about Jim Morris.
2. What led Jim Morris to try out for the major leagues?
3. What distinguished Morris from the other Tampa Bay Devil Rays?

Applying the Reading Strategy

Evaluating Evidence for an Author's Conclusions

4. What conclusion(s) has the author drawn about the likelihood of Morris's baseball career?
5. What reasons does the author give for his conclusion(s)?

Activity

Investigate a Conclusion

Do research to discover whether the author's conclusions turned out to be valid. Use the Internet to find online information. Use the *Readers' Guide to Periodical Literature* (print or electronic) to find magazine articles. If you don't know how to use the *Readers' Guide*, ask the reference librarian to help you. Compare what has happened in Jim Morris's baseball career with the author's conclusions.

Contrasting Informational Materials

Articles and Autobiographies

Autobiographical writing is writing in which the subject writes about all or part of his or her own life. In **biographical articles,** such as "Throw and Tell," the author writes about all or part of someone else's life. Look at the chart that shows characteristics of biographical articles and autobiographical writing. Contrast the two types of informational materials by answering the questions.

1. What is one reason a reader might choose an article over an autobiography?
2. What is one reason a reader might choose an autobiography over an article?
3. What details in "Throw and Tell" might not be included in an autobiographical account by Jim Morris?

	Biographical Article	Autobiography
Purpose	To tell about someone else's life	To tell about one's own life
Details	What the writer observes or is told about the subject	What the writer knows about his or her own actions, thoughts, and feelings
Audience	People interested in the person's life	People interested in the author's life

Answers for p. 335

Check Your Comprehension

1. Possible responses: Jim Morris was a science teacher and baseball coach at Reagan County High School in Texas; he has a fast pitch (98 mph); he was a minor league baseball player who was injured; he tried out for the major leagues after his team won state playoffs; he was picked up by the Tampa Bay Devil Rays; he struck out Royce Clayton.
2. Morris told his students that if they made it to the state playoffs, he would try out for the major leagues.
3. Morris was the oldest major league rookie to take to the playing field in nearly thirty years, and he struck out a player on the Texas Rangers team in four pitches.

Applying the Reading Strategy

4. The author makes it seem as though Jim Morris has a promising pitching career ahead of him.
5. The author mentions that Morris's pitches went as fast as 98 mph, that Morris was picked up by the Tampa Bay Devil Rays within a week of performing for scouts, and that Morris struck out a major league batter on his first trip to the pitching mound.

Activity

Before students begin their searches, ask each student to state the purpose of his or her search in the form of a question, such as "What has happened to Jim Morris since October 1999?" Then, suggest that students identify key words or phrases in the article to use in their searches. (Students will have the best results if they search for Morris's name, baseball, and for the Tampa Bay Devil Rays.) Also, remind students that they will find the best information in periodicals and Internet sites devoted to baseball. Finally, ask each student to write a brief report that details Jim Morris's career and compares it to the conclusions made in the article "Throw and Tell." Have students identify the facts and other forms of evidence in their papers by using different colored highlighters or by writing brief notes in the margins of their reports.

continued

Answers continued

Contrasting Informational Materials

Articles and Autobiographies

1. An article is much shorter than an autobiography. If a reader has limited time or only a passing interest in the subject, then he or she would probably prefer an article.
2. Because an autobiography is written by its subject, it will have information that cannot be found anywhere else, and it may cover the subject's entire life. If a reader is very interested in a particular person, he or she will probably want to read an autobiography rather than an article.
3. In an autobiography, comments made by Jim Morris would not appear in quotes.

Lesson Objectives

1. To identify the characteristics of persuasive speeches
2. To understand the purpose of a persuasive speech

About Persuasive Speeches

- Have students read "About Persuasive Speeches." Then, ask them to think of persuasive speeches they have heard or read and to comment on the effectiveness of the speeches. Guide students to see that a speech's effectiveness depends on the characteristics mentioned on p. 336.
- Ask students to identify the kinds of persuasive speeches they have heard or read and their purposes. Possible responses: Students may mention political speeches whose purpose is to get votes for the candidates. They may mention speeches by parents, doctors, or police officials trying to persuade kids to wear bicycle helmets or obey laws.
- Discuss whether students were persuaded by the speeches.

Reading Strategy

Understanding a Writer's Purpose

- Have students read the information about the Reading Strategy.
- Ask students why they think speakers clarify their purpose in the first paragraphs. Possible response: Because listeners are usually attentive during the beginning, speakers will make their purpose clear in the opening.
- Explain the distinction between facts and arguments. Fact can be proved, such as a date or a name. Arguments are ideas that come from a point of view. An argument must be supported by facts, evidence, and logic in order to be considered valid.
- Ask students to copy the graphic organizer on p. 336 onto a sheet of paper, leaving space to answer the questions. Ask students to complete the organizer as they read pp. 337–338.

READING INFORMATIONAL MATERIALS

Persuasive Speeches

About Persuasive Speeches

A persuasive speech is a public presentation that argues for or against a particular position. People who use persuasive speeches to sway an audience's opinion include politicians and business people. A powerful persuasive speech can change the way an audience thinks and feels about an issue. Most persuasive speeches have the following characteristics:

- An issue with two sides
- A clear statement of the speaker's purpose and position
- Clear organization, including an introduction, a body, and a conclusion
- Powerful language intended to persuade

Reading Strategy

Understanding a Writer's Purpose

When a speaker writes and delivers a persuasive speech, the basic purpose is always the same. To understand a writer's purpose, consider these points:

- The speaker is trying to persuade you to accept his or her position.
- His or her position can usually be determined by reading the opening paragraphs of the speech.
- The rest of the speech is devoted to supporting the position with facts and arguments.

When reading the speech, determine the writer's possible purpose and whether the speech achieves this purpose.

Writer's Purpose	Was it achieved?
The writer was trying to persuade me to believe that ______	Did the writer present accurate facts?
	Did the writer support a position with convincing arguments?
	Were the arguments presented clearly, in a logical order?
	Did the writer convince me to accept that position?

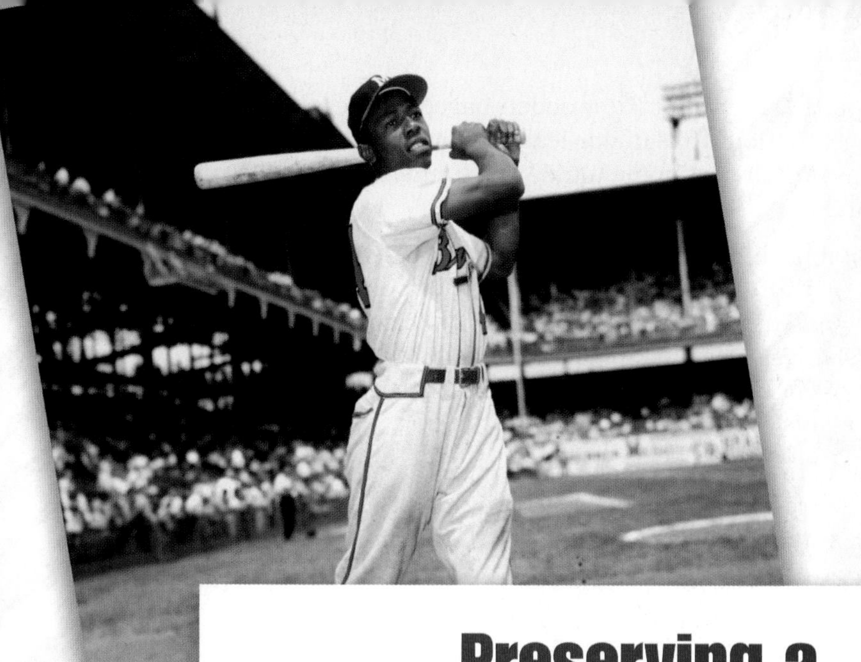

Preserving a Great American Symbol

Richard Durbin

Congressman Richard Durbin gave the following humorous speech in the House of Representatives on July 26, 1989. While most speeches to Congress are serious, Durbin's is humorous yet persuasive and "drives home" the point that wooden baseball bats should not be replaced with metal ones.

In his introduction, Durbin clearly introduces his topic and his purpose for delivering the speech.

Mr. Speaker, I rise to condemn the desecration of a great American symbol. No, I am not referring to flagburning; I am referring to the baseball bat.

Preserving a Great American Symbol

- Before students begin reading, tell them that the speech is presented in a humorous or sarcastic way.
- Point out that the speaker's introduction is actually the first two paragraphs. The first paragraph serves as an attention-getting device and does focus on the subject, but the true purpose (calling for the outlawing of aluminum baseball bats) does not become clear until the second paragraph.
- Talk to students about the speaker's use of humor. The humor is very specific to baseball fans and so might not appeal to all people. Discuss the speaker's choice of humor. Why might he risk losing the interest of listeners who do not care for baseball?
  Possible response: Because the speaker's topic is baseball, he addresses baseball fans, although he might hope that his humor also appeals to nonbaseball fans.
- Ask students to focus on the dramatic comparison made between baseball players and the president of the United States. What is its effect?
  Possible response: The comparison grabs the listeners' or readers' attention, and it makes clear that the expense of wooden bats is not an issue.

CUSTOMIZE INSTRUCTION FOR UNIVERSAL ACCESS

For Special Needs Students	For Gifted/Talented Readers
Some of the word usage in "Preserving a Great American Symbol" may be difficult for special needs students. Direct students to the words *desecration, extinction, indignities,* and *heinous sacrilege.* Have students use a dictionary to understand how the words are used in this context. Be sure that students grasp the humor and sarcasm of Durbin's intent.	Have students work in pairs to rewrite Durbin's speech. Students should develop a list of reasons that Durbin uses for his argument against aluminum baseball bats. Then, have students write a new speech that either bypasses the humor or contains the students' own humor. Allow volunteers to read their new speeches to the class.

continued from p. 337

- Invite students to list the arguments the speaker makes against aluminum bats. Then, ask students whether they think the evidence is reasonable. Point out that the speaker uses emotional appeal as well as appeals to reason.
- Talk to students about the final paragraph of the speech. What do students notice about its tone? What emotion does the speaker suggest here?
  Possible response: The speaker sounds disappointed and sad. He makes it sound as if the use of aluminum bats reflects poorly on the United States.

Several experts tell us that the wooden baseball bat is doomed to extinction, that major league baseball players will soon be standing at home plate with aluminum bats in their hands.

Baseball fans have been forced to endure countless indignities by those who just cannot leave well enough alone: designated hitters,[1] plastic grass, uniforms that look like pajamas, chicken clowns dancing on the base lines, and, of course, the most heinous sacrilege, lights in Wrigley Field.[2]

> Durbin uses humor to persuade and entertain.

Are we willing to hear the crack of a bat replaced by the dinky ping? Are we ready to see the Louisville Slugger replaced by the aluminum ping dinger? Is nothing sacred?

Please do not tell me that wooden bats are too expensive, when players who cannot hit their weight are being paid more money than the President of the United States.

Please do not try to sell me on the notion that these metal clubs will make better hitters.

What will be next? Teflon baseballs? Radar-enhanced gloves? I ask you.

I do not want to hear about saving trees. Any tree in America would gladly give its life for the glory of a day at home plate.

I do not know if it will take a constitutional amendment to keep our baseball traditions alive, but if we forsake the great Americana of broken-bat singles and pine tar,[3] we will have certainly lost our way as a nation.

> Durbin closes with a dramatic statement, which serves as a final persuasive argument.

1. **designated hitter** player who bats in place of the pitcher and does not play any other position. The position was created in 1973 in the American League. Some fans argue it has changed the game for the worse.
2. **Wrigley Field** historic baseball field in Chicago. It did not have lights for night games until 1988. Some fans regretted the change.
3. **broken-bat singles . . . pine tar** When a batter breaks a wooden bat while hitting the ball and makes it to first base, it is a notable event in a baseball game. Pine tar is a substance used to improve the batter's grip on a wooden bat.

CUSTOMIZE INSTRUCTION FOR UNIVERSAL ACCESS

For English Learners	For Advanced Readers
Help students understand the tone of the speech by reading it aloud to them, emphasizing the sarcasm. Then, explain that the humor occurs when the speaker raises the matter of baseball to great national importance. Allow students to work together to figure out the facts and essential arguments of the speech and to separate them from the tone.	Students may recognize the sarcastic or ironic tone of the work. Invite them to think of other works—speeches, books, stories, or essays—that they have read that have used a similar tone. Then, ask students to write a short statement about the effect of the tone on them as listeners or readers. Ask volunteers to share their responses with the class. Students may suggest that the tone makes the speech more interesting, and it captures the interest of baseball fans.

Check Your Comprehension

1. To which "American symbol" does Durbin refer in his opening statement?
2. Why does Durbin favor wooden bats and dislike aluminum bats?
3. How does the author tie baseball to America's national well-being?

Applying the Reading Strategy

Analyzing the Writer's Purpose

4. What is Richard Durbin's purpose in delivering this speech?
5. Summarize the arguments he uses to achieve his purpose.
6. Why do you think Durbin chose to use humor in his speech?
7. **(a)** Did Durbin persuade you with his arguments? Explain. **(b)** Did he leave out any details that would have been more persuasive? Explain.

Activity

Persuasive Speech

Write and present a persuasive speech that takes the opposite side of the position taken by Durbin. In other words, try to convince an audience that baseball teams should replace their wooden bats with aluminum ones.

- State your main position and purpose clearly in the opening and closing portions of the speech.
- Back up your main position with appropriate evidence and arguments that make sense.

To learn more about how to deliver a persuasive speech, see the Listening and Speaking Workshop on page 344.

Comparing Informational Materials

Political Speeches and Advertisements

Richard Durbin's persuasive speech supporting wooden bats is a political speech that uses humor as a persuasive tool. He also uses images that have emotional appeal and language that evokes strong emotions. Find examples of each persuasive technique in this speech and in an advertisement. Complete the chart with the examples you find.

	Political Speech	Advertisement
Purpose	(Persuasion) To convince enough voters to support a particular position.	(Persuasion) To convince customers to buy a particular product or service.
Methods		

Answers for p. 339

Check Your Comprehension

1. The baseball bat is the symbol Durbin refers to in his speech.
2. Durbin thinks that aluminum baseball bats are cheap and that they detract from the tradition and dignity of the game.
3. The author suggests that the state of baseball directly reflects on the United States as a nation. If we allow aluminum bats to ruin the tradition of baseball, he argues, then the United States does not care about its traditions.

Applying the Reading Strategy

4. Durbin's purpose is to make a humorous statement about the use of aluminum bats in baseball.
5. Durbin argues that aluminum bats lack dignity, make a dinky pinging sound, are cheap, and go against tradition.
6. The humor attracts listeners' or readers' attention and hides the fact that the speaker is actually serious about wanting to remove aluminum bats from baseball.
7. **(a)** Possible responses: Some students may say that he did persuade them. Others may say that the issue does not concern them, despite the author's efforts. **(b)** Students may say that the facts presented in the argument were a little thin; the author's main argument is that the bats are cheap and tacky and do not represent the tradition of baseball.

Activity

Students should follow the guidelines that appear on p. 339 when writing their persuasive speeches. Students who are not sports fans may have trouble deciding where to begin. Suggest that they talk to someone knowledgeable, such as a baseball fan or the owner of a sports equipment shop. You also may guide students to respond point-by-point to Durbin's argument.

Ask students to practice their speeches before delivering them. They may work with a partner to rehearse. Remind students to maintain eye contact with the audience and to speak in strong voices.

Answers continued

Comparing Persuasive Speeches

Before students complete the chart, ask them to think about examples of political speeches and advertisements they have seen or heard that used humor. Discuss how the humor was used and the effect it had on the audience. Then, turn to the chart on p. 339.

Possible answers:

Humorous Political Speech:

Uses humor to show that the politician is friendly and down-to-earth, make the issues understandable, and put listeners at ease.

Humorous Advertisement:

Uses humor to engage the audience and show that the product is fun.

continued

Lesson Objectives

1. To write a persuasive composition
2. To use writing strategies to generate ideas, plan, organize, evaluate, and revise the composition

Model From Literature

In "Lob's Girl" on p. 279, Mrs. Pearce, the main character's grandmother, makes a persuasive argument for allowing a German shepherd dog into the hospital to see the hurt girl.

Prewriting

- Consider working as a class to brainstorm for a list of topics that have at least two sides. Challenge students to identify the sides of each issue. Steer students away from controversial issues, such as capital punishment; instead, guide them toward local, school, or personal issues, like the one addressed in the student model, which can be more easily addressed in a short persuasive paper.
- Discuss with students the different kinds of evidence. Draw a five-column chart on the board or overhead transparency, and label each of the columns: *Facts, Examples, Statistics, Quotations,* and *Personal Observations.* Take a position on a topic, and then generate examples of each kind of evidence. Encourage students to include an example of each type of evidence in their papers.
- Remind students that counterarguments are very important to consider because they reveal both sides of the argument. If students have trouble identifying a counterargument, have them return to the brainstorming they did with the class at the beginning of the workshop.
- Before students draft their essays, have them review the Rubric for Self-Assessment (p. 343), so they know what is expected.

Writing WORKSHOP

Persuasion: Persuasive Composition

A **persuasive composition** presents an argument for or against a particular position. In this workshop, you will write a persuasive composition in support of a proposition, or proposal.

Assignment Criteria. Your persuasive composition should have the following characteristics:

- An issue with two sides
- A clear thesis statement—a statement of your position on an issue, a proposition, or proposal
- Evidence that supports your position and anticipates the readers' concerns and counter-arguments
- A clear organization, including an introduction, a body, and a strong conclusion
- Powerful images and language

See the Rubric on page 343 for the criteria on which your persuasive composition may be assessed.

Prewriting

Choose a topic. Choose a topic that has at least two sides. Your purpose will be to show that your position, or side, is stronger than the opposing position.

Gather evidence. Identify facts, examples, statistics, quotations, and personal observations that support your position. Take notes on the sources of your information. You may need to recheck facts, and you will need to credit any ideas or words that are not your own.

Anticipate counterarguments. Anticipate readers' concerns, questions, and arguments against your position. Identify facts that can be included in the composition to address opposing positions.

Arguments	Counterarguments
It isn't music.	It is a group of organized sounds. It has a rhythmic pattern
There's no variety; all the same key.	The old standby key of E is gone. Guitarists are experimenting with techniques for changing keys.

TEACHING RESOURCES

The following resources can be used to enrich or extend the instruction for pp. 340–343.

Writing and Grammar, Copper Level, Chapter 7, pp. 124–149

Performance Assess. and Portfolio Mgmt., p. 11

Writing Models and Graphic Organizers on Transparencies, p. 73

Writing and Grammar iText CD-ROM
Students can use the following tools as they complete their persuasive compositions.

- Persuasion Topic Bank
- Interactive Pros and Cons Chart
- Outliner
- Vague Adjectives Revision Checker

Student Model

Before you begin drafting your persuasive composition, read this student model and review the characteristics of a successful persuasive composition.

Isaac Tetenbaum
Reseda, CA

Modern Rock Is Music, Too

Maybe you think Chopin is really cool—the blissful tones of the piano, played to serenade and mesmerize, the dazzling cadenzas and glistening high notes. For a change, though, why don't you pop in a modern rock CD? Contemporary music gets very little respect, yet most of the people who put it down haven't even listened to it. Modern rock deserves to be regarded and respected as music.

The writer clearly established the two sides—those who like contemporary music and those who prefer classical.

The last sentence in the introduction is the thesis.

Music can be classified as any group of organized sounds. Yet while the roars of today's lead vocalists don't seem to make sense, even they are organized and related to the message of the song. Is it music? Yes. It follows a precise rhythmic pattern. It repeats. Just because howls from a modern vocalist don't follow any pitches doesn't mean they can't be classified as perfectly good music. You might not like the style, but you cannot deny it is music.

The writer provides evidence that contemporary artists would be considered musical even by classical definitions.

Once you've accepted rock as music, you might say all rock songs are in the same key—E. Just because the lowest string of the guitar is an E doesn't mean modern rock musicians continuously strum that string and open and end a tune with it. Nowadays, as new musicians experiment with different pitches, the common E of rock has almost disappeared.

Here, the writer realizes that readers might argue that all rock music is written in the same key—an argument he says used to be true but isn't anymore.

In a technique called "dropping," guitarists and bassists of modern rock bands have been able to use lower pitches in their songs. In fact, a well-known modern-style guitarist has successfully created a seven-string guitar. Its seventh string has the default pitch of a B. Although you might have to listen a little harder to hear the evidence, the musicians of contemporary bands know their music. How else could they come up with "dropping" and the seven-string guitar?

I think anyone, even the most classic of classical music lovers, can appreciate today's sounds if given a chance. (Notice I didn't say love, just appreciate.) I listen to Chopin and modern rock. I respect both kinds of music because each one has its place. Chopin is like elegant figure skating—rock is like snowboarding. I feel free when I listen to my favorite rock group. Why don't you listen with me?

A powerful image helps readers understand the difference in the effect of the two kinds of music and to recognize that one person can like two different things for two different occasions.

CUSTOMIZE INSTRUCTION FOR UNIVERSAL ACCESS

For Less Proficient Readers	For English Learners	For Advanced Readers
If students have trouble gathering evidence, suggest that they choose a topic, such as recycling, that has ample factual evidence available. Guide students to evaluate their sources and use only convincing and relevant evidence. Ask students if the evidence would convince *them.*	For students using the Internet to conduct their research, help them narrow their searches by using the most effective keywords and phrases. Ensure that the librarian can assist students in areas such as reference materials if students conduct their research in the library.	Challenge students to gather a variety of evidence, such as an interview with a person who has first-hand knowledge or experience of the topic. Encourage students also to use strong sources when examining the counterargument for their topics.

Student Model

- Explain that the Student Model is a sample and that essays may be longer.
- Have students identify the topic or issue and its counterargument. **Answer:** The topic is the musical merit of contemporary rock music. Some people prefer the melodic sound of classical music and think that rock music is not musical.
- Talk with students about how Isaac supports his idea with evidence. Students should notice that Isaac provides facts ("the lowest string of the guitar is an E") and personal observations ("Chopin is like elegant figure skating"). Challenge students to think of other forms of evidence, such as quotations or statistics, that would help the argument.
- Then, have students identify the evidence that the writer gives that disproves the counterargument. **Answer:** The writer explains that rock musicians have developed techniques to help change the pitch and key of songs, so that songs no longer sound the same.
- Point out how Isaac saves most of his evidence for the fourth paragraph where he disproves his counterargument. By saving his strongest ideas for the end, Isaac makes a lasting impression.
- Discuss how Isaac describes the two kinds of music—comparing them to sports. Point out how these images make the reader see the differences between the two types of music.

Real-World Connection

Persuasive writing in the real world: Persuasive writing has many uses in the real world. Businesses use it in advertisements, hoping to convince people to buy and use their products or services. Politicians use persuasion in campaigns to get people to vote for them and the issues they support. Editorial writers in newspapers and magazines use persuasion to change people's minds. Challenge students to think of issues that affect their local communities. Discuss persuasive arguments about these issues.

Drafting

- Remind students that the one-sentence thesis statement is very important. It clearly tells readers exactly what the writer thinks about an issue. Students should make sure that the thesis statement appears at the beginning or the end of the introductory paragraph.
- Students should realize that a strong persuasive paper takes readers step-by-step through each idea and supports each idea with evidence. Remind students that they should save their strongest piece of evidence for the end, where it will have the greatest impact. If students are not sure which piece of evidence is strongest, have them discuss their evidence with a partner and ask the partner for his or her opinion.
- Encourage students to use a wide range of evidence, but remind them that the majority probably are examples and personal observations. Although these are valid forms of evidence, explain that expert opinions and statistics carry more clout because they come from respected sources.
- If students have trouble organizing their papers, remind them that their introductions should include not only the thesis statement but an attention-grabbing beginning and some background about the topic of their papers.

Revising

- Supply students with colored pencils, pens, or highlighters to use as they follow the revising instructions in the text.
- Remind students that, ideally, they should have three supporting points for each idea. In a short assignment such as this one, however, suggest that students offer at least two.
- Tell students to identify the type of evidence they offer for support. Remind them that they should have as many different types of evidence as possible to strengthen their arguments.

(continued on page 343)

Drafting

Write a thesis statement. Review your notes, and write a strong one-sentence statement of your position. Include this sentence early in your composition.

Example: Our school should have a recycling bin next to every trash can.

Support each point. To support and clarify your points, use the following techniques.

- Find and use examples.
- Use facts or statistics.
- Make a specific observation.
- Include quotes and expert opinions.

Create a clear organization. Organize your thoughts clearly and concisely. Include your thesis statement in your introduction. Support your thesis statement in the body. Organize facts, details, and other support into paragraphs. Each paragraph should focus on one reason you give for your position. Conclude with a restatement of your thesis.

Introduction
Thesis statement

Body
Main point followed by facts, details, arguments, statistics, expert opinions. Explanations and evidence for readers' concerns and counterarguments.

Conclusion
Summary of arguments
Strong restatement of position

Revising

Revise to strengthen support. Look over your draft to find places where you can strengthen your support.

1. Underline your thesis statement in red.
2. Put a star next to each supporting point. Add more support if you have few stars.

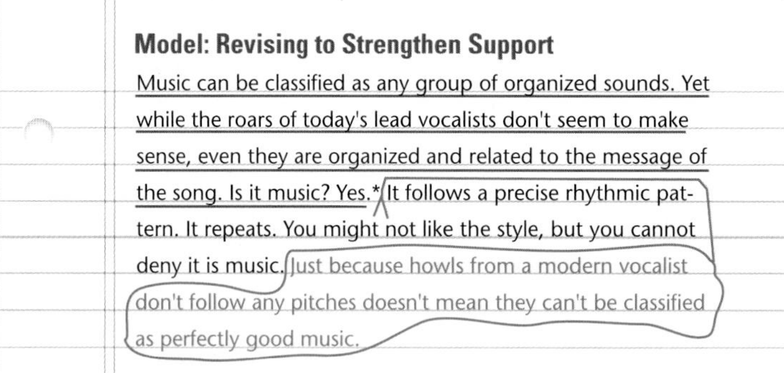

Model: Revising to Strengthen Support

Music can be classified as any group of organized sounds. Yet while the roars of today's lead vocalists don't seem to make sense, even they are organized and related to the message of the song. Is it music? Yes.* It follows a precise rhythmic pattern. It repeats. You might not like the style, but you cannot deny it is music. Just because howls from a modern vocalist don't follow any pitches doesn't mean they can't be classified as perfectly good music.

USING TECHNOLOGY IN WRITING

If students have access in class to a computer with a word-processing program, suggest that they work with a partner to revise each other's papers. Have students read their partner's papers on the computer screen and make their comments in marginal comment boxes or electronic "sticky" notes. Students should comment on the clarity of the thesis statement, the strength and types of evidence, and the strength of the counter-argument. Students should use the "Save As" function to preserve their comments in another file. Students can also use the sentence openers and transition words checkers on **Writing and Grammar iText.**

Revise to strengthen images. Look for places where you can add or improve an image that illustrates your point. Use words that call specific pictures or sensory details to mind.

Compare the model and the nonmodel. Why is the model more effective than the nonmodel?

Nonmodel	Model
I think anyone, even the most classic of classical music lovers, can appreciate today's sounds if given a chance. I listen to Chopin and modern rock. I respect both kinds of music because each one has its place.	I think anyone, even the most classic of classical music lovers, can appreciate today's sound if given a chance. (Notice I didn't say love, just appreciate.) I listen to Chopin and modern rock. I respect both kinds of music because each one has its place. Chopin is like elegant figure skating—rock is like snowboarding.

Publishing and Presenting

Choose one of these ways to share your writing with classmates or a larger audience.

Deliver a speech. Use your persuasive composition as the basis for a speech that you give to your classmates.

Post your essay. Use a word-processing program to format your composition. Post your persuasive composition on a class bulletin board so that classmates can read it and discuss your position.

WG Prentice Hall Writing and Grammar Connection: Chapter 7, Section 6

Speaking Connection
To learn more about delivering a persuasive composition as a speech, see the **Listening and Speaking Workshop: Delivering a Persuasive Speech**, page 344.

Rubric for Self-Assessment

Evaluate your persuasive composition using the following criteria and rating scale:

Criteria	Rating Scale Not very				Very
Does the issue have two sides?	1	2	3	4	5
How clear and focused is the thesis statement?	1	2	3	4	5
How well are readers' concerns anticipated and addressed?	1	2	3	4	5
How effectively are arguments organized?	1	2	3	4	5
How powerful is the persuasive language?	1	2	3	4	5

TEST-TAKING TIP

Students should remember to be practical when arguing an issue on a test—even if they do not agree with it. Students should spend most of their limited time considering evidence and support. Because students will not be able to do research during a test, evidence is limited to examples and personal observations. Tell students that outlining their ideas is always a good idea before they begin to write. Students should always make sure that their strongest ideas appear at the end of their essay, just before the conclusion.

Revising (continued)

- Help students understand the impact of images by writing the following two sentences on the board:

  To me, classical music is boring.

  To me, classical music is like a glass of warm tap water.

  Ask students to explain the difference in the impact of each sentence.
  Answer: The first sentence is just an opinion. The second one creates an image that leaves an impression on the reader.
- Work with students to see how the nonmodel and the model are worded differently. Discuss how the model's ideas are clearer and more memorable than the ideas in the nonmodel.
  Answer: By citing "even Mozart lovers," the writer is strengthening the argument. Also, the writer uses clear visual images when comparing the sounds of the two kinds of music—the "elegant footwork" of classical music versus the "enthusiastic and energetic leaping" of rock.
- Have students return to their essays to find places where they can illustrate their points with specific images or sensory details.

Publishing and Presenting

- Have students write brief statements about the audience they think will be interested in their essays.
- Then, ask students to think about how they would deliver their papers as speeches. Would they change anything? Ask volunteers to read their papers aloud and, as a class, talk about the issues that were raised and identify any common themes or concerns.

Assessment

- Review the assessment criteria in class.
- Have students practice assessment skills by comparing the Student Model on p. 341 to the rubric here. Remind students to be objective in their evaluations.
- For further practice, have students evaluate a partner's paper.
- The rubric on this page, and another rubric in an alternative format, can be found on p. 11 of **Performance Assessment and Portfolio Management.**

Lesson Objectives

1. To deliver a persuasive speech that presents a clear position and supporting evidence
2. To engage listeners with a strong beginning and good eye contact
3. To convince listeners by repeating key points and using visuals

Engage Listeners

- Remind students that a strong speech contains interesting ideas and a clear position with solid evidence.
- Explain to students that they should open their speeches with engaging language. Suggest that students work with partners to test the opening of their speeches.
- Next, students should read aloud the entire speech to partners or into a tape recorder. They should find that their sentences are not too long and that their listener does not lose interest.

Convince Listeners

- A key difference between a persuasive composition and a persuasive speech is the repetition of key phrases or ideas. Students should work with their partners to identify key points to reinforce through repetition.
- Remind students that key points can also be repeated with visual aids. Informing the audience while pointing to a visual aid reinforces the information. Visual aids are most effective when their wording is more succinct than what the speaker says. For example, the speaker might tell the audience "One way to make sure that people recycle on a regular basis is to reward the most active participants. You could offer them coupons to their favorite restaurants, for example." The visual aid would say merely "Reward the most active participants."

Listening and Speaking WORKSHOP

Delivering a Persuasive Speech

A **persuasive speech** shares many of the characteristics of a persuasive composition. (To review the characteristics of successful persuasive compositions, see the Writing Workshop, pp. 340–343.) The following speaking strategies will help you engage and convince your listeners.

Engage Listeners

Like compositions, persuasive speeches provide clear position statements and include supporting evidence in logical order. Follow these guidelines to plan and deliver a persuasive speech.

Start strong. Begin with a startling comparison or an anecdote that will capture your audience's attention.

Example: Animal shelters across the country are full of unwanted pets that have been thrown away like garbage.

Make contact. Your audience will hear your presentation only once—make sure they hear each and every word.

- Speak loudly and slowly enough to be heard and understood.
- Make eye contact.
- Move around the room as you speak.
- Pause after key points.

Convince Listeners

To convince an audience of listeners, use speaking strategies that will highlight your strongest support.

Repeat key points. An audience of listeners cannot reread a point they have missed. As a speaker, make sure your audience does not miss your most important evidence and support. After explaining a key point, repeat it in a single sentence. After explaining several points, pause and restate the points in order.

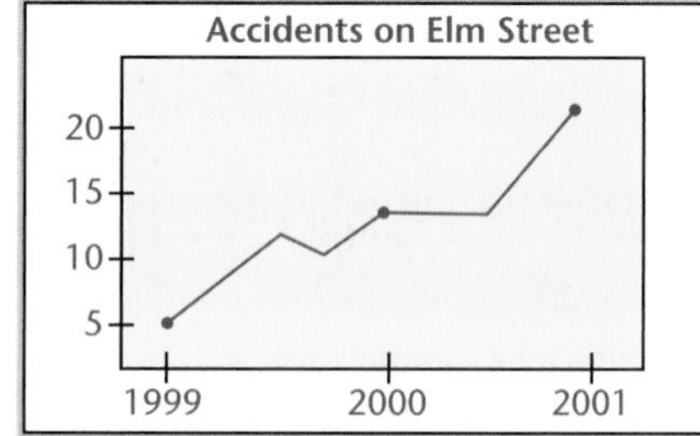

Use visuals. A picture or chart can be a dramatic illustration of a point you are making. If you claim that overcrowding is a problem, show a picture of the overcrowding. If you say accidents are increasing, use a bar graph or a line graph to show the increase. The line graph at right shows how an increase can be shown to an audience rather than just described.

Plan and deliver your speech to the class. Ask for feedback on how you can improve your delivery.

CUSTOMIZE INSTRUCTION FOR UNIVERSAL ACCESS	
For Special Needs Students	**For English Learners**
Students may benefit from working in groups of four or six to evaluate and revise their written speeches. Suggest that students identify strengths and weaknesses in both the written speeches and the deliveries. Then, students can work in pairs to help each other create their visuals; they can even help out by displaying the visuals during a group member's speech.	Students may be reluctant to deliver their own speeches to the class. Ask students to exchange speeches with a partner and to deliver the partner's speech instead. Students may not feel shy about delivering another student's speech, and they will probably work harder to make a good presentation on behalf of another student. The speakers may consult the writers as they prepare their deliveries.

Assessment WORKSHOP

Identifying Cause and Effect

The reading sections of some tests require you to read a passage and answer multiple-choice questions about cause and effect. Use what you have learned about cause and effect to help you answer such questions.

To answer a cause-and-effect test item, ask yourself, "Why did something happen?" or "What happened as a result of something?"

Test-Taking Strategies

- Look for signal words such as *because, why, the reason for, as a result of, in order to,* and *so that.*
- Watch out for distractors—choices that state an event that is from the passage but that is not the cause or effect.

Sample Test Item

Directions: Read the passage and answer the questions.

The Cabrera children liked their new home in the United States. Their parents had good jobs, the neighbors were friendly, and their house was pleasant. Still, they missed their relatives in the Dominican Republic and looked forward to a long summer vacation on the island.

1. Why were the Cabrera children happy in the United States?
   A The neighbors were friendly.
   B They could go to the Dominican Republic for the summer.
   C Their mother didn't have to work.
   D Their new house was like their old one.
2. The children missed their relatives, so they—
   A planned to move back to the Dominican Republic
   B asked their parents to quit their jobs
   C looked forward to summer vacation
   D sold their new home in the United States

Answers and Explanations

1. **C** and **D** are not stated. **B** is not the reason they were happy. ***A*** is the answer.
2. **A** and **B** are not stated. **D** does not make sense in the sentence. ***C*** is the answer.

Practice

Directions: Read the passage and answer the questions.

Immigrants have come to the United States for many reasons. Some have come to escape war, famine, or religious persecution. Others have come to make a better life for their families.

In the early twentieth century, millions of immigrants came from southern and eastern Europe. Many of them stayed in the coastal cities where they landed. As a result, these cities experienced growth and overcrowding.

1. Immigrants came to the United States to—
   A lose their old identity
   B escape war, famine, and persecution
   C avoid prosecution in their old country
   D escape political conditions
2. What contributed to the growth of cities in the United States in the early twentieth century?
   A overcrowding
   B famine
   C immigration
   D progress

TEACHING RESOURCES

The following resources can be used to enrich or extend the instruction for p. 345.

Workbook　　Transparencies

Skill Book　　CD-ROM

Lesson Objective

To identify a cause-and-effect relationship in a text

Applying Reading Strategies

Explain to students that determining the main idea of a passage may help them identify cause and effect. When answering the sample test item, students should try to identify the main idea of the passage. For example, the sample passage can be restated as: "The Cabrera children liked living in the United States, but because they missed their relatives, they looked forward to summer in the Dominican Republic." This statement of the main idea identifies a cause-and-effect relationship in the passage and points to the answer to question 2.

Test-Taking Skills

- Have students read the sample test item. Then, ask them to make a list of the details in the two paragraphs.
  Possible answers: Reasons that people come to the United States include: to escape war, famine, or religious persecution, and to live a better life. Often, immigrants move to the cities, and the cities become crowded.
- Then, ask students to figure out the main idea that is supported by the details. Challenge students to include a cause-and-effect signal word in their statement of the main idea.
  Possible answer: Because immigrants have left their native countries in order to live in the United States, many U.S. cities have become overcrowded.
- Once students have generated a main idea, ask them to answer the sample test item.

Answer

1. The correct answer is *B*. The passage says nothing about *A* or *C*. *D* is implied but not stated. The only answer that is a clear cause of people moving to the United States is *B*.
2. The correct answer is *C*. *A* is the result, not the cause, of immigration to United States cities. *B* is a cause of immigration but not of growth in cities. *D* is not mentioned in the passage.

Unit Objectives

1. To read selections in different genres that develop the theme "Mysterious Worlds"
2. To apply a variety of reading strategies, particularly strategies for reading critically, appropriate for reading these selections
3. To analyze literary elements
4. To use a variety of strategies to build vocabulary
5. To learn elements of grammar, usage, and style
6. To use recursive writing processes to write in a variety of forms
7. To develop listening and speaking skills
8. To express and support responses to various types of texts
9. To prepare, organize, and present literary interpretations

Meeting the Objectives

With each selection, you will find instructional materials through which students can meet these objectives. Further, you will find additional practice pages for reading strategies, literary analysis, vocabulary, and grammar in the **Selection Support: Skills Development Workbook** in your **Teaching Resources.**

Background

Art

This, That, There by Pat Adams

Have students link the painting to the theme of Mysterious Worlds by asking the following questions.

1. What details in the painting are mysterious?
   Possible response: The dark colors and the bumpy-textured spheres, which seem to represent unknown planets, are mysterious.
2. What type of story might use this painting as an illustration?
   Possible response: The painting could illustrate a science fiction story with a space-related theme.

UNIT 5 Mysterious Worlds

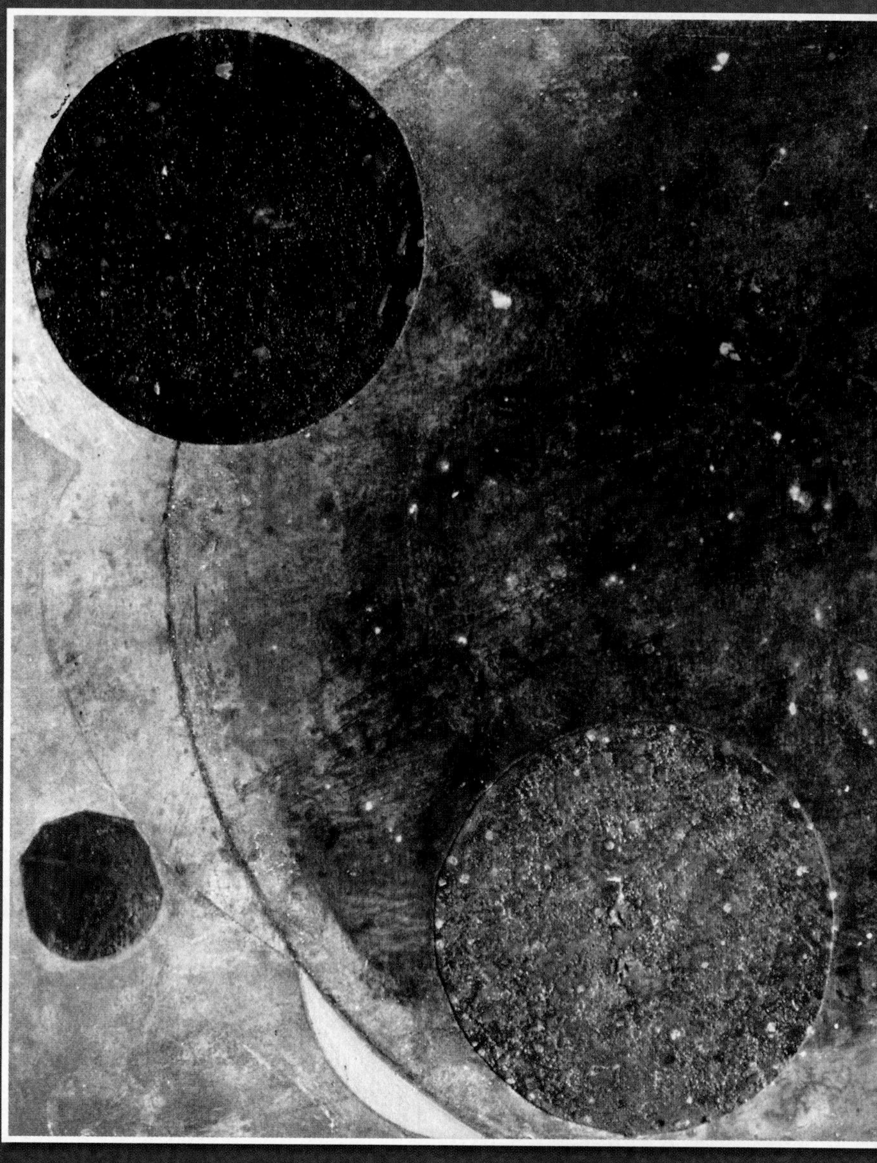

This, That, There, 1993, Pat Adams. Courtesy of Eleanor Munro

UNIT FEATURES

Connections	Reading Informational Material
Every unit contains a feature that connects literature to a related topic, such as art, science, or history. In this unit, students will read an excerpt from *Esperanza Rising* by Pam Muñoz Ryan about the struggles of Mexican immigrants during the Great Depression. The main character's yearning for the past connects thematically to "The Fun They Had." Use the information and questions on the Connections page to enrich students' understanding of the selections presented within the unit.	These selections will help students learn to analyze and evaluate informational texts, such as workplace documents, technical directions, and consumer materials. They will expose students to the organization and features unique to nonnarrative texts. In this unit, students learn to read a Web site and a social studies article for information.

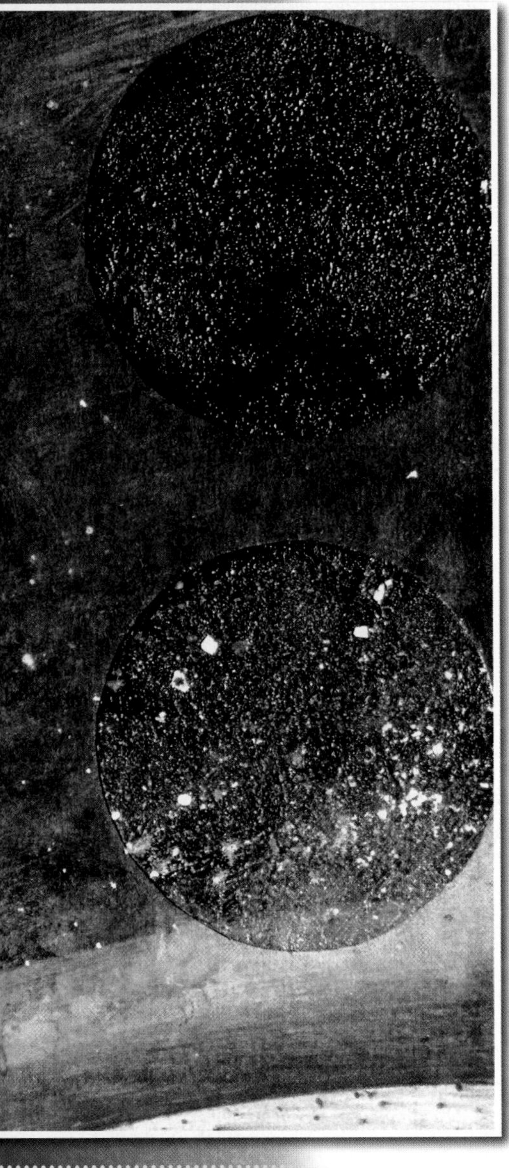

Exploring the Theme

The picture on these pages could be a view of distant planets as seen through a telescope, or it could be a view of microorganisms as seen through a microscope. The stories, poems, and essays in this unit give you a lens through which you can examine mysteries near and far. Through the literature you can explore the mysteries of the past, search for answers to the unexplained, and appreciate the mysteries in the everyday world around you.

◀ **Critical Viewing** How does the artist suggest mystery and the unknown? **[Analyze]**

ASSESSMENT RESOURCES

- **Selection Support: Skills Development Workbook**
- **Formal Assessment**
- **Open Book Tests**
- **Performance Assess. and Portfolio Mgmt.**
- **Extension Activities**

Assessing Student Progress

Listed below are the tools that are available to measure the degree to which students meet the unit objectives.

Informal Assessment

The questions in the Review and Assess sections are a first level of response to the concepts and skills presented within the selections. Students' responses are a brief, informal measure of their grasp of the material. These responses can indicate where further instruction and practice are needed. Follow up with the practice pages in the **Selection Support: Skills Development Workbook.**

Formal Assessment

The **Formal Assessment** booklet contains the Selection Tests and Unit Tests.

- Selection Tests measure comprehension and skills acquisition for each selection or group of selections.
- Each Unit Test provides students with thirty multiple-choice questions and five essay questions designed to assess students' knowledge of the literature and skills taught in the unit.

The **Open-Book Tests** ask students to demonstrate their ability to synthesize and communicate information from selections or groups of selections.

To assess student writing, you will find rubrics and scoring models in the **Performance Assessment and Portfolio Management** booklet. In this booklet, you will also find scoring rubrics for listening and speaking activities.

Alternative Assessment

The **Extension Activities** booklet contains writing activities, listening and speaking activities, and research and technology activities that are appropriate for students with different ability levels. You may also use these activities as an alternative measurement of students' growth.

▶Critical Viewing

The artist suggests mystery and the unknown by using dark colors for the spheres that could be perceived as undiscovered planets.

Why Read Literature?

The "Why Read Literature?" page in each unit presents a list of possible purposes for reading. Each purpose for reading is connected to one or more of the selections in the unit. Good readers set a purpose before reading in order to help them read actively and focus on meaningful details.

Unit 5 introduces three purposes for reading. "Read for Information" leads students to the mystery of the Loch Ness Monster and the story of the *Titanic*. "Read for the Love of Literature" encourages students to read an African folk tale and the story in a poem by Jack Prelutsky. Finally, "Read to be Entertained" guides students to read an eye-opening science fiction story by Isaac Asimov.

How to Use This Page

- Tell students that before reading each selection in this unit, they should set a purpose for reading. This will help them read in an active and focused manner.
- Explain that reading works about other cultures, such as "Why the Tortoise's Shell Is Not Smooth" (p. 411) and "Breaker's Bridge" (p. 392) will increase students' appreciation of literature.
- When reading for information, students want the answers to particular questions, such as "Does the Loch Ness Monster exist?" or "When was the *Tyrannosaurus Rex* called Sue discovered?" Answers to these and other questions appear in "The Loch Ness Monster" (p. 406) and on the "Life and Times of Sue" Web page (p. 376).
- Another reason to read is for entertainment. Remind students as they read Isaac Asimov's science fiction story "The Fun They Had" (p. 352) to enjoy the futuristic descriptions.

Why Read Literature?

This unit explores mysterious worlds—looking into the past and the future at unsolved mysteries and worlds to be discovered. While reading about the mysteries we can or cannot explain, you may have other purposes for reading these works. Preview three of the purposes you might set before reading the selections in this unit.

1 Read for information.

Sightings of the Loch Ness monster and monsters in other large lakes around the world have been reported for more than 1,400 years. Today, scientists use sonar, underwater photography, and other technological equipment to search for proof that these creatures do or do not exist. So far, clues found through technological means have only deepened the mystery. Learn what scientists have done to try to find "Nessie" when you read **"The Loch Ness Monster,"** page 406.

Only seven skeletons that are more than half complete of Tyrannosaurus Rex have ever been discovered. The most complete skeleton was discovered by an amateur fossil hunter. Learn interesting facts about this dinosaur discovery when you read information from the Web page **"The Life and Times of Sue,"** page 376.

The *Titanic* was one of three luxury liners in a fleet built by the White Star Line. The *Olympic,* one of the other two, survived four submarine attacks and made hundreds of transatlantic crossings without accident. Although the *Titanic* was the one people called "unsinkable," the *Olympic* eventually earned the nickname "Old Reliable." Find out why the *Titanic* could not live up to its unsinkable reputation when you read the excerpt from **"Exploring the *Titanic*,"** page 380.

2 Read for the love of literature.

When Jack Prelutsky was a boy, he hated poetry. When he grew up, he became a poet. Read a poem by this former poetry hater: **"Ankylosaurus,"** page 370.

A tortoise's shell has approximately fifty bones covered by twenty-six "scutes." The scutes are the separate sections that you can see on a tortoise's shell. Long before scientists came up with an explanation for these markings, storytellers in Africa were offering an entertaining explanation of their own. Read this humorous explanation in **"Why the Tortoise's Shell Is Not Smooth,"** page 411.

3 Read to be entertained.

The first general-purpose electronic digital computer was built in 1946. It was called ENIAC, for *E*lectronic *N*umerical *I*ntegrator *A*nd *C*omputer. It weighed thirty tons and took up more than 1,500 square feet. Isaac Asimov's story about computers, **"The Fun They Had,"** page 352, was written during ENIAC's time. Read it to see whether Asimov's vision of the future was accurate.

Take It to the Net

Visit the Web site for online instruction and activities related to each selection in this unit.

www.phschool.com

ENRICHMENT: Further Reading

Have students choose one or more of the works below to extend the unit theme "Mysterious Worlds" or to read more by the unit authors.

Time and Again by Jack Finney

This novel about one New Yorker's travel through time from the 1970s to the 1880s is considered a science fiction classic.

The Stars My Destination by Alfred Bester

This well-loved science fiction novel, first published in 1956, has thrilled generations of readers with the story of Gulliver Foyle, a man stranded in outer space.

The New Kid on the Block by Jack Prelutsky

This book offers students a chance to view more than 100 additional humorous poems by unit author Jack Prelutsky.

A Wrinkle in Time by Madeleine L'Engle

This Newbery Medal winner about a clever sister and brother who must hunt through time and space for their lost father can be found in the **Prentice Hall Literature Library.**

How to Read Literature

Strategies for Reading Critically

Every day we receive countless messages through the media. In addition, we read texts that are fiction and nonfiction. To get the most from our reading, we need to read critically—to make decisions about what we believe and what we question. In this unit, you will learn strategies that will help you read critically.

1. Evaluate the author's message.

A good reader thinks about the writer's ideas and views and evaluates the author's message. Evaluating means making a critical judgment using questions like these:

- Does the writer present accurate information?
- Does the writer support opinions with sound reasons?
- Do I agree with the writer's message? Why or why not?

As you read the selections in this unit, you will practice asking and answering these questions to evaluate authors' messages.

2. Distinguish between fact and opinion.

Use the evidence the author presents to distinguish between fact and opinion. A fact can be proved. An opinion can be supported by facts, but a different opinion might also be supported. A statement of opinion is based on interpretation of evidence. A statement of fact is based on evidence alone.

Fact
Can be proved.
The radio room had received a total of seven ice warning messages in one day.

Opinion
Can be supported but not proved.
The atmosphere in the radio room was chaotic.

3. Evaluate logic and reasoning.

As you read, determine whether the author's conclusions are logical by identifying the specific facts that support each conclusion. Look for explanations, evidence, and arguments the author uses as reasons for statements about the topic.

4. Determine cause and effect.

Nonfiction writing, such as works about science and history, often explains the causes and effects of events. Fiction is also based on events with causes and effects. One way to determine cause and effect is to look for words that signal the cause—for example, *because, as a result, therefore,* and *so that.*

Example: The emperor asked Breaker to build a bridge *because* he believed that Breaker was a clever man.

As you read the selections in this unit, review the reading strategies and look at the notes in the side columns. Use the suggestions to apply the strategies for reading critically.

How to Read Literature

The "How to Read Literature" page in each unit presents a set of strategies to help readers understand authors' words and ideas. Each reading strategy is taught in conjunction with one or more of the selections within the unit. Good readers develop a bank of strategies from which they can draw as needed.

Unit 5 introduces four strategies for reading critically. To understand a selection fully, students must be able to understand and evaluate the writer's message and the techniques he or she uses to convey it. The strategies on this page help readers examine a text with a critical eye.

How to Use This Page

Introduce the strategies for reading critically, presenting each as a tool for developing understanding when reading the selections in this unit.

- As students read the story "The Fun They Had" (p. 352), they will consider the author's message about mixing computers and education.
- As students read from *Exploring the* Titanic (p. 380), they will learn to identify statements made by the author and by his subjects as facts or opinions.
- As students read "The Loch Ness Monster" (p. 406), they will question the reasoning offered by the scientists and by the writer.
- As students read "Breaker's Bridge" (p. 392), they will see how events in the story cause other events to happen.

MODEL A READING STRATEGY: Evaluate the Author's Message

Demonstrate how to ask critical questions about George Laycock's "The Loch Ness Monster" (pp. 406–410) by modeling your thinking.

The author of the selection spends a lot of time talking to scientists who have explored the mystery of the Loch Ness Monster without reaching any final conclusions. The author's efforts to present the findings and explain the history of the search for the monster suggest that he thinks that solving the mystery is a good idea. Does he offer enough evidence? Clearly he is not alone in his thinking. He interviews several scientists who are intrigued by the possibility that ancient creatures live deep in Loch Ness. He also presents compelling evidence, such as photographs that possibly show parts of the creature and the results of a sophisticated study of the lake's geography. He also mentions sightings of the monster over a 50-year period. This evidence suggests that the author thinks the search is worthwhile. I am curious, too, so I agree.

The Fun They Had

Lesson Objectives

1. **To analyze and respond to literary elements**
   - Literary Analysis: Science Fiction
   - Connecting Literary Elements: Short Story
2. **To read, comprehend, analyze, and critique a short story**
   - Reading Strategy: Evaluating the Author's Message
   - Reading Check Questions
   - Review and Assess Questions
   - Assessment Practice (ATE)
3. **To develop word analysis skills, fluency, and systematic vocabulary**
   - Vocabulary Development Lesson: Word Analysis: Latin Prefix *non-*
4. **To understand and apply written and oral language conventions**
   - Spelling Strategy
   - Grammar Lesson: Simple Subjects and Predicates
5. **To understand and apply appropriate writing and research strategies**
   - Writing Lesson: Comparison of School Then and Now
   - Extension Activity: Multimedia Report
   - Extension Activity: Journal
6. **To understand and apply listening and speaking strategies**
   - Extension Activity: Speech

STEP-BY-STEP TEACHING GUIDE	PACING GUIDE
PRETEACH	
Motivate Students and Provide Background	
Use the Motivation activity (ATE p. 350)	5 min.
Read and discuss the Preview material and Background information (SE/ATE p. 350) [A]	5 min.
Introduce the Concepts	
Introduce the Literary Analysis and Reading Strategy (SE/ATE p. 351) [A]	15 min.
Pronounce the vocabulary words and read their definitions (SE p. 351)	5 min.
TEACH	
Monitor Comprehension	
Informally monitor comprehension by circulating while students read independently or in groups [A]	10–15 min.
Monitor students' comprehension with the Reading Check notes (SE/ATE pp. 353, 355)	as students read
Develop vocabulary with Vocabulary notes (SE pp. 353, 355; ATE p. 355)	as students read
Develop Understanding	
Develop students' understanding of science fiction with the Literary Analysis annotations (SE/ATE pp. 353, 354, 355) [A]	5 min.
Develop students' ability to evaluate the author's message with the Reading Strategy annotations (ATE p. 354)	5 min.
ASSESS	
Assess Mastery	
Assess students' mastery of the Reading Strategy and Literary Analysis by having them answer the Review and Assess questions (SE/ATE p. 357)	15 min.
Use one or more of the print and media Assessment Resources (ATE p. 359) [A]	up to 45 min.
EXTEND	
Apply Understanding	
Have students complete the Vocabulary Development Lesson and the Grammar Lesson (SE p. 358) [A]	20 min.
Apply students' ability to compare and contrast using the Writing Lesson (SE/ATE p. 359) [A]	30–45 min.
Apply students' understanding using one or more of the Extension Activities (SE p. 359)	20–90 min.

ACCELERATED INSTRUCTION:
Use the strategies and activities identified with an [A].

UNIVERSAL ACCESS
● = Below Level Students
▲ = On-Level Students
■ = Above Level Students

Time and Resource Manager

Reading Level: Average
Average Number of Instructional Days: 4

	RESOURCES		
	PRINT	**TRANSPARENCIES**	**TECHNOLOGY**
	• **Beyond Literature,** Career Connection: Teacher, p. 21 ▲ ■		• **Interest Grabber Videotapes,** Tape 3 ● ▲ ■
	• **Selection Support Workbook:** ● ▲ ■ Literary Analysis, p. 105 Reading Strategy, p. 104 Build Vocabulary, p. 101	• **Literary Analysis and Reading Transparencies,** pp. 41 and 42 ● ▲ ■	
	• **Adapted Reader's Companion** ● • **Reader's Companion** ●		• **Listening to Literature** ● ▲ ■ Audiocassettes, Side 13 Audio CDs, CD 6
	• **English Learner's Companion** ● ▲ • **Literatura en español** ● ▲ • **Literary Analysis for Enrichment** ■		
	• **Formal Assessment:** Selection Test, pp. 93–95 ● ▲ ■ • **Open Book Test,** pp. 61–63 ● ▲ ■ • **Performance Assessment and Portfolio Management,** pp. 29, 89 ● ▲ ■ • Prentice Hall Assessment System ● ▲ ■	• Prentice Hall Assessment System ● ▲ ■ Skills Practice Answers and Explanations on Transparencies	• **Test Bank Software** ● ▲ ■ • **Got It! Assessment Videotapes,** Tape 3 ● ▲
	• **Selection Support Workbook:** ● ▲ ■ Build Spelling Skills, p. 102 Build Grammar Skills, p. 103 • **Writing and Grammar,** Copper Level ● ▲ ■ • **Extension Activities,** p. 21 ● ▲ ■	• **Daily Language Practice Transparencies** ● ▲ • **Writing Models and Graphic Organizers on Transparencies** ● ▲ ■	• **Writing and Grammar iText CD-ROM** ● ▲ ■ *Take It to the Net* www.phschool.com

BLOCK SCHEDULING: Use one 90-minute class period to preteach the selection and have students read it. Use a second 90-minute class period to assess students' mastery of skills and have them complete one of the Extension Activities.

PRETEACH

Step-by-Step Teaching Guide for pp. 350–351

Motivation

Ask students to discuss what they think school might be like two centuries from now. What will teachers be like? How will electronic equipment be used? Then, read aloud the following passage:

> Margie went into her schoolroom. It was right next to her bedroom, and the mechanical teacher was on and waiting for her.

Tell students that this story is set more than one hundred years in the future and is one author's vision of schools in the future.

Interest Grabber Video

As an alternative, play "Education: Past, Present, and Future" on Tape 3 to engage student interest.

❶ Background

Technology

In this story, computers have replaced teachers and schools. Although many people think that mechanical computing devices are recent inventions, they have been in use for many years. The earliest computers were simple calculating devices. The first to be invented was an adding machine devised in the mid-1600s by mathematician Blaise Pascal. He designed the machine to help his father who collected taxes. A few decades later, Gottfried Wilhelm von Leibnitz invented a machine that could also multiply. The first commercially produced adding machine would not appear until two hundred years later.

Prepare to Read

❶ The Fun They Had

 ***Take It to the Net***

Visit www.phschool.com for interactive activities and instruction related to "The Fun They Had," including

- background
- graphic organizers
- literary elements
- reading strategies

Preview

Connecting to the Literature

In "The Fun They Had," by Isaac Asimov, two schoolchildren in the year 2155 find a relic of the past. Think about objects you associate with the past—such as record albums, which have been replaced by CDs. Read the story to find out what surprising item these children think of as outdated—in fact, antique!

Background

Isaac Asimov published "The Fun They Had" in 1957. At that time, the technology that led to the invention of computers was "science fiction." Personal computers were introduced in 1975, but it was not until 1992 that the World Wide Web was available to everyone. As you read "The Fun They Had," keep in mind that it was written long before computers were used in schools.

TEACHING RESOURCES

The following resources can be used to enrich or extend the instruction for pp. 350–351.

Motivation

Interest Grabber Video, Tape 3

Background

Beyond Literature, p. 21 ■

Take It to the Net

Visit www.phschool.com for Background and hotlinks for "The Fun They Had."

Literary Analysis

Literary Analysis and Reading Transparencies, Science Fiction, p. 42

Reading

Selection Support: Reading Strategy, p. 104; Build Vocabulary, p. 101

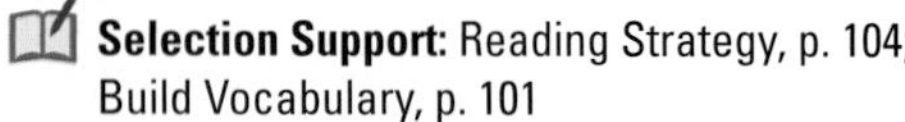

Literary Analysis and Reading Transparencies, Evaluating the Author's Message, p. 41 ■

■ **BLOCK SCHEDULING:** Resources marked with this symbol provide varied instruction during 90-minute blocks.

❷ Literary Analysis

Science Fiction

Science fiction is writing that tells about imaginary events that involve science or technology. Often, science fiction is set in the future. In "The Fun They Had," Asimov takes an idea from the present—teaching—and imagines what it will be like in the future. In this excerpt, he describes a mechanical teacher of the future:

> . . . large and ugly, with a big screen on which all the lessons were shown and the questions were asked.

As you read, notice the elements of science fiction in this story by looking for answers to the following focus questions:

1. What elements of science does Asimov incorporate in his story?
2. What details did Asimov create from his imagination?

Connecting Literary Elements

Like other short stories, science fiction stories have the following elements:

- **plot**: a series of related events that tell a story
- **characters**: the "actors" in a story
- **setting**: the time and place of the story
- **theme**: the message or insight about life that the work conveys

Identify these elements in "The Fun They Had."

❸ Reading Strategy

Evaluating the Author's Message

When you **evaluate the author's message,** you make a judgment. You decide whether the author's points are logical. As you read "The Fun They Had," consider what point Asimov is making. That point is his message. Then, evaluate whether his message makes sense and whether you agree or disagree. The graphic organizer at right shows some points you might consider as you evaluate Asimov's message in "The Fun They Had."

Author's Message:
Learning in a group from real people is better than learning from computers.
I like discussing ideas with classmates.
With computers, kids learn at their own pace.
Computers can't explain everything.
Points to Consider

Vocabulary Development

calculated (kal′ kyo͞o lāt′ id) *v.* determined by using math (p. 353)

loftily (lôf′ tə lē) *adv.* in a superior way (p. 355)

dispute (di spyo͞ot′) *v.* argue; debate (p. 355)

nonchalantly (nän′ shə lant′ lē) *adv.* without concern or interest (p. 355)

CUSTOMIZE INSTRUCTION FOR UNIVERSAL ACCESS

For Special Needs Students	For Less Proficient Readers	For English Learners
Have students read the adapted version of "The Fun They Had" in the **Adapted Reader's Companion.** This version provides basic-level instruction in an interactive format with questions and write-on lines. Completing the adapted version will prepare students to read the selection in the Student Edition.	Have students read "The Fun They Had" in the **Reader's Companion.** This version provides basic-level instruction in an interactive format with questions and write-on lines. After students finish the selection in the Reader's Companion, have them complete the questions and activities in the Student Edition.	Have students read the adapted version of "The Fun They Had" in the **English Learner's Companion.** This version provides basic-level instruction in an interactive format with questions and write-on lines. Completing the adapted version will prepare students to read the selection in the Student Edition.

❷ Literary Analysis

Science Fiction

- Ask students to name some of their favorite science fiction stories, books, movies, or television shows. Briefly, talk about what their examples all have in common.
- Then, read aloud the instruction and explain that students will read a science-fiction story about schools of the future.
- Point out that science fiction stories contain the same elements as other stories and that these elements are discussed in the Connecting Literary Elements instruction.
- Finally, offer students the Science Fiction transparency on p. 42 in **Literary Analysis and Reading Transparencies.** Students may use the organizer on the transparency to identify the story elements of "The Fun They Had."

❸ Reading Strategy

Evaluating the Author's Message

- After students read the instruction on p. 351, tell them how to identify an author's message. Remind students that the author's message may be implied rather than stated directly.
- Make sure students understand that the points the author makes are directly related to their overall message.
- Explain that an author's message can be found in the details of the story, such as the actions and dialogue of the characters, and images or ideas that are repeated several times.
- The Evaluating the Author's Message transparency on p. 41 of **Literary Analysis and Reading Transparencies** will help students identify the message.

Vocabulary Development

- Pronounce each vocabulary word for students, and read the definitions as a class. Have students identify any words with which they are already familiar.

E-Teach

Visit E-Teach at www.phschool.com for teachers' essays on how to teach, with questions and answers.

TEACH

Step-by-Step Teaching Guide for pp. 352–356

CUSTOMIZE INSTRUCTION
For Intrapersonal Learners

Invite students to write a journal entry in which they write about their ideal school experience. Students should be sure to cover the subjects they would learn, the classroom in which they would learn them, and the teacher they would have. Ask volunteers to share their visions with the class.

1 About the Selection

The year is 2155, and Tommy finds a relic of the past in his attic—a real book printed on paper—which he shows to Margie. Both Tommy and Margie are intrigued by reading a book in which the words stand still instead of moving across a television screen. Margie is even more surprised to learn that the book is about a school long ago where children were taught by humans rather than machines, and in schools rather than at home. As the children explore the past in the book, Margie thinks about all the fun that kids must have had in the old days.

TEACHING RESOURCES

The following resources can be used to enrich or extend the instruction for pp. 352–356.

Literary Analysis

- **Selection Support:** Literary Analysis, p. 105
- **Literary Analysis for Enrichment**
- **Writing Models and Graphic Organizers on Transparencies,** p. 93

Reading

- **Reader's Companion**
- **Adapted Reader's Companion**
- **English Learner's Companion**
- **Literatura en español**
- **Listening to Literature Audiocassettes,** Side 13 ■
- **Listening to Literature Audio CDs,** CD 6 ■

■ **BLOCK SCHEDULING:** Resources marked with this symbol provide varied instruction during 90-minute blocks.

2 Margie even wrote about it that night in her diary. On the page headed May 17, 2155, she wrote, "Today Tommy found a real book."

It was a very old book. Margie's grandfather once said that when he was a little boy, *his* grandfather told him that there was a time when all stories were printed on paper.

They turned the pages, which were yellow and crinkly, and it was awfully funny to read words that stood still instead of moving the way they were supposed to—on a screen, you know. And then, when they turned back to the page before, it had the same words on it that it had had when they read it the first time.

"Gee," said Tommy, "what a waste. When you're through with the book, you just throw it away, I guess. Our television screen must have had a million books on it and it's good for plenty more. I wouldn't throw *it* away."

"Same with mine," said Margie. She was eleven and hadn't seen as many telebooks as Tommy had. He was thirteen.

She said, "Where did you find it?"

"In my house." He pointed without looking, because he was busy reading. "In the attic."

"What's it about?"

"School."

Margie was scornful. "School? What's there to write about school? I hate school." Margie always hated school, but now she hated it more than ever. The mechanical teacher had been giving her test after test in geography, and she had been doing worse and worse until her mother had shaken her head sorrowfully and sent for the county inspector.

He was a round little man with a red face and a whole box of tools with dials and wires. He smiled at her and gave her an apple, then took the teacher apart. Margie had hoped he wouldn't know how to put it together again, but he knew how all right, and after an hour or so, there it was again, large and ugly, with a big screen
3 on which all the lessons were shown and the questions were asked. That wasn't so bad. The part she hated most was the slot where she had to put homework and test papers. She always had to write them out in a punch code they made her learn when she was six years old, and the mechanical teacher calculated the mark 4
in no time.

Literary Analysis
Science Fiction This story was written in the mid-twentieth century. What detail at the opening suggests that it is science fiction?

calculated (kal´ kyo͞o lāt´ id) *v.* determined by using math

4 **Reading Check**
What does Tommy find?

5 ◀ **Critical Viewing** In what ways does this picture combine imagination and technology? **[Analyze]**

2 Literary Analysis

Science Fiction

- Ask students the Literary Analysis question on this page.
  Answer: The date of the diary entry suggests that this story is science fiction.
- Ask students whether they think Margie is used to seeing printed books. why or why not?
  Answer: Students will say that Margie is not used to seeing printed books because she writes in her diary about finding a "real" book. She also mentions that "real" books used to be printed on paper, suggesting that the books Margie knows are not printed.
- Point out that Margie's diary is probably not a book with pages and that she probably types her entries.

3 Literary Analysis

Science Fiction

- Ask students to explain what is happening in this passage.
  Answer: The county inspector is taking apart the computer teacher.
- Then, ask students to explain what is odd about technology in this passage.
  Answer: The mechanical teacher, which is a computer, handles all of Margie's homework, as a real teacher would.

4 Reading Check

Answer: Tommy finds an old book with paper pages in the attic of his house.

5 ▶ Critical Viewing

Possible response: The computers represent technology and look realistic, but they are arranged imaginatively, as if they were floating in space, each one inside the previous one, and surrounded by brightly colored objects.

CUSTOMIZE INSTRUCTION FOR UNIVERSAL ACCESS

For Special Needs Students	For English Learners
Explain to students that instead of focusing on what happens in the story, they should try focusing on what characters say and think. Give students a copy of an Open Mind diagram, like the one on p. 93 of **Writing Models and Graphic Organizers on Transparencies.** Have students label it either *Margie* or *Tommy.* As students read, have them write down the character's key thoughts throughout the story. After the story, discuss students' overall impressions of the two characters.	Students unfamiliar with the difference between past tense and past-perfect tense may be confused when the scene shifts from reading the book with Tommy to the appearance of the county inspector. Help students follow the narrative by telling them that the story takes place while Tommy and Margie are reading the book together. Encourage students to fill out a timeline with the events in the order that they happen in the story.

6 Literary Analysis

Science Fiction

- Have students make a list of the details in this paragraph.
  Answer: **Details:** the inspector fixes the teacher, the inspector tells Margie's mother that it wasn't Margie's fault that the teacher broke; the inspector changes the teaching level for geography inside the teacher.
- Then, ask them the Literary Analysis question on p. 354: How do these details indicate that the setting of the story is the future?
  Answer: The details of the mechanical teacher and the way in which the inspector adjusts the gears on the "geography sector" of the machine point to the story's setting in the future.

7 Reading Strategy

Evaluating the Author's Message

- Remind students that one way an author gets his or her message across is to show it through the thoughts and words of a character.
- Then, ask students to describe Margie's attitude toward the mechanical teacher.
  Answer: Margie hates her mechanical teacher and wishes the inspector would take it away.
- Then, challenge students to consider whether the author agrees or disagrees with Margie.
  Possible response: Students may think that the author agrees with her because he does not make the mechanical teacher sound very interesting.
- Ask students to keep track of the author's message throughout the story.

8 ▶Critical Viewing

Answer: Students may respond that the school of the past might be fun because it is different from their school, and they might like dressing up to go to school. Others may say that they would not like it because the teacher looks stern, or that the classroom does not appear to have any computers.

6 The inspector had smiled after he was finished and patted her head. He said to her mother, "It's not the little girl's fault, Mrs. Jones. I think the geography sector was geared a little too quick. Those things happen sometimes. I've slowed it up to an average ten-year level. Actually, the overall pattern of her progress is quite satisfactory." And he patted Margie's head again.

7 Margie was disappointed. She had been hoping they would take the teacher away altogether. They had once taken Tommy's

Literary Analysis
Science Fiction and Setting How do these details indicate that the setting of the story is the future?

8 ▼ **Critical Viewing** Do you think it would be fun to go to a school of the past, such as the one shown in the picture? **[Make a Judgment]**

CUSTOMIZE INSTRUCTION FOR UNIVERSAL ACCESS

For English Learners

Students who are from different cultures may understand very well Margie's disbelief and confusion about how school can be different. Ask students to meet in pairs or in small groups to talk about schools in their native countries. Students in the groups should use a Venn diagram, like the one on p. 89 of **Writing Models and Graphic Organizers on Transparencies,** to show the differences and similarities between their school now and other schooling they have had.

For Gifted/Talented Students

Have students consult the science or technology sections of newspapers and magazines to find examples of recent scientific advances or discoveries. Then, have them create a story set 200 years in the future, based on the possibilities raised by new scientific development. Suggest that students develop their stories by using if/then statements, such as "If life were discovered on Mars, then . . ."

teacher away for nearly a month because the history sector had blanked out completely.

So she said to Tommy, "Why would anyone write about school?"

Tommy looked at her with very superior eyes. "Because it's not our kind of school, stupid. This is the old kind of school that they had hundreds and hundreds of year ago." He added loftily, pronouncing the word carefully, "*Centuries* ago."

loftily (lof´ tə lē) *adv.* in a superior way

9 Margie was hurt. "Well, I don't know what kind of school they had all that time ago." She read the book over his shoulder for a while, then said, "Anyway, they had a teacher."

"Sure they had a teacher, but it wasn't a *regular* teacher. It was a man."

Literary Analysis
Science Fiction How can you tell that the school of the future is different from yours?

"A man? How could a man be a teacher?"

"Well, he just told the boys and girls things and gave them homework and asked them questions."

"A man isn't smart enough."

"Sure he is. My father knows as much as my teacher."

"He can't. A man can't know as much as a teacher."

"He knows almost as much I betcha."

Margie wasn't prepared to dispute that. She said, "I wouldn't want a strange man in my house to teach me."

dispute (di spyo͞ot´) *v.* argue; debate

Tommy screamed with laughter. "You don't know much, Margie. The teachers didn't live in the house. They had a special building and all the kids went there."

"And all the kids learned the same thing?"

"Sure, if they were the same age."

"But my mother says a teacher has to be adjusted to fit the mind of each boy and girl it teaches and that each kid has to be taught differently."

"Just the same, they didn't do it that way then. If you don't like it, you don't have to read the book."

"I didn't say I didn't like it," Margie said quickly. She wanted to read about those funny schools.

They weren't even half finished when Margie's mother called, "Margie! School!"

Margie looked up. "Not yet, Mamma."

"Now," said Mrs. Jones. "And it's probably time for Tommy, too."

Margie said to Tommy, "Can I read the book some more with you after school?"

10 "Maybe," he said, nonchalantly. He walked away whistling, the dusty old book tucked beneath his arm.

nonchalantly (nän´ shə lant´ lē) *adv.* without concern or interest

Margie went into the schoolroom. It was right next to her bedroom, and the mechanical teacher was on and waiting for her. It was always on at the same time every day except Saturday and

11 **Reading Check**

What do Tommy and Margot learn from the book?

9 Literary Analysis

Science Fiction

- Ask students the Literary Analysis question on p. 355.
  Answer: Students should understand that Margie's idea of a regular teacher is a machine. Students' experience of a regular teacher is a human being.

▶ **Monitor Progress** Point out that the author set the word *regular* in italic type in order to draw attention to it. Ask students what importance the emphasis on *regular* has in the story.
Answer: The emphasis on the word *regular* shows that having a mechanical teacher is the only kind of teacher they know.

▶ **Reteach** If students have trouble with the concept of science fiction, ask them a few focusing questions like the ones below. Then, have students return to the selection in order to answer the questions.

- Do computers or other examples of technology appear in the story?
- Is there a conflict in the story between the use of technology and traditional ways of doing things?
- Does the writer suggest that technology is good or bad?

Point out that if the first two questions can be answered "yes," then the story is a science-fiction story.

10 Vocabulary Development

Latin Prefix *non-*

- Call students' attention to the word *nonchalantly*. Tell students that the root of the word is *calere*, which is Latin for "warmth." The prefix *non-*, meaning "not" or "no," changes the word from implying warmth to implying coolness.
- Then, ask students to think of words they use regularly that begin with the prefix *non-*.

11 Reading Check

Answer: They learn that schooling was very different—people were teachers, and students went to a building together to learn from books that were made of paper.

CUSTOMIZE INSTRUCTION FOR UNIVERSAL ACCESS

For Special Needs Students	For Less Proficient Readers
Students may have trouble identifying and evaluating the author's message. Remind them that the author's message is often the same as the main idea. Offer students the Main Idea and Supporting Details organizer on p. 73 of **Writing Models and Graphic Organizers on Transparencies.** Allow students to work in pairs to complete the organizer and identify the main idea. Tell students that one possible main idea is "Learning with a group of people is better than learning alone from a computer."	Students may feel intimidated or tempted to use harsh criticism when evaluating a writer's message. Help them achieve a balanced approach by drawing a scale on the board. Draw a horizontal line with three hatchmarks, one at each end and one in the middle. Label the ends "I hated It" and "I loved it." Label the middle "This did/did not work for me." Ask for students' reactions to a story they have already read. Guide students toward making remarks in the middle range.

ASSESS

Answers for p. 356

Review and Assess

1. Possible responses: Some may enjoy learning at their own pace; others may prefer the social aspect of present-day school.
2. **(a)** Margie writes that Tommy found a paper book. **(b)** Margie is amazed. **(c)** She has never seen a paper book before.
3. **(a)** Margie writes homework in a punch code and puts it into the computer. **(b)** Now homework is written by hand or by computer and given to a teacher to grade. **(c)** Some may agree; others may say that the teacher's input is important.
4. **(a)** Tommy and Margie are the main characters. **(b)** The author wanted the story to show what school in the future might be like. **(c)** Some may believe that such inventions could happen because technology is more advanced now.
5. **(a)** School involves sitting in front of a television screen. **(b)** Margie thinks that school was fun because students spent time with one another. **(c)** Possible response: Both schools use computers and give homework. Margie's is different because there is not a classroom with other students.
6. **(a)** Possible response: Students will receive schooling by computer. Students will learn at their own pace. **(b)** Possible response: Computers may transmit facts, but human teachers inspire and help.

Sunday, because her mother said little girls learned better if they learned at regular hours.

The screen was lit up, and it said: "Today's arithmetic lesson is on the addition of proper fractions. Please insert yesterday's homework in the proper slot."

Margie did so with a sigh. She was thinking about the old schools they had when her grandfather's grandfather was a little boy. All the kids from the whole neighborhood came, laughing and shouting in the schoolyard, sitting together in the schoolroom, going home together at the end of the day. They learned the same things so they could help one another on the homework and talk about it.

And the teachers were people. . . .

The mechanical teacher was flashing on the screen: "When we add the fractions 1/2 and 1/4 . . ."

Margie was thinking about how the kids must have loved it in the old days. She was thinking about the fun they had.

Review and Assess

Thinking About the Selection

1. **Respond:** Would you like to go to school the way Margie and Tommy do? Why or why not?
2. (a) **Recall:** What does Margie write in her diary about the book? (b) **Infer:** What does she think of the book? (c) **Draw Conclusions:** Why does she have such a strong reaction to the book?
3. (a) **Recall:** How does Margie hand in her homework? (b) **Compare and Contrast:** How is this activity different in 2155 than it is now? (c) **Speculate:** Do you think homework could be corrected mechanically in the future? Why or why not?
4. (a) **Recall:** Who are the main characters in this story? (b) **Infer:** Why do you think the author shows his ideas about the future through these characters? (c) **Assess:** Is the author successful in convincing you that his inventions of the future could really happen? Why or why not?
5. (a) **Recall:** Describe what school is like for the main characters. (b) **Draw Conclusions:** Why does Margie think that school in the past was fun? (c) **Compare and Contrast:** How is Margie's school the same as and different from your school?
6. (a) **Apply:** Describe the school of the future using science or technology. Give two examples of what the day will be like and what students will do. (b) **Make a Judgment:** Are human teachers or computerized teachers more effective? Why?

Isaac Asimov

(1920–1992)

Check any section of the library and you will probably find a book by Isaac Asimov. He wrote fiction, medical books, humor, autobiography, essays, a guide to Shakespeare, and science books. Although he was an expert in many subjects, his main interest was science. Asimov taught biochemistry at Boston University for thirteen years before becoming a full-time writer. He is best known for his science-fiction work, a kind of writing his father regarded as "trash" and would not—until convinced—allow the young Isaac to read as a child.

ASSESSMENT PRACTICE: Reading Comprehension

Draw Inferences **(For more practice, see Test Preparation Workbook, p. 32.)**

Tell students to combine information from the text with their own knowledge and experience to draw inferences. Use the following passage.

> Margie did so with a sigh. She was thinking about the old schools they had when her grandfather's grandfather was a little boy. . . .
>
> Margie was thinking about how the kids must have loved it in the old days. She was thinking about the fun they had.

Which of the following best describes Margie's feelings about schools of the past?

A She would rather go to an old school.
B She thinks the old schools were boring.
C She would rather go to her new school.
D She wishes she were older.

B, C, and *D* are not supported by the passage. Margie is thinking longingly of schools of the past, so *A* is correct.

Review and Assess

Literary Analysis

Science Fiction

1. What are two uses of technology that Asimov imagines for the future?
2. How does technology change education by the year 2155?
3. Asimov creates **science fiction** with his imagination and technology. In the diagram shown, list details or events from the story to show how Asimov used his imagination and technology to create science fiction.

Imagination
1. ___________
2. ___________
3. ___________

Technology
1. ___________
2. ___________
3. ___________

Science Fiction

Connecting Literary Elements

4. What elements do science fiction stories share with other short stories?
5. Retell the plot of "The Fun They Had."
6. On an organizer like the one shown, write details from the story that indicate the time and the place.

Time	Place

Reading Strategy

Evaluating the Author's Message

7. What does Asimov appear to say is the main difference between the schools of the past and the schools of 2155?
8. Which methods of education does Asimov prefer: those of 2155 or those of the past? Which story details help you draw this conclusion?
9. Explain Asimov's **message.** Do you agree with him? Explain why or why not.

Extending Understanding

10. **Career Connection:** How do teachers today use computers in the classroom?

Quick Review

Science fiction is writing that tells about imaginary events that involve science or technology. It is often set in the future. To review science fiction, see page 351.

The elements of a **short story** are plot, characters, setting, and theme. To review these elements, see page 351.

The **author's message** is the point or lesson of the work.

Take It to the Net
www.phschool.com
Take the interactive self-test online to check your understanding of the selection.

ENRICHMENT: Further Reading

Other Works by Isaac Asimov

Foundation

I, Robot

Fantastic Voyage

Take It to the Net
Visit www.phschool.com for more information on Isaac Asimov.

Answers for p. 357

Review and Assess

1. Computers will teach children and correct homework.
2. Technology has made schools unnecessary; students learn with a mechanical teacher.
3. Imagination: mechanical teachers, county inspectors, scarcity of paper and books; schools unnecessary.

   Technology: punch cards, slots, computer grading, TV screens with lessons.
4. Science fiction shares the elements of plot, characters, setting, and theme.
5. Margie is amazed by an old book. As she and Tommy read, Margie remembers how her mechanical teacher had to be taken apart. They discuss differences between old-fashioned school and school in 2155. At the end, Margie sits in front of her mechanical teacher, daydreaming about the fun kids had.
6.

Time	Place
diary entry: May 17, 2155; books are described as rare; schools with books and human teachers are described as having existed centuries ago; homework is assigned and graded by a machine.	Tommy points to his house; Mrs. Jones calls Margie inside for school; Margie's schoolroom is right next to her bedroom.

7. Students miss human contact by having machines as teachers and no classmates.
8. He prefers the past. Mechanical teachers sound boring; Margie hates her teacher.
9. Mechanical teachers are not better than human ones. Possible responses: Some may prefer contact with others. Some prefer to learn on their own.
10. Computers help to drill students with skills, do research, and write.

EXTEND

Answers for p. 358

1 Vocabulary Development

Word Analysis

1. not violent
2. does not make sense
3. not toxic, or not poisonous
4. does not stop

Spelling Strategy

1. pistachio
2. machine
3. chef
4. chauffeur

Fluency: Definitions

1. d
2. a
3. b
4. c

1. nonchalantly
2. calculated
3. loftily
4. dispute

2 Grammar

1. It (S), was a very old book (P); It; was
2. They (S); turned the pages of the book (P); They; turned
3. Tommy (S); had been looking in the attic (P); Tommy; had been looking
4. The inspector (S); had smiled at Margie (P); inspector; had smiled
5. All the children (S); learned the same thing (P); the children; learned

Writing Application

Make sure that students have accurately identified the subject and predicate in each sentence.

Integrate Language Skills

1 Vocabulary Development Lesson

Word Analysis: Latin Prefix *non-*

You can add the Latin prefix *non-* to many words in English to form words that mean "not" or "without." For example, *nonbreakable* means "not breakable," and the story word *nonchalant* means "without concern or interest." On your paper, write a meaning for each word.

1. nonviolent
2. nonsense
3. nontoxic
4. nonstop

Spelling Strategy

The *sh* sound has many different spellings. In some words the *sh* sound is spelled *ch*, as in *nonchalant*, a story word. For each definition, write a word on your paper that contains the *sh* sound spelled with a *ch*.

1. a type of nut: pi _ _ _ _ _ io
2. equipment that does work: m _ _ _ ine
3. a head cook: _ _ _ _
4. a driver: _ _ au _ _ eu _

Fluency: Definitions

On your paper, write the word in the first column that matches the meaning of each word in the second column.

1. calculated	a. proudly
2. loftily	b. argue
3. dispute	c. casually
4. nonchalantly	d. figured out

Use each word in one of the following sentences.

1. Tommy wanted to appear casual, so he spoke ___?___.
2. As she added up one row of numbers, he ___?___ the other.
3. Feeling superior, he spoke ___?___.
4. There was no argument at recess, but a ___?___ occurred after school.

2 Grammar Lesson

Simple Subjects and Predicates

A **simple subject** is the person, place, or thing about which a sentence is written. A **simple predicate** is the verb or verb phrase that tells the action or states the condition of the subject. Look at the examples below. The complete subject is underlined once and the complete predicate twice. The simple subject is highlighted in blue. The simple predicate is highlighted in green.

Margie even wrote about it in her diary.

The mechanical teacher had been giving her tests in geography.

▶ *For more practice, see page R28, Exercise A.*

Practice Copy these sentences. Underline the complete subject once and label it *S*. Underline the complete predicate twice and label it *P*. Circle the simple subject and the simple predicate.

1. It was a very old book.
2. They turned the pages of the book.
3. Tommy had been looking in the attic.
4. The inspector had smiled at Margie.
5. All the children learned the same thing.

Writing Application On your paper, write four or five sentences about your school day. Draw one line under the simple subject and two lines under the simple predicate in each sentence.

WG Prentice Hall Writing and Grammar Connection: Chapter 19, Section 1

TEACHING RESOURCES

The following resources can be used to enrich or extend the instruction for pp. 358–359.

Vocabulary

- **Selection Support:** Build Vocabulary, p. 101; Build Spelling Skills, p. 102
- **Vocabulary and Spelling Practice Book** (Use this booklet for skills enrichment) ■

Grammar

- **Selection Support:** Build Grammar Skills, p. 103
- **Writing and Grammar,** Copper Level, p. 380

- **Daily Language Practice Transparencies**

Writing

- **Writing and Grammar,** Copper Level, p. 154 ■
- **Writing Models and Graphic Organizers on Transparencies,** p. 89
- **Writing and Grammar iText CD-ROM**

■ **BLOCK SCHEDULING:** Resources marked with this symbol provide varied instruction during 90-minute blocks.

❸ Writing Lesson

Comparison of School Then and Now

Learn more about school in the 1950s, when "The Fun They Had" was written. Write a comparison-and-contrast essay that shows how school then is similar to and different from school now.

Prewriting Write a list of categories that relate to school, such as subjects taught, books used, rules, equipment in the classroom, teachers, homework, and sports. Review "The Fun They Had" to gather preliminary details in each category. Gather further information by asking older adults in your family and by using library resources.

Drafting Organize details into paragraphs based on your categories. For each category, give the details of then and the details of now.

Revising On a draft of your essay, highlight all the details of "Then" with one color and all the details of "Now" with another. If you have far more of one color than the other, revise to add details for a better balance.

Model: Revising for Balance

Most students wrote with a fountain pen. They wrote their homework on paper. ^*Now many students do homework on a computer.* Most students today have never even seen a fountain pen.

This paragraph should be revised for balance. Add a detail about "Now" to create balance.

WG Prentice Hall Writing and Grammar Connection: Chapter 8, Section 2

❹ Extension Activities

Listening and Speaking Give a **speech** presenting the advantages and disadvantages of technological advances.

1. Divide a paper into two columns, labeled *Advantages* and *Disadvantages*. List examples in each column.
2. Prepare a graph or chart to illustrate the growth of technology.
3. Give your speech.

Research and Technology In a group, prepare a **multimedia report** that shows some of the major technological advances made during the past fifty years.

Writing The story opens with one sentence from Margie's journal. As Margie, write the rest of the journal entry. Include details from the story about events and your reaction, as Margie, to these events.

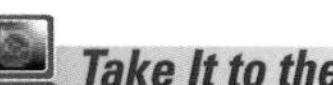

Take It to the Net www.phschool.com

Go online for an additional research activity using the Internet.

ASSESSMENT RESOURCES

The following resources can be used to assess students' knowledge and skills.

Selection Assessment

- **Formal Assessment,** pp. 93–95
- **Open Book Test,** pp. 61–63
- **Got It! Assessment Videotapes,** Tape 3
- **Test Bank Software**

Take It to the Net

Visit www.phschool.com for self-tests and additional questions on "The Fun They Had."

Writing Rubric

- **Performance Assess. and Portfolio Mgmt.,** p. 16

Listening and Speaking Rubric

- **Performance Assess. and Portfolio Mgmt.,** p. 29

PRENTICE HALL ASSESSMENT SYSTEM

- **Workbook**
- **Transparencies**
- **Skill Book**
- **CD-ROM**

Lesson Support for p. 359

❸ Writing Lesson

- After students read the instruction on p. 359 and before they begin to work, explain the two ways to organize a comparison-and-contrast essay: (1) to alternate paragraphs, with each focused on details about one of the two objects of comparison, (2) or to devote each paragraph to one of the details.
- Ask students to use the Venn diagram on p. 89 of **Writing Models and Graphic Organizers on Transparencies** in their brainstorming process.
- Encourage students to exchange their drafts with partners to revise and proofread.
- Finally, use the Exposition rubric on p. 16 of **Performance Assessment and Portfolio Management** to evaluate students' papers.

❹ Listening and Speaking

- Remind students that a presentation that incorporates visual aids can be tricky because it involves moving materials around while talking and maintaining eye contact with the audience.
- As students prepare, tell them to vary what they say from what the visual aids say. This technique helps listeners retain information.
- Encourage students to practice their presentations in front of a mirror or with others.
- Finally, have students use the Speaking rubric on p. 29 in **Performance Assessment and Portfolio Management.**

CUSTOMIZE INSTRUCTION For Universal Access

To address different learning styles, use the activities suggested in the **Extension Activities** booklet, p. 21.

- For Logical/Mathematical Learners, use Activity 5.
- For Interpersonal and Verbal/Linguistic Learners, use Activity 6.
- For Bodily/Kinesthetic and Interpersonal Learners, use Activity 7.

Lesson Objectives

1. To understand the thematic connection between a work of historical fiction and a science fiction story
2. To understand that works in different genres can explore similar themes

Connections

In the excerpt from *Esperanza Rising,* the main character wishes she could return to the life she lived in Mexico before her family moved to the United States. Before the move, she lived the life of a wealthy rancher's daughter; now she must learn to do household chores. Her longing for a happier time is similar to that of the children in Isaac Asimov's story "The Fun They Had." Have students reread "The Fun They Had" (p. 352) after they read the excerpt here. What similarities and differences between the two stories do students notice?

CONNECTIONS

Science Fiction and Historical Fiction

Fact and Fantasy

Esperanza Rising is a novel about the past. "The Fun They Had" is a story about the future. What these two fictional works have in common is that the time of the setting and the circumstances of the characters make them completely unfamiliar with objects and a lifestyle that seems ordinary to most readers. In "The Fun They Had," the characters are unfamiliar with books. In *Esperanza Rising,* the character is unfamiliar with a broom.

Different but the same. When you read about characters in the past or in the future, you might think that their feelings and reactions would be very different from yours. In fact, if a writer does his or her job correctly, you can understand the feelings of story characters even if they are living on Mars! Although people and characters come from different backgrounds, cultures, and time periods, most people share a desire to feel as if they belong, as if they are part of a group. These common feelings make it possible for readers to relate to fictional characters who live in different times or places.

Find out more. When you read historical fiction, you might want to do a little background research to get an even greater understanding of a character's circumstances. For example, the political circumstances in Mexico during the early 1900s and the Great Depression in the United States have an impact on the way characters act and think in *Esperanza Rising.* Because of the upheaval caused by both sets of circumstances, it is believable that a character could go from riches to rags, as Esperanza does. This sudden change in her fortune provides a logical explanation for why she is unable to sweep. As you read, look for other details of Esperanza's circumstances that make it possible for you to understand and believe her feelings, actions, and reactions.

Esperanza Rising
BY THE AUTHOR OF RIDING FREEDOM
PAM MUÑOZ RYAN

from Esperanza Rising

Pam Muñoz Ryan

Esperanza is the thirteen-year-old daughter of a wealthy Mexican rancher. When she emigrates to the United States, she is no longer a rich aristocrat, but a laborer in the fields. Esperanza struggles to learn how to work to be a support to her mother.

Isabel sat with the babies while Esperanza went to sweep the platform. The camp was quiet and even though it was late in the day, the sun was unrelenting. She retrieved the broom and stepped onto the wooden floor. Dried and brittle onion skins were everywhere.

In her entire life, Esperanza [es´pə rän´zə] had never held a broom in her hand. But she had seen Hortensia [hôr´ten sē ə] sweep and she tried to visualize the memory. It couldn't possibly be that hard. She put both hands near the middle of the broomstick and moved it back and forth. It swung wildly. The motion seemed awkward and the fine dirt on the wooden planks lifted into a cloud. Onion jackets[1] flew into the air instead of gathering together in a neat pile like Hortensia's. Esperanza's elbows did not know what to do. Neither did her arms. She felt streams of perspiration sliding down her neck. She stopped for a moment and stared at the broom, as if willing it to behave. Determined, she tried again. She hadn't noticed that several trucks were already unloading workers nearby. Then she heard it. First a small tittering and then louder. She turned around. A group of women were laughing at her. And in the middle of the group was Marta, pointing.

¡*La Cenicienta!* Cinderella!" she laughed.

Burning with humiliation,[2] Esperanza dropped the broom and ran back to the cabin.

In her room, she sat on the edge of the cot. Her face flushed again at the thought of the ridicule. She was still sitting there, staring at the wall, when Isabel found her.

Thematic Connection
To what extent is Esperanza's inability to sweep realistic? What details of the situation make her character believable?

1. **onion jackets** the outer skins of the onion
2. **humiliation** (hyo͞o mil´ē ā shən) a feeling of hurt, or loss of pride or dignity

Background

Social Studies

The story of the main character in *Esperanza Rising* is based on the life of the author's grandmother. Like the character Esperanza, Ryan's grandmother, who was also named Esperanza, had been the daughter of a wealthy rancher and, after his death, had moved with her mother to the United States to find work. Finding work was not easy, as the two women had moved to California during the Great Depression, a time when people from many areas of the United States were also heading west to find jobs picking fruits and vegetables. Because there was so much competition for work, Esperanza, her family, and other immigrants often were treated badly and were refused work because they were not citizens of the United States. When Ryan was a little girl, her grandmother told her many stories about those desperate times in California. Ryan was nearly grown before her grandmother talked about the happier years in Mexico. Ryan's novel brings both elements of her grandmother's life together.

CUSTOMIZE INSTRUCTION FOR UNIVERSAL ACCESS

For Special Needs Students	For English Learners
Students may have trouble understanding what is happening in the excerpt from *Esperanza Rising*. Help students by previewing the excerpt. First, review the information on p. 360 and the introductory paragraph on p. 361. Then, go through the excerpt and identify the characters that are mentioned. Explain that the main character is Esperanza. The others are only important in that they can teach her something. Tell students to focus on Esperanza as they read the excerpt.	Students may be able to identify with the difficulties Esperanza experiences as she settles into a new life in the United States. Ask each student to write a short journal entry describing one particular problem he or she had in learning to live in the United States. The problem can be something small, such as Esperanza's struggle to sweep. Students should also mention how they resolved the problem. Ask volunteers to share their stories with the group. Have the English learners make connections between one another's stories and Esperanza's story.

Fact and Fantasy

- Explain to students that the selection here is an excerpt from the novel *Esperanza Rising.* As they read or listen, ask students to identify the things that Esperanza wishes for and the things she must learn to do. Have a volunteer read aloud the text on p. 361.
- Point out the scene on p. 361 in which Esperanza struggles to perform a menial task. Help students relate to Esperanza by inviting them to share a time when they felt frustrated when they had to do something for the first time.
- Ask students to respond to the Thematic Connection question on p. 361.
  Possible response: The effort that Esperanza makes in learning to sweep with a broom suggests that she is unused to simple housekeeping tasks. However, her complete inability to sweep seems a little exaggerated. Marta's calling her "Cinderella" suggests that Esperanza is now reduced to sweeping whereas she once had a fairy-tale life.

Fact and Fantasy

- Offer students two copies of an Open Mind Organizer like the one on p. 93 of **Writing Models and Graphic Organizers on Transparency.** Have students label one organizer *Esperanza* and the other *Miguel.* As they read further, instruct students to fill in the organizers with words, symbols, or pictures that reveal what the characters think and feel.
- Finally, have each student write a couple of sentences that make a generalization about what the two characters have in common. Then, ask them to identify ways in which they are different.
- When students have finished reading the selection, challenge them to sum up in a single sentence the similarities and differences between the two characters. You may offer them the following sentence to fill in: "Although Esperanza and Miguel both ________, they also ________."

▲ **Critical Viewing**
What details in this picture seem familiar and recognizable to you? Which seem strange and unfamiliar? Explain.
[Compare and Contrast]

"I said I could work. I told Mama I could help. But I cannot even wash clothes or sweep a floor. Does the whole camp know?"

Isabel sat down on the bed next to her and patted her back. "Yes."

Esperanza groaned. "I will never be able to show my face." She put her head in her hands until she heard someone else come into the room.

Esperanza looked up to see Miguel, holding a broom and a dustpan. But he wasn't laughing. She looked down and bit her lip so she wouldn't cry in front of him.

He shut the door, then stood in front of her and said, "How would you know how to sweep a floor? The only thing you ever learned was how to give orders. That is not your fault. Anza, look at me."

She looked up.

"Pay attention," he said, his face serious. "You hold the broom like this. One hand here and the other here."

Esperanza watched.

"Then you push like this. Or pull it toward you like this. Here, you try," he said, holding out the broom.

Slowly, Esperanza got up and took the broom from him. He positioned

ENRICHMENT: Social Studies Connection

Mexican Repatriation

During the Great Depression in the United States, millions of people were devastated by the loss of their jobs, homes, businesses, and farms. Many people became migrants, wandering around the country in search of seasonal work such as harvesting fruits and vegetables. Of course, Americans were not the only ones hit by the economic downturn, and immigrants from around the world, including Mexico, came to the United States. However, many Americans resented the loss of needed jobs to immigrants. In 1929, the U.S. government passed a law that was intended to help American workers. The Repatriation Act of 1929 allowed states to force immigrants to return to their countries of origin. The reasoning behind this act was that without the competition for jobs, Americans would find work and economic stability. In California, the act had devastating effects. Thousands of people of Mexican heritage were dispatched to Mexico. Many were actually native-born American citizens.

her hands on the handle. She tried to copy him but her movements were too big.

"Smaller strokes," said Miguel, coaching. "And sweep all in one direction."

She did as he said.

"Now, when you get all the dirt into a pile, you hold the broom down here, near the bottom, and push the dirt into the pan."

Esperanza collected the dirt.

"See, you can do it." Miguel raised his thick eyebrows and smiled. "Someday, you just might make a very good servant."

Isabel giggled.

Esperanza could not yet find humor in the situation. Somberly[3] she said, "Thank you, Miguel."

He grinned and bowed. "At your service, *mi reina*." But this time, his voice was kind.

She remembered that he had gone to look for work at the railroad. "Did you get a job?"

His smile faded. He put his hands in his pockets and shrugged his shoulders. "It is frustrating. I can fix any engine. But they will only hire Mexicans to lay track and dig ditches, not as mechanics. I've decided to work in the fields until I can convince someone to give me a chance."

Esperanza nodded.

After he left the room, Isabel said, "He calls you *mi reina!* Will you tell me about your life as a queen?

Esperanza sat on the mattress and patted the spot next to her. Isabel sat down.

"Isabel, I will tell you all about how I used to live. About parties and private school and beautiful dresses. I will even show you the beautiful doll my papa bought me, if you will teach me how to pin diapers, how to wash, and . . ."

Isabel interrupted her. "But that is so easy!"

Esperanza stood up and carefully practiced with the broom. "It is not easy for me."

3. **somberly** (säm′bər lē) in a dark, gloomy, or dull way

Pam Muñoz Ryan

Pam Muñoz Ryan grew up in the San Joaquin Valley of California. She now lives with her family near San Diego. The story of *Esperanza Rising* is based on the experiences of her grandmother on her mother's side.

Connecting Science Fiction and Historical Fiction

1. What kinds of challenges do you think Esperanza is going to face besides learning how to work?
2. Why does Esperanza find a different life difficult, but the characters in "The Fun They Had" find a different life appealing?
3. Do you find the characters in *Esperanza Rising* or in "The Fun They Had" more realistic and believable? Explain.
4. In what ways are Esperanza's challenges similar to and different from the challenges of the students in "The Fun They Had"?

▶Critical Viewing

Answer: Students might say that the vegetables and the pots on the stove seem familiar, but the clothing, the oven, and the woman's chore seem unfamiliar.

Answers

Connecting Science Fiction and Historical Fiction

1. Possible response: Esperanza will probably have to face the challenges of learning English and living on little money.
2. Esperanza must adopt a very different lifestyle, whereas the characters in "The Fun They Had" only read about life in a different time period.
3. Possible responses: Some students may say that the characters in the excerpt from *Esperanza Rising* are more realistic because they experience things that people really have experienced. Others may say that they relate more to the characters in "The Fun They Had" and that the idea of technology eliminating schools is more realistic to them than the description of Esperanza's former fairy-tale life.
4. Esperanza and the students in "The Fun They Had" all understand that life in the present moment seems harder and less enjoyable than it was in the past. The difference is that Esperanza actually experiences the abrupt change of circumstances. The students only read about what school was like centuries before.

CUSTOMIZE INSTRUCTION FOR UNIVERSAL ACCESS

For Advanced Readers

The conflict a character faces as he or she becomes used to a new culture or new living situation is common in literature. Invite students to think of other stories, books, plays, movies, or television programs that deal with a character's learning to live in a new place. After making a list, ask each student to choose one or two of the characters that have been mentioned and to compare him or her to Esperanza. What do they have in common? How are their situations different? How do they each react to their new surroundings? Students may use a Venn diagram like the one on p. 89 in **Writing Models and Graphic Organizers on Transparencies** to make their comparisons. Then, have each student write an essay comparing and contrasting the two characters. Tell students that they will have to summarize each story briefly in their essays before they begin to compare and contrast the characters. Challenge students to create interesting introductory paragraphs and to compose solid concluding paragraphs that state what can be learned from the two characters they analyzed.

A Dream Within a Dream ✦ The Spring and the Fall ✦ Ankylosaurus

Lesson Objectives

1. **To analyze and respond to literary elements**
   - Literary Analysis: Rhyme
   - Comparing Literary Works
2. **To read, comprehend, analyze, and critique three poems**
   - Reading Strategy: Drawing Inferences
   - Reading Check Questions
   - Review and Assess Questions
   - Assessment Practice (ATE)
3. **To develop word analysis skills, fluency, and systematic vocabulary**
   - Vocabulary Development Lesson: Word Analysis: Latin Prefix *in-*
4. **To understand and apply written and oral language conventions**
   - Spelling Strategy
   - Grammar Lesson: Complete Sentences
5. **To understand and apply appropriate writing and research strategies**
   - Writing Lesson: Dinosaur Description
   - Extension Activity: Research Summary
   - Extension Activity: Interpretation
6. **To understand and apply listening and speaking strategies**
   - Extension Activity: Choral Reading

STEP-BY-STEP TEACHING GUIDE	PACING GUIDE
PRETEACH	
Motivate Students and Provide Background	
Use the Motivation activity (ATE p. 364)	5 min.
Read and discuss the Preview material and Background information (SE/ATE p. 364) [A]	10 min.
Introduce the Concepts	
Introduce the Literary Analysis and Reading Strategy (SE/ATE p. 365) [A]	15 min.
Pronounce the vocabulary words and read their definitions (SE p. 365)	5 min.
TEACH	
Monitor Comprehension	
Informally monitor comprehension by circulating while students read independently or in groups [A]	5 min.
Develop vocabulary with Vocabulary notes (SE pp. 367, 369, 370)	as students read
Develop Understanding	
Develop students' understanding of rhyme with the Literary Analysis annotations (ATE p. 368) [A]	5 min.
Develop students' ability to draw inferences with the Reading Strategy annotations (ATE p. 367)	5 min.
ASSESS	
Assess Mastery	
Assess students' mastery of the Reading Strategy and Literary Analysis by having them answer the Review and Assess questions (SE/ATE p. 371)	15 min.
Use one or more of the print and media Assessment Resources (ATE p. 373) [A]	up to 45 min.
EXTEND	
Apply Understanding	
Have students complete the Vocabulary Development Lesson and the Grammar Lesson (SE p. 372) [A]	20 min.
Apply students' ability to write about a dinosaur using the Writing Lesson (SE/ATE p. 373) [A]	30–45 min.
Apply students' understanding of the selection using one or more of the Extension Activities (SE p. 373)	20–90 min.

ACCELERATED INSTRUCTION:
Use the strategies and activities identified with an [A].

UNIVERSAL ACCESS
● = Below Level Students
▲ = On-Level Students
■ = Above Level Students

Time and Resource Manager

Reading Level: Challenging, Average, Easy
Average Number of Instructional Days: 3

RESOURCES		
PRINT	**TRANSPARENCIES**	**TECHNOLOGY**
• **Beyond Literature,** Cross-Curricular Connection: History, p. 22 ▲ ■		• **Interest Grabber Videotapes,** Tape 3 ● ▲ ■
• **Selection Support Workbook:** ● ▲ ■ Literary Analysis, p. 110 Reading Strategy, p. 109 Build Vocabulary, p. 106	• **Literary Analysis and Reading Transparencies,** pp. 43 and 44 ● ▲ ■	
		• **Listening to Literature** ● ▲ ■ Audiocassettes, Side 13 Audio CDs, CD 6
• **Literary Analysis for Enrichment** ■		
• **Formal Assessment:** Selection Test, pp. 96–98 ● ▲ ■ • **Open Book Test,** pp. 64–66 ● ▲ ■ • **Performance Assessment and Portfolio Management,** p. 23 ● ▲ ■ • PRENTICE HALL ASSESSMENT SYSTEM ● ▲ ■	• PRENTICE HALL ASSESSMENT SYSTEM ● ▲ ■ Skills Practice Answers and Explanations on Transparencies	• **Test Bank Software** ● ▲ ■ • **Got It! Assessment Videotapes,** Tape 3 ● ▲
• **Selection Support Workbook:** ● ▲ ■ Build Spelling Skills, p. 107 Build Grammar Skills, p. 108 • **Writing and Grammar,** Copper Level ● ▲ ■ • **Extension Activities,** p. 22 ● ▲ ■	• **Daily Language Practice Transparencies** ● ▲ • **Writing Models and Graphic Organizers on Transparencies** ● ▲ ■	• **Writing and Grammar iText CD-ROM** ● ▲ ■ ***Take It to the Net*** www.phschool.com

BLOCK SCHEDULING: Use one 90-minute class period to preteach the selection and have students read it. Use a second 90-minute class period to assess students' mastery of skills and have them complete one of the Extension Activities.

PRETEACH

Step-by-Step Teaching Guide for pp. 364–365

Motivation

Ask students what they think of when they hear the word *poetry*. Some students may say that they think of rhymes or of expressions of sad or sentimental feelings. Tell students that they will read three poems that explore the past. All include rhymes. One is humorous, but the other two express sad, sentimental feelings.

Interest Grabber Video

As an alternative, play "Animal Extinction" on Tape 3 to engage student interest.

❶ Background

Film

Except for cartoons, most early dinosaur movies were made by filming models of dinosaurs in "stop-action." Filming stopped and restarted each time the dinosaur model was repositioned, creating a choppy motion. Occasionally, actual lizards were used to portray dinosaurs—not very successfully. In 1957, the first mechanical dinosaurs appeared in a movie. They were a slight improvement over stop-action. Finally, computer graphics allowed moviemakers to create realistic-looking dinosaurs and dinosaur-type creatures like in the movies today.

Prepare to Read

❶ A Dream Within a Dream ◆ The Spring and the Fall ◆ Ankylosaurus

Take It to the Net

Visit www.phschool.com for interactive activities and instruction related to these selections, including

- background
- graphic organizers
- literary elements
- reading strategies

Preview

Connecting to the Literature

The poets in this group show that the past has a way of leaving its mark on the present. Your world may change unexpectedly when a friend moves or an event upsets you. Yet no friend or experience ever completely leaves you. Look back at past people and events in your life and think about what you have learned from them or what memories they have left with you.

Background

Fossil remains reveal the lives of dinosaurs, such as the Ankylosaurus in Prelutsky's poem. Ankylosaurus (aŋ´ kə lō sôr əs) had small jaws and weak teeth suitable only for chewing soft plants. For protection, an Ankylosaurus had tough, leathery skin and a heavy tail shaped like a club. Its short, stubby legs kept the ankylosaurus close to the ground, protecting its soft underbelly. The picture on page 370 shows what scientists believe an Ankylosaurus looked like.

TEACHING RESOURCES

The following resources can be used to enrich or extend the instruction for pp. 364–365.

Motivation

Interest Grabber Video, Tape 3

Background

Beyond Literature, p. 22

Take It to the Net

Visit www.phschool.com for Background and hotlinks for the selections.

Literary Analysis

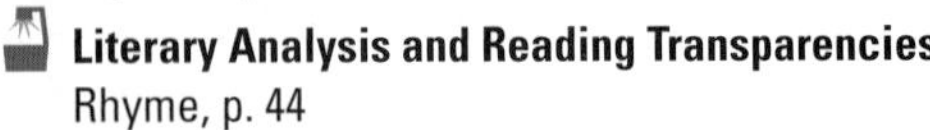

Literary Analysis and Reading Transparencies, Rhyme, p. 44

Reading

Selection Support: Reading Strategy, p. 109; Build Vocabulary, p. 106

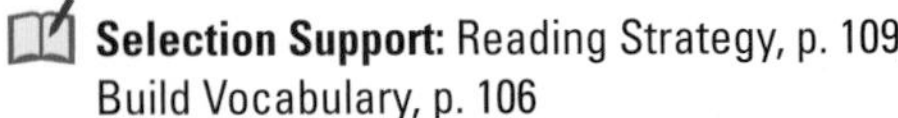

Literary Analysis and Reading Transparencies, Drawing Inferences, p. 43

BLOCK SCHEDULING: Resources marked with this symbol provide varied instruction during 90-minute blocks.

❷ Literary Analysis

Rhyme

Rhyme is the repetition of sounds at the ends of words. Many poems have rhyming words at the ends of lines. To identify the pattern of rhyme in a poem, use letters. For example, lines ending in *sing, last, ring, past* have an *abab* rhyme scheme, or pattern. The following lines from Prelutsky's poem shown below have an *aabb* pattern.

Clankity Clankity Clankity Clank!
Ankylosaurus was built like a tank,
its hide was a fortress as sturdy as steel,
it tended to be an inedible meal.

The choice of words that rhyme in this poem reinforces the writer's amused attitude toward the subject. As you read, notice the rhymes.

Comparing Literary Works

In addition to the words that rhyme, the poet's choice of words can also reveal the **tone**, or author's attitude toward the subject. In "A Dream Within a Dream," the formal word choice conveys a serious, dramatic tone.

Take this kiss upon the brow!
And, in parting from you now,
Thus much let me avow—

Compare and contrast the tones of these poems. Think about these focus questions:

1. Which two of these three poems have a more serious tone?
2. Which poem has the most humorous tone?

❸ Reading Strategy

Drawing Inferences

The poems in this group hint at past events and circumstances rather than directly stating them. You can **draw inferences** about past events, that is, make logical guesses about them, based on details that are provided in the poem. As you read, look for details that you can put together to draw inferences. The organizer shows one example of details that can be used to draw an inference.

Detail
Someone is leaving

Detail
The speaker weeps

Inference
The speaker is sad because the person is leaving

Vocabulary Development

deem (dēm) *v.* judge (p. 367)

bough (bou) *n.* tree branch (p. 369)

raucous (rô´ kəs) *adj.* loud and rowdy (p. 369)

inedible (in ed´ ə bəl) *adj.* not fit to be eaten (p. 370)

cudgel (kuj´ əl) *n.* short, thick stick or club (p. 370)

❷ Literary Analysis

Rhyme

- Before students read the instruction, explain that they probably are already familiar with the concept of rhyme. Ask them to think of as many words as they can that rhyme with the word *sing*. Students should offer plenty of examples. Then, ask them whether they associate any feelings with any of the words they mentioned.
- Read the instruction on rhyme and the Comparing Literary Works feature aloud to them. Point out how the lines from the poems convey two very different feelings—silliness and sadness.
- The Rhyme transparency on p. 44 of **Literary Analysis and Reading Transparencies** will help reinforce the concept of rhyme.

❸ Reading Strategy

Drawing Inferences

- Before asking students to read the instruction, ask them to identify some basic differences between poetry and other types of writing. Guide students to see that ideas in poetry are not always stated directly, but are implied.
- Then, ask a volunteer to read the instruction.
- Point out how the graphic organizer helps make connections between ideas in a poem. Practice using the organizer by filling in information from a poem students are familiar with.

Vocabulary Development

- Review the words and definitions on the vocabulary list.
- Explain that *raucous* means "loud and rowdy." Ask students to identify places where raucous behavior would be acceptable.
  Possible responses: athletic competition; an outdoor party. Then ask students to name some events where raucous behavior would be inappropriate.
  Possible responses: library; movie theater.

CUSTOMIZE INSTRUCTION FOR UNIVERSAL ACCESS

For Less Proficient Readers	For English Learners	For Advanced Readers
Allow students to listen to a recording of a poem before they read it. Recordings are available on **Listening to Literature Audiocassettes,** Side 19 or **Listening to Literature Audio CDs,** CD 7. Have students listen to the recording three times and recall out loud or write down as many of the rhyming words as they can.	Students may have trouble with Poe's word choice and syntax. Help students interpret metaphors and draw inferences about meaning. Then, have students write a one-sentence paraphrase of the poem. Read aloud and discuss the paraphrases as a class.	Edgar Allan Poe was noted for using rhyme, repetition, and other poetic devices to give his poems a musical quality. Have students locate another poem by Poe that demonstrates this musical quality. Have students read the poems aloud in class.

E-Teach

Visit E-Teach at www.phschool.com for teachers' essays on how to teach, with questions and answers.

TEACH

Step-by-Step Teaching Guide for pp. 366–370

CUSTOMIZE INSTRUCTION For Verbal/Linguistic Learners

To help students understand the imagery of the poem "A Dream Within a Dream," have them think of an image, in addition to the grains of sand, that could be an analogy for the movement of time.

❶ About the Selection

In "A Dream Within a Dream," Edgar Allan Poe describes how the speaker feels after having lost a love. The speaker experiences life as if it were a dream, as he or she desperately wishes to hold onto the past.

❷ ▶Critical Viewing

Possible responses: Students may say the sand suggests that time cannot be stopped or that it slips away one minute at a time, just as each grain of sand runs through the hourglass.

❶

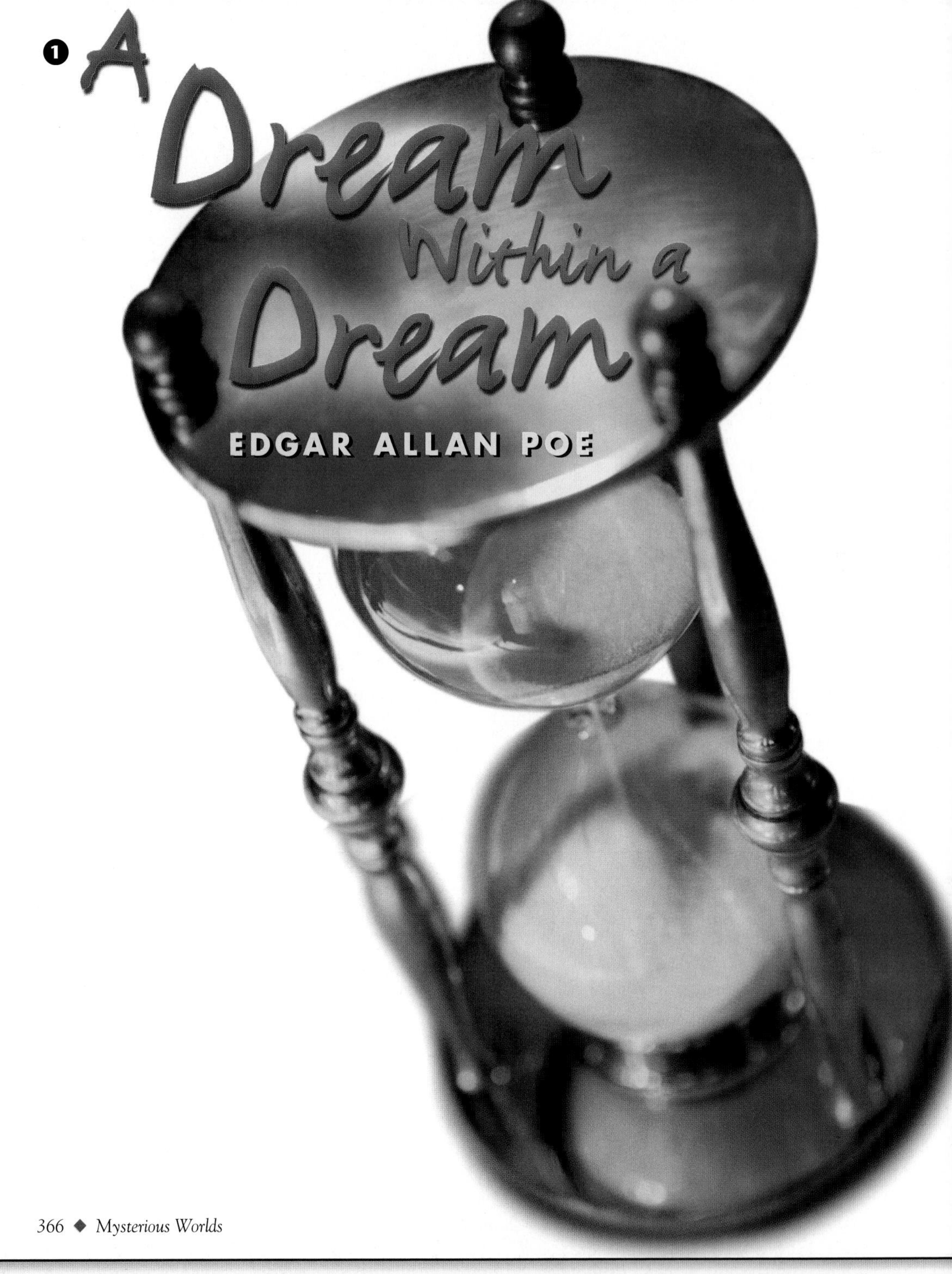

TEACHING RESOURCES

The following resources can be used to enrich or extend the instruction for pp. 366–370.

Literary Analysis

- **Selection Support:** Literary Analysis, p. 110
- **Literary Analysis for Enrichment**

Reading

- **Literatura en español**
- **Listening to Literature Audiocassettes,** Side 13 ■
- **Listening to Literature Audio CDs,** CD 6 ■

■ **BLOCK SCHEDULING:** Resources marked with this symbol provide varied instruction during 90-minute blocks.

Take this kiss upon the brow!
And, in parting from you now,
Thus much let me avow—
You are not wrong, who deem
That my days have been a dream;
Yet if hope has flown away
In a night, or in a day,
In a vision, or in none,
Is it therefore the less *gone*?
All that we see or seem
Is but a dream within a dream.
I stand amid the roar
Of a surf-tormented shore,
And I hold within my hand
Grains of the golden sand—
❸ How few! yet how they creep
Through my fingers to the deep,
While I weep—while I weep!
O God! can I not grasp
Them with a tighter clasp?
O God! can I not save
One from the pitiless wave?
Is *all* that we see or seem
But a dream within a dream?

deem (dēm) *v.* judge

❷ ◀ **Critical Viewing** What does the sand running through the hourglass suggest about time? **[Interpret]**

Review and Assess

Thinking About the Selections

1. **Respond:** Do you think you would enjoy meeting the speaker in Poe's poem?
2. **(a) Analyze:** What happens in the first two lines of "A Dream Within a Dream"? **(b) Interpret:** Who is *you* in lines 2 and 4? **(c) Connect:** What does the person in lines 2 and 4 have to do with the dream?
3. **(a) Analyze:** What is the speaker doing in lines 13–19? **(b) Connect:** How are these actions related to the idea of dreaming? **(c) Interpret:** Explain the title. What dream is within what dream?
4. **Interpret:** What is the "pitiless wave" that washes away the "grains" of experiences that the speaker tries to hold in his or her hand?

Edgar Allan Poe

(1809–1849)

Edgar Allan Poe, one of America's best-known writers, led a troubled life plagued by poverty and the loss of people he loved. His father deserted him, his mother died before he was three, and his wife died while she was still young. Despite his problems, Poe produced a large body of work, including short stories, essays, and poems. He died in Baltimore at the age of forty, but his stories and poems live on, read by millions in America and around the world.

❸ Reading Strategy

Drawing Inferences

- Point out that the speaker refers to the sand as "golden," and that he says the grains of sand are "few." Ask students what is implied when something is called "golden."
  Answer: When something is called "golden," it usually means that it is valuable.
- Ask students what these few grains of sand might represent to the speaker.
  Answer: The grains of sand might represent the brief but precious time that he spent with his love.

Answers for p. 367

Review and Assess

1. Possible responses: Some students may say that they would not like to meet the speaker because he or she sounds sad. Others may say that they might like to offer the speaker some advice about love.
2. **(a)** The speaker kisses his or her love upon the forehead as they are about to part. **(b)** "You" is the person the speaker loves. **(c)** The person suggests that the speaker is living a dream.
3. **(a)** The speaker is standing at the seashore contemplating grains of sand slipping between his or her fingers. **(b)** The sand falling is like time slipping away, just as life does when we dream. **(c)** Life itself is like a dream, and when we dream, we are dreaming within a dream.
4. The "pitiless wave" may be time passing, or it may be death.

CUSTOMIZE INSTRUCTION FOR UNIVERSAL ACCESS

For Special Needs Students	For English Learners
Have students read the poem once and write a journal entry in response. Then, offer students the following cloze-type statements, and have them fill in the statements during their second reading of the poem. At the beginning of the poem, I think the speaker feels ______ because ______. I think the speaker is located ______ because ______. I think the dream is ______. At the end of the poem, I think the speaker feels ______ because ______.	Students may benefit from reading the poem in small sections. Ask students to take out several sheets of paper and copy the poem, writing five lines on each side of a page. Read aloud a section of the poem. Then, allow students time to write questions and notes about words they do not know. Talk for a moment about the metaphors and syntax. After students complete the poem, ask them to write a summary of it.

❹ About the Selections

In Edna St. Vincent Millay's "The Spring and the Fall" (p. 369), the speaker describes how her love was bright and fresh in springtime, but by fall it had begun to slip away.

Jack Prelutsky's poem "Ankylosaurus" (p. 370) uses humor to give the reader a look into the past at the heavily armored dinosaur, the ankylosaurus.

❺ Literary Analysis

Rhyme

- Remind students that rhyme reinforces the author's attitude toward the poem.
- Have students look at the rhyming words at the end of each line. Ask them this question: What do the rhyming words seem to say about the poet's attitude?
  Possible responses: The repetition of the word *year* suggests awareness of passing time; rhyming with *dear* shows an amorous tone; *peach* and *reach* seem to show growth and striving; and *falling* and *calling* seem to indicate the fall of emotions, as well as a reference to the fall season, and a sense of loneliness ("calling"). Although Millay refers to various feelings while describing her loss, she seems to realize that the loss of love, like the passage of time, is part of life, but the *manner* of love's loss is what is saddest to her.

▷ **Monitor Progress** To help students understand the author's references to spring and fall, ask students to find words that refer to each season.
Answer: The references to spring include the wet bark and the blossoming peach; the references to fall include the trill of the rooks and the word *falling*.

▷ **Reteach** Guide students to see Millay's attitude about the loss of love in the last line of the poem, where the little losses along the way to losing her love are the most painful of all.

❻ ▶Critical Viewing

Answer: The woman seems to be sad, lonely, or mourning for something she has lost.

CUSTOMIZE INSTRUCTION FOR UNIVERSAL ACCESS

For Gifted/Talented Students

Students may benefit from taking on the roles of the poets and the speakers in the poems in the format of a panel or round-table discussion. Place students in groups of four to six, and ask them to choose the role of poet, speaker, or discussion moderator. Give students time to reread the poems and do research, if they like, into the lives of the poets. Students should be able to explain in a minute who their characters are and what concerns they have. They should also work together to write questions they would like the moderator to ask during the discussion. When students are ready, ask them to perform their discussions for the class. After the initial discussion, students should answer questions from the class in character.

❹ # The Spring and the Fall

Edna St. Vincent Millay

In the spring of the year, in the spring of the year,
I walked the road beside my dear.
The trees were black where the bark was wet.
I see them yet, in the spring of the year.
He broke me a bough of the blossoming peach
That was out of the way and hard to reach.

In the fall of the year, in the fall of the year,
I walked the road beside my dear.
❺ The rooks[1] went up with a raucous trill.
I hear them still, in the fall of the year.
He laughed at all I dared to praise,
And broke my heart, in little ways.

Year be springing or year be falling,
The bark will drip and the birds be calling.
There's much that's fine to see and hear
In the spring of a year, in the fall of a year.
'Tis not love's going hurts my days,
But that it went in little ways.

bough (bou) *n.* branch of a tree

raucous (rô´ kəs) *adj.* loud and rowdy

1. **rooks** (ro͝oks) *n.* European crows.

❻ ◀ **Critical Viewing** What emotions do you think this woman is feeling? **[Infer]**

Edna St. Vincent Millay

(1892–1950)

Edna St. Vincent Millay was born in Rockland, Maine. Raised by her mother, who encouraged her creativity, she published her first poem in a children's magazine when she was only fourteen. Her first book of poetry came out when she was twenty-five. Just six years later, in 1923, she won a Pulitzer Prize for poetry. Like "The Spring and the Fall," many of Millay's poems and sonnets are about love and the loss of love.

Review and Assess

Thinking About the Selections

1. **Respond:** What questions would you like to ask Edna St. Vincent Millay about the poem?
2. **(a) Recall:** What happens to the couple in spring in this poem? **(b) Connect:** How does the idea of a new love connect with the idea of spring?
3. **(a) Recall:** What happens to the couple in fall in this poem? **(b) Connect:** How does the idea of love's departure connect with the idea of fall? **(c) Draw Conclusions:** Do you think "The Spring and the Fall" is an appropriate title? Why or why not?

Answers for p. 369

Review and Assess

1. **Possible responses:** Students might like to ask whether the speaker ever got over the feelings of sadness or perhaps found a new love.
2. **(a)** In spring, the couple walks along a road, and the man breaks off a branch from a peach tree. **(b)** Both new love and spring suggest newness, freshness, and possibility.
3. **(a)** The couple fall out of love in the fall. **(b)** Fall and lost love are about reaching an end of something; both are opportunities for reflection. **(c) Possible responses:** Students may think it is an appropriate title; they may even see the wordplay in the use of the word *fall* in the title; the speaker experiences fall, the season, as well as an emotional fall.

CUSTOMIZE INSTRUCTION FOR UNIVERSAL ACCESS

For Special Needs Students	For Advanced Readers
Remind students that when reading poetry, they should pay more attention to punctuation than to line endings. Explain that poets often break lines in the middle of a thought in order to emphasize a word or a sound. Remind students that they should find meaning in each sentence, not necessarily in each line. Help students by asking them to rewrite "The Spring and the Fall" in sentence and paragraph forms. Ask a volunteer to read the paragraphs aloud. Then, ask the class whether that reading made more sense to them and why.	Explain that because so much meaning in poetry is implied, readers must figure out what is going on with the characters or speakers in the poems. Ask students to select one of the characters or speakers in one of the poems and to write a short character sketch. Students should make up names, imagine the characters' biographies, and fill in the background to the poem. Ask volunteers to read their sketches aloud.

ASSESS

Answers for p. 370

Review and Assess

1. Possible responses: Some students may be amused by the poet's comparison to a metal tank that clanks when it moves; others may find the description strange or intimidating.
2. **(a)** The animal was built like an armored tank. **(b)** The words that reinforce the image of the tank are *clank, tank, fortress, steel,* and *armored.* **(c)** Possible responses: The poet may want to give the impression of the ankylosaurus approaching, or he may want to emphasize that the creature is like a tank.
3. **(a)** The ankylosaurus made a poor meal because it was so tough. **(b)** Since no other creature could eat the ankylosaurus, it survived very nicely.
4. **(a)** The tail was like a club or hammer. **(b)** Another animal was not likely to have a chance of winning against the ankylosaurus. The ankylosaurus was not necessarily an aggressive fighter, but it could certainly defend itself. **(c)** The dinosaur was best left alone because it would not make a good meal and it was too tough to fight with.

Ankylosaurus

Jack Prelutsky

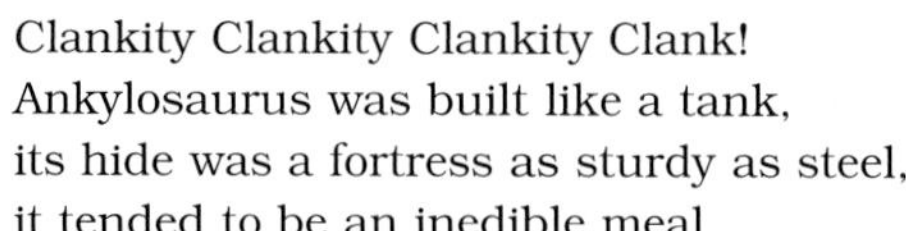

Clankity Clankity Clankity Clank!
Ankylosaurus was built like a tank,
its hide was a fortress as sturdy as steel,
it tended to be an inedible meal.

It was armored in front, it was armored behind,
there wasn't a thing on its minuscule mind,
it waddled about on its four stubby legs,
nibbling on plants with a mouthful of pegs.

Ankylosaurus was best left alone,
its tail was a cudgel of gristle and bone,
Clankity Clankity Clankity Clank!
Ankylosaurus was built like a tank.

inedible (in ed′ ə bəl) *adj.* not fit to be eaten

cudgel (kuj′ əl) *n.* short, thick stick or club

Review and Assess

Thinking About the Selection

1. **Respond:** Do you find the description of Ankylosaurus amusing or frightening? Why?
2. (a) **Recall:** What was Ankylosaurus built like? (b) **Analyze:** Which sound words help reinforce this image? (c) **Speculate:** Why do you think Prelutsky begins the poem with these words and this image?
3. (a) **Recall:** What kind of meal did Ankylosaurus make? (b) **Hypothesize:** How did this help ensure the survival of Ankylosaurus?
4. (a) **Recall:** What was the tail of Ankylosaurus like? (b) **Speculate:** What was likely to happen in a fight between Ankylosaurus and another animal? (c) **Generalize:** Why was Ankylosaurus "best left alone"?

Jack Prelutsky

(b. 1940)

Jack Prelutsky was born in Brooklyn, New York. His writing career began when he showed a friend some poems he had written to accompany drawings of imaginary creatures. With his friend's encouragement, Prelutsky soon published his first book of poems. He went on to write many more books and to win numerous awards for his humorous verse.

ASSESSMENT PRACTICE: Reading Comprehension

Draw Inferences (For more practice, see Test Preparation Workbook, p. 32.)

Have students use this passage to draw inferences.

Clankity Clankity Clankity Clank!
Ankylosaurus was built like a tank,
its hide was a fortress as sturdy as steel
it tended to be an inedible meal.
It was armored in front, it was armored behind, / . . . / it waddled about on its four stubby legs, / nibbling on plants with a mouthful of pegs.

Other dinosaurs find the ankylosaurus inedible because—

A it has large teeth
B it is poisonous
C it is armored
D it eats plants

The passage does not support *B. A* and *D* do not explain why the ankylosaurus is inedible. *C* is correct. The ankylosaurus has armor that makes it difficult to attack and eat.

Review and Assess

Literary Analysis

Rhyme

1. Where do the rhyming words in these three poems usually fall?
2. Complete a chart like the one shown to give examples of rhyming words each poet uses.

Poem	Rhyming Words
"Dream Within a Dream"	
"The Spring and the Fall"	
"Ankylosaurus"	

3. Use letters to show the **rhyme scheme** of the first stanza of "The Spring and the Fall."

Comparing Literary Works

4. Which two of these three poems have the most serious **tone**? Explain.
5. Which poem has the most humorous tone? Explain.
6. Identify the similarities and differences in word choice that reveal the similarities and differences in tone.
7. How do the similarities and differences in tone affect your reactions to the poems?

Reading Strategy

Drawing Inferences

8. What inferences do you draw about the couple's relationship in "The Spring and the Fall"?
9. What details from "Ankylosaurus" help you make inferences about the world in which the dinosaur lived?

Extending Understanding

10. **Career Connection:** People who explore the past by studying dinosaurs are called paleontologists. What other careers are available to people who enjoy studying the past?

Quick Review

Rhyme is the repetition of sounds at the ends of words. Rhyme often occurs at the ends of lines of poetry. To review rhyme, see page 365.

Tone is the author's attitude toward the subject. To review tone, see page 365.

Drawing inferences is forming ideas or coming to conclusions that are based on the reading.

Take It to the Net

www.phschool.com

Take the interactive self-test online to check your understanding of these selections.

ENRICHMENT: Further Reading

Other Works by the Poets

Works by Edgar Allan Poe

Complete Poems

The Black Cat and Other Stories

Works by Edna St. Vincent Millay

Selected Poems

Collected Lyrics

Works by Jack Prelutsky

Imagine That! Poems of Never-Was

A. Nonny Mouse Writes Again: Poems

Take It to the Net

Visit www.phschool.com for more information on the poets.

Answers for p. 371

Review and Assess

1. The rhymes tend to fall at the ends of the lines.
2.

Poem	Rhyming Words
"Dream"	now, brow, avow
	creep, deep, weep
"Spring"	year, dear, hear
	falling, calling
"Ankylo-saurus"	clank, tank
	steel, meal

3. The rhyme scheme of the first stanza of "The Spring and the Fall" is *aabacc.*
4. "A Dream Within a Dream" and "The Spring and the Fall" have the most serious tone. Both are about lost or dying love.
5. "Ankylosaurus" is the most humorous. It is a poem that compares a dinosaur to a tank with words that make the dinosaur seem humorous.
6. The words *kiss, spring, dream,* and *blossoming peach* give "Dream" and "Spring" a sweet tone that in the end becomes bittersweet with *tighter clasp, pitiless wave, hurts my days,* and *little ways.* The tone of "Ankylosaurus" is humorous, as shown in the use of the words *clankity, hide was a fortress,* and *a cudgel of gristle and bone.*
7. The seriousness and the bitter-sweet tone of "Dream" and "Spring" lead the reader to reflect on the poems, and the humor in "Ankylosaurus" imparts a lightheartedness.
8. Possible responses: Students may infer that the couple's relationship was happy and new in the spring and then sad and falling apart in the fall.
9. The words and phrases *"fortress," "inedible meal," "nibbling on plants,"* and *"gristle* and *bone"* suggest a world where plant-eating dinosaurs were targets of meat-eaters.
10. Possible responses: Students may suggest the careers of historian or archaeologist for those who enjoy studying the past.

EXTEND

Answers for p. 372

❶ Vocabulary Development

Word Analysis

1. incomplete: The sentence makes sense because the speaker misses a loved one.
2. indefinite: This sentence does not make sense because a year is an exact amount of time.
3. inaccurate: This sentence does not make sense because he is giving exact details of a real type of dinosaur.

Fluency: Context

1. No, he thinks it is stupid.
2. No, it liked to eat plants.
3. No, a raucous song would be too loud and noisy for a lullaby.
4. Yes, a bough is a branch that would make a good club.

Spelling Strategy

1. plough
2. crowd
3. drought
4. frown

❷ Grammar

1. subordinate; As it nibbled on plants, the dinosaur smiled.
2. complete
3. subordinate; If hope has flown away, I will be sad.
4. complete
5. subordinate; Because it was an inedible meal, we left.

Writing Application

Students should demonstrate their understanding of complete sentences with the writing application.

Integrate Language Skills

❶ Vocabulary Development Lesson

Word Analysis: Latin Prefix *in-*

The Latin prefix *in-* means "not" or "the opposite of." Combined with *edible,* which means "fit to eat," it forms a word that means "not fit to eat." Copy the following sentences. Add the Latin prefix *in-* to the italicized word to change its meaning to the opposite. Then, explain whether the rewritten sentence makes sense.

1. The speaker of "A Dream Within a Dream" feels *complete.*
2. A year is a(n) *definite* period of time.
3. Prelutsky's description of Ankylosaurus is *accurate.*

Fluency: Context

On your paper, answer the following questions, explaining your answers.

1. Does Prelutsky *deem* Ankylosaurus thoughtful?
2. Did Ankylosaurus find plants *inedible?*
3. Would a *raucous* song make a good lullaby?
4. Would a *bough* make a good *cudgel?*

Spelling Strategy

The word *bough* is one example of the *ow* sound spelled with *ough*. *Brow* is an example of the *ow* sound spelled with *ow*. On your paper, unscramble the letters to spell words that have the *ow* sound.

1. glopuh 2. dworc 3. dogruth 4. wronf

❷ Grammar Lesson

Complete Sentences

A **complete sentence** is a group of words that expresses a complete thought and contains at least one subject and one predicate (verb).

Example: I (S) walked (P) the road beside my dear.

The following is not a complete sentence: "While I weep—While I weep!" Although it contains a subject and predicate, it does not express a complete thought. "While I weep" is a subordinate thought. The following example is a complete sentence because it tells what happens.

Example: The grains of sand (S) run (P) through my fingers while I weep.

▶ *For more practice, see page R28, Exercise B.*

Practice Copy the following sentences. If an item is a subordinate thought, add the information needed to make a complete sentence.

1. As it nibbled on plants.
2. You are not wrong.
3. If hope has flown away.
4. The bark will drip, and the birds will call.
5. Because it was an inedible meal.

Writing Application Add your own words to make each of the following complete sentences.

1. As I walked along the road
2. If he had stayed
3. Although it was strong and sturdy at first

WG Prentice Hall Writing and Grammar Connection: Chapter 21, Section 4

TEACHING RESOURCES

The following resources can be used to enrich or extend the instruction for pp. 372–373.

Vocabulary

- **Selection Support:** Build Vocabulary, p. 106; Build Spelling Skills, p. 107
- **Vocabulary and Spelling Practice Book** (Use this booklet for skills enrichment)

Grammar

- **Selection Support:** Build Grammar Skills, p.108 ■
- **Writing and Grammar,** Copper Level, p. 454

- **Daily Language Practice Transparencies** ■

Writing

- **Writing and Grammar,** Copper Level, p. 102 ■
- **Writing Models and Graphic Organizers on Transparencies,** p. 81
- **Writing and Grammar iText CD-ROM**

■ **BLOCK SCHEDULING:** Resources marked with this symbol provide varied instruction during 90-minute blocks.

❸ Writing Lesson

Dinosaur Description

Although Jack Prelutsky includes factual information in his poem, his primary purpose is to entertain. Describe another dinosaur. Decide what your primary purpose is, then choose the form of writing that best suits your purpose.

Prewriting Do research to find facts that will help you achieve your purpose. For example, if your purpose is to entertain, look for unusual facts or details you can present in a humorous way. Use this chart to consider how to match your form to your purpose.

Model: Match Form to Purpose

Purpose	Possible Form
Entertain	poem, dialogue
Inform	essay, description, report
Explore ideas	imaginary journal entry, short story including dinosaurs

Drafting If you write a poem, dialogue, or imaginary journal entry, you can use contractions and informal language. If you write a story, relate events in chronological or time order. If you write an essay, report, or description, structure your writing with an introduction, a body, and a conclusion.

Revising Review your writing to make sure you have included descriptive details—no matter what your form or purpose. Circle words that you can make more exact.

WG *Prentice Hall Writing and Grammar Connection: Chapter 2*

❹ Extension Activities

Listening and Speaking With a small group, prepare a **choral reading** of one of the poems. Read the poem together, deciding what you want to emphasize and where you want to add special effects. Evaluate each other's reading on

- rise and fall of the voice.
- emphasis on rhyme and rhythm.
- adjustment of pace to punctuation.

Perform the poem for the class. **[Group Activity]**

Research and Technology Write a **research summary** of an encyclopedia article about Ankylosaurus. Include points that are mentioned in the article and in the poem.

Writing Write an **interpretation** in which you explain in your own words the meaning of one of the poems.

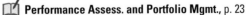

 ***Take It to the Net*** www.phschool.com

Go online for an additional research activity using the Internet.

ASSESSMENT RESOURCES

The following resources can be used to assess students' knowledge and skills.

Selection Assessment

- **Formal Assessment,** pp. 96–98
- **Open Book Test,** pp. 64–66
- **Got It! Assessment Videotapes,** Tape 3
- **Test Bank Software**

Take It to the Net

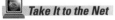

Visit www.phschool.com for self-tests and additional questions on the selections.

Listening and Speaking Rubric

- **Performance Assess. and Portfolio Mgmt.,** p. 23

Prentice Hall Assessment System

- **Workbook**
- **Transparencies**
- **Skill Book**
- **CD-ROM**

Lesson Support for p. 373

❸ Writing Lesson

- After students read the instruction on p. 373, talk with them about the elements that appear in each form of writing. You may wish to assign a particular form to students.
- Encourage students to research before they write. Ask the librarian at your school to offer suggestions for appropriate sources.
- As students begin writing, review the concept of sensory details. Request that students include at least two or three in their descriptions. Have them use the Sensory Language chart on p. 81 in **Writing Models and Graphic Organizers on Transparencies.**

❹ Listening and Speaking

- After students read the instruction, explain that choral reading is more than the simple act of reading aloud together. Tell students that having a different number of people reciting lines from the poem will have different effects on the listeners. Explain that the challenge of choral reading is finding the right mixture and balance of voices for each line or thought in the poem.
- As students prepare their readings, suggest that they copy the poem on a separate sheet of paper so that they have room between the lines to take notes and make comments.
- Allow students to use notes as they perform but challenge them to be familiar with the material.
- Have students use the Understanding, Tone, Mood, and Emotion rubric on p. 23 in **Performance Assessment and Portfolio Management.**

CUSTOMIZE INSTRUCTION For Universal Access

To address different learning styles, use the activities suggested in the **Extension Activities** booklet, p. 22.

- For Visual/Spatial and Mathematical/Logical Learners, use Activity 5.
- For Visual/Spatial and Interpersonal Learners, use Activity 6.
- For Intrapersonal, Verbal/Linguistic, and Visual/Spatial Learners, use Activity 7.

Lesson Objectives

1. To use structural features of Web sites to gather information
2. To understand the purpose of the features of a Web site
3. To read a Web site

About Web Sites

- Before students read "About Web Sites," invite them to name some of their favorite Web sites. Then, ask students what they already know about the Internet and how Web sites work. Write students' responses on the board or on an overhead transparency. Make a note if any responses contradict one another.
- Next, have students read "About Web Sites." Then, have them explain the difference between a Web site and a Web page. **Answer:** A Web site is a location on the Internet that is made up of many Web pages. A Web page is one screen or page on a Web site.

Reading Strategy

Using Structural Features of Web Sites

- Have students read the information about the Reading Strategy.
- Then, review the definitions of Web-site features that appear in the chart. Ask students whether these terms are familiar to them. Students may say that they knew how the features worked but did not know what the features were called.
- If you have access to the Internet in your classroom, pull up an appropriate Web site, and ask students to identify the features that are described in the chart.

READING INFORMATIONAL MATERIALS

Web Sites and Web Pages

About Web Sites

Web sites are specific locations on the Internet. If you think of the Internet as a giant library, Web sites are individual books within that library. As you explore a Web site on a computer, what you see on the screen is a part of the site called a Web page. A Web site can have many Web pages, just as a book has many pages. You can move from one Web page to another easily (or from one part of a long Web page to another) by using the mouse to click on a picture, a "button," or a highlighted or underlined word or phrase, called a *link*.

Reading Strategy

Using Structural Features of Web Sites

Use the special features of Web sites to move quickly around the site and find the information you need. Web sites and Web pages have some of the same structural features as textbooks and magazines, such as headings and graphics, but they have some special features unique to electronic texts as well. Learn to navigate, or find your way from place to place, in a Web site by using these special features. The features will make your searches for information more efficient by getting you to the right place in the shortest amount of time.

The chart shows some of the special features of Web sites and Web pages.

Web Site Features	
Link	A connection to another spot on the same Web page or to a different Web page or Web site. A link can be underlined or highlighted text, or an image or photograph. Links are what make the Web a "web."
Icon	An image or small drawing that may appear by itself or with accompanying text. Icons are often links as well.
Graphics	Pictures, maps, tables, and other graphic sources are often featured on a Web site. These graphics are often sources of information in themselves, but they may also be links to other Web pages.

Use bookmarks to "save" useful Web sites so that you can quickly return to them when you need to verify or find additional information. Most Web browsers—the software that allows you to get to the material on the Web—have a "bookmark" or "favorites" feature that creates an easy-to-access list of your favorite sites.

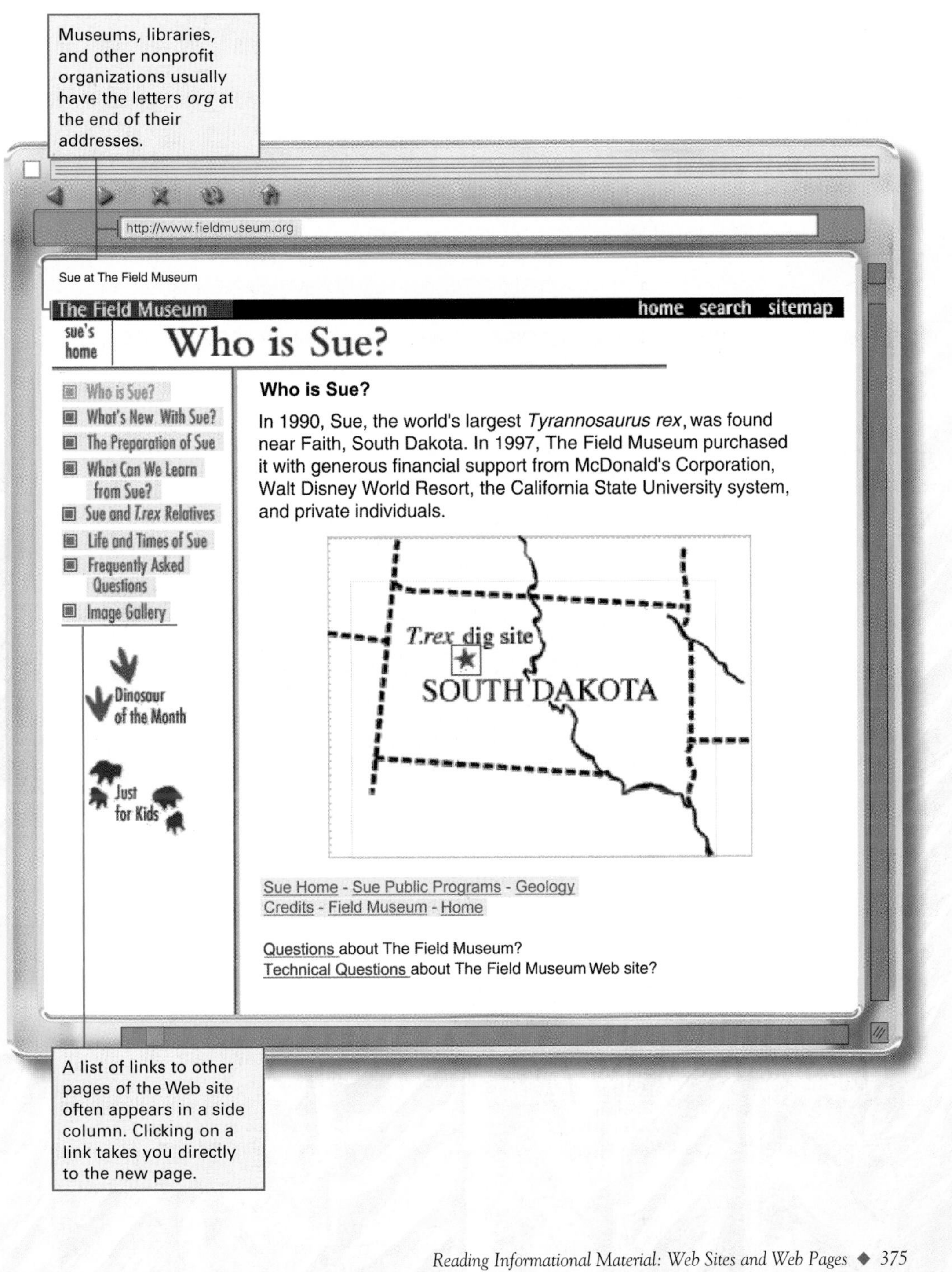

Who is Sue?

- Introduce the Web site that appears on pp. 375–376 by explaining that it is devoted to the story of the largest *Tyrannosaurus Rex* fossil in the world, which was discovered in South Dakota in 1990.
- Have students read the Web site and the notes that identify the elements of the site.
- If you have access to the Internet in your classroom, access an appropriate museum Web site. Point out the features that are discussed in the margin notes on p. 375.
- As you discuss each feature of the Web site, remind students that every Web site and Web page is arranged in a slightly different way and with different graphics and fonts. Ask students to think about why the person who designed this site made the choices that he or she did.
- Ask students whether they think the page has too much, too little, or just enough information. Do they find that there are too many items on the bulleted list? Do they find the graphics helpful or distracting? **Possible response:** Students may suggest that the site has a good mixture of text, colorful graphics, and links.

CUSTOMIZE INSTRUCTION FOR UNIVERSAL ACCESS

For Less Proficient Readers	For Gifted/Talented Students
Ask students to record a journal entry in "real-time" as they look at the Web site shown on pp. 375–376. Have them take notes about how they look at a Web page. For example, students may write a chronology like this: "First, I look at the graphics and try to figure out what is going on. Then, I look at the links," and so on. Then, ask students to talk about how they look at the sites and to compare their approaches. Talk as a class about the most logical way to look for information on a Web site.	Ask students to write a short essay about how they would create a Web site and how they would decide which features to include in it. Encourage students to write about the process of choosing a topic, selecting images, writing text, and programming the page. Then, have students compare their approaches in small groups. One student in the group should serve as secretary to take notes about what students agree on and what new ideas are raised.

continued from p. 375

- Ask students to name organizations that usually use the letters *org* at the end of their Web addresses.
  Possible responses: Students should name museums, libraries, and other nonprofit organizations.
- Ask students to point out the elements of the two Web pages shown on pp. 375–376 that are the same.
  Answer: Students should notice that the links to other pages of the Web site (in the side column) and the links to frequently used places on the site (on the bottom of the page) stay the same.
- Challenge students to explain why the pages repeat this information.
  Answer: The links stay the same so that the person searching the page does not have to return to the home page in order to move around on the site. Because the same links appear on every Web page, the person searching can move anywhere on the site from any page.

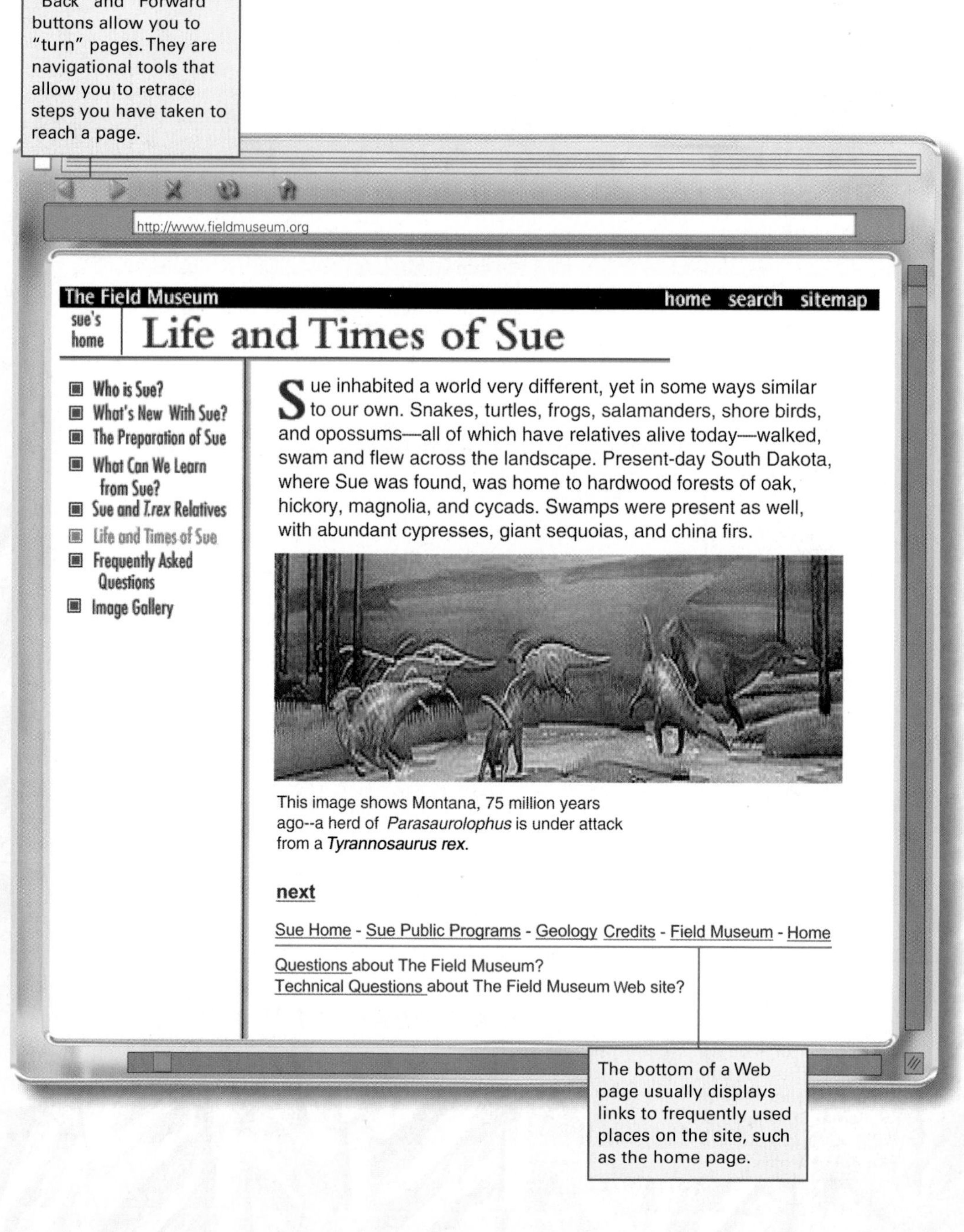
"Back" and "Forward" buttons allow you to "turn" pages. They are navigational tools that allow you to retrace steps you have taken to reach a page.
http://www.fieldmuseum.org
The Field Museum
home search sitemap
sue's home
Life and Times of Sue
Who is Sue?
What's New With Sue?
The Preparation of Sue
What Can We Learn from Sue?
Sue and T.rex Relatives
Life and Times of Sue
Frequently Asked Questions
Image Gallery
Sue inhabited a world very different, yet in some ways similar to our own. Snakes, turtles, frogs, salamanders, shore birds, and opossums—all of which have relatives alive today—walked, swam and flew across the landscape. Present-day South Dakota, where Sue was found, was home to hardwood forests of oak, hickory, magnolia, and cycads. Swamps were present as well, with abundant cypresses, giant sequoias, and china firs.
This image shows Montana, 75 million years ago--a herd of Parasaurolophus is under attack from a Tyrannosaurus rex.
next
Sue Home - Sue Public Programs - Geology Credits - Field Museum - Home
Questions about The Field Museum?
Technical Questions about The Field Museum Web site?
The bottom of a Web page usually displays links to frequently used places on the site, such as the home page.

CUSTOMIZE INSTRUCTION FOR UNIVERSAL ACCESS

For English Learners

Although many cultures have adopted English technological terms, some students may have trouble with the terms used to describe features of Web sites. Have students make a list of unfamiliar terms and then work with a computer-terminology dictionary or a proficient speaker to determine the terms' definitions. Challenge students to find and write down the terms that are used in their native languages. Students may make a three-column chart that shows the two terms as well as the literal definition of the non-English term. Have students share their charts with the class and talk as a class about how the English term and the non-English term convey the same idea.

Check Your Comprehension

1. Where was Sue found?
2. When was Sue found?
3. Describe the environment in which Sue lived.

Applying the Reading Strategy

Using Web Site Features

4. To what page can you link to learn about the most recent findings on Sue?
5. How do you know that the star on the map of South Dakota will take you to a new page or section of the site?

Activity

Web Site Evaluation

With a partner or group, find two different Web sites related to a topic you are currently studying in social studies or science, or find two Web sites on an author whose work you have read. Evaluate the two Web sites based on the following criteria

- reliability of source
- amount of information
- navigability (how easy it is to find your way around)
- use of graphics

Give each Web site a rating in each category. Then, give each Web site an overall rating. Explain your ratings to the class.

Comparing Informational Materials

Web Sites and Encyclopedias

Compare the structural features of Web sites and pages to the structural features of an encyclopedia article. In an encyclopedia, find an article on a topic of interest. Find a Web site on the same or a very similar topic. Make a chart like the one shown. In each category, write brief notes that show how the encyclopedia and the Web site are similar and different.

Feature	Web Site	Encyclopedia Article
Links	10 hot links	5 cross references to other articles
Headings		
Bullets, Numerals, and Other Organizing Elements		
Icons		
Graphics		

Answers for p. 377

Check Your Comprehension

1. Sue was found near Faith, South Dakota.
2. Sue was found in 1990.
3. Sue lived in a land of hardwood forests and swamps, cypresses, sequoias, and firs. She lived among other animals that walked, swam, and flew across the land.

Apply the Reading Strategy

4. The What's New With Sue? page gives information about the most recent findings on Sue.
5. You know that the star will take you to a new page or section of the site because it is highlighted.

Activity

You may wish to search the Internet yourself in order to identify appropriate Web sites and then ask students to limit their searches to these sites. Review the criteria listed on p. 377 with students so they understand what they are measuring the Web sites against. Once students have evaluated two sites based on the criteria, have them give each site a rating in each category. Finally, have students share their findings with the class.

Comparing Informational Materials

Web Sites and Encyclopedias: Again, you may wish to limit students' searches. Or, you may photocopy an encyclopedia article on the same topic as the Web sites you had students evaluate in the activity on p. 377. As a class, discuss the main differences between a Web page and an encyclopedia article. Then, ask students which medium they prefer. Finally, talk with students about the benefits of both sources.

from Exploring the Titanic

Lesson Objectives

1. **To analyze and respond to literary elements**
   - Literary Analysis: Suspense
   - Connecting Literary Elements: Atmosphere
2. **To read, comprehend, analyze, and critique nonfiction**
   - Reading Strategy: Distinguishing Between Fact and Opinion
   - Reading Check Questions
   - Review and Assess Questions
   - Assessment Practice (ATE)
3. **To develop word analysis skills, fluency, and systematic vocabulary**
   - Vocabulary Development Lesson: Concept Development: Compound Adjectives
4. **To understand and apply written and oral language conventions**
   - Spelling Strategy
   - Grammar Lesson: Types of Sentences
5. **To understand and apply appropriate writing and research strategies**
   - Writing Lesson: Investigative Report
   - Extension Activity: Create a Timeline
6. **To understand and apply listening and speaking strategies**
   - Extension Activity: Identify False and Misleading Information

STEP-BY-STEP TEACHING GUIDE	PACING GUIDE
PRETEACH	
Motivate Students and Provide Background	
Use the Motivation activity (ATE p. 378)	5 min.
Read and discuss the Preview material and Background information (SE/ATE p. 378) [A]	10 min.
Introduce the Concepts	
Introduce the Literary Analysis and Reading Strategy (SE/ATE p. 379) [A]	25 min.
Pronounce the vocabulary words and read their definitions (SE p. 379)	5 min.
TEACH	
Monitor Comprehension	
Informally monitor comprehension by circulating while students read independently or in groups [A]	25–30 min.
Monitor students' comprehension with the Reading Check notes (SE/ATE pp. 381, 383, 385)	as students read
Develop vocabulary with Vocabulary notes (SE pp. 381, 385; ATE p. 384)	as students read
Develop Understanding	
Develop students' understanding of suspense with the Literary Analysis annotations (SE pp. 382, 385; ATE pp. 381, 382, 383, 385) [A]	5 min.
Develop students' ability to distinguish between fact and opinion with the Reading Strategy annotations (SE p. 385; ATE pp. 384, 385)	5 min.
ASSESS	
Assess Mastery	
Assess students' mastery of the Reading Strategy and Literary Analysis by having them answer the Review and Assess questions (SE/ATE p. 386)	25 min.
Use one or more of the print and media Assessment Resources (ATE p. 389) [A]	up to 45 min.
EXTEND	
Apply Understanding	
Have students complete the Vocabulary Development Lesson and the Grammar Lesson (SE p. 388) [A]	20 min.
Apply students' ability to write an investigative report using the Writing Lesson (SE/ATE p. 389) [A]	45 min.
Apply students' understanding using one or more of the Extension Activities (SE p. 389)	20–90 min.

ACCELERATED INSTRUCTION:
Use the strategies and activities identified with an [A].

UNIVERSAL ACCESS
● = Below Level Students
▲ = On-Level Students
■ = Above Level Students

Time and Resource Manager

Reading Level: Average
Average Number of Instructional Days: 4

RESOURCES		
PRINT	**TRANSPARENCIES**	**TECHNOLOGY**
• **Beyond Literature,** Cross-Curricular Connection: Science, p. 23 ▲ ■		• **Interest Grabber Videotapes,** Tape 3 ● ▲ ■
• **Selection Support Workbook:** ● ▲ ■ Literary Analysis, p. 115 Reading Strategy, p. 114 Build Vocabulary, p. 111	• **Literary Analysis and Reading Transparencies,** pp. 45 and 46 ● ▲ ■	
• **Adapted Reader's Companion** ● • **Reader's Companion** ●		• **Listening to Literature** ● ▲ ■ Audiocassettes, Side 14 Audio CDs, CD 6
• **English Learner's Companion** ● ▲ • **Literary Analysis for Enrichment** ■		
• **Formal Assessment:** Selection Test, pp. 99–101 ● ▲ ■ • **Open Book Test,** pp. 67–69 ● ▲ ■ • **Performance Assessment and Portfolio Management,** pp. 14, 22 ● ▲ ■ • Prentice Hall Assessment System ● ▲ ■	• Prentice Hall Assessment System ● ▲ ■ Skills Practice Answers and Explanations on Transparencies	• **Test Bank Software** ● ▲ ■ • **Got It! Assessment Videotapes,** Tape 3 ● ▲
• **Selection Support Workbook:** ● ▲ ■ Build Spelling Skills, p. 112 Build Grammar Skills, p. 113 • **Writing and Grammar,** Copper Level ● ▲ ■ • **Extension Activities,** p. 23 ● ▲ ■	• **Daily Language Practice Transparencies** ● ▲ • **Writing Models and Graphic Organizers on Transparencies** ● ▲ ■	• **Writing and Grammar iText CD-ROM** ● ▲ ■ ***Take It to the Net*** www.phschool.com

BLOCK SCHEDULING: Use one 90-minute class period to preteach the selection and have students read it. Use a second 90-minute class period to assess students' mastery of skills and have them complete one of the Extension Activities.

PRETEACH

Step-by-Step Teaching Guide for pp. 378–379

Motivation

Ask students if they have ever seen the same suspenseful movie more than once. Ask them why they have watched it again, knowing what will happen. Elicit from students that even though they know what is coming, the sense of suspense still keeps them interested. Tell students that this selection is about the ship *Titanic*. Even though most people know that the ship hit an iceberg and sank, the suspenseful story of its voyage continues to hold people's interest.

Interest Grabber Video

As an alternative, play "The *Titanic*" on Tape 3 to engage student interest.

❶ Background

Science

The wreckage of the *Titanic* fascinates many. Robert D. Ballard's intense curiosity about what lay under the water led him to develop a special camera called ANGUS. This camera could stay on the ocean floor up to fourteen hours and take as many as 16,000 pictures in a single dive. Later, in the early 1980s, Ballard developed a remote-controlled robot that could move about underwater and take pictures on command.

Prepare to Read

❶ *from* Exploring the *Titanic*

 ***Take It to the Net***

Visit www.phschool.com for interactive activities and instruction related to "*from* Exploring the *Titanic*," including

- background
- graphic organizers
- literary elements
- reading strategies

Preview

Connecting to the Literature

This excerpt from *Exploring the* Titanic by Robert D. Ballard narrates the events that led to one of the most famous disasters of all time. The sinking of the *Titanic* has been covered in movies, books, and documentaries. Think about what you already know about the *Titanic* from these and other sources. Then, read the selection to see if what you know is accurate and complete.

Background

The *Titanic* was the largest and most luxurious ocean liner of its time. Huge watertight doors between sections and a construction believed to be "unbreakable" made the *Titanic* seem safer than other ships. According to the publicity, it was "unsinkable." Perhaps the owners of the *Titanic* did not supply enough lifeboats for all the passengers because they were sure lifeboats would never be needed.

TEACHING RESOURCES

The following resources can be used to enrich or extend the instruction for pp. 378–379.

Motivation

Interest Grabber Video, Tape 3

Background

Beyond Literature, p. 23

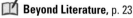

 ***Take It to the Net***

Visit www.phschool.com for Background and hotlinks for *Exploring the* Titanic.

Literary Analysis

Literary Analysis and Reading Transparencies, Suspense, p. 46

Reading

Selection Support: Reading Strategy, p. 114; Build Vocabulary, p. 111

Literary Analysis and Reading Transparencies, Distinguishing Between Fact and Opinion, p. 45

BLOCK SCHEDULING: Resources marked with this symbol provide varied instruction during 90-minute blocks.

❷ Literary Analysis

Suspense

Suspense is the feeling of anxious uncertainty about upcoming events. In literature, writers create suspense by keeping you wondering *what* will happen or *when* an event will happen.

When you read this excerpt from *Exploring the* Titanic, you know that the *Titanic* will hit an iceberg, but you do not know when. Ballard builds suspense by constantly reminding you that icebergs are out there and by keeping you wondering when the ship will hit one. Add details that increase the suspense to an organizer like the one shown.

Caronia reports iceberg

Captain is unconcerned

Connecting Literary Elements

Atmosphere, or mood, is the feeling created in a work or passage. One way writers create atmosphere is with images—words and phrases that appeal to one or more of the five senses. In the following example, the two details of *calm* and *cold* create an atmosphere of uncomfortable waiting, as if something is about to happen.

The sea was dead calm. The air bitterly cold.

As you read, keep these focus questions in mind.

1. Why does Ballard include descriptions of the calm, moonless night?
2. What other details contribute to the atmosphere?

❸ Reading Strategy

Distinguishing Between Fact and Opinion

Nonfiction works often include an author's opinions as well as facts.

- A **fact** is information that can be proved true or false: Harold Bride was only 22 years old.
- An **opinion** expresses a belief that can be supported, but not proved: He was quite pleased with himself . . .

Although the opinions Ballard includes cannot be proven, they are logical conclusions based on the facts. By including them, Ballard makes the characters and events more real to readers. As you read, distinguish between actual facts and the author's opinions.

Vocabulary Development

majestically (mə jesʹ tik lē) *adv.* grandly (p. 381)

collision (kə lizhʹ ən) *n.* coming together with a sudden violent force; a crash (p. 381)

novelty (nävʹ əl tē) *n.* something new or unusual (p. 381)

watertight *adj.* put together so that no water can get through (p. 385)

CUSTOMIZE INSTRUCTION FOR UNIVERSAL ACCESS

For Special Needs Students	For Less Proficient Readers	For English Learners
Have students read the adapted version of the excerpt from the adapted version of *Exploring the* Titanic in the **Adapted Reader's Companion.** This version provides basic-level instruction in an interactive format with questions and write-on lines. Completing the adapted version will prepare students to read the selection in the Student Edition.	Have students read the excerpt from *Exploring the* Titanic in the **Reader's Companion.** This version provides basic-level instruction in an interactive format with questions and write-on lines. After students finish the selection in the Reader's Companion, have them complete the questions and activities in the Student Edition.	Have students read and complete the adapted version of the excerpt from the adapted version of *Exploring the* Titanic in the **English Learner's Companion.** This version provides basic-level instruction in an interactive format with questions and write-on lines that will prepare students to read the selection in the Student Edition.

❷ Literary Analysis

Suspense

- Before students read the instruction on p. 379, ask them to talk about what they feel or think when they watch a scary movie or read a mystery.
- Then, read aloud the section on suspense. Demonstrate how to use the graphic organizer by filling in information based on students' experiences with suspenseful movies or books.
- Ask a volunteer to read aloud the Connecting Literary Elements instruction. Then, ask students to reflect on their experiences as readers or viewers to decide if certain kinds of atmosphere are inherently more suspenseful than others.
- Use the Suspense transparency on p. 46 in **Literary Analysis and Reading Transparencies** to help students with the concept of suspense.

❸ Reading Strategy

Distinguishing Between Fact and Opinion

- Before students read, ask them for some examples of facts and opinions. Write their responses on the board. Then, ask students to read the instruction on p. 379.
- Students should be made aware that some written works include both facts and opinions. They should be careful not to accept opinions as if they were facts.
- Ask students to use their new understanding of fact and opinion to decide which of the responses you wrote on the board are facts and which are opinions.

Vocabulary Development

- Review the words and definitions on the vocabulary list.
- Explain that *majestically* means "grandly" and ask students to hypothesize about the word's origins.
  Possible response: *Majestically* is related to *majesty,* a word used to describe royalty or grandeur.

 ***E-Teach***

Visit E-Teach at www.phschool.com for teachers' essays on how to teach, with questions and answers.

TEACH

Step-by-Step Teaching Guide for pp. 380–386

CUSTOMIZE INSTRUCTION
For Musical/Rhythmic Learners

Invite students to think of musical compositions that would make an appropriate soundtrack for the reading selection. If possible, ask students to find music to bring in and play for the class. Students should be able to explain their choices of music.

❶ About the Selection

In this excerpt from *Exploring the* Titanic, the author gives a suspenseful narrative of the last hours of the *Titanic.* Using historical records and first-person accounts, the author skillfully interweaves the stories of passengers and crew, keeping his readers in suspense, even though they know the tragic fate of the *Titanic.*

❶ from Exploring the TITANIC

Robert D. Ballard

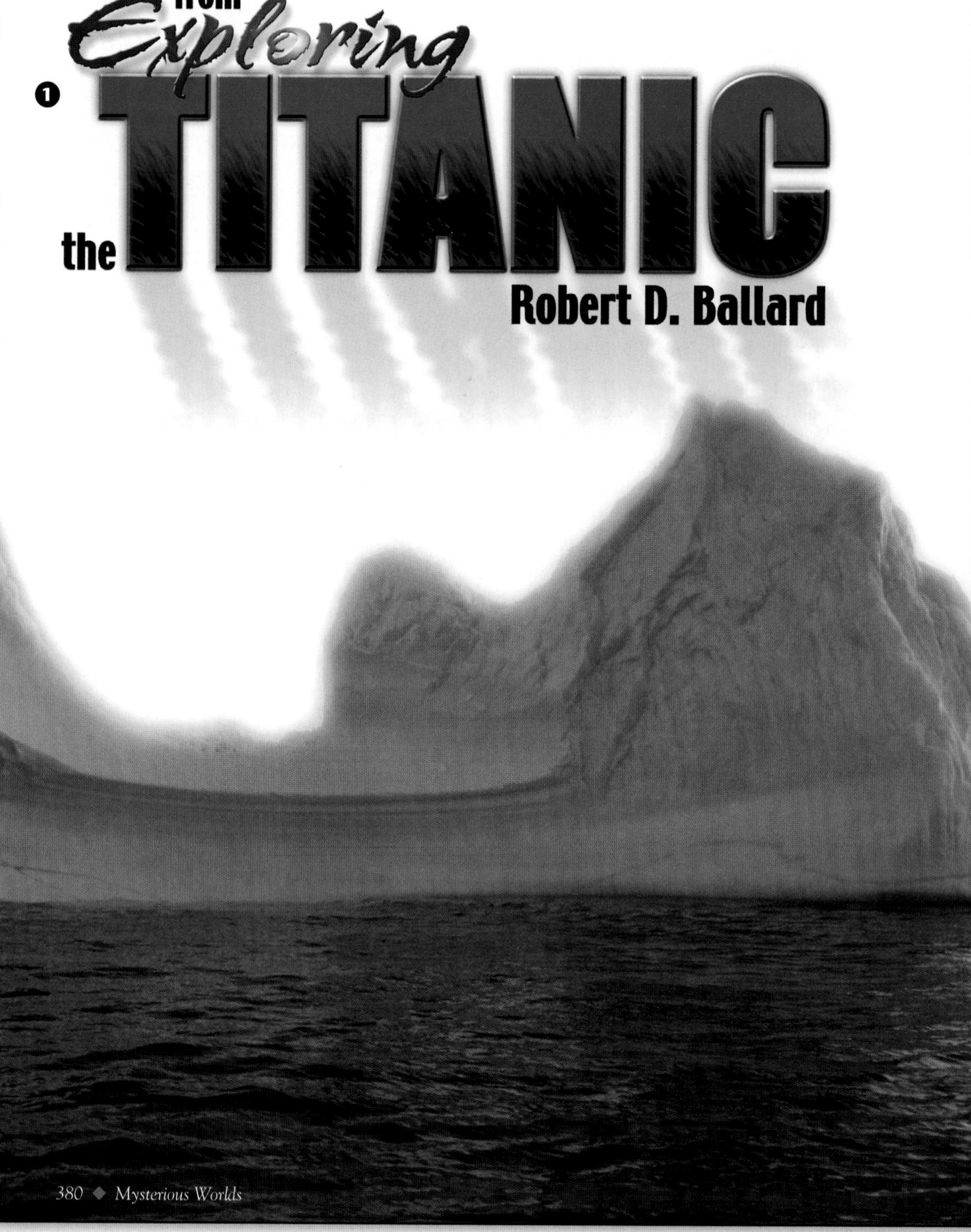

TEACHING RESOURCES

The following resources can be used to enrich or extend the instruction for pp. 380–386.

Literary Analysis

- **Selection Support:** Literary Analysis, p. 115
- **Literary Analysis for Enrichment**
- **Writing Models and Graphic Organizers on Transparencies,** p. 69

Reading

- **Reader's Companion**
- **Adapted Reader's Companion**
- **English Learner's Companion**
- **Listening to Literature Audiocassettes,** Side 14 ■
- **Listening to Literature Audio CDs,** CD 6 ■

■ **BLOCK SCHEDULING:** Resources marked with this symbol provide varied instruction during 90-minute blocks.

At noon on Wednesday, April 10, the *Titanic* cast off. The whistles on her huge funnels were the biggest ever made. As she began her journey to the sea, they were heard for miles around.

2 Moving majestically down the River Test, and watched by a crowd that had turned out for the occasion, the *Titanic* slowly passed two ships tied up to a dock. All of a sudden, the mooring ropes holding the passenger liner *New York* snapped with a series of sharp cracks like fireworks going off. The enormous pull created by the *Titanic* moving past her had broken the *New York*'s ropes and was now drawing her stern toward the *Titanic.* Jack Thayer watched in horror as the two ships came closer and closer. "It looked as though there surely would be a collision," he later wrote. "Her stern could not have been more than a yard or two from our side. It almost hit us." At the last moment, some quick action by Captain Smith and a tugboat captain nearby allowed the *Titanic* to slide past with only inches to spare.

It was not a good sign. Did it mean that the *Titanic* might be too big a ship to handle safely? Those who knew about the sea thought that such a close call at the beginning of a maiden voyage was a very bad omen.

Jack Phillips, the first wireless operator on the *Titanic,* quickly jotted down the message coming in over his headphones. "It's another iceberg warning," he said wearily to his young assistant, Harold Bride. "You'd better take it up to the bridge." Both men had been at work for hours in the *Titanic*'s radio room trying to get caught up in sending out a large number of personal messages. In 1912, passengers on ocean liners thought it was a real novelty to send postcard-style messages to friends at home from the middle of the Atlantic.

Bride picked up the iceberg message and stepped out onto the boat deck. It was a sunny but cold Sunday morning, the fourth day of the *Titanic*'s maiden voyage. The ship was steaming at full speed across a calm sea. Harold Bride was quite pleased with himself at having landed a job on such a magnificent new ship. After all, he was only twenty-two years old and had just nine months' experience at operating a "wireless set," as a ship's radio was then called. As he entered the bridge area, he could see one of the crewmen standing behind the ship's wheel steering her course toward New York.

Captain Smith was on duty in the bridge, so Bride handed the message to him. "It's from the *Caronia,* sir. She's reporting icebergs

majestically (mə jes′ tik lē) *adv.* grandly

collision (kə lizh′ ən) *n.* coming together with a sudden violent force; a crash

novelty (näv′ əl tē) *n.* something new or unusual

3 **Reading Check**

What happens to the *Titanic* at the beginning of her maiden voyage?

4 **Critical Viewing** Why might an iceberg like this one be difficult to spot from far away? **[Analyze]**

2 Literary Analysis

Suspense

- After students read the bracketed passage, ask them to locate the language that conveys suspense.
  Answer: The writer conveys suspense by using words and phrases that suggest sudden change and fear, such as "all of a sudden," "watched in horror," and "only inches to spare."
- Then, ask students why they think the author included the account of the incident that almost resulted in a collision.
  Possible response: Students may say that the incident prepares the reader for what will happen later.

Monitor Progress Ask students how the incident adds to the suspense of the selection.
Answer: It builds suspense by making the reader think about the collision that is coming.

Reteach If students have trouble with the concept of suspense, try the following activity. Retell a short but suspenseful story backwards, from the ending to the beginning. Then, ask students if they were interested in the story. Explain that knowing the ending often makes a story less interesting. Stories such as the one of the sinking of the *Titanic* are still interesting even though the ending is known, in part because of its horrifying subject matter.

3 Reading Check

Answer: The Titanic nearly collides with another ship at the beginning of its first voyage.

4 Critical Viewing

Answer: The iceberg is a bluish color that blends in with the water and the sky.

CUSTOMIZE INSTRUCTION FOR UNIVERSAL ACCESS

For Special Needs Students	For Gifted/Talented Students
Students may need to be reminded that the selection is nonfiction, not a fictional story. Help them understand this distinction by asking them to list the facts mentioned by the author. After students create their lists, they should test the items on it by asking the following question about each one: "Can this fact be confirmed by another person or source?" Remind students that the answer to the question will be *yes* if the item is a fact.	Ask students to compare the factual information provided in the selection with information from other stories or films they have seen that involve the *Titanic.* Students should work on the assumption that the facts as stated by Ballard are true. How do the other stories or films stand up to these facts? Have students write a short comparison-and-contrast paper, pointing to how well or how badly other authors or filmmakers have used the facts about the sinking of the ship.

5 Literary Analysis

Suspense

- Have a volunteer read the bracketed passage. Then, ask students the Literary Analysis question on p. 382: How does the question about an "unsinkable ship" increase suspense?
  Answer: Because it is a question, the reader has to think about a possible answer, which leads the reader to wonder whether the ship really could be facing danger from the ice.
- Then, ask students to think about why the sentence is a question instead of a statement.
- Explain that if the sentence were declarative, it would sound like a statement of fact; however, because the thought could not be confirmed by another source, the author could not treat the idea as a statement. The question is not in quotation marks, even though it is clearly supposed to be the thought of Harold Bride.

6 Critical Thinking

Compare and Contrast

- Have students identify the first-class, second-class, and third-class areas on the cutaway illustration of the ship.
- Then, ask students to explain how the three areas compare in size.
  Answer: First class takes up most of the space on the ship; second class and third class each take up about one quarter of the area of first class.
- Finally, ask students to draw conclusions based on their analysis of the distribution and location of the different classes.
  Answer: Students should understand that first-class passengers were clearly the most important on the ship.

and pack ice ahead." The captain thanked him, read the message, and then posted it on the bulletin board for other officers on watch to read. On his way back to the radio room, Bride thought the captain had seemed quite unconcerned by the message. But then again, he had been told that it was not unusual to have ice floating in the sea lanes during an April crossing. 5 Besides, what danger could a few pieces of ice present to an unsinkable ship?

Elsewhere on board, passengers relaxed on deck chairs, reading or taking naps. Some played cards, some wrote letters, while

Literary Analysis
Suspense How does the question about an "unsinkable ship" increase suspense?

The Grand Staircase was one of the most elegant and extraordinary features of *Titanic*'s interior design.

In luxurious rooms such as this, first-class passengers read, wrote letters, socialized.

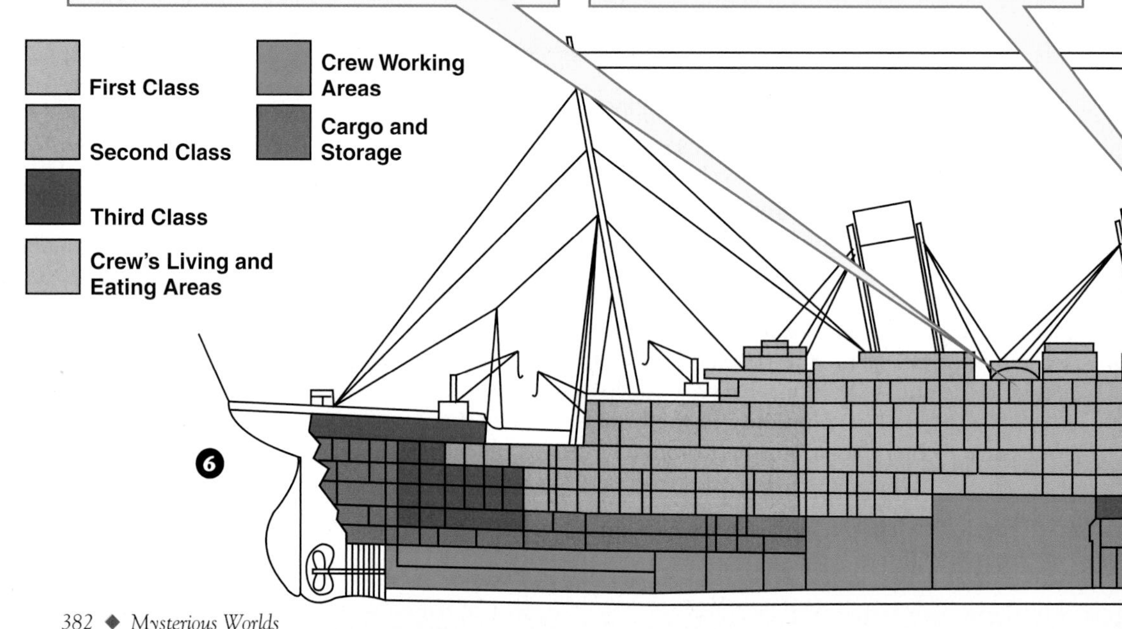

ENRICHMENT: Social Studies Connection

Iceberg Alley

Icebergs found in the North Atlantic, like the one that the *Titanic* struck, originate in Greenland, the large island that lies near the Arctic Circle between northern Europe and the northeast territories of Canada. Most of Greenland is covered with an enormous ice sheet, which is an average of 5,000 feet thick. Pieces of this ice sheet extend out into the sea and sometimes crack and break off, forming icebergs. The icebergs that reach the North Atlantic usually float across Baffin Bay to Labrador, where currents carry them into the Atlantic Ocean. There they melt in the sun and warmer water. Icebergs usually make it no farther south than about 400 miles south of Newfoundland. Most icebergs reach the North Atlantic during April (the month that the *Titanic* tragedy occurred), May, and June. Ships sailing across the Atlantic during those months usually travel farther south to avoid the danger of icebergs.

others chatted with friends. As it was Sunday, church services had been held in the morning, the first-class service led by Captain Smith. Jack Thayer spent most of the day walking about the decks getting some fresh air with his parents.

7 Two more ice warnings were received from nearby ships around lunch time. In the chaos of the radio room, Harold Bride only had time to take one of them to the bridge. The rest of the day passed quietly. Then, in the late afternoon, the temperature began to drop rapidly. Darkness approached as the bugle call announced dinner.

8 **Reading Check**

What message does Bride give to the captain?

9

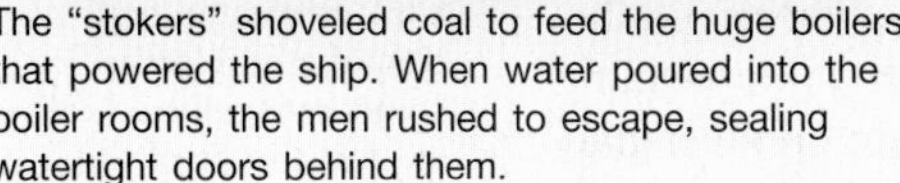

The "stokers" shoveled coal to feed the huge boilers that powered the ship. When water poured into the boiler rooms, the men rushed to escape, sealing watertight doors behind them.

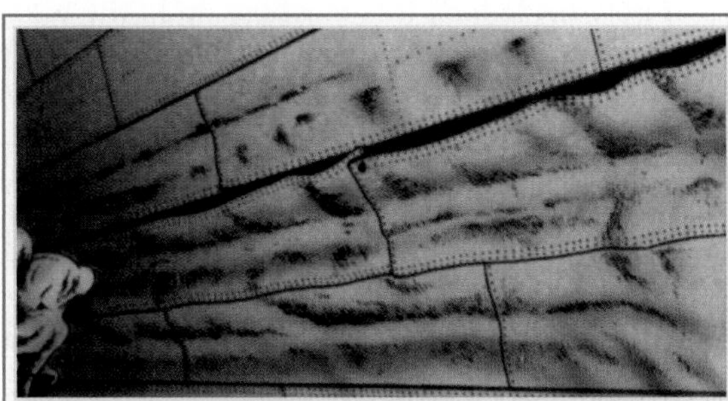

The pressure of the iceberg scraping the side of *Titanic*'s hull caused the plates to buckle, allowing huge amounts of water to flow into the ship.

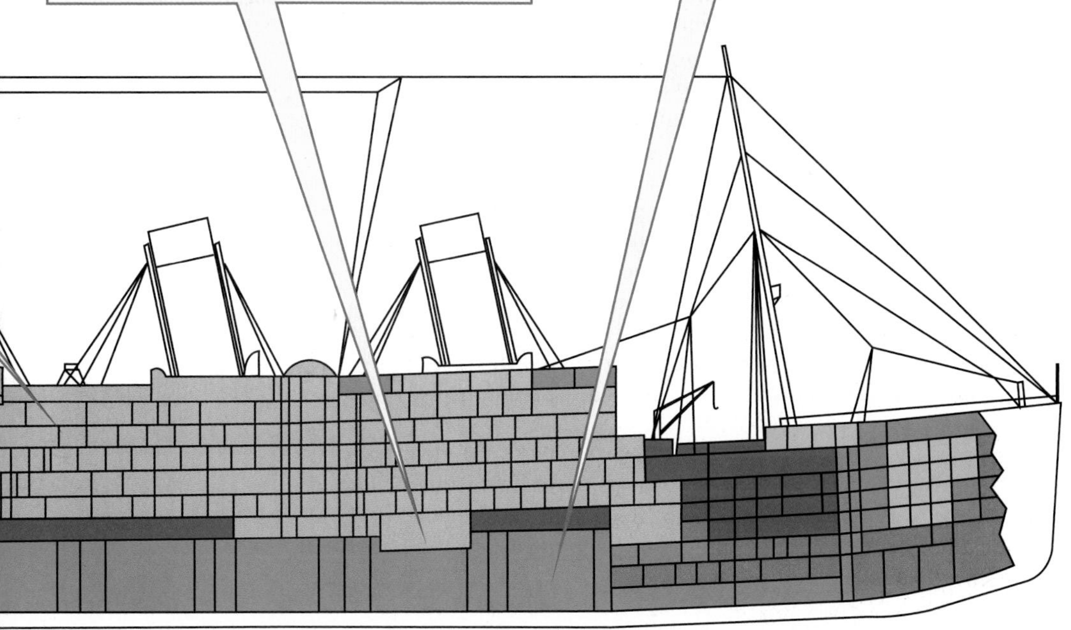

7 Literary Analysis

Suspense

- Refer students to the bracketed passage on p. 383. Ask students to identify at least three details in this paragraph that help build suspense. As a hint, tell students that two of the details are related to atmosphere.

  Answer: Students should identify the two additional ice warnings, the sudden drop in temperature, and the approach of darkness.

8 Reading Check

Answer: Bride gives the captain one of the two messages that warn of ice in nearby waters.

9 Background

Technology

Early shipboard radios, like those used on the *Titanic,* did not transmit voice sounds. The signal was not strong enough. Two radio operators could not have a conversation, such as happens today between ham radio operators. Instead, messages were sent in Morse Code, which required only long and short beeps, but this method was time-consuming. The *Titanic's* radio operators were so busy because they had to translate all of the outgoing messages from the passengers into code. Incoming messages had to be decoded as well.

CUSTOMIZE INSTRUCTION FOR UNIVERSAL ACCESS

For Gifted/Talented Students

Challenge students to write journal entries in the voice of one of the people in Ballard's account. To do this, students will have to get an idea of the person's viewpoint. To help, have students fill in the following information:

- My name is ____________.
- I am on the *Titanic* because ____________.
- When the ship hit the iceberg, I ____________.

For Advanced Readers

Ballard presents information from journals and personal accounts of *Titanic* survivors. Because such sources tend to be subjective, Ballard needed to separate fact from opinion. Have students practice this skill by choosing a passage from a personal narrative and writing a factual account of the event it describes. Have students share their writings with the class.

the river. The piers would support the bridge like miniature stone islands.

From the forests of the south came huge logs that were as tough and heavy as iron. From the quarries of the west came large, heavy stones of granite. The workers braved the cold water to sink the logs in the muddy riverbed. Breaker had to change the teams of workers often. The cold numbed anyone who stayed too long in the river.

8 Once the logs had been pounded into the mud, he tried to set the stones on top of the logs. But the river did not want to be tamed. It bucked and fought like a herd of wild stallions. It crushed the piles of stones into pebbles. It dug up the logs and smashed them against the rocky sides until they were mounds of soggy toothpicks.

Over the next month, Breaker tried every trick he knew; and each time the river defeated him. With each new failure, Breaker suspected more and more that he had met his match. The river flowed hard and strong and fast like the lifeblood of the earth itself. Breaker might as well have tried to tame the mountains.

In desperation, he finally tried to build a dam to hold back the river while he constructed the biggest and strongest piers yet. As he was supervising the construction, an official came by from the emperor.

Reading Strategy
Determining Cause and Effect What is the effect of the river's wild rushing?

9 **Reading Check**
How does Breaker feel about building the bridge when he sees the river?

10 **◀Critical Viewing**
What details of this scene seem magical and mysterious? **[Analyze]**

8 Reading Strategy

Determining Cause and Effect

- Point out that one way to locate cause-and-effect relationships in a story is to look for the action. A character's actions will usually have consequences.
- Before asking the Reading Strategy question, remind students that the river might be considered a character in the story.
- Then, ask the Reading Strategy question on p. 395: What is the effect of the river's wild rushing? Answer: The river smashes the attempts to build a foundation for the bridge; the stones are smashed into small pebbles, and logs are dug up and shattered into tiny pieces.

9 Reading Check

Answer: Breaker thinks that it will be impossible to build a bridge across the river.

10 ▶Critical Viewing

Possible response: Students may point out the strangely shaped, dark-colored landscape, the deep cliff, and the animals grazing.

CUSTOMIZE INSTRUCTION FOR UNIVERSAL ACCESS

For Less Proficient Readers	For Gifted/Talented Students
Students may benefit from a discussion of the figurative language in the story. After defining the terms *personification* and *simile*, point out at least one example of each. On p. 394, point to the personification "it raced faster than a tiger" and the simile "boulders thrust up like fangs." Ask students to list in a two-column chart all the examples of personification and simile that they find in the story. After students read the story, review their charts and discuss the effectiveness of the figurative language.	Have students point out several examples of simile and personification in the story. Discuss with students the effect of such comparisons in the story. Students should notice that the figurative language makes the landscape seem alive and menacing, like a wild animal. Challenge students to write a brief description of a natural scene or landscape with which they are familiar. Students should use at least three examples of simile and personification. Invite them to read their descriptions to the class. Elicit responses from the class.

11 Reading Strategy

Determining Cause and Effect

- Ask students to think about the effect the emperor's power has on people.
- Then, ask the Reading Strategy question on p. 396: What feeling about the emperor causes the workers to drop to their knees here?
  Answer: The workers fall to their knees out of respect, honor, and probably fear when they see the emperor's letter.

12 Critical Thinking

Analyze

- Ask students why they think the emperor threatened such a severe punishment if Breaker failed in his task.
  Possible responses: Some students may respond that the emperor was simply unfair; some may say that the emperor wanted to frighten Breaker; others may say that the emperor needed to be harsh to keep his people obedient to him.
- Then, ask students to predict how this threat will affect how Breaker works.
  Answer: Some students may respond that the threat will make Breaker work harder because he wants to live; others may say that Breaker's work will suffer because the threat will make him nervous and distracted.

"This bridge has already cost a lot of money," he announced to the wrecker. "What do you have to show for it?"

Breaker pointed to the two piers.♦ They rose like twin towers toward the top of the gorge. "With a little luck, the emperor will have his bridge."

Suddenly, they heard a distant roar. The official looked up at the sky. "It sounds like thunder, but I don't see a cloud in the sky."

Breaker cupped his hands around his mouth to amplify his voice. "Get out," he shouted to his men. "Get out. The river must have broken our dam."

His men slipped and slid on the muddy riverbed, but they all managed to scramble out just as a wall of water rolled down the gorge. The river swept around the two piers, pulling and tugging at the stones.

Everyone held their breath. Slowly the two piers began to rock back and forth on their foundations until they toppled over with a crash into the river. Water splashed in huge sheets over everyone, and when the spray finally fell back into the river, not one sign of the piers remained.

11 "All this time and all this money, and you have nothing to show for it." The official took a soggy yellow envelope from his sleeve.

Breaker and the other workers recognized the imperial color of the emperor. They instantly dropped to their knees and bowed their heads.

12 Then, with difficulty, Breaker opened the damp envelope and unfolded the letter. "In one month," it said, "I will have a bridge or I will have your head." It was sealed in red ink with the official seal of the emperor.

Breaker returned the letter and bowed again. "I'll try," he promised.

"You will do more than try," the official snapped. "You will build that bridge for the emperor. Or the executioner will be sharpening his sword." And the official left.

Wet and cold and tired, Breaker made his way along a path toward the room he had taken in an inn. It was getting late, so the surrounding forest was black with shadows. As he walked, Breaker tried to come up with some kind of new scheme, but the dam had been his last resort. In a month's time, he would feel the "kiss" of the executioner's sword.

13 "Hee, hee, hee," an old man laughed in a creaky voice that

Literature in context

♦ *Piers and Bridges*

The **piers** of a bridge are the columns that support the bridge over the water. (The structure that supports the bridge where it touches land is an **abutment** or **anchorage**.) Most kinds of bridges require piers to keep them from collapsing. The Golden Gate Bridge, shown below, is one of the world's longest suspension bridges. Below the roadway it is supported by two piers. Above the piers rise the towers, which help to distribute the weight.

Golden Gate Bridge

Reading Strategy
Determining Cause and Effect What feeling about the emperor causes the workers to drop to their knees here?

executioner
(ek′ si kyo͞o′ shən ər) *n.* one who carries out a death penalty imposed by the courts or a ruler

CUSTOMIZE INSTRUCTION FOR UNIVERSAL ACCESS

For Advanced Readers

Suggest that students read additional works by Laurence Yep. Provide students with the titles listed in the Enrichment box, ATE p. 401. You might also use **Authors In Depth**, Copper Level, which contains the following selections:

- "The Old Jar" (fiction, p. 82)
- from "The Pearl Apartments" (nonfiction, p. 87)
- from "The Great Silkie" from "Sweetwater" (fiction, p. 92)
- from "Dragon's Gate" (fiction, p. 96)

After students have read these or other works by Yep, have them form discussion groups in which they compare and contrast the selections they have read. Then, have students write essays discussing how Yep's interest in other worlds is reflected in his work. Students might also include commentary on Yep's character traits as he presents them in his works.

sounded like feet on old, worn steps. "You never liked hats anyway. Now you'll have an excuse not to wear them."

13 Breaker turned and saw a crooked old man sitting by the side of the road. He was dressed in rags, and a gourd hung from a strap against his hip. One leg was shorter than the other.

"How did you know that, old man?" Breaker wondered.

"Hee, hee, hee. I know a lot of things: the softness of clouds underneath my feet, the sounds of souls inside bodies." And he shook his gourd so that it rattled as if there were beans inside. "It is the law of the universe that all things must change; and yet Nature hates change the most of all."

"The river certainly fits that description." Although he was exhausted and worried, Breaker squatted down beside the funny old man. "But you better get inside, old man. Night's coming on and it gets cold up in these mountains."

"Can't." The old man nodded to his broken crutch.

14 Breaker looked all around. It was growing dark, and his stomach was aching with hunger. But he couldn't leave the old man stranded in the mountains, so Breaker took out his knife. "If I make you a new crutch, can you reach your home?"

"If you make me a crutch, we'll all have what we want." It was getting so dim that Breaker could not be sure if the old man smiled.

Although it was hard to see, Breaker found a tall, straight sapling and tried to trim the branches from its sides; but being Breaker, he dropped his knife several times and lost it twice among the old leaves on the forest floor. He also cut each of his fingers. By the time he was ready to cut down the sapling, he couldn't see it. Of course, he cut his fingers even more. And just as he was trimming the last branch from the sapling, he cut the sapling right in two.

He tried to carve another sapling and broke that one. It was so dark by now that he could not see at all. He had to find the next sapling by feel. This time he managed to cut it down and began to trim it. But halfway through he dropped his knife and broke it. "He'll just have to take it as it is," Breaker said.

When he finally emerged from the forest, the moon had come out. Sucking on his cut fingers, Breaker presented the new crutch to the funny old man.

The old man looked at the branches that grew from the sides of his new crutch. "A little splintery."

Breaker angrily took his cut finger from his mouth. "Don't insult someone who's doing you a favor."

The crooked old man lifted his right arm with difficulty and managed to bring it behind his neck. "Keep that in mind yourself." He began to rub the back of his neck.

Literary Analysis
Character Traits What character trait shows in Breaker's concern for the old man?

15  **Reading Check**

What will happen to Breaker if he does not finish constructing the bridge by the end of the month?

13 Critical Thinking

Speculate

- Ask students who or what they think the old man might be.
  Answer: Students may respond that the old man could be a magical being or a god in disguise. Others may say that he is just a confused old man.
- As they read more about the old man, ask students to draw conclusions about his identity. Students should be able to defend their conclusions with evidence from the story. For example, they may point to how he suddenly appears in the story, keeps repeating unusual sayings, and has unusual strength.

14 Literary Analysis

Character Traits

- Ask students the Literary Analysis question on p. 397.
  Answer: Breaker is showing the character trait of kindness or concern for others.

Monitor Progress Take a moment to have students orally list all the character traits that Breaker has demonstrated so far. Then, ask them to sum up his character in a few words.
Possible answer: Students may suggest that Breaker is a determined, kind, lucky, and able man.

15 Reading Check

Answer: Breaker will be executed if he does not complete the bridge by the end of the month.

CUSTOMIZE INSTRUCTION FOR UNIVERSAL ACCESS

For Special Needs Students	For English Learners
Tell students that they will understand the characters better by role-playing conversations. Have students review the story and look for details that explain each character. Encourage students to jot the ideas on note cards, and tell them to use the notes on the cards as motivation for their characters. Then, as they get more comfortable role-playing their characters, they should role-play a scene for the class.	Help students understand the story's characters by having them act out a scene from the story. Arrange students in groups of four, assigning the roles of Breaker, the Emperor, the River, and the Old Man. Have students engage in conversations in character. Students may consult the story, but they should improvise as much as possible. After the conversations, have each student write a journal entry explaining what he or she learned about the characters.

16 Critical Thinking

Analyze

- Tell students that in retelling this folk tale, the author carefully develops Breaker's character to make him a sympathetic figure. His negative traits, such as his clumsiness, are balanced by positive ones, such as his kindness to the old man.
- Ask students whether Breaker is demonstrating a positive or negative trait in the bracketed paragraph.
  Answer: Students may say that Breaker is acting impatiently here, which is a negative trait. Others may say he is afraid, which is neither negative nor positive.

17 Literary Analysis

Character Traits and Theme

- Have students read the bracketed passage.
- Then, ask students the Literary Analysis question.
  Answer: The mysterious character seems to say that Breaker and the river are tied together by the same laws of nature.

18 Background

Culture

The old man in the story is one of the *Ba Xian*, the Chinese name of the eight immortal gods who are said to have been born as human beings, but who became immortal through the practice of Daoism (or Taoism). According to Chinese legend, the immortals live on a mythical island named Penglai Shan. The island is surrounded by water that will not support ships and that only immortals can cross. Each of the immortals has a unique character and a unique story.

Breaker thrust the crutch at the old man. "Here, old man. This is what you wanted."

But the old man kept rubbing the back of his neck. "Rivers are like people: Every now and then, they have to be reminded that change is the law that binds us all."

16 "It's late. I'm tired and hungry and I have to come up with a new plan. Here's your crutch." And Breaker laid the crutch down beside the old man.

But before Breaker could straighten, the old man's left hand shot out and caught hold of Breaker's wrist. The old man's grip was as strong as iron. "Even the least word from me will remind that river of the law."

Breaker tried to pull away, but as strong as he was, he could not break the old man's hold. "Let me go."

17 But the crooked old man lowered his right hand so that Breaker could see that he had rubbed some of the dirt and sweat from his skin. "We are all bound together," the old man murmured, "and by the same laws." He murmured that over and over until he was almost humming like a bee. At the same time, his fingers quickly rolled the dirt and sweat into two round little pellets.

Literary Analysis
Character Traits and Theme What do the words of this mysterious character seem to be telling Breaker?

Frightened, Breaker could only stare at the old man. "Ar-ar-are you some mountain spirit?"♦ he stammered.

The old man turned Breaker's palm upward and deposited the two little pellets on it. Then he closed Breaker's fingers over them. "Leave one of these at each spot where you want a pier. Be sure not to lose them."

"Yes, all right, of course," Breaker promised quickly.

The old man picked up the crutch and thrust himself up from the ground. "Then you'll have what you want too." And he hobbled away quickly.

Breaker kept hold of the pellets until he reached the inn. Once he was among the inn's bright lights and could smell a hot meal, he began to laugh at himself. "You've let the emperor's letter upset you so much that you let a harmless old man scare you."

Even so, Breaker didn't throw away the pellets but put them in a little pouch. And the next morning when he returned to the gorge, he took along the pouch.

The canyon widened at one point so that there was a small beach. Breaker kept his supplies of stone and logs there. Figuring that he had nothing to lose, Breaker walked down the steep path. Then he took the boat and rowed out onto the river.

As he sat in the bobbing boat, he thought of the funny old man again. "You and I," he said to the river, "are both part of the same scheme of things. And it's time you faced up to it."

CUSTOMIZE INSTRUCTION FOR UNIVERSAL ACCESS

For English Learners	For Advanced Readers
Invite students to retell or summarize folk tales or other stories from their original cultures that involve mysterious characters like the Old Man. Ask students to work together to identify the purposes of these characters. Students should realize that the characters tend to make things right in a story or help the main character achieve his or her goals. Based on this discussion, ask students to predict what will happen in "Breaker's Bridge."	Review with students the elements of folk and fairy tales—the hero's or heroine's nearly impossible quest, the evil king or queen, and the mysterious stranger who offers help. Ask each student to write a brief comparison of "Breaker's Bridge" and a favorite fairy or folk tale. Then, ask students to make predictions about the outcome of "Breaker's Bridge" based on these comparisons.

Although it was difficult to row at the same time, he got out the pouch with the two pellets. "I must be even crazier than that old man." He opened the pouch and shook one of the pellets into his hand.

When he was by the spot where the first pier should be, Breaker threw the pellet in. For a moment, nothing happened. There was only the sound of his oars slapping at the water.

And suddenly the surface began to boil. Frantically, he tried to row away, but the water began to whirl and whirl around in circles. Onshore, the workers shouted and ran to higher ground as waves splashed over the logs and stones.

From beneath the river came loud thumps and thuds and the grinding of stone on stone. A rock appeared above the surface. The water rose in another wave. On top of the wave another stone floated as if it were a block of wood. The river laid the first stone by the second.

Open-mouthed, Breaker watched the river lay stone after stone. The watery arms reached higher and higher until the first pier rose to the top of the gorge.

As the waters calmed, Breaker eagerly rowed the boat over to the second spot. At the same time that he tried to row enough to keep himself in the right place, Breaker reached for the pouch and opened it.

19 But in his hurry, his clumsy fingers crushed part of the pellet. He threw the remainder of the pellet into the water and then shook out the contents of the pouch. But this time, the river only swirled and rippled.

Breaker leaned over the side and peered below. He could just make out the pale, murky shape of a mound, but that was all. Even so, Breaker wasn't upset. His workers could easily build a second pier and meet the emperor's deadline.

So Breaker finished the bridge, and that summer the emperor reached his hunting palace with ease. When the emperor finished hunting and returned to his capital, he showered Breaker with gold and promised him all the work he could ever want.

However, winter brought deep snows once again to the mountains. That spring, when the snow thawed, the river grew strong and wild again. It roared down the gorge and smashed against the first pier. But the first pier was solid as a mountain.

Literature in context Cultural Connection

18 ♦ ***The Eight Immortals***
The old man in the story is one of the Eight Immortals, the Ba Xian of Chinese mythology. The Eight Immortals are symbols of good fortune. They are often featured in Chinese art and literature.

The Eight Immortals Crossing the Sea (detail), illustration from "Myths and Legends of China" by Edward T.C. Werner, pub. by George G. Harrap & Co., 1922, Private Collection

One of The Eight Immortals

Literary Analysis
Character Traits
How does Breaker's clumsiness affect what happens to the bridge?

20 **Reading Check**
What happens when Breaker throws the first pellet into the water?

19 Literary Analysis

Character Traits

- Ask students whether they were surprised to see Breaker's childhood trait of clumsiness appear again in the story.
  Answer: Some students may be surprised because the story made it sound as if he had outgrown that trait.
- Then, ask them the Literary Analysis question on p. 399.
  Answer: His clumsiness causes one pier of the bridge to form only partway, which means that it will not be as strong as the other pier.

Reteach If students have trouble identifying character traits, offer them a series of events organizer on p. 69 of **Writing Models and Graphic Organizers on Transparencies.** Have students fill the organizer with the events from the story in the order in which they occur. Then, under each event box, ask students to write one or two words to describe the character involved in the event. Finally, ask students to generate a statement about each of the characters from these descriptive words.

20 Reading Check

Answer: The first pellet forms into a pier for the bridge.

CUSTOMIZE INSTRUCTION FOR UNIVERSAL ACCESS

For English Learners	For Gifted/Talented Students
Once students have finished reading the story, ask them to compile a list of all of Breaker's character traits. Then, have each student work with a partner and, using a dictionary and thesaurus, generate a list of words that mean the exact opposite of the traits. Challenge each pair to use the antonyms in sentences and to share the words and their sentences with the class.	Invite students to consider Breaker's character traits and then to generate a list of antonyms from it. Challenge students to work in small groups to retell Breaker's story orally, this time giving Breaker and the other characters these opposite traits. Have students tell their stories to the class and then talk about the challenges of turning the story into its opposite.

ASSESS

Answers for p. 400

Review and Assess

1. Some students may say that the emperor is unfair in demanding that Breaker build the bridge or lose his head. Others may say that the emperor is generous to give Breaker such an opportunity to prove himself.
2. **(a)** The emperor wants Breaker because he has a reputation for building excellent bridges. **(b)** Breaker accepts the challenge because he has no other choice. **(c)** The advantages are that Breaker can meet a great challenge and receive gold for it. The disadvantages are that the task may be impossible, and if Breaker fails he will die.
3. **(a)** The old man laughs and makes a joke about Breaker's possible execution. **(b)** The old man grasps Breaker's arm in an iron grip and gives Breaker two magic pellets made of his sweat and dirt. **(c)** The pellets turn out to have magical powers; the old man appears suddenly at the emperor's court and even the emperor bows to him.
4. **(a)** Breaker builds a bridge that respects the power of nature. **(b)** They both have a respect for nature's power.
5. **(a)** Possible response: We all experience change. **(b)** Students will probably agree with the idea. **(c)** Students' examples should illustrate how life is always changing.

However, the second pier had not been built with magic. The river swept away the second pier as if it were nothing but twigs.

The bridge was repaired before the summer hunting, but the emperor angrily summoned Breaker to his hunting palace. "You were supposed to build a bridge for me," the emperor declared.

"Hee, hee, hee," laughed a creaky old voice. "He did, but you didn't say how long it was supposed to stay up."

Breaker turned around and saw it was the crooked old man. He was leaning on the crutch that Breaker had made for him. "How did you get here?" he asked the old man. But from the corner of his eye, he could see all the court officials kneeling down. And when Breaker looked back at the throne, he saw even the emperor kneeling.

"How can we serve you and the other eight immortals?" the emperor asked the crooked old man.

immortals (im môrt′ əlz) *n.* beings who live forever

"We are all bound by the same laws," the old man croaked again, and then vanished.

And then Breaker knew the old man for what he truly was—a saint and a powerful magician.

So the emperor spared Breaker and sent him to build other projects all over China. And the emperor never regretted that he had let Breaker keep his head. But every year, the river washed away part of the bridge and every year it was rebuilt. And so things change and yet do not change.

Review and Assess

Thinking About the Selection

1. **Respond:** Do you think the emperor was fair to Breaker? Explain.
2. (a) **Recall:** Why did the emperor want Breaker instead of other builders to build the bridge? (b) **Infer:** Why does Breaker accept the challenge? (c) **Assess:** What are the advantages and disadvantages of his situation?
3. (a) **Recall:** How does the crooked old man first appear to Breaker? (b) **Analyze:** What clues indicate that the old man is more than he seems? (c) **Support:** What events prove that the old man is more than he seems?
4. (a) **Recall:** What does Breaker accomplish? (b) **Synthesize:** What do you think Breaker and the old man have in common?
5. (a) **Interpret:** In your own words, explain the meaning of "change is the law that binds us all." (b) **Assess:** Do you agree or disagree with this idea? (c) **Support:** Give examples from life, movies, and literature that support your position.

Laurence Yep

(b. 1948)

Laurence Yep was born and raised in San Francisco, California. A third-generation Chinese American, he began writing in high school, selling his first story when he was just eighteen years old. Since then, he has written many books for young people and won numerous honors and awards. Much of Yep's subject matter comes from his interest in other worlds. His books of science fiction and fantasy tell of strange events in mysterious lands. He has also researched and written novels about the experiences of Chinese immigrants and their descendants.

ASSESSMENT PRACTICE: Reading Comprehension

Draw Conclusions **(For more practice, see Test Preparation Workbook, p. 35.)**

Many tests require students to draw conclusions. Use the following sample to help students practice this skill.

But Breaker was as clever as he was clumsy. When he grew up, he managed to outlive his nickname. He could design a bridge to cross any obstacle. No canyon was too wide. No river was too deep. Somehow the clever man always found a way to bridge them all.

It can be concluded from this passage that—

A Breaker grew into his nickname.
B Breaker's nickname suited him in youth.
C Breaker's nickname never suited him.
D Breaker changed his name when he grew up.

A, *C*, and *D* are not supported by the passage. Breaker outlived his nickname, so it probably suited him in his youth. *B* is correct.

Review and Assess

Literary Analysis

Character Traits

1. What is one **character trait** of the emperor? Give an example of an action that demonstrates this trait.
2. What action shows that one of the old man's character traits is mischievousness?

Connecting Literary Elements

3. What qualities are shown in Breaker's actions?
4. Complete the organizer to connect character traits to actions to the message of the work.

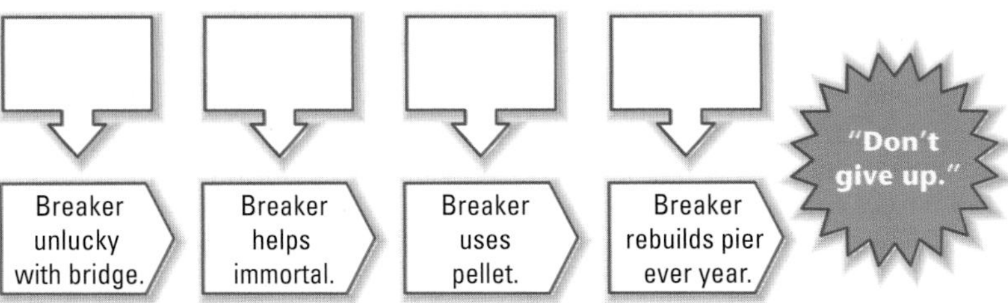

Breaker unlucky with bridge.
Breaker helps immortal.
Breaker uses pellet.
Breaker rebuilds pier ever year.
"Don't give up."

Reading Strategy

Determining Cause and Effect

5. What **effect** would take place if Breaker fails to build the bridge?
6. Copy the chart. Connect the **causes and effects** by drawing arrows between them. Do not connect events that simply follow each other.

1. Breaker tries to build bridge.	2. River washes out first bridge.	3. Breaker gets letter.	4. Breaker makes crutch for old man.	5. Old man gives Breaker pellets.

Extending Understanding

7. **Make a Judgment:** Did Breaker meet the emperor's demands? Explain.
8. **Math Connection:** In what way would a bridge builder use measurements of distance and weight?

Quick Review

Character traits are the qualities that determine a person's or character's personality and actions. To review character traits, see page 391.

Theme is the message in a literary work. To review theme, see page 391.

A **cause** is the reason something happens. An effect is the result.

 ***Take It to the Net***

www.phschool.com

Take the interactive self-test online to check your understanding of the selection.

Answers for p. 401

Review and Assess

1. Possible response: The emperor is self-centered. He demonstrates this trait by ordering Breaker to build the bridge or die.
2. The old man presents himself as weak and helpless but really has an iron grip. Also, the man appears where no one expects him, makes cryptic jokes, and disappears without answering questions.
3. Breaker demonstrates cleverness by being able to build bridges almost anywhere; he demonstrates kindness by making the old man a crutch.
4. Breaker's character traits are determination, kindness, belief, and consistency.
5. Breaker would be executed if he failed to build the bridge.
6. 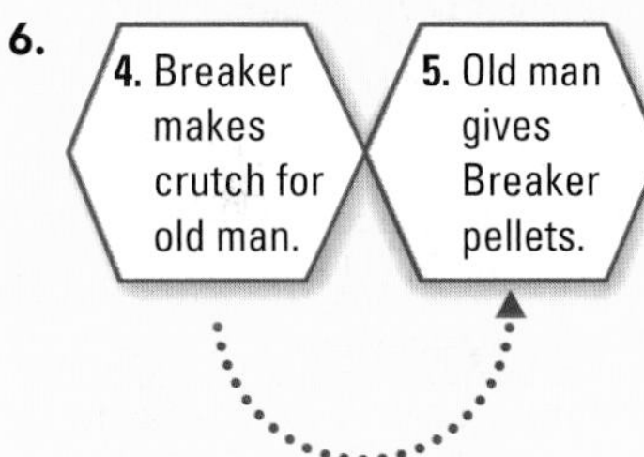

4. Breaker makes crutch for old man.
5. Old man gives Breaker pellets.

7. Breaker met the emperor's demands when he built the bridge. Even though Breaker had to repair the bridge annually, the emperor had a bridge to help him reach his hunting place.
8. A builder would use distance measurements to determine the length, width, and height of the bridge and would use weight measurements to determine the load limit, or how much weight the bridge could hold.

 **ENRICHMENT: Further Reading**

Other Works by Laurence Yep

The Case of the Goblin Pearls

Dragonwings

Child of the Owl

 ***Take It to the Net***

Visit www.phschool.com for more information on Laurence Yep.

EXTEND

Answers for p. 402

❶ Vocabulary Development

Word Analysis

1. executioner
2. executive
3. execute
4. execution

Spelling Strategy

1. belief
2. deceive
3. weight

Concept Development: Analogies

1. executioner
2. immortal
3. obstacle
4. writhing
5. piers

❷ Grammar

1. indirect object: Breaker
   direct object: letter
2. indirect object: him
   direct object: pellets
3. direct object: Breaker
4. direct object: solution
5. indirect object: emperor
   direct object: bridge

Writing Application

Students should write four sentences about "Breaker's Bridge." Two sentences should include direct objects, and two should include indirect objects and direct objects.

Integrate Language Skills

❶ Vocabulary Development Lesson

Word Analysis: Forms of *execute*

In your notebook, use a form of *execute* to complete each sentence. Choose from *execute*, *executive*, *execution*, or *executioner*.

1. Breaker did not want the ___?___ to carry out the emperor's threat.
2. An ___?___ carries out business plans.
3. This plan is not easy to ___?___.
4. The ___?___ of the plan is complicated.

Spelling Strategy

Words with the vowel combination *ie* such as *pier* follow this spelling rule: Use *i* before *e* except after *c* or when sounded like *a*, as in *neighbor* and *weigh*. Add letters to correctly spell words

1. A strong opinion: b_l_ _f
2. To trick or lie: d_c_ _ _e
3. How heavy something is: w_ _gh_

Concept Development: Analogies

Analogies are comparisons between things that are in most ways not alike, but which share one main quality. Word pairs are sometimes called analogies because the first pair and the second pair share one main quality. The quality may be that they both name opposites. It may be that the first word in each pair is a part and the second word names the whole. On your paper, write a vocabulary word that completes the second pair of words.

1. Bake is to baker as kill is to ___?___.
2. Natural is to mortal as supernatural is to ___?___.
3. Help is to assistance as problem is to ___?___.
4. Motionless is to still as twisting is to ___?___.
5. Table is to legs as bridge is to ___?___.

❷ Grammar Lesson

Direct and Indirect Objects

A **direct object** is a noun or pronoun that receives the action of the verb and answers the question *what* or *whom*.

> He could design a bridge to cross any obstacle. (Design what? a *bridge*)

An **indirect object** is a noun or pronoun that names the person or thing to whom or for whom an action is done. The indirect object immediately follows the verb and precedes the direct object.

> If I make *you* a new crutch, can you reach your home? (Make what? *a crutch* For whom? *you*)

▶ *For more practice, see page R28, Exercise B*

Practice On your paper, copy the following sentences. Write DO over each direct object and IO over each indirect object.

1. The official handed Breaker the letter.
2. The old man gave him the pellets.
3. The emperor summoned Breaker.
4. Breaker found an unusual solution.
5. Breaker built the emperor a bridge.

Writing Application Write four sentences about the story. Two should include direct objects, and two should include indirect and direct objects.

WG Prentice Hall Writing and Grammar Connection: Chapter 19, Section 5

TEACHING RESOURCES

The following resources can be used to enrich or extend the instruction for pp. 402–403.

Vocabulary

- **Selection Support:** Build Vocabulary, p. 116
  Build Spelling Skills, p. 117
- **Vocabulary and Spelling Practice Book**
  (Use this booklet for skills enrichment)

Grammar

- **Selection Support:** Build Grammar Skills, p. 118
- **Writing and Grammar,** Copper Level, p. 398

- **Daily Language Practice Transparencies** ■

Writing

- **Writing and Grammar,** Copper Level, p. 226
- **Writing and Grammar iText CD-ROM**

■ **BLOCK SCHEDULING:** Resources marked with this symbol provide varied instruction during 90-minute blocks.

❸ Writing Lesson

Proposal for Research

While reading "Breaker's Bridge," you might have wondered how bridge builders get the foundation for a bridge into the water. Write a **research proposal** to study a question about bridge building. A research proposal is an overview of what you want to learn, why you want to learn it, and what you will need to complete your research.

Prewriting Make a chart like the one shown to plan the details of your proposal.

Model: Proposal

Question	Reason	Resources	Time
How do bridge builders get the foundation set into the water?	I have always wondered what holds a bridge in place.	Interviews with engineers	Two afternoons
	My research will teach me about practical applications of some principles of gravity, force, and matter.	Internet search	Two evenings
		Encyclopedia	One hour for encyclopedia review

Drafting Use an excerpt from "Breaker's Bridge" to explain why your question interests you. Then, explain the resources and time you will need.

Revising Look for places where you can be more specific about times and resources. Add the needed details.

WG *Prentice Hall Writing and Grammar Connection: Chapter 11, Section 2*

❹ Extension Activities

Listening and Speaking In a group, prepare a **dramatization** of "Breaker's Bridge" using these guidelines.

1. First, decide which scenes to enact and write a brief script.
2. Determine the mood of each scene and how it should be interpreted. Highlight parts of the script that can help create the mood.
3. Perform the dramatization for the class.

Research and Technology Conduct research on the "immortals" of Chinese lore. Use what you learn to write an **essay** giving background that will help readers understand the significance of the old man in the story.

Writing Write a **letter** from Breaker to the emperor explaining why it is difficult to complete the bridge.

www.phschool.com

Go online for an additional research activity using the Internet.

ASSESSMENT RESOURCES

The following resources can be used to assess students' knowledge and skills.

Selection Assessment

- **Formal Assessment,** pp. 102–104
- **Open Book Test,** pp. 70–72
- **Got It! Assessment Videotapes,** Tape 3
- **Test Bank Software**

Visit www.phschool.com for self-tests and additional questions on "Breaker's Bridge."

Writing Rubric

- **Performance Assess. and Portfolio Mgmt.,** p. 14

Listening and Speaking Rubric

- **Performance Assess. and Portfolio Mgmt.,** p. 24

- **Workbook**
- **Transparencies**
- **Skill Book**
- **CD-ROM**

❸ Writing Lesson

- After students read the instruction on p. 403, have them generate a list of possible questions. You may wish to approve the questions before students begin researching and writing.
- Before students research their resources, invite the school librarian to talk to the class about some of the resources available to students.
- Use the Research rubric on p. 14 of **Performance Assessment and Portfolio Management** to evaluate students' proposals.

❹ Listening and Speaking

- After students read the instruction on p. 403, you may wish to assign scenes to groups of students so that the entire story is dramatized.
- Next, review with students the basic elements of a successful scene—character, action, climax, and resolution.
- Then, help students deal with the challenge of bringing mood into a scene that features only characters. Suggest that characters talk about their surroundings, or encourage students to treat the river and woods as characters in their scenes.
- Finally, have students use the Engaging Listeners form on p. 24 in **Performance Assessment and Portfolio Management**.

CUSTOMIZE INSTRUCTION For Universal Access

To address different learning styles, use the activities suggested in the **Extension Activities** booklet, p. 24.

- For Visual/Spatial Learners, use Activity 5.
- For Bodily/Kinesthetic and Interpersonal Learners, use Activity 6.
- For Verbal/Linguistic and Interpersonal Learners, use Activity 7.

The Loch Ness Monster ✦ Why The Tortoise's Shell Is Not

Lesson Objectives

1. **To analyze and respond to literary elements**
   - Literary Analysis: Oral Tradition
   - Comparing Literary Works
2. **To read, comprehend, analyze, and critique nonfiction and a folk tale**
   - Reading Strategy: Evaluating Logic and Reasoning
   - Reading Check Questions
   - Review and Assess Questions
   - Assessment Practice (ATE)
3. **To develop word analysis skills, fluency, and systematic vocabulary**
   - Vocabulary Development Lesson: Word Analysis: Using Forms of *orate*
4. **To understand and apply written and oral language conventions**
   - Spelling Strategy
   - Grammar Lesson: Subject Complements
5. **To understand and apply appropriate writing and research strategies**
   - Writing Lesson: Invitation to a Feast
   - Extension Activity: Loch Ness Theory Update
6. **To understand and apply listening and speaking strategies**
   - Extension Activity: Presentation

STEP-BY-STEP TEACHING GUIDE	PACING GUIDE
PRETEACH	
Motivate Students and Provide Background	
Use the Motivation activity (ATE p. 404)	5 min.
Read and discuss the Preview material and Background information (SE/ATE p. 404) [A]	10 min.
Introduce the Concepts	
Introduce the Literary Analysis and Reading Strategy (SE/ATE p. 405) [A]	25 min.
Pronounce the vocabulary words and read their definitions (SE p. 405)	5 min.
TEACH	
Monitor Comprehension	
Informally monitor comprehension by circulating while students read independently or in groups [A]	35–40 min.
Monitor students' comprehension with the Reading Check notes (SE/ATE pp. 407, 409, 411, 413)	as students read
Develop vocabulary with Vocabulary notes (SE pp. 407, 412, 413)	as students read
Develop Understanding	
Develop students' understanding of oral tradition with the Literary Analysis annotations (SE pp. 407, 412, 413; ATE pp. 407, 412, 413) [A]	5 min.
Develop students' ability to evaluate logic with the Reading Strategy annotations (SE pp. 408, 409; ATE pp. 408, 409)	5 min.
ASSESS	
Assess Mastery	
Assess students' mastery of the Reading Strategy and Literary Analysis by having them answer the Review and Assess questions (SE/ATE p. 414)	25 min.
Use one or more of the print and media Assessment Resources (ATE p. 417) [A]	up to 45 min.
EXTEND	
Apply Understanding	
Have students complete the Vocabulary Development Lesson and the Grammar Lesson (SE p. 416) [A]	20 min.
Apply students' ability to write an invitation using the Writing Lesson (SE/ATE p. 417) [A]	30–45 min.
Apply students' understanding of the selection using one or more of the Extension Activities (SE p. 417)	20–90 min.

ACCELERATED INSTRUCTION:
Use the strategies and activities identified with an [A].

UNIVERSAL ACCESS
● = Below Level Students
▲ = On-Level Students
■ = Above Level Students

Time and Resource Manager

Reading Level: Challenging, Average
Average Number of Instructional Days: 4

RESOURCES		
PRINT	**TRANSPARENCIES**	**TECHNOLOGY**
• **Beyond Literature,** Multimedia Connection: Documentary, p. 25 ▲ ■		• **Interest Grabber Videotapes,** Tape 3 ● ▲ ■
• **Selection Support Workbook:** ● ▲ ■ Literary Analysis, p. 125 Reading Strategy, p. 124 Build Vocabulary, p. 121	• **Literary Analysis and Reading Transparencies,** pp. 49 and 50 ● ▲ ■	
• **Adapted Reader's Companion** ● • **Reader's Companion** ●		• **Listening to Literature** ● ▲ ■ Audiocassettes, Side 15 Audio CDs, CD 7
• **English Learner's Companion** ● ▲ • **Literatura en español** ● ▲ • **Literary Analysis for Enrichment** ■	• **Fine Art Transparencies, Volume 1,** Transparency 8 ● ▲ ■	
• **Formal Assessment:** Selection Test, pp. 105–107 ● ▲ ■ • **Open Book Test,** pp. 73–75 ● ▲ ■ • **Performance Assessment and Portfolio Management,** p. 28 ● ▲ ■ • PRENTICE HALL ASSESSMENT SYSTEM ● ▲ ■	• PRENTICE HALL ASSESSMENT SYSTEM ● ▲ ■ Skills Practice Answers and Explanations on Transparencies	• **Test Bank Software** ● ▲ ■ • **Got It! Assessment Videotapes,** Tape 3 ● ▲
• **Selection Support Workbook:** ● ▲ ■ Build Spelling Skills, p. 122 Build Grammar Skills, p. 123 • **Writing and Grammar,** Copper Level ● ▲ ■ • **Extension Activities,** p. 25 ● ▲ ■	• **Daily Language Practice Transparencies** ● ▲ • **Writing Models and Graphic Organizers on Transparencies** ● ▲ ■	• **Writing and Grammar iText CD-ROM** ● ▲ ■ ***Take It to the Net*** www.phschool.com

BLOCK SCHEDULING: Use one 90-minute class period to preteach the selection and have students read it. Use a second 90-minute class period to assess students' mastery of skills and have them complete one of the Extension Activities.

PRETEACH

Step-by-Step Teaching Guide for pp. 404–405

Motivation

Help students understand how stories evolve in the oral tradition by having them tell a "growing story." The first student starts by stating aloud a simple three-sentence plot. The next student builds on that, either by adding a plot event or details about one of the characters. The third student must try to include all the information from the first two, and add at least one detail. When all students have had a chance to add to the story, point out that the stories they are about to read also contain details and events passed on by many storytellers.

Interest Grabber Video

As an alternative, play "Nessie of Loch Ness" on Tape 3 to engage student interest.

❶ Background

Social Studies

Although scientists have given the Loch Ness Monster serious consideration since the 1930s, people have claimed to see mysterious creatures in the lochs of Scotland for more than a thousand years. The first news of a mysterious and dangerous creature was recorded in A.D. 565 by a man who claimed to have attended the funeral of a man who was bitten by a monster in the loch. In the Middle Ages, people often claimed to have seen a creature they called a "water horse." These sightings could not be proved, of course; it was not until the invention of photography that people could begin to provide (or manufacture) proof that these mysterious water creatures exist.

Prepare to Read

❶ The Loch Ness Monster ◆ Why the Tortoise's Shell Is Not Smooth

 ***Take It to the Net***

Visit www.phschool.com for interactive activities and instruction related to these selections, including

- background
- graphic organizers
- literary elements
- reading strategies

Preview

Connecting to the Literature

You know that it is important to think for yourself—to evaluate information and come to your own conclusion or decision. "The Loch Ness Monster" and "Why the Tortoise's Shell Is Not Smooth" both deal with the problems people and characters face when they must make judgments based on incomplete or faulty information.

Background

Some scientists believe that the depths of the ocean may still hold undiscovered species—or members of species thought to be extinct. Many wonder if Loch Ness, a deep murky lake that may be connected to the ocean by underwater tunnels, may also contain an unidentified species.

TEACHING RESOURCES

The following resources can be used to enrich or extend the instruction for pp. 404–405.

Motivation

Interest Grabber Video, Tape 3

Background

Beyond Literature, p. 25

 ***Take It to the Net***

Visit www.phschool.com for Background and hotlinks for the selections.

Literary Analysis

Literary Analysis and Reading Transparencies, Oral Tradition, p. 50

Reading

Selection Support: Reading Strategy, p. 124; Build Vocabulary, p. 121

Literary Analysis and Reading Transparencies, Evaluating Logic and Reasoning, p. 49

BLOCK SCHEDULING: Resources marked with this symbol provide varied instruction during 90-minute blocks.

❷ Literary Analysis

Oral tradition

Oral tradition is the passing along of songs, stories, and poems by word of mouth. For example, "Why the Tortoise's Shell Is Not Smooth" was originally told orally. Because oral storytelling is not as common as it was once, writers have preserved many of the works in written texts. Think about these focus questions as you read:

1. In what way is the story of the Loch Ness monster part of the oral tradition?
2. Which detail in "Why the Tortoise's Shell Is Not Smooth" indicates that it is part of the oral tradition?

Comparing Literary Works

Both of these works offer explanations of something in nature. However, "Why the Tortoise's Shell Is Not Smooth" is **fiction.** The details come from the storyteller's imagination. On the other hand, "The Loch Ness Monster" is **nonfiction.** While the Loch Ness monster itself may or may not be a creature of the imagination, the details are factual. Compare and contrast the two works by supplying specific examples of the description on the diagram.

Tortoise
- imaginative details
- ancient story
- made up of events
- fantasy

Both
- Explanation of something in nature

Loch Ness Monster
- scientific details
- contemporary author
- actual events
- facts

❸ Reading Strategy

Evaluating Logic and Reasoning

Faulty reasoning is reasoning that seems logical because it contains facts, but it uses or interprets the facts in an illogical way.

- **Unsupported inferences:** Conclusions that are based on too few examples or facts.
  Example: Mark was frowning when he walked out of math class. *Mark doesn't like math.*
  Sound reasoning: Mark was frowning when he walked out of math class. *Mark was unhappy about something that happened in math class.*
- **Fallacious reasoning:** False or incorrect interpretation of facts
  Example: Many people have dogs. *Dogs are the best pets.*

As you read, evaluate whether the reasoning in each work is logical or faulty.

Vocabulary Development

elusive (ē lo͞o′ siv) *adj.* always escaping (p. 407)

abundant (ə bun′ dənt) *adj.* plentiful; more than enough (p. 407)

famine (fa′ min) *n.* shortage of food (p. 412)

orator (ôr′ ə tər) *n.* speaker (p. 412)

eloquent (el′ ə kwint) *adj.* persuasive and expressive (p. 413)

❷ Literary Analysis

Oral Tradition

- Before students read the instruction on p. 405, explain that for thousands of years, before a time when most people could read and write, telling stories to the next generations was a way of passing on the history of a people or culture. This is known as oral tradition.
- Ask volunteers to share a story that they were told by a family member about their family's history. Explain to students that this is the way to begin an oral tradition.
- Ask students to read the instruction. Explain that students cannot answer the questions at this point but will have a chance to do so on p. 415.
- Offer students the Oral Tradition transparency on p. 50 of **Literary Analysis and Reading Transparencies** to help them identify the elements that qualify a story or history as part of oral tradition.

❸ Reading Strategy

Evaluating Logic and Reasoning

- Before students read the instruction, ask them whether they have ever been told "Don't believe everything you read or hear." Ask students what this message means. Possible response: Not everything that is written down or said on television is necessarily true.
- After students read, point out that they should develop a habit of looking for flaws in the arguments or ideas presented in stories.

Vocabulary Development

- Review the words and definitions on the vocabulary list.
- Explain that *eloquent* means "persuasive and expressive" and ask students to identify occasions in which it is important to speak eloquently. Possible responses: speeches, formal toasts, or debates.

CUSTOMIZE INSTRUCTION FOR UNIVERSAL ACCESS

For Special Needs Students	For Less Proficient Readers	For English Learners
Have students read the adapted version of "Why the Tortoise's Shell Is Not Smooth" in the **Adapted Reader's Companion.** This version provides basic-level instruction in an interactive format with questions and write-on lines. Completing the adapted version will prepare students to read the selection in the Student Edition.	Have students read "Why the Tortoise's Shell Is Not Smooth" in the **Reader's Companion.** This version provides basic-level instruction in an interactive format with questions and write-on lines. After students finish the selection in the Reader's Companion, have them complete the questions and activities in the Student Edition.	Have students read the adapted version of "Why the Tortoise's Shell Is Not Smooth" in the **English Learner's Companion.** This version provides basic-level instruction in an interactive format with questions and write-on lines. Completing the adapted version will prepare students to read the selection in the Student Edition.

E-Teach

Visit E-Teach at www.phschool.com for teachers' essays on how to teach, with questions and answers.

TEACH

Step-by-Step Teaching Guide for pp. 406–414

CUSTOMIZE INSTRUCTION For Logical/Mathematical Learners

A logical purpose for reading "The Loch Ness Monster" is to determine whether the author believes there is or is not a monster. As students read, have them gather evidence about the existence of the monster, noting whether the author accepts the evidence or questions it. After identifying the author's opinion, students can use the same body of evidence to draw their own conclusions.

1 About the Selection

For centuries, the Loch Ness Monster was thought to be just a legend. Recent scientific studies have found good reason to believe that "Nessie" may be a giant plesiosaur thought to be extinct for over fifty million years. As scientists introduce modern technology to seek the unknown, they are beginning to think that what people claimed to have seen in the cold waters was not just an illusion.

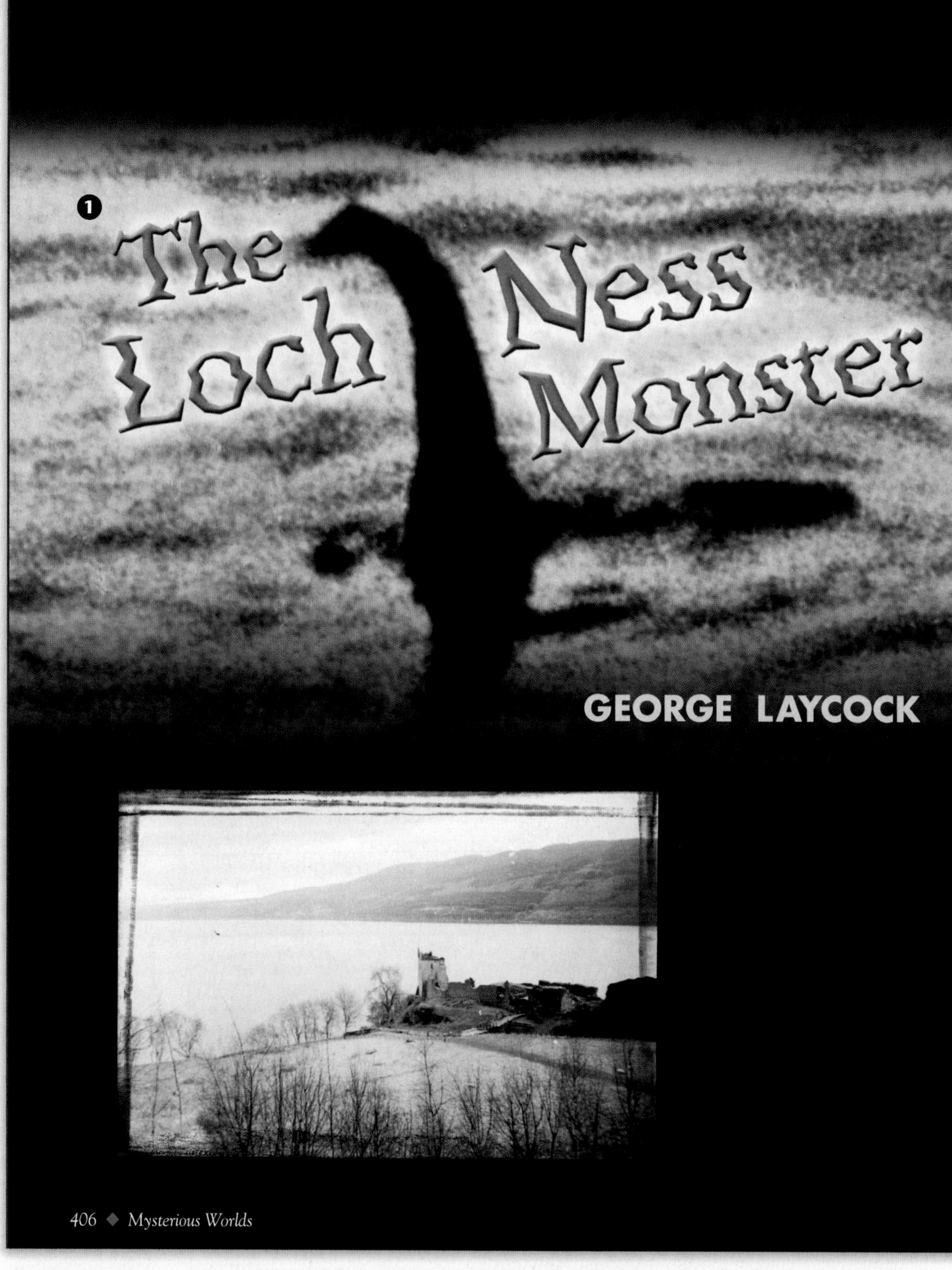

TEACHING RESOURCES

The following resources can be used to enrich or extend the instruction for pp. 406–414.

Literary Analysis

- **Selection Support:** Literary Analysis, p. 125
- **Literary Analysis for Enrichment**
- **Writing Models and Graphic Organizers on Transparencies,** p. 69 ■

Reading

- **Reader's Companion**
- **Adapted Reader's Companion**
- **English Learner's Companion**
- **Literatura en español**
- **Listening to Literature Audiocassettes,** Side 15 ■
- **Listening to Literature Audio CDs,** CD 7
- **Fine Art Transparencies, Volume 1,** Art Transparency 8 (Have students discuss whether they think any of the creatures in the picture could be the Loch Ness Monster. Have students describe what they think the monster might look like.)

■ **BLOCK SCHEDULING:** Resources marked with this symbol provide varied instruction during 90-minute blocks.

In 1938, a tugboat captain was steering his boat across Loch Ness. Everything seemed to be in order. The sky was cloudy just as it is much of the time around Loch Ness. The water was rough from the wind. The tug plowed on mile after mile, its engines laboring normally. The captain was not thinking about monsters. He didn't believe in Nessie anyhow. He made this plain enough to anyone who asked him if he'd ever seen the beast. Then, beside the boat, a creature like nothing the captain had ever seen before stuck its long humped back out of the water. It had a long, slender neck and a little head. The monster rushed ahead, gained speed on the tug, and disappeared far out in front of the boat. This was enough to change the captain's mind. As far as he was concerned, Nessie was real, after all.

Other sightings even included an observation by a driver who saw Nessie in the beam of his headlights on a dark night as the monster crossed the highway near the loch.

Literary Analysis
Oral Tradition How does news about Nessie spread?

❷ These stories were told and retold. Word of Nessie spread around the world. This did a marvelous thing for Scotland. Tourists began to visit Loch Ness, hoping for a glimpse of the elusive lake monster. Tourism can be good for a country's economy. Nessie, real or not, became the most valuable animal in all Scotland.

elusive (ē lo͞o′ siv) *adj.* always escaping

But the lecturer who was to tell us about the Loch Ness monster that night in Oxford, Ohio, had brought scientific methods to the search for Nessie, and people were eager to hear his message. All the seats were filled and students stood around the walls and sat in the aisles to listen to the story Robert H. Rines had to tell.

Dr. Rines, president of the Boston Academy of Applied Science, led his first scientific expedition to Loch Ness in 1970. He took along modern sonar equipment and used this to "see" into the murky depths. Sonar works by sending high-intensity sound impulses into the water and measuring the echoes sent back as the sound waves bounce off the bottom or off objects between it and the bottom. It can reveal the depth of objects in the water, their size, and whether or not they are moving. That summer the sonar equipment showed the researchers important facts. There were large moving objects in the loch. Also there were abundant fish to feed monsters.

abundant (ə bun′ dənt) *adj.* plentiful; more than enough

Dr. Rines meanwhile was consulting with his colleagues, searching for still better equipment for gathering information about the monster of Loch Ness. He worked with Dr. Harold E. Edgerton, who, as a professor at Massachusetts Institute of Technology, had pioneered in the development of high-speed underwater photography. Dr. Edgerton

❸ **✓Reading Check**
Who is Nessie?

❹ ◀ **Critical Viewing** Describe the "creature" you see in the photographs. **[Describe]**

❷ Literary Analysis

Oral Tradition

- Point out how the writer begins the selection by retelling a famous sighting of the Loch Ness Monster.
- Next, ask students the Literary Analysis question on p. 407: How does news about Nessie spread? **Answer:** Students should understand that news about the monster spreads first by word of mouth and eventually in print.
- Ask students how these stories of Nessie are part of an oral tradition. **Answer:** Students may respond that because these stories about the captain's sighting on the lake and the driver's sighting on the highway were "told and retold" all around the world, they are part of an oral tradition.

▶ **Monitor Progress** Ask students why stories are told and retold. **Answer:** Guide students to realize that stories are told again and again because they interest, comfort, or puzzle listeners.

▶ **Reteach** To demonstrate the way oral tradition grows and changes, invite students to play a game of "telephone." Quietly tell one student two or three sentences that you have written down. Ask each student in turn to tell the sentences to the next. Ask the last student to tell the class what he or she heard. Then, compare the final retelling to the original. Finally, explain that in the oral tradition, every retelling is slightly different.

❸ ✓Reading Check

Answer: Nessie is a mysterious water creature or monster that has been sighted in the murky waters of Loch Ness in Scotland.

❹ ▶Critical Viewing

Possible responses: Students may say that they see in the larger picture what looks like a large creature underwater with a flipper or fin protruding from the water; in the inset is a creature that looks as if it has a long neck rising up from the water.

CUSTOMIZE INSTRUCTION FOR UNIVERSAL ACCESS

For Special Needs Students	For Less Proficient Readers
Help students keep track of the anecdotes and evidence presented in the selection by offering them a Series of Events organizer, like the one on p. 69 of **Writing Models and Graphic Organizers on Transparencies.** In each box, students may write notes about each sighting of Nessie and each attempt to find the creature. Have students distinguish the two by labeling the example in each box as a sighting or as science. After students complete the organizer, ask them whether sightings or science prevails in the author's evidence.	A logical purpose for reading is to determine whether the author believes there is or is not a monster. As students read, have them gather and write down evidence about the existence of the monster, noting whether the author seems to accept the evidence or whether he denies its validity. After identifying the author's opinion, students can use the same body of evidence to draw their own conclusions.

5 Reading Strategy

Evaluating Logic and Reasoning

- Before asking students the Reading Strategy direction on p. 408, ask them to think of some reasons for the sand on the camera lens.
- Then, have students respond to the Reading Strategy instruction: Explain why assuming that "Nessie had been there" would be an example of fallacious reasoning. **Answer**: There is absolutely no evidence that Nessie or any creature kicked sand on the lens. The author is conveying what the divers might have thought.
- Finally, point out that the author is simply raising a question; he is not suggesting that he believes that any creature was frightened or kicked sand on the camera.

6 Critical Thinking

Analyze

- Ask students how the passage supports the belief in the existence of the Loch Ness Monster. **Answer:** Because the photograph could not be proved false, people have believed that it is proof of the monster's existence.
- Point out the author's language here: "No one was ever able to prove that this picture had been faked." Ask students whether they think the author is convinced that the photograph is real. **Answer:** The author does not say that the photograph was real; he is careful to say that no one ever proved it wrong, which is different from saying it is authentic.

had also developed remarkable strobe lights for making pictures in dingy water. Now, he designed a system of lights Dr. Rines might use to obtain closeup pictures in Loch Ness.

Dr. Rines linked his camera to the sonar and set it so that it would begin making pictures automatically as soon as any large object passed through the sonar field. It would continue to make pictures every fifteen seconds as long as the sonar told it to.

For their first test, the crew of monster seekers chose the bay where Nessie had most often been sighted. They carefully cleaned the camera lens, then began lowering it gently toward the lake bottom. Divers checked it there and found it clean and ready to make monster pictures.

Another camera was suspended under the research boat and pointed downward into the dark water. All that was needed now was to wait for Nessie to come nosing around.

5 But a strange thing happened. The lens of the camera on the bottom of the loch was suddenly covered with sand, apparently kicked onto it by some large frightened creature. Had Nessie been there and kicked up the silt?

That camera, with its sand-covered lens, made no pictures. But the other camera, hanging beneath the boat, was still in working order. It yielded pictures that to some looked plainly like parts of a huge unknown monster swimming in the water. These color pictures were perhaps the best evidence yet that there really is a Nessie. In 1975 Dr. Rines and his crew were back in Scotland with still better photographic equipment, and the pictures they took were among those shown to the audience in Oxford.

6 One famous picture, believed by some to be Nessie, was made in 1934 by a noted physician who was vacationing on Loch Ness. It showed a large, dark creature swimming on the surface. Its long slender neck and small head stuck out of the water. No one was ever able to prove that this picture had been faked. Neither could anyone suggest a reason why the photographer would want to set up such a hoax. But this picture, like others made later, was rather indistinct. So, for that matter, were those made by Dr. Rines and his crew in 1972 and 1975.

But, sitting in the darkened auditorium, we saw the head of a monster in murky water as it filled the screen before us. It was lumpy and appeared to have a wide mouth where the mouth should be. It also seemed to have two small horns on the top of the head. But perhaps these were not horns. Some believe that they may, instead, have been breathing tubes. This supports the theory that Nessie is a huge reptile that must come to the surface to breathe.

Another picture revealed a large angular object that could have

Reading Strategy
Evaluate Logic Explain why assuming that "Nessie had been there" would be an example of fallacious reasoning.

ENRICHMENT: Cultural Connection

Urban Legends

A modern-day kind of oral tradition is known as an urban legend. An urban legend is a tale of humor or horror about contemporary life passed around by word-of-mouth. Most urban legends have several versions, all of which have evolved from a small, single (if any) grain of truth. One of the most famous urban legends is the one about alligators in the sewers of New York City. One version tells of alligators slipping up through storm drains to eat pets. Others tell of sewer workers mysteriously disappearing, later to be discovered to have been eaten by the sewer alligators. In most versions, the alligators are at least six feet long. The many versions of the urban legend can be traced back to a news report that appeared in the *New York Times* on February 10, 1935. The article reported that a young boy claimed to have seen an alligator in a sewer near the Harlem River.

been a flipper, four to six feet across. It was attached to the side of what may have been the body of Nessie.

But the research team also wanted to know more about the nature of the lake deep below the surface. They hoped to learn whether there really were places where large creatures could hide.

This search was concentrated on Urquhart Bay, where Nessie has been most often reported. On the research vessel *Narwhal* the scientists cruised back and forth over the bay, taking soundings and pictures and transferring the information to a map.

7 For the first time they began to understand the truth about this arm of Loch Ness. Underwater, along both sides of the bay, were deep hidden ravines, rocky canyons and caves, dark recesses far below the surface. This excited the research team. The hiding places made the whole story of Nessie more believable. Nessie, it was agreed, could cruise about down there among those dark caves without sending a ripple to the surface.

This is also the area in which one earlier investigator heard strange underwater sounds the year before, tapping sounds that no biologist has yet been able to successfully identify.

8 These are the bits of evidence that help convince a growing number of people that there really is some "large animal" living deep in Loch Ness. Studying the accumulated evidence, Dr. George R. Zug, curator of amphibians and reptiles at the Smithsonian Institution in Washington, D.C., said, "I started as a skeptic. Now I believe there is a population of large animals in the loch. I don't have any idea of what they are." But he is convinced that research should continue and that the mystery of the Loch Ness monster should be solved.

Another scientist calling for more such research is Dr. Alfred W. Crompton, professor of biology at Harvard University. He, too, believes that the evidence points to a large aquatic animal living in Loch Ness.

What kind of animal this might be is little more than a guess. The most frequent speculation is that Nessie is an ancient reptile, a plesiosaur◆ believed extinct for fifty million years or more.

This is not the only such monster reported from deep lakes over the years. For more than half a century people around Montana's Flathead Lake have thought there might be something very large and unidentified living in the depths of that cold lake. Indians told

Literature in context — History Connection

◆***Plesiosaurs***
One theory about the creature in Loch Ness is that it is a plesiosaur: a large, long-necked water reptile with four paddle-like flippers. The problem with this theory is that plesiosaurs are believed to have become extinct millions of years ago. Although there are explanations for and against this theory, it has not been conclusively proved or disproved.

Picture of the unidentified creature photographed in Loch Ness

Reading Strategy
Evaluate Logic Explain whether the examples offered should be called evidence or not.

9 **Reading Check**
What evidence is used to convince people of Nessie's existence?

7 Critical Thinking

Generalize

- Students may not realize that one reason it has been so difficult to verify the existence of the Loch Ness Monster is that the lake is so large and deep. Loch Ness is about 23 miles long, with a maximum depth of 788 feet.
- Ask students to stop at this point in the selection and make a generalization about the efforts of people to find the Loch Ness Monster.
  Possible response: For years, scientists had only oral accounts of the monster. Now they have technology, but even the best technology is hindered by nature. Even with all of the obstacles hindering scientists, their wills are so strong that they don't give up.

8 Reading Strategy

Evaluating Logic and Reasoning

- Before asking the Reading Strategy question on this page, have students list the recent developments or discoveries that may provide evidence of the monster.
  Answer: Scientists have provided photographs of a head and fin, information about the depth and geography of the lake, and evidence of mysterious tapping sounds.
- Then, read the following Reading Strategy direction: Explain whether the examples offered should be called evidence or not.
  Answer: The fact that the scientists who provide the information are legitimate suggests that the examples should be considered evidence.

9 Reading Check

Answer: Photographs of a face and fin have effectively convinced people of Nessie's existence.

CUSTOMIZE INSTRUCTION FOR UNIVERSAL ACCESS

For English Learners	For Gifted/Talented Students
Invite students to think of urban legends or mysterious creatures that have been featured in stories from their original cultures. Ask students for examples. Then, as a class, use a Venn diagram, such as the one on p. 89 of **Writing Models and Graphic Organizers on Transparencies,** to draw comparisons between the urban legends or mysteries of two cultures.	Students may enjoy making a comparison between the story of the search for Nessie and a popular urban legend. Both have elements of oral history, and both are believed and disbelieved in equal numbers. Read aloud the Enrichment feature on p. 408, and then challenge students to write a brief comparison of the sightings of the Loch Ness Monster and an urban legend like the one discussed. After students complete their work, ask them whether they are now less inclined to believe in the existence of the Loch Ness Monster.

Answers for p. 410

Review and Assess

1. Possible responses: Students may say they would feel frightened. Others may say they would be amazed or excited.
2. **(a)** Scientists have used underwater photography, sonar equipment, and recording devices to find evidence of the monster. **(b)** The loch is cold, deep, and murky.
3. **(a)** Nessie supposedly looks like a big dinosaur, with a long neck; a wide, round body; fins; and a tiny head with breathing tubes or horns. **(b)** The photographs have shown a face, long neck, and a side with a fin. **(c)** The photos are too fuzzy to provide good evidence. The photos also could have been faked.
4. **(a)** Possible responses: Students may or may not believe in the creature's existence. Those who do will cite the photographs and the recent scientific discoveries. Those who do not will suggest that the evidence is fake. **(b)** The loch and the creature might be in danger if the creature were proved to exist. People would come from around the world to look at it and disturb its habitat and habits. If the creature were proved not to exist, people might lose interest in visiting Scotland. **(c)** Possible responses: Students may say that the creature should be left in the lake; to disturb or remove it may endanger it.

the earliest white people about this monster. The monster of Flathead Lake is said to be at least twenty-five feet long and uniformly black, and to swim on the surface, sometimes creating huge waves even when the rest of the lake is calm.

In 1922 scientists in Argentina were choosing sides on the question of whether there could be a similar monster in Patagonia. An American mining engineer was among those who had sighted such a creature. What he described had the size, outline, and features of the ancient plesiosaurs. But there has been little heard of this population of monsters in recent times, and if they were indeed there, they may by now have become extinct.

The mystery locked in the depths of Loch Ness may be closer to an answer than ever before. Dr. Rines and Sir Peter Scott of England have even given Nessie a proper scientific name, *Nessiteras rhombopteryx*, meaning "Ness marvel with a diamond-shaped fin." Some believe that science will soon solve the ancient mystery.

Meanwhile, officials in Scotland have taken steps to protect Nessie. They warn that their famous monsters, if they are really out there in the cold water of Loch Ness, must be among the world's most endangered wildlife. Anyone harming, or even teasing, a Loch Ness monster can be arrested.

Review and Assess

Thinking About the Selection

1. **Respond:** How would you feel if you saw a strange creature like Nessie? Explain.
2. (a) **Recall:** What techniques have scientists used to try to prove Nessie's existence? (b) **Apply:** What features of the loch prevent scientists from conclusively proving that Nessie does or does not exist?
3. (a) **Recall:** What is Nessie reported to look like? (b) **Distinguish:** Which parts of Nessie do the photographs seem to show? (c) **Synthesize:** Why don't people accept the photographs as evidence of Nessie's existence?
4. (a) **Make a Judgment:** Do you believe that an unidentified creature lives in Loch Ness? Why or why not? (b) **Predict:** What would happen to Loch Ness and Nessie if scientists prove that the creature exists? What would happen if scientists prove that the creature definitely does not exist? (c) **Take a Position:** If such a creature does exist, should it be captured or left in the lake? Explain.

George Laycock

(b. 1921)

George Laycock is an avid photographer who often illustrates his writing with his photographs. He lives in Cincinnati, Ohio, not far from the town of Zanesville, where he was born. His interest in nature, wildlife, and the environment is evident in the books and magazine articles he writes. As a professional writer, Laycock has received many honors, including five Science Teacher of America awards for outstanding books for young people.

CUSTOMIZE INSTRUCTION FOR UNIVERSAL ACCESS

For Advanced Readers

Ask students to research and recommend books, articles, movies or television programs, and Internet sites that deal with the Loch Ness Monster and other mysterious creatures. Have students work in teams, with each team member researching a different medium. Before researching, students should generate a list of criteria that qualify a resource as good or interesting. Make sure that they consider the reliability of the sources. Students should find materials that are suited to different reading levels. Their final lists should show the works by medium and in alphabetical order and should contain comments about the materials. Distribute the lists to all the students in your class. Be sure to preview any Internet sites before directing students to view them.

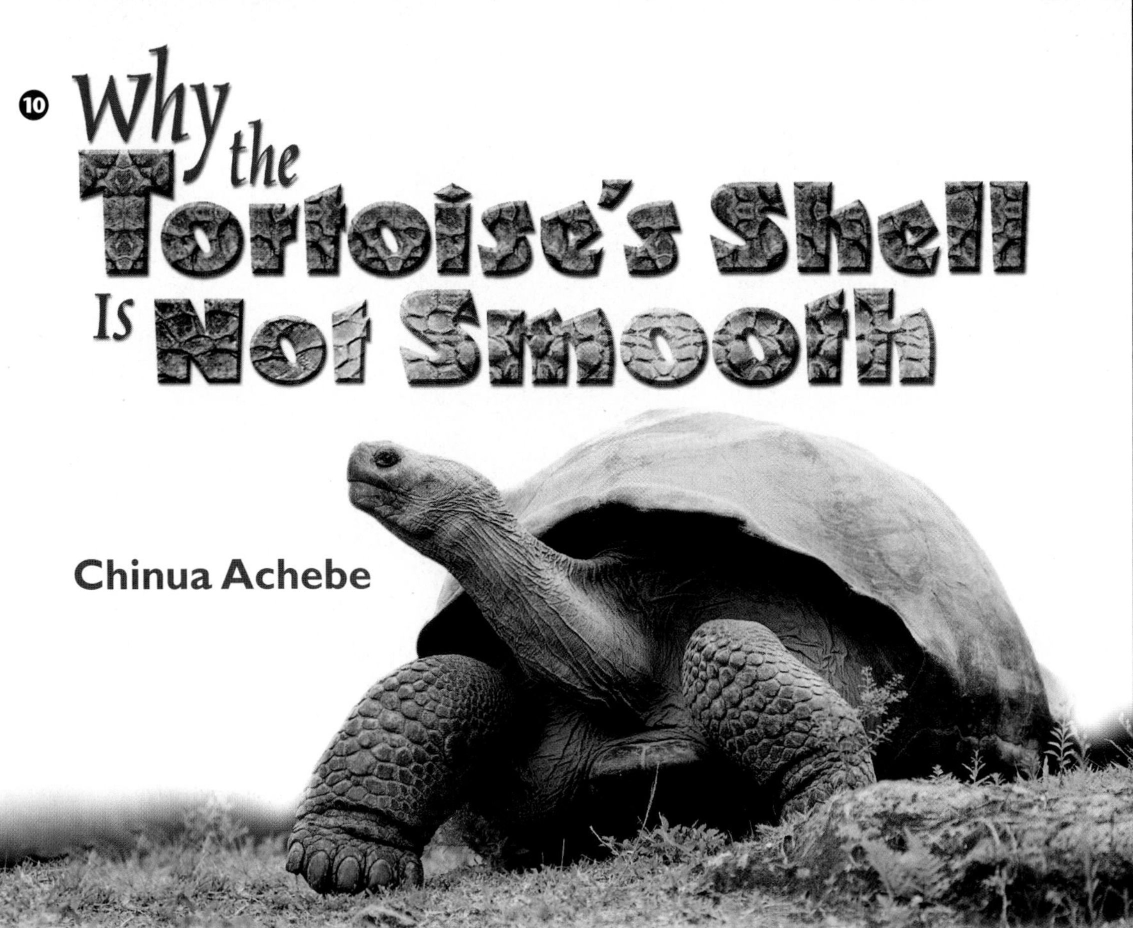

10 Why the Tortoise's Shell Is Not Smooth

Chinua Achebe

Low voices, broken now and again by singing, reached Okonkwo (ō kōn´ kwō) from his wives' huts as each woman and her children told folk stories. Ekwefi (e kwe´ fē) and her daughter, Ezinma (e zēn´ mä), sat on a mat on the floor. It was Ekwefi's turn to tell a story.

"Once upon a time," she began, "all the birds were invited to a feast in the sky. They were very happy and began to prepare themselves for the great day. They painted their bodies with red cam wood[1] and drew beautiful patterns on them with dye.

"Tortoise saw all these preparations and soon discovered what it all meant. Nothing that happened in the world of the animals ever escaped his notice; he was full of cunning. As

11 ▲ **Critical Viewing**
What details in this picture might lead to questions about a tortoise's appearance? **[Connect]**

12 **Reading Check**
Who is telling stories?

1. **red cam** (cam) **wood** hard West African wood that makes red dye.

10 About the Selection

In "Why the Tortoise's Shell Is Not Smooth," Tortoise convinces the birds to lend him some feathers so that he can fly with them to a great banquet in the sky. Tortoise uses his cunning to trick the birds and eat all the food at the banquet. The birds get their revenge by taking back the feathers that Tortoise has used to fly. Tortoise falls to the ground, shattering his shell in pieces. This tale teaches a lesson about not believing everything you see and offers an ancient explanation for the markings on a tortoise's shell.

11 ▶Critical Viewing

Possible response: Some may wonder why the shell is lumpy and looks patched together. The shell also has lines that make it look as if it had been shattered and put back together.

12 Reading Check

Answer: Ekwefi, one of Okonkwo's wives, is telling this story. Okonkwo's other wives and their children have also been telling stories.

CUSTOMIZE INSTRUCTION FOR UNIVERSAL ACCESS

For Special Needs Students	For Less Proficient Readers
Remind students that most tales in the oral tradition have a moral, either stated or implied. Help students identify the moral of this story by analyzing character traits. Ask students to draw a cluster diagram with the words *Tortoise* and *Birds* in two circles in the center. Have students draw and fill in additional bubbles with words that describe the characters. Work with students to make a generalization about the characters based on their diagrams.	Students may have difficulty understanding that this story opens in an African village and that the body of the story is actually told by a woman in the village. Help students identify the three human characters (Okonkwo, his wife Ekwefi, and her daughter Ezinma) and see where the story of the tortoise actually begins. Point out to students that the entire story of the Tortoise appears in quotation marks.

13 ▶ Critical Viewing

Possible responses: The storyteller might get very close to his audience, speak directly to the listeners, or use different voices for each of the characters.

14 Literary Analysis

Oral Tradition

- Point out to students that at this point, the narrator of the story becomes less important and that the tortoise's story becomes the focal point.
- Next, ask students this question: How does the writer suggest the oral tradition? Who is the narrator?
Answer: The writer suggests the oral tradition by having the woman's daughter interrupt the story to ask a question. The narrator is the mother. Also, the writer explains that Okonkwo hears his wife telling stories to her daughter.

13 ▲ **Critical Viewing** What techniques might a storyteller like the one in this picture use to keep an audience interested? **[Speculate]**

soon as he heard of the great feast in the sky his throat began to itch at the very thought. There was a famine in those days and Tortoise had not eaten a good meal for two moons. His body rattled like a piece of dry stick in his empty shell. So he began to plan how he would go to the sky."

famine (fa´ min) *n.* shortage of food

"But he had no wings," said Ezinma.

"Be patient," replied her mother. "That is the story. Tortoise had no wings, but he went to the birds and asked to be allowed to go with them.

14 "'We know you too well,' said the birds when they had heard him. 'You are full of cunning and you are ungrateful. If we allow you to come with us you will soon begin your mischief.'

"'You do not know me,' said Tortoise. 'I am a changed man. I have learned that a man who makes trouble for others is also making it for himself.'

"Tortoise had a sweet tongue, and within a short time all the birds agreed that he was a changed man, and they each gave him a feather, with which he made two wings.

"At last the great day came and Tortoise was the first to arrive at the meeting place. When all the birds had gathered together, they set off in a body. Tortoise was very happy as he flew among the birds, and he was soon chosen as the man to speak for the party because he was a great orator.

orator (ôr´ ə ter) *n.*: speaker

CUSTOMIZE INSTRUCTION FOR UNIVERSAL ACCESS

For English Learners

To help students understand the way oral tradition causes tales to change and grow, try the following activity. Divide students into two teams. Ask the two team leaders to work together to brainstorm four sentences about an imaginary event. Each leader should then memorize the sentences and take them back to his or her team. One team's members will pass along the four sentences orally, "telephone-style," from one member to the next. The other team's members will write the sentences, and then dictate them to the next member, who will write them. After both teams have completed a circuit, ask the last members of each team to recite or read the version of the sentences that they received. Ask both teams to compare the differences between the written and the spoken versions.

"'There is one important thing which we must not forget,' he said as they flew on their way. 'When people are invited to a great feast like this, they take new names for the occasion. Our hosts in the sky will expect us to honor this age-old custom.'

"None of the birds had heard of this custom but they knew that Tortoise, in spite of his failings in other directions, was a widely traveled man who knew the customs of different peoples. And so they each took a new name. When they had all taken, Tortoise also took one. He was to be called *All of you.*

"At last the party arrived in the sky and their hosts were very happy to see them. Tortoise stood up in his many-colored plumage and thanked them for their invitation. His speech was so eloquent that all the birds were glad they had brought him, and nodded their heads in approval of all he said. Their hosts took him as the king of the birds, especially as he looked somewhat different from the others.

eloquent (el′ ə kwint) *adj.* persuasive and expressive

15 "After kola nuts[2] had been presented and eaten, the people of the sky set before their guests the most delectable dishes Tortoise had ever seen or dreamed of. The soup was brought out hot from the fire and in the very pot in which it had been cooked. It was full of meat and fish. Tortoise began to sniff aloud. There was pounded yam[3] and also yam pottage[4] cooked with palm oil and fresh fish. There were also pots of palm wine. When everything had been set before the guests, one of the people of the sky came forward and tasted a little from each pot. He then invited the birds to eat. But Tortoise jumped to his feet and asked: 'For whom have you prepared this feast?'

Literary Analysis
Oral Tradition Why might a storyteller include names of specific foods in a tale?

"'For all of you,' replied the man.

"Tortoise turned to the birds and said: 'You remember that my name is *All of you.* The custom here is to serve the spokesman first and the others later. They will serve you when I have eaten.'

"He began to eat and the birds grumbled angrily. The people of the sky thought it must be their custom to leave all the food for their king. And so Tortoise ate the best part of the food and then 16 drank two pots of palm wine, so that he was full of food and drink and his body grew fat enough to fill out his shell.

"The birds gathered round to eat what was left and to peck at the bones he had thrown all about the floor. Some of them were too angry to eat. They chose to fly home on an empty stomach. But before they left, each took back the feather he had lent to Tortoise. And there he stood in his hard shell full of food and wine but without any wings to fly home. He asked the birds to take a

17 **Reading Check**
Why do the birds change their names?

2. **kola** (kō′ lə) **nuts** the seeds of the African cola tree. These seeds contain caffeine and are used to make soft drinks and medicines.
3. **yam** (yam) *n.* sweet potato.
4. **pottage** (pät′ ij) *n.* thick soup or stew.

15 Literary Analysis
Oral Tradition

- Explain that every oral tale is rooted in the culture it comes from. Point out to students that the animals in the story would be totally different if the story had originated in Canada instead of Africa. Tell students that the moral, however, is universal and applies to all people.
- Next, ask students the Literary Analysis question on p. 413: Why might a storyteller include names of specific foods in a tale?
  Answer: The specific foods let the reader know which culture the story comes from; also, the foods are familiar to the story's original listeners.

16 Background
Science

A tortoise is a turtle that lives only on land. Like other turtles, tortoises have a shell. In general, tortoises and other turtles that live on land have high, domed shells. Turtles that live in water have flatter shells. The shell is made of two layers. The inner layer is made of bony plates and is actually part of the skeleton. The outer layer consists of tough "scales," skin tissue called *scutes.* Because the shell is connected to the backbone, a broken or cracked shell usually means death for the turtle or tortoise.

17 Reading Check

Answers: They change their names because Tortoise tells them to, and they believe him to be wiser than they are.

CUSTOMIZE INSTRUCTION FOR UNIVERSAL ACCESS

For Gifted/Talented Students	For Advanced Readers
Have students compare the mysterious world of Nessie and the imaginary world of the Tortoise. Students may consider these questions: What do we know about the world of Nessie and the world of Tortoise? What elements of each world appeal to storytellers? What is it about these stories that causes people to want to retell them? Have students explore these questions in a short essay.	Tell students that the Tortoise in "Why the Tortoise's Shell Is Not Smooth" is a trickster, a mischievous but smart character who appears in folk tales from around the world. Invite students to research at least one other trickster figure and to compare him or her to the Tortoise. Students should also be able to define the role of the trickster in their brief reports.

ASSESS

Answers for p. 414

Review and Assess

1. Possible responses: Some students may agree that Tortoise got what he deserved because he had tricked the birds; others may say that he should have been punished more severely.
2. **(a)** Tortoise has not eaten in two months, so he wants to go to the feast. **(b)** The birds do not trust Tortoise.
3. **(a)** Tortoise convinces the birds to take him by using his "sweet tongue" to tell them he is a "changed man." **(b)** The birds choose Tortoise because he is an eloquent speaker. **(c)** Tortoise takes advantage of his privilege and upsets the birds by eating the best part of the food.
4. **(a)** Because his new name is "All of you," he can ask the question "For whom have you prepared this feast?" The answer, of course, is his new name. **(b)** The birds learn that Tortoise has not changed at all. **(c)** Everyone would have eaten, and Tortoise would have kept his smooth shell.
5. **(a)** Possible response: Some students may say that the birds should have forgiven Tortoise and helped him return home. **(b)** Possible response: Students may think that the birds' actions are justified because the birds were also hungry, and they had been betrayed by Tortoise. **(c)** Students' examples should show a clear difference between revenge and justice.

message for his wife, but they all refused. In the end Parrot, who had felt more angry than the others, suddenly changed his mind and agreed to take the message.

"'Tell my wife,' said Tortoise, 'to bring out all the soft things in my house and cover the compound[5] with them so that I can jump down from the sky without very great danger.'

"Parrot promised to deliver the message, and then flew away. But when he reached Tortoise's house he told his wife to bring out all the hard things in the house. And so she brought out her husband's hoes, machetes,[6] spears, guns, and even his cannon. Tortoise looked down from the sky and saw his wife bringing things out, but it was too far to see what they were. When all seemed ready he let himself go. He fell and fell and fell until he began to fear that he would never stop falling. And then like the sound of his cannon he crashed on the compound."

"Did he die?" asked Ezinma.

"No," replied Ekwefi. "His shell broke into pieces. But there was a great medicine man in the neighborhood. Tortoise's wife sent for him and he gathered all the bits of shell and stuck them together. That is why Tortoise's shell is not smooth."

5. **compound** (käm´ pound) *n.* grounds surrounded by buildings.
6. **machetes** (mə shet´ ēz) *n.* large heavy-bladed knives.

Review and Assess

Thinking About the Selection

1. **Respond:** Do you think the tortoise got what he deserved? Why or why not?
2. (a) **Recall:** Why does the tortoise want to go to the great feast? (b) **Infer:** Why don't the birds want to take him?
3. (a) **Analyze:** Why do the birds decide to help Tortoise go to the feast? (b) **Deduce:** Why do they choose him to speak for the group? (c) **Assess:** How does Tortoise make use of this privilege?
4. (a) **Interpret:** Explain how Tortoise's new name allows him to eat before the birds. (b) **Apply:** What lesson have the birds learned about Tortoise? (c) **Speculate:** How might the story have ended if the Tortoise had behaved himself at the feast?
5. (a) **Make a Judgment:** Should the birds have helped Tortoise return home? Why or why not? (b) **Extend:** Do you consider the birds' actions to be revenge or justice? Explain. (c) **Apply:** Use a situation from real life to illustrate the difference between justice and revenge.

Chinua Achebe

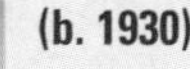

(b. 1930)

Chinua Achebe likes to retell stories that originated in his native country of Nigeria many years ago. Achebe writes, "Our ancestors created their myths and legends and told their stories for a purpose. Any good story, any good novel, should have a message."

Achebe studied broadcasting in London after graduating from college. Then, he became a professional writer. Although he has written poetry, short stories, and essays, he is best known for his novels, which have won many honors and awards. His favorite topics for writing are Nigerian history and culture and African politics.

ASSESSMENT PRACTICE: Reading Comprehension

Draw Conclusions (For more practice, see Test Preparation Workbook, p. 37.)

Many tests require students to draw conclusions. Use the following passage to help students practice drawing conclusions.

The mystery locked in the depths of Loch Ness may be closer to an answer than ever before. Dr. Rines and Sir Peter Scott of England have even given Nessie a proper scientific name. . . . Some believe that science will soon solve the ancient mystery.

You can conclude from this passage that Rines and Scott __________ .

A have solved the ancient mystery
B have proof that Nessie is real
C believe that Nessie is real
D think that Nessie is a joke

A, B, and *D* are not supported by the passage. The men gave Nessie a scientific name because they thought Nessie was real. The correct answer is *C*.

Review and Assess

Literary Analysis

Oral Tradition

1. Why can the story of the Loch Ness monster be considered part of the **oral tradition**?
2. What details at the beginning of "Why the Tortoise's Shell Is Not Smooth" indicate that it is part of the oral tradition?
3. Identify three details from "Why the Tortoise's Shell Is Not Smooth" that reflect ancient Nigerian customs and culture.

Comparing Literary Works

4. Use an organizer like the one shown to record details that reflect the difference between **fiction and nonfiction**. Explain your choices.

Reading Strategy

Evaluating Logic and Reasoning

5. What examples of photographic evidence of Nessie's existence does George Laycock include in "The Loch Ness Monster"?
6. What are two possible interpretations of these pictures?
7. What is one example of **faulty reasoning** in "The Loch Ness Monster"?
8. Based on the fact that Tortoise eats first, the people of the sky infer that it is a custom to let the leader or spokesperson eat first. Explain whether this inference is supported or unsupported.

Extending Understanding

9. **Science Connection:** Explain how Dr. Rines proved that the food web in Loch Ness could support a creature such as Nessie.
10. **Take a Position:** Do you think scientists should continue to spend money and time searching for Nessie? Explain.

Quick Review

Oral tradition is the passing along of songs, stories, and poems by word of mouth. To review oral tradition, see page 405.

Fiction is prose writing that tells about imaginary characters and events.
Nonfiction is prose writing that presents and explains ideas or that tells about real people, places, objects, or events. To review fiction and nonfiction, see page 405.

Faulty reasoning looks logical because it contains facts, but it uses or interprets the facts in an illogical way. To review faulty reasoning, see page 405.

 ***Take It to the Net***
www.phschool.com
Take the interactive self-test online to check your understanding of these selections.

ENRICHMENT: Further Reading

Other Works by the Authors

Works by George Laycock
The Mountain Men
Grizzly: Wilderness Legend

 ***Take It to the Net***
Visit www.phschool.com for more information on the authors.

Works by Chinua Achebe
Chike and the River
How the Leopard Got His Claws
Anthills of the Savannah

Answers for p. 415

Review and Assess

1. The story can be considered part of the oral tradition because sightings of the monster have been shared and retold for many years.
2. The details that indicate the story is part of the oral tradition are the details about who was telling the story, where it was being told, and to whom it was being told.
3. The oral tradition of storytelling, the specific foods mentioned in the story, and the animals in the story reflect ancient Nigerian customs and culture.
4. **Loch Ness:**
   1. explanation of how sonar works
   2. essay based on lecture by scientist, Dr. Rines
   3. description of photographs taken by Dr. Rines

   Tortoise:
   1. a group of women and children are sharing folk stories
   2. animals converse like humans
   3. storyteller is frequently interrupted, so reader is reminded that it is a story
5. Laycock includes early photos of the monster, which are fuzzy. He mentions more recent ones that show the face and fin of a creature.
6. They may be evidence of the monster's existence, or they may be fakes.
7. One example of faulty reasoning is the assumption that the sand covering the underwater camera was kicked there by Nessie.
8. The inference is not supported. Tortoise knew that the food was prepared for all the guests, so he named himself "All of you." When he asks for whom the food has been prepared, the answer is his new name.
9. Dr. Rines's sonar readings of the lake show plenty of fish to feed a monster.
10. Possible responses: Some may think that money would be better spent on problems that affect people in need. Others may suggest that we can learn more about life by solving the riddle of the Loch Ness Monster.

EXTEND

Answers for p. 416

❶ Vocabulary Development

Word Analysis

1. oratorical
2. orator
3. oration

Concept Development: Word Groups

1. *eloquent* and *orator*
2. *abundant* and *famine*
3. *elusive*

Spelling Strategy

1. eloquent
2. Abundant
3. frequent

❷ Grammar

1. predicate noun: orator; renames: Tortoise
2. predicate adjective: eloquent; describes: speech
3. predicate noun: bird; renames: Parrot
4. predicate adjective: cheated; describes: birds
5. predicate noun: reason; renames: That

Writing Application

Possible responses: Tortoise is a trickster. Tortoise is a changed man. Tortoise is clever. Tortoise is selfish.

Integrate Language Skills

❶ Vocabulary Development Lesson

Word Analysis: Forms of *orate*

The story word *orator* comes from the word *orate*, which means "deliver a speech." Other words that are forms of *orate* also relate to speaking.

On your paper, write each sentence and complete it with one of these forms of *orate*:

orator oration oratorical

1. Tortoise's __?__ skills were admired by all.
2. He is considered a great __?__ by the birds.
3. His eloquent __?__ was applauded.

Concept Development: Word Groups

Answer each question with a vocabulary word.

1. Which two words deal with speaking?
2. Which two words could describe opposite amounts of food?
3. Which word describes something that keeps escaping?

Spelling Strategy

The ending sound in the story words *eloquent* and *abundant* is the same, but the words have different spellings. Use *eloquent*, *abundant*, and *frequent* in these sentences to practice spelling the endings.

1. The Tortoise gave an __?__ speech.
2. __?__ fish were available in the loch.
3. There were __?__ sightings of the Loch Ness Monster.

❷ Grammar Lesson

Subject Complements

A **subject complement** is a word that comes after a linking verb and identifies or describes the subject. A subject complement may be either a predicate noun or a predicate adjective.

A predicate noun (or pronoun) follows a linking verb and identifies or renames the subject.

I am a changed man. (*Man* renames *I*.)

A predicate adjective follows a linking verb and describes the subject.

Tortoise was very happy as he flew among the birds. (*Happy* describes *Tortoise*.)

▶ *For more practice, see page R28, Exercise B*

Practice Copy the following sentences. Underline each subject complement. Identify it as a predicate noun or predicate adjective. Then, draw an arrow to the word it renames or describes.

1. Tortoise is a great orator.
2. His speech was eloquent
3. Parrot seemed to be a bird of great intelligence.
4. The birds felt cheated.
5. That is the reason.

Writing Application Write four sentences about Tortoise. In the first two, use predicate nouns to rename him. In the second two, use predicate adjectives to describe him.

WG Prentice Hall Writing and Grammar Connection: Chapter 19, Section 5

TEACHING RESOURCES

The following resources can be used to enrich or extend the instruction for pp. 416–417.

Vocabulary

- **Selection Support:** Build Vocabulary, p. 121; Build Spelling Skills, p. 122
- **Vocabulary and Spelling Practice Book** (Use this booklet for skills enrichment)

Grammar

- **Selection Support:** Build Grammar Skills, p. 123
- **Writing and Grammar,** Copper Level, p. 398

- **Daily Language Practice Transparencies** ■

Writing

- **Writing and Grammar,** Copper Level, p. 102 ■
- **Writing and Grammar iText CD-ROM**

■ **BLOCK SCHEDULING:** Resources marked with this symbol provide varied instruction during 90-minute blocks.

❸ Writing Lesson

Invitation to the Feast

Based on details from "Why the Tortoise's Shell Is Not Smooth," make an invitation to the feast. Use a word-processing program to make your invitation. Use tabs, spacing, special fonts, and page orientation to format your invitation.

Prewriting Review the story to identify details that can be used in your invitation. Make up additional details, such as time and date, that are not provided in the story. The basic information to be included on any invitation is time, date, and place. Some invitations will tell whether the guest should RSVP (respond).

Drafting Begin your invitation with a paragraph that describes the activities and food at the feast. Use vivid verbs that tell what guests will do and precise nouns to tell what things and foods will be at the feast. Use text formatting to highlight the words *date*, *time*, and *place*. Decide whether your page orientation will be vertical (called *portrait*) or horizontal (called *landscape*).

> **Come to the Feast**
>
> Celebrate with us! Stuff yourself with yams, kola nuts, and fish.
>
> *Date: March 26* — *Place: The Palace of the Sky People*
> *Time: 4:00 p.m.* — *RSVP: The Sky King: 555-4141*

Revising If the date, time, and place are not the most noticeable information on your invitation, revise to make them more visible.

WG *Prentice Hall Writing and Grammar Connection: Chapter 6, Section 2*

❹ Extension Activities

Listening and Speaking Prepare and deliver a brief **presentation** on the history of and current research related to Nessie. Explain how it confirms or refutes the evidence in this selection.

1. Develop a sentence outline of your most important points.
2. Use this general organization to highlight the most important ideas and information in your presentation.

Research and Technology Write a one-page **summary** that updates the latest scientific information on the Loch Ness monster. Use electronic sources such as the Internet and electronic library catalogs to research current sightings and scientific theories.

www.phschool.com

Go online for an additional research activity using the Internet.

Lesson Support for p. 417

❸ Writing Lesson

- After students read the instruction, make sure they understand the essential information that should appear on an invitation.
- As students brainstorm for the design for their invitations, explain that the art and design of invitations should be appropriate to the event. If possible, have students bring in examples of invitations to different events, such as weddings and parties.
- Also, remind students that the event dictates the tone of the language. Invitations may be briefly stated or they may be conversational.

❹ Listening and Speaking

- After students read the instruction, talk to them about how to limit the topic of their presentations. Suggest that they address just one point in history or one development in research.
- As students research, remind them to use only sources that are reliable. Show students how to document their sources.
- Allow students to present their talks from written notes, but caution them about reading directly from the notes.
- Have students use the Speaking rubric on p. 28 in **Performance Assessment and Portfolio Management.**

CUSTOMIZE INSTRUCTION For Universal Access

To address different learning styles, use the activities suggested in the **Extension Activities** booklet, p. 25.

- For Visual/Spatial Learners, use Activity 5.
- For Bodily/Kinesthetic and Verbal/Linguistic Learners, use Activity 6.
- For Musical/Rhythmic Learners, use Activity 7.

ASSESSMENT RESOURCES

The following resources can be used to assess students' knowledge and skills.

Selection Assessment

- **Formal Assessment,** pp. 105–107
- **Open Book Test,** pp. 73–75
- **Got It! Assessment Videotapes,** Tape 3
- **Test Bank Software**

Visit www.phschool.com for self-tests and additional questions on the selections.

Listening and Speaking Rubric

- **Performance Assess. and Portfolio Mgmt.,** p. 28

PRENTICE HALL ASSESSMENT SYSTEM

- **Workbook**
- **Skill Book**
- **Transparencies**
- **CD-ROM**

Lesson Objectives

1. To watch for unknown words when reading an article on a specialized topic
2. To understand what social studies texts are

About Social Studies Texts

- After students read "About Social Studies Texts," ask them to make a list of the reasons they might consult social studies texts.
- Then, invite students to think of some magazines that carry social studies articles.
  Possible response: Students may suggest magazines such as *Smithsonian* or *National Geographic.*
- Finally, ask students whether they have ever read social studies texts on their own outside of school assignments. If so, what do they like about them?
  Possible response: Students may say that they enjoy reading about ancient civilizations in magazine articles because the articles have interesting photographs.

Reading Strategy

Watching for Unknown Words

- Have students read the information about the Reading Strategy.
- Then, work with students to brainstorm for possible reasons to watch for unknown words in an article.
  Possible responses: Students may suggest these reasons: to learn new vocabulary, to learn the pronunciations of new words, to have a better understanding of a topic.
- Explain to students that they will be taking notes on unknown words, names, and terms in "Human Footprints at Chauvet Cave" on pp. 419–420. Show them the graphic organizer on p. 418 as an example of how to do this.

READING INFORMATIONAL MATERIALS

Social Studies Texts

About Social Studies Texts

Information about social studies topics can be found in a variety of texts. For any given topic you can probably find a full-length nonfiction book, an anthology in which the writings of several experts are collected, magazine articles, and Web pages. You might consult social studies texts other than your social studies textbook for several reasons, including the following:

- **General interest**—to find out more about a specific topic you have studied in class.
- **Background**—to improve your understanding of a specific event or topic.
- **Perspective**—to look at an event or topic from several different angles or viewpoints to get a clear picture of it.
- **Research**—to find facts and details that support a thesis or proposition.

Reading Strategy

Watch for Unknown Words

When you read an article on a specialized topic, watch for unknown words, names, and terms. Decide which ones to look up immediately, which to check later, and which to take notes on.

- Knowing the pronunciation of a name will not affect your understanding of the text, so you can wait until you are done reading to look it up.
- Knowing the meaning of a specialized term may make a difference to the meaning of the text, so you might want to look it up right away.
- Take notes on unfamiliar words, names, and specialized terms. You may run into them again in related texts.

March 26, 20__

"Human Footprints at Chauvet Cave"
by Spencer Harrington

Summary:
Scientists discover oldest human footprints in a cave in France. More than 447 paintings have also been found in this cave.

Names:
* Aldene, Montespan, Niaux, Pech Merle = other caves
* Jean-Marie Chauvet = He discovered the cave with the footprints

New Words:
* upper paleolithic— 40,000–10,000 BC
* "ca." = "circa" = about; approximately

Section of the paintings found in Chauvet Cave.

Human Footprints at Chauvet Cave

Spencer P.M. Harrington

Recent exploration of the Chauvet [shō vā′] Cave near Vallon-Pont-d'Arc [valoŋ′ poŋ dark] in southern France has yielded the oldest footprints of *Homo sapiens sapiens* and a cavern with a dozen new animal figures. The footprints appear to be those of an eight-year-old boy, according to prehistorian Michel-Alain Garcia [mē shel′ a lan′ gär sē′ ä] of the Centre National de la Recherche Scientifique, Nanterre.[1] They are between 20 and 30 thousand years old, perhaps twice as old as those discovered previously at Aldene, Montespan [mon tə span], Niaux [nē o′], Pech Merle [pesh merl], and other Upper Palaeolithic sites.[2]

Garcia estimates that the boy was about four-and-a-half feet tall, his feet more than eight inches long and three-and-a-half inches wide. First spotted in 1994 by Jean-Marie [zhäŋ mä rē′] Chauvet, the cave's discoverer,

The translation of this name does not affect your immediate understanding of the article. You can wait until you have finished reading to check the footnote.

The words "Upper Palaeolithic sites" affect your understanding of the significance and age of the footprints. You should read the footnote before continuing.

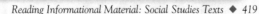

1. **Centre National de la Recherche Scientifique, Nanterre** French for "National Center for Scientific Research [at] Nanterre."
2. **Upper Palaeolithic sites** places believed to have artifacts from the period of time between approximately 40,000 and 10,000 B.C.

Human Footprints at Chauvet Cave

- Introduce the social studies text that appears on pp. 419–420 by explaining that it describes the contents of an ancient cave in southern France. The cave is thought to contain the oldest set of human footprints in the world.
- Have students read the text and the notes that identify the elements of the text.
- Point out how each of the paragraphs in the article answers different questions. For example, the first paragraph explains "Where are the caves?"; "Who made the footprints?"; and "How old are the footprints?" Challenge students to identify the questions that are answered in the second and third paragraphs.
- Explain to students that some unknown words will not affect their immediate understanding of a text. Students can wait to look up these words until they are finished reading the article. Ask students to find one example of this type of unknown word in the first paragraph.
  Possible response: Students may say that the name *Michel-Alain Garcia* does not affect their immediate understanding of the text.
- Have students find an example of an unknown word or term on p. 419 that does affect their understanding of the text. Have students find the word's definition.
  Possible response: Students may say that the term *Upper Paleolithic* affects their immediate understanding of the text.

continued on p. 420

CUSTOMIZE INSTRUCTION FOR UNIVERSAL ACCESS

For Special Needs Students	For Less Proficient Readers
Explain to students that when they do research, they will have more success if they have a particular purpose for reading. Illustrate this point by having students think of a topic that interests them. Then, ask them to complete a KWL organizer like the one on p. 61 of **Writing Models and Graphic Organizers on Transparencies.** Have students fill out the first two columns. Explain that the second column essentially is their purpose for reading.	Students may be confused by the terms and names in the article. Preview the article with students in order to identify categories of terms, such as place names, scientific terms, animal names, and discoverers. Have students make a four-column chart and label each of the columns with a category. As students read the first time, they should identify unfamiliar words or names and place them in the appropriate category. Tell students as they reread to substitute generic terms, such as *scientist* or *animal,* for the specific word.

continued from p. 419

- Explain to students that watching for unknown words and terms in a text will help them better understand other types of text. For example, if students learn the meaning of the term *Upper Paleolithic* from this social studies text, they will understand the term when it is used in an article for another subject area.
- Help students brainstorm for other subject areas in which they might find articles containing the unknown words mentioned in "Human Footprints at Chauvet Cave." Write students' suggestions on the board.
  Possible responses: Students might suggest the subject areas of art, history, and anthropology.
- Allow students time to look up the words, names, and terms from their charts that they designated as not affecting their immediate understanding of the text.

the footsteps stretch perhaps 150 feet and at times cross those of bears and wolves. The steps lead to the so-called room of skulls, where a number of bear skulls have been found. In a few places, there is evidence that the boy slipped on the soft clay floor, though Garcia says the prints show the boy was not running, but walking normally. The boy appears at one point to have stopped to clean his torch, charcoal from which has been dated to ca. 26,000 years ago. The prints from the Chauvet Cave, like nearly all footprints thus far discovered in Palaeolithic caves, are from bare feet, which has led scholars to speculate that people of the time either left footwear at cave entrances or carried them.

> If you don't know the meaning of *ca.*, look it up to see how it affects the meaning of the number that follows. You will see *ca.* in many informational materials.

Meanwhile, a team of 15 specialists directed by French prehistorian Jean Clottes recently investigated an uninventoried room originally discovered by Chauvet. There they found a dozen new paintings of mammoth, bison, and horses, among other animals. Clottes' team has so far documented 447 animals of 14 different species. By comparison, Niaux Cave in the French Pyrenees, cited by the French Palaeolithic specialist Abbé Breuil [ä bā′ brool] as one of the half-dozen great caves containing prehistoric art, has 110 images of six species.

> Make connections to other studies. In what other subject areas might you read articles containing the names of people and places mentioned in this article?

CUSTOMIZE INSTRUCTION FOR UNIVERSAL ACCESS

For Advanced Readers

Invite students to read more about the ancient footprints found in Chauvet Cave. Encourage students to think of at least three questions that are left unanswered by the article "Human Footprints at Chauvet Cave." Then, ask them to find and read other social studies articles and books on the subject and to search the Internet so they can write a brief report about the topic. Students should be sure to explain why these particular footprints are so extraordinary. Distribute students' reports to the class. Ask readers to repeat the steps of this workshop and to identify unknown words, names, and terms in the reports.

Check Your Comprehension

1. How much older are the footprints found in the Chauvet Cave compared to ones previously found?
2. Who do scientists believe made the footprints? How do you think they came to that conclusion?
3. Where do the footprints lead?
4. What do scientists believe is the reason for all the footprints found that were made by bare feet?
5. How many animal paintings have been found in Chauvet Cave?

Applying the Reading Strategy

Watch for Unknown Words

6. What are four significant place names in this text? Why are they significant?
7. What is one new word you noted that is not a place or person's name? Why did you take notes on it?
8. Compare your notes with a partner. Do your lists contain the same words or different words? Explain why you might have some of the same notes and some different notes.

Activity

Use one of the names of people or places that you took notes on as a key word in an Internet search or look the name up in an encyclopedia. Explain to a partner or small group what the significance of the person or place is beyond a connection with the Chauvet Cave.

Contrasting Informational Materials

Articles Written From Different Perspectives

Compare this social studies article to an article on the Chauvet Cave that is written for an art magazine or an art Web site. Use a Venn diagram to compare and contrast the types of information included in the two articles.

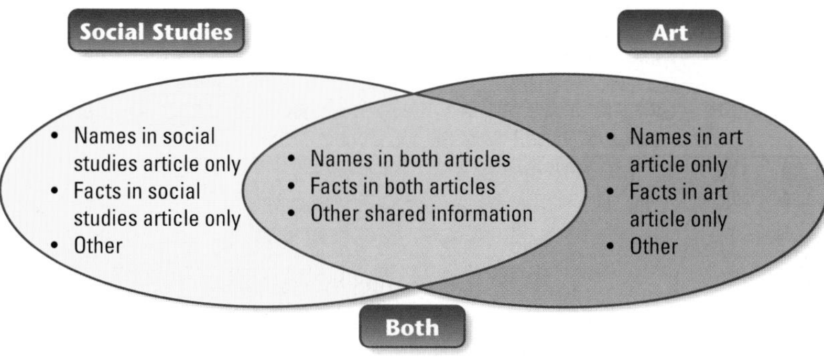

Answers for p. 421

Check Your Comprehension

1. The footprints are probably twice as old as the ones previously discovered.
2. Scientists believe the footprints were made by an eight-year-old boy. They based their guess on the measurements of the prints.
3. The footprints lead to the room of skulls.
4. Scientists believe that people either left their shoes at the opening of the cave or that they carried their shoes with them.
5. One dozen animal paintings have been found in Chauvet Cave.

Applying the Reading Strategy

6. Possible response: Four significant place names are *Aldene*, *Montespan*, *Niaux*, and *Pech Merle*. They are all significant because they are excavation sites discovered before Chauvet Cave.
7. Possible response: Students might have taken notes on the word *bison* to find out what type of animal was discovered in the Chauvet Cave paintings.
8. Possible response: Students might attribute the similarities to both students not knowing the same words. They might attribute the differences to both students believing different words affected their understanding of the text.

Activity

Allow students time to look up their names on the Internet or in an encyclopedia. Then, have them write and present their information to a partner or small group. After students complete their presentations, discuss their experience of watching for unknown words.

continued

Answers continued

Contrasting Informational Materials

Articles Written From Different Perspectives: Remind students that one of the reasons they might consult a social studies text is to look at an event or topic from a different perspective or viewpoint. Present students with a range of art articles on Chauvet Cave or a list of appropriate Web sites, or allow them time to visit the library. Show students how to create a Venn diagram by walking them through the example shown on p. 421. After students have completed their research and diagrams, have them compare their results in small groups.

Lesson Objectives

1. To write a cause-and-effect essay
2. To use writing strategies to generate ideas, plan, organize, evaluate, and revise the composition

Model From Literature

In the excerpt from *Exploring the Titanic* (p. 380), writer Robert D. Ballard explains the causes and effects of the ship hitting an iceberg.

Prewriting

- As students consider topics, remind them that it will be easier for them to decide on a topic if they have some specific questions they want to answer. Draw their attention to the three bulleted topic possibilities on p. 422. Allow time for them to brainstorm for questions about specific subtopics that come to mind when they read each of these general topics. Finally, instruct students to choose the topic that interests them the most for their essays.
- After students do preliminary research, they should see that they are trying to answer one particular question, such as "What are the effects of water pollution on people and animals?" Students can use their focus question as the basis for their thesis. They merely need to turn it into a statement. Here is an example: "Water pollution has many terrible effects on humans and animals."
- Before students draft their essays, have them review the **Rubric for Self-Assessment** (p. 425) so they know what is expected.

Writing WORKSHOP

Expository Writing: Cause-and-Effect Essay

Expository writing is writing that informs. In an expository composition, you explain, analyze, or describe. This workshop will give you tips and strategies for writing a **cause-and-effect essay**—a composition in which you explain and analyze the specific reasons for and results of an event or a situation.

Assignment Criteria. Your expository composition should have the following characteristics:

- A clearly stated thesis about the causes and effects of a situation
- Facts and details that support the thesis statement
- An organizational pattern that emphasizes the cause-and-effect relationships
- Transitions that make connections between ideas

See the rubric on page 425 for the criteria on which your cause-and-effect essay may be assessed.

Prewriting

Choose a topic. Consider the following topic possibilities:

- an event or situation you are learning about in social studies
- a natural phenomenon such as erosion or lightning
- an event currently in the news

Write a thesis statement. Use your notes to write a clear statement that introduces the topic or purpose of your expository composition.

Model: Thesis Statement

Sunscreen should always be worn when you are out in the sun because the effects of the sun can be dangerous to your skin.

In his thesis statement, Bryson identifies the cause-and-effect relationship he will analyze: The *effects* of the sun are a *cause* for wearing sunscreen.

TEACHING RESOURCES

The following resources can be used to enrich or extend the instruction for pp. 422–425.

- **Writing and Grammar,** Copper Level, Chapter 7, pp. 124–145
- **Performance Assess. and Portfolio Mgmt.,** p. 18
- **Writing Models and Graphic Organizers on Transparencies,** p. 51

Writing and Grammar iText CD-ROM

Students can use the following tools as they complete their descriptive essays:

- KWL Chart
- Unity and Coherence
- Comparatives
- Transition Words

Student Model

Before you begin drafting your composition, read this student model and review the characteristics of a successful explanation.

Bryson McCollum
Cumming, Georgia

Sunscreen should always be worn when you are out in the sun because the sun can be very dangerous to your skin. If your skin is exposed to the sun's ultraviolet rays without sunscreen, it will turn red, burn, and hurt. Many people believe that burning their skin is one step closer to their desire of getting a tan. They do not realize that both burning and tanning your skin can damage it. Once you burn or tan and the redness or color begins to fade, the damaged skin may begin to peel, leaving a new, unhealthy, thin, and sensitive layer of skin.

> The writer begins by stating his thesis, the cause-and-effect relationship he will show.

> Details about the sun's ability to damage the skin help support the writer's purpose.

What you do to your skin as a child and as a young adult will affect your skin in the future. Doctors recommend that children apply sunscreen often and at least 30 minutes before going out in the sun. Adults, children, and young adults will benefit from using sunscreens with sun protection factor (SPF) numbers 15 or more. The SPF number gives some idea of how long you can stay out in the sun without burning. For example, an SPF of 15 should protect you for approximately 150 minutes in the sun. While some sunscreens say they are waterproof, they do not give you total protection from water and sweat. As a result, it is also recommended that sunscreen be applied often.

> The writer uses examples to make doctor recommendations clear.

Nobody's skin is immune to skin cancer. If your skin is damaged a lot by the sun during your childhood and adult years, your chances of getting skin cancer are great. Some signs of skin cancer are leathery scab-like patches of skin that may be discolored, bleed, or burn. If you have been burned several times in a short period of time, you should be checked by a doctor because some forms of skin cancer cannot be detected.

> Each paragraph focuses on a cause or an effect related to Bryson's thesis.

So, next time you are at the beach or the pool without sunscreen, hoping to absorb the sun, be careful and apply sunscreen. Remember that even though a tan may look nice, it may cause you health problems and unhealthy looking skin in the future.

CUSTOMIZE INSTRUCTION FOR UNIVERSAL ACCESS

For Less Proficient Readers	For English Learners	For Advanced Readers
Have students use the Main Idea and Supporting Details Organizer on p. 73 in **Writing Models and Graphic Organizers on Transparencies.** After students have listed the main ideas, tell them to develop their details so that they have enough information to dedicate a paragraph to each main idea.	Suggest that students focus on a topic that is already familiar to them. Suggest that students make a list of words that are associated with their topics. Then, have them work with partners proficient in English to make sure they are using the correct words or words with the appropriate connotations.	Challenge students to explain a chain of causes and effects in their papers. To help them organize their ideas and information, offer the Cause-and-Effect organizer on p. 65 in **Writing Models and Graphic Organizers on Transparencies.** Remind students that in a series of causes and effects some effects are also causes.

Student Model

- Explain that the Student Model is a sample, and that essays may be longer.
- Have a volunteer read aloud the first paragraph of the Student Model. Check students' comprehension by asking them to identify the thesis statement.
  Answer: "Sunscreen should always be worn when you are out in the sun because the sun can be very dangerous to your skin."
- Draw students' attention to the second boxed annotation. Emphasize the importance of providing details or evidence to support the thesis statement in an essay.
- Have a volunteer read aloud the second paragraph of the Student Model, and draw students' attention to the sentence that is bracketed by the third boxed annotation. Point out that the writer has summarized information from his research in this sentence. Explain to students that they will have to paraphrase and summarize the research they find for their essays.
- Read aloud the final two paragraphs of the Student Model. Point out that the writer clearly explains the cause-and-effect relationship of sun exposure and that this adds weight to the writer's message.

Real-World Connection

Expository writing in the real world: Expository writing—particularly how-to writing or instructions—can be found almost everywhere. Discuss with the class the kinds of instructions they see every day. For example, they may find written instructions on subway cars and buses, in hospitals and libraries, on mail boxes and cereal boxes, and on bills and reading tests. Have students find at least three examples of instructions that appear in public places and bring them to class. Challenge students to find unusual examples.

Drafting

- Focus students' attention on the cause-and-effect organizer on p. 424. Discuss the importance of establishing an organization for writing.
- Tell students that each paragraph in a composition should have a clear topic sentence and include at least three forms of evidence, including facts, quotations, examples, or statistics.
- Explain that students should place their paragraphs in the order that suits the type of exposition they are writing. For this assignment, causes should come before effects. Tell students that the use of logical organization will make it easier for them to insert transitional words and phrases into their essays.

Revising

- Suggest that students work in pairs as they revise. Each student should read aloud his or her paper to a partner, stopping after each paragraph. Tell students that the listening partner should be able to easily identify the strongest sentence in the paragraph.
- Remind students that each topic sentence should present an idea that is then supported by every other sentence in the paragraph. Students should cross out sentences that do not support the topic sentence, or move them to another paragraph.

continued on p. 425

Drafting

Write from a plan. Use an organizer to plan the sections of your essay. As you draft, group details in paragraphs based on the sections of your organizer.

Develop paragraphs. Write a topic sentence, or main idea sentence, for each paragraph. Organize supporting information under each topic sentence.

Connect with transitions. Use transitional words and phrases to make cause-and-effect relationships clear.

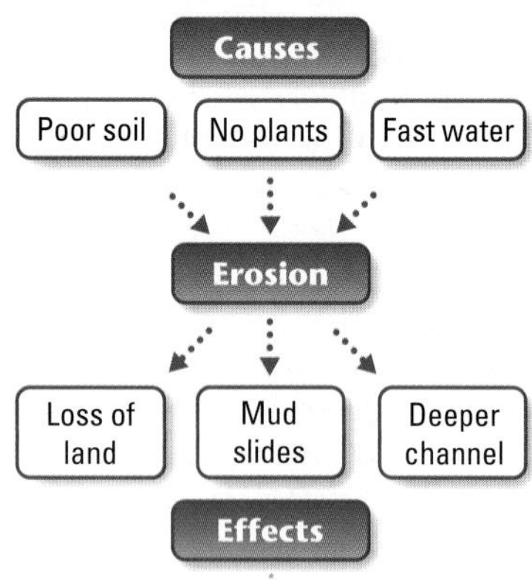

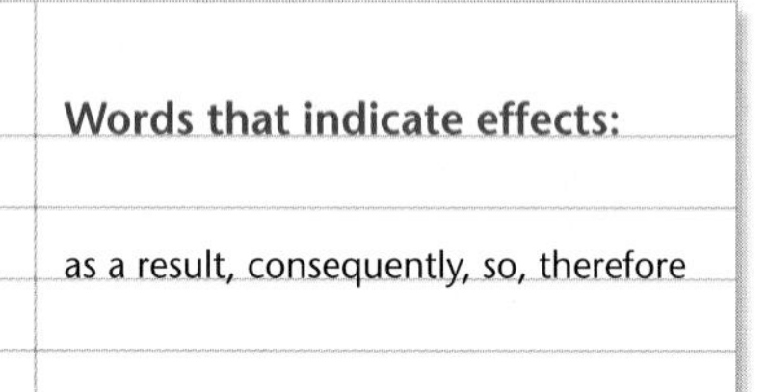

Words that indicate a cause:	Words that indicate effects:
due to, because, for this reason	as a result, consequently, so, therefore

Revising

Revise for logical organization. Check the overall organization of your essay by checking the connections between paragraphs as well as the order of your paragraphs.

1. Highlight the topic sentence of each paragraph.
2. Read the topic sentences in the order in which they appear.
3. Label each topic sentence's connection to the topic as cause or effect.

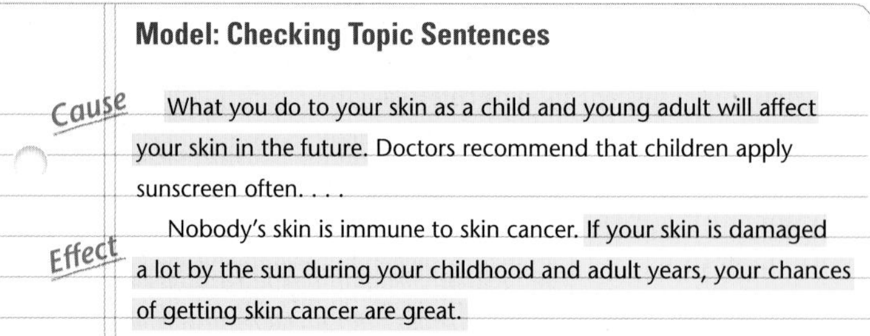

Model: Checking Topic Sentences

Cause What you do to your skin as a child and young adult will affect your skin in the future. Doctors recommend that children apply sunscreen often. . . .

Effect Nobody's skin is immune to skin cancer. If your skin is damaged a lot by the sun during your childhood and adult years, your chances of getting skin cancer are great.

USING TECHNOLOGY IN WRITING

Suggest that students use different fonts or colored text to highlight the topic sentences in each of their paragraphs. Students should have a highlighted sentence in each paragraph. Students may also benefit from highlighting transition words to show the connections between ideas within paragraphs and across paragraphs. For a list of transition words and their functions, refer students to p. 38 in **Writing and Grammar,** Copper Level.

Students can also use the Transition Word Bin on the **Writing and Grammar iText CD-ROM.**

Revise for transitions. Look for places to add transitions to make connections between ideas. In the following example, *because* connects two related ideas.

Draft: We were late. We did not see the movie beginning.
Revision: We could not see the movie beginning *because* we were late.

Compare the model and the nonmodel. Why is the model more effective than the nonmodel?

Nonmodel	Model
If your skin is exposed to the sun's ultraviolet rays without sunscreen, it will turn red, burn, and hurt. The burning damages the skin. The top layers peel off. Thin, raw, unprotected skin is exposed.	Without sunscreen, your skin is exposed to the sun's ultraviolet rays. As a result, your skin will tun red, burn, and hurt. The burning damages the skin. Consequently, the top layers peel off.

Publishing and Presenting

Choose one of these ways to share your writing with classmates or a larger audience.

Make a movie. Treat your expository composition as if it were the script for a short film. Make a storyboard that shows the images that you would choose to go with it.

Deliver instructions. Read your composition to a small group as a way of having listeners follow multiple-step oral directions.

WG *Prentice Hall Writing and Grammar Connection: Chapter 9*

Speaking Connection

To learn how to get information from an expository presentation, see **Listening and Speaking Workshop: Following Oral Directions,** page 426.

Rubric for Self-Assessment

Evaluate your expository composition using the following criteria and rating scale:

Criteria	Rating Scale Not very				Very
How clearly is the cause-and-effect relationship identified in the thesis statement?	1	2	3	4	5
How well do the facts and details support the thesis?	1	2	3	4	5
How clearly does the organization link cause-and-effect relationships?	1	2	3	4	5
How well do transitions connect related ideas?	1	2	3	4	5

TEST-TAKING TIP

The key to writing an expository composition in a test situation is to identify the type of exposition that is required. The test prompt should make clear which form of exposition students will need to concentrate on, including comparison and contrast, cause and effect, problem and solution, or how-to. Once students identify their purposes for writing, they should sketch appropriate graphic organizers to organize their ideas in the prewriting stage. They should also jot down a list of appropriate transition words that come to mind. Remind students to budget their time in a test situation. Explain that, if they have 45 minutes, they should spend at least 15 on planning their papers, 15 to 20 on writing, and five to ten minutes on proofreading.

Revising (continued)

- Tell students that transitions show the relationship between ideas and paragraphs. For example, transitions can show that ideas have something in common, that ideas contrast, that ideas follow one another in time order, or that ideas are causes or effects. Explain that readers might have trouble figuring out the connections between ideas if a composition lacks transitions.
- Review the nonmodel and model with students. Point out that transitions can be used to connect ideas between sentences in addition to ideas between paragraphs.
- Have students identify the transition words and phrases in the model.
  Answer: The model includes the transitions *as a result* and *consequently.*

Publishing and Presenting

- Ask each student to write a brief journal entry about the purpose of his or her essay and the audience that would be interested in reading it.
- Students may be confused by the notion of turning an essay into a film. Explain that their films would be instructional. For example, if they wrote about how to fix a flat bicycle tire, their film would need visuals to show the steps they described in their papers.
- Remind students that turning a written paper into an oral speech is not always simple. Have students practice reading their papers aloud. Students should notice whether their sentences are too long or whether their word choice does not sound as clear as it appears on paper. Guide students to make adjustments as necessary.

Assessment

- Write the following in a bulleted list on the board to summarize the four criteria for students: *clear thesis, sufficient support, logical organization,* and *transitions.* Describe for students the importance of each of these criteria in an essay.
- The rubric on this page, and another rubric in an alternative format, can be found on p. 18 of **Performance Assessment and Portfolio Management.**

Lesson Objectives

1. To follow oral directions
2. To identify key action words in oral directions
3. To restate oral directions, emphasizing action words and transitions

Listen Carefully

- To emphasize the point of this workshop, have students listen without following along in their books as you read aloud the Listen Carefully instruction.
- After students have listened, ask them to review with a partner what they heard. Ask volunteers to share the key points they remember from the reading.
  Possible responses: Most students will remember the following key points: ask questions, notice action words, and look for visual clues.
- Allow time for students to read the instruction silently. Then, discuss with students how watching the speaker aids comprehension.
- Review with students the concept of action words. Make a list of some typical action words that students are likely to hear or use when giving directions, such as *stop, turn left, turn on,* or *turn off.*
- Ask students to comment on whether or not they find visuals helpful when they listen for information.

Restate Directions

- Allow students to read the Restate Directions instruction section aloud to a partner. Afterwards, the reader should listen as the partner rereads the section aloud.
- After both partners have read aloud the instruction, ask students to recall the action words included in this section.
  Answer: Students should recall the words *repeat, restate, listen,* and *use.*
- Review the checklist on p. 426. Tell students to use this checklist as a guide as they complete the Activity.

Listening and Speaking WORKSHOP

Following Oral Directions

Every day, you hear and follow oral directions and instructions. To understand and carry out **multiple-step oral directions**, or spoken directions with several steps, you need to listen carefully to the speaker and restate the directions in the correct sequence. The following strategies will help you demonstrate effective listening skills.

Listen Carefully

Following oral directions correctly requires understanding the speaker's message. To understand directions, follow these guidelines.

Notice action words and time-order words. Pay special attention to the key action word in each step. The key action words will help you remember what to do. For example, in these directions for a fire drill, the action words are underlined.

> First, <u>close</u> the doors and windows. Then, <u>walk</u> to the nearest exit. When you are outside, <u>stand</u> with your class until the teacher counts the group.

Most directions are stated in chronological order and include words such as *first, then, next, finally,* and *last.*

Ask questions. Do not assume that the speaker will give you all the information you need. Identify missing information and ask questions to clarify. Some questions you might ask to clarify information are

- How far?
- How much?
- How long?
- How many?

Restate Directions

Repeating the directions allows the directions-giver to correct any misunderstanding.

Use the action words and transition words. Repeat or restate the directions in your own words using the action words to recall the action required. Use the transition words at the beginning of each step to restate multiple-step directions. The example below shows a restatement of the fire drill directions in the example above.

> First, shut the windows. After the windows are shut, walk to the closest door. Once you get out, stand with the rest of the class. Don't move until the teacher counts you.

Checklist for Restating and Following Directions

Listen Carefully
- ☑ Focus on the speaker. Listen for main ideas and details.
- ☑ Notice the action word in each step of the directions.
- ☑ Notice words that tell time order.
- ☑ Ask questions.

Restate Directions
- ☑ Repeat the directions using the action words.
- ☑ Use words that tell chronological order.

Activity: Directions Ask a partner to give you oral directions for an unfamiliar activity, such as a new sports technique or a way of getting from school to another place. Restate the directions. With adult permission, follow the directions to check your understanding.

CUSTOMIZE INSTRUCTION FOR UNIVERSAL ACCESS

For Special Needs Students	For English Learners
Remind students that some people learn well from oral instructions and remember them easily. Others may need to take notes. Have students practice taking notes while you read aloud simple instructions or directions. Tell students that they may write words or draw symbols or pictures. After students listen, ask them to compare their notes with those of a partner. As a class, discuss different ways of taking notes and strategies for making them more effective.	English learners may not recognize spoken words that they would otherwise recognize on the page. Students may benefit from tape recording the oral directions that are given in the Activity on p. 426. That way, they can listen to the directions as many times as they need. Students may be tempted to memorize the words of the directions, without completely understanding their meanings. Challenge students to change partners and to use their own words to retell the directions they hear to another person.

Assessment WORKSHOP

Draw Conclusions

The reading sections of some tests require you to read a passage and answer multiple-choice questions about inferences and conclusions. Use what you have learned in this unit about evaluating logic and reasoning to answer these questions.

Test-Taking Strategies

- Read the questions related to a passage before reading the passage.
- After making your choice, quickly scan the passage to make sure your choice is logically supported.

Sample Test Items

Directions: Read the passage and answer the questions that follow.

Sam checked his backpack once again. He didn't want to arrive too early at the bus stop to stand with kids he didn't know. After fidgeting for five more minutes, Sam said good-bye to his mother and walked out the front door. Seven or eight boys and girls were waiting at the corner. "Hi," said one of them. "Are you new in town?"

1. Which word best describes Sam?
   A cheerful
   B nervous
   C relaxed
   D sloppy

2. The passage gives you reason to believe that—
   A Sam is unfriendly
   B Sam and his mother don't communicate well
   C Sam lives near his new school
   D this is Sam's first day at a new school

Answers and Explanations

1. There are no details to support choices **A**, **C**, or **D**. Answer ***B*** is correct.
2. There is no evidence to support choices **A** or **B**. Sam is taking a bus, so **C** is not correct. ***D*** is the correct answer.

Practice

Directions: Read the passage and answer the questions that follow.

For years, people have dreamed of having robots to do household chores. While this has not happened, robots are doing many important jobs. Surgeons use robots to make precise movements that are difficult for a human hand. Robots pick apples from the tops of trees without bruising them. Security robots warn of fires and intruders. Scientists have used robots to explore places too dangerous for humans, for example, inside active volcanoes, on the ocean floor, and on the surface of Mars.

1. Information in the passage suggests that—
   A robots are cheaper than human surgeons
   B Mars is too cold for humans
   C robots are not as reliable as humans
   D robots can survive higher temperatures than humans

2. From this passage, you can conclude that—
   A robots will never do household chores
   B robots have expanded scientific knowledge
   C the idea for robots came from science fiction
   D robots would not be useful in schools

Lesson Objective

To draw conclusions from a text in a test situation

Applying Reading Strategies

Explain to students that evaluating the logic and reasoning of a writer's ideas will help them draw conclusions that are accurate. A good writer will present information in a logical and clear way, so even if the writer's conclusion is implied, students will be able to figure it out. Mention that test items that require students to draw conclusions will contain details and information that clearly point to one logical conclusion.

Test-Taking Skills

- Have students read the sample test item passage. Then, tell students to focus on the details in the passage. Ask students what the details have in common.
  Answer: Most of the details are about Sam. They show how he is acting before going to school. The details suggest that he is nervous about something related to school.
- Invite students to talk about possible reasons that Sam might be nervous. Remind them to base their speculations on the information given in the passage.
  Answer: Students should understand that Sam is nervous about going to school, probably because he is a new student.
- Finally, have students answer the sample test item questions.

Answer

1. The correct answer is D. It is clear that if a robot can explore inside a live volcano, it can withstand higher temperatures than humans. The passage suggests nothing about the cost of robots *(A)* or the cold temperatures on Mars *(B)*. It is also clear from the passage that robots can be *more* reliable than humans *(C)*.
2. The correct answer is B. The passage does not suggest that robots will not be used in households *(A)*, and it makes no mention of science fiction *(C)* or of the role of robots in schools *(D)*.

TEACHING RESOURCES

The following resources can be used to enrich or extend the instruction for p. 427.

Prentice Hall Assessment System

Workbook | Transparencies
Skill Book | CD-ROM

Unit Objectives

1. To develop skill in reading short stories
2. To apply a variety of reading strategies, particularly strategies for reading fiction, appropriate for reading these selections
3. To analyze literary elements
4. To use a variety of strategies to build vocabulary
5. To learn elements of grammar, usage, and style
6. To use recursive writing processes to write in a variety of forms
7. To develop listening and speaking skills
8. To express and support responses to various types of texts
9. To prepare, organize, and present literary interpretations

Meeting the Objectives

With each selection, you will find instructional materials through which students can meet these objectives. Further, you will find additional practice pages for reading strategies, literary analysis, vocabulary, and grammar in the **Selection Support: Skills Development Workbook** in your **Teaching Resources.**

Background

Art

The Storyteller

by Adolphe Tidemand

Have students link this painting with the focus of Unit 6 ("Short Stories") by asking these questions:

1. What kind of story is the woman telling?
   Possible response: The story is suspenseful or even frightening because the children's faces look frightened and the adults have stopped to listen.
2. What was a storyteller's role before books were widely available?
   Answer: A storyteller entertained and kept stories alive by telling them and teaching them to younger people.

UNIT 6 Short Stories

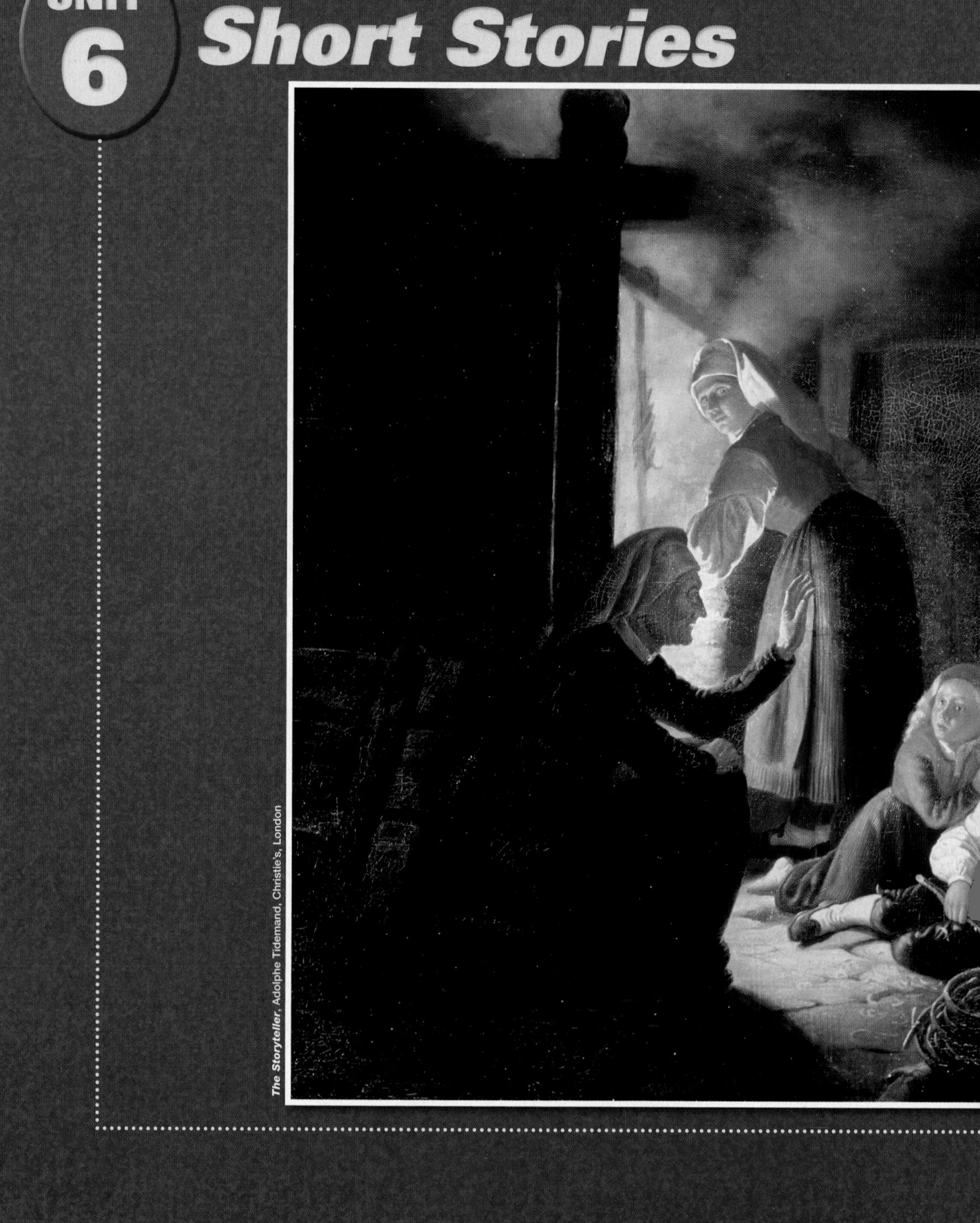

The Storyteller, Adolphe Tidemand, Christie's, London

UNIT FEATURES	
Connections	**Reading Informational Material**
Every unit contains a feature that connects literature to a related topic, such as art, science, or history. In this unit, the birthdays in "Eleven" on p. 465 and "Obie's Gift" on p. 472 link different feelings about birthdays. Use the information and questions on the Connections page to enrich students' understanding of the selections presented within the unit.	These selections will help students learn to analyze and evaluate informational texts, such as workplace documents, technical directions, and consumer materials. They will expose students to the organization and features unique to nonnarrative texts. In this unit, students will learn strategies for reading and understanding magazine articles and book reviews.

Exploring the Genre

A short story is a doorway into another world. The world of a short story may be another town or city similar to yours or it may be a distant planet. A short story may introduce you to new ideas or remind you of events in your own life. Although short stories cover a wide range of possibilities, they all share certain elements.

- **Plot:** the sequence of events that keeps the story moving.
- **Characters:** the people or animals in the story.
- **Setting:** the time and place in which the characters live and the events occur.
- **Theme:** the central message expressed in the story.

You will learn more about these elements as you read the short stories in this unit.

◀ **Critical Viewing** Which person in this picture is telling a story? How do you know? **[Analyze]**

Assessing Student Progress

Listed below are the tools that are available to measure the degree to which students meet the unit objectives.

Informal Assessment

The questions in the Review and Assess sections are a first level of response to the concepts and skills presented within the selections. Students' responses are a brief, informal measure of their grasp of the material. These responses can indicate where further instruction and practice are needed. Follow up with the practice pages in the **Selection Support: Skills Development Workbook**.

Formal Assessment

The **Formal Assessment** booklet contains Selection Tests and Unit Tests.

- Selection Tests measure comprehension and skills acquisition for each selection or group of selections.
- Each Unit Test provides students with thirty multiple-choice questions and five essay questions designed to assess students' knowledge of the literature and skills taught in the unit.

The **Open Book Tests** ask students to demonstrate their ability to synthesize and communicate information from selections or groups of selections.

To assess student writing, you will find rubrics and scoring models in the **Performance Assessment and Portfolio Management** booklet. In this booklet you will also find scoring rubrics for listening and speaking activities.

Alternative Assessment

The **Extension Activities** booklet contains writing activities, listening and speaking activities, and research and technology activities that are appropriate for students with different ability levels. You may also use these activities as an alternative measurement of students' growth.

▶Critical Viewing

Answer: The old woman is telling a story. The reader can see that everyone is paying attention to her.

ASSESSMENT RESOURCES

- **Selection Support:** Skills Development Workbook
- **Formal Assessment**
- **Open Book Test**
- **Performance Assessment and Portfolio Management**
- **Extension Activities**

Why Read Literature?

The "Why Read Literature?" page in each unit presents a list of possible purposes for reading. Each purpose for reading is connected to one or more of the selections in the unit. Good readers set a purpose before reading in order to help them read actively and focus on meaningful details.

Unit 6 introduces three purposes for reading. "Read for the love of literature" encourages students to enjoy two humorous tales from the nineteenth century. "Read for information" introduces two accounts of animal life. Students are invited to "Read to consider another point of view" in unusual stories about a dragon slayer and a young girl's birthday.

How to Use This Page

- Tell students that before reading each selection in this unit, they should set a purpose for reading. This will help them read in an active and focused manner.
- This unit includes works by two nineteenth-century literary giants. Explain that reading about a lawyer's argument with a ghost in "The Lawyer and the Ghost" (p. 478) and a cold ride across a desolate Russian landscape in "Overdoing It" (p. 460) will increase their love of literature.
- Predict that students will find fascinating information about life among wolves in "The Wounded Wolf" (p. 482). They will also understand more about the aftermath of an oil spill from reading "Can Oiled Seabirds Be Rescued, Or Are We Just Fooling Ourselves?" (p. 491).
- One of the many benefits of reading is seeing the world from a different perspective. John Gardner's "Dragon, Dragon" (p. 434) is a new take on an old tale. People who think that birthdays are always happy can gain insight by reading "Eleven" (p. 465).

Why Read Literature?

This unit presents a variety of short stories by authors from different cultures. Your purpose for reading each selection may be different, depending on the content. You might want to read to consider another point of view, read for information, or read for the love of literature. Preview the three purposes you might set before reading the works in this unit.

Read for the love of literature.

Charles Dickens is one of the "Top Ten" authors of all time. Along with Shakespeare, Dickens is one of the five authors who have had more books published about them than any other authors. Read a sample of the work the world finds so fascinating and enjoy a tale of ghostly humor when you read **"The Lawyer and the Ghost,"** page 476.

You may think a nineteenth-century Russian author who suffered from disease much of his life would have a poor sense of humor, but you would be wrong. Discover the laughter in literature when you read Anton Chekhov's humorous story **"Overdoing It,"** page 460.

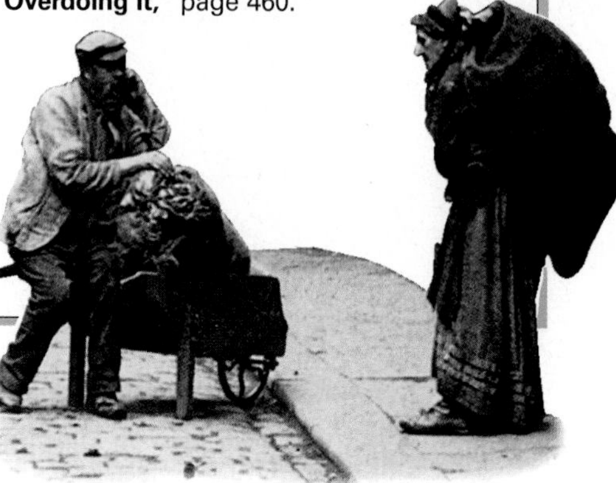

Read for information.

You have probably heard about the devastating effects of oil spills on wildlife. Find out what can and cannot be done to help water birds that have been covered with oil during a spill. Read **"Can Oiled Seabirds Be Rescued?"** page 491.

Wolves have been observed "decorating" the outsides of their dens with flowers. Jean Craighead George spent months in Alaska studying the behavior of wolves before writing her novel *Julie of the Wolves*. During her study, she once saw a wolf bring a bunch of flowers to the outside of its den and carefully place them at the entrance. Find out more about the unexpected qualities of wolves when you read **"The Wounded Wolf,"** page 482.

Read to consider another point of view.

You may think that all dragon slayers are strong and brave and that all birthdays are happy. Read two stories that consider other possibilities. Read about a meek and humble dragon slayer in **"Dragon, Dragon,"** page 434, and an unhappy birthday in **"Eleven,"** page 465.

Take It to the Net

Visit the Web site for online instruction and activities related to each selection in this unit.
www.phschool.com

ENRICHMENT: Further Reading

Have students choose one or more of the works below to extend the unit theme "Short Stories" or to read more by the unit authors.

My Side of the Mountain by Jean Craighead George
The writer of "The Wounded Wolf" tells the tale of a 13-year-old who spends a year in the wilderness trying to become self-reliant like his hero, Thoreau.

About the B'nai Bagels by E. L. Konigsburg
Mark Setzer plays on the Little League team called the B'nai Bagels. With his mother as manager and his brother as coach, he has many problems. In addition, he has to worry about his bar mitzvah.

Grendel by John Gardner
The writer of "Dragon, Dragon" retells the tale of Beowulf with a novel twist: The narrator is Grendel!

The Wizard in the Tree by Lloyd Alexander
Lloyd Alexander, who wrote "The Stone," also wrote this fantasy about a servant who frees an incompetent wizard from a tree.

How to Read Literature

Strategies for Reading Fiction

Fiction, which includes short stories and novels, is filled with made-up characters and events. Reading a work of fiction is like exploring a new world. As you read, your imagination creates a map of this world. The following strategies will help you find your way in a work of fiction.

1. Compare and contrast characters.

Looking at the similarities and differences between characters can help you understand them more fully. This unit will give you opportunities to compare and contrast characters from a variety of cultures and time periods.

2. Predict.

A map tells you what you will see around the next turn. As you read, make predictions about what might happen farther along the "road" of the story. Base predictions on your experience or on information in the story. In the same way that a rock in the road may cause you to choose a new path, new information can lead to new predictions.

3. Draw inferences.

Draw inferences, that is, make logical guesses or assumptions, based on details in a story. Strategies you will learn in this unit will help you "read between the lines" of fiction, to understand both what is stated and what is implied or suggested.

4. Picture the setting.

Use details provided in the story to create an image in your mind of a setting—the time and place in which the action of a story occurs.

- In this unit, you will learn to notice sensory details—words that appeal to the senses of sight, sound, smell, taste, and touch. These details will help you picture a variety of settings, including historical time periods and distant places.

As you read the selections in this unit, review the reading strategies and look at the notes in the side columns. Use the suggestions to apply the strategies for reading fiction.

How to Read Literature

The "How to Read Literature" page in each unit presents a set of strategies to help readers understand authors' words and ideas. Each reading strategy is taught in conjunction with one or more of the selections within the unit. Good readers develop a bank of strategies from which they can draw as needed.

Unit 6 introduces four strategies for reading fiction. To understand fiction, students must use elements of the genre within each of the stories. The strategies on this page help readers use textual elements to find the meaning of reading material.

How to Use This Page

Introduce the strategies for reading fiction, presenting each as a tool for reading the selections in this unit.

- As they read "Dragon, Dragon" (p. 434), students will compare and contrast characters in order to understand them more fully.
- As they read "Becky and the Wheels-and-Brake Boys" (p. 448), students will learn techniques for predicting a story's progress.
- As students read "The All-American Slurp" (p. 496) and "The Stone" (p. 505), they will gain experience in making inferences about characters and settings.
- As they read "The Lawyer and the Ghost" (p. 478) and "The Wounded Wolf" (p. 482), students will use details in the story to picture the setting.

MODEL A READING STRATEGY: Predict

Tell students to interact with the story they are reading by predicting what will happen as the story unfolds. They should use what they know and what they learn from a story to predict events.

Illustrate prediction by using a passage from "Becky and the Wheels-and-Brake Boys":

> Over and over I told my mum I wanted a bike.
> Over and over she looked at me as if I was crazy.

These sentences summarize the conflict between mother and daughter. Early in the story, students will want to predict whether Becky will change her mother's mind. As they read, students may revise their predictions.

Model the prediction strategy: "I know that Becky wants a bike, and her mother does not think she should have one. I will read more to see whether or not Becky can convince her mother to change her mind. I understand Becky's point of view better, so I predict that she will get the bike."

Dragon, Dragon

Lesson Objectives

1. **To analyze and respond to literary elements**
   - Literary Analysis: Plot
   - Connecting Literary Elements: Theme
2. **To read, comprehend, analyze, and critique a short story**
   - Reading Strategy: Comparing and Contrasting
   - Reading Check Questions
   - Review and Assess Questions
   - Assessment Practice (ATE)
3. **To develop word analysis skills, fluency, and systematic vocabulary**
   - Vocabulary Development Lesson: Word Analysis: Forms of *tyrant*
4. **To understand and apply written and oral language conventions**
   - Spelling Strategy
   - Grammar Lesson: Clauses
5. **To understand and apply appropriate writing and research strategies**
   - Writing Lesson: Help-Wanted Ad
   - Extension Activity: Compare-and-Contrast Chart
6. **To understand and apply listening and speaking strategies**
   - Extension Activity: Dramatic Reading

STEP-BY-STEP TEACHING GUIDE	PACING GUIDE
PRETEACH	
Motivate Students and Provide Background	
Use the Motivation activity (ATE p. 432)	5 min.
Read and discuss the Preview material and Background information (SE/ATE p. 432) [A]	5 min.
Introduce the Concepts	
Introduce the Literary Analysis and Reading Strategy (SE/ATE p. 433) [A]	20 min.
Pronounce the vocabulary words and read their definitions (SE p. 433)	5 min.
TEACH	
Monitor Comprehension	
Informally monitor comprehension by circulating while students read independently or in groups [A]	25 min.
Monitor students' comprehension with the Reading Check notes (SE/ATE pp. 435, 437, 439, 441)	as students read
Develop vocabulary with Vocabulary notes (SE pp. 435, 436, 440, 441)	as students read
Develop Understanding	
Develop students' understanding of plot with the Literary Analysis annotations (SE pp. 438, 441; ATE pp. 435, 438, 441) [A]	5 min.
Develop students' ability to compare and contrast with the Reading Strategy annotations (SE pp. 437, 440; ATE pp. 437, 440)	5 min.
ASSESS	
Assess Mastery	
Assess students' mastery of the Reading Strategy and Literary Analysis by having them answer the Review and Assess questions (SE/ATE p. 443)	25 min.
Use one or more of the print and media Assessment Resources (ATE p. 445) [A]	up to 45 min.
EXTEND	
Apply Understanding	
Have students complete the Vocabulary Development Lesson and the Grammar Lesson (SE p. 444) [A]	20 min.
Apply students' ability to write a help-wanted ad using the Writing Lesson (SE/ATE p. 445) [A]	45 min.
Apply students' understanding using one or more of the Extension Activities (SE p. 445)	20–90 min.

ACCELERATED INSTRUCTION:
Use the strategies and activities identified with an [A].

UNIVERSAL ACCESS
● = Below Level Students
▲ = On-Level Students
■ = Above Level Students

Time and Resource Manager

Reading Level: Average
Average Number of Instructional Days: 4

RESOURCES		
PRINT	**TRANSPARENCIES**	**TECHNOLOGY**
• **Beyond Literature,** Humanities Connection: Fairy Tales, p. 26 ▲ ■		• **Interest Grabber Videotapes,** Tape 3 ● ▲ ■
• **Selection Support Workbook:** ● ▲ ■ Literary Analysis, p. 130 Reading Strategy, p. 129 Build Vocabulary, p. 126	• **Literary Analysis and Reading Transparencies,** pp. 51 and 52 ● ▲ ■	
• **Adapted Reader's Companion** ● • **Reader's Companion** ●		• **Listening to Literature** ● ▲ ■ Audiocassettes, Side 16 Audio CDs, CD 8
• **English Learner's Companion** ● ▲ • **Literatura en español** ● ▲ • **Literary Analysis for Enrichment** ■		
• **Formal Assessment:** Selection Test, pp. 116–118 ● ▲ ■ • **Open Book Test,** pp. 76–78 ● ▲ ■ • **Performance Assessment and Portfolio Management,** p. 9 ● ▲ ■ • Prentice Hall Assessment System ● ▲ ■	• Prentice Hall Assessment System ● ▲ ■ Skills Practice Answers and Explanations on Transparencies	• **Test Bank Software** ● ▲ ■ • **Got It! Assessment Videotapes,** Tape 3 ● ▲
• **Selection Support Workbook:** ● ▲ ■ Build Spelling Skills, p. 127 Build Grammar Skills, p. 128 • **Writing and Grammar,** Copper Level ● ▲ ■ • **Extension Activities,** p. 26 ● ▲ ■	• **Daily Language Practice Transparencies** ● ▲ • **Writing Models and Graphic Organizers on Transparencies** ● ▲ ■	• **Writing and Grammar iText CD-ROM** ● ▲ ■ *Take It to the Net* www.phschool.com

BLOCK SCHEDULING: Use one 90-minute class period to preteach the selection and have students read it. Use a second 90-minute class period to assess students' mastery of skills and have them complete one of the Extension Activities.

PRETEACH

Step-by-Step Teaching Guide for pp. 432–433

Motivation

Read the Cobbler's poem:

Dragon, dragon, how do you do?
I've come from the king to murder you.

Tell students the poem was created by an old shoemaker to help his sons frighten and slay a horrible dragon who is destroying the kingdom where they live. Ask them whether they think it will work, and whether they would risk facing a dragon with this rhyme as their major weapon. Tell students they will have to read the story to find out whether the poem worked.

Interest Grabber Video

As an alternative, play "Suma, the Fire Dragon" on Tape 3 to engage student interest.

❶ Background

Culture

Dragons are mythological beasts that can be considered both helpful and fearsome. The Chinese associate dragons with water; four dragon kings rule the oceans of the world. Early Middle-Eastern literature attributes destructive qualities to the reptilian monsters. Dragons had more redeeming qualities in ancient Greek and Roman times, when they were thought to teach people secrets. Romans used dragons as part of their military insignia because the beasts were thought to both protect the troops and scare the enemy.

Prepare to Read

❶ Dragon, Dragon

Take It to the Net

Visit www.phschool.com for interactive activities and instruction related to "Dragon, Dragon," including

- background
- graphic organizers
- literary elements
- reading strategies

Preview

Connecting to the Literature

In "Dragon, Dragon," author John Gardner illustrates the power of advice—even advice that does not seem at first to make much sense. How has advice helped you work through problems?

Background

Since ancient times, dragon stories have been told all over the world. Different cultures have different beliefs about these imaginary creatures. Although Asian dragons are believed to be wise and good, in other cultures, dragons are greedy, evil creatures. In most Western folklore, the hero who kills a dragon is a brave, strong warrior who is rewarded with marriage to the king's daughter.

TEACHING RESOURCES

The following resources can be used to enrich or extend the instruction for pp. 432–433.

Motivation

Interest Grabber Video, Tape 3

Background

Beyond Literature, p. 26 ■

Take It to the Net

Visit www.phschool.com for Background and hotlinks for "Dragon, Dragon."

Literary Analysis

Literary Analysis and Reading Transparencies, Plot, p. 52

Selection Support: Literary Analysis, p. 130 ■

Reading

Literary Analysis and Reading Transparencies, Comparing and Contrasting, p. 51

■ **BLOCK SCHEDULING:** Resources marked with this symbol provide varied instruction during 90-minute blocks.

❷ Literary Analysis

Plot

The **plot** of a story is the sequence of events arranged around a problem, or conflict. In "Dragon, Dragon," the problem is introduced in the first sentence:

> There was once a king whose kingdom was plagued by a dragon.

As characters attempt to solve the problem, events build to a climax, or turning point. The resolution, or conclusion, of the story follows the climax. As you read "Dragon, Dragon," identify the following parts of the plot:

- **Exposition** (introduction of the problem)
- **Rising Action** (development of the problem)
- **Climax** (turning point)
- **Falling Action** (after the problem is solved)
- **Resolution** (how the problem turns out)

Connecting Literary Elements

The **theme**, or central idea, of a story is an insight about life or human nature. Sometimes, the theme is stated directly. Other times, you must figure it out for yourself by thinking about the characters and their actions. Determine the theme of "Dragon, Dragon" by looking for the lesson behind the outcome of each character's actions. While reading, keep the following focus questions in mind.

1. Which of the sons is successful at solving the problem, and why?
2. What theme, or message, is suggested by his success?

❸ Reading Strategy

Comparing and Contrasting

When you **compare and contrast**, you examine similarities and differences. Comparing and contrasting characters and their actions can provide a clue to the meaning of a story. As you read, make an organizer like this one. Then, compare and contrast the three brothers in this story, all of whom act differently when given the chance to become a hero.

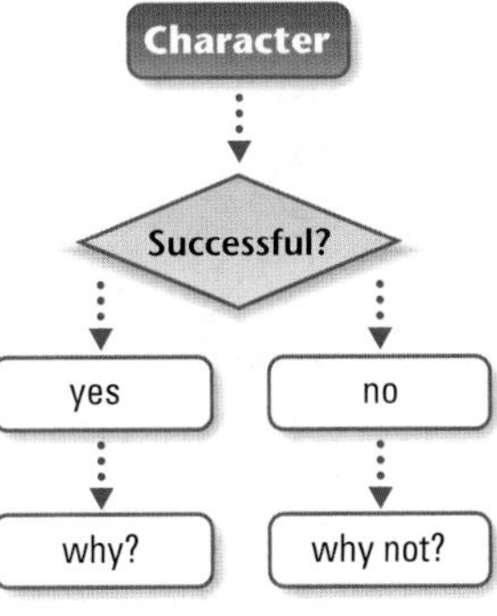

Vocabulary Development

plagued (plāgd) *v.* tormented (p. 435)

ravaged (rav′ ijd) *v.* violently destroyed; ruined (p. 435)

tyrant (tī′ rənt) *n.* cruel, unjust ruler (p. 436)

reflecting (ri flekt′ iŋ) *adj.* thinking seriously (p. 440)

craned (krānd) *v.* stretched out (one's neck) for a better view (p. 441)

CUSTOMIZE INSTRUCTION FOR UNIVERSAL ACCESS

For Special Needs Students	For Less Proficient Readers	For English Learners
Have students read the adapted version of "Dragon, Dragon" in the **Adapted Reader's Companion.** This version provides basic-level instruction in an interactive format with questions and write-on lines. Completing the adapted version will prepare students to read the selection in the Student Edition.	Have students read "Dragon, Dragon" in the **Reader's Companion.** This version provides basic-level instruction in an interactive format with questions and write-on lines. After students finish the selection in the Reader's Companion, have them complete the questions and activities in the Student Edition.	Have students read the adapted version of "Dragon, Dragon" in the **English Learner's Companion.** This version provides basic-level instruction in an interactive format with questions and write-on lines. Completing the adapted version will prepare students to read the selection in the Student Edition.

❷ Literary Analysis

Plot

- Explain to students that they will be studying plot, or the sequence of events that happen in a story, as they read "Dragon, Dragon."
- Have students think about the plots of favorite books or films. Then, ask a few volunteers to share the plots with the class.
- Point out that plot follows a pattern, beginning with exposition and ending with resolution. Clarify each of the terms with students.
- Discuss the theme in Connecting Literary Elements, and explain the relationship between the plot of a story and the theme. To help students understand the theme of "Dragon, Dragon," tell them to pay attention to the main characters' actions.

❸ Reading Strategy

Comparing and Contrasting

- Remind students that *comparing* involves finding similarities and *contrasting* involves finding differences.
- Tell students that comparing and contrasting the characters in a story can provide clues to the story's meaning. Using a few of the examples of plot given in the Reading Strategy notes, ask students to compare and contrast two of the characters.
- Suggest that students use the organizer to compare the brothers in the story. Point out that the information in the diagram will help them understand why each character was or was not successful.

Vocabulary Development

- Review the words and definitions on the vocabulary list.
- Point out the word *plagued* and explain that it has a negative connotation, or set of feelings associated with it.
- Ask students to identify other words on the vocabulary list with negative connotations. Possible responses: ravaged, tyrant.

 ***E-Teach***

Visit E-Teach at www.phschool.com for teachers' essays on how to teach, with questions and answers.

TEACH

Step-by-Step Teaching Guide for pp. 434–442

CUSTOMIZE INSTRUCTION
For Visual/Spatial Learners

In "Dragon, Dragon," most of the characters agree that the kingdom would be better off without the dragon. There are many references to things the dragon has done and is about to do, and many descriptions of his reactions to other characters. However, there is no description of what the dragon looks like. Have students take notes about the dragon or make sketches of it as they read the story. When they have finished reading, ask students to either draw or write a description of the dragon based on what they learn about it in the story.

❶ About the Selection

The kingdom in John Gardner's story "Dragon, Dragon" is plagued by a tremendous dragon that outsmarts anyone sent to kill it. The kingdom's cobbler, who thinks he is the least important person in the land, is perhaps the smartest. His two eldest sons volunteer to slay the dragon, but they fail because they refuse to take his advice. It is only the unassuming youngest son who decides that an older, more experienced person might know best. He takes his father's advice and slays the dragon. Gardner tells the story with humor and in the style of a fable.

❶ Dragon,

John Gardner

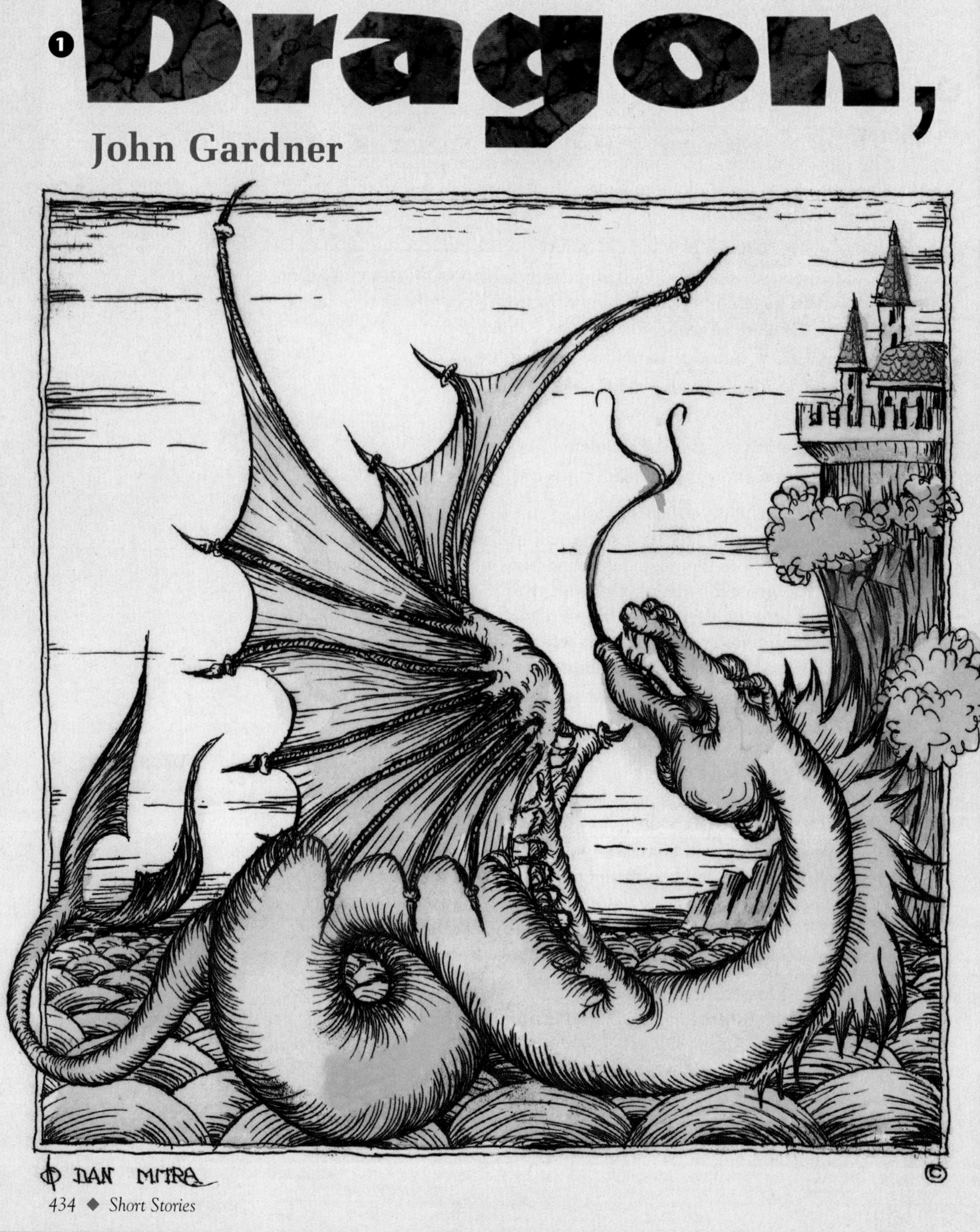

TEACHING RESOURCES

The following resources can be used to enrich or extend the instruction for pp. 434–442.

Literary Analysis
- **Literary Analysis for Enrichment** ▪
- **Writing Models and Graphic Organizers on Transparencies,** p. 89

Reading
- **Selection Support:** Reading Strategy, p. 129; Build Vocabulary, p. 126
- **Reader's Companion**
- **Adapted Reader's Companion**
- **English Learner's Companion**
- **Literatura en español**
- **Listening to Literature Audiocassettes,** Side 16 ▪
- **Listening to Literature Audio CDs,** CD 8 ▪

▪ **BLOCK SCHEDULING:** Resources marked with this symbol provide varied instruction during 90-minute blocks.

There was once a king whose kingdom was plagued by a dragon. The king did not know which way to turn. The king's knights were all cowards who hid under their beds whenever the dragon came in sight, so they were of no use to the king at all. And the king's wizard could not help either because, being old, he had forgotten his magic spells. Nor could the wizard look up the spells that had slipped his mind, for he had unfortunately misplaced his wizard's book many years before. The king was at his wit's end.

plagued (plāgd) *v.* tormented

Every time there was a full moon the dragon came out of his lair and ravaged the countryside. He frightened maidens and stopped up chimneys and broke store windows and set people's clocks back and 2 made dogs bark until no one could hear himself think.

ravaged (rav′ ijd) *v.* violently destroyed; ruined

He tipped over fences and robbed graves and put frogs in people's drinking water and tore the last chapters out of novels and changed house numbers around so that people crawled into bed with their neighbors.

He stole spark plugs out of people's cars and put firecrackers in people's cigars and stole the clappers from all the church bells and sprung every bear trap for miles around so the bears could wander wherever they pleased.

And to top it all off, he changed around all the roads in the kingdom so that people could not get anywhere except by starting out in the wrong direction.

"That," said the king in a fury, "is enough!" And he called a meeting of everyone in the kingdom.

Now it happened that there lived in the kingdom a wise old cobbler who had a wife and three sons. The cobbler and his family came to the king's meeting and stood way in back by the door, for the cobbler had a feeling that since he was nobody important there had probably been some mistake, and no doubt the king had intended the meeting for everyone in the kingdom except his family and him.

"Ladies and gentlemen," said the king when everyone was present, "I've put up with that dragon as long as I can. He has got to be stopped."

3 ✓Reading Check

What is the problem in the kingdom?

2 Literary Analysis

Plot

- Ask students to recall the plot term that introduces the problem in a story.
  Answer: The term is *exposition*.
- Have students find one sentence in the bracketed passage that summarizes the exposition of the story.
  Answer: Students should identify the first sentence as a summary of the exposition.
- Ask students to note information that supports the exposition.
  Answer: Among other things, the dragon has frightened maidens, tipped over fences and robbed graves, changed house numbers around, and changed around all the roads.

3 ✓Reading Check

Answer: The kingdom is "plagued" by a dragon.

CUSTOMIZE INSTRUCTION FOR UNIVERSAL ACCESS

For Less Proficient Readers	For English Learners	For Advanced Readers
To assist students with tracking character development in the story, have them make a list of characters as each one is introduced. As the plot progresses, students should take notes about each character's actions and attitudes.	Tell students that they should read the story not only for its literal events but also for its humor and its message. Ask them to recall other stories or fables that need to be read on more than one level, perhaps even in another language more familiar to them. Thinking about this as they read should improve their understanding.	Advanced students may benefit from close analysis of the story's dialogue. Gardner's characters use contemporary language, even though the story takes place long ago. Have students note modern language (such as "I've put up with") and explain its effect on the pace of the story and on the readers.

❹ Background

Literature

Beowulf is thought to date from the eighth century, although the earliest manuscript version of it is at least two centuries older than the story itself. The tale was originally told by bards, men who sang epic poems. It centers on the heroic achievements of a prince named Beowulf, who slays both the monster Grendel and Grendel's mother. In the process of killing the dragon, Beowulf, who has become king, receives a fatal injury. This epic poem is well known for its powerful language and metaphors.

❺ Background

Art

Frontispiece of *The Boy's King Arthur*, by N. C. Wyeth

N. C. Wyeth developed a naturalistic style, which he used in his drawings for historical novels and for children's literature classics.

Have students look at the picture. Then, ask the following questions:

1. What details in the picture of the king make him appear to be powerful?
   Answer: He is standing with his right hand forcefully placed on his sword and his left hand clutching his belt.
2. How do you think N. C. Wyeth would have portrayed the king in this story?
   Possible responses: Students may say Wyeth would have made the king look friendly, and he would be small and not imposing. His hands might be carefully folded in front of him. Wyeth may have made the king look worried.

All the people whispered amongst themselves, and the king smiled, pleased with the impression he had made.

But the wise cobbler said gloomily, "It's all very well to talk about it—but how are you going to do it?"

And now all the people smiled and winked as if to say, "Well, King, he's got you there!"

The king frowned.

"It's not that His Majesty hasn't tried," the queen spoke up loyally.

"Yes," said the king, "I've told my knights again and again that they ought to slay that dragon. But I can't *force* them to go. I'm not a tyrant."

"Why doesn't the wizard say a magic spell?" asked the cobbler.

"He's done the best he can," said the king.

The wizard blushed and everyone looked embarrassed. "I used to do all sorts of spells and chants when I was younger," the wizard explained. "But I've lost my spell book, and I begin to fear I'm losing my memory too. For instance, I've been trying for days to recall one spell I used to do. I forget, just now, what the deuce it was for. It went something like—

Bimble,
Wimble,
Cha, cha
CHOOMPF!

Suddenly, to everyone's surprise, the queen turned into a rosebush.

"Oh dear," said the wizard.

"Now you've done it," groaned the king.

"Poor Mother," said the princess.

"I don't know what can have happened," the wizard said nervously, "but don't worry, I'll have her changed back in a jiffy." He shut his eyes and racked his brain for a spell that would change her back.

But the king said quickly, "You'd better leave well enough alone. If you change her into a rattlesnake we'll have to chop off her head."

Meanwhile the cobbler stood with his hands in his pockets, sighing at the waste of time. "About the dragon . . . " he began.

"Oh yes," said the king. "I'll tell you what I'll do. I'll give the princess's hand in marriage to anyone who can make the dragon stop."

"It's not enough," said the cobbler. "She's a nice enough girl, you understand. But how would an ordinary person support her?

Literature in context — Humanities Connection

❹ ***Traditional Dragon Stories***

Much of the humor in "Dragon, Dragon" comes from the way it turns traditional dragon stories upside down. For example, in one of the most famous dragon stories of all time, *Beowulf*, the king is a wise and noble man. A terrible dragon has been attacking his hall and killing his warriors. When brave Beowulf, a true hero, learns the king needs help, he sails quickly to the rescue, humbly yet courageously presenting himself as the man for the job.

❺

Frontispiece of The Boy's King Arthur, N.C. Wyeth

tyrant (tī′ rənt) *n.* cruel, unjust ruler

ENRICHMENT: Social Studies Connection

Fables and Legends

John Gardner's story is unusual because it overturns the reader's expectations of traditional folk heroes and legends. Traditionally, such stories are thought to be based on the beliefs, values, and historical events of people in long-ago times, and they often reflect important aspects of the early history of a community.

Some students may be interested in learning about people in the early periods of American, European, or Asian history as it is reflected in this type of literature.

Tell students to look for collections of tales from the regions in which they are interested. They can use the school's media center, the local library, or the Internet for their research.

Have students make notes so they can retell or summarize one of their favorite fables or legends for the class. Sharing what they have read will give all of them some insights into different cultures.

Also, what about those of us that are already married?"

"In that case," said the king, "I'll offer the princess's hand or half the kingdom or both—whichever is most convenient."

The cobbler scratched his chin and considered it. "It's not enough," he said at last. "It's a good enough kingdom, you understand, but it's too much responsibility."

"Take it or leave it," the king said.

6 "I'll leave it," said the cobbler. And he shrugged and went home.

But the cobbler's eldest son thought the bargain was a good one, for the princess was very beautiful and he liked the idea of having half the kingdom to run as he pleased. So he said to the king, "I'll accept those terms, Your Majesty. By tomorrow morning the dragon will be slain."

"Bless you!" cried the king.

"Hooray, hooray, hooray!" cried all the people, throwing their hats in the air.

The cobbler's eldest son beamed with pride, and the second eldest looked at him enviously. The youngest son said timidly, "Excuse me, Your Majesty, but don't you think the queen looks a little unwell? If I were you I think I'd water her."

"Good heavens," cried the king, glancing at the queen who had been changed into a rosebush, "I'm glad you mentioned it!"

Now the cobbler's eldest son was very clever and was known far and wide for how quickly he could multiply fractions in his head. He was perfectly sure he could slay the dragon by somehow or other playing a trick on him, and he didn't feel that he needed his wise old father's advice. But he thought it was only polite to ask, and so he went to his father, who was working as usual at his cobbler's bench, and said, "Well, Father, I'm off to slay the dragon. Have you any advice to give me?"

The cobbler thought a moment and replied, "When and if you come to the dragon's lair, recite the following poem:

Dragon, dragon, how do you do?
I've come from the king to murder you.

Say it very loudly and firmly and the dragon will fall, God willing, at your feet."

"How curious!" said the eldest son. And he thought to himself, "The old man is not as wise as I thought. If I say something like that to the dragon, he will eat me up in an instant. The way to kill a dragon is to out-fox him." And keeping his opinion to himself, the eldest son set forth on his quest.

When he came at last to the dragon's lair, which was a cave, the eldest son slyly disguised himself as a peddler and knocked on the door and called out, "Hello there!"

"There's nobody home!" roared a voice.

Reading Strategy
Comparing and Contrasting Which character, the cobbler or his eldest son, seems more sensible? **[Explain]**

7 **Reading Check**
What does the father tell his eldest son to do when he gets to the dragon's lair?

6 Reading Strategy

Comparing and Contrasting

- Assign four students the parts of the king, the cobbler, the eldest son, and the narrator. Have them read their parts in the bracketed passage to the class.
- Write *Father* and *Son* on the board. Ask students how each character reacts to the king's offer. Record student answers.
  Answer: The father does not take the king's offer, but the son accepts it.
- Ask the Reading Strategy question on p. 437: Which character, the cobbler or his eldest son, is more sensible? Explain.
  Answer: The cobbler is more sensible because he does not take on a challenge that he cannot live up to, but the son makes a promise that he may not be able to keep.

7 Reading Check

Answer: The father gives his son a rhyme to recite when the son gets to the dragon's lair.

CUSTOMIZE INSTRUCTION FOR UNIVERSAL ACCESS

For Less Proficient Readers	For Gifted/Talented Students	For Advanced Readers
To help students understand the story line, have them read along with the tape or audio CD version of the story. Stop the recording after key scenes, and have students discuss what has happened. Invite them to predict further plot developments, record their predictions, and check the accuracy of their predictions as they read further.	The wizard and his spell and the cobbler's rhyme provide some of the comedy in "Dragon, Dragon." Challenge students to write additional spells for the wizard or rhymes for the cobbler, using the rhythm and rhyme scheme that Gardner uses in the story. Ask volunteers to read their spells to the class.	The eldest son prides himself on the knowledge he has acquired. However, he also discounts his father's wisdom. Have students write a paragraph defining knowledge, a paragraph defining wisdom, and then a paragraph contrasting them. Challenge students to show the relationship between being smart and being wise.

❽ Background

Culture

Explain to students that the eldest son is pretending to be a traveling salesman. Traveling salesmen are contemporary and commonly go from door to door in neighborhoods, selling anything from brooms to encyclopedias. The son is mimicking a salesman for the Fuller Brush Company, a company that was famous for selling brushes from house to house and through a catalogue.

❾ Literary Analysis

Plot and Theme

- Ask students to recall the relationship between plot and theme.
  Answer: The plot is a series of events in a story; the theme is the main idea of a story.
- Then, ask the Literary Analysis question on p. 438: What lesson does the cobbler's son learn as events unfold?
  Answer: The son learns that his father is wise and that he should have taken his father's advice.

Monitor Progress Ask students if the son's conclusion is a statement about the plot or about the theme of the story.
Answer: It is a statement about the theme.

Reteach If students have difficulty grasping the difference between plot and theme, point out that the actions that lead up to the son's realization are part of the plot. The son's realization is the main idea the author wants readers to understand, so it is the theme.

The voice was as loud as an earthquake, and the eldest son's knees knocked together in terror.

❽ "I don't come to trouble you," the eldest son said meekly. "I merely thought you might be interested in looking at some of our brushes. Or if you'd prefer," he added quickly, "I could leave our catalogue with you and I could drop by again, say, early next week."

"I don't want any brushes," the voice roared, "and I especially don't want any brushes next week."

"Oh," said the eldest son. By now his knees were knocking together so badly that he had to sit down.

❾ Suddenly a great shadow fell over him, and the eldest son looked up. It was the dragon. The eldest son drew his sword, but the dragon lunged and swallowed him in a single gulp, sword and all, and the eldest son found himself in the dark of the dragon's belly. "What a fool I was not to listen to my wise old father!" thought the eldest son. And he began to weep bitterly.

"Well," sighed the king the next morning, "I see the dragon has not been slain yet."

"I'm just as glad, personally," said the princess, sprinkling the queen. "I would have had to marry that eldest son, and he had warts."

Literary Analysis
Plot and Theme What lesson does the cobbler's son learn as events unfold?

Now the cobbler's middle son decided it was his turn to try. The middle son was very strong and he was known far and wide for being able to lift up the corner of a church. He felt perfectly sure he could slay the dragon by simply laying into him, but he thought it would be only polite to ask his father's advice. So he went to his father and said to him, "Well, Father, I'm off to slay the dragon. Have you any advice for me?"

The cobbler told the middle son exactly what he'd told the eldest.

"When and if you come to the dragon's lair, recite the following poem:

Dragon, dragon, how do you do?
I've come from the king to murder you.

Say it very loudly and firmly, and the dragon will fall, God willing, at your feet."

"What an odd thing to say," thought the middle son. "The old man is not as wise as I thought. You have to take these dragons by surprise." But he kept his opinion to himself and set forth.

When he came in sight of the dragon's lair, the middle son spurred his horse to a gallop and thundered into the entrance swinging his sword with all his might.

But the dragon had seen him while he was still a long way off, and being very clever, the dragon had crawled up on top of the door so that when the son came charging in he went under the

CUSTOMIZE INSTRUCTION FOR UNIVERSAL ACCESS

For Less Proficient Readers

Students may benefit from trying to identify with important characters. By understanding a character's thoughts and motives, readers gain a better understanding of a story plot. It will also improve their ability to use other strategies, such as inferring and predicting. If readers have personal experiences similar to those of story characters, their understanding is further strengthened. Model this thinking about the cobbler's eldest son to help students learn this strategy:

In "Dragon, Dragon," the narrator tells the reader that the cobbler's eldest son is too sure of his own cleverness to think through his father's advice. He then shares the thoughts that make this son believe he is wiser than his father. By putting myself in the son's place and thinking about a time when I rejected good advice from someone because I thought I was smarter, I understood the son's problem. I also could predict the younger sons' failure or success.

Dick Whittington on his way to London from My Nursery Story Book, Private Collection

11 ◀ **Critical Viewing**
Does the boy in this picture look like a dragon slayer? Explain. **[Evaluate]**

dragon and on to the back of the cave and slammed into the wall. Then the dragon chuckled and got down off the door, taking his time, and strolled back to where the man and the horse lay unconscious from the terrific blow. Opening his mouth as if for a yawn, the dragon swallowed the middle son in a single gulp and put the horse in the freezer to eat another day.

12 
Reading Check
What happens to the middle son when he arrives at the dragon's lair?

CUSTOMIZE INSTRUCTION FOR UNIVERSAL ACCESS

For Gifted/Talented Students	For Advanced Readers
Point out to students that writers use words to create images in readers' minds, whereas artists and film-makers use visual effects to create images. Have them brainstorm for ways to produce the images of the eldest or second son's attempts to slay the dragon. Students could create a mural of the image, or animate the encounter. Provide materials for them to create murals or animation.	Explain to students that rite-of-passage themes are about the transition of young men and women into adulthood. Slaying the dragon is a mythical rite-of-passage theme found in the literature of many cultures. Challenge students to locate texts with themes about rites of passage for young men and women. Have the school librarian assist students as they search the stacks or the Internet. Students should describe the results of their searches to the class.

10 Background

Art

Dick Whittington on his way to London from *My Nursery Story Book*

This illustration is a good representation of the cobbler's youngest son. The boy is fearful about his tasks, and the picture captures how uncertain he is about proceeding. Although the drawing was not done specifically for this story, its rich colors and impressionistic style capture the period and background of traditional folklore.

Have students examine the illustration, and then ask the following questions:

1. What do you think the boy in the drawing is thinking about?
   Possible response: Students may suggest that he is wondering why he agreed to try to slay the dragon, and he may be trying to think of a way to get out of doing this task.
2. Do you think he will continue or turn back?
   Possible responses: Students may suggest that, although his demeanor is fearful and uncertain, there does seem to be a look of purpose on his face and in the bend of his knees and right foot. They may also say that he is about to rise and go forward. Others may say he looks too fearful and will turn back to reconsider his choice.

11 ▶ Critical Viewing

Possible responses: Some students may say that the boy looks nothing like a dragon slayer. He is frail and appears to be fearful. He seems to be sitting on the stump thinking of a way to get out of his task. Other students may say he has a very calm and friendly appearance.

12 Reading Check

Answer: The middle son charges into the cave's wall, is knocked unconscious, and then is eaten by the dragon.

Even my own cousin Ben was there—riding away, in the ringing of bicycle bells down the road. Every time I came to watch them—see them riding round and round enjoying themselves—they scooted off like crazy on their bikes.

They can't keep doing that. They'll see!

I only want to be with Nat, Aldo, Jimmy, and Ben. It's no fair reason they don't want to be with me. Anybody could go off their head for that. Anybody! A girl can not, not, let boys get away with it all the time.

Bother! I have to walk back home, alone.

I know total-total that if I had my own bike, the Wheels-and-Brake Boys wouldn't treat me like that. I'd just ride away with them, wouldn't I?

3 Over and over I told my mum I wanted a bike. Over and over she looked at me as if I was crazy. "Becky, d'you think you're a boy? Eh? D'you think you're a boy? In any case, where's the money to come from? Eh?"

4 Of course I know I'm not a boy. Of course I know I'm not crazy. Of course I know all that's no reason why I can't have a bike. No reason! As soon as I get indoors I'll just have to ask again—ask Mum once more.

Literary Analysis
Conflict What is the conflict in the story?

At home, indoors, I didn't ask my mum.

It was evening time, but sunshine was still big patches in yards and on housetops. My two younger brothers, Lenny and Vin, played marbles in the road. Mum was taking measurements of a boy I knew, for his new trousers and shirt. Mum made clothes for people. Meggie, my sister two years younger than me, was helping Mum on the veranda. Nobody would be pleased with me not helping. I began to help.

veranda (və ran′ də) *n.* open porch, usually with a roof, along the outside of a building

Granny-Liz would always stop fanning herself to drink up a glass of ice water. I gave my granny a glass of ice water, there in her rocking chair. I looked in the kitchen to find shelled coconut pieces to cut into small cubes for the fowls' morning feed. But Granny-Liz had done it. I came and started tidying up bits and pieces of cut-off material around my mum on the floor. My sister got nasty, saying she was already helping Mum. Not a single good thing was happening for me. 5

With me even being all so thoughtful of Granny's need of a cool drink, she started up some botheration[1] against me.

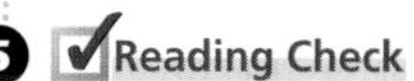

What does Becky want and what are some reasons she cannot have it?

1. **botheration** (bäth′ ər ā′ shən) *n.* trouble.

2 ◀ **Critical Viewing** Based on the expression and posture of the girl in this picture, what kind of personality do you think she has? **[Analyze]**

Opposite page: Daddy's Girl, 1992, Carlton Murrell, Courtesy of the artist

3 Literary Analysis

Conflict

- Remind students that they will be studying conflict as they read this story. Ask them to explain what *conflict* means in literature.
  Answer: *Conflict* is a struggle between two opposing forces.
- After students have read the bracketed passage, ask the Literary Analysis question on p. 449: What is the conflict in the story?
  Answer: The conflict is that Becky has asked her mother for a bike over and over, but her mother always says "no."

4 Reading Strategy

Predicting

- Help students understand how to make predictions based on a story's details.
- Select significant details and ask students what importance these details may have. Call attention to what characters say and do.
- After reading aloud the bracketed passage, ask students what details they might use to predict the eventual outcome of the story.
  Answer: Students may include Becky's early intense statements about owning a bike, the opposition of Becky's mother to her daughter's owning one, and Becky's determination in the face of this opposition.

5 Reading Check

Answer: Becky wants a bike, but she can't have it because her mother doesn't think bikes are for girls, and they don't have enough money to buy a bike.

CUSTOMIZE INSTRUCTION FOR UNIVERSAL ACCESS

For Special Needs Students	For Less Proficient Readers	For Advanced Readers
Have students read the selection in pairs. Tell pairs to take turns reading aloud and to help each other with pronunciations. Have each pair make a list of words they had difficulty pronouncing and/or understanding. Then, have students discuss their lists with their classmates.	Have students list statements or events from the story and make predictions based on each statement or event. They can fill in what actually happens as the plot unfolds. Have them use the Predicting transparency on p. 53 in **Literary Analysis and Reading Transparencies.**	Challenge students to make inferences based on information in the story. For example, the family cannot afford a bike; Becky's brothers play marbles in the road. What do these facts tell about the family? Have students construct inferences and test them as they acquire new information.

6 Critical Thinking

Compare and Contrast

- Ask students to explain what Becky's mother thinks about the Wheels-and-Brake Boys and why she thinks that way.
  Answer: She thinks they are a nuisance because they ride their bikes in a way that bothers other people.
- Based on what Becky has said about the boys, what does she think about them?
  Answer: She envies them and wants to be part of their group.
- Ask students to speculate on why Becky and her mother have such different views of the boys.
  Possible responses: Becky and her mother are different ages and have different ideas of what is important. They have different perspectives on the boys' behavior.

7 Reading Strategy

Predicting

- Ask the Reading Strategy question on p. 450: Do you think Becky will give up her idea of getting a bike? Why or why not?
  Possible answer: No; she will not give up her idea of getting a bike because she is determined to get what she wants.
- Ask students to cite examples from the text that support their answers.
  Possible answer: Becky shows her determination by continuing to pursue her dream of owning a bike, even after her mother has said "no" time and time again.

Listen to Granny-Liz: "Becky, with you moving about me here on the veranda, I hope you dohn have any centipedes or scorpions[2] in a jam jar in your pocket."

"No, mam," I said sighing, trying to be calm. "Granny-Liz," I went on, "you forgot. My centipede and scorpion died." All the same, storm broke against me.

6 "Becky," my mum said. "You know I don't like you wandering off after dinner. Haven't I told you I don't want you keeping company with those awful riding-about bicycle boys? Eh?"

"Yes, mam."

"Those boys are a menace. Riding bicycles on sidewalks and narrow paths together, ringing bicycle bells and braking at people's feet like wild bulls charging anybody, they're heading for trouble."

menace (men′ əs) *n.* threat; a troublesome or annoying person

"They're the Wheels-and-Brake Boys, mam."

"The what?"

"The Wheels-and-Brake Boys."

"Oh! Given themselves a name as well, have they? Well, Becky, answer this. How d'you always manage to look like you just escaped from a hair-pulling battle? Eh? And don't I tell you not to break the backs down and wear your canvas shoes like slippers? Don't you ever hear what I say?"

"Yes, mam."

"D'you want to end up a field laborer? Like where your father used to be overseer?"[3]

"No, mam."

"Well, Becky, will you please go off and do your homework?"

Everybody did everything to stop me. I was allowed no chance whatsoever. No chance to talk to Mum about the bike I dream of day and night! And I knew exactly the bike I wanted. I wanted a bike like Ben's bike. Oh, I wished I still had even my scorpion on a string to run up and down somebody's back!

I answered my mum. "Yes, mam." I went off into Meg's and my bedroom.

7 I sat down at the little table, as well as I might. Could homework stay in anybody's head in broad daylight outside? No. Could I keep a bike like Ben's out of my head? Not one bit. That bike took me all over the place. My beautiful bike jumped every log, every rock, every fence. My beautiful bike did everything cleverer than a clever cowboy's horse, with me in the saddle. And the bell, the bell was such a glorious gong of a ring!

Reading Strategy
Predicting Do you think Becky will give up her idea of getting a bike? Why or why not?

If Dad was alive, I could talk to him. If Dad was alive, he'd give me money for the bike like a shot.

---

2. **scorpions** (skôr′ pē ənz) *n.* close relatives of spiders, with a poisonous stinger at the end of their tails; found in warm regions.
3. **overseer** (ō′ vər sē′ ər) *n.* supervisor of laborers.

8

Mother, I Love to Ride, 1992, Carlton Murrell, Courtesy of the artist

I sighed. It was amazing what a sigh could do. I sighed and tumbled on a great idea. Tomorrow evening I'd get Shirnette to come with me. Both of us together would be sure to get the boys interested to teach us to ride. Wow! With Shirnette they can't just ride away!

Next day at school, everything went sour. For the first time, Shirnette and me had a real fight, because of what I hated most.

Shirnette brought a cockroach to school in a shoe-polish tin. At playtime she opened the tin and let the cockroach fly into my blouse. Pure panic and disgust nearly killed me. I crushed up the cockroach in my clothes and practically ripped my blouse off, there in open sunlight. Oh, the smell of a cockroach is the nastiest ever to block your nose! I started running with my blouse to go and wash it. Twice I had to stop and be sick.

9 ▲ **Critical Viewing**
What do you think the girl in this picture would tell Becky's mother about riding a bike? **[Speculate]**

10 ✓ **Reading Check**
How does Becky's mother feel about the Wheels-and-Brake Boys?

CUSTOMIZE INSTRUCTION FOR UNIVERSAL ACCESS

For English Learners	For Gifted/Talented Students
Becky's description of her daydream about the bicycle she wants (p. 450) is an excellent beginning point for students to learn bicycle terminology. Have them read the paragraph aloud. Then, demonstrate the parts of a bike with either a diagram or, if possible, a real bike. To reinforce the vocabulary lesson, have students draw pictures of a bicycle, and instruct them to label the parts.	Have students dramatize the action on pp. 449–450 with Becky and her family members. The student who portrays Becky should also be the narrator. Students may read from the book or construct their own scripts based on the story. In addition to reading the dialogue and narration, encourage students to use body language and facial expressions to show the characters' actions and emotions.

8 Background

Art

Biking for Fun, Daddy's Girl, and **Mother, I Love to Ride,** by Carlton Murrell

In these brightly colored works, the artist has used an impressionistic style, which is especially good for portraying the bicycling scenes. For example, the pictures on pp. 446 and 451 show people riding their bikes. The picture *Daddy's Girl* (p. 448) shows a friendly girl who is self-assured. Have students carefully look at these pictures, and then ask them whether the pictures have been helpful in understanding the story.

Discuss the following questions.

1. Does *Biking for Fun* (p. 446) portray the way the Wheels-and-Brake Boys feel when they are on their bikes? Explain your answer.
   Possible response: Yes; the colors used by the artist and the positions of the riders portray the independence and power of the bike group.
2. Do *Daddy's Girl* (p. 448) and *Mother, I Love to Ride* (p. 451) provide any clues about whether or not Becky will pursue her dream against the wisdom of her mother?
   Answer: *Daddy's Girl* is a good reflection of Becky's strength and personality; the other picture shows a girl riding a bike, which is Becky's dream.

9 ▶ Critical Viewing

Answer: The girl would tell Becky's mother that people feel a sense of joy and freedom when they are on a bike, and those who watch are envious of the rider.

10 ✓ Reading Check

Answer: Becky's mother considers the Wheels-and-Brake Boys a menace. She wants Becky to avoid them.

11 Critical Thinking

Infer

- Recall with students that *inferring* means using clues in a story to come to a conclusion about a character or an incident.
- After reading the bracketed passage, ask students to infer why Becky wants to join this group of bike riders.
  Answer: Becky wants to join them because she admires their independence, their bike-riding skills, their friendship with one another, and the fun they have together.

12 Reading Strategy

Predicting

- As narrator, Becky has told the readers a lot about her views of the Wheels-and-Brake Boys. Ask students how they think the boys view Becky. Have students explain their answers.
  Possible answer: From the way they avoid her and make fun of her, the boys probably do not want to have much to do with her.
- Have a volunteer read the bracketed passage. Ask the Reading Strategy question on p. 452: Will the boys include Becky? Why or why not?
  Possible response: They probably will not; it is an all-boy group, and Becky is not a good bike rider.

I washed away the crushed cockroach stain from my blouse. Then the stupid Shirnette had to come into the toilet, falling about laughing. All right, I knew the cockroach treatment was for the time when I made my centipede on a string crawl up Shirnette's back. But you put fair-is-fair aside. I just barged into Shirnette.

When it was all over, I had on a wet blouse, but Shirnette had one on, too.

Then, going home with the noisy flock of children from school, I had such a new, new idea. If Mum thought I was scruffy, Nat, Aldo, Jimmy, and Ben might think so, too. I didn't like that.

After dinner I combed my hair in the bedroom. Mum did her machining[4] on the veranda. Meggie helped Mum. Granny sat there, wishing she could take on any job, as usual.

I told Mum I was going to make up a quarrel with Shirnette. I went, but my friend wouldn't speak to me, let alone come out to keep my company. I stood alone and watched the Wheels-and-Brake Boys again.

This time the boys didn't race away past me. I stood leaning against the tall coconut palm tree. People passed up and down.
11 The nearby main road was busy with traffic. But I didn't mind.
I watched the boys. Riding round and round the big flame tree, Nat, Aldo, Jimmy, and Ben looked marvelous.

Reading Strategy
Predicting Will the boys include Becky? Why or why not?

At first each boy rode round the tree alone. Then each boy raced each other round the tree, going round three times. As he won, the winner rang his bell on and on, till he stopped panting and could
12 laugh and talk properly. Next, most reckless and fierce, all the
boys raced against each other. And, leaning against their bicycles, talking and joking, the boys popped soft drinks open, drank, and ate chipped bananas.

reckless (rek′ lis) *adj.* not careful; taking chances

I walked up to Nat, Aldo, Jimmy, and Ben and said, "Can somebody teach me to ride?"

"Why don't you stay indoors and learn to cook and sew and wash clothes?" Jimmy said.

I grinned. "I know all that already," I said. "And one day perhaps I'll even be mum to a boy child, like all of you. Can you cook and sew and wash clothes, Jimmy? All I want is to learn to ride. I want you to teach me."

I didn't know why I said what I said. But everybody went silent and serious.

One after the other, Nat, Aldo, Jimmy, and Ben got on their bikes and rode off. I wasn't at all cross with them. I only wanted to be riding out of the playground with them. I knew they'd be heading into the town to have ice cream and things and talk and laugh.

4. **machining** (mə shēn′ iŋ) *v.* sewing.

ENRICHMENT: Sports Connection

Bikes, Boards, and Skates

Bikes, boards, and skates are all forms of recreation, that have been around for a surprisingly long time. Bicycles are related to scooters—wheeled vehicles without pedals. Foot pedals were added (creating the first official bicycle) in 1839. The first in-line skates were invented in 1819. Because of poor performance, they were abandoned in favor of roller skates. They were reinvented by the Chicago Roller Skate Company in 1960. This company also produced wheels for the first skateboards, which appeared in 1958. These land-surfing boards were invented by a surf-shop owner in California.

Have students use the Timeline on p. 77 in **Writing Models and Graphic Organizers on Transparencies** to show the development of bicycles, skateboards, or in-line skates. They should gather maps, charts, photographs, and other materials, label them, and then assemble the materials into a classroom exhibit.

Mum was sitting alone on the veranda. She sewed buttons onto a white shirt she'd made. I sat down next to Mum. Straightaway, "Mum," I said, "I still want to have a bike badly."

"Oh, Becky, you still have that foolishness in your head? What am I going to do?"

Mum talked with some sympathy. Mum knew I was honest. "I can't get rid of it, mam," I said.

Mum stopped sewing. "Becky," she said, staring in my face, "how many girls around here do you see with bicycles?"

"Janice Gordon has a bike," I reminded her.

"Janice Gordon's dad has acres and acres of coconuts and bananas, with a business in the town as well."

I knew Mum was just about to give in. Then my granny had to come out onto the veranda and interfere. Listen to that Granny-Liz. "Becky, I heard your mother tell you over and over she cahn[5] afford to buy you a bike. Yet you keep on and on. Child, you're a girl."

"But I don't want a bike because I'm a girl."

"D'you want it because you feel like a bwoy?" Granny said.

"No. I only want a bike because I want it and want it and want it."

Granny just carried on. "A tomboy's like a whistling woman and a crowing hen, who can only come to a bad end. D'you understand?"

I didn't want to understand. I knew Granny's speech was an awful speech. I went and sat down with Lenny and Vin, who were making a kite.

13 By Saturday morning I felt real sorry for Mum. I could see Mum really had it hard for money. I had to try and help. I knew anything of Dad's—anything—would be worth a great mighty hundred dollars.

I found myself in the center of town, going through the busy Saturday crowd. I hoped Mum wouldn't be too cross. I went into the fire station. With lots of luck I came face to face with a round-faced man in uniform. He talked to me. "Little miss, can I help you?"

I told him I'd like to talk to the head man. He took me into the office and gave me a chair. I sat down. I opened out my brown paper parcel. I showed him my dad's sun helmet. I told him I thought it would make a good fireman's hat. I wanted to sell the helmet for some money toward a bike, I told him.

The fireman laughed a lot. I began to laugh, too. The fireman put me in a car and drove me back home.

Mum's eyes popped to see me bringing home the fireman. The round-faced fireman laughed at my adventure. Mum laughed, too, which was really good. The fireman gave Mum my dad's hat back. Then—mystery, mystery—Mum sent me outside while they talked.

Literary Analysis
Conflict and Resolution
In what way does Becky try to resolve the conflict on her own?

14  **Reading Check**
What does Becky do to try to get money for a bike?

5. **cahn** can't.

13 Literary Analysis

Conflict and Resolution

- Ask students to define the relationship between conflict and resolution in literature.
  Answer: *Conflict* is the struggle in the story; *resolution* is the way in which the struggle is resolved, or ended.

Monitor Progress If students have difficulty answering the question, use the Conflict transparency on p. 54 in **Literary Analysis and Reading Transparencies** to refresh their memories.

- Have a student read the bracketed text. Ask the Literary Analysis question on p. 453: In what way does Becky try to resolve the conflict on her own?
  Answer: Becky decides that the only way she'll ever get a bike is to sell her father's sun helmet.

Reteach Ask: How would this be a resolution to the problem?
Answer: It would be a resolution because she would have money to buy a bike.

14 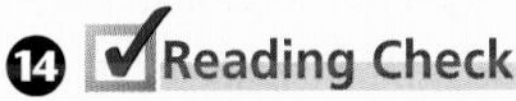 Reading Check

Answer: Becky tries to sell her father's sun helmet to a fireman.

CUSTOMIZE INSTRUCTION FOR UNIVERSAL ACCESS	
For Less Proficient Readers	**For Advanced Readers**
If students are still having difficulty understanding the dialect used by Becky and her family, have them read along in their books while listening to it on the **Listening to Literature Audiocassettes,** Side 23, or the **Listening to Literature Audio CDs,** CD 8. Then, help students rephrase sections of the dialogue and Becky's narrative, using vocabulary more familiar to them. For example, "It's no fair reason they don't want to be with me" can be rephrased as "They had no reason for not wanting to spend time with me."	Have students think about the bike Becky wants in the story as a symbol. Suggest to them that the object of her desire could have been anything—a new pair of shoes or another toy, for example. Ask them to write a brief essay explaining what the bicycle represents in this story. Students should offer ideas such as independence, freedom, or growing up (leaving childhood behind). Ask volunteers to share their essays with the class.

ASSESS

Answers for p. 454

Review and Assess

1. Possible responses: Some may say no, because it wasn't hers. Others may say that Becky thought her father would have understood.
2. **(a)** They are a group of boys who ride their bikes and have fun together. **(b)** Becky wants to join them because she wants the independence they have. **(c)** They represent freedom and fun.
3. **(a)** Becky's mother and grandmother think that the boys are troublemakers. **(b)** They do not think a girl should have a bike. **(c)** Becky's family cannot afford one.
4. **(a)** Mr. Dean, a fireman, offers to sell her a bike. **(b)** Becky's mother knows Becky wants it, and Mr. Dean says that they can make small payments. **(c)** Becky is happy because she has a bike; her mother is happy because she has a new friend.
5. **(a)** Becky is fun-loving, confident, and persistent. **(b)** Becky's self-confidence, persistence, creativity, and boldness help her realize her dream.
6. People who are determined do whatever it takes to get what they want, just as Becky is willing to sell something to get money. People who are stubborn refuse to change—Becky's mother is stubborn until she realizes how Becky feels.

My mum was only a little cross with me. Then—mystery and more mystery—my mum took me with the fireman in his car to his house.

The fireman brought out what? A bicycle! A beautiful, shining bicycle! His nephew's bike. His nephew had been taken away, all the way to America. The bike had been left with the fireman-uncle for him to sell it. And the good, kind fireman-uncle decided we could have the bike—on small payments. My mum looked uncertain. But in a big, big way, the fireman knew it was all right. And Mum smiled a little. My mum had good sense to know it was all right. My mum took the bike from the fireman Mr. Dean.

And guess what? Seeing my bike much, much newer than his, my cousin Ben's eyes popped with envy. But he took on the big job. He taught me to ride. Then he taught Shirnette.

I ride into town with the Wheels-and-Brake Boys now. When she can borrow a bike, Shirnette comes too. We all sit together. We have patties and ice cream and drink drinks together. We talk and joke. We ride about, all over the place.

And, again, guess what? Fireman Mr. Dean became our best friend, and Mum's especially. He started coming around almost every day.

James Berry

(b. 1925)

In his writing, James Berry often celebrates the richness of his West Indian heritage. His characters speak with the sounds and rhythms of Jamaican dialects, and many of his stories are set in his island birthplace.

Although he moved to England as an adult, James Berry's imagination seems to live in Jamaica. His young-adult fiction includes a novel called *Ajeemah and His Son*, the story of an African man and his son who are snatched by slave traders and taken to Jamaica. Another book, *A Thief in the Village and Other Stories*, is a collection of stories about life in Jamaica. "Becky and the Wheels-and-Brake Boys" comes from this collection.

Review and Assess

Thinking About the Selection

1. **Respond:** Do you think Becky should have taken her father's sun helmet to sell? Why or why not?
2. **(a) Recall:** Who are the Wheels-and-Brake Boys? **(b) Interpret:** Why does Becky want to join them? **(c) Analyze:** For Becky, what do the Wheels-and-Brake Boys represent?
3. **(a) Recall:** What do Becky's mother and grandmother think of the Wheels-and-Brake Boys? **(b) Infer:** Why don't they want Becky to get a bike and join the group? **(c) Analyze:** What additional reasons keep Becky from getting a bike?
4. **(a) Recall:** Who offers to sell Becky a bicycle? **(b) Infer:** Why does Becky's mother finally consent to buying Becky a bike? **(c) Analyze:** In what ways does the story end happily for both Becky and her mother?
5. **(a) Infer:** How would you describe Becky's personality? **(b) Analyze:** Which parts of Becky's personality help her to achieve her goal?
6. **Distinguish:** What is the difference between being determined and being stubborn? Use details from the story to illustrate your points.

ASSESSMENT PRACTICE: Reading Comprehension

Describing Character **(For more practice, see Test Preparation Workbook, p. 41.)**

Many tests require students to describe characters in literary selections. Students are expected to examine characters' traits, feelings, and motives. Write this sample test item on the board:

> Over and over I told my mum I wanted a bike. Over and over she looked at me as if I was crazy. . . . Everybody did everything to stop me. I was allowed no chance whatsoever. No chance to talk to Mum about the bike I dream of day and night!

Which of the following best describes Becky's feelings about not having a bicycle?

A content
B indifferent
C relieved
D frustrated

Becky's determination to have her own bicycle makes *A, B,* and *C* incorrect. Becky expresses her frustration. *D* is the best answer.

Review and Assess

Literary Analysis

Conflict

1. What does Becky want, and why?
2. What characters or conditions prevent Becky from getting what she wants?
3. How does the **conflict** intensify, and how is it solved? Show your answer on an organizer like this one.

Connecting Literary Elements

4. What is the **resolution** of the story? In other words, how is the conflict resolved?
5. On a web like the one below, list some of Becky's qualities that contribute to the resolution of the story.

6. Which other characters influence the resolution? How?

Reading Strategy

Predicting

7. (a) What **prediction** did you make about Becky's getting a bike? (b) On what details did you base your prediction?
8. Did you change any predictions? Why or why not?

Extend Understanding

9. **Science Connection:** Explain the relationship between the pedals on a bike and the wheels.

Quick Review

The **conflict** in a story is the struggle between two opposing forces. To review conflict, see page 447.

The **resolution** is the way the story turns out. To review resolution, see page 447.

A **prediction** is a logical guess based on past experience and information in the story.

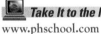

Take It to the Net

www.phschool.com

Take the interactive self-test online to check your understanding of the selection.

Answers for p. 455

Review and Assess

1. Becky wants a bicycle so she can ride with the Wheels-and-Brake Boys.
2. Becky's mother and grandmother do not want her to get a bike. In addition, her family cannot afford to buy one.
3. Possible response: Becky wants the boys to teach her to ride./The boys ride away. Becky tries to sell her father's sun helmet./Mr. Dean sells a bike to her mother.
4. The conflict is resolved when Mr. Dean sells the bike to Becky and her mother.
5. Possible response:

6. Mr. Dean influences the resolution by offering to sell the bike. Becky's mother influences the resolution by agreeing to buy the bike.
7. **(a)** Possible response: Students may say that they predicted Becky would get a bike.
   (b) Possible details include Becky's persistence and her mother's listening to Becky's ideas.
8. Students should be able to demonstrate reasons for any revision of their predictions.
9. When the pedals on a bike are pushed down, the chain moves; the chain then moves the wheels that move the bike.

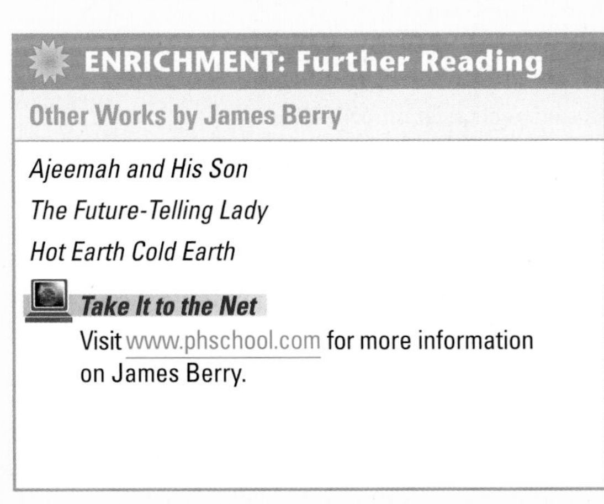

ENRICHMENT: Further Reading

Other Works by James Berry

Ajeemah and His Son

The Future-Telling Lady

Hot Earth Cold Earth

Take It to the Net

Visit www.phschool.com for more information on James Berry.

EXTEND

Answers for p. 456

❶ Vocabulary Development

Concept Development: Regional Synonyms

1. c
2. a
3. b

Spelling Strategy

1. necklace
2. surface
3. menace

Concept Development: Analogies

1. danger
2. reckless
3. menace
4. reckless
5. veranda

❷ Grammar

Possible responses:

1. When I open my book again, I will find the answer.
2. Becky begged and begged because she wanted a bike.
3. Becky went to see Mr. Dean, and he laughed at her idea.
4. The boys laughed as they rode.
5. Becky smiled at her new bike; her mother was pleased, too.

Writing Application

Possible responses:

1. Becky played a trick on Shirnette; she put a bug down Shirnette's back.
2. Those two girls are best friends; they like to spend time together.

Integrate Language Skills

❶ Vocabulary Development Lesson

Concept Development: Regional Synonyms

Regional synonyms are the words used in different places to describe or name the same thing. For example, Becky uses the word *veranda* to refer to a porch. On your paper, match the regional synonyms.

1. soda
2. trousers
3. hoagie

a. pants
b. hero
c. soft drink

Spelling Strategy

The *is* sound at the end of a word is sometimes spelled *ace*. Unscramble the letters to spell words that end in *ace*.

1. lanckece 2. secrauf 3. ceneam

Concept Development: Analogies

In word **analogies**, the pairs of words have the same relationship. In the following example, both first words are opposites of the second words.

fear : courage joy : sadness

Complete each analogy to create word pairs that are synonyms.

1. certain : sure :: menace : _________
2. happy : glad :: careless : _________

Use a vocabulary word from the list on page 447 to complete each sentence.

3. *Precipice* is to *danger* as *wildfire* is to __?__.
4. *Prudent* is to *sensible* as *irresponsible* is to __?__.
5. *Basement* is to *cellar* as *porch* is to __?__.

❷ Grammar Lesson

Independent Clauses

An **independent clause** is a group of words that has a subject and a verb and that can stand on its own. A **simple sentence** consists of a single independent clause:

The boys ride their bikes.

A **compound sentence** consists of two or more independent clauses. To join two independent clauses, use a comma and a coordinating conjunction or a semicolon:

I will ask, but she might say no.
He has a bike; I do not.

Practice Complete each of the following sentences with an independent clause. If the resulting sentence has two independent clauses, be sure to join them correctly.

1. When I open my book again, __?__.
2. __?__ because she wanted a bike.
3. Becky went to see Mr. Dean __?__.
4. __?__ as they rode.
5. Becky smiled at her new bike __?__.

Writing Application Add an independent clause to each independent clause below. Connect your new sentences with semicolons.

1. Becky played a trick on Shirnette.
2. Those two girls are best friends.

WG Prentice Hall Writing and Grammar Connection: Chapter 20, Section 2

TEACHING RESOURCES

The following resources can be used to enrich or extend the instruction for pp. 456–457.

Vocabulary

Selection Support: Build Vocabulary, p. 131; Build Spelling Skills, p. 132

Vocabulary and Spelling Practice Book (Use this booklet for skills enrichment) ■

Grammar

Selection Support: Build Grammar Skills, p. 133

Writing and Grammar, Copper Level, p. 424 ■

Daily Language Practice Transparencies

Writing

Writing and Grammar, Copper Level, p. 84

Writing and Grammar iText CD-ROM

■ **BLOCK SCHEDULING:** Resources marked with this symbol provide varied instruction during 90-minute blocks.

❸ Writing Lesson

Journal Entry

Write a journal entry as one of the characters in "Becky and the Wheels-and-Brake Boys." In the journal entry, describe an event from the story and include your own thoughts and feelings (as the character) about the event.

Prewriting Choose a moment in the story as the topic of your journal entry. Review the story, and jot down notes about your character's reaction to the occurrences.

Drafting Tell what happened, but do not stop there. Explain how you feel about the events, rather than just reporting them.

Model: Include Thoughts and Feelings

I sat down at the little table, as well as I might. Could homework stay in anybody's head in broad daylight outside? No. Could I keep a bike like Ben's out of my head? Not one bit.

Becky tells how she cannot keep her mind off her bike. She does this by asking and answering questions.

Revising Ask a partner to comment on whether your journal entry reflects the feelings of the character you have chosen. Keep your partner's suggestions in mind as you revise.

WG *Prentice Hall Writing and Grammar Connection: Chapter 5, Section 4*

❹ Extension Activities

Research and Technology Imagine that Becky has asked you to recommend a bicycle. Prepare a **chart** that compares and contrasts at least three different kinds of bikes.

1. To begin finding information, use the word *bicycle* to do a keyword search on the Internet.
2. Prepare a chart with the following categories: price, features, and condition.
3. Do comparisons in each category on retail Web sites. Then, based on your data, decide which one is the best buy.

Listening and Speaking Becky will need to learn how to take care of her bike. Present a set of **directions** for good bicycle maintenance. Obtain information in books or magazines about bikes. In your presentation, include the following:

- a list of materials needed
- a series of steps explained in logical order
- details that tell *when, how much, how often,* or *to what extent*

Take It to the Net www.phschool.com

Go online for an additional research activity using the Internet.

ASSESSMENT RESOURCES

The following resources can be used to assess students' knowledge and skills.

Selection Assessment

- **Formal Assessment,** pp. 119–121
- **Open Book Test,** pp. 79–81
- **Got It! Assessment Videotapes,** Tape 3
- **Test Bank Software**

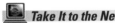

Take It to the Net

Visit www.phschool.com for self-tests and additional questions on "Becky and the Wheels-and-Brake Boys."

Writing Rubric

- **Performance Assess. and Portfolio Mgmt.,** p. 13

Listening and Speaking Rubric

- **Performance Assess. and Portfolio Mgmt.,** p. 14

PRENTICE HALL ASSESSMENT SYSTEM

- **Workbook**
- **Skill Book**
- **Transparencies**
- **CD-ROM**

Lesson Support for p. 457

❸ Writing Lesson

- Remind students that a journal is a type of diary that can be used to record actions, thoughts, and feelings.
- Use the steps in the Writing Lesson to help students develop a journal entry based on a character in the story.
- Remind students to include information about the setting and other characters. Tell them to make their descriptions vivid by choosing colorful words that precisely express the meaning they are trying to convey.
- As students review each other's entries, advise them to make constructive comments about their peers' work.
- Use the Narration rubric on p. 13 in **Performance Assessment and Portfolio Management** to evaluate students' journal entries.

❹ Listening and Speaking

- Have students work in small groups for this activity. Remind them that they are writing these directions for first-time bicycle owners. Tell students to make their instructions clear and specific.
- With your school librarian, assist students in finding resources about bicycle maintenance.
- Evaluate students' work with the Research rubric on p. 14 in **Performance Assessment and Portfolio Management.**

CUSTOMIZE INSTRUCTION
For Universal Access

To address different learning styles, use the activities suggested in the **Extension Activities** booklet, p. 27.

- For Visual/Spatial Learners, use Activity 5.
- For Verbal/Linguistic Learners, use Activity 6.
- For Musical/Rhythmic Learners, use Activity 7.

Overdoing It ✦ Eleven

Lesson Objectives

1. **To analyze and respond to literary elements**
   - Literary Analysis: Characterization
   - Comparing Literary Works
2. **To read, comprehend, analyze, and critique two short stories**
   - Reading Strategy: Recognizing Word Origins
   - Reading Check Questions
   - Review and Assess Questions
   - Assessment Practice (ATE)
3. **To develop word analysis skills, fluency, and systematic vocabulary**
   - Vocabulary Development Lesson: Word Analysis: Recognizing Commonly Used Foreign Words
4. **To understand and apply written and oral language conventions**
   - Spelling Strategy
   - Grammar Lesson: Subordinate Clauses
5. **To understand and apply appropriate writing and research strategies**
   - Writing Lesson: Character Description
   - Extension Activity: Chart
6. **To understand and apply listening and speaking strategies**
   - Extension Activity: Discussion

STEP-BY-STEP TEACHING GUIDE	PACING GUIDE
PRETEACH	
Motivate Students and Provide Background	
Use the Motivation activity (ATE p. 458)	5 min.
Read and discuss the Preview material and Background information (SE/ATE p. 458) [A]	5 min.
Introduce the Concepts	
Introduce the Literary Analysis and Reading Strategy (SE/ATE p. 459) [A]	25 min.
Pronounce the vocabulary words and read their definitions (SE p. 459)	5 min.
TEACH	
Monitor Comprehension	
Informally monitor comprehension by circulating while students read independently or in groups [A]	25 min.
Monitor students' comprehension with the Reading Check notes (SE/ATE pp. 461, 463, 465, 467)	as students read
Develop vocabulary with Vocabulary notes (SE pp. 461, 462, 463, 464)	as students read
Develop Understanding	
Develop students' understanding of characterization with the Literary Analysis annotations (SE pp. 462, 467; ATE pp. 462, 467) [A]	5 min.
Develop students' ability to recognize word origins with the Reading Strategy annotations (SE p. 463; ATE p. 463)	5 min.
ASSESS	
Assess Mastery	
Assess students' mastery of the Reading Strategy and Literary Analysis by having them answer the Review and Assess questions (SE/ATE p. 469)	25 min.
Use one or more of the print and media Assessment Resources (ATE p. 471) [A]	up to 45 min.
EXTEND	
Apply Understanding	
Have students complete the Vocabulary Development Lesson and the Grammar Lesson (SE p. 470) [A]	20 min.
Apply students' ability to write a character description using the Writing Lesson (SE/ATE p. 471) [A]	45 min.
Apply students' understanding using one or more of the Extension Activities (SE p. 471)	20–90 min.

ACCELERATED INSTRUCTION:
Use the strategies and activities identified with an [A].

UNIVERSAL ACCESS
● = Below Level Students
▲ = On-Level Students
■ = Above Level Students

Time and Resource Manager

Reading Level: Challenging, Easy
Average Number of Instructional Days: 4

RESOURCES		
PRINT	**TRANSPARENCIES**	**TECHNOLOGY**
• **Beyond Literature,** Workplace Connection: Dealing With Injustice, p. 28 ▲ ■		• **Interest Grabber Videotapes,** Tape 3 ● ▲ ■
• **Selection Support Workbook:** ● ▲ ■ Literary Analysis, p. 140 Reading Strategy, p. 139 Build Vocabulary, p. 136	• **Literary Analysis and Reading Transparencies,** pp. 55 and 56 ● ▲ ■	
• **Adapted Reader's Companion** ● • **Reader's Companion** ●		• **Listening to Literature** ● ▲ ■ Audiocassettes, Side 17 Audio CDs, CD 8
• **English Learner's Companion** ● ▲ • **Literatura en español** ● ▲ • **Literary Analysis for Enrichment** ■		
• **Formal Assessment:** Selection Test, pp. 122–124 ● ▲ ■ • **Open Book Test,** pp. 82–84 ● ▲ ■ • **Performance Assessment and Portfolio Management,** pp. 9, 29 ● ▲ ■ • PRENTICE HALL ASSESSMENT SYSTEM ● ▲ ■	• PRENTICE HALL ASSESSMENT SYSTEM ● ▲ ■ Skills Practice Answers and Explanations on Transparencies	• **Test Bank Software** ● ▲ ■ • **Got It! Assessment Videotapes,** Tape 3 ● ▲
• **Selection Support Workbook:** ● ▲ ■ Build Spelling Skills, p. 137 Build Grammar Skills, p. 138 • **Writing and Grammar,** Copper Level ● ▲ ■ • **Extension Activities,** p. 28 ● ▲ ■	• **Daily Language Practice Transparencies** ● ▲ • **Writing Models and Graphic Organizers on Transparencies** ● ▲ ■	• **Writing and Grammar iText CD-ROM** ● ▲ ■ *Take It to the Net* www.phschool.com

BLOCK SCHEDULING: Use one 90-minute class period to preteach the selection and have students read it. Use a second 90-minute class period to assess students' mastery of skills and have them complete one of the Extension Activities.

PRETEACH

Step-by-Step Teaching Guide for pp. 458–459

Motivation

Call students' attention to the photograph of the birthday cake on this page. Ask for words and phrases that come to mind when students think about birthdays. Write student responses on the board. Explain that in "Eleven," a girl has a birthday that does not turn out the way she would have hoped.

Interest Grabber Video

As an alternative, play "The Art of Anton Chekhov" on Tape 3 to engage student interest.

❶ Background

Social Studies

In the second half of the nineteenth-century, when "Overdoing It" was written, life in Russia was hard for many. The imperial czars tried to unite their vast empire by imposing the Russian language and Russian customs on all their people. This policy, known as Russification, antagonized various peoples within the ethnically diverse empire. The czars, however, feared that a multi-ethnic population could undermine their authority and cause the dissolution of the empire.

Prepare to Read

❶ Overdoing It ◆ Eleven

 ***Take It to the Net***

Visit www.phschool.com for interactive activities and instruction related to these selections, including

- background
- graphic organizers
- literary elements
- reading strategies

Preview

Connecting to the Literature

Sometimes, it seems that nothing goes well, and you just have to hope that tomorrow will be better. As you read these stories, ask yourself how you would react to the difficulties the characters face.

Background

In Anton Chekov's story "Overdoing It," a character's fear leads him to say and do foolish things. Fear caused many problems for Russians in the late nineteenth century. Because the czars (rulers of Russia) feared losing their power, they passed harsh laws prohibiting people from disagreeing with them. Sometimes people were imprisoned for suspected rather than real crimes.

TEACHING RESOURCES

The following resources can be used to enrich or extend the instruction for pp. 458–459.

Motivation

Interest Grabber Video, Tape 3

Background

Beyond Literature, p. 28 ■

 ***Take It to the Net***

Visit www.phschool.com for Background and hotlinks for the selections.

Literary Analysis

Literary Analysis and Reading Transparencies, Characterization, p. 56

Selection Support: Literary Analysis, p. 140 ■

Reading

Literary Analysis and Reading Transparencies, Recognizing Word Origins, p. 55 ■

■ **BLOCK SCHEDULING:** Resources marked with this symbol provide varied instruction during 90-minute blocks.

❷ Literary Analysis

Characterization

Characterization is the art of developing a character. Authors reveal characters' traits or qualities through their words, thoughts, and actions. Here, Chekhov uses the words and actions of the surveyor in "Overdoing It" to reveal the surveyor's faultfinding nature:

> "What kind of a wagon do you have here!" grumbled the surveyor as he climbed into the wagon. "You can't tell the front from the rear."

Comparing Literary Works

With **direct characterization**, a writer makes direct statements about a character. With **indirect characterization,** a writer reveals a character's traits through his or her thoughts, words, and actions and through what other characters say and think about the character. Use the focus questions to compare and contrast characterization in "Overdoing It" and "Eleven":

1. How much direct characterization does each writer use?
2. In which story did you learn more about a character?

❸ Reading Strategy

Recognizing Word Origins

Word origins are a word's roots—where a word comes from. English words often share origins with words from other languages. Some words used in English were borrowed from foreign languages and have changed over time. Others are spelled and used in their original form. The chart shows English and French for some travel-related words you will read in "Overdoing It." Notice similarities that indicate shared origins or borrowed words. Look for the English words in the story.

English	French
vehicle	véhicule
passenger	passager
station	station
mile	mille

Vocabulary Development

prolonged (prō lôŋd) *adj.* long and drawn out (p. 461)

emaciated (ē mā′ shē āt id) *adj.* thin and bony as a result of starvation or disease (p. 461)

wry (rī) *adj.* twisted (p. 462)

foresee (fôr sē′) *v.* know beforehand (p. 463)

emerged (ē merjd′) *v.* came out from; came into view (p. 464)

meditated (med′ i tāt id) *v.* thought deeply (p. 464)

CUSTOMIZE INSTRUCTION FOR UNIVERSAL ACCESS

For Special Needs Students	For Less Proficient Readers	For English Learners
Have students read the adapted version of "Eleven" in the **Adapted Reader's Companion.** This version provides basic-level instruction in an interactive format with questions and write-on lines. Completing the adapted version will prepare students to read the selection in the Student Edition.	Have students read "Eleven" in the **Reader's Companion.** This version provides basic-level instruction in an interactive format with questions and write-on lines. After students finish the selection in the Reader's Companion, have them complete the questions and activities in the Student Edition.	Have students read the adapted version of "Eleven" in the **English Learner's Companion.** This version provides basic-level instruction in an interactive format with questions and write-on lines. Completing the adapted version will prepare students to read the selection in the Student Edition.

❷ Literary Analysis

Characterization

- Have each student name a favorite character from TV, a book, or from a film. Then, have them write down five adjectives that describe the character. Finally, have students give examples of the character's actions.
- Explain to students that characters are developed through their words, their thoughts, and their actions.
- Use the characterization example from the story to show how authors develop characters. Ask students to describe the surveyor's comment. What does his comment say about him? **Answer:** The surveyor seems overly critical.
- Use the Characterization transparency on p. 56 in **Literary Analysis and Reading Transparencies** to show students how to gather information about characters.

❸ Reading Strategy

Recognizing Word Origins

- Remind students that English contains words from many other languages.
- Tell students that as they read "Overdoing It," they will encounter several travel-related words with foreign origins.
- After reading the Reading Strategy instruction to the students, suggest that they be alert for these expressions as they read.

Vocabulary Development

- Review the words and definitions on the vocabulary list.
- Point out that two words on the list describe an extreme. *Emaciated* means more than just skinny. It means "bony" or "starved to near death." *Meditated* means more than just thought. It means "thought deeply" or "reflected."

E-Teach

Visit E-Teach at www.phschool.com for teachers' essays on how to teach, with questions and answers.

TEACH

Step-by-Step Teaching Guide for pp. 460–468

CUSTOMIZE INSTRUCTION
For Bodily/Kinesthetic Learners

Have students read the text on p. 463 from "Because . . . because four . . ." through the paragraph beginning "Help!" Ask whether they can see why the surveyor should have realized the peasant was about to run away. Students should discuss the surveyor's final boast, which made the peasant so nervous that he ran away to save himself. Ask a pair of students to role-play this sequence for the class and demonstrate the characters' motivations.

❶ About the Selection

When the land surveyor Gleb Smirnov arrives in the Gnilushka train station, he hires a peasant to take him to the estate he must survey. It is twilight when they begin the journey, and the surveyor is afraid of being alone with Klim, the peasant, in the deserted countryside. To mask his fears, Smirnov exaggerates his physical strength and says that he has three revolvers. Klim fears for his life and runs off into the forest, leaving the surveyor lost and alone in the carriage. Smirnov calls for Klim for nearly two hours, and finally Klim returns. Smirnov assures Klim that there are no revolvers. Klim feels that Smirnov almost made him die of fright and wishes he had not agreed to take Smirnov to the country.

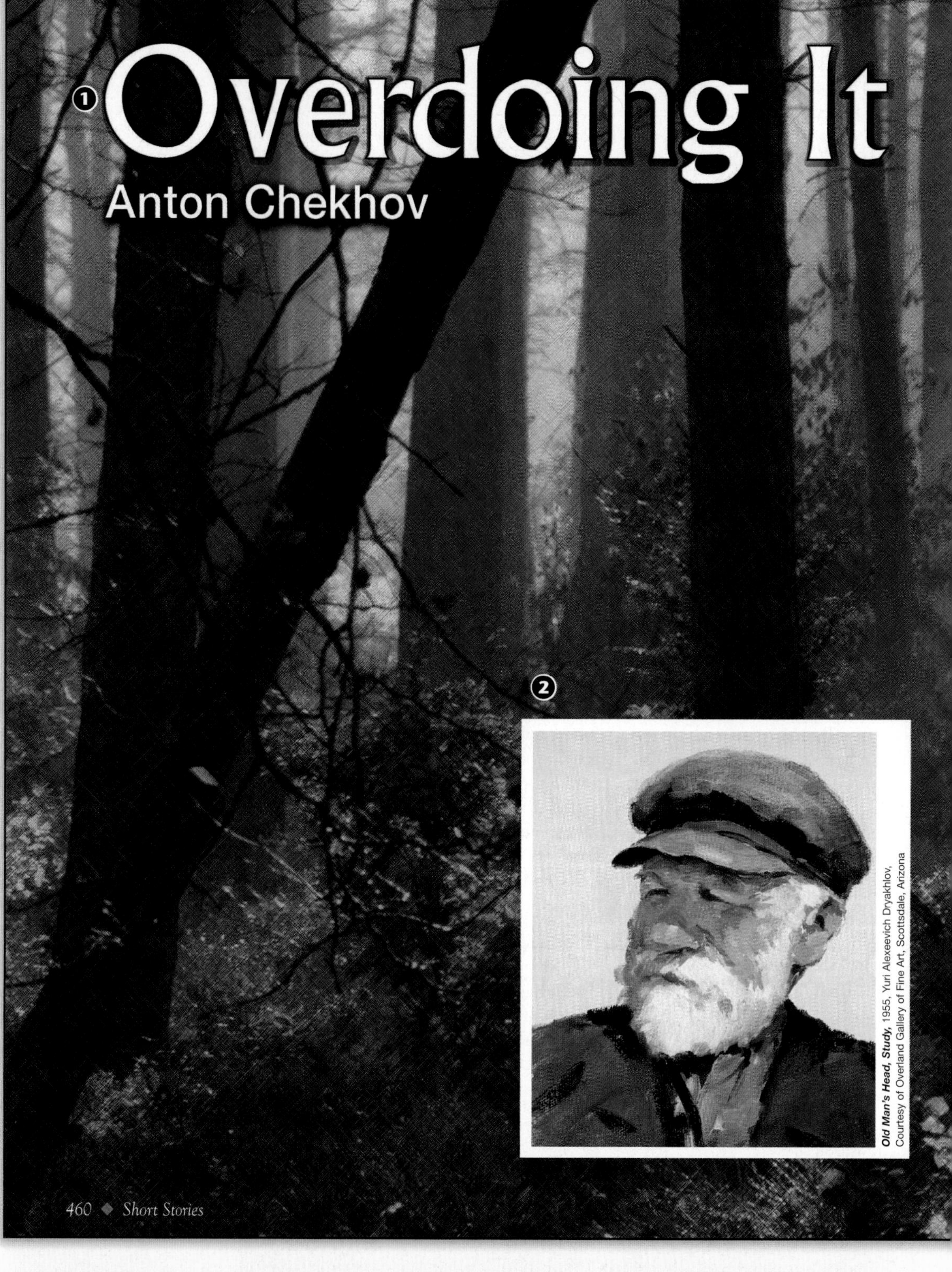

① Overdoing It

Anton Chekhov

②

Old Man's Head, Study, 1955, Yuri Alexeevich Dryakhlov, Courtesy of Overland Gallery of Fine Art, Scottsdale, Arizona

TEACHING RESOURCES

The following resources can be used to enrich or extend the instruction for pp. 460–468.

Literary Analysis

- **Literary Analysis for Enrichment**
- **Literary Analysis and Reading Transparencies,** p. 70 ■
- **Writing Models and Graphic Organizers on Transparencies,** p. 77

Reading

- **Selection Support:** Reading Strategy, p. 139; Build Vocabulary, p. 136

- **Adapted Reader's Companion**
- **Reader's Companion**
- **English Learner's Companion**
- **Literatura en español**
- **Listening to Literature Audiocassettes,** Side 17 ■
- **Listening to Literature Audio CDs,** CD 8 ■

■ **BLOCK SCHEDULING:** Resources marked with this symbol provide varied instruction during 90-minute blocks.

The land surveyor[1] Gleb Smirnov got off the train at Gnilushka. The station was some twenty miles from the estate he came to survey, and he had to cover that distance in a horse-drawn vehicle of some sort.

"Tell me, please, where could I find post horses and a carriage around here?" the surveyor said to the station guard.

"What kind? . . . Post horses? . . . Here for fifty miles around you couldn't even find a sled dog, let alone post horses. . . . Where are you bound for?"

"For Devkino—the estate of General Khokhotov."

"Well," the guard yawned, "try on the other side of the station. You may find some peasants over there who haul passengers."

The land surveyor made his way across from the station. After looking for some time, then after prolonged negotiations and hesitations, he engaged a husky peasant—glum, pockmarked, and dressed in a tattered gray coarse wool coat and bast-bark shoes.

prolonged (prō lôŋd) *adj.* long and drawn out

"What kind of a wagon do you have here!" grumbled the surveyor as he climbed into the wagon. "You can't tell the front from the rear."

"What is there to tell? Near the horse's tail it's the front, and where your lordship is now sitting is the rear."

The horse was young but emaciated, with splayed hoofs and nicked ears. When the driver, raising himself, struck her with his hemp whip, she merely shook her head. When he cursed and struck her a second time, the wagon creaked and shook as if with a bad chill. After the third stroke, the wagon lurched and swayed from side to side, and after the fourth, it moved.

emaciated (ē māʹ shē āt id) *adj.* thin and bony as a result of starvation or disease

"Is this how we'll proceed all the way?" the surveyor asked, feeling a violent jolting and amazed at the ability of Russian drivers to combine a snail's pace with a jolting that turned one's insides upside down.

"We-e-'ll get there . . . ," the driver assured him. "The mare is a young one, and spirited. Just let her get started at her own pace, then there'll be no stopping her . . . . Giddy-up, you accursed one!"

It was dusk when the wagon drew away from the station. To the right of the surveyor stretched the dark, frozen plain—broad and endless. Try to cross it and you'll come to the end of the world. On the horizon, where the plain merged with the sky and disappeared, the autumn sun was lazily sinking in the mist. To the left of the road, in the darkening space, loomed oddly shaped mounds, and it was hard to tell whether they were last year's haystacks or the

3 **✓Reading Check**

Who are the two men and why are they traveling together?

1. **land surveyor** one who measures land boundaries.

2 Background

Art

Old Man's Head, Study
by Yuri Alexeevich Dryakhlov

Yuri Alexeevich Dryakhlov was born in Nitzhni Novgorod, Russia, in 1928. He studied art at the Gorki Art College and the Vilnyus Art Institute. Dryakhlov specializes in landscapes and historical paintings. This study is a good example of his perception of human character.

After students have read p. 461, discuss the following questions:

1. What aspects of the work *Old Man's Head, Study* make you think that the artist is portraying a peasant?
   Answer: His very lined and weathered face makes him look as if he has had a hard life, and it might suggest that his work keeps him outdoors most of the time.
2. How is the man in the picture similar to the peasant in the story?
   Answer: His weathered face and dark clothes are similar to those of the man in the story.

3 ✓Reading Check

Answer: One is a surveyor and one is a peasant. The surveyor has asked the peasant to drive him to an estate that he must survey.

CUSTOMIZE INSTRUCTION FOR UNIVERSAL ACCESS

For Special Needs Students	For Less Proficient Students	For English Learners
To help students understand the development of events in the story, invite them to fill in the Timeline transparency on p. 77 in **Writing Models and Graphic Organizers on Transparencies.** Students should begin with the events at the train station and continue to the resolution of the story.	Encourage students to set a purpose for reading. Help students see the humor in "Overdoing It" by reading the surveyor's remark about the wagon on p. 461. As students read, have them look for and write down humorous passages and share them with the class.	Students may benefit from hearing **Listening to Literature on Audiocassettes,** Side 17, and pausing from time to time to clarify what is happening. They can then reread the story from beginning to end on their own to get the true experience Chekhov gives them of the surveyor's growing fear.

❹ Literary Analysis

Characterization

- Ask students to put themselves in the surveyor's place. What concerns would they have traveling in a strange place?
  Answer: They may be concerned about safety and about getting to the place where they were headed.
- Have a volunteer read the bracketed passage. Ask the Literary Analysis question on p. 462.
  Answer: The words show that he is worried about his own safety on the journey.

Monitor Progress Have students read to the end of the page. Ask: What is Chekhov showing in this passage? How is this passage a clue to the surveyor's character?
Answer: Chekhov is showing the surveyor's thoughts. They show his fears more clearly than his words will show them.

Reteach If students have difficulty answering the questions, continue the discussion about how characters are revealed. Ask whether they know more about the surveyor or the peasant driver, and why.
Answer: The reader knows more about the surveyor because Chekhov reveals his thoughts, but he describes only the driver's actions and words.

huts of a village. What there was ahead of them the surveyor could not tell because his field of vision was completely obstructed by the massive back of the driver. It was still, cold, frosty.

"What a God-forsaken place this is!" thought the surveyor as he tried to cover his ears with the collar of his greatcoat. "Not a man or beast in sight! Who knows what could happen in a place like this—they can attack you and rob you and no one will be the wiser for it. And this driver—he's not very reassuring. . . . Some husky back he's got! And he has the mug of a beast . . . yes, it's all very frightening."

"Tell me, my dear man," the surveyor asked, "what is your name?"

"Mine? Klim."

"Well, tell me, Klim, is it safe around here? No ruffians?"

"No, thank God! What kind of ruffians could there be here?"

"That's good that there are none. But, just the same, to play it safe, I brought along three revolvers," the surveyor lied. "And with a gun, as you know, it's bad business to joke. I can handle ten cutthroats with them!"

❹ It grew dark. The wagon suddenly creaked, squeaked, shook, and, as though against its will, turned left.

"Where is he taking me?" the surveyor thought. "He's driving straight ahead and suddenly he turns left. What is he up to? He'll take me, the wretch, into some thicket and . . . and. . . . One hears of such things happening!"

"Listen here," he called to the driver. "You say there's no danger around here? That's too bad! I like to fight off cutthroats. In appearance I'm thin, sickly looking, but I have the strength of a bull! Once three highwaymen threw themselves upon me. And what do you think happened? One of them I socked so hard that he gave up his soul to the Lord, and the other two were sentenced to Siberia to do hard labor because of me. And where I get all this power, I really couldn't tell you. I can grab a husky fellow—like you—and knock him down flat!"

Klim looked around at the surveyor, made a wry face, and struck the horse with the whip.

"Yes, brother . . . ," continued the surveyor, "may God help those who tangle with me! Not only will the cutthroat remain without arms and without legs, but he will be dragged off to court as well. I'm acquainted with every district judge and police inspector. I'm a civil servant, you know, and an important one at that. I'm in transit now, but the officials know about this journey . . . they're watching that no one does me any harm. Everywhere along the way, behind the bushes over there, are deputized village police inspectors and policemen. St-o-o-o-p!" the surveyor suddenly screamed. "Where did you drive into now? Where are you taking me?"

Literary Analysis
Characterization What do the surveyor's words reveal about him?

wry (rī) *adj.* twisted

CUSTOMIZE INSTRUCTION FOR UNIVERSAL ACCESS

For Gifted/Talented Students

Have students read aloud or play the audiocassette of the story, focusing on the description of the vast Russian plains and forests and the small cart carrying the peasant and the surveyor through them. Point out to students that writers use words to create images in reader's minds, whereas artists and filmmakers use visual effects to create them. Have students brainstorm for ways to produce images of Chekhov's landscape and the cart, perhaps even researching additional information about Russian land features. Students may decide to create murals or animation.

Divide students into small groups. Have each group create an aspect of the mural or animation. Provide the materials and/or equipment they need to create their projects. Have the groups present their visual representations to the class and explain their choice of media.

"Can't you see? Into the forest."

"That's right—it's a forest . . . ," thought the surveyor. "And I got scared! However, I must not show my fear. He's noticed already that I'm scared. Why has he been looking around at me so much? He's probably planning something. . . . Before he crawled along, and now look at him speed!"

"Listen, Klim, why are you hurrying your horse this way?"

"I'm not hurrying her. She is speeding of her own free will. I suppose she herself isn't pleased to have legs that make her go that fast."

"You're lying! I can see that you're lying! But I'd advise you not to rush that way. Rein in your horse! Do you hear me? Rein it in!"

"Why?"

5 "Because . . . because four pals of mine are joining me here . . . from the station. We must let them catch up with us. They promised to catch up with me in this forest. . . . It will be merrier to travel with them. . . . They are tough fellows, thick-set . . . each one is armed with a pistol. . . . Why do you keep looking around and fidgeting as if you were on pins and needles? Why? There is nothing to look at . . . there is nothing especially interesting about me . . . just my guns, perhaps . . . if you want me to, I'll get them out and show them to you . . . if you want . . ."

Reading Strategy
Recognizing Word Origins
Why do you think the word *station* has the same meaning and spelling in French and English?

The surveyor dug into his pockets for the imaginary guns. And then something unexpected, something that he did not foresee in
6 all his cowardice, happened. Klim suddenly rolled off the wagon and almost on all fours rushed into a thicket.

foresee (fôr sē′) *v.* know beforehand

"Help!" he wailed. "Help! Take the horse and the wagon, but don't kill me! Help!"

The surveyor heard the departing steps of the driver, the crackling of the underbrush—then complete silence. Not expecting such a verbal attack, the surveyor first of all stopped the horse, then sat back more comfortably in the wagon and gave himself over to thought.

"He ran off . . . got scared, the fool! What'll I do now? I can't go on by myself because I don't know the way, and also, I might be suspected of stealing his horse. . . . What had I better do?"

"Klim! Klim!"

"Klim!" answered the echo.

The thought that he might have to spend the night sitting there in the cold dark forest, hearing only the wolves, their echo, and the neighing of the emaciated mare, sent shivers up and down the surveyor's spine, as though it were being scraped with a cold file.

"Klimushka!" he cried. "My dear man! Where are you, Klimushka?"

The surveyor called for about two hours, and only after he

7 

What does Klim think the surveyor will do?

5 Reading Strategy

Recognizing Word Origins

- Explain to students that the English language developed from the combination of several different languages.
- Have a student read the first bracketed passage. Ask the Reading Strategy question on p. 463: Why do you think the word *station* has the same meaning and spelling in French and English?
  Answer: Students may theorize that the English language borrowed the word from French or that the words came from a common ancestor language.

6 Critical Thinking

Interpret

- Ask students what causes the driver to run into the woods.
  Answer: The driver gets scared because he thinks that the surveyor puts his hands into his pockets to pull out his guns.
- Discuss the surveyor's point of view. Why is he surprised when the driver runs off?
  Answer: The surveyor does not realize how the driver interpreted his remarks.

7 Reading Check

Answer: Klim probably thinks that the surveyor will hurt or kill him.

CUSTOMIZE INSTRUCTION FOR UNIVERSAL ACCESS

For Less Proficient Readers	For Advanced Readers
Chekhov's goal in "Overdoing It" is to give the reader a strong sense of how a character's imagination clouds his judgment. To help readers understand that the dialogue between the two characters is the result of the surveyor's imaginings, have students read p. 462 aloud. Then, discuss with them key words and phrases that will help them understand what is happening. Possible phrases for discussion include "Who knows what could happen in a place like this?" and "Where is he taking me?"	In the story, a supposedly intelligent person puts himself into an impossible situation, while an uneducated peasant acts reasonably. After they have read, have students review the language and devices Chekhov uses to set up the two characters, particularly on pp. 461–463. Have each student write a brief story that reverses the events: one of the characters is a crafty peasant who is thinking of robbing the surveyor and who is undone by his imagination, and the events are set in motion by the surveyor's innocent conversation.

Answers for p. 464

Review and Assess

1. Some students may say that they thought Smirnov would have to spend the night in the forest.
2. **(a)** The surveyor is looking for a driver and a carriage. **(b)** Students learn that the surveyor must travel twenty miles to get to an estate and that he needs a driver. They also can infer that he is unfamiliar with the area. **(c)** The narrator tells the reader that the surveyor must go twenty miles. The reader can see that he is unfamiliar with the area when he asks for a horse and carriage and the station guard is amused.
3. **(a)** The surveyor reacts to the setting by imagining he will be hurt or robbed. **(b)** He has heard about dangers in isolated areas and notices that the driver is a large person. **(c)** He copes with his fear by telling the driver he is armed, he is strong, and he is to meet some friends.
4. **(a)** The driver jumps out of the wagon and runs off into the forest. **(b)** The surveyor is surprised because he has not considered the effects of his remarks on the driver. **(c)** The surveyor assumed that the driver was a dangerous person and that he would not harm the surveyor if the surveyor made himself appear prepared for danger.
5. **(a)** In the end, the driver comes back and starts driving the cart again. **(b)** Yes, the surveyor benefits because he is no longer afraid, but his bragging almost backfires because the driver might not have come back. **(c)** The surveyor has learned that his words can create unanticipated effects.

became hoarse and resigned himself to spending the night in the forest, did a soft wind carry to him the sound of someone's groaning.

"Klim! Is that you, my dear man? Let's go on!"

"You'll ki-i-i-ill me!"

"I was just joking, my man! May God punish me if I wasn't joking! I have no guns! I lied because I was scared! Do me a favor, let's go on! I'm freezing to death!"

Klim, having perhaps decided that a real cutthroat would have long since got away with his horse and wagon, emerged from the thicket and hesitantly approached his passenger.

"What was there to get scared about, you fool? I . . . I was just kidding, and got scared. . . . Get in!"

"I'll have nothing more to do with you, master," Klim muttered, climbing up into the wagon. "Had I known, I wouldn't have taken you on, not for a hundred rubles. You nearly made me die of fright."

Klim struck the horse with his whip. The wagon trembled. Klim struck again, and the wagon lurched. After the fourth time, when the wagon moved, the surveyor covered his ears with his collar, and meditated. The road and Klim no longer seemed to him threatening.

emerged (ē merjd′) *v.* came out from; came into view

meditated (med′ i tāt id) *v.* thought deeply

Review and Assess

Thinking About the Selection

1. **Respond:** What was your reaction when the driver ran into the woods?
2. **(a) Recall:** What is the surveyor looking for when he gets off the train? **(b) Interpret:** What do you learn about the surveyor before he meets the driver? **(c) Support:** Which of his words and actions support your answer?
3. **(a) Recall:** What is the surveyor's reaction to the isolated setting? **(b) Interpret:** Why is the surveyor so fearful? **(c) Analyze Cause and Effect:** How does the surveyor cope with his fear?
4. **(a) Recall:** How does the driver react to the surveyor's bragging? **(b) Infer:** Why is the surveyor surprised by the driver's reaction? **(c) Deduce:** What assumptions do you think the surveyor had made about the driver?
5. **(a) Recall:** What happens at the end of the story? **(b) Evaluate:** Does the surveyor benefit from bragging? **(c) Speculate:** What do you think the surveyor has learned from this experience?

Anton Chekhov

(1860–1904)

Anton Chekhov was born in the middle of a family of six children. The family lived in a small coastal town of Southern Russia, where Chekhov's father ran a grocery business. When the business failed, the family moved to Moscow. There, Chekhov enrolled in medical school. By writing short stories and humorous articles, he earned enough money to help support his family.

Although Chekhov had tuberculosis for most of his adult life, he didn't allow his struggles against illness to limit him. In Chekhov's short lifetime, he wrote more than 400 short stories. He is considered one of Russia's greatest writers.

CUSTOMIZE INSTRUCTION FOR UNIVERSAL ACCESS

For Gifted/Talented Students

Tell students that the author of this selection, Anton Chekhov, wrote plays as well as short stories. Have them analyze how the dialogue shows the influence of his dramatic talents. Then, invite students to rewrite a portion of "Overdoing It" as a scene from a play. Possible scenes include the two men meeting at the station and the traveling scene in which the surveyor boasts of his strength and weapons. Suggest that students use the dialogue and descriptive sentences from the story that are appropriate for a play. Also tell them that they may need to add some explanatory stage directions and character descriptions as well as additional dialogue. Remind them that their audience will understand what is happening only through the dialogue and actions of the characters. Finally, as students rehearse, remind them that the story hinges on how the characters react to one another. The students taking the parts of the two men should interact as they say their lines in order to convey the mounting tension in the story.

8 # Eleven

Sandra Cisneros

9

Orange Sweater, 1955, Elmer Bischoff, San Francisco Museum of Modern Art, San Francisco, California

What they don't understand about birthdays and what they never tell you is that when you're eleven, you're also ten, and nine, and eight, and seven, and six, and five, and four, and three, and two, and one. And when you wake up on your eleventh birthday you expect to feel eleven, but you don't. You open your eyes and everything's just like yesterday, only it's today. And you don't feel eleven at all. You feel like you're still ten. And you are—underneath the year that makes you eleven.

10 ▲ **Critical Viewing**
Why might the girl in the picture be sitting alone?

11 ✓ **Reading Check**
How does the narrator feel about her eleventh birthday?

8 About the Selection

"Eleven" begins with Rachel, the narrator, saying that when she wakens on her eleventh birthday, she "doesn't feel eleven at all." When she goes to school, her teacher, Mrs. Price, makes Rachel wear an old red sweater that is not hers. Rachel is unable to tell Mrs. Price that the unattractive sweater does not belong to her, and she ends up crying. Rachel thinks about birthdays and how you do not feel different on the very day of your birthday, but in time you do feel older. She also realizes that people have all their birthdays and ages within themselves. After the incident at school, Rachel wishes she were far, far away instead of celebrating her birthday with people whom she knows.

9 Background

Art

Orange Sweater, by Elmer Bischoff

Elmer Bischoff (1916–1991) was known for his bold brush strokes, which enhance his use of color.

Use the following questions for discussion:

1. How would you describe the girl in the painting?
   Answer: She seems sensitive, lonely, or insecure, and she may be unhappy about something.
2. Why do you think the painter chose to place the girl in such a large space?
   Answer: He probably wanted to create a feeling of loneliness.

10 ▶ Critical Viewing

Possible response: She might be sitting alone because she is feeling sad and wants to be by herself. Another possibility is that she is trying to concentrate without distractions.

11 ✓ Reading Check

Answer: The narrator seems disappointed that she does not feel different on her birthday and that she does not seem a year older.

CUSTOMIZE INSTRUCTION FOR UNIVERSAL ACCESS

For Less Proficient Readers	For English Learners	For Advanced Students
Preview the story with students. Help them decode the long sentences. Then, have students read the story aloud, stopping to discuss sentences that are confusing. Help students break sentences into meaningful sections as they read. Students may benefit from reading the story fully a second time.	Some students may benefit from additional sentence study with this selection. Write some of the more confusing sentences on sentence strips, separating subject, predicate, objects, prepositional phrases, and so on. Help students reorder these into more familiar syntax.	Encourage students to consider their opinions of the characters. Have them list traits of the two main characters as they read, adding more traits when they finish reading. They can record their observations in a three-column chart using headings of *Character/ Beginning Traits/Ending Traits.*

⓬ ▶Critical Viewing

Possible response: Students may say they think the girl is feeling much older than she actually is and is having to cope with a lot of problems.

⓭ Background

Art

Portrait, by Eloy Blanco

Eloy Blanco was born in Aguadilla, Puerto Rico, in 1933. As part of therapeutic exercises he underwent for a speech problem during his childhood, he started to draw. He began to study at the Brooklyn Museum of Art School in 1948, and he had a one-person show a year later. This was a remarkable achievement for a young artist. The oval shapes of some of the figures in Blanco's paintings may have been inspired by Picasso's style.

1. Do you think that the girl in the painting represents Rachel? Possible responses: Some students may say that she looks like Rachel because she appears to be very serious; others may think that the girl in the painting is too old to be Rachel.
2. Would you want to get to know the person depicted in the painting? Why or why not? Possible responses: Some students may say that she looks too unfriendly and set in her ways for them to want to know her. Others may say that despite her serious expression, she is probably a very nice person.

Like some days you might say something stupid, and that's the part of you that's still ten. Or maybe some days you might need to sit on your mama's lap because you're scared, and that's the part of you that's five. And one day when you're all grown up maybe you will need to cry like if you're three, and that's okay. That's what I tell Mama when she's sad and needs to cry. Maybe she's feeling three.

Because the way you grow old is kind of like an onion or like the rings inside a tree trunk or like my little wooden dolls that fit one inside the other, each year inside the next one. That's how being eleven years old is.

You don't feel eleven. Not right away. It takes a few days, weeks even, sometimes even months before you say eleven when they ask you. And you don't feel smart eleven, not until you're almost twelve. That's the way it is.

Only today I wish I didn't have just eleven years rattling inside me like pennies in a tin Band-Aid box. Today I wish I was one-hundred-and-two instead of eleven because if I was one-hundred-and-two I'd have known what to say when Mrs. Price put the red sweater on my desk. I would've known how to tell her it wasn't mine instead of just sitting there with that look on my face and nothing coming out of my mouth.

"Whose is this?" Mrs. Price says, and she holds the red sweater up in the air for all the class to see. "Whose? It's been sitting in the coatroom for a month."

"Not mine," says everybody. "Not me."

"It has to belong to somebody," Mrs. Price keeps saying, but nobody can remember. It's an ugly sweater with red plastic buttons and a collar and sleeves all stretched out like you could use it for a jump rope. It's maybe a thousand years old and even if it belonged to me I wouldn't say so.

Maybe because I'm skinny, maybe because she doesn't like me, that stupid Felice Garcia says, "I think it belongs to Rachel." An ugly sweater like that, all raggedy and old, but Mrs. Price believes her. Mrs. Price takes the sweater and puts it

⓬ ▼Critical Viewing How old do you think the girl in this painting feels? **[Speculate]**

Portrait, From the Estate of Eloy Blanco, Collection of El Museo del Barrio, New York, NY

⓭

CUSTOMIZE INSTRUCTION FOR UNIVERSAL ACCESS

For Gifted/Talented Learners

Ask students to reread the paragraphs that describe Mrs. Price putting the sweater on Rachel's desk. Then, discuss how they would illustrate the setting of the schoolroom. Tell students to analyze the writer's words and come up with images for the setting, including the schoolroom's furniture and important props such as the sweater. Point out that their choice of colors will help enhance the mood in the schoolroom. Have students make an illustration of the classroom, showing Mrs. Price, Rachel, and Felice Garcia. Encourage them to try to portray the action of the main characters and how they are feeling at this time. Provide a variety of materials for students to create visual effects, such as paint, colored paper, and tissue paper.

Invite students to display their illustrations in the classroom. Have the class respond by describing the mood depicted in each illustration.

right on my desk, but when I open my mouth nothing comes out.

"That's not, I don't, you're not . . . not mine," I finally say in a little voice that was maybe me when I was four.

"Of course it's yours," Mrs. Price says, "I remember you wearing it once." Because she's older and the teacher, she's right and I'm not.

Not mine, not mine, not mine, but Mrs. Price is already turning to page 32, and math problem number four. I don't know why but all of a sudden I'm feeling sick inside, like the part of me that's three wants to come out of my eyes, only I squeeze them shut tight and bite down on my teeth real hard and try to remember today I am eleven, eleven. Mama is making a cake for me for tonight, and when Papa comes home everybody will sing happy birthday, happy birthday to you.

But when the sick feeling goes away and I open my eyes, the red sweater's still sitting there like a big red mountain. I move the red sweater to the corner of my desk with my ruler. I move my pencil and books and eraser as far from it as possible. I even move my chair a little to the right. Not mine, not mine, not mine.

In my head I'm thinking how long till lunch time, how long till I can take the red sweater and throw it over the schoolyard fence, or leave it hanging on a parking meter, or bunch it up into a little ball and toss it in the alley. Except when math period ends Mrs. Price says loud and in front of everybody, "Now, Rachel, that's enough," because she sees I've shoved the red sweater to the tippy-tip corner of my desk and it's hanging all over the edge like a waterfall, but I
14 don't care.

"Rachel," Mrs. Price says. She says it like she's getting mad. "You put that sweater on right now and no more nonsense."

"But it's not . . ."

"Now!" Mrs. Price says.

This is when I wish I wasn't eleven, because all the years inside of me—ten, nine, eight, seven, six, five, four, three, two, and one—are all pushing at the back of my eyes when I put one arm through one sleeve of the sweater that smells like cottage cheese, and then the other arm through the other and stand there with my arms apart as if the sweater hurts me and it does, all itchy and full of germs that aren't even mine.

That's when everything I've been holding in since this morning, since when Mrs. Price put the sweater on my desk, finally lets go, and all of a sudden I'm crying in front of everybody. I wish I was invisible but I'm not. I'm eleven and it's my birthday today and I'm crying like I'm three in front of everybody. I put my head down on the desk and bury my face in my stupid clown sweater arms. My face all hot and spit coming out of my mouth because I can't stop the little animal noises from coming out of me, until there aren't

Literary Analysis
Characterization How do Mrs. Price's actions show that she is not a patient or sympathetic character?

15  **Reading Check**
What does Rachel do after putting on the sweater?

14 Literary Analysis

Characterization

- Ask students to recall the difference between direct characterization and indirect characterization.
  Answer: With direct characterization, the author tells readers *about* the character. With indirect characterization, the author reveals characters through their speech and actions.
- Ask the Literary Analysis question on p. 467: How do Mrs. Price's actions show that she is not a patient or sympathetic character?
  Answer: She does not listen when Rachel tells her that the sweater is not hers; she gets angry when Rachel hangs the sweater over the side of her desk; she makes Rachel put on the sweater when Rachel does not want to.

15 Reading Check

Answer: Rachel begins to cry after putting on the sweater.

CUSTOMIZE INSTRUCTION FOR UNIVERSAL ACCESS

For Special Needs Students	For Advanced Students
Invite students to return to the text in order to study the plot more closely. Have them make illustrations on cards that show key events in the story. Possibilities include: Rachel waking up on her birthday, Mrs. Price asking about the red sweater, and Rachel hanging the sweater over the edge of her desk. Students can write a sentence describing the illustration on the back of the card. After they have completed the illustrations, have students mix the cards up and then put them in the correct order.	Students may enjoy investigating and expanding upon Rachel's analogies for aging. Have students read the paragraph on p. 466 that begins "Because the way you grow old is . . . ." Invite students to explain the analogies, using actual onions, tree trunks, or nesting dolls. Encourage them to come up with other analogies for aging or other processes with which they are familiar. Have them present their analogies to the class and invite comment on their effectiveness.

ASSESS

Answers for p. 468

Review and Assess

1. Possible responses: Students may want Rachel to express her feelings about the sweater to Mrs. Price. Others would express disappointment with Felice.
2. **(a)** It is Rachel's eleventh birthday. **(b)** Rachel thinks that aging happens like a tree grows: You add another layer every year. **(c)** Events may make her feel and react as if she were younger.
3. **(a)** Mrs. Price sees the sweater as lost clothing; Rachel thinks it is ugly and knows it isn't hers. **(b)** Rachel cannot speak up because she is too upset. **(c)** She knows that the sweater is not hers.
4. **(a)** Phyllis Lopez claims the sweater. **(b)** Rachel is still upset. **(c)** It is satisfactory because it proves that the sweater is not Rachel's; it is unsatisfactory because Rachel is still upset.
5. **(a)** Rachel wants to be "anything but eleven" so the day would be a memory. **(b)** The story suggests that her theory about aging is true because she feels younger than she is.
6. **(a)** Possible responses: Advantages of growing up include freedom. Disadvantages include more responsibility. **(b)** Rachel's experiences show that being older means she must speak up. **(c)** Yes, Rachel's reactions are understandable because she is a sensitive person.

any more tears left in my eyes, and it's just my body shaking like when you have the hiccups, and my whole head hurts like when you drink milk too fast.

But the worst part is right before the bell rings for lunch. That stupid Phyllis Lopez, who is even dumber than Felice Garcia, says she remembers the red sweater is hers! I take it off right away and give it to her, only Mrs. Price pretends like everything's okay.

Today I'm eleven. There's a cake Mama's making for tonight, and when Papa comes home from work we'll eat it. There'll be candles and presents and everybody will sing happy birthday, happy birthday to you, Rachel, only it's too late.

I'm eleven today. I'm eleven, ten, nine, eight, seven, six, five, four, three, two, and one, but I wish I was one-hundred-and-two. I wish I was anything but eleven, because I want today to be far away already, far away like a tiny kite in the sky, so tiny-tiny you have to close your eyes to see it.

Review and Assess

Thinking About the Selection

1. **Respond:** What would you like to say to Rachel? To Mrs. Price? To Felice Garcia?
2. **(a) Recall:** What is special about the day in this story? **(b) Interpret:** What is Rachel's theory about a person's age? **(c) Analyze:** Explain how Rachel can be eleven, but also all her younger ages as well.
3. **(a) Recall:** How do Mrs. Price and Rachel react differently to the red sweater? **(b) Infer:** Why can't Rachel speak up to tell Mrs. Price that the sweater is not hers? **(c) Analyze:** Why does Rachel react so strongly to being given the sweater?
4. **(a) Recall:** How is the mix-up straightened out? **(b) Describe:** How does Rachel feel after the problem is solved? **(c) Distinguish:** In what ways is this a satisfactory or unsatisfactory solution?
5. **(a) Analyze:** Why does Rachel wish she were "anything but eleven"? **(b) Connect:** In what way do the story events suggest that Rachel's theory about ages has some truth to it?
6. **(a) Assess:** What are some advantages and disadvantages to "growing up"? **(b) Apply:** What disadvantages do Rachel's experiences illustrate? **(c) Make a Judgment:** Are Rachel's reactions understandable? Explain.

Sandra Cisneros

(b. 1954)

Sandra Cisneros was born in Chicago and stayed in her hometown through college. Then, she moved to Iowa and began to write about her life, her family, and her Mexican heritage. She writes about real-life experiences.

Cisneros creates characters who are distinctly Hispanic and who are often isolated from mainstream culture. The themes of isolation, divided cultural loyalties, and alienation appear in many of her works. They reflect Cisneros's own feeling of being an "outsider" as a Hispanic American youth growing up in the United States.

ASSESSMENT PRACTICE: Reading Comprehension

Describing Setting (For more practice, see Test Preparation Workbook, p. 40.)

Many tests require students to describe the setting of a literary work. Write the following sample test item on the board:

It was dusk when the wagon drew away from the station. To the right of the surveyor stretched the dark, frozen plain—broad and endless. Try to cross it and you'll come to the end of the world.

Which of the following best describes the setting of the story?

A the cold countryside at twilight
B early morning in the city
C early afternoon at the train station
D afternoon on the estate

The city and the estate are not mentioned in the passage, so *B* and *D* are incorrect. The station is mentioned, but the time is at twilight, not early afternoon. Thus, *C* is also incorrect. It is "dusk" when the men set off across the "frozen plain." The correct answer is *A*.

Review and Assess

Literary Analysis

Characterization

1. On a chart like the one shown, identify some of the key details of **characterization** for each character.

Character	Words	Thoughts	Actions
Klim			
Surveyor			
Rachel			
Mrs. Price			

2. Describe each character in your own words.

Comparing Literary Works

3. Use organizers like these to record details of **direct** and **indirect characterization** of Klim, the surveyor, Rachel, and Mrs. Price.

4. How much direct characterization does each writer use?
5. Which character from these stories seems the most believable? Explain why.
6. In which story did you learn more about a character? Why?

Reading Strategy

Recognizing Word Origins

7. Use a dictionary to find the **origins** of the following words: (a) mile (b) station (c) vehicle (d) passenger.
8. The French word *bon* means *good*. Explain the meaning of *bon voyage*.
9. If Rachel invited classmates to a birthday party, the invitation would probably say *RSVP*. Use a dictionary to find the origin and meaning of this expression. Explain what language it comes from, what the full expression is, and what it means.

Extend Understanding

10. **Career Connection:** The land surveyor's job requires that he visit unfamiliar places. In what other careers do people often travel to unfamiliar places?

Quick Review

Characterization is the art of creating and developing a character. To review characterization, see page 463.

Direct characterization results when an author directly states information about a character.

Indirect characterization results when the character's traits are revealed through what the character does, says, and thinks, as well as through the words and thoughts of other characters.

Word origins are a word's roots—where a word comes from. To review word origins, see page 463.

Take It to the Net

www.phschool.com

Take the interactive self-test online to check your understanding of these selections.

Answers for p. 469

Review and Assess

1. Klim **Words:** "Near the horse's tail it's the front, and where your lordship is now sitting is the rear." "Take the horse and wagon, but don't kill me!" **Thoughts:** not given **Actions:** jumps off cart and runs into the forest Surveyor **Words:** "Is it safe around here?" "I was just kidding, and got scared." **Thoughts:** "What a God-for-saken place this is!" "He ran off . . . got scared, the fool!" **Actions:** digs into his pocket for imaginary guns Rachel **Words:** "That's not, I don't, you're not . . . not mine." **Thoughts:** "Not mine, not mine, not mine." **Actions:** pushes sweater off desk; puts sweater on when told Mrs. Price **Words:** "I remember you wearing it once." "You put that sweater on right now." "Now!" **Thoughts:** not given **Actions:** puts sweater on Rachel's desk
2. Possible response: Klim is simple and reacts reasonably. The surveyor is foolish. Rachel is sensitive. Mrs. Price is thoughtless.
3. Klim: **Direct:** husky, glum, poorly dressed, decided that a real cut-throat would have run away already **Indirect:** talks back to surveyor, runs away, regrets taking on the passenger Surveyor: **Direct:** occupation, afraid of staying out alone all night **Indirect:** uncomfortable in wagon, afraid of Klim, lies about weapons and strength, says he was joking Rachel: **Direct:** none **Indirect:** her theory of aging, feels sick inside about the sweater, cries Mrs. Price: **Direct:** none **Indirect:** says she thinks Rachel owns the sweater, pretends that everything is okay
4. Chekhov uses direct characterization, but Cisneros does not.
5. The character that seems to be most believable is Rachel because her shame and frustration are described vividly.
6. The reader learns more about Rachel in "Eleven" because she tells the reader her thoughts.
7. **(a)** *Mile* is from the Latin for *thousand.* **(b)** *Station* is from Latin and French for *standing place.* **(c)** *Vehicle* is from French

Answers continued

and Latin *to carry.* **(d)** *Passenger* is from French *to carry.*

8. If *bon* means "good" in French, then *bon voyage* means "good voyage."
9. *RSVP* is from the French phrase *repondez s'il vous plaît,* which means "please respond."
10. People in the military often travel, as do sales representatives, travel industry employees, and people who manage employees in different locations.

ENRICHMENT: Further Reading

Other Works by the Authors

Works by Anton Chekhov

The Fiancee and Other Stories

The Duel and Other Stories

Works by Sandra Cisneros

The House on Mango Street

Woman Hollering Creek and Other Stories

Take It to the Net

Visit www.phschool.com for more information on the authors.

EXTEND

Answers for p. 470

❶ Vocabulary Development

Word Analysis

1. *Faux pas* is a French term meaning a "social blunder."
2. *Rendezvous* is a French word for "present yourself" (for a meeting or an appointment).
3. *Siesta* is a Spanish word meaning "afternoon nap."
4. *Mañana* is a Spanish word for "tomorrow."

Spelling Strategy

1. wrap
2. wring
3. wrest
4. write
5. wry

Fluency: Sentence Completions

1. emaciated
2. prolonged
3. wry
4. emerged
5. meditated
6. foresee

❷ Grammar

1. when the wagon left the station
2. that I'm scared
3. before you say eleven
4. until she saw the sweater
5. After Rachel left school

Writing Application

Possible answers:

1. The wagon lurched because the road was uneven.
2. Kim hid until the game was over.
3. It was clear that he was afraid.

Integrate Language Skills

❶ Vocabulary Development Lesson

Word Analysis: Recognizing Commonly Used Foreign Words

Many words used by English speakers are words from other languages. For example, *cliché* (which means "unoriginal") is from the French verb *clicher*, meaning "to stereotype." Use a dictionary to determine the origins and meanings of the following foreign words commonly used in English.

1. faux pas **2.** rendezvous **3.** siesta **4.** mañana

Spelling Strategy

Sometimes, the *r* sound is spelled *wr*, as in *wry*. For each word below, write the homophone—another word that sounds the same but has a different meaning and spelling—that begins with *wr*.

1. rap **2.** ring **3.** rest **4.** right **5.** rye

Fluency: Sentence Completions

Copy each sentence on your paper. Use one of the following words to complete each one.

prolonged, meditated, emaciated, wry, foresee, emerged

1. The hungry dog looked __?__.
2. The ceremony was __?__ by lengthy speeches.
3. He made a __?__ face.
4. The butterfly __?__ from its cocoon.
5. The professor __?__ on the question.
6. I cannot __?__ the future.

❷ Grammar Lesson

Subordinate Clauses

A **subordinate clause** is a group of words that has a subject and a verb but cannot stand alone as a sentence. It is dependent on an independent clause to complete its meaning. Subordinate clauses usually begin with words such as *who, which, that, after, because, before, when,* and *until.* In the following examples, the subordinate clauses are shown in italics. Notice that they do not express complete thoughts.

> "You may find some peasants over there *who haul passengers.*"
>
> *When Papa comes home from work,* we will eat cake.

▶ *For more practice, see page R29, Exercise C.*

Practice Copy these sentences on your paper. Underline the subordinate clause in each sentence.

1. It was dusk when the wagon left the station.
2. He's noticed already that I'm scared.
3. It takes a few days before you say eleven.
4. She was not upset until she saw the sweater.
5. After Rachel left school, she went home.

Writing Application In your notebook, complete each sentence with a subordinate clause. The first word in the clause is given in parentheses.

1. The wagon lurched (because) __?__.
2. Kim hid (until) __?__.
3. It was clear (that) __?__.

WG Prentice Hall Writing and Grammar Connection: Chapter 20, Section 2

TEACHING RESOURCES

The following resources can be used to enrich or extend the instruction for pp. 470–471.

Vocabulary

- **Selection Support:** Build Vocabulary, p. 136; Build Spelling Skills, p. 137
- **Vocabulary and Spelling Practice Book** (Use this booklet for skills enrichment)

Grammar

- **Selection Support:** Build Grammar Skills, p. 138
- **Writing and Grammar,** Copper Level, p. 425 ■

- **Daily Language Practice Transparencies**

Writing

- **Writing and Grammar,** Copper Level, p. 106 ■
- **Writing Models and Graphic Organizers on Transparencies,** p. 85
- **Writing and Grammar iText CD-ROM**

■ **BLOCK SCHEDULING:** Resources marked with this symbol provide varied instruction during 90-minute blocks.

❸ Writing Lesson

Character Description

A **character description** is a written sketch of a character. It conveys a main impression about a character by focusing on his or her major traits. Write a character description about one of the characters in "Overdoing It" or "Eleven."

Prewriting Choose your character, and then review the story to find his or her three main character traits. Support each trait with details from the text. Use a web like the one below to organize your thoughts.

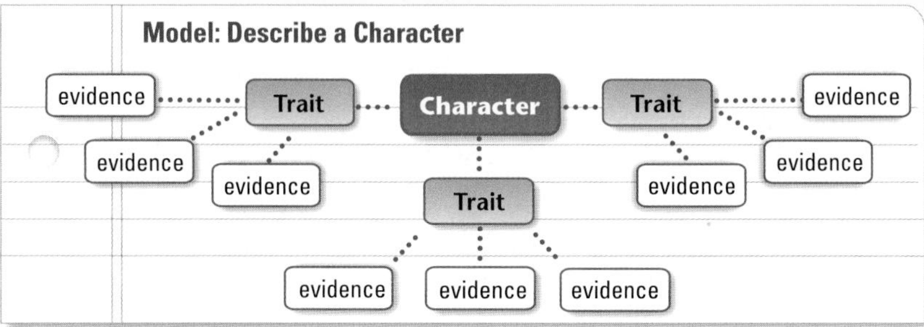

Drafting Write your description, discussing the three traits you listed above. Include brief quotations as part of the evidence that illustrates your points.

Revising Make sure you have provided evidence for all three traits. Then, proofread for spelling, grammar, and mechanics.

WG Prentice Hall Writing and Grammar Connection: Chapter 6, Sections 3

❹ Extension Activities

Listening and Speaking In "Overdoing It," the surveyor's fear leads him to believe false information. When people intentionally mislead others by playing on their fears, the false information is called **propaganda**. With a group, research an example of propaganda in history or current events. In a **group discussion**, talk about the following:

- the example of propaganda
- the fear that fuels people's acceptance of it
- the results of this acceptance

Research and Technology Make a **chart** comparing and contrasting modern-day Russia with nineteenth-century Russia—the setting of "Overdoing It." Use electronic resources to find information about the country and its people during both time periods. Discuss with your class how the story might have turned out differently in a modern setting. **[Group Activity]**

www.phschool.com

Go online for an additional research activity using the Internet.

ASSESSMENT RESOURCES

The following resources can be used to assess students' knowledge and skills.

Selection Assessment

- **Formal Assessment,** pp. 122–124
- **Open Book Test,** pp. 82–84
- **Got It! Assessment Videotapes,** Tape 3
- **Test Bank Software**

Take It to the Net

Visit www.phschool.com for self-tests and additional questions on the selections.

Writing Rubric

- **Performance Assess. and Portfolio Mgmt.,** p. 9

Listening and Speaking Rubric

- **Performance Assess. and Portfolio Mgmt.,** p. 29

- **Workbook**
- **Transparencies**
- **Skill Book**
- **CD-ROM**

Lesson Support for p. 471

❸ Writing Lesson

- Discuss the different effects that indirect characterization has on the stories "Overdoing It" and "Eleven."
- Tell students that they will be taking information from the stories and using it to write a description of a character.
- Use the instructions for the Writing Lesson to assist students in developing a character description.
- You may wish to use the Cluster organizer on p. 85 in **Writing Models and Graphic Organizers on Transparencies** to help students organize their descriptions.
- Use the Description rubric on p. 9 in **Performance Assessment and Portfolio Management** to assess student work.

❹ Listening and Speaking

- Divide the class into groups. Have each group decide on an example of propaganda that they will research.
- With your school librarian, help students find examples of propaganda, the reasons that people accepted it, and its effects.
- As students discuss the propaganda, use the Speaking rubric on p. 29 in **Performance Assessment and Portfolio Management** to assess their presentations.

CUSTOMIZE INSTRUCTION
For Universal Access

To address different learning styles, use the activities suggested in the **Extension Activities** booklet, p. 28

- For Interpersonal and Verbal/Linguistic Learners, use Activity 5.
- For Musical/Rhythmic Learners, use Activity 6.
- For Visual/Spatial and Verbal/Linguistic Learners, use Activity 7.

Lesson Objectives

1. To understand the connection between birthdays as depicted in short stories and birthdays as depicted in novels
2. To understand the significance of birthday customs

Connections

The short story "Eleven" depicts an eleven-year-old girl's reaction to a difficult birthday. This excerpt from the novel *Little Obie and the Flood* takes a different view of a family's celebration of a grandmother's special day. After students have read "Obie's Gift," review the key points in "Eleven." Ask students to compare and contrast the views of birthdays from the two selections.

Birthdays as a Time of Change

- Point out to students that they are growing and changing every day; however, there are certain days, more than others, when people stop to notice these changes. Have students suggest days when they feel great changes in their lives.
  Possible response: Students may suggest birthdays, first or last days of school, or days when they are weighed or measured for clothes or physical examinations.
- Discuss with students Rachel's attitude toward her birthday in "Eleven." Ask whether students feel the same way Rachel does about birthdays.
  Possible response: Most students will say that they enjoy their birthdays and do not share Rachel's feelings about the day.
- Ask students to suggest qualities of short stories and novels. Write their suggestions on the board, and use the lists to compare and contrast short stories and novels as literature.
  Possible response: The major difference between the two genres is length. Both genres include characters, plot, setting, and literary devices.

CONNECTIONS
Short Stories and Novels
Birthdays as a Time of Change

Birthdays are a time when people can measure the changes in their lives and in themselves since the previous year. In the short story "Eleven," Rachel is confused because, although her age is changing, she still feels all the fears and insecurities of a younger child. "Obie's Gift" is an excerpt from the novel *Little Obie and the Flood.* The characters have more time to grow and change because a novel is longer than a short story. Both forms of fiction, however, communicate messages, or themes, through events and actions. In this excerpt from *Little Obie and the Flood,* a grandson's birthday gift lovingly illustrates the changes in the family.

Obie's Gift

Martin Waddell

The following selection is from the book Little Obie and the Flood. *The story begins on the day of Effie's birthday. Effie's grandson has been working very hard on a present for her. He has made a puppet that consists of four wooden dolls that are connected together. The dolls' hips and knees are also connected by string; when you move the dolls, they look like they are dancing. Each doll represents a member of the family, including Marty, an orphan who lives with Effie's family.*

The next day Effie got her presents.

"Well, I declare!" said Effie, when she saw the spread.

"That's from Marty and me," said Grandad.

"Not from me," said Little Obie. "I made you something all by myself. I made it 'cause I haven't got no money."

And he gave it to her.

"That's you," said Little Obie, "the one with the big nose. The one with the humpy sort of back is Grandad, and the two little ones, either side, are me and Marty."

"Is that so?" said Effie, fingering her nose and wondering.

And he fitted the stick from the creek in the back of the figures, put the barrel-plank on his knee and put the figures on it, and then . . .

Tap-tap-tap he tapped the plank with his knuckles, and . . . *tap-tap-tap* the four figures danced, all stiff in a row, with their legs jerking up and down. Little Obie had jointed the knees with yarn, and the ankles and the hips, so that all eight wooden legs skipped around just like people dancing.

"That's real nice, Little Obie," Effie said, and she was so pleased she forgot all about having a big nose.

Effie took the plank and put it on her knee and danced the doll family.

Then Grandad did it.

Then Marty did it.

Then Effie did it again.

Martin Waddell
LITTLE OBIE
and the
FLOOD
Illustrated by
Elsie Lennox

"Thank you!" she said, and she gave Little Obie a hug, which was something she didn't often do.

"They're us," Little Obie explained again, in case Effie hadn't understood. "That one is me and this one is Marty . . ."

"And that's me! "said Effie. "And the big one is Obadiah!"

"Don't look like me," said Grandad, holding his old bones as straight as he could, because no one had ever called him humpy before.

"It's got your wooden head!" said Effie.

When it was late and all the family had gone to bed, Effie heard a noise coming from the big room.

Tap-tap-tap.

She put on her wrap and went to look.

Marty was out of bed, sitting in Grandad's old chair in the firelight, with Effie's new stitched spread around her to keep her warm.

She had the barrel-plank on her knee and she was *tap-tap-tapping* to make the dolls dance.

Background

Social Studies

The family in "Obie's Gift" is observing birthdays as they are celebrated in many countries around the world: Family members gather to wish the grandmother well and give her presents. In Europe long ago, birthday celebrations were held only for important leaders. Eventually, birthdays of all people were celebrated in many cultures. Many people think that giving gifts and gathering well-wishers to feast together will bring the birthday celebrant good luck in the coming year.

Critical Thinking

Infer

- Tell students that a careful reader can find several clues about Obie's family in the text.
- Have students read pp. 472–473. Ask: Why did Obie have to make a present for Effie?
  Answer: He made the present because he did not have the money to buy one.
- Discuss with students how Effie feels about the present and how she shows those feelings through her words and actions.
  Answer: Effie likes the present. She shows her feelings by saying that it is nice, by forgetting that it shows her with a big nose, and by hugging Little Obie.
- Challenge students to notice how members of the family treat one another.
  Possible response: The family members show that they care about one another by giving Effie presents and by taking turns with the dolls to see how they work.

ENRICHMENT: Social Studies Connection

Birthdays Around the World

Tell students that although birthday customs vary from country to country, almost all birthday traditions center around making a happy day for the celebrant. For example:

In Japan, children enjoy birthday cake decorated with floral designs. Rice and beans or rice and vegetables are favorite party foods. Favorite presents for young children include toys or clothes, while older children often receive money. An old Italian birthday custom is to send flowers to the birthday celebrant. In England, charms are baked into birthday cakes. Each charm has a meaning; for example, if you receive a charm shaped like a coin, you will be rich. In Germany, Russia, and Denmark, children wake up to a display of presents on the morning of their birthday.

Invite students to research birthday customs for a particular region of the United States or for a foreign country. Have students present their findings to the class.

Critical Thinking

Connect

- Remind students that Marty is an orphan who lives with Effie's family.
- Have students read p. 475. Then, ask them why Marty is up so late. **Answer:** Marty is playing with the dolls.
- Discuss what Marty says to the dolls. Ask students what her statement tells about her feelings for the others in the family. **Answer:** Marty names the dolls, just as Little Obie did. Her statement shows that she is happy to belong to this family.

▶Critical Viewing

Answer: Based on the picture, the story "Obie's Gift" is set in the early 1800s.

▲**Critical Viewing** Based on this picture, during what time period do you think "Obie's Gift" is set? **[Speculate]**

CUSTOMIZE INSTRUCTION FOR UNIVERSAL ACCESS

For English Learners

Students may be confused by some of the expressions used in the excerpt. Point out the double negative, "I haven't got no money," in Little Obie's first speech. Explain to students that this is grammatically incorrect, but that some people, nevertheless, speak this way. The author uses this expression, as well as Effie's "Time we was all in bed," to show some qualities of the speakers without directly stating them. Help students see that these expressions are dialect that is characteristic of rural speakers who have not had the opportunity to learn and practice standard English. Have students rephrase these sentences using correct grammar. Then, have them list other unfamiliar words and phrases from the excerpt and work with dictionaries and proficient speakers to determine the meanings.

"Marty?" Effie said, but she said it very softly because she didn't want to frighten her.

Marty never heard her. She was talking to the dolls.

"You're our family," she said. "You're me, and that one's Grandma with her big nose, and that one is Grandad with the humpy back, and the little skinny one down at the end, that's Little Obie."

"A-hem!" said Effie, clearing her throat.

Marty looked up.

"Back to bed, Marty!" Effie said.

Marty went back to bed.

Effie didn't.

She sat down in the firelight in her own chair, with the new spread around her to keep the hog-bite warm. She picked up the barrel-plank, and rested it on her knee. Then she stuck the stick in the back and let the doll family dance and dance.

Tap-tap-tap. Tap-tap-tap.

The Marty doll danced, and the Effie doll danced, and the Obadiah doll danced, and the Little Obie doll danced.

Tap-tap-tap. Tap-tap-tap.

Then Effie stopped tapping the plank and the doll family stopped dancing.

"Time we was all in bed!" Effie told them, and then she looked up, quick-like, to make sure no one had heard her.

No one had, so she laid the dolls on the table and, gathering her new, all-the-colors-of-the-rainbow spread around her, she went back to bed, a year older but years younger as well.

Effie went to sleep.

Everybody slept.

A whole family, together in their cabin at Cold Creek on the Rock River.

Martin Waddell

(b. 1941)

Martin Waddell was born in Belfast, Ireland, in 1941 during the bombing of that city by the Germans. He grew up in Newcastle, County Down, where he still lives today. Waddell is a successful author of children's books, having written more than ninety books—both picture books and novels. *Can't You Sleep, Little Bear?* won the Smarties Grand Prix in 1988. *The Park in the Dark* was awarded the Kurt Maschler/Emil Award in 1989, and *Farmer Duck* won the Smarties Grand Prix in 1991. Waddell has written a number of books for older children on the situation in Northern Ireland. Waddell's advice for budding writers is "to write about things that you feel passionate about."

Connecting Short Stories and Novels

1. In what ways does Effie's family try to make her feel special on her birthday?
2. How are Effie's feelings about her birthday different from Rachel's in "Eleven"?
3. Compare the realizations Effie and Rachel come to on their birthdays.
4. In what ways does this novel excerpt seem like a short story? In what ways is it different?
5. Would you like to read more about these characters? Why or why not?

Answers

Connecting Novels and Short Stories

1. Effie's family has presents for her on her birthday. She receives a spread and a set of dolls.
2. Effie loved her birthday because she felt loved and treasured by her family. In contrast, Rachel did not enjoy her birthday because a terrible experience at school overshadowed the joy she should have felt on her special day.
3. Rachel realizes that even though she is eleven, it will take her a while to feel that she is really as old as her true age. Effie seems to be younger as the day passes because she plays with the dolls before she goes to bed.
4. Possible response: This excerpt seems like a short story because it tells one specific incident in the life of the family. It is different from most short stories in that it does not have a lot of information about the characters and relationships between them; this information is probably somewhere else in the book.
5. Possible response: Some students may say that they want to read more about these characters to find out how Marty came to live with the family and why Effie rarely hugs Little Obie.

CUSTOMIZE INSTRUCTION FOR UNIVERSAL ACCESS

For Less Proficient Readers	For Advanced Readers
Have students isolate from the passage the information that describes the set of dolls. Have students use the information to write a description of the dolls. The description should include the number of dolls, their relative size, and any identifying features for each specific doll. Have students use their written descriptions as a basis for drawing the set of dolls. Display the drawings on a bulletin board.	Little Obie's gift for Effie is a version of a classic handmade toy. Students may enjoy researching different types of folk toys, such as rocking horses, dollhouses, and spinning tops. Have students use print or Internet resources to find descriptions of different types of folk toys, how they are made, and how they are operated. Or, students may wish to focus on the toys' histories. Have students make posters to share their findings with the class.

The Lawyer and the Ghost ✦ The Wounded Wolf

Lesson Objectives

1. **To analyze and respond to literary elements**
   - Literary Analysis: Setting
   - Comparing Literary Works
2. **To read, comprehend, analyze, and critique two short stories**
   - Reading Strategy: Picturing the Setting
   - Reading Check Questions
   - Review and Assess Questions
   - Assessment Practice (ATE)
3. **To develop word analysis skills, fluency, and systematic vocabulary**
   - Vocabulary Development Lesson: Word Analysis: Latin Prefix *in-*
4. **To understand and apply written and oral language conventions**
   - Spelling Strategy
   - Grammar Lesson: Simple and Compound Sentences
5. **To understand and apply appropriate writing and research strategies**
   - Writing Lesson: Annotated Bibliography
   - Extension Activity: Oral Report on Historical Setting
6. **To understand and apply listening and speaking strategies**
   - Extension Activity: Persuasive Presentation

STEP-BY-STEP TEACHING GUIDE	PACING GUIDE
PRETEACH	
Motivate Students and Provide Background	
Use the Motivation activity (ATE p. 476)	5 min.
Read and discuss the Preview material and Background information (SE/ATE p. 476) [A]	10 min.
Introduce the Concepts	
Introduce the Literary Analysis and Reading Strategy (SE/ATE p. 477) [A]	25 min.
Pronounce the vocabulary words and read their definitions (SE p. 477)	5 min.
TEACH	
Monitor Comprehension	
Informally monitor comprehension by circulating while students read independently or in groups [A]	20–25 min.
Monitor students' comprehension with the Reading Check notes (SE/ATE pp. 479, 483, 485)	as students read
Develop vocabulary with Vocabulary notes (SE pp. 479, 480, 483, 485, 486)	as students read
Develop Understanding	
Develop students' understanding of setting with the Literary Analysis annotations (SE pp. 481, 483, 485; ATE pp. 480, 483, 485) [A]	5 min.
Develop students' ability to picture the setting with the Reading Strategy annotations (SE p. 479; ATE p. 479)	5 min.
ASSESS	
Assess Mastery	
Assess students' mastery of the Reading Strategy and Literary Analysis by having them answer the Review and Assess questions (SE/ATE p. 487)	25 min.
Use one or more of the print and media Assessment Resources (ATE p. 489) [A]	up to 45 min.
EXTEND	
Apply Understanding	
Have students complete the Vocabulary Development Lesson and the Grammar Lesson (SE p. 488) [A]	20 min.
Apply students' ability to write an annotated bibliography using the Writing Lesson (SE/ATE p. 489) [A]	45 min.
Apply students' understanding using one or more of the Extension Activities (SE p. 489)	20–90 min.

ACCELERATED INSTRUCTION:
Use the strategies and activities identified with an [A].

UNIVERSAL ACCESS
● = Below Level Students
▲ = On-Level Students
■ = Above Level Students

Time and Resource Manager

Reading Level: Challenging, Average
Average Number of Instructional Days: 4

RESOURCES		
PRINT	**TRANSPARENCIES**	**TECHNOLOGY**
• **Beyond Literature,** Cross-Curricular Connection: Science, p. 29 ▲ ■		• **Interest Grabber Videotapes,** Tape 3 ● ▲ ■
• **Selection Support Workbook:** ● ▲ ■ Literary Analysis, p. 145 Reading Strategy, p. 144 Build Vocabulary, p. 141	• **Literary Analysis and Reading Transparencies,** pp. 57 and 58 ● ▲ ■	
• **Adapted Reader's Companion** ● • **Reader's Companion** ● • **Authors In Depth,** Copper Level, p. 106 ■		• **Listening to Literature** ● ▲ ■ Audiocassettes, Side 17 Audio CDs, CD 8
• **English Learner's Companion** ● ▲ • **Literatura en español** ● ▲ • **Literary Analysis for Enrichment** ■		
• **Formal Assessment:** Selection Test, pp. 125–127 ● ▲ ■ • **Open Book Test,** pp. 85–87 ● ▲ ■ • **Performance Assessment and Portfolio Management,** p. 27 ● ▲ ■ • PRENTICE HALL ASSESSMENT SYSTEM ● ▲ ■	• PRENTICE HALL ASSESSMENT SYSTEM ● ▲ ■ Skills Practice Answers and Explanations on Transparencies	• **Test Bank Software** ● ▲ ■ • **Got It! Assessment Videotapes,** Tape 3 ● ▲
• **Selection Support Workbook:** ● ▲ ■ Build Spelling Skills, p. 142 Build Grammar Skills, p. 143 • **Writing and Grammar,** Copper Level ● ▲ ■ • **Extension Activities,** p. 29 ● ▲ ■	• **Daily Language Practice Transparencies** ● ▲ • **Writing Models and Graphic Organizers on Transparencies** ● ▲ ■	• **Writing and Grammar iText CD-ROM** ● ▲ ■ ***Take It to the Net*** www.phschool.com

BLOCK SCHEDULING: Use one 90-minute class period to preteach the selection and have students read it. Use a second 90-minute class period to assess students' mastery of skills and have them complete one of the Extension Activities.

PREACH

Step-by-Step Teaching Guide for pp. 476–477

Motivation

Play an audio recording of wolves howling. Ask students to describe the emotional effect of listening to the sounds and to compare the sounds to similar sounds. Most students will suggest that the howls have a mournful or eerie sound. Guide students to compare the wolf calls to the howls and groans that moviemakers use for the cry of a ghost. Lead students to recognize that these sounds contribute to the mood of a story's setting. Then, tell students that they will be reading a ghost story and a story about wolves. Instruct them to watch for descriptions of sounds that contribute to the mood of each story.

Interest Grabber Video

As an alternative, play "The Gray Wolf of Yellowstone" on Tape 3 to engage student interest.

❶ Background

Social Studies

The lawyer in "The Lawyer and the Ghost" (p. 478), by Charles Dickens lives in one of London's Inns of Court. There are four Inns of Court in London: Gray's Inn, Lincoln Inn, Inner Temple, and Middle Temple. The Inns are legal societies that have the right to declare that a law student knows enough to become a barrister, or lawyer. The Inns were first established in the Middle Ages and have had an educational function ever since. Their current relationship with students is to provide library resources and other support. The buildings that house the societies are also called the Inns of Court. The Inn buildings house offices for different types of lawyers.

Prepare to Read

❶ The Lawyer and the Ghost ◆ The Wounded Wolf

Take It to the Net

Visit www.phschool.com for interactive activities and instruction related to these selections, including

- background
- graphic organizers
- literary elements
- reading strategies

Preview

Connecting to the Literature

Anything that takes away your healthy appearance, such as worry or illness, can make you seem pale, weak, and ghostly. These stories show how worry and injury make "ghosts." When has worry or injury made you a ghost?

Background

In "The Lawyer and the Ghost," the lawyer lives in nineteenth-century London in a centuries-old building known as an Inn of Court. Lawyers ate, slept, and studied in these buildings. Lawsuits could last for years, leaving only papers and a ghostly memory of the original complaint.

TEACHING RESOURCES

The following resources can be used to enrich or extend the instruction for pp. 476–477.

Motivation

Interest Grabber Video, Tape 3

Background

Beyond Literature, p. 29

Take It to the Net

Visit www.phschool.com for Background and hotlinks for the selections.

Literary Analysis

Literary Analysis and Reading Transparencies, Setting, p. 58

Reading

Selection Support: Reading Strategy, p. 144; Build Vocabulary, p. 141

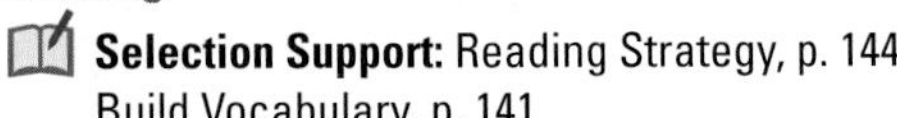

Literary Analysis and Reading Transparencies, Picturing the Setting, p. 57

BLOCK SCHEDULING: Resources marked with this symbol provide varied instruction during 90-minute blocks.

❷ Literary Analysis

Setting

The **setting** is the time and place of a story's events. The "time" may be established as a historical era, the present, or the future, the season of the year, or the hour of the day. The "place" can be as general as "outer space" or as specific as a particular street. The following line from "The Lawyer and the Ghost" describes the gloomy building in which the story takes place.

> "I knew a man . . . who took an old, damp, rotten set of chambers, in one of the most ancient Inns, that had been shut up and empty for years and years before."

Comparing Literary Works

In many stories, the setting influences the **conflict,** or problem, and its **resolution,** or the way the problem is settled. In "The Wounded Wolf," the harsh winter setting contributes to the problem, but some physical features of the setting also contribute to the solution.

Compare and contrast the settings of these two stories and the ways each setting influences the problem and its solution. Think about the following focus questions as you read.

1. In what ways are the two settings similar and different?
2. Do the settings make problems or solutions?

❸ Reading Strategy

Picturing the Setting

You can see the setting of a movie because the director has filmed the right details. When you read, be your own director. **Picture the setting** by making a movie of the story in your mind. With your senses, try to see, hear, touch, taste, and smell the surroundings. Use an organizer like this one to help you.

Detail	Sense
"damp, rotten rooms"	touch, smell

Vocabulary Development

sufficient (sə fish′ ənt) *adj.* enough, satisfactory (p. 479)

expend (ek spend′) *v.* spend (p. 480)

inconsistent (in′ kən sis′ tənt) *n.* contradictory; not making sense (p. 480)

massive (mass′ iv) *adj.* huge; large and impressive (p. 483)

stoic (stō ik) *adj.* showing no reaction to good or bad events; calm and unaffected by hardship (p. 485)

gnashes (nash′ iz) *v.* bites with grinding teeth (p. 486)

❷ Literary Analysis

Setting

- Write the words "a sunny day in the park" and "a dark, rainy street" on the board. Then, ask students to think about what kind of story would take place in each of these locations.
  Possible response: Students may say that the first might be about a picnic, a sports game, or a vacation. The second might be a mystery or a sad story of some sort.
- Explain to students that the setting of a story can be as important as the characters.
- Tell students that as they read the selections, they should be aware of the setting, which is the time and place of the story.
- Read the instructions about setting to the class. Call attention to the example. Ask volunteers to describe some details of the room that they read on this page.
- Use the Setting transparency on p. 58 in **Literary Analysis and Reading Transparencies** to demonstrate for students the elements of setting in the selection.

❸ Reading Strategy

Picturing the Setting

- Point out to students that good readers try to imagine, or picture, the setting of a story to help them grasp the action and characters.
- Remind students that authors use details that appeal to each of the senses to help readers envision the time and place of the story.
- Encourage students to make a graphic organizer like the one pictured on p. 477 to track details in the settings.

Vocabulary Development

- Review the words and definitions on the vocabulary list.
- Explain that *sufficient* means "enough" or "satisfactory." Ask students to identify what is sufficient and what is more than enough in categories such as sleep, meals, allowance, or other categories of their choice.

CUSTOMIZE INSTRUCTION FOR UNIVERSAL ACCESS

For Special Needs Students	For Less Proficient Readers	For English Learners
Have students read the adapted version of "The Wounded Wolf" in the **Adapted Reader's Companion.** This version provides basic-level instruction in an interactive format with questions and write-on lines. Completing the adapted version will prepare students to read the selection in the Student Edition.	Have students read "The Wounded Wolf" in the **Reader's Companion.** This version provides basic-level instruction in an interactive format with questions and write-on lines. After students finish the selection in the Reader's Companion, have them complete the questions and activities in the Student Edition.	Have students read the adapted version of "The Wounded Wolf" in the **English Learner's Companion.** This version provides basic-level instruction in an interactive format with questions and write-on lines. Completing the adapted version will prepare students to read the selection in the Student Edition.

E-Teach

Visit E-Teach at www.phschool.com for teachers' essays on how to teach, with questions and answers.

TEACH

Step-by-Step Teaching Guide for pp. 478–486

CUSTOMIZE INSTRUCTION For Logical/Mathematical Learners

Have students read for reasoning and arguments in "The Lawyer and the Ghost." Encourage them to make pro-and-con charts to demonstrate the sense of the lawyer's arguments. Recording the advantages and disadvantages of the ghost's decision to remain or to leave will help students appreciate the logic of the lawyer's point.

❶ About the Selection

In "The Lawyer and the Ghost," a poor lawyer moves into a gloomy, spooky set of rooms. The rooms turn out to be haunted by a ghost who was bankrupted by a lawsuit and who died in these very rooms. In a humorous twist on the usual ghost story, the lawyer remains calm and convinces the ghost that the ghostly habit of inhabiting the dark, uncomfortable places is against the ghost's own interests. The ghost agrees and disappears.

❶ The Lawyer and the Ghost

Charles Dickens

❷

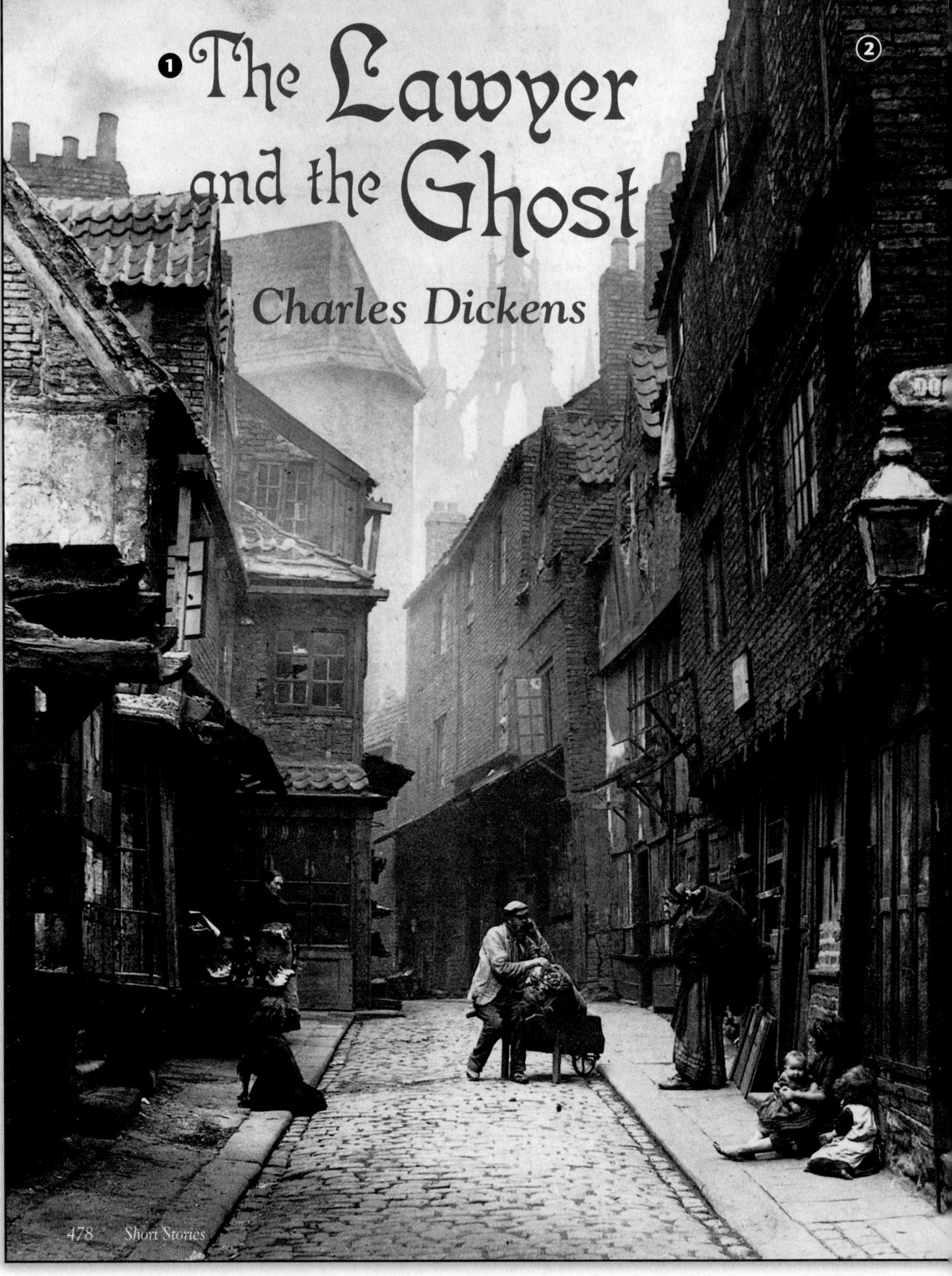

TEACHING RESOURCES

The following resources can be used to enrich or extend the instruction for pp. 478–486.

Literary Analysis
- **Selection Support:** Literary Analysis, p. 145
- **Literary Analysis for Enrichment**

Reading
- **Adapted Reader's Companion**
- **Reader's Companion**
- **English Learner's Companion**

- **Literatura en español**
- **Listening to Literature Audiocassettes,** Side 17 ▪
- **Listening to Literature Audio CDs,** CD 8 ▪

Extention
- **Authors In Depth,** Copper Level, p. 106 (The collection includes three additional selections by Jean Craighead George for extended reading.) ▪

▪ **BLOCK SCHEDULING:** Resources marked with this symbol provide varied instruction during 90-minute blocks.

I knew [a] man—let me see—it's forty years ago now—who took an old, damp, rotten set of chambers, in one of the most ancient Inns, that had been shut up and empty for years and years before. There were lots of old women's stories about the place, and it certainly was very far from being a cheerful one; but he was poor, and the rooms were cheap, and that would have been quite a sufficient reason for him, if they had been ten times worse than they really were. He was obliged to take some moldering fixtures that were on the place, and, among the rest, was a great lumbering wooden press for papers, with large glass doors, and a green curtain inside; a pretty useless thing for him, for he had no papers to put in it; and as to his clothes, he carried them about with him, and that wasn't very hard work, either.

3

Well, he had moved in all his furniture—it wasn't quite a truck-full—and sprinkled it about the room, so as to make the four chairs look as much like a dozen as possible, and was sitting down before the fire at night, . . . when his eyes encountered the glass doors of the wooden press. "Ah!" says he— "If I hadn't been obliged to take that ugly article at the old broker's valuation, I might have got something comfortable for the money. I'll tell you what it is, old fellow," he said, speaking aloud to the press, just because he had got nothing else to speak to— "If it wouldn't cost more to break up your old carcass, than it would ever be worth afterwards, I'd have a fire out of you, in less than no time."

He had hardly spoken the words, when a sound resembling a faint groan, appeared to issue from the interior of the case. It startled him at first, but thinking, on a moment's reflection, that it must be some young fellow in the next chambers, who had been dining out, he put his feet on the fender, and raised the poker to stir the fire. At that moment, the sound was repeated: and one of the glass doors slowly opening, disclosed a pale and emaciated figure in soiled and worn apparel, standing erect in the press. The figure was tall and thin, and the countenance expressive of care and anxiety; but there was something in the hue of the skin, and gaunt and unearthly appearance of the whole form, which no being of this world was ever seen to wear.

"Who are you?" said the new tenant, turning very pale, poising the poker in his hand, however, and taking a very decent aim at the countenance[1] of the figure— "Who are you?"

"Don't throw that poker at me," replied the form— "If you hurled

sufficient (sə fish´ ənt) *adj.* enough; satisfactory

Reading Strategy
Picturing the Setting What details help you picture the time and place of the story?

4 **Reading Check**
What does the man see coming out of the old wooden press?

1. **countenance** (koun´ tə nəns) *n.* face; also, the look on a person's face.

5 ◀ **Critical Viewing** Does this photograph of nineteenth-century London capture the same mood as the story? Explain using details. **[Support]**

2 Background

Art

Photograph of London Street Scene

Have students look carefully at the photograph on p. 478. Tell them that this old photograph depicts a street scene as it looked in nineteenth-century London. Point out the mother and her children sitting on the sidewalk. They are poor and are possibly begging. The other woman and the man with the wheelbarrow may be carrying items they have found on the streets.

Use these questions for discussion:

1. How does this picture add to your appreciation of the story?
Possible response: Students may say that the photograph gives a better sense of the time and place than they might have had if they had only read the description.
2. What details in the picture indicate that it shows a scene from the past?
Answer: Clues include the style of the buildings, the cobblestone streets, the lack of cars, and the clothing worn by the people.

3 Reading Strategy

Picturing the Setting

- Ask students to recall the elements of a setting.
Answer: The elements are the time and place.
- Read the bracketed passage. Then, ask the Reading Strategy question on p. 479: What details help you picture the time and place of the story?
Answer: The story takes place "forty years" before it was written in "damp and rotten" rooms in an "ancient" inn. The furnishings are old and falling apart.

4 Reading Check

Answer: A tall, thin, unearthly looking man comes out of the press.

5 ▶ Critical Viewing

Answer: Students might say that both the story and the photograph convey a grim, dreary mood.

CUSTOMIZE INSTRUCTION FOR UNIVERSAL ACCESS

For Special Needs Students	For English Learners	For Gifted/Talented Students
Use the picture on this page to help students identify the elements of the setting in "The Lawyer and The Ghost." Have students discuss what they see in the picture that is similar to what is described in the first paragraph on p. 479. Ask students to consider how the setting for the story could be the scene in this photograph.	The outdated words and expressions in "The Lawyer and the Ghost" may be difficult for students to decode. Have them follow along in the text as they listen to a recorded version of the story. Stop the tape or CD occasionally to discuss questions students may have or to allow students to check definitions in the dictionary.	Students may enjoy researching photographs of London in the nineteenth century. They can use library or Internet resources to find images. Have students make copies of images that pertain to "The Lawyer and the Ghost," analyze the images, and share the images and their interpretations with the class.

6 ▶**Critical Viewing**

Answer: The ghosts in the picture and in the story are both emaciated, thin, gaunt, and unearthly.

7 Critical Thinking

Interpret

- Point out that lawyers are expected to make arguments that will persuade people.
- Ask students to explain the lawyer's argument in their own words.
  Answer: The lawyer suggests that the ghost has power to be anywhere he wants to be and that he should not limit himself to the place where he was troubled in life.

8 Literary Analysis

Setting

- Remind students that a story's setting can influence its resolution.
- Have a volunteer read the bracketed passage. Ask the Literary Analysis question on p. 481: What details of the setting help the man solve the problem?
  Answer: The lawyer uses the condition of the room, the "appearance of the press," and London's weather to convince the ghost to leave.

it with ever so sure an aim, it would pass through me, without resistance, and expend its force on the wood behind. I am a spirit."

"And, pray, what do you want here?" faltered the tenant.

"In this room," replied the apparition, "my worldly ruin was worked, and I and my children beggared. In this press, the papers in a long, long suit,[2] which accumulated for years, were deposited. In this room, when I had died of grief, and long-deferred hope, two wily harpies[3] divided the wealth for which I had contested during a wretched existence, and of which, at last, not one farthing was left for my unhappy descendants. I terrified them from the spot, and since that day have prowled by night—the only period at which I can re-visit the earth—about the scenes of my long-protracted misery. This apartment is mine: leave it to me."

"If you insist upon making your appearance here," said the tenant, who had had time to collect his presence of mind during this prosy statement of the ghost's— "I shall give up possession with greatest pleasure; but I should like to ask you one question, if you will allow me."

"Say on," said the apparition, sternly.

"Well," said the tenant,

7 "I don't apply the observation personally to you, because it is equally applicable to all the ghosts I ever heard of; but it does appear to me, somewhat inconsistent, that when you have an opportunity of visiting the fairest spots of earth—for I suppose space is nothing to

6 ◀ **Critical Viewing** What adjectives used to describe the apparition in the story could be used to describe the ghost in this picture? **[Compare and Contrast]**

expend (ek spend′) *v.* spend

inconsistent (in′ kən sis′ tənt) *n.* contradictory; not making sense

2. **suit** (so͞ot) *n.* lawsuit; a court case in which two or more persons or businesses argue over a matter.
3. **harpies** (här′ pēz) *n.* greedy people (originally the name of hideous mythological monsters with women's heads and birds' wings and claws).

CUSTOMIZE INSTRUCTION FOR UNIVERSAL ACCESS

For Gifted/Talented Readers

Explain to students that a storyboard is a visual representation of the main events in a story. Like a comic strip, it is divided into frames, with each frame representing one event. Each frame may have a caption explaining the event or providing dialogue from the story "The Lawyer and the Ghost." Have students make a list of the events in the story. Tell them that a line of dialogue can be shown as an event by creating an illustration of the speaker and using the dialogue as a caption below the frame. Students should be sure to include the most important events and dialogue so that the entire story can be understood from the storyboard. Because they must draw a picture for each event, however, they should avoid including too many details. Provide students with large pieces of posterboard and drawing tools. Have them make a storyboard with one frame for each event on their lists, printing a caption below each frame. Post the storyboards in your room or a hallway. Evaluate storyboards based on how effectively they convey the meaning of Dickens's story.

7 you—you should always return exactly to the very places where you have been most miserable."

"Egad, that's very true; I never thought of that before," said the ghost.

"You see, Sir," pursued the tenant, "this is a very uncomfortable room. From the appearance of that press, I should be disposed to
8 say that it is not wholly free from bugs; and I really think you might find much more comfortable quarters: to say nothing of the climate of London, which is extremely disagreeable."

"You are very right, Sir," said the ghost, politely, "it never struck me till now; I'll try a change of air directly"—and, in fact, he began to vanish as he spoke: his legs, indeed, had quite disappeared.

"And if, Sir," said the tenant, calling after him, "if you *would* have the goodness to suggest to the other ladies and gentlemen who are now engaged in haunting old empty houses, that they might be much more comfortable elsewhere, you will confer a very great benefit on society."

"I will," replied the ghost; "we must be dull fellows—very dull fellows, indeed; I can't imagine how we can have been so stupid." With these words, the spirit disappeared; and what is rather remarkable, . . . he never came back again.

Literary Analysis
Setting What details of the setting help the man solve the problem?

Charles Dickens

(1812–1870)

The stories of English author Charles Dickens remain popular today. You may be familiar with *A Christmas Carol* and its main character, Ebenezer Scrooge.

Dickens's early life was difficult. When Dickens was just a boy, his father went to prison, and Dickens had to work long hours pasting labels on bottles.

At fourteen, Dickens became a law clerk. He taught himself shorthand and became a court reporter. His observations of lawyers helped him to write novels such as *Great Expectations*. They also helped him describe the damp, dusty lawyer's room in "The Lawyer and the Ghost."

Review and Assess

Thinking About the Selection

1. **Respond:** What would you have said to the ghost if it asked you to leave?
2. **(a) Recall:** What piece of furniture comes with the room? **(b) Describe:** What is the condition of the piece?
3. **(a) Recall:** Who is the ghost that haunts these rooms? **(b) Infer:** What does the ghost want? **(c) Analyze:** Why do you think the ghost returns to the scene of his "misery"?
4. **(a) Recall:** What question does the man ask the ghost? **(b) Infer:** For what purpose does he ask the question? **(c) Compare and Contrast:** How is the man's behavior with the ghost similar to or different from what you expected?
5. **(a) Recall:** How does the ghost respond to the man's question? **(b) Analyze:** What is surprising about the end of this story? **(c) Draw Conclusions:** How does the interaction between the man and the ghost make this story a humorous one?

Review and Assess

1. Some students may want to tell the ghost to leave, as he is an uninvited guest.
2. **(a)** A "press," or bookcase, comes with the room. **(b)** The press is old and ugly.
3. **(a)** The ghost is the person who had lived in the room while he was involved in a lengthy lawsuit over money. **(b)** The ghost wants the apartment. **(c)** Possible response: The ghost believes that the apartment is his and that somehow it should make him feel better to return to the scene of his "misery."
4. **(a)** Why do you want to return to the very place where you have been most miserable? **(b)** He is asking the question to make the ghost think about his choices and possibly leave. **(c)** The lawyer's behavior is not what the reader would expect because the lawyer does not fear the ghost and challenges him with a question.
5. **(a)** The ghost agrees to leave. **(b)** It is surprising that the ghost quickly agreed to vanish from the apartment. **(c)** It is humorous because of the casual interaction between the lawyer and the ghost—the lawyer does not seem at all frightened by the ghost, and the ghost readily agrees with the lawyer and leaves.

CUSTOMIZE INSTRUCTION FOR UNIVERSAL ACCESS

For Special Needs Students	For Advanced Learners
To help students sequence the events in "The Lawyer and the Ghost," suggest that they use the Series of Events Chain transparency on p. 69 in **Writing Models and Graphic Organizers on Transparencies.** Invite students to start at the beginning of the story and track each of the major events to the end. The first event occurs when the lawyer rents the set of chambers; the last is when the ghost vanishes. Have students fill in the remaining events.	The photograph on p. 480 appears to be that of a ghost. Have students investigate developments of photographic techniques that could have been used to produce these effects. Possible resources for this investigation include local photographers, library resources such as art books and the Internet, and art teachers. Students should also note the inventor and/or artist who developed the various techniques. Invite volunteers to share their findings with the class.

❾ About the Selection

In "The Wounded Wolf," the wolf Roko is injured when he leaps in front of a caribou to protect Kiglo, the pack leader. The weakened Roko falls and is attacked by ravens and a fox, but he fights them off. Roko remains too hurt to respond to the call of Kiglo, the leader of his pack. Kiglo finds Roko and brings him meat. Finally, Roko is able to return to his pack. The events of the story demonstrate the cooperative social behavior of wolves.

❿ ▶Critical Viewing

Answer: In addition to his thick coat, the wolf has fur between the pads of his feet and inside his ears.

❾ The Wounded Wolf

Jean Craighead George

❿ ▲ **Critical Viewing** What physical features help this wolf survive in a cold, harsh environment? **[Analyze]**

ENRICHMENT: Science Connection

Wolves

The wolf family has two branches: red wolves and gray wolves. Red wolves live only in the southern United States. The wolves in this story are probably gray wolves, which live in northern climates and other regions such as the Pacific Northwest, Canada, and Alaska. They are also called timber wolves.

In "The Wounded Wolf," Jean Craighead George realistically depicts the social behavior of timber wolves. They travel in packs, and in the winter they hunt for food as a group. The caribou that injures Roko would be common prey for wolves, although they most often hunt smaller animals and occasionally eat berries. Wolves serve a valuable purpose in the food web because they help control the populations of other animals. The dominant, or alpha, male leads the pack. This is Kiglo's role in the story. The howling to assemble the pack is part of wolf social rituals. Howling also serves as a communication device between packs and as a warning to animals encroaching on a pack's territory.

A wounded wolf climbs Toklat Ridge, a massive spine of rock and ice. As he limps, dawn strikes the ridge and lights it up with sparks and stars. Roko, the wounded wolf, blinks in the ice fire, then stops to rest and watch his pack run the thawing Arctic valley.

11 They plunge and turn. They fight the mighty caribou that struck young Roko with his hoof and wounded him. He jumped between the beast and Kiglo, leader of the Toklat pack. Young Roko spun and fell. Hooves, paws, and teeth roared over him. And then his pack and the beast were gone.

Gravely injured, Roko pulls himself toward the shelter rock. Weakness overcomes him. He stops. He and his pack are thin and hungry. This is the season of starvation. The winter's harvest has been taken. The produce of spring has not begun.

Young Roko glances down the valley. He droops his head and stiffens his tail to signal to his pack that he is badly hurt. Winds wail. A frigid blast picks up long shawls of snow and drapes them between young Roko and his pack. And so his message is not read.

A raven scouting Toklat Ridge sees Roko's signal. "Kong, kong, kong," he bells—death is coming to the ridge; there will be flesh and bone for all. His voice rolls out across the valley. It penetrates the rocky cracks where the Toklat ravens rest. One by one they hear and spread their wings. They beat their way to Toklat Ridge. They alight upon the snow and walk behind the wounded wolf.

"Kong," they toll[1] with keen excitement, for the raven clan is hungry, too. "Kong, kong"—there will be flesh and bone for all.

Roko snarls and hurries toward the shelter rock. A cloud of snow envelops him. He limps in blinding whiteness now.

A ghostly presence flits around. "Hahahahahahaha," the white fox states—death is coming to the Ridge. Roko smells the fox tagging at his heels.

The cloud whirls off. Two golden eyes look up at Roko. The snowy owl has heard the ravens and joined the deathwatch.

Roko limps along. The ravens walk. The white fox leaps. The snowy owl flies and hops along the rim of Toklat Ridge. Roko stops. Below the ledge out on the flats the musk-ox herd is circling. They form a ring and all face out, a fort of heads and horns and fur that sweeps down to their hooves. Their circle means to Roko that an enemy is present. He squints and smells the wind. It carries scents of thawing ice, broken grass—and earth. The grizzly bear is up! He has awakened from his winter's sleep. A craving need for flesh will drive him.

1. **toll** (tōl) *v.* announce.

massive (mass´iv) *adj.* huge; large and impressive

Literary Analysis
Setting In what region of the world and at what time of year is the story set?

12 **Reading Check**
What is Roko's problem?

11 Literary Analysis

Setting

- Ask students to listen for details of the setting as you read aloud the first three paragraphs of the selection.
- Ask the Literary Analysis question on p. 483: In what region of the world and at what time of year is the story set?
  Answer: The story is set in the Arctic, near the end of winter.

Monitor Progress Ask students to identify the details that helped them specify the place and season.
Answer: The author says Roko is in a thawing Arctic valley and indicates that winter's harvest is over but spring's food is not yet available.

Reteach If students have difficulty finding the information, use the following question to model finding setting details: What time of day is it when the story begins?
Answer: In the second line of the story, the author mentions dawn, so it must be early morning.

12 Reading Check

Answer: Roko was injured when he was hunting a caribou.

CUSTOMIZE INSTRUCTION FOR UNIVERSAL ACCESS

For Special Needs Students	For Less Proficient Readers	For Advanced Readers
Students may need help visualizing the animals mentioned in "The Wounded Wolf." Help them find photographs in encyclopedias and other library resources. Make copies of the photographs for students. Have students point to each animal as they read about it.	Students who need assistance following the sequence of events in the story may benefit from hearing it read aloud or listening to a recorded version. Play the tape or CD version, pausing occasionally to clarify a point or summarize the action. Invite students to ask questions.	Students may be interested in learning about the reintroduction of wolves into national parks in the United States during the 1990s. Direct them to resources that will detail the debates between naturalists and local farmers that preceded the reintroduction. Have students report on the results of the program.

13 Critical Thinking

Criticize

- Tell students that sentence structure influences how the story's content affects the reader.
- Call students' attention to the short sentences in the bracketed passage.
- Point out that the author is building tension with this style.
- Ask students to describe the effect of this sentence style and how longer sentences would alter the effect.
  Answer: The short sentences are direct, listing the animals' actions, producing the effect of the animals' forming a procession. The style helps build tension as one animal after another moves in to take turns at Roko. Longer sentences would take longer to read and would thus detract readers' attention fron the action.

14 ▶Critical Viewing

Answer: Students should apply what they have learned in the story to recognize that this howling wolf is probably communicating with others in his pack. Knowing this information, students can infer that there are other wolves in the area—probably a large group.

Roko sees the shelter rock. He strains to reach it. He stumbles. The ravens move in closer. The white fox boldly walks beside him.
13 "Hahaha," he yaps. The snowy owl flies ahead, alights, and waits.
The grizzly hears the eager fox and rises on his flat hind feet. He twists his powerful neck and head. His great paws dangle at his

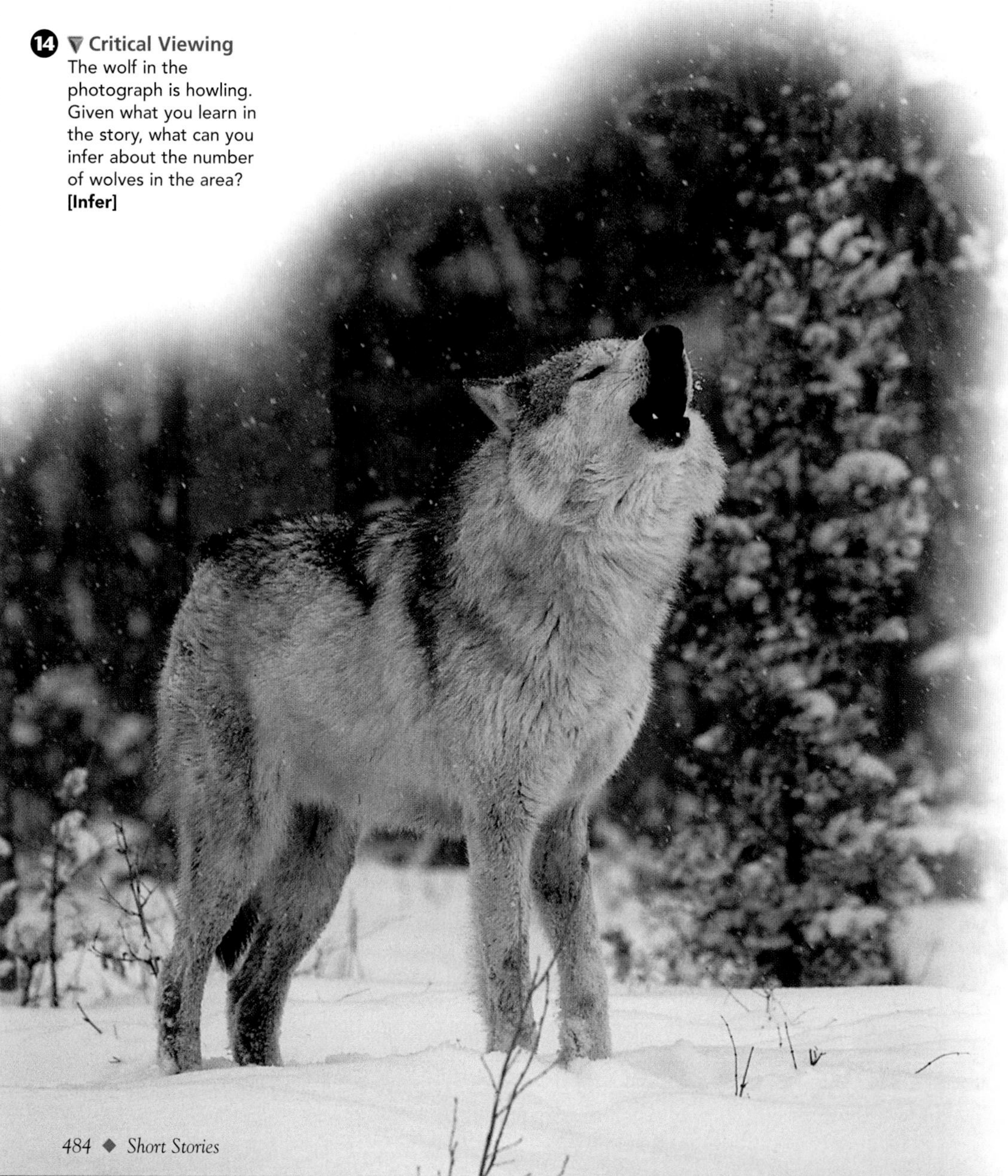

14 ▼ **Critical Viewing** The wolf in the photograph is howling. Given what you learn in the story, what can you infer about the number of wolves in the area? **[Infer]**

CUSTOMIZE INSTRUCTION FOR UNIVERSAL ACCESS

For Advanced Readers

Suggest that students read additional works by Jean Craighead George. Provide students with the titles listed in the Enrichment box, ATE p. 487. You may also wish to use **Authors In Depth,** Copper Level, which contains the following selections:

- from *The Tarantula in My Purse*
- from *The Wild, Wild Cookbook*
- from *The Moon of the Mountain Lions*

After students have read these or other works by Jean Craighead George, have them form groups to present some of her works to the class. Students can dramatize key scenes from her writing, using narration that preserves her style. After the presentations, have the presenters comment on George's style, subject matter, and use of settings.

chest. He sees the animal procession and hears the ravens' knell[2] of death. Dropping to all fours, he joins the march up Toklat Ridge.

Roko stops; his breath comes hard. A raven alights upon his back and picks the open wound. Roko snaps. The raven flies and circles back. The white fox nips at Roko's toes. The snowy owl inches closer. The grizzly bear, still dulled by sleep, stumbles onto Toklat Ridge.

Only yards from the shelter rock, Roko falls.

Instantly the ravens mob him. They scream and peck and stab at his eyes. The white fox leaps upon his wound. The snowy owl sits and waits.

Young Roko struggles to his feet. He bites the ravens. Snaps the fox. And lunges at the stoic owl. He turns and warns the grizzly bear. Then he bursts into a run and falls against the shelter rock. The wounded wolf wedges down between the rock and barren ground. Now protected on three sides, he turns and faces all his foes.

stoic (stō′ ik) *adj.* showing no reaction to good or bad events; calm and unaffected by hardship

The ravens step a few feet closer. The fox slides toward him on his belly. The snowy owl blinks and waits, and on the ridge rim roars the hungry grizzly bear.

Roko growls.

The sun comes up. Far across the Toklat Valley, Roko hears his pack's "hunt's end" song. The music wails and sobs, wilder than the bleating wind. The hunt song ends. Next comes the roll call. Each member of the Toklat pack barks to say that he is home and well.

"Kiglo here," Roko hears his leader bark. There is a pause. It is young Roko's turn. He cannot lift his head to answer. The pack is silent. The leader starts the count once more. "Kiglo here."—A pause. Roko cannot answer.

The wounded wolf whimpers softly. A mindful raven hears. "Kong, kong, kong," he tolls—this is the end. His booming sounds across the valley. The wolf pack hears the raven's message that something is dying. They know it is Roko, who has not answered roll call.

The hours pass. The wind slams snow on Toklat Ridge. Massive clouds blot out the sun. In their gloom Roko sees the deathwatch
15 move in closer. Suddenly he hears the musk-oxen thundering into their circle. The ice cracks as the grizzly leaves. The ravens burst into the air. The white fox runs. The snowy owl flaps to the top of the shelter rock. And Kiglo rounds the knoll.

Literary Analysis
Setting Which features of the setting create a problem, and which features help solve a problem?

In his mouth he carries meat. He drops it close to Roko's head and wags his tail excitedly. Roko licks Kiglo's chin to honor him. Then Kiglo puts his mouth around Roko's nose. This gesture says "I am your leader." And by mouthing Roko, he binds him and all the wolves together.

 **Reading Check**
What makes the animals run away from Roko?

2. **knell** (nel) *n.* mournful sound, like a slowly ringing bell—usually indicating a death.

15 Literary Analysis

Setting

- Remind students that the setting often influences the conflict and its resolution in a story. Have students review the story so far to think of when the setting influenced the action.
- Ask the Literary Analysis question on p. 485.
  Answer: Problems that occur because of the setting include Roko's injury, the weather that keeps the other wolves from seeing his signs of distress, and the distance he must cross in open space before he can get to shelter. Solutions that are a result of the setting include the rock that gives him shelter and the knoll around which Kiglo appears.

16 

Answer: The animals run away from Roko because Kiglo, a strong wolf, is approaching.

CUSTOMIZE INSTRUCTION FOR UNIVERSAL ACCESS

For English Learners	For Gifted/Talented Students
Point out to students that all of the sentences in the paragraph beginning "Instantly the ravens mob him" are simple sentences. Help students identify the simple sentences with compound verbs: "They scream and peck and stab at his eyes." "The snowy owl sits and waits." Tell students that there are many sentences with compound verbs in this story. They will also discover a few simple sentences that have compound subjects: more than one subject with the same verb.	By now, students should be familiar with the style of the authors of these selections. Have them write a paragraph comparing Charles Dickens's and Jean Craighead George's use of language to create setting and mood. They may wish to investigate the authors' use of adjectives and verbs, for example. Encourage them to cite specific words and phrases in their paragraphs. They may also want to note the relationship between the formality of the language and the subject matter of each story.

ASSESS

Answers for p. 486

Review and Assess

1. Have students support their opinions with story details.
2. **(a)** Trying to protect his leader, Roko jumped between the caribou and Kiglo. **(b)** Possible responses: He may climb the ridge to find protection from other animals and the weather, or it may be easier for the pack to find him. **(c)** Roko is loyal and intelligent.
3. **(a)** Roko is threatened by the hungry ravens that pick at him, by the fox that leaps upon his wound, and by the snow. **(b)** They are similar because they hunt weakened animals. **(c)** Possible responses: Some may suggest that the wolves are the "good guys," and the ravens and the fox are the "bad guys." Others may say that there are no "good" or "bad" guys because the animals act according to nature.
4. **(a)** Kiglo hears the call of the raven signaling a weak animal and knows that Roko is missing. **(b)** Kiglo brings food to Roko. **(c)** The wolves demonstrate "teamwork" by hunting together, responding to roll call, and helping one another.
5. **(a)** The wolves celebrate Roko's return. **(b)** It means that Roko has returned to the pack. **(c)** Wolves have social relationships similar to those of people.

The wounded wolf wags his tail. Kiglo trots away.

Already Roko's wound feels better. He gulps the food and feels his strength return. He shatters bone, flesh, and gristle and shakes the scraps out on the snow. The hungry ravens swoop upon them. The white fox snatches up a bone. The snowy owl gulps down flesh and fur. And Roko wags his tail and watches.

For days Kiglo brings young Roko food. He gnashes, gorges, and shatters bits upon the snow.

gnashes (nash′ iz) *v.* bites with grinding teeth

A purple sandpiper winging north sees ravens, owl, and fox. And he drops in upon the feast. The long-tailed jaeger gull flies down and joins the crowd on Toklat Ridge. Roko wags his tail.

One dawn he moves his wounded leg. He stretches it and pulls himself into the sunlight. He walks—he romps. He runs in circles. He leaps and plays with chunks of ice. Suddenly he stops. The "hunt's end" song rings out. Next comes the roll call.

"Kiglo here."

"Roko here," he barks out strongly.

The pack is silent.

"Kiglo here," the leader repeats.

"Roko here."

Across the distance comes the sound of whoops and yips and barks and howls. They fill the dawn with celebration. And Roko prances down the Ridge.

Review and Assess

Thinking About the Selection

1. **Respond:** Do you admire the wolves in this story? Why?
2. (a) **Recall:** What action did Roko take that caused him to be wounded? (b) **Infer:** Why does he climb the ridge? (c) **Draw Conclusions:** Based on these actions, how would you describe Roko's personality?
3. (a) **Recall:** Describe the threats that Roko faces. (b) **Compare and Contrast:** In what way are animals that follow Roko similar to the wolves? (c) **Evaluate:** Are there "good-guy" and "bad-guy" animals in this story? Explain.
4. (a) **Recall:** How does Kiglo learn that Roko is hurt? (b) **Infer:** What does Kiglo do when he finds out Roko is hurt? (c) **Synthesize:** How do the wolves demonstrate "teamwork"?
5. (a) **Recall:** What happens at the end of the story? (b) **Interpret:** What does the celebration at the end mean? (c) **Generalize:** Based on what you have read, what general statement can you make about wolf relationships?

Jean Craighead George

(b. 1919)

Jean Craighead George has been a reporter, illustrator, teacher, and editor. She is the author of more than 100 books, including *My Side of the Mountain* and *Julie of the Wolves*.

Nearly all of George's books are about nature. She grew up on land that her family had farmed since the 1700s. Her experiences of rural life, wild animals, and family pets fostered the love of nature shown in her writing. George calls her fiction "documentary novels" because the facts about nature that they contain are scientifically accurate.

ASSESSMENT PRACTICE: Reading Comprehension

Describing a Character (For more practice, see Test Preparation Workbook, p. 41.)

Many tests require students to describe characters in a selection. Students will often have to infer traits of a character from information given in the selection. Write the following text on the board:

> "Well," said the tenant, "... it does appear to me, somewhat inconsistent that when you have an opportunity of visiting the fairest spots on earth ... you should always return exactly to the very places where you have been most miserable."

In this story, the tenant points out that the ghost—

A likes to be happy
B has a sense of humor
C likes to be miserable
D is logical

Ask what the passage reveals about the ghost's personality. By focusing on how the tenant talks to the ghost, students should see that *C* is correct.

Review and Assess

Literary Analysis

Setting

1. List four details in "The Wounded Wolf" that reveal the amount of time that passes. Record them on a chart like the one shown.

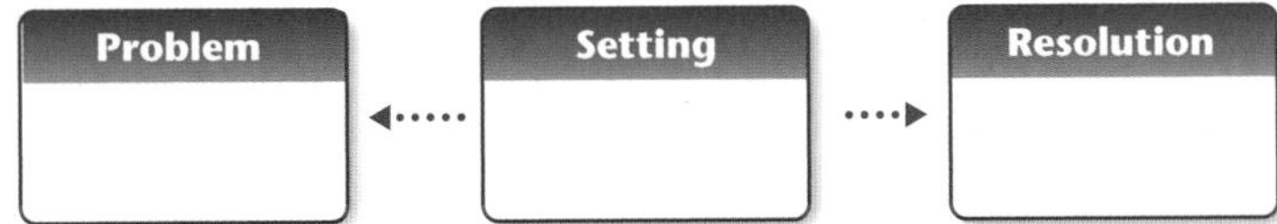

Setting: Details that show the passage of time
1.
2.
3.
4.

2. In "The Lawyer and the Ghost," what are three clues that suggest the story does not take place in contemporary London?

Comparing Literary Works

3. In what ways are the settings similar and different?
4. Do the settings make problems or solutions? Explain.
5. Make a chart to show how setting influences the problem and the resolution.

Story:________________________________

Problem ◄····· **Setting** ·····► **Resolution**

6. Which setting do you think is more important to the resolution of the story? Explain why.

Reading Strategy

Picturing the Setting

7. In your own words, describe the place where "The Lawyer and the Ghost" occurs.
8. What sensory details do you associate with the setting of "The Wounded Wolf?"

Extend Understanding

9. **Cultural Connection:** What does "The Lawyer and the Ghost" suggest about lawyers and law in Dickens's England?

Quick Review

The **setting** is the time and place of a story's events. To review setting, see page 477.

The **conflict** is the problem in a story. The **resolution** is the way the problem is settled. To review conflict and resolution, see page 477.

When **picturing the setting** of a story, you use sensory details to experience it.

Take It to the Net

www.phschool.com

Take the interactive self-test online to check your understanding of these selections.

ENRICHMENT: Further Reading

Other Works by the Authors

Works by Charles Dickens

Oliver Twist

Great Expectations

A Christmas Carol

Works by Jean Craighead George

Julie

My Side of the Mountain

Water Sky

The Talking Earth

Take It to the Net

Visit www.phschool.com for more information on the authors.

Answers for p. 487

Review and Assess

1. "The sun comes up."
   "The hours pass."
   "For days, Kiglo brings young Roko food."
   "One dawn he moves his wounded leg."
2. The story takes place "over forty years ago"; fireplaces are used for warmth; papers are stored in "presses."
3. Both settings are cold and unfamiliar. They are different because one story is set in a nineteenth-century city and the other is set in the Arctic winter.
4. The settings make both problems and solutions.
5. "The Lawyer and the Ghost": **Problem:** Ghost haunts the chambers **Setting:** Depressing chambers **Resolution:** Ghost decides to leave for a more pleasant place; "The Wounded Wolf": **Problem:** Roko is wounded **Setting:** Hostile animals, sheltering rock **Resolution:** Roko finds shelter and gets well
6. Possible responses: Students may say that the setting of "The Lawyer and the Ghost" is more important to the resolution because the setting is what causes the ghost to leave. Others may say that the setting of "The Wonderful Wolf" is more important because the setting helps protect Roko.
7. "The Lawyer and the Ghost" is set in very old, dirty, haunted chambers in a building used by lawyers.
8. Sensory details include cold, wet, snow; howling wolves and cawing ravens; red blood on white snow; cracking ice; and the sound of wolves eating raw meat.
9. "The Lawyer and the Ghost" suggests that lawyers lived and practiced in the same set of rooms and that not all lawyers were well off.

EXTEND

Answers for p. 488

❶ Vocabulary Development

Word Analysis

1. inexpensive room—changes from a costly room to a cheap one
2. inconsistent reason—changes from a reason that makes sense to one that does not
3. indigestible food—changes from food that can be easily absorbed by the body to food that cannot be absorbed
4. inefficient methods—changes from methods that produce results to ones that do not

Spelling Strategy

1. proficient 2. deficient

Fluency: Definitions

1. d 4. e
2. f 5. a
3. b 6. c

❷ Grammar

1. (He); stops; looks; CV
2. (Kiglo and the other wolves); helped; CS
3. (Hooves, paws, and teeth); roared; CS
4. (raven); hops; flaps; CV
5. (snowy owl); has heard; joined; CV

Writing Application

Possible response: Students should write sentences demonstrating their mastery of compound subjects and verbs.

Integrate Language Skills

❶ Vocabulary Development Lesson

Word Analysis: Latin Prefix *in-*

The Latin prefix *in-* can mean "no, not, without, the lack of, or the opposite of." In "The Lawyer and the Ghost," for example, *inconsistent* means "not consistent." On your paper, add *in-* to the first word in each phrase. Then, explain the change in meaning.

1. expensive room
2. consistent reason
3. digestible food
4. efficient methods

Spelling Strategy

The *shent* sound is often spelled *cient,* as in *sufficient*. On your paper, correct the following misspelled words.

1. profishent (skillful in doing something)
2. defishent (lacking in something)

Fluency: Definitions

On your paper, match each word in the first column with its lettered meaning in the second column. Then, write a sentence in which you use each word.

1. sufficient	a. not reacting to good or bad events
2. expend	b. not making sense
3. inconsistent	c. bites with grinding teeth
4. massive	d. enough
5. stoic	e. large and impressive
6. gnashes	f. use up; spend

❷ Grammar Lesson

Simple and Compound Sentences

A **simple sentence** is made of a single independent clause—a group of words that contains a subject and a verb and can stand by itself as a sentence. A simple sentence can contain a **compound subject** (a subject made up of two or more nouns) or a **compound verb** (two or more verbs that name actions done by the same subject) and still be a simple sentence.

Compound subject
The ghost and the lawyer talked about the situation.
Compound verb
Kiglo watched and waited.

▶ *For more practice, see page R29, Exercise F.*

Practice Copy the sentences on your paper. Circle each subject. Underline each verb. Then, label the compound subjects and verbs.

1. He stops and looks.
2. Kiglo and the other wolves helped Roko.
3. Hooves, paws, and teeth roared over him.
4. The raven hops and flaps its wings.
5. The snowy owl has heard the ravens and joined the deathwatch.

Writing Application Write five sentences to describe a scene from "The Wounded Wolf." Include two sentences with compound verbs and one sentence with a compound subject.

WG Prentice Hall Writing and Grammar Connection: Chapter 20, Section 2

TEACHING RESOURCES

The following resources can be used to enrich or extend the instruction for pp. 488–489.

Vocabulary

- **Selection Support:** Build Vocabulary, p. 141; Build Spelling Skills, p. 142
- **Vocabulary and Spelling Practice Book** (Use this booklet for skills enrichment)

Grammar

- **Selection Support:** Build Grammar Skills, p. 143
- **Writing and Grammar,** Copper Level, p. 426

- **Daily Language Practice Transparencies** ■

Writing

- **Writing and Grammar,** Copper Level, p. 226 ■
- **Writing and Grammar iText CD-ROM**

■ **BLOCK SCHEDULING:** Resources marked with this symbol provide varied instruction during 90-minute blocks.

❸ Writing Lesson

Annotated Bibliography

An **annotated bibliography** is a list of materials on a given topic, along with publication information and summaries. Write down five questions about wolves that you have after reading "The Wounded Wolf." Then, compile an **annotated bibliography**—a source list with comments—of materials that could answer these questions.

Prewriting Write your questions and then go to the library to gather useful sources. Record the publication information and write a summary of each source.

Drafting After writing your summaries, write a bibliography entry for each source. See the model for help in formatting your bibliography.

Model: Bibliography Format

Full-Length Book: Carpenter, Albert, *Football, Now and Then.* Upper Saddle River, NJ: Prentice Hall, 1997.

Encyclopedia Entry: "Football." World Book. Vol. 7, pp. 365, 366.

Magazine Article: Taylor, Beth. "Glory Days." *Football Journal,* July 1995, pp. 40–45.

Revising Make sure all of your publication information is accurate and that you have used the correct format.

WG Prentice Hall Writing and Grammar Connection: Chapter 11, Section 5

❹ Extension Activities

Listening and Speaking Prepare a **persuasive presentation** in which you state and support an opinion on the issue of whether or not efforts should be made to protect wolves. Do research to learn about both sides of the issue. Support your opinion with detailed evidence arranged in a visual display. For example, you might

- make a graph that shows the declining population of wolves.
- use photographs to show the damage caused by wolves.

Check your facts for accuracy, and then present your findings.

Research and Technology With a partner, research what London was like during Charles Dickens's life. What details from "The Lawyer and the Ghost" are historically accurate? To show what you learned, give your class **an oral report on the historical setting** of the story. In your oral report, include visuals such as diagrams, drawings, or reproductions of photographs. Try to find representations of the Inns of Court and the paper press that are described in the story. [Group Activity]

www.phschool.com

Go online for an additional research activity using the Internet.

ASSESSMENT RESOURCES

The following resources can be used to assess students' knowledge and skills.

Selection Assessment

- **Formal Assessment,** pp. 125–127
- **Open Book Test,** pp. 85–87
- **Got It! Assessment Videotapes,** Tape 3
- **Test Bank Software**

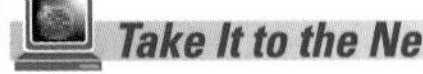

Visit www.phschool.com for self-tests and additional questions on the selections.

Listening and Speaking Rubric

- **Performance Assess. and Portfolio Mgmt.,** p. 27

PRENTICE HALL ASSESSMENT SYSTEM

- **Workbook**
- **Skill Book**
- **Transparencies**
- **CD-ROM**

Lesson Support for p. 489

❸ Writing Lesson

- You may want to work with your school librarian to set aside research resources that will be appropriate for this lesson.
- Point out to students that annotated bibliographies are useful to researchers because they provide names, publication information, and summaries of the sources.
- Use the instructions to guide students through the writing lesson.
- Have students report to the class on the most useful research resources they found.

❹ Listening and Speaking

- Divide the class into groups. Then, have each group research the issue of protecting wolves.
- After students have done sufficient research to form an opinion, have them decide which side they wish to take.
- Direct students to organize the information for their presentation and prepare any visual aids that they may need.
- As students make their presentations, use the Speaking rubric on p. 27 in **Performance Assessment and Portfolio Management** to assess their work.

CUSTOMIZE INSTRUCTION For Universal Access

To address different learning styles, use the activities suggested in the **Extension Activities** booklet, p. 29.

- For Visual/Spatial Learners, use Activity 5.
- For Bodily/Kinesthetic and Interpersonal Learners, use Activity 6.
- For Verbal/Linguistic and Interpersonal Learners, use Activity 7.

Lesson Objectives

1. To recognize supported and unsupported claims in magazine articles
2. To understand the purposes and limitations of magazine articles

About Magazine Articles

- Have students read "About Magazine Articles." Then, discuss magazine articles that students have read. Ask students why people read magazine articles. Possible responses: People read magazines to get information about people, events, or issues that interest them; to do research on products they want to buy; to get information on topics they are researching for class assignments; to find out opinions on topics.
- Ask students about the differences between the information in books and in magazine articles. Possible response: Magazines have more current information than books because magazines are published more often than books. Books usually cover topics in greater depth because there is more space in a book than in most magazine articles.
- Point out to students that magazines are often published by organizations that have specific goals, such as entertainment or scientific research.

Reading Strategy

Recognizing Supported and Unsupported Claims

- Have a volunteer read aloud the information about the Reading Strategy.
- Ask students why they need to evaluate claims in magazine articles. Possible response: They need to read closely to determine whether all of the claims made in the article are supported by facts.
- Using the bulleted information, discuss how students can determine whether claims are supported. Have volunteers give examples of facts and opinions.
- Have students apply these strategies as they read the magazine article on pp. 491–492.

READING INFORMATIONAL MATERIALS

Magazine Articles

About Magazine Articles

Magazine articles are nonfiction texts written for various reasons: to inform readers about a person or topic, to state a viewpoint, or to convince readers to take a specific action. Whatever the purpose, the writer should include statements that support the claims made in the text. When you read magazine articles, evaluate whether claims are supported and whether they are logically presented.

Reading Strategy

Recognizing Supported and Unsupported Claims

To reach your own conclusions about the information in a magazine article, read carefully, noting claims unsupported by the text. As you read, ask yourself these questions:

- Does the writer support the statement with facts (information that can be proved to be true) or with opinions (the writer's or someone else's viewpoint)?
- Are citations (quotes and sources of information) accurate and related to the claims?
- Is the reasoning logical and appropriate to the claims made by the writer?

As you read the article on the next two pages, use a chart like the one shown to identify and analyze the writer's statements that are not supported by the text. Write the statement and the supporting text. If there is no supporting text, explain the support that is needed.

Analyzing Support

Statement	Support	Support Needed
Rehabilitation techniques have come a long way in the past quarter century.	None	The writer needs to tell *how* techniques have improved.

Can Oiled Seabirds Be Rescued, Or Are We Just Fooling Ourselves?

Sharon Levy

Like dozens of other volunteers, I felt compelled to help when a cargo ship spilled 5,000 gallons of fuel oil in Humboldt Bay, near my home on California's north coast. When we released rehabilitated birds, we all felt great. Later, I learned that what we had done was controversial. Many biologists believe that rescuing oiled birds serves more to soothe human feelings than to help wildlife and some studies show that many cleaned birds survive for only a few days. But there are a number of encouraging success stories.

Look for examples in the article that support the claim that there are encouraging success stories.

Plumage normally keeps a seabird warm and dry even as it dives far below the surface. When oil coats feathers, the plumage loses its ability to insulate, leaving a bird susceptible to hypothermia. Beached birds also suffer from dehydration, anemia and pneumonia.

Rehabilitation techniques have come a long way in the past quarter century. But critics contend that the surviving birds represent an insignificant proportion

National Wildlife Feb-Mar 1999

Can Oiled Seabirds Be Rescued, Or Are We Just Fooling Ourselves?

- Explain that students may read a magazine article like this one for a school assignment or because they have a personal interest in the topic.
- Point out that the magazine in which the article appears can give clues to the objectivity of the article. For example, an article on oiled seabirds in an oil-industry publication might present information differently than would an article published by an environmental group. News magazines may have another perspective on the issue.
- Have students read the article and the notes.
- The introduction alerts readers to the topics that will be covered. Some writers and editors may not include support for claims in the introduction, so readers should look further for them.
- Encourage students to evaluate the quote in the third paragraph. What could be the relationship between the opinion and the statistic that follows it?
  Answer: The opinion shows that the biologist does not trust the oil companies, so he may be citing statistics that are especially unfavorable to the oil companies.

continued on p. 492

CUSTOMIZE INSTRUCTION FOR UNIVERSAL ACCESS

For Special Needs Students	For Less Proficient Readers	For Advanced Students
Acquaint students with the title, cover, table of contents, articles, and advertisements in magazines. Show where to find the date of an issue. Note that magazines are published at regular intervals and that recent issues contain the most current information on a topic. Supply several magazines, and challenge students to find the basic parts.	Students may benefit from learning the differences between nonfiction articles and fiction often included in magazines. Point out key features of nonfiction articles and fiction, including the topics and types of illustrations. Make several articles available, and have students determine which are nonfiction and which are fiction.	Have students compare how two news magazines treat a controversial topic. Ask students to note the opinions and the supporting details. Encourage them to note unsupported claims or claims that are supported only by opinions. Have students write essays that compare and contrast the treatment of the issue.

continued from p. 491

- Have students finish reading the article and the notes.
- Recall with students the introductory paragraph. Note that the second full paragraph on p. 492 supports the claim that some oiled birds have been treated successfully.
- Call attention to the third full paragraph on p. 492. Ask whether any information in this paragraph is based on fact.
  Answer: Specific cases of rescued penguins in South Africa, as well as information that includes statistics about penguin survival in oil spills, appear to be based on fact, although no sources are cited.
- Discuss the author's personal commitment to cleaning oiled birds. Does this make her a biased or an unbiased source?
  Possible responses: She may be considered biased by some students because of her personal involvement in projects; others may note that she reports on both sides of the cleaning issue, so she is not biased.

of the bird populations affected in most spills. "Future oil company support for bird rescue should be considered a public relations effort to counteract negative public opinion," wrote Oregon biologist Brian Sharp in a 1995 report. He estimates that only 4 percent of cleaned birds live for a year in the wild.

> Here, an opinion is quoted. Do not mistake quoted opinions for factual support.

"Bird survival will be quite different from spill to spill," says David Jessup, a veterinarian with the California Department of Fish and Game's Office of Spill Prevention and Response, which has established regional facilities to provide rapid response during such catastrophes. "The species involved, the toxicity of the oil, the weather and length of time between oiling and being picked up, all influence survival."

After the Platform Irene oil spill near Santa Barbara last winter, researchers conducted one of the first studies using radiotelemetry to directly compare the survival of oiled and unoiled western gulls. "It was a sticky, nasty crude oil that pasted the birds' feathers, wings and legs to their bodies," recalls veterinarian Jonna Mazet, director of the state's Oiled Wildlife Care Network. "Following release, all of the rehabilitated gulls survived for the life of their radio transmitters [more than eight months] and did as well or better than a control group of unoiled birds."

> A specific example of a scientific study directly supports the earlier claim of success stories.

The most successful cases of oiled-bird rescue have occurred at the tip of South Africa, where African penguin colonies have suffered from several serious oil spills over the last decade. Penguins have a better chance of surviving oiling and rehabilitation then most other seabirds. They have a layer of blubber to keep them warm. And their normal life cycle involves periods of fasting. Following a spill in 1994, more than 65 percent of the 4,076 penguins that were cleaned were later resighted in good health.

Dee Boersma, a University of Washington biologist who works with Magellanic penguins in Argentina, hasn't experienced the same success. "The reason South Africa worked is they had a huge aquarium and fire department that delivered water free so that they could really wash the birds. In Argentina, it's a desert. The nearest town is many miles from the large penguin colonies and there's no water."

During a major spill off Argentina in 1991, Boersma estimates 17,000 birds were oiled. "Perhaps 360 birds were recovered, giving a false impression that the population was being rescued," she says.

> Here, the writer presents facts about a failure and the reasons for the failure.

At the Humboldt spill, I experienced the joy of seeing birds recover as well as the sorrow of seeing them suffer. If an oil spill does hit here again, chances are I'll go back to the wildlife care center to help out. I'll do this for some good reasons and for some bad ones. I'll do it because I know action is an effective antidote to the grief I'll feel. I'll do it in the hope that a majority of the birds that go through rehabilitation will survive. That's a goal that seems far more attainable here than on the remote beaches of Argentina.

> This conclusion is logical, because conditions in California more closely resemble conditions in successful areas than conditions in Argentina.

Yes, I'd work at the center again. But I'd know as I started up my car engine to go there that I was applying a Band-Aid, not solving the problem of oil pollution. Like everyone else in our oil-addicted society, I am still part of that dilemma.

Californian Sharon Levy specializes in topics relating to science and nature.

National Wildlife Feb-Mar 1999

Check Your Comprehension

1. Where did the writer volunteer to help out with the oil spill?
2. Using details from the article, explain the phrase "rehabilitated birds."
3. How does oil affect a bird's plumage?
4. What species of bird has a better chance of surviving oiling than most other seabirds? Why?
5. Why does the writer feel that she is part of the oil-spill problem?

Applying the Reading Strategy

Recognizing Supported and Unsupported Claims

6. Identify one claim that is not supported by the text. Tell what kind of information is needed to support the claim.
7. Choose a claim made by the writer that is supported by the text. Write the statement and the supporting text.

Activity

Support Search

With a group, conduct a "support search" to analyze both sides of the question this article explores. Prepare two empty bulletin boards or display areas to represent the two possible answers. Over the course of a week, look for articles, studies, and examples that support either answer. Post photocopies of your findings on the bulletin boards. At the end of the week, discuss and evaluate the evidence the group has found.

Comparing Informational Materials

Magazine and Online Articles

Find an article on the Internet about rescuing oiled seabirds. Compare and contrast the amount, type, and presentation of information in the online article and "Oiled Seabirds." Use a chart like the one at right. After you have completed your chart, write a one-paragraph evaluation explaining which medium you found to be more effective. Use details from your chart for support.

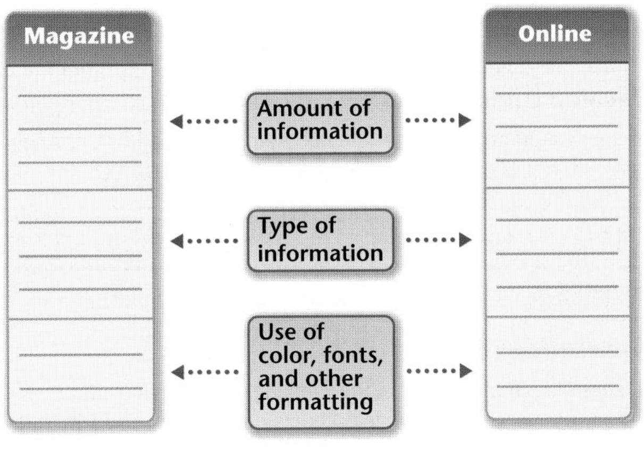

Answers for p. 493

Check Your Comprehension

1. She volunteered at Humboldt Bay, in northern California.
2. "Rehabilitated birds" are birds that have been cleaned after being covered in oil from oil spills.
3. Oil affects the bird's ability to keep warm and dry.
4. Penguins have a better chance of surviving a spill because they have blubber to keep them warm and are able to go for long periods without food.
5. The writer feels that she is part of the problem because she is a member of a society that uses too much oil, which indirectly causes oil spills.

Applying the Reading Strategy

6. "Rehabilitation techniques have come a long way in the past quarter century." To support this, the author should either provide details of previous and current techniques or give statistics that show improvement over time. "Future oil company support . . . counteract[s] negative public opinion." This opinion needs the support of information that reveals oil company executives' motives or their lack of support for the reclamation programs.
7. "The most successful cases of oiled-bird rescue have occurred at the tip of South Africa . . . " is supported at the end of the same paragraph with statistics showing the success rate.

Activity

Students should provide relevant articles and objectively evaluate the opinions and support presented in the articles. They should clearly state which opinions have sufficient support and which need further information or support. You might wish to divide the class into two groups, with each group taking a side on this issue. Require students to use facts and well-supported opinions in their presentations.

continued

Answers continued

Comparing Informational Materials

The source of the Internet article will tell students a great deal about the reliability of its information. In addition, the Internet article will probably be more current than the article in the book, because Internet information can be revised often. Most Internet articles may be more complete and have illustrations, graphs, and other features that will make the articles appealing to readers.

The All-American Slurp ✦ The Stone

Lesson Objectives

1. **To analyze and respond to literary elements**
   - Literary Analysis: Theme
   - Comparing Literary Works
2. **To read, comprehend, analyze, and critique two short stories**
   - Reading Strategy: Drawing Inferences
   - Reading Check Questions
   - Review and Assess Questions
   - Assessment Practice (ATE)
3. **To develop word analysis skills, fluency, and systematic vocabulary**
   - Vocabulary Development Lesson: Word Analysis: Forms of *migrate*
4. **To understand and apply written and oral language conventions**
   - Spelling Strategy
   - Grammar Lesson: Compound and Complex Sentences
5. **To understand and apply appropriate writing and research strategies**
   - Writing Lesson: Story Plot
   - Extension Activity: Human Growth Report
6. **To understand and apply listening and speaking strategies**
   - Extension Activity: Oral Response to Theme

STEP-BY-STEP TEACHING GUIDE	PACING GUIDE
PRETEACH	
Motivate Students and Provide Background	
Use the Motivation activity (ATE p. 494)	5 min.
Read and discuss the Preview material and Background information (SE/ATE p. 494) [A]	5 min.
Introduce the Concepts	
Introduce the Literary Analysis and Reading Strategy (SE/ATE p. 495) [A]	25 min.
Pronounce the vocabulary words and read their definitions (SE p. 495)	5 min.
TEACH	
Monitor Comprehension	
Informally monitor comprehension by circulating while students read independently or in groups [A]	40 min.
Monitor students' comprehension with the Reading Check notes (SE/ATE pp. 497, 499, 501, 503, 505, 507, 509, 511)	as students read
Develop vocabulary with Vocabulary notes (SE pp. 496, 501, 507, 508, 512)	as students read
Develop Understanding	
Develop students' understanding of theme with the Literary Analysis annotations (SE pp. 499, 503, 507, 510; ATE pp. 499, 503, 507, 510) [A]	5 min.
Develop students' ability to draw inferences with the Reading Strategy annotations (SE pp. 497, 498, 502, 503, 506, 510; ATE pp. 497, 498, 502, 503, 506, 510)	5 min.
ASSESS	
Assess Mastery	
Assess students' mastery of the Reading Strategy and Literary Analysis by having them answer the Review and Assess questions (SE/ATE p. 513)	25 min.
Use one or more of the print and media Assessment Resources (ATE p. 515) [A]	up to 45 min.
EXTEND	
Apply Understanding	
Have students complete the Vocabulary Development Lesson and the Grammar Lesson (SE p. 514) [A]	20 min.
Apply students' knowledge of story plot using the Writing Lesson (SE/ATE p. 515) [A]	30–45 min.
Apply students' understanding of the selection using one or more of the Extension Activities (SE p. 515)	20–90 min.

ACCELERATED INSTRUCTION:
Use the strategies and activities identified with an [A].

UNIVERSAL ACCESS
● = Below Level Students
▲ = On-Level Students
■ = Above Level Students

Time and Resource Manager

Reading Level: Average, Average
Average Number of Instructional Days: 4

RESOURCES		
PRINT	**TRANSPARENCIES**	**TECHNOLOGY**
• **Beyond Literature,** Community Connection: Diversity, p. 30 ▲ ■		• **Interest Grabber Videotapes,** Tape 3 ● ▲ ■
• **Selection Support Workbook:** ● ▲ ■ Literary Analysis, p. 150 Reading Strategy, p. 149 Build Vocabulary, p. 146	• **Literary Analysis and Reading Transparencies,** pp. 59 and 60 ● ▲ ■	
• **Adapted Reader's Companion** ● • **Reader's Companion** ●		• **Listening to Literature** ● ▲ ■ Audiocassettes, Side 18 Audio CDs, CD 9
• **English Learner's Companion** ● ▲ • **Literary Analysis for Enrichment** ■		
• **Formal Assessment:** Selection Test, pp. 128–130 ● ▲ ■ • **Open Book Test,** pp. 88–90 ● ▲ ■ • **Performance Assessment and Portfolio Management,** pp. 13, 29 ● ▲ ■ • PRENTICE HALL ASSESSMENT SYSTEM ● ▲ ■	• PRENTICE HALL ASSESSMENT SYSTEM ● ▲ ■ Skills Practice Answers and Explanations on Transparencies	• **Test Bank Software** ● ▲ ■ • **Got It! Assessment Videotapes,** Tape 3 ● ▲
• **Selection Support Workbook:** ● ▲ ■ Build Spelling Skills, p. 147 Build Grammar Skills, p. 148 • **Writing and Grammar,** Copper Level ● ▲ ■ • **Extension Activities,** p. 30 ● ▲ ■	• **Daily Language Practice Transparencies** ● ▲ • **Writing Models and Graphic Organizers on Transparencies** ● ▲ ■	• **Writing and Grammar iText CD-ROM** ● ▲ ■ ***Take It to the Net*** www.phschool.com

BLOCK SCHEDULING: Use one 90-minute class period to preteach the selection and have students read it. Use a second 90-minute class period to assess students' mastery of skills and have them complete one of the Extension Activities.

PRETEACH

Step-by-Step Teaching Guide for pp. 494–495

Motivation

On the board, write the words "Unwritten Rules." Ask students to help you make a list of unwritten rules that they know and follow. Some of these rules may be acts of courtesy or manners; others may deal with styles of dress. Help students recognize that only a person living with a group that practices these rules would know them. Ask students how someone would learn some of these rules. Most students will understand that a person has to make mistakes and get help from friends to fully understand the customs of a society or a group.

Interest Grabber Video

As an alternative, play "Make A Wish" on Tape 3 to engage student interest.

❶ Background

Social Studies

Students will read about different eating customs when a Chinese family is invited to dinner at an American home. In addition to eating certain foods unknown or unusual in the U.S., people in other parts of the world have eating customs that Americans might find as surprising as others would find Americans'. For example, in France bread and cheese generally follow a meal. They are considered neither appetizers nor quick meals in themselves. In Italy, pasta is a first course rather than a main course as it generally is in the United States. Similarly, French and Italian visitors think it strange that Americans eat eggs for breakfast, whereas in Japan breakfast usually consists of soup, rice, salad, and grilled fish.

Prepare to Read

❶ The All-American Slurp ◆ The Stone

Take It to the Net

Visit www.phschool.com for interactive activities and instruction related to these selections, including
- background
- graphic organizers
- literary elements
- reading strategies

Preview

Connecting to the Literature

These selections share insights into growth and change. As you read, notice how the characters deal with the challenges that change brings. Then, consider how you might have reacted to similar situations.

Background

In "The All-American Slurp," a Chinese family newly arrived in the United States must deal with unfamiliar eating habits. The following are some Chinese customs concerning food that the family in this story observes:

- Food is usually served "family style" on large platters in the center of the table.
- Food is scooped up or handled with slender sticks called chopsticks.

TEACHING RESOURCES

The following resources can be used to enrich or extend the instruction for pp. 494–495.

Motivation

Interest Grabber Video, Tape 3 

Background

Beyond Literature, p. 30

Take It to the Net

Visit www.phschool.com for Background and hotlinks for the selections.

Literary Analysis

Literary Analysis and Reading Transparencies, Theme, p. 60

Reading

Selection Support: Reading Strategy, p. 149; Build Vocabulary, p. 146

Literary Analysis and Reading Transparencies, Drawing Inferences, p. 59

BLOCK SCHEDULING: Resources marked with this symbol provide varied instruction during 90-minute blocks.

❷ Literary Analysis

Theme

The theme is the central message of a literary work. The theme of a story can be either stated or implied.

- A **stated theme** is expressed directly by the author.
- An **implied theme** is suggested, or stated indirectly.

Often, you can figure out the implied theme by paying attention to the characters' actions. To figure out the implied theme in these stories, think about the following:

- The ways in which the Lin family changes
- What Maibon learns from getting his wish

Comparing Literary Works

As you read these stories, think about what each one says about change.

Compare and contrast the themes in these selections by answering these focus questions as you read:

1. What does each story say about change?
2. What themes do these stories share? What themes are unique to each story?

❸ Reading Strategy

Drawing Inferences

Sometimes you need to figure out an implied theme by **drawing inferences**, or reaching conclusions based on evidence. Evidence may include unusual events, as well as characters' words, actions, and reactions. Use a chart like the one here to help you draw inferences about the important details in these stories.

Story Detail

The Lins sit "stiffly in a row" on the Gleasons' couch.

My Thoughts

People sit stiffly when they are nervous.

My Inference

New to the United States, the Lins are afraid of making a mistake.

Vocabulary Development

emigrated (em i grāt′ id) *v.* left one country to settle in another (p. 496)

etiquette (et′ i ket) *n.* acceptable social manners (p. 501)

consumption (kən sump′ shen) *n.* eating; drinking; using up (p. 501)

plight (plīt) *n.* awkward, sad, or dangerous situation (p. 507)

jubilation (jo͞o bə lā′ shen) *n.* great joy; triumph(p. 508)

rue (ro͞o) *v.* regret (p. 508)

fallow (fal′ ō) *adj.* inactive; unproductive (p. 512)

CUSTOMIZE INSTRUCTION FOR UNIVERSAL ACCESS

For Special Needs Students	For Less Proficient Readers	For English Learners
Have students read the adapted version of "The All-American Slurp" in the **Adapted Reader's Companion.** This version provides basic-level instruction in an interactive format with questions and write-on lines. Completing the adapted version will prepare students to read the selection in the Student Edition.	Have students read "The All-American Slurp" in the **Reader's Companion.** This version provides basic-level instruction in an interactive format with questions and write-on lines. After students finish the selection in the Reader's Companion, have them complete the questions and activities in the Student Edition.	Have students read the adapted version of "The All-American Slurp" in the **English Learner's Companion.** This version provides basic-level instruction in an interactive format with questions and write-on lines. Completing the adapted version will prepare students to read the selection in the Student Edition.

❷ Literary Analysis

Theme

- Tell students that as they read the selections, they will be learning about the themes, or central messages, of these stories.
- Review the meaning of plot, the chain of events in a literary work. Help students distinguish plot from theme by explaining that the plot is what happens in a selection, whereas the theme is a general idea that the author wants readers to understand.
- Use the Theme transparency on p. 60 in **Literary Analysis and Reading Transparencies** to show how events in a story contribute to its theme.
- Read aloud the instruction about Comparing Literary Works. Point out the difference between stated and implied themes.

❸ Reading Strategy

Drawing Inferences

- To help students understand how to make inferences, write on the board an example sentence such as the following: "The boy ran away from the dog." Ask students why they think the boy ran away. Possible response: Most students will say that the boy was probably scared of the dog. Then, point out to students that they have just made an inference.
- Tell students that making inferences will help them find an implied theme.
- Explain that a character's words, actions, and reactions will help the reader draw inferences.
- Have students make simple charts to record their observations and their inferences.

Vocabulary Development

- Review the words on the vocabulary list.
- Explain that *consumption,* the noun form of the verb *consume,* means "eating, drinking, or using up." Work with students to identify several items that people consume each day.

E-Teach

Visit E-Teach at www.phschool.com for teachers' essays on how to teach, with questions and answers.

TEACH

Step-by-Step Teaching Guide for pp. 496–512

CUSTOMIZE INSTRUCTION For Bodily/Kinesthetic Learners

Have students role-play having dinner at a friend's home. Some students can act as the host family and others can play the part of guests. What happens when the guests do not know the customs in the host's home? Have students take turns in each role. Ask students to explain how eating away from home can be a much different experience than eating at home.

1 About the Selection

In "The All-American Slurp," readers follow the events of the story through the voice of the narrator. The narrator and her family encounter table manners that are much different from their Chinese customs, such as eating raw vegetables and not slurping their soup. Various events during their first few months in America illustrate how the family members learn the customs of their new country. After the Lins have been in America for about three months, they invite their neighbors to dinner. Unaware of Chinese eating customs, Mrs. Gleason dumps her rice onto the dinner plate and mixes the rice with the prawns, and Mr. Gleason has a hard time with chopsticks. The Lins watch their guests in amazement, but the dinner ends happily when the narrator and her best friend, Meg Gleason, go down the street for a milkshake. Meg finishes her shake first and toward the end she slurps and explains, "All Americans slurp." The narrator and her family may still have a lot to learn about American customs, but they have already found some common ground in everyday life.

1 The All-American Slurp

Lensey Namioka

The first time our family was invited out to dinner in America, we disgraced ourselves while eating celery. We had emigrated to this country from China, and during our early days here we had a hard time with American table manners.

emigrated (em´ i grāt´ id) *v.* left one country to settle in another

In China we never ate celery raw, or any other kind of vegetable raw. We always had to disinfect the vegetables in boiling water first. When we were presented with our first relish tray, the raw celery caught us unprepared.

We had been invited to dinner by our neighbors, the Gleasons. After arriving at the house, we shook hands with our hosts and packed ourselves into a sofa. As our family of four sat stiffly in a row, my younger brother and I stole glances at our parents for a clue as to what to do next.

Mrs. Gleason offered the relish tray to Mother. The tray looked pretty, with its tiny red radishes, curly sticks of carrots, and long, slender stalks of pale green celery. "Do try some of the celery, Mrs. Lin," she said. "It's from a local farmer, and it's sweet."

Mother picked up one of the green stalks, and Father followed suit. Then I picked up a stalk, and my brother did too. So there we sat, each with a stalk of celery in our right hand.

Mrs. Gleason kept smiling. "Would you like to try some of the dip, Mrs. Lin? It's my own recipe: sour cream and onion flakes, with a dash of Tabasco sauce."

Most Chinese don't care for dairy products, and in those days I wasn't even ready to drink fresh milk. Sour cream sounded perfectly revolting. Our family shook our heads in unison.

TEACHING RESOURCES

The following resources can be used to enrich or extend the instruction for pp. 496–512.

Literary Analysis

- **Selection Support:** Literary Analysis, p. 150
- **Literary Analysis for Enrichment** ■
- **Writing Models and Graphic Organizers on Transparencies,** p. 85

Reading

- **Adapted Reader's Companion**
- **Reader's Companion**

- **English Learner's Companion**
- **Listening to Literature Audiocassettes,** Side 18 ■
- **Listening to Literature Audio CDs,** CD 9 ■

■ **BLOCK SCHEDULING:** Resources marked with this symbol provide varied instruction during 90-minute blocks.

Mrs. Gleason went off with the relish tray to the other guests, and we carefully watched to see what they did. Everyone seemed to eat the raw vegetables quite happily.

Mother took a bite of her celery. *Crunch.* "It's not bad!" she whispered.

Father took a bite of his celery. *Crunch.* "Yes, it is good," he said, looking surprised.

I took a bite, and then my brother. *Crunch, crunch.* It was more than good; it was delicious. Raw celery has a slight sparkle, a zingy taste that you don't get in cooked celery. When Mrs. Gleason came around with the relish tray, we each took another stalk of celery, except my brother. He took two.

There was only one problem: long strings ran through the length of the stalk, and they got caught in my teeth. When I help my mother in the kitchen, I always pull the string out before slicing celery.

I pulled the strings out of my stalk. *Z-z-zip, z-z-zip.* My brother followed suit. *Z-z-zip, z-z-zip, z-z-zip.* To my left, my parents were taking care of their own stalks. *Z-z-zip, z-z-zip, z-z-zip.*

Suddenly I realized that there was dead silence except for our zipping. Looking up, I saw that the eyes of everyone in the room were on our family. Mr. and Mrs. Gleason, their daughter Meg, who was my friend, and their neighbors the Badels—they were all staring at us as we busily pulled the strings of our celery.

That wasn't the end of it. Mrs. Gleason announced that dinner was served and invited us to the dining table. It was lavishly covered with platters of food, but we couldn't see any chairs around the table. So we helpfully carried over some dining chairs and sat down. All the other guests just stood there.

Mrs. Gleason bent down and whispered to us, "This is a buffet dinner. You help yourselves to some food and eat it in the living room."

Our family beat a retreat back to the sofa as if chased by enemy soldiers. For the rest of the evening, too mortified to go back to the dining table, I nursed a bit of potato salad on my plate.

Reading Strategy
Drawing Inferences
What can you infer based on the Lins' surprised reactions to the raw vegetables?

3 **Reading Check**
Why is the narrator embarrassed?

2 Reading Strategy

Drawing Inferences

- Ask a volunteer to define the word *inference*.
  Answer: An inference is a conclusion that is based on evidence.
- After students have read the bracketed text, ask the Reading Strategy question on p. 497: What can you infer based on the Lins' surprised reaction to the raw vegetables?
  Answer: The Lins are not used to eating raw vegetables.
- What can you infer from the reaction of the other guests to the Lins?
  Possible response: The other guests are probably surprised, and wonder what they are doing.

3 Reading Check

Answer: The narrator is embarrassed because her family takes chairs to the dining room table instead of sitting in the other room.

CUSTOMIZE INSTRUCTION FOR UNIVERSAL ACCESS

For Special Needs Students	For Less Proficient Readers	For English Learners
Students may benefit from both reading and listening to the story at the same time. Invite students to read along while you play the story on the **Listening to Literature Audiocassettes** or **Audio CD**. As each important episode ends, turn off the playing device, and have students discuss the plot developments.	Have students read aloud the first two pages. Point out sentences that are clues to the theme: "As our family of four . . . what to do next," and "For the rest . . . potato salad on my plate." Explain that these sentences help readers determine the theme: that people worry about making mistakes in unusual or difficult situations.	Terms such as *z-z-zip* may not be familiar to students. Point out that the author is using these words to convey sounds. The italic font is a clue that the word is meant to portray a sound. Invite students to imitate the sound *z-z-zip*. Suggest that they preview the text to acquaint themselves with other such sounds.

4 Reading Strategy

Drawing Inferences

- Have students read the paragraph beginning "Meg was . . ." on p. 498.
- Ask students the Reading Strategy question.
  Answer: It is probably difficult for the narrator to make friends because she is in a new school.

5 Critical Thinking

Analyze

- Invite students to share their observations about the narrator up to this point in the story.
  Answer: The narrator is from China and is going to school in the United States. She is trying hard to fit in and understand American ways.
- Have a volunteer read aloud the bracketed passage. Ask students what the passage reveals about the narrator.
  Answer: She is worried about making mistakes, so she speaks slowly.

6 Critical Thinking

Compare and Contrast Characters

- After students have read p. 498, draw a Venn diagram on the board. Label one circle *mother* and the other *father*. Have students describe what these two characters have in common and what qualities are specific to each character. Record their responses in the diagram.
  Answer: Both want to learn English and studied only written English in China. The father uses charts and diagrams to learn English. The mother memorizes polite phrases to use in social situations.
- Ask the following question: Do you think the mother would have a difficult time carrying on a conversation with Mrs. Gleason? Have students explain their answers.
  Possible answer: Yes, because the mother studied only written English in school and has memorized a list of polite phrases. She would be unable to ask complicated questions or talk about everyday events.

Next day Meg and I got on the school bus together. I wasn't sure how she would feel about me after the spectacle our family made at the party. But she was just the same as usual, and the only reference she made to the party was, "Hope you and your folks got enough to eat last night. You certainly didn't take very much. Mom never tries to figure out how much food to prepare. She just puts everything on the table and hopes for the best."

I began to relax. The Gleasons' dinner party wasn't so different from a Chinese meal after all. My mother also puts everything on the table and hopes for the best.

4 Meg was the first friend I had made after we came to America. I eventually got acquainted with a few other kids in school, but Meg was still the only real friend I had.

Reading Strategy
Drawing Inferences
What can you infer about the narrator after reading this paragraph?

My brother didn't have any problems making friends. He spent all his time with some boys who were teaching him baseball, and in no time he could speak English much faster than I could—not better, but faster.

5 I worried more about making mistakes, and I spoke carefully, making sure I could say everything right before opening my mouth. At least I had a better accent than my parents, who never really got rid of their Chinese accent, even years later. My parents had both studied English in school before coming to America, but what they had studied was mostly written English, not spoken.

6 Father's approach to English was a scientific one. Since Chinese verbs have no tense, he was fascinated by the way English verbs changed form according to whether they were in the present, past imperfect, perfect, pluperfect,[1] future, or future perfect tense. He was always making diagrams of verbs and their inflections,[2] and he looked for opportunities to show off his mastery of the pluperfect and future perfect tenses, his two favorites. "I shall have finished my project by Monday," he would say smugly.[3]

Mother's approach was to memorize lists of polite phrases that would cover all possible social situations. She was constantly muttering things like "I'm fine, thank you. And you?" Once she accidentally stepped on someone's foot, and hurriedly blurted, "Oh, that's quite all right!" Embarrassed by her slip, she resolved to do better next time. So when someone stepped on *her* foot, she cried, "You're welcome!"

1. **pluperfect** (plo͞o´ pʉr´ fikt) *adj.* the past perfect tense of verbs in English.
2. **inflections** (in flek´ shən) *n.* the changes in the forms of words to show different tenses.
3. **smugly** (smug´ lē) *adv.* in a way that shows satisfaction with oneself.

CUSTOMIZE INSTRUCTION FOR UNIVERSAL ACCESS

For Advanced Readers

Tell students that people from different countries have settled in communities across the United States. In addition to learning a new language, these people have had to learn the customs of their new country, which can vary from community to community.

Ask students whether they have classmates, friends, or family members who have come to the United States from another country. Tell students to interview one or two of these people, asking them to relate their experiences during their first months in this country. (Some of your students may be from another country. If so, they may choose to relate their own experiences.) Have the students write short reports based on their interviews.

Have students read their reports in class. Then have a question-and-answer discussion. Encourage students to talk about how they might have reacted to similar incidents.

In our own different ways, we made progress in learning English. But I had another worry, and that was my appearance. My brother didn't have to worry, since Mother bought him blue jeans for school, and he dressed like all the other boys. But she insisted that girls had to wear skirts. By the time she saw that Meg and the other girls were wearing jeans, it was too late. My school clothes were bought already, and we didn't have money left to buy new outfits for me. We had too many other things to buy first, like furniture, pots, and pans.

The first time I visited Meg's house, she took me upstairs to her room, and I wound up trying on her clothes. We were pretty much the same size, since Meg was shorter and thinner than average. Maybe that's how we became friends in the first place. Wearing Meg's jeans and T-shirt, I looked at myself in the mirror. I could almost pass for an American—from the back, anyway. 7 At least the kids in school wouldn't stop and stare at me in my white blouse and navy blue skirt that went a couple of inches below the knees.

When Meg came to my house, I invited her to try on my Chinese dresses, the ones with a high collar and slits up the sides. Meg's eyes were bright as she looked at herself in the mirror. She struck several sultry poses, and we nearly fell over laughing.

The dinner party at the Gleasons' didn't stop my growing friendship with Meg. Things were getting better for me in other ways too. Mother finally bought me some jeans at the end of the month, when Father got his paycheck. She wasn't in any hurry about buying them at first, until I worked on her. This is what I did. Since we didn't have a car in those days, I often ran down to the neighborhood store to pick up things for her. The groceries cost less at a big supermarket, but the closest one was many blocks away. One day, when she ran out of flour, I offered to borrow a bike from our neighbor's son and buy a ten-pound bag of flour at the supermarket. I mounted the boy's bike and waved to Mother. "I'll be back in five minutes!"

Before I started pedaling, I heard her voice behind me. "You can't go out in public like that! People can see all the way up to your thighs!"

"I'm sorry," I said innocently. "I thought you were in a hurry to get the flour." For dinner we were going to have pot-stickers (fried Chinese dumplings), and we needed a lot of flour.

"Couldn't you borrow a girl's bicycle?" complained Mother. "That way your skirt won't be pushed up."

"There aren't too many of those around," I said. "Almost all the girls wear jeans while riding a bike, so they don't see any point buying a girl's bike."

Literary Analysis
Theme What does the narrator's statement about almost passing for an American suggest that the theme might revolve around?

8  **Reading Check**
What does the speaker think is wrong with her appearance?

7 Literary Analysis

Theme

- Remind students that the *theme* is the main idea that the author tries to convey.
- Ask students the Literary Analysis question on p. 499: What does the narrator's statement about almost passing for an American suggest that the theme might revolve around?
  Answer: The theme might revolve around trying to fit in with American life.

Monitor Progress Ask students to describe the two types of themes and the difference between them.
Answer: *Stated themes* are expressed directly in the story. *Implied themes* are themes that the reader must infer, based on information that the author supplies.

Reteach If students do not understand the difference between stated and implied themes, you may wish to review a theme from a recent selection with which students are familiar.

8 

Answer: The narrator thinks she does not look American enough.

CUSTOMIZE INSTRUCTION FOR UNIVERSAL ACCESS

For Less Proficient Readers	For Gifted/Talented Students
Students may be able to understand the sequence of events in "All-American Slurp" more clearly if they use a timeline. Have them record the events of the story on their time lines. As students read, encourage them to add not only the events from the story, but also the inferences that they make from these events and the narrator's comments about them. As the story progresses, invite students to share their time lines and their inferences with the class.	Have students choose parts and dramatize the actions of the main characters in this story. Key scenes that they may want to portray include the dinner at the Gleasons' and the afternoon that Meg and the narrator try on each other's clothes. In addition to reading the dialogue and narration, encourage students to use body language and facial expressions to show the characters' actions and attitudes. Have the class share what they learn about the characters from watching the dramatization.

9 Critical Thinking

Connect

- Invite students to recall how the Lin family behaves in the beginning of the story. You may wish to have students reread the second paragraph on p. 496 to refresh their memories.
  Answer: They are just beginning to learn American ways.
- Next, have students read the bracketed passage. Ask them how the narrator's and her family's attitudes have changed since the beginning of the story.
  Answer: They had an awkward experience the first time they were invited to dinner. By now, the narrator has begun to think that they might become a normal American family. For example, the brother is on the baseball team, the father is taking driving lessons, the narrator is able to wear jeans, and the mother is shopping at rummage sales.

10 Critical Thinking

Analyze

- Ask students to describe the father's character.
  Answer: He is methodical and precise. He studies things in a very organized manner.
- Have a volunteer read aloud the passage beginning "Father, being an engineer. . . ." Ask: Does the father's behavior surprise you? Why or why not?
  Possible response: No, because he studied English by using diagrams and is the sort of person who would prepare for a new experience in this way.

9 We didn't eat pot-stickers that evening, and Mother was thoughtful. Next day we took the bus downtown and she bought me a pair of jeans. In the same week, my brother made the baseball team of his junior high school, Father started taking driving lessons, and Mother discovered rummage sales.

We soon got all the furniture we needed, plus a dart board and a 1,000-piece jigsaw puzzle (fourteen hours later, we discovered that it was a 999-piece jigsaw puzzle). There was hope that the Lins might become a normal American family after all.

Then came our dinner at the Lakeview restaurant.

The Lakeview was an expensive restaurant, one of those places where a headwaiter dressed in tails conducted you to your seat, and the only light came from candles and flaming desserts. In one corner of the room a lady harpist played tinkling melodies.

Father wanted to celebrate, because he had just been promoted. He worked for an electronics company, and after his English started improving, his superiors decided to appoint him to a position more suited to his training. The promotion not only brought a higher salary but was also a tremendous boost to his pride.

Up to then we had eaten only in Chinese restaurants. Although my brother and I were becoming fond of hamburgers, my parents didn't care much for western food, other than chow mein.[4] But this was a special occasion, and Father asked his coworkers to recommend a really elegant restaurant. So there we were at the Lakeview, stumbling after the headwaiter in the murky dining room.

At our table we were handed our menus, and they were so big that to read mine I almost had to stand up again. But why bother? It was mostly in French, anyway.

10 Father, being an engineer, was always systematic.[5] He took out a pocket French dictionary. "They told me that most of the items would be in French, so I came prepared." He even had a pocket flashlight, the size of a marking pen. While Mother held the flashlight over the menu, he looked up the items that were in French.

"*Pâté en croûte,*" (pä tā′ än kro͞ot) he muttered. "Let's see . . . *pâté* is paste . . . *croûte* is crust . . . hmm . . . a paste in crust."

---

4. **chow mein** (chou′ mān′) *n.* thick stew of meat, celery, and Chinese vegetables.
5. **systematic** (sis′ tə mat′ ik) *adj.* orderly.

CUSTOMIZE INSTRUCTION FOR UNIVERSAL ACCESS

For Advanced Readers

Discuss the differences in customs that are central to the setting and plot of this story. Then, have students research other Chinese customs. Have each student focus on one topic, such as food, clothing, or leisure-time activities. Tell students to use encyclopedias and textbooks in their research.

Have each student write several paragraphs presenting their findings. Each student should compare and contrast the customs. If more than one student chooses the same topic, have them work together on their presentations.

Invite students to present their findings to the class. After the presentations, ask students whether they think they would have a difficult time adopting Chinese customs. Have them explain their answers.

11 The waiter stood looking patient. I squirmed and died at least fifty times.

At long last Father gave up. "Why don't we just order four complete dinners at random?" he suggested.

"Isn't that risky?" asked Mother. "The French eat some rather peculiar things, I've heard."

12 "A Chinese can eat anything a Frenchman can eat," Father declared.

The soup arrived in a plate. How do you get soup up from a plate? I glanced at the other diners, but the ones at the nearby tables were not on their soup course, while the more distant ones were invisible in the darkness.

Fortunately my parents had studied books on western etiquette before they came to America. "Tilt your plate," whispered my mother. "It's easier to spoon the soup up that way."

etiquette (et′ i ket) *n.* acceptable social manners

She was right. Tilting the plate did the trick. But the etiquette book didn't say anything about what you did after the soup reached your lips. As any respectable Chinese knows, the correct way to eat your soup is to slurp. This helps to cool the liquid and prevent you from burning your lips. It also shows your appreciation.

We showed our appreciation. *Shloop*, went my father. *Shloop* went my mother. *Shloop, shloop*, went my brother, who was the hungriest.

The lady harpist stopped playing to take a rest. And in the silence, our family's consumption of soup suddenly seemed unnaturally loud. You know how it sounds on a rocky beach when the tide goes out and the water drains from all those little pools? They go *shloop, shloop, shloop*. That was the Lin family, eating soup.

consumption (kən sump′ shen) *n.* eating; drinking; using up

At the next table a waiter was pouring wine. When a large *shloop* reached him, he froze. The bottle continued to pour, and red wine flooded the tabletop and into the lap of a customer. Even the customer didn't notice anything at first, being also hypnotized by the *shloop, shloop, shloop*.

It was too much. "I need to go to the toilet," I mumbled, jumping to my feet. A waiter, sensing my urgency, quickly directed me to the ladies' room.

I splashed cold water on my burning face, and as I dried myself with a paper towel, I stared into the mirror. In this perfumed ladies' room, with its pink-and-silver wallpaper and marbled sinks, I looked completely out of place. What was I doing here? What was our family doing in the Lakeview restaurant? In America?

13 ✓Reading Check

Why does the Lin family slurp their soup?

11 Critical Thinking

Relate

- Point out to students that even if they have lived in America all their lives, they may have felt out of place in certain situations.
- Read aloud the bracketed text. Ask students to relate this situation to something that may have happened to them or to someone they know.
  Possible response: Ordering food that you have never eaten can be a strange experience. It can be hard to tell what it is when you have never eaten it before.

12 Reading Strategy

Drawing Inferences

- Have students read the bracketed passage.
- Ask the following question: What does this remark suggest about Father's attitude about fitting in with the ways of another country?
  Answer: Father's attitude is that he is capable of adapting to any unusual circumstance.

13 ✓Reading Check

Answer: The Lins slurp their soup because in China, slurping is a sign of good manners.

CUSTOMIZE INSTRUCTION FOR UNIVERSAL ACCESS

For Special Needs Students	For Less Proficient Readers	For Advanced Readers
To help students think in an organized way about this story, have them take turns retelling "The All-American Slurp." Have them relate events in the story in the order in which they are presented in the selection. Point out that writers deliberately put events in a certain order.	Have students make a comic strip about the major events in the story. Invite them to choose incidents and make line drawings with captions illustrating the incidents. Post the illustrations on a bulletin board, or bind them into a book that will be available for student review.	Borrow several etiquette books from the library, and make them available to students. Have students read the sections about table manners from the viewpoint of the Lin family. Ask each student to write a brief summary about what the Lins might have learned from the books.

14 Reading Strategy

Drawing Inferences

- Ask students where the narrator goes while her family are eating their soup.
  Answer: She goes to the ladies' room.
- Then, ask the Reading Strategy question on p. 502.
  Answer: The narrator is deeply embarrassed by her family's behavior.

15 Critical Thinking

Evaluate

- Have a volunteer read aloud the bracketed text. Ask how long the incident bothers the narrator.
  Answer: The narrator says that it bothers her for at least several weeks.
- Ask students to talk about why the incident bothers the narrator for weeks. Do they think they would have had the same reaction as the narrator? Why or why not?
  Possible responses: Some students may say that the narrator's reaction was a typical one. They, too, would have been very embarrassed and would try not to think about it later. Some students may say they might have been a little amused as well as embarrassed.

16 Critical Thinking

Connect

- Ask students to infer what all of the incidents in the story have in common.
  Answer: The incidents are about a Chinese family and how its members are becoming more familiar with life in America.
- Read aloud the passage beginning "The day came." Ask the following question: What does this passage reveal about the Lins?
  Answer: They now feel comfortable enough in America to invite the Gleasons into their home.

The door to the ladies' room opened. A woman came in and glanced curiously at me. I retreated into one of the toilet cubicles and latched the door.

Time passed—maybe half an hour, maybe an hour. Then I heard the door open again, and my mother's voice. "Are you in there? You're not sick, are you?"

There was real concern in her voice. A girl can't leave her
14 family just because they slurp their soup. Besides, the toilet
cubicle had a few drawbacks as a permanent residence. "I'm all right," I said, undoing the latch.

Mother didn't tell me how the rest of the dinner went, and I didn't want to know. In the weeks following, I managed to push
15 the whole thing into the back of my mind, where it jumped out
at me only a few times a day. Even now, I turn hot all over when I think of the Lakeview restaurant.

But by the time we had been in this country for three months, our family was definitely making progress toward becoming Americanized. I remember my parents' first PTA meeting. Father wore a neat suit and tie, and Mother put on her first pair of high heels. She stumbled only once. They met my homeroom teacher and beamed as she told them that I would make honor roll soon at the rate I was going. Of course Chinese etiquette forced Father to say that I was a very stupid girl and Mother to protest that the teacher was showing favoritism toward me. But I could tell they were both very proud.

The day came when my parents announced that they wanted to give a dinner party. We had invited Chinese friends to eat with us before, but this dinner was going to be different. In
16 addition to a Chinese-American family, we were going to invite
the Gleasons.

"Gee, I can hardly wait to have dinner at your house," Meg said to me. "I just *love* Chinese food."

That was a relief. Mother was a good cook, but I wasn't sure if people who ate sour cream would also eat chicken gizzards stewed in soy sauce.

Mother decided not to take a chance with chicken gizzards. Since we had western guests, she set the table with large dinner plates, which we never used in Chinese meals. In fact we didn't use individual plates at all, but picked up food from the platters in the middle of the table and brought it directly to our rice bowls. Following the practice of Chinese-American restaurants, Mother also placed large serving spoons on the platters.

Reading Strategy
Drawing Inferences
How does the narrator feel about her family's behavior?

CUSTOMIZE INSTRUCTION FOR UNIVERSAL ACCESS

For English Learners

Students may have difficulty identifying the theme of "The All-American Slurp." Point out that phrases and sentences throughout the story are clues to the theme. Examples include "I worried more about making mistakes . . . " and "I looked completely out of place. What was I doing here? What was our family doing in the Lakeview Restaurant? In America?"

Help students trace the narrator's changing feelings about living in America. Have them find and record the narrator's statements about her feelings about living in America. Students should note whether the narrator has any setbacks and what those setbacks might be.

These clues help readers identify the theme (different cultures have different customs, but all people have similar feelings). The narrator and her family worry about making mistakes in speaking the language and are adopting new customs, just as all people do when they are in a new country.

The dinner started well. Mrs. Gleason exclaimed at the beautifully arranged dishes of food: the colorful candied fruit in the sweet-and-sour pork dish, the noodle-thin shreds of chicken meat stir-fried with tiny peas, and the glistening pink prawns in a ginger sauce.

At first I was too busy enjoying my food to notice how the guests were doing. But soon I remembered my duties. Sometimes guests were too polite to help themselves and you had to serve them with more food.

I glanced at Meg, to see if she needed more food, and my eyes nearly popped out at the sight of her plate. It was piled with food: the sweet-and-sour meat pushed right against the chicken shreds, and the chicken sauce ran into the prawns. She had been taking food from a second dish before she finished eating her helping from the first!

Horrified, I turned to look at Mrs. Gleason. She was dumping rice out of her bowl and putting it on her dinner plate. Then she ladled prawns and gravy on top of the rice and mixed everything together, the way you mix sand, gravel, and cement to make concrete.

I couldn't bear to look any longer, and I turned to Mr. Gleason. He was chasing a pea around his plate. Several times he got it to the edge, but when he tried to pick it up with his chopsticks, it rolled back toward the center of the plate again. Finally he put down his chopsticks and picked up the pea with his fingers. He really did! A grown man!

All of us, our family and the Chinese guests, stopped eating to watch the activities of the Gleasons. I wanted to giggle. Then I caught my mother's eyes on me. She frowned and shook her head slightly, and I understood the message: the Gleasons were not used to Chinese ways, and they were just coping the best they could. For some reason I thought of celery strings.

When the main courses were finished, Mother brought out a platter of fruit. "I hope you weren't expecting a sweet dessert," she said. "Since the Chinese don't eat dessert, I didn't think to prepare any."

"Oh, I couldn't possibly eat

Reading Strategy
Drawing Inferences What can you infer about the Lins' dinner customs based on the narrator's reaction to the Gleasons' actions? (17)

Literary Analysis
Theme What lesson is the narrator learning about people's experiences?

 **Reading Check**

What happens when the Gleasons come over to the Lins' for dinner?

17 Reading Strategy

Drawing Inferences

- Remind students to watch for clues that the author uses to help the reader make inferences about the characters and the theme of the story.
- Ask a volunteer to read aloud the bracketed passage. Ask the Reading Strategy question on p. 503: What can you infer about the Lins' dinner customs based on the narrator's reaction to the Gleasons' actions?
  Answer: The Lins put one type of food on their plate and eat all of it before putting on another type of food. The Lins use chopsticks easily and do not like to mix foods together.

18 Literary Analysis

Theme

- Point out to students that the Gleasons are learning Chinese ways, just as the Lins are learning American ways.
- Ask the Literary Analysis question on p. 503: What lesson is the narrator learning about people's experiences?
  Answer: The narrator is learning that everyone has new experiences that can be embarrassing and that everyone has feelings. She is learning to be more accepting of others and herself.

19 Reading Check

Answer: When the Gleasons come over for dinner, they are unfamiliar with Chinese customs, so they mix their foods together and have difficulty using chopsticks.

CUSTOMIZE INSTRUCTION FOR UNIVERSAL ACCESS

For English Learners	For Advanced Readers
Have students role-play ordering dinner in a fancy restaurant. Students can create menus with explanations of certain dishes. Have some students act as staff and others as patrons. Make sure each patron asks at least one question that members of the staff must answer. Then have students switch roles. Ask students to explain how eating in a fancy restaurant is different from eating at home.	Have students plan a mock interview with the author for a live TV broadcast. Suggest some resources for getting information about the author, such as library publications and Internet resources. They could also read her other works. Each student should use the resources to write a list of questions to ask the author. Then, have students work in pairs to role-play the interview. Have one student play the interviewer and the other play the author. Have pairs of students perform their interviews for the class.

Answers for p. 504

Review and Assess

1. Possible response: Don't worry about making mistakes in English or table manners because people born in the U.S. make similar, or worse, mistakes.
2. **(a)** The narrator worries about everything and makes sure she says everything right. The brother learns English from his friends. The father takes a scientific approach and concentrates on English verb forms. The mother memorizes lists of polite phrases. **(b)** The narrator is worried about what other people think of her and her family. The brother is not concerned with details but wants to communicate with his new friends. The father thinks he can cope with any situation. The mother is polite, proper, and easily embarrassed.
3. **(a)** The narrator convinces her mother to buy jeans by getting on a boy's bike while wearing a skirt. **(b)** Jeans are important because the narrator wants to dress like an American. **(c)** The narrator is in school and sees what American children are like. The mother is usually at home and less familiar with American ways.
4. **(a)** The Lins slurp their soup. **(b)** The narrator runs to the ladies' room because she is embarrassed.
5. **(a)** The Gleasons put food from every dish on their plates all at once. Mrs. Gleason dumps rice out of her bowl. Mr. Gleason picks up a pea with his fingers. **(b)** Both families are in new situations and do the best they can.
6. **(a)** Meg says that all Americans slurp milkshakes. **(b)** Meg's comment is funny and reassuring because of the soup-slurping incident. **(c)** Possible responses: Some students may say the narrator has a good sense of humor because she and Meg have fun dressing in each other's clothing. She is also able to have a good time with Meg. Other students may say that the narrator does not have a good sense of humor until the end of the story. Earlier, every time she or her family did anything "not American," she would be embarassed.

dessert!" cried Mrs. Gleason. "I'm simply stuffed!"

Meg had different ideas. When the table was cleared, she announced that she and I were going for a walk. "I don't know about you, but I feel like dessert," she told me, when we were outside. "Come on, there's a Dairy Queen down the street. I could use a big chocolate milkshake!"

Although I didn't really want anything more to eat, I insisted on paying for the milkshakes. After all, I was still hostess.

Meg got her large chocolate milkshake and I had a small one. Even so, she was finishing hers while I was only half done. Toward the end she pulled hard on her straws and went *shloop, shloop*.

"Do you always slurp when you eat a milkshake?" I asked, before I could stop myself.

Meg grinned. "Sure. All Americans slurp."

Review and Assess

Thinking About the Selection

1. **Respond:** What advice would you give the narrator about adjusting to life in the United States? Why?
2. **(a) Recall:** Describe the way in which each family member learns English. **(b) Infer:** What does each person's way of learning English reveal about his or her personality?
3. **(a) Recall:** How does the narrator convince her mother to buy jeans? **(b) Infer:** Why are jeans so important to the narrator? **(c) Compare and Contrast:** How is the narrator's experience in adjusting to life in the U.S. different from her mother's experience?
4. **(a) Recall:** What do the Lins do with their soup at a restaurant? **(b) Interpret:** Why does the narrator run to the ladies' room?
5. **(a) Recall:** Name two things the Gleasons do at the Lins' dinner party that shock the narrator. **(b) Compare and Contrast:** In what way are the Gleasons' actions at the Lins' dinner party similar to the Lins' actions at the Gleasons' party?
6. **(a) Recall:** What does Meg say that all Americans do? **(b) Infer:** Why does Meg's comment seem funny and reassuring to the narrator? **(c) Evaluate:** Do you think the narrator has a good sense of humor about her family's difficulties in adjusting to life in the U.S.? Why?

Lensey Namioka

(b. 1929)

Lensey Namioka is a Chinese American who uses her Chinese heritage in her writing. Her novel *Who's Hu?*, the story of a Chinese girl learning the ways of Americans, is among her most popular works. The novel's heroine, Emma Hu, is a math whiz who has to battle prejudice against girls in math.

Namioka's main character in "The All-American Slurp" is based on Namioka herself. Like her character, she was born in China and moved with her family to the United States as a teenager. Also like her character, she discovered big differences between Chinese and American eating habits.

20 # The Stone

Lloyd Alexander

Walk in the Country, Javran

There was a cottager named Maibon, and one day he was driving down the road in his horse and cart when he saw an old man hobbling along, so frail and feeble he doubted the poor soul could go many more steps. Though Maibon offered to take him in the cart, the old man refused; and Maibon went his way home, shaking his head over such a pitiful sight, and said to his wife, Modrona:

"Ah, ah, what a sorry thing it is to have your bones creaking and cracking, and dim eyes, and dull wits. When I think this might come to me, too! A fine, strong-armed, sturdy-legged fellow like me?

21 ▲ **Critical Viewing** What impression of old age does the picture give? **[Support]**

22 **Reading Check** Who is Maibon?

20 About the Selection

In Lloyd Alexander's "The Stone," the cottager Maibon passes an ancient man on the road and starts thinking about the physical problems of old age. Later in his journey he frees a red-haired dwarf from under a log and asks that one of his wishes be granted by the dwarf. He decides to ask for a stone that will stop him from growing old. The dwarf tries to persuade Maibon to ask for a more useful reward, but Maibon insists on the stone. The stone keeps Maibon and everything around him from changing, so that his crops do not grow, his cow does not have a calf, and his baby's teeth do not come in. He tries to get rid of the stone, but it keeps coming back, as if by magic. Finally, he meets the dwarf again, who tells him the stone will always return until Maibon stops hoping that he will never grow old. When Maibon does this, he is able to throw the stone away.

21 ▶Critical Viewing

Answer: The picture gives the impression that old age is an unhappy time, because the old man is frowning, has patched clothes, and needs a tree branch to serve as a cane. Even his pet has a very serious expression.

22 Reading Check

Answer: Maibon is a cottager who feels sorry for an old man.

CUSTOMIZE INSTRUCTION FOR UNIVERSAL ACCESS

For Less Proficient Readers	For English Learners	For Advanced Readers
Use the art on pp. 505 and 509 to help students understand the setting of the story. Have students preview the art, and then ask them to infer answers to questions such as the following: Where does Maibon live? What does he do for a living? Have them check their inferences as the story progresses.	Maibon uses two hyphenated words, "strong-armed" and "sturdy-legged" to describe himself. Explain to students that hyphens are used to join two words that are used together as one adjective. Encourage students to make a short list of hyphenated adjectives and to watch for them in other selections.	The author uses alliteration in the phrases "frail and feeble" and "creaking and cracking" on p. 505. Have students look up *alliteration* in a dictionary. Challenge them to find examples of it and comment on its use in the story. Encourage them to use alliteration in their own creative writing where appropriate.

23 Reading Strategy

Drawing Inferences

- Have students relate how they draw inferences.
  Possible response: Inferences are drawn by making conclusions based on the clues that an author provides in a story.
- Read aloud the bracketed passage on p. 506.
- Ask students the Reading Strategy question: What can you infer about Maibon's feelings about growing old? Have students explain their answers.
  Possible response: Maibon is saddened at the prospect of growing older because he sees only the negative aspects of old age, such as creaking bones, poor eyesight, and a decrease in alertness.
- Ask students what other inferences they can make about Maibon.
  Possible response: He is a peasant, he is a farmer, and he is married.

24 Critical Thinking

Analyze

- Have a student read aloud the passage beginning "At this, the dwarf." Then, have students analyze the dwarf's anger.
- Ask students whether they think Doli is more upset about not being able to disappear or about being caught under a log.
  Possible responses: Some students may say that Doli is more upset about not being able to disappear because everyone else in his family can do it, and this hurts his pride. Others may say that he is more concerned about being caught beneath a log.

One day to go tottering, and have his teeth rattling in his head, and live on porridge, like a baby? There's no fate worse in all the world."

"There is," answered Modrona, "and that would be to have neither teeth nor porridge. Get on with you, Maibon, and stop borrowing trouble. Hoe your field or you'll have no crop to harvest, and no food for you, nor me, nor the little ones."

Sighing and grumbling, Maibon did as his wife bade him. Although the day was fair and cloudless, he took no pleasure in it. His ax-blade was notched, the wooden handle splintery; his saw had lost its edge; and his hoe, once shining new, had begun to rust. None of his tools, it seemed to him, cut or chopped or delved[1] as well as they once had done.

"They're as worn out as that old codger I saw on the road," Maibon said to himself. He squinted up at the sky. "Even the sun isn't as bright as it used to be, and doesn't warm me half as well. It's gone threadbare as my cloak. And no wonder, for it's been there longer than I can remember. Come to think of it, the moon's
23 been looking a little wilted around the edges, too.

"As for me," went on Maibon, in dismay, "I'm in even a worse state. My appetite's faded, especially after meals. Mornings, when I wake, I can hardly keep myself from yawning. And at night, when I go to bed, my eyes are so heavy I can't hold them open. If that's the way things are now, the older I grow, the worse it will be!"

In the midst of his complaining, Maibon glimpsed something bouncing and tossing back and forth beside a fallen tree in a corner of the field. Wondering if one of his piglets had squeezed out of the sty and gone rooting for acorns, Maibon hurried across the turf. Then he dropped his ax and gaped in astonishment.

There, struggling to free his leg which had been caught under the log, lay a short, thickset figure: a dwarf with red hair bristling in all directions beneath his round, close-fitting leather cap. At the sight of Maibon, the dwarf squeezed shut his bright red eyes and began holding his breath. After a moment, the dwarf's face went redder than his hair; his cheeks puffed out and soon turned purple. Then he opened one eye and blinked rapidly at Maibon, who was staring at him, speechless.

"What," snapped the dwarf, "you can still see me?"

"That I can," replied Maibon, more than ever puzzled, "and I can see very well you've got yourself tight as a wedge under that log, and all your kicking only makes it worse."

At this, the dwarf blew out his breath and shook his fists. "I can't
 do it!" he shouted. "No matter how I try! I can't make myself invisible! Everyone in my family can disappear—Poof! Gone! Vanished! But not

Reading Strategy
Drawing Inferences What can you infer about Maibon's feelings about growing old? Explain.

1. **delved** (delvd) *v.* dug.

CUSTOMIZE INSTRUCTION FOR UNIVERSAL ACCESS

For Advanced Readers

After students have read this story, it would be a good time for them to find and read other stories about magic and magicians, such as "Aladdin and the Wonderful Lamp" from *The Arabian Nights* and the stories in T. H. White's *The Once and Future King.*

Have students check the library for stories involving magic. Then each student should select his or her favorite story to summarize in a written report. The report should include the main character(s), the plot, the theme, the setting, and the main events. Instruct students to be sure to list the events in the proper order.

Have students read their reports to the class. Then, have a class discussion about the reports. You may want to ask students to comment on the similarities between "The Stone" and the stories in their reports.

me! Not Doli! Believe me, if I could have done, you never would
24 have found me in such a plight. Worse luck! Well, come on. Don't
stand there goggling like an idiot. Help me get loose!"

At this sharp command, Maibon began tugging and heaving at the log. Then he stopped, wrinkled his brow, and scratched his head, saying:

"Well, now, just a moment, friend. The way you look, and all your talk about turning yourself invisible—I'm thinking you might be one of the Fair Folk."

"Oh, clever!" Doli retorted. "Oh, brilliant! Great clodhopper! Giant beanpole! Of course I am! What else! Enough gabbling. Get a move on. My leg's going to sleep."

"If a man does the Fair Folk a good turn," cried Maibon, his excitement growing, "it's told they must do one for him."

"I knew sooner or later you'd come round to that," grumbled the
dwarf. "That's the way of it with you ham-handed, heavy-footed
25 oafs. Time was, you humans got along well with us. But nowadays,
you no sooner see a Fair Folk than it's grab, grab, grab! Gobble,
gobble, gobble! Grant my wish! Give me this, give me that! As if we
had nothing better to do!

"Yes, I'll give you a favor," Doli went on. "That's the rule, I'm obliged to. Now, get on with it."

Hearing this, Maibon pulled and pried and chopped away at the log as fast as he could, and soon freed the dwarf.

Doli heaved a sigh of relief, rubbed his shin, and cocked a red eye at Maibon, saying:

"All right. You've done your work, you'll have your reward. What do you want? Gold, I suppose. That's the usual. Jewels? Fine clothes? Take my advice, go for something practical. A hazelwood twig to help you find water if your well ever goes dry? An ax that never needs sharpening? A cook pot always brimming with food?"

"None of those!" cried Maibon. He bent down to the dwarf and
whispered eagerly, "But I've heard tell that you Fair Folk have
26 magic stones that can keep a man young forever. That's what I
want. I claim one for my reward."

Doli snorted. "I might have known you'd pick something like that. As to be expected, you humans have it all muddled. There's nothing can make a man young again. That's even beyond the best of our skills. Those stones you're babbling about? Well, yes, there are such things. But greatly overrated. All they'll do is keep you from growing any older."

"Just as good!" Maibon exclaimed. "I want no more than that!"

Doli hesitated and frowned. "Ah—between the two of us, take the cook pot. Better all around. Those stones—we'd sooner not give them away. There's a difficulty—"

plight (plit) *n.* awkward, sad, or dangerous situation

Literary Analysis
Theme What kind of lesson do stories about wishes usually teach?

27 **Reading Check**

What does Maibon ask for?

25 Literary Analysis

Theme

- Ask students to recall other stories about wishes. How do such stories usually end?
  Answer: These stories usually end with the person who made the wish wanting things to return to the way they had been before the wish was granted.
- Ask the Literary Analysis question on p. 507: What kind of lesson do stories about wishes usually teach?
  Answer: They usually teach that people are regretful about getting what they thought they wanted, and that people should be happy with their lives as they are.

26 Critical Thinking

Analyze

- Assign three students to read the parts of Maibon, Doli, and the narrator.
- Ask students why the dwarf is advising Maibon to "go for something practical" instead of the stones, which "are greatly overrated."
  Answer: He is trying to explain to Maibon that it is better to wish for something that will make his life better in some small way than to wish for something that will make his life drastically different.

27 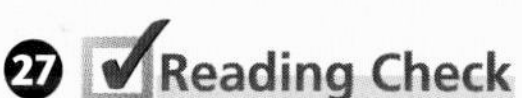

Answer: Maibon asks for a magic stone that will let him be young forever.

CUSTOMIZE INSTRUCTION FOR UNIVERSAL ACCESS

For Special Needs Students	For Less Proficient Readers	For Advanced Readers
Guide students to read for entertainment by helping them understand the imaginary world depicted in "The Stone." Explain that this story contains elements of real life as well as elements of magic. After students finish, ask which feature of the story—characters, mood, or setting—they enjoyed the most.	Have students work with a story partner to learn the sequence of events in the story. As students read, have the pairs work together to note each event in the story on a separate card. When the cards are complete, have one student shuffle the cards and the other put the cards in the correct order. Then, have the students trade tasks.	In "The Stone," the author uses similes and analogies to express Maibon's feelings. His tools are "as worn out as that old codger." The sun has "gone threadbare as my cloak." Have students take notes about other similes and analogies they find in the story, and ask them to explain why they are more effective than simple adjectives.

28 Critical Thinking

Compare and Contrast

- Have a volunteer read aloud the first paragraph of the bracketed passage. Ask students to describe Maibon's feelings about getting the stone from the dwarf.
  Answer: He is happy because he will not get old.
- Ask another student to read aloud the remaining two paragraphs of the bracketed passage. Ask the following question: What does Modrona think about Maibon's choosing the rock?
  Answer: Modrona thinks that Maibon is dumb for asking for the rock. She thinks he should have asked for more practical things, like clothing, treasures, and repairs to their home.
- Ask students whether they agree with Maibon or Modrona.
  Possible responses: Some students may agree with Maibon because he can get practical things anytime, but the rock is a special gift. Others may agree with Modrona, because they know that a gift such as the rock will cause only trouble.

"Because you'd rather keep them for yourselves," Maibon broke in. "No, no, you shan't cheat me of my due. Don't put me off with excuses. I told you what I want, and that's what I'll have. Come, hand it over and not another word."

Doli shrugged and opened a leather pouch that hung from his belt. He spilled a number of brightly colored pebbles into his palm, picked out one of the larger stones, and handed it to Maibon. The dwarf then jumped up, took to his heels, raced across the field, and disappeared into a thicket.

Laughing and crowing over his good fortune and his cleverness, Maibon hurried back to the cottage. There, he told his wife what had happened, and showed her the stone he had claimed from the Fair Folk.

"As I am now, so I'll always be!" Maibon declared, flexing his arms and thumping his chest. "A fine figure of a man! Oho, no gray beard and wrinkled brow for me!"

Instead of sharing her husband's jubilation, Modrona flung up her hands and burst out:

jubilation (jo͞o′ bə lā′ shən) *n.* great joy; triumph

28 "Maibon, you're a greater fool than ever I supposed! And selfish into the bargain! You've turned down treasures! You didn't even ask that dwarf for so much as new jackets for the children! Nor a new apron for me! You could have had the roof mended. Or the walls plastered. No, a stone is what you ask for! A bit of rock no better than you'll dig up in the cow pasture!"

Crestfallen[2] and sheepish, Maibon began thinking his wife was right, and the dwarf had indeed given him no more than a common field stone.

"Eh, well, it's true," he stammered, "I feel no different than I did this morning, no better nor worse, but every way the same. That redheaded little wretch! He'll rue the day if I ever find him again!"

rue (ro͞o) *v.* regret

So saying, Maibon threw the stone into the fireplace. That night he grumbled his way to bed, dreaming revenge on the dishonest dwarf.

Next morning, after a restless night, he yawned, rubbed his eyes, and scratched his chin. Then he sat bolt upright in bed, patting his cheeks in amazement.

"My beard!" he cried, tumbling out and hurrying to tell his wife. "It hasn't grown! Not by a hair! Can it be the dwarf didn't cheat me after all?"

"Don't talk to me about beards," declared his wife as Maibon went to the fireplace, picked out the stone, and clutched it safely in both hands. "There's trouble enough in the chicken roost. Those eggs should have hatched by now, but the hen is still brooding on her nest."

2. **crestfallen** (krest′ fôl′ ən) *adj.* made sad or humble; disheartened.

CUSTOMIZE INSTRUCTION FOR UNIVERSAL ACCESS

For Special Needs Students

Some students may benefit from extended work in visualizing segments of the story.

Have students read aloud or listen to the audiocassette or audio CD of the paragraphs on p. 506, where Maibon discovers the dwarf trying to free his leg from under the log. Discuss the reactions of Maibon and the dwarf to each other.

Point out to students that writers use words to create images in readers' minds, just as artists use visual effects to create images. Have students brainstorm for a list of ways to produce images from the paragraphs, such as creating a sequential mural or a comic strip.

Divide students into small groups, and have each group create a visual representation of the paragraphs. Provide materials for their representations.

Have each group present its visual representation to the class and explain its choice of medium.

Harvesting the Fruit Crop, Javran

"Let the chickens worry about that," answered Maibon. "Wife, don't you see what a grand thing's happened to me? I'm not a minute older than I was yesterday. Bless that generous-hearted dwarf!"

"Let me lay hands on him and I'll bless him," retorted Modrona. "That's all well and good for you. But what of me? You'll stay as you are, but I'll turn old and gray, and worn and wrinkled, and go doddering into my grave! And what of our little ones? They'll grow up and have children of their own. And grandchildren, and great-grandchildren. And you, younger than any of them. What a foolish sight you'll be!"

But Maibon, gleeful over his good luck, paid his wife no heed, and only tucked the stone deeper into his pocket. Next day, however, the eggs had still not hatched.

32 "And the cow!" Modrona cried. "She's long past due to calve, and no sign of a young one ready to be born!"

30 **▲Critical Viewing**
Find three details that suggest the people in the painting live a life similar to that of Maibon and his wife. **[Support]**

31 
Reading Check

What does Maibon realize when he wakes up in the morning?

29 Background

Art

Walk in the Country and **Harvesting the Fruit Crop,** by Javran

Have students carefully examine the art on this page and on p. 505. Then, point out the similarities and differences between the two works. Both show families in their fields. In the picture on this page, the family is shown harvesting its crop. The focal point in the picture on p. 505 is an old man with a walking stick rather than the family members, who appear to be standing in the fields rather than working.

Discuss the following questions with the class:

1. Do you think the painting *Harvesting the Fruit Crop* is a good choice for this story? Explain your answer.
   Possible responses: Some students may say it is a good choice because it shows a family at harvest time. Others may say that most of the story takes place before harvest time; in the story the corn should be sprouting and the apple tree should have small, green fruit, so the season is probably late summer.
2. The title of the painting on p. 505 is *Walk in the Country*. Why do you think this painting was chosen to illustrate this page?
   Possible response: The painting depicts an old man hobbling down the road. He could very well be the old man that Maibon encounters.

30 ▶Critical Viewing

Answer: The painting depicts a life similar to that of Maibon's because the subject of the painting seems to be a group of family members harvesting crops on their small farm.

31 Reading Check

Answer: Maibon realizes that he has not aged.

CUSTOMIZE INSTRUCTION FOR UNIVERSAL ACCESS

For English Learners	For Advanced Students
Identify the last sentence on p. 508 ("Those eggs should . . . on her nest.") as a compound sentence. Tell students that a compound sentence is made up of two or more clauses and may be joined by a coordinating conjunction. Point out that the coordinating conjunction in this sentence is *but*. Ask students to find another compound sentence on this page. ("I told you what I want . . ." or "Crestfallen and sheepish . . .")	Dwarfs and fairies have prominent places in folk tales from many countries. Ask students to investigate the traditions surrounding these characters. Make library or Internet resources available to students, and have them take notes on the powers and limitations such characters have. Students may also be interested in comparing and contrasting the roles these characters play in the folklore of two or more countries.

32 Reading Strategy

Drawing Inferences

- Before reading aloud the bracketed passage, tell students to listen for details that reveal information about the stone's effects.
- Ask the Reading Strategy question on p. 510: What inference can you make about the stone's effects based on these details?
  Answer: The stone is not only keeping Maibon from aging, it is also keeping the things around him from getting older.

33 Literary Analysis

Theme

- Read aloud the bracketed passage, and ask students why Maibon gets rid of the stone.
  Answer: Maibon's wife wants him to get rid of it.
- Ask students how Maibon feels about the stone. Have students explain their conclusions.
  Possible response: Maibon does not really want to get rid of the stone. He throws it "reluctantly," digs a hole that is "not a very deep one," and "regretfully and unwillingly" throws it in the well.
- Ask the Literary Analysis question on p. 510: What clue to the story's message is provided by Maibon's inability to get rid of the stone?
  Answer: Maibon cannot get rid of the stone because he does not want to. The message is that we should be careful of what we wish for, because sometimes what we want is not good for us.

"Don't bother me with cows and chickens," replied Maibon. "They'll all come right, in time. As for time, I've got all the time in the world!"

32 Having no appetite for breakfast, Maibon went out into the field. Of all the seeds he had sown there, however, he was surprised to see not one had sprouted. The field, which by now should have been covered with green shoots, lay bare and empty.

"Eh, things do seem a little late these days," Maibon said to himself. "Well, no hurry. It's that much less for me to do. The wheat isn't growing, but neither are the weeds."

Some days went by and still the eggs had not hatched, the cow had not calved, the wheat had not sprouted. And now Maibon saw that his apple tree showed no sign of even the smallest, greenest fruit.

"Maibon, it's the fault of that stone!" wailed his wife. "Get rid of the thing!"

"Nonsense," replied Maibon "The season's slow, that's all."

Nevertheless, his wife kept at him and kept at him so much that Maibon at last, and very reluctantly, threw the stone out the cottage window. Not too far, though, for he had it in the back of his mind to go later and find it again.

Next morning he had no need to go looking for it, for there was the stone sitting on the window ledge.

"You see?" said Maibon to his wife. "Here it is back again. So, it's a gift meant for me to keep."

"Maibon!" cried his wife. "Will you get rid of it! We've had nothing but trouble since you brought it into the house. Now the baby's fretting and fuming. Teething, poor little thing. But not a tooth to

33 be seen! Maibon, that stone's bad luck and I want no part of it!"

Protesting it was none of his doing that the stone had come back, Maibon carried it into the vegetable patch. He dug a hole, not a very deep one, and put the stone into it.

Next day, there was the stone above ground, winking and glittering.

"Maibon!" cried his wife. "Once and for all, if you care for your family, get rid of that cursed thing!"

Seeing no other way to keep peace in the household, Maibon regretfully and unwillingly took the stone and threw it down the well, where it splashed into the water and sank from sight.

But that night, while he was trying vainly to sleep, there came such a rattling and clattering that Maibon clapped his hands over his ears, jumped out of bed, and went stumbling into the yard. At the well, the bucket was jiggling back and forth and up and down at the end of the rope; and in the bottom of the bucket was the stone.

Reading Strategy
Drawing Inferences What inference can you make about the stone's effects based on these details?

Literary Analysis
Theme What clue to the story's message is provided by Maibon's inability to get rid of the stone?

CUSTOMIZE INSTRUCTION FOR UNIVERSAL ACCESS

For Gifted/Talented Students	For Advanced Readers
Fantasy stories provide excellent material for visual representations. Have gifted/talented students work in pairs or small groups to select a scene from "The Stone" and create a small three-dimensional stage set for their selection. Students can use construction paper to cover grocery cartons for their models. Have students design appropriate costumes for the characters, create an original backdrop, and furnish their sets with appropriate props.	Ask students to research and recommend books and movies about problems that may arise when someone is granted a wish. Point out that the themes of many fairy tales show the problems that come from magical wishes. Provide students several such tales to read. Have students find evidence that certain themes have been passed down and remembered because they teach about life. Then, ask students to write a paragraph explaining what inferences they can draw from the existence of so many warnings.

Now Maibon began to be truly distressed, not only for the toothless baby, the calfless cow, the fruitless tree, and the hen sitting desperately on her eggs, but for himself as well.

"Nothing's moving along as it should," he groaned. "I can't tell one day from another. Nothing changes, there's nothing to look forward to, nothing to show for my work. Why sow if the seeds don't sprout? Why plant if there's never a harvest? Why eat if I don't get hungry? Why go to bed at night, or get up in the morning, or do anything at all? And the way it looks, so it will stay for ever and ever! I'll shrivel from boredom if nothing else!"

"Maibon," pleaded his wife, "for all our sakes, destroy the dreadful thing!"

Maibon tried now to pound the stone to dust with his heaviest mallet;◆ but he could not so much as knock a chip from it. He put it against his grindstone without so much as scratching it. He set it on his anvil and belabored it with hammer and tongs, all to no avail.

At last he decided to bury the stone again, this time deeper than before. Picking up his shovel, he hurried to the field. But he suddenly halted and the shovel dropped from his hands. There, sitting cross-legged on a stump, was the dwarf.

"You!" shouted Maibon, shaking his fist. "Cheat! Villain! Trickster! I did you a good turn, and see how you've repaid it!"

The dwarf blinked at the furious Maibon. "You mortals are an ungrateful crew. I gave you what you wanted."

"You should have warned me!" burst out Maibon.

"I did," Doli snapped back. "You wouldn't listen. No, you yapped and yammered, bound to have your way. I told you we didn't like to give away those stones. When you mortals get hold of one, you stay just as you are—but so does everything around you. Before you know it, you're mired in time like a rock in the mud. You take my advice. Get rid of that stone as fast as you can."

"What do you think I've been trying to do?" blurted Maibon. "I've buried it, thrown it down the well, pounded it with a hammer—it keeps coming back to me!"

 35 "That's because you really didn't want to give it up," Doli said. "In the back of your mind and the bottom of your heart, you didn't want to change along with the rest of the world. So long as you feel that way, the stone is yours."

"No, no!" cried Maibon. "I want no more of it. Whatever may happen, let it happen. That's better than nothing happening at all.

Literature in context Vocabulary Connection

34 ◆ *Mallet*

The word *mallet* comes from the Old French word *maillet.* A mallet is a kind of hammer that usually has a heavy wooden head and a short handle. Mallets are used for driving things, such as chisels to shape wood. In the days before electricity and power tools, a mallet would have had a lot of uses, especially in a rural life like Maibon's.

36 Reading Check

What is the stone doing to everything on Maibon's farm?

34 Background

Vocabulary

Maibon's tools tell us quite a bit about his life. Although he is a farmer, he also has tools for other professions. The *hammer* and *tongs* would be useful when performing smithing duties, such as shoeing horses or repairing metal. He would also hammer metalwork against his *anvil,* a heavy metal block that has a flat top. The *grindstone* was probably made of a hard stone and would be used for either polishing or sharpening tools. Other types of grindstones, called *millstones,* would be used to grind grain into flour.

35 Critical Thinking

Analyze Causes and Effects

- Have students read the bracketed passage. Ask the students what caused the stone to return.
  Answer: Maibon did not really want it to go away, because he did not want to change.
- Ask students to predict what will happen next.
  Possible response: The stone will not come back, because Maibon does not want it back.

36 Reading Check

Answer: The stone makes everything on Maibon's farm stay the same age.

CUSTOMIZE INSTRUCTION FOR UNIVERSAL ACCESS

For Less Proficient Readers	For Gifted/Talented Students
To help students understand the descriptive words used in the story (for example, *ham-handed, splintery, bristling,* and *threadbare as my cloak*), have them read the first two pages carefully and note these words or phrases as they read. They may also note context clues that hint at meanings. Help them define words that they may find difficult, and have students list these in a story vocabulary list.	Have students work in pairs on this activity. Ask students to act out the last meeting between the dwarf and Maibon. Have each pair write a short script based on this scene from the story. Encourage them to improvise any actions that would illustrate the feelings of these characters. Students may want to consider using accents and postures they imagine the characters having.

ASSESS

Answers for p. 512

Review and Assess

1. Possible responses: Students who identify with Maibon's fear of growing old may understand and agree with Maibon's desire to keep it. Others may realize the benefits of change and would not wish to remain the same age forever.
2. **(a)** Maibon gets the stone because he frees a red-headed dwarf. **(b)** He chooses the stone because he does not want to grow older.
3. **(a)** Possessing the stone causes problems for Maibon and all that surrounds him. His hen's eggs do not hatch; his cow does not have her calf; and his baby's teeth do not come in. **(b)** Maibon says he will "shrivel from boredom" because everything around him will always be the same. **(c)** This remark shows that Maibon has come to value change and to see that there is a good side to aging.
4. **(a)** The stone comes back. **(b)** He cannot get rid of it because he does not really want to. **(c)** Maibon's new belief is that getting old is better than always staying the same.
5. **(a)** Maibon feels relieved when the stone is gone. **(b)** He realizes that it is natural to grow old and that he does not wish to give up that part of his life.

I've had my share of being young, I'll take my share of being old. And when I come to the end of my days, at least I can say I've lived each one of them."

"If you mean that," answered Doli, "toss the stone onto the ground, right there at the stump. Then get home and be about your business."

Maibon flung down the stone, spun around, and set off as fast as he could. When he dared at last to glance back over his shoulder, fearful the stone might be bouncing along at his heels, he saw no sign of it, nor of the redheaded dwarf.

Maibon gave a joyful cry, for at that same instant the fallow field was covered with green blades of wheat, the branches of the apple tree bent to the ground, so laden they were with fruit. He ran to the cottage, threw his arms around his wife and children, and told them the good news. The hen hatched her chicks, the cow bore her calf. And Maibon laughed with glee when he saw the first tooth in the baby's mouth.

fallow (fal′ ō) *adj.* inactive; unproductive

Never again did Maibon meet any of the Fair Folk, and he was just as glad of it. He and his wife and children and grandchildren lived many years, and Maibon was proud of his white hair and long beard as he had been of his sturdy arms and legs.

"Stones are all right, in their way," said Maibon. "But the trouble with them is, they don't grow."

Review and Assess

Thinking About the Selection

1. **Respond:** Would you have given up the stone? Explain.
2. (a) **Recall:** Describe how Maibon gets the stone.
   (b) **Infer:** Why does Maibon choose the stone over all the other gifts that Doli suggests?
3. (a) **Recall:** How does the stone cause problems for Maibon, his family, and his farm? (b) **Analyze:** Why does Maibon say he will "shrivel from boredom"? (c) **Compare and Contrast:** How does this remark suggest that Maibon's opinion of the stone is different from his initial opinion of it?
4. (a) **Recall:** What happens when Maibon tries to get rid of the stone? (b) **Interpret:** Why can't Maibon get rid of the stone? (c) **Analyze:** What new belief does Maibon have that finally allows him to get rid of the stone?
5. (a) **Infer:** How does Maibon feel when the stone is gone?
   (b) **Draw Conclusions:** How has the stone changed Maibon's feelings about growing old?

Lloyd Alexander

(b. 1924)

Lloyd Alexander has written stories and novels about an imaginary kingdom called Prydain.

Alexander found in creating this kingdom that "a writer could know and love a fantasy world as much as his real one."

Perhaps the best-known Prydain novel is *The High King* (1968), winner of a Newbery medal. "The Stone" also takes place in Prydain, where fantastic happenings are a part of everyday life.

ASSESSMENT PRACTICE: Reading Comprehension

Describing Mood (For more practice, see Test Preparation Workbook, p. 43.)

Many tests have students describe the mood in a passage. Write the following text on the board:

> [Father] took out a pocket French dictionary. . . . He even had a pocket flashlight, the size of a marking pen. While Mother held the flashlight over the menu, he looked up the items that were in French. . . . The waiter stood looking patient. I squirmed and died at least fifty times.

Which adjective best describes the mood?

A angry **C** confident
B joyous **D** tense

The pocket dictionary shows that the family is uncertain about what to eat. The narrator's squirming indicates embarrassment. These details add to a mood of tension. The correct answer is *D*.

Review and Assess

Literary Analysis

Theme

1. Provide three specific actions in "The All-American Slurp" that reveal the story's **theme.** Use a graphic organizer like the one here to organize your thoughts.

Theme:
Different cultures have different customs, but all people have similar feelings and needs.

Action:	Action:	Action:

2. What is the theme of "The Stone"?

Comparing Literary Works

3. Make a chart like the one here to show how the main characters of both stories change.

"The All-American Slurp"	"The Stone"
At the beginning, the narrator • • By the end, the narrator • •	At the beginning, Maibon • • By the end, Maibon • •

4. What does each story say about change?
5. (a) What themes do these stories share? (b) What themes are unique to each story?

Reading Strategy

Drawing Inferences

6. In "The All-American Slurp," what is one thing you can infer about the narrator from her way of getting jeans?
7. Based on Maibon's wish, what can you infer about how he feels about aging?

Extend Understanding

8. **Cultural Connection:** What agencies or services are available in your area to help recent immigrants?

Quick Review

A **theme** is the central message of a literary work and often is an insight about life. To review theme, see page 495.

A **stated theme** is expressed directly.

An **implied theme** is suggested, or stated indirectly.

Drawing inferences means reaching conclusions about something based on evidence and your own thoughts.

Take It to the Net

www.phschool.com

Take the interactive self-test online to check your understanding of these selections.

ENRICHMENT: Further Reading

Other Works by the Authors

Works by Lensey Namioka

Den of the White Fox

April and the Dragon Lady

Yang the Second and Her Secret Admirers

Works by Lloyd Alexander

The Arkadians

The Cat Who Wished to Be a Man

The Book of Three

Take It to the Net

Visit www.phschool.com for more information on the authors.

Answers for p. 513

Review and Assess

1. Action 1: The Lins are embarrassed when they move their chairs to the table. Action 2: The narrator is embarrassed when her family slurps soup. Action 3: The Gleasons do not know how to eat Chinese food.
2. The theme of "The Stone" is that it is important to let life take its natural course.
3.

"The All-American Slurp"	"The Stone"
beginning: • does not know American customs • worries about mistakes **end:** • has learned American customs • understands that people make mistakes	**beginning:** • is afraid of getting old • wants a gift from the dwarf **end:** • is not afraid of getting old • is happy he has not seen any Fairy Folk

4. Each story says that change is a necessary part of life that we must accept.
5. **(a)** Both stories address the theme of self-acceptance. In both stories, the narrators' dissatisfaction with themselves is replaced with acceptance. **(b)** In "The All-American Slurp," the narrator learns to accept the mistakes that one makes while learning a new culture, while in "The Stone," Maibon learns that change is better than eternal youth.
6. Students can infer that she is resourceful and logical and understands her mother.
7. Maibon fears aging.
8. Possible response: Government and church agencies help recent immigrants.

EXTEND

Answers for p. 514

❶ Vocabulary Development

Word Analysis

1. *Emigrated* means "left one's country to live elsewhere."
2. *Immigrated* means "moved to a country."
3. *Immigrants* are people who come to a country to live.

Spelling Strategy

The words are *raquet* and *physique*.

Concept Development

1. **F.** People *emigrate* from a country.
2. **T.** The rules of *etiquette* are rules of conduct.
3. **T.** *Consumption* is the amount of food you eat.
4. **F.** A *plight* is a difficult situation.
5. **T.** *Jubilation* means great joy.
6. **F.** *Rue* means regret.
7. **F.** A *fallow* field has not been cultivated.

❷ Grammar

1. The old man refused, so Maibon left. *compound*
2. Maibon saw that wheat grew. *complex*
3. We had a hard time with manners when we arrived in the U.S. *complex*
4. The table was covered, but we couldn't see chairs around it. *compound*
5. In China we never ate celery; we never ate any kinds of raw vegetables. *compound*

Writing Application

Students should demonstrate mastery of compound and complex sentences.

Integrate Language Skills

❶ Vocabulary Development Lesson

Word Analysis: Forms of *migrate*

Some forms of the word *migrate*, "to travel from one place to another," have to do with settling in a new land. For example, *emigrated* means "left one country to settle in another." Explain the meaning of each italicized word.

1. The Lins *emigrated* from China.
2. They *immigrated* to their new home, the United States.
3. Here, they were known as *immigrants*.

Spelling Strategy

In some words, the *k* sound is spelled *qu*, as in *plaque* and *etiquette*. On your paper, select the words that reflect this rule.

1. cost 2. racquet 3. ache 4. kin 5. physique

Concept Development: True or False

On your paper, answer each question **true** or **false.** Then, explain your answer.

1. People settle in the country from which they *emigrated*.
2. Different countries have different rules of *etiquette*.
3. Your food *consumption* affects your weight.
4. A *plight* is something you would enjoy.
5. Winning a prize inspires people with *jubilation*.
6. People *rue* great achievements.
7. A *fallow* field is ready to be harvested.

❷ Grammar Lesson

Compound and Complex Sentences

A **compound sentence** is made of two or more independent clauses. The clauses are joined by a semicolon or by a comma and a coordinating conjunction, such as *and, but, for, or, yet,* or *so*.

> **Example:** [Mother picked up one of the green stalks] (Ind. Clause), and [Father followed suit] (Ind. Clause).

A **complex sentence** consists of one independent clause and one or more subordinate clauses.

> **Example:** [That is the first dinner party] (Ind. Clause) [that she attends in the story] (Sub. Clause).

▶ *For more practice, see page R29, Exercise F.*

Practice Write the following sentences. Underline independent clauses once and subordinate clauses twice. Label each sentence *compound* or *complex*.

1. The old man refused, so Maibon left.
2. Maibon saw that wheat grew.
3. We had a hard time with manners when we arrived in the U.S.
4. The table was covered, but we couldn't see chairs around it.
5. In China, we never ate celery; we never ate any kinds of raw vegetables.

Writing Application Write two compound and two complex sentences about American eating habits.

WG Prentice Hall Writing and Grammar Connection: Chapter 20, Section 2

TEACHING RESOURCES

The following resources can be used to enrich or extend the instruction for pp. 514–515.

Vocabulary

- **Selection Support:** Build Vocabulary, p. 146; Build Spelling Skills, p. 147
- **Vocabulary and Spelling Practice Book** (Use this booklet for skills enrichment)

Grammar

- **Selection Support:** Build Grammar Skills, p. 148
- **Writing and Grammar,** Copper Level, pp. 427–428

- **Daily Language Practice Transparencies** ■

Writing

- **Writing and Grammar,** Copper Level, p. 78 ■
- **Writing and Grammar iText CD-ROM**

■ **BLOCK SCHEDULING:** Resources marked with this symbol provide varied instruction during 90-minute blocks.

❸ Writing Lesson

Story Plot

One theme or message can be communicated by a variety of events. Write a plot proposal—a plan of story events—that illustrates the theme of one of these selections.

Prewriting Write a statement of the theme. Then, identify the problem and the resolution that will show the message.

Model: Identify the Problem and the Resolution

Main Character	What Main Character Wants	Who or What Gets in the Way
Twyla	Wants to fit in at a new school	She has trouble meeting other students who share her interests.

Drafting Tell the basic events and explain what the character learns.

Revising If necessary, add a sentence or two that explains how events illustrate the theme.

WG *Prentice Hall Writing and Grammar Connection: Chapter 5, Section 2*

❹ Extension Activities

Listening and Speaking Present an **oral response** to the theme of one of the stories.

1. Clearly state the story's theme.
2. Explain how you came to this conclusion.
3. Support your interpretation of the theme with details from the text.
4. Use examples from other literature and from your own experience to explain whether you agree or disagree with the message of the story.

Rehearse your presentation after you have prepared it. Make sure to organize your ideas logically and speak in a slow, clear manner.

Research and Technology "The Stone" concerns human aging. With a group, use technology resources to prepare a written and visual **report** on human growth. Prepare charts and diagrams that share exciting facts about these and other topics:

- how many cells are in a human body
- how often in a lifetime cells change
- what happens to skin as we age

When you finish, present your findings to your class. **[Group Activity]**

 ***Take It to the Net*** www.phschool.com

Go online for an additional research activity using the Internet.

ASSESSMENT RESOURCES

The following resources can be used to assess students' knowledge and skills.

Selection Assessment

- **Formal Assessment,** pp. 128–130
- **Open Book Test,** pp. 88–90
- **Got It! Assessment Videotapes,** Tape 3
- **Test Bank Software**

 ***Take It to the Net***

Visit www.phschool.com for self-tests and additional questions on the selections.

Writing Rubric

- **Performance Assess. and Portfolio Mgmt.,** p. 13

Listening and Speaking Rubric

- **Performance Assess. and Portfolio Mgmt.,** p. 29

PRENTICE HALL ASSESSMENT SYSTEM

- **Workbook**
- **Skill Book**
- **Transparencies**
- **CD-ROM**

Lesson Support for p. 515

❸ Writing Lesson

- Explain to students that a plot outline gives the basic framework of the story. It supports a story the same way that a skeleton supports a body.
- Model a plot outline for students by using the chart on this page.
- Use the writing lesson to guide students in developing the plot outline.
- Have students exchange papers to evaluate one another's outlines.
- Use the Narration rubric on p. 13 in **Performance Assessment and Portfolio Management** to evaluate students' plot outlines.

❹ Listening and Speaking

- After students read the instruction, make sure they use relevant details from the story to support their interpretations.
- Then, tell students that an effective presentation involves preparation and rehearsal.
- Finally, make sure students understand that their own life experiences will influence whether or not they agree with the message of the story.
- Have each student give his or her presentation in front of the class. Refer to the Speaking rubric on p. 29 in **Performance Assessment and Portfolio Management.**

CUSTOMIZE INSTRUCTION For Universal Access

To address different learning styles, use the activities suggested in the **Extension Activities** booklet, p. 30.

- For Body/Kinesthetic and Musical/Rhythmic Learners, use Activity 5.
- For Intrapersonal and Verbal/Linguistic Learners, use Activity 6.
- For Visual/Spatial Learners, use Activity 7.

Lesson Objectives

1. To understand how to read to take action
2. To learn the structure of book reviews
3. To learn how to evaluate book reviews

About Book Reviews

- Have students read "About Book Reviews." Then, ask the class when it might be helpful to consult a book review.
  Possible responses: Students may want to consult a nonfiction book review to see whether a book will be useful for research assignments or to find information about personal interests.
- Point out that a review includes a summary of the book. Ask: Is this always a useful addition to a review?
  Answer: Students may note that if a summary goes into great detail about a work of fiction, it might give away too much of the plot.
- Ask: What is the value of finding a review with an excerpt?
  Possible responses: By giving an example of the author's style, an excerpt reveals what the book might be like. Having an idea of what to expect helps readers determine whether they will enjoy the book.

Reading Strategy

Reading to Take Action

- Have students read the information about reading to take action.
- Ask students how reading could help them on a project.
  Answer: Reading with a purpose may help someone decide what course of action to take. Once a reader has found necessary information on a topic, he or she is better prepared to decide how to act.
- Ask: How could relevant questions and a graphic organizer help readers take action?
  Answer: Relevant questions will help a reader know what to look for in a review. A graphic organizer helps record information so that important questions and corresponding answers can be seen at a glance.

READING INFORMATIONAL MATERIALS

Book Reviews

About Book Reviews

If you want to learn more about a book before you decide whether to read it, you can find useful information in a *book review*. A book review is an article which gives you a brief summary of a book, tells you about its author, and sometimes presents a short excerpt. Reading the excerpt gives you a chance to see if you would enjoy the style and content of the book. If you like the excerpt and want to read more, you can locate the book in a bookstore or library.

Most book reviews include

- an opening paragraph introducing the book, including title and author.
- a brief summary of the book.
- a description of the background of the author or authors.
- an opinion about the quality of the book.
- an excerpt from the book.

Reading Strategy

Reading to Take Action

When you read to take action, you focus on finding specific information in order to help you do something. This is especially important if the activity is unfamiliar to you. To help guide your reading, begin by asking one or two questions. Then, look for answers as you read. For example, if you were planning a snorkeling trip, you might ask, "How can I protect the wildlife I encounter?" As you read to take action, take notes on the information that answers your question. Then organize the information in a graphic organizer like the one shown.

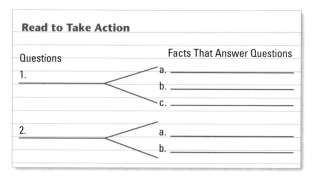

Read to Take Action

Questions	Facts That Answer Questions
1.	a.
	b.
	c.
2.	a.
	b.

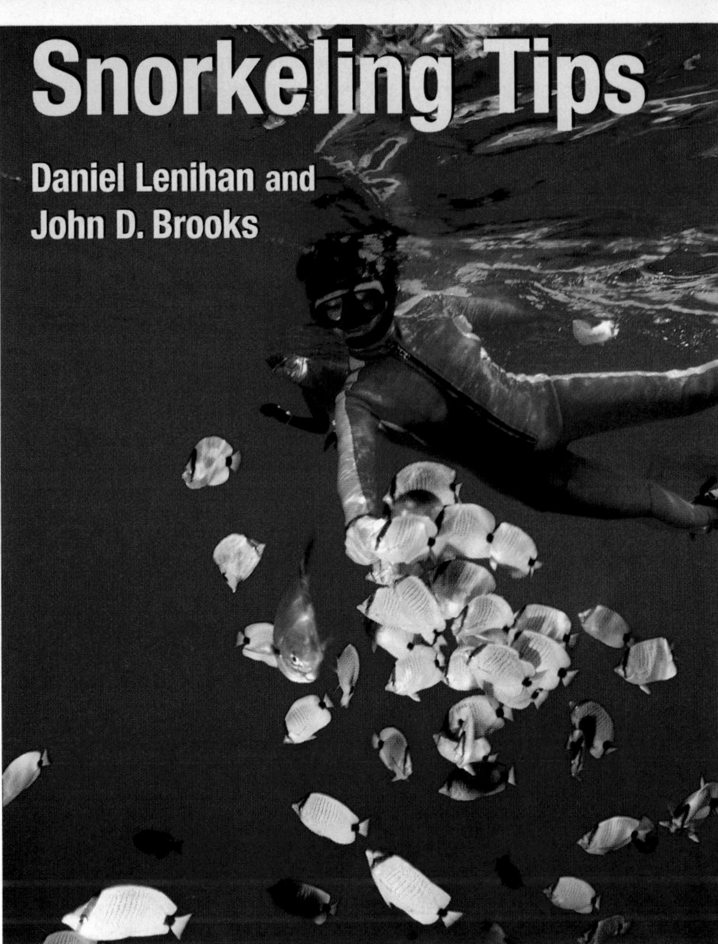

This picture makes snorkeling look like an interesting thing to do.

Underwater Wonders of the National Parks, published last year, is an indispensable resource for anyone considering a snorkeling trip. Written by Daniel Lenihan, director of the NPS Submerged Cultural Resource Unit, and John D. Brooks, an underwater photographer with the unit, the book details the watery wonders of the park system, from the coral reefs of the Caribbean to the icebergs in Alaska.

This paragraph provides the title and authors of the book. It also includes a brief summary.

The two have gone snorkeling and scuba diving at every park mentioned in the book and include detailed suggestions on where to go, how to get there, and what you might find. They also have some sound advice for making your snorkeling excursion more enjoyable and helping to protect the fragile reef environment, including these tips:

This paragraph discusses the authors' backgrounds.

Snorkeling Tips

- Point out to students that they might find a review like this one in a magazine. Ask: What might be a good way to find more reviews like this one?
  Possible responses: Students might search an index of periodicals, use an online search engine, or ask a reference librarian for assistance to find topics of interest.
- After students read the first paragraph of the review, call their attention to the callout box. Ask: Why would this information be included in the opening paragraph?
  Answer: This information is included to show who the authors are and what the book is about. This information could help readers decide whether they would like to read the rest of the review.
- Have a student volunteer read the second paragraph of the review and the second callout box. Ask: What is the function of the second paragraph?
  Answer: The second paragraph introduces a list of tips from the book and gives additional information about the authors' experience with snorkeling.

CUSTOMIZE INSTRUCTION FOR UNIVERSAL ACCESS

For Less Proficient Students	For Advanced Readers
Help students recognize the components of a book review. Have them reread the bulleted list of features in the "About Book Reviews" on p. 516. Then, have students locate each of the items on the list in "Snorkeling Tips." Point out that most reviews will contain the features listed but that they will not necessarily appear in the same order.	Students may benefit from evaluating a reviewer's bias. Point out that some book reviewers never mention the quality of the book. For example, a review in a bookstore newsletter may be written favorably just to sell the book. This type of review may be biased. Have students find examples of book reviews, including those that appear in books, magazines, professional publications, and publishers' Web sites. Then, have students evaluate each source for possible bias.

- Have a student volunteer read aloud the first four bulleted items. Point out that these items explain how to protect the wildlife when snorkeling. Ask: Why it is important to protect underwater wildlife?
  Possible responses: We should protect the wildlife because some underwater plants and animals are endangered and will become extinct without the conservation efforts of concerned individuals. Also, if one animal is endangered or becomes extinct, the rest of the wildlife in the reef will suffer because the plants and animals need each other to survive.
- Have a volunteer read aloud the rest of the list. Ask: What is the purpose of the second part of the list?
  Answer: In this part of the list, the reader learns some safety tips to use while snorkeling.
- Discuss the organization of the list. Ask students why it might help to have the two different types of information in two different parts of the list.
  Possible response: The information is divided in a logical way, so it is easy for the reader to understand. In addition, this type of organization helps readers who need to use the text as a quick reference guide.

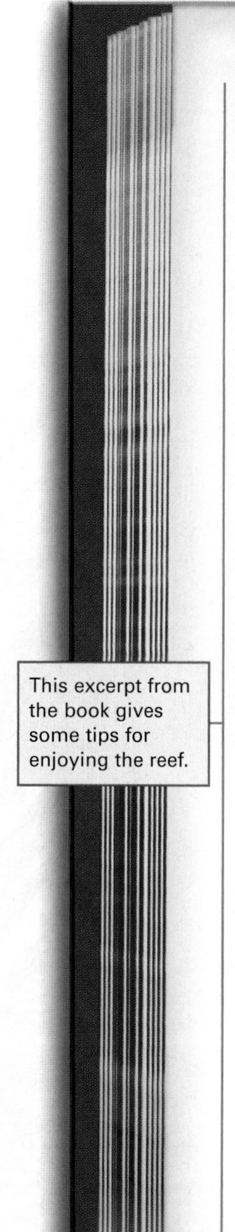

- Do not touch the animals. Even a gentle caress can disturb the mucous coating that helps protect fish from disease.
- Do not feed the fish. If fed by humans, after a while they become dependent on handouts and lose the ability to forage. Also, they lose their natural wariness, which makes them easy prey for poachers. Even though harvesting fish for tropical collectors is illegal in the national parks, it still goes on.
- Do not touch the coral. The tiny jelly-like polyps that live inside the hard calcium casing are fragile. One swipe of the hand can kill hundreds of them. Many popular shallow reefs have been decimated by careless swimmers who stand on them when they get tired.
- Swim gently and avoid kicking up a lot of sand when near a reef. The sediment can eventually smother the coral and block vital sunlight.
- Wear a liberal coating of waterproof sunscreen on your back and the backs of your legs. The thin film of water over you acts as a magnifier, and because the water keeps your skin cool, you may not realize your skin is burning until it is too late. People who are especially sun-sensitive should wear a covering.
- Keep an eye out for stinging organisms like jellyfish and fire coral.
- Do not reach into holes or crevices in the reef. They could turn out to be the lair of a moray eel.
- Take off your jewelry. While barracuda attacks are almost unheard of, the toothy fish are attracted to shiny objects.
- Shark spottings are rare on the shallow reefs that snorkelers frequent, but if you see a shark, do not panic. Most reef sharks are passive types, not man-eaters, and they usually ignore swimmers. If one acts aggressively or pays undue attention to you, calmly and slowly leave the water.
- Do not walk in shallow water near the reef; sea urchin spines can cause nasty puncture wounds to the bottom of your feet.
- Shuffle your feet across the bottom as you wade through the shallow sandy areas on your way to and from the reef. Stingrays lying on the bottom will swim off if you bump into them, but sometimes sting when they are stepped on.
- Be aware of currents. Unless you plan to do a "drift dive" where you start in one spot and let the current carry you to an exit point, it's usually best to swim into the current first and then let it carry you back at the end of your dive when you are most tired.

This excerpt from the book gives some tips for enjoying the reef.

CUSTOMIZE INSTRUCTION FOR UNIVERSAL ACCESS

For Gifted/Talented Students

Note that some items on the list on p. 518 do not fully explain the danger involved. As an example, read aloud the seventh bulleted item. Invite students to identify incomplete warnings and then do further research to find out the full story behind the warning. For example, students researching the moray eel warning would need to find out more information about moray eels and why they should be avoided. Students could use library resources or search online to find the necessary information. They may also want to illustrate their research. Have students present their findings to the class in poster form or as oral reports.

Check Your Comprehension

1. Why are the authors of this book well qualified to write about snorkeling?
2. Who might find this book useful?
3. What type of information could a reader find in this book?
4. Why do the authors advise snorkelers not to touch the coral?
5. Why should you shuffle your feet when you are walking in shallow water?

Applying the Reading Strategy

Reading to Take Action

6. How can you protect the wildlife you encounter when snorkeling?
7. What can you do to protect your skin?
8. What measures can you take to avoid a dangerous encounter with a jellyfish, moray eel, or barracuda?
9. Why should you avoid walking in shallow water near the reef without anything protecting your feet?
10. What steps can you take to avoid being carried off by ocean currents?

Activity

Write a Book Review

Select a book you have read and enjoyed. Write a book review to persuade others to read the book. Introduce the book and identify the intended audience. Include an excerpt that is interesting.

To learn more about writing about literature, see the Writing Workshop: Response to Literature on page 694.

Comparing Informational Texts

Positive and Negative Book Reviews

Look in newspapers, magazines, or online to find two book reviews by different people on the same book. The book reviews should express different opinions of the book. Read the reviews and fill out a chart like the one shown. Then, answer the questions.

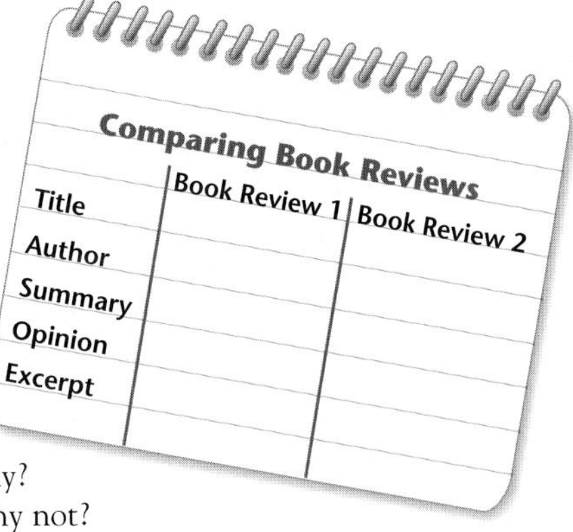

Comparing Book Reviews

	Book Review 1	Book Review 2
Title		
Author		
Summary		
Opinion		
Excerpt		

1. (a) Which book review is more complete? (b) What information is missing from the less complete review?
2. (a) Which book review is more effective? Why? (b) Do you want to read the book? Why or why not?

Answers continued

a summary of the book, an excerpt from the book, and an opinion of the book. Each student may also wish to include a brief statement explaining why he or she chose to review the book.

Comparing Informational Materials

Students should find two different opinions of the book. Enlist the aid of your school librarian or media assistant to help students find reviews. You may want to have students turn in copies of the book reviews with their answers to the questions and their completed charts. If students have difficulty finding two opposite reviews, have them examine two reviews of the same book to see whether the reviewers comment on the same features of the book and what they say about each feature. Students' answers should explain which review seems more complete, what might be missing, and which review seems more effective.

Answers for p. 519

Check Your Comprehension

1. The authors are qualified to write about snorkeling because they have gone snorkeling and scuba diving at the parks mentioned in the book. Also, one author is director of an underwater unit of the National Parks Service, and the other is an underwater photographer.
2. People who are interested in snorkeling would find this book useful.
3. Readers could find out which parks permit scuba diving, how to reach them, and what to expect when they arrive. They could also find information about protecting the underwater environment and how to snorkel safely.
4. The authors warn against touching coral because this damages the coral's habitat and kills the tiny polyps that live inside the hard calcium.
5. You should shuffle your feet when walking in shallow water to scare off stingrays.

Applying the Reading Strategy

6. You can protect wildlife by not touching anything, by not feeding animals you may encounter, and by swimming slowly and carefully.
7. You can protect your skin by wearing waterproof sunscreen.
8. You can protect yourself by watching where you go, by not reaching into holes, and by taking off your jewelry.
9. You should avoid walking in shallow water near the reef without foot protection because stepping on sea urchin spines can cause severe puncture wounds.
10. You should swim into the current first, and then swim with the current at the end. Otherwise, an ocean current can carry off a fatigued diver.

Activity

Students should include all the requested information in their reviews. This includes the title, the author and his or her background, the intended audience for the book,

continued

Lesson Objectives

1. To write a short story
2. To use writing strategies to generate ideas, plan, organize, evaluate, and revise the short story

Model From Literature

This unit contains many short stories; you may want to feature a class favorite as an example as you work through the writing process in this workshop.

Prewriting

- Identify and discuss the topics of students' favorite stories from this unit. For example, "Eleven" is about a girl's birthday.
- As students begin their freewriting, encourage them to write a topic that interests them at the top of their paper. This will help them focus on the topic. Point out to students that if they do not have a topic they like at the end of the first freewriting session, they can repeat the technique.
- Point out that a topic is not enough to carry a story. Plot is also important. The plot is what happens. For example, the plot in "Eleven" arises from the narrator's feelings that she did not respond in the right way to a teacher's question.
- Have students share their conflict maps with a partner and comment upon each other's work.
- Point out to students that they must make certain that their topic and plot are consistent with their purpose for writing the story. For example, they would not want to write a humorous story about a person getting hurt.
- Before students draft their essays, have them review the Rubric for Self-Assessment (p. 523) so that they know what is expected.

Writing WORKSHOP

Narration: Short Story

A **short story** is a brief, fictional account of an event or series of events with a beginning, middle, and end. In this workshop, you will write a short story.

Assignment Criteria. Your short story should have the following characteristics:

- One or more well-drawn **characters**
- An interesting **conflict** or problem
- A **plot**, or series of events that move toward the resolution of the conflict
- A consistent **point of view**, or perspective
- Sensory details and concrete language that establish the **setting**, the time and place
- **Dialogue**; conversations between characters

See the Rubric on page 523 for criteria on which your short story may be assessed.

Prewriting

Choose a topic. Set a timer and freewrite for five minutes. Start with an image—a bus, a snowshoe, a bank robber—or an idea—*jealousy* or *a lie*. During freewriting, focus more on the flow of ideas than on spelling, grammar, or punctuation. After five minutes, go back and circle ideas to use in your story.

Identify conflict. Establish **conflict**—a struggle between opposing forces. To identify the conflict, ask yourself these questions.

- What does your main character want?
- Who or what is getting in the way?
- What will the main character do to overcome the person or thing getting in the way?

Consider your purpose. Some short story writers want to make readers laugh. Others want to give their readers goosebumps. Still others want to deliver an important message about life. Decide your purpose for writing a short story.

TEACHING RESOURCES

The following resources can be used to enrich or extend the instruction for pp. 520–523.

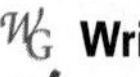 **Writing and Grammar,** Copper Level, pp. 72–94

Performance Assess. and Portfolio Mgmt., pp. 13, 46

 **Writing Models and Graphic Organizers on Transparencies,** p. 23

 **Writing and Grammar iText CD-ROM**
Students can use the following tools as they complete their short stories.

- Story Map
- Story Wheels
- Sensory Word Bin

Student Model

Before you begin drafting your short story, read this portion of the student model and review the characteristics of a successful short story. To read the full short story, visit www.phschool.com.

Jocelyn Meyer
St. Leon, IN

Pharaoh's Peak

Terri looked around as she knocked on the door of her best friend Sara's house. Sara's mom opened the door.

> Jocelyn introduces her main characters in the first sentence.

"Well, hello, Terri," Mrs. Duncan said.

"Hello, Mrs. Duncan. Is Sara ready yet?" Terri asked.

"She will be down in a minute. So where are you two going riding today?" Mrs. Duncan asked.

"Maybe up to Pharaoh's Peak."

"Oh, well, be careful. Make sure you both wear your riding helmets."

* * *

It was a beautiful summer day. The sun was hot on the dusty trail, but the temperature cooled off suddenly as the girls turned the horses onto the trail that entered the cool darkness of the pine woods. The girls were about to the top of the hill when both horses stopped. As Terri tried to nudge Cajun along, Sara asked, "Terri, what's wrong?"

> Sensory details describe the setting.

"I don't know. Maybe they heard some . . ." Before she could finish, there was a movement in the bushes and a mountain lion stepped out.

> The writer introduces a problem.

"Terri," Sara said in a whisper, "what should we do?"

"I don't know," Terri replied. "Just don't move and scare the horses more."

But it was too late. . . . She hit the ground with a thud as O.T. galloped off down the trail.

> The plot moves forward toward the climax.

"Sara, Sara! Are you all right?" Terri cried.

There was no reply. Through tears, Terri turned Cajun and charged the mountain lion. The suddenness of this attack sent the mountain lion running into the bushes. Terri looked around. Sara was still breathing, but she was not moving. . . .

> The writer includes an exciting climax.

* * *

Three days later, Terri walked into a hospital room. . . .

"Sara, are you awake?" she whispered into the darkness.

"Terri, is that you?" said a faint voice. . . .

CUSTOMIZE INSTRUCTION FOR UNIVERSAL ACCESS

For Less Proficient Writers	For English Learners	For Advanced Writers
Remind students that a conflict occurs between two opposing forces. Encourage students to write about an external conflict rather than an internal one because this will make it easier to identify and describe the two opposing forces.	Help students make a question-and-answer chart to outline the conflict in their stories. Students should write the following questions: Who is the main character? What does this character want? Why can't this character get what he or she wants? How will the conflict be resolved? Have students answer these questions specifically.	Give students several copies of the Series of Events Chain on p. 69 in **Writing Models and Graphic Organizers on Transparencies.** Have them jot down different plots and choose their favorites for further work. Students should be able to identify the theme of their stories at this stage.

Student Model

- Explain that the student model is an excerpt and that stories may be longer.
- After students have read the Student Model, ask them how dialogue helps advance the plot of a story.
  Answer: Dialogue tells what people are thinking and helps to show action. In this story, it predicts trouble when Mrs. Duncan says to be careful.
- Ask students to identify the topic and the conflict of the story.
  Answer: The topic is a horseback ride on a mountain. The conflict is that one of the girls is injured after an encounter with a mountain lion.
- Discuss how Jocelyn creates suspense by having Terri's dialogue trail off in the first paragraph beginning "I don't know."
  Answer: When the dialogue trails off, it alerts the reader that something unusual has happened.
- Point out that Terri is not telling the story, but we know what she is thinking and feeling. This is called limited third-person point of view. This point of view is described as "third-person" because someone outside the story (a third party) is narrating the events, and it is "limited" because the narrator can report the thoughts and feelings of only one character.

Real-World Connection

Short-story writing in the real world: Let students know that there will be many times when they can use short-story writing skills. Magazines and newspapers often have story writing contests, and many high schools and colleges have literary magazines that print student works. In addition, the skills used to write stories can be transferred easily to writing for the stage, television, and movies. News reporters use narration to tell stories that are true.

Drafting

- Before students begin drafting their stories, use the plot diagram on p. 522 to help them visualize how a plot rises, reaches a climax, and falls.
- Have students make their own copies of the plot diagram and put the events in their stories in order on the diagram. Tell students to follow their diagrams as they draft their stories.
- Point out that suspense is essential to keep readers interested in the rising action of a plot. For example, in "The Wounded Wolf," the writer created suspense by describing the wolf's injury and the animals surrounding the wolf. Readers want to finish the story because they want to know what will happen to the wolf.
- Remind students that the setting plays a vital part in a short story. Ask students why setting is important in "The Lawyer and the Ghost."
  Answer: The setting is important because the description of the damp, gloomy room sets up an appropriate environment for a ghost to appear.
- Discuss point of view with students. Point out that in a third-person narrative, all characters are referred to in the third person. A limited point of view reports on one person's thoughts and feelings. First-person point of view, which was used in "Becky and the Wheels-and-Brake Boys," is useful for understanding the story from the narrator's perspective. Tell students to consider the pros and cons of each point of view and then choose a point of view for their stories.

Revising

- After students are satisfied with the development of their stories, suggest that they highlight places where dialogue would move the plot along better than narration does. Have students revise the stories to add the dialogue.

continued on p. 523

Drafting

Develop a plot. Organize the plot—the arrangement of events in sequence in a short story. Plot often follows this pattern:

- **Exposition** introduces characters and their situation, including the central conflict.
- The **conflict** develops during the **rising action,** which leads to the climax of the story
- The **climax,** or point of greatest tension, is when the story turns out one way or another.
- In the **falling action,** events and emotions wind down.
- In the **resolution,** the conflict is resolved and loose ends are tied up.

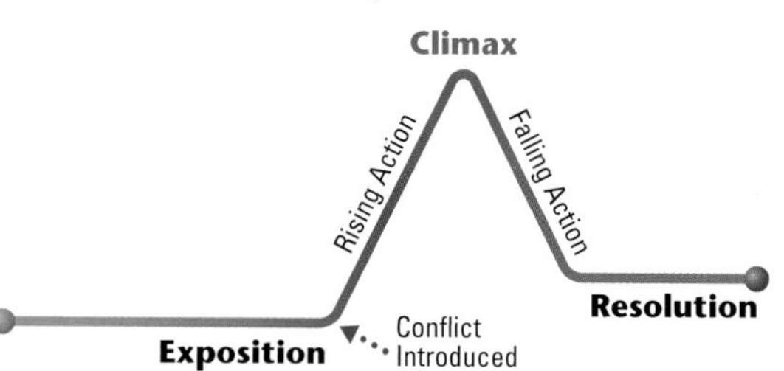

Build suspense. Writers build suspense by creating uncertainty about future events and developing tension about how a problem will be resolved. On your plot diagram, make notes about how you can raise questions that build suspense into the story's rising action.

Establish setting with sensory details. Use each of the five senses (taste, touch, smell, sight, and hearing) to describe details of the setting. For example, instead of just saying "It's a cold day," use sensory images to show your reader how cold it is.

Write from a specific point of view. Tell your story from a single point of view, either as a participant or an observer.

First-person point of view: participant

Example: I stood by the door, wondering how long I should wait.

Third-person point of view: observer

Example: Matt stood by the door checking his watch and looking uncertain.

Revising

Revise to add dialogue. You can bring your story to life by using dialogue. Review your draft for places to add characters speaking to each other.

We were near the top of the hill when both horses
"What do you think they see?" I asked. "Who knows. . ." said Sarah.
stopped. ^ Then we saw a movement in the trees.

USING TECHNOLOGY IN WRITING

If students are using word processors, they might want to use the "search" or "find" feature to find repeated words in their stories. For example, students may discover from doing a search for the word *said* that they use this word almost every time dialogue is introduced. Students should consider using other words, such as *replied, yelled,* or *whispered,* to give readers a better sense of the tone or mood in which something is said. Students also can use the editing tools and revision checkers on the **Writing and Grammar iText CD-ROM.**

Revise to strengthen setting. You can make your story more realistic by adding sensory details to the description of the setting.

Compare the model and nonmodel. Why is the model more interesting than the nonmodel?

Nonmodel	Model
It was a beautiful summer day. The girls rode up the trail then took the turnoff into the woods. They were about to the top of the hill when both horses stopped.	It was a beautiful summer day. The sun was hot on the dusty trail, but the temperature cooled off suddenly as the girls turned the horses onto the trail that entered the cool darkness of the pine woods. The girls were about to the top of the hill when both horses stopped.

Publishing and Presenting

Choose one of these ways to share your writing with classmates or a larger audience.

Storytelling. Perform your story as a live reading. Use gestures and tone of voice to give it pizzazz. If possible, tape record or videotape your storytelling.

Submit your story to a magazine. Send your story to a school or local literary magazine that publishes student writing.

 *Prentice Hall Writing and Grammar Connection: Chapter 5*

Speaking Connection
For instruction about narrative presentations, see the **Listening and Speaking Workshop,** p. 94.

Rubric for Self-Assessment

Evaluate your short story using the following criteria and rating scale:

Criteria	Rating Scale: Not very				Very
How well drawn are the characters?	1	2	3	4	5
Is the conflict interesting?	1	2	3	4	5
How well does the plot move toward resolving the conflict?	1	2	3	4	5
How consistent is the point of view?	1	2	3	4	5
How effectively are sensory details used to describe setting?	1	2	3	4	5
How often is dialogue used?	1	2	3	4	5

Revising (continued)

- Use the nonmodel and model on p. 523 to contrast a weak setting and a strong one. Ask students to describe the major difference between the two settings.
  Answer: The model contains more vivid details that help readers feel the heat of the sun and the coolness of the forest.

Publishing and Presenting

- Have students consider who might be interested in hearing oral presentations of their stories. Libraries, park districts, and other organizations often have storytelling gatherings. Encourage students to seek out venues for performing their stories.
- Find out from your principal, school board, or local newspaper whether any local publications solicit student fiction. Encourage students to consider submitting their stories to these publications.
- Out-of-town friends and family members also may enjoy reading your students' fiction.

Assessment

- Review the assessment criteria with students in class.
- Before students assess their own work, have them score the Student Model in class using one or more of the rubric categories. This will help them see how to apply the criteria. For example, have students score the Model in terms of how often dialogue is used. What score would they give it, and why?
- The rubric on this page, and another rubric in an alternative format, can be found on pp. 13 and 46 of **Performance Assessment and Portfolio Management.**

TEST-TAKING TIP

When taking a test that includes a narrative writing prompt, students should be careful to use realistic dialogue. In order to make characters sound like real people, writers use elements such as contractions, colloquialisms, and interrupted speech. Have students practice using these techniques in timed writing assignments in order to gain the expertise necessary in testing situations.

Lesson Objectives

1. To identify tone, mood, and emotion in presentations
2. To analyze verbal clues in order to determine the speaker's attitude toward a subject
3. To understand the effect of nonverbal clues on the presentation of a message
4. To describe verbal and nonverbal clues used in a presentation

Using Verbal Clues

- Explain that speakers use their voices in different ways to deliver their ideas and get people's attention.
- Speakers alter their tone depending on whether the content is lighthearted or serious. Ask students to brainstorm for examples of lighthearted and serious topics, and guide them to explain how the content would affect the presentation of each one.
- The audience is influenced by layers of meaning in the words used by the speaker; alert students to connotations, or hidden meanings. For example, a speaker arguing against censorship might refer to it as an "assault on people's freedom of speech." The word *assault*, which is associated with serious physical harm, indicates that the speaker feels strongly about the issue and wants audience members to defend themselves against censorship.

Using Nonverbal Clues

- Invite students to discuss speakers they have enjoyed hearing, or speakers who have a distinctive style.
- Give students an example of the effect of nonverbal communication by reading the instruction for Using Nonverbal Clues without using body language. Then, reread the instruction using gestures and facial expressions. Have students comment on how the second reading was more engaging.
- After students have completed the Activity, invite them to record observations in their charts.

Listening and Speaking WORKSHOP

Identifying Tone, Mood, and Emotion

Understanding oral communication involves more than just listening to the speaker's words. It means being able to identify the tone, mood, and emotion.

- **Tone:** the speaker's attitude toward the subject and the listeners
- **Mood:** the overall feeling of the presentation
- **Emotion:** the speaker's feelings

Using Verbal Clues

The way a person speaks is closely connected with the words he or she chooses. Verbal clues are the spoken indications of tone, mood, and emotion.

Listen to tone of voice. In an oral presentation, a speaker conveys his or her attitude through tone of voice as well as through words. A serious speaker might speak slowly and deliberately in a quiet voice. A speaker who is enthusiastically trying to persuade you might use a high-pitched voice and talk faster than in normal speech.

Consider content. The mood of a presentation is often a result of *what* is said in addition to *how* it is said. The feeling the audience gets from a presentation will be influenced by the subject.

Notice word choice. The specific words a speaker uses can indicate attitude and emotion. The intensity of a word is a clue to the speaker's emotion. The connotations, or associations, of a word can indicate attitude.

Using Nonverbal Clues

Motion. A speaker who moves with energy and purpose has a positive attitude toward his or her subject and listeners. Watch how a speaker stands, gestures, and leans to get a sense of the feelings they have and the feelings they want listeners to have.

Expression. Facial expressions are a clear clue to emotions. Smiles, frowns, and thoughtful looks are meant to communicate feelings. Watch expressions to connect the speaker's feelings with the words being spoken.

Activity: Speech Watching Watch a news interview program in which one or two people speak for at least five minutes. Keep a chart like the one shown here to record verbal and nonverbal clues to the speakers' tone, mood, and emotion.

	Verbal	Nonverbal
Tone		
Mood		
Emotion		

CUSTOMIZE INSTRUCTION FOR UNIVERSAL ACCESS

For Special Needs Students	For English Learners
Encourage students to experiment with tone as a way of understanding its impact on listeners. Use a simple sentence, such as "I have had enough" or "Do you want some more?" Have students work in pairs to practice saying the sentence with varying tones, such as an angry tone or a polite tone. As students coach each other, help them see that tone assists listeners with interpreting the speaker's meaning.	Obtain a videotape of Martin Luther King Jr.'s "I Have A Dream" speech or another speech by a famous American. Have students analyze the verbal and nonverbal clues that the speaker uses. What is effective? What is ineffective? If an audience is shown, what effect does the speaker have on listeners? Have students discuss the speech and its delivery in a group and report their findings to the class.

Assessment WORKSHOP

Describing Plot, Setting, Character, and Mood

The reading sections of some tests require you to read a passage and answer multiple-choice questions about such literary elements as plot, setting, character, and mood. Use the following strategies to help you answer such questions:

- When you are asked about plot, choose the answer that most accurately tells what happens.
- You may have to infer the time and place based on information in the story.
- You may have to draw inferences about character based on words and actions.
- You can identify the mood based on your feelings and descriptive details.

Test-Taking Strategies

- Read the questions first to focus your attention on the most important elements of the passage.
- Before answering, scan the passage (run your eyes quickly over the text to find specific details) to find the correct answer.

Sample Test Item

Use the strategies you have learned to answer the question on the passage.

With a deep sigh, Dulcie drifted toward the window. In the fading light, she could barely see the figure riding up the path. As soon as he sprang from his horse and strode to the front door, Dulcie knew it was Lance. Quickly, she thrust the letter she had been reading into her dress pocket. The door to the drawing room swung open.

"What have you done with our son?" Lance bellowed, his face distorted with rage.

"He is in a safe place," Dulcie replied, and with a sudden movement, she yanked at the bell cord to summon the servant.

1. Before Lance arrived, Dulcie had been—
   A waiting for him
   B saying good-bye to their son
   C reading a letter
   D staring out the window

Answer and Explanation

The text supports choice ***C***. The text does not say that Dulcie was doing **A**, **B**, or **D**.

Practice

Use the strategies you have learned to answer these questions on the passage.

1. Dulcie and Lance are in conflict over—
   A their home
   B their son
   C the servant
   D money
2. The story takes place in—
   A a foreign country
   B the United States
   C the past
   D the present
3. Lance can be described as—
   A angry
   B unhappy
   C supportive
   D distant
4. At the beginning of the passage, the mood is—
   A eerie
   B energetic
   C quiet
   D romantic

TEACHING RESOURCES

The following resources can be used to enrich or extend the instruction for p. 525.

PRENTICE HALL ASSESSMENT SYSTEM

Workbook **Transparencies**
Skill Book **CD-ROM**

Lesson Objective

To describe plot, setting, character, and mood in a test situation

Applying Reading Strategies

Point out that picturing the setting will help students identify details and make inferences.

Test-Taking Skills

- Have students read the sample test item. Encourage them to visualize the characters and setting as they read and to notice details that they can use to make inferences.
- If they have visualized the passage, students will remember that Dulcie was standing by the window and reading a letter. Ask students to point out a detail that helps them answer question 1.
  Answer: The writer states that Dulcie "thrust the letter she had been reading in her dress pocket."

Answers

1. *B* is correct. The son is specifically mentioned by Lance. Options *A* and *D* are not mentioned, and servants are mentioned only because Dulcie summons one.
2. *C* is correct. There is not enough evidence to support *A* or *B*. The facts that Lance arrived on a horse and Dulcie called servants using a bell rather than an electric buzzer should help students infer that more evidence supports *C* than *D*.
3. *A* is correct. Lance's outburst cannot be described as "supportive" or "distant," so *C* and *D* are incorrect. "Unhappy" is too mild for someone who bellows and has a "face distorted with rage," so *B* is incorrect.
4. *C* is correct. "Eerie" has a connotation of spooky or scary, which does not fit the beginning of the passage, so *A* is not correct. Similarly, "energetic," option *B*, is not supported by the text. Of the remaining choices, *C* is better because *romantic* implies a happy relationship, and there is no evidence of one.

Unit Objectives

1. To read selections in nonfiction genres
2. To apply a variety of reading strategies, particularly strategies for reading critically, appropriate for reading these selections
3. To analyze literary elements
4. To use a variety of strategies to build vocabulary
5. To learn elements of grammar, usage, and style
6. To use recursive writing processes to write in a variety of forms
7. To develop listening and speaking skills
8. To express and support responses to various types of texts
9. To prepare, organize, and present literary interpretations

Meeting the Objectives

With each selection, you will find instructional materials through which students can meet these objectives. Further, you will find additional practice pages for reading strategies, literary analysis, vocabulary, and grammar in the **Selection Support: Skills Development Workbook** in your **Teaching Resources.**

Background

Art

Desk Set by Wayne Thiebaud

Help students connect the painting to the theme "Exploring the Genre" by asking the following question:

Why is this painting a good choice to illustrate the genre of nonfiction? Answer: Students may note the realistic rendering of real-life objects, such as pencils and pens. The envelopes, pen, pencils, and blotter imply that someone is about to write a letter, which is one form of nonfiction.

UNIT 7 Nonfiction

Desk Set, 1972, Wayne Thiebaud, Courtesy of the artist

UNIT FEATURES

Connections	Reading Informational Material
Every unit contains a feature that connects literature to a related topic, such as art, science, or history. In this unit, students will read an article about the environmental problems facing birds that depend on California's Salton Sea. Students will compare the plight of those birds with that of endangered turkeys described in Bailey White's essay "Turkeys" on p. 580. Use the information and questions on the Connections page to enrich students' understanding of the selections presented within each unit.	These selections will help students learn to analyze and evaluate informational texts, such as workplace documents, technical directions, and consumer materials. They will expose students to the organization and features unique to nonnarrative texts. In this unit, students learn strategies for reading textbooks and research reports.

Exploring the Genre

You will discover in this unit that nonfiction tells true stories that are as interesting and unique as any you will find in fiction. Nonfiction is about real people and real events. In this unit, you will read the following types of nonfiction:

- **Letters and journals** contain personal thoughts and reflections.
- **Biographies and autobiographies** are life stories. A biography is the life story of someone written by someone else. An autobiography is a writer's own life story.
- **Media accounts** are nonfiction works written for newspapers, magazines, television, or radio.
- **Essays** are short nonfiction works about a particular subject. Types of essays include historical essays, persuasive essays, informational essays, narrative essays, and visual essays.

As you read the nonfiction works in this unit, you will learn the characteristics of this genre, meet a variety of authors and styles, and learn facts and other information on a variety of subjects.

◀ **Critical Viewing** What details of this picture suggest factual details and accuracy? **[Analyze]**

ASSESSMENT RESOURCES

- **Selection Support: Skills Development Workbook**
- **Formal Assessment**
- **Open-Book Tests**
- **Performance Assessment and Portfolio Mangement**
- **Extension Activities**

Assessing Student Progress

Listed below are the tools that are available to measure the degree to which students meet the unit objectives.

Informal Assessment

The questions in the Review and Assess sections are a first level of response to the concepts and skills presented within the selections. Students' responses are a brief, informal measure of their grasp of the material. These responses can indicate where further instruction and practice are needed. Follow up with the practice pages in the **Selection Support: Skills Development Workbook.**

Formal Assessment

The **Formal Assessment** booklet contains the Selection Tests and Unit Tests.

- Selection Tests measure comprehension and skills acquisition for each selection or group of selections.
- Each Unit Test provides students with thirty multiple-choice questions and five essay questions designed to assess students' knowledge of the literature and skills taught in the unit.

The **Open-Book Tests** ask students to demonstrate their ability to synthesize and communicate information from selections or groups of selections.

To assess student writing, you will find rubrics and scoring models in the **Performance Assessment and Portfolio Management** booklet. In this booklet, you will also find scoring rubrics for listening and speaking activities.

Alternative Assessment

The **Extension Activities** booklet contains writing activities, listening and speaking activities, and research and technology activities that are appropriate for students with different ability levels. You may also use these activities as an alternative measurement of students' growth.

▶Critical Viewing

Answer: The clarity of the details suggests that the artist looked very carefully at his subject as he painted it. His attention to detail in recreating the setting of a desk suggests factual detail and accuracy.

Why Read Literature?

The "Why Read Literature?" page in each unit presents a list of possible purposes for reading. Each purpose for reading is connected to one or more of the selections in the unit. Good readers set a purpose before reading in order to help them read actively and focus on meaningful details.

Unit 7 introduces three purposes for reading. "Read for the Love of Literature" encourages students to meet a famous writer through an informal letter. "Read to Be Entertained" offers students a glimpse of a bittersweet experience in the adolescence of a well-known author. "Read for Information" introduces students to some facts they probably did not know about baseball and Native American writing.

How to Use This Page

- Tell students that before reading each selection in this unit, they should set a purpose for reading. This will help them read in an active and focused manner.
- Explain that reading "Letter to Scottie" (p. 542), which writer F. Scott Fitzgerald wrote to his young daughter, will increase students' appreciation of literature. By reading Patricia and Fredrick McKissack's "The Shutout" (p. 532) and Joseph Bruchac's "Restoring the Circle" (p. 572), students will learn about aspects of African American and Native American cultures that have been lost, confused, or ignored.
- Students can read to learn as well as to be entertained. When they read Gary Soto's "The Drive-In Movies" (p. 558), they will learn about and be entertained by a day in the life of the author as a teenager.

Why Read Literature?

This unit presents a variety of material called nonfiction. Your purpose for reading each selection may be different, depending on the type of nonfiction and the content. You might want to read for information, read to be entertained, or read for the love of literature. Preview the three purposes you might set before reading the works in this unit.

1 Read for the love of literature.

Francis Scott Key Fitzgerald began writing at an early age. One of his teachers at St. Paul Academy encouraged him to write because he "did not shine in his other subjects." During his life, he was not highly regarded by critics, but since his death, he is considered one of this country's most important writers. Enjoy Fitzgerald's letter to his daughter in **"Letter to Scottie,"** page 542.

2 Read to be entertained.

As a Mexican American from a working-class family, Gary Soto understands and connects with the emotions and experiences of Latino teenagers. His poetry and stories depict the world of young people learning, growing, and changing with humor and sensitivity, for which his works are admired. Read Soto's **"The Drive-In Movies,"** page 558, to get a glimpse of life during the 1950s.

3 Read for information.

Textbooks provide in-depth material on many topics. In "Populations," a section from a science textbook on page 592, you will read about environmental issues and how they affect humans and animals in different parts of the globe.

Patricia and Fredrick McKissack have written many books individually and together and won many awards for their children's books. Fredrick McKissack was a general contractor but found writing more satisfying because he met wonderful children. The McKissacks' books cover a range of topics, including a **"Great African Americans"** series. Read **"The Shutout"** for information about the origins of baseball.

Take It to the Net

Visit the Web site for online instruction and activities related to each selection in this unit.

www.phschool.com

ENRICHMENT: Further Reading

Have students choose one or more of the works below to extend the unit theme "Nonfiction" or to read more by the unit authors.

Long Hard Journey: The Story of the Pullman Porter by Patricia and Fredrick McKissack

This book tells the stories of African American train porters after the Civil War.

Color Me Dark: The Diary of Nellie Lee Love, The Great Migration North by Patricia McKissack

This novel tells of a family's attempt to escape racism in the South in the 1920s.

Nothing to Do But Stay: My Pioneer Mother by Carrie Young

This biography describes the life of the author's mother, who lived and worked during the Great Depression in America's Great Plains.

Dawn Land by Joseph Bruchac

This novel tells of a Native American people who lived thousands of years ago.

How to Read Literature

Strategies for Reading Nonfiction

Nonfiction writing, such as biographies and encyclopedia articles, gives you facts and explanations concerning real people, places, and events. When you read nonfiction, choose the facts you need and judge the connections between them. The following strategies, which you will learn in this unit, will help you read nonfiction.

1. Understand the author's purpose.

A nonfiction writer gives facts about a subject. What the writer does with the facts depends on his or her purpose. For example, a writer may present facts to provide information, to entertain you, or perhaps to persuade you of a particular viewpoint. In this unit, you will learn to recognize an author's purpose and how it is presented.

"It is papa I am writing about, and I shall have no trouble in not knowing what to say about him, as he is a *very* striking character."

The author's purpose is to inform.

2. Use context to determine meaning.

In nonfiction works, the author often includes vocabulary that is specialized, or specific to the topic of the work, and therefore unfamiliar to readers. Context—the situation in which the word is used—can help you get an idea of the word's meaning.

3. Clarify the author's meaning.

Sometimes, you need to clarify, or make clear to yourself, what the author's statements mean. Read the following statements from Amanda Borden's "Olympic Diary."

"I look back now and the injuries seem so small. When I had to deal with them, I felt like I was holding the world. After I competed, I felt I was on top of it."

She follows with examples of situations that will help you clarify what she means.

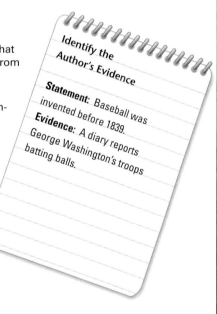

4. Identify the author's evidence.

The author should give evidence—facts or arguments—supporting the statements he or she makes. In this unit, you will practice identifying and evaluating evidence.

As you read the selections in this unit, review the reading strategies and look at the notes in the side columns. Use the suggestions to help you apply strategies for reading nonfiction.

Identify the Author's Evidence

Statement: Baseball was invented before 1839.
Evidence: A diary reports George Washington's troops batting balls.

How to Read Literature

The "How to Read Literature" page in each unit presents a set of strategies to help readers understand authors' words and ideas. Each reading strategy is taught in conjunction with one or more of the selections within the unit. Good readers develop a bank of strategies from which they can draw as needed.

Unit 7 introduces four strategies for reading nonfiction. To understand a selection fully, students must understand how to find and analyze the information presented in nonfiction. The strategies on this page help readers to examine a nonfiction text.

How to Use This Page

Introduce the strategies for reading nonfiction, presenting each as a tool for developing understanding when reading the selections in this unit.

- As students read "The Shutout" (p. 532), they may find that some ideas are unfamiliar to them and will need clarification.
- As students read "Letter to Scottie" (p. 542) and "Olympic Diary" (p. 545), they will be encouraged to think about the authors' purposes for writing.
- As students read "My Papa, Mark Twain" (p. 554), "The Drive-In Movies" (p. 558), and "Space Shuttle *Challenger*" (p. 562), they will learn to identify the different types of evidence presented by the authors.
- As students read "Restoring the Circle" (p. 572), "How the Internet Works" (p. 576), and "Turkeys" (p. 580), they will learn how context clues help explain the meanings of unfamiliar words.

MODEL A READING STRATEGY: Understand the Author's Purpose

Good readers understand that writers have a purpose, which might be to inform, to persuade, or to entertain. Demonstrate how to discover the purpose of authors Patricia and Fredrick McKissack by reading aloud the introductory paragraph of "The Shutout" (p. 532). Then, model your thinking for students. The first paragraph explains that it is difficult to understand the history of baseball because there are many stories, or myths, that are entertaining but not true.

The next sentence about the Doubleday story provides supporting evidence for this research. The authors provide more evidence when they explain that people played stick-and-ball games before 1839. This paragraph not only provides information, but also instructs. The author's purpose must be to inform the reader about the history of baseball.

The Shutout

Lesson Objectives

1. **To analyze and respond to literary elements**
   - Literary Analysis: Historical Essay
   - Connecting Literary Elements: Nonfiction
2. **To read, comprehend, analyze, and critique nonfiction**
   - Reading Strategy: Clarifying the Author's Meaning
   - Reading Check Questions
   - Review and Assess Questions
   - Assessment Practice (ATE)
3. **To develop word analysis skills, fluency, and systematic vocabulary**
   - Vocabulary Development Lesson: Word Analysis: Latin Prefix *ir-*
4. **To understand and apply written and oral language conventions**
   - Spelling Strategy
   - Grammar Lesson: Compound and Complex Sentences
5. **To understand and apply appropriate writing and research strategies**
   - Writing Lesson: Researched Response
   - Extension Activity: Baseball History Timeline
   - Extension Activity: Summary
6. **To understand and apply listening and speaking strategies**
   - Extension Activity: Presentation

STEP-BY-STEP TEACHING GUIDE	PACING GUIDE
PRETEACH	
Motivate Students and Provide Background	
Use the Motivation activity (ATE p. 530)	5 min.
Read and discuss the Preview material and Background information (SE/ATE p. 530) [A]	5 min.
Introduce the Concepts	
Introduce the Literary Analysis and Reading Strategy (SE/ATE p. 531) [A]	15 min.
Pronounce the vocabulary words and read their definitions (SE p. 531)	5 min.
TEACH	
Monitor Comprehension	
Informally monitor comprehension by circulating while students read independently or in groups [A]	15–20 min.
Monitor students' comprehension with the Reading Check notes (SE/ATE pp. 533, 535)	as students read
Develop vocabulary with Vocabulary notes (SE pp. 532, 533, 535; ATE p. 535)	as students read
Develop Understanding	
Develop students' understanding of historical essays with the Literary Analysis annotations (SE p. 534; ATE pp. 533, 534) [A]	5 min.
Develop students' ability to clarify the author's meaning with the Reading Strategy annotations (SE p. 534; ATE p. 534)	5 min.
ASSESS	
Assess Mastery	
Assess students' mastery of the Reading Strategy and Literary Analysis by having them answer the Review and Assess questions (SE/ATE p. 537)	15 min.
Use one or more of the print and media Assessment Resources (ATE p. 539) [A]	up to 45 min.
EXTEND	
Apply Understanding	
Have students complete the Vocabulary Development Lesson and the Grammar Lesson (SE p. 538) [A]	20 min.
Apply students' ability to write about the history of sports using the Writing Lesson (SE/ATE p. 539) [A]	30–45 min.
Apply students' understanding using one or more of the Extension Activities (SE p. 539)	20–90 min.

ACCELERATED INSTRUCTION:
Use the strategies and activities identified with an [A].

UNIVERSAL ACCESS
● = Below Level Students
▲ = On-Level Students
■ = Above Level Students

Time and Resource Manager

Reading Level: Average
Average Number of Instructional Days: 3

RESOURCES		
PRINT	**TRANSPARENCIES**	**TECHNOLOGY**
• **Beyond Literature,** Study Skills: Using a Timeline, p. 31 ▲ ■		• **Interest Grabber Videotapes,** Tape 4 ● ▲ ■
• **Selection Support Workbook:** ● ▲ ■ Literary Analysis, p. 155 Reading Strategy, p. 154 Build Vocabulary, p. 151	• **Literary Analysis and Reading Transparencies,** pp. 61 and 62 ● ▲ ■	
• **Adapted Reader's Companion** ● • **Reader's Companion** ●		• **Listening to Literature** ● ▲ ■ Audiocassettes, Side 19 Audio CDs, CD 9
• **English Learner's Companion** ● ▲ • **Literatura en español** ● ▲ • **Literary Analysis for Enrichment** ■		
• **Formal Assessment:** Selection Test, pp. 139–141 ● ▲ ■ • **Open Book Test,** pp. 91–93 ● ▲ ■ • **Performance Assessment and Portfolio Management,** pp. 14, 29 ● ▲ ■ • PRENTICE HALL ASSESSMENT SYSTEM ● ▲ ■	• PRENTICE HALL ASSESSMENT SYSTEM ● ▲ ■ Skills Practice Answers and Explanations on Transparencies	• **Test Bank Software** ● ▲ ■ • **Got It! Assessment Videotapes,** Tape 4 ● ▲
• **Selection Support Workbook:** ● ▲ ■ Build Spelling Skills, p. 152 Build Grammar Skills, p. 153 • **Writing and Grammar,** Copper Level ● ▲ ■ • **Extension Activities,** p. 31 ● ▲ ■	• **Daily Language Practice Transparencies** ● ▲ • **Writing Models and Graphic Organizers on Transparencies** ● ▲ ■	• **Writing and Grammar iText CD-ROM** ● ▲ ■ ***Take It to the Net*** www.phschool.com

BLOCK SCHEDULING: Use one 90-minute class period to preteach the selection and have students read it. Use a second 90-minute class period to assess students' mastery of skills and have them complete one of the Extension Activities.

PRETEACH

Step-by-Step Teaching Guide for pp. 530–531

Motivation

Have students examine the picture on p. 530, and ask them to draw conclusions about who is pictured and why they are posed this way. Then, ask students what makes this picture different from the baseball-team portraits of today. Help students understand that baseball's Major Leagues were racially segregated until 1947 when the Brooklyn Dodgers called up Jackie Robinson from their farm team, the Montreal Royals. Then, tell students that "The Shutout" will explain how segregation in baseball evolved.

Interest Grabber Video

As an alternative, play "Breaking Down Barriers" on Tape 4 to engage student interest.

1 Background

Sports

Since African Americans were refused admittance into the National Association of Base Ball Players, they formed their own baseball leagues. Leroy ("Satchel") Paige was a legendary player known for his remarkable pitching ability. In 1948, the year after African American Jackie Robinson joined the Major Leagues, Paige joined the Cleveland Indians. His thirty-year baseball career included at least 2,500 games and fifty-five no-hitters. In 1971, Paige was the first African American inducted into the Baseball Hall of Fame.

Prepare to Read

1 The Shutout

Take It to the Net

Visit www.phschool.com for interactive activities and instruction related to "The Shutout," including

- background
- graphic organizers
- literary elements
- reading strategies

Preview

Connecting to the Literature

You have probably used the expression "That's not fair!" when you feel you are being unjustly punished or made to follow a rule with which you do not agree. In "The Shutout," authors Patricia C. and Fredrick McKissack describe an unfair situation that African American ballplayers faced in the early days of major league baseball.

Background

In the earliest days of baseball, African Americans played alongside white players. Eventually, however, baseball was segregated, or separated, into teams of "blacks" and teams of "whites." As this essay shows, though, segregation could not shut out African Americans from playing the game and creating baseball legends as amazing as those of their white counterparts.

TEACHING RESOURCES

The following resources can be used to enrich or extend the instruction for pp. 530–531.

Motivation

Interest Grabber Video, Tape 4

Background

Beyond Literature, p. 31

Take It to the Net

Visit www.phschool.com for Background and hotlinks for the "The Shutout."

Literary Analysis

Literary Analysis and Reading Transparencies, Historical Essay, p. 62

Reading

Selection Support: Reading Strategy, p. 154; Build Vocabulary, p. 151

Literary Analysis and Reading Transparencies, Clarifying the Author's Meaning, p. 61

BLOCK SCHEDULING: Resources marked with this symbol provide varied instruction during 90-minute blocks.

❷ Literary Analysis

Historical Essay

An essay is a short nonfiction work about a particular subject. A **historical essay** gives facts, explanations, and interpretations of historical events. For example, in "The Shutout," the authors provide facts about a variety of stick-and-ball games from different cultures. They interpret these facts by stating:

> Although baseball is a uniquely American sport, it was not invented by a single person.

As you read "The Shutout," use a graphic organizer like the one shown to take notes on the facts, explanations, and interpretations you find in the essay.

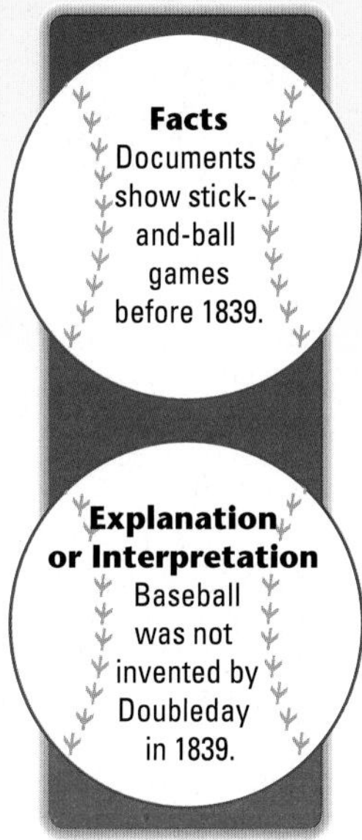

Facts
Documents show stick-and-ball games before 1839.
Explanation or Interpretation
Baseball was not invented by Doubleday in 1839.

Connecting Literary Elements

The **author's purpose** is his or her reason for writing. In a historical essay, the author's general purpose is to give information about events from history. The author's more specific purpose is often to show the significance or effects of the events. To achieve this purpose, an author may draw conclusions. Read critically to determine whether facts in the essay support the conclusions. Begin with the following focus questions.

1. What conclusion does the author draw about the origins of baseball?
2. Which facts in the essay support this conclusion?

❸ Reading Strategy

Clarifying the Author's Meaning

Often a nonfiction writer will state a conclusion or offer an opinion or interpretation. This general statement will be followed by details, examples, and explanations that will help you **clarify the author's meaning,** that is, make the author's meaning clear. As you read "The Shutout," notice general statements made by the authors. Then, look for details that explain, elaborate on, or support these statements.

Vocabulary Development

anecdotes (an′ ik dōts′) *n.* short, entertaining tales (p. 532)

evolved (ē vôlvd′) *v.* grew gradually; developed (p. 533)

diverse (də vʉrs′) *adj.* various; with differing characteristics (p. 533)

composed (kəm pōzd′) *adj.* made up (of) (p. 535)

irrational (ir rash′ ə nəl) *adj.* unreasonable; not making sense (p. 535)

❷ Literary Analysis

Historical Essay

- Explain to students that a historical essay is a type of writing that combines exposition and persuasion. Writers draw conclusions from the facts in order to argue an idea persuasively. "The Shutout" is an example of a historical essay.
- Ask a volunteer to read aloud the instruction and the Connecting Literary Elements feature. You may wish to write the Connecting Literary Elements questions on the board. Remind students to stop and consider the questions as they read the selection.
- Introduce students to the graphic organizer by using the Historical Essay transparency on p. 62 in **Literary Analysis and Reading Transparencies.**

❸ Reading Strategy

Clarifying the Author's Meaning

- Have a volunteer read the instruction about clarifying the author's meaning as the class follows along. Then, write the words *Facts* and *Conclusions* on the board.
- Explain that as students read, they should note the facts presented in the selection. Then, they should draw conclusions about what point the authors are supporting with each fact.
- To illustrate this point further, show students the Clarifying the Author's Meaning transparency in p. 61 of **Literary Analysis and Reading Transparencies.**

Vocabulary Development

- Pronounce each vocabulary word for students, and read the definitions as a class. Have students identify any words with which they are already familiar.

CUSTOMIZE INSTRUCTION FOR UNIVERSAL ACCESS

For Special Needs Students	For Less Proficient Readers	For English Learners
Have students read the adapted version of "The Shutout" in the **Adapted Reader's Companion.** This version provides basic-level instruction in an interactive format with questions and write-on lines. Completing the adapted version will prepare students to read the selection in the Student Edition.	Have students read "The Shutout" in the **Reader's Companion.** This version provides basic-level instruction in an interactive format with questions and write-on lines. After students finish the selection in the Reader's Companion, have them complete the questions and activities in the Student Edition.	Have students read the adapted version of "The Shutout" in the **English Learner's Companion.** This version provides basic-level instruction in an interactive format with questions and write-on lines. Completing the adapted version will prepare students to read the selection in the Student Edition.

 ***E-Teach***

Visit E-Teach at www.phschool.com for teachers' essays on how to teach, with questions and answers.

TEACH

Step-by-Step Teaching Guide for pp. 532–536

CUSTOMIZE INSTRUCTION
For Visual/Spatial Learners

To help all students gain a broader view of baseball's history, have them bring to class illustrations, photographs, or other memorabilia that tell the story of baseball before World War II. Encourage students to search the Internet, check out illustrated books from the library, and talk to those who collect baseball treasures. Have the class create a bulletin board or display table that features the works collected.

❶ About the Selection

In "The Shutout" Patricia and Fredrick McKissack begin by describing the history of baseball. The authors then point out that after the Civil War, baseball became a segregated sport. African American players turned to barnstorming, where demonstrations of their skill and dedication kept the Negro Leagues alive. After Jackie Robinson broke into the major leagues in 1947, ball clubs began admitting all ethnic groups. Once again, baseball became common ground for fans and players.

❶ The Shutout

Patricia C. McKissack and Fredrick McKissack, Jr.

The history of baseball is difficult to trace because it is embroidered with wonderful anecdotes that are fun but not necessarily supported by fact. There are a lot of myths that persist about baseball—the games, the players, the owners, and the fans—in spite of contemporary research that disproves most of them. For example, the story that West Point cadet Abner Doubleday "invented" baseball in 1839 while at Cooperstown, New York, continues to be widely accepted, even though, according to his diaries, Doubleday never visited Cooperstown. A number of records and documents show that people were playing stick-and-ball games long before the 1839 date.

anecdotes (an′ ik dōts′) *n.* short, entertaining tales

❷ Albigence Waldo, a surgeon with George Washington's troops at Valley Forge, wrote in his diary that soldiers were "batting balls and running bases" in their free time. Samuel Hopkins Adams (1871–1958), an American historical novelist, stated that his grandfather "played baseball on Mr. Mumford's pasture" in the 1820's.

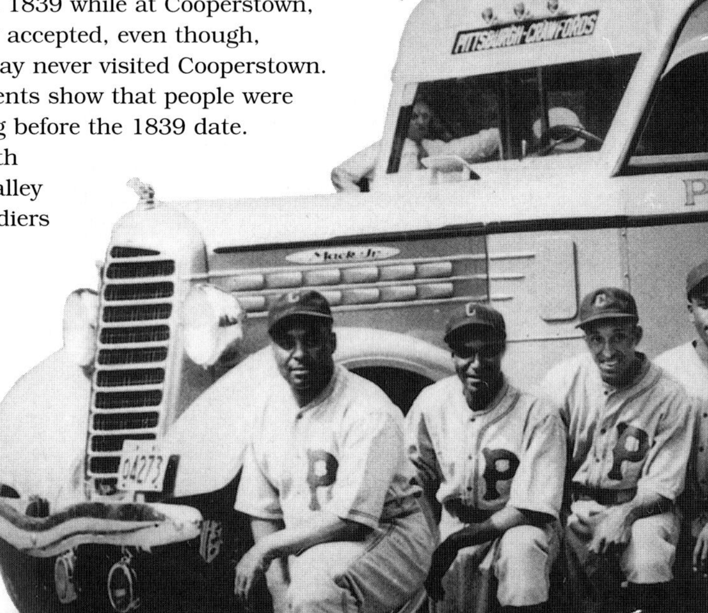

TEACHING RESOURCES

The following resources can be used to enrich or extend the instruction for pp. 532–536.

Literary Analysis
- **Selection Support:** Literary Analysis, p. 155
- **Literary Analysis for Enrichment** ▪
- **Writing Models and Graphic Organizers on Transparencies,** p. 77

Reading
- **Reader's Companion**
- **Adapted Reader's Companion**
- **English Learner's Companion**
- **Literatura en español**
- **Listening to Literature Audiocassettes,** Side 19 ▪
- **Listening to Literature Audio CDs,** CD 9 ▪

▪ **BLOCK SCHEDULING:** Resources marked with this symbol provide varied instruction during 90-minute blocks.

Although baseball is a uniquely American sport, it was not invented by a single person. Probably the game evolved from a variety of stick-and-ball games that were played in Europe, Asia, Africa, and the Americas for centuries and brought to the colonies by the most diverse group of people ever to populate a continent. More specifically, some historians believe baseball is an outgrowth of its first cousin, *rounders*, an English game. Robin Carver wrote in his *Book of Sports* (1834) that "an American version of rounders called *goal ball* was rivaling cricket in popularity."

It is generally accepted that by 1845, baseball, as it is recognized today, was becoming popular, especially in New York. In that year a group of baseball enthusiasts organized the New York Knickerbocker Club. They tried to standardize the game by establishing guidelines for "proper play."

The Knickerbockers' rules set the playing field—a diamond-shaped infield with four bases (first, second, third, and home) placed ninety feet apart. At that time, the pitching distance was forty-five feet from home base and the "pitch" was thrown underhanded. The three-strikes-out rule, the three-out inning, and the ways in which a player could be called out were also specified. However, the nine-man team and nine-inning game were not established until later. Over the years, the Knickerbockers' basic rules of play haven't changed much.

evolved (ē vôlvd′) *v.* grew gradually; developed

diverse (də vʉrs′) *adj.* various; with differing characteristics

3 **Reading Check**

Why is the history of baseball difficult to trace?

2 Literary Analysis

Historical Essay

- Point out to students that in the preceding paragraph, the authors state that baseball existed before 1839, the accepted date of invention.
- Then, ask students what facts are presented in the bracketed paragraph.
  Answer: A surgeon with George Washington wrote about people playing a baseball-like game at Valley Forge, and an American novelist states that his grandfather played baseball in the 1820s.
- Finally, ask students why they think the authors included these facts.
  Answer: The facts are evidence that people were playing baseball before it was "invented" in 1839.

3 Reading Check

Answer: The history of baseball is difficult to trace because baseball lore contains many myths and stories but little factual evidence.

CUSTOMIZE INSTRUCTION FOR UNIVERSAL ACCESS

For Special Needs Students	For Less Proficient Readers
Students may have trouble keeping track of the different events in the history of baseball in regards to African Americans. Ask each student to prepare a timeline for African American players. Students should write significant dates and events on their timelines. You may wish to use the Timeline transparency on p. 77 in **Writing Models and Graphic Organizers on Transparencies.**	Students may benefit from an organizer that helps them see the role that race played in the forming of the present-day Major League Baseball association. Suggest that each student prepare a two-column chart with the headings *National Association of BaseBall Players* and *the Negro League.* As they read, encourage students to jot notes in each column. After they complete the reading, ask them to write summaries of each of the columns. Discuss the different information presented in the two columns.

4 Literary Analysis

Historical Essay

- Before asking students the Literary Analysis question, ask them what is the subject of the bracketed paragraph.
  Answer: The subject of the paragraph is the history of the National Association of Base Ball Players.
- Then, ask students the Literary Analysis question on p. 534.
  Answer: Students may point out any part of this passage, because every sentence in the paragraph states a fact that can be proved true.

Monitor Progress Ask students to identify the two elements that are key to a historical essay.
Answer: Facts and explanations or interpretations are key elements of a historical essay.

Reteach If students struggle to understand the elements of a historical essay, you might help them by reading a portion of "The Shutout" and an excerpt from a story about baseball, such as Gary Soto's "Baseball in April," or from a recent newspaper article about a baseball game. Before you read, make sure students understand that a fact is something that can be proved true. As you read, ask students to listen for key facts. Read the excerpts aloud, and then discuss how factual material is used differently in each excerpt.

5 Reading Strategy

- Ask a volunteer to read aloud the bracketed paragraph.
- Remind students that they can clarify an author's meaning by looking for details that further explain, elaborate on, or support a particular statement.
- Ask students to respond to the Reading Strategy question on p. 534.
  Possible responses: Students may suggest that the last sentence of the preceding paragraph or the last sentence of the bracketed paragraph clarify the meaning of the statement.

4 In 1857–1858, the newly organized National Association of Base Ball Players was formed, and baseball became a business. Twenty-five clubs—mostly from eastern states—formed the Association for the purpose of setting rules and guidelines for club and team competition. The Association defined a professional player as a person who "played for money, place or emolument (profit)." The Association also authorized an admission fee for one of the first "all-star" games between Brooklyn and New York. Fifteen hundred people paid fifty cents to see that game. Baseball was on its way to becoming the nation's number-one sport.

Literary Analysis
Historical Essay What are two facts in this paragraph that can be proven true?

By 1860, the same year South Carolina seceded from the Union, there were about sixty teams in the Association. For obvious reasons none of them were from the South. Baseball's development was slow during the Civil War years, but teams continued to compete, and military records show that, sometimes between battles, Union soldiers chose up teams and played baseball games. It was during this time that records began mentioning African-American players. One war journalist noted that black players were "sought after as teammates because of their skill as ball handlers."

Information about the role of African Americans in the early stages of baseball development is slight. Several West African cultures had stick-and-ball and running games, so at least some blacks were familiar with the concept of baseball. Baseball, however, was not a popular southern sport, never equal to boxing, wrestling, footracing, or horse racing among the privileged landowners.

5 Slave owners preferred these individual sports because they could enter their slaves in competitions, watch the event from a safe distance, pocket the winnings, and personally never raise a sweat. There are documents to show that slave masters made a great deal of money from the athletic skills of their slaves.

Reading Strategy
Clarify the Author's Meaning What details clarify the meaning of the statement that slave owners preferred individual sports?

Free blacks, on the other hand, played on and against integrated[1] teams in large eastern cities and in small midwestern hamlets. It is believed that some of the emancipated[2] slaves and runaways who served in the Union Army learned how to play baseball from northern blacks and whites who had been playing together for years.

After the Civil War, returning soldiers helped to inspire a new interest in baseball all over the country. Teams sprung up in northern and midwestern cities, and naturally African Americans

1. **integrated** (inˊ tə grā tid) *adj.* open to both African Americans and whites.
2. **emancipated** (ē manˊ sə pāˊ tid) *adj.* freed from slavery.

Union Prisoners at Salisbury, N.C., National Baseball Library and Archive, Cooperstown, NY

were interested in joining some of these clubs. But the National Association of Base Ball Players had other ideas. They voted in December 1867 not to admit any team for membership that "may be composed of one or more colored persons." Their reasoning was as irrational as the racism that shaped it: "If colored clubs were admitted," the Association stated, "there would be in all probability some division of feeling whereas, by excluding them no injury could result to anyone . . . and [we wish] to keep out of the convention the discussion of any subjects having a political bearing as this [admission of blacks on the Association teams] undoubtedly would."

So, from the start, organized baseball tried to limit or exclude African-American participation. In the early days a few black ball players managed to play on integrated minor league teams. A few even made it to the majors, but by the turn of the century, black players were shut out of the major leagues until after World War II. That doesn't mean African Americans didn't play the game. They did.

composed (kəm pōzd′) *v.* made up (of)

irrational (ir rash′ ə nəl) *adj.* unreasonable; not making sense

8 **Reading Check**
What was the National Association of Baseball Players rule about African American players?

6 Background

Art

Union Prisoners at Salisbury, N.C., by unknown artist

The color lithograph, a popular medium in the mid-1800s, pictures Union soldiers caught in play at a Confederate prison. Lithography is a printing process in which ink is applied to an image on a flat surface, such as a sheet of zinc or aluminum. Grease placed on the image retains the ink while the nonimage, or blank area, repels it. This lithograph highlights the spirit of baseball. The game is common ground on which all can meet. Discuss these questions.

1. In what ways does the lithograph show common ground among those pictured?
   Possible responses: Some will say that Union and Confederate soldiers enjoy the sport together, even during a war. Others may say that soldiers are sharing the same field.
2. How does baseball provide common ground in your community?
   Possible response: Baseball draws people together, and for a moment they can forget their differences.

7 Vocabulary Development

Latin Prefix *ir-*

- Remind students that when the prefix *ir-* is used, the word's meaning is changed to its opposite. Explain that in this passage, the Association's reasoning was *irrational,* or "not rational or reasonable."
- Work with students to paraphrase the Association's statement.
  Possible response: If African American clubs joined the Association, it is certain there would be a conflict. If they were not permitted to join, no one would be hurt.

8 Reading Check

Answer: The rule was that no African Americans would be allowed to play in the National Association of Base Ball Players.

CUSTOMIZE INSTRUCTION FOR UNIVERSAL ACCESS

For Gifted/Talented Students	For Advanced Readers
Have students participate in a panel discussion based on this selection. Students should be divided into groups of fans, players from the Negro League, and players from the National Association. Students should support their opinions with information from the essay.	Invite students to examine the history of baseball and hypothesize about why certain myths persist about the sport. Then, have students write essays explaining why they think events of history are often confused by anecdotes, beliefs, or fictional tales. Ask students to publish their essays in the school newspaper or on the school Web page, if one exists.

ASSESS

Answers for p. 536

Review and Assess

1. Possible response: Students may say that they would feel angry and frustrated because they might be able to play as well as any other player.
2. **(a)** It probably began before 1839. **(b)** Baseball probably came from the game rounders.
3. **(a)** Baseball became popular around 1845, at which point the New York Knickerbocker Club formed rules. **(b)** The National Association of Base Ball Players was formed. It set rules and guidelines for teams and clubs. **(c)** Rules were formed to make the games fair and uniform.
4. **(a)** The Civil War slowed baseball's development. **(b)** Soldiers who returned from the Civil War created enthusiasm for the game; teams were formed in the North and Midwest.
5. **(a)** The National Association of Base Ball Players thought that no one would get hurt if African Americans were excluded. **(b)** The decision meant that African Americans had to form their own league in order to play. **(c)** Racism and segregation contributed to this exclusion.
6. **(a)** Possible response: Sports are segregated by gender and social class. Girls often are prohibited from participating with boys. Sports that require expensive equipment exclude those who cannot afford it. **(b)** Possible response: Excluding female players from any sport would be unfair.

Black people organized their own teams, formed leagues, and competed for championships. The history of the old "Negro Leagues" and the players who barnstormed[3] on black diamonds is one of baseball's most interesting chapters, but the story is a researcher's nightmare. Black baseball was outside the mainstream of the major leagues, so team and player records weren't well kept, and for the most part, the white press ignored black clubs or portrayed them as clowns. And for a long time the Baseball Hall of Fame didn't recognize any of the Negro League players. Because of the lack of documentation, many people thought the Negro Leagues' stories were nothing more than myths and yarns, but that is not the case. The history of the Negro Leagues is a patchwork of human drama and comedy, filled with legendary heroes, infamous owners, triple-headers, low pay, and long bus rides home—not unlike the majors.

3. **barnstormed** *v.* went from one small town to another, putting on an exhibition.

Patricia C. McKissack Fredrick McKissack, Jr.

Patricia McKissack **(b. 1944)** and Fredrick McKissack **(b. 1939)** are husband and wife. Both were born in Nashville, Tennessee, and they have been writing books since 1984. Their works, including *Christmas in the Big House, Christmas in the Quarters*, honor the struggles of African Americans. The McKissacks try to "build bridges with books." By showing young readers the sometimes "forgotten" parts of history, they hope to encourage understanding between different groups. As a team and individually, the McKissacks have written more than 100 books.

Review and Assess

Thinking About the Selection

1. **Respond:** How might you have felt as an African American baseball player who was denied the chance to play in the major leagues?
2. (a) **Recall:** When did baseball probably begin? (b) **Connect:** From what English game did baseball probably grow?
3. (a) **Recall:** When did baseball become popular, and who created the playing rules? (b) **Analyze:** Give specific examples of the changes that occurred following the creation of baseball as a professional sport. (c) **Generalize:** What is one reason that rules and regulations were created as baseball moved from an informal game to a professional sport?
4. (a) **Identify Cause and Effect:** What effect did the Civil War have on baseball? (b) **Infer:** In what way did the end of the Civil War help the growth of baseball?
5. (a) **Recall:** What were the National Association of Base Ball Players' reasons for not letting African Americans play? (b) **Identify Cause and Effect:** What effect did this exclusion have on the history of baseball? (c) **Connect:** What attitudes and conditions contributed to this exclusion?
6. (a) **Make a Judgment:** Do you think that sports today are segregated in any way? (b) **Take a Position:** Do you think there are any sports from which girls and women should be excluded? Why or why not?

ASSESSMENT PRACTICE: Reading Comprehension

Distinguishing Between Fact and Nonfact (For more practice, see Test Preparation Workbook, p. 44.)

Many tests ask students to distinguish facts from nonfacts. Write this text from the selection on the board.

> In 1857–1858, the newly organized National Association of Base Ball Players was formed, and baseball became a business. . . . The Association defined a professional player as [one who] "played for money, place, or emolument (profit)." . . . Baseball was on its way to becoming the nation's number-one sport.

Which is a FACT from the passage?

A Baseball is an exciting game.
B The National Association of Base Ball Players was formed in 1857–1858.
C Professional baseball players were rich.
D Baseball was more popular than football.

Point out that *A* is an opinion, and *C* and *D* are not statements found in the passage. Choice *B* is correct.

Review and Assess

Literary Analysis

Historical Essay

1. Explain why researchers are not completely sure about the origins of baseball.
2. One insight the authors offer is that the Negro leagues were filled with "drama and comedy." What historical evidence is provided to support this insight?

Connecting Literary Elements

3. Make an organizer like the one below to record facts and conclusions about the conditions faced by African American ball players.

Facts	Conclusions

4. Do the facts provide adequate evidence for the authors' conclusions?

Reading Strategy

Clarifying the Author's Meaning

5. In your own words, explain the meaning of the statement "The history of baseball is difficult to trace because it is embroidered with wonderful anecdotes that are fun, but not necessarily supported by fact."
6. What details are grouped together to communicate this meaning?
7. On an organizer like the one below, list details from the selection that help you clarify the meaning of the statement given. In the last box, explain the meaning.

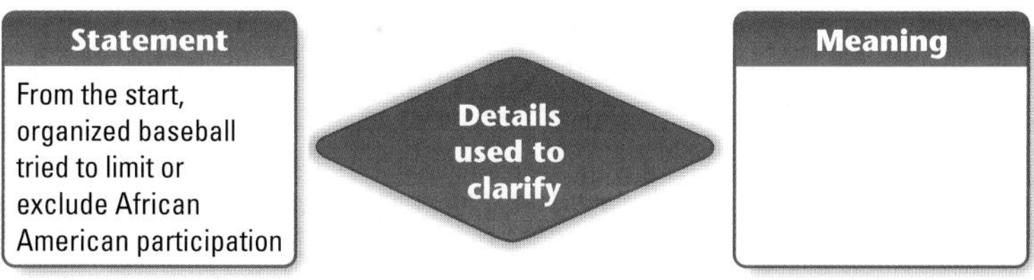
Statement
From the start, organized baseball tried to limit or exclude African American participation
Details used to clarify
Meaning

Extending Understanding

8. **Take a Position:** Do you think that baseball is truly "the great American pastime"? Explain.

Quick Review

Nonfiction explains ideas or tells about real people, places, or events.

A **historical essay** is nonfiction that gives facts, explanations, and interpretations of historical events. To review nonfiction and historical essays, see p. 531.

When you **clarify the author's meaning,** you look for details that make clear the writer's point. To review clarifying the author's meaning, see p. 531.

 ***Take It to the Net***

www.phschool.com

Take the interactive self-test online to check your understanding of the selection.

ENRICHMENT: Further Reading

Other Works by the Authors

African-American Inventors

The Civil Rights Movement in America

Rebels Against Slavery: American Slave Revolts

Take It to the Net

Visit www.phschool.com for more information on the authors.

Answers for p. 537

Review and Assess

1. Researchers are not sure about the origins of baseball because there are many stories, but there is little factual evidence.
2. Possible response: Evidence of drama includes the players' experiences with segregation. Evidence of comedy includes the sheer fun of the game.
3. **Facts:** Slave owners did not like African Americans to participate in group sports. Free African Americans played with Caucasians in the North. After the Civil War, African American players were excluded. Records from the Negro League games were not well kept. For many years, the Baseball Hall of Fame did not recognize Negro League players. **Conclusions:** Many people thought the stories about the Negro Leagues were myths. Many people did not take the Negro Leagues seriously. The Negro Leagues were full of comedy and tragedy. Racism kept many African Americans from participating in baseball.
4. The authors' conclusions are derived from the facts they present.
5. Possible response: The history of baseball is hard to pinpoint because its stories are not all supported by facts.
6. Details of the accepted history are grouped together and followed by details that support the idea that baseball is older than 1839.
7. **Details:** In 1867, the National Association refused to admit African American players. Players were shut out of the Major Leagues. **Meaning:** Racist attitudes kept African American players from playing.
8. Possible response: Students may say that baseball's popularity shows that it is "the great American pastime." Others may say that, because so many were excluded, baseball's history was not "great" for all Americans.

EXTEND

Answers for p. 538

❶ Vocabulary Development

Word Analysis

1. cannot be substituted for
2. cannot fight against
3. cannot be retrieved

Spelling Strategy

1. irregular; The apple had an irregular shape.
2. irrelevant; Her comment was irrelevant to our conversation.
3. irresponsible; My little brother is irresponsible.

Concept Development

1. d; The anecdote of Paige's perfect pitch has been told often.
2. c; The rules evolved over a short period of time.
3. a; Keeping black players from the major leagues was irrational.
4. b; Fans come from diverse backgrounds.
5. e; The baseball diamond is composed of three bases and home plate.

❷ Grammar

1. complex
2. compound
3. complex
4. compound
5. complex

Writing Application

Possible responses:

Complex: There are a lot of stories about baseball because people love it. Many people get excited when the season begins.

Compound: Many high-school athletes hope to make the Major Leagues, but only the best players make it. Baseball has a long tradition, and it will continue to be popular.

Integrate Language Skills

❶ Vocabulary Development Lesson

Word Analysis: Latin Prefix *ir-*

The Latin prefix *ir-*, as in the word *irrational*, turns a word meaning into its opposite. Define each italicized word:

1. You broke an *irreplaceable* vase!
2. I find chocolate *irresistible*.
3. The lost money is *irrecoverable*.

Spelling Strategy

The prefix *ir-* is used only with words that begin with *r*. When adding the prefix *ir-*, keep both *r*'s. For example: *ir-* + *rational* = *irrational*.

Write the word for each numbered definition. Underline the base word before *ir-* is added. Then, use each word in a complete sentence.

1. not regular
2. not relevant
3. not responsible

Concept Development: Definitions

For each numbered item below, match the word with its meaning.

1. anecdote	**a.** unreasonable
2. evolved	**b.** varied
3. irrational	**c.** grew gradually
4. diverse	**d.** tale
5. composed	**e.** made up

Use each vocabulary word in a sentence that restates its meaning.

Examples: The anecdote she told was an amusing tale of camping.

The diverse species of the rain forest are more varied than most ecosystems.

❷ Grammar Lesson

Compound and Complex Sentences

A **compound sentence** consists of two or more independent clauses. In most cases, the independent clauses are joined by a comma and a coordinating conjunction such as *and*, *but*, *for*, *nor*, *or*, *so*, or *yet*.

IND: I wanted to go to the game, | but | IND: I had the flu.

A **complex sentence** consists of one independent clause—called the main clause—and one or more subordinate clauses. The subordinate clause can appear at the beginning or end of the sentence.

IND: They left | SUB: when the game ended.

SUB: When the game ended, | IND: they left.

Practice Copy the sentences below. Label each sentence as compound or complex.

1. Bring your glove to the picnic because we might play ball.
2. Brad is a great pitcher, but he can't field the ball.
3. Since Nolan gave his report, everyone is interested in the Negro leagues.
4. Maya signed up for the baseball clinic, and Ashley signed up for gymnastics.
5. Put your cap on sideways when you want your team to rally.

Writing Application Write two compound sentences and two complex sentences about baseball.

WG *Prentice Hall Writing and Grammar Connection: Chapter 20, Section 2*

TEACHING RESOURCES

The following resources can be used to enrich or extend the instruction for pp. 538–539.

Vocabulary

- **Selection Support:** Build Vocabulary, p. 151; Build Spelling Skills, p. 152
- **Vocabulary and Spelling Practice Book** (Use this booklet for skills enrichment)

Grammar

- **Selection Support:** Build Grammar Skills, p. 153
- **Writing and Grammar,** Copper Level, pp. 427–428

- **Daily Language Practice Transparencies**

Writing

- **Writing and Grammar,** Copper Level, p. 226
- **Writing Models and Graphic Organizers on Transparency,** p. 61
- **Writing and Grammar iText CD-ROM**

BLOCK SCHEDULING: Resources marked with this symbol provide varied instruction during 90-minute blocks.

❸ Writing Lesson

Researched Response

"The Shutout" ends with the statement beginning "The history of the Negro Leagues is a patchwork of human drama and comedy . . ." Conduct research on the Negro Leagues and use the information you find in a response to that statement.

Prewriting Identify questions that you will investigate during your research. For example, who were some of the heroes of the league? What legends and anecdotes are told about players and games?

Drafting In your introduction, cite the quotation by the McKissacks. In the body of your essay, organize details around each part of the quotation: heroes, owners, games, and so on.

Model: Crediting a Quotation

In "The Shutout," Patricia and Fredrick McKissack explain the circumstances leading to the formation of the Negro Leagues. With the following comment, they leave readers wanting to learn more. "The history of the Negro Leagues is a patchwork of human drama and comedy, filled with legendary heroes, infamous owners, triple-headers, low pay, and long bus rides home—not unlike the majors." (McKissack 10)

After giving the quotation, the writer cites the author of the source and the page number. Complete information about sources is given in a "Works Cited" list at the end of the essay.

Revising Check that you have correctly punctuated and credited any quotations you have used. Use quotation marks before and after each quotation. In parentheses, give the author of the source and the page number.

WG Prentice Hall Writing and Grammar Connection: Chapter 11, Section 2

❹ Extension Activities

Listening and Speaking Plan and deliver a brief **presentation** about the origins of baseball.

1. Review the general information provided in "The Shutout."
2. List questions you will research when looking for additional details.
3. Use a variety of resources to find answers to your questions.
4. Deliver your presentation to the class.

Research and Technology With a small group, create a **timeline** on a specific era in the history of baseball.

Writing Write a **summary** of "The Shutout." Identify and explain the main events and ideas.

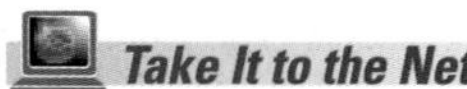

www.phschool.com

Go online for an additional research activity using the Internet.

Lesson Support for p. 539

❸ Writing Lesson

- After students have read the instruction on p. 539, have a short discussion about what kinds of questions students will ask in their research. Write the questions on the board.
- You may want to research the Internet before giving the students this assignment in order to find appropriate Web sites.
- Use the Research rubric on p. 14 in **Performance Assessment and Portfolio Management** to assess students' research reports.

❹ Listening and Speaking

- After students read the instruction, talk to them about focusing their questions on one aspect of the origins of baseball, such as the New York Knickerbocker Club or the Negro Leagues.
- Once students begin their research, encourage them to work together in groups. Students can share the resources they find.
- Remind students as they rehearse that they should know the material well enough that they do not have to rely completely on their notes as they speak.
- Have students review the Speaking rubric on p. 29 in **Performance Assessment and Portfolio Management** before they give their presentations.

CUSTOMIZE INSTRUCTION For Universal Access

To address different learning styles, use the activities suggested in the **Extension Activities** booklet, p. 31

- For Visual/Spatial Learners, use Activity 6.
- For Visual/Spatial and Logical/Mathematical Learners, use Activity 7.

ASSESSMENT RESOURCES

The following resources can be used to assess students' knowledge and skills.

Selection Assessment

- **Formal Assessment,** pp. 139–141
- **Open Book Test,** pp. 91–93
- **Got It! Assessment Videotapes,** Tape 4
- **Test Bank Software**

Take It to the Net
Visit www.phschool.com for self-tests and additional questions on "The Shutout."

Writing Rubric

- **Performance Assess. and Portfolio Mgmt.,** p. 14

Listening and Speaking Rubric

- **Performance Assess. and Portfolio Mgmt.,** p. 29

- **Workbook**
- **Skill Book**
- **Transparencies**
- **CD-ROM**

Letter to Scottie ✦ Olympic Diary

Lesson Objectives

1. **To analyze and respond to literary elements**
   - Literary Analysis: Letters and Journals
   - Comparing Literary Works
2. **To read, comprehend, analyze, and critique nonfiction**
   - Reading Strategy: Understanding the Author's Purpose
   - Reading Check Questions
   - Review and Assess Questions
   - Assessment Practice (ATE)
3. **To develop word analysis skills, fluency, and systematic vocabulary**
   - Vocabulary Development Lesson: Word Analysis: Forms of *document*
4. **To understand and apply written and oral language conventions**
   - Spelling Strategy
   - Grammar Lesson: Subject and Object Pronouns
5. **To understand and apply appropriate writing and research strategies**
   - Writing Lesson: Letter to an Author
   - Extension Activity: Olympic Presentation
6. **To understand and apply listening and speaking strategies**
   - Extension Activity: Oral Presentation
   - Extension Activity: Journal Entry

STEP-BY-STEP TEACHING GUIDE	PACING GUIDE
PRETEACH	
Motivate Students and Provide Background	
Use the Motivation activity (ATE p. 540)	5 min.
Read and discuss the Preview material and Background information (SE/ATE p. 540) A	10 min.
Introduce the Concepts	
Introduce the Literary Analysis and Reading Strategy (SE/ATE p. 541) A	25 min.
Pronounce the vocabulary words and read their definitions (SE p. 541)	5 min.
TEACH	
Monitor Comprehension	
Informally monitor comprehension by circulating while students read independently or in groups A	15–20 min.
Monitor students' comprehension with the Reading Check notes (SE/ATE pp. 543, 545)	as students read
Develop vocabulary with Vocabulary notes (SE pp. 543, 545, 546; ATE p. 543)	as students read
Develop Understanding	
Develop students' understanding of letters and journals with the Literary Analysis annotations (SE p. 547; ATE p. 547) A	5 min.
Develop students' ability to understand the author's purpose with the Reading Strategy annotations (SE pp. 543, 547; ATE pp. 543, 547)	5 min.
ASSESS	
Assess Mastery	
Assess students' mastery of the Reading Strategy and Literary Analysis by having them answer the Review and Assess questions (SE/ATE p. 549)	25 min.
Use one or more of the print and media Assessment Resources (ATE p. 551) A	up to 45 min.
EXTEND	
Apply Understanding	
Have students complete the Vocabulary Development Lesson and the Grammar Lesson (SE p. 550) A	20 min.
Apply students' ability to write letters to authors using the Writing Lesson (SE/ATE p. 551) A	45 min.
Apply students' understanding using one or more of the Extension Activities (SE p. 551)	30–90 min.

ACCELERATED INSTRUCTION:
Use the strategies and activities identified with an A.

UNIVERSAL ACCESS
● = Below Level Students
▲ = On-Level Students
■ = Above Level Students

Time and Resource Manager

Reading Level: Easy, Average
Average Number of Instructional Days: 4

	RESOURCES		
	PRINT	TRANSPARENCIES	TECHNOLOGY
	• **Beyond Literature,** Workplace Skills: Setting Priorities, p. 32 ▲ ■		• **Interest Grabber Videotapes,** Tape 4 ● ▲ ■
	• **Selection Support Workbook:** ● ▲ ■ Literary Analysis, p. 160 Reading Strategy, p. 159 Build Vocabulary, p. 156	• **Literary Analysis and Reading Transparencies,** pp. 63 and 64 ● ▲ ■	
			• **Listening to Literature** ● ▲ ■ Audiocassettes, Side 19 Audio CDs, CD 9
	• **Literary Analysis for Enrichment** ■	• **Fine Art Transparencies, Volume 1,** Transparency 4 ● ▲ ■	
	• **Formal Assessment:** Selection Test, pp. 142–144 ● ▲ ■ • **Open Book Test,** pp. 94–96 ● ▲ ■ • **Performance Assessment and Portfolio Management,** pp. 15, 27 ● ▲ ■ • PRENTICE HALL ASSESSMENT SYSTEM ● ▲ ■	• PRENTICE HALL ASSESSMENT SYSTEM ● ▲ ■ Skills Practice Answers and Explanations on Transparencies	• **Test Bank Software** ● ▲ ■ • **Got It! Assessment Videotapes,** Tape 4 ● ▲
	• **Selection Support Workbook:** ● ▲ ■ Build Spelling Skills, p. 157 Build Grammar Skills, p. 158 • **Writing and Grammar,** Copper Level ● ▲ ■ • **Extension Activities,** p. 32 ● ▲ ■	• **Daily Language Practice Transparencies** ● ▲ • **Writing Models and Graphic Organizers on Transparencies** ● ▲ ■	• **Writing and Grammar iText CD-ROM** ● ▲ ■ ***Take It to the Net*** www.phschool.com

BLOCK SCHEDULING: Use one 90-minute class period to preteach the selection and have students read it. Use a second 90-minute class period to assess students' mastery of skills and have them complete one of the Extension Activities.

PRETEACH

Step-by-Step Teaching Guide for pp. 540–541

Motivation

Ask students why people write friendly letters and keep daily journals. Encourage the class to explain what people write in these documents. Then, pose this question: If you could read the letters or journals of anyone, who would it be and why? Steer the discussion toward famous people. Ask students what they might hope to learn from reading the private documents and why they would enjoy it. Then tell students that they are about to read a letter by a famous writer and a journal entry by an Olympic gold medalist.

Interest Grabber Video

As an alternative, play "History of the Modern Olympics" on Tape 4 to engage student interest.

❶ Background

Social Studies

In "Olympic Diary" (p. 545), Amanda Borden uses her journal entries as a means to chronicle what she considers important events in her life. Many famous people, such as Captain James Cook and Anne Frank, documented their lives and thoughts in journals that have been published.

Prepare to Read

❶ Letter to Scottie ◆ Olympic Diary

Take It to the Net

Visit www.phschool.com for interactive activities and instruction related to these selections, including

- background
- graphic organizers
- literary elements
- reading strategies

Preview

Connecting to the Literature

The letter and journal entries in this group capture the personal side—the thoughts and feelings—of two famous people, in this case, a well-known author and an athlete. While reading, look for ways in which the cares and concerns of these famous people are similar to those of "ordinary" people.

Background

Letters and journals are not usually written for a public audience. Sometimes, however, a person may keep a journal when traveling or during an interesting time period with the intention of allowing others to read it. Letters of historical or literary figures are sometimes published (with permission) to give personal insights into the person's life.

TEACHING RESOURCES

The following resources can be used to enrich or extend the instruction for pp. 540–541.

Motivation

Interest Grabber Video, Tape 4

Background

Beyond Literature, p. 32

Take It to the Net

Visit www.phschool.com for Background and hotlinks for the selections.

Literary Analysis

Literary Analysis and Reading Transparencies, Letters and Journals, p. 64

Reading

Selection Support: Reading Strategy, p. 159; Build Vocabulary, p. 156

Literary Analysis and Reading Transparencies, Understanding the Author's Purpose, p. 63

BLOCK SCHEDULING: Resources marked with this symbol provide varied instruction during 90-minute blocks.

❷ Literary Analysis

Letters and Journals

A **letter** is a written communication, usually from one person to another. In personal letters, the writer shares information, thoughts, and feelings with one other person. A **journal** is a daily account of events and the writer's thoughts and feelings about those events. As you read these two works, notice that the language is less formal than in most other kinds of writing.

Comparing Literary Works

The letter and the journal in this group are both examples of personal writing—they include details about the writers' thoughts and feelings. However, the works are intended for different **audiences,** or readers. Although now published, "Letter to Scottie" was originally written by F. Scott Fitzgerald to his daughter. Amanda Borden's Olympic Diary was written for a wider audience. She kept a record of her experiences to publish and share with the general public. Compare and contrast the letter and the journal by answering the following focus questions:

1. How much or how little background information does each writer give about his or her experiences?
2. In what way might the difference in the amount of background material be related to the intended audience for each work?

❸ Reading Strategy

Understanding the Author's Purpose

An **author's purpose** is his or her reason for writing. Fitzgerald's purposes in writing his letter to his daughter, Scottie, are to encourage her to do her best and also to show his affection. The following example includes details and language that indicate his purpose of encouraging his daughter to do her best.

Example: I feel very strongly about you doing [your] duty. Would you give me a little more documentation about your reading in French?

Use an organizer like the one shown here to record details that will help you understand each author's purpose.

Vocabulary Development

documentation (däk´ yōō mən tā´ shən) *n.* supporting evidence (p. 543)

intrigued (in trēgd´) *adj.* fascinated (p. 545)

compulsory (kəm pul´ sə rē) *adj.* must be done; having specific requirements (p. 546)

CUSTOMIZE INSTRUCTION FOR UNIVERSAL ACCESS

For Less Proficient Readers	For English Learners	For Advanced Readers
To increase students' understanding of the writer's voice in a letter or journal entry, play recordings of the reading selections. Ask students as they listen to imagine what kind of person wrote the letter or journal entry. Have students write a short description of the writer, and discuss students' impressions.	To help students get more comfortable with less formal writing, have each student write either a letter to a friend or a journal entry including actual or imaginary events for a recent day. Tell students to save the letters or journal entries and to read them after they finish the selection, noting similar elements between the selection and their writing.	Before students read, ask them to identify a few purposes or reasons for writing letters or journal entries. Engage students in a discussion of how people write in letters and journals, as opposed to essays or novels. Have students research the style of a published author of journals or letters, and then have them share their findings with the class.

❷ Literary Analysis

Letters and Journals

- Before asking students to read the instruction, ask them to tell what they would include in 9 letters to 9 friends.
  Possible response: Students will probably say that they would include details about what is happening in their lives.
- Then, ask students what they would write in a journal.
  Possible response: Students will probably say that they would write about their thoughts and feelings, special events in their lives, and their hopes and dreams.
- Have students read the instruction about letters and journals. Make sure that they understand the differences.
- Use the Letters and Journals transparency on p. 64 in **Literary Analysis and Reading Transparencies** to show how writers reveal their feelings through letters and journals.

❸ Reading Strategy

Understanding the Author's Purpose

- Point out that every writer, your students included, has a purpose when he or she writes. A common purpose is to share ideas. Another purpose is to teach or instruct.
- After students read the instruction, guide them through the graphic organizer in the margin of p. 541. Point out that, as readers, they should pay attention not only to what the writer says but also to the way he or she says it.

Vocabulary Development

- Review the words and definitions on the vocabulary list.
- Call students' attention to the word *documentation,* and ask them to think of a similiar word with a related meaning. Help students understand that a *documentary* is a program that presents and supports facts about a subject.

E-Teach

Visit E-Teach at www.phschool.com for teachers' essays on how to teach, with questions and answers.

TEACH

Step-by-Step Teaching Guide for pp. 542–548

CUSTOMIZE INSTRUCTION
For Musical/Rhythmic Learners

Point out to students that the text of F. Scott Fitzgerald's letter to his daughter contains repetition that would lend itself nicely to the lyrics of a song or to a verse of poetry. Challenge students to write a brief song or rhythmic poem that incorporates Fitzgerald's words into the lyrics or stanzas. Ask students to perform or read the work for the class.

❶ About the Selection

In "Letter to Scottie," F. Scott Fitzgerald advises his daughter to live a virtuous life and develop her talents. While keeping a humorous tone, Fitzgerald supplies Scottie with a thoughtful and practical list of "Things to worry about" and "Things not to worry about." He ends his correspondence with a witty reprimand for Scottie, who refers to him as "Pappy." If she persists, Fitzgerald says, he may peg her with the name "Egg," an embarrassing title she will have difficulty shaking off.

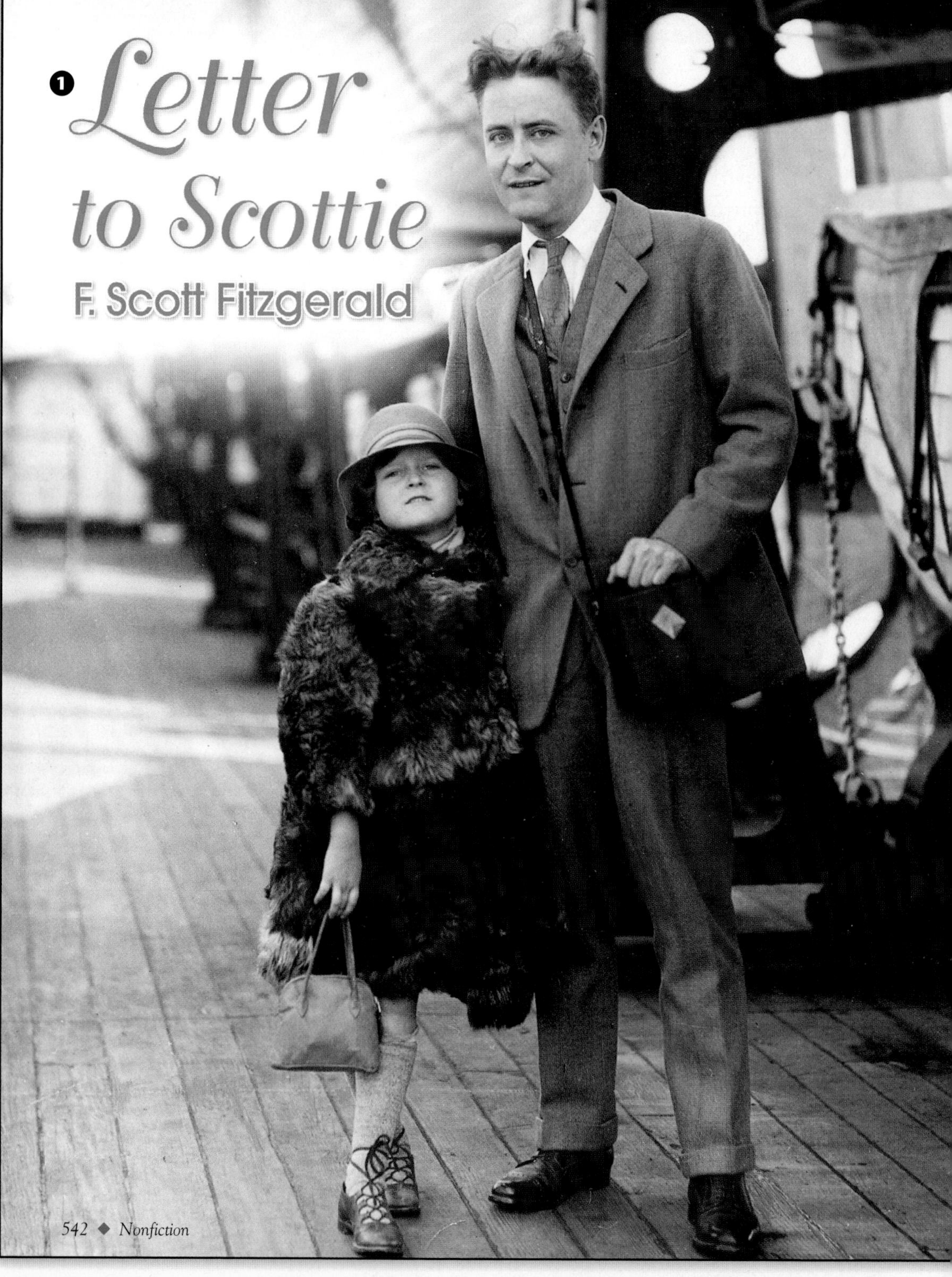

542 ◆ *Nonfiction*

TEACHING RESOURCES

The following resources can be used to enrich or extend the instruction for pp. 542–548.

Literary Analysis

- **Selection Support:** Literary Analysis, p. 160
- **Literary Analysis for Enrichment**
- **Writing Models and Graphic Organizers on Transparencies,** p. 77 ▪

Reading

- **Literatura en español**
- **Listening to Literature Audiocassettes,** Side 19
- **Listening to Literature Audio CDs,** CD 9

Enrichment

- **Fine Art Transparencies, Volume 1,** Art Transparency 4 (Have students discuss the ways in which the artist uses color and form to show the energy of the gymnast.) ▪

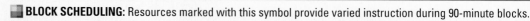

▪ **BLOCK SCHEDULING:** Resources marked with this symbol provide varied instruction during 90-minute blocks.

La Paix, Rodgers' Forge
Towson, Maryland
August 8, 1933

Dear Pie:[1]

2 3 I feel very strongly about you doing [your] duty. Would you give me a little more documentation about your reading in French? I am glad you are happy—but I never believe much in happiness. I never believe in misery either. Those are things you see on the stage or the screen or the printed page, they never really happen to you in life.

All I believe in in life is the rewards for virtue (according to your talents) and the *punishments* for not fulfilling your duties, which are doubly costly. If there is such a volume in the camp library, will you ask Mrs. Tyson to let you look up a sonnet of Shakespeare's in which the line occurs *"Lilies that fester smell far worse than weeds."*

Have had no thoughts today, life seems composed of getting up a *Saturday Evening Post*[2] story. I think of you, and always pleasantly; but if you call me "Pappy" again I am going to take the White Cat out and beat his bottom *hard, six times for every time you are impertinent.* Do you react to that?

I will arrange the camp bill.

Halfwit, I will conclude.

Things to worry about:

Worry about courage
Worry about cleanliness
Worry about efficiency
Worry about horsemanship
Worry about . . .

Things not to worry about:

Don't worry about popular opinion
Don't worry about dolls
Don't worry about the past
Don't worry about the future
Don't worry about growing up
Don't worry about anybody getting ahead of you
Don't worry about triumph
Don't worry about failure unless it comes through your own fault
Don't worry about mosquitoes
Don't worry about flies
Don't worry about insects in general

documentation (däk′ yoo mən tā′ shən) *n.* supporting evidence

Reading Strategy
Understanding the Author's Purpose
How does the first sentence of the letter establish the author's purpose for writing the letter?

4 **Reading Check**
Who is writing to whom?

1. **Pie** affectionate nickname for his daughter, Frances Scott Fitzgerald, also known as Scottie, who was away at summer camp.
2. ***Saturday Evening Post*** a weekly magazine.

5 **Critical Viewing** What details in the letter indicate the affection that is shown between Fitzgerald and his daughter in this picture? **[Support]**

2 Reading Strategy

Understanding the Author's Purpose

- Remind students that in a letter the writer uses the first-person *I*. Tell students that in a letter, the writer will be clear about why he or she is writing.
- Ask students the Reading Strategy question on p. 543: How does the first sentence of the letter establish the author's purpose for writing the letter?
  Answer: Clearly, Fitzgerald wants to talk to his daughter about the concept of duty.
- Explain to students that a letter may have more than one purpose, especially if it is an informal one. A letter writer may wish to instruct, to express ideas or feelings, or to persuade. Challenge students to find other purposes in this letter.

3 Vocabulary Development

Forms of *document*

- Point out that the word *document*, the root of *documentation*, can be used as a verb or a noun. The suffix *–ation*, which means "state or condition," makes the word *document* a noun.
- Ask students to identify the documentation that Scottie might give to her father.
  Possible responses: Students may say that she could give him assignments, tests, homework, grades, or a letter from her teacher.

4 Reading Check

Answer: F. Scott Fitzgerald is writing to his daughter Scottie.

5 Critical Viewing

Answer: The loving insults that the father and daughter pass on to one another ("Pappy," "Halfwit," and "Egg") suggest that they are close to one another, just as they are in the photograph.

CUSTOMIZE INSTRUCTION FOR UNIVERSAL ACCESS

For Special Needs Students	For English Learners	For Gifted/Talented Students
After reading Fitzgerald's "worry" list, have students form small teams to list five things today's young people should worry about and five things they should not. Suggest that students use a two-column chart to list their ideas.	Encourage students to pretend that their own parents or guardians revised one of the lists from the selection "Letter to Scottie." Ask them what would be the same and what would be different on these lists. Discuss the differences among cultures represented in the class.	Have students look at the photograph on p. 542 and make generalizations about Fitzgerald, his daughter, and his life, basing opinions on what they see. Encourage students to use the posture, expressions, clothing, background, and time of day shown to build a story about the moment captured in the photograph.

Answers for p. 544

Review and Assess

1. Students may suggest that they would enjoy receiving a letter that offered advice in such a playful and affectionate way.
2. **(a)** Scottie's nickname for her father is "Pappy." **(b)** He is clearly insulted by the name and threatens to beat her cat and to call her "Egg" if she ever calls him by the name again. **(c)** The relationship seems honest, affectionate, and playful.
3. **(a)** The main message is not to worry about little things but to be a good and healthy person. **(b)** Fitzgerald indicates that virtue and duty are important. He also mentions courage, cleanliness, efficiency, horsemanship, scholarship, and health as important qualities. **(c)** Possible responses: Scottie would probably think the letter has good advice because it can help guide her in life. The letter may even be in response to a question she had and may provide her with an answer.
4. Possible response: Students may suggest that courage is the most important item on the list because it is something everyone needs in order to make the right choices in life.

Don't worry about parents
Don't worry about boys
Don't worry about disappointments
Don't worry about pleasures
Don't worry about satisfactions
Things to think about:
What am I really aiming at?
How good am I really in comparison to my contemporaries in regard to:
(a) Scholarship
(b) Do I really understand about people and am I able to get along with them?
(c) Am I trying to make my body a useful instrument or am I neglecting it?

With dearest love,
[Daddy]

P.S. My come-back to your calling me Pappy is christening you by the word Egg, which implies that you belong to a very rudimentary state of life and that I could break you up and crack you open at my will and I think it would be a word that would hang on if I ever told it to your contemporaries. "Egg Fitzgerald." How would you like that to go through life with—"Eggie Fitzgerald" or "Bad Egg Fitzgerald" or any form that might occur to fertile minds? Try it once more and I swear I will hang it on you and it will be up to you to shake it off. Why borrow trouble?

Love anyhow.

Review and Assess

Thinking About the Selections

1. **Respond:** How would you react if you received this letter?
2. **(a) Recall:** What is Scottie's nickname for her father? **(b) Infer:** How does he feel about this, and how do you know? **(c) Speculate:** What kind of relationship do you think Fitzgerald had with his daughter?
3. **(a) Recall:** What is Fitzgerald's main message to Scottie? **(b) Infer:** What qualities does Fitzgerald indicate are important? **(c) Speculate:** How do you think Scottie would respond to this letter? Why?
4. **Evaluate:** Which item on Fitzgerald's list of things to worry about do you think is most important? Explain.

F. Scott Fitzgerald

(1896–1940)

A descendant of the author of "The Star-Spangled Banner," Francis Scott Key Fitzgerald was born in Minnesota, educated at Princeton University, and served in the army. At the age of twenty-three, he published his first novel, *This Side of Paradise.* Fitzgerald married and had a daughter, Scottie. Frances (Scottie) spent much of her childhood in boarding schools and at camps. F. Scott Fitzgerald died at the age of forty-four.

CUSTOMIZE INSTRUCTION FOR UNIVERSAL ACCESS

For Less Proficient Readers	For Gifted/Talented Students
Bring in examples of different types of letters, such as solicitations, invitations, business letters, and informal letters. Place students in small groups, and hand out the letters randomly. Offer students several categories of letters to choose from, including persuasive, expressive, and informational. Then, ask students to read the letters and identify the purpose of each one. Ask each group to talk about its letter[s]. Guide students to understand how tone and word choice shape the purpose of a letter.	Each student will have a better understanding of the letter's writer if he or she performs the letter as a dramatic monologue. Invite students to read the letter for clues to the life of F. Scott Fitzgerald. Students may also do outside research. Then, individual students should practice delivering the letter in a voice that fits the writer's own character. After students perform, ask them about the choices they made in their delivery.

6 # OLYMPIC DIARY

Amanda Borden

March 22, 1996

Growing up, I couldn't decide which sport I liked the best. My first sport was T-ball. I wasn't very good. I had trouble hitting the ball and even more trouble catching it. So I moved on to soccer. I was pretty good at that, but I got bored when I didn't have the ball. Then came ballet. When I saw the girls leaping and jumping in beautiful tutus, I fell in love. I really enjoyed dancing and performing. But
7 after many recitals and shows, I was ready for a new challenge.

A friend of the family suggested gymnastics. Wow, did my life change! I was 7 years old when I started and absolutely intrigued with Mary Lou Retton. I watched her in the 1984 Olympics and thought she was amazing. I never really thought I could do the things she did or even have a chance to be in the Olympics like she was. All I knew is that it looked like a lot of fun.

intrigued (in trēgd′) *adj.* fascinated

8 **✓Reading Check**

What is Amanda Borden's sport?

9 **▼Critical Viewing** What qualities do you think these gymnasts share that helped them become Olympic gold medalists? **[Speculate]**

6 About the Selection

In "Olympic Diary," gymnast Amanda Borden recalls the efforts it has taken her to reach the 1996 Olympics. She describes her childhood gymnastics experiences as well as injuries and setbacks. In the end, her persistence and courage pay off.

7 Critical Thinking

Analyze

- After students read the first two paragraphs, ask them to characterize Borden's feelings about the sports and activities she has tried. Answer: She has fun at first, even when she is not very good, but she quickly tires of them and moves on.
- Then, ask students to predict what will happen when Borden tries gymnastics. Possible responses: Students may suggest that Borden will find gymnastics to be exactly what she has been looking for.
- If students have trouble with the prediction, suggest they use the photograph on p. 545 to help them.

8 ✓Reading Check

Answer: Amanda Borden's sport is gymnastics.

9 ▶Critical Viewing

Answer: Students may suggest qualities such as determination, strength, endurance, and athletic ability.

CUSTOMIZE INSTRUCTION FOR UNIVERSAL ACCESS

For Less Proficient Readers	For English Learners
Explain to students that Amanda Borden's journal is a chronology of events. Have students complete a timeline of the events mentioned in the journal. Offer them the Timeline transparency on p. 77 in **Writing Models and Graphic Organizers on Transparencies,** and ask them to plot out key events in Borden's life. Point out that the diary format helps by providing dates for the timeline. To reinforce the learning, encourage students to add symbols, slogans, and graphics that represent ideas and events.	Students may struggle with the specialized vocabulary in the selection. Have students work in pairs and read p. 545 for unfamiliar or difficult words. After students jot down the words, allow them time to consult the dictionary and define the words. As they read the rest of the selection, have students continue to add words to their list. Then, bring students together and ask them to form a master list from their definitions.

⑩ Background

Sports

Although the Olympic games have their roots in ancient Greece, the games we know today have been a tradition for only about one hundred years. The original Olympic games were held to honor the Greek gods, and they featured foot races, spear throwing, and wrestling contests. The last of these games was held in A.D. 394 when the Roman emperor decided that the games glorified human achievement too much. Fifteen hundred years later, in 1896, a French noble inaugurated the first of the modern Olympic games in Athens, Greece. Gymnastics was among the sports featured there (men's gymnastics only—women did not compete in early modern games).

⑪ Reinforcing Skills

Drawing Inferences

- Ask students to consider the tone of this part of the entry.
- Remind students to look at the choice of words and the feelings Amanda may be expressing or trying not to express.
  Answer: Amanda sounds as though she may have been a little bitter but is trying to put a good face on her feelings. Of course, she must have been disappointed, but it sounds as if the experience has made her stronger.

In the beginning, I practiced one hour, one day a week. That lasted one week. My coaches moved me up to training two hours a day, three days a week. I was in the Junior Elite Testing program, where they measured physical strength and flexibility as well as basic gymnastics skills. If your scores were high enough, you qualified for a national-level training camp.

I went to Tennessee for a week. It was my first time away from home and I didn't like it.

By the time I was 10, gymnastics had become a part of me. I was in the gym 12 hours a week—and loving every minute of it. I began competing at the compulsory level, traveling around my home state of Ohio as well as Kentucky, Indiana and Michigan. My family went along. My older brother Bryan usually brought a friend to play in the hotel.

[Amanda began training with a new coach, and soon qualified for the USA Championships.]

I was training really hard for the biggest competition of the year. But 12 weeks before the meet, I broke my elbow. The doctors said I could compete as long as I let it heal, so I had my arm in a cast for six weeks. But when the doctor gave me the OK to start again, I pulled my hamstring. I know, it sounds like bad luck. I couldn't compete, so I began to get my body healthy again for the next year.

I was now 15 and had to compete at the Senior Elite level. That meant going up against all the big guys like Kim Zmeskal. I made the U.S. Championships and did great—finishing fifth. That qualified me for the 1992 Olympic Trials.♦ It wasn't until that point that I realized I really had a chance to make the Olympic team. I had a really good competition and finished seventh. Seven girls make the Olympic team. So you would've thought I'd have been in Barcelona.

⑪ Well, I wasn't. There were a lot of politics involved, but to make it short and sweet they put two injured athletes, who didn't compete at the trials, on the team, and bumped Kim, Kelly and me off. It was disappointing, but life goes on. I didn't quit.

[At the end of 1995, Amanda broke her toe and her hand. Once again, she had to stop training and competing to allow her body to heal.]

Literature in context — Social Studies Connection

⑩ ♦ ***Qualifying for the Olympics*** In competition for gymnastics, the sessions are given numbers, and each session is judged by different rules. The sessions, in order, are the Team compulsories, Team optionals, All-around finals, and Event finals. A gymnast is required to do more difficult exercises in the last competitions to achieve the "start value" of 10.0. A start value is the maximum score that a gymnast can receive for a routine before any deductions are taken for errors.

In the Olympic Games, the top 36 gymnasts qualify for all-around finals with three gymnasts per country. In the event finals, the top eight qualify on each apparatus, with a maximum of two gymnasts per country. In the all-around and event finals, the gymnasts start over with a score of zero.

compulsory (kəm pulʹ sə rē) *adj.* must be done; having specific requirements

CUSTOMIZE INSTRUCTION FOR UNIVERSAL ACCESS

For Gifted/Talented Readers	For Advanced Readers
Have students invite a gymnast or a gymnastics instructor from their school or community center to the class to demonstrate a gymnastic routine and to answer questions. Ask students to prepare questions in advance. After the demonstration and interview, ask students to write an article about the event for the school newspaper. As a follow-up, have students write thank-you letters to the guest.	Encourage interested students to search the Internet for information about the Olympic sport of their choice. Then, ask each student to write a brief essay about the history of the selected sport. Students should address the following points in their essays: • When the sport was accepted into the Olympics • What athletes/countries have won medals in it • Why the sport interests them Ask students to post their essays in the classroom.

April 12, 1996

12 Four weeks ago, I got the go-ahead to start practicing again and, let me tell you, I was more than ready to get back on the mat. I began training and—slowly—I got everything back. Two weeks later, I was able to compete at the Budget Gymnastics Invitational (United States vs. France). It was going to be my first competition in a year. I was so excited I could not wait!

I flew to Miami and had a wonderful time. The women only were able to compete on bars, beam and floor—and you didn't have to compete in every event if you didn't want to.

We had four people on the team, and three had to compete in each event. I had planned on competing on the beam and floor.

The day before the competition, I was asked to compete on bars. I had only been practicing for two weeks, but I was honored to compete for the USA.

The competition was great! On bars, I got a 9.725. I had to water down my routine a little because I had not been training for my full routine, so I was pleased with that score—even with an easy dismount.

We then went to the beam. I was second up and extremely confident. I went up and rocked a set—my score was 9.775.

13 Our next event was the floor. I have a new routine and was excited to let everybody see it. I had to water down my tumbling passes, too, because I did not have enough time to get them ready. My first pass was a double Arabian, which is two flips in the air with a half-twist on the first flip. I had a little too much energy and ran out of bounds—but I was happy to be on my feet. My second pass was a two-and-a-half twist. That went great! I finished with a front full punch front, and that was good, too. I received a 9.512, which isn't the best score I've ever received, but I was happy to be back in competition.

I did it! I had a great meet! I felt so good! I was back, the people still remembered me and I did wonderfully!

I look back now and the injuries seem so small. When I had to deal with them, I felt like I was holding the world. After I competed, I felt I was on top of it.

Unfortunately, everyone goes through tough times, but those tough times only make the good times even better. You may think I have had my share of bad luck. I have thought that at some times, too. But when I look back on my gymnastics career, the places I've been, the people I've met and the things I've learned—the good far outweighs the bad.

Reading Strategy
Understand the Author's Purpose What was the author's purpose in recording these entries?

Literary Analysis
Letters and Journals and Author's Style What word choices and expressions give Amanda's journal a style that reflects her personality?

14 **✓Reading Check**
What prevents Amanda from doing her full routine at the meet in Miami?

CUSTOMIZE INSTRUCTION FOR UNIVERSAL ACCESS

For Special Needs Students	For English Learners
Students may benefit from a quick review of what makes language informal. Explain that informal language involves the use of the first person, contractions, and words one would use in conversation. Ask students to list all the examples of conversational language they can find on pp. 546–547. After students compile their lists, ask them what they can infer about the writer from her choices of words.	Students will benefit from a discussion of word choice and connotation. Select a few words from pp. 546–547, and ask students to think about the feelings that are associated with the words. Then, challenge them to think of synonyms that have different connotations. Ask them to plug the synonyms into the sentences and to talk about the effect the new word has on the meaning of the sentence. You might wish to have students start with the word *great,* which Amanda uses frequently.

12 Reading Strategy
Understanding the Author's Purpose

- Remind students that usually when an individual is writing in a journal, he or she does not think about how others will react to his or her thoughts. Although Amanda wrote her journal with publication in mind, it was also important for her to be honest and open about her experiences.
- Then, ask students the Reading Strategy question on p. 547.
  Possible response: Amanda may be writing to deal with her disappointment. She may also be writing to remind herself of what is important.

13 Literary Analysis
Letters and Journals

- After reading the bracketed passage, ask students to consider the way Amanda expresses herself.
- Then, ask them the Literary Analysis question on p. 547: What word choices and expressions give Amanda's journal a style that reflects her personality?
  Possible response: Students may point to Amanda's use of exclamation points and the word *great* as indicators of her enthusiasm.

Monitor Progress Ask students to define at least two differences and one similarity between a letter and a diary entry.
Possible responses: A letter is written to another person, and its purpose is to convey ideas or feelings. A journal entry is a private record written about feelings or an event. Letters and journal entries are often written in informal language.

Reteach To help students understand the informal style of letters and journals, have them choose an informal paragraph from one of the selections and rewrite it as if it were part of a formal essay.

14 ✓Reading Check

Answer: Women were allowed to compete only on bars, beam, and floor.

ASSESS

Answers for p. 548

Review and Assess

1. Possible responses: Some students may say they enjoy the challenge of a gymnastics competition. Other students may say that they lack the strength or the stamina.
2. **(a)** Amanda became involved in gymnastics. **(b)** Bad luck in the form of injuries set Amanda back in her career, but it also forced her to slow down until she was better prepared for the Olympics. **(c)** Amanda did not quit her sport even after she was bumped from the Olympic team in 1992. She also competed in the Budget Gymnastics Invitational, even though she was recovering from a previous injury.
3. **(a)** Amanda is disappointed but realistic. **(b)** She knows that life is not always fair, so she does not take the setback too hard.
4. Possible responses: Some students will say that it is worth the effort because they get to represent the United States and they are recognized for their athletic ability. Others may disagree because the training is difficult and can cause injuries.

Of course, I would like to never have to deal with problems, but I know that it will only make me a better person.

[Amanda's Olympic dream finally came true. In 1996, at the Olympic trials in Boston, Amanda claimed one of seven spots on the women's gymnastic team.]

July 21, 1996

What a whirlwind I've been on since the Olympic trials! We arrived in Atlanta at 1:30 P.M. and had processing, which took seven hours. We received lots of great clothes and other goodies. We were also measured for Olympic uniforms, which we will receive later. We finally got to our home at Emory University at 9 P.M. We're staying in a fraternity house until we are competing and then can move into the Olympic Village after that. Jaycie and I are rooming together, sharing a bathroom with Shannon Miller. We decorated our room to make it a little more "homey."

Training is going very well. We train at a private club, except when we have podium training. Tuesday, we had 22,000 cheering fans at our training. I was totally overwhelmed. You just can't imagine the feeling.

Here we are in the Georgia Dome and the Dream Team will be using the other side. I'm hoping to meet some of them. Too bad Michael Jordan isn't here. Oh well.

I was honored by being named captain of our team. I think we will do just great—everyone gets along so well and supports each other. Here's hoping we bring home the gold!

[Amanda Borden and her teammates did bring home the gold medal in 1996. The picture on page 545 shows the 1996 women's team after receiving their gold medals.]

Review and Assess

Thinking About the Selections

1. **Respond:** Would you enjoy gymnastic competition? Why or why not?
2. **(a) Recall:** What sport did Amanda Borden play? **(b) Infer:** How did bad luck play a role in her career? **(c) Support:** In what two ways did Amanda show her determination to succeed?
3. **(a) Recall:** What is Amanda's reaction to being bumped from the 1992 Olympic team? **(b) Infer:** Why does she react as she does?
4. **Make a Judgment:** Do you think becoming an Olympic gymnast is worth the effort? Why or why not?

Amanda Borden

(b. 1977)

At age seven, this Olympic-gymnast-to-be was training two hours a day, three days a week. By age ten, Borden spent twelve hours a week in the gym. By nineteen, she was the captain of the gold-medal-winning 1996 U.S. Olympic gymnastic team.

ASSESSMENT PRACTICE: Reading Comprehension

Distinguishing Between Fact and Nonfact (For more practice, see Test Preparation Workbook, p. 45.)

Many tests require students to recognize statements of fact and nonfact from written texts. Write this text on the board:

> All I believe in in life is the rewards for virtue (according to your talents) and the *punishments* for not fulfilling your duties, which are doubly costly.

Which of the following is an OPINION expressed by F. Scott Fitzgerald?

A He believes only in rewards for virtue.
B Life is difficult.
C It is important to be talented.
D It is necessary to fulfill one's duties in life.

Point out that choice *A* is a statement of fact, where *B* and *C* are not statements from the text. The correct answer is *D* because it conveys Fitzgerald's opinion.

Review and Assess

Literary Analysis

Letters and Journals

1. How can a **letter** or a **journal** be personal in ways that other kinds of writing cannot?
2. Identify examples of the language in "Letter to Scottie" and "Olympic Diary" that distinguish letters and journals from other kinds of writing.

Examples of Language	"Letter to Scottie"	"Olympic Diary"
informal		
humorous		
personal		

Comparing Literary Works

3. What is the difference between the **audiences** for which the works were written?
4. On a Venn diagram, show similarities and differences in the types of details Fitzgerald and Borden include. Consider background information, thoughts and feelings, and factual details.

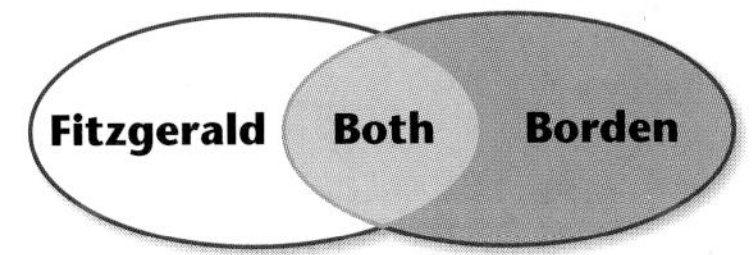

5. How do the different audiences affect the details included in each work?

Reading Strategy

Understanding the Author's Purpose

6. Explain the **purpose** for the "Letter to Scottie." Do you think Fitzgerald achieves his purpose? What details does he include to achieve that purpose?
7. What are two purposes Amanda Borden may have for writing her "Olympic Diary"? What does she include in her diary to achieve the purpose?

Extending Understanding

8. **Take a Position:** Do you think professional athletes should be allowed to compete in the Olympics? Why or why not?

Quick Review

Letters and journals are forms of communication that a writer uses to share information, thoughts, and feelings with another person. To review letters and journals, see p. 541.

Audience is the readers for whom a work is intended.

To **understand an author's purpose,** notice the language and details supported by quotes or cited material.

Take It to the Net

www.phschool.com

Take the interactive self-test online to check your understanding of these selections.

ENRICHMENT: Further Reading

Other Works by and About the Authors

Works by F. Scott Fitzgerald

The Ice Palace and Other Stories

The Great Gatsby

Works About Amanda Borden

The Magnificent Seven: The Authorized Story of American Gold

Take It to the Net

Visit www.phschool.com for more information on the authors.

Answers for p. 549

Review and Assess

1. Letters or journals allow writers to express feelings and opinions. Writers can use informal, conversational language.
2. **"Letter to Scottie" informal:** "Things to worry about: Worry about courage." **humorous:** "but if you call me 'Pappy' again I am going to take the White Cat out and beat his bottom *hard, six times for every time you are impertinent.* Do you react to that?" **personal:** "Would you give me a little more documentation about your reading in French?" **"Olympic Diary" informal:** "That lasted one week." **humorous:** "I had trouble hitting the ball and even more trouble catching it." **personal:** "Wow, did my life change!"
3. "Letter to Scottie" was written for the author's daughter. "Olympic Diary" was written for the author herself with publication in mind.
4. Fitzgerald reveals that he is busy but still able to think about his daughter away at camp. His list reveals concern. His response to "Pappy" suggests playfulness and perhaps vanity. Borden's exclamation points suggest enthusiasm. Descriptions of her schedule show dedication. "It was disappointing, but life goes on. I didn't quit" shows commitment. Unlike Fitzgerald, Borden includes background information. Both works include details about the authors' thoughts and feelings.
5. Since"Letter to Scottie" is a letter from the author to his daughter, there is no background information. "Olympic Diary" is Borden's attempt to record her life story, so she includes background information in addition to her thoughts and feelings.
6. Possible responses: "Letter to Scottie" may have several purposes: to share wisdom, to show concern, and to let her know not to call him certain names. He achieves his first purpose in his list. He achieves his other purposes by reminding her that he thinks of her "pleasantly" and by threatening to give her a nickname.
7. Possible response: Amanda wrote to record events and feelings. She includes statements of excitement and expressions of disappointment.
8. Possible responses: All excellent athletes should compete. Or, professionals should step aside to allow newcomers to compete.

EXTEND

Answers for p. 550

❶ Vocabulary Development

Word Analysis

1. document
2. documentary
3. documentation

Spelling Strategy

1. plague 2. vague

Concept Development: Synonyms

1. c 1. documentation
2. c 2. intrigued
3. a 3. compulsory

❷ Grammar

1. Despite setbacks, (I) continued to compete in the trials. *I*—subject
2. (They) bumped Kim, Kelly, and me off. *They*—subject; *me*—direct object
3. The doctor told her the news. *her*—indirect object
4. Would (you) give me more documentation? *You*—subject; *me*—indirect object
5. (It) is she the crowd wants to see perform. *It*—subject; *she*—renames subject

Writing Application

Students should respond using at least four of the listed object pronouns and identify each as a direct or indirect object.

Integrate Language Skills

❶ Vocabulary Development Lesson

Word Analysis: Forms of *document*

Words that are related to *document*, such as *documentary* and *documentation*, usually have something to do with a record, or proof. Write the form of *document* that fits each description.

1. A piece of written proof
2. A visual record of an event or time period
3. A collection of evidence

Spelling Strategy

In some words, like *intrigue*, the *g* sound is spelled *gue*. On your paper, unscramble the letters to make words that end with *gue*.

1. disease: gluape
2. unclear: vugae

Concept Development: Synonyms

Synonyms are words that have almost the same meaning. On your paper, write the synonym of the vocabulary word.

1. documentation: **(a)** paper, **(b)** interest, **(c)** proof
2. compulsory: **(a)** suggested, **(b)** interesting, **(c)** required
3. intrigued: **(a)** curious, **(b)** disgusted, **(c)** confused

Rewrite each sentence, replacing the underlined word with a synonym from the vocabulary words.

1. We need records of her scores.
2. They were fascinated by her story.
3. The mandatory exercises are difficult.

❷ Grammar Lesson

Subject and Object Pronouns

To name or rename the subject of a sentence, use a **subject pronoun**. The subject pronouns are *I, you, he, she, it, we, you,* and *they*. The object pronouns are *me, you, him, her, them,* and *us*.

Subject: *They* tried to standardize the game.
Rename Subject: It was *I* who batted last.
Direct Object: That qualified *her* for the Olympics.
Indirect Object: The doctor gave *her* the okay to start again.

Use an **object pronoun** for a **direct object** (receives the action of the verb) or an **indirect object** (person or thing to which or for which an action is performed).

Prentice Hall Writing and Grammar Connection: Chapter 23

Practice Copy the following sentences. Circle each subject pronoun. Underline each object pronoun. Then, tell how each pronoun is used.

1. Despite setbacks, I continued to compete in the trials.
2. They bumped Kim, Kelly, and me off.
3. The doctor told her the news.
4. Would you give me more documentation?
5. Is it she the crowd wants to see perform?

Writing Application Write a brief journal entry that uses at least four subject and object pronouns. Use the object pronouns as direct and indirect objects. State how each pronoun is used.

TEACHING RESOURCES

The following resources can be used to enrich or extend the instruction for pp. 550–551.

Vocabulary

Selection Support: Build Vocabulary, p. 156; Build Spelling Skills, p. 157

Vocabulary and Spelling Practice Book (Use this booklet for skills enrichment) ■

Grammar

Selection Support: Build Grammar Skills, p. 158

Writing and Grammar, Copper Level, pp. 508–509

Daily Language Practice Transparencies

Writing

Writing and Grammar, Copper Level, p. 250 ■

Writing Models and Graphic Organizers on Transparencies, p. 3

Writing and Grammar iText CD-ROM

■ **BLOCK SCHEDULING:** Resources marked with this symbol provide varied instruction during 90-minute blocks.

❸ Writing Lesson

Letter to an Author

One way to respond to literature is to write a letter to an author. Even if you never mail your letter, the form allows you to express your reactions in a direct way. Write a letter to F. Scott Fitzgerald in which you respond to the letter he wrote to his daughter. Tell whether or not you find his advice useful for students your age.

Prewriting On a photocopy of Fitzgerald's letter, mark parts you will use as examples of advice that is or is not useful.

Drafting Begin with a sentence that states your overall reaction. Do not use the words "I am writing to you because . . ." In the body of your letter, develop the reasons for your overall reaction and give examples.

Model: Appropriate Beginnings

Dear Mr. Fitzgerald,

Your advice to your daughter may have been useful in the 1930s, but some of your ideas just don't apply in the twenty-first century.

In the first sentence, the writer directly states the overall reaction. In later sentences and paragraphs she will support her response with examples from the work.

Revising Look for statements that are not supported by examples, and revise by adding an example.

WG Prentice Hall Writing and Grammar Connection: Chapter 12, Section 2

❹ Extension Activities

Listening and Speaking The list of things to worry about and not worry about identifies potential problems F. Scott Fitzgerald's daughter, Scottie, may be trying to solve. Identify one of the problems and give an **oral presentation** on how she or another student her age might solve the problem.

Writing As Amanda Borden, write a **journal entry** about how you feel after your team wins the gold medal. Include details about how you, as Amanda, have worked to achieve this goal.

Research and Technology With a group, prepare a **presentation** on the Olympics. Group members can choose from the following tasks:

- research the history of the Olympics
- create a map of Olympic sites
- prepare posters showing athletic events
- research new sports and future changes

Use a variety of electronic resources, such as the library card catalog, CD-ROMs, and the Internet, to conduct research.

Take It to the Net www.phschool.com

Go online for an additional research activity using the Internet.

ASSESSMENT RESOURCES

The following resources can be used to assess students' knowledge and skills.

Selection Assessment

- **Formal Assessment,** pp. 142–144
- **Open Book Test,** pp. 94–96
- **Got It! Assessment Videotapes,** Tape 4
- **Test Bank Software**

Take It to the Net

Visit www.phschool.com for self-tests and additional questions on the selections.

Writing Rubric

- **Performance Assess. and Portfolio Mgmt.,** p. 15

Listening and Speaking Rubric

- **Performance Assess. and Portfolio Mgmt.,** p. 27

PRENTICE HALL ASSESSMENT SYSTEM

- **Workbook**
- **Transparencies**
- **Skill Book**
- **CD-ROM**

Lesson Support for p. 551

❸ Writing Lesson

- After students read the instruction on p. 551, remind them about the elements of a letter—date, greeting, body, closing, signature. Bring in examples of informal letters for students to see and use as models. Or use the Personal Letter transparency on p. 3 of **Writing Models and Graphic Organizers on Transparencies.**
- Point out that the letter for this assignment has the purpose of expressing a personal reaction and supporting it with details. Suggest that before writing, students talk to a partner or write a journal entry about their reactions to "Letter to Scottie."
- As students begin to write, talk about the tone of their letters. Students should express themselves with respect.
- Use the Response to Literature rubric on p. 15 in **Performance Assessment and Portfolio Management** to assess students' responses.

❹ Listening and Speaking

- Have students review the list of things to worry and not worry about in "Letter to Scottie."
- For their presentations, tell students to choose the problems they have the best solutions for.
- Use the Speaking rubric on p. 27 in **Performance Assessment and Portfolio Management** to assess persuasiveness.

CUSTOMIZE INSTRUCTION For Universal Access

To address different learning styles, use the activities suggested in the **Extension Activities** booklet, p. 32.

- For Visual/Spatial Learners, use Activity 5.
- For Logical/Mathematical Learners, use Activity 6.
- For Verbal/Linguistic and Musical/Rhythmic Learners, use Activity 7.

My Papa, Mark Twain ✦ The Drive-In Movies ✦ Space Shuttle *Challenger*

Lesson Objectives

1. **To analyze and respond to literary elements**
   - Literary Analysis: Biography and Autobiography
   - Comparing Literary Works
2. **To read, comprehend, analyze, and critique nonfiction**
   - Reading Strategy: Identifying Author's Evidence
   - Reading Check Questions
   - Review and Assess Questions
   - Assessment Practice (ATE)
3. **To develop word analysis skills, fluency, and systematic vocabulary**
   - Vocabulary Development Lesson: Word Analysis: Latin Root *-sequi-*
4. **To understand and apply written and oral language conventions**
   - Spelling Strategy
   - Grammar Lesson: Writing Proper Nouns
5. **To understand and apply appropriate writing and research strategies**
   - Writing Lesson: Autobiographical Narrative
   - Extension Activity: Character Poster
   - Extension Activity: Response
6. **To understand and apply listening and speaking strategies**
   - Extension Activity: Informal Presentation

STEP-BY-STEP TEACHING GUIDE	PACING GUIDE
PRETEACH	
Motivate Students and Provide Background	
Use the Motivation activity (ATE p. 552)	5 min.
Read and discuss the Preview material and Background information (SE/ATE p. 552) [A]	10 min.
Introduce the Concepts	
Introduce the Literary Analysis and Reading Strategy (SE/ATE p. 553) [A]	15 min.
Pronounce the vocabulary words and read their definitions (SE p. 553)	5 min.
TEACH	
Monitor Comprehension	
Informally monitor comprehension by circulating while students read independently or in groups [A]	35–40 min.
Monitor students' comprehension with the Reading Check notes (SE/ATE pp. 555, 559, 563, 565)	as students read
Develop vocabulary with Vocabulary notes (SE pp. 555, 563–565; ATE p. 555)	as students read
Develop Understanding	
Develop students' understanding of biography and autobiography with the Literary Analysis annotations (SE pp. 555, 556, 560, 563, 565; ATE pp. 555, 556, 560, 563, 565) [A]	5 min.
Develop students' understanding of author's evidence with the Reading Strategy annotations (SE p. 564; ATE pp. 555, 559, 564)	5 min.
ASSESS	
Assess Mastery	
Assess students' mastery of the Reading Strategy and Literary Analysis by having them answer the Review and Assess questions (SE/ATE p. 567)	25 min.
Use one or more of the print and media Assessment Resources (ATE p. 569) [A]	up to 45 min.
EXTEND	
Apply Understanding	
Have students complete the Vocabulary Development Lesson and the Grammar Lesson (SE p. 568) [A]	20 min.
Apply students' ability to write an autobiographical narrative using the Writing Lesson (SE/ATE p. 569) [A]	45 min.
Apply students' understanding using one or more of the Extension Activities (SE p. 569)	20–90 min.

ACCELERATED INSTRUCTION:
Use the strategies and activities identified with an [A].

UNIVERSAL ACCESS
● = Below Level Students
▲ = On-Level Students
■ = Above Level Students

Time and Resource Manager

Reading Level: Average, Easy, Challenging
Average Number of Instructional Days: 4

RESOURCES		
PRINT	**TRANSPARENCIES**	**TECHNOLOGY**
• **Beyond Literature,** Humanities Connection: Comic Movies, p. 33 ▲ ■		• **Interest Grabber Videotapes,** Tape 4 ● ▲ ■
• **Selection Support Workbook:** ● ▲ ■ Literary Analysis, p. 165 Reading Strategy, p. 164 Build Vocabulary, p. 161	• **Literary Analysis and Reading Transparencies,** pp. 65 and 66 ● ▲ ■	
• **Adapted Reader's Companion** ● • **Reader's Companion** ● • **Authors In Depth,** Copper Level, p. 132 ■		• **Listening to Literature** ● ▲ ■ Audiocassettes, Sides 19, 20 Audio CDs, CDs 9, 10
• **English Learner's Companion** ● ▲ • **Literary Analysis for Enrichment** ■		
• **Formal Assessment:** Selection Test, pp. 145–147 ● ▲ ■ • **Open Book Test,** pp. 94–96 ● ▲ ■ • **Performance Assessment and Portfolio Management,** p. 8 ● ▲ ■ • PRENTICE HALL ASSESSMENT SYSTEM ● ▲ ■	• PRENTICE HALL ASSESSMENT SYSTEM ● ▲ ■ Skills Practice Answers and Explanations on Transparencies	• **Test Bank Software** ● ▲ ■ • **Got It! Assessment Videotapes,** Tape 4 ● ▲
• **Selection Support Workbook:** ● ▲ ■ Build Spelling Skills, p. 162 Build Grammar Skills, p. 163 • **Writing and Grammar,** Copper Level ● ▲ ■ • **Extension Activities,** p. 33 ● ▲ ■	• **Daily Language Practice Transparencies** ● ▲ • **Writing Models and Graphic Organizers on Transparencies** ● ▲ ■	• **Writing and Grammar iText CD-ROM** ● ▲ ■ ***Take It to the Net*** www.phschool.com

BLOCK SCHEDULING: Use one 90-minute class period to preteach the selection and have students read it. Use a second 90-minute class period to assess students' mastery of skills and have them complete one of the Extension Activities.

PRETEACH

Step-by-Step Teaching Guide for pp. 552–553

Motivation

Ask students to think about a person they know who has a good side few people see—for example, a neighbor who may be grouchy to kids but donates books to the children's library. Have each student write a short character sketch that highlights this person's positive side. Ask a volunteer to read aloud his or her work. Then, turn to "My Papa, Mark Twain." Tell the class that Susy Clemens writes about her father, a man she thinks few people really know. Tell students to compare their character sketches to Susy's.

Interest Grabber Video

As an alternative, play "Gary Soto on Childhood Memories" or "Apollo 13: Disaster Avoided" on Tape 4 to engage student interest.

❶ Background

Social Studies

In the second selection, you will read Gary Soto's account of his experience at the drive-in movies. The first drive-in movie theater in the United States was opened in 1935 in Camden, New Jersey. The "theater" was a large field with 400 parking places facing a 1,200 square-foot screen. The early theaters broadcast the movies' soundtrack from one huge speaker that could disturb people living a mile away. By the mid-1940s, individual car speakers had been invented. In the 1950s, there were more than two thousand drive-in movie theaters in the country, but by 1980, the number had dropped by more than half. Today, there are only about 850 left.

Prepare to Read

❶ My Papa, Mark Twain ◆ The Drive-In Movies Space Shuttle *Challenger*

El Auto Cinema, Roberto Gil de Montes, Jan Baum Gallery

Take It to the Net

Visit www.phschool.com for interactive activities and instruction related to these selections, including

- background
- graphic organizers
- literary elements
- reading strategies

Preview

Connecting to the Literature

In these three works, the writers share important experiences from childhood and adult life. As you read, use the author's experiences and your own to think about what makes a moment or experience memorable.

Background

In the 1950s and 1960s, many people saw movies at the "drive-in," where people parked in front of a large, outdoor screen, hooked up to a listening box, and enjoyed the show. The drive-in movie was an economical way for an entire family to see a movie.

TEACHING RESOURCES

The following resources can be used to enrich or extend the instruction for pp. 552–553.

Motivation

Interest Grabber Video, Tape 4

Background

Beyond Literature, p. 33

Take It to the Net

Visit www.phschool.com for Background and hotlinks for the selections.

Literary Analysis

Literary Analysis and Reading Transparencies, Biography and Autobiography, p. 66

Reading

Selection Support: Reading Strategy, p. 164; Build Vocabulary, p. 161

Literary Analysis and Reading Transparencies, Author's Evidence, p. 65

BLOCK SCHEDULING: Resources marked with this symbol provide varied instruction during 90-minute blocks.

❷ Literary Analysis

Biography and Autobiography

A **biography** is the story of all or part of someone's life. An **autobiography** is a person's account of his or her own life and experiences. In a biography, the subject is shown from the perspective of an observer, someone who can report only how the subject acts, looks, and speaks. In autobiographical writing, the subject writes about himself or herself. The Venn diagram shows the main similarity and difference between biographical and autobiographical writing.

Biography
- The writer observes the subject

Both
- Narrative writing tells part of the subject's (person's) life.

Autobiography
- The writer is the subject

Comparing Literary Works

Both of these works are written in the **first-person point of view**—by a narrator who participates in the action. Compare the two works by answering the following focus questions.

1. How is the amount you learn influenced by who the first-person narrator is in each work?
2. How is the first-person narrator in a biography different from the first-person narrator of an autobiography?

❸ Reading Strategy

Identifying Author's Evidence

When you read a general statement by the author of a biography, autobiography, or other work of nonfiction, decide whether or not you accept the statement as true. Make your decision based on examples, observations, or details that show the truth of the statement. In "My Papa, Mark Twain," Susy Clemens writes that her father is "a *very* striking character." The following example shows some of the evidence she provides for that general statement.

> He has beautiful gray hair, not any too thick or any too long, but just right; a Roman nose which greatly improves the beauty of his features; . . .

Vocabulary Development

incessantly (in ses´ ənt lē) *adv.* never ceasing (p. 555)

consequently (kän´ si kwent´ lē) *adv.* as a result (p. 555)

monitoring (män´ i tər iŋ) *v.* watching or listening to (p. 563)

accumulations (ə kyo͞om´ yo͞o lā´ shənz) *n.* buildups over a period of time (p. 564)

moot (mo͞ot) *adj.* not worthy of thought or discussion because it has already been resolved (p. 564)

peripheral (pə rif´ ər əl) *adj.* lying on the outside edge (p. 565)

catastrophic (kat´ ə sträf´ ik) *adj.* causing a complete disaster (p. 565)

CUSTOMIZE INSTRUCTION FOR UNIVERSAL ACCESS

For Special Needs Students	For Less Proficient Readers	For English Learners
Have students read the adapted version of "The Drive-In Movies" in the **Adapted Reader's Companion.** This version provides basic-level instruction in an interactive format with questions and write-on lines. Completing the adapted version will prepare students to read the selection in the Student Edition.	Have students read "The Drive-In Movies" in the **Reader's Companion.** This version provides basic-level instruction in an interactive format with questions and write-on lines. After students finish the selection in the Reader's Companion, have them complete the questions and activities in the Student Edition.	Have students read the adapted version of "The Drive-In Movies" in the **English Learner's Companion.** This version provides basic-level instruction in an interactive format with questions and write-on lines. Completing the adapted version will prepare students to read the selection in the Student Edition.

❷ Literary Analysis

Biography and Autobiography

- Before having students read the instruction on page 553, explain that biographies and autobiographies tell the stories of people's lives. They are nonfictional, or true, narratives.
- After asking a volunteer to read aloud the instruction, make sure that students understand the difference between first- and third-person narrators.
- Write the Comparing Literary Works questions on the board. Students should think about the questions as they read; the questions will appear again on page 567.
- You may also use the Biography and Autobiography transparency on p. 66 in **Literary Analysis and Reading Transparencies** to point out the differences and similarities between biographies and autobiographies.

❸ Reading Strategy

Identifying Author's Evidence

- After students read the instruction on this page, talk to them about how writers of biographies and autobiographies probably feel about their subjects. Direct students toward understanding that writers who know their subjects personally may be more careful or sensitive in their choice of evidence. Tell students that a person writing his or her autobiography may present only certain evidence and leave out other details.
- Also, point out the kinds of details likely to appear in a biographical or an autobiographical narrative, such as quotations, anecdotes, sensory details, thoughts, and personal reactions.

Vocabulary Development

- Pronounce each vocabulary word for students, and read the definitions as a class. Have students identify any words with which they are already familiar.

 ***E-Teach***

Visit E-Teach at www.phschool.com for teachers' essays on how to teach, with questions and answers.

TEACH

Step-by-Step Teaching Guide for pp. 554–566

CUSTOMIZE INSTRUCTION
For Intrapersonal Learners

Invite students to write a short biographical sketch of someone they are close to. The subject may be a family member or close personal friend. Then, have each student compare the way he or she described the subject to the way Susy Clemens describes her father. Ask volunteers to talk about the similarities and differences in their approaches.

1 About the Selection

Susy Clemens's description of her father in "My Papa, Mark Twain" shows the private side of the author and humorist. Susy is bothered that few people seem to understand Twain, and she is overjoyed that his recent novels show his kind, sympathetic nature. Susy wrote this biographical account in her journal when she was only thirteen years old. When Mark Twain read the account, he said, "I have had no compliment, no praise, no tribute from any source that was so precious to me as this one was and still is."

2 ▶Critical Viewing

Answer: The family is seated casually on the steps. Family members seem focused on the pet dog. The youngest child rests her arm on her mother's lap.

1 My Papa, Mark Twain

Susy Clemens

2 ◀**Critical Viewing** What details in the picture show that the Clemens family enjoys spending time together? **[Analyze]**

We are a very happy family. We consist of Papa, Mamma, Jean, Clara and me. It is papa I am writing about, and I shall have no trouble in not knowing what to say about him, as he is a *very* striking character.

3 Papa's appearance has been described many times, but very incorrectly. He has beautiful gray hair, not any too thick or any too long, but just right; a Roman nose which greatly improves the beauty of his features; kind blue eyes and a small mustache. He has a wonderfully shaped head and profile. He has a very good figure—in short, he is an extrodinarily fine looking man. All his features are perfect except that he hasn't extrodinary teeth. His complexion is very fair, and he doesn't ware a beard. He is a very good man and a very funny one. He has got a temper, but we all of us have in this family. He is the loveliest man I ever saw or ever hope to see—and oh, so absentminded.

TEACHING RESOURCES

The following resources can be used to enrich or extend the instruction for pp. 554–566.

Literary Analysis
- **Selection Support:** Literary Analysis, p. 165
- **Literary Analysis for Enrichment**
- **Writing Models and Graphic Organizers on Transparencies,** pp. 69, 81, 97 ■

Reading
- **Reader's Companion**
- **Adapted Reader's Companion**
- **English Learner's Companion**
- **Listening to Literature Audiocassettes,** Sides 19, 20
- **Listening to Literature Audio CDs,** CDs 9, 10

Extension
- **Authors In Depth,** Copper Level (The collection includes five additional selections by Gary Soto for extended reading.) ■

■ **BLOCK SCHEDULING:** Resources marked with this symbol provide varied instruction during 90-minute blocks.

Papa's favorite game is billiards, and when he is tired and wishes to rest himself he stays up all night and plays billiards, it seems to rest his head. He smokes a great deal almost incessantly. He has the mind of an author exactly, some of the simplest things he can't understand. Our burglar alarm is often out of order, and papa had been obliged to take the mahogany room off from the alarm altogether for a time, because the burglar alarm had been in the habit of ringing even when the mahogany-room window was closed. At length he thought that perhaps the burglar alarm might be in order, and he decided to try and see; accordingly he
4 put it on and then went down and opened the window; consequently the alarm bell rang, it would even if the alarm had been in order. Papa went despairingly upstairs and said to mamma, "Livy the mahogany room won't go on. I have just opened the window to see."

"Why, Youth," mamma replied. "If you've opened the window, why of course the alarm will ring!"

"That's what I've opened it for, why I just went down to see if it would ring!"

5 Mamma tried to explain to papa that when he wanted to go and see whether the alarm would ring while the window was closed he *mustn't go* and open the window—but in vain, papa couldn't understand, and got very impatient with mamma for trying to make him believe an impossible thing true.

Papa has a peculiar gait we like, it seems just to suit him, but most people do not; he always walks up and down the room while thinking and between each coarse at meals.

Papa is very fond of animals particularly of cats, we had a dear little gray kitten once that he named "Lazy" (papa always wears gray to match his hair and eyes) and he would carry him around on his shoulder, it was a mighty pretty sight! the gray cat sound asleep against papa's gray coat and hair. The names that he has give our different cats are really remarkably funny, they are named Stray Kit, Abner, Motley, Fraeulein, Lazy, Buffalo Bill, Soapy Sall, Cleveland, Sour Mash, and Pestilence and Famine.

Papa uses very strong language, but I have an idea not nearly so strong as when he first married mamma. A lady acquaintance of his is rather apt to interrupt what one is saying, and papa told mamma he thought he should say to the lady's husband "I am glad your wife wasn't present when the Deity said Let there be light."

Papa said the other day, "I am a mugwump[1] and a mugwump is pure from the marrow out." (Papa knows that I am writing this biography of him, and he said this for it.) He doesn't like to go to

incessantly (in ses′ ənt lē) *adv.* never ceasing

consequently (kän′ si kwent′ lē) *adv.* as a result

Literary Analysis
Biography and Autobiography
What details make Susy's account different from one Mark Twain himself may have given?

6 **Reading Check**
What is the relationship between the writer and the subject?

1. **mugwump** (mug′ wump′) *n.* a Republican who refused to support the candidates of the party in the 1884 election.

3 Reading Strategy
Author's Evidence

- Point out to students that Susy provides evidence that her father is "striking."
- Then, ask students what evidence she gives that suggests Twain has unimpressive characteristics, too.
  Answer: Students should notice that Twain's teeth are not beautiful and he is quick to anger.

4 Vocabulary Development
Word Analysis

- Ask students to guess or look up the meaning of the word root *-sequi-*.
  Answer: The word root means "follow."
- Then, ask for the meaning of the word *consequently*.
  Answer: The word means "as a result."
- Ask students to list other words that include the root.
  Possible responses: Other words include *sequence* and *sequel*.
- Have students write sentences using each word. Students should make sure that the sentence relates to "following."

5 Literary Analysis
Biography and Autobiography

- Before asking the Literary Analysis question on p. 555, ask students to summarize the anecdote Susy has just related about her father.
  Answer: Twain and his wife have a disagreement over their burglar alarm because of Twain's inability to understand how it works.
- Then, ask the Literary Analysis question.
  Answer: Susy's account of her father's confusion and her mother's futile explanations about the burglar alarm probably would not appear in Twain's own version.

6 Reading Check

Answer: The writer is the subject's (Mark Twain's) daughter.

CUSTOMIZE INSTRUCTION FOR UNIVERSAL ACCESS

For Special Needs Students	For Gifted/Talented Students
Students may have trouble keeping track of all the details and anecdotes Susy Clemens uses to describe her father, Mark Twain. Offer students a Sunburst diagram, like the one on p. 97 of **Writing Models and Graphic Organizers on Transparencies.** Have students write "Mark Twain" in the center circle and then fill in the surrounding rectangles with information they learn about the man from his daughter's account. Ask students to compare their diagrams and to discuss their overall impressions of Mark Twain.	Point out that the works of Mark Twain are full of wit, humor, and ironic observations about people. Call attention to humorous passages in his daughter's biography, and have students discuss their favorite anecdote. Then, challenge students to find an example of humor from Twain himself and to contrast it with his daughter's. Ask each student to write a short comparison-and-contrast essay of the two writers' styles and approaches to humor.

7 ▶ **Critical Viewing**

Possible responses: Susy will write about how the sisters play with the dog. She may explain how they get along with each other or what they think of their father. She might also include humorous stories about them.

8 Literary Analysis

Biography and Autobiography

- Ask students what Susy Clemens is discussing here.
  Answer: Susy is discussing a review of her father's book *The Prince and the Pauper*.
- Then, ask students whether they think her review is fair.
  Possible responses: Some students may say that her review is biased because Susy thinks her father is wonderful. Others will point out that Susy does say that the book is full of fine ideas and language.
- Next, ask students the Literary Analysis question on this page: What details on this page show how the writer's role of daughter helps her as a biographer?
  Answer: One detail is Twain's admission that he does not like to listen to others talk. Only Twain's family would know such details. Another detail is Susy's knowledge of Twain's tender side.

church at all, why I never understood, until just now, he told us the other day that he couldn't bear to hear anyone talk but himself, but that he could listen to himself talk for hours without getting tired, of course he said this in joke, but I've no dought it was founded on truth. **7**

8 One of papa's latest books is "The Prince and the Pauper" and it is unquestionably the best book he has ever written, some people want him to keep to his old style, some gentleman wrote him, "I enjoyed Huckleberry Finn immensely and am glad to see that you have returned to your old style." That enoyed me, that enoyed me greatly, because it trobles me to have so few people know papa, I mean realy know him, they think of Mark Twain as a humorist joking at everything; "And with a mop of reddish brown hair which sorely needs the barbar brush, a roman nose, short stubby mustache, a sad care-worn face, with maney crows' feet" etc. That is the way people picture papa, I have wanted papa to write a book that would reveal something of his kind sympathetic nature, and "The Prince and the Pauper" partly does it. The book is full of lovely charming ideas, and oh the language! It is perfect. I think that one of the most touching scenes in it is where the pauper is riding on horseback with his nobles in the "recognition procession" and he

▲ **Critical Viewing**
Susy is observing her two sisters in this picture. What do you think she might write about them in her journal? **[Speculate]**

Literary Analysis
Biography and Autobiography
What details on this page show how the writer's role of daughter helps her as a biographer?

ENRICHMENT: Language Arts Connection

Samuel Clemens aka Mark Twain

Samuel Clemens, known by his pen name Mark Twain, is considered one of the best American writers of the nineteenth century. He is perhaps best known for his tales of the Mississippi River in books such as *Tom Sawyer* and *The Adventures of Huckleberry Finn*. Twain traveled around the world looking for ideas and subjects to write about. He explored the western United States, Hawaii, and Europe but found his best material in the world of his childhood—Missouri and the Mississippi River. Late in his life, he suffered from severe money troubles as well as the deaths of his wife and his daughter Susy. At this point, his writing became dark and pessimistic, lacking the humor and sympathy that his daughter had noticed in his earlier writings as well as in his own character.

Invite students to read a short essay or an excerpt from one of Twain's novels and to look for the characteristics his daughter described in "My Papa, Mark Twain." Students should explain why the piece or excerpt would or would not be one of Susy's favorites.

sees his mother oh and then what followed! How she runs to his side, when she sees him throw up his hand palm outward, and is rudely pushed off by one of the King's officers, and then how the little pauper's conscience troubles him when he remembers the shameful words that were falling from his lips when she was turned from his side "I know you not woman" and how his grandeurs were stricken valueless and his pride consumed to ashes. It is a wonderfully beautiful and touching little scene, and papa has described it so wonderfully. I never saw a man with so much variety of feeling as papa has; now the "Prince and the Pauper" is full of touching places, but there is always a streak of humor in them somewhere. Papa very seldom writes a passage without some humor in it somewhere and I don't think he ever will.

Clara and I are sure that papa played the trick on Grandma about the whipping that is related in "The Adventures of Tom Sawyer": "Hand me that switch." The switch hovered in the air, the peril was desperate—"My, look behind you Aunt!" The old lady whirled around and snatched her skirts out of danger. The lad fled on the instant, scrambling up the high board fence and disappeared over it.

We know papa played "Hookey" all the time. And how readily would papa pretend to be dying so as not to have to go to school! Grandma wouldn't make papa go to school, so she let him go into a printing office to learn the trade. He did so, and gradually picked up enough education to enable him to do about as well as those who were more studious in early life.

Review and Assess

Thinking About the Selection

1. **Respond:** What questions do you have about Mark Twain after reading Susy Clemens's account?
2. **(a) Recall:** What does Susy think of her father's appearance? **(b) Infer:** If Susy Clemens were to use three words to describe her father, what would they be? **(c) Synthesize:** What three words would you use to describe Mark Twain?
3. **(a) Recall:** What details does the author give about her father's education? **(b) Deduce:** Explain how you think she feels about her father's lack of formal education. **(c) Support:** What do you think Susy Clemens feels about her father's books? What details does the account provide?
4. **Speculate:** This essay contains many misspelled words. Why do you think it was published without correcting the errors?

Susy Clemens

(1872–1896)

The oldest of Mark Twain's three daughters, Susy Clemens grew up in a luxurious home in Hartford, Connecticut, where her parents entertained some of the most prominent people of the time. As a girl, Susy adored her father; as she grew older, she began to resent his showy public image. She died at the age of twenty-four.

Answers for p. 557

Review and Assess

1. Possible responses: Students may want to ask about Twain's job at the printing office. Others might want to know how Mark Twain got his ideas for writing.
2. **(a)** Susy thinks her father is handsome. **(b)** Possible responses: The three words might be *funny, impatient,* and *honest.* **(c)** Possible responses: Twain is humorous, absent-minded, and hard-working.
3. **(a)** Susy recalls how her father left school so he could learn the trade of printing and, in doing so, educated himself. **(b)** Possible response: She seems proud of her father's ability to do as well as those who went to school when they were young. **(c)** Possible response: Susy enjoys and is proud of her father's books. She seems to have read and admired them. She knows important scenes from *The Prince and the Pauper* and thinks that the language in the book is lovely.
4. Students should realize that the essay was published as it was written.

CUSTOMIZE INSTRUCTION FOR UNIVERSAL ACCESS

For English Learners	For Advanced Readers
To help students grasp Susy's love for her father, have them listen to "My Papa, Mark Twain" on **Listening to Literature Audiocassettes,** Sides 19 and 20, or **Listening to Literature Audio CDs,** CDs 9 and 10. As they listen, tell students to note the pride, devotion, and support for Twain that Susy's words convey through the reader's voice.	Urge students to read different excerpts from *The Prince and the Pauper* and *Tom Sawyer.* After they read, invite them to talk about Twain's use of humor in his writing. Then, ask them to give informal book talks, create book jackets, or make advertisements in order to persuade their classmates to read the books, too.

❾ About the Selection

In "The Drive-In Movies," young Gary Soto wants his mother to take him and his siblings to the drive-in movies. His plan is to be very good and to do lots of chores one Saturday morning and afternoon in order to impress his mother. Unfortunately, he works so hard at weeding, mowing, and waxing the car, that he falls asleep during the film.

❾ The Drive-In Movies

GARY SOTO

CUSTOMIZE INSTRUCTION FOR UNIVERSAL ACCESS

For Advanced Readers

Suggest that students read additional works by Gary Soto. Provide students with the titles listed in the Enrichment box, ATE p. 567. You may also wish to use **Authors In Depth,** Copper Level, which contains the following selections:

- "Mother and Daughter" (fiction, p. 139)
- "Ode to Mi Perrito" (poem, p. 145)
- "Where We Could Go" (poem, p. 147)
- "Tortillas Like Africa" (poem, p. 148)

After students have read the selections, have each student write a brief essay about Soto's viewpoint, listing descriptive phrases that convey what shapes his experiences. Have them include his reasons for choosing to write in first-person when relating events that happened in his boyhood.

For our family, moviegoing was rare. But if our mom, tired from a week of candling eggs,[1] woke up happy on a Saturday morning, there was a chance we might later scramble to our blue Chevy and beat nightfall to the Starlight Drive-In. My brother and sister knew this. I knew this. So on Saturday we tried to be good. We sat in the cool shadows of the TV with the volume low and watched cartoons, a prelude of what was to come.

10 One Saturday I decided to be extra good. When she came out of the bedroom tying her robe, she yawned a hat-sized yawn and blinked red eyes at the weak brew of coffee I had fixed for her. I made her toast with strawberry jam spread to all the corners and set the three boxes of cereal in front of her. If she didn't care to eat cereal, she could always look at the back of the boxes as she drank her coffee.

I went outside. The lawn was tall but too wet with dew to mow. I picked up a trowel and began to weed the flower bed. The weeds were really bermuda grass, long stringers that ran finger-deep in the ground. I got to work quickly and in no time crescents of earth began rising under my fingernails. I was sweaty hot. My knees hurt from kneeling, and my brain was dull from making the trowel go up and down, dribbling crumbs of earth. I dug for half an hour, then stopped to play with the neighbor's dog and pop ticks from his poor snout.

I then mowed the lawn, which was still beaded with dew and noisy with bees hovering over clover. This job was less dull because as I pushed the mower over the shaggy lawn, I could see it looked tidier. My brother and sister watched from the window. Their faces

11 **Reading Check**

Why is the narrator being extra good?

1. **candling eggs** examining uncooked eggs for freshness by placing them in front of a candle.

12 **Critical Viewing** What are some reasons people might enjoy watching a movie from their car? **[Speculate]**

10 Reading Strategy

Author's Evidence

- Point out that the narrator in this selection is the author and that he is retelling an event from his childhood.
- Show students that in the first paragraph, the narrator sets up a conflict—being allowed to go to the movies means that the narrator must behave well.
- Then, ask students what evidence the author provides in the bracketed paragraph to support his statement that he acted "extra good."
  Answer: The author prepared coffee and toast for his mother. He thoughtfully provided her with three boxes of cereal to eat or to read.

11 Reading Check

Answer: The narrator is being extra good because he wants to go to the drive-in movies that night.

12 Critical Viewing

Possible responses: People enjoy the privacy of a car. They can wear casual clothing, eat their own food, talk during the movie, and bring young children.

CUSTOMIZE INSTRUCTION FOR UNIVERSAL ACCESS

For Less Proficient Readers	For English Learners
Help students keep track of the events in the narrative by asking them to create cartoon strips based on the selection. Have students work alone or in pairs to select three or four key scenes and to figure out how to render them visually. Help them get started by suggesting that they draw a picture of Gary making toast with jam while his mother yawns in the background. Remind students to look at the details and dialogue to gather ideas. Post students' work where the class may view it.	Gary Soto uses figures of speech and idioms that may be unfamiliar to students. Assign excerpts to pairs of students, and have the students select and copy confusing passages. Then, challenge them to write paraphrases of the passages to clarify the expressions. Read aloud the original passage and then ask students to read aloud their paraphrases. Allow students to discuss and evaluate which wording they prefer and why.

13 Literary Analysis

Biography and Autobiography

- Point out that the narrator of the selection is the author when he was younger.
- Ask students to consider the effects of time on his memory of the day he describes in this selection.
  Possible response: Some students may say that time may have caused the writer to forget some details. Others may say that the events are memorable enough to withstand the passing of time.
- Next, ask students the Literary Analysis question on p. 560: What autobiographical details would only the writer know about his own childhood?
  Answer: Only the writer would know most of the details in this passage—all the chores he has completed, including plucking ticks off a dog's nose and using his grandmother's remedy for bee stings.

14 Literary Analysis

Autobiography and First-Person Narrator

- Ask a volunteer to read aloud the paragraph that begins "My brother joined me . . ."
- Draw students' attention to the description of the mother's reaction in the bracketed passage. Pantomime her reaction for students as you read aloud her words.
- Ask students to respond to the second Literary Analysis question on p. 560.
  Possible response: Details about what Soto's mother was thinking and feeling would be included.

were fat with cereal, a third helping. I made a face at them when they asked how come I was working. Rick pointed to part of the lawn. "You missed some over there." I ignored him and kept my attention on the windmill of grassy blades.

While I was emptying the catcher, a bee stung the bottom of my foot. I danced on one leg and was ready to cry when Mother showed her face at the window. I sat down on the grass and examined my foot: the stinger was pulsating. I pulled it out quickly, ran water over the sting and packed it with mud, Grandmother's remedy.

13 Hobbling, I returned to the flower bed where I pulled more stringers and again played with the dog. More ticks had migrated to his snout. I swept the front steps, took out the garbage, cleaned the lint filter to the dryer (easy), plucked hair from the industrial wash basin in the garage (also easy), hosed off the patio, smashed three snails sucking paint from the house (disgusting but fun), tied a bundle of newspapers, put away toys, and, finally, seeing that almost everything was done and the sun was not too high, started waxing the car.

My brother joined me with an old gym sock, and our sister watched us while sucking on a cherry Kool-Aid ice cube. The liquid wax drooled onto the sock, and we began to swirl the white slop on the chrome. My arms ached from buffing, which though less boring than weeding, was harder. But the beauty was evident. 14 The shine, hurting our eyes and glinting like an armful of dimes, brought Mother out. She looked around the yard and said, "Pretty good." She winced[2] at the grille and returned inside the house.

We began to wax the paint. My brother applied the liquid and I followed him rubbing hard in wide circles as we moved around the car. I began to hurry because my arms were hurting and my stung foot looked like a water balloon. We were working around the trunk when Rick pounded on the bottle of wax. He squeezed the bottle and it sneezed a few more white drops.

We looked at each other. "There's some on the sock," I said. "Let's keep going."

We polished and buffed, sweat weeping on our brows. We got scared when we noticed that the gym sock was now blue. The paint was coming off. Our sister fit ice cubes into our mouths and we worked harder, more intently, more dedicated to the car and our mother. We ran the sock over the chrome, trying to pick up extra wax. But there wasn't enough to cover the entire car. Only half got waxed, but we thought it was better than nothing and went inside for lunch. After lunch, we returned outside with tasty sandwiches.

Literary Analysis
Biography and Autobiography
What autobiographical details would only the writer know about his own childhood?

Literary Analysis
Autobiography and First-Person Narrator
What different details might be included if the first-person narrator were Soto's mother?

2. **winced** (winst) *v.* drew back slightly, as if in pain.

CUSTOMIZE INSTRUCTION FOR UNIVERSAL ACCESS

For Less Proficient Readers	For English Learners
Explain to students that sensory details in the story help the reader to enjoy Gary Soto's memorable day. Ask students to keep track of the sensory details by creating a chart like the one provided on p. 81 in **Writing Models and Graphic Organizers on Transparencies.** Students may work in groups of five, so that each group member is responsible for finding details that relate to one sense. After students complete the reading, have the groups compare charts.	Invite each student to write a brief journal entry describing a day from when he or she was younger. Challenge students to use sensory details like those Gary Soto uses in "The Drive-In Movies." Remind students that sensory details are details relating to one of the five senses. After writing, each student should meet with a partner and summarize his or her entry. Then, each student should tell his or her partner at least two sensory details from the entry.

Rick and I nearly jumped. The waxed side of the car was foggy white. We took a rag and began to polish vigorously and nearly in tears, but the fog wouldn't come off. I blamed Rick and he blamed me. Debra stood at the window, not wanting to get involved. Now, not only would we not go to the movies, but Mom would surely snap a branch from the plum tree and chase us around the yard.

Mom came out and looked at us with hands on her aproned hips. Finally, she said, "You boys worked so hard." She turned on the garden hose and washed the car. That night we did go to the drive-in. The first feature was about nothing, and the second feature, starring Jerry Lewis,[3] was *Cinderfella*. I tried to stay awake. I kept a wad of homemade popcorn in my cheek and laughed when Jerry Lewis fit golf tees in his nose. I rubbed my watery eyes. I laughed and looked at my mom. I promised myself I would remember that scene with the golf tees and promised myself not to work so hard the coming Saturday. Twenty minutes into the movie, I fell asleep with one hand in the popcorn.

3. **Jerry Lewis** comedian who starred in many movies during the 1950s and 1960s.

Review and Assess

Thinking About the Selections

1. **Respond:** How would you have felt if you had worked so hard and had then fallen asleep at the movies?
2. **(a) Recall:** How does Soto convince his mother to take the family to the drive-in movies? **(b) Draw Conclusions:** Why do you think the boys' mother does not get angry with them for making a mess of the car with the wax? **(c) Relate:** Do you think it was worth the hard work? Why or why not?
3. **Deduce:** Do you think the narrator is older or younger than his brother and sister? Use evidence from the story to support your answer.
4. **(a) Recall:** What two things does the narrator promise himself to remember? **(b) Assess:** As an adult, do you think he still has fond memories about that day and night? Why or why not?
5. **Speculate:** Do you think children should have to work hard on chores before their parents allow them to do something enjoyable? Why or why not?

Gary Soto

(b. 1952)

This popular writer of poetry and prose was once a farm worker in California's San Joaquin Valley. Some of his work—including the poetry collection *The Elements of San Joaquin*—explores the lives of migrant farm workers. Other books—such as the collection of essays *Living Up the Street* and *Baseball in April and Other Stories*—focus on the large and small events in the lives of family and friends. Today, Gary Soto lives and teaches in Berkeley, California.

Answers for p. 561

Review and Assess

1. **Possible responses:** Students might say that even though they missed the movie, they would feel proud of the work they accomplished.
2. **(a)** Soto makes his mother breakfast and then works hard doing household chores in order to convince her. **(b)** The mother realizes that the boys did not intend to make a mess. They worked hard to correct the problem. **(c)** **Possible responses:** Some students may say that it was worth the hard work because Soto really did help out his mother. Others may say that he worked too hard and could not enjoy his reward.
3. **Possible response:** Students may say that the narrator is older. He takes responsibility for the household chores while his brother and sister watch for the most part.
4. **(a)** The narrator promises that he will remember the scene with the golf tees and that he will not work so hard the following Saturday. **(b)** **Possible response:** Soto probably remembers that experience fondly because as an adult he can better appreciate its humor.
5. **Possible response:** Students might say that children will learn to value their free time if they have to work hard to earn it.

CUSTOMIZE INSTRUCTION FOR UNIVERSAL ACCESS

For Special Needs Students	For Gifted/Talented Students
For students having difficulty understanding the difference between biography and autobiography, provide or have each student draw a four-column table. The columns should be labeled *Title, Author, Subject,* and *Type*. Have students fill in the first two columns with titles and authors of selections in this unit as well as some other well-known works. Then, allow students to work in pairs to figure out who the subject of each work is and whether each work is a biography or an autobiography.	After discussing with students the differences between biography and autobiography, challenge students to rewrite a section of Gary Soto's first-person narrative as a third-person narrative. Before students begin, they should think about details that only Soto would know and figure out how changing them will change the narrative. Ask students to read aloud their narratives. Then, ask the class to comment on how the change from first- to third-person makes a difference.

⓯ About the Selection

"Space Shuttle *Challenger*" is William Harwood's dramatic eyewitness account of the ill-fated mission. From the Kennedy Space Center press site, Harwood records his initial feelings of unease: A valued colleague is absent; there is a two-hour flight delay. When *Challenger* launches, Harwood wires his story to UPI, but within minutes he witnesses the shuttle's fatal explosion. He tries to make sense of it. At 4.2 miles away, his vision is impaired. Had he been watching NASA TV, he would have clearly seen the disaster. Harwood is caught up in the rush to file an accurate report. Later, he faces the event's full impact when he remembers the seven astronauts waving and smiling as they made their way to the *Challenger* launch pad.

ENRICHMENT: Science Connection

The History of the Space Shuttle

In 1972, the National Air and Space Administration (NASA) decided that the space shuttle, a reusable spacecraft, would replace the traditional rocket and take U.S. space exploration into a new era. Designed to be launched like a rocket and land on a runway like a plane at the end of its flight, the first shuttle took to the air in 1981. The purpose of the shuttle was to launch satellites, test new space-age equipment, and allow scientists to conduct experiments in space. The design of the space shuttle also allowed for a larger and more varied crew. Pilots and scientists and even school teachers could ride into space. The space shuttle *Challenger* had had ten successful missions before the fatal explosion on January 28, 1986. The cause of the crash was a deformed O-ring seal, which allowed the hydrogen fuel to ignite during take-off. The space shuttle program was placed on hold for two years but started again with success in 1988.

15 # SPACE SHUTTLE *Challenger*

William Harwood

I witnessed the launch from the Kennedy Space Center press site just 4.2 miles from pad 39B. It was my 19th shuttle launch but my first without the comforting presence of UPI Science Editor Al Rossiter Jr., a space veteran with all of the experience I lacked. He was in Pasadena, California, at the Jet Propulsion Laboratory covering *Voyager 2*'s flyby of Uranus.

I arrived at the UPI trailer around 11:30 P.M. Monday night, January 27. I always came to work before the start of fueling on the theory that anytime anyone loaded a half-million gallons of liquid oxygen and liquid hydrogen into anything it was an event worth staffing.

It was bitterly cold that night. I remember cranking up the drafty UPI trailer's baseboard heaters in a futile attempt to warm up while I started banging out copy. I was writing for afternoon, or PM, newspapers that would hit the streets the following afternoon. Because *Challenger*'s launch was scheduled for that morning, the PM cycle was where the action was, the closest thing to "live" reporting that print journalists ever experience. . . . I had written my launch copy the day before and as usual, I spent most of the early morning hours tweaking the story, checking in periodically with NASA public affairs and monitoring the chatter on the bureau's radio scanner. I would occasionally glance toward the launch pad where *Challenger* stood bathed in high power spotlights, clearly visible for dozens of miles around. Off to the side, a brilliant tongue of orange

Literary Analysis
Biography and Autobiography
What details about the author's experience of preparing for the launch do you learn about in this section?

monitoring (män′ i tər iŋ) *v.* watching or listening to

Reading Check 17
What is the narrator's job?

16 Literary Analysis

Biography and Autobiography

- Before asking students the Literary Analysis question on page 563, make sure that students realize that the author is a reporter for UPI, the United Press International, a wire organization that provides up-to-the-minute news to newspapers around the world.
- Then, ask the Literary Analysis question: What details about the author's experience of preparing for the launch do you learn about in this section?
  Answer: Students should note Harwood's early arrival to watch the fueling of the shuttle; his writing and revising of "copy," or news text, for the afternoon editions of newspapers; and his listening for news on the radio scanner.

17 

Answer: The narrator is a reporter.

CUSTOMIZE INSTRUCTION FOR UNIVERSAL ACCESS

For Special Needs Students	For English Learners
Help students connect to the scene set by Harwood and illustrated by the photograph on page 562. First, ask students to imagine that they are at the shuttle launch. Then, have them write their reactions and reflections in journal entries. Encourage students to write sensory descriptions by asking them the following questions: How does the glare from the flames affect your eyes? What do you hear? What can you feel in the air? Finally, ask students to sum up their reactions in a few words.	Help students follow the chronology of events in "Space Shuttle *Challenger*" by using the Series of Events Chain on p. 69 of **Writing Models and Graphic Organizers on Transparencies.** After completing the parts of the chain, students should list phrases from each link that need clarification, such as "cranking up" "banging out copy," "tweaking the story," or "brilliant tongue of orange flame." Allow students time to figure out the meanings of these and other phrases. Explain any phrases that are too difficult for students.

18 Critical Thinking

Connect

- Ask students to summarize what has happened so far in the narrative.
- Then, ask students to draw a comparison between the preparations for the launch of the shuttle and the writer's preparation of his news story. Ask: What similarities exist between the two?
  Possible response: Both the shuttle and the news story have been carefully attended to; both are delayed; both are "launched" at the same time.

19 Reading Strategy

Author's Evidence

- Before asking students the Reading Strategy question on p. 564, make sure students realize that Harwood is dropping clues about the crisis he is about to witness and describe.
- Then, ask the Reading Strategy question on p. 564: What details does the author provide as evidence that his view of the launch was marvelous?
  Answer: Students should point to the sensory details of "puffs of smoke," "crackling roar of the boosters," and "shaking and rattling."

Monitor Progress Ask students to identify at least two ways that authors of biographies or autobiographies provide evidence to support their ideas.
Possible response: They can provide details, quotations, facts, and anecdotes or stories.

Reteach If students struggle with the concept of authors' evidence, choose a paragraph or passage from any of the selections in this grouping. Before reading it aloud to students, write these question words on the board: *Who? What? Where? When? Why?* and *How?* Read aloud the passage, and then ask students to answer each one of the questions. Explain that evidence in the text should answer these basic questions.

flame periodically flared in the night as excess hydrogen was vented harmlessly into the atmosphere. Back in the UPI trailer, radio reporter Rob Navias rolled in around 4 A.M. A veteran shuttle reporter with an encyclopedic memory for space trivia, Rob and I had covered 14 straight missions together. In keeping with long-standing launch-day tradition, Rob's first comment after stomping into the trailer was "Will it go?" to which I would respond: "Or will it blow?" It was a grim little charade we carried out to mask our constant fear of catastrophe.

As night gave way to day, the launch team was struggling to keep the countdown on track. Problems had delayed fueling and launch—originally scheduled for 9:38 A.M.—for two hours to make sure no dangerous accumulations of ice had built up on *Challenger*'s huge external tank. Finally, all systems were "go" and the countdown resumed at the T-minus nine-minute mark for a liftoff at 11:38 A.M. Battling my usual pre-launch jitters, I called UPI national desk editor Bill Trott in Washington about three minutes before launch. I had already filed the PM launch story to UPI's computer and Trott now called it up on his screen. We shot the breeze. I reminded him not to push the send button until I confirmed vertical motion; two previous launches were aborted at the last second and we didn't want to accidentally "launch" a shuttle on the wire when it was still firmly on the ground. But there were no such problems today. *Challenger*'s three main engines thundered to life on schedule, belching blue-white fire and billowing clouds of steam. Less than seven seconds later, the shuttle's twin boosters ignited with a ground-shaking roar and the spacecraft vaulted skyward.

accumulations (ə kyo͞om′ yo͞o lā′ shənz) *n.* buildups occurring over a period of time

18 "And liftoff . . . liftoff of the 25th space shuttle mission, and it has cleared the tower!" said NASA commentator Hugh Harris.

"OK, let it go," I told Trott when Harris started talking. He pushed the SEND button and my story winged away on the A-wire.

19 Four miles away, *Challenger* was climbing majestically into a cloudless blue sky. We could not see the initial puffs of smoke indicating a fatal booster flaw. A few seconds later, the crackling roar of those boosters swept over the press site and the UPI trailer started shaking and rattling as the ground shock arrived. I marveled at the view, describing it to Trott in Washington. We always kept the line open for the full eight-and-a-half minutes it took for a shuttle to reach orbit; should disaster strike, the plan went, I would start dictating and Trott would start filing raw copy to the wire.

Reading Strategy
Author's Evidence
What details does the author provide as evidence that his view of the launch was marvelous?

But for the first few seconds, it was a moot point. The roar was so loud we couldn't hear each other anyway. But the sound quickly faded to a dull rumble as *Challenger* wheeled about and arced over behind its booster exhaust plume, disappearing from view. NASA television, of course, carried the now-familiar closeups of the

moot (mo͞ot) *adj.* not worthy of thought or discussion because it has already been resolved

CUSTOMIZE INSTRUCTION FOR UNIVERSAL ACCESS

For Gifted/Talented Students

Invite students to interview older people they know regarding their memories of the day the space shuttle *Challenger* exploded. Suggest that students prepare interview questions that elicit memories of where interviewees were when they first heard the news, as well as their emotional reactions. Have students compile the information into written interviews. Make sure they include important questions such as the following: What were you doing when you first heard the news? Where and when did you hear it? How did the news of the *Challenger* tragedy make you feel? Ask students to read aloud their interviews for the class. Then, ask the class to compare the different perspectives revealed by the interviews.

orbiter, but I wasn't watching television. I was looking out the window at the exhaust cloud towering into the morning sky.

"Incredible," I murmured.

And then, in the blink of an eye, the exhaust plume seemed to balloon outward, to somehow thicken. I recall a fleeting peripheral impression of fragments, of debris flying about, sparkling in the morning sunlight. And then, in that pregnant instant before the knowledge that something terrible has happened settled in, a single booster emerged from the cloud, corkscrewing madly through the sky.

I sat stunned. I couldn't understand what I was seeing.

"Wait a minute . . . something's happened . . ." I told Trott. A

20 booster? Flying on its own? "They're in trouble," I said, my heart pounding. "Lemme dictate something!"

"OK, OK, hang on," Trott said. He quickly started punching in the header material of a one-paragraph "story" that would interrupt the normal flow of copy over the wire and alert editors to breaking news.

I still didn't realize *Challenger* had actually exploded. I didn't know what had happened. For a few heartbeats, I desperately reviewed the crew's options: Could the shuttle somehow have pulled free? Could the crew somehow still be alive? Had I been watching television, I would have known the truth immediately and my copy would have been more final.

But I wasn't watching television.

"Ready," Trott said.

The lead went something like this: "The space shuttle *Challenger* apparently exploded about two minutes after launch today (pause for Trott to catch up) and veered wildly out of control. (pause) The fate of the crew was not known."

"Got it . . ." Trott said, typing as I talked. Bells went off seconds later as the story started clattering out on the bureau's A-wire printer behind me.

Out in Pasadena, Rossiter had watched the launch on NASA television. He ran to his computer, checked the wire and urgently called the bureau. He wanted to know why we had "apparently" blown up the shuttle in the precede. On television, there was no "apparently" about it.

Trott and I quickly corrected the time of the accident (my sense of time was distorted all day) and clarified that *Challenger* had, in fact, suffered a catastrophic failure. While we did not yet know what had happened to the crew, we all knew the chances for survival were virtually zero and the story began reflecting that belief.

For the next half hour or so, I simply dictated my impressions and background to Trott, who would file three or four paragraphs

peripheral (pə rif′ ər əl) *adj.* lying on the outside edge

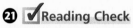

Literary Analysis
Autobiography and First-Person Narrator
How do the narrator's thoughts and feelings appear in this account?

catastrophic (kat′ ə sträf′ ik) *adj.* causing a complete disaster

21  **Reading Check**

What happens to the shuttle?

20 Literary Analysis

Autobiography and First-Person Narrator

- Ask students the Literary Analysis question on page 565: How do the narrator's thoughts and feelings appear in this account?
  Possible responses: The narrator expresses his confusion, his concern for the shuttle's crew, and his frenzy to find out what happened to the shuttle. He is too stunned to comprehend the disaster that has occurred.
- As students continue reading, ask them to watch for more insight into the narrator's emotional state.
  Answer: He will not pause to think about anything more than reporting the story until later in the afternoon, when he nearly cries.

21 Reading Check

Answer: The shuttle explodes two minutes after its launch.

CUSTOMIZE INSTRUCTION FOR UNIVERSAL ACCESS

For Special Needs Students	For Advanced Readers
Help students in their comprehension of the selection by asking them to summarize it orally, round-robin style. Start by pointing to a student and saying "The first thing that happened was . . ." The student should complete the sentence and end the statement with "and then . . ." Then, point to another student or have the students continue this around the room. If the summary is complete before all students have a chance to participate, start another round.	Clarify that Rossiter wants to know why Harwood's precede, or lead, leaves doubt that *Challenger* blew up. Those who watched NASA television were certain that it had. Ask students to rewrite Harwood's precede as if he had seen the explosion on television. Then, have each student write the precede as if the shuttle's launch had been successful. Afterwards, ask students to discuss the different tone and word choice in the two precedes.

ASSESS

Answers for p. 566

Review and Assess

1. **(a)** Harwood describes arriving at the UPI trailer and working on his writing while waiting for the shuttle to be launched. **(b)** The mood is a little suspenseful.
2. **(a)** The two reporters joke about whether the shuttle will be launched or if it will explode: "Will it go?" "Or will it blow?" **(b)** Details include the fact that Harwood makes sure that the shuttle is in the air before he allows his editor to submit his report; Harwood always chats with his editor for eight minutes after a launch just in case of disaster; Harwood had prepared profiles of the shuttle's crew that he knew might have to serve as obituaries. **(c)** The biographies are intended to serve as obituaries in case of disaster.
3. **(a)** The observation post is 4.2 miles from the launch pad. **(b)** The view of the launch on television clearly shows that the shuttle has exploded, but Harwood could not see it. **(c)** The television view is more accurate.
4. **(a)** Possible responses: Harwood may have felt disbelief, great concern, and excitement. **(b)** Harwood has difficulty understanding what happens because he is too stunned to believe that disaster has hit the shuttle.

of "running copy" to the wire at a time. At one point, I remember yelling "Obits! Tell somebody to refile the obits!" Before every shuttle mission, I wrote detailed profiles of each crew member. No one actually printed these stories; they were written to serve as instant obits in the event of a disaster. Now, I wanted to refile my profiles for clients who had not saved them earlier. At some point—I have no idea when—I put the phone down and started typing again, filing the copy to Washington where Trott assembled all the pieces into a more-or-less coherent narrative. Dozens of UPI reporters swung into action around the world, later funneling reaction and quotes into the evolving story.

For the next two hours or so I don't remember anything but the mad rush of reporting. Subconsciously, I held the enormity of the disaster at bay; I knew if I relaxed my guard for an instant it could paralyze me. I was flying on some kind of mental autopilot. And then, around 2 P.M. or so, I recall a momentary lull. My fingers dropped to the keyboard and I stared blankly out the window toward the launch pad. I saw those seven astronauts. I saw them waving to the photographers as they headed for the launch pad. I remembered Christa McAuliffe's smile and Judy Resnik's flashing eyes. Tears welled up. I shook my head, blinked rapidly and turned back to my computer. I'll think about it all later, I told myself. I was right. I think about it every launch.

Review and Assess

Thinking About the Selections

1. **(a) Recall:** What kinds of activities does Harwood describe taking place before the launch? **(b) Describe:** How would you describe the mood, or feeling, of the reporters before the launch?
2. **(a) Recall:** What nervous joke do Harwood and another reporter make before every launch? **(b) Analyze:** What details reveal that the reporters know the launch could go either way? **(c) Deduce:** Why does Harwood write detailed biographies of the astronauts before every launch?
3. **(a) Recall:** How far away is *Challenger* from Harwood's observation post? **(b) Contrast:** How is the view on television different from Harwood's eyewitness view? **(c) Evaluate:** Which view gives a more reliable view of events?
4. **(a) Speculate:** What do you think Harwood felt when he saw the booster come out of the cloud from the explosion? **(b) Synthesize:** Why does Harwood have difficulty understanding what has happened?

William Harwood

(b. 1952)

William Harwood's first article about the space program was written for his school newspaper at the University of Tennessee. Since then, he has covered more than eighty-five shuttle flights, working for United Press International, CBS News, and the *Washington Post*. In addition to writing about the space program, Harwood has written astronomy articles for *Ciel et Espace* (a French astronomy magazine) and *Astronomy Now*.

ASSESSMENT PRACTICE: Reading Comprehension

Distinguishing Between Fact and Nonfact (For more practice, see Test Preparation Workbook, p. 46.)

Many tests ask students to identify facts and opinions in a written text. Write this text on the board:

> Papa's appearance has been described many times, but very incorrectly. He has beautiful gray hair, not any too thick or any too long, but just right; a Roman nose which greatly improves the beauty of his features; kind blue eyes and a small mustache.
>
> Which statement from the passage does NOT express an opinion?

A Mark Twain has beautiful gray hair.
B Mark Twain's nose improves the beauty of his features.
C Mark Twain has kind blue eyes.
D Mark Twain has a small mustache.

Answers *A, B,* and *C* contain words such as "kind" and "beautiful," which express the author's judgment. Only *D* is a statement of fact that can be verified, so *D* is the correct answer.

Review and Assess

Literary Analysis

Biography and Autobiography

1. Identify two details that Susy Clemens includes in her **biography** "My Papa, Mark Twain" that Twain might not tell about himself.
2. Name three details in "The Drive-In Movies" that an author besides Soto would not know or include.
3. What would be different about "Space Shuttle *Challenger*" if it were narrated by someone who did not actually witness the event?

Comparing Literary Works

4. Complete an organizer like the one here to compare these works.

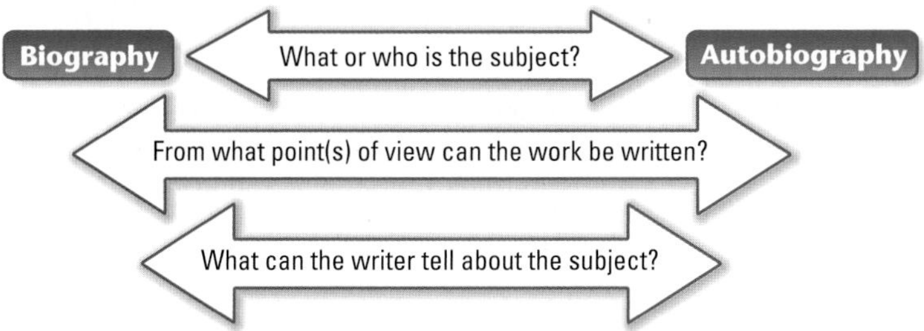

5. How is the **first-person narrator** in a biography different from the first-person narrator of an autobiography?
6. How is the amount you learn about the thoughts and feelings of each subject influenced by who the first-person narrator is in each work?

Reading Strategy

Identifying Author's Evidence

7. Make a chart like the one shown to record author's evidence for each statement.

Selection	Statement	Evidence
"My Papa, Mark Twain	"We are a happy family."	
"The Drive-In Movies"	"So on Saturday we tried to be good."	
"Space Shuttle *Challenger*"	"I couldn't understand what I was seeing."	

Extending Understanding

8. **Take a Position:** How much or how little personal information should the media publish about celebrities' lives?

Quick Review

A **biography** is the story of someone's life written by another person. An **autobiography** is a person's own account of his or her life. To review biography and autobiography, see p. 553.

A **first-person narrator** participates in the events being narrated. To review first-person narrator, see p. 553.

Author's evidence is details and information that support the author's statements.

 ***Take It to the Net***

www.phschool.com

Take the interactive self-test online to check your understanding of these selections.

ENRICHMENT: Further Reading

Other Work by the Authors

Works by Susy Clemens

Papa: An Intimate Biography of Mark Twain

Works by Gary Soto

Baseball in April

The Cat's Meow

Living Up the Street

 ***Take It to the Net***

Visit www.phschool.com for more information on the authors.

Answers for p. 567

Review and Assess

1. Possible responses: Twain might not say that he is handsome or sympathetic.
2. Possible responses: Another author would not know that going to the drive-in depends on Gary's mother's mood, his grandmother's remedy for bee stings, or that Gary falls asleep at the drive-in.
3. The selection would be less exciting, and it might convey less confusion and suspense.
4. **Biography:** subject: another person; point of view: as an observer; what writer can tell: subject's actions, words, and looks **Autobiography:** subject: the writer himself or herself; point of view: first-person; what writer can tell: subject's experiences, thoughts, and feelings
5. The first-person narrator of a biography can give only his or her own point of view, commenting only on what the subject does or says. The first-person narrator of an autobiography can share personal thoughts and feelings.
6. "My Papa, Mark Twain" was written by Twain's daughter, so the reader gets an insider's view of Twain as a family man. However, the author can report only her observation of Twain's actual thoughts and feelings. The subject of "The Drive-In Movies" is the narrator himself, so the reader knows the subject's thoughts and feelings. "Space Shuttle *Challenger*" is an eye-witness account of the explosion.
7. "My Papa": Susy thinks her father has a striking character; the family likes Twain's walk; family members all love cats. "Drive-In": The children watch television quietly; Gary makes his mother breakfast; Gary does household chores. "Shuttle": Harwood could not see the smoke and debris; he tells his editor that the shuttle "apparently" exploded.
8. Possible responses: The media should publish no personal information about celebrities' lives. Or, the price of celebrity is the loss of privacy.

EXTEND

Answers for p. 568

❶ Vocabulary Development

Word Analysis

1. as a result
2. next part
3. order

Concept Development: Synonyms

1. incessantly
2. peripheral
3. monitoring
4. catastrophic
5. moot
6. consequently
7. accumulations

Spelling Strategy

1. accumulations
2. incessantly
3. vigorously
4. peripheral

❷ Grammar

1. The article was written by William Harwood.
2. We read The Prince and the Pauper.
3. The film starred Jerry Lewis.
4. We watched the launch at the Kennedy Space Center.
5. The science editor was in Pasadena, California, covering Voyager 2.

Writing Application

Possible responses:

1. Mark Twain's daughter Susy wrote a biography of her father.
2. Gary Soto loved drive-in movies when he was a kid.
3. The space shuttle *Challenger* had flown many missions.

Integrate Language Skills

❶ Vocabulary Development Lesson

Word Analysis: Latin Root *-sequi-*

When you see the Latin root *-sequi-*, as in the word *consequently* found in "My Papa, Mark Twain," remember that *sequi* means "follow." Thus, a word with this root means "following" or "coming after."

On your paper, explain the meaning of each italicized word.

1. The alarm didn't ring; *consequently*, I was late.
2. We liked the *sequel* to the movie more than the first one because it was funnier and more action-packed.
3. In the *sequence* for this pattern, a blue dot follows three red dots.

Concept Development: Synonyms

On your paper, write the vocabulary word that could be used as a synonym for each word below.

1. steadily
2. on the edge
3. watching
4. disastrous
5. unimportant
6. therefore
7. buildups

Spelling Strategy

Words with several syllables may have more letters than you expect. Copy the sentences below, completing each one with the words provided. Pronounce each syllable of the word before writing.

ac•cum•u•la•tions　　vig•or•ous•ly
per•i•pher•al　　in•cess•ant•ly

1. There were large _________ of snow.
2. The rain drummed _______ on the roof.
3. They exercised _________.
4. The ________ colors are fading.

❷ Grammar Lesson

Writing Proper Nouns

In the selections you have just read, there are many kinds of proper nouns. All proper nouns begin with a capital letter. Titles are proper nouns. Each word in a title, unless it is an article or a preposition with fewer than four letters, begins with a capital letter. In addition, titles have special punctuation and formatting. Short works are set off by quotation marks. Full-length works are italicized.

Titles of short works, such as stories and essays: "My Papa, Mark Twain," "The Drive-In Movies," "The Circuit"
Titles of full-length works, such as novels, plays, and movies: *Cinderfella*, *The Adventures of Tom Sawyer*

Practice Copy each sentence, and use capital letters and quotation marks where needed. Then, underline any words that should be printed in italics.

1. The article was written by William Harwood.
2. We read the prince and the pauper.
3. The film starred jerry lewis.
4. We watched the launch at the kennedy space center.
5. The science editor was in pasadena, california, covering voyager 2.

Writing Application Write three sentences using proper nouns.

WG *Prentice Hall Writing and Grammar Connection: Chapter 27*

TEACHING RESOURCES

The following resources can be used to enrich or extend the instruction for pp. 568–569.

Vocabulary
- **Selection Support:** Build Vocabulary, p. 161; Build Spelling Skills, p. 162
- **Vocabulary and Spelling Practice Book** (Use this booklet for skills enrichment) ■

Grammar
- **Selection Support:** Build Grammar Skills, p. 163
- **Writing and Grammar,** Copper Level, p. 600
- **Daily Language Practice Transparencies** ■

Writing
- **Writing and Grammar,** Copper Level, p. 82
- **Writing Models and Graphic Organizers on Transparencies,** pp. 69, 77, 81
- **Writing and Grammar iText CD-ROM**

■ **BLOCK SCHEDULING:** Resources marked with this symbol provide varied instruction during 90-minute blocks.

❸ Writing Lesson

Autobiographical Narrative

Gary Soto wrote an autobiographical account to share his memories of going to drive-in movies. Write an autobiographical narrative to tell about an event, period, or person in your life.

Prewriting Brainstorm for ideas from your life experience. Then, narrow your topic to a single event or experience you can thoroughly cover.

Drafting Write your draft, putting the details and events together as you remember them. Then, put the paragraphs in order to create a story with a beginning, middle, and end.

Revising Revise your draft, using concrete language—language that names or describes things that can be perceived through the senses. Where possible, replace words with ones that give a more specific sensory impression.

Model: Concrete Language

clanging, yapping, and howling
As we drove up to the shelter, we heard ~~a lot of noise.~~ Inside
squirming bundle of brown fur that barked.
the volunteer handed me a ~~puppy~~.

Prentice Hall Writing and Grammar Connection: Chapter 5, Section 3

❹ Extension Activities

Listening and Speaking William Harwood, as a newspaper reporter, communicates through words only. In contrast, television newscasters use their voices and expressions as well as words. In a small group, watch a newscast and observe the reporter. In an **informal presentation,** share your observations in the following areas:

- **Tone of voice:** Is the reporter sympathetic, concerned, unconcerned, objective?
- **Mood or atmosphere:** Do the descriptions, examples, and quotations create a positive or negative feeling?

Research and Technology With a partner, research some of Mark Twain's characters. Make a **poster** or chart that shows some of Twain's best known works and characters.

Writing Write a **response** in which you explain which of these nonfiction works you found most realistic. Give examples from the work to support your answer.

www.phschool.com

Go online for an additional research activity using the Internet.

ASSESSMENT RESOURCES

The following resources can be used to assess students' knowledge and skills.

Selection Assessment

- **Formal Assessment,** pp. 145–147
- **Open Book Test,** pp. 94–96
- **Got It! Assessment Videotapes,** Tape 4
- **Test Bank Software**

Take It to the Net

Visit www.phschool.com for self-tests and additional questions about the selections.

Writing Rubric

- **Performance Assess. and Portfolio Mgmt.,** p. 8

PRENTICE HALL ASSESSMENT SYSTEM

- **Workbook**
- **Transparencies**
- **Skill Book**
- **CD-ROM**

Lesson Support for p. 569

❸ Writing Lesson

- Before students brainstorm, remind them that the incident that they relate need not be important.
- Suggest that students use a Series of Events Chain or Timeline organizer such as those on p. 69 and p. 77 in **Writing Models and Graphic Organizers on Transparencies** when outlining their autobiographical accounts.
- They may also benefit from the Sensory Language chart on p. 81 in **Writing Models and Graphic Organizers on Transparencies** as they revise. They can keep track of the sensory details they include in their narratives.
- Finally, use the Autobiographical Narration rubric on p. 8 in **Performance Assessment and Portfolio Management** to evaluate students' narratives.

❹ Listening and Speaking

- Make a checklist of the criteria students are to consider as they watch and listen.
- To save time, show students a videotaped excerpt from a news broadcast that you have viewed previously.
- Talk with students before they give their presentations. Make sure that students are objective. Direct them away from comments about newscasters' appearances.
- Remind students to maintain eye contact and to speak clearly to their audience.

CUSTOMIZE INSTRUCTION
For Universal Access

To address different learning styles, use the activities suggested in the **Extension Activities** booklet, p. 33.

- For Visual/Spatial Learners, use Activity 5.
- For Bodily/Kinesthetic and Interpersonal Learners, use Activity 6.
- For Logical/Mathematical Learners, use Activity 7.

Restoring the Circle ✦ How the Internet Works ✦ Turkeys

Lesson Objectives

1. **To analyze and respond to literary elements**
   - Literary Analysis: Types of Essays
   - Comparing Literary Works
2. **To read, comprehend, analyze, and critique nonfiction**
   - Reading Strategy: Using Context to Determine Meaning
   - Reading Check Questions
   - Review and Assess Questions
   - Assessment Practice (ATE)
3. **To develop word analysis skills, fluency, and systematic vocabulary**
   - Vocabulary Development Lesson: Word Analysis: Forms of *tolerate*
4. **To understand and apply written and oral language conventions**
   - Spelling Strategy
   - Grammar Lesson: Punctuation and Capitalization in Dialogue
5. **To understand and apply appropriate writing and research strategies**
   - Writing Lesson: Compare-and-Contrast Composition
   - Extension Activity: Research Native American Authors
   - Extension Activity: Letter
6. **To understand and apply listening and speaking strategies**
   - Extension Activity: Oral Directions

STEP-BY-STEP TEACHING GUIDE	PACING GUIDE
PRETEACH	
Motivate Students and Provide Background	
Use the Motivation activity (ATE p. 570)	5 min.
Read and discuss the Preview material and Background information (SE/ATE p. 570) [A]	10 min.
Introduce the Concepts	
Introduce the Literary Analysis and Reading Strategy (SE/ATE p. 571) [A]	25 min.
Pronounce the vocabulary words and read their definitions (SE p. 571)	5 min.
TEACH	
Monitor Comprehension	
Informally monitor comprehension by circulating while students read independently or in groups [A]	25–30 min.
Monitor students' comprehension with the Reading Check notes (SE/ATE pp. 573, 577)	as students read
Develop vocabulary with Vocabulary notes (SE pp. 575, 582, 584)	as students read
Develop Understanding	
Develop students' understanding of types of essays with the Literary Analysis annotations (SE pp. 576, 582; ATE pp. 572, 576, 582) [A]	5 min.
Develop students' ability to use context clues to determine meaning with the Reading Strategy annotations (SE pp. 578, 581; ATE pp. 578, 581)	5 min.
ASSESS	
Assess Mastery	
Assess students' mastery of the Reading Strategy and Literary Analysis by having them answer the Review and Assess questions (SE/ATE p. 585)	25 min.
Use one or more of the print and media Assessment Resources (ATE p. 587) [A]	up to 45 min.
EXTEND	
Apply Understanding	
Have students complete the Vocabulary Development Lesson and the Grammar Lesson (SE p. 586) [A]	20 min.
Apply students' knowledge of compare and contrast compositions using the Writing Lesson (SE/ATE p. 587) [A]	45 min.
Apply students' understanding using one or more of the Extension Activities (SE p. 587)	20–90 min.

ACCELERATED INSTRUCTION:
Use the strategies and activities identified with an [A].

UNIVERSAL ACCESS
● = Below Level Students
▲ = On-Level Students
■ = Above Level Students

Time and Resource Manager

Reading Level: Easy, Average, Challenging
Average Number of Instructional Days: 4

RESOURCES		
PRINT	**TRANSPARENCIES**	**TECHNOLOGY**
• **Beyond Literature,** Cross-Curricular Connection: Science, p. 34 ▲ ■		• **Interest Grabber Videotapes,** Tape 4 ● ▲ ■
• **Selection Support Workbook:** ● ▲ ■ Literary Analysis, p. 170 Reading Strategy, p. 169 Build Vocabulary, p. 166	• **Literary Analysis and Reading Transparencies,** pp. 67 and 68 ● ▲ ■	
• **Adapted Reader's Companion** ● • **Reader's Companion** ●		• **Listening to Literature** ● ▲ ■ Audiocassettes, Side 20 Audio CDs, CD 10
• **English Learner's Companion** ● ▲ • **Literary Analysis for Enrichment** ■		
• **Formal Assessment:** Selection Test, pp. 148–150 ● ▲ ■ • **Open Book Test,** pp. 100–102 ● ▲ ■ • **Performance Assessment and Portfolio Management,** pp. 16, 21 ● ▲ ■ • PRENTICE HALL ASSESSMENT SYSTEM ● ▲ ■	• PRENTICE HALL ASSESSMENT SYSTEM ● ▲ ■ Skills Practice Answers and Explanations on Transparencies	• **Test Bank Software** ● ▲ ■ • **Got It! Assessment Videotapes,** Tape 4 ● ▲
• **Selection Support Workbook:** ● ▲ ■ Build Spelling Skills, p. 167 Build Grammar Skills, p. 168 • **Writing and Grammar,** Copper Level ● ▲ ■ • **Extension Activities,** p. 34 ● ▲ ■	• **Daily Language Practice Transparencies** ● ▲ • **Writing Models and Graphic Organizers on Transparencies** ● ▲ ■	• **Writing and Grammar iText CD-ROM** ● ▲ ■ ***Take It to the Net*** www.phschool.com

BLOCK SCHEDULING: Use one 90-minute class period to preteach the selection and have students read it. Use a second 90-minute class period to assess students' mastery of skills and have them complete one of the Extension Activities.

PRETEACH

Step-by-Step Teaching Guide for pp. 570–571

Motivation

Before reading the selections, have students scan the pictures and graphics that accompany them. After they have examined the images, ask students what they predict each essay will be about. Ask them what tone the artwork sets for each essay. Does the art make them want to read the essays? Why or why not? What else do they see that gives them clues about the selections?

Interest Grabber Video

As an alternative, play "Joseph Bruchac on the Art of Persuasion" on Tape 4 to engage student interest.

❶ Background

Social Studies

Conservation efforts waned after the 1920s until the mid-1960s and 1970s. After the publication of Rachel Carson's *Silent Spring*, which detailed the horrific effects of deadly chemicals on wildlife and the environment, people became aware again of the risks of thoughtless development and industry. Young people in particular became supporters of the environmental movement, as it came to be known. College students across the country celebrated the first Earth Day on April 22, 1970.

Prepare to Read

❶ Restoring the Circle ◆ How the Internet Works Turkeys

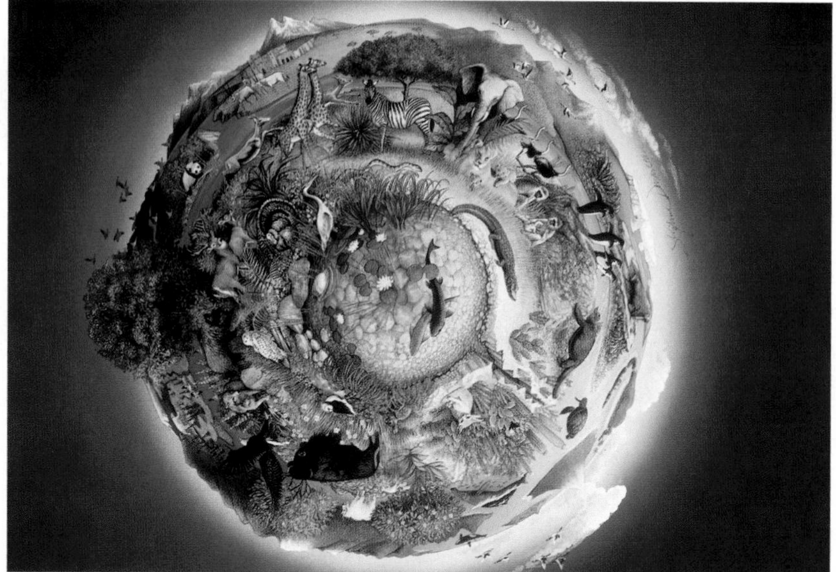

Paradise #1, Suzanne Duranceau, Illustratrice

Take It to the Net

Visit www.phschool.com for interactive activities and instruction related to these selections, including

- background
- graphic organizers
- literary elements
- reading strategies

Preview

Connecting to the Literature

"Restoring the Circle" by Joseph Bruchac, "How the Internet Works" by Kerry Cochrane, and "Turkeys" by Bailey White are all essays in this grouping. Each essay shows how people make connections between themselves and the world around them. As you read, think about where you find connections between your own experience and the rest of the world.

Background

"Turkeys" tells of the efforts of conservationists to preserve a population of wild turkeys. Conservation became an issue in the United States in the early 1900s. President Theodore Roosevelt established the first federal wildlife refuge at Pelican Island in Florida and set aside more than 140 million acres to be national forest reserves.

TEACHING RESOURCES

The following resources can be used to enrich or extend the instruction for pp. 570–571.

Motivation

Interest Grabber Video, Tape 4

Background

Beyond Literature, p. 34

Take It to the Net

Visit www.phschool.com for Background and hotlinks for the selections.

Literary Analysis

Literary Analysis and Reading Transparencies, Types of Essays, p. 68

Reading

Selection Support: Reading Strategy, p. 169; Build Vocabulary, p. 166

Literary Analysis and Reading Transparencies, Using Context to Determine Meaning, p. 67

BLOCK SCHEDULING: Resources marked with this symbol provide varied instruction during 90-minute blocks.

❷ Literary Analysis

Types of Essays

An **essay** is a nonfiction work about a particular subject.

- "Restoring the Circle" is a **persuasive essay:** it presents reasons or arguments in favor of something and provides supporting evidence.
- "How the Internet Works" is an **informational essay:** it presents facts, information, and explanations about a topic.
- "Turkeys" is a **narrative essay:** it tells about real-life experiences using the elements of storytelling.

Comparing Literary Works

An informational essay and a persuasive essay both provide facts. However, because the two types of essays have different **purposes,** or goals, different types of facts may be used or the facts may be presented in different ways. Compare and contrast the essays in this group by thinking about the following focus questions.

1. What characteristics do all essays share?
2. How do the different purposes of essays influence the kinds of details they include?

❸ Reading Strategy

Using Context to Determine Meaning

Nonfiction works often include words that are unfamiliar or that are used in a way that is specific to the topic of the work. Use **context**—the situation in which the word is used—to help determine the meaning. Look for clues in the surrounding words, sentences, and paragraphs. The chart at right shows clues from the selection that can help you figure out the meaning of the word *ornithologist*. As you read, use a chart like it to record unfamiliar words and clues to their meanings.

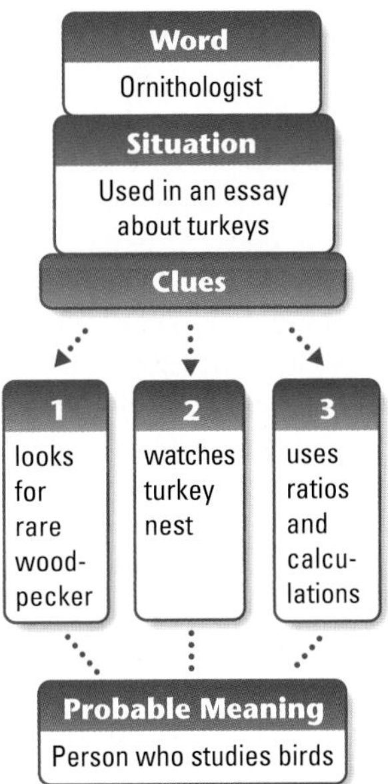

Vocabulary Development

tolerance (täl′ ər əns) *n.* respect for something different (p. 575)

detrimental (de′ trə ment′ əl) *adj.* harmful (p. 575)

dilution (di lo͞o′ shən) *n.* weakening by mixing with something else (p. 582)

vigilance (vij′ ə ləns) *n.* watchfulness (p. 584)

❷ Literary Analysis

Types of Essays

- Explain to students that there are several types of essays—persuasive, informational, and narrative. Each type has a different purpose and uses different techniques to present information.
- Invite a volunteer to read aloud the instruction about types of essays. Then, tell students that they will be reading three different essays, each of which has a distinct purpose.
- Use the Types of Essays transparency on p. 68 in **Literary Analysis and Reading Transparencies** to show students the differences between persuasive, informational, and narrative essays.

❸ Reading Strategy

Using Context to Determine Meaning

- After students read the instruction on p. 571, explain that in nonfiction essays, authors often have to introduce unfamiliar words. These words are key to understanding a particular idea.
- Next, explain that context clues may appear in the same sentence as a restatement or in sentences around the unfamiliar word.
- Use the chart on p. 571 to show students how to use context clues. If time permits, use context clues with another word from one of the essays to demonstrate how to determine meaning.

Vocabulary Development

- Review the words and definitions on the vocabulary list.
- Point out the word *dilution* to students. Ask students to name situations in which a person might *dilute* something.
  Answer: Students might suggest working on a science project, mixing a cleaning solution, or cooking.

CUSTOMIZE INSTRUCTION FOR UNIVERSAL ACCESS

For Special Needs Students	For Less Proficient Readers	For English Learners
Have students read the adapted versions of these selections in the **Adapted Reader's Companion.** These versions provide basic-level instruction in an interactive format with questions and write-on lines. Completing the adapted versions will prepare students to read the selections in the Student Edition.	Have students read these selections in the **Reader's Companion.** These versions provide basic-level instruction in an interactive format with questions and write-on lines. After students finish the selections in the Reader's Companion, have them complete the questions and activities in the Student Edition.	Have students read the adapted versions of these selections in the **English Learner's Companion.** These versions provide basic-level instruction in an interactive format with questions and write-on lines. Completing the adapted versions will prepare students to read the selections in the Student Edition.

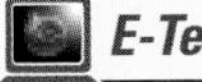

E-Teach

Visit E-Teach at www.phschool.com for teachers' essays on how to teach, with questions and answers.

TEACH

Step-by-Step Teaching Guide for pp. 572–584

CUSTOMIZE INSTRUCTION
For Musical/Rhythmic Learners

Ask volunteers to give oral interpretations of Native American folk tales, stories, or poems. First, have students practice giving their interpretations before a small group. Ask them to present their oral interpretations to the class.

1 About the Selection

In "Restoring the Circle," Joseph Bruchac cautions that the Native American way of life, the circle, is threatened. The history of the Native Americans has been distorted, causing shame among the people. Now it is time to return respect and honor to the culture. Today, leading Native American writers work to present the truth and give back pride to those who have lost it. Through their efforts, they preserve the heritage and enhance the self-worth of their people. Their literature helps develop understanding and create tolerance among all people, thus restoring the circle.

2 Literary Analysis

Types of Essays

- Ask students to paraphrase the first paragraph.
  Possible response: For Native Americans, life goes in cycles, with the elders teaching the children about their culture.
- Explain that the point Bruchac makes in the first paragraph is an important part of his essay. He will argue that the circle has been broken for Native Americans for too long and needs to be closed.

1 Restoring The Circle

Native American Literature as a Means of Preserving Cultural Traditions

Joseph Bruchac

2 In many Native American traditions life is seen as a circle. We enter that circle when we are born and as we travel around that circle we come back, as elders, to the place where we began. The elders, who have spent a lifetime learning their cultural traditions, are the ones who are supposed to be the closest to the children, passing on their traditions through the teaching to be found in stories. As long as that circle remains unbroken, the people will survive.

Imagine what it would be like if someone who never met you and knew nothing about the circle of your life wrote a story about you. Even if that person was a good writer, you probably would not agree with what he wrote. As interesting as imagination may be, it cannot take the place of experience and firsthand knowledge. In a similar way, imaginative portrayals of Native American people and Native American cultures became painful stereotypes and distorted history. Native American men were pictured as savage and dangerous people who were aggressive for no good reason. Yet it is historically true that none of America's so-called "Indian wars" were ever begun by the Indians. Native American women were pictured as nothing more than

TEACHING RESOURCES

The following resources can be used to enrich or extend the instruction for pp. 572–584.

Literary Analysis
- **Selection Support:** Literary Analysis, p. 170
- **Literary Analysis for Enrichment** ■
- **Writing Models and Graphic Organizers on Transparencies,** pp. 69, 73, 77, 89, 93

Reading
- **Reader's Companion**
- **Adapted Reader's Companion**

- **English Learner's Companion**
- **Literatura en español**
- **Listening to Literature Audiocassettes,** Side 20 ■
- **Listening to Literature Audio CDs,** CD 10 ■

■ **BLOCK SCHEDULING:** Resources marked with this symbol provide varied instruction during 90-minute blocks.

beasts of burden. Yet in many Native American cultures, such as that of the Iroquois, the women were the heads of families, the owners of the houses, and the ones who chose the chiefs. Details of Native cultures were badly confused. For example, the famous poem *Hiawatha* by Henry Wadsworth Longfellow actually tells the story of Managozho, a trickster hero of the Chippewa people. The real Hiawatha was a political leader of the Iroquois people. It would be like calling the hero of the Anglo-Saxon epic *Beowulf* Julius Caesar. More than 400 different languages are spoken by the various Native American nations of North America, but instead of showing the complexity and variety of Native American cultures, much of the literature by non-Native people made all Indians look and sound alike.

4

Many Native Americans chose to become writers because they wanted to restore the circle through more accurate portrayals of themselves and their people. In many cases, too, they hoped to restore a sense of pride in their own heritage. Because of the inaccurate and unpleasant ways Native Americans have been portrayed in books by non-Indian authors, Native children have

3 ▲ **Critical Viewing** In what two ways does the picture reflect the title? **[Identify]**

5 ✓ **Reading Check**

What problem bothers the writer?

3 ▶ Critical Viewing

The picture reflects the title because of the image of a half circle and because the sand painting is an example of Native American art being preserved.

4 Critical Thinking

Analyze

- After students have read the bracketed passage, ask them to point out two mistakes that writers from outside Native American cultures have made.
  Answer: Longfellow tells the story of Managozho, a Chippewa trickster figure, but calls the character Hiawatha, an Iroquois leader. Also, 400 Native American languages have been presented as one.
- Then, pose the following question: What example does Bruchac use to persuade you that Native American cultures are rich and valuable?
  Answer: Students should point out that the Native American nations in North America speak over 400 different languages.

5 ✓ Reading Check

Answer: The fact that Native American cultures have been misrepresented by non-Native Americans bothers the author.

CUSTOMIZE INSTRUCTION FOR UNIVERSAL ACCESS

For Special Needs Students

Students may understand Bruchac's essay better if they can identify his main idea and the details that support it. Offer students the Main Idea and Supporting Details organizer on p. 73 in **Writing Models and Graphic Organizers on Transparencies.** Help students by identifying the main idea—that Bruchac believes that modern Native American writers can help mend the broken circle of Native American tradition. Ask students to work in pairs and fill in the supporting details as they read.

For English Learners

Because English language learners may be able to identify with Bruchac and his experience as a Native American, ask them to complete an Open Mind Diagram like the one on p. 93 in **Writing Models and Graphic Organizers on Transparencies.** Have students use pictures, words, and symbols to represent their ideas about the essay. Then, ask them to write a brief journal entry explaining the meanings behind their images.

6 Literary Analysis

Types and Purposes of Essays

- Ask students to freewrite in their journals a response to this question: How could connecting with your history make you a stronger person?
- Then, ask volunteers to summarize their responses.
  Possible responses: When you know what your culture has accomplished, you have confidence in yourself. History unites people through a common ground. People find role models in their history. Since history is passed down, it makes the family stronger.
- Read aloud the bracketed passage. Then, invite students to respond to the Literary Analysis question on p. 574.
  Possible response: The detail shows a concrete way in which the Native American way of life has been threatened.

7 ▶Critical Viewing

Possible responses: Students should understand that Bruchac enjoys nature. Their reasons may include the following: Bruchac believes in preserving Native American cultures, which are closely tied to nature; Bruchac respects nature; he appears relaxed and natural in this photograph.

sometimes felt ashamed of themselves and decided that it would be better for them to forget their own cultures and try to be "just like everyone else." Today, because of the writing of such Native American authors as Michael Dorris or Linda Hogan, young Native people can read stories and poems in which Native Americans are presented as fully-rounded characters from accurately described tribal traditions. As portrayed by Native American authors, Indians are sometimes good, sometimes not so good, but no longer one-dimensional stereotypes.

6 In the period between 1850 and 1950, many Native American children were sent away to Indian boarding schools where they were not allowed to speak their own Native languages. Whether they wanted to or not, they were expected to no longer "be Indian" and, removed completely from the circle of their families, denied contact with their elders. It was felt by many well-meaning people in the United States government that the only way to "help the Indians" was by making them be more like European Americans. Today, of course, we see things differently. In a multicultural world we understand how important cultural traditions are in maintaining a sense of self-worth. It is now believed that whoever you are, whether you are Jewish American, African American, Italian American, or Native American, knowing about your own 7 history and culture can make you a stronger person. Today, many Native American people are discovering that Native American literature can help them find their way back to that old circle of knowledge. In some cases, people who were not taught their tribal languages as children are learning those languages again through literature. In Arizona, a successful project helped Pima and Papago children learn their native O'odham language by reading traditional songs in O'odham and then writing poems in O'odham. Those songs, which had been preserved as literature, and the new poems worked together to help strengthen traditions.

One of the most prominent Native American writers is N. Scott Momaday, who is of Kiowa Indian ancestry. His first novel, *House Made of Dawn*, tells the story of a young Native American man who returns home after fighting as an American soldier in a foreign war. He feels divided between the white world and the Indian world, and that division in himself makes him sick. It is only by understanding his own traditions and returning to them that he is able to restore his health and self-respect. That novel, which won a Pulitzer Prize in 1969, is a good example of the kind of Native American writing which helps preserve cultural traditions. It contains authentic and very well-written descriptions of Native American life around the time of the late 1940's and early

Literary Analysis
Types and Purposes of Essays How does the detail about native languages add to the persuasive power of the essay?

▼ Critical Viewing Based on the essay and this picture of Bruchac, explain whether you think Bruchac enjoys nature. **[Speculate]**

ENRICHMENT: Social Studies Connection

The Abenaki People

Joseph Bruchac is part Abenaki, a Native American people in the northeastern United States. The name *Abenaki* is an Algonquian word for "easterner." Eastern Woodland Indians, of which the Abenaki are a part, at first welcomed the European settlers. The growing European populations, though, decreased the game supply and made it difficult for these Native Americans to continue their traditional lifestyles.

Eventually, the hunters became farmers, and by 1800, the Abenaki, who had once ranged over much of the Northeast, found themselves limited to Maine.

Invite students to find out more about the traditional and contemporary culture of another group of Native Americans from the Eastern Woodlands. Have students explain their findings to the class.

1950's. Many Native Americans who have read this book have felt deeply inspired by it because its main character, caught between the white and Indian worlds, experiences some of the confusion and pain which they have also felt. It is hard to be a stranger in your own country, but that is the way many Native Americans sometimes feel. By reading Momaday's novel, they gained a better understanding of their own feelings, and it strengthened their convictions about the importance of preserving their own traditions.

Native American literature, like all literatures, is also a way to speak to the world. In some cases, novels by Native American writers are now being used as textbooks in college courses in history and sociology. Writing can become a window into another reality, offering to non-Natives the opportunity to authentically experience something of Native American culture. If you read a book about another culture, you may be more likely to have understanding and tolerance for that culture. When you have respect for another culture, then you are much less likely to do things which will be detrimental to that culture and to the people of that culture. Perhaps, because of the cultural understanding offered through Native American literature, the circle of Native American cultural traditions will be less threatened in the generations to come.

tolerance (täl′ ər əns) *n.* respect for something different

detrimental (de′ trə ment′ əl) *adj.* harmful

Review and Assess

Thinking About the Selection

1. **Respond:** What questions would you like to ask Joseph Bruchac about his heritage?
2. **(a) Recall:** Describe how some Native Americans use a circle to explain life. **(b) Interpret:** Explain the title "Restoring the Circle." **(c) Support:** In what ways do Native American writers help to restore the circle?
3. **(a) Recall:** What are two examples of ways in which Native American people have been misunderstood by those who are not Native American? **(b) Generalize:** Why is it important to Bruchac that Native American culture be portrayed accurately and sensitively?
4. **(a) Recall:** What does Bruchac say happens when people read about another culture? **(b) Apply:** How do writers of all cultures help to build people's understanding of a multicultural world?
5. **Make a Judgment:** Do you think an understanding of one's heritage makes a person stronger? Explain why.

Joseph Bruchac

(b. 1942)

A writing instructor once said to Joseph Bruchac, "Give it up. You'll never write a good poem." Since that awful prediction, Bruchac has written and edited many collections of poetry, winning numerous writing awards. His poems, stories, and essays have been translated into Russian, Italian, Polish, German, and many other languages. Among many other things, Bruchac is committed to preserving and celebrating his Native American heritage.

Answers for p. 575

Review and Assess

1. **Possible responses:** Students may want to ask Bruchac questions about the history, culture, and religion of his or other Native American nations.
2. **(a)** People enter the circle when they are born and travel the circle until they return, as elders, to the beginning. **(b)** **Possible response:** Students may say that the circle represents Native American culture. Restoring it means respecting Native American heritage, teaching the truth about American history, and passing on the traditions of the people. **(c)** They present a more realistic picture of their people and generate pride in Native American heritage.
3. **(a)** In *Hiawatha*, Hiawatha is portrayed as a Chippewa trickster when he is really an Iroquois leader. Also, no "Indian wars" were started by Native Americans, as many people believe. **(b)** If a culture is acknowledged and respected, people will be more tolerant of and less harmful to it.
4. **(a)** When people read about another culture, they are more understanding and respectful of it. **(b)** By writing honestly about their cultures, writers of all cultures help readers understand the complicated and multicultural world in which they live.
5. **Possible response:** Students may say "yes," because understanding one's heritage gives a person pride and a feeling of self-worth.

CUSTOMIZE INSTRUCTION FOR UNIVERSAL ACCESS

For Less Proficient Readers	For Gifted/Talented Students
Students may have trouble finding the thread of the argument in Bruchac's essay. Point out that his argument is subtle; he does not say outright what people should do. Help students by having them read the selection in sections. After each section, have them write the answers to these questions: What is the author's point here? What does he want me to think? What does he want me to do? Do I agree with him? Why or why not? Have students compare answers after they read.	Bruchac says that Momaday's novel inspires many Native Americans because its main character experiences the same emotions they do. Ask students which book characters have inspired them for the same reason. Ask them what effect the literature has had on them. Remind students that we study literature to share our experiences and learn from one another.

❽ About the Selection

In her informational essay "How the Internet Works," Kerry Cochrane compares the way the Internet transmits information to the way the postal service delivers mail. Both systems rely on a set of rules or protocols. Once people learn the protocols for a system, information can be shared. Cochrane defines the general rules, basic structure, and worldwide scope of the postal service and then uses similar terms to explain features of the Internet. By presenting several specific examples of Internet addresses and translating the individual parts of the addresses, she helps clarify some of the Net's language.

❾ Literary Analysis

Types of Essays

- After students read the first two paragraphs, ask them to explain which type of essay they are reading and why.
  Answer: Students should understand that the essay is informational. The writer is explaining how Internet protocols are like the rules of a game and how the Internet operates like the post office.
- Next, ask students the Literary Analysis question on p. 576.
  Answer: By comparing the Internet to the post office, the author is comparing the Internet to something readers are already familiar with. The author helps readers by making connections between something new and something familiar.

❽

How the Internet Works

Kerry Cochrane

The central problem in designing the Internet was finding a way for different kinds of computers all over the country to talk to one another. ARPA solved this problem with Internet protocols. Protocols are sets of rules that standardize how something is done, so that everyone knows what to expect. For example, think of any game you've played and the rules that went with that game. The rules of the game tell you how many players you can have, what order you play in, what's allowed and what's not allowed, and how to keep score. Once you know the rules, you can play with people very different from you. Internet protocols are like game rules: they set up standard procedures for computers to follow so that they can communicate with each other.

❾ The Internet is often compared to the postal service. They both seem to work like one big organization, but are actually made up of smaller parts that work together. There are local post offices in small towns, regional postal systems in big cities, and national postal services for countries. They all use different machinery to handle the mail, and different equipment to deliver it, from bicycles to trucks to airplanes. Postal workers all over the world speak hundreds of different languages. But they all manage to work together because of certain rules, or protocols. Postal protocols say that mail must be in envelopes or packages, there must be postage, and every piece of mail must have an address. As long as you know these rules, you can send mail to anyone in the world.

Literary Analysis
Types of Essays How does this comparison to the post office help you learn about the Internet?

The Internet works in a similar way. As long as everyone knows the protocols, information can travel easily between machines and the people using them worldwide. The basic group of protocols that governs the Internet is the TCP/IP set of protocols. This stands for Transmission Control Protocol (TCP)

CUSTOMIZE INSTRUCTION FOR UNIVERSAL ACCESS

For Less Proficient Readers	For English Learners
Within the first two paragraphs, the writer has compared the Internet to a game and to the post office. Help students keep track of comparisons by asking them to make a two-column chart with the headings *Post Office* and *Internet.* As students read, they should record examples the writer gives of how both systems work. After students finish reading and compiling facts about the two systems, have them read across the columns to see the parallels.	Have students make a list of computer terms used in the selection and define each one using the information in the text. Then, help students compare these definitions with dictionary definitions of the same term. It may help students if you have a dictionary of computer or technological terms on hand, too. Finally, talk to students about whether, in their own experiences, new technical language is harder or easier to learn than other types of vocabulary.

❸ Writing Lesson

Compare-and-Contrast Composition

In "How to Use the Internet," Kerry Cochrane compares the postal service to the Internet. Write a composition comparing and contrasting two Internet sites.

Prewriting Choose a topic and find two Web sites with information on the topic. Use an organizer like this one to gather details.

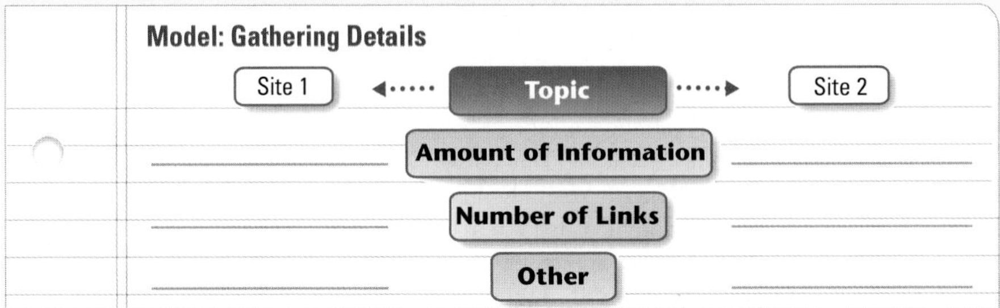

Drafting Begin with an introductory paragraph in which you identify your two sites. Then, organize paragraphs around the categories on the chart.

Revising Highlight all the details about the first site in one color. Highlight all the details about the second site in a second color. If there are many more details in one color than in the other, add details that will improve the balance.

WG *Prentice Hall Writing and Grammar Connection: Chapter 8, Section 3*

❹ Extension Activities

Listening and Speaking Deliver **oral directions** to the class for starting a computer, logging on to e-mail, or doing an Internet search.

1. Present the steps in order.
2. Be clear and specific in identifying each part of the computer for each step of the directions.
3. Define any terms that may be unfamiliar.
4. Speak clearly, and pause after explaining each step so that listeners can remember what you have said.

Research and Technology Joseph Bruchac calls for respect and honor for Native American cultures through literature that develops understanding and tolerance. Compile a list of Native American authors and works that students your age might enjoy. Share your list with the class.

Writing Write a letter to one of the authors. Tell the author what you think are the strengths and weaknesses of the work. Use examples from the text.

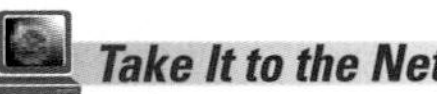

Take It to the Net www.phschool.com

Go online for an additional research activity using the Internet.

ASSESSMENT RESOURCES

The following resources can be used to assess students' knowledge and skills.

Selection Assessment

- **Formal Assessment,** pp. 148–150
- **Open Book Test,** pp. 100–102
- **Got It! Assessment Videotapes,** Tape 4
- **Test Bank Software**

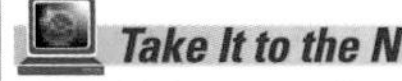

Take It to the Net

Visit www.phschool.com for self-tests and additional questions on the selections.

Writing Rubric

- **Performance Assess. and Portfolio Mgmt.,** p. 16

Listening and Speaking Rubric

- **Performance Assess. and Portfolio Mgmt.,** p. 21

PRENTICE HALL ASSESSMENT SYSTEM

- **Workbook**
- **Skill Book**
- **Transparencies**
- **CD-ROM**

Lesson Support for p. 587

❸ Writing Lesson

- Remind students that they must compare the Web sites in at least three ways.
- As students search for sites, suggest that they look for two sites that cover the same topic. If you wish to restrict the sites that students visit, offer them several pairs that you have researched and downloaded.
- Remind students that there are two ways to present information in a comparison-and-contrast paper. They may alternate paragraphs, devoting each paragraph exclusively to one site, or they may alternate information within the paragraphs, devoting each paragraph to a particular detail.
- Use the Exposition rubric on p. 16 in **Performance Assessment and Portfolio Management** to evaluate students' work.

❹ Listening and Speaking

- After students read the instruction for the activity, suggest that they choose the topic with which they are least familiar. That way, they must learn the steps before they can teach others. Or, you may wish to assign topics randomly.
- Suggest that students adapt the Series of Events Chain organizer on p. 69 in **Writing Models and Graphic Organizers on Transparencies** as they plan their directions. The chart will help them keep the steps in order.
- As students practice their presentations, have them follow their own steps to ensure that the steps are accurate and in the correct order.
- Remind students that they should speak slowly and clearly when giving instructions to the audience.
- Have students use the Listening rubric on p. 21 in **Performance Assessment and Portfolio Management.**

CUSTOMIZE INSTRUCTION
For Universal Access

To address different learning styles, use the activities suggested in the **Extension Activities** booklet, p. 34.

- For Mathematical/Logical and Verbal/Linguistic Learners, use Activity 7.

Lesson Objectives

1. To understand the connection between conserving animal life and conserving a habitat that sustains certain animals
2. To understand that writers can write eloquently and descriptively about scientific phenomena

Connections

In "Turkeys" (p. 580), Bailey White describes some scientists' often comical efforts to preserve the wild turkeys that lived in the woods near her house when she was a girl. Today, the wild turkey thrives. The article on this page discusses the decline of the Salton Sea habitat and the resulting ill effects on birds and other wildlife. Have students reread "Turkeys" after they read the article here. What similarities and differences do students notice between these two pieces in terms of the writers' content, purpose, and tone?

Environmental Emergencies

- Before students begin reading, point out that the article combines elements of a descriptive essay, a research report, and a first-person narrative. By combining these elements, the writer provides the information necessary to give the reader a good sense of the place described.
- Have students begin reading the article. Ask them to identify the vivid details in the first two paragraphs.
  Answer: Vivid details include the dying fish, the ferocious heat, and the waiting birds.

continued on p. 589

CONNECTIONS

Literature and Science

Environmental Emergencies

In "Turkeys," Bailey White gives a personal account of her experience with efforts to save populations of wild turkeys. At the turn of the twentieth century, wild turkeys had disappeared from 18 of the 39 states they had inhabited. In 1937, the Federal Aid in Wildlife Restoration Act began funding the acquisition of wildlife habitats. In the early 1950s, wildlife biologists in South Carolina trapped healthy wild turkeys and released them in habitats where there were few wild turkeys. When the National Wild Turkey Federation was founded in 1973, the restoration of wild turkeys was underway in many states. Today, more than five million wild turkeys roam the fields and forests of North America.

This article discusses another wildlife "emergency." Saving the many species of migrating birds and fish from the increasingly polluted Salton Sea is a challenge facing engineers and scientists. The Salton Sea is a landlocked lake in Southern California's Imperial Valley. This popular, 360-mile-square saltwater lake has become polluted by agricultural runoff, including chemicals and silt. Lacking a steady supply of fresh water, it is becoming more salty and polluted every day and increasingly dangerous for wildlife.

California's Much-Maligned Salton Sea— Is a Desert Oasis for Wildlife

National Wildlife
August-Sept. 2000

Joby Warrick

To appreciate the beauty of the Salton Sea you first have to look past some very big warts. Dennis Imhoff, state park ranger and booster for California's biggest inland lake, is trying to steer a visitor away from the sea's gnarliest features but they keep popping up, like the dying fish now floating in clumps near the shoreline.

The midday heat is ferocious, a blistering 100 degrees F. The sand whines with millions of insects. The public beach is deserted, except for a few dozen black cormorants keeping sullen watch over the rotting fish. As Imhoff watches, a young couple in a Volvo cruises slowly through the parking lot and then drives away without even cracking a window. . . .

Yet this ugly duckling of a lake harbors surprises, some of which are only now becoming fully appreciated. Recent biological surveys of this much-maligned water body have revealed an astonishing richness in wildlife. The 90-degree water churns with fish in such abundance that some locals describe scooping them up in trash bags. The fish in turn attract birds by the millions. Indeed, this unusual lake attracts more species of migrating birds than any other location in the contiguous United States, except for the Texas coastline.

Thematic Connection
Why is the Salton Sea worth saving?

That's why, say the lake's supporters, the Salton Sea has become a natural wonder. The problem is convincing government officials and a less-than-eager public that it is a treasure worth saving.

"That smell—it's the smell of life," says Steven Horvitz, superintendent of the state's Salton Sea Recreation Area. With nearly 95 percent of California's inland wetlands lost to development in the past 150 years, the sea has taken on critical importance as a feeding ground for birds migrating north along the Pacific flyway, he says. "If the sea can no longer support the bird population," he adds, "many of the birds that use the lake as a feeding ground will no longer be able to survive."

The lake itself is a tear-shaped body of water that lies 227 feet below sea level, in a natural and utterly barren depression that

continued from p. 588

- Point out that the author describes several cause-and-effect relationships on this page of the article. Offer students a cause-and-effect organizer like the one on p. 65 of **Writing Models and Graphic Organizers on Transparencies.** Challenge students to find at least two cause-and-effect relationships and to include them in their organizers.
  Answer: Students should understand that poor water quality will have a negative effect on the bird population. Also, the lake lacks an outlet, so farm runoff is steadily accumulating. Finally, students should understand that deteriorating conditions stopped tourists from coming to the lake.

Thematic Connection

Answer: The Salton Sea is worth saving because it is still rich in wildlife. An abundance of fish and birds lives there. However, if conditions continue to deteriorate, wildlife will become endangered.

ENRICHMENT: Science Connection

The Greatest Lake in the World

Lake Baikal, which is a crescent-shaped lake in the heart of Russia's Siberian region, is the largest, oldest, deepest, and purest freshwater lake in the world. It contains one-fifth of the world's freshwater supply, which is more water than in all the Great Lakes combined. Yet, the lake has many characteristics in common with the Salton Sea. Like the Salton Sea, Lake Baikal is an ancient site and is home to diverse forms of wildlife and organisms. It is also a popular resort area, attracting people from all around Russia. Unfortunately, like the Salton Sea, the ancient lake is showing the effects of pollution. Factories and refineries that sit around the lake are changing the chemistry of the water, putting the fish and animals that depend on it at risk.

Tell students to find information about a local lake, pond, river, or stream. Students should focus on the role of the body of water in their community. Is it a natural body of water, or is it the result of human planning? Encourage students to share their information with the class.

Environmental Emergencies

- In this article, the writer is careful to point out the positive and negative aspects of the Salton Sea. Ask students to draw a two-column chart, labeling one column *Positive* and the other *Negative*. Then, have them fill in the chart. If students have difficulty, direct their attention to the description of the sea during autumn.
- Next, ask students what the writer can accomplish by showing both the positive and negative aspects of the Salton Sea.
  Answer: By giving an objective picture of the sea, the writer lets the reader make his or her own judgment about the value of the sea and what should be done to save it.

Thematic Connection

Answer: The problems are similar because conservationists need to find ways to help the wildlife populations of both environments survive.

Spanish explorers once called "the palm of the hand of God." To the east and west are rugged hills; to the south is one of California's most productive agricultural regions, a former desert that exploded to life at the turn of the last century with the arrival of irrigated water from the Colorado River.

It was an irrigation accident that brought the Salton Sea into existence. In 1905, a flood-swollen Colorado River crashed through a poorly made dike, sending billions of gallons of water surging into the Imperial Valley. The flow continued unchecked for 18 months, creating a new freshwater sea larger than Lake Tahoe.

Stocked with game fish in the 1950s, the sea's shores sprouted fish clubs and motels that drew hundreds of thousands of visitors a year. But ultimately the sea was doomed by its own geography. Lacking an outlet, the lake became increasingly salty, with each day bringing new deposits of minerals and silt in the form of farm runoff. Slowly, many of the businesses in the new area dried up. In the former resort known as Salton Sea, a dilapidated yacht club and a few rusted trailers are all that's left of a bustling waterfront that once was the stomping ground of the Beach Boys and Hollywood's infamous Rat Pack.

Thematic Connection
Are the environmental problems that are dooming the Salton Sea similar to those facing the wild turkey? Explain.

Despite the sea's odd origins and seemingly harsh environment, birds are continually drawn to the area. "It is a crown jewel of avian biodiversity," says Milton Friend, executive director of the Salton Sea Science Subcommittee, a multiagency task force.

Science Subcommittee researchers recently completed the most comprehensive survey ever of the sea's biological assets, and pronounced it "incredibly rich" with life in all its variety. The study found 200 new species of plants, animals and microbes that previously had not been recorded at Salton Sea. In addition, it reported that more than 400 kinds of birds—nearly half the total number of known species in North America—have been spotted around the lake, drawn by prey both large and small. And the fish population, widely believed to be in decline, is actually vibrant. Highly prized game fish such as corvina and other species such as croaker and tilapia are not only plentiful, but apparently also safe to eat. "The Salton Sea," the report noted, "may be the most productive fishery in the world."

But it also may be doomed. Eventually, the rising salt levels could destroy the fish—and that's only if farm chemicals fail to do the job first. Nutrients from fertilizers accelerate the life cycle of tiny plants called algae, and the runaway growth strips the water of the oxygen fish need to live. Last year, eight million fish died of asphyxiation on a single day.

Reversing the sea's decline will require major feats in both engineering and public relations. "It represents one of the greatest challenges I've seen in 40 years of studying damaged ecosystems, says

CUSTOMIZE INSTRUCTION FOR UNIVERSAL ACCESS

For Less Proficient Readers	For English Learners
Because the article is fairly long, students may not understand its main point. Have students work as partners and take turns reading several paragraphs. After one student reads, the listening partner should summarize the paragraphs. Then, the partners should switch roles. If partners disagree on the summaries, they should stop and reread the passage. Make sure that students understand that the article describes a natural wonder and expresses concern over its decline.	Students may have trouble understanding some of the technical vocabulary in the article. Have students search the article and list any unfamiliar words. Then, work with students to identify some general categories of words, such as animal names, place names, geographical names, and scientific terms. Help students define these words and place them in the appropriate categories.

Friend. Several proposals are being studied that would reverse the rising salt levels, but launching any of them would require generating large amounts of money and equally large amounts of political capital—a not-so-easy feat for supporters of a lake that generates relatively little income and doesn't always put on its best face for visitors.

But with the arrival of fall the sea turns into a different place. Daytime temperatures drop into the 60s and 70s. The algal blooms cease, the fish stop dying and the birds begin to arrive-by the millions. Egrets, herons, ducks and pelicans feed and roost along the shores, along with such rarely seen creatures as the frigate bird and booby. The annual migrations draw serious birders from across the West to Sonny Bono National Wildlife Refuge, a reserve recently renamed to honor the former California congressman who led efforts to restore the sea before his death in a Sierra Nevada skiing accident.

Some who visit never leave and grow to love the place, warts and all. The beauty of the desert sunsets and the endless variety of wildlife convinced Los Angeles bartender John White to trade his city apartment eight years ago for a small bungalow in Bombay Beach, one of the largest of a half-dozen villages of trailers and cottages scattered along the 60 miles of waterfront. As he fishes from the town pier, his head wrapped in a sweaty bandana to muffle the sun's intensity, a pair of large pelicans take flight behind him with a great whooshing sound like a helicopter's rotor.

"Sometimes when I come here early in the morning, there will be hundreds of birds scattered out in the weeds," White says. "I like to just sit here and listen to the noises they make."

The chattering of birds is getting fainter, and Imhoff, the park ranger, worries that it may eventually disappear. If the Salton Sea goes, the birds go, too.

"Only now, we've destroyed so many wetlands there's no place else for them to go," he says. "There won't be anything left when this is gone."

Joby Warrick, a staff writer for The Washington Post, *visited the Salton Sea while reporting for this article.*

Thematic Connection
What challenges face scientists working to preserve the Salton Sea habitat? How are these challenges similar to and different from those that scientists working with wild turkey habitats?

Connecting Literature and Science

1. Compare the conditions for saving the wild turkey with the conditions for saving the birds and fish that inhabit the Salton Sea. Why would it be more difficult to save the wildlife at the Salton Sea?
2. If the turkey hen abandoned her eggs today rather than in 1950, how would the ornithologists save the eggs? What measures or procedures do scientists and conservationists have today to save other kinds of wildlife?

Thematic Connection

Answer: Scientists struggle to find a way to reverse the the rising salt levels and to secure money to fund this project. The scientists working with wild turkey habitats are also trying to save wildlife populations, but they do not have to struggle as much for publicity or financing.

Answers

Connecting Literature and Science

1. In the last half of the twentieth century, the wild turkey was the focus of federal wildlife programs and many concerned individuals worked to save the bird from extinction. During that time, ornithologists studied the wild turkeys, protected their habitat, and carefully monitored their reproduction. The birds that depend on the Salton Sea to survive are migrating birds, and they are not the focus of much organized concern. Part of the problem is that the wildlife population is very diverse there, so the effort to save the Salton Sea would be very complicated and also costly.
2. Modern ornithologists would have portable incubator equipment with them to help hatch eggs. Today, scientists and conservationists have better methods to help them save wildlife. Because of modern technology, scientists possess the necessary equipment to save wildlife from extinction.

Lesson Objectives

1. To create an outline from a textbook section
2. To learn the purpose of textbooks
3. To read a textbook section for information

About Textbooks

- Before students read "About Textbooks," ask them to brainstorm for a list of words—qualities, descriptions, and so on—that they associate with textbooks. Encourage them to suggest words that focus on the areas of content, purpose, and design.
  Possible responses: Students may suggest words such as *units, section reviews, terms, charts,* and *education.*
- Then, have students read "About Textbooks." Discuss the section as a class.
- Next, have students work in pairs or small groups to identify the types of information and visual aids that are offered in this or another textbook.
  Possible response: This textbook provides information about reading, writing, speaking, listening, and viewing. The book is divided into units, and each section has a page that introduces concepts, a reading selection, and questions. The book contains art and graphic organizers.

Reading Strategy

Making an Outline

- Have students read the Reading Strategy instruction.
- Show students a copy of a completed outline for an unrelated article so they can see how to fill in the model shown on p. 592. Tell students to use complete sentences in their outlines.
- Point out that an outline shows how a writer moves from the general to the specific within the overall composition and within each paragraph. Tell students that the statements under the main headings should be more general and comprehensive than the statements under the subheads. The statements that identify the details should be the most specific.

READING INFORMATIONAL MATERIALS

Textbooks

About Textbooks

Since you first started school, you have read and used many textbooks. Though they covered different topics, they were alike in some ways.

- A textbook gives information about a particular subject, such as literature, math, science, geography, or American history.
- The purpose of a textbook is to help students learn new materials. The material is divided into units, chapters, and sections, usually by topic. Within the text, boldface heads, color, and other graphic devices highlight important ideas. Questions at the end of a unit or section help you review what you have read.
- Textbooks also include visual aids such as photos, graphs, charts, and fine art. Visuals work with the text by illustrating concepts, showing examples, or summarizing information.

Reading Strategy

Making an Outline

An outline is an organized list of main ideas and significant details. Its organization shows the relationship between ideas and information. Outlines can be used to take notes on informational materials.

Outlines usually follow a form like the one shown here. Each main heading is listed under a Roman numeral: I, II, III, and so on. Each subhead is identified by a capital letter: A, B, C. Supporting details are numbered: 1, 2, 3. In a formal outline structure, there must be at least two of each type of head. For example, if you have a subhead A, you must also have a subhead B.

In a textbook, the organization of the material itself helps shape your outline. Boldface heads and subheads point out the main ideas. These heads are the "skeleton" of your outline.

Model: Outline

I. First main topic or idea
- **A.** Subheading #1
- **B.** Subheading #2
  - **1.** Supporting detail 1
    - (a) smaller detail
    - (b) smaller detail
  - **2.** Supporting detail 2
  - **3.** Supporting detail 3

II. Second main topic or idea
- **A.** Subheading #1
- **B.** Subheading #2
- **C.** Subheading #3

Populations and Communities

The section head states the topic of this section of the textbook.

Populations

In 1900, travelers saw a prairie dog town in Texas covering an area twice the size of the city of Dallas. The sprawling town contained more than 400 million prairie dogs! These prairie dogs were all members of one species, or single kind, of organism. A **species** (SPEE sheez) is a group of organisms that are physically similar and can reproduce with each other to produce fertile offspring.

New terms are defined and their pronunciation given.

All the members of one species in a particular area are referred to as a **population**. The 400 million prairie dogs in the Texas town are one example of a population. All the pigeons in New York City make up a population, as do all the daisies in a field. In contrast, all the trees in a forest do not make up a population, because they do not all belong to the same species. There may be pines, maples, birches, and many other tree species in the forest.

A different style or size of the type indicates an important idea or term.

The area in which a population lives can be as small as a single blade of grass or as large as the whole planet. Scientists studying a type of organism usually limit their study to a population in a defined area. For example, they might study the population of bluegill fish in a pond, or the population of alligators in the Florida Everglades.

Some populations, however, do not stay in a contained area. For example, to study the population of finback whales, a scientist might need to use the entire ocean.

☑ **CHECKPOINT** *What is the difference between a species and a population?*

Questions in the text make sure the student is learning the most important ideas.

Figure 1
A single organism

Figure 2
A population

Science Textbook

- Have students read the section from the science textbook and the notes that identify the elements of the textbook.
- Invite volunteers to read aloud the first four paragraphs of the textbook section. Then, ask students to point out features of the section that probably would not be found in a magazine article or a book.
  Possible responses: Students might note the heading, the key words in boldface, the definitions of the key terms, and the pronunciation guide set in parentheses.
- Next, ask students how the features help them learn the material presented.
  Possible responses: Students may suggest that the use of boldface helps them understand which terms are most important. The pronunciation guide and definition give them an immediate understanding of the terms. The headings tell them the topic of each section.

CUSTOMIZE INSTRUCTION FOR UNIVERSAL ACCESS

For Special Needs Students	For Less Proficient Readers
Offer students the Main Idea and Supporting Details organizer on p. 73 in **Writing Models and Graphic Organizers on Transparencies.** Then, have them work in pairs to read aloud to each other the section on populations. After each paragraph, have students discuss what they read and then pinpoint the main idea. After students have read the excerpt, tell them to figure out what idea is supported in each section. Then, have them fill in the graphic organizer.	Write the letters and numerals for an outline on the board. Then, fill in the first main heading—Populations. Explain to students that the subheading will be the main idea of the section. Remind them that they are already familiar with the process of finding a main idea. Offer them the Main Idea and Supporting Details organizer on p. 73 in **Writing Models and Graphic Organizers on Transparencies** as a review. Then, fill in the rest of the outline on the board as a class.

Science Textbook continued from p. 593

- Point out the Checkpoint question on p. 594. Explain that the question helps readers make sure they understand important terms.
- Next, ask students how the artwork on this textbook page helps them as readers.
  Possible response: Students might say that the artwork provides a clear picture of what a prairie dog looks like and how it moves and behaves.

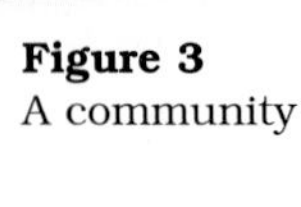

Figure 3
A community

Communities

Of course, most ecosystems contain more than one type of organism. The prairie, for instance, includes prairie dogs, hawks, grasses, badgers, and snakes, along with many other organisms. All the different populations that live together in an area make up a **community**.

The smallest unit of organization is a single **organism** *(figure 1)*. The organism belongs to a **population** of other members of its species *(figure 2)*. The population belongs to a **community** of different species *(figure 3)*. The community and abiotic factors together form an **ecosystem** *(figure 4)*.

References to pictures, charts, and photographs give you another way to look at concepts described or explained in the text.

To be considered a community, the different populations must live close enough together to interact. One way the populations in a community may interact is by using the same resources, such as food and shelter. For example, the tunnels dug by the prairie dogs also serve as homes for burrowing owls and black-footed ferrets. The prairie dogs share the grass with other animals. Meanwhile, prairie dogs themselves serve as food for many species.

☑ **CHECKPOINT** ***What is a community? How is it different from an ecosystem?***

Figure 4
An ecosystem

Check Your Comprehension

1. What is an example of a population?
2. Where could you go to study an alligator habitat?
3. What is one way that populations in a community interact?

Applying the Reading Strategy

Creating an Outline

4. What two terms or concepts would you assign to Roman numerals in an outline of this section?
5. How do the section title and subheads help you decide what the main categories on your outline will be?
6. Make an outline of this textbook section that you could keep in your notebook for study.

Activity

Identify Features of Textbooks

In addition to headings, visual aids, and formatting, textbooks include other features that help readers find and organize information.

- The table of contents provides a quick reference to locate each topic.
- The index is a kind of outline of all the smaller categories of information listed alphabetically with page numbers.
- A glossary defines specialized vocabulary at the end of the book. Choose a textbook you use in any class. Identify as many features as you can using this checklist and include an example or description of each feature.

Feature	Example
Photos, fine art, charts, graphs, tables, other visuals	
Chapter, unit, or section titles	
Subheads	
Color bars with type	
Word definitions at page bottom	
Table of contents	
Index	
Glossary	

Contrasting Informational Materials

Textbooks and Magazines

Using library resources, find a magazine article related to environmental issues. Look in magazines such as *National Geographic World* and *National Wildlife*. Compare the article with this textbook section in terms of **(a)** text organization, **(b)** text features such as boldface heads and vocabulary, **(c)** use of graphics like photographs and graphs or charts. Write a brief explanation of the similarities and differences in each category.

Answers for p. 595

Check Your Comprehension

1. Possible response: Pigeons in New York City are a population.
2. A swampy area, like the Florida Everglades, is a good place to study an alligator habitat.
3. One way populations interact is by sharing resources, such as food or shelter.

Applying the Reading Strategy

4. I would assign "Populations" and "Communities" Roman numerals.
5. The section title and subheads reveal the main topics of the textbook section.
6. Possible response:

I. Populations

A. All the members of one species in a particular area make up a population.

1. 400 million prairie dogs are a population.
2. All the pigeons in New York City are a population.
3. All the daisies in a field are a population.

B. Scientists study populations in limited areas.

1. They might study the bluegill fish in a pond.
2. They might study alligators in the Florida Everglades.
3. They might study finback whales in the world's oceans.

II. Communities

A. Different populations living together are called communities.

1. On the prairie, prairie dogs live among hawks, snakes, grasses, and badgers.
2. Different animals in a community share resources.

B. An ecosystem is a community of different species that share resources and depend on one another.

1. Ferrets and owls use prairie-dog holes for shelter.
2. Prairie dogs share grasses with other animals.
3. Prairie dogs serve as food for other animals.

continued

Answers continued

Activity

If possible, encourage students to consult a wide variety of textbooks representing different subjects and grade levels. Ask them to create checklists like the one on p. 595, allowing room for comments about the usefulness of each feature. After they complete their checklists, have each student write a brief paragraph about the purpose, design, and appeal of the textbook. Then, lead a class discussion about students' findings.

Contrasting Informational Materials

To save time, you may wish to provide the articles for this activity. Have each student draw a two-column chart with a column for comments about the textbook and a column for comments about the magazine article. Ask each student to write a short paragraph that sums up the similarities and differences between the two categories.

Lesson Objectives

1. To ask questions while reading a research report
2. To understand the characteristics of a research report

About Research Reports

- After students read the section "About Research Reports," ask them whether they have used research reports in the past and how they have used them. Answer: Students may have used research reports in answering questions or in writing for class assignments.
- Point out that research reports may take several forms. Most often, however, they are published as articles in journals or periodicals and as chapters in books.
- Review with students the characteristics of a typical research report. Make sure that students notice that the characteristics are the same as an expository report. Tell students that a research report is a form of expository writing or writing that *explains* something.

Reading Strategy

Asking Questions

- Have students read the information about the Reading Strategy.
- Discuss with students why asking questions before and while reading a research report is important.
- Tell students that they should preview a research report before deciding to read it. Students should look at the title of the report, its length, the level of its vocabulary, and the graphics and subheadings. Remind students that when researching, they should avoid reading research reports that will not answer their questions.

READING INFORMATIONAL MATERIALS

Research Reports

About Research Reports

A research report presents detailed factual information about a subject. There are many reasons people use research reports. A heart surgeon might turn to a research report to learn about new surgical techniques. A new parent might turn to research to find out about good methods for raising children. As a student, you might use a research report to increase your level of knowledge about an interesting subject. Most research reports have the following characteristics:

- a well-defined topic
- a clear organization
- information from a variety of sources
- facts and details supporting each main point

Reading Strategy

Asking Questions

To understand a research report better, ask questions *before*, *while*, and *after* you read:

Before you read, you may not know very much about the subject. Your questions will be very general. For instance, you might ask, "What types of sharks are there?"

While you read, your questions should be geared toward understanding the information the author is presenting. If the author has just claimed that sharks have more to fear from people than the reverse, you might reasonably ask, "Why is that?" These questions can usually be answered by reading further.

After you read, you might ask two types of questions, "What did I just learn?" and "What more do I still want to know?" For the first type of question, go back to the reading material. For the second question, choose another book or article on the subject to find out more. Use the Works Cited list or the Bibliography to find additional resources.

Research Phase	General Questions You Can Ask
Before you read . . .	What do I already know about a subject? What would I like to learn?
While you read . . .	What is the main point the author is making? How does the author support the main point with evidence?
After you read . . .	What new information did I learn? Do I agree with the author's conclusions? Do I have additional questions that this research report does not answer?

SHARKS

Susan McGrath

In the opening paragraph, the author asks two questions for you to consider as you read. Find the answers in the rest of the article.

They're big, they're ugly, they're vicious, and the only good one is a dead one. That's what some people say about sharks. Is their bad reputation based on truth? "Not!" say the experts. But is time running out for sharks?

The blue shark looks like any typical shark: streamlined, powerful, bluish gray–more fighter jet than fish. But shark experts are quick to tell you that, among the 370 species of sharks, there simply *isn't* a "typical" shark (Springer 52–53).

A whale shark is as long as a school bus, while a cigar shark would fit neatly in a pencil case. A frilled shark looks like an eel with a lacy collar. A Pacific angel shark is as flat as a pancake. And the megamouth shark's gums glow in the dark.

Sharks

- Tell students that they might encounter an article about sharks in science magazines, which often include articles about animals and nature.
- Point out that although the article is a research report, the writer makes a persuasive argument. Explain that research reports often contain persuasive writing. The writer has specific ideas about the facts and information that influences his or her perspective on the report.
- Before students begin reading the report, have them notice its title. What do they think the report will be about?
  Answer: Students should notice that the title is general, so they cannot predict exactly what the report will be about. They might guess it will be about different kinds of sharks.
- Ask students to identify the well-defined topic in the first paragraph of the report.
  Answer: The topic is that not all sharks are dangerous and that they are in danger of becoming extinct.
- Ask students why they think the writer waited until the fifth paragraph before answering the questions she raised in the first paragraph.
  Answer: Students should be able to tell from reading that the writer had a large amount of information to bring up before answering the questions.

continued on p. 598

CUSTOMIZE INSTRUCTION FOR UNIVERSAL ACCESS

For Special Needs Students	For Less Proficient Readers
Help students identify the questions that "Sharks" raises and answers. After they read the report once, pair students and have them go through the report again looking for actual questions. Students should identify four questions. Have students then return to the text to find the answers to these questions. (Three questions are answered. The question "Surprised?" can be answered only by the reader.) Finally, have students discuss with the class what they learned from the research report.	Students may have trouble following the organization of ideas of the research report. Suggest that students use the outlining skills they learned in the previous **Reading Informational Materials** feature on pp. 592–595. After students read the article once, allow them to work in pairs to go through the article again, this time looking for the main ideas and key details in each paragraph. After students complete their outlines, discuss what the research report says about sharks.

"Sharks" *(continued from p. 597)*

- Challenge students to identify what each paragraph in the report is about. Students should notice that the paragraphs either ask questions or provide background information and answers. Tell students that raising questions in a research report allows readers to know exactly what answers will appear in the report.
- Make sure students do not ignore the list of sources at the bottom of p. 598. Show students how the sources are cited in the body of the research report (in parentheses, after statements of fact). Explain that a good research report gives full credit to the sources that provide its information.
- You might explain how source citations work and how bibliographies or Works Cited pages are arranged.

Not mindless monsters, sharks are more intelligent than once thought (Allen, *Shadows* 24). They possess highly developed senses, also (Parker 90–91). And a chemical compound that seems to help sharks fight off infections may someday help doctors treat humans (Springer 90).

As for their killer reputation, very few shark species attack humans, and then only under certain conditions (Taylor 50–51). Sharks have more reason to be afraid of people than the reverse. Surprised? Just look at the numbers. Sharks kill between five and ten people a year (Allen, *Almanac* 44–46). People kill more than 100 *million* sharks a year (Perrine 17). Placed snout-to-tail-fins, that many sharks would circle the Earth five times. So many sharks have been killed that scientists fear some species may be wiped out.

In this paragraph, McGrath provides answers to the questions, "Are sharks' bad reputation based on truth?" and "Is time running out for sharks?"

Why are sharks on the hit list? They are fished for food—shark steak has taken the place of more expensive tuna and swordfish on many menus (Perrine 144–148). Also, in a cruel practice called "finning," sharks are hooked; their fins are sliced off; and the animals are tossed back into the sea to die. The sail-shaped fins are used to make shark-fin soup (Allen 240). Other sharks are killed after being trapped in nets intended for other fish (*Reader's* 133–134).

The author cites her source of information using the appropriate style. The full citation can be found at the end of the article in the Works Cited list.

When you figure that many sharks don't breed until they are more than 12 years old and that only about half of all sharks born survive (Allen *Shadows* 17–23), you can see how overfishing could eventually threaten sharks with extinction.

The oceans would be a very different place without sharks. As predators at the top of the oceans' food chain, large sharks play an important role in keeping the population of other species in check. Part of their job is to weed out weak and injured animals, leaving the healthiest to reproduce.

Concerned scientists are working with government officials to put reasonable limits on shark fishing (Taylor 35). If they succeed, sharks will survive and maintain a useful place in the oceans of the world.

McGrath uses her final paragraphs to emphasize the positive role sharks play. She also makes the argument that sharks need our help.

Works Cited

Allen, Thomas B. *Shadows in the Sea.* New York: Lyons & Burford Publishers, 1996.
The Shark Almanac. New York: The Lyons Press, 1999.
Parker, Steve and Jane. *The Encyclopedia of Sharks.* Buffalo, NY: Firefly Books, 1999.
Perrine, Doug. *Sharks.* Stillwater, MN: Voyageur Press, Inc., 1995.
Reader's Digest Explores Sharks. Pleasantville, NY: Reader's Digest, 1998.
Sharks, Silent Hunters of the Deep. Pleasantville, NY: Reader's Digest, 1986-1995.
Springer, Victor G., and Joy P. Gold. *Sharks in Question: The Smithsonian Answer Book.* Washington, DC: Smithsonian Institution Press, 1989.
Taylor, Leighton, ed. *Sharks and Rays: The Nature Company Guides.* New York: Time-Life Books. 1997.

This section lists McGrath's sources.

CUSTOMIZE INSTRUCTION FOR UNIVERSAL ACCESS

For Advanced Readers

Challenge students to find one of the sources the writer cites in her research report. Have students choose a title from her list of sources and locate it at the school or local library. Students should look up the page the writer cites in the body of the report and determine exactly how she used the information. For example, did the writer quote the source directly, or did she paraphrase? Did she use the main point of the source, or did she use facts that were less central to the source? Students may wish to read the entire source and compare the information in it to the research report on pp. 597–598. Ask students to present their findings to the class.

Check Your Comprehension

1. Why does the author say that sharks have more to fear from humans than the reverse?
2. Approximately how many species of sharks exist?
3. What are two reasons sharks are killed?

Applying the Reading Strategy

Asking Questions

4. What views and knowledge did you have of sharks before reading this article?
5. What questions occurred to you as you read? Why?
6. What are the main questions McGrath poses in this article?
7. What information would you like to know about sharks that is not included in this article?

Activity

Problem Investigation

In the article on sharks, the author mentions the problem of overfishing of ocean species. This is a problem with many other fish species as well, including salmon, cod, and bluefin tuna. Research and write a report on the problem of overfishing. Be sure to ask yourself questions as you prepare. Consult multiple sources in your research and cite them appropriately in your report. To learn more about how to write a research report, use the Writing Workshop on page 600 to guide you.

Comparing Informational Texts

Research Reports and Newspaper Articles

Research reports follow a specific format for citing information from sources and providing information to help readers find the source materials. Newspaper articles, while often research based, do not follow a set format for crediting sources. In fact, newspaper articles sometimes do not tell source information at all.

Find two newspaper articles about sharks, shark populations, or shark hunting. Use a chart like the one shown to compare and contrast the characteristics of the two informational materials.

	Research	Newspaper
Main Ideas		
Number of Sources Created		
Similar Facts		
Different Facts		

Answers for p. 599

Check Your Comprehension

1. Each year, far more sharks are killed by humans (100 million) than humans are by sharks (5–10).
2. There are 370 species of sharks.
3. Sharks are fished for food and killed after being trapped in nets set for other fish.

Applying the Reading Strategy

4. Possible responses: Some students may say that they thought sharks were dangerous and bad. Others may say that they already knew much of the information that appeared in the article.
5. Possible responses: Some students may have asked why so many sharks are killed by humans. Others may have asked why people practice "finning."
6. The main questions are "Do sharks deserve their bad reputation?"; "Is time running out for sharks?"; and "Why are sharks on the hit list?"
7. Possible responses: Students may suggest that they would like to know the exact statistics for the recent decline in shark populations. They also may like to know when the shark may become extinct.

Activity

To save time, have students work in groups as they research sources for their reports. As a class, identify some specific questions about the topic of overfishing to guide students to narrow their questions. Challenge students to find at least three sources for their reports. When students have researched and written drafts of their reports, have them work with a partner to revise. In revising, students should make sure that their sources support their main ideas. Explain how to write citations that appear within and at the end of a text. Finally, ask students to submit copies of their sources with their writing.

Comparing Informational Texts

Ask students to submit copies of the newspaper articles they used when they submit their completed charts.

Lesson Objectives

1. To write a research report
2. To use writing strategies to generate ideas, plan, organize, evaluate, and revise the composition

Model From Literature

In "The Shutout" (p. 532), writers Patricia C. McKissack and Frederick McKissack Jr. present their research on the true beginnings of baseball and the history of African American baseball players.

Prewriting

- Suggest that students identify topic ideas by asking themselves the following questions:
  - *What interesting people do I know or have I heard about?*
  - *What fascinating places would I like to visit?*
  - *What interesting events would I like to know more about?*
  - *What discoveries interest me?*
- Next, have students narrow their topics by using a Cluster organizer like the one on p. 85 of **Writing Models and Graphic Organizers on Transparencies.** Students should write their topics in the center circle in the diagram and then fill in the remaining ovals with words that are related to or associated with the topic. Each student should focus on one of these ideas as his or her narrowed topic.
- Tell students to consult the school or local librarian about sources for their research. Remind students that although the Internet is a convenient resource for information, many of the sources found there are questionable.
- Suggest that students make two sets of cards: bibliography cards and note cards. Bibliography cards should be numbered. The number of the appropriate bibliography card can be written at the top of the note card that contains information from that source. Source information should be written on note cards, not on bibliography cards. Clipping the bibliography cards to the appropriate stack of note cards will also be helpful.
- Before students draft their essays, have them review the Rubric for Self-Assessment (p. 605), so they know what is expected.

Writing WORKSHOP

Research: Research Report

A **research report** presents facts and information gathered from several credible sources, such as public records, reference books, and periodicals. In this workshop, you will choose a subject, gather information, and write a report, citing your sources in a bibliography.

Assignment Criteria Your research report should have the following characteristics:

- A topic that is narrow enough in scope to thoroughly cover in the course of the report
- Facts, details, examples, and explanations from multiple authoritative sources to support the main ideas
- A clear method of organization
- Accurate and complete citations identifying sources
- A complete and accurate bibliography

See the Rubric on page 605 for the criteria on which your research report may be assessed.

Prewriting

Choose and narrow a topic. Browse through reference sources or magazines at the library to find topics you are interested in. Narrow broad topics by asking questions about particular areas of your topic. Then, circle parts of your answers to consider as possibilities for the focus of your research report.

- What are the causes or effects?
- Who is the most important or influential person?
- How is it similar to something else?

Locate authoritative sources. Use a variety of sources to find information about your topic: speeches, periodicals, newspapers, online information, videotapes, interviews, books, and brochures. Keep careful track of the source you use for each piece of information. Write down title, author, publication date, and place. You'll need this information to write your bibliography.

Take notes. Take careful notes about information you can use. Use quotation marks when you copy words directly. Otherwise, use your own words.

Sample Source Card

Connolly, Peter, and Hazel Dodge. *The Ancient City.* New York: Oxford University Press, 1998. p. 28

Sample Note Card

Connolly, 28	Construction
Colosseum construction begins — A. D. 75	

TEACHING RESOURCES

The following resources can be used to enrich or extend the instruction for pp. 600–605.

- **Writing and Grammar,** Copper Level, Chapter 11, pp. 222–241
- **Performance Assessment and Portfolio Management,** p. 14
- **Writing Models and Graphic Organizers on Transparency,** p. 51

Writing and Grammar iText CD-ROM
Students can use the following tools as they complete their descriptive essays:

- Unity and Coherence
- Comparatives
- Sentence Openers Variety
- Transition Words

Student Model

Before you begin drafting your research report, read this portion of a student model and review the characteristics of a successful research report. To read the full report, see www.phschool.com.

Elizabeth Cleary,
Maplewood, New Jersey

Ice Ages

Ice ages occur every two hundred million years or so. An ice age is defined as a long period of cold where large amounts of water are trapped under ice. Although ice ages happened long ago, studing their causes and effects helps contemporary scientists understand geological conditions of the world today.

> The author defines her topic clearly in this sentence.

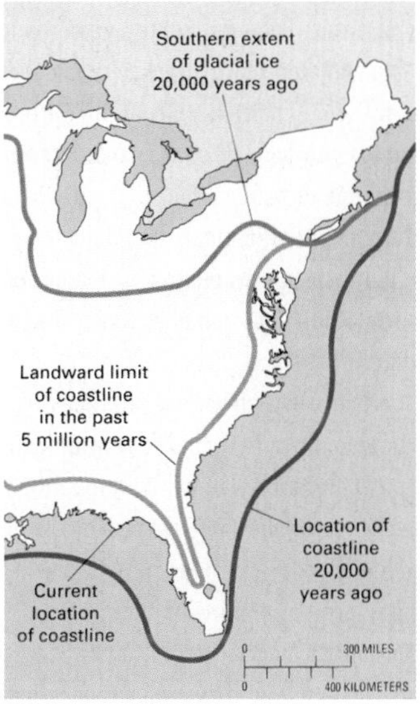

Effects of Ice Ages on Eastern Coastline of United States

> This map illustrates the writer's point that ice ages caused current conditions.

When an ice age does occur, ice covers much of the Earth. This ice forms when the climate changes. The polar regions become very cold and the temperatures drop everywhere else. The ice is trapped in enormous mountains of ice called glaciers. Glaciers can be as large as a continent in size. When the Earth's temperature warms up, the glaciers start to melt, forming rivers and lakes. Glaciers' tremendous weight and size can actually wear away mountains and valleys as the glaciers melt and move. The melting ice also raises ocean levels.

There are many different theories to explain why ice ages occur, but no one knows for sure. Many scientists agree that it is probably due to a combination of causes, including changes in the sun's intensity, the distance of the Earth from the sun, changes in ocean currents, the continental plates rubbing up against each other, and the varying amounts of carbon dioxide in the atmosphere (*PBS Nova* Web site "The Big Chill").

> Here the author presents factual information related to the possible causes of ice ages.

Student Model

- Explain that the Student Model is a sample, and that research reports may be longer.
- Ask students to identify the broad topic of the Student Model and then its narrowed topic.
  Answer: The broad topic is the ice age. The narrowed topic is the causes and effects of ice ages on Earth and on human beings.
- Guide students to notice how the writer uses each paragraph to explain one idea. The second paragraph, for example, focuses on the definition of an ice age. Challenge students to identify the topics of other paragraphs.

CUSTOMIZE INSTRUCTION FOR UNIVERSAL ACCESS

For Less Proficient Readers	For English Learners	For Advanced Readers
Once students have selected a topic, suggest that they use a KWL organizer like the one on p. 61 of **Writing Models and Graphic Organizers on Transparencies.** Students can use the questions in the second column to guide their research.	Students who are overwhelmed by the prospect of researching sources written in English can select a topic with which they are already somewhat familiar. They can consult sources, such as their relatives, friends, or neighbors, recording their interviews and citing them in their research papers.	Group students to work together to research different aspects of a broad topic, such as the environment. Each student in the group can be responsible for researching and writing about one aspect of the larger issue, but all of their papers should connect to the larger issue.

Student Model (continued)

- Review with students the proper way to use citations in the text of a research paper. Here, the student writer simply puts the source in parentheses after the information. Talk to students about how to incorporate a source in the actual sentence. Here is an example: "According to *National Geographic* writer David Roberts, scientists were able to learn a lot about this ancient period."
- Discuss the use of direct quotations in students' research reports. Explain that quoting knowledgeable sources is a way to add authority to their papers. Students should quote only sources that explain an idea better than they can.

During the last ice age, or the Wisconsin Ice Age, people lived on the Earth. These people saw ice and snow all the time. It was never warm enough for it to melt, so it piled up. In the summertime, women fished in chilly streams. The men hunted year-round.

The skeleton of one person who lived and hunted during this time was found by some hikers in 1901 in the European Alps. He had been buried in the ice for nearly 5,000 years. Nicknamed "The Iceman," scientists believe that perhaps he was suddenly caught by a blizzard or that he possibly ran out of food, became weak, and died.

Elizabeth clearly and accurately cites her sources to show where she obtained a set of specific details.

Scientists were able to learn a lot about this ancient period from the leather clothes and animal skins he was wearing and the tools he was carrying (Roberts, p. 38).

Ice ages also affect our life today. The ice sheets that formed weighed a huge amount. When the ice retreated, it left behind large rocks and other debris which otherwise would not be there. Also, without ice ages, large bodies of water like the Great Lakes simply wouldn't exist. We depend on these bodies of water every day for fresh drinking water, recreation, and shipping large quantities of materials.

In each section, Elizabeth explores a different aspect of the ice ages. Here she is explaining scientific discovery.

Scientists discovered ice ages because of Louis Agassiz, a nineteenth-century scientist who is sometimes called the "Father of Glaciology." In Switzerland, he saw boulders or granite far from where any granite should be. He also noticed scrapes and grooves, or striae. He theorized that glaciers had caused all of these geologic features (University of California Museum of Paleontology Web page).

Many animals that are extinct now lived during the Ice Age. The saber-toothed tiger and the mastodon, an elephantlike animal, formerly lived in North America. They became extinct because of climate change and hunting. Other animals became extinct as well because they could not adapt to the way the Earth was changing.

Baron Gerard de Geer, a Swedish geologist, did pioneering work which estimated the end of the last Ice Age. In a similar way to the way we count

CUSTOMIZE INSTRUCTION FOR UNIVERSAL ACCESS

For Less Proficient Readers	For Gifted/Talented Students
Students may not have a well-developed sense of a source's reliability. Remind students to answer the following questions: **1.** Is the author well known? **2.** Is the author an expert in this field? **3.** Was the source published recently? **4.** Is the source produced or published by a recognized publisher? Explain that students have consulted a reliable source if they can answer the questions with "yes."	Challenge students to use sources other than books, articles, or the Internet for their papers. Suggest that students conduct interviews with experts or people who experienced an event firsthand or consult primary documents, such as personal papers or public documents in local archives. Remind students that the school or local librarian can help them find the sources they need.

tree rings to estimate a tree's age, De Geer used layers of sediment left by glaciers' summer melts to calculate the history of the Ice Age. He did much of his work in Sweden, but he also visited areas that had been affected by glaciers in New England.

Thanks to scientists like De Geer and Agassiz, we know a great deal about that remote age when glaciers roamed the Earth. We can now estimate the history of ice ages and determine what features—valleys, inland seas, mountains, lakes, rocks—were caused by glaciers. We are even able to determine where the large glaciers were, as you can see by the map displayed here of the Eastern United States. There is still a lot more to be discovered about the causes of ice ages, but one thing is clear: Glaciers had a powerful effect on the world as we know it today.

The author restates the main idea that she presented in the introduction and supported in the body of the paper.

Bibliography

Department of Geosciences, University of Arizona. 10 Nov. 2000. <http://www.geo.arizona.edu/Antevs/degeer.html>

History of the Universe. 11 Nov. 2000. <http://www.historyoftheuniverse.com/iceage.html>

Ice Age. Compton's Interactive Encyclopedia © The Learning Company, Inc. [CD-ROM] (1998).

Roberts, David. "The Iceman." *National Geographic Magazine,* June 1993: 37–49

University of California Museum of Paleontology. 11 Nov. 2000 <http://www.ucmp.berkeley.edu/history/aggassiz.html>

PBS Nova "The Big Chill." 10 Nov. 2000. <http://www.pbs.org/wgbh/nova/ice/chill.html>

In her bibliography, Elizabeth cites all the sources used to research her paper.

Student Model continued

- Have students notice how Web sites are cited in the student's bibliography. Point out that this is a standard way of citing Web sites. Students should see that the title of the Web site is set in italics (it would be underlined if the students wrote the citation by hand or typed it on a typewriter), that the date is set with the day first, and that the entire Web address is set inside triangular brackets.
- Talk with the class about the differences among the citations of the Web sites, the CD-ROM, and the article from *National Geographic.* You may wish to make a handout of the different citation forms. Include one for a book by one author, as well.

Real-World Connection

Research reports in the workplace: Students may associate research papers with school. Explain that research reports are essential to most professional fields, including science, medicine, and engineering. Tell students that every field of work requires new knowledge and answers to questions that can be reached only through research. For example, new medicines cannot be produced without research. Research is almost always shared in writing. Every field has professional journals in which researchers share their ideas and their findings. Their papers are written in formats similar to what students learn here. As a class, brainstorm for some professions in which research is used.

CUSTOMIZE INSTRUCTION FOR UNIVERSAL ACCESS

For Special Needs Students	For Advanced Readers
Students may have a difficult time understanding the distinctions between the citation styles of various sources. Offer students a handout that clearly shows how different types of sources should appear in a bibliography. Remind students that the items listed in a bibliography should appear in alphabetical order. Allow students to work in pairs or small groups to proofread their bibliographies.	Students may already be familiar with the formats for citations in a research paper. In that case, have these students work with partners who are less familiar with writing bibliographies. Suggest that students design and make a handout or poster that shows the different types of sources and the way they are cited in a bibliography. Then, have students work with their partners to proofread each other's bibliography.

Drafting

- If students need a reminder about how to prepare an outline, refer them to the Reading Instructional Materials feature on p. 592.
- Tell students that an outline often shows a movement from a general idea to a specific one. Also, tell students that outlines must be balanced; if they have a subhead A, they must also have a subhead B.
- Explain to students that an outline serves as a guide, but it is not written in stone. Students may find that ideas that made sense in the outline really do not work well in their papers. Encourage students to adjust their outlines as they write.
- Remind students that any information—any fact, detail, example, or explanation—that comes from a source needs to be cited in their paper. This might be a good time to discuss plagiarism with students.

Revising

- Suggest that students work with partners to identify the different types of sentences in their drafts (topic sentence, restatement, or illustration). It may help students to work with copies of their papers and highlight the different sentences with colored markers or highlighters.
- Challenge students to watch for particular grammatical or mechanical errors, such as sentence fragments or inconsistent verb tense. Have students work in pairs to read each other's papers and identify the errors you mention.

Drafting

Organize your research report. Group your notes by categories that break your topic into subtopics. For example, if you are writing about the Colosseum, you might use these topics in your notes:

- architecture of Colosseum
- construction of Colosseum
- events held in Colosseum
- spectators at Colosseum

Use Roman numerals (I, II, III) to number topics and A, B, C to indicate subtopics, as in the outline shown here.

I. Introduction
II. Architecture of Colosseum
A. measurements
B. building material
III. Construction of Colosseum
A. beginning date
B. workers

Match your draft to your outline. A solid, detailed outline will guide you through writing your draft. The headings with Roman numerals indicate sections of your report. You will need to write several paragraphs to fully cover each Roman numeral. Organize your paragraphs around the topics with capital letters. You can even include headings in your draft if you want to guide your reader through complex subjects.

Support main ideas with facts. Using your outline, jot down sentences about each of the main ideas in your report. Leave spaces between sentences, and add wide margins. Then, fill in supporting facts, details, examples, and explanations drawn from your reference sources.

Prepare to cite sources. Part of "drafting" a research report is making a bibliography or Works Cited list.

Model: Making a Bibliography

1. Organize your source cards in alphabetical order by author's or editor's last name. If the work has no author or editor, use the first word of the entry to alphabetize.
2. Write or keyboard information on a separate page.
3. Refer to Citing Sources and Preparing Manuscripts, page R12, to check styles of different kinds of entries.

USING TECHNOLOGY IN WRITING

Students may use different fonts and colors available in their word-processing programs to identify the types of sentences in their drafts. Suggest that students use boldface for their topic sentences, red italics for their restatements, and blue for their illustration sentences. Students will then be able to tell at a glance whether their papers have a good balance.

Students also can use the organizing tools and revision checkers on the **Writing and Grammar iText CD-ROM.**

Revising

Revise for effective paragraph structure. In a research report, most paragraphs will be built like this:

- a **topic sentence** (T) stating the paragraph's main idea
- a **restatement** or elaboration (R) of the topic sentence
- **illustrations** (I), facts, examples, or details about the main idea

Review your draft. Label each of your sentences with *T*, *R*, or *I*. If you find a group of *I*'s, make sure there is a *T* they support. If you find a *T* by itself, add *I*'s to support it.

Model: Balancing Your Paragraphs

R These people saw ice and snow all the time. R It was never warm enough for it to melt, so it piled up.

T During the last ice age, or the Wisconsin Ice Age, people lived on the Earth. I In the summertime, women fished in chilly streams. I The men hunted year-round.

Elizabeth adds sentences that restate her topic sentence to achieve balance in the paragraph.

Publishing and Presenting

Use the following suggestion to share your writing with classmates or a larger audience.

Present a Mini-Lesson Use your report as the basis for an oral presentation on your topic for your classmates. Make a poster announcing your presentation.

WG *Prentice Hall Writing and Grammar Connection: Chapter 11*

Speaking Connection
To learn more about delivering a research report as a speech, see the **Listening and Speaking Workshop: Delivering a Research Presentation,** page 606.

Rubric for Self-Assessment

Evaluate your research report using the following criteria and rating scale:

Criteria	Rating Scale Not very				Very
How well defined is the topic?	1	2	3	4	5
How well do facts, details, examples, and explanations support the main ideas?	1	2	3	4	5
How well does the writer use a variety of credible sources?	1	2	3	4	5
How clear is the method of organization?	1	2	3	4	5
How accurate and complete are citations in the bibliography?	1	2	3	4	5

Publishing and Presenting

- If you would like students to present their papers orally, refer them to the Listening and Speaking Workshop on p. 606. The workshop offers tips on adapting research reports and delivering oral reports.
- Have students write brief responses to their papers in which they identify the audience they hope to reach and share their thoughts about how effective their papers are in reaching that audience.
- Finally, encourage students to submit their research reports to the school or local newspaper or to local organizations that might be interested in their research.

Assessment

- Review the assessment criteria in class.
- Encourage students to practice using the rubric for self-assessment to evaluate the Student Model that appears on pp. 601–603. Tell students to pay close attention to the student writer's citations.
- The rubric on this page, and another rubric in an alternative format, can be found on p. 14 of **Performance Assessment and Portfolio Management.**

TEST-TAKING TIP

It is not likely that students will be asked to write a research report in a test situation because of time constraints and the lack of resources; however, students may be asked to write an explanation or an expository essay. Students should approach such an essay as they did their research report, by selecting a topic, narrowing it, and identifying key points of information and supporting details. Before students settle on a possible topic, they should make sure that they can offer at least three details, facts, examples, or quotations to support their ideas. Tell students to make a general outline in a test situation. Suggest that students identify a suitable topic and its key ideas in about 10 minutes, write an outline in about 5 minutes, and then spend 20 minutes writing. Students should always spend the last 5 minutes of their testing time proofreading their writing.

Lesson Objectives

1. To prepare and deliver a research presentation
2. To use multiple sources and visual aids to support a topic presented orally
3. To pose relevant questions in an oral presentation of research
4. To use effective speaking techniques in delivering an oral presentation of research

Effective Preparation

- Suggest that students introduce ideas they have pulled from a source. For example, students might begin sentences with phrases such as "According to marine biologist Selma Jones . . ." or "In her book *Shark Attack!* writer Selma Jones says. . . ." Tell students that they do not give the page numbers in an oral presentation.
- Explain that visual aids are useful for listeners but can be distracting for speakers. Remind students to practice showing and referring to their visuals before they give their presentations.

Effective Delivery

- If students wonder how to incorporate questions into their presentations, remind them of how Susan McGrath, the author of "Sharks" (Reading Informational Materials, pp. 596–599), uses questions to engage her readers' interest. Point out how the writer places her questions and her answers throughout the article so that readers are always either considering a question or evaluating its answer.
- The pace at which speakers speak is crucial to a good presentation. Have students time their presentations while practicing in order to gauge how much to slow down.

Listening and Speaking WORKSHOP

Delivering a Research Presentation

Delivering an effective **research presentation** has many of the same characteristics as preparing a research report. (To review the characteristics of a successful research report, see the Writing Workshop, pp. 600–605.) For hints on preparing and delivering a research report, use some of the strategies suggested here.

Effective Preparation

Before giving a research presentation, take time to go over your material and organize your notes and any visual aids you plan to use. Have on hand a list of reliable sources, including Web site addresses that you used.

Draw from multiple sources. Make the audience aware that your information is drawn from a number of reliable sources, such as expert interviews, books, newspapers, videotapes, periodicals, and online sites. Keep in mind that some sources, such as government Web sites, are more reliable than others.

Support your topic. Develop your topic so that you introduce your main ideas and then support them with interesting facts, details, and explanations from a variety of sources. Providing examples will further enhance your presentation.

Use visual aids. As often as possible, present photographs, charts, and diagrams. Use slides and videotapes when appropriate. These aids will give your presentation variety.

Using Visual Aids

- **Maps**
  Use **maps** when presenting a report on a country or region.
- **Charts and Graphs**
  Use **charts and graphs** to show statistics or changes in amount.
- **Diagrams**
  Use **diagrams** with explanations of parts or processes.

Effective Delivery

Before giving a research presentation, take time to rehearse, practicing ways to use your voice for emphasis. Be sure that your topic is not so broad that you cannot adequately cover it in the allotted time.

Pose relevant questions. It's a good idea to begin your presentation with a few good questions, sufficiently narrow in scope to be completely and thoroughly answered in your presentation. This technique will let your audience know exactly what you will cover.

Slow down; take your time. Sometimes, presenters speak too quickly because they are nervous. Pause for a moment before you begin and take a deep breath.

Activity: Presentation Choose a subject related to a current event in the news. Research the background, as well as the importance of the event, using newspapers, magazines, and Web sites. Prepare and deliver a research presentation on your topic.

CUSTOMIZE INSTRUCTION FOR UNIVERSAL ACCESS

For Less Proficient Readers	For Gifted/Talented Students
Consider asking students to adapt a section of their research reports for this assignment. This decision will allow students to concentrate on their presentation rather than on doing more research and writing. Suggest that students work in teams of three or four to adapt their presentation topics, write and practice delivering their presentations, and create visual aids. Work with students to generate a rubric of points that every presenter and presentation must demonstrate or include.	Group students together to develop related presentations that focus on different aspects of a larger, more complicated issue. Groups should select an issue and then figure out which four or five aspects to cover in their individual presentations. Students may research and write together. Each presentation should fit clearly into the overall scheme, and each should include clear transitions from one presentation to the next.

Assessment WORKSHOP

Distinguishing Fact From Opinion

The reading sections of some tests require you to read a passage and answer multiple-choice questions about distinguishing fact from opinion. Use the following strategies to help you answer such questions:

- A *fact* is a statement that can be proved by consulting a reliable source, such as a book or an expert on the topic. When you are asked to identify a statement as a fact, ask yourself, "Could this statement be proved?"
- An *opinion* may sound like a fact but cannot be proved. To determine if a statement is an opinion, ask yourself if it reflects the writer's belief and whether it can be proved.

Test-Taking Strategies

- Look for certain words that signal an opinion, such as "think" or "believe."
- Ask yourself if the statement could be seen from another point of view. If so, it is probably an opinion.

Sample Test Item

Directions: Read the following passage, and then choose the letter of the best possible answer.

"Be careful," warned the dealer. "That's the most valuable stamp in the shop. It's the prettiest, too. You'll never see another one of those. There are only five in the world. I never get tired of telling the story of how I found that stamp. It happened when I was traveling in North Africa. Stamp collecting is a hobby for the adventurous."

1. Which of these is a FACT from the passage?
   - **A** You'll never see another one of those.
   - **B** That's the most valuable stamp in the shop.
   - **C** It's the prettiest one, too.
   - **D** Stamp collecting is for the adventurous.

Answer and Explanation

The correct answer is *B*. Answers **A, C,** and **D** cannot be proved. An exact value can be found for the stamp.

Practice

Directions: Read the following passage, and then choose the letter of the best possible answer.

It is illegal to hunt and sell wild chimpanzees. Captured chimps often get sick in captivity. Then, their owners give them up. Concerned people have set up sanctuaries to shelter chimps who cannot be returned to the wild. Some wildlife experts think the money used to run the sanctuaries should be spent on enforcing the hunting laws instead. Famous chimpanzee specialist Jane Goodall says, "I cannot turn my back on an individual."

1. Which of these statements is an OPINION?
   - **A** It is illegal to hunt chimpanzees.
   - **B** Chimps often get sick in captivity.
   - **C** Money spent on sanctuaries should be used to enforce the hunting laws.
   - **D** Goodall cannot turn her back on chimps.

TEACHING RESOURCES

The following resources can be used to enrich or extend the instruction for p. 607.

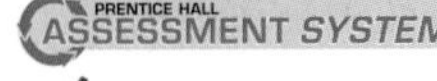

Workbook

Transparencies

Skill Book

CD-ROM

Lesson Objective

To distinguish fact from opinion in a test situation

Applying Reading Strategies

Explain to students that the strategy of identifying an author's evidence is directly related to distinguishing between fact and opinion. Remind students that when they read any passage for information, they should try to figure out how the writer is supporting his or her ideas. Writers may offer facts, statistics, and examples as evidence. Opinions do not count as evidence because they cannot be proved. When students read a sample test item, they should try to figure out the types of evidence that are provided to support the main idea.

Test-Taking Skills

- Have students read the sample test item.
- Then, have them make a three-column chart, with the first column labeled *Sentence Number*, the second labeled *Type of Evidence*, and the third labeled *Opinion*.
- Next, ask students to work alone or with a partner to review each sentence and determine what kind of evidence it is—fact, statistic, example, or detail. Students should write the type of evidence in the second column. If the sentence is an opinion, they should note that in the third column.
- As a class, review students' answers. If students have trouble with a particular sentence, ask them "Can the writer prove the idea in this sentence? If so, how?"

Answer

The answer is C. *A, B,* and *D* are facts. *A* can be proved by a law book. *B* can be proved by a chimp expert. *D* is a direct quotation from a chimpanzee specialist herself. Only *C* is an opinion that cannot be proved.

Unit Objectives

1. To develop skill in reading drama
2. To apply a variety of reading strategies, particularly strategies for reading drama, appropriate for reading these selections
3. To analyze literary elements
4. To use a variety of strategies to read unfamiliar words and to build vocabulary
5. To learn elements of grammar, usage, and style
6. To use recursive writing processes to write in a variety of forms
7. To develop listening and speaking skills
8. To express and support responses to various types of texts
9. To prepare, organize, and present literary interpretations

Meeting the Objectives

With each selection, you will find instructional materials through which students can meet these objectives. Further, you will find additional practice pages for reading strategies, literary analysis, vocabulary, and grammar in the **Selection Support: Skills Development Workbook** in your **Teaching Resources.**

Background

Art

Theatre Scene by Edgar Degas

Edgar Degas (1834–1917) is usually considered an Impressionist painter, although he favored theatrical subjects over the natural subjects that the Impressionists generally painted. He often presented his subjects from interesting angles. Connect this painting to the theme of drama by asking this question:

What is unusual about the point of view of this painting?

Answer: It is presented from the vantage point of a performer on stage rather than from that of the audience.

UNIT 8 Drama

Theatre Scene, Edgar Degas

UNIT FEATURES	
Connections	**Reading Informational Material**
Every unit contains a feature that connects literature to a related topic, such as art, science, or history. In this unit, the drama beginning on p. 684 connects students' understanding and appreciation of literature beyond the language arts curriculum. Use the information and questions on the Connections page to enrich students' understanding of the selections presented within the unit.	These selections will help students learn to analyze and evaluate informational texts, such as workplace documents, technical directions, and consumer materials. They will expose students to the organization and features unique to nonnarrative texts. In this unit, students will learn strategies for making assertions about the text and identifying cause-and-effect relationships.

Exploring the Genre

Drama is different from other forms of literature—it is written to be performed. When you read a drama, you should imagine that you see and hear the action of the performance. The following elements help readers and performers create the magic of drama:

- **Dialogue** is the conversation among characters.
- **Stage directions** are the words that tell readers and performers about the action, the sets, and the way in which the dialogue should be spoken.
- Scenery, costumes, props, sound effects, and lighting help create the world in which the actors perform. Playwrights usually give directions about these elements in the stage directions.

As you read the dramas in this unit, notice these features that make drama a unique form of literature.

◀ **Critical Viewing** What elements of drama are captured in the picture? **[Connect]**

Assessing Student Progress

Listed below are the tools that are available to measure the degree to which students meet the unit objectives.

Informal Assessment

The questions in the Review and Assess sections are a first level of response to the concepts and skills presented within the selections. Students' responses are a brief, informal measure of their grasp of the material. These responses can indicate where further instruction and practice are needed. Follow up with the practice pages in the **Selection Support: Skills Development Workbook.**

Formal Assessment

The **Formal Assessment** booklet contains the Selection Tests and Unit Tests.

- Selection Tests measure comprehension and skills acquisition for each selection or group of selections.
- Each Unit Test provides students with thirty multiple-choice questions and five essay questions designed to assess students' knowledge of the literature and skills taught in the unit.

The **Open Book Tests** ask students to demonstrate their ability to synthesize and communicate information from selections or groups of selections.

To assess student writing, you will find rubrics and scoring models in the **Performance Assessment and Portfolio Management** booklet. In this booklet, you will also find scoring rubrics for listening and speaking activities.

Alternative Assessment

The **Extension Activities** booklet contains writing activities, listening and speaking activities, and research and technology activities that are appropriate for students with different ability levels. You may also use these activities as an alternative measurement of students' growth.

▶Critical Viewing

Some details of drama that are captured in this picture include a stage, an audience, a conductor, and actors.

ASSESSMENT RESOURCES

- Selection Support: Skills Development Workbook
- Formal Assessment
- Open Book Tests
- Performance Assessment and Portfolio Management
- Extension Activities

Why Read Literature?

The "Why Read Literature?" page in each unit presents a list of possible purposes for reading. Each purpose for reading is connected to one or more of the selections in the unit. Good readers set a purpose before reading in order to help them read actively and focus on meaningful details.

Unit 8 introduces three purposes for reading. "Read for the Love of Literature" encourages students to witness a change of heart experienced by an elderly man. "Read to Be Entertained" introduces a clever fantasy with witty wordplay. "Read for Information" relates real-life experiences of immigrants.

How to Use This Page

- Tell students that before reading each selection in this unit, they should set a purpose for reading. This will help them read in an active and focused manner.
- Explain to students that reading a play about how an immigrant views the United States will increase their love of literature.
- Predict that students will be entertained by a fantastic journey to a fictional land in "The Phantom Tollbooth."
- Informational reading, such as "Chinese Immigrants Remember Detention at Angel Island," will give students a new perspective on the experiences of immigrants arriving in the United States.

Why Read Literature?

As you read drama, visualize how the words and actions might be performed on a stage or onscreen. To help you understand and remember dramatic works, set different purposes for your reading. Preview three purposes you might set before reading the works in this unit.

1 Read for the love of literature.

Renowned American playwright Arthur Miller was an impressionable teenager in 1929 when the New York Stock Exchange crashed and the Great Depression began. His family was forced to sell off their home and all their possessions to pay the bills. The experience deeply affected Miller, leading him to question what things in life have lasting value and permanence. Read **"Grandpa and the Statue,"** page 666, in which a stingy grandfather resists seeing any lasting value in the Statue of Liberty.

2 Read to be entertained.

Norton Juster started out as an architect but ended up as a writer. Unlike his character Milo, who says, "It seems to me that almost everything is a waste of time," Juster pursued many interests. Enjoy the humor in Juster's ingenious fantasy **"The Phantom Tollbooth,"** page 614. Step into Milo's car and ride through the secret tollbooth into the Land Beyond.

3 Read for information.

Known as the Ellis Island of the West, Angel Island in San Francisco Bay, California, opened in 1910 as an immigration station. Thousands of Chinese immigrants were detained and processed at Angel Island. Today, it is a National Historic Landmark. Read **"Chinese Immigrants Remember Detention at Angel Island,"** page 687, for personal accounts of some who were held there.

Take It to the Net

Visit the Web site for online instruction and activities related to each selection in this unit.

www.phschool.com

610 ◆ Drama

ENRICHMENT: Further Reading

Have students choose one or more of the works below to extend the unit theme or to read more by the unit authors.

The Phantom Tollbooth by Norton Juster

This is the original novel version of Milo's adventure in search of Rhyme and Reason.

Journey Home by Yoshiko Uchida

This selection from the **Prentice Hall Literature Library** tells of a Japanese American girl and her family encountering prejudice.

The Lion, the Witch, and the Wardrobe by C. S. Lewis

In this first book in the Chronicles of Narnia, children travel through a wardrobe to a fantastic land.

The Complete Nonsense Book by Edward Lear

This is a delightful collection of poems, prose, and drawings by a master of wordplay.

How to Read Literature

Strategies for Reading Drama

The story of a drama is told mostly through performance—what actors say and what they do. Stage directions in the script give other helpful information about the setting and about how actors should move and speak. When you read a drama, keep in mind that it is written to be performed. The following strategies will help you as you read a drama.

1. Summarize.

Dramas are frequently broken into parts called acts, which may be broken into smaller parts called scenes. To clarify your understanding of the drama, pause at the end of an act or a scene to summarize what has happened so far—restate what you have read briefly in your own words.

- If the play is not broken into acts or scenes, pause to summarize when an episode or event is over.
- Include main events of the scene or episode expressed in the order in which they occurred.

Use an organizer like the one shown to summarize in notes that you can use to review the play.

Act	Scene	Known Characters	New Characters	Main Events
I	1	none	Milo Clock	Milo is bored until he gets the tollbooth
II	2	Milo	Dischord Dynne Dodecahedron	

Summarizing a Scene

1. Name the characters.
2. Identify the key events.
3. Explain the meaning or significance.

2. Distinguish fact from fantasy.

Sometimes writers combine imaginary characters, situations, and events with real-life elements. In this passage, Grandpa and his dialogue are fantasy—made-up details—but the Statue of Liberty and the inscription on it are factual—details that can be proved true.

> MONAGHAN. . . . I'll try it with me spectacles, just a minute. Why, it's a poem, I believe. . . . "Give me your tired, your poor, your huddled masses yearning to breathe free, the wretched refuse of your teeming shore. . . ."

In this unit, you will learn strategies for distinguishing fact from fantasy.

As you read the plays in this unit, review the reading strategies and look at the notes in the side columns. Use the suggestions to apply the strategies for reading drama.

How to Read Literature

The "How to Read Literature" page in each unit presents a set of strategies to help readers understand authors' words and ideas. Each reading strategy is taught in conjunction with one or more of the selections within the unit. Good readers develop a bank of strategies from which they can draw as needed.

Unit 8 introduces two strategies for reading drama. To understand a selection fully, students must interact with the text to discover its meaning. The strategies on this page help readers interpret drama texts.

How to Use This Page

Introduce the strategies for reading drama, presenting each as a tool for reading the selections in this unit.

- As they read Act I of *The Phantom Tollbooth* (p. 614), students will be asked to summarize action in a play.
- As they read *Grandpa and the Statue* (p. 666), students will learn to find facts in a fictional drama.

MODEL A READING STRATEGY: Distinguish Fact and Fantasy

Tell students that sometimes a drama writer will mix fact and fantasy to achieve a dramatic effect. The effect helps make the play come alive for the audience.

Illustrate this strategy by using a passage from *Grandpa and the Statue*. These lines are spoken by Sheean, a neighbor of Grandpa's:

> This here Frenchman has gone and built a fine Statue of Liberty. It costs who knows how many millions to build. All they're askin' us to do is contribute enough to put up a base for the statue to stand on. . . . People all over the United States are puttin' in for it. Butler Street is doin' the same. We'd like to hang up a flag on the corner saying—"Butler Street, Brooklyn, is one hundred percent behind the Statue of Liberty."

Point out that Sheean is a fictional character, but some of what he says may be true. One way to prove what Sheean says is to use an encyclopedia or a book about the Statue of Liberty to find out whether it was built by a Frenchman and whether Americans contributed money to build the base. Students can also check a map to find a Butler Street in Brooklyn.

The Phantom Tollbooth, Act I

Lesson Objectives

1. **To analyze and respond to literary elements**
   - Literary Analysis: Elements of Drama
   - Connecting Literary Elements: Stage Directions
2. **To read, comprehend, analyze, and critique drama**
   - Reading Strategy: Summarizing
   - Reading Check Questions
   - Review and Assess Questions
3. **To develop word analysis skills, fluency, and systematic vocabulary**
   - Vocabulary Development Lesson: Word Analysis: Latin Prefix *pre-*
4. **To understand and apply written and oral language conventions**
   - Spelling Strategy
   - Grammar Lesson: Subject and Verb Agreement
   - Assessment Practice (ATE)
5. **To understand and apply appropriate writing and research strategies**
   - Writing Lesson: Letter
6. **To understand and apply listening and speaking strategies**
   - Extension Activity: Speech

STEP-BY-STEP TEACHING GUIDE	PACING GUIDE
PRETEACH	
Motivate Students and Provide Background	
Use the Motivation activity (ATE p. 612)	5 min.
Read and discuss the Preview material and Background information (SE/ATE p. 612) A	10 min.
Introduce the Concepts	
Introduce the Literary Analysis and Reading Strategy (SE/ATE p. 613) A	25 min.
Pronounce the vocabulary words and read their definitions (SE p. 613)	5 min.
TEACH	
Monitor Comprehension	
Informally monitor comprehension by circulating while students read independently or in groups A	50 min.
Monitor students' comprehension with the Reading Check notes (SE/ATE pp. 615, 617, 619, 621, 623, 625, 627, 629, 631)	as students read
Develop vocabulary with Vocabulary notes (SE pp. 615, 616, 625; ATE p. 616)	as students read
Develop Understanding	
Develop students' understanding of elements of drama with the Literary Analysis annotations (SE/ATE pp. 615, 618, 620, 624–632) A	5 min.
Develop students' ability to summarize with the Reading Strategy annotations (SE/ATE pp. 617, 618, 621–623, 628, 630, 632)	5 min.
ASSESS	
Assess Mastery	
Assess students' mastery of the Reading Strategy and Literary Analysis by having them answer the Review and Assess questions (SE/ATE p. 635)	25 min.
Use one or more of the print and media Assessment Resources (ATE p. 635) A	up to 45 min.
EXTEND	
Apply Understanding	
Have students complete the Vocabulary Development Lesson and the Grammar Lesson (SE p. 635) A	30 min.
Apply students' ability to write a letter using the Writing Lesson (SE/ATE p. 635) A	45 min.
Apply students' understanding of the selection using one or more of the Extension Activities (SE p. 635)	30–90 min.

ACCELERATED INSTRUCTION:
Use the strategies and activities identified with an A.

UNIVERSAL ACCESS
● = Below Level Students
▲ = On-Level Students
■ = Above Level Students

Time and Resource Manager

Reading Level: Average
Average Number of Instructional Days: 5

RESOURCES		
PRINT	**TRANSPARENCIES**	**TECHNOLOGY**
• **Beyond Literature,** Cross-Curricular Connection: Math, p. 35 ▲ ■		• **Interest Grabber Videotapes,** Tape 4 ● ▲ ■
• **Selection Support Workbook:** ● ▲ ■ Literary Analysis, p. 175 Reading Strategy, p. 174 Build Vocabulary, p. 171	• **Literary Analysis and Reading Transparencies,** pp. 69 and 70 ● ▲ ■	
• **Adapted Reader's Companion** ● • **Reader's Companion** ● • **Authors In Depth,** Copper Level, p. 154 ■		• **Listening to Literature** ● ▲ ■ Audiocassettes, Sides 21–22 Audio CDs, CD 11
• **English Learner's Companion** ● ▲ • **Literatura en español** ● ▲ • **Literary Analysis for Enrichment** ■		
• **Formal Assessment:** Selection Test, pp. 159–161 ● ▲ ■ • **Open Book Test,** pp. 103–105 ● ▲ ■ • **Performance Assessment and Portfolio Management,** p. 25 ● ▲ ■ • Prentice Hall ASSESSMENT SYSTEM ● ▲ ■	• Prentice Hall ASSESSMENT SYSTEM ● ▲ ■ Skills Practice Answers and Explanations on Transparencies	• **Test Bank Software** ● ▲ ■ • **Got It! Assessment Videotapes,** Tape 4 ● ▲
• **Selection Support Workbook:** ● ▲ ■ Build Spelling Skills, p. 172 Build Grammar Skills, p. 173 • **Writing and Grammar,** Copper Level ● ▲ ■ • **Extension Activities,** p. 35 ● ▲ ■	• **Daily Language Practice Transparencies** ● ▲ • **Writing Models and Graphic Organizers on Transparencies** ● ▲ ■	• **Writing and Grammar iText CD-ROM** ● ▲ ■ ***Take It to the Net*** www.phschool.com

BLOCK SCHEDULING: Use one 90-minute class period to preteach the selection and have students read it. Use a second 90-minute class period to assess students' mastery of skills and have them complete one of the Extension Activities.

MERCHANT 4. I knew you'd like it. "A" is one of our best-sellers. All of them aren't that good, you know. The "Z," for instance—very dry and sawdusty. And the "X"? Tastes like a trunkful of stale air. But most of the others aren't bad at all. Here, try the "I."

28 **MILO.** [*Tasting.*] Cool! It tastes icy.

MERCHANT 4. [*To* TOCK.] How about the "C" for you? It's as crunchy as a bone. Most people are just too lazy to make their own words, but take it from me, not only is it more fun, but it's also *de*-lightful, [*Holds up a "D."*] *e*-lating, [*Holds up an "E."*] and extremely *u*seful! [*Holds up a "U."*]

MILO. But isn't it difficult? I'm not very good at making words.

[*The* SPELLING BEE, *a large colorful bee, comes up from behind.*]

SPELLING BEE. Perhaps I can be of some assistance . . . a-s-s-i-s-t-a-n-c-e. [*The Three turn around and see him.*] Don't be alarmed . . . a-l-a-r-m-e-d. I am the Spelling Bee. I can spell anything. Anything. A-n-y-t-h-i-n-g. Try me. Try me.

MILO. [*Backing off,* TOCK *on his guard.*] Can you spell goodbye?

SPELLING BEE. Perhaps you are under the misapprehension . . . m-i-s-a-p-p-r-e-h-e-n-s-i-o-n that I am dangerous. Let me assure you that I am quite peaceful. Now, think of the most difficult word you can, and I'll spell it.

misapprehension (mis´ ap rē hen´ shən) *n.* misunderstanding

29 **MILO.** Uh . . . o.k. [*At this point,* MILO *may turn to the audience and ask them to help him choose a word or he may think of one on his own.*] How about . . . "Curiosity"?

SPELLING BEE. [*Winking.*] Let's see now . . . uh . . . how much time do I have?

MILO. Just ten seconds. Count them off, Tock.

30 **SPELLING BEE.** [As TOCK counts.] Oh dear, oh dear. [*Just at the last moment, quickly.*]
C-u-r-i-o-s-i-t-y.

MERCHANT 4. Correct! [ALL *Cheer.*]

MILO. Can you spell anything?

SPELLING BEE. [*Proudly.*] Just about. You see, years ago, I was an ordinary bee minding my own business, smelling flowers all day, occasionally picking up part-time work in people's bonnets. Then one day, I realized that I'd never amount to anything without an education, so I decided that . . .

HUMBUG. [*Coming up in a booming voice.*] BALDERDASH! [*He wears a lavish coat, striped pants, checked vest, spats and a derby*

Literary Analysis
Elements of Drama What do the dialogue and the stage directions reveal about Spelling Bee?

31 **✓Reading Check**
What is sold in the marketplace of Dictionopolis?

29 Critical Thinking

Speculate

- Ask students how Milo thinks of a word for the bee to spell.
  Answer: He asks the audience to help him or thinks of one on his own.
- Ask students to speculate on why the author included audience involvement in the play.
  Answer: This technique is used to keep the audience's attention and to make audience members feel involved in the play.

30 Literary Analysis

Elements of Drama

- Point out to students that all parts of a play must work together for drama to succeed.
- Have a student read aloud the bracketed stage direction and dialogue for Spelling Bee. Ask the Literary Analysis question on p. 625.
  Answer: Spelling Bee winks and spells words to show that he or she is playful and not harmful.

31 ✓Reading Check

Answer: Words and letters are sold in the Word Market.

CUSTOMIZE INSTRUCTION FOR UNIVERSAL ACCESS

For Special Needs Students	For Advanced Readers
Students may need help understanding what the author has done in naming and depicting the characters. Refer students to the cast list on p. 614, or have them list the characters they have already met. Have students think about the names as words; for example, is a spelling bee usually a creature? Tell students that many of these names are puns, or plays on words. Have each student write interpretations of the names and share those interpretations with the class.	Norton Juster, the author of the novel upon which this play is based, packs his pages with wordplay. Have each student record and explain examples of the wordplay on just one page of this play to emphasize the cleverness of the writing. Then, have individuals compare their lists with those of several other students to see whether they identified the same examples. It is likely that students' lists will differ.

32 ▶ Critical Viewing

Answer: The picture of the bee shows qualities similar to those of Spelling Bee—both seem proud, triumphant, and quick.

33 Critical Thinking

Speculate

- Have students analyze the exchange between Humbug and Spelling Bee. Ask: What is happening between Humbug and Spelling Bee?
  Answer: The two characters are fighting to get Milo's attention.
- Ask students what they do when they are trying to get someone's attention in a chaotic atmosphere.
  Possible responses: Students might say they raise their hands, raise their voices, or move right in front of the person so the person sees them.
- Ask: Why would Humbug say so much about his family history?
  Answer: He may want to make himself sound important and reliable, because Spelling Bee is saying mean things about him.

34 Literary Analysis

Elements of Drama

- Have students describe the names of the characters in this play.
  Answer: The characters have names that describe their characteristics.
- Ask the Literary Analysis question on p. 626: In what one way are the characters of Humbug and Spelling Bee similar to their names?
  Answer: They are both depicted as bugs. Spelling Bee spells words as he speaks. Humbug claims to be someone that he really isn't.

hat.] Let me repeat . . . BALDERDASH! [*Swings his cane and clicks his heels in the air.*] Well, well, what have we here? Isn't someone going to introduce me to the little boy?

SPELLING BEE. [*Disdainfully.*] This is the Humbug. You can't trust a word he says.

HUMBUG. NONSENSE! Everyone can trust a Humbug. As I was saying to the king just the other day . . .

SPELLING BEE. You've never met the king. [*To* MILO.] Don't believe a thing he tells you.

HUMBUG. Bosh, my boy, pure bosh. The Humbugs are an old and noble family, honorable to the core. Why, we fought in the Crusades with Richard the
33 Lionhearted, crossed the Atlantic with Columbus, blazed trails with the pioneers. History is full of Humbugs.

34 **SPELLING BEE.** A very pretty speech . . . s-p-e-e-c-h. Now, why don't you go away? I was just advising the lad of the importance of proper spelling.

HUMBUG. BAH! As soon as you learn to spell one word, they ask you to spell another. You can never catch up, so why bother? [*Puts his arm around* MILO.] Take my advice, boy, and forget about it. As my great-great-great-grandfather George Washington Humbug used to say. . .

SPELLING BEE. You, sir, are an impostor i-m-p-o-s-t-o-r who can't even spell his own name!

HUMBUG. What? You dare to doubt my word? The word of a Humbug? The word of a Humbug who has direct access to the ear of a King? And the king shall hear of this, I promise you . . .

VOICE 1. Did someone call for the King?

VOICE 2. Did you mention the monarch?

VOICE 3. Speak of the sovereign?

VOICE 4. Entreat the Emperor?

VOICE 5. Hail his highness?

32 ▲ Critical Viewing How does this picture of Spelling Bee compare to the description of him in the play? (Compare)

Literary Analysis
Elements of Drama In what one way are the characters of Humbug and Spelling Bee similar to their names?

CUSTOMIZE INSTRUCTION FOR UNIVERSAL ACCESS

For Less Proficient Readers

Students may need assistance in developing their summarizing skills. Tell students that a good summary will retell the story in fewer words than the original. However, a good summary will also answer most of the basic questions that all writing must answer:

- **Who** is in the story?
- **What** are the characters doing?
- **Why** are the characters doing what they are doing?
- **How** are the characters doing what they are doing?
- **Where** does the story take place?
- **When** does the story take place?

Encourage students to check the drafts of their summaries against this list. If any of the questions are left unanswered, students should be able to explain why.

[*Five tall, thin gentlemen regally dressed in silks and satins, plumed hats and buckled shoes appear as they speak.*]

MILO. Who are they?

SPELLING BEE. The King's advisors. Or in more formal terms, his cabinet.

MINISTER 1. Greetings!

MINISTER 2. Salutations!

MINISTER 3. Welcome!

MINISTER 4. Good Afternoon!

MINISTER 5. Hello!

MILO. Uh . . . Hi.

[*All the* MINISTERS, *from here on called by their numbers, unfold their scrolls and read in order.*]

MINISTER 1. By the order of Azaz the Unabridged . . .

MINISTER 2. King of Dictionopolis . . .

MINISTER 3. Monarch of letters . . .

MINISTER 4. Emperor of phrases, sentences, and miscellaneous figures of speech . . .

MINISTER 5. We offer you the hospitality of our kingdom . . .

35 **MINISTER 1.** Country

36 **MINISTER 2.** Nation

MINISTER 3. State

MINISTER 4. Commonwealth

MINISTER 5. Realm

MINISTER 1. Empire

MINISTER 2. Palatinate

MINISTER 3. Principality.

MILO. Do all those words mean the same thing?

MINISTER 1. Of course.

MINISTER 2. Certainly.

MINISTER 3. Precisely.

MINISTER 4. Exactly.

MINISTER 5. Yes.

MILO. Then why don't you use just one? Wouldn't that make a lot more sense?

Literary Analysis

Elements of Drama How do the characters' words indicate the importance of words in the kingdom of Dictionopolis?

37 

Reading Check

Which characters does Milo meet in Dictionopolis?

35 Critical Thinking

Analyze

- Point out to students that sometimes characters act in a pattern to make a point. Ask students to glance down pp. 626–627 and note which characters speak in a pattern.
  Answer: The five ministers always speak one after the other and use words that mean the same thing.
- Ask students what the pattern tells them about the ministers.
  Answer: They are similar characters.

36 Literary Analysis

Elements of Drama

- Call attention to the ministers' excessive use of words.
- Ask the Literary Analysis question on p. 627: How do the characters' words indicate the importance of words in the kingdom of Dictionopolis?
  Answer: The use of many words indicates that words are plentiful and important in Dictionopolis.

37 Reading Check

Answer: In Dictionopolis, Milo meets a gatekeeper, merchants, Humbug, Spelling Bee, and the ministers.

CUSTOMIZE INSTRUCTION FOR UNIVERSAL ACCESS

For Less Proficient Readers	For English Learners
Have students compare and contrast the Doldrums and Dictionopolis. Have them use the Venn Diagram on p. 89 in **Writing Models and Graphic Organizers on Transparencies** to organize their thoughts. Students may want to compare the types of costumes and characters seen in the two settings.	Help students expand their vocabularies by telling them that the ministers are using different words to say the same things. Discuss their words and their meanings as necessary. You may then want to suggest a concept, such as parting, and have students come up with different words and phrases: for example, *farewell, so long, see you later,* and *take it easy.*

38 Literary Analysis

Elements of Drama

- Call students' attention to the first three examples of stage directions on p. 628. Then ask the Literary Analysis question: Which characters' actions are described in the stage directions?
  Answer: The actions of the Ministers and Milo are described.
- Have students explain how they know this information.
  Answer: Stage directions that appear in the same block of text as a character's speech usually refer to that character. If the directions apply to a different character, that character's name appears in capital letters.

39 Reading Strategy

Summarizing

- Review with students the purpose of summarizing literature.
  Answer: Summaries give the basic idea or plot of the writing.

Monitor Progress Ask students the Reading Strategy question on p. 628.
Answer: The most significant events are these: Milo has arrived at Dictionopolis; he has met Humbug, Spelling Bee, and the ministers; and he has been invited to the royal banquet.

Reteach Evaluate the summaries that students suggest. If there are too many details, have students reflect on what is necessary and revise their work. If there are not enough details, have students look at their work to decide what else to include.

MINISTER 1. Nonsense!

MINISTER 2. Ridiculous!

MINISTER 3. Fantastic!

MINISTER 4. Absurd!

MINISTER 5. Bosh!

MINISTER 1. We're not interested in making sense. It's not our job.

MINISTER 2. Besides, one word is as good as another, so why not use them all?

MINISTER 3. Then you don't have to choose which one is right.

MINISTER 4. Besides, if one is right, then ten are ten times as right.

38 **MINISTER 5.** Obviously, you don't know who we are. [*Each presents himself and* MILO *acknowledges the introduction.*]

MINISTER 1. The Duke of Definition.

MINISTER 2. The Minister of Meaning.

MINISTER 3. The Earl of Essence.

MINISTER 4. The Count of Connotation.

MINISTER 5. The Undersecretary of Understanding.

ALL FIVE. And we have come to invite you to the Royal Banquet.

39 **SPELLING BEE.** The banquet! That's quite an honor, my boy. A real h-o-n-o-r.

HUMBUG. DON'T BE RIDICULOUS! Everybody goes to the Royal Banquet these days.

SPELLING BEE. [*To the* HUMBUG.] True, everybody does go. But some people are invited and others simply push their way in where they aren't wanted.

HUMBUG. HOW DARE YOU? You buzzing little upstart, I'll show you who's not wanted . . . [*Raises his cane threateningly.*]

SPELLING BEE. You just watch it! I'm warning w-a-r-n-i-n-g you! [*At that moment, an ear-shattering blast of TRUMPETS, entirely off-key, is heard, and a* PAGE *appears.*]

PAGE. King Azaz the Unabridged is about to begin the Royal banquet. All guests who do not appear promptly at the table will automatically lose their place. [*A huge Table is carried out with* KING AZAZ *sitting in a large chair, carried out at the head of the table.*]

AZAZ. Places. Everyone take your places. [*All the characters, including the* HUMBUG *and the* SPELLING BEE, *who forget their quarrel,*

Literary Analysis
Elements of Drama Which characters' actions are described in the stage directions?

Reading Strategy
Summarizing What are the most significant events that have occurred since Milo learned about Rhyme and Reason?

ENRICHMENT: Language Arts Connection

Alliteration

Tell students that the writers choose to characterize the five ministers as a group of similarly minded characters. Therefore, every time they are asked a question, they answer with responses that may not be identical but that all have the same general meaning.

The first time the ministers speak, the authors use the literary technique of *alliteration* to unify these five characters. Remind students that alliteration is the repetition of initial consonant sounds, as in "call for the King," "mention the monarch," and "speak of the sovereign."

Point out that in addition to emphasizing the similarities between the ministers—they each respond in the same, cunning way—alliteration makes the play fun to read and hear.

As students read, tell them to look for other examples of alliteration, and to share these examples with the class.

rush to take their places at the table. MILO *and* TOCK *sit near the king.* AZAZ *looks at* MILO.] And just who is this?

MILO. Your Highness, my name is Milo and this is Tock. Thank you very much for inviting us to your banquet, and I think your palace is beautiful!

MINISTER 1. Exquisite.

MINISTER 2. Lovely.

MINISTER 3. Handsome.

MINISTER 4. Pretty.

MINISTER 5. Charming.

AZAZ. SILENCE! Now tell me, young man, what can you do to entertain us? Sing songs? Tell stories? Juggle plates? Do tumbling tricks? Which is it?

MILO. I can't do any of those things.

AZAZ. What an ordinary little boy. Can't you do anything at all?

MILO. Well . . . I can count to a thousand.

40 **AZAZ.** AARGH, numbers! Never mention numbers here. Only use them when we absolutely have to. Now, why don't we change the subject and have some dinner? Since you are the guest of honor, you may pick the menu.

MILO. Me? Well, uh . . . I'm not very hungry. Can we just have a light snack?

AZAZ. A light snack it shall be!

41 [AZAZ *claps his hands. Waiters rush in with covered trays. When they are uncovered, Shafts of Light pour out. The light may be created through the use of battery-operated flashlights which are secured in the trays and covered with a false bottom. The Guests help themselves.*]

HUMBUG. Not a very substantial meal. Maybe you can suggest something a little more filling.

MILO. Well, in that case, I think we ought to have a square meal . . .

AZAZ. [*Claps his hands.*] A square meal it is! [*Waiters serve trays of Colored Squares of all sizes. People serve themselves.*]

SPELLING BEE. These are awful. [HUMBUG *Coughs and all the Guests do not care for the food.*]

AZAZ. [*Claps his hands and the trays are removed.*] Time for speeches. [*To* MILO.] You first.

Literary Analysis
Elements of Drama What do Azaz's words contribute to the development of the plot?

Literary Analysis
Elements of Drama How do the stage directions help you realize that Milo's light snack is something unusual?

42 **Reading Check**
What does the king forbid Milo to talk about?

40 Literary Analysis

Elements of Drama

- Have students recall the conflict between Azaz and the Mathemagician. Have them summarize the problem.
  Answer: The problem is that the brothers can't agree on whether words or numbers are more important.
- Ask a volunteer to read aloud the bracketed passage. Then, ask the first Literary Analysis question on p. 629: What do Azaz's words contribute to the development of the plot?
  Answer: His words show that Azaz is still angry with his brother.

41 Literary Analysis

Elements of Drama

Direct students' attention to the bracketed stage directions. Ask the second Literary Analysis question on p. 629: How do the stage directions help you realize that Milo's light snack is something unusual?
Answer: The directions show that shafts of light are the snack. This is a literal meaning of *light* that Milo did not intend.

42 

Reading Check

Answer: The king forbids Milo to talk about numbers.

CUSTOMIZE INSTRUCTION FOR UNIVERSAL ACCESS

Special Needs Students	Less Proficient Readers
Students may be able to understand plot developments better if they act out characters' lines with gestures. For example, ask students to read and think of gestures for King Azaz's first line on p. 629: "SILENCE! Now tell me, young man, what can you do to entertain us? Sing songs? Tell stories? Juggle plates? Do tumbling tricks? Which is it?" When they have practiced the gestures, have students perform for the class.	Students may benefit from a closer analysis of Humbug and Spelling Bee and their relationship. Have students use stage directions and dialogue to draw illustrations of each character. Then, ask students to write brief descriptions of each character and the ways in which they interact with one another. What is the basis of their antagonism? Which character appeals more to students? Why?

43 Literary Analysis

Elements of Drama

- Ask students the first part of the Literary Analysis question on p. 630: What happens to Milo each time he tries to talk?
  Answer: He is interrupted by the other characters.
- Then, ask the second part of the question.
  Answer: Milo is told he must eat his words. That is why the king chides Milo for the "poor taste" of his words.

44 Reading Strategy

Summarizing

- Tell students to review the summaries they have been writing.
- Allow students to reread p. 630 if necessary before asking the Reading Strategy question.
  Possible response: At the banquet, when Milo tries to speak, the other characters cut him off. The other characters' speeches consist of lists of food items. Milo learns that the guests at the banquet are expected to eat their words.

MILO. [*Hesitantly.*] Your Majesty, ladies and gentlemen, I would like to take this opportunity to say that . . .

AZAZ. That's quite enough. Mustn't talk all day.

MILO. But I just started to . . .

AZAZ. NEXT!

HUMBUG. [*Quickly.*] Roast turkey, mashed potatoes, vanilla ice cream.

43 SPELLING BEE. Hamburgers, corn on the cob, chocolate pudding p-u-d-d-i-n-g. [*Each Guest names two dishes and a dessert.*]

AZAZ. [*The last.*] Pâté de foie gras, soupe à l'oignon, salade endives, fromage et fruits et demi-tasse. [*He claps his hands. Waiters serve each Guest his Words.*] Dig on. [*To* MILO.] Though I can't say I think much of your choice.

MILO. I didn't know I was going to have to eat my words.

AZAZ. Of course, of course, everybody here does. Your speech should have been in better taste.

MINISTER 1. Here, try some somersault. It improves the flavor.

MINISTER 2. Have a rigamarole. [*Offers breadbasket.*]

MINISTER 3. Or a ragamuffin.

MINISTER 4. Perhaps you'd care for a synonym bun. 44

MINISTER 5. Why not wait for your just desserts?

AZAZ. Ah yes, the dessert. We're having a special treat today . . . freshly made at the half-bakery.

MILO. The half-bakery?

AZAZ. Of course, the half-bakery! Where do you think half-baked ideas come from? Now, please don't interrupt. By royal command, the pastry chefs have . . .

MILO. What's a half-baked idea?

[AZAZ *gives up the idea of speaking as a cart is wheeled in and the Guests help themselves.*]

HUMBUG. They're very tasty, but they don't always agree with you. Here's a good one. [HUMBUG *hands one to* MILO.]

MILO. [*Reads.*] "The earth is flat."

SPELLING BEE. People swallowed that one for years. [*Picks up one and reads.*] "The moon is made of green cheese." Now, there's a half-baked idea.

[*Everyone chooses one and eats. They include: "It Never Rains But*

Literary Analysis
Elements of Drama What happens to Milo each time he tries to talk? How does this relate to the action that follows?

Reading Strategy
Summarizing How would you summarize the events at the banquet so far?

ENRICHMENT: Language Arts Connection

Wordplay

The writer of *The Phantom Tollbooth* employs many types of wordplay; in fact, many of the settings, characters, and situations are based on wordplay.

A pun is a humorous use of words, playing on different uses of the same word or on a similar sense or sound of different words. For example, banquet guests eat synonym buns, rigamaroles, and just desserts.

Another type of wordplay is the literal rendering of figurative or idiomatic expressions. For example, Milo is given a light snack—it consists of rays of light—and a square meal—in the shape of a square.

Related to literal renderings are personifications of expressions, such as Rhyme and Reason and the Spelling Bee.

Encourage students to point out clever uses of language and explain how they differ from ordinary usage.

44 *Pours," "Night Air Is Bad Air," "Everything Happens for the Best," "Coffee Stunts Your Growth."*]

AZAZ. And now for a few closing words. Attention! Let me have your attention! [*Everyone leaps up and Exits, except for* MILO, TOCK, *and the* HUMBUG.] Loyal subjects and friends, once again on this gala occasion, we have . . .

MILO. Excuse me, but everybody left.

AZAZ. [*Sadly.*] I was hoping no one would notice. It happens every time.

HUMBUG. They're gone to dinner, and as soon as I finish this last bite, I shall join them.

MILO. That's ridiculous. How can they eat dinner right after a banquet?

AZAZ. SCANDALOUS! We'll put a stop to it at once. From now on, by royal command, everyone must eat dinner before the banquet.

MILO. But that's just as bad.

HUMBUG. Or just as good. Things which are equally bad are also equally good. Try to look at the bright side of things.

MILO. I don't know which side of anything to look at. Everything is so confusing, and all your words only make things worse.

AZAZ. How true. There must be something we can do about it.

HUMBUG. Pass a law.

AZAZ. We have almost as many laws as words.

45 **HUMBUG.** Offer a reward. [AZAZ *shakes his head and looks madder at each suggestion.*] Send for help? Drive a bargain? Pull the switch? Lower the boom? Toe the line?

[*As* AZAZ *continues to scowl, the* HUMBUG *loses confidence and finally gives up.*]

46 **MILO.** Maybe you should let Rhyme and Reason return.

AZAZ. How nice that would be. Even if they were a bother at times, things always went so well when they were here. But I'm afraid it can't be done.

HUMBUG. Certainly not. Can't be done.

MILO. Why not?

HUMBUG. [*Now siding with* MILO.] Why not, indeed?

AZAZ. Much too difficult.

HUMBUG. Of course, much too difficult.

Literary Analysis
Elements of Drama What is the problem that must be settled as the plot unfolds?

47  **Reading Check**

What does Milo suggest Azaz should do to solve his problems?

45 Critical Thinking

Connect

- Ask a volunteer to read aloud the bracketed passage. Then, ask students to comment on Humbug's suggestions.
  Possible response: Students should note that Humbug uses idioms, language that has a meaning that differs from its literal meaning, in his suggestions.
- Then, ask students what other characters reply with answers that show some similarities to Humbug's.
  Answer: The ministers also use wordplay, but their wordplay is in the form of puns.

46 Literary Analysis

Elements of Drama

- Ask students to recall why the kingdoms are without Rhyme and Reason.
  Answer: The princesses were banished because the kings did not like the way the princesses tried to settle the kings' argument.
- Ask the Literary Analysis question on p. 631: What is the problem that must be settled as the plot unfolds?
  Answer: The princesses Rhyme and Reason must be returned to the kingdoms.

47 Reading Check

Answer: Milo suggests that Azaz let Rhyme and Reason return.

CUSTOMIZE INSTRUCTION FOR UNIVERSAL ACCESS

For Special Needs Students	For Advanced Readers
To help students check their summaries, suggest that each student make a storyboard showing the main events in the play. First, they might want to organize the events using the Series of Events Chain on p. 69 in **Writing Models and Graphic Organizers in Transparencies.** Then, have students work in groups to make an illustration for each major event. Have them add captions or titles to the events. Display students' illustrations in the classroom.	Challenge students to create wordplay in connection with some of their everyday school and classroom activities. They might enjoy literally rendering figurative or idiomatic expressions. For example, many students eat a bag lunch. Do they actually eat bags for lunch? Suggest these phrases to help students start their wordplay: heavy schedule, cold facts, and hard test. Have them illustrate their choices as personification, like the characters in *The Phantom Tollbooth.*

48 Literary Analysis

Elements of Drama

- Ask students to restate the main problem in the play.
  Answer: The princesses Rhyme and Reason have been banished.
- After students have read the bracketed passage, have them answer the Literary Analysis question on p. 632.
  Answer: Milo's problem is that he must free the princesses. The difficulties he faces include crossing the countryside to Digitopolis, persuading the Mathemagician to release the princesses, entering the Mountain of Ignorance, climbing a two-thousand-foot staircase without railings in a high wind at night to the Castle-in-the-Air, and returning through the chaotic crags.

49 Reading Strategy

Summarizing

- Remind students that they are to be keeping track of the main events in the play.
- Ask the Reading Strategy question on p. 632.
  Answer: Milo, a bored child, receives and assembles a tollbooth. Through it, he enters the Lands Beyond. First, Milo meets the Whether Man in the Land of Expectations. Then, he enters the Doldrums, where he encounters the Lethargarians. Next, Tock the Watchdog arrives and tells Milo that he must think hard to get out of the Doldrums. On their way to Dictionopolis, Tock tells Milo about the princesses Rhyme and Reason, who were banished when they could not settle a dispute between the warring brother kings, Azaz, King of Words, and the Mathemagician, King of Numbers. When they get to Dictionopolis, Milo and Tock meet Spelling Bee, Humbug, and the king's cabinet, who invite everyone to the banquet of King Azaz. There, the King suggests that Milo, Tock, and Humbug go to rescue the princesses.

MILO. You could, if you really wanted to.

HUMBUG. By all means, if you really wanted to, you could.

AZAZ. [*To* HUMBUG.] How?

MILO. [*Also to* HUMBUG.] Yeah, how?

HUMBUG. Why . . . uh, it's a simple task for a brave boy with a stout heart, a steadfast dog and a serviceable small automobile.

AZAZ. Go on.

48 **HUMBUG.** Well, all that he would have to do is cross the dangerous, unknown countryside between here and Digitopolis, where he would have to persuade the Mathemagician to release the Princesses, which we know to be impossible because the Mathemagician will never agree with Azaz about anything. Once achieving that, it's a simple matter of entering the Mountains of Ignorance from where no one has ever returned alive, an effortless climb up a two thousand foot stairway without railings in a high wind at night to the Castle-in-the-Air. After a pleasant chat with the Princesses, all that remains is a leisurely ride back through those chaotic crags where the frightening fiends have sworn to tear any intruder from limb to limb and devour him down to his belt buckle. And finally after doing all that, a triumphal parade! If, of course, there is anything left to parade . . . followed by hot chocolate and cookies for everyone.

Literary Analysis
Elements of Drama What problem does Milo have to solve? What difficulties will he face as the plot unfolds?

AZAZ. I never realized it would be so simple.

MILO. It sounds dangerous to me.

TOCK. And just who is supposed to make that journey?

AZAZ. A very good question. But there is one far more serious problem.

MILO. What's that?

AZAZ. I'm afraid I can't tell you that until you return.

MILO. But wait a minute, I didn't . . .

AZAZ. Dictionopolis will always be grateful to you, my boy, and your dog. [AZAZ *pats* TOCK *and* MILO.] 49

Reading Strategy
Summarizing What are the main events of the first act?

TOCK. Now, just one moment, sire . . .

AZAZ. You will face many dangers on your journey, but fear not, for I can give you something for your protection. [AZAZ *gives* MILO *a box.*] In this box are the letters of the alphabet. With them you can form all the words you will ever need to help you overcome

CUSTOMIZE INSTRUCTION FOR UNIVERSAL ACCESS

For Gifted/Talented Students

Have students imagine that they have been given the mission of rescuing the banished princesses. Divide the class into groups of four or five. Have each group designate a "Rescue Mission" leader, under whose direction the rescue mission will be executed. Taking into consideration the ideas of other members, have the leader designate other group members' titles: archivist (to document the mission), computer genius, chemist, or any other titles they come up with. Have the group make a list of items they will need and a strategy of how they will achieve their mission. Then, have each group present their list and strategy to the class. Allow the class time to discuss the pros and cons of the information presented.

the obstacles that may stand in your path. All you must do is use them well and in the right places.

MILO. [*Miserably.*] Thanks a lot.

AZAZ. You will need a guide, of course, and since he knows the obstacles so well, the Humbug has cheerfully volunteered to accompany you.

HUMBUG. Now, see here . . . !

AZAZ. You will find him dependable, brave, resourceful and loyal.

HUMBUG. [*Flattered.*] Oh, your Majesty.

MILO. I'm sure he'll be a great help. [*They approach the car.*]

TOCK. I hope so. It looks like we're going to need it.

[*The lights darken and the* KING *fades from view.*]

AZAZ. Good luck! Drive carefully! [*The three get into the car and begin to move. Suddenly a thunderously loud NOISE is heard. They slow down the car.*]

MILO. What was that?

TOCK. It came from up ahead.

HUMBUG. It's something terrible, I just know it. Oh, no. Something dreadful is going to happen to us. I can feel it in my bones. [*The NOISE is repeated. They all look at each other fearfully as the lights fade.*]

Review and Assess

Thinking About the Selection

1. **Respond:** Which character would you most like to meet?
2. **(a)Recall:** Who are Rhyme and Reason? **(b) Identify Cause and Effect:** What effect does their absence have on Dictionopolis?
3. **(a) Recall:** Why were Rhyme and Reason banished? **(b) Infer:** Why do you think Milo is chosen to rescue them?
4. **(a) Recall:** How does the Humbug describe the journey Milo must make? **(b) Speculate:** Describe what you think Milo's journey will be like, and give three details from the story to support your answer.
5. **(a) Recall:** What gift does King Azaz give Milo? **(b) Hypothesize:** Describe a situation in which the gift might help Milo.

Answers for p. 633

Review and Assess

1. Possible responses: Some students may be intrigued by Milo; others may prefer one of the more unusual characters.
2. **(a)** Rhyme and Reason are the princesses who have been banished from the kingdom. **(b)** Their absence has made Dictionopolis unruly.
3. **(a)** The princesses were banished because they said that words and numbers were equally important. **(b)** Milo is chosen because he has a stout heart, a steadfast dog, and an automobile.
4. **(a)** Humbug makes the journey sound perilous. **(b)** Possible response: Students may say that it will be a dangerous journey because Milo will enter mountains from which no one has ever returned alive, climb a dangerous staircase, and get past frightening fiends.
5. **(a)** The king gives Milo a box of alphabet letters. **(b)** Possible response: They might help him make a sign to ask for help.

ASSESSMENT PRACTICE: Reading Comprehension

Sentence Construction (For more practice, see Test Preparation Workbook, p. 49.)

Some tests require students to recognize appropriate sentence construction. Use the sample item below to help students identify run-on sentences. Write the following on the board:

Norton Juster was an architect and he also taught design to college students.

Choose the best way to write the underlined section:

A Norton Juster was an architect; and he also taught design to college students.

B Norton Juster was an architect—and he also taught design—to college students.

C Norton Juster was an architect, and he also taught design to college students.

D Correct as is.

A comma must precede a coordinating conjunction that separates two independent clauses. Therefore, *C* is the correct choice.

ASSESS

Answers for p. 634

Review and Assess

1. Dialogue reveals a character's thoughts and actions. Possible responses: **Tock:** "KILLING TIME! It's bad enough wasting time without killing it." Shows: Tock wants Milo to use time wisely. **Humbug:** "Bosh, my boy, pure bosh. The Humbugs are an old and noble family, honorable to the core." Shows: He is vain and self-important.
2. **(a)** Tock explains the problem. **(b)** Tock's name is related to keeping time, and his explanation highlights the absurdities of wasting time.
3. **Expectations:** A "lonely road in the middle of nowhere"; a little man who lives there speaks fast and excitedly. **The Doldrums:** Everything moves slowly; the Lethargarians blend in with the road or the trees. **Dictionopolis:** The Word Market is a busy place; Dictionopolis is guarded by a gate.
4. **(a)** Possible response: On p. 620 the Watchdog is described as having the body of a clock. This explains that he is both a watch and a dog. **(b)** Students' stage directions should be written in brackets and should help readers envision the scene.
5. **(a)** Through a tollbooth, Milo enters the Lands Beyond. He meets Whether Man in the Land of Expectations. Then, he enters the Doldrums, where he thinks hard to escape. On the way to Dictionopolis, Tock tells Milo about the princesses. **(b)** These events are the most important because they reveal the play's themes.
6. Milo, a bored child, enters the Lands Beyond through a tollbooth. There, he visits the Land of Expectations, the Doldrums, and Dictionopolis. He meets many interesting characters, and is asked to rescue the two banished princesses.
7. Possible response: Make a to-do list, prioritize tasks, and know how much time to allot.

Review and Assess

Literary Analysis

Elements of Drama

1. How does the dialogue in the play show you what kind of people the characters are? Copy and complete a chart like the one below to track how the dialogue shows a character's qualities.

Dialogue	Shows about the character
Milo: Well, it doesn't matter anyway. Dictionopolis. That's a weird name. I might as well go there.	He is a bored and indifferent person.
Tock:	
The Humbug:	

2. **(a)** Which character explains the problem in the play? **(b)** What is the effect of this character explaining the problem?

Connecting Literary Elements

3. What details of each setting do you learn in the stage directions? Record them on a chart like the one below.

Places	Details
Expectations	
The Doldrums	
Dictionopolis	

4. **(a)** Describe one place in the play where stage directions were necessary to understanding the events. **(b)** Find one place in the play that has no stage direction. Using your imagination, write your own stage directions for that scene.

Reading Strategy

Summarizing

5. **(a)** What are the most important events in Act I? **(b)** Why do you think they are the most important events?
6. Use the most important events to **summarize** Act I.

Extending Understanding

7. **Study Skills Connection:** What are three strategies for using time well?

Quick Review

The elements of drama—characters, setting, and plot—are developed mainly through dialogue. To review elements of drama, see page 613.

Stage directions are the explanations of how the characters move, look and talk and how the setting looks. To review setting, see page 613.

Summarizing is restating key events or ideas in your own words. To review summarizing, see page 613.

Take It to the Net

www.phschool.com

Take the interactive self-test online to check your understanding of the selection.

TEACHING RESOURCES

The following resources can be used to enrich or extend the instruction for pp. 634–635.

Vocabulary

- **Selection Support:** Build Vocabulary, p. 171; Build Spelling Skills, p. 172
- **Vocabulary and Spelling Practice Book** (Use this booklet for skills enrichment)

Grammar

- **Selection Support:** Build Grammar Skills, p. 173
- **Writing and Grammar,** Copper Level, p. 520
- **Daily Language Practice Transparencies**

BLOCK SCHEDULING: Resources marked with this symbol provide varied instruction during 90-minute blocks.

Integrate Language Skills

❶ Vocabulary Development Lesson

Word Analysis: Latin Prefix *pre-*

The Latin prefix *pre-* means "before." Using the meaning of *pre-*, write a definition for each italicized word.

1. I wonder if Milo's trip was *prearranged?*
2. None of the food at the banquet was *precooked*.
3. I want to *preview* the next act.

Fluency: Sentence Completions

Fill in each blank with a vocabulary word.

The ___?___ directions helped Milo avoid danger. He had the ___?___ that the Humbug could be trusted. He soon regretted his ___?___ .

Spelling Strategy

Some of the words below are misspelled. On your paper, correctly spell the misspelled words.

1. quotation
2. discussion
3. subtracsion
4. tention

❷ Grammar Lesson

Subject and Verb Agreement

The verb in a sentence must **agree** in number with the subject. A singular subject is one person, place, or thing. A plural subject is more than one. Verbs in the present tense change form to agree with a singular or plural subject. Singular verbs add an *s*, while plural verbs do not.

The chart shows rules for **compound subjects**—subjects with two or more nouns.

Rules	Examples
Parts of a compound subject joined by *and* usually take a plural verb.	Milo and Tock drive to Dictionopolis.
Singular subjects joined by *or* or *nor* use a singular verb.	Neither Reason **nor** Rhyme lives in Dictionopolis.
Plural subjects joined by *or* or *nor* use a plural verb.	Neither words **nor** numbers are superior.
When a compound subject is made up of one singular subject and one plural subject joined by *or* or *nor,* the verb agrees with the subject closer to it.	Neither Milo **nor** his friends are fearless. Neither his friends **nor** Milo is fearless.

▶ *For more practice, see page R30, Exercise D.*

Practice Write the verb to agree with the subject.

1. A tollbooth (is, are) in the package.
2. The Lethargarians (is, are) sleepy.
3. A word or number (means, mean) a lot.
4. The ministers (say, says), "Hello!"
5. Milo and Tock (is, are) learning.

WG Prentice Hall Writing and Grammar Connection: Chapter 6, Section 3

❸ Extension Activities

Listening and Speaking Write and deliver to classmates a brief **speech** that Milo might have given at the banquet about his experiences so far. Rehearse the speech before presenting it to the class, using gestures and tone of voice to reinforce the feeling and meaning of your words.

Writing As Milo, write a **letter** to friends at home. In the letter, describe your experiences so far. Include details about the thoughts and feelings that you, as Milo, have about events. End your letter with a prediction about the adventure you are about to begin with Tock and Humbug.

ASSESSMENT RESOURCES

The following resources can be used to assess students' knowledge and skills.

Selection Assessment

- **Formal Assessment,** pp. 159–161
- **Open Book Test,** pp. 103–105
- **Got It! Assessment Videotapes,** Tape 4
- **Test Bank Software**

Take It to the Net

Visit www.phschool.com for self-tests and additional questions on *The Phantom Tollbooth*, Act I.

Listening and Speaking Rubric

- **Performance Assess. and Portfolio Mgmt.,** p. 25

PRENTICE HALL ASSESSMENT SYSTEM

- **Workbook**
- **Skill Book**
- **Transparencies**
- **CD-ROM**

EXTEND

Answers for p. 635

❶ Vocabulary Development

Word Analysis

1. *Prearranged* means "set up in advance."
2. *Precooked* means "already cooked."
3. To *preview* means "to look at something in advance."

Fluency: Sentence Completions

The precautionary directions helped Milo avoid danger. He had the misapprehension that the Humbug could be trusted. He soon regretted his ignorance.

Spelling Strategy

1. correct as is
2. correct as is
3. subtraction
4. tension

❷ Grammar

1. A tollbooth is in the package.
2. The Lethargarians are sleepy.
3. A word or number means a lot.
4. The ministers say, "Hello!"
5. Milo and Tock are learning.

❸ Listening and Speaking

- Point out that students' speeches will summarize Milo's experiences before the banquet.
- Have students consult their notes as they develop their speeches.
- Remind students to bring out the most interesting points about Milo's journey.
- Use the Speaking rubric on p. 25 in **Performance Assessment and Portfolio Management** to assess students' speeches.

CUSTOMIZE INSTRUCTION For Universal Access

To address different learning styles, use the activities suggested in the **Extension Activities** booklet, p. 35.

- For Bodily/Kinesthetic and Interpersonal Learners, use Activity 5.
- For Musical/Rhythmic and Verbal/Linguistic Learners, use Activity 6.
- For Visual/Spatial and Mathematical/Logical Learners, use Activity 7.

The Phantom Tollbooth, Act II

Lesson Objectives

1. **To analyze and respond to literary elements**
    - Literary Analysis: Theme
    - Connecting Literary Elements: Images
2. **To read, comprehend, analyze, and critique drama**
    - Reading Strategy: Recognizing Wordplay
    - Reading Check Questions
    - Review and Assess Questions
3. **To develop word analysis skills, fluency, and systematic vocabulary**
    - Vocabulary Development Lesson: Word Analysis: Latin Root *-son-*
4. **To understand and apply written and oral language conventions**
    - Spelling Strategy
    - Grammar Lesson: Indefinite Pronouns
    - Assessment Practice (ATE)
5. **To understand and apply appropriate writing and research strategies**
    - Writing Lesson: Drama Review
    - Extension Activity: Number Research
6. **To understand and apply listening and speaking strategies**
    - Extension Activity: Debate
    - Extension Activity: Summary

STEP-BY-STEP TEACHING GUIDE	PACING GUIDE
PRETEACH	
Motivate Students and Provide Background	
Review the Preview material and Background information (SE/ATE p. 612) [A]	10 min.
Introduce the Concepts	
Introduce the Literary Analysis and Reading Strategy (SE/ATE p. 636) [A]	25 min.
Pronounce the vocabulary words and read their definitions (SE p. 636)	5 min.
TEACH	
Monitor Comprehension	
Informally monitor comprehension by circulating while students read independently or in groups [A]	50 min.
Monitor students' comprehension with the Reading Check notes (SE/ATE pp. 637, 639, 641, 643, 645, 647, 649, 651, 653, 655, 657, 659)	as students read
Develop vocabulary with Vocabulary notes (SE pp. 637, 642, 644, 651; ATE p. 637)	as students read
Develop Understanding	
Develop students' understanding of theme with the Literary Analysis annotations (SE/ATE pp. 638–643, 647, 649, 650, 651, 652, 653, 655, 658, 659) [A]	5 min.
Develop students' ability to recognize wordplay with the Reading Strategy annotations (SE/ATE pp. 643, 645, 647, 649, 652, 658)	5 min.
ASSESS	
Assess Mastery	
Assess students' mastery of the Reading Strategy and Literary Analysis by having them answer the Review and Assess questions (SE/ATE p. 661)	30 min.
Use one or more of the print and media Assessment Resources (ATE p. 663) [A]	up to 45 min.
EXTEND	
Apply Understanding	
Have students complete the Vocabulary Development Lesson and the Grammar Lesson (SE p. 662) [A]	30 min.
Apply students' ability to write drama reviews using the Writing Lesson (SE/ATE p. 663) [A]	45 min.
Apply students' understanding of the selection using one or more of the Extension Activities (SE p. 663)	30–90 min.

ACCELERATED INSTRUCTION:
Use the strategies and activities identified with an [A].

UNIVERSAL ACCESS
● = Below Level Students
▲ = On-Level Students
■ = Above Level Students

Time and Resource Manager

Reading Level: Average
Average Number of Instructional Days: 5

RESOURCES			
	PRINT	**TRANSPARENCIES**	**TECHNOLOGY**
	• **Beyond Literature,** Workplace Skills: Learning From Mistakes, p. 36 ▲ ■		
	• **Selection Support Workbook:** ● ▲ ■ Literary Analysis, p. 180 Reading Strategy, p. 179 Build Vocabulary, p. 176	• **Literary Analysis and Reading Transparencies,** pp. 71 and 72 ● ▲ ■	
	• **Authors In Depth,** Copper Level, p. 154 ■		• **Listening to Literature** ● ▲ ■ Audiocassettes, Sides 23–24 Audio CDs, CD 12
	• **Literatura en español** ● ▲ • **Literary Analysis for Enrichment** ■		
	• **Formal Assessment:** Selection Test, pp. 162–164 ● ▲ ■ • **Open Book Test,** pp. 106–108 ● ▲ ■ • **Performance Assessment and Portfolio Management,** pp. 15, 22 ● ▲ ■ • PRENTICE HALL ASSESSMENT SYSTEM ● ▲ ■	• PRENTICE HALL ASSESSMENT SYSTEM ● ▲ ■ Skills Practice Answers and Explanations on Transparencies	• **Test Bank Software** ● ▲ ■ • **Got It! Assessment Videotapes,** Tape 4 ● ▲
	• **Selection Support Workbook:** ● ▲ ■ Build Spelling Skills, p. 177 Build Grammar Skills, p. 178 • **Writing and Grammar,** Copper Level ● ▲ ■ • **Extension Activities,** p. 36 ● ▲ ■	• **Daily Language Practice Transparencies** ● ▲ • **Writing Models and Graphic Organizers on Transparencies** ● ▲ ■	• **Writing and Grammar iText CD-ROM** ● ▲ ■ *Take It to the Net* www.phschool.com

BLOCK SCHEDULING: Use one 90-minute class period to preteach the selection and have students read it. Use a second 90-minute class period to assess students' mastery of skills and have them complete one of the Extension Activities.

PRETEACH

Step-by-Step Teaching Guide for p. 636

❶ Literary Analysis

Theme

- Tell students that the theme of a literary work is its central idea, which can also be a lesson. Then, read the instruction for Theme.
- Recall with students some of the descriptions and action in Act I of the drama. Use the Connecting Literary Elements text to show the relationship between the theme and the language that shows action and description.
- Use the Theme transparency on p. 72 in **Literary Analysis and Reading Transparencies** to demonstrate for students how to identify the theme.

❷ Reading Strategy

Recognizing Wordplay

- Discuss with students how humor in *The Phantom Tollbooth* helps convey the theme. Ask students to think of a time in their own lives when humor made a difficult situation bearable.
- Point out to students that wordplay is a specific device used by the writers not only to amuse the audience but also to help convey the theme.
- Instruct students to take notes showing examples of wordplay as they read Act II.

Vocabulary Development

- Review the words and definitions on the vocabulary list.
- Ask students to describe the relationship between *malicious* and *admonishing*.
  Possible response: They both suggest bad behavior—A *malicious* action may be met with an *admonishing* response.

E-Teach

Visit E-Teach at www.phschool.com for teachers' essays on how to teach, with questions and answers.

Prepare to Read

The Phantom Tollbooth, Act II

❶ Literary Analysis

Theme

The **theme**, or central idea, of a literary work is the idea or insight about life that the events in the work suggest. The lessons Milo learns from his experiences are clues to the theme of *The Phantom Tollbooth*. As you read, think about these focus questions:

1. What are two lessons Milo learns on his travels?
2. How can these lessons be applied in real life?

Connecting Literary Elements

Images are the "word pictures" created by language that appeals to the senses—sight, sound, smell, taste, touch. They can be used to reinforce the author's theme, or message. For example, at the opening of Act II, images are used to reinforce the message that Milo should be using his imagination or powers of observation.

VOICE: Have you ever heard a whole set of dishes dropped from the ceiling onto a hard stone floor? [. . . MILO *shakes his head.* VOICE *happily.*] Have you ever heard an ant wearing fur slippers walk across a thick wool carpet? [MILO *shakes his head again.*] . . . Just as I expected . . . You're all suffering from a severe lack of noise.

❷ Reading Strategy

Recognizing Wordplay

In addition to mental pictures, this play provides mental exercise. Through **word play**, the author calls readers' attention to the richness of language by playing with several meanings of the same word. In the example, notice that the two meanings of *fork* lead to a shift in the conversation.

MILO. But wait! The fork in the road . . . You didn't tell us where it is . . .

HUMBUG. I could use a fork of my own at the moment . . . All of a sudden I feel very hungry.

Vocabulary Development

dissonance (dis´ ə nəns) *n.* harsh combination of sounds (p. 637)

admonishing (ad män´ ish iŋ) *adj.* disapproving (p. 642)

iridescent (ir´ ə des´ ənt) *adj.* showing different colors when seen from different angles (p. 644)

malicious (mə lish´ əs) *adj.* showing evil intentions (p. 651)

TEACHING RESOURCES

The following resources can be used to enrich or extend the instruction for p. 636.

Background

Beyond Literature, p. 36

Take It to the Net

Visit www.phschool.com for Background and hotlinks for *The Phantom Tollbooth,* Act II.

Literary Analysis

Literary Analysis and Reading Transparencies, Theme, p. 72

Reading

Selection Support: Reading Strategy, p. 179; Build Vocabulary, p. 176

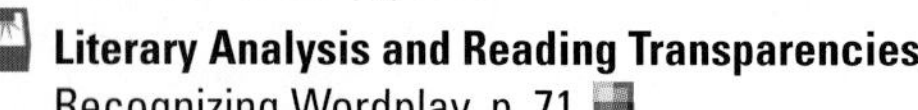
Literary Analysis and Reading Transparencies, Recognizing Wordplay, p. 71

BLOCK SCHEDULING: Resources marked with this symbol provide varied instruction during 90-minute blocks.

Review and Anticipate

In Act I, Milo is lifted from his boredom into a strange kingdom in conflict over the importance of letters and numbers. After traveling through Dictionopolis, he agrees to rescue the princesses who can settle the conflict. As Act II opens, Milo enters Digitopolis with Tock and Humbug—characters who will help him rescue the princesses.

Act II

Scene i

2 *The set of Digitopolis glitters in the background, while Upstage Right near the road, a small colorful Wagon sits, looking quite deserted. On its side in large letters, a sign reads: "KAKAFONOUS A. DISCHORD Doctor of Dissonance" Enter* MILO, TOCK *and* HUMBUG, *fearfully. They look at the wagon.*

TOCK. There's no doubt about it. That's where the noise was coming from.

HUMBUG. [*To* MILO.] Well, go on.

MILO. Go on what?

HUMBUG. Go on and see who's making all that noise in there. We can't just ignore a creature like that.

MILO. Creature? What kind of creature? Do you think he's dangerous?

HUMBUG. Go on, Milo. Knock on the door. We'll be right behind you.

MILO. O.K. Maybe he can tell us how much further it is to Digitopolis.

[MILO *tiptoes up to the wagon door and KNOCKS timidly. The moment he knocks, a terrible CRASH is heard inside the wagon, and* MILO *and the others jump back in fright. At the same time, the Door Flies Open, and from the dark interior, a Hoarse* VOICE *inquires.*]

VOICE. Have you ever heard a whole set of dishes dropped from the ceiling onto a hard stone floor? [*The Others are speechless with fright.* MILO *shakes his head.* VOICE *happily.*] Have you ever heard an ant wearing fur slippers walk across a thick wool carpet? [MILO *shakes his head again.*] Have you ever heard a blindfolded octopus unwrap a cellophane-covered bathtub? [MILO *shakes his*

1 ▼ **Critical Viewing** How do you think a character like the one shown will fit into Milo's adventures? **[Speculate]**

dissonance (dis′ ə nəns) *n.* harsh combination of sounds

3 **Reading Check** Where do Milo, Tock, and Humbug find themselves?

TEACH

Step-by-Step Teaching Guide for pp. 637–660

1 ▶ Critical Viewing

Possible response: The man looks like a doctor or a medical scientist because he is wearing a lab coat and a stethoscope, and he carries a mortar and pestle, which are used to make medicines. Also, his sense of hearing must be important because he has big ears. Perhaps Milo will need the help of a doctor who specializes in sound or hearing.

2 Vocabulary Development

The Latin Root *-son-*

- Point out the word *dissonance* and its definition. Tell students that the Latin root *-son-* shows that a word relates to sound.
- Advise students that words with *-son-* do not always require a prefix and a suffix. A suffix alone may be sufficient, as in *sonar* and *sonorous*. Challenge students to think of words that contain *-son-*.

3 Reading Check

Answer: Milo, Tock, and Humbug are outside Digitopolis.

CUSTOMIZE INSTRUCTION FOR UNIVERSAL ACCESS

For Less Proficient Readers	For English Learners	For Advanced Readers
As students begin Act II, they are likely to be comfortable reading the play format. Allow time for sustained silent reading so they can develop fluency without interruption. Provide time for questions and clarification, but only after students have completed a significant portion of Act II.	Students may benefit from previewing the vocabulary terms and other difficult words throughout Act II. Have them check the definitions of unfamiliar vocabulary words in a dictionary. Challenge them to use the new words in sentences.	Have students predict how this drama will unfold. Ask them to use the timeline on p. 77 in **Writing Models and Graphic Organizers on Transparencies** to record their predictions. Have each student record the events that have already taken place and list his or her predictions for the remainder of the play.

❹ Literary Analysis

Theme and Images

- Direct students to read Dischord's bracketed speech and the accompanying stage directions. Then, ask the first Literary Analysis question on p. 638.
  Answer: Students may say they picture a man who behaves like a doctor as he examines the travelers and mixes medicines. However, this doctor is unusual because he is using sounds to make medicines.

❺ Literary Analysis

Theme

- Remind students that characters' speeches give clues for recognizing the theme of a play. Then, read aloud the bracketed speech.
- Ask the second Literary Analysis question on p. 638: What message about noise is suggested by Dischord's speech?
  Possible responses: Noise is louder, more common, and more constant than it used to be.

head a third time.] Ha! I knew it. [*He hops out, a little man, wearing a white coat, with a stethoscope around his neck, and a small mirror attached to his forehead, and with very huge ears, and a mortar and pestle in his hands. He stares at* MILO, TOCK *and* HUMBUG.] None of you looks well at all! Tsk, tsk, not at all. [*He opens the top or side of his Wagon, revealing a dusty interior resembling an old apothecary shop, with shelves lined with jars and boxes, a table, books, test tubes and bottles and measuring spoons.*]

MILO. [*Timidly.*] Are you a doctor?

DISCHORD. [VOICE.] I am KAKAFONOUS A. DISCHORD, DOCTOR OF DISSONANCE! [*Several small explosions and a grinding crash are heard.*]

HUMBUG. [*Stuttering with fear.*] What does the "A" stand for?

❹ **DISCHORD.** AS LOUD AS POSSIBLE! [*Two screeches and a bump are heard.*] Now, step a little closer and stick out your tongues. [DISCHORD examines them.] Just as I expected. [*He opens a large dusty book and thumbs through the pages.*] You're all suffering from a severe lack of noise. [DISCHORD *begins running around, collecting bottles, reading the labels to himself as he goes along.*] "Loud Cries." "Soft Cries." "Bangs, Bongs, Swishes. Swooshes." "Snaps and Crackles." "Whistles and Gongs." "Squeeks, Squacks, and Miscellaneous Uproar." [*As he reads them off, he pours a little of each into a large glass beaker and stirs the mixture with a wooden spoon. The concoction smokes and bubbles.*] Be ready in just a moment.

Literary Analysis
Theme and Images What images come to mind as you read Dischord's words?

MILO. [*Suspiciously.*] Just what kind of doctor are you?

DISCHORD. Well, you might say, I'm a specialist. I specialize in noises, from the loudest to the softest, and from the slightly annoying to the terribly unpleasant. For instance, have you ever heard a square-wheeled steamroller ride over a street full of hard-boiled eggs? [*Very loud CRUNCHING SOUNDS are heard.*]

MILO. [*Holding his ears.*] But who would want all those terrible noises?

❺ **DISCHORD.** [*Surprised at the question.*] Everybody does. Why, I'm so busy I can hardly fill all the orders for noise pills, racket lotion, clamor salve and hubbub tonic. That's all people seem to want these days. Years ago, everyone wanted pleasant sounds and business was terrible. But then the cities were built and there was a great need for honking horns, screeching trains, clanging bells and all the rest of those wonderfully unpleasant sounds we use so much today. I've been working overtime ever since and my medicine here is in great demand. All you have to do is

Literary Analysis
Theme What message about noise is suggested by Dischord's speech?

TEACHING RESOURCES

The following resources can be used to enrich or extend the instruction for pp. 637–660.

Literary Analysis

- **Selection Support:** Literary Analysis, p. 180 ▪
- **Writing Models and Graphic Organizers on Transparencies,** pp. 61, 70, 77
- **Literary Analysis for Enrichment**

Reading

- **Literatura en español**

- **Listening to Literature Audiocassettes,** Sides 23–24 ▪
- **Listening to Literature Audio CDs,** CD 12 ▪

Extension

- **Authors In Depth,** Copper Level, p. 154 (The collection includes two additional selections by Norton Juster.)

▪ **BLOCK SCHEDULING:** Resources marked with this symbol provide varied instruction during 90-minute blocks.

MILO. Maybe if you discussed it with him . . .

MATHEMAGICIAN. He's just too unreasonable! Why just last month, I sent him a very friendly letter, which he never had the courtesy to answer. See for yourself. [*Puts the letter on the easel. The letter reads:*]

4738 1919,

667 394107 5841 62589 85371 14

39588 7190434 203 27689 57131 481206.

5864 98053,

62179875073

MILO. But maybe he doesn't understand numbers.

31 **MATHEMAGICIAN.** Nonsense! Everybody understands numbers. No matter what language you speak, they always mean the same thing. A seven is a seven everywhere in the world.

MILO. [*To* TOCK *and* HUMBUG.] Everyone is so sensitive about what he knows best.

TOCK. With your permission, sir, we'd like to rescue Rhyme and Reason.

MATHEMAGICIAN. Has Azaz agreed to it?

TOCK. Yes, sir.

MATHEMAGICIAN. THEN I DON'T! Ever since they've been banished, we've never agreed on anything, and we never will.

MILO. Never?

MATHEMAGICIAN. NEVER! And if you can prove otherwise, you have my permission to go.

MILO. Well then, with whatever Azaz agrees, you disagree.

MATHEMAGICIAN. Correct.

MILO. And with whatever Azaz disagrees, you agree.

32 **MATHEMAGICIAN.** [*Yawning, cleaning his nails.*] Also correct.

MILO. Then, each of you agrees that he will disagree with whatever each of you agrees with, and if you both disagree with the same thing, aren't you really in agreement?

MATHEMAGICIAN. I'VE BEEN TRICKED! [*Figures it over, but comes up with the same answer.*]

TOCK. And now may we go?

MATHEMAGICIAN. [*Nods weakly.*] It's a long and dangerous journey. Long before you find them, the demons will know you're there.

Literary Analysis
Theme What real-life situations support the Mathemagician's statement?

Reading Strategy
Wordplay How does Milo use words and logic to get the Mathemagician to agree to the rescue?

33 **Reading Check**
To what does Milo get the Mathemagician to agree?

31 Literary Analysis

Theme

- Call students' attention to the bracketed statement on p. 649, and read it aloud.
- Then, ask the Literary Analysis question: What real-life situations support the Mathemagician's statement?
  Answer: When people speak different languages, they do not always understand one another. However, written numbers are the same across many languages, so people can understand them and the ideas that they represent even if they speak different languages.

32 Reading Strategy

Recognizing Wordplay

- Have students read the second bracketed passage several times, as it is difficult to understand.
- Point out that this passage contains a paradox—an idea that contains contradictions. Then, ask the Reading Strategy question: How does Milo use words and logic to get Mathemagician to agree to the rescue?
  Answer: Milo tricks Mathemagician with a paradox: the kings' agreement to disagree shows that they really do agree on something.
- Lead students to understand that Milo's logic and ability to see the paradox in this situation are important tools in understanding mathematics. Milo does have the ability to solve problems.

33 Reading Check

Answer: Milo gets Mathemagician to agree that the princesses can be freed.

CUSTOMIZE INSTRUCTION FOR UNIVERSAL ACCESS

For Special Needs Students	For Gifted/Talented Students	For Advanced Readers
To help students understand the play's events, have them listen to the recorded version on **Listening to Literature Audiocassettes,** Sides 23–24, or **Listening to Literature Audio CDs,** CD 12. Instruct students to take notes as they listen, pausing the recording when necessary so that they can write their notes and questions.	Mathemagician shows a range of emotions as Milo tries to persuade him to allow Tock, Humbug, and himself to rescue Rhyme and Reason. Have students perform this dialogue using gestures and expressions that convey such emotions. Remind them to exaggerate their gestures and to raise their voices slightly, as if they were on stage.	Challenge students to imagine themselves in Milo's position by having them write journal entries about the attempt to rescue the princesses. They should write about the places Milo has seen, the people he has met, and his plan for using the gifts that others have given him. Tell students to support their observations and plans with details from the play.

34 Literary Analysis

Theme

- Ask students what Mathemagician gives to Milo.
  Answer: Mathemagician gives Milo a small magic staff that is a pencil.
- Then, ask the Literary Analysis question on p. 650: What can Milo do with the Mathemagician's gift?
  Answer: Milo can use the gift to solve problems.

35 Critical Thinking

Analyze

- Have all but two students close their books. As the rest of the class listens, have the two volunteers read Rhyme's and Reason's opening lines.
- Ask students what they can tell about the lines just by listening to them.
  Answer: Rhyme speaks in poetry, and Reason speaks in prose.
- Ask students how Rhyme's and Reason's dialogue reveals their characters.
  Answer: Rhyme talks in rhymes. Reason tries to reason with Rhyme; she tells Rhyme not to worry and advocates reasonable thinking, which can make Rhyme feel more hopeful.

Watch out for them, because if you ever come face to face, it will be too late. But there is one other obstacle even more serious than that.

MILO. [*Terrified.*] What is it?

34 **MATHEMAGICIAN.** I'm afraid I can't tell you until you return. But maybe I can give you something to help you out. [*Claps hands. ENTER the* DODECAHEDRON, *carrying something on a pillow. The* MATHEMAGICIAN *takes it.*] Here is your own magic staff. Use it well and there is nothing it can't do for you. [*Puts a small, gleaming pencil in* MILO'S *breast pocket.*]

Literary Analysis
Theme What can Milo do with the Mathemagician's gift?

HUMBUG. Are you sure you can't tell about that serious obstacle?

MATHEMAGICIAN. Only when you return. And now the Dodecahedron will escort you to the road that leads to the Castle-in-the-Air. Farewell, my friends, and good luck to you. [*They shake hands, say goodbye, and the* DODECAHEDRON *leads them off.*] Good luck to you! [*To himself.*] Because you're sure going to need it. [*He watches them through a telescope and marks down the calculations.*]

DODECAHEDRON. [*He re-enters.*] Well, they're on their way.

MATHEMAGICIAN. So I see. . . [DODECAHEDRON *stands waiting.*] Well, what is it?

DODECAHEDRON. I was just wondering myself, your Numbership. What actually *is* the serious obstacle you were talking about?

MATHEMAGICIAN. [*Looks at him in surprise.*] You mean you really don't know?

BLACKOUT

Scene ii

The Land of Ignorance

LIGHTS UP on RHYME *and* REASON, *in their castle, looking out two windows.*

RHYME. *I'm worried sick, I must confess*
I wonder if they'll have success
All the others tried in vain,
35 *And were never seen or heard again.*

REASON. Now, Rhyme, there's no need to be so pessimistic. Milo, Tock, and Humbug have just as much chance of succeeding as they do of failing.

ENRICHMENT: Language Arts Connection

Literature

In *The Phantom Tollbooth,* the princess Rhyme speaks in rhyme. Review with students the fact that end rhyme is the most common type of rhyme. As the name suggests, this type of rhyme occurs at the end of a verse line:

I'm worried sick, I must confess
I wonder if they'll have success

Write the lines on the board; have a student underline the rhyming words.

Then, write on the board other lines spoken by Rhyme, and allow volunteers to come to the board and underline the rhyming words.

Encourage interested students to write additional rhyming lines for Rhyme or for another character in the play. Allow students to read aloud what they have written.

 **RHYME.** *But the demons are so deadly smart*
They'll stuff your brain and fill your heart
With petty thoughts and selfish dreams
And trap you with their nasty schemes.

REASON. Now, Rhyme, be reasonable, won't you? And calm down, you always talk in couplets when you get nervous. Milo has learned a lot from his journey. I think he's a match for the demons and that he might soon be knocking at our door. Now come on, cheer up, won't you?

RHYME. I'll try.

[*LIGHTS FADE on the* PRINCESSES *and COME UP on the little Car, traveling slowly.*]

MILO. So this is the Land of Ignorance. It's so dark. I can hardly see a thing. Maybe we should wait until morning.

VOICE. They'll be mourning for you soon enough. [*They look up and see a large, soiled, ugly* BIRD *with a dangerous beak and a malicious expression.*]

MILO. I don't think you understand. We're looking for a place to spend the night.

BIRD. [*Shrieking.*] It's not yours to spend!

MILO. That doesn't make any sense, you see . . .

BIRD. Dollars or cents, it's still not yours to spend.

37 **MILO.** But I don't mean . . .

BIRD. Of course you're mean. Anybody who'd spend a night that doesn't belong to him is very mean.

TOCK. Must you interrupt like that?

BIRD. Naturally, it's my job. I take the words right out of your mouth. Haven't we met before? I'm the Everpresent Wordsnatcher.

MILO. Are you a demon?

BIRD. I'm afraid not. I've tried, but the best I can manage to be is a nuisance. [*Suddenly gets nervous as he looks beyond the three.*] And I don't have time to waste with you. [*Starts to leave.*]

TOCK. What is it? What's the matter?

MILO. Hey, don't leave. I wanted to ask you some questions. . . . Wait!

Literary Analysis
Theme How can the princess's rhyme be applied to real life?

malicious (mə lish′ əs) *adj.* showing evil intentions

Literary Analysis
Theme and Images What message is suggested by the image of a loud, annoying, unattractive bird that interrupts?

38 **Reading Check**
What are the princesses worried about?

36 Literary Analysis
Theme
- Ask a student to read Rhyme's rhyme aloud. Have another student paraphrase the rhyme.
Possible response: Demons will try to make you think about and want things that are not good for you.
- Then, ask the Literary Analysis question on p. 651: How can the princess's rhyme be applied to real life?
Answer: There are people and things that may be smart enough to distract us from our real goals, and we will have to outsmart them.

37 Literary Analysis
Theme and Images
- Have students read the bracketed passage. Be sure students realize that the travelers have entered the Land of Ignorance.
- Then, ask the Literary Analysis question: What message is suggested by the image of a loud, annoying, unattractive bird that interrupts?
Possible response: The image is that of an ignorant, impolite person.

38 Reading Check
Answer: The princesses are worried that the demons will capture or delay the travelers.

CUSTOMIZE INSTRUCTION FOR UNIVERSAL ACCESS

For Less Proficient Readers	For Gifted and Talented Students
To help students see the connection between Rhyme's fears on pp. 650–651 and what takes place between Milo and Bird, offer them the KWL organizer on p. 61 in **Writing Models and Graphic Organizers on Transparencies.** Help students fill in the columns with what they think Rhyme means and with how they interpret the general confusion of the discussion between Milo and Bird. Students should then fill in the middle column with questions. Have students complete the organizer when they have finished reading.	Most of the scenery in Digitopolis and Dictionopolis is described in great detail, but the castle in which Rhyme and Reason are living is barely mentioned. Have students think about the nature of these two princesses and their brothers, Azaz and the Mathemagician, and design the setting for the Castle-in-the-Air. The route to the castle mentioned in Scene i gives some clues. Students can use their imaginations to fill in what is missing. Invite students to sketch their designs and display them.

39 Reading Strategy

Recognizing Wordplay

- Remind students that homophones are words that sound alike but have different spellings and meanings.
- Then, ask students the Reading Strategy question on p. 652. **Answer:** Milo wants Bird to *wait,* or stay where he is. Bird responds with "twenty-seven pounds," a *weight,* or unit of measure.

Monitor Progress Have students describe other kinds of wordplay in the exchange between Milo and Bird.
Answer: Other examples of wordplay include the *mean/mean* puns and the idea that Bird "takes the words right out of your mouth."

Reteach If students have difficulty finding and identifying these examples of wordplay, have them think of pairs of homonyms and write their own wordplays with them. An example might be "cake batter that hits a home run." Have students share and explain their wordplays with the class.

40 Literary Analysis

Theme

- Ask a volunteer to read Man's dialogue.
- Then, ask students the Literary Analysis question. **Answer:** Man asks them to do tedious and meaningless work for the purpose of wasting time, which is one of the themes in the play.

39 **BIRD.** Weight? Twenty-seven pounds. Bye-bye. [*Disappears.*]

MILO. Well, he was no help.

MAN. Perhaps I can be of some assistance to you? [*There appears a beautifully dressed man, very polished and clean.*] Hello, little boy. [*Shakes* MILO'S *hand.*] And how's the faithful dog? [*Pats* TOCK.] And who is this handsome creature? [*Tips his hat to* HUMBUG.]

HUMBUG. [*To others.*] What a pleasant surprise to meet someone so nice in a place like this.

MAN. But before I help you out, I wonder if first you could spare me a little of your time, and help me with a few small jobs?

HUMBUG. Why, certainly.

TOCK. Gladly.

MILO. Sure, we'd be happy to.

40 **MAN.** Splendid, for there are just three tasks. First, I would like to move this pile of sand from here to there. [*Indicates through pantomime a large pile of sand.*] But I'm afraid that all I have is this tiny tweezers. [*Hands it to* MILO, *who begins moving the sand one grain at a time.*] Second, I would like to empty this well and fill that other, but I have no bucket, so you'll have to use this eyedropper. [*Hands it to* TOCK, *who begins to work.*] And finally, I must have a hole in this cliff, and here is a needle to dig it. [HUMBUG *eagerly begins. The man leans against a tree and stares vacantly off into space. The LIGHTS indicate the passage of time.*]

MILO. You know something? I've been working steadily for a long time, now, and I don't feel the least bit tired or hungry. I could go right on the same way forever.

MAN. Maybe you will. [*He yawns.*]

MILO. [*Whispers to* TOCK.] Well, I wish I knew how long it was going to take.

TOCK. Why don't you use your magic staff and find out?

MILO. [*Takes out pencil and calculates. To* MAN.] Pardon me, sir, but it's going to take 837 years to finish these jobs.

MAN. Is that so? What a shame. Well then you'd better get on with them.

MILO. But . . . it hardly seems worthwhile.

MAN. WORTHWHILE! Of course they're not worthwhile. I wouldn't ask you to do anything that was worthwhile.

Reading Strategy
Wordplay What is the wordplay used with the words "wait" and "weight"?

Literary Analysis
Theme How would you describe the work the man is asking them to do? How might it relate to a theme in the play?

CUSTOMIZE INSTRUCTION FOR UNIVERSAL ACCESS

For Advanced Readers

Suggest that students read additional works by Norton Juster. Provide students with the titles listed in the Enrichment box, ATE p. 661. You may also wish to use **Authors In Depth,** Copper Level, which contains the following selections:

- "It's All in How You Look at Things" from *The Phantom Tollbooth*
- *Alberic the Wise*

After students have read these or other works by Juster, have them write reports that compare and contrast the play version of *The Phantom Tollbooth* with the novel of the same name. Suggest criteria, such as setting, dialogue, and characters, for the comparisons. To extend the activity, have students present their reports to the class.

TOCK. Then why bother?

MAN. Because, my friends, what could be more important than doing unimportant things? If you stop to do enough of them, you'll never get where you are going. [*Laughs villainously.*]

MILO. [*Gasps.*] Oh, no, you must be . . .

MAN. Quite correct! I am the Terrible Trivium, demon of petty tasks and worthless jobs, ogre of wasted effort and monster of habit. [*They start to back away from him.*] Don't try to leave, there's so much to do, and you still have 837 years to go on the first job.

MILO. But why do unimportant things?

41 **MAN.** Think of all the trouble it saves. If you spend all your time doing only the easy and useless jobs, you'll never have time to worry about the important ones which are so difficult. [*Walks toward them whispering.*] Now do come and stay with me. We'll have such fun together. There are things to fill and things to empty, things to take away and things to bring back, things to pick up and things to put down . . . [*They are transfixed by his soothing voice. He is about to embrace them when a* VOICE *screams.*]

Literary Analysis
Theme What message about laziness is revealed through Terrible Trivium's words?

VOICE. Run! Run! [*They all wake up and run with the Trivium behind. As the* VOICE *continues to call out directions, they follow until they lose the Trivium.*] RUN! RUN! This way! This way! Over here! Over here! Up here! Down there! Quick, hurry up!

TOCK. [*Panting.*] I think we lost him.

VOICE. Keep going straight! Keep going straight! Now step up! Now step up!

MILO. Look out! [*They all fall into a Trap.*] But he said "up!"

VOICE. Well, I hope you didn't expect to get anywhere by listening to me.

HUMBUG. We're in a deep pit! We'll never get out of here.

42 **VOICE.** That is quite an accurate evaluation of the situation.

MILO. [*Shouting angrily.*] Then why did you help us at all?

VOICE. Oh, I'd do as much for anybody. Bad advice is my specialty. [*A Little Furry Creature appears.*] I'm the demon of Insincerity. I don't mean what I say; I don't mean what I do; and I don't mean what I am.

Literary Analysis
Theme What lesson have Milo and the others learned?

MILO. Then why don't you go away and leave us alone!

INSINCERITY. (VOICE) Now, there's no need to get angry. You're a very clever boy and I have complete confidence in you. You can certainly climb out of that pit . . . come on, try. . .

43 **✓Reading Check**
Where are Milo and the others stuck, and how did they get there?

41 Literary Analysis
Theme

- Have students read the Terrible Trivium's speech and ask them what he wants the travelers to do with their time.
  Answer: He wants them to waste their time doing pointless tasks.
- Then, ask the first Literary Analysis question on p. 653.
  Answer: The message is that people who waste their time doing useless jobs will not complete important tasks.

42 Literary Analysis
Theme

- Have volunteers read aloud the dialogue that occurs after the characters fall into the trap. Then, have students look for the name of the character who is giving bad advice to the travelers.
- Next, ask the second Literary Analysis question on p. 653.
  Answer: They have learned not to listen to insincere people.

43 ✓Reading Check

Answer: Milo and his friends are in a pit. They ended up there because they listened to bad advice.

CUSTOMIZE INSTRUCTION FOR UNIVERSAL ACCESS

For Special Needs Students	For English Learners	For Advanced Readers
Ask students whether they find themselves doing unimportant things when they are bored. Then, have them make a list of things they think are unimportant. Next, draw the connection between students' examples and Man's description of the tasks he needs completed, found on p. 652.	Voice, the demon of Insincerity, tries to trick Milo, Humbug, and Tock. Have students look up the definition of *insincerity* in a dictionary. Help them recognize that the *in-* prefix signifies an opposite. Reinforce the idea of the prefix by having them look up the definition of *sincerity.*	Note for students that Man's speech beginning "Think of all the trouble it saves" on p. 653 almost convinces the travelers to stay with the Trivium. Have students write a paragraph explaining why the Trivium's ideas are so attractive. Encourage students to explore whether the ideas are also destructive and why.

44 Literary Analysis

Theme and Images

- Remind students that the theme of *The Phantom Tollbooth* deals with insights about life.
- Ask a volunteer to read aloud the bracketed passage.
- Then, ask students how Milo's statement applies to real life. Possible response: Bad advice is worse than no advice, and it is best to work together through a tough situation.

45 Reinforcing Skills

Drawing Inferences

- Have a volunteer read aloud the bracketed passage. Then, ask the question: What does Tock say about resting? Answer: He says that they should not rest but should get out as soon as possible.
- Ask students to infer why Tock wants to leave quickly. Answer: Tock senses that there is still danger around them.

46 ▶Critical Viewing

Answer: The image reveals how each of them requires the help of the other two in order to climb out of the hole.

MILO. I'm not listening to one word you say! You're just telling me what you think I'd like to hear, and not what is important.

INSINCERITY. Well, if that's the way you feel about it . . .

44 **MILO.** That's the way I feel about it. We will manage by ourselves without any unnecessary advice from you.

INSINCERITY. [*Stamping his foot.*] Well, all right for you! Most people listen to what I say, but if that's the way you feel, then I'll just go home. [*Exits in a huff.*]

HUMBUG. [*Who has been quivering with fright.*] And don't you ever come back! Well, I guess we showed him, didn't we?

MILO. You know something? This place is a lot more dangerous than I ever imagined.

TOCK. [*Who's been surveying the situation.*] I think I figured a way to get out. Here, hop on my back. [MILO *does so.*] Now, you, Humbug, on top of Milo. [*He does so.*] Now hook your umbrella onto that tree and hold on. [*They climb over* HUMBUG, *then pull him up.*]

HUMBUG. [*As they climb.*] Watch it! Watch it, now. Ow, be careful of my back! My back! Easy, easy . . . oh, this is so difficult. Aren't you finished yet?

TOCK. [*As he pulls up* HUMBUG.] There. Now, I'll lead for a while. Follow me, and we'll stay out of trouble. [*They walk and climb higher and higher.*]

HUMBUG. Can't we slow down a little?

45 **TOCK.** Something tells me we better reach the Castle-in-the-Air as soon as possible, and not stop to rest for a single moment. [*They speed up.*]

MILO. What is it, Tock? Did you see something?

TOCK. Just keep walking and don't look back.

MILO. You *did* see something!

46 ▲ **Critical Viewing** How does this image show that Milo, Tock and Humbug need each other to succeed?

ENRICHMENT: Psychology Connection

Leadership

Leadership skills, such as those Tock reveals in the pit, are beneficial skills to have in the workplace. Leaders must be good decision makers and have strong logic and reasoning skills so that they can make choices quickly but keenly. In addition, leaders must feel comfortable taking responsibility for both the successes and the failures of the group. Most important, a leader must understand that without the group, he or she could never attain the goal. Hence, the leader must always trust and communicate with members of the group and support each member individually and as part of a team effort. Point out to students that not everyone enjoys being a leader; there can be a lot of pressure in a leadership position, and it is just as important to be a good follower—a loyal, dedicated individual who respects authority and follows directions.

Ask students to discuss with partners their favorite leaders. What qualities do they most admire in the leaders? Why?

HUMBUG. What is it? Another demon?

TOCK. Not just one, I'm afraid. If you want to see what I'm talking about, then turn around. [*They turn around. The stage darkens and hundreds of Yellow Gleaming Eyes can be seen.*]

47 **HUMBUG.** Good grief! Do you see how many there are? Hundreds! The Overbearing Know-it-all, the Gross Exaggeration, the Horrible Hopping Hindsight, . . . and look over there! The Triple Demons of Compromise! Let's get out of here! [*Starts to scurry.*] Hurry up, you two! Must you be so slow about everything?

MILO. Look! There it is, up ahead! The Castle-in-the-Air! [*They all run.*]

HUMBUG. They're gaining!

MILO. But there it is!

HUMBUG. I see it! I see it!

[*They reach the first step and are stopped by a little man in a frock coat, sleeping on a worn ledger. He has a long quill pen and a bottle of ink at his side. He is covered with ink stains over his clothes and wears spectacles.*]

TOCK. Shh! Be very careful. [*They try to step over him, but he wakes up.*]

SENSES TAKER. [*From sleeping position.*] Names? [*He sits up.*]

HUMBUG. Well, I . . .

SENSES TAKER. *NAMES?* [*He opens book and begins to write, splattering himself with ink.*]

HUMBUG. Uh . . . Humbug, Tock and this is Milo.

SENSES TAKER. Splendid, splendid. I haven't had an "M" in ages.

MILO. What do you want our names for? We're sort of in a hurry.

48 **SENSES TAKER.** Oh, this won't take long. I'm the official Senses Taker and I must have some information before I can take your sense. Now if you'll just tell me: [*Handing them a form to fill. Speaking slowly and deliberately.*] When you were born, where you were born, why you were born, how old you are now, how old you were then, how old you'll be in a little while . . .

MILO. I wish he'd hurry up. At this rate, the demons will be here before we know it!

SENSES TAKER. . . . Your mother's name, your father's name, where you live, how long you've lived there, the schools you've attended, the schools you haven't attended . . .

HUMBUG. I'm getting writer's cramp.

Literary Analysis

Theme and Images Why are these qualities shown as scary creatures that cannot be completely seen?

49 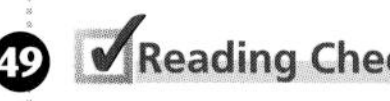

Why are Milo and the others in a hurry?

47 Literary Analysis

Theme and Images

- Ask volunteers to repeat some of the images and names from the passage.
  Answer: Images include gleaming eyes that represent unseen demons, including the Overbearing Know-it-all, the Gross Exaggeration, the Horrible Hopping Hindsight, and the Triple Demons of Compromise.
- Then, ask the Literary Analysis question on p. 655.
  Possible response: Perhaps the qualities cannot be seen because they are part of our imaginations and never really take form; or perhaps when they are revealed in the light of day, the qualities lose their powers, so they stay in the dark.

48 Background

Language Arts

The Senses Taker has a very dated appearance, and some of the items associated with his character might need to be clarified. Tell students that a *frock coat* is typically a man's double-breasted coat that comes to the knees. A *ledger* is a book or register that contains written accounts of varying subjects. A *quill pen* is a pen made from the quill of a feather. A quill is the hollow shaft that runs down the center of a feather. *Spectacles* is an old-fashioned term for eyeglasses.

49 Reading Check

Answer: Milo and the others are in a hurry because they have almost reached their destination and because the demons are close behind.

CUSTOMIZE INSTRUCTION FOR UNIVERSAL ACCESS

For Special Needs Students	For English Learners	For Gifted/Talented Students
Call students' attention to the illustration on p. 654. Have students identify the scene that is being illustrated and answer the following questions: Who is on the bottom? Who is in the middle? Who is on top? What are they trying to do? Why are they trying to do it?	Have volunteers read the dialogue on p. 654 in which the characters get out of the pit. Have students use the characters' dialogue to figure out what is happening. Then, ask a student to write stage directions that tell what each character is to do to get out of the pit. Have students share their directions with the class.	Students may enjoy the challenge of figuring out how to design scenery for the play. For example, the *Yellow Gleaming Eyes* would pose interesting problems. Have students make a plan for designing the scenery of their choice. Students should test the plan's feasibility by making a model of their design.

50 Critical Thinking

Analyze

- Have two volunteers read the Senses Taker's lines and the stage directions within the bracketed passage.
- Direct students to pay attention to how the Senses Taker stops the travelers.
- Then, ask students what puts each of the individual travelers in a trance.
  Answer: Circus music puts Milo in a trance; smells put Tock in a trance; and cheers and applause put Humbug in a trance.
- Lead students in a discussion about how the trap for each traveler is uniquely effective: Most children like circuses, so circus music is a good trap for Milo. Dogs have a strong sense of smell, so good smells are an effective trap for Tock. Humbug is very vain, so cheers and applause stop him effectively.

51 Reinforcing Skills

Drawing Inferences

- Ask a volunteer to read the bracketed stage directions. Then, ask students what breaks the Senses Taker's spell.
  Answer: Milo drops the gifts, and the laughter box opens up to release the laughter.
- Have students infer why the laughter stops the spell.
  Possible response: The laughter stops the spell because it shows that the Senses Taker was playing a joke on the travelers; it could also show that if you keep your sense of humor, you can get past most of life's problems.

52 ▶ Critical Viewing

Possible response: Students are likely to say that this image resembles the Senses Taker as he is portrayed in the play. He wears eyeglasses and is covered with ink as if the speed with which he is writing answers to his questions is creating a mess.

TOCK. I smell something very evil and it's getting stronger every second. [*To* SENSES TAKER.] May we go now?

SENSES TAKER. Just as soon as you tell me your height, your weight, the number of books you've read this year . . .

MILO. We have to go!

SENSES TAKER. All right, all right, I'll give you the short form. [*Pulls out a small piece of paper.*] Destination?

MILO. But we have to . . .

SENSES TAKER. *DESTINATION?*

MILO, TOCK AND HUMBUG. The Castle-in-the-Air! [*They throw down their papers and run past him up the first few stairs.*]

50 **SENSES TAKER.** Stop! I'm sure you'd rather see what I have to show you. [*Snaps his fingers; they freeze.*] A circus of your very own. [*CIRCUS MUSIC is heard.* MILO *seems to go into a trance.*] And wouldn't you enjoy this most wonderful smell? [TOCK *sniffs and goes into a trance.*] And here's something I know you'll enjoy hearing . . . [*To* HUMBUG. *The sound of CHEERS and APPLAUSE for* HUMBUG *is heard, and he goes into a trance.*] There we are. And now, I'll just sit back and let the demons catch up with you.

51 [MILO *accidentally drops his package of gifts. The Package of Laughter from* DR. DISCHORD *opens and the Sounds of Laughter are heard. After a moment,* MILO, TOCK *and* HUMBUG *join in laughing and the spells are broken.*]

MILO. There was no circus.

TOCK. There were no smells.

HUMBUG. The applause is gone.

SENSES TAKER. I warned you I was the Senses Taker. I'll steal your sense of Purpose, your sense of Duty, destroy your sense of Proportion—and but for one thing, you'd be helpless yet.

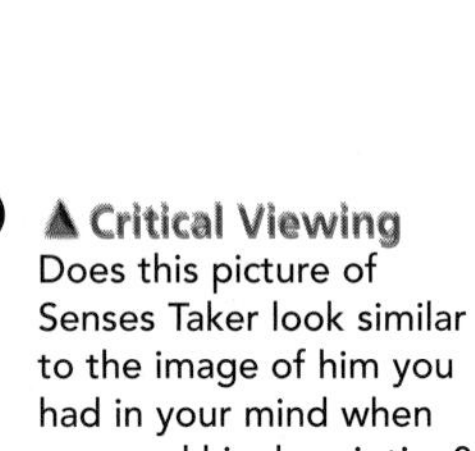

52 ▲ Critical Viewing
Does this picture of Senses Taker look similar to the image of him you had in mind when you read his description?

CUSTOMIZE INSTRUCTION FOR UNIVERSAL ACCESS

For Less Proficient Readers

Have students make a list of questions to ask Milo in an interview. Encourage students to use the basic questions (who, why, what, where, when, and how) as a starting point. Model the following questions to ask Milo:

- Whom were you trying to rescue?
- Why did you want to rescue them?
- What troubles did you find on the way?
- Where did your journey take you?
- When did you start and finish your journey?
- How did you get out of traps?

After they have composed their lists, have students taking on the role of Milo answer the questions by finding relevant passages in the text. Give all students a chance to participate as either Milo or the interviewer.

MILO. What's that?

SENSES TAKER. As long as you have the sound of laughter, I cannot take your sense of Humor. Agh! That horrible sense of humor.

HUMBUG. HERE THEY COME! LET'S GET OUT OF HERE!

[*The demons appear in nasty slithering hordes, running through the audience and up onto the stage, trying to attack* TOCK, MILO *and* HUMBUG. *The three heroes run past the* SENSES TAKER *up the stairs toward the Castle-in-the-Air with the demons snarling behind them.*]

MILO. Don't look back! Just keep going! [*They reach the castle. The two* PRINCESSES *appear in the windows.*]

PRINCESSES. Hurry! Hurry! We've been expecting you.

MILO. You must be the Princesses. We've come to rescue you.

HUMBUG. And the demons are close behind!

TOCK. We should leave right away.

PRINCESSES. We're ready anytime you are.

MILO. Good, now if you'll just come out. But wait a minute—there's no door! How can we rescue you from the Castle-in-the-Air if there's no way to get in or out?

HUMBUG. Hurry, Milo! They're gaining on us.

53 **REASON.** Take your time, Milo, and think about it.

MILO. Ummm, all right . . . just give me a second or two. [*He thinks hard.*]

HUMBUG. I think I feel sick.

MILO. I've got it! Where's that package of presents? [*Opens the package of letters.*] Ah, here it is. [*Takes out the letters and sticks them on the door, spelling:*] E-N-T-R-A-N-C-E. Entrance. Now, let's see. [*Rummages through and spells in smaller letters:*] P-u-s-h. Push. [*He pushes and a door opens. The* PRINCESSES *come out of the castle. Slowly, the demons ascend the stairway.*]

HUMBUG. Oh, it's too late. They're coming up and there's no other way down!

MILO. Unless . . . [*Looks at* TOCK.] Well . . . Time flies, doesn't it?

TOCK. Quite often. Hold on, everyone, and I'll take you down.

HUMBUG. Can you carry us all?

TOCK. We'll soon find out. Ready or not, here we go! [*His alarm begins to ring. They jump off the platform and disappear. The demons, howling with rage, reach the top and find no one there. They see the* PRINCESSES *and the heroes running across the stage*

54 

Reading Check

What prevents Senses Taker from taking Milo's sense of humor?

53 Literary Analysis

Theme

- Read aloud the bracketed passage. Remind students that the problem that Milo and the other travelers face is that there is no door to get into the Castle-in-the-Air.
- Discuss with students what happens after Milo considers the problem: Milo comes up with a solution.
- Then, ask students this question: What do Reason's words indicate people should do when faced with a difficult problem?
  Answer: People should take time to think about how to solve the problem.

54 Reading Check

Answer: The sound of laughter prevents Senses Taker from taking Milo's sense of humor.

CUSTOMIZE INSTRUCTION FOR UNIVERSAL ACCESS

For English Learners	For Advanced Readers
Point out to students that Milo, Tock, and Humbug can enter the Castle-in-the-Air because Milo made signs saying "Entrance" and "Push." Challenge students to think of other words or phrases that could be used to get into the castle or, alternatively, to stop the demons from coming up the stairs after the travelers. Possibilities include "Stop," "Travelers Only," "No Demons Allowed," and "Invited Guests Only." Then, have students make signs for their phrases.	Students may be interested to research the United States census in order to understand the humor behind the character Senses Taker. With the help of your school librarian, compile a list of resources, including encyclopedias, books, periodicals, and Internet resources. Have students compile a list of research questions about the census and then try to answer them as a class. Students may enjoy comparing a list of the questions on the most recent census with the questions asked by the Senses Taker.

55 Reading Strategy

Recognizing Wordplay

- Remind students to listen for wordplay while a volunteer reads the bracketed passage.
- Then, ask students the Reading Strategy question: What wordplay is used when the Mathemagician says, "their days are numbered?" **Answer:** Usually, the saying "their days are numbered" means that someone does not have long to live. Coming from the Mathemagician, however, it is a play on words, because everything he does has something to do with numbers.

56 Literary Analysis

Theme

- Read aloud the bracketed dialogue.
- Then, ask the Literary Analysis question: What does Reason mean by "what you can do is often a matter of what you *will* do"? **Possible response:** You can do anything you are willing to do. If you are not willing, the action can never happen.

and bound down the stairs after them and into the audience. There is a mad chase scene until they reach the stage again.]

HUMBUG. I'm exhausted! I can't run another step.

MILO. We can't stop now . . .

TOCK. Milo! Look out there! [*The armies of* AZAZ *and* MATHEMAGICIAN *appear at the back of the theater, with the Kings at their heads.*]

AZAZ. [*As they march toward the stage.*] Don't worry, Milo, we'll take over now.

55 **MATHEMAGICIAN.** Those demons may not know it, but their days are numbered!

SPELLING BEE. Charge! C-H-A-R-G-E! Charge! [*They rush at the demons and battle until the demons run off howling. Everyone cheers. The* FIVE MINISTERS *of* AZAZ *appear and shake* MILO'S *hand.*]

MINISTER 1. Well done.

MINISTER 2. Fine job.

MINISTER 3. Good work!

MINISTER 4. Congratulations!

MINISTER 5. CHEERS! [*Everyone cheers again. A fanfare interrupts. A* PAGE *steps forward and reads from a large scroll:*]

PAGE.

Henceforth, and forthwith,
Let it be known by one and all,
That Rhyme and Reason
Reign once more in Wisdom.

[*The* PRINCESSES *bow gratefully and kiss their brothers, the Kings.*]

And furthermore,
The boy named Milo,
The dog known as Tock,
And the insect hereinafter referred to as the Humbug
Are hereby declared to be Heroes of the Realm.

[*All bow and salute the heroes.*]

MILO. But we never could have done it without a lot of help.

56 **REASON.** That may be true, but you had the courage to try, and what you can do is often a matter of what you *will* do.

AZAZ. That's why there was one very important thing about your quest we couldn't discuss until you returned.

Reading Strategy
Recognizing Wordplay What wordplay is used when Mathemagician says "their days are numbered"?

Literary Analysis
Theme What does Reason mean by "what you can do is often what you will do"?

MILO. I remember. What was it?

AZAZ. Very simple. It was impossible!

MATHEMAGICIAN. *Completely* impossible!

57 **HUMBUG.** Do you mean . . . ? [*Feeling faint.*] Oh . . . I think I need to sit down.

AZAZ. Yes, indeed, but if we'd told you then, you might not have gone.

MATHEMAGICIAN. And, as you discovered, many things are possible just as long as you don't know they're impossible.

MILO. I think I understand.

RHYME. I'm afraid it's time to go now.

REASON. And you must say goodbye.

MILO. To everyone? [*Looks around at the crowd. To* TOCK *and* HUMBUG.] Can't you two come with me?

HUMBUG. I'm afraid not, old man. I'd like to, but I've arranged for a lecture tour which will keep me occupied for years.

TOCK. And they do need a watchdog here.

MILO. Well, O.K., then. [MILO *hugs the* HUMBUG.]

HUMBUG. [*Sadly.*] Oh, bah.

MILO. [*He hugs* TOCK, *and then faces everyone.*] Well, goodbye. We all spent so much time together, I know I'm going to miss you. [*To the* PRINCESSES.] I guess we would have reached you a lot sooner if I hadn't made so many mistakes.

REASON. You must never feel badly about making mistakes, Milo, as long as you take the trouble to learn from them. Very often you learn more by being wrong for the right reasons than you do by being right for the wrong ones.

MILO. But there's so much to learn.

RHYME. That's true, but it's not just learning that's important. It's learning what to do with what you learn and learning why you learn things that matters.

MILO. I think I know what you mean, Princess. At least, I hope I do. [*The car is rolled forward and* MILO *climbs in.*] Goodbye! Goodbye! I'll be back someday! I will! Anyway, I'll try. [*As* MILO *drives the set of the Land of Ignorance begins to move offstage.*]

AZAZ. Goodbye! Always remember. Words! Words! Words!

MATHEMAGICIAN. And numbers!

AZAZ. Now, don't tell me you think numbers are as important as words?

Literary Analysis
Theme Do you agree with Mathemagician's statement?

58 **Reading Check**

How do they get rid of the demons?

57 Literary Analysis

Theme

- Review with students the various themes thus far in Act II of *The Phantom Tollbooth.*
- Then, have students silently read the bracketed passage, and ask them what lesson Milo has learned.
  Answer: Milo learns that we can do more than we think we can and that we should not let the idea that something is impossible keep us from trying to do it.
- Ask students the Literary Analysis question.
  Answer: Many students may agree with the Mathemagician's statement. Whatever their points of view, students should support their answers.

58 **Reading Check**

Answer: The armies of Azaz and Mathemagician battle the demons until they retreat.

CUSTOMIZE INSTRUCTION FOR UNIVERSAL ACCESS

For Less Proficient Readers

The play is full of images for readers to envision. To teach the skill of envisioning and describing mental images, have students imagine that they are stage managers working on a production of the play. Have each student choose one page of the play. For their pages, students should describe all aspects of the stage setting. Tell them to use a two-column chart and in the left-hand column list the following: *physical setting (scenery, backdrop, etc.), lighting, props,* and *action.* In the right-hand column next to each entry, have students write instructions for the people who are responsible for each item on their chart. For example, students should give instructions to the stage hands about which props are needed, when they are needed, and where they are to be placed. Challenge students to give instructions to the actors, as well.

ASSESS

Answers for p. 660

Review and Assess

1. Possible response: Some students will want to keep their sense of purpose, because that has the most to do with who they are as individuals.
2. **(a)** Knowledge of numbers is most important. **(b)** The Mathemagician is similar to Azaz because they are both kings and are both stubborn.
3. **(a)** The Terrible Trivium wants Milo, Tock, and Humbug to do meaningless tasks that will waste their time. **(b)** They will not achieve their goal. **(c)** Milo learns to use time wisely.
4. **(a)** The Senses Taker's spell is broken by the sound of laughter. **(b)** Milo learns that you can never take away a person's sense of humor.
5. **(a)** Milo does not waste time waiting for something to excite him anymore. **(b)** Possible response: Most students will say that time passes more quickly when they are doing something they enjoy and more slowly when they are bored. **(c)** Possible response: Time goes quickly when a person is playing a sport he or she enjoys or reading a good book. In the play, Milo feels that time moves slowly when he is bored but that it moves faster when he has learned to keep himself busy with worthwhile tasks.

MATHEMAGICIAN. Is that so? Why I'll have you know . . . [*The set disappears, and* MILO'S *Room is seen onstage.*]

MILO. [*As he drives on.*] Oh, oh, I hope they don't start all over again. Because I don't think I'll have much time in the near future to help them out. [*The sound of loud ticking is heard.* MILO *finds himself in his room. He gets out of the car and looks around.*]

THE CLOCK. Did someone mention time?

MILO. Boy, I must have been gone for an awful long time. I wonder what time it is. [*Looks at clock.*] Five o'clock. I wonder what day it is. [*Looks at calendar.*] It's still today! I've only been gone for an hour! [*He continues to look at his calendar, and then begins to look at his books and toys and maps and chemistry set with great interest.*]

CLOCK. An hour. Sixty minutes. How long it really lasts depends on what you do with it. For some people, an hour seems to last forever. For others, just a moment, and so full of things to do.

MILO. [*Looks at clock.*] Six o'clock already?

CLOCK. In an instant. In a trice. Before you have time to blink. [*The stage goes black in less than no time at all.*]

Susan Nanus

Susan Nanus has won several awards for her scripts. Like other screenwriters, she sometimes adapts novels to create screenplays for movies and scripts for stage plays. Her script for *The Phantom Tollbooth* is an adaptation of Norton Juster's novel.

Norton Juster

(b. 1929)

Norton Juster's first career was as an architect, designing buildings and other structures. He took up creative writing in his spare time "as a relaxation" from architecture. He began writing what he thought was just a short story for his own pleasure. Yet before long, Juster says, "it had created its own life and I was hooked." As a writer and as an architect, he puts words and ideas together in creative ways, as in *The Phantom Tollbooth*, the novel on which this play is based.

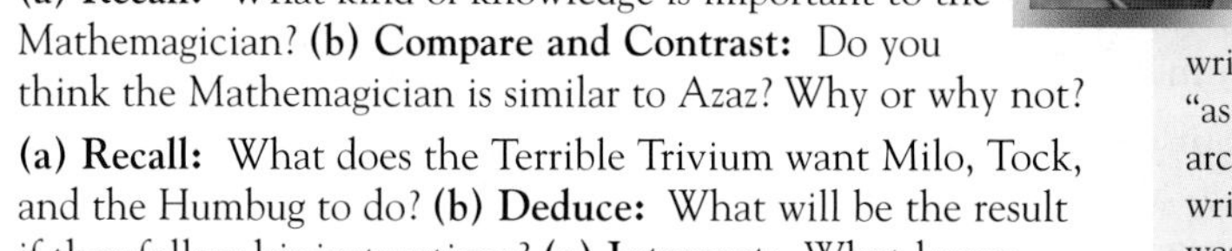

Review and Assess

Thinking About the Selection

1. **Respond:** Of all the senses that the Senses Taker wants to steal, which do you think is most important? Why?
2. **(a) Recall:** What kind of knowledge is important to the Mathemagician? **(b) Compare and Contrast:** Do you think the Mathemagician is similar to Azaz? Why or why not?
3. **(a) Recall:** What does the Terrible Trivium want Milo, Tock, and the Humbug to do? **(b) Deduce:** What will be the result if they follow his instructions? **(c) Interpret:** What lesson does Milo learn as a result of their meeting?
4. **(a) Recall:** How is the Senses Taker's spell broken? **(b) Draw Conclusions:** What does Milo learn about humor from his encounter with the Senses Taker?
5. **(a) Recall:** How is Milo different when he returns to his own room? **(b) Evaluate:** Do you agree that how time passes depends on what you are doing? **(c) Support:** Support your answer with examples from the play or from your own experience.

ASSESSMENT PRACTICE: Writing Skills

Sentence Construction (For more practice, see Test Preparation Workbook, p. 50.)

Many tests require students to recognize appropriate sentence construction. Use the sample item below to help students identify run-on sentences. Write the following on the board, and have students answer the question that follows:

<u>An important aspect of a performance. Staging includes the use of props.</u>

Choose the best way to rewrite the underlined section.

A An important aspect of a performance, staging includes the use of props.

B An important aspect of a performance staging includes the use of props.

C An important aspect. Of a performance staging includes the use of props.

D Correct as is

The sentence begins with an appositive, which should be set off from the noun it modifies by a comma. Therefore, *A* is the correct answer.

Review and Assess

Literary Analysis

Theme

1. What message does the author suggest by having demons run through the audience to reach the stage?
2. What theme is expressed in Milo's farewell to Rhyme and Reason at the end of the play?

Connecting Literary Elements

3. Make a chart like the one shown to analyze the images associated with each character and the message suggested by each character's qualities.

Character	Quality Represented	Images Associated	Suggested Message
Trivium	Doing meaningless tasks	Well-dressed, soothing voice	Some bad habits can sneak up on you
Word Snatcher			
Insincerity			

Reading Strategy

Recognizing Wordplay

4. Review the scene with the Bird in Act II, Scene ii. Use an organizer like the one below to show the two meanings used for each word (or pair of words that sound the same).

Word(s)	Milo's Meaning	Bird's Meaning
morning/mourning		
spend		
sense/cents		
mean		
wait/weight		

5. The Dodecahedron asks Milo, "And did you know that narrow escapes come in different widths?" How does the wordplay lead you to recognize the bigger message behind the statement?

Extending Understanding

6. **Social Studies Connection:** Name two examples from history that show that "many things are possible just as long as you don't know they're impossible."

Quick Review

The **theme** of a work is the central idea or message about life. To review theme, see p. 636.

Images are word pictures made by language that appeals to the senses.

Through **wordplay,** the author calls readers' attention to the richness of language by playing with several meanings of the same word. To review word play, see p. 636.

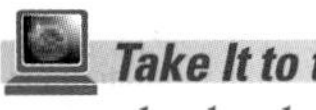

www.phschool.com

Take the interactive self-test online to check your understanding of the selection.

ENRICHMENT: Further Reading

Other Works by the Authors

Works by Norton Juster

As: A Surfeit of Similes

Works by Susan Nanus

Five in One: Holiday Plays for Children

(and Marc Kornblatt) *Mission to World War II*

Take It to the Net

Visit www.phschool.com for more information on the authors.

Answers for p. 661

Review and Assess

1. The author suggests that such demons are always among us.
2. Milo's farewell expresses the theme that people learn through their mistakes and that using knowledge is as important as acquiring it.
3. **Word Snatcher**
   Quality: Quarrelsome, ill-mannered **Images:** Large, soiled, ugly bird **Message:** Ignorance will not wait to find out the truth or be helpful.

   Insincerity
   Quality: Meaningless flattery **Images:** Little, furry creature, is angry when disbelieved **Message:** Beware of those who tell you what you want to hear rather than what is important.
4. ***morning/mourning***

Milo's meaning: early part of the day; **Bird's meaning:** sorrow for a loss or death

spend

Milo's meaning: to pass time; **Bird's meaning:** to exchange money for something

sense/cents

Milo's meaning: logical thought; **Bird's meaning:** money

mean

Milo's meaning: the idea behind a thought; **Bird's meaning:** malicious

wait/weight

Milo's meaning: to delay; **Bird's meaning:** the measurement of mass

5. Possible response: The wordplay helps readers realize that sometimes we escape easily from a problem, but other times we barely escape at all.
6. Possible responses: The American Revolution and the moon landing are good examples.

EXTEND

Answers for p. 662

❶ Vocabulary Development

Word Analysis

1. consonant
2. resonate
3. dissonant

Spelling Strategy

1. precious
2. gracious
3. spacious
4. delicious

Fluency: Sentence Completions

iridescent; dissonance; malicious; admonishing

1. The singer's dissonance was unbelievable. The sentence now means the singer sounded bad.
2. The color was iridescent. The sentence now means that the color was no longer dull.
3. He spoke with an admonishing tone. The sentence now means that the speaker was scolding.
4. The malicious act did not go unnoticed. The sentence now describes a destructive act.

❷ Grammar

1. Each
2. Nobody
3. everyone
4. everything
5. Somebody

Writing Application

Possible responses: In Digitopolis, everyone loves numbers. Each has a few of his or her own. Among the residents, some have number-related names.

Integrate Language Skills

❶ Vocabulary Development Lesson

Word Analysis: Latin Root *-son-*

Words with the Latin root *-son-* include the idea of sound in their meaning. *Dissonance* means "a harsh or disagreeable combination of sounds."

On your paper, fill in the blanks to match each definition. Hint: The root *-son-* is in each word.

1. A letter that is not a vowel: c ________ nt
2. Vibrate with sound: re ________ te
3. Sounding harsh: dis _______a __ t

Spelling Strategy

The sound *shus* at the end of a word is often spelled *cious*, as in *malicious*. On your paper, add *cious* to make a word that matches the definition.

1. Valuable: pre
2. Well-mannered: gra
3. Roomy: spa
4. Tasty: deli

Fluency: Sentence Completions

On your paper, write out this paragraph. Choose from the following vocabulary words to fill in the blanks.

dissonance   admonishing
iridescent   malicious

Though the peacock's ___?___ tail feathers are beautiful, its song is of unbelievable ___?___. When the seemingly ___?___ bird wakes you up at night, your lecture to the bird's owner is likely to be ___?___.

Replace the underlined word in each sentence with a vocabulary word that is the same part of speech. Explain how the meaning of the sentence changes. Use each word only once.

1. The singers' harmony was unbelievable.
2. The color was dull.
3. He spoke with an appreciative tone.
4. The helpful act did not go unnoticed.

❷ Grammar Lesson

Indefinite Pronouns

An **indefinite pronoun** is a word that refers to a person, place, or thing in a general way. Use singular verbs with singular indefinite pronouns. Use plural verbs with plural indefinite pronouns.

Indefinite Pronouns	Examples
Singular: each, everyone, everything, much, nobody, somebody	Somebody has the answer.
Plural: both, few, many, others, several	Others have tried to rescue the princesses.

Practice On your paper, write the indefinite pronoun that correctly completes each sentence.

1. (Each, Many) agrees to disagree.
2. (Few, Nobody) understands the king.
3. Is (everyone, others) called Milo?
4. Here (everything, both) is called what it is.
5. (Several, Somebody) help Milo.

Writing Application On your paper, write three sentences describing the inhabitants of Digitopolis. Use an indefinite pronoun in each.

Prentice Hall Writing and Grammar Connection: Chapter 24, Section 2

TEACHING RESOURCES

The following resources can be used to enrich or extend the instruction for pp. 662–663.

Vocabulary

- **Selection Support:** Build Vocabulary, p. 176
  Build Spelling Skills, p. 177
- **Vocabulary and Spelling Practice Book** (Use this booklet for skills enrichment)

Grammar

- **Selection Support:** Build Grammar Skills, p. 178
- **Writing and Grammar,** Copper Level, p. 524
- **Daily Language Practice Transparencies** ■

Writing

- **Writing and Grammar,** Copper Level, p. 250 ■
- **Writing Models and Graphic Organizers on Transparencies,** p. 73
- **Writing and Grammar iText CD-ROM**

■ **BLOCK SCHEDULING:** Resources marked with this symbol provide varied instruction during 90-minute blocks.

❸ Writing Lesson

Drama Review

Be a drama critic and share your opinions with others! Write a review of *The Phantom Tollbooth,* explaining whether or not the play is well written and entertaining.

Prewriting Use a graphic organizer such as the one shown to help you gather details about what happened in the act you are reviewing.

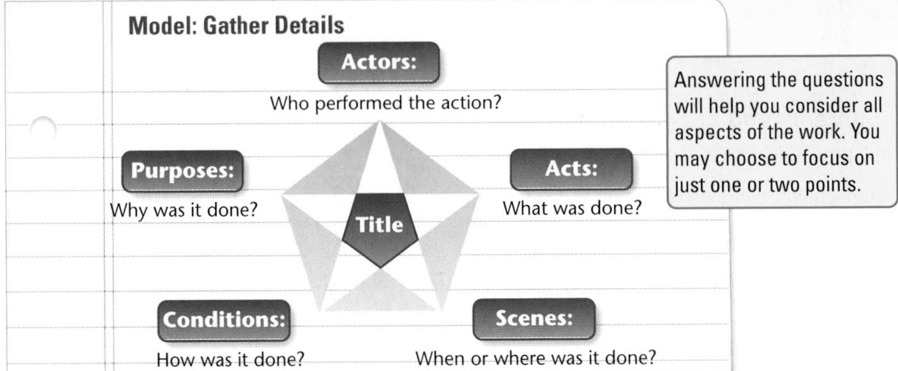

Model: Gather Details
Actors:
Who performed the action?
Purposes:
Why was it done?
Title
Acts:
What was done?
Conditions:
How was it done?
Scenes:
When or where was it done?
Answering the questions will help you consider all aspects of the work. You may choose to focus on just one or two points.

Drafting Begin by stating your overall impression. Then, organize your review around several clear premises, or statements about the work. With each statement you write, ask yourself "What is my evidence?" Add supporting details to answer the question.

Revising Reread your review. Be sure you support your opinions with examples and textual evidence such as quotations or descriptions of settings.

WG *Prentice Hall Writing and Grammar Connection: Chapter 12, Section 2*

❹ Extension Activities

Listening and Speaking As part of a group, **debate** the following: Numbers are more important and more fun than words. Divide into two teams, one speaking for numbers and one for words. In the debate, use details and examples in the play and in your experience that support your points.

Writing Write a **summary** of Act II. Identify the key events, and retell them, in order, in your own words.

Research and Technology Use print and electronic resources to **research** the ideas of infinity and of the biggest and smallest numbers. Display your findings in a chart or other visual. Prepare a written summary to accompany your visual.

Take It to the Net

www.phschool.com

Go online for an additional research activity using the Internet.

ASSESSMENT RESOURCES

The following resources can be used to assess students' knowledge and skills.

Selection Assessment

- **Formal Assessment,** pp. 162–164
- **Open Book Test,** pp. 106–108
- **Got It! Assessment Videotapes,** Tape 4
- **Test Bank Software**

Take It to the Net

Visit www.phschool.com for self-tests and additional questions on *The Phantom Tollbooth,* Act II.

Writing Rubric

- **Performance Assess. and Portfolio Mgmt.,** p. 15

Listening and Speaking Rubric

- **Performance Assess. and Portfolio Mgmt.,** p. 22

PRENTICE HALL ASSESSMENT SYSTEM

- **Workbook**
- **Skill Book**
- **Transparencies**
- **CD-ROM**

❸ Writing Lesson

- Supply students with copies of reviews of books or dramatic presentations. Suggest that students read the reviews to become familiar with their format and content.
- Tell students that when they write reviews, they must consider many aspects of the piece that they are reviewing. Use the Main Idea and Supporting Details organizer on p. 73 in **Writing Models and Graphic Organizers on Transparencies** to aid organization.
- Guide students through writing a review with the instructions for the Writing Lesson.
- Use the Response to Literature rubric on p. 15 in **Performance Assessment and Portfolio Management** to evaluate students' reviews.

❹ Listening and Speaking

- Arrange the class in groups of four. Have each group decide which two students are proponents of numbers and which two are proponents of words.
- Encourage students to generate ideas that will support their position. Also, suggest that they anticipate and prepare responses to the arguments used by the other side.
- Point out to students that good reasons are not personal opinions but are important points backed up by solid facts.
- Have students use the Listening rubric on p. 22 in **Performance Assessment and Portfolio Management** to assess their peers' work.

CUSTOMIZE INSTRUCTION For Universal Access

To address different learning styles, use the activities suggested in the **Extension Activities** booklet, p. 36.

- For Visual/Spatial Learners, use Activity 5.
- For Bodily/Kinesthetic Learners, use Activity 6.
- For Logical/Mathematical Learners, use Activity 7.

Grandpa and the Statue

Lesson Objectives

1. **To analyze and respond to literary elements**
   - Literary Analysis: Dialogue
   - Connecting Literary Elements: Characterization
2. **To read, comprehend, analyze, and critique drama**
   - Reading Strategy: Distinguishing Fact From Fantasy
   - Reading Check Questions
   - Review and Assess Questions
3. **To develop word analysis skills, fluency, and systematic vocabulary**
   - Vocabulary Development Lesson: Word Analysis: Latin Root *-scrib-*
4. **To understand and apply written and oral language conventions**
   - Spelling Strategy
   - Grammar Lesson: Pronoun and Antecedent Agreement
   - Assessment Practice (ATE)
5. **To understand and apply appropriate writing and research strategies**
   - Writing Lesson: Position Paper
   - Extension Activity: Liberty Island Fair
6. **To understand and apply listening and speaking strategies**
   - Extension Activity: Reader's Theater
   - Extension Activity: Explanation

STEP-BY-STEP TEACHING GUIDE	PACING GUIDE
PRETEACH	
Motivate Students and Provide Background	
Use the Motivation activity (ATE p. 664)	5 min.
Read and discuss the Preview material and Background information (SE/ATE p. 664) [A]	10 min.
Introduce the Concepts	
Introduce the Literary Analysis and Reading Strategy (SE/ATE p. 665) [A]	25 min.
Pronounce the vocabulary words and read their definitions (SE p. 665)	5 min.
TEACH	
Monitor Comprehension	
Informally monitor comprehension by circulating while students read independently or in groups [A]	50 min.
Monitor students' comprehension with the Reading Check notes (SE/ATE pp. 667, 669, 671, 673, 675, 677, 679)	as students read
Develop vocabulary with Vocabulary notes (SE pp. 669, 670, 673, 679)	as students read
Develop Understanding	
Develop students' understanding of dialogue with the Literary Analysis annotations (SE pp. 668–672, 675–677; ATE pp. 668–672, 675–677) [A]	5 min.
Develop students' ability to distinguish between fact and fantasy with the Reading Strategy annotations (SE pp. 668, 673, 674, 679; ATE pp. 668, 673, 674, 679)	5 min.
ASSESS	
Assess Mastery	
Assess students' mastery of the Reading Strategy and Literary Analysis by having them answer the Review and Assess questions (SE/ATE p. 681)	25 min.
Use one or more of the print and media Assessment Resources (ATE p. 683) [A]	up to 45 min.
EXTEND	
Apply Understanding	
Have students complete the Vocabulary Development Lesson and the Grammar Lesson (SE p. 682) [A]	30 min.
Apply students' ability to write a position paper using the Writing Lesson (SE/ATE p. 683) [A]	45 min.
Apply students' understanding using one or more of the Extension Activities (SE p. 683)	20–90 min.

ACCELERATED INSTRUCTION:
Use the strategies and activities identified with an [A].

UNIVERSAL ACCESS
● = Below Level Students
▲ = On-Level Students
■ = Above Level Students

Time and Resource Manager

Reading Level: Average
Average Number of Instructional Days: 5

RESOURCES		
PRINT	**TRANSPARENCIES**	**TECHNOLOGY**
• **Beyond Literature,** Humanities Connection: Monuments, p. 37 ▲ ■		• **Interest Grabber Videotapes,** Tape 4 ● ▲ ■
• **Selection Support Workbook:** ● ▲ ■ Literary Analysis, p. 185 Reading Strategy, p. 184 Build Vocabulary, p. 181	• **Literary Analysis and Reading Transparencies,** pp. 73 and 74 ● ▲ ■	
• **Adapted Reader's Companion** ● • **Reader's Companion** ●		• **Listening to Literature** ● ▲ ■ Audiocassettes, Side 25 Audio CDs, CD 13
• **English Learner's Companion** ● ▲ • **Literatura en español** ● ▲ • **Literary Analysis for Enrichment** ■		
• **Formal Assessment:** Selection Test, pp. 165–167 ● ▲ ■ • **Open Book Test,** pp. 106–108 ● ▲ ■ • **Performance Assessment and Portfolio Management,** pp. 11, 23 ● ▲ ■ • PRENTICE HALL ASSESSMENT SYSTEM ● ▲ ■	• PRENTICE HALL ASSESSMENT SYSTEM ● ▲ ■ Skills Practice Answers and Explanations on Transparencies	• **Test Bank Software** ● ▲ ■ • **Got It! Assessment Videotapes,** Tape 4 ● ▲
• **Selection Support Workbook:** ● ▲ ■ Build Spelling Skills, p. 182 Build Grammar Skills, p. 183 • **Writing and Grammar,** Copper Level ● ▲ ■ • **Extension Activities,** p. 37 ● ▲ ■	• **Daily Language Practice Transparencies** ● ▲ • **Writing Models and Graphic Organizers on Transparencies** ● ▲ ■	• **Writing and Grammar iText CD-ROM** ● ▲ ■ ***Take It to the Net*** www.phschool.com

BLOCK SCHEDULING: Use one 90-minute class period to preteach the selection and have students read it. Use a second 90-minute class period to assess students' mastery of skills and have them complete one of the Extension Activities.

PRETEACH

Step-by-Step Teaching Guide for pp. 664–665

Motivation

Call students' attention to the Statue of Liberty shown here. Ask them to list the things that come to mind when they look at the statue. What feelings does the statue seem to convey? Tell them to notice how the statue is posed and what she is holding in each of her hands. Then, ask students to pretend that they are portraying the character of the Statue of Liberty in a play. What kind of person would she be? How would she talk? What would she say? Ask volunteers to present their character to the class. Tell students that this is a drama about someone who forgets why it is important to share common ground.

Interest Grabber Video

As an alternative, play "The Statue of Liberty" on Tape 4 to engage student interest.

❶ Background

Social Studies

In *Grandpa and the Statue,* the dialogue revolves around the worthiness and the stability of the Statue of Liberty. French sculptor Auguste Bartholdi designed the statue, and American architect Richard Morris Hunt designed the pedestal. Gustave Eiffel, the same man who designed the Eiffel Tower in Paris, designed the metal framework that supports the statue. Here are some other statue statistics:

Height: 305 feet, 1 inch from foundation to torch

Weight: 225 tons

Steps from ground to the top: 354

Prepare to Read

❶ Grandpa and the Statue

Take It to the Net

Visit www.phschool.com for interactive activities and instruction related to "Grandpa and the Statue," including

- background
- graphic organizers
- literary elements
- reading strategies

Literature in Your Life

Connecting to the Literature

This play tells a story from the Statue of Liberty's early days. The only way to see the statue then was "in person." Even if you've never visited the Statue of Liberty, you've probably seen it in a movie, a book, or on television. What thoughts or feelings do you have when you see it?

Background

The Statue of Liberty was dedicated in 1886. Although the statue itself was a gift from France, money for the pedestal on which it stands was raised in the United States. It was placed on a small island in New York Harbor, and, at the time, stood taller than any building in New York City.

TEACHING RESOURCES

The following resources can be used to enrich or extend the instruction for pp. 664–665.

Motivation

Interest Grabber Video, Tape 4

Background

Beyond Literature, p. 37

Take It to the Net

Visit www.phschool.com for Background and hotlinks for *Grandpa and the Statue.*

Literary Analysis

Literary Analysis and Reading Transparencies, Dialogue, p. 74

Reading

Selection Support: Reading Strategy, p. 184; Build Vocabulary, p. 181

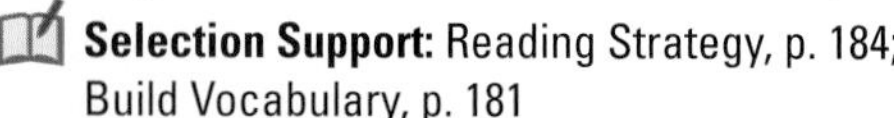

Literary Analysis and Reading Transparencies, Distinguishing Fact From Fantasy, p. 73

BLOCK SCHEDULING: Resources marked with this symbol provide varied instruction during 90-minute blocks.

❷ Literary Analysis

Dialogue

Grandpa and the Statue was written in 1945 as a radio play—a play to be listened to, not watched. (At the time, radios were very popular, and few people had television sets or could afford to see a play on Broadway.) In a radio play, most of the action must be conveyed through dialogue—the conversations among characters—because the audience cannot view what the characters are doing.

Connecting Literary Elements

In radio plays as well as stage plays, much of the **characterization**—how the characters' personalities are revealed—occurs through dialogue. The audience learns about a character through what the character says, the way in which he or she says it, and what other characters say about him or her. The characters' words also reveal the **plot**—the set of events that move the story forward.

As you read, pay attention to what the dialogue reveals about the characters and the plot. Think about whether these elements seem realistic or believable. Use these focus questions to guide you:

1. Do the characters act like real people? (Keep in mind that the play is set in the 1800s.)
2. How well-developed and realistic are the characters' personalities?

❸ Reading Strategy

Distinguishing Fact From Fantasy

This play is an example of historical fiction—literature set in a specific period in history. It deals with the building of the Statue of Liberty in the 1800s. Like other works of historical literature, it includes factual as well as made-up details.

- **Facts** are true details that can often be found through research in an encyclopedia or other reference work.
- **Fantasy** is made up of details that are fictional and do not exist in real life.

Use a chart like the one here to track details from the play as you read, and record whether or not you find that they are factual.

Detail	Fact or Fiction?
People collected dimes and nickels	**Fact:** Even school children made contributions

Vocabulary Development

subscribed (səb skrībd′) *adj.* signed up to give money (p. 669)

peeved (pēvd) *adj.* bad-tempered or annoyed (p. 670)

uncomprehending (ən cäm prē hend′ iŋ) *adj.* not understanding (p. 673)

tempest (tem′ pist) *n.* violent storm with high winds (p. 679)

CUSTOMIZE INSTRUCTION FOR UNIVERSAL ACCESS

For Special Needs Students	For Less Proficient Readers	For English Learners
Have students read the adapted version of *Grandpa and the Statue* in the **Adapted Reader's Companion.** This version provides basic-level instruction in an interactive format with questions and write-on lines. Completing the adapted version will prepare students to read the selection in the Student Edition.	Have students read *Grandpa and the Statue* in the **Reader's Companion.** This version provides basic-level instruction in an interactive format with questions and write-on lines. After students finish the selection in the Reader's Companion, have them complete the questions and activities in the Student Edition.	Have students read the adapted version of *Grandpa and the Statue* in the **English Learner's Companion.** This version provides basic-level instruction in an interactive format with questions and write-on lines. Completing the adapted version will prepare students to read the selection in the Student Edition.

❷ Literary Analysis

Dialogue

- Tell students that one of the major differences between stories and plays is the amount of dialogue, or speaking. Stories can be told through narration and dialogue, but dramatic works depend on the characters' dialogue to tell the story.
- Read the Dialogue instructions aloud. Emphasize that as a radio play *Grandpa and the Statue* is especially dependent upon dialogue to tell the story, because listeners are meant to see neither actors nor scenery.
- Use the instructions for Connecting Literary Elements to help students understand characterization. Instruct students to consider the focus questions as they read the play.

❸ Reading Strategy

Distinguishing Fact From Fantasy

- Remind students that literature can either be fact or fantasy, or a mixture of the two.
- Encourage students to determine the parts of the play that are factual, which are primarily those about the statue, and those that are fictitious.
- Invite students to make charts such as the one on p. 665 to help them keep track of the factual and fictitious elements in the play.

Vocabulary Development

- Review the words and definitions on the vocabulary list.
- Point out the word *peeved* to students. After discussing the word's definition, "bad-tempered" or "annoyed," introduce the related phrase "pet peeve," an action or idea that annoys someone. Explain that pet peeves are individualized so that what bothers one person may not bother another; for example, a person may dislike when others tap their pens or crack their knuckles. Ask students to identify some of their own pet peeves.

E-Teach

Visit E-Teach at www.phschool.com for teachers' essays on how to teach, with questions and answers.

TEACH

Step-by-Step Teaching Guide for pp. 666–680

CUSTOMIZE INSTRUCTION
For Intrapersonal Learners

Parts of this play center on a man's efforts to rally his neighborhood to contribute to the cause of erecting the Statue of Liberty. Ask students what they would do to convince someone to contribute. Have them outline arguments and a plan of action for convincing people who have refused or who are undecided. As students read, have them compare their plan to Sheean's actions.

❶ About the Selection

In *Grandpa and the Statue,* the character of Grandpa is revealed through the recollections of his grandson, Monaghan, a disabled war veteran. As a child, Monaghan is clearly affected by Grandpa. Every word that Grandpa speaks is a word Monaghan remembers, especially when Grandpa voices his opinion on the uselessness of the Statue of Liberty. During the late 1800s, when the drama takes place, subscriptions were being taken to fund the Statue of Liberty, but Grandpa—convinced that the statue is a waste of money—will not contribute a dime. Years later, his grandson's young and inquisitive nature starts to break down Grandpa's stubbornness, and at last, Grandpa understands that the Statue of Liberty is symbolic of the unity and common ground for which all immigrants come to America.

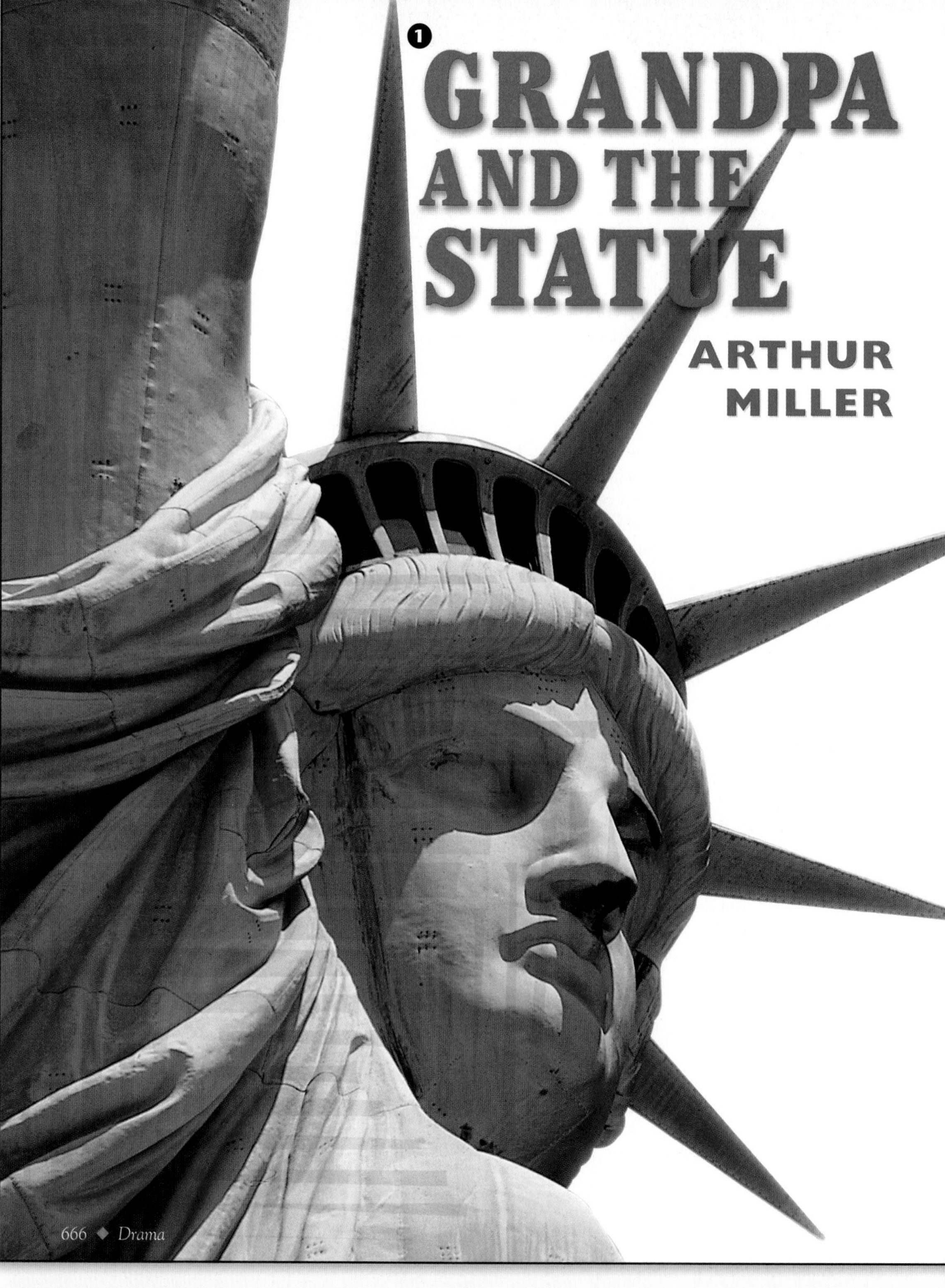

❶ GRANDPA AND THE STATUE

ARTHUR MILLER

TEACHING RESOURCES

The following resources can be used to enrich or extend the instruction for pp. 666–680.

Literary Analysis
- **Selection Support:** Literary Analysis, p. 185
- **Literary Analysis for Enrichment**

Reading
- **Reader's Companion**
- **Adapted Reader's Companion**
- **English Learner's Companion**

- **Literatura en español**
- **Listening to Literature Audiocassettes,** Side 35
- **Listening to Literature Audio CDs,** CD 13

BLOCK SCHEDULING: Resources marked with this symbol provide varied instruction during 90-minute blocks.

CHARACTERS

CHARACTERS IN THE PRESENT TIME OF THE PLAY

* ANNOUNCER
* AUGUST
* MONAGHAN *(Young Monaghan, a soldier)*

CHARACTERS FROM THE PAST

(Heard in the flashback scenes that Young Monaghan remembers)

* SHEEAN
* MONAGHAN *(Grandfather of Young Monaghan)*
* CHILD MONAGHAN *(Young Monaghan himself, as a child)*
* GEORGE, CHARLEY, JACK, MIKE, JOE *(Neighborhood children, Child Monaghan's friends)*
* ALF, GIRL, YOUNG MAN *(Passengers on the Statue of Liberty boat)*
* MEGAPHONE VOICE
* VETERAN *(Visitor to the statue)*

[*Music: Theme*]

ANNOUNCER. The scene is the fourth floor of a giant army hospital overlooking New York Harbor. A young man sitting in a wheel chair is looking out a window—just looking. After a while another young man in another wheel chair rolls over to him and they both look.

[*Music out*]

AUGUST. You want to play some checkers with me, Monaghan?

MONAGHAN. Not right now.

2 **AUGUST.** Okay. [*Slight pause*] You don't want to go feeling blue, Monaghan.

MONAGHAN. I'm not blue.

AUGUST. All you do most days is sit here looking out this window.

MONAGHAN. What do you want me to do, jump rope?

3 **Reading Check**

Where are these characters?

4 ◄ **Critical Viewing** In what way does the angle of this picture make the statue look very impressive? **[Analyze]**

2 Reinforcing Skills

Drawing Inferences

- Point out to students that the dialogue in a play will give them clues they can use for making inferences, or educated guesses, about the characters.
- Have two students read the bracketed passage, one reading the part of August and one reading the part of Monaghan.
- Ask: What character traits of Monaghan's are revealed through this dialogue?
  Answer: Monaghan is being sarcastic. Because he is in a wheelchair, he cannot skip rope. His dialogue also reveals his unhappiness and what he does with his time.

3 Reading Check

Answer: August and Monaghan are patients in a big army hospital that overlooks New York Harbor.

4 ► Critical Viewing

Answer: The angle makes the statue look very powerful. It also makes Lady Liberty's face look serious, but also very sure of herself. The crown that she is wearing stands out from this angle, and its design contributes to how powerful she looks.

CUSTOMIZE INSTRUCTION FOR UNIVERSAL ACCESS

For Special Needs Students	For Less Proficient Readers	For Advanced Readers
Because some of the dialogue is in an Irish dialect, students may benefit from reading the story aloud in small groups. Have students pause in their reading from time to time to discuss and clarify what the characters are saying.	Have students preview the play's title, the illustrations, and the list of characters. Then, have them generate a list of questions about the play. Possible questions include: "Why is Monaghan staring out the window?" and "What is Grandpa's connection with the statue?" As students read, have them record details that relate to their questions.	Have students research what may have influenced Arthur Miller to write *Grandpa and the Statue.* Ask the school librarian to help students either conduct an Internet search or look through the stacks for information on the author and his play. Students should share their findings with the class.

5 Literary Analysis

Dialogue

- Have students recall what type of play this is.
  Answer: It is a radio play.
- Have students discuss what the playwright will need to reveal in the dialogue.
  Answer: The playwright will need to reveal setting, characters, and action in the dialogue.
- As volunteers read the dialogue on p. 668, have them listen for details about the time and setting of the play.
- Then, ask the Literary Analysis question: What does the dialogue on this page reveal about the time and place of the play's beginning?
  Answer: The dialogue shows that the hospital is close to Monaghan's childhood home in Brooklyn. The time is not specified, but the play takes place in the daytime, probably after a war, because the characters are in an army hospital.

6 Reading Strategy

Distinguishing Fact From Fantasy

- Remind students that the author has mixed facts and fantasy in this play—what may appear realistic could indeed be fantasy.
- Then, ask the Reading Strategy question on p. 668: Which part of Monaghan's explanation is a fact about the time period?
  Answer: The cost of the trolley is a fact about the time period.

AUGUST. No, but what do you get out of it?

MONAGHAN. It's a beautiful view. Some companies make millions of dollars just printing that view on postcards.

AUGUST. Yeh, but nobody keeps looking at a postcard six, seven hours a day.

MONAGHAN. I come from around here, it reminds me of things. My young days.

5 **AUGUST.** That's right, you're from Brooklyn, aren't you?

MONAGHAN. My house is only about a mile away.

AUGUST. That so. Tell me, are you looking at just the water all the time? I'm curious. I don't get a kick out of this view.

MONAGHAN. There's the Statue of Liberty out there. Don't you see it?

AUGUST. Oh, that's it. Yeh, that's nice to look at.

MONAGHAN. I like it. Reminds me of a lot of laughs.

AUGUST. Laughs? The Statue of Liberty?

MONAGHAN. Yeh, my grandfather. He got all twisted up with the Statue of Liberty.

AUGUST. [*Laughs a little*] That so? What happened?

MONAGHAN. Well. My grandfather was the stingiest man in Brooklyn. "Mercyless" Monaghan, they used to call him. He even used to save umbrella handles.

AUGUST. What for?

MONAGHAN. Just couldn't stand seeing anything go to waste. After a big windstorm there'd be a lot of broken umbrellas laying around in the streets.

AUGUST. Yeh?

6 **MONAGHAN.** He'd go around picking them up. In our house the closets were always full of umbrella handles. My grandma used to say that he would go across the Brooklyn Bridge on the trolley just because he could come back on the same nickel. See, if you stayed on the trolley they'd let you come back for the same nickel.

AUGUST. What'd he do, just go over and come back?

MONAGHAN. Yeh, it made him feel good. Savin' money. Two and a half cents.

AUGUST. So how'd he get twisted up with the Statue of Liberty?

MONAGHAN. Well, way back in 1887 around there they were living on Butler Street. Butler Street, Brooklyn, practically runs right down to the river. One day he's sitting on the front porch, reading

Literary Analysis

Dialogue What does the dialogue on this page reveal about the time and place of the play's beginning?

Reading Strategy

Distinguishing Fact and Fantasy Which part of Monaghan's explanation is a fact about the time period?

CUSTOMIZE INSTRUCTION FOR UNIVERSAL ACCESS

For English Learners

Students may benefit from a quick review of the basis upon which the United States was founded. Tell students that the British colonized North American land in the 1700s. Early British settlers, who moved to North America to make a new life for themselves, were mostly escaping the British government, which allowed its people very few liberties. The British colonists eventually fought the Revolutionary War to gain their independence from the British. After the war, the United States of America outlined the Constitution and the Bill of Rights, which guaranteed U.S. citizens the freedoms they sought. Once the United States was established, immigrants from all over the world poured into this young and promising nation. Ellis Island was the port that processed some twenty million immigrants and welcomed them to U.S. soil. Ellis Island is next to Liberty Island, where the statue was erected.

a paper he borrowed from the neighbors, when along comes this man Jack Sheean who lived up the block.

[*Music: Sneak into above speech, then bridge, then out*]

SHEEAN. [*Slight brogue*[1]] A good afternoon to you, Monaghan.

MONAGHAN. [*Grandfather*] How're you, Sheean, how're ya?

SHEEAN. Fair, fair. And how's Mrs. Monaghan these days?

MONAGHAN. Warm. Same as everybody else in summer.

SHEEAN. I've come to talk to you about the fund, Monaghan.

7 **MONAGHAN.** What fund is that?

SHEEAN. The Statue of Liberty fund.

MONAGHAN. Oh, that.

SHEEAN. It's time we come to grips with the subject, Monaghan.

MONAGHAN. I'm not interested, Sheean.

SHEEAN. Now hold up on that a minute. Let me tell you the facts. This here Frenchman has gone and built a fine statue of Liberty. It costs who knows how many millions to build. All they're askin' us to do is contribute enough to put up a base for the statue to stand on.

MONAGHAN. I'm not . . . !

SHEEAN. Before you answer me. People all over the whole United States are puttin' in for it. Butler Street is doin' the same. We'd like to hang up a flag on the corner saying—"Butler Street, Brooklyn, is one hundred per cent behind the Statue of Liberty." And Butler Street *is* a hundred per cent subscribed except for you. Now will you give us a dime, Monaghan? One dime and we can put up the flag. Now what do you say to that?

8 **MONAGHAN.** I'm not throwin' me good money away for somethin' I don't even know exists.

SHEEAN. Now what do you mean by that?

MONAGHAN. Have you seen this statue?

SHEEAN. No, but it's in a warehouse. And as soon as we get the money to build the pedestal they'll take it and put it up on that island in the river, and all the boats comin' in from the old country will see it there and it'll raise the hearts of the poor immigrants to see such a fine sight on their first look at this country.

MONAGHAN. And how do I know it's in this here warehouse at all?

SHEEAN. You read your paper, don't you? It's been in all the papers for the past year.

Literary Analysis
Dialogue What action does the dialogue here reveal?

Literary Analysis
Dialogue and Characterization Are Monaghan's and Sheean's different reactions realistic for the situation? Explain.

subscribed (səb skrībd′) *adj.* signed up to give money

9 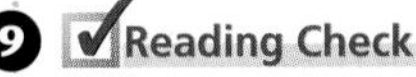

What does Sheean want Monaghan to do?

1. **brogue** (brōg) *n.* Irish accent.

7 Literary Analysis

Dialogue

- Remind students that dialogue is occasionally used in the play to show what is happening.
- Have two students read the bracketed passage.
- Then, ask students the first Literary Analysis question on p. 669.
  Answer: The dialogue shows that two neighbors are meeting on the street.

Monitor Progress Ask students what the dialogue reveals in addition to the action.
Answer: The dialogue shows that the men have spoken about this issue before, and that they do not agree about it.

8 Literary Analysis

Dialogue and Characterization

- Have students continue to read the dialogue on the page.
- Ask the second Literary Analysis question on p. 669: Are Monaghan's and Sheean's different reactions realistic for the situation? Explain.
  Answer: Yes; Monaghan probably has a belief that was common among people at that time that the statue may not exist, whereas Sheean knows the facts about the Statue of Liberty.

9 Reading Check

Answer: Sheean wants Monaghan to contribute money to build the base for the Statue of Liberty.

CUSTOMIZE INSTRUCTION FOR UNIVERSAL ACCESS

For Special Needs Students	For Gifted/Talented Students
Pair up students to help them keep the play's events in sequence. Have students write key events on cards as they read *Grandpa and the Statue*. After the set of cards is complete, have one student shuffle the set and the other student put the cards back into the correct time order for the events. After the first student has correctly sequenced the cards, have students trade duties. The student who put the cards in order should shuffle them, and the student who shuffles the cards should put the events in order.	Point out to students that Sheean is trying to sell an idea to Grandpa. Have students speculate on the difficulty of selling ideas as opposed to physical products. Ask students to study the methods Sheean uses to try to persuade Grandpa to subscribe to the Statue of Liberty fund. Then, have students pair up and try to "sell" something to each other. Remind students to pick an object or an idea that they really believe in and to try to find out what angle or aspect of the product or idea would persuade their partner to buy it.

❸ Writing Lesson

Position Paper

Write a position paper from Grandpa's or Sheean's viewpoint at the beginning of the play—either for or against the statue.

Prewriting Find details in the play related to your character's position. Evaluate whether these are convincing facts or details. Add more supporting evidence to your notes, as needed.

Drafting Begin by stating your position. Then, give your reasons. Follow each of your reasons with examples and details that support your position. Remember to speak in the voice of your character. Conclude with a summary that reemphasizes your position.

Model: Supporting Evidence

People all over the whole United States are puttin' in for it. Butler Street is doin' the same. We'd like to hang a flag on the corner saying—"Butler Street, Brooklyn, is one hundred percent behind the Statue of Liberty."

Sheean provides supporting evidence for his position. He gives examples (people contributing to the fund) and a reason (putting up a flag) to persuade Grandpa.

Revising Ask a partner to review your draft. Add more examples and details if your reviewer is unconvinced of one of your points.

WG *Prentice Hall Writing and Grammar Connection: Chapter 7, Section 3*

❹ Extension Activities

Listening and Speaking In a group, plan a **reader's theater** production of *Grandpa and the Statue*, or of an excerpt from the play.

- Assign parts.
- Practice the reading.
- After each rehearsal, provide feedback for each other on how well you have interpreted the characters' speech and actions.

When you are satisfied with the reading, perform it for the class.

Writing Write a brief **explanation** of Grandpa's change of heart. Use examples of his actions and words as well as your own inferences.

Research and Technology With a group, create a **Liberty Island Fair** in your classroom. Use the Internet and other sources to gather information, then write overviews and create visuals on the computer. Group members can choose to make diagrams of the island, describe its history, prepare factual charts, or make posters that show the Statue and display facts about it. **[Group Activity]**

www.phschool.com

Go online for an additional research activity using the Internet.

Lesson Support for p. 683

❸ Writing Lesson

- Tell students that a position paper summarizes a person's opinion about an issue.
- Have students return to the opening pages of the play to recall the opinions that the two men had about the statue.
- Use the Writing Lesson instructions to guide students through the assignment.
- Use the Persuasion rubric on p. 11 in **Performance Assessment and Portfolio Management** to assess student work.

❹ Listening and Speaking

- Divide the class into groups. You may wish to assign a portion of the play to each group.
- Guide each group to work together to bring the script to life. If possible, provide class time for organization and rehearsals.
- As groups present their readings, use the Understanding, Tone, Mood, and Emotion rubric on p. 23 in **Performance Assessment and Portfolio Management** to assess their work.

CUSTOMIZE INSTRUCTION For Universal Access

To address different learning styles, use the activities suggested in the **Extension Activities** booklet, p. 37.

- For Visual/Spatial Learners, use Activity 5.
- For Verbal/Linguistic and Interpersonal Learners, use Activity 6.
- For Musical/Rhythmic Learners, use Activity 7.

ASSESSMENT RESOURCES

The following resources can be used to assess students' knowledge and skills.

Selection Assessment

- **Formal Assessment,** pp. 165–167
- **Open Book Test,** pp. 106–108
- **Got It! Assessment Videotapes,** Tape 4
- **Test Bank Software**

Take It to the Net

Visit www.phschool.com for self-tests and additional questions on *Grandpa and the Statue*.

Writing Rubric

- **Performance Assess. and Portfolio Mgmt.,** p. 11

Listening and Speaking Rubric

- **Performance Assess. and Portfolio Mgmt.,** p. 23

PRENTICE HALL ASSESSMENT SYSTEM

- **Workbook**
- **Skill Book**
- **Transparencies**
- **CD-ROM**

Lesson Objectives

1. To understand the connection between immigration themes used in drama and nonfiction
2. To gain insight into how a writer views inquiries from readers

Connections

In a play, a writer uses characters to make statements for the audience to agree or disagree with. In an essay, a writer states opinions for readers to consider. After students have read the essay by Julia Alvarez, have them review the drama *Grandpa and the Statue* by Arthur Miller, paying close attention to Grandpa's statements before and after reading the poem at the base of the statue. How are Grandpa's and Alvarez's statements similar?

Making Statements

- Point out to students that "Something to Declare" is the introduction to a book of essays by Julia Alvarez. After students read the essay, have them speculate about why authors write introductions.
Possible responses: Authors might write introductions to explain why they wrote something or to set the tone for a longer work. Some authors might use introductions to thank people who have helped them write a book.
- Discuss why writers might not answer inquiries from readers. Ask students whether the reason Alvarez gives for not writing back makes sense and whether they understand why Alvarez doesn't adhere to this reasoning when it comes to her own writing.
Possible response: The reason makes sense, but it is a selfish one, and Alvarez does not seem selfish.
- Ask students the Thematic Connection question on p. 685: Why can't Julia resist answering questions from her readers?
Possible response: Alvarez seems to like interacting with readers and explaining her writing. In addition, she seems to want to help organizations that ask for assistance and seems eager to explain what she thinks and how she feels about different topics related to her life.

CONNECTIONS
Themes in Drama and Nonfiction
Making Statements

Both Julia Alvarez's essay from her book *Something to Declare* and Arthur Miller's drama *Grandpa and the Statue* explore the theme of having something to say, a statement to make, something to declare. Grandpa's "statement" changes after he finds out what the Statue of Liberty "says" or declares to immigrants entering the United States. Julia Alvarez explains that she has many statements to make, many things to declare. As you read Alvarez's essay, which is the introduction to her book *Something to Declare*, think about the statements each writer is making. Ask yourself why each writer connects his or her theme to the idea of immigration. Identify ways in which the writers' ideas are connected to each other.

from
Something to Declare
Julia Alvarez

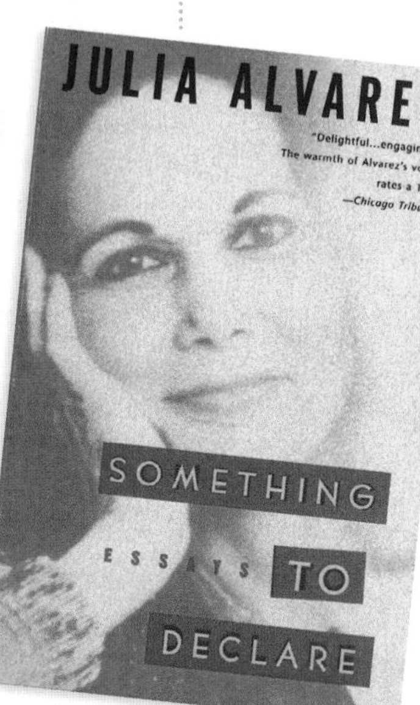

The title of Julia Alvarez's book Something to Declare *is based on a question that travelers entering the United States are asked, whether they are coming to live or to visit. The question is "Do you have anything to declare?" The literal meaning of the question is "Do you have any statement to make about taxable items or other things you are bringing into the country?" Alvarez recalls being asked that question when she entered the United States. Since much of what Alvarez has to say is related to her experience as an immigrant, she uses the question to make a connection between her life and her work.*

The first time I received a letter from one of my readers, I was surprised. I had just published my first book of poems, *Homecoming*, which concludes with a sonnet sequence titled "33." My reader wanted to know why I had included forty-one sonnets when the title of the sequence was "33."

I considered not answering. Often, it is the little perplexities and curiosities and quandaries that remain after I have finished reading a book that send me to buy another book by that author. If I want to know more, the best way to find out is to read all the books that the author has written.

In the end, though, I couldn't resist. I wrote back, explaining how thirty-three represented my age at the time I wrote the sequence, how I had meant to include only thirty-three sonnets but I kept writing them and writing them, how the sonnets were not sonnets in the traditional sense. . . . Before I knew it, I had written my reader not just a note on my sonnet sequence but a short essay.

Many of the essays in this book began in just that way—as answers to such queries. Jessica Peet, a high-school student, read my first novel, *How the García Girls Lost Their Accents*, in her Vermont Authors class and wanted to know if I considered myself a Vermonter. The Lane Series, our local arts and entertainment series, wanted to know what I might have to say about opera. Share Our Strength was putting together a fund-raising anthology. Did I have anything at all to declare about food?

I could not really say to any of them, "Read my novels or my poems or my stories." These folks wanted what my boarding-school housemother used to call a straight answer. Which is where essays start. Not that they obey housemothers. Not that they list everything you are supposed to list on that Customs Declaration form. (How could the wild, multitudinous, daily things in anyone's head be inventoried in a form?) But that is the pretext of essays: *we have something to declare.*

And so this essay book is dedicated to you, my readers, who have asked me so many good questions and who want to know more than I have told you in my novels and poems. About my experience of immigration, about switching languages, about the writing life, the teaching life, the family life, about all of those combined.

Your many questions boil down finally to this one question: Do you have anything more to declare?

Yes, I do.

Thematic Connection
Why can't Julia resist answering questions from her readers?

Julia Alvarez

(b. 1950)

Julia Alvarez was born in New York City, but raised until the age of ten in the Dominican Republic. She is the author of three critically acclaimed novels: *¡Yo!*, *In the Time of the Butterflies*, and *How the García Girls Lost Their Accents*. She is also the author of four books of poetry, including *The Other Side/El Otro Lado* and *Homecoming*.

Connecting Drama and Nonfiction

1. What theme or message about making statements do Arthur Miller and Julia Alvarez communicate in their works?
2. Explain how the message is revealed in each work.
3. Do you find the theme of Alvarez's nonfiction or Miller's drama easier to understand? Why?

Background

Customs Declarations

Point out to students the necessity of customs declarations. Explain that every country has certain items that it does not want to let in, or that it will only let in after the owner pays a fee. Thus, someone traveling into a country must declare whether any of the items he or she is bringing into the country are prohibited or subject to duty, a type of tax on imports.

Answers

Connecting Drama and Nonfiction

1. Arthur Miller and Julia Alvarez both state that there are some things that need to be said, things that people need to understand.
2. Through *Grandpa and the Statue,* Miller illustrates why immigrants came to the United States, and he expresses the importance of symbols such as the Statue of Liberty. Alvarez, through her response to her readers, expresses the importance of explaining things further, and she states that she has more to "declare."
3. Ask students to support their answers with specific reasons.

ENRICHMENT: Social Studies Connection

Customs Declarations

Students may be interested in finding out more about regulations concerning items that may or may not be brought into the United States. Students should be aware that some items can be brought into the country after duties are paid; this is done for economic purposes. Animals and plants are sometimes prohibited from entering a country altogether or are subject to quarantines, which means that they must be kept isolated for a period of time to be certain that they are not bringing diseases into the country. Point out that regulations such as these are usually based on scientific and medical reasons, not merely the ideas of lawmakers.

Have students research how customs laws are made and enforced. They can use library resources and the Internet to find out current regulations and challenges faced by border agents. They may also be interested in getting customs forms from the United States Customs Service. Another possible avenue of investigation would be the history of trade laws. Have students share their findings with the class.

Lesson Objectives

1. To learn about newspaper feature articles
2. To learn to make assertions about a text

About Newspaper Feature Articles

- Have a student volunteer to read "About Newspaper Feature Articles" aloud. Ask students how a feature article is different from a news article.
  Answer: A news article is about recent newsworthy events. A feature article can be historical (the anniversary of an event), a timely topic (education at the beginning of the school year), or biographical.
- Bring samples of feature and news articles to class for students to compare. Discuss why newspapers run feature articles.
  Answer: Newspapers run features for additional depth and insight into the news. Features also expand the newspaper's coverage to areas that are not strictly news but that are interesting or useful to readers.

Reading Strategy

Making Assertions About the Text

- Have a volunteer read the information about making assertions. Ask: What is an assertion?
  Answer: An assertion is a statement of opinion that is backed up by evidence.
- Discuss the type of evidence that is available in a feature article; explain that it is not always scientific evidence, and it is information that supports or elaborates on the writer's opinion.
- Discuss why it is important to find information from the text that supports your assertion.

READING INFORMATIONAL MATERIALS

Newspaper Feature Articles

About Newspaper Feature Articles

Most of a newspaper is news articles about very recent events. However, articles that are on topics or issues of current *interest* may or may not be on current *events*. These are called feature articles. The list shows a few types of feature articles you will encounter in newspapers.

At the time this article was written, Angel Island had recently been declared a National Landmark, and money was being assigned to restore the buildings. These events stirred public interest in the topic of the article.

A Few Types of Feature Articles

- Historical articles on the anniversary of an event
- Articles on education at the beginning of a school year
- Biographical articles on a famous person's birthday

Reading Strategy

Making Assertions About the Text

An assertion is a statement of opinion. When you make an assertion about a text, you give an opinion. For example, when you say "The article was interesting," you are making an assertion. However, the statement "The article is 2,000 words long" is simply a statement of fact. It is not an assertion. When you make an assertion about a text, you should be prepared to support it by citing evidence from the text.

In the model, two assertions are underlined in blue. The assertions are supported by a quotation from the text, underlined in red.

Model: Citing Evidence From Text

The article highlights the difficulties faced by Chinese immigrants who were processed through Angel Island. The details are specific and vivid, giving readers a clear understanding of the conditions. For example, the situation of Dale Ching shows how trivial the reasons that people were detained. "Days after he arrived on the island, Ching learned that he could not leave because his description of his family's house in China did not match what his uncle had told immigration authorities."

The title of a feature article identifies the subject of the article. The title is always worded in the present tense.

from Chinese Immigrants Remember Detention at Angel Island

Newspaper articles often begin with a label telling you where the article was written.

The writer uses the experiences of one man to personalize the situation she will analyze.

By Esther Wu
The Dallas Morning News,
May 19, 2000

ANGEL ISLAND, Calif. Dale Ching was a teenager in 1937 when he rode on a steamer bound for America from China. For 22 days, he dreamed about San Francisco, fortified by the knowledge that his father was waiting for him there.

But when his boat docked in San Francisco's bay, he didn't see his father. Instead, his welcoming committee was a group of armed guards who ordered him and other Chinese immigrants to board a boat bound for Angel Island, where he was detained.

Ching was one of 175,000 Chinese immigrants who entered this country between 1910 and 1940 through the Angel Island Immigration Station, often called the Ellis Island of the West. They came to escape war and famine in their homeland. But once in America, they were subjected to interrogations, and some were held for as long as three to four years.

"Life here was harsh," Ching said recently during a tour of the immigration station.

"When we landed at Angel Island, the guards took away our suitcases. We were allowed the clothes we had on and one change of underwear."

Days after he arrived on the island, Ching learned that he could not leave because his description of his family's house in China did not match what his uncle had told immigration authorities. Officials, suspicious of immigrants entering the United States using false identity papers, detained Ching for three months before his father successfully petitioned officials for his release.

While immigrants coming to America through Ellis Island were welcomed by the Statue of Liberty, Chinese immigrants here had no such symbol, and many felt the

from Chinese Immigrants Remember Detention at Angel Island

- Remind students that feature articles are found in newspapers. Like all newspaper articles, features have a title that describes them.
- Point out the other introductory information for the story, including the byline and the date. Ask: Why does the article begin "Angel Island, Calif."?
  Answer: The article was written at Angel Island, California.
- Discuss how the author tries to interest the reader as the article begins by using a real person's story. This approach ties a personal element to the story and the reader will want to know what happened to Dale Ching at Angel Island.
- Have students read the first column of the article. Then, ask: What makes Dale Ching an authority on Angel Island?
  Answer: He lived there for several months.

(continued on p. 688)

CUSTOMIZE INSTRUCTION FOR UNIVERSAL ACCESS

For Less Proficient Readers	For English Learners	For Advanced Readers
Challenge students to find a feature article and a news article about the same topic. For example, a news article might be about a new park in the students' town; a related feature article could be about an artist who designed sculpture that is in the park. Have students read the articles and note the differences between them.	To help students understand the essence of this article, challenge them to look up the meaning of difficult words on this page. Words such as *detained, interrogations,* and *petitioned* help convey the challenges that immigrants at Angel Island experienced. Then, have students discuss the relevance of these words to the passage.	Challenge students to find out more information about Angel Island and the immigrants who were detained there. Students can check library resources or the Internet. Have students share their findings with the class.

from *Chinese Immigrants Remember Detention at Angel Island (continued)*

- Have students finish reading the feature.
- Then, ask students why Angel Island is being preserved.
  Answer: Angel Island is being preserved to memorialize the difficult welcome that many immigrants experienced.
- Discuss how the author proves her assertions in the first column of this page.
  Answer: The author refers to specific pieces of legislation that prove the discrimination against Chinese people in the nineteenth and twentieth centuries.
- Next, ask students why "Outcry for Preservation" is set in bolder type than the rest of the article.
  Answer: It is a heading, or subhead, for a particular section that the author chooses to highlight.
- What evidence at the end of the article lets readers know how Angel Island is used today?
  Answer: The last paragraph gives a statistic about how many people visit the island each year and describes what they do there.

sting of scorn and discrimination.

"The stories of Angel Island are not as welcoming, obviously, as it is on the East Coast," said Nick Franco, Angel Island park superintendent. "But it is still a symbolic place, and the stories need to be preserved. It's uncomfortable, but that's all the more why they need to be told."

Quotations may be used to give individual viewpoints or expert opinions.

Today, visitors to the island can experience the immigrants' despair in poems written and carved on barracks walls. More than 135 poems from the barracks have been recorded, most undated and unsigned.

Some voice resentment at being confined and bitterness over the political process that imprisoned the immigrants on the island. Most simply record a writer's anguish. Others reflect on being homesick and longing for freedom.

Some of the immigrants' despair can be traced to the early history of Chinese immigration to this country.

Long before the Angel Island Immigration Station was opened in 1910, officials tried to stem the flow of Chinese immigration to America.

The Chinese Exclusion Act of 1882 barred immigration of Chinese laborers to the United States and prohibited Chinese immigrants from becoming naturalized U.S. citizens. The National Origins Act of 1924 banned all Chinese from coming to America but was later amended to allow a small number, determined by the number of immigrants already in the United States.

The Exclusion Act was the first and only time the United States restricted immigration by ethnicity. It was not repealed until 1943, when China was a U.S. ally in World War II, and Congress established a set quota of 105 Chinese immigrants into the country annually. The quota system was banned in 1965.

Outcry for Preservation

Angel Island, in the western part of San Francisco Bay a few miles beyond the Golden Gate Bridge and Alcatraz, served as a military base as early as the Civil War. The base was active during World War II, when the threat of a West Coast invasion by the Japanese was a possibility. After the war, however, the hilly island was deserted and became covered with lush vegetation.

U.S. officials closed the island's immigration station in 1940 after a fire destroyed the administration building. And in 1962, the abandoned island was given to California's state park system. The barracks were about to be demolished in 1970 when a park ranger discovered the poems on the walls.

Public outcry persuaded state officials to preserve what was left of the immigration station, and it became a National Historic Landmark in 1997. Last year, the National Trust named it one of 11 endangered historic sites.

Feature articles often link historical information to current-day information.

In March, Californians approved a $15 million bond issue that will help restore some of the buildings and preserve the writings. Preliminary renovation studies are being done, and work may start as early as 2001 and take as long as eight years to complete.

What's left of the immigration station is basically the hospital and barracks. What remained of a two-story administration building, kitchen and dining hall has been demolished.

A few small houses that were once used as officers' private quarters have been refurbished as offices for park officials.

Public tours have been conducted since 1982, and schoolchildren take field trips here. Groups often come to boat, hike or camp overnight. An estimated 200,000 people visit the island each year.

Check Your Comprehension

1. Where is Angel Island?
2. Why is Angel Island called the Ellis Island of the West?
3. Why did thousands of people leave China for the United States between 1910 and 1940?
4. Why were Chinese immigrants detained at Angel Island?
5. What happened in 1970 to change plans to demolish the barracks on Angel Island?

Applying the Reading Strategy

Making Assertions About the Text

6. Make an assertion about the writer's position regarding the problems of the Chinese immigrants. Cite two details that support your assertion.
7. Which of the following is an assertion?
   - Preserving the immigration station on Angel Island is important to Californians.
   - Ching is one of 175,000 Chinese immigrants.
8. What assertion can you make about the balance of fact and opinion in this text? Cite one example of a fact and one of an opinion.

Activity

Media Investigation

Find two media sources that give an update on the plans to restore the buildings and preserve the writings at Angel Island. Give an oral summary of the information you find.

Comparing Informational Materials

Characteristics of Newspaper Feature Articles

Compare feature articles in newspapers to special features on television newscasts. Watch a special-interest or feature story on a newscast. Then, read a newspaper feature article on the same or a closely related topic. Use a chart like the one shown to record similarities and differences.

	Newspaper	Television
Uses facts?		
Includes opinions?		
Connects to a current event or issue?		
Uses images?		
Other?		

Answers for p. 689

Check Your Comprehension

1. Angel Island is in San Francisco Bay, near Alcatraz and the Golden Gate Bridge.
2. Angel Island is called the Ellis Island of the West because many immigrants entered the United States through Ellis Island in the nineteenth and twentieth centuries.
3. Chinese immigrants came to the United States to escape war and famine.
4. Chinese immigrants were detained because officials were suspicious that some immigrants were entering with false papers.
5. In 1970, a park ranger discovered poetry on the walls.

Applying the Reading Strategy

6. Possible response: The writer believes many of the Chinese immigrants were detained at Angel Island unfairly and is sympathetic toward their anguish. Her position is shown when she says the Chinese immigrants came to the United States to escape war and famine, but they were subjected to interrogation and detainment. She also says "many felt the sting of scorn and discrimination." Although these are facts, she seems to believe that Chinese immigrants were treated unfairly.
7. The first statement is an assertion.
8. Possible response: The article by Wu is primarily fact-based. The opinions in the article are expressed through quoted information. Wu, herself, does not express any opinions. Fact: The quota system was banned in 1965. Opinion: "Life here was harsh."

Activity

Students should locate and summarize two different kinds of media sources concerning the restoration of the buildings on Angel Island. Consult the school librarian to assist students in using microfiche and other media resources. Remind students of the importance of including facts in their oral reports. Before students give their reports to the class, allow them to practice giving their reports to a partner.

continued

Answers continued

Comparing Informational Materials

Newspaper and Television Features: Students should select one newspaper feature article and one special feature in a television newscast, and use the given chart to record similarities and differences between the two. To help students easily compare the two features, encourage them to take detailed notes.

Lesson Objectives

1. To learn the purposes of and elements of how-to essays
2. To learn to identify cause-and-effect relationships

About How-to Essays

- Have a volunteer read aloud "About How-to Essays." Ask students to name three things they can learn from a how-to essay.
Possible response: A how-to essay can show students how to do or make something, how to improve a skill, or how to achieve a desired result.
- Ask students to explain the difference between a how-to essay and a recipe or a set of instructions.
Answer: A how-to essay includes more detailed information about the way steps should be accomplished to achieve the desired results. Instructions usually are just steps to complete a task; a recipe includes a list of materials and brief directions.

Reading Strategy

Identifying Cause-and-Effect Relationships

- Have students read the Reading Strategy instruction.
- Talk with students about cause-and-effect relationships in their lives. Point out that one cause can have multiple effects. Ask: What will happen if you forget to set your alarm clock?
Possible responses: The first effect would be getting up late. Other possible effects would be having no time for breakfast and arriving late to school.
- Tell students that they will be recording the cause and effect of each step described in "Twist and Shout." They will use a chart like the one on p. 690.

READING INFORMATIONAL MATERIALS

How-to Essay

About How-to Essays

A how-to essay presents a step-by-step process for completing a certain task. Examples of how-to writing include directions for how to build and fly a model airplane or how to get a short story published. How-to essays teach you how to do or make something new, how to improve a skill, or how to achieve a desired result.

The elements of a how-to essay include

- a specific result that the reader can accomplish by following the directions or explanation.
- a list of the materials needed.
- a series of steps explained in logical order.
- details that tell when, how much, how often, or to what extent.

Reading Strategy

Identifying Cause-and-Effect Relationships

When a baseball hits a glass window, everyone knows what happens. The glass breaks. This is an example of a simple cause-and-effect relationship. The ball hitting the window is the cause, or reason. The glass breaking is the effect, or result.

In a how-to essay or a set of instructions, each step is a cause that, if the step is performed correctly, results in a particular effect. In the following example, the fold is the cause, the legs are the effect.

Cause	Effect
Step 1	
Step 2	
Step 3	
Step 4	
Step 5	
Step 6	
Step 7	
Step 8	

Example: Fold the long bubble over again and twist against the two new bubbles (another locking twist). Now you have two front legs.

Identify the cause-and-effect relationships in "Twist and Shout" by completing a chart like the one shown here.

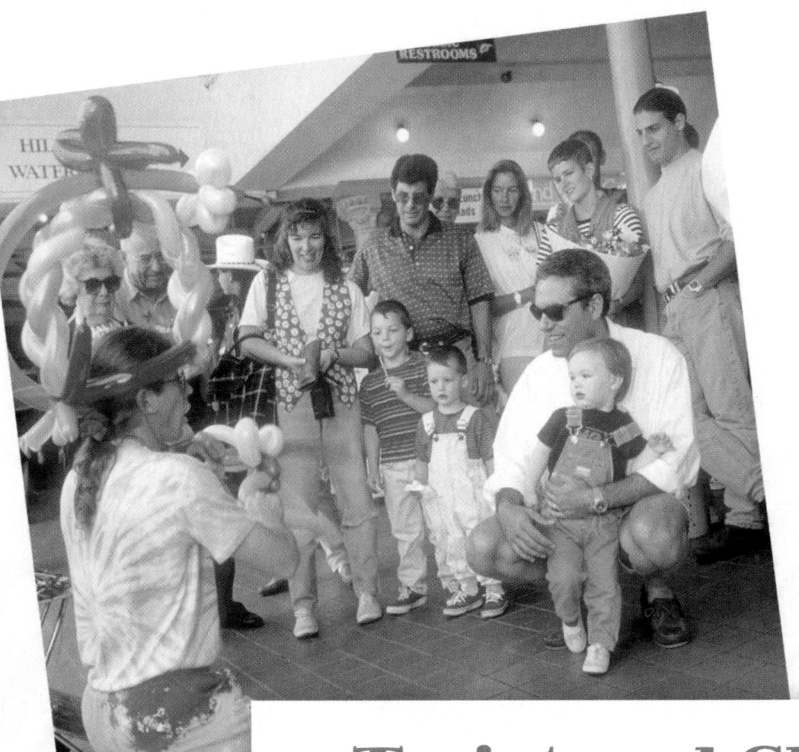

Twist and Shout

K. Wayne Wincey

The essay begins by identifying the final, specific result that the essay will help the reader accomplish.

A pinch here, a twist there, and you've made a balloon animal! Creating balloon animals is easy. All you need is a bag of balloons and the desire to have some fun. You can usually master the basics in about a week.

The best part of balloon twisting is that most animal sculptures follow the same 10-step order: nose, ear, ear, neck, leg, leg, body, leg, leg, and tail. What varies is the size of the bubbles and the amount of uninflated balloon (tail) that you start with.

Here, the writer identifies the materials.

Supplies are cheap. A gross of animal balloons, that's 144 of 'em, costs about $10. Find the balloons (also called 260's, twisties, or pencil balloons) at party supply stores or magic shops. While there, consider paying about $4 for a palm pump that helps blow up the balloons. (It'll save time and heavy breathing.)

Twist and Shout

- Before students read the article, review the elements of a how-to essay on p. 690.
- Have students read the how-to essay and the notes that identify the elements of the essay.
- Ask a volunteer to read aloud the first sentence of the essay. Ask: What will be the result of following the directions in this essay? Then, ask students to identify the purpose of this essay.
  Answer: A person who follows the directions will make a balloon animal. The purpose of this essay is to teach a person how to do or make something new.
- Have students check the text to find out what materials are needed. Ask: Does the author think that materials are expensive?
  Answer: Materials include balloons and a pump. The author thinks that the materials are cheap.
- Challenge students to explain why the author would suggest starting with an easy animal.
  Possible response: Starting with an easy project will keep the learner from getting frustrated.

(continued on p. 692)

CUSTOMIZE INSTRUCTION FOR UNIVERSAL ACCESS

For Less Proficient Readers	For Advanced Readers
Students may need help understanding cause-and-effect relationships. Distribute copies of the Cause-and-Effect Organizer on p. 66 in **Writing Models and Graphic Organizers on Transparencies.** Point out that triangles indicate causes and that squares indicate effects. Have students suggest examples for each of the situations pictured in the organizer. Work with them to complete an organizer for each situation.	Introduce students to the Latin phrase *post hoc, ergo propter hoc* and its translation, "after it, therefore because of it." Explain that this phrase refers to a common error in reasoning: confusing time relationships. Point out that one event may follow another without being caused by it. Encourage students to find an example of a text that uses both chronology and cause and effect to describe the same series of events.

Twist and Shout (continued)

- Discuss with students why the writer divided the essay into steps instead of using paragraphs.
  Answer: The author used steps to show how the task is done by following a logical, orderly sequence. In addition, numbered steps make it easy for someone making a balloon animal to keep track of where he or she is in the process.
- Have students identify the effect of not keeping a firm grip on all the bubbles in Step 4.
  Answer: The effect would be that the bubbles would come undone.
- Challenge students to discover how each step is a cause-and-effect relationship.
  Answer: Each step is a cause-and-effect relationship because if someone follows the directions, the effect will be that another step is accomplished in making a balloon animal.
- Discuss one effect of learning to make balloon animals.
  Possible responses: One effect of learning to make balloon animals could be earning money by making animals at children's parties. Another effect could be making children in a hospital happy by visiting them and giving them balloon animals.

Start with an easy balloon animal, like the dog shown here. Experiment a little, and you'll soon have a whole zoo of critters!

Numbered steps create a logical order.

Details in the directions identify how much balloon to pinch and how many times to pinch and how many times to twist.

The writer identifies the effect of not completing the step correctly.

1. Blow up a balloon, leaving about three inches uninflated. This is called the tail; the open end is the nozzle. Tie off the nozzle in an overhand knot. Note: The more twists in your sculpture, the more uninflated the balloon must be.

2. Using your thumb and forefinger, pinch or squeeze off three inches of the balloon from the nozzle for the dog's nose. Twist the body of the balloon around at least three times. Don't worry about pops—they happen, but not often with this type of balloon.

3. Pinch off another three inches of balloon and twist. This will be one ear of your dog.

4. Fold the first two bubbles against the rest of the balloon. Squeeze the long segment against the twist of the two shorter segments. Keep a firm grip on all the bubbles at this point or they'll come undone. Twist the long bubble and the two short bubbles together. Now your critter has two ears and a nose.

5. Pinch off and twist three more inches for the neck, followed by three additional inches for one front leg.

6. Fold the long bubble over again and twist against the two new bubbles (another locking twist). Now you have two front legs.

7. Another three inches and a twist gives your dog a body. Squeeze and twist off three more.

8. Now give your canine one last locking twist with the rest of the balloon. You've got two hind legs, a tail, and finally, a dog!

CUSTOMIZE INSTRUCTION FOR UNIVERSAL ACCESS

For Gifted/Talented Students

Encourage each student to write a how-to essay explaining a hobby, activity, or process that he or she enjoys. For example, students might use the following topics: how to play a sport, how to play an instrument, how to sing in harmony, how to compose music, how to give a dramatic monologue, or how to paint with watercolors. Have students write their essays in the format of "Twist and Shout." Work with students to combine their completed essays into a booklet called "How to Do Almost Everything." Have one student make a table of contents, and have another student write an introduction. Display the anthology in your school or local library, where people can make copies of essays that interest them.

Check Your Comprehension

1. Which materials does Wincey suggest for creating your own balloon animals?
2. Why does the author say it is easy to create other balloon animals once you have completed one?
3. Why does the author include the note about making sure your balloons are uninflated?
4. What is a split or locking twist?

Applying the Reading Strategy

Identifying Cause-and-Effect Relationships

5. If you did not let air out of the balloon and you twisted it several times, what might be the effect?
6. What would be the effect of pinching off ten inches instead of three in Step 3?
7. Why do the steps have to be performed in order?

Activity

Balloon Animal Demonstration

Use what you have learned in the essay to give a demonstration in which you orally explain how to make balloon animals while you make one.

Comparing Informational Texts

How-to Essays and User's Guides

A user's guide is like a how-to essay for a specific product or piece of equipment. Find a user's guide and compare its format and contents to this how-to essay.

	How-to Essay	User's Guide
Purpose		
Contents		
Format or Presentation		

Answers for p. 693

Check Your Comprehension

1. Wincey suggests using long, thin balloons and a pump to make balloon animals.
2. The author says it is easy to make other balloon animals after you have completed one because once you understand the basic principle, you can apply it to other balloon animals.
3. The author says to underinflate the balloons to keep them from popping when they are twisted.
4. A split or locking twist is one that holds a folded-over part (such as a leg) in place by twisting it with another part of the animal (such as the other leg).

Applying the Reading Strategy

5. If you did not let air out of the balloon and you twisted it several times, it might pop.
6. If you pinch off ten inches instead of three inches in step 3, one of the dog's ears will be too long, and you will run out of balloon too soon.
7. If the steps are not performed in order, the dog might be poorly proportioned or might fall apart because the twists will not hold.

Activity

Encourage students to use their completed cause-and-effect charts when they are planning their oral presentations. The chart will remind them of the correct sequence of steps. Review with students proper speaking techniques, such as using a clear, strong voice and making eye contact with the audience.

continued

Answers continued

Comparing Informational Texts

How-to Essays and User's Guides: Help students brainstorm for user's guides for different types of products, such as computers, bicycles, microwaves, stereos, and games. Bring in copies of user's guides for students to use for their comparisons, or suggest that they bring in user's guides from their homes. Have students record their comparisons in a chart like the one on p. 693.

Lesson Objectives

1. To write a response to literature
2. To use writing strategies to generate ideas, and to plan, organize, evaluate, and revise the composition

Model From Literature

Point out that when students read *Grandpa and the Statue* (p. 664), they may have been surprised by how Grandpa Monaghan changed his mind about the Statue of Liberty. Their surprise is a response to the play. Tell students that they will be writing a more formal response to literature in this assignment.

Prewriting

- Divide the class into groups. Have students discuss works of literature that they have read in class or on their own. Suggest that they consult the table of contents in this book to help stimulate discussion.
- Point out the value of choosing for this assignment a work that students feel strongly about. Ask students why they might benefit from choosing such a work. Possible response: Students might suggest that they will benefit because their feelings will give them many ideas for the composition.
- Call students' attention to the pentad on p. 694. Discuss how using it can help students gather and organize information. Point out that in answering the questions on the pentad, students will analyze most of the topics within a story, and they will be able to determine what they want to emphasize in their responses.
- Before students draft their essays, have them review the Rubric for Self-Assessment (p. 697), so they know what is expected.

Writing WORKSHOP

Response to Literature

A **response to literature** is a work that expresses the writer's feelings and thoughts about what he or she has read—a book, short story, essay, article, or poem. Using examples from the literature, you can explain why you reacted to the work as you did. In this workshop, you will choose a piece of literature and write a response to it.

Assignment Criteria. Your response to literature should have the following characteristics:

- A clear organization, based on several clear ideas, premises, or images
- Your interpretation, based on careful reading, understanding, and insight
- Relevant examples and textual evidence that support and justify your interpretation
- A brief summary of important features of the literature
- Your own feelings or judgments about the literature

To see the criteria on which your response to literature may be assessed, see the Rubric on page 697.

Prewriting

Choose a topic. With a small group of readers, hold a round-table discussion of literary works you all have enjoyed. Each member should offer the title, author, and special qualities of a work. Jot down titles. Choose one of these works that you had a strong reaction to as the subject for your writing.

Use a pentad. To help you focus your topic, fill in a pentad like the one shown by answering these questions:

- **Actors**: Who performs the action?
- **Acts**: What is done?
- **Scenes**: When or where is it done?
- **Conditions**: How is it done?
- **Purposes**: Why is it done?

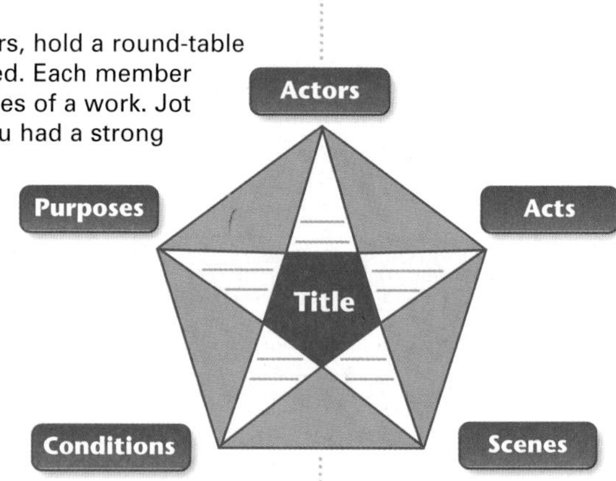

After answering the questions, highlight the most interesting points and choose your specific topic.

TEACHING RESOURCES

The following resources can be used to enrich or extend the instruction for pp. 694–697.

- **Writing and Grammar,** Copper Level, Chapter 12, pp. 246–271
- **Performance Assessment and Portfolio Management,** pp. 15, 57
- **Writing Models and Graphic Organizers on Transparencies,** p. 43

Writing and Grammar iText CD-ROM
Students can use the following tools as they complete their responses to literature:

- Pentad
- Sentence Openers Variety
- Transition Word Bin

Student Model

Before you begin drafting your response to literature, read this student model and review the characteristics of a successful response to literature.

Chris Harshfield
Louisville, Kentucky

Response to *Tuck Everlasting*

Imagine finding a way to stay young forever! That's what the characters in *Tuck Everlasting,* a novel by Natalie Babbit, do. The novel makes the idea especially interesting by presenting it in a story that makes a realistic situation out of a very unrealistic idea.

> In the introduction, the writer indicates what the focus of his response will be.

Winnie, the main character, meets a strange family, the Tucks. She soon discovers that they have a secret: All of them have drunk from a spring of water that makes them live forever. Because Winnie has a crush on Jesse, one of the Tucks, she is tempted to drink from the spring, too, when she is old enough to marry him. Based on things the characters say and do, we know that this will not be an easy decision for Winnie.

> Enough of a summary is given so that readers can understand the response that follows.

The theme of this story is not a new one, but the way it is presented is better than in other stories. Like most of the other writers, Babbit suggests that living forever is not a good idea. Unlike other stories I have read about this theme, however, *Tuck Everlasting* really convinced me by showing examples I could understand and by doing it with characters who seem like real people. Even though I know there is no spring like the one in the book, the book made it seem real enough to get me thinking about the problem Winnie faces.

> As identified in the introduction, the response is organized mainly around the theme.

> Here, the writer gives his interpretation of the theme and supports it with an example from the novel.

The final outcome of the story settles the question as far as Winnie is concerned. When Jesse returns years later, he finds her marker in the cemetery. Because she is dead, we know that she decided to not drink from the spring. The words on her marker suggest that she had a happy life, and that she got over Jesse. For Winnie, in any case, Mr. Tuck's words prove true: ". . .the stream keeps moving on, taking it all back again" (Babbit 31).

The questions that do not get answered left me a little disappointed. I would have preferred to know how Winnie reached her decision, not just what she decided. Overall, though, *Tuck Everlasting* tells a good story and raises interesting questions. In the end, Tuck gives the answer, "Life. Moving, growing, changing, never the same two minutes together" (Babbit 30).

> In the conclusion, the writer shares his own feelings and judgments. He finishes with a general impression and a quotation from the novel. The page number where the quotation is found is given in parentheses after the author's name.

CUSTOMIZE INSTRUCTION FOR UNIVERSAL ACCESS

For Less Proficient Writers	For English Learners	For Advanced Writers
Have students reread the introduction to the student essay. Point out the interest-grabbing first sentence and the way that the writer links the idea to the novel being discussed. In the last sentence of the paragraph, the writer states what will be proven in the evaluation. Challenge students to use a similar structure in their introductions.	Point out that the opening sentence in the student essay is an exclamation. Tell students that this punctuation mark shows surprise or alarm. Have students work with proficient readers to discern the difference in reading two sentences that are identical except that one ends in a period and the other in an exclamation point.	Encourage students to be creative with the openings of their essays. Tell them that the opening paragraph states a writer's final evaluation, but a good critical response also invites people to read on. Challenge them to experiment with their topics from interesting angles.

Student Model

- Explain that the student model is an excerpt, and that essays may be longer.
- Ask students what the first paragraph tells them about the writer's response to *Tuck Everlasting.*
  Answer: The writer liked the book, and the response will concentrate on how the author of the book made the plot believable.
- Have students read the second paragraph of the essay. Discuss whether the writer has included the proper amount of details for readers.
  Possible response: Enough details are included so that readers can understand the plot and decide whether they are interested in reading the book.
- Help students recall that the theme is the main idea or lesson in a book. Ask: What do you learn about the theme in the introduction? How is the theme used later in the composition?
  Answer: The theme of what happens when people stay young forever is introduced in the first paragraph. It is repeated in later paragraphs of the composition. The theme is used to organize the response, so the writer restates the theme and uses examples from the book to support his points.
- Have students read the conclusion. Ask them to comment on whether it is an effective conclusion.
  Possible responses: Some students may feel that the conclusion jumps around too much. Other students may feel that it is a balanced assessment of the novel.

Real-World Connection

Writing responses to literature in the real world: Point out to students that many jobs require employees to write responses to different types of literature. Businesses require their employees to evaluate resource books, reports, and other professional publications. Personnel directors often must evaluate and respond to résumés and letters of application. Discuss with students other jobs or job situations in which a response to literature might be needed, such as a writer reviewing a book for a magazine.

Drafting

- Explain to students that if they have used the pentad effectively, they should have several ideas that will be useful for their compositions.
- Point out to students that their writing will be stronger if everything in the composition points back to one idea. This idea should be expressed in the introduction, body, and conclusion of the composition.
- Discuss the necessity of a strong introduction to bring a reader into the composition. Reassure students that they do not need to polish the introduction before going on with the body and conclusion of the composition. They can change the introduction in the revision stage.
- Encourage students to arrange their ideas in an order that will make sense to the reader. Tell them that support for each point should usually be in the same paragraph as the interpretation.
- Discuss ways of making the conclusion as strong as the introduction. Again, note that students can improve the conclusion during the revision stage.
- Emphasize that interpretations contained in the essay must be backed up with evidence. Support can be in the form of quotations, plot summaries, or references to events in the story.

Revising

- Distribute colored pencils or markers for the color-coding exercise. Have students follow the directions to check the organization of their ideas. Use the revision sample to model color-coding.
- Have each student trade papers with a partner to see whether the ideas are clear and are organized in a logical fashion. Have partners make constructive suggestions for reorganizing each other's papers.
- As students are reading each other's papers, encourage them to mark places where additional support is needed to clarify or strengthen points. Students should then revisit these areas and add evidence to support their statements.

(continued on p. 697)

Drafting

Organize your interpretation. Your draft should develop around several clearly expressed ideas, premises, or images. A well-organized draft has these connected parts:

- **Introduction** that includes your brief summary and states your main idea about the literature
- **Body** that offers a variety of supporting evidence, including quotations, examples, and specific references to the text
- **Conclusion** that restates your interpretation and may include feelings or opinions about what you have read

Justify your interpretation. Elaborate on your general ideas by pushing yourself to go deeper to reach new insights. A sentence such as "This story is full of suspense" needs details to support it. Ask, "*Why* is it suspenseful?" or "*In what way* is it suspenseful?"

Revising

Revise your draft to make sure your ideas will be clearly organized.

Color-code related details. Reread what you have written. Circle each of your main points in a different color. Underline the sentences supporting each main point in the same color as the main point. Use the following suggestions for revision.

1. If a paragraph contains marks of a few different colors, revise by moving sentences to the paragraph they support.
2. If a sentence is neither circled nor underlined, delete it or use it in a new paragraph.

Model: Color-coding Details

The theme of this story is not a new one, but the way it is presented is better than in other stories. Many stories, folk tales, and books have been written about characters who want to live forever or end up living forever. Like most of the other writers, Babbit suggests that living forever is not a good idea. ~~Although at the end, we find out whether Winnie agrees, I was disappointed that some questions were not answered.~~ Unlike other stories I have read about this theme, however, *Tuck Everlasting* really convinced me by showing examples I could understand and by doing it with characters who seem like real people.

The sentence underlined in red was deleted here because it did not relate to the main point of the paragraph.

USING TECHNOLOGY IN WRITING

Have students identify the parts of their essays—introduction, body, and conclusion—using the highlight mode, boldface, or italics of a word-processing program. Tell them to read each part and make sure it follows the description on p. 696. Then, have students check to be sure that the parts of the essays are connected with smooth transitions. Brainstorm for a list of transitions that students might use. Then, allow them time to revise their essays as needed.

Students can also use the revision tools on the **Writing and Grammar iText CD-ROM.**

Add a quotation—or two. Go back to the text as you revise. Now that you have written your response, find quotations that leap out as good examples. Using the writer's exact words will strengthen your interpretation of the work.

Example: "The Geese" is an uplifting poem. When I read it, I felt my "earthbound soul take flight."

Compare the model and nonmodel. Why is the model more effective than the nonmodel?

Nonmodel	Model
Because she is dead, we know that she decided to not drink from the spring. The words on her marker suggest that she had a happy life, and that she got over Jesse.	Because she is dead, we know that she decided to not drink from the spring. The words on her marker suggest that she had a happy life, and that she got over Jesse. For Winnie, in any case, Mr. Tuck's words prove true: ". . .the stream keeps moving on, taking it all back again" (Babbit 31).

Publishing and Presenting

Choose one of these ways to share your writing with classmates or a larger audience.

Organize a Book Day. Arrange a day on which you and your classmates present your responses to literature and hold discussions about the works you have enjoyed.

Write a letter to an author. Turn your written response to a work into a letter to the author. Share your letter and any response you get to it with your classmates.

WG Prentice Hall Writing and Grammar Connection: Chapter 12.

Speaking Connection

To learn more about delivering a response to literature, see the **Listening and Speaking Workshop: Delivering an Oral Response to Literature,** p. 698.

Rubric for Self-Assessment

Evaluate your response to literature, using the following criteria and rating scale:

Criteria	Rating Scale Not very				Very
How clearly and logically organized is the response?	1	2	3	4	5
How well does the response express understanding and insight into the work?	1	2	3	4	5
How relevant and effective are the examples?	1	2	3	4	5
How well are the necessary points summarized?	1	2	3	4	5
How well does the response express the writer's feelings or judgments about the work?	1	2	3	4	5

TEST-TAKING TIP

When taking a test that includes a response to literature, students should be aware of the need to support their assertions with evidence from the text. Help students get into the habit of supplying evidence by telling them that for every assertion they make about a literary work, they must include evidence from the text to support the assertion. Review the different types of evidence that will support assertions, including quotations, references to specific incidents, and summaries of actions.

Revising (continued)

- Ask two volunteers to read aloud the model and the nonmodel. Then, ask students to discern the difference between the two and suggest why the model is more effective than the nonmodel. Answer: The model adds a quotation that helps the reader see the connection between the reader's interpretation and a specific part of the book.
- Allow students time to find quotations from the text that they can use to strengthen their responses.

Publishing and Presenting

- Ask students to consider an audience that would enjoy reading their literary responses.
- Encourage students to think of ways of presenting the responses to an audience. Consider inviting younger students to attend oral presentations of the responses or displaying written responses in the school library.
- If students wish to recast their responses as letters to authors, you may wish to contact your school or community librarian for suggestions on where to send the letters.

Assessment

- Review the assessment criteria in class.
- Before students continue with self-assessment, have them evaluate the Student Model on p. 695 using one or more of the criteria in the rubric. This will familiarize them with the rubric and its application. Have students work in small groups and explain their scoring to the class.
- The rubric on this page, and another rubric in an alternative format, can be found on pp. 15 and 57 of **Performance Assessment and Portfolio Management.**

Lesson Objectives

1. To develop an interpretation of a literary work
2. To prepare an oral response to literature based on the opinion
3. To deliver the response confidently

Develop an Interpretation

- Tell students that all responses to literature begin with students understanding what they have read. Impress upon students that good notes on the plot, characters, setting, and literary devices will help them develop a response.
- Help students clarify their ideas. Point out that a few well-developed ideas will be easier for listeners to understand than many ideas that lack support. Emphasize the need for being selective in choosing what to include.
- Remind students that this assignment centers on a literary work. Their opinions will be most easily supported with evidence from the text, including examples and quotations. If students are using quotations, remind them to choose short, direct quotations, and to have the exact quotation in their notes.

Deliver With Confidence

- Ask volunteers to model speaking with different tones, volume levels, and pacing to show the impact of these changes on listeners' interest in a presentation.
- Remind students to include vital information about the work they are responding to. Also, they should have a clear statement of their evaluation of the work at the beginning of the presentation.
- Coach students to take a deep breath before beginning their presentations and to consciously slow down their delivery.
- Challenge students to maintain eye contact with the audience, using notes only for main ideas and direct quotations.

Listening and Speaking WORKSHOP

Delivering an Oral Response to Literature

After you have read a literary work, you may be asked to deliver an **oral response to literature**. An oral response includes many of the characteristics of a successful written response. (To review response to literature, see the Writing Workshop, pp. 694–697.) The speaking strategies that follow will help you develop and deliver an organized response that your audience will appreciate. Use the checklist on this page to improve your performance.

Develop an Interpretation

The first step toward a successful oral response is to read carefully and thoughtfully to develop an interpretation.

Organize around clear ideas. Organize your response around a number of clear ideas, premises, or images. Do not try to cover everything. Your introduction should include your interpretation of the work. The body of the speech should support those ideas with good reasons. Conclude by restating your interpretation and voicing your opinion.

Use examples and textual evidence. To give your oral response credibility, pull out quotations and examples from the literature to support your response. Keep yourself focused on what the text has to say.

Deliver with Confidence

To deliver an effective response to literature, use speaking techniques such as tone, volume, and pacing to engage the audience and win them over to your interpretation of the literature.

Use a strong speaking voice. Speak clearly, confidently, and loudly enough to be heard by everyone. Include the title and author and mention where the work can be found in case your audience wants to read it, too.

Speak slowly. Too many speakers rush through their presentations because they are nervous and want the presentation to be over! Do not make this mistake. Speak slowly and enunciate clearly. You want your audience to hear every word. Do not be afraid to pause before reading a quotation or starting a new thought.

Activity: Videotape a review Suppose you have been asked to deliver a two- to three-minute review of a piece of literature to be broadcast on your local television station. With a partner, prepare and rehearse your review. While one of you speaks, the other should videotape. Then, exchange roles. Share your videotapes with your classmates.

Tips for Engaging the Audience

Show the work
Hold up the novel or the collection in which you read the work.

Read from the work
When reading a quotation or passage, read directly from the work. Use sticky notes to mark pages before the presentation.

Use props
Hold up an object mentioned in your presentation.

CUSTOMIZE INSTRUCTION FOR UNIVERSAL ACCESS

For Special Needs Students	For Less Proficient Readers
As students prepare their oral responses to literature, they may need help organizing their presentations. Have students work with graphic organizers from **Writing Models and Graphic Organizers on Transparencies,** such as the Main Idea and Supporting Details organizer on p. 73. They can use this chart to organize and develop the major points of the response. Model for students the use of the organizer.	Remind students that the success of their presentations depends on how they deliver them. Encourage students to practice their deliveries in a way that is comfortable for them. Some students may prefer practicing in front of a mirror; others may benefit from having a partner critique them. Another possibility is to have students record their presentations on audiocassettes or videocassettes. They can then review the tapes to find areas that need polishing.

Assessment WORKSHOP

Sentence Construction

The writing sections of some tests require you to read a passage and answer multiple-choice questions about sentence construction. Use the following strategies to help you answer such questions:

- **Recognize incomplete sentences and run-on sentences.** An incomplete sentence is lacking a subject or a predicate or both. It is not a complete thought. Run-on sentences are two or more sentences without the correct punctuation.
- **Combine sentences.** Sometimes two short, closely related sentences can be combined into one sentence. When you are given this option as a test-answer choice, make sure the answer you choose is a complete sentence. Look at the following sample test item:

Test-Taking Strategies

- Identify the problem in the underlined section before choosing a replacement.
- Proofread the replacement you choose to make sure new errors are not introduced.

Sample Test Item

Directions: Choose the best way to write the underlined section. If it needs no change, choose "Correct as is."

According to Thomas Edison, genius is one percent inspiration and ninety-nine percent perspiration. (1) By his own definition, he certainly qualified during his lifetime he patented 1,093 inventions.

A He certainly qualified by his own definition during his lifetime he patented 1,093 inventions.

B By his own definition, he certainly qualified. During his lifetime, he patented 1,093 inventions.

C By his own definition. He certainly qualified during his lifetime he patented 1,093 inventions.

D Correct as is

Answer and Explanation

A is a run-on sentence. **C** contains an incomplete sentence and a run-on sentence. ***B*** is correct. It turns a run-on sentence into two complete sentences.

Practice

Directions: Choose the best way to write the underlined section. If it needs no change, choose "Correct as is."

(1) Scientists have been studying bubbles. The bubbles were trapped in the Antarctic ice for thousands of years. Studies show a connection between the amount of carbon dioxide in the air and the temperature. (2) This is important for people today. Because the amount of carbon dioxide in the air is increasing yearly.

1. A Scientists have been studying Antarctic ice for thousands of years.

B Scientists have been in Antarctic ice for thousands of years.

C Bubbles were trapped in Antarctic ice.

D Correct as is

2. A This is important for people today because the amount of carbon dioxide in the air is increasing yearly.

B This is important. For people today because carbon dioxide is increasing yearly.

C This is important for people today the amount of carbon dioxide in the air increasing yearly.

D Correct as is

Lesson Objective

To identify and correct sentence construction in a test situation

Applying Reading Strategies

Explain to students that correcting incomplete sentences can help students clarify the facts presented in their writing.

Test-Taking Skills

- Have students read the sample item. Then, ask them to determine which option is the best way to write the underlined words. Some students may find it helpful to determine first which options are incorrect in order to rule them out.
- Review the answer with students. Make certain that they understand why *B* is the correct choice.
- Next, ask students to read the practice test items. Ask: What is the test item asking for?
  Answer: The test item is asking for the best way to rewrite the underlined words.
- Remind students to use the Test-Taking Strategies listed on p. 699 as they determine the answer to the question.

Answers

The correct answer for item 1 is *D*. Option A makes it sound as though the scientists have been studying the ice for thousands of years, and it does not mention the bubbles. Option *B* also distorts the meaning of the sentences, and option *C* tells only some of the ideas.

The correct answer for item 2 is *A*. Option *B* contains a fragment. Option *C* is a run-on sentence. Option *D* is incorrect because the original passage contains a fragment.

TEACHING RESOURCES

The following resources can be used to enrich or extend the instruction for p. 699.

PRENTICE HALL ASSESSMENT SYSTEM

- Workbook
- Skill Book
- Transparencies
- CD-ROM

Unit Objectives

1. To develop skill in reading poetry
2. To apply a variety of reading strategies, particularly strategies for reading poetry
3. To analyze literary elements
4. To use a variety of strategies to read unfamiliar words and to build vocabulary
5. To learn elements of grammar, usage, and style
6. To use recursive writing processes to write in a variety of forms
7. To develop listening and speaking skills
8. To express and support responses to various types of texts
9. To prepare, organize, and present literary interpretations

Meeting the Objectives

With each selection, you will find instructional materials through which students can meet these objectives. Further, you will find additional practice pages for reading strategies, literary analysis, vocabulary, and grammar in the **Selection Support: Skills Development Workbook** in your **Teaching Resources.**

Background

Art

Waves of Matsushima

Edo Period

Connect this eighteenth-century folding screen to the topic of poetry by asking the following question:

How is this screen like a poem?

Possible responses: It is a creative work of art that captures a beautiful image. The image can generate different feelings in different people who look at it, just as a poem can.

UNIT 9 Poetry

Waves of Matsushima, Endo period, early 18th century, six-panel folding screen, Korin Ogata, Courtesy, Museum of Fine Arts, Boston, MA

UNIT FEATURES

Connections	Reading Informational Material
Every unit contains a feature that connects literature to a related topic, such as art, science, or history. In this unit, students will compare the way two writers write about trees. Use the information and questions on the Connections page to enrich students' understanding of the selections presented within the unit.	These selections will help students learn to analyze and evaluate informational texts, such as workplace documents, technical directions, and consumer materials. They will expose students to the organization and features unique to nonnarrative texts. In this unit, students learn how to take notes on literary backgrounds and how to identify the main points of a comparison-and-contrast article.

Exploring the Genre

Poems can tell stories, describe natural events, and express feelings. Some poems are shaped to look like their subjects, and others follow strict patterns of rhyme, rhythm, or syllables. Through the use of images, or word pictures, poets paint vivid pictures for readers to see with their minds as well as their eyes. By reading poems, you can learn a new way to see something that you have looked at hundreds of times before.

As you read the poems in this unit, notice how the poets blend language and feeling to convey new ideas to you.

◀ **Critical Viewing** Which details in the painting seem poetic? **[Connect]**

ASSESSMENT RESOURCES

- **Selection Support: Skills Development Workbook**
- **Formal Assessment**
- **Open Book Tests**
- **Performance Assessment and Portfolio Management**
- **Extension Activities**

Assessing Student Progress

Listed below are the tools that are available to measure the degree to which students meet the unit objectives.

Informal Assessment

The questions in the Review and Assess sections are a first level of response to the concepts and skills presented within the selections. Students' responses are a brief, informal measure of their grasp of the material. These responses can indicate where further instruction and practice are needed. Follow up with the practice pages in the **Selection Support: Skills Development Workbook.**

Formal Assessment

The **Formal Assessment** booklet contains the Selection Tests and Unit Tests.

- Selection Tests measure comprehension and skills acquisition for each selection or group of selections.
- Each Unit Test provides students with thirty multiple-choice questions and five essay questions designed to assess students' knowledge of the literature and skills taught in the unit.

The **Open Book Tests** ask students to demonstrate their ability to synthesize and communicate information from selections or groups of selections.

To assess student writing, you will find rubrics and scoring models in the **Performance Assessment and Portfolio Management** booklet. In this booklet, you will also find scoring rubrics for listening and speaking activities.

Alternative Assessment

The **Extension Activities** booklet contains writing activities, listening and speaking activities, and research and technology activities that are appropriate for students with different ability levels. You may also use these activities as an alternative measurement of students' growth.

▶Critical Viewing

Answer: Like poetry, the artwork appeals to the senses—you can almost hear, smell, and feel the waves. The picture conveys a strong feeling of the artist's love of the sea.

Why Read Literature?

The "Why Read Literature?" page in each unit presents a list of possible purposes for reading. Each purpose for reading is connected to one or more of the selections in the unit. Good readers set a purpose before reading in order to help them read actively and focus on meaningful details.

Unit 9 introduces three purposes for reading. "Read for the Love of Literature" encourages students to read poems about a clever walrus, the resilience of a ginkgo tree, and riding a skateboard on an "asphalt sea." "Read to Be Entertained" suggests that two poets' silliness will provide students with amusement as well as insight. Students can even "Read for Information" when reading poems to learn facts and details about unfamiliar places.

How to Use This Page

- Tell students that before reading each selection in this unit, they should set a purpose for reading. This will help them read in an active and focused manner.
- Explain that reading the silly "The Walrus and the Carpenter" (p. 708) by Lewis Carroll, the evocative "April Rain Song" (p. 742) by Langston Hughes, and the action-packed "The Sidewalk Racer" (p. 718) by Lillian Morrison will increase students' appreciation of literature.
- As they read the limerick on p. 720 and Shel Silverstein's "Jimmy Jet and His TV Set" (p. 707), students will be entertained by word play and impossibly silly events.
- Students can even learn from poems. When they read Eve Merriam's "Simile: Willow and Ginkgo" (p. 740) and Emily Dickinson's "Fame Is a Bee" (p. 741), they will learn about the differences between two kinds of trees as well as the true meaning of fame.

Why Read Literature?

When you read poems, make sure you put your mind, your voice, and all of your senses to work to get the full meaning. Often, how words sound and look is just as important as what they mean. To help you understand and remember poems, set different purposes for your reading. Review the three purposes you might set before reading the poems in this unit.

1 Read for the love of literature.

Did you know that an adult walrus eats about 6,000 clams per day? For a humorous and imaginative spin on a scientific fact, read **"The Walrus and the Carpenter,"** page 708.

Some people think that the ginkgo is the hardest tree to destroy. In fact, a 350-year-old ginkgo survived the atom bomb that was dropped on Hiroshima, Japan, in 1945. Note the special qualities that poet Eve Merriam sees in the ginkgo when you read **"Simile: Willow and Ginkgo,"** page 740.

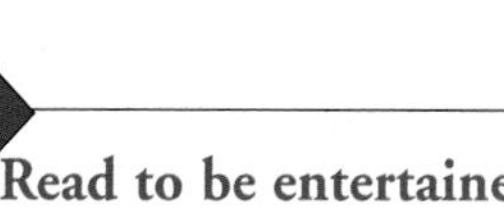

Imagine a poem that looks like a skateboard and makes you feel as if you are skateboarding on an "asphalt sea." Read Lillian Morrison's **"The Sidewalk Racer"** for its look and its feeling, page 718.

2 Read to be entertained.

The first limericks, written in the 1820s, were part of a collection called *Book of Nonsense.* It was a perfect name, since limericks are supposed to be fun and even silly. Read **"Limerick"** to see how the poet mixes funny ideas with plays on words, page 720.

Did you know that your brain is more active when it is asleep than when it is awake but watching television? It's true! Read how TV affects a little boy in **"Jimmy Jet and His TV Set,"** page 707.

3 Read for information.

Shakespeare lived in a world of danger, excitement, and change. Learn details about Shakespeare's world when you read **"Shakespeare's London,"** page 735.

You may think from its name that the Dead Sea is a sea, but did you know that it is actually a lake? To learn more about the Dead Sea, read **"More Than a Pinch,"** page 749.

Take It to the Net

Visit the Web site for online instruction and activities related to each selection in this unit.

www.phschool.com

ENRICHMENT: Further Reading

Have students choose one or more of the works below to extend the unit theme "Poetry" or to read more by the unit authors.

Cricket Songs: Japanese Haiku translated by Harry Behn

This is a classic collection of Japanese haiku.

I'm Nobody! Who Are You? Poems of Emily Dickinson for Children by Emily Dickinson

Most of Dickinson's poems were not published or even discovered until after her death.

The Dream Keeper and Other Poems by Langston Hughes

These poems for children were originally published in 1932.

How Pleasant to Know Mr. Lear! by Edward Lear

This is a collection of nonsense verse with the author's own illustrations.

Poem Stew by William Cole

This is a book of comical poems about food and eating.

How to Read Literature

Strategies for Reading Poetry

In a poem, even plain, everyday words seem to stand out and mean more than they usually do in other types of writing. The unique arrangements and combinations of words can, at times, seem like unfamiliar territory. The following strategies that you will learn in this unit will help you understand the poetry you read.

1. Identify the speaker.

The voice that "says" a poem is its speaker, but the speaker is not necessarily the poet. Sometimes, the poet takes on an imaginary voice to describe what is going on. In this unit, you will learn to recognize the speaker of a poem.

Poet's words

The willow is sleek as a velvet-nosed calf;

The ginkgo is leathery as an old bull.

—from "Simile: Willow and Ginkgo"

My words

A willow is smooth and soft to the touch.

A ginkgo is tough and rough feeling.

2. Use your senses.

Poets often include details that appeal to your five senses—sight, hearing, smell, touch, or taste. To get the full meaning of a poem, put all of your senses to work to help you paint a mental picture of what the poet is describing. To which of your senses do the following lines appeal?

A frog jumps into the pond,
Splash! Silence again.
—from "Haiku"

3. Read lines according to punctuation.

Do not sound like a stiff computer voice by automatically stopping after each line. Keep going when a line has no punctuation mark at the end. Pause at commas and semicolons; stop longer at end marks. In this unit, you will practice using reading clues provided by punctuation. Look at the punctuation in the lines to the right:

Cockades at every horse's head — Keep going.
Will nod, and riders dressed in red — Pause. / Keep going.
Or blue trot by. — Stop.

—from "Parade"

4. Paraphrase the lines.

If you are unsure of a poem's meaning, you may want to restate a line or a passage in your own words to help you understand it. Notice the example above.

As you read the selections in this unit, review the strategies for reading poetry and look at the examples. Use the suggestions to help you understand the text.

How to Read Literature

The "How to Read Literature" page in each unit presents a set of strategies to help readers understand authors' words and ideas. Each reading strategy is taught in conjunction with one or more of the selections within the unit. Good readers develop a bank of strategies from which they can draw as needed.

Unit 9 introduces four strategies for reading poetry. To understand a poem fully, students must enter the poem and get a sense of its speaker and what is happening. The strategies on this page will help readers examine a poem.

How to Use This Page

Introduce the strategies for reading poetry, presenting each as a tool for developing understanding when reading the selections in this unit.

- As students read the poems "The Geese," "Jimmy Jet and His TV Set," and "The Walrus and the Carpenter" (pp. 706–712), they will need to figure out who is speaking and what are his or her characteristics.
- As students read "The Sidewalk Racer," "Haiku," and "Limerick" (pp. 718–720), they will identify which of their five senses are engaged by the poems.
- As students read "Wind and water and stone," "February Twilight," "The Fairies' Lullaby," "Cynthia in the Snow," and "Parade" (pp. 726–730), they will learn to read a poem according to its punctuation, rather than line by line.
- As students read "Simile: Willow and Ginkgo," "Fame Is a Bee," and "April Rain Song" (pp. 740–742), they will learn how to restate poems in their own words.

MODEL A READING STRATEGY: Read Lines According to Punctuation

The unpredictable punctuation included in many poems, as well as the practice of beginning each line of many poems with a capital letter, may cause some students to get lost when they read. Show students the places in the poem "February Twilight" (p. 727) that should have longer pauses. Point out not only the end marks but also the dash at the end of line 6. Then, point out places where no pause is indicated, such as the ends of lines 1, 3, 5, and 7. Explain that a reader should not pause at the ends of these lines because there is no punctuation. Finally, model how to pay close attention to the punctuation in the poem by reading the poem aloud for the class. After you read, you may want to point out that careful attention to punctuation not only helps clarify the meaning of a poem but also helps bring the beauty and rhythm of a poem to life.

The Geese ✦ Jimmy Jet and His TV Set ✦ The Walrus and the Carpenter

Lesson Objectives

1. **To analyze and respond to literary elements**
   - Literary Analysis: Narrative and Lyric Poetry
   - Comparing Literary Works
2. **To read, comprehend, analyze, and critique three poems**
   - Reading Strategy: Identifying the Speaker
   - Reading Check Questions
   - Review and Assess Questions
3. **To develop word analysis skills, fluency, and systematic vocabulary**
   - Vocabulary Development Lesson: Concept Development: Using Multiple Meanings
4. **To understand and apply written and oral language conventions**
   - Spelling Strategy
   - Grammar Lesson: Comparisons with Adjectives and Adverbs
   - Assessment Practice (ATE)
5. **To understand and apply appropriate writing and research strategies**
   - Writing Lesson: Story With Dialogue
   - Extension Activity: Invention of the Television
   - Extension Activity: Literary Response
6. **To understand and apply listening and speaking strategies**
   - Extension Activity: Persuasive Presentation

STEP-BY-STEP TEACHING GUIDE	PACING GUIDE
PRETEACH	
Motivate Students and Provide Background	
Use the Motivation activity (ATE p. 704)	5 min.
Read and discuss the Preview material and Background information (SE/ATE p. 704) [A]	10 min.
Introduce the Concepts	
Introduce the Literary Analysis and Reading Strategy (SE/ATE p. 705) [A]	15 min.
Pronounce the vocabulary words and read their definitions (SE p. 705)	5 min.
TEACH	
Monitor Comprehension	
Informally monitor comprehension by circulating while students read independently or in groups [A]	10 min.
Monitor students' comprehension with the Reading Check notes (SE/ATE pp. 709, 711)	as students read
Develop vocabulary with Vocabulary notes (SE pp. 707, 709; ATE p. 709)	as students read
Develop Understanding	
Develop students' understanding of narrative and lyric poetry with the Literary Analysis annotations (SE pp. 709, 711; ATE pp. 709, 711) [A]	5 min.
Develop students' ability to identify the speaker in the poem with the Reading Strategy annotations (SE p. 710; ATE pp. 707, 710)	5 min.
ASSESS	
Assess Mastery	
Assess students' mastery of the Reading Strategy and Literary Analysis by having them answer the Review and Assess questions (SE/ATE p. 713)	25 min.
Use one or more of the print and media Assessment Resources (ATE p. 715) [A]	up to 45 min.
EXTEND	
Apply Understanding	
Have students complete the Vocabulary Development Lesson and the Grammar Lesson (SE p. 714) [A]	20 min.
Apply students' ability to write a story with dialogue using the Writing Lesson (SE/ATE p. 715) [A]	30–45 min.
Apply students' understanding using one or more of the Extension Activities (SE p. 715)	20–90 min.

ACCELERATED INSTRUCTION:
Use the strategies and activities identified with an [A].

UNIVERSAL ACCESS
● = Below Level Students
▲ = On-Level Students
■ = Above Level Students

Time and Resource Manager

Reading Level: Average, Average, Average
Average Number of Instructional Days: 3

RESOURCES		
PRINT	**TRANSPARENCIES**	**TECHNOLOGY**
• **Beyond Literature,** Cross-Curricular Connection: Science, p. 38 ▲ ■		• **Interest Grabber Videotapes,** Tape 5 ● ▲ ■
• **Selection Support Workbook:** ● ▲ ■ Literary Analysis, p. 190 Reading Strategy, p. 189 Build Vocabulary, p. 186	• **Literary Analysis and Reading Transparencies,** pp. 75 and 76 ● ▲ ■	
• **Adapted Reader's Companion** ● • **Reader's Companion** ● • **Authors In Depth,** Copper Level, p. 174 ■		• **Listening to Literature** ● ▲ ■ Audiocassettes, Side 25 Audio CDs, CD 13
• **English Learner's Companion** ● ▲ • **Literary Analysis for Enrichment** ■	• **Fine Art Transparencies, Volume 1,** Transparency 12 ● ▲ ■	
• **Formal Assessment:** Selection Test, pp. 176–178 ● ▲ ■ • **Open Book Test,** pp. 112–114 ● ▲ ■ • **Performance Assessment and Portfolio Management,** pp. 13, 27 ● ▲ ■ • PRENTICE HALL ASSESSMENT SYSTEM ● ▲ ■	• PRENTICE HALL ASSESSMENT SYSTEM ● ▲ ■ Skills Practice Answers and Explanations on Transparencies	• **Test Bank Software** ● ▲ ■ • **Got It! Assessment Videotapes,** Tape 5 ● ▲
• **Selection Support Workbook:** ● ▲ ■ Build Spelling Skills, p. 187 Build Grammar Skills, p. 188 • **Writing and Grammar,** Copper Level ● ▲ ■ • **Extension Activities,** p. 38 ● ▲ ■	• **Daily Language Practice Transparencies** ● ▲ • **Writing Models and Graphic Organizers on Transparencies** ● ▲ ■	• **Writing and Grammar iText CD-ROM** ● ▲ ■ ***Take It to the Net*** www.phschool.com

BLOCK SCHEDULING: Use one 90-minute class period to preteach the selection and have students read it. Use a second 90-minute class period to assess students' mastery of skills and have them complete one of the Extension Activities.

PRETEACH

Step-by-Step Teaching Guide for pp. 704–705

Motivation

Before students read the selections, ask them to spend a few moments remembering an experience they have had outdoors that left them with a strong feeling. Offer them a few examples, such as feeling warm, sleepy, and content while sitting in the sun. Tell students to jot down vivid details from their experiences and then write brief journal entries about their experiences. Encourage each interested student to write a poem that captures the feeling he or she wants to express.

Interest Grabber Video

As an alternative, play "Reading and Student Response" on Tape 5 to engage student interest.

❶ Background

Music

Lyric poetry, like the poem "The Geese," was popular in ancient Greece. The Greeks were the first people to create myths and accompany them on lyre, but they were not the first people to use the lyre. They believed that the instrument was invented by the messenger god Hermes, who used the shell of a tortoise and the horns of an antelope to create the lyre's sound box and arms. The Greeks strung their lyres with eleven strings and played them by plucking some strings while holding down, or damping, the others.

Prepare to Read

❶ The Geese ◆ Jimmy Jet and His TV Set ◆ The Walrus and the Carpenter

Take It to the Net

Visit www.phschool.com for interactive activities and instruction related to these selections, including

- background
- graphic organizers
- literary elements
- reading strategies

Preview

Connecting to the Literature

You probably use different tones of voice to express humor, sadness, and other thoughts and feelings. The poems in this section have distinctly different voices too. In "The Walrus and the Carpenter" and "Jimmy Jet and His TV Set," the poets Lewis Carroll and Shel Silverstein sound like stand-up comics. In "The Geese," Richard Peck sounds more like the singer of a sad ballad. Listen to these different voices as you read.

Background

The poem "The Geese" is a lyric poem. The word *lyric* comes from the word *lyre*, the name of a stringed instrument. This instrument was used in ancient Greece to accompany poets as they performed their poetry.

TEACHING RESOURCES

The following resources can be used to enrich or extend the instruction for pp. 704–705.

Motivation

Interest Grabber Video, Tape 5

Background

Beyond Literature, p. 38

 **_Take It to the Net_**

Visit www.phschool.com for Background and hotlinks for the selections.

Literary Analysis

Literary Analysis and Reading Transparencies, Narrative and Lyric Poetry, p. 76

Reading

Selection Support: Reading Strategy, p. 189; Build Vocabulary, p. 186

Literary Analysis and Reading Transparencies, Identifying the Speaker, p. 75

BLOCK SCHEDULING: Resources marked with this symbol provide varied instruction during 90-minute blocks.

❷ Literary Analysis

Narrative and Lyric Poetry

Narrative poetry tells a story in verse. "The Walrus and the Carpenter" and "Jimmy Jet and His TV Set" are narrative poems. Notice how the following lines from "The Walrus and the Carpenter" suggest the beginning of a story.

"O Oysters, come and walk with us!"
The Walrus did beseech.

In contrast, **lyric poetry** is highly musical verse that expresses a speaker's personal thoughts and feelings. A lyric poem usually focuses on a single powerful emotion, event, or image. "The Geese" is a lyric poem.

Comparing Literary Works

Each of these poems has a regular **rhythm,** or pattern of beats. The chart shows how to mark accented and unaccented syllables to discover the pattern of beats. Although all three of the poems have a regular rhythm, the rhythm is not the same in all three poems. Compare and contrast the rhythms of the poems by answering the following focus questions:

1. In which two poems does the rhythm go back and forth between a line with four beats and a line with three beats?
2. In what three ways are these two poems different from the third poem in the group?

Accented ´ Unaccented ˘
O Oysters come and walk with us (4)
The Walrus did beseech. (3)

❸ Reading Strategy

Identifying the Speaker

The imaginary voice you hear when you read a poem is the **speaker.** The speaker can be, but is not always, the same "person" as the poet. When you read a poem, think about what the word choice, details, and language level suggest about the age, personality, and outlook of the speaker.

Vocabulary Development

lean (lēn) *adj.* thin (p. 707)

antennae (an ten´ ē) *n.* metal rods that receive TV or radio signals (p. 707)

beseech (bi sēch´) *v.* beg (p. 709)

❷ Literary Analysis

Narrative and Lyric Poetry

- Before students read, ask them what they already know about narratives and lyrics. Explain that a poem can tell a series of events, as a story does, and that a poem can express ideas in a musical fashion, as a song does.
- Next, have students read the instruction on p. 705 to themselves. Spend a moment explaining the concepts of rhyme and rhythm that are discussed in the Comparing Literary Works feature. Demonstrate how to use the graphic organizer by filling in rhymes from a familiar nursery rhyme or song.
- Also, use the Narrative and Lyric Poetry transparency on p. 76 of **Literary Analysis and Reading Transparencies** to show students the elements of a narrative poem.

❸ Reading Strategy

Identifying the Speaker

- Have a volunteer read aloud the instruction on p. 705.
- Then, show students the Identifying the Speaker in a Poem transparency on p. 75 of **Literary Analysis and Reading Transparencies**. The transparency offers several key questions that will help students identify the speakers of the poems in this grouping.

Vocabulary Development

- Review the words and definitions on the vocabulary list.
- Point out the word *lean* and with students generate a bank of synonyms.
  Possible responses: skinny, thin, gaunt, emaciated.
- For each one, determine whether the word has positive or negative connotations or feelings associated with it.

CUSTOMIZE INSTRUCTION FOR UNIVERSAL ACCESS

For Special Needs Students	For Less Proficient Readers	For English Learners
Have students read the adapted version of "The Walrus and the Carpenter" in the **Adapted Reader's Companion.** This version provides basic-level instruction in an interactive format with questions and write-on lines. Completing the adapted version will prepare students to read the selection in the Student Edition.	Have students read "The Walrus and the Carpenter" in the **Reader's Companion.** This version provides basic-level instruction in an interactive format with questions and write-on lines. After students finish the selection in the Reader's Companion, have them complete the questions and activities in the Student Edition.	Have students read the adapted version of "The Walrus and the Carpenter" in the **English Learner's Companion.** This version provides basic-level instruction in an interactive format with questions and write-on lines. Completing the adapted version will prepare students to read the selection in the Student Edition.

E-Teach

Visit E-Teach at www.phschool.com for teachers' essays on how to teach, with questions and answers.

TEACH

Step-by-Step Teaching Guide for pp. 706–712

CUSTOMIZE INSTRUCTION For Musical/Rhythmic Learners

The poems in this selection have very regular rhythms and short stanzas that lend themselves to musical interpretation. Encourage students to imagine what kind of simple melodies would go with the poems as they read. Alternatively, have students pick a favorite song and imagine singing or speaking the poems over the melody or rhythm of the song.

❶ About the Selections

The speaker in Richard Peck's poem "The Geese," on p. 706, describes his or her father's reaction to the migration of geese each fall. The father is reminded of the long passage of the years and his own longing for things far away.

In "Jimmy Jet and His TV Set" (p. 707), Shel Silverstein tells a humorous story about a boy who watches so much television that he becomes transformed into one.

❷ ▶Critical Viewing

Answer: The geese may be migrating, which means that the seasons are changing and time is passing. Thinking about the passage of time might cause someone to remember events from the past or dream of events in the future.

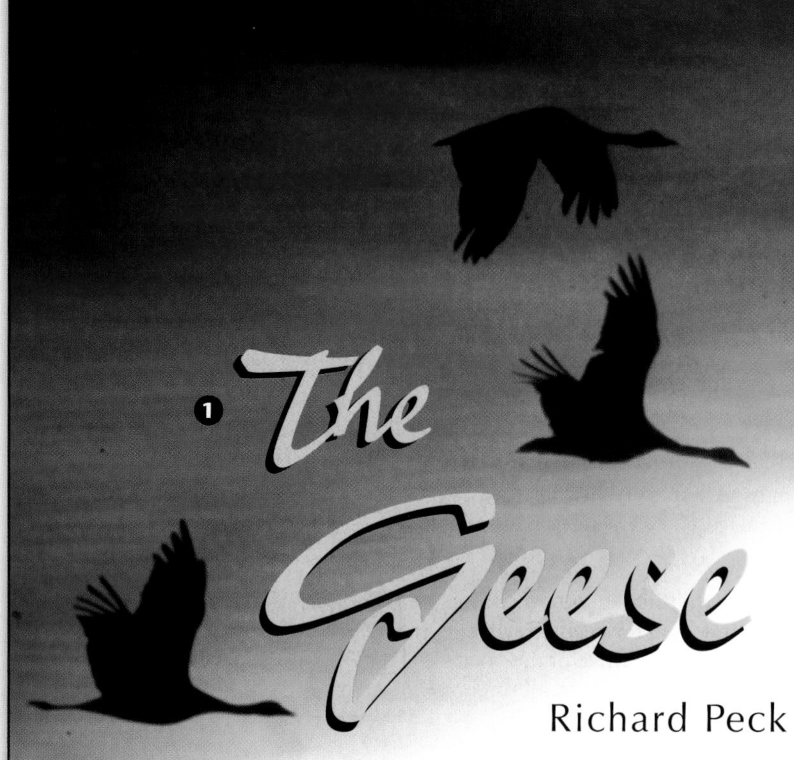

❶ # The Geese

Richard Peck

❷ ▲Critical Viewing Why might a sight like this one cause someone to think of the past or the future? **[Infer]**

❸

My father was the first to hear
The passage of the geese each fall,
Passing above the house so near
He'd hear within his heart their call.

And then at breakfast time he'd say:
"The geese were heading south last night,"
For he had lain awake till day,
Feeling his earthbound soul take flight.

Knowing that winter's wind comes soon
After the rushing of those wings,
Seeing them pass before the moon,
Recalling the lure of faroff things.

Richard Peck

(b. 1934)

Born in Illinois, Richard Peck grew up listening to dramas and stories presented on the radio, which stimulated his imagination. Peck has written poetry and won awards for some of his many young-adult novels, which include *Ghosts I Have Been*, *Secrets of the Shopping Mall*, and *The Last Safe Place on Earth*.

TEACHING RESOURCES

The following resources can be used to enrich or extend the instruction for pp. 706–712.

Literary Analysis
- **Selection Support:** Literary Analysis, p. 190
- **Literary Analysis for Enrichment** ▦
- **Writing Models and Graphic Organizers on Transparencies,** pp. 69, 89, 93

Reading
- **Reader's Companion**
- **Adapted Reader's Companion**
- **English Learner's Companion**

- **Listening to Literature Audiocassettes,** Side 25
- **Listening to Literature Audio CDs,** CD 13

Enrichment
- **Fine Art Transparencies, Volume 1,** Art Transparency 12 (Have students compare and contrast the transparency with the illustration in the book. Discuss how both tell a story.) ▦
- **Authors In Depth,** Copper Level, p. 174 (The collection includes two additional selections by Lewis Carroll for extended reading.) ▦

▦ **BLOCK SCHEDULING:** Resources marked with this symbol provide varied instruction during 90-minute blocks.

Jimmy Jet and His TV Set

SHEL SILVERSTEIN

I'll tell you the story of Jimmy Jet—
And you know what I tell you is true.
He loved to watch his TV set
Almost as much as you.

He watched all day, he watched all night
Till he grew pale and lean,
From *The Early Show* to *The Late Late Show*
And all the shows between.

He watched till his eyes were frozen wide,
And his bottom grew into his chair.
And his chin turned into a tuning dial,
And antennae grew out of his hair.

And his brains turned into TV tubes,
And his face to a TV screen.
And two knobs saying "VERT." and "HORIZ."
Grew where his ears had been.

And he grew a plug that looked like a tail
So we plugged in little Jim.
And now instead of him watching TV
We all sit around and watch him.

lean (lēn) *adj.* thin

antennae (an ten′ ē) *n.* metal rods that receive TV or radio signals

Shel Silverstein

(1932–1999) Chicago-born Shel Silverstein was a talented poet, cartoonist, playwright, and songwriter. His tremendously popular poetry collections, *Where the Sidewalk Ends* and *A Light in the Attic*, show Silverstein's imaginative sense of humor, which both children and adults enjoy. He also wrote the classic children's book *The Giving Tree*.

Review and Assess

Thinking About the Selections

1. **Respond:** Have you ever felt "the lure of faroff things"? Explain your answer.
2. **(a) Recall:** Why does the father lie awake all night in "The Geese"? **(b) Infer:** Why do the sounds of geese going south have a strong effect on him? **(c) Relate:** Describe something in the change of seasons that, for you, brings certain memories or feelings.
3. **(a) Recall:** Describe Jimmy's TV-watching habits.
   (b) Interpret: What is funny about what happens to Jimmy?
   (c) Draw Conclusions: What is the poet saying about the effects of watching television?

CUSTOMIZE INSTRUCTION FOR UNIVERSAL ACCESS

For Less Proficient Readers	For English Learners
Students may be confused by the abstract aspects of "The Geese." First, show how the poet used the rhyme scheme and the rhythm, or beat, to make the poem very regular. Then, ask students to paraphrase the poem by retelling it in their own words to a partner. Ask students to comment on how their version sounds different from the poet's version.	Students may notice that "The Geese" uses several gerunds and participles. Have students make a list of all the *-ing* words. Students should identify *passing, heading, feeling, knowing, rushing, seeing,* and *recalling.* Explain that the *-ing* ending suggests something that is still happening or an action that is not complete. Ask students to talk about how this sense of incompleteness correlates with the tone of the poem.

❸ Reading Strategy

Identifying the Speaker

- After students read the first stanza of "The Geese," ask them what they know about the poem. Answer: Students should notice that the poem is set in the fall and that the speaker's father heard the geese passing.
- Next, ask students what they know about the speaker of the poem. Answer: Students should figure out that the speaker has a father who lives in a northern climate where geese fly over his house.
- Finally, help students realize that the word *my* is the only clue to the identity of the speaker—he or she is the son or daughter of the subject of the poem.

Answers for p. 707

Review and Assess

1. Possible responses: Students may say that they dream about traveling to a distant place or doing something adventuresome; others may mention places or people they miss.
2. **(a)** The father lies awake all night because he hears geese flying overhead. **(b)** The sounds of the geese seem to remind the father of time passing and slipping away. **(c)** Possible responses: Students may suggest that the change of summer to fall fills them with feelings of regret about the end of the summer and excitement about the start of a new school year.
3. **(a)** Jimmy Jet watches television all day and all night. **(b)** Jimmy's transformation is funny because it is something that could never happen in real life and because of the way the poet describes the details, such as the plug that looked like a tail. **(c)** The poet seems to suggest that watching too much television can have harmful effects.

❹ About the Selection

In "The Walrus and the Carpenter," Lewis Carroll combines nonsense and narrative to tell how a walrus tricks some young oysters into taking a walk with him and his companion, the Carpenter. In the end, the Walrus and the Carpenter eat the trusting oysters.

❺ ▶Critical Viewing

Answer: The Walrus is wearing clothes and looks like a proud but silly gentleman. The Carpenter's face is exaggerated; his head is too big and his nose seems to be stretching out to smell the Oysters. The Oysters have legs and are wearing shoes.

❹ The Walrus and the Carpenter

Lewis Carroll

From *Alice Through the Looking Glass* by Lewis Carroll, Illustration by John Tenniel

❺ ▲ Critical Viewing How does the picture help you predict that this poem will be funny? **[Connect]**

CUSTOMIZE INSTRUCTION FOR UNIVERSAL ACCESS

For Advanced Readers

Suggest that students read additional works by Lewis Carroll. Provide students with the titles listed in the Enrichment box, ATE p. 713. You may also wish to use **Authors In Depth,** Copper Level, which contains the following selections:

- "Down the Rabbit-hole" and "The Pool of Tears" from *Alice's Adventures in Wonderland* (fiction, p 174)
- "Humpty Dumpty" from *Through the Looking-Glass* (fiction, p. 183)

After students have read these or other works by Carroll, have them form discussion groups in which they compare and contrast the selections they have read. Suggest criteria for comparison, such as setting, theme, and characters. To extend the activity, have volunteers present to the class brief oral reports on their favorite Carroll selections.

The sun was shining on the sea,
Shining with all his might:
He did his very best to make
The billows smooth and bright—
And this was odd, because it was
The middle of the night.

The moon was shining sulkily,
Because she thought the sun
Had got no business to be there
After the day was done—
"It's very rude of him," she said,
"To come and spoil the fun!"

6 The sea was wet as wet could be,
The sands were dry as dry.
You could not see a cloud, because
No cloud was in the sky:
No birds were flying overhead—
There were no birds to fly.

Literary Analysis
Narrative and Lyric Poetry, Rhyme, and Rhythm
How many lines in each stanza, or group of lines, rhyme with one another?

The Walrus and the Carpenter
Were walking close at hand:
They wept like anything to see
Such quantities of sand:
"If this were only cleared away,"
They said, "it would be grand!"

"If seven maids with seven mops
Swept it for half a year,
Do you suppose," the Walrus said,
"That they could get it clear?"
7 "I doubt it," said the Carpenter,
And shed a bitter tear.

"O Oysters, come and walk with us!"
The Walrus did beseech.
"A pleasant walk, a pleasant talk,
Along the briny beach:
We cannot do with more than four,
To give a hand to each."

beseech (bi sēch′) *v.* beg

8 **Reading Check**
With whom do the Walrus and Carpenter want to walk?

6 Literary Analysis

Narrative and Lyric Poetry, Rhyme, and Rhythm

- You may wish to read a stanza or two aloud so that students can hear how the line breaks do not interrupt the flow of the words.
- After reading, pose the Literary Analysis question on p. 709: How many lines in each stanza, or group of lines, rhyme with one another?
  Answer: Three lines (the second, fourth, and sixth lines) in each stanza rhyme with one another.
- You may wish to introduce or review the concept of rhythm by having students tap quietly on their desks in time with the poem. Students should understand that the rhythm of the poem alternates between lines of four beats and three beats.

7 Vocabulary Development

Using Multiple Meanings

- Tell students that some words, such as *shed,* have more than one meaning.
- Ask students to define *shed* in this context, and encourage them to think of another meaning.
  Answer: *Shed* can mean "to let something, such as a tear, fall or drop." It can also mean "a small storage building."

8 Reading Check

Answer: The Walrus and the Carpenter want to walk with the Oysters.

CUSTOMIZE INSTRUCTION FOR UNIVERSAL ACCESS

For Special Needs Students	For Less Proficient Readers
Students may be distracted by the nonsensical aspects of the poem "The Walrus and the Carpenter." Remind students that the poem is a narrative; it tells a story. Offer them a Series of Events Chain organizer, like the one on p. 69 of **Writing Models and Graphic Organizers on Transparencies.** Have students work in pairs to identify each event in the poem. When they have completed the diagram, ask them to retell the story to a partner, event by event.	Students may be confused by the nonsensical details in "The Walrus and the Carpenter." Help them find a focus by suggesting that they consider the motives of the characters. Offer students an Open Mind diagram, like the one on p. 93 of **Writing Models and Graphic Organizers on Transparencies.** Tell students to select a character from the poem and to put the character's name on the diagram. Then, have students fill in the diagram with words, symbols, and images that convey the thoughts, wishes, and motives of the character.

9 Background

Art

Illustration from *Alice Through the Looking Glass,* John Tenniel

John Tenniel was well known in nineteenth-century England as a humorist and illustrator. His specialty was caricature, a type of drawing that exaggerates natural features and makes subjects look silly or ridiculous. Discuss the following question:

Do you think this caricature is effective in portraying these characters? Why or why not?
Possible response: Students may say that the Carpenter is grumpy in this picture and grumpy in the story, and the Walrus is holding up a handkerchief to dry his tears as he gobbles up the oysters.

10 ▶Critical Viewing

Answer: The empty oyster shells lying on the ground indicate that the oysters have been eaten. The Walrus is greedily slurping down an oyster, while the Carpenter looks at him shocked and unhappy. Perhaps the Walrus has eaten more than his share of oysters.

11 Reading Strategy

Identifying the Speaker

- Before asking the Reading Strategy question on p. 710, talk with students about the speaker of the poem. What do students already know about him or her?
  Answer: Students should point out that they know that the speaker is not in the poem and has a sense of humor.
- Next, ask the Reading Strategy question.
  Answer: The speaker's humorous comment reveals a wild imagination that provides oysters with clothes, faces, hair, and feet.

9

From *Alice Through the Looking Glass* by Lewis Carroll, Illustration by John Tenniel

10 ▲ **Critical Viewing** Explain how this picture tells a story by itself. **[Interpret]**

The eldest Oyster looked at him,
    But never a word he said:
The eldest Oyster winked his eye,
    And shook his heavy head—
Meaning to say he did not choose
    To leave the oyster-bed.

But four young Oysters hurried up,
    All eager for this treat:
11 Their coats were brushed, their faces
    washed,
    Their shoes were clean and neat—
And this was odd, because, you know,
    They hadn't any feet.

Four other Oysters followed them,
    And yet another four;
And thick and fast they came at last,
    And more, and more, and more—
All hopping through the frothy waves,
    And scrambling to the shore.

Reading Strategy
Identifying the Speaker
What does this humorous comment reveal about the speaker's personality?

CUSTOMIZE INSTRUCTION FOR UNIVERSAL ACCESS

For Gifted/Talented Students	For Advanced Readers
Suggest that students recast one of the narrative poems as lyrical, or vice versa. Invite students either to find a thoughtful moment in one of the narrative poems and write a short poem about it or to invent plot, characters, and dialogue to expand the lyrical poem. Students can borrow language from the original poems, but they should try to make the poems their own. Have students read their poems to the class, and ask listeners to comment on how effective the changes were.	Challenge students to rewrite "The Walrus and the Carpenter" from the point of view of one of the characters: the Walrus, the Carpenter, the Oysters, or even the moon. Encourage students to brainstorm for a list of qualities of their chosen speaker before they begin to write. Students should cover the same events and include the same dialogue but change the perspective to that of the one who is speaking. Have students read their poems to the class. Invite listeners to respond to the changes.

⓬

The Walrus and the Carpenter
Walked on a mile or so,
And then they rested on a rock
Conveniently low:
And all the little Oysters stood
And waited in a row.

"The time has come," the Walrus said,
"To talk of many things:
Of shoes—and ships—and sealing wax—
Of cabbages—and kings—
And why the sea is boiling hot—
And whether pigs have wings."

"But wait a bit," the Oysters cried,
"Before we have our chat;
For some of us are out of breath,
And all of us are fat!"
"No hurry!" said the Carpenter.
They thanked him much for that.

"A loaf of bread," the Walrus said,
"Is what we chiefly need:
Pepper and vinegar besides
Are very good indeed—
Now, if you're ready, Oysters dear,
We can begin to feed."

"But not on us!" the Oysters cried,
Turning a little blue.
"After such kindness, that would be
A dismal thing to do!"
"The night is fine," the Walrus said.
"Do you admire the view?"

"It was so kind of you to come!
And you are very nice!"
The Carpenter said nothing but
"Cut us another slice.

Literary Analysis
Narrative and Lyric Poetry, Rhyme, and Rhythm. How many syllables should you pronounce in *conveniently* to maintain the poem's regular rhythm?

⓭ **Reading Check**

What are the Walrus and Carpenter going to do with the Oysters?

⓬ Literary Analysis

Narrative and Lyric Poetry, Rhyme, and Rhythm

- Ask a volunteer to read aloud the first stanza on p. 711.
- Then, ask students the Literary Analysis question: How many syllables should you pronounce in *conveniently* to maintain the poem's regular rhythm?
  Answer: Students should pronounce the word as if it had five syllables rather than four.

Monitor Progress Ask students to explain the difference between a narrative poem and a lyric poem.
Answer: A narrative poem tells a story using storytelling devices, such as characters, plot, and dialogue; a lyric poem is more like a song and focuses on the speaker's feelings or thoughts.

Reteach On the board, write a jumbled list of terms that are associated with narrative and lyric poems. Your list might include *story, feelings, plot, speaker, song, stanza, characters, dialogue,* and so on. Then, draw a Venn diagram like the one on p. 89 of **Writing Models and Graphic Organizers on Transparencies** next to the list on the board. Label one circle *narrative* and the other *lyric*. Have students direct you to put the terms in the correct circles or in the area where the circles overlap.

⓭ Reading Check

Answer: The Walrus and the Carpenter are going to eat the Oysters.

CUSTOMIZE INSTRUCTION FOR UNIVERSAL ACCESS

For Special Needs Students	For Advanced Readers
Remind students that sometimes the speaker in a poem is inside the action, and other times the speaker is watching and describing the action. Encourage students to discuss whether the speaker in the first two stanzas of "The Walrus and the Carpenter" is inside or outside the action and to say what clues they used to determine the speaker's position.	Students may already be familiar with the works of Lewis Carroll. Invite students to talk about what they know about Carroll and his famous stories of Alice. Then, have them think of a list of words that would best describe Carroll's works. If students are not familiar with Carroll or his works, suggest that they do some research about the Alice stories and their creator and then share their findings with the class.

Review and Assess

Literary Analysis

Special Forms of Poetry

1. Would "The Sidewalk Racer" be more or less effective if it were written in a different shape? Explain your answer.
2. What image is presented in each line of the haiku? Use a web like this one to record your answer.

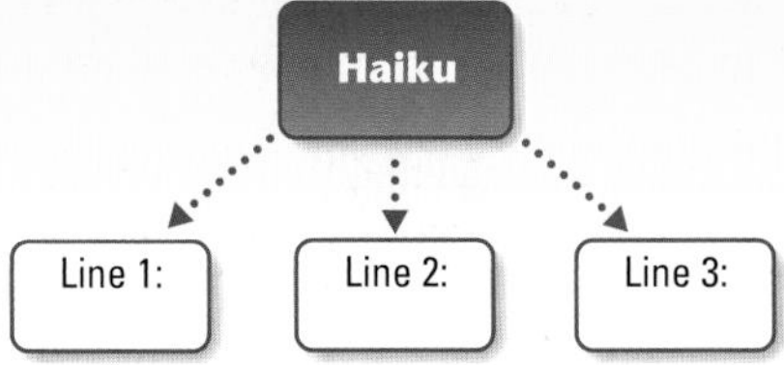

3. Would it be possible to write a serious limerick? Explain.

Comparing Literary Works

4. **(a)** Which poem has the shortest lines? **(b)** What is the effect created by the short lines?
5. What are the similarities and differences in the ways the poems organize ideas into sentences?

Poem	Line Length	Sentences	Effect
"The Sidewalk Racer"	Short	All ideas in poem expressed in one long sentence	Captures the effect of continuous motion
"Haiku"			
"Limerick"			

Reading Strategy

Using Your Senses

6. Which two senses does the haiku appeal to?
7. Which three senses help you experience "The Sidewalk Racer"?
8. Which senses does the limerick engage?

Extending Understanding

9. **Extend:** Why do you think there are many different forms of poetry?

Quick Review

In a **concrete poem,** words take the shape of the poem's subject. A **haiku** is a three-line poem in which line 1 has five syllables, line 2 has seven, and line 3 has five. A **limerick** is a short, funny poem of five lines with a distinct pattern of rhyme and rhythm.
To review each form of poetry, see page 717.

Using your senses while reading a poem will help you imagine seeing, hearing, tasting, smelling, and touching what the words describe.

Take It to the Net

www.phschool.com

Take the interactive self-test online to check your understanding of these selections.

ENRICHMENT: Further Reading

Other Works by the Poets

Works by Lillian Morrison

At the Crack of the Bat

I Scream, You Scream

Other Collections of Poetry

Cricket Never Dies: A Collection of Haiku and Tanka by Myra Cohn Livingston

Daffy Down Dillies: Silly Limericks by Edward Lear

Take It to the Net

Visit www.phschool.com for more information on the poets.

Answers for p. 721

Review and Assess

1. Possible responses: Some may say that the poem does not look much like a skateboard anyway, so the poem would still be effective if it were written in a different shape. Others may say that the shape makes the poem interesting.
2. **line 1:** a silent pond

   line 2: a jumping frog

   line 3: a splash followed by silence
3. Possible response: Some may say that it would be impossible to write a serious limerick because the pattern of the rhythm and rhyme is so bouncy that even serious words would sound lighthearted.
4. **(a)** "The Sidewalk Racer" has the shortest lines, although it is the longest poem. **(b)** The short lines convey action and speed.
5. **Haiku:**

   Line length: short

   Sentences: Each image has its own sentence.

   Effect: Three images unfold quickly.

   Limerick:

   Line length: medium

   Sentences: There are four sentences in five lines.

   Effect: The first sentence is the longest (two lines) and is followed by three shorter sentences, which creates a comic effect.
6. The haiku appeals to the senses of sight and sound.
7. The senses of sight, touch, and sound help readers experience the poem.
8. The limerick engages the senses of sight and sound.
9. Possible responses: Students may suggest that there are many forms of poetry because there are so many possible ideas, images, and sounds to express. Each form is suited to a particular mood or idea.

EXTEND

Answers for p. 722

❶ Vocabulary Development

Concept Development: Homophones

1. flea, flee
2. flew
3. flue
4. their
5. there
6. They're
7. see, sea

Fluency: Word Replacement

A fly and a flea were *skimming* along when a frog jumped out of a pond to chase them. The fly said to the flea, "We don't have to *flee* from the *flue* to get away from this beast." Turning to the frog, the fly said calmly, "There's a *flaw* in your thinking. You're in the wrong poem!"

Spelling Strategy

Possible answers:

1. true
2. to
3. flew
4. resume

❷ Grammar

1. better
2. worst
3. less
4. best
5. more

Writing Application

Possible sentences:

"The Skateboard Racer" is the *best* poem of the three. It is a *better* poem than the haiku because it describes an experience I know. I read it *more* times than I read the limerick.

Integrate Language Skills

❶ Vocabulary Development Lesson

Concept Development: Homophones

Homophones are words that sound the same but have different meanings and that may be spelled differently. For example, *their, there,* and *they're* are homophones.

On your paper, choose the homophone that best completes each sentence.

1. Pursued by a (flee, flea), he had to (flea, flee) the room.
2. The fly and the flea (flue, flew) speedily.
3. Those two creatures went up the (flue, flew).
4. We went to (there, their) house.
5. Over (there, their) is the park.
6. (They're Their) my friends.
7. When you (see, sea) him on the skateboard, he sails so high you think he could fly over the (see, sea).

Fluency: Word Replacement

On your paper, replace each italicized word or phrase with a vocabulary word.

A fly and a flea were *gliding* along when a frog jumped out of a pond to chase them. The fly said to the flea, "We don't have to *escape* from the *chimney-tube* to get away from this beast." Turning to the frog, the fly said calmly, "There's a *mistake* in your thinking. You're in the wrong poem!"

Spelling Strategy

The *oo* sound in words can be spelled in different ways. For each word, write a rhyming word that uses the same spelling for the *oo* sound.

1. flue
2. do
3. new
4. assume

❷ Grammar Lesson

Irregular Comparisons

Depending on your opinion, you might say the first limerick is *good,* but the second one is *better*. A few modifiers, such as *good* and *bad*, are irregular. You must memorize their comparative and superlative forms.

Positive	Comparative	Superlative
good	better	best
bad	worse	worst
well	better	best
little	less	least
many	more	most

Practice On your paper, change the positive form of the modifier to the correct comparative or superlative form.

1. Sarita is (good) at skateboarding than Sasha is.
2. Of my three tries at skateboarding, the second was the (bad) one.
3. My stunts are (little) dramatic than hers.
4. She is the (good) skateboarder in our class.
5. She has practiced for (many) hours than I have.

Writing Application Write a series of sentences in which you use three irregular modifiers to compare the poems in this section.

WG Prentice Hall Writing and Grammar Connection: Chapter 25, Section 1

TEACHING RESOURCES

The following resources can be used to enrich or extend the instruction for pp. 722–723.

Vocabulary

- **Selection Support:** Build Vocabulary, p. 191; Build Spelling Skills, p. 192 ■
- **Vocabulary and Spelling Practice Book** (Use this booklet for skills enrichment)

Grammar

- **Selection Support:** Build Grammar Skills, p. 193
- **Writing and Grammar,** Copper Level, p. 538

Daily Language Practice Transparencies

Writing

- **Writing and Grammar,** Copper Level, p. 78 ■
- **Writing Models and Graphic Organizers on Transparencies,** p. 81
- **Writing and Grammar iText CD-ROM**

■ **BLOCK SCHEDULING:** Resources marked with this symbol provide varied instruction during 90-minute blocks.

❸ Writing Lesson

Limerick

Now that you have read a limerick—a five-line poem with a comical twist at the end—try writing your own limerick.

Prewriting Brainstorm for a list of possible topics, which might include silly animals or unusual people. Think of rhyming words to go with each one. Then, choose the funniest character as your topic.

Drafting In the first line, introduce the character. Then, describe the situation, and in the last line or two, add a twist of humor. Follow the pattern of rhyme and rhythm that characterizes a limerick.

Model: Rhyme and Rhythm in a Limerick

Line 1: 3 beats	There was a young fellow named Hall,	a
Line 2: 3 beats	Who fell in the spring in the fall;	a
Line 3: 2 beats	'Twould have been a sad thing	b
Line 4: 2 beats	If he'd died in the spring	b
Line 5: 3 beats	But he didn't—he died in the fall.	a

To write a limerick, follow the rhyme scheme (shown by letters), and provide the correct number of beats (stressed syllables) in each line.

Revising Read your limerick aloud to check for the correct rhyme scheme and rhythm. Tap the beat as you go. Mark lines where there are too many or too few syllables or beats, or where the beats fall in the wrong place. Rewrite marked lines.

Prentice Hall Writing and Grammar Connection: Chapter 5, Section 2

❹ Extension Activities

Listening and Speaking Prepare and deliver an **oral response** to one of the poems in this section. Include the following in your response.

- a clear, careful oral reading of the poem
- your interpretation of the poem's meaning
- examples and clear ideas to support your interpretation
- selected images that support your interpretation
- your opinion of how successful the poem is

After you deliver your response, ask your classmates for feedback.

Research and Technology Choose one of the poems to format. On the computer, develop a well-designed presentation of a poem. Since lines of poetry must break as they are originally written, set wide enough margins. Choose a font that will make the poem easy to read. Use tabs to set off indented lines, and set the title in larger type. Use spacing to enhance the appearance of the poem.

Take It to the Net www.phschool.com

Go online for an additional research activity using the Internet.

ASSESSMENT RESOURCES

The following resources can be used to assess students' knowledge and skills.

Selection Assessment

- **Formal Assessment,** pp. 179–181
- **Open Book Test,** pp. 115–117
- **Got It! Assessment Videotapes,** Tape 5
- **Test Bank Software**

Take It to the Net

Visit www.phschool.com for self-tests and additional questions on the selections.

Listening and Speaking Rubric

- **Performance Assess. and Portfolio Mgmt.,** p. 28

PRENTICE HALL ASSESSMENT SYSTEM

- **Workbook**
- **Transparencies**
- **Skill Book**
- **CD-ROM**

Lesson Support for p. 723

❸ Writing Lesson

- Help students brainstorm for rhyming names and words. Offer examples like *Charlie* and *barley* or *Mary* and *scary*. Have students test the rhymes by offering opening limerick phrases using these or their own pairs.
- Students may include word play in their limericks. Invite students to list humorous homophones. Write the list on the board so that students may refer to it.
- Allow students to work with partners to revise their limericks. Students may benefit from hearing their limericks read aloud.
- Prepare a rubric for evaluating students' poems. Consider sharing the rubric with students before they complete the assignment, so they know what is expected of their poems.

❹ Listening and Speaking

- Suggest that each student copy the poem of his or her choice in the center of a blank sheet of paper. Encourage students to write notes about the language and images.
- Remind students that an interpretation must have a main idea or thesis. Offer them this sentence to fill in with their own ideas: "I think the poem means _____ because _____."
- Students may prefer to write their interpretations first. Have students work in pairs or small groups to practice.
- Have students use the Speaking rubric on p. 28 in **Performance Assessment and Portfolio Management.**

CUSTOMIZE INSTRUCTION For Universal Access

To address different learning styles, use the activities suggested in the **Extension Activities** booklet, p. 39.

- For Visual/Spatial Learners, use Activity 5.
- For Musical/Rhythmic Learners, use Activity 6.
- For Mathematical/Logical and Visual/Spatial Learners, use Activity 7.

Wind and water and stone ✦ February Twilight ✦ The Fairies' Lullaby ✦ Cynthia in the Snow ✦ Parade

Lesson Objectives

1. **To analyze and respond to literary elements**
   - Literary Analysis: Sound Devices
   - Comparing Literary Works
2. **To read, comprehend, analyze, and critique five poems**
   - Reading Strategy: Reading According to Punctuation
   - Reading Check Questions
   - Review and Assess Questions
3. **To develop word analysis skills, fluency, and systematic vocabulary**
   - Vocabulary Development Lesson: Word Analysis: Suffix *-ly*
4. **To understand and apply written and oral language conventions**
   - Spelling Strategy
   - Grammar Lesson: Commas and Semicolons
   - Assessment Practice (ATE)
5. **To understand and apply appropriate writing and research strategies**
   - Writing Lesson: Response to a Poem
   - Extension Activity: Résumé
6. **To understand and apply listening and speaking strategies**
   - Extension Activity: Respond to an Oral Presentation

STEP-BY-STEP TEACHING GUIDE	PACING GUIDE
PRETEACH	
Motivate Students and Provide Background	
Use the Motivation activity (ATE p. 724)	5 min.
Read and discuss the Preview material and Background information (SE/ATE p. 724) [A]	10 min.
Introduce the Concepts	
Introduce the Literary Analysis and Reading Strategy (SE/ATE p. 725) [A]	15 min.
Pronounce the vocabulary words and read their definitions (SE p. 725)	5 min.
TEACH	
Monitor Comprehension	
Informally monitor comprehension by circulating while students read independently or in groups [A]	5–10 min.
Develop vocabulary with Vocabulary notes (SE pp. 728, 730)	as students read
Develop Understanding	
Develop students' ability to read according to punctuation with the Reading Strategy annotations (ATE p. 728)	5 min.
ASSESS	
Assess Mastery	
Assess students' mastery of the Reading Strategy and Literary Analysis by having them answer the Review and Assess questions (SE/ATE p. 731)	15 min.
Use one or more of the print and media Assessment Resources (ATE p. 733) [A]	up to 45 min.
EXTEND	
Apply Understanding	
Have students complete the Vocabulary Development Lesson and the Grammar Lesson (SE p. 732) [A]	20 min.
Apply students' ability to write a response to a poem using the Writing Lesson (SE/ATE p. 733) [A]	30–45 min.
Apply students' understanding of the selection using one or more of the Extension Activities (SE p. 733)	20–90 min.

ACCELERATED INSTRUCTION:
Use the strategies and activities identified with an [A].

UNIVERSAL ACCESS
● = Below Level Students
▲ = On-Level Students
■ = Above Level Students

Time and Resource Manager

Reading Level: Average, Average, Challenging, Average, Average
Average Number of Instructional Days: 4

RESOURCES		
PRINT	**TRANSPARENCIES**	**TECHNOLOGY**
• **Beyond Literature,** Cultural Connection: The Circus, p. 40 ▲ ■		• **Interest Grabber Videotapes,** Tape 5 ● ▲ ■
• **Selection Support Workbook:** ● ▲ ■ Literary Analysis, p. 200 Reading Strategy, p. 199 Build Vocabulary, p. 196	• **Literary Analysis and Reading Transparencies,** pp. 79 and 80 ● ▲ ■	
• **Adapted Reader's Companion** ● • **Reader's Companion** ●		• **Listening to Literature** ● ▲ ■ Audiocassettes, Side 26 Audio CDs, CD 13
• **English Learner's Companion** ● ▲ • **Literatura en español** ● ▲ • **Literary Analysis for Enrichment** ■	• **Fine Art Transparencies, Volume 1,** Transparency 10 ● ▲ ■	
• **Formal Assessment:** Selection Test, pp. 182–184 ● ▲ ■ • **Open Book Test,** pp. 118–120 ● ▲ ■ • **Performance Assessment and Portfolio Management,** p. 15 ● ▲ ■ • Prentice Hall Assessment System ● ▲ ■	• Prentice Hall Assessment System ● ▲ ■ Skills Practice Answers and Explanations on Transparencies	• **Test Bank Software** ● ▲ ■ • **Got It! Assessment Videotapes,** Tape 5 ● ▲
• **Selection Support Workbook:** ● ▲ ■ Build Spelling Skills, p. 197 Build Grammar Skills, p. 198 • **Writing and Grammar,** Copper Level ● ▲ ■ • **Extension Activities,** p. 40 ● ▲ ■	• **Daily Language Practice Transparencies** ● ▲ • **Writing Models and Graphic Organizers on Transparencies** ● ▲ ■	• **Writing and Grammar iText CD-ROM** ● ▲ ■ ***Take It to the Net*** www.phschool.com

BLOCK SCHEDULING: Use one 90-minute class period to preteach the selection and have students read it. Use a second 90-minute class period to assess students' mastery of skills and have them complete one of the Extension Activities.

PRETEACH

Step-by-Step Teaching Guide for pp. 724–725

Motivation

Ask students to recite the tongue twisters "Peter Piper picked a peck of pickled peppers" or "Rubber baby buggy bumpers." Tell them that one reason these phrases are so difficult to say is *alliteration*—the repetition of the same sounds at the beginnings of words. Tell students that although poets would not begin every word with the same sound, they do use alliteration and other sound devices to add emphasis to certain words or ideas in their poetry. Have students watch for alliteration in the poems in this grouping.

Interest Grabber Video

As an alternative, play "How to Build a Snowman" on Tape 5 to engage student interest.

❶ Background

Social Studies

Like in the poem "Parade," the traveling circus, with its elephants, trapeze acts, and clowns, is a relatively recent development. The circus as we know it today was established in the 1700s. Circuses were essentially horse shows, with daring riders doing tricks on horseback in a single ring. It was not until the mid-1800s that circus owners like P.T. Barnum took to the road with tents large enough to cover three rings. The three-ring circus is an American phenomenon; European audiences still attend single-ring shows.

Prepare to Read

❶ Wind and water and stone ◆ February Twilight ◆ The Fairies' Lullaby ◆ Cynthia in the Snow ◆ Parade

Take It to the Net

Visit www.phschool.com for interactive activities and instruction related to these selections, including

- background
- graphic organizers
- literary elements
- reading strategies

Preview

Connecting to the Literature

The poets who wrote the next five poems stopped to listen to the world's music. They captured what they saw and heard and stored it up in words on the silent page. What words would you use to describe the music around you—a cough, the squeak of a chair, or the ticking of a clock?

Background

"Parade" describes a circus tradition more than 100 years old—the circus parade. In the days before television and radio, a parade down the main street of town was the best way to advertise the performances to come: clowns on stilts, cages of wild animals, and a giant musical instrument called the calliope.

TEACHING RESOURCES

The following resources can be used to enrich or extend the instruction for pp. 724–725.

Motivation

Interest Grabber Video, Tape 5 ■

Background

Beyond Literature, p. 40

Take It to the Net

Visit www.phschool.com for Background and hotlinks for the selections.

Literary Analysis

Literary Analysis and Reading Transparencies, Sound Devices, p. 80

Reading

Selection Support: Reading Strategy, p. 199; Build Vocabulary, p. 196

Literary Analysis and Reading Transparencies, Reading According to Punctuation, p. 79 ■

■ **BLOCK SCHEDULING:** Resources marked with this symbol provide varied instruction during 90-minute blocks.

❷ Literary Analysis

Sound Devices

Poets use the **sound** of words—the musical quality of words—to express images and feelings in poetry. In addition to rhyme, poets use the following sound devices.

- **Onomatopoeia:** The use of words to imitate sounds, such as *clash*.
- **Alliteration:** The repetition of initial consonant sounds, as in the *wh* sound in "whitely whirs."
- **Repetition:** The use, more than once, of any element of language, such as a sound, word, phrase, or sentence. A **refrain** is a line or group of lines that is repeated at regular intervals.

Comparing Literary Works

Whether they are impressions of magic and mystery or natural beauty, the sounds created by the words in a poem form various impressions and impact the reader in different ways. Compare and contrast the use of sound in these poems by answering the following focus questions:

1. Which poem uses the greatest variety of sound devices?
2. Which poem makes the strongest impression through sound?

❸ Reading Strategy

Reading According to Punctuation

In reading poetry, read according to **punctuation**—follow the set of instructions to stop or pause or read on. The punctuation groups words to reflect a specific meaning or sound. Notice in the example how changing the punctuation would change the meaning of the words, as well as the sound of how they are read.

As written:	With different punctuation:
It hushes	It hushes.
The loudness in the road.	The loudness in the road—
It flitter-twitters . . .	It flitter-twitters!

Use the punctuation guide at right to review how you should use punctuation when reading.

Punctuation Guide

STOP after
periods (.)
question marks (?)
exclamation marks (!)
PAUSE after
commas (,)
semicolons (;)
dashes (—)

Vocabulary Development

nigh (nī) *adv.* near (p. 728)

offense (ə fens´) *n.* harmful act (p. 728)

hence (hens) *adv.* away (p. 728)

gilded (gild´ id) *adj.* coated with a thin layer of gold (p. 730)

leisurely (lē´ zhər lē) *adv.* in an unhurried way (p. 730)

CUSTOMIZE INSTRUCTION FOR UNIVERSAL ACCESS

For Special Needs Students	For Less Proficient Readers	For English Learners
Have students read the adapted version of "Parade" and "The Fairies' Lullaby" in the **Adapted Reader's Companion.** This version provides basic-level instruction in an interactive format with questions and write-on lines. Completing the adapted version will prepare students to read the selection in the Student Edition.	Have students read "Parade" and "The Fairies' Lullaby" in the **Reader's Companion.** This version provides basic-level instruction in an interactive format with questions and write-on lines. After students finish the selection in the Reader's Companion, have them complete the questions and activities in the Student Edition.	Have students read the adapted version of "Parade" and "The Fairies' Lullaby" in the **English Learner's Companion.** This version provides basic-level instruction in an interactive format with questions and write-on lines. Completing the adapted version will prepare students to read the selection in the Student Edition.

❷ Literary Analysis

Sound Devices

- Ask students to think of the lyrics to a nursery rhyme or lullaby. Discuss what makes the lyrics memorable. Help students see that the repetition of sounds and words is part of the appeal.
- Read the instruction aloud. Challenge students to think of other examples of the three sound devices.
- Then, write the Comparing Literary Works questions on the board so that students can refer to them as they read the poems.
- Finally, have students create a chart like the one on the Sound Devices transparency on p. 80 in **Literary Analysis and Reading Transparencies** to help them keep track of the three sound devices.

❸ Reading Strategy

Reading According to Punctuation

- Review with students the purposes of punctuation marks such as commas, semicolons, and dashes.
- After students read the instruction, guide them through the information in the chart on p. 725. Demonstrate the hints given in the chart by reading a poem students are already familiar with—first without paying attention to punctuation and then paying attention to punctuation.

Vocabulary Development

- Review the words and definitions on the vocabulary list.
- Point out the noun *offense,* meaning "harmful act." Ask students to differentiate between *offense* and *defense* as used in the world of sports.
  Possible responses: *Offense* describes the act of scoring for a team; *defense* involves protecting the team against scoring.

 ***E-Teach***

Visit E-Teach at www.phschool.com for teachers' essays on how to teach, with questions and answers.

TEACH

Step-by-Step Teaching Guide for pp. 726–730

CUSTOMIZE INSTRUCTION
For Verbal/Linguistic Learners

Each of the poems in this grouping creates a different scene and mood. Challenge students to read or listen to the poems and then to try to describe in a journal entry the scene or mood and their effect. Or, you might ask students to write quick responses on the backs of index cards. Collect and redistribute the cards and ask students to identify the poem based on the notes on the cards.

❶ About the Selection

"Wind and water and stone" describes the interaction of these three elements and how they shape one another.

❷ Critical Thinking

Interpret

- Ask students to explain in their own words what the poet is describing in these lines. **Answer:** The water runs over the stone and makes hollow places in it; the wind blows away the water that gathers in the hollows; the stone blocks the wind from blowing.
- Challenge students to see the interactive relationships that exist between the wind, water, and stone.
- Explain that without one of these elements, the others would not be the same or would not serve the same function.

❶ Wind and water and stone

Octavio Paz

❷
The water hollowed the stone,
the wind dispersed the water,
the stone stopped the wind.
Water and wind and stone.

The wind sculpted the stone,
the stone is a cup of water,
the water runs off and is wind.
Stone and wind and water.

The wind sings in its turnings,
the water murmurs as it goes,
the motionless stone is quiet.
Wind and water and stone.

One is the other, and is neither:
among their empty names
they pass and disappear,
water and stone and wind.

Octavio Paz

(1914–1998)

Mexican poet Octavio Paz (ok täv´yō päs) traveled widely and used his experiences and memories in his poetry.

Although he lived in and visited many countries, he remained deeply committed to his Mexican heritage. In "Wind and water and stone," he captures the beauty of a Mexican landscape and uses it to suggest how a culture changes and yet stays the same. In 1990, Paz received the Nobel Prize for Literature.

TEACHING RESOURCES

The following resources can be used to enrich or extend the instruction for pp. 726–730.

Literary Analysis
- **Selection Support:** Literary Analysis, p. 200
- **Literary Analysis for Enrichment**

Reading
- **Reader's Companion**
- **Adapted Reader's Companion**
- **English Learner's Companion**

- **Literatura en español**
- **Listening to Literature Audiocassettes,** Side 26 ▪
- **Listening to Literature Audio CDs,** CD 13 ▪

Enrichment
-  **Fine Art Transparencies, Volume 1,** Art Transparency 10 (Using the picture, lead a discussion connecting the colors, shapes, and mood of the artwork to "Parade.")

▪ **BLOCK SCHEDULING:** Resources marked with this symbol provide varied instruction during 90-minute blocks.

3 # February Twilight

Sara Teasdale

I stood beside a hill
Smooth with new-laid snow,
A single star looked out
From the cold evening glow.

There was no other creature
That saw what I could see—
I stood and watched the evening star
As long as it watched me.

Sara Teasdale

(1884–1933)

Teasdale had a very protected childhood in St. Louis, Missouri. Perhaps that's why her highly musical poems seem so delicate. Her book *Love Songs* (1917) received a Columbia Poetry Prize, now known as the Pulitzer Prize.

Review and Assess

Thinking About the Selections

1. Which poem gives a view of nature that is more familiar to you?
2. (a) **Recall:** What does each natural element named in the title of "Wind and water and stone" do? (b) **Relate:** How do these activities make the elements related to one another? (c) **Interpret:** Explain the meaning of the last stanza.
3. (a) **Recall:** Where is the speaker of "February Twilight"? (b) **Speculate:** Why do you think the speaker is there? (c) **Infer:** Does the speaker enjoy the experience he or she describes?

3 About the Selection

In "February Twilight," the poet uses simple words and a delicate, musical rhythm to capture an experience in nature. Her description of standing outside gazing at the evening star evokes a feeling of peacefulness and contemplation. Teasdale's unique perspective highlights the beauty to be found in a cold winter's evening.

Answers for p. 727

Review and Assess

1. Possible responses: Students may say that they are more familiar with the stargazing in "February Twilight," but others may have seen the effects of wind and water on stone described in "Wind and water and stone."
2. **(a)** The wind disperses water, sculpts stone, and sings; the water hollows stone, runs off, and murmurs; the stone stops wind, holds water, and is quiet. **(b)** The actions of each object depend on the presence of the others. For example, the wind cannot disperse the water if there is no water. **(c)** Possible response: Alone, each of the elements is nothing. Their names mean nothing. They exist only to interact.
3. **(a)** The speaker is standing on a snowy hill on a cold evening. **(b)** Possible response: The speaker is there to watch the evening star. He or she may be needing inspiration. **(c)** The speaker enjoys the experience and stays as long as the star is in the sky, which may be all night long.

CUSTOMIZE INSTRUCTION FOR UNIVERSAL ACCESS

For Special Needs Students	For Gifted/Talented Students
Students may have trouble reading "Wind and water and stone" because it lacks standard punctuation and uses incomplete sentences. Suggest that students listen to the poem on **Listening to Literature Audiocassettes,** Side 26 or **Listening to Literature Audio CDs,** CD 13. Students should listen to get an idea of the poem's mood and ideas. They should write down notes about what they think is happening. Assure students that the poem is more about describing a scene and setting a mood than about telling a story.	Invite students to write their own version of Paz's poem. Challenge students to think of three elements or objects that are common to their experience and to write a poem about how the elements or objects interact. Students should try to create a mood and suggest the effects of the interaction of the elements. Ask volunteers to read their work aloud or post students' work on a bulletin board where all students can read them.

❹ About the Selection

In "The Fairies' Lullaby," fairies warn snakes, newts, spiders, and other unpleasant creatures to stay away from their queen. Shakespeare uses sounds and images to share the magic of the unknown with readers.

❺ Reading Strategy

Reading According to Punctuation

- Ask a volunteer to read aloud the chorus of the poem before asking the Reading Strategy question below.
- Then, ask students the following question: After which words in the chorus should you stop?
  Answer: Students should stop after the words *lullaby* in line 7, *nigh* in line 10, and *lullaby* in line 11.

▶ **Monitor Progress** Ask students to review the punctuation marks that call for a full stop when reading and those that call for only a pause.
Answer: Periods, question marks, and exclamation points require readers to stop; commas, semicolons, and dashes require only a pause.

▶ **Reteach** Borrow the reading technique of comic and musician Victor Borge. Invent, or ask students to invent, appropriate sounds and assign them to each of the punctuation marks in the punctuation guide on p. 725. Then, read, or ask a volunteer to read, one of the poems in this grouping, using the sounds whenever they see the corresponding punctuation. Then, ask the entire class to read with the sounds and then without any sounds. Students should get a sense of the relationship between punctuation and rhythm in a poem.

❹ The Fairies' Lullaby
from A Midsummer Night's Dream

William Shakespeare

Fairies. You spotted snakes with double tongue,
Thorny hedgehogs, be not seen.
Newts and blindworms,[1] do no wrong,
Come not near our fairy Queen.

Chorus. Philomel,[2] with melody
Sing in our sweet lullaby;
Lulla, lulla, lullaby, lulla, lulla, lullaby.
❺ Never harm,
Nor spell, nor charm,
Come our lovely lady nigh.
So, good night, with lullaby.

Fairies. Weaving spiders, come not here.
Hence, you long-legged spinners, hence!
Beetles black, approach not near.
Worm nor snail do no offense.

Chorus. Philomel, with melody
Sing in our sweet lullaby;
Lulla, lulla, lullaby, lulla, lulla, lullaby.
Never harm,
Nor spell, nor charm,
Come our lovely lady nigh.
So, good night, with lullaby.

nigh (nī) *adv.* near

hence (hens) *adv.* away

offense (ə fens′) *n.* harmful act

William Shakespeare

(1564–1616)

William Shakespeare is the most highly regarded poet and playwright in the English language. He was born in the English town of Stratford-on-Avon and went to London when he was a young man. There, he began writing and acting in plays. Shakespeare wrote at least thirty-seven plays, as well as several long, narrative poems and more than one hundred and fifty shorter poems called sonnets.

"The Fairies' Lullaby" appears in *A Midsummer Night's Dream*, a comedy written around 1600.

1. **newts** (nōōts) **and blindworms** *n.* newts are salamanders, animals that look like lizards but are related to frogs. Blindworms are legless lizards.
2. **Philomel** (fil′ ō mel′) *n.* nightingale.

CUSTOMIZE INSTRUCTION FOR UNIVERSAL ACCESS

For Gifted/Talented Students	For Advanced Readers
Have students practice at home, reciting the poem aloud in a rhythmical manner. If students are musicians, encourage them to provide their own background music for the poem or create a melody for the poem. If possible, students should tape-record their readings at home, or tape-record them in class, and then play them for an audience.	Have students read a prose version of Shakespeare's play *A Midsummer Night's Dream.* Then, have them give an oral summary of the play to the class, explaining the role of fairies in the play and describing the scene in which "The Fairies' Lullaby" is sung. If students wish, have them write their own poem based on another scene from the prose version of *A Midsummer Night's Dream.* Students may share their poems with the class.

6 # Cynthia in the Snow

Gwendolyn Brooks

It SUSHES.
It hushes
The loudness in the road.
It flitter-twitters,
And laughs away from me.
It laughs a lovely whiteness,
And whitely whirs away,
To be
Some otherwhere,
Still white as milk or shirts.
So beautiful it hurts.

Gwendolyn Brooks

(1917–2000)

Gwendolyn Brooks wrote many poems about her neighbors in Chicago, the city she lived in most of her life. She included "Cynthia in the Snow" in a book titled *Bronzeville Boys and Girls* (1956). Bronzeville refers to an African American community in Chicago.

When she was only seven, Brooks started writing poetry. As a teenager, her poetry was published in a well-known magazine. Her poems were also published in a local newspaper, the *Chicago Defender*. Brooks became a well-respected poet who received the Pulitzer Prize for *Annie Allen* (1949).

Review and Assess

Thinking About the Selections

1. **Respond:** Which poem presents a scene that is more appealing to you? Why?
2. **(a) Recall:** What do the fairies tell the snakes and hedgehogs to do? **(b) Infer:** What tone of voice do you think the fairies would use?
3. **(a) Recall:** Name all the creatures the fairies address. **(b) Classify:** What do all these creatures have in common?
4. **(a) Recall:** Whom does the chorus ask to join them? **(b) Contrast:** How is this creature different from the others? **(c) Infer:** Why do you think they ask this creature to sing with them?
5. **(a) Recall:** In "Cynthia in the Snow," what five things does the snow do? **(b) Analyze:** How is the snow something that the speaker cannot hold or keep?
6. **Assess:** What is unusual about the speaker's description of the snow?

6 About the Selections

In "Cynthia in the Snow" the poet creates the vision and sound of falling snow, recalling the almost painful beauty of that memorable moment.

In "Parade" (p. 730), Rachel Field, the poet, uses vivid images and the sound device of onomatopoeia to express the thrill and delight of one child's memory of a circus parade marching through town.

Answers for p. 729

Review and Assess

1. Possible responses: Students may prefer "Cynthia in the Snow" because it describes an ordinary moment in an extraordinary way; others may prefer "The Fairies' Lullaby" because it describes a fantasy world.
2. **(a)** The fairies tell them to be quiet and to stay away from the sleeping queen. **(b)** They would probably use soft, gentle tones of voice.
3. **(a)** The fairies address snakes, hedgehogs, newts, blindworms, spiders, beetles, worms, and snails. **(b)** The creatures all live outside and on or in the ground.
4. **(a)** The chorus members ask Philomel to join them in song. **(b)** This creature sings in a sweet voice. **(c)** They want the nightingale to sing with them because its song will be sweet and it will help the queen to sleep.
5. **(a)** The snow "sushes," "hushes," "flitter-twitters," "laughs," and "whirs." **(b)** The snow seems to laugh and slip away when the speaker tries to grasp it.
6. The speaker's description of the snow is unusual because it gives the snow human qualities.

CUSTOMIZE INSTRUCTION FOR UNIVERSAL ACCESS

For Less Proficient Readers	For English Learners
Students may benefit from participating in a choral reading of Shakespeare's poem. Have students form groups of four or six. Ask students to take a few minutes to figure out an effective way to read the poem together. Students may divide themselves into two groups—fairies and chorus. Or they may think of other combinations. Have students practice their readings briefly and then perform them for the class. After students perform, ask them to write a journal entry about what they learned from the reading.	Students may focus on the meaning of the words and so have problems with the purpose of repetition in "The Fairies' Lullaby" and onomatopoeia in "Cynthia in the Snow." Discuss with students that it is the sound as much as the meaning that contributes to the overall effect in some poems. Have students form small groups in which to listen to the poem on the **Listening to Literature Audiocassettes,** Side 26 or **Listening to Literature Audio CDs,** CD 13, and then have them read the poem aloud to one another.

ASSESS

7 ▶Critical Viewing

Answer: The clown shown here appeals mostly to the sense of sight.

Answers for p. 730

Review and Assess

1. Possible responses: Students may mention a circus or a Fourth of July or Mardi Gras parade because of the colors, animals, and excitement.
2. **(a)** Possible responses: Students might see a marching band, horses with fancy headdresses, floats shaped like dragons, and clowns on stilts. **(b)** Words such as *blare, clashing,* and *roar* suggest action and excitement. **(c)** The speaker sounds like a child who is excited and full of wonder, but the poem's language is in many instances sophisticated; therefore, the speaker could be an adult.
3. **(a)** The speaker's mention of the town limits and the town's elm trees and grass suggests that the town is small and suburban. **(b)** It is extraordinary because exotic animals and people are parading down an ordinary street.
4. **(a)** Possible responses: A baseball game or a concert might generate the same kind of excitement. Both are special events that bring many people together. **(b)** Communities are often large and busy with cars and other traffic—it would be inconvenient or dangerous to have a circus parade.

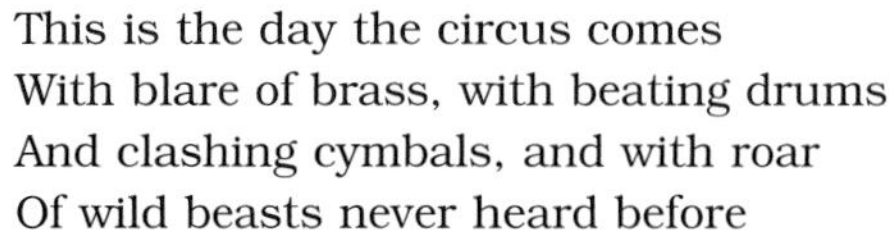

PARADE

RACHEL FIELD

This is the day the circus comes
With blare of brass, with beating drums,
And clashing cymbals, and with roar
Of wild beasts never heard before
Within town limits. Spick and span
Will shine each gilded cage and van;
Cockades at every horse's head
Will nod, and riders dressed in red
Or blue trot by. There will be floats
In shapes like dragons, thrones and boats,
And clowns on stilts; freaks big and small,
Till leisurely and last of all
Camels and elephants will pass
Beneath our elms, along our grass.

7 ▲ Critical Viewing To which senses do sights like this one appeal? **[Analyze]**

gilded (gild′ id) *adj.* coated with a thin layer of gold

leisurely (lē′ zhər lē) *adv.* in an unhurried way

Review and Assess

Thinking About the Selections

1. **Respond:** Does "Parade" remind you of any procession that you have seen? Explain why or why not.
2. **(a) Recall:** What are four attractions you would see if you were watching the circus procession in "Parade"? **(b) Infer:** Which details suggest that the speaker is excited? **(c) Infer:** Is the speaker in "Parade" an adult or a child? Explain.
3. **(a) Recall:** Which details in "Parade" describe the town? **(b) Infer:** In what way is the procession an extraordinary event in ordinary surroundings?
4. **(a) Compare:** What contemporary event generates the excitement in a community that a circus parade once did? **(b) Contrast:** In what ways have communities changed to make holding a circus parade more difficult than it once was?

Rachel Field

(1894–1942)

Rachel Field could not read until she was ten. However, this late reader became a well-known writer of books for adults and children. She also became the first woman to receive the Newbery medal for children's literature. One reason for her success as a writer was her "camera memory," which stored up details such as those described in "Parade."

ASSESSMENT PRACTICE: Writing Skills

Recognize Appropriate Usage (For more practice, see Test Preparation Workbook, p. 56.)

Many tests require students to identify the correct usage of pronouns. Tell students that pronouns and their antecedents must agree in number (singular and plural). Help students practice this skill by giving them the following sample test item.

Gwendolyn Brooks writes poems about Chicago, and _________ reflect her life in the city.

Choose the word that belongs in the space.

A she **C** they
B it **D** you

The antecedent of the missing pronoun is poems, so the pronoun will need to be plural. *A* and *B* are singular. *D* could be plural, but it does not make sense in the sentence. The correct answer is *C*.

Review and Assess

Literary Analysis

Sound Devices

1. On a chart like this one, record examples of sound devices in the poems and categories indicated.

Onomatopoeia	Alliteration	Repetition
"Parade" "Cynthia in the Snow"	"Cynthia in the Snow"	"Wind and water and stone" "The Fairies' Lullaby"

2. Which poems could be listed under more than one column in the chart? Why?

Comparing Literary Works

3. Which poem uses the greatest variety of sound devices? Explain.
4. Which poem makes the strongest impression through sound? Explain.
5. Which poems have the most similar effects based on their use of sound? Explain and give examples.

Reading Strategy

Reading According to Punctuation

6. In what way do the commas in lines 1–3 of "The Fairies' Lullaby" help you understand the meaning?
7. Read aloud "Parade." How does the punctuation affect the pace of the poem?
8. Read aloud "Cynthia in the Snow." How does the punctuation affect the pace and meaning of this poem?

Extending Understanding

9. **Science Connection:** "The Fairies' Lullaby" mentions four classes of vertebrates—animals that have a backbone. Identify one example of a reptile, a mammal, a bird, and an amphibian in the poem. Which vertebrate class is missing from this list?

Quick Review

Onomatopoeia is the use of words to imitate sounds. **Alliteration** is the repetition of initial consonant sounds. **Repetition** is the use, more than once, of any element of language—a sound, word, phrase, or sentence. To review sound devices, see page 725.

Punctuation is the set of symbols that give specific directions to the reader, such as when to pause or stop.

Take It to the Net

www.phschool.com

Take the interactive self-test online to check your understanding of these selections.

ENRICHMENT: Further Reading

Other Works by the Poets

Works by Octavio Paz
"Exclamation"

Works by Sara Teasdale
Flame and Shadow

Works by William Shakespeare
Complete Sonnets

Works by Gwendolyn Brooks
Selected Poems
The Near Johannesburg Boy and Other Poems

Works by Rachel Field
Calico Bush
If Once You Have Slept on an Island

Take It to the Net

Visit www.phschool.com for more information on the poets.

Answers to p. 731

Review and Assess

1. **Onomatopoeia:** blare, beating, clashing, roar, spick and span, trot; sushes, hushes, whirs

   Alliteration: loudness, laughs, lovely; whiteness, whitely whirs

   Repetition: stone, wind, water; lulla, lulla, lullaby; never harm, nor spell, nor charm
2. Possible responses: "The Fairies' Lullaby" could be listed under onomatopoeia (*lulla* and *lullaby*) and alliteration (*long-legged* and *Beetles black*). "Cynthia in the Snow" also includes repetition (*laughs* and *whitely whiteness*). "Parade" includes alliteration (*blare of brass* and *spic and span*).
3. "The Fairies' Lullaby" uses the greatest variety of sound devices. It contains alliteration ("spotted snakes," "sing in our sweet," "lovely lady . . . lullaby"), onomatopoeia ("Lulla, lulla, lullaby"), and repetition ("Never harm, nor spell, nor charm.")
4. "Cynthia in the Snow" probably makes the strongest impression by its made-up words that capture the sound of falling snow.
5. Possible response: "Parade" and "The Fairies' Lullaby" sound most similar because of their use of alliteration, onomatopoeia, and a regular rhyme scheme. Field uses loud, crashing words such as *blare* and *beating* to suggest the excitement of a parade. Shakespeare uses alliteration by having the fairies sing the sleepy, soft phrase *lulla, lulla lullaby*, which reminds readers that they are reading a lullaby.
6. The commas set off the creatures addressed by the fairies.
7. Punctuation makes the poem sound like a marching band.
8. The punctuation highlights the images of the snow, and it affects the pace by causing the reader to pause and stop at certain moments while reading.
9. A snake is a reptile; a hedgehog is a mammal; Philomel is a bird; a newt is an amphibian. Fish are missing.

EXTEND

Answers for p. 732

❶ Vocabulary Development

Word Analysis

1. cleverly
2. stubbornly
3. affectionately
4. slyly

Possible answers:

1. The cat behaved cleverly.
2. My brother stubbornly held on to the ball.
3. She spoke to her daughter affectionately.
4. The fox slyly disappeared with the food.

Spelling Strategy

1. freight
2. weird
3. weight
4. receive

Concept Development

1. gilded
2. leisurely
3. nigh
4. offense
5. hence

❷ Grammar

1. The spiders weave webs, but they do not draw near.
2. The nightingale sings, and the fairy queen sleeps.
3. The snowstorm was blinding; she could not see the road.
4. The band and floats are in view; everyone starts to clap.
5. The band blares, and the trumpets blast.

Writing Application

Possible sentences:

Octavio Paz wrote poetry for many years, and he won the Nobel Prize for Literature in 1990.

William Shakespeare is considered the greatest poet in the English language; even today people read and admire his work.

Integrate Language Skills

❶ Vocabulary Development Lesson

Word Analysis: Suffix *-ly*

The suffix *-ly* often turns adjectives into adverbs that tell *when, how,* or *in what way* an action happens. Add *-ly* to each adjective. Use each new word in a sentence.

1. clever
2. stubborn
3. affectionate
4. sly

Spelling Strategy

When you spell a word that has the letters *i* and *e* next to each other, you can often follow this rule: *i* before *e* except after *c (ceiling)* and in words with a long *a* sound *(weigh)*. Among the exceptions to the rule are *leisure, weird, seize, height,* and *neither.* Write the word that is spelled correctly in each pair.

1. freight, frieght
2. weird, wierd
3. wieght, weight
4. receive, recieve

Concept Development: Analogies

An **analogy** makes a comparison between two or more things that are similar in some ways but otherwise unalike.

Write the vocabulary word that best completes each analogy. To help you, review the vocabulary list on page 725.

1. *Solid* is to *soft* as *plain* is to __?__.
2. *Anxiously* is to *uneasily* as *unhurriedly* is to __?__.
3. *Enormous* is to *miniature* as *far* is to __?__.
4. *Generosity* is to *kindness* as *insult* is to __?__.
5. *Forward* is to *backward* as *come* is to __?__.

❷ Grammar Lesson

Commas and Semicolons

The clauses in a compound sentence can be connected in one of two ways—with a comma or with a semicolon. Use a **comma** to separate two independent clauses that are linked by a conjunction, such as *and, or, yet,* or *but.* Add the comma before the conjunction. Use a **semicolon** to link two independent clauses that are closely connected in meaning.

Examples:
Cynthia has seen snow before, yet she is dazzled by its whiteness.
Cynthia has never seen snow before; she is dazzled by its whiteness.

Practice On your paper, write each sentence with the correct punctuation.

1. The spiders weave webs but they do not draw near.
2. The nightingale sings and the fairy queen sleeps.
3. The snowstorm was blinding she could not see the road.
4. The band and floats are in view everyone starts to clap.
5. The band blares and the trumpets blast.

Writing Application On your paper, write two compound sentences, one connected by a comma and the other connected by a semicolon.

WG Prentice Hall Writing and Grammar Connection: Chapter 26, Sections 2 and 3

TEACHING RESOURCES

The following resources can be used to enrich or extend the instruction for pp. 732–733.

Vocabulary

Selection Support: Build Vocabulary, p. 196
Build Spelling Skills, p. 197

Vocabulary and Spelling Practice Book
(Use this booklet for skills enrichment)

Grammar

Selection Support: Build Grammar Skills, p. 198

Writing and Grammar, Copper Level, pp. 564, 574

Daily Language Practice Transparencies ■

Writing

Writing and Grammar, Copper Level, p. 257 ■

Writing and Grammar iText CD-ROM

■ **BLOCK SCHEDULING:** Resources marked with this symbol provide varied instruction during 90-minute blocks.

❸ Writing Lesson

Response to a Poem

Write an essay in which you respond to one of the poems you just read. Choose a poem that you had a strong response to, either positive or negative.

Prewriting Jot down reasons why you respond to the poem as you do. For example, you may have a negative response because you think the images or comparisons are too far outside your experience. Identify specific examples that illustrate your point. Find examples that support your response.

Drafting As you draft, pause at the end of each paragraph. Circle the main point. If necessary, add supporting details that answer the question.

Model: Justify Interpretation with Examples and Textual Evidence

Writer circles main point of paragraph.

Rachel Field's "Parade" is a masterful poem that brings a parade to life. You can hear the band and animals as you read. The poet uses onomatopoeic words such as *blare, beating, clashing,* and *roar.*

Writer adds an example (in blue) as support.

Revising Reread your draft. Strengthen support for your points by adding specific quotations from the poem.

WG Prentice Hall Writing and Grammar Connection: Chapter 12, Section 4

❹ Extension Activities

Listening and Speaking With a small group, **respond to an oral presentation** of a poem or character's speech from Shakespeare. Listen carefully to a recording of the poem or speech. Notice especially the sound devices used.

- Explain which sound devices are used and provide examples of each.
- Describe the effect created by the sound devices.

After working in your small groups, share your response with your class. **[Group Activity]**

Research and Technology A **résumé** is a summary that includes important information about a person's career and education. Prepare a résumé for your favorite poet! Go online to find examples of résumés and to collect important facts about the poet you choose, such as

- schools attended
- awards received.
- books and poems written

Turn these facts into a "résumé" for your poet.

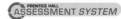

 ***Take It to the Net*** www.phschool.com

Go online for an additional research activity using the Internet.

ASSESSMENT RESOURCES

The following resources can be used to assess students' knowledge and skills.

Selection Assessment

- **Formal Assessment,** pp. 182–184
- **Open Book Test,** pp. 118–120
- **Got It! Assessment Videotapes,** Tape 5
- **Test Bank Software**

Take It to the Net

Visit www.phschool.com for self-tests and additional questions on the selections.

Writing Rubric

- **Performance Assess. and Portfolio Mgmt.,** p. 15

PRENTICE HALL ASSESSMENT SYSTEM

- **Workbook**
- **Transparencies**

- **Skill Book**
- **CD-ROM**

Lesson Support for p. 733

❸ Writing Lesson

- After students read the instruction, tell them that a response to a poem is more than just an expression of their feelings; it must have a main idea. Point to the main idea that is circled in the model on p. 733: "Rachel Field's 'Parade' is a masterful poem that brings a parade to life."
- Remind students to explore all possible sound devices in the poem, including alliteration, onomatopoeia, repetition, and refrain.
- When students revise, review how to quote poems. Show students how to include line numbers in parentheses at the ends of sentences that incorporate quotations.
- Use the Response to Literature rubric on p. 15 of **Performance Assessment and Portfolio Management** to assess students' responses.

❹ Listening and Speaking

- You may wish to choose in advance the selection from Shakespeare that students will hear. You may also use a recording, such as those provided in **Listening to Literature Audiocassettes** or **Listening to Literature Audio CDs,** or you may wish to read the work aloud.
- Before students listen, have them create a checklist of items to notice as they listen.
- Allow students to listen to the poem or reading more than once.
- Students should be able to offer articulate responses in discussion. Guide them away from "I liked it" or "It was good." Ask students to give concrete reasons for their responses.

CUSTOMIZE INSTRUCTION
For Universal Access

To address different learning styles, use the activities suggested in the **Extension Activities** booklet, p. 40.

- For Visual/Spatial and Verbal/Linguistic Learners, use Activity 5.
- For Musical/Rhythmic Learners, use Activity 6.
- For Verbal/Linguistic Learners, use Activity 7.

Lesson Objectives

1. To read a literary background for information
2. To take notes on background information about literature

About Literary Backgrounds

- Before students read "About Literary Backgrounds," ask them to think of the questions they usually have when they read something by an unknown author. Guide students to identify questions such as "Who is the author?"; "When did he or she live?"; "What was his or her life like?"; and "Is the writing based on the author's own experiences?"
- Ask a volunteer to read aloud the section. Have students think of examples of literary backgrounds that have helped them in the past. (If students need help here, suggest that they look back at the author information in the reading selections they have already completed.)

Reading Strategy

Taking Notes

- Before students read the "Reading Strategy" section, discuss with them the importance of taking notes as they read. Explain that this section will offer three strategies for taking effective notes.
- Have students read the information in the Reading Strategy section. Review with them the differences between writing outlines and writing summaries.
- As a class, discuss the benefits and possible drawbacks of taking notes. For example, students may say that the process of writing prevents them from listening carefully to the teacher. Others may say that notes help them remember what they heard.
- As an exercise, randomly assign one of the three note-taking strategies to each of the students in the class. Ask students to use the strategy as they read "Shakespeare's London." After they have read, ask students to comment on how effective the note-taking strategy was.

READING INFORMATIONAL MATERIALS

Literary Backgrounds

About Literary Backgrounds

The background information given in the introduction to a text is an important type of informational material. It can provide information about the author, the setting, or even the history of the time when the text was written. Literary backgrounds include facts, statistics, and interesting or unusual information that enriches your understanding and appreciation by providing details that put the work in context. When reading literary backgrounds, pay attention to important details.

Reading Strategy

Taking Notes

Taking notes is one of the best ways to remember what you have read. Everyone takes notes differently. There are a variety of note-taking methods, including the following:

- Outlines
- Highlighted photocopies
- Summaries

When you use an outline, you should break down the information into the main points followed by the major and supporting details. The outline shown gives you the basic structure you can use to take notes on almost any topic.

Highlighting a photocopy is also an effective note-taking tool. After highlighting sentences that state main ideas, you can underline or circle supporting details.

Another way to take notes is to summarize. Summaries are an excellent tool to help you review the stories or information you have read. Summaries are created by stating in your own words the main ideas and major details of what you have read.

Outline

1. **Sentence about first main idea**
   - Sentence or phrase about major detail
     Words and phrases related to supporting details
   - Sentence or phrase about major detail
     Words and phrases related to supporting details
2. **Sentence about second main idea**
   - Sentence or phrase about major detail
   - Sentence or phrase about major detail

The Globe Theater is shown in the lower right corner of the picture.

Pictures can help you envision places and people.

Shakespeare's London

Anna Claibourne and Rebecca Treays

Shakespeare's poem "The Fairies' Lullaby" comes from his play A Midsummer Night's Dream. *In Shakespeare's time, most people believed that fairies and goblins lived among the humans. The following background gives more information about the times in which Shakespeare lived.*

"All the World's a Stage"

The world Shakespeare knew was full of danger, excitement and change. Elizabethan London was filthy, crowded, crime-ridden, hazardous, thrilling and inspiring. The theatres, situated in the seedier parts of town, were among the most popular places of entertainment, and the best plays to see were Shakespeare's. . . .

"Shakespeare's London"

- Tell students that they may find literary backgrounds in the introductions of literature.
- Before students read, point out that this short excerpt is ideal for practicing the outline form of note taking. Each paragraph has a distinct main idea and several details. Consider modeling the outline of the first paragraph. Answers appear below.

Sentence about first main idea: The London of Shakespeare's time was dirty, dangerous, and exciting.

Sentence or phrase about major detail: Visiting the theatre was among the most popular forms of entertainment.

Sentence or phrase about major detail: Shakespeare's plays were the best.

- Work as a class to summarize sections of "Shakespeare's London" and then to summarize the whole piece.

continued on p. 736

CUSTOMIZE INSTRUCTION FOR UNIVERSAL ACCESS

For Special Needs	For English Learners
Remind students that they are already familiar with the concept of identifying main ideas and details. Offer students a copy of the Main Idea and Supporting Details Organizer that appears on p. 73 in **Writing Models and Graphic Organizers on Transparencies.** Work with students to fill in the information from one of the paragraphs in the literary background on pp. 735–736. Then, work as a class to transfer the information from the organizer to the outline format shown on p. 734.	Before students prepare an outline based on the literary background that appears on pp. 735–736, give them additional information about Shakespeare and his times. For example, students may not know about the Tower of London or the plague. Allow students time to preview the reading and make a list of unfamiliar terms or phrases. Work with students, using illustrations if possible, to explain the terms. Then, ask students to complete an outline and to compare it with those of their classmates.

continued from p. 735

- Point out how the use of subheadings in the literary background gives readers clues about what kind of information will appear in the paragraphs that follow. For example, the subheading "From Tower to Temple" is about the geography of the city of London.
- Discuss with students how the subtopics on p. 736 explain in more detail what was introduced in the first paragraph on p. 735.
- Ask students what events and situations, based on this reading, most likely influenced Shakespeare.
  Answer: Shakespeare most likely was influenced by the crowds, plague and disease, extremes of wealth and poverty, science lectures, and nightlife.

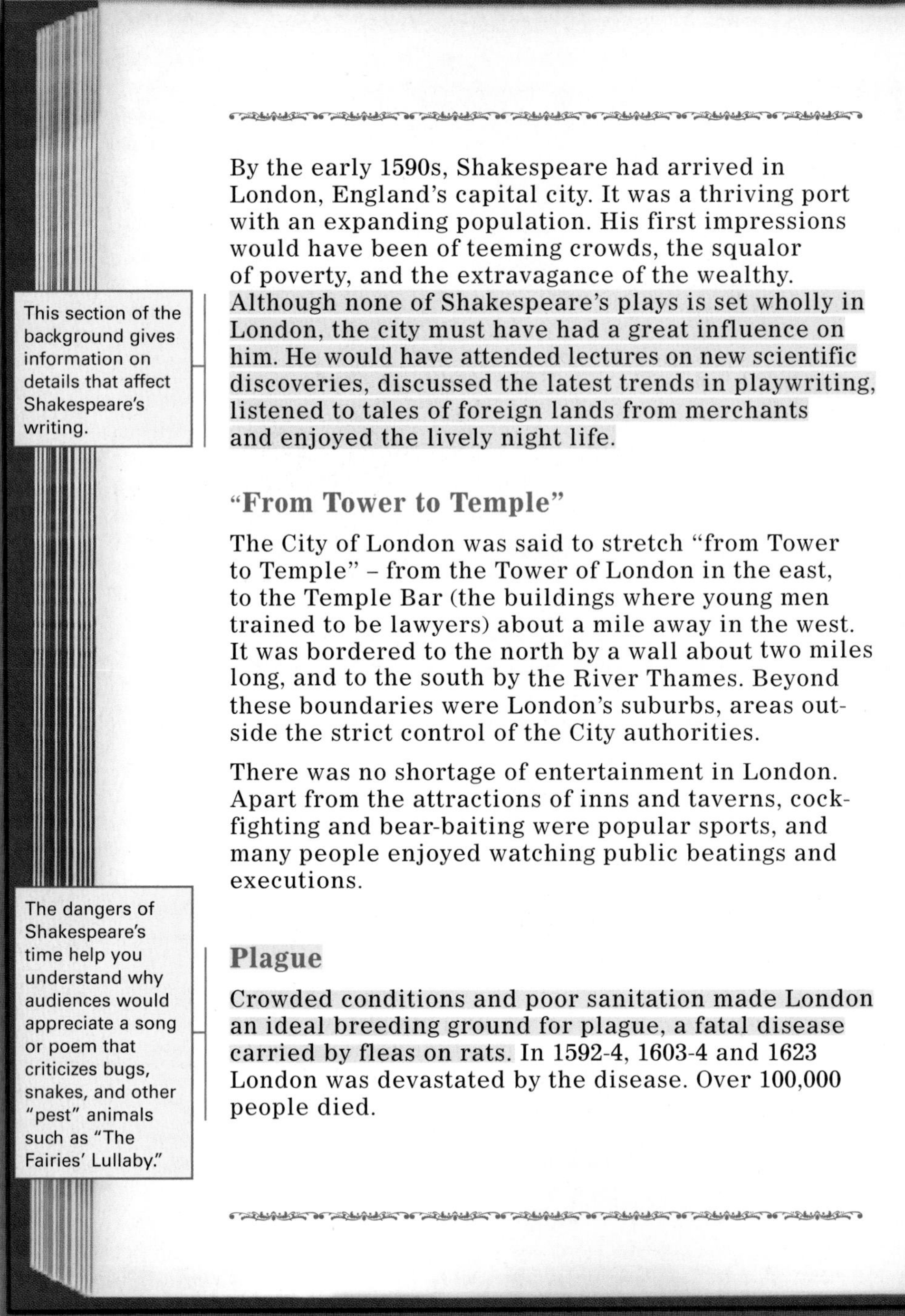

This section of the background gives information on details that affect Shakespeare's writing.
By the early 1590s, Shakespeare had arrived in London, England's capital city. It was a thriving port with an expanding population. His first impressions would have been of teeming crowds, the squalor of poverty, and the extravagance of the wealthy. Although none of Shakespeare's plays is set wholly in London, the city must have had a great influence on him. He would have attended lectures on new scientific discoveries, discussed the latest trends in playwriting, listened to tales of foreign lands from merchants and enjoyed the lively night life.
"From Tower to Temple"
The City of London was said to stretch "from Tower to Temple" – from the Tower of London in the east, to the Temple Bar (the buildings where young men trained to be lawyers) about a mile away in the west. It was bordered to the north by a wall about two miles long, and to the south by the River Thames. Beyond these boundaries were London's suburbs, areas outside the strict control of the City authorities.
There was no shortage of entertainment in London. Apart from the attractions of inns and taverns, cock-fighting and bear-baiting were popular sports, and many people enjoyed watching public beatings and executions.
The dangers of Shakespeare's time help you understand why audiences would appreciate a song or poem that criticizes bugs, snakes, and other "pest" animals such as "The Fairies' Lullaby."
Plague
Crowded conditions and poor sanitation made London an ideal breeding ground for plague, a fatal disease carried by fleas on rats. In 1592-4, 1603-4 and 1623 London was devastated by the disease. Over 100,000 people died.

CUSTOMIZE INSTRUCTION FOR UNIVERSAL ACCESS

For Advanced Learners

Students who are interested in literature or history may wish to explore more about Shakespeare or his time. Suggest that these students read another, more in-depth source about Shakespeare or about London during the Renaissance. Invite students to give a brief presentation based on their readings. In their presentations, students should show how they took notes as they researched. Ask listeners to take notes during the student presentations.

Check Your Comprehension

1. What would Shakespeare's first impressions have been of London?
2. How would London have influenced Shakespeare?
3. What kinds of entertainment could be found in London?

Applying the Reading Strategy

Taking Notes

4. What three main ideas would you include in an **outline** of this background?
5. Which sentences would you **highlight** or **underline** on a photocopy?
6. Write a **summary** of the background.

Activity

Build a Background

"Shakespeare's London" provides information about London during the time when Shakespeare was writing his plays. It helps the reader get a better understanding of the time and setting of England before reading the works of Shakespeare. Choose a story that you have recently read. Find information about the author and the time that the story was written. Then, write a brief background for the story.

Comparing and Contrasting Informational Materials

Background and Biography

Both literary backgrounds and author biographies give factual information about the author of a piece of literature. A literary background provides information on all or some of the following:

- the time and place
- the customs
- the politics
- the problems

Information in an author biography is more focused on the author only. It will include dates, places, and details specific to the author. Compare and contrast background and biography by making a chart like the one shown. Use the author biography on page 728 and the background in this feature to complete the chart.

What information do you find in each source?

	Background	Biography
Shakespeare's occupations	playwright	writer and actor
Birth and death	None	
London	• England's capital • a port city • poor and rich	Shakespeare
Entertainment		

Answers for p. 737

Check Your Comprehension

1. His first impressions would have been of a busy city with extreme poverty and extreme wealth.
2. While in London, Shakespeare would have learned about scientific discoveries, literature, and travel.
3. The entertainment included violent sports, such as bear baiting, cock fighting, and viewing public beatings and executions. Other entertainments included visits to taverns and inns, and listening to tales of foreign lands.

Applying the Reading Strategy

4. The three main ideas are the following: The London that Shakespeare encountered in the early 1590s was dirty, crowded, and full of excitement; London was bordered by the Tower of London, The Temple Bar, the River Thames, and a wall two miles long; and the plague spread rapidly in the city.
5. The sentences include the following: "The world Shakespeare knew was full of danger, excitement and change"; "Although none of Shakespeare's plays is set wholly in London, the city must have had a great influence on him"; "The City of London was said to stretch 'from Tower to Temple'"; "Crowded conditions and poor sanitation made London an ideal breeding ground for plague."
6. Shakespeare gleaned much inspiration from London, which offered overcrowding, disease, poverty, wealth, and scientific discoveries. The theatres provided an outlet for creativity, an escape from squalor, and a venue for portraying city life.

continued

Answers continued

Activity

Choose the story and author for students to research, or have students revisit any of the stories they have read in this book. Resources that can be useful when writing backgrounds include reference books that focus on writers. If students cannot find specific information about the writer's life that ties to the story, encourage them to speculate about connections. Have students take notes in outline form for their research and submit the outline with their completed background.

Comparing and Contrasting Informational Materials

Background and Biography: Explain to students that book-length biographies often contain a lot of information about the author's life and the environment in which he or she lived and wrote. In contrast, a background includes a short summary of the biography that gives the reader just enough information necessary to enjoy the author's work.

Simile: Willow and Ginkgo ✦ Fame Is a Bee ✦ April Rain Song

Lesson Objectives

1. **To analyze and respond to literary elements**
   - Literary Analysis: Figurative Language
   - Comparing Literary Works
2. **To read, comprehend, analyze, and critique three poems**
   - Reading Strategy: Paraphrasing
   - Reading Check Questions
   - Review and Assess Questions
3. **To develop word analysis skills, fluency, and systematic vocabulary**
   - Vocabulary Development Lesson: Concept Development: Musical Words
4. **To understand and apply written and oral language conventions**
   - Spelling Strategy
   - Grammar Lesson: Colons
   - Assessment Practice (ATE)
5. **To understand and apply appropriate writing and research strategies**
   - Writing Lesson: Description
   - Extension Activity: Multimedia Report
   - Extension Activity: Poem
6. **To understand and apply listening and speaking strategies**
   - Extension Activity: Speech

STEP-BY-STEP TEACHING GUIDE	PACING GUIDE
PRETEACH	
Motivate Students and Provide Background	
Use the Motivation activity (ATE p. 738)	5 min.
Read and discuss the Preview material and Background information (SE/ATE p. 738) [A]	10 min.
Introduce the Concepts	
Introduce the Literary Analysis and Reading Strategy (SE/ATE p. 739) [A]	15 min.
Pronounce the vocabulary words and read their definitions (SE p. 739)	5 min.
TEACH	
Monitor Comprehension	
Informally monitor comprehension by circulating while students read independently or in groups [A]	5 min.
Develop vocabulary with Vocabulary notes (SE p. 740)	as students read
Develop Understanding	
Develop students' understanding of figurative language with the Literary Analysis annotations (ATE p. 740) [A]	5 min.
Develop students' ability to paraphrase with the Reading Strategy annotations (ATE p. 741)	5 min.
ASSESS	
Assess Mastery	
Assess students' mastery of the Reading Strategy and Literary Analysis by having them answer the Review and Assess questions (SE/ATE p. 743)	15 min.
Use one or more of the print and media Assessment Resources (ATE p. 745) [A]	up to 45 min.
EXTEND	
Apply Understanding	
Have students complete the Vocabulary Development Lesson and the Grammar Lesson (SE p. 744) [A]	20 min.
Apply students' ability to write a description using the Writing Lesson (SE/ATE p. 745) [A]	30–45 min.
Apply students' understanding of the selection using one or more of the Extension Activities (SE p. 745)	20–90 min.

ACCELERATED INSTRUCTION:
Use the strategies and activities identified with an [A].

UNIVERSAL ACCESS
● = Below Level Students
▲ = On-Level Students
■ = Above Level Students

Time and Resource Manager

Reading Level: Challenging, Average, Average
Average Number of Instructional Days: 3

RESOURCES		
PRINT	**TRANSPARENCIES**	**TECHNOLOGY**
• **Beyond Literature,** Cross-Curricular Connection: Science, p. 41 ▲ ■		• **Interest Grabber Videotapes,** Tape 5 ● ▲ ■
• **Selection Support Workbook:** ● ▲ ■ Literary Analysis, p. 205 Reading Strategy, p. 204 Build Vocabulary, p. 201	• **Literary Analysis and Reading Transparencies,** pp. 81 and 82 ● ▲ ■	
• **Adapted Reader's Companion** ● • **Reader's Companion** ●		• **Listening to Literature** ● ▲ ■ Audiocassettes, Side 26 Audio CDs, CD 13
• **English Learner's Companion** ● ▲ • **Literary Analysis for Enrichment** ■		
• **Formal Assessment:** Selection Test, pp. 185–187 ● ▲ ■ • **Open Book Test,** pp. 121–123 ● ▲ ■ • **Performance Assessment and Portfolio Management,** p. 29 ● ▲ ■ • PRENTICE HALL ASSESSMENT SYSTEM ● ▲ ■	• PRENTICE HALL ASSESSMENT SYSTEM ● ▲ ■ Skills Practice Answers and Explanations on Transparencies	• **Test Bank Software** ● ▲ ■ • **Got It! Assessment Videotapes,** Tape 5 ● ▲
• **Selection Support Workbook:** ● ▲ ■ Build Spelling Skills, p. 202 Build Grammar Skills, p. 203 • **Writing and Grammar,** Copper Level ● ▲ ■ • **Extension Activities,** p. 41 ● ▲ ■	• **Daily Language Practice Transparencies** ● ▲ • **Writing Models and Graphic Organizers on Transparencies** ● ▲ ■	• **Writing and Grammar iText CD-ROM** ● ▲ ■ ***Take It to the Net*** www.phschool.com

BLOCK SCHEDULING: Use one 90-minute class period to preteach the selection and have students read it. Use a second 90-minute class period to assess students' mastery of skills and have them complete one of the Extension Activities.

PRETEACH

Step-by-Step Teaching Guide for pp. 738–739

Motivation

Ask students to look at the picture of the tree on this page. Then, write the following sentence on the board: A tree is like (a/an) ________. Have students brainstorm as many words and phrases as they can to complete the sentence. Then, tell them that the sentences they have created are similes. Finally, explain that the writers of the poems in this grouping use similes, metaphors, and personification that will help readers look at common things in a new and unique way.

Interest Grabber Video

As an alternative, play "Giants of the Forest" on Tape 5 to engage student interest.

❶ Background

Science

The ginkgo tree that is the subject of Eve Merriam's poem "Simile: Willow and Ginkgo," is the last remaining species of a tree that flourished millions of years ago. Scientists have unearthed fossils that are 200 million years old which have the distinctive fan-shaped leaves of this tree. The tree, native to China, has spread around the world even as other varieties of trees have become extinct. The ginkgo grows in climates with harsh weather and is valued by some people for its medicinal qualities.

Prepare to Read

❶ Simile: Willow and Ginkgo ◆ Fame Is a Bee ◆ April Rain Song

Take It to the Net

Visit www.phschool.com for interactive activities and instruction related to these selections, including

- background
- graphic organizers
- literary elements
- reading strategies

Preview

Connecting to the Literature

Poets may write about ordinary subjects—trees, bees, or rain—but they use imagination to surprise you into seeing things in a new way. As you read, ask yourself what words you would use to make an ordinary object unique.

Background

Willow trees and ginkgo trees are very different from each other. A willow tree has long, slender branches with long, narrow leaves. The ginkgo, on the other hand, is a large tree with fan-shaped leaves.

TEACHING RESOURCES

The following resources can be used to enrich or extend the instruction for pp. 738–739.

Motivation

Interest Grabber Video, Tape 5 

Background

Beyond Literature, p. 41

Take It to the Net

Visit www.phschool.com for Background and hotlinks for the selections.

Literary Analysis

Literary Analysis and Reading Transparencies, Figurative Language, p. 82

Reading

Selection Support: Reading Strategy, p. 204; Build Vocabulary, p. 201

Literary Analysis and Reading Transparencies, Paraphrasing, p. 81

BLOCK SCHEDULING: Resources marked with this symbol provide varied instruction during 90-minute blocks.

❷ Literary Analysis

Figurative Language

Figurative language is language that uses comparisons to help you see or feel things in a new way.

- **Simile** uses *like* or *as* to make a direct comparison between unlike things, as in "The willow is like an etching."
- **Metaphor** compares unlike things by describing one as if it were the other, without using *like* or *as*. An example is "peace is a dove," which means "peace is like a dove."
- **Personification** gives human characteristics to a nonhuman subject as if it were human, as in "Let the rain kiss you."

As you read, find examples of figurative language, and record and analyze each in an organizer like the one shown.

Passage from Poem
The ginkgo is like a crude sketch . . .

↓

Figurative Language
Simile

↓

What it Means
The ginkgo is not attractive to look at.

Comparing Literary Works

All of these poems use figurative language. The things being compared, however, are very different and give each poem a distinct mood or feeling. Compare and contrast the poems by answering the following focus questions:

1. Which two poems make comparisons that emphasize grace or beauty?
2. How does the comparison in "Fame Is a Bee" make its mood different from that of the other poems? What other characteristics set it apart from the other two poems?

❸ Reading Strategy

Paraphrasing

Paraphrasing is restating an author's words in your own words. Paraphrasing difficult or confusing passages in a poem helps you clarify the meaning. Look at the following example from "The Fairies' Lullaby," and notice how it can be paraphrased.

Example: Beetles black, approach not near.
Worm nor snail do no offense.

Paraphrased: Don't come near, you black beetles; don't do any harm, you worm and snail.

As you read confusing or difficult lines, paraphrase them in your own words.

Vocabulary Development

soprano (sə pran′ ō) *n.* the highest singing voice of women, girls, or young boys (p. 740)

chorus (kôr′ əs) *n.* the part of a song sung by many voices at once (p. 740)

❷ Literary Analysis

Figurative Language

- Tell students that they are already familiar with figurative language from music, books, stories, and poems. Add that figurative language is a tool writers use to connect ideas.
- Then, ask a volunteer to read aloud the instruction and the description of each type of figurative language. Walk students through the graphic organizer on p. 739.
- Take a moment to talk about the Comparing Literary Works questions. Write the questions on the board along with this additional question: What two things are compared in the poem? Ask students to consider these questions as they read.
- Encourage students to use the graphic organizer on the Figurative Language transparency on p. 82 of **Literary Analysis and Reading Transparencies** as they read.

❸ Reading Strategy

Paraphrasing

- Explain that paraphrasing is helpful when reading poetry. Because poems often imply ideas or use unusual words or syntax, paraphrasing allows readers to express ideas in their own words.
- Offer these steps for paraphrasing: If a line or passage is difficult to understand, stop and reread it. Then, say it in your own words.
- Explain that paraphrases will differ, depending on interpretation.

Vocabulary Development

- Pronounce each vocabulary word for students, and read the definitions as a class. Have students identify any words with which they are already familiar.

CUSTOMIZE INSTRUCTION FOR UNIVERSAL ACCESS

For Special Needs Students	For Less Proficient Readers	For English Learners
Have students read the adapted version of "April Rain Song" in the **Adapted Reader's Companion.** This version provides basic-level instruction in an interactive format with questions and write-on lines. Completing the adapted version will prepare students to read the selection in the Student Edition.	Have students read "April Rain Song" in the **Reader's Companion.** This version provides basic-level instruction in an interactive format with questions and write-on lines. After students finish the selection in Reader's Companion, have them complete the questions and activities in the Student Edition.	Have students read the adapted version of "April Rain Song" in the **English Learner's Companion.** This version provides basic-level instruction in an interactive format with questions and write-on lines. Completing the adapted version will prepare students to read the selection in the Student Edition.

 ***E-Teach***

Visit E-Teach at www.phschool.com for teachers' essays on how to teach, with questions and answers.

TEACH

Step-by-Step Teaching Guide for pp. 740–743

CUSTOMIZE INSTRUCTION
For Bodily/Kinesthetic Learners

Challenge students to act out the ideas in the poems in this grouping. Allow students to work in pairs or small groups to read the poems and identify clear actions that are described. Have each student act out the poems while another student reads them, or have group members act out the poems in silence and ask the class to guess which poem they are performing.

❶ About the Selections

In "Simile: Willow and Ginkgo," the poet compares the delicate beauty of the willow tree and the sturdy toughness of the ginkgo. In the end, the poet sees that the unique qualities of the ginkgo are closer to her heart.

In "Fame Is a Bee," (p. 741) Emily Dickinson describes the characteristics of fame—its attraction, its pain, and its tendency to arrive and depart quickly.

In "April Rain Song" (p. 742), Langston Hughes paints a vivid picture of gentle rain.

❷ Literary Analysis

Figurative Language

- Write the following sentence on the board before students read the poems in this grouping: The poet is comparing ________ and ________.
- Then, after students read this poem, ask them to complete the sentence.
  Answer: The poet is comparing a willow tree and a ginkgo tree.

❶ *Simile:* Willow *and* Ginkgo

Eve Merriam

❷
The willow is like an etching,[1]
Fine-lined against the sky.
The ginkgo is like a crude sketch,
Hardly worthy to be signed.

The willow's music is like a soprano,
Delicate and thin.
The ginkgo's tune is like a chorus
With everyone joining in.

The willow is sleek as a velvet-nosed calf;
The ginkgo is leathery as an old bull.
The willow's branches are like silken thread;
The ginkgo's like stubby rough wool.

The willow is like a nymph[2] with streaming hair;
Wherever it grows, there is green and gold and fair.
The willow dips to the water,
Protected and precious, like the king's favorite daughter.

The ginkgo forces its way through gray concrete;
Like a city child, it grows up in the street.
Thrust against the metal sky,
Somehow it survives and even thrives.

My eyes feast upon the willow,
But my heart goes to the ginkgo.

soprano (sə pran′ ō) *n.* the highest singing voice of women, girls, or young boys

chorus (kôr′ əs) *n.* the part of a song sung by many voices at once

1. **etching** (ech′ iŋ) *n.* a print of a drawing or design made on metal, glass, or wood.
2. **nymph** (nimf) *n.* goddess of nature thought of as a beautiful maiden.

Eve Merriam

(1916–1992)

Eve Merriam was bitten by the word bug early in life, falling in love with the music of language. Among her many books of poems is the award-winning *Family Circle*.

TEACHING RESOURCES

The following resources can be used to enrich or extend the instruction for pp. 740–743.

Literary Analysis
- **Selection Support:** Literary Analysis, p. 205
- **Literary Analysis for Enrichment**

Reading
- **Reader's Companion**
- **Adapted Reader's Companion**
- **English Learner's Companion**

- **Listening to Literature Audiocassettes,** Side 26
- **Listening to Literature Audio CDs,** CD 13

BLOCK SCHEDULING: Resources marked with this symbol provide varied instruction during 90-minute blocks.

Fame Is a Bee

Emily Dickinson

Fame is a bee.
It has a song—
3 It has a sting—
Ah, too, it has a wing.

Reading Strategy
Paraphrasing State the third line in your own words.

Emily Dickinson

(1830–1886)

Only a handful of Dickinson's poems appeared in print during her lifetime. However, together with Walt Whitman, she is considered a founder of American poetry. Her poems are a kind of lifelong diary of her deepest guesses and wonderings. The daughter of a lawyer in Amherst, Massachusetts, Emily Dickinson lived quietly in her family's home all her life. All the while, she was writing and saving away over 1,700 of her brief lyrics.

Review and Assess

Thinking About the Selections

1. **Respond:** Which poem do you think makes the most powerful comparison? Why?
2. (a) **Recall:** To what three things are the willow and ginkgo compared in "Simile: Willow and Ginkgo"?
(b) **Compare and Contrast:** Contrast the general impression you get of the willow and the ginkgo. (c) **Interpret:** Explain the meaning of the last two lines in the poem. (d) **Assess:** Based on the rest of the poem, is the last line surprising?
3. (a) **Recall:** What three things does Fame have in "Fame Is a Bee"? (b) **Interpret:** What is Fame's song? (c) **Assess:** Is a bee a good image to suggest fame? Explain.
4. **Take a Position:** Celebrities often have details of their private lives analyzed in the media. What is your stand on the following questions (a) At what point, if any, is publishing information on a celebrity's life an invasion of privacy?
(b) What strategies, if any, should reporters be prohibited from using when gathering information?

CUSTOMIZE INSTRUCTION FOR UNIVERSAL ACCESS

For Special Needs	For Gifted/Talented Students
Students may have trouble with the implied comparisons of metaphor and personification. Allow students to work in pairs to read the poems aloud. After reading each poem, the partners should discuss what comparison is being made and whether they think it works. Tell students to compare the ideas in the poems with their own personal experiences.	Explain to students that Emily Dickinson is known for her ability to condense surprising insights into very few words. Point out how she does this in "Fame Is a Bee." Explain how the poem uses a simple image from nature to make an abstract idea, fame, concrete. Challenge students to write short poems of their own that compare another abstract idea to something found in nature. Students may follow Dickinson's poem as a model or develop their own styles.

3 Reading Strategy

Paraphrasing

- Remind students that paraphrasing means telling something in your own words.
- Ask students the Reading Strategy question on p. 741.
Answer: The third line literally means that a bee has both a stinger and causes pain. In regards to fame, the line means that fame can cause one pain just as it can bring happiness.

Answers for p. 741

Review and Assess

1. Possible response: "Simile: Willow and Ginkgo" is a fuller, more detailed comparison, but "Fame Is a Bee" is more powerful because it is simple and clear.
2. **(a)** The trees are compared to drawings, singers, animals, humans, and fabrics. **(b)** The willow sounds delicate, elegant, slim, and fine; the ginkgo sounds rough, tough, and brave. **(c)** The poet suggests that there is reason to care about both trees; one demands admiration, and the other deserves love and hope. **(d)** The last line is somewhat surprising as the speaker paints a lovely picture of the willow; however, the speaker hints where her sympathies lie when she refers to the ginkgo as a struggling city child.
3. **(a)** Fame has a song, a sting, and wings. **(b)** Fame's song, like the buzzing of a bee, is the allure that attracts attention to a famous person. **(c)** Possible response: The bee is a good image because fame has a sweet song that attracts people, is painful like a bee sting when it exacts its price, and is fleeting like a bee when it flies away quickly.
4. **(a)** Possible responses: The invasion of celebrities' privacy is the price they pay for fame; celebrities deserve the same privacy as anyone else.
(b) Possible responses: Using telephoto lenses to gather information when celebrities are in a private area should be prohibited; reporters should have the freedom to ask questions and get information in any way necessary no matter who their subject is.

ASSESS

4 ▶Critical Viewing

Answer: Students might suggest line 1, because the rain has "kissed" the leaf.

Answers for p. 742

Review and Assess

1. Possible responses: Students may or may not share the speaker's feelings about rain. They may enjoy the rain or find it to be an inconvenience instead of a musical treat.
2. **(a)** The rain sings a lullaby or sleep-song. **(b)** The poet clearly loves the sound and sight of falling rain. **(c)** The poem would probably not describe rain as kissing or as liquid silver; it would probably describe the coldness and the dampness that late autumn rain produces.
3. **(a)** The speaker tells the readers to let the rain kiss them, beat upon their heads, and sing them a lullaby. **(b)** One positive aspect would be to see the rain as a gentle, caring being.

April Rain Song

Langston Hughes

4 ◀Critical Viewing Which line from the poem would you use as a caption for this picture? **[Connect]**

Let the rain kiss you.
Let the rain beat upon your head with silver liquid drops.
Let the rain sing you a lullaby.

The rain makes still pools on the sidewalk.
The rain makes running pools in the gutter.
The rain plays a little sleep-song on our roof at night—

And I love the rain.

Langston Hughes

(1902–1967)

Langston Hughes brought the rhythms of African American music and speech to American poetry. Raised in the Midwest, Hughes traveled as a young man before settling in New York City's African American community of Harlem. There he felt the influence of musical styles such as jazz and the blues. Among his best-known collections of poetry are *The Weary Blues* (1926) and *The Dream Keeper and Other Poems* (1932).

Review and Assess

Thinking About the Selections

1. **Respond:** Do you share the speaker's feelings about rain? Why or why not?
2. **(a) Recall:** In "April Rain Song," what kind of songs does the rain sing? **(b) Infer:** What is revealed about the poet's thoughts about rain? **(c) Evaluate:** How would the poem be different if it were about a late autumn rain in a cold climate?
3. **(a) Recall:** What three things does the speaker tell the reader to let the rain do? **(b) Apply:** What would be the positive aspects of experiencing these three things?

ASSESSMENT PRACTICE: Writing Skills

Recognize Appropriate Usage **(For more practice, see Test Preparation Workbook, p. 57.)**

Many tests require students to distinguish between correct and incorrect usage of comparatives and superlatives. Explain that adjectives and adverbs are called comparatives when they are used to compare two items, and they are called superlatives when they are used to compare more than two objects or qualities. Help students practice recognizing these forms by giving them the following sample test item.

Emily Dickinson is the _____ American female poet.

Choose the word or group of words that belongs in the space.

A greater **C** more great
B greatest **D** most greatest

Because there are more than two American female poets, the sentence requires a superlative. The correct answer is *B*. *A* and *C* are the comparative forms, and *C* and *D* are grammatically incorrect.

Review and Assess

Literary Analysis

Figurative Language

1. (a) What is being compared in lines 5–8 in "Simile: Willow and Ginkgo"? (b) What is meant by this comparison?
2. What type of figurative language is used in "Fame Is a Bee"?
3. Explain the figurative language in line 2 of "April Rain Song."

Comparing Literary Works

4. (a) Using a chart like this one, compare the animal comparisons used in "Simile: Willow and Ginkgo" and "Fame Is a Bee." (b) Have both poems used effective comparisons? Explain.

"Simile: Willow and Ginkgo"	"Fame Is a Bee"
Line: Type of Figurative Language:	Line: Type of Figurative Language:

5. What types of figurative language does each poet use?
6. Which poem uses figurative language most effectively to help convey the meaning of the poem?

Reading Strategy

Paraphrasing

7. Restate lines 9–10 of "Simile: Willow and Ginkgo" in your own words. Record your answer in a graphic organizer like the one shown.

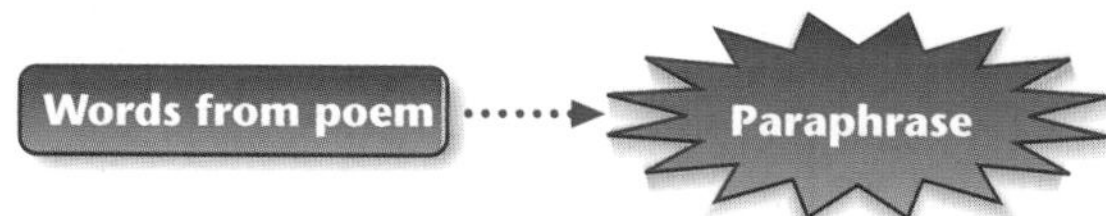

8. Restate "Fame Is a Bee" in your own words.
9. How would you paraphrase line 2 of "April Rain Song"?

Extending Understanding

10. **Cultural Connection:** Langston Hughes was part of an African American cultural movement in the 1920s called the Harlem Renaissance, which included aspiring writers, artists, and musicians. Find out what Hughes contributed to the movement.

Quick Review

Figurative language is language that uses comparisons to help you see or feel things in a new way. A **simile** uses *like* or *as* to compare two apparently unlike items. A **metaphor** compares one thing to another without using *like* or *as*. **Personification** gives human characteristics to a nonhuman subject.
To review figurative language, see page 739.

Paraphrasing is restating an author's words in your own words.

Take It to the Net

www.phschool.com

Take the interactive self-test online to check your understanding of these selections.

ENRICHMENT: Further Reading

Other Works by the Poets

Works by Eve Merriam

The Singing Green: New and Selected Poems for All Seasons

Works by Emily Dickinson

The Complete Poems of Emily Dickinson

Works by Langston Hughes

Selected Poems of Langston Hughes

Take It to the Net

Visit www.phschool.com for more information on the poets.

Answers for p. 743

Review and Assess

1. **(a)** The trees are compared to singers. The willow is compared to a soprano; the ginkgo is compared to a chorus. **(b)** Possible response: The speaker means that willows, like sopranos' voices, are delicate and beautiful, while ginkgoes, like choruses, are noisy and rough.
2. The poem features a metaphor.
3. The poet uses personification; rain will fall or beat upon the reader in silver droplets.
4. **(a) "Simile":** "The willow is sleek as a velvet-nosed calf." (simile) "The ginkgo is leathery as an old bull" (simile) **"Fame":** "Fame is a bee." (metaphor) **(b)** Possible responses: The comparisons are effective. The choices in "Simile: Willow and Ginkgo" may be more vivid, but the comparison in "Fame Is a Bee" may be easier to understand.
5. Merriam uses simile. Dickinson uses metaphor. Hughes uses personification.
6. Possible response: The metaphor in "Fame Is a Bee" most effectively and concisely conveys the poem's meaning.
7. **Words from poem:** "The willow is sleek as a velvet-nosed calf;/The ginkgo is leathery as an old bull."
   Paraphrase: The willow tree is sleek, smooth, and young like a calf. The ginkgo is tough like an old bull.
8. Possible response: Fame sings an attractive song, can cause pain, and can go away as quickly as it comes.
9. Possible response: Let the rain fall gently on your head with its silvery droplets.
10. Students should discover that Hughes contributed to the Harlem Renaissance as a poet and playwright. His career and influence far outlasted the movement, however. While he continued to write poetry, he also wrote his autobiography, *The Big Sea;* edited anthologies of African American poetry; wrote opera lyrics; translated poetry from Spanish; and wrote a regular newspaper column.

EXTEND

Answers for p. 744

❶ Vocabulary Development

Concept Development

soprano, alto, tenor, bass

Word Analysis: Special Terms

1. A woman should be cast as a soprano because her voice would be higher.
2. A chorus would sing the loudest because many voices singing together are louder than one.

Spelling Strategy

altos; sopranos; banjos; cellos

❷ Grammar

1. To whom it may concern:
2. Bees do things such as the following: sing, sting, and fly away.
3. Sentence is correct.
4. Dear Sir:
5. Warning: Keep Out of Reach of Children

Writing Application

Possible answer:

Dear Sir or Madam:

I am writing to find out whether you have any of the following books: *The Singing Green: New and Selected Poems for All Seasons, The Complete Poems of Emily Dickinson,* and *Selected Poems of Langston Hughes*. Note: I need these books as soon as possible.

Thank you.

Integrate Language Skills

❶ Vocabulary Development Lesson

Concept Development: Musical Words

"Simile: Willow and Ginkgo" uses words from the world of music. One of these is *soprano*, which means "the highest singing voice." Another music term is *chorus*, which means "a singing group."

Write these terms for the singers in a chorus in order. List the highest voice first and the lowest voice last. Use a dictionary to check definitions as needed.

bass soprano
alto tenor

Word Analysis: Special Terms

Explain your answer to each question.

1. Would you cast a woman or a man to sing a *soprano* part?
2. Would a *soloist*, a *chorus*, or a *songbird* sing the loudest?

Spelling Strategy

When a consonant precedes a final *o*, you usually add *es* to the end of the word to form the plural. Exceptions include all musical terms, such as *sopranos*. Correctly write the italicized words that are misspelled:

The *altoes* and *sopranoes* sang to the accompaniment of *banjoes*, *celloes*, and *pianos*.

❷ Grammar Lesson

Colons

A **colon** (:) is a punctuation mark with a number of uses. The chart shown here explains how to use colons and gives examples.

Use Colons	Examples
After the salutation, or greeting, in a business letter	Dear Ms. Tang: Gentlemen:
To introduce an example or illustration	Simile: Willow and Ginkgo
After an independent clause to introduce a list of items. (Note: An independent clause that comes before a colon often includes *the following, as follows, these,* or *those*.)	The following trees grow in the park: maples, oaks and elms. These are my favorite kinds of weather: snowstorms and gentle rain.
To separate hours and minutes	3:15 P.M.
On warnings and labels	Warning: Thin ice

Practice Rewrite each item below, adding colons where necessary. If the item is correct as is, write *Correct*.

1. To whom it may concern
2. Bees do things such as the following sing, sting, and fly away.
3. Jed eats lunch at 12:30 P.M.
4. Dear Sir
5. Warning Keep Out of Reach of Children

Writing Application Write a three-sentence business letter to request information about ordering books from a publisher. Correctly use two colons in your letter.

WG Prentice Hall Writing and Grammar Connection: Chapter 26, Section 3

TEACHING RESOURCES

The following resources can be used to enrich or extend the instruction for pp. 744–745.

Vocabulary

Selection Support: Build Vocabulary, p. 201
Build Spelling Skills, p. 202

Vocabulary and Spelling Practice Book
(Use this booklet for skills enrichment)

Grammar

Selection Support: Build Grammar Skills, p. 203

Writing and Grammar, Copper Level, p. 574

Daily Language Practice Transparencies ■

Writing

Writing and Grammar, Copper Level, p. 102 ■

Writing Models and Graphic Organizers on Transparencies, p. 81

Writing and Grammar iText CD-ROM

■ **BLOCK SCHEDULING:** Resources marked with this symbol provide varied instruction during 90-minute blocks.

❸ Writing Lesson

Description

The writers in this group describe their topics largely through figurative language. The effect of the figurative language is a fanciful picture that focuses on a mood or feeling. Choose one of the topics from the poems and write a practical description.

Prewriting Choose the poem and topic you will re-describe. Identify the main qualities on which the poet focuses. Then make a list of qualities you will describe in your more practical description. Some may be the same as those in the poem, with a different emphasis.

Model: Identifying Qualities

In poem	In my description
• like an etching	• brittle, thin, easily broken branches
• fine-lined	

Drafting Begin by identifying the topic you are describing. In the body of your description, develop the description with details that show the "reality" of your subject. Refer to the qualities mentioned in the poem and give your own description of these qualities.

Revising Add detail to your description by elaborating on statements with examples.

WG Prentice Hall Writing and Grammar Connection: Chapter 6, Section 2

❹ Extension Activities

Research and Technology Work with a small group to conduct research and prepare a **multimedia report** on trees. Prepare the following to accompany your report:

- Printouts, slides, photos, or drawings of trees
- Leaves mounted on posterboard
- Labeled diagram showing the parts of a tree

Present your report to the class. **[Group Activity]**

Writing Write a poem of your own about a topic from nature. Choose one of the poems in this group as a model of figurative language. For example, you might use personification in your poem as Langston Hughes does in his.

Listening and Speaking Prepare and give a **speech** to explain to classmates how advertisers and the media use famous people to promote products in print and on television. Identify persuasive techniques used in ads, such as presenting a celebrity's image to give false or misleading information on a product.

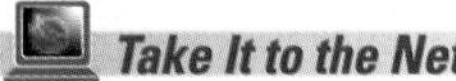

www.phschool.com

Go online for an additional research activity using the Internet.

ASSESSMENT RESOURCES

The following resources can be used to assess students' knowledge and skills.

Selection Assessment

- **Formal Assessment,** pp. 185–187
- **Open Book Test,** pp. 121–123
- **Got It! Assessment Videotapes,** Tape 5
- **Test Bank Software**

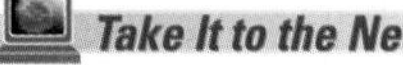

Visit www.phschool.com for self-tests and additional questions on the selections.

Research and Technology Rubric

- **Performance Assess. and Portfolio Mgmt.,** p. 29

- **Workbook**
- **Skill Book**
- **Transparencies**
- **CD-ROM**

Lesson Support for p. 745

❸ Writing Lesson

- Talk to students about the possible forms of writing they can use. Suggest that students write a letter or a descriptive scene.
- Encourage students to draw a chart similar to the one on p. 745 and to add details, including at least one detail for each sense. Have them add examples of each type of figurative language, as well.
- As students revise, have them underline examples of figurative language and discuss with a writing partner the effectiveness of the figurative language. Guide students away from clichés.
- Use or adapt the appropriate rubric from **Performance Assessment and Portfolio Management** to evaluate students' work.

❹ Research and Technology

- Discuss with students how to select and narrow topics. For example, students may wish to focus on one particular tree that grows in their area.
- Next, students should work in their groups to decide the areas of research and to divide research tasks. Consider asking the school librarian to suggest or provide resources.
- Every student should participate in all aspects of the report: researching, writing, finding and preparing art, and presenting material.
- After students present their reports, they should use the Speaking rubric on p. 29 in **Performance Assessment and Portfolio Management.**

CUSTOMIZE INSTRUCTION For Universal Access

To address different learning styles, use the activities suggested in the **Extension Activities** booklet, p. 41.

- For Visual/Spatial and Interpersonal Learners, use Activity 5.
- For Musical/Rhythmic and Interpersonal Learners, use Activity 6.
- For Bodily/Kinesthetic Learners, use Activity 7.

Lesson Objectives

1. To understand the connection between a poem that compares trees and a story that describes kinds of wood
2. To understand how writers compare a similar object in poetry and prose

Connections

In her poem "Simile: Willow and Ginkgo" (p. 740), poet Eve Merriam compares two types of trees to people and to objects. In "La Leña Buena," writer John Phillip Santos discusses the value and qualities of two types of wood. After students read the excerpt here, have them reread the poem "Simile: Willow and Ginkgo." What similarities and differences do students notice in the way trees and wood are compared to other objects?

Comparisons From Nature

- Before students begin reading, explain that even in the 1920s, wood was the fuel that many people used to heat their homes and cook their food, so both the quality and the quantity of firewood were important.
- After students read the excerpt, ask them to create a Venn diagram like the one on p. 89 of **Writing Models and Graphic Organizers on Transparencies.** Have students label one circle *Huisache* and one circle *Mesquite*. Allow students to work as partners to identify the similarities and differences between the characteristics of the two woods.
  Answer: *Differences:* Huisache burns fast, in bright yellow flames, and does not burn hot. Mesquite burns slowly, with great heat, and smells good. *Similarities:* Both types of wood are found in Mexico and are used for fuel.
- After students complete the reading and questions here, have them turn to "Simile: Willow and Ginkgo" and complete a Venn diagram for the two types of trees described there.

CONNECTIONS

Poetry and Prose

Comparisons from Nature

Both Eve Merriam and John Phillip Santos compare and contrast trees. Merriam writes in poetry, focusing mostly on the appearance of the trees. Santos writes in prose, writing that is not in verse. He considers the function as well as the appearance. As you read, notice that the writing is organized to emphasize the similarities and differences. Think about the point Santos is making when he compares and contrasts the qualities of the trees.

La Leña Buena

John Phillip Santos

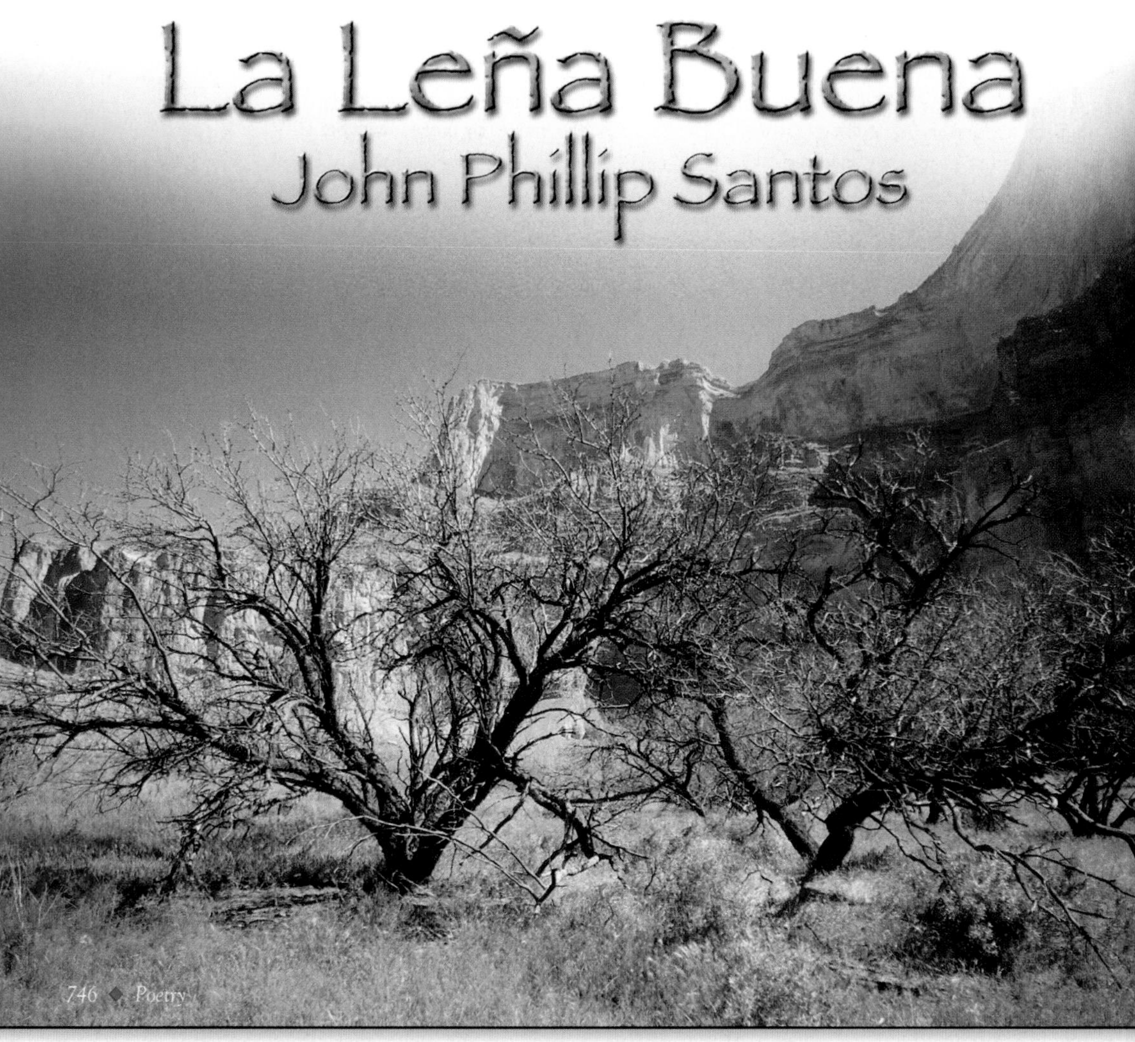

Good wood is like a jewel, Tío Abrán, my great-grandfather Jacobo's twin brother, used to say. Huisache burns fast, in twisting yellow flames, engulfing the log in a cocoon of fire. It burns brightly, so it is sought after for Easter bonfires. But it does not burn hot, so it's poor wood for home fires. On a cold morning in the sierra, you can burn a whole tree by noon. Mesquite, and even better, cedar—these are noble, hard woods. They burn hot and long. Their smoke is fragrant. And if you know how to do it, they make exquisite charcoal.

"La leña buena es como una joya"

Good wood is like a jewel. And old Tío Abrán knew wood the way a jeweler knows stones, and in northern Coahuila, from Múzquiz to Rosita, his charcoal was highly regarded for its sweet, long-burning fire.

Abrán was one of the last of the Garcias to come north. Somewhere around 1920, he finally had to come across the border with his family. He was weary of the treacheries along the roads that had become a part of life in the sierra towns since the beginning of the revolution ten years earlier. Most of the land near town had been deforested and the only wood he could find around Palaú was huisache. To find any of the few pastures left with arbors of mesquite trees, he had to take the unpaved mountain road west from Múzquiz, along a route where many of the militantes had their camps. Out by the old Villa las Rusias, in a valley far off the road, there were mesquite trees in every direction as far as you could see. He made an arrangement with the owner of the villa to give him a cut from the sale of charcoal he made from the mesquite. But many times, the revolucionarios confiscated his day's load of wood, leaving him to return home, humiliated, with an empty wagon.

Aside from Tía Pepa and Tío Anacleto, who had returned to Mexico by then, he had been the last of the Garcias left in Mexico, and he had left reluctantly. On the day he arrived in San Antonio with his family, he had told his brother Abuelo Jacobo, "If there was still any mesquite that was easy to get to, we would've stayed."

◀ **Critical Viewing** What details from Santos's description can you identify in this picture of mesquite trees? **[Compare]**

Connecting Poetry and Prose

1. Why does Santos think mesquite or cedar trees are "noble"?
2. What tree does Merriam use to represent noble qualities?
3. What role did trees play in Santos's family immigrating to the United States?
4. What are two reasons Santos and Merriam might have picked the trees they compared?
5. Explain how each author's comparisons and contrasts are developed either through poetry or prose.

John Phillip Santos

Author John Phillip Santos was the first Mexican American Rhodes Scholar. He has won numerous awards for his writing. His works include reviews, opinion pieces, and features for magazines and newspapers such as the *New York Times* and the *Los Angeles Times*. He has also written and produced more than forty television documentaries. Santos has received Emmy nominations for two of his films. He currently works for the Ford Foundation.

Background

Social Studies

The period in Mexico that Santos describes in "La Leña Buena" is during the Mexican Revolution of 1910, which lasted for eleven years. The revolution was the result of years of upheaval in millions of Mexicans' lives. The roots of the revolution were formed much earlier, during the late nineteenth century, as Mexico developed into an industrialized nation. Yet, despite increasing wealth for some, most workers in the cities and farmers and peasants in the countryside remained desperately poor. Finally, in 1910, the leadership collapsed, and Mexico fell into a violent civil war.

▶Critical Viewing

Answer: Students might mention that the trees seem strong and "noble."

Answers for Connecting Poetry and Prose

1. Santos thinks these trees are noble because they burn hot and for a long time, and they have a lovely smell.
2. Merriam uses a willow to represent noble qualities.
3. Because Santos's uncle did not have access to mesquite trees to burn into charcoal, he could not support his family, and he had to move to the United States.
4. Santos and Merriam might have chosen the trees they compared because they have both similarities and differences.
5. Merriam uses a series of similes to compare and contrast the trees in her poem. Santos compares and contrasts the trees through descriptive prose. In his prose, he includes similes, such as "Good wood is like a jewel," and metaphors, such as "a cocoon of fire."

ENRICHMENT: Science Connection

Charcoal and Its Many Uses

Although most people may associate charcoal with barbecue cookouts, it has been an important fuel for thousands of years. Charcoal can be made from any number of substances, including wood, bone, coal, and peat. The process of making charcoal is time-consuming. Appropriate materials are packed in a pit and burned slowly for weeks at a time. Today, charcoal is rarely used for fuel. It has been replaced by more easily produced fuels such as oil and gas. It still has many uses, however. It is used in the process of finishing metals and is a valued drawing tool used by artists. Because charcoal is so absorbent, it is also used to filter and purify water and air.

Have students research the different uses for charcoal today. They may explore the uses of charcoal in the fields of art and science. Then, have students share their findings with the class.

Lesson Objectives

1. To identify main points in a comparison-and-contrast article
2. To understand the characteristics of a comparison-and-contrast article

About Comparison-and-Contrast Articles

- Ask students to discuss the way two trees are described in Eve Merriam's poem "Simile: Willow and Ginkgo" (p. 740). Guide students to see that the comparisons in the poem are not direct but implied. No sentence actually reads "The willow tree is different from the ginkgo tree." Then, explain that comparison-and-contrast articles tend to be more direct and explicit in their comparisons.
- Review with students some of the words writers use to indicate comparison and contrast: Comparison words are *also, too, similar to, similarly,* and *like.* Contrast words are *unlike, on the other hand, in contrast, but,* and *yet.*

Reading Strategy

Identify Main Points

- Have students read the information about the Reading Strategy.
- Explain how a writer uses generalizations to compare or contrast two things or ideas. For example, the sentence "The two salt lakes have two very different histories" is not specific. The writer saves the details for the supporting evidence.
- Demonstrate for students how to use the chart on p. 748. Remind students that each sentence in the organizer should contain the names of both lakes.

Comparison-and-Contrast Articles

About Comparison-and-Contrast Articles

A comparison-and-contrast article uses factual details to analyze the similarities and differences between two or more persons, places, or things. For example, a newspaper might feature a comparison-and-contrast article about the policies of two presidential candidates or the talents of two sports teams. Comparison-and-contrast articles include

- a topic involving two or more things that are similar in some ways and different in other ways.
- an organized presentation of details that illustrate similarities and differences.

Reading Strategy

Identify Main Points

In a comparison-and-contrast article, the main points are the main similarities and differences that the writer examines. By identifying the writer's main points, you can more easily grasp the information he or she provides. For instance, in "More Than a Pinch: Two Salt Lakes," the first main idea is a similarity—the Dead Sea and the Great Salt Lake have similar percentages of salt.

As you identify each main point, decide whether it is a similarity or a difference. Record these main points on a Venn diagram.

Paragraph	Main Point
1	Both the Dead Sea and the Great Salt Lake contain uncommonly high percentages of salt.
2	
3	
4	
5	

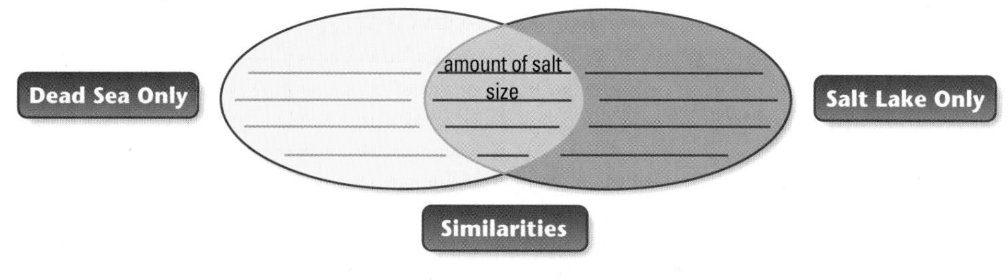

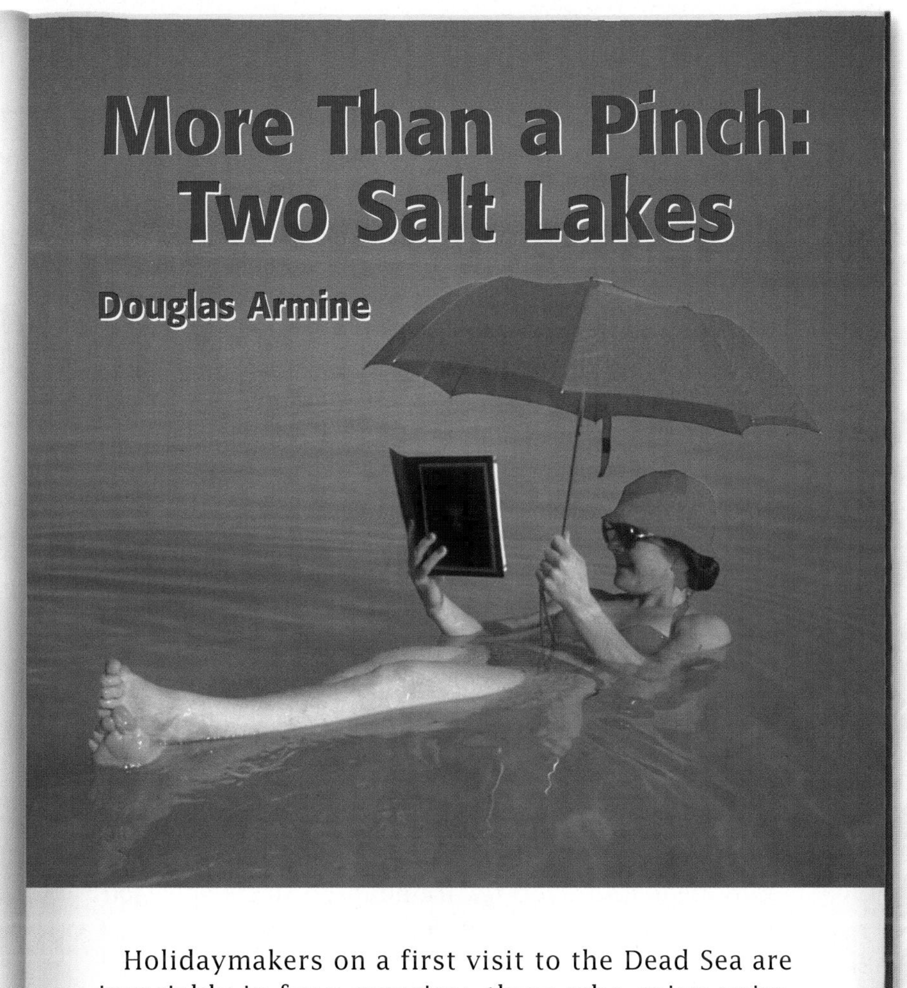

Holidaymakers on a first visit to the Dead Sea are invariably in for a surprise: those who enjoy swimming underwater in town pools at home have great difficulty in just staying below the surface. This is because the Dead Sea contains 25 to 30 percent salt, compared to 4 to 6 percent in ocean water. Similar readings have been recorded at Utah's Great Salt Lake in the United States, where it is equally difficult to sink.

In the first paragraph, the writer introduces two things to be compared: the Dead Sea and the Great Salt Lake.

The two salt lakes have very different histories. The spectacular trench occupied by the Dead Sea

Travel Section

More Than a Pinch: Two Salt Lakes

- Explain that the writer draws in the reader with the first sentence; the sentence arouses curiosity about the difficulty of staying under water.
- Point out how the writer does not identify both places being compared in the article until the last sentence of the first paragraph. Tell students to notice the pattern of naming first one body of water and then the other.
- Ask what is special about the Dead Sea.
  Answer: The salt content is about 20 to 25 percent higher than it is in the ocean; there is so much salt in the water that people can float effortlessly.

CUSTOMIZE INSTRUCTION FOR UNIVERSAL ACCESS

For Special Needs Students

Help students find the comparisons and contrasts in the first paragraph of "More Than a Pinch: Two Salt Lakes." Students should divide a sheet of paper lengthwise and write *Similarities* on the top of the left column and *Differences* on the top of the right column. Guide students to list the author's supporting details in the appropriate columns.

For Less Proficient Readers

Suggest that students use the outlining skills they learned in the **Reading Informational Materials** feature on p. 734 to identify the main idea and details of each paragraph in the article "More Than a Pinch: Two Salt Lakes." Once students have reduced the article to outline form, they can use the information in the outline to complete the graphic organizer on p. 748. Discuss students' answers as a class.

- Point out that the first sentence of the second paragraph serves as the topic sentence for both the second and third paragraphs. Each paragraph focuses on one of the bodies of water.
- Tell students to notice the general nature of the first sentence of the second paragraph. The details within the paragraph offer more specific information.
- Ask students how they think the Dead Sea earned its name.
  Possible response: It is called "dead" because few forms of life can live in it.
- Then, ask students how the author compares the contents of both lakes.
  Answer: Both lakes contain single-cell organisms. The Great Salt Lake, however, also contains shrimp and flies.

and the Jordan River, which flows into it, was created some 26 million years ago by an upheaval on the seabed at a time when the Mediterranean covered the Holy Land. At 1300 feet below sea level, the Dead Sea is the lowest body of water on Earth.

Here the writer identifies and explains a main difference—age.

The Great Salt Lake is of more recent origin, being the remnant of the glacial Lake Bonneville which came into existence 18,000 to 25,000 years ago. Having shrunk, through evaporation, to one-twentieth of its original size, it now, like the Dead Sea, has no outlet. But rivers still feed the lake, bearing minerals dissolved from surrounding rocks. As the water evaporates, the minerals remain–66 million tons of them, including magnesium, lithium, boron, and potash.

At 1300 feet below sea level, the Dead Sea is the lowest body of water on Earth.

Salt lakes are conventionally seen as barren, because they support no fish, but the Dead Sea is not completely dead: certain algae and bacteria are adapted to its salt-rich environment. The Great Salt Lake, too, has its single-cell organisms, most noticeably the algae that color the northern part of the lake pink. There are also larger life forms: brine shrimps and flies, whose larvae develop in the water. The shrimps are eaten by gulls, and shrimp eggs are harvested for sale as tropical fish food.

A significant similarity is that the lakes have similar life forms.

This business is miniscule compared to trade in the lake's great mineral wealth, such as the valuable potash used for fertilizer. The Dead Sea also yields potash, and the Israelis run health spas where tourists can coat themselves in rich, black mineral mud.

Travel Section

CUSTOMIZE INSTRUCTION FOR UNIVERSAL ACCESS

For Advanced Readers

Students who read poetry and literature may be aware that the most interesting comparisons are of things that are not immediately perceived to be alike. To review the idea of comparing unlike things, refer students back to Emily Dickinson's poem "Fame Is a Bee" on p. 741. Challenge students to write their own poem or short descriptive piece about two objects that appear, at first sight, to be unlike. Encourage students to use descriptive detail and figurative language, such as metaphors, similes, and personification, to make their points. Invite students to read their works to the class, and ask listeners to discuss the comparisons.

Check Your Comprehension

1. Why do swimmers in the Dead Sea have difficulty staying below the surface?
2. How was the trench occupied by the Dead Sea created?
3. How and when did Lake Bonneville become the Great Salt Lake?
4. What are two life forms that exist in the Great Salt Lake?
5. In what ways do the lakes contribute to the mineral trade?

Applying the Reading Strategy

Identify Main Points

6. What are the main points about similarities between the Dead Sea and the Salt Lake?
7. Name two ways in which the lakes' histories are different.
8. Why do you think the writer organized the article point by point rather than writing all about one lake and then all about the other?

Activity

Travel Brochures

Choose two vacation spots that have something in common, such as two beaches or ski lodges. On the Internet or in the library, find a brochure for each destination. Read the brochures and then compare and contrast the two destinations in a chart like the one shown here. Make sure to focus on main points that would be helpful to someone planning a trip.

	Destination A:	Destination B:
Activities Available		
Where to Stay		
Cost		
Distance		

Contrasting Informational Materials

Comparison-and-Contrast Articles and Consumer Reports

Consumer reports offer information on different brands of a single product, such as cars or computers. Consumers often use these reports to compare and contrast products or services before deciding which one to purchase. Examine a consumer report and contrast it with the comparison-and-contrast article you read here. Answer the following questions:

1. What is the purpose of each document?
2. How does its purpose affect what information is included?
3. How does its purpose affect the way the information is organized and presented?

Answers for p. 751

Check Your Comprehension

1. The high salt content of the Dead Sea keeps swimmers afloat.
2. The trench was formed by "an upheaval on the seabed" or a shift in the plates on the ocean floor.
3. The Great Salt Lake formed when Lake Bonneville evaporated and formed a smaller lake.
4. The Great Salt Lake contains single-cell organisms as well as shrimp and flies.
5. Both provide minerals such as valuable potash that is used for fertilizer.

Applying the Reading Strategy

6. Both bodies of water have high salt levels. Both contain tiny organisms that have adapted to salt water; both are mined for minerals.
7. The Dead Sea is millions of years old and was formed by shifts in the ocean floor. The Great Salt Lake is thousands of years old and was formed when a larger body of water shrank.
8. The writer organized the article this way to highlight points of comparison. By alternating details of each body of water, the writer gives each equal treatment.

Activity

Provide students with travel brochures. Encourage students to research two similar destinations for their vacations. Model the process of identifying details for comparison and contrast. After students complete the chart on p. 751, ask them to write a statement that sums up similarities and differences of the two destinations, and have them say which they would prefer to visit and why.

continued

Answers continued

Contrasting Informational Materials

Comparison-and-Contrast Articles and Consumer Reports: Before students begin the activity, remind them that consumer researchers prepare a list of standard criteria about a product's quality and price. In contrast, a writer often will not see points of comparison and contrast until he or she has researched the subjects. Then, ask students to answer the questions on p. 751.

1. The purpose is to inform, but the article may also try to entertain.
2. The purpose of the text almost always directs the information that is presented. For instance, the consumer report is consulted as a resource for buyers, so it will give clear, factual, and statistical evidence to support its claims.
3. The report makes its case point by point, so it most likely will present the analysis for one product at a time and then compare both products at the end. The article has more freedom.

Lesson Objectives

1. To write a comparison-and-contrast essay
2. To use writing strategies to generate ideas, and to plan, organize, evaluate, and revise the composition

Model From Literature

In the poem "Simile: Willow and Ginkgo" (p. 740), writer Eve Merriam uses the poetic device of simile to compare the characteristics of two types of trees.

Prewriting

- Consider working as a class to brainstorm for possible topics. Suggest that students focus on physical objects that they can observe and describe in detail.
- Tell students that when narrowing their topics, they should consider which information will be of the most value to their audiences.
- Remind students that if they are comparing two physical objects they should use sensory language and details to describe them. Offer students the Sensory Language Chart on p. 81 in **Writing Models and Graphic Organizers on Transparencies,** which will help them identify details that appeal to the five senses.
- Remind students that the thesis of a comparison-and-contrast essay should state similarities and differences. Offer students the following sentence as a model for the thesis statement: "_______ and _______ both are/have/do _______, but one is/has/does _______ and the other is/has/does _______."
- Finally, before students draft their essays, have them review the Rubric for Self-Assessment (p. 755) so that they know what is expected.

Writing WORKSHOP

Exposition: Comparison-and-Contrast Essay

A **comparison-and-contrast essay** is a work in which a writer uses factual details to analyze similarities and differences between two or more persons, places, or things. In this workshop, you will choose a topic involving two related things and discuss each one by considering how it is like and unlike the other.

Assignment Criteria. Your comparison-and-contrast essay should have the following characteristics:

- A **thesis** or purpose that states how two or more things are alike and different
- An **organizational pattern** appropriate for a comparison-contrast composition
- Specific and **concrete details** to support each main point

See the rubric on page 755 for the criteria on which your comparison-and-contrast essay may be assessed.

Prewriting

Choose a topic. To write a comparison-and-contrast essay, choose two things that have noticeable similarities and differences. Choose two subjects for which there is a reason to make a comparison, such as

- to show benefits.
- to make a choice.
- to persuade.

Gather Details. Gather facts, descriptions, and examples that you can use to make comparisons and contrasts. Organize your details in a Venn diagram like the one shown here. In the two outside sections, write details about how each is different. In the overlapping middle section, write details about how the subjects are alike.

Different Kinds of Pets

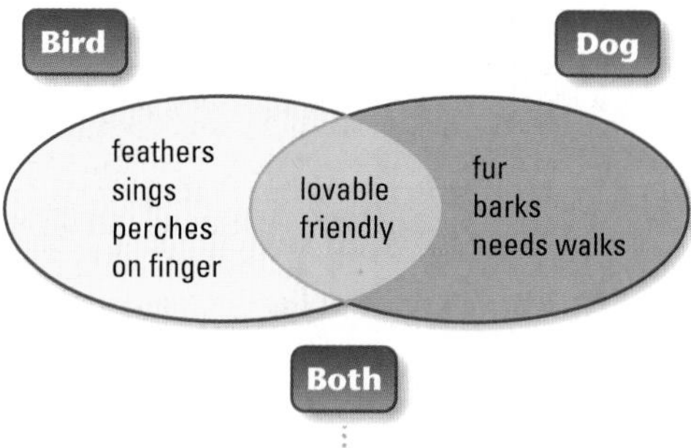

State a thesis. Review your notes and thoughts, and write one good sentence that states the purpose of your essay. Consider this a "working thesis" that may change.

Example: Birds and dogs are very different animals, but both make lovable pets.

TEACHING RESOURCES

The following resources can be used to enrich or extend the instruction for p. 752.

- **Writing and Grammar,** Copper Level, Chapter 8, pp. 150–167
- **Performance Assessment and Portfolio Management,** p. 16
- **Writing Models and Graphic Organizers on Transparencies,** p. 89

 **Writing and Grammar iText CD-ROM**
Students can use the following tools as they complete their comparison-and-contrast essays:

- Unity and Coherence
- Comparatives
- Sentence Openers Variety
- Transition Words

Student Model

Before you begin drafting your comparison-and-contrast essay, read this student model and review the characteristics of a successful comparison-and-contrast essay.

Elizabeth Leanard
Fort Wayne, Indiana

Which Instrument Is Better for You?

Have you ever wanted to play a musical instrument? Children all over the United States learn to play musical instruments in the band. Here is a look at the similarities and differences of two of the most popular instruments children play—trumpets and clarinets. Trumpets and clarinets are similar in cost and function, but they differ in their sound and the way they are played. Each of these facts will help in making a decision about which instrument to play.

The thesis states how a clarinet and a trumpet are similar and different.

The trumpet is part of the brass family, while the clarinet belongs to the woodwinds. However, although they are from different musical families, clarinets and trumpets are similar in that they both use the treble scale. This similarity also makes them quite different from other brass and woodwind instruments, which play only the bass scale. This means that they can share the same sheet music. It also means that clarinets and trumpets have the same pitch.

The essay is organized point by point—each point of similarity or difference is explained for each instrument.

Another way clarinets and trumpets are similar is in their cost. The cost of a basic clarinet is around four hundred eighty-five dollars. An average trumpet costs a little more, usually around five hundred ninety-five dollars. If cost is an important factor, then clarinets are less costly.

Another difference is the way in which each instrument is played. With trumpets, you must change your lips to play each note. This is called buzzing. For clarinets, you simply change your key position. Trumpets are played this way because they have only three valves, while clarinets have seventeen buttons.

The writer states how the trumpet and clarinet are different and then follows with supporting details.

Clarinets and trumpets also sound quite different. Clarinets can sound serious or happy. For example, the low notes sound grim, while the higher notes sound happy and bubbly. Trumpets may sound military or festive, but they can also show a range of moods.

In conclusion, based on these facts, I would pick the clarinet over the trumpet. The clarinet is less costly, easier to play, and I like the way it sounds better than the trumpet. However, whichever instrument you choose, I'm sure you will enjoy it.

Customize Instruction for Universal Access

For Less Proficient Readers	For English Learners	For Advanced Readers
Suggest that students limit their topics to objects or ideas from their own experiences. This choice will allow them to focus on their writing rather than on researching facts and details. Remind students that they should identify at least three similarities and differences between their topics.	Challenge students to compare and contrast one object or idea from their native cultures with one from American culture. Students may focus on something simple, such as food or music, or they may try to explain larger cultural differences.	Suggest that students compare and contrast two ideas or issues rather than two objects. This choice would require them to go beyond straightforward description and to seek information from outside sources, such as newspapers and books.

Student Model

- Explain that the Student Model is a sample and that essays may be longer.
- Ask students to identify the two objects compared in the Student Model and the key points of comparison.
  Answer: Trumpets and clarinets are compared. The points of comparison are the costs, functions, sounds, and playing techniques.
- Challenge students to complete a Venn diagram like the one on p. 89 in **Writing Models and Graphic Organizers on Transparencies** as they read the Student Model.
- To show students how Elizabeth organized her essay, outline it as a class. Ask students to identify the topic sentence of each paragraph. Point out how each topic sentence mentions an area of comparison or contrast and how the details support it.
  Answer: The instruments' musical families are described in the second paragraph; the costs are discussed in the third paragraph; the way the instruments are played is described in the fourth paragraph; and the sounds of the instruments are described in the fifth paragraph.
- Point out that the final paragraph offers a recommendation. Students may state a preference or identify the advantages or disadvantages of one item over another.

Real-World Connection

Comparison-and-contrast essays in the workplace: Managers, business owners, and others in the workforce need to know the pros and cons of an idea or situation to make informed decisions. Decision makers may ask for a report that compares and contrasts two ideas or items, like prices of office supplies or productivity of two departments. These reports, like the students' papers, must provide accurate facts and details in an organized manner.

Drafting

- Provide students with the Main Idea and Supporting Details organizer on p. 73 in **Writing Models and Graphic Organizers on Transparencies.** Students may use the organizer to identify their topic sentences and supporting details. Students also can use the organizer after they write their drafts to check whether they have comprehensive topic sentences and appropriate details.
- Remind students that their introductions of the subjects and their characteristics should be general. They also might include some background information or pose a question that readers might have about the topics.
- Explain to students that details are important in a comparison-and-contrast essay. Remind them that specific details create images in the reader's mind and are interesting to read. Challenge students to use vivid language, such as concrete nouns and colorful adjectives, in their papers.

Revising

- Provide students with highlighters, and ask them to follow the instructions in the text.
- Tell students that their papers should be balanced and fair in their coverage of the topics. Providing details about only one of the topics would suggest that students either did not do enough research or are biased in their writing. Point out how in the fifth paragraph of the Student Model on p. 753, the writer included details about the sound of the clarinet but not about that of the trumpet. This suggests that she prefers the clarinet, which is her recommendation in the final paragraph.

continued on p. 755

Drafting

Follow an organizational pattern. Develop a draft that organizes information logically so the reader clearly understands similarities and differences. Use the point-by-point method in which you discuss each aspect of your subject in turn.

- First, discuss one aspect of both subjects.
- Next, discuss another aspect of both subjects.

For example, first compare and contrast physical characteristics of birds and dogs; then compare and contrast the personalities of each.

Organizational Pattern for Compare/Contrast
Introduce the subjects you are comparing.
Identify a feature or aspect you are comparing and contrasting.
Provide specific details that support similarities and differences.
Identify another feature you are comparing and contrasting.
Provide specific details that support similarities and differences.
State your conclusion about your subjects.

State your thesis. Draft an introductory paragraph that clearly states the subject and the aspects of two things that you plan to compare and contrast.

Use specific details. The more specific and concrete your examples, the better your reader will understand your comparisons and contrasts. As you draft, review what you have written and add concrete details wherever possible.

Revising

Check organizational pattern and balance. Your essay should give equal space to each thing being compared. Reread your essay. Use one color to highlight the details about one of your subjects. Use another color to highlight details about the other subject. Check the balance.

1. If you find more highlight of one color than another, add more details to the subject with fewer highlights.
2. If you find large chunks of a color and places where colors alternate, revise to follow the point-by-point method of organization.

USING TECHNOLOGY IN WRITING

Students may use the character color and font features of their word-processing programs to color-code their papers, as suggested at the bottom of p. 754.

Also, students may find it helpful to use the thesaurus feature to find more vivid or appropriate adjectives to use in the descriptions of their topics.

Students also can use the organizing tools and revision checkers on the **Writing and Grammar iText CD-ROM.**

Check subject-verb agreement. Look over your draft for agreement between subjects and verbs. Check to see that sentences with singular subjects have the singular form of the verb. Check that plural subjects have plural verbs.

Example: Both football and hockey *are* fast-paced.
Hockey *is* played both indoors and outdoors.

Compare the model and nonmodel. Why is the model correct?

Nonmodel	Model
What do you notice about these sentences? It also means that clarinets and trumpets has the same pitch. The clarinet are less costly.	*Read these sentences aloud. What do you notice about the revisions that were made?* It also means that clarinets and trumpets have the same pitch. The clarinet is less costly.

Publishing and Presenting

Choose one of these ways to share your writing with classmates or a larger audience.

Make an audiotape. Practice reading your essay aloud several times. Then, record it using a tape recorder. Play the recording for your classmates. Have them evaluate its effectiveness.

Make a two-part poster. Turn your essay into a poster that compares and contrasts two subjects. Provide illustrations, photographs, or drawings. Use your main points to write captions that state similarities and differences. Display your poster in your classroom.

WG *Prentice Hall Writing and Grammar Connection: Chapter 8*

Speaking Connection

To learn tips for engaging listeners during a reading or presentation, see the **Listening and Speaking Workshop,** Engaging Listeners, p. 756.

Rubric for Self-Assessment

Evaluate your comparison-and-contrast essay using the following criteria and rating scale:

Criteria	Rating Scale: Not very				Very
How clearly does the thesis state how two or more subjects are similar and different?	1	2	3	4	5
How consistent and appropriate is the organizational pattern?	1	2	3	4	5
How effectively are concrete details used to illustrate similarities and differences?	1	2	3	4	5
How balanced is the support of both subjects?	1	2	3	4	5

TEST-TAKING TIP

When facing a comparison-and-contrast prompt, students first should reread the prompt to see whether it specifies the items to be compared. If not required to write on a given topic, students should select two items that have clear points of comparison and contrast. If possible, students should consider items that have physical characteristics, which are easier to describe than ideas. Students should set aside half of their time for prewriting and use a Venn diagram to plan their essays.

Revising (continued)

- Ask students to identify the subjects and verbs in the nonmodel and the model.
  Answer: In the nonmodel, the subjects are *clarinets* and *trumpets*; the verb is *has*. In the model, the subjects are *clarinets* and *trumpets*; the verb is *have*.
- Then, ask why the model is correct.
  Answer: The model is correct because the plural verb "have" agrees with its plural subject.
- Explain that subject-verb agreement mistakes occur because the verb must agree with the subject, not with the word that precedes the verb. Often, the word that precedes the verb is the object of a prepositional phrase.
- Have students check subjects and verbs in their sentences and make sure they agree.

Publishing and Presenting

- After students record their essays, have them evaluate their recordings before sharing them with the class. If they have not spoken slowly and clearly, encourage them to redo parts or all of the recording.
- As a class, talk about ways that students can reach larger audiences. Encourage students to submit work to school or local newspapers.
- Challenge students who are familiar with presentation software to turn their papers (or posters) into computer-based presentations and to deliver them to the class.

Assessment

- Review the assessment criteria as a class.
- Encourage students to use the self-assessment criteria after you have modeled their use in evaluating the Student Model on p. 753. Students should focus on the writer's use of a consistent and appropriate organizational pattern.
- The rubric on this page, and another rubric in an alternative format, can be found on p. 16 in **Performance Assessment and Portfolio Management.**

Lesson Objectives

1. To engage listeners during an oral presentation
2. To identify an audience and appeal to it directly with eye contact and questions
3. To use nonverbal cues to engage and persuade listeners

Engage the Audience

- Ask students to brainstorm for a list of various audiences. Then, ask students to suggest how a speaker might appeal to each one. Possible responses: For young children, a speaker should make a presentation that is simple and lively; for teens, the speaker might need to cover subjects that interest audience members; for adults, the speaker might use more formal language.
- Students may be reluctant to address the audience directly. Assure students that most audience members appreciate being drawn into a speaker's presentation.
- Making eye contact is an important way speakers can show their interest and engage listeners.

Build Acceptance for Your Proposal

- To demonstrate the different messages that body language can send, ask volunteers to read aloud sections of this workshop while assuming different postures and using different body movements.
- Similarly, ask volunteers to demonstrate voice quality. Have volunteers read aloud in a monotone, a whisper, a nervous quiver, and a steady voice. Ask students to comment on the difference volume, pitch, and pace can make in a speech.
- Suggest ways that students can practice. For example, they might practice in front of a mirror, or family members, or they might tape-record or videotape their rehearsals.
- Finally, review the Self-Evaluation Form in the margin. Point out that the form is designed to help students identify and address weaknesses and strengths in their presentations.

Listening and Speaking WORKSHOP

Engaging Listeners

Being a good speaker in an empty room is easy. Being an effective, persuasive speaker in front of an audience is a challenge. In delivering a persuasive presentation, you want to **engage the listener**—grab and hold the attention of the audience from your first words to your closing statement. If you can keep your listeners interested, you have a good chance of convincing them to accept your opinion or proposal. Use some of the strategies suggested here. Practice your speech, using the Self-Evaluation Form to assess your performance.

Engage the Audience

Identify your audience. If you want to convince your listeners, you must determine who they are—classmates, the whole student body, or teachers and students. Once you know your audience, you can tailor what you say to their interests. Lead off with a target statement that you know will hook them—a surprising fact, an amusing statement, or an opening that will touch them personally.

Address your audience. Speak directly to your audience by saying "you." For example, when you say, "You might be wondering why a gecko makes a better pet than a hamster," you make listeners feel that you are speaking directly to them.

Self-Evaluation Form for Engaging Listeners

Self-Rating System:
+ = Very well ✔ = Needs improvement
– = Not very well

How well did I . . .
- identify my audience? ______
- hook the audience in my introduction? ______
- speak directly to my audience? ______
- use appropriate gestures and movements? ______
- vary my voice pitch and pace? ______

Build Acceptance for Your Proposal

To convince your listeners to accept your idea or proposal, you need to use more than just persuasive language. You also need to win them over by using nonverbal techniques—your voice, posture, facial expressions, body movements, and gestures. Here are some tips.

Use body language. Your body language—posture, movement, and gestures—should send the same message that your words convey. When you deliver a powerful message, stand up straight and look confident.

Vary the pitch and pace of your voice. Speak in a strong voice so you appear sure of yourself. It will help to keep your audience engaged if you vary the pitch and volume of your voice to emphasize important points. Speak clearly so you will be understood.

Activity: Presentation Choose a topic on which you have an opinion. For example, paper bags are better than plastic bags or vice-versa. Develop a proposal and deliver a presentation that is engaging and persuasive. Rehearse your persuasive presentation and evaluate your performance using the checklist shown here.

CUSTOMIZE INSTRUCTION FOR UNIVERSAL ACCESS

For Special Needs Students	For English Learners
Students may benefit from seeing a videotape of a professional speaker. Ask the school librarian to find an example of a videotaped seminar or public event on a topic that is likely to interest students. As you show the video to students, point out the speaker's techniques, particularly his or her use of eye contact and confident physical gestures. Encourage students to use the speaker in the video as a model for their own presentations.	Some cultures put less emphasis on signs of confidence in public speaking. For example, eye contact or speaking in a strong voice may not be considered polite or persuasive. Ask students to write brief journal entries about the role of public speaking in their native cultures and about their experiences as public speakers. Ask students to submit their journals to you. Use the journals to get a sense of students' abilities to complete the assignment for this workshop.

Assessment WORKSHOP

Identifying Appropriate Usage

The writing sections of some tests require you to read a passage and answer multiple-choice questions about appropriate usage. Use the following strategies to help you answer such questions:

Use the Correct Form of a Word Some test questions ask you to choose the correct part of speech, the appropriate form of an adjective or adverb, the correct pronoun, or the correct form of a negative. Use what you have learned about usage to answer these questions.

Test-Taking Strategy

After selecting an answer, read the sentence with your selected answer in place. If it does not seem correct in context, read the sentence with the other choices in place.

Sample Test Items

1. Get the teacher's _____ for your topic.
   A approve
   B approving
   C approval
   D approved

2. The first problem is _____ than the second.
   A simple
   B simply
   C more simpler
   D simpler

Answers and Explanations

1. A noun is needed, so ***C*** is correct.

2. Two things are compared, so the comparative form of the adjective is needed. ***D*** is correct.

Practice

Read the passage and choose the word or words that belong in each space.

Christopher Wolfe __(1)__ believe his eyes. Sticking out of a hillside __(2)__ dinosaur horns! Chris and his dad, who is a paleontologist, __(3)__ up the fossils and took __(4)__ to a museum. Imagine their excitement when they learned that the fossils were a ninety-million-year-old dinosaur!

1. **A** couldn't hardly
   B could hardly
   C could never hardly
   D didn't hardly
2. **A** has been
   B was
   C were
   D is
3. **A** dug
   B dugged
   C had digged
   D digged
4. **A** it
   B him
   C themselves
   D them

Lesson Objective

To identify appropriate usage in a test situation

Applying Reading Strategies

Tell students that the skill of paraphrasing may help them identify incorrect usage in test passages. Explain that the ability to restate a sentence in their own words will help students identify what the sentence is missing. Students also should pay attention to the punctuation of the test samples. For example, a question mark or an exclamation point instead of a period may provide necessary clues.

Test-Taking Skills

- Have students read the first sample test item.
- Then, suggest that they try to paraphrase the sentence—even though they are not certain what is missing from it.
  Possible response: The sentence is a command that tells somebody to get something from the teacher. The missing word must be a noun. That means that the correct answer is *C*.

Answers

1. The correct answer is *B*. All the other answers are double negatives.
2. The correct answer should be a plural verb in the past tense. Only *C* is plural.
3. *A* is the correct answer. *A* is the only correct past-tense form of the word *dig*.
4. What is missing is a plural pronoun that refers to the fossils. *A* and *B* are singular pronouns. *C* is reflexive and would refer to Chris and his father. *D* is the correct answer.

TEACHING RESOURCES

The following resources can be used to enrich or extend the instruction for p. 757.

PRENTICE HALL ASSESSMENT SYSTEM

 **Workbook** | **Transparencies**

 **Skill Book** | **CD-ROM**

Unit Objectives

1. To develop skills in reading folk tales and myths
2. To apply a variety of reading strategies, particularly strategies for reading folk literature, appropriate for reading these selections
3. To analyze literary elements
4. To use a variety of strategies and to build vocabulary
5. To learn elements of grammar, usage, and style
6. To use recursive writing processes to write in a variety of forms
7. To develop listening and speaking skills
8. To express and support responses to various types of texts
9. To prepare, organize, and present literary interpretations

Meeting the Objectives

With each selection, you will find instructional materials through which students can meet these objectives. Further, you will find additional practice pages for reading strategies, literary analysis, vocabulary, and grammar in the **Selection Support: Skills Development Workbook** in your **Teaching Resources.**

Background

Art

The Story of the War Robe,
by Joseph H. Sharp

Joseph H. Sharp (1859–1953) was one of several artists who started the Taos Society of Artists based in Taos, New Mexico. Sharp is noted for his depictions of life around New Mexico in the early 1900s and for his paintings of Pueblo Indians. Connect this painting to the oral tradition by asking the following questions:

1. How do you know Sharp has depicted Native Americans?
Possible response: The subjects wear Native American dress; the painting depicts feathers; a Native American symbol is on the wall.
2. Aside from orally, how might people in the picture tell stories?
Possible response: They might create artworks or garments.

UNIT 10 The Oral Tradition

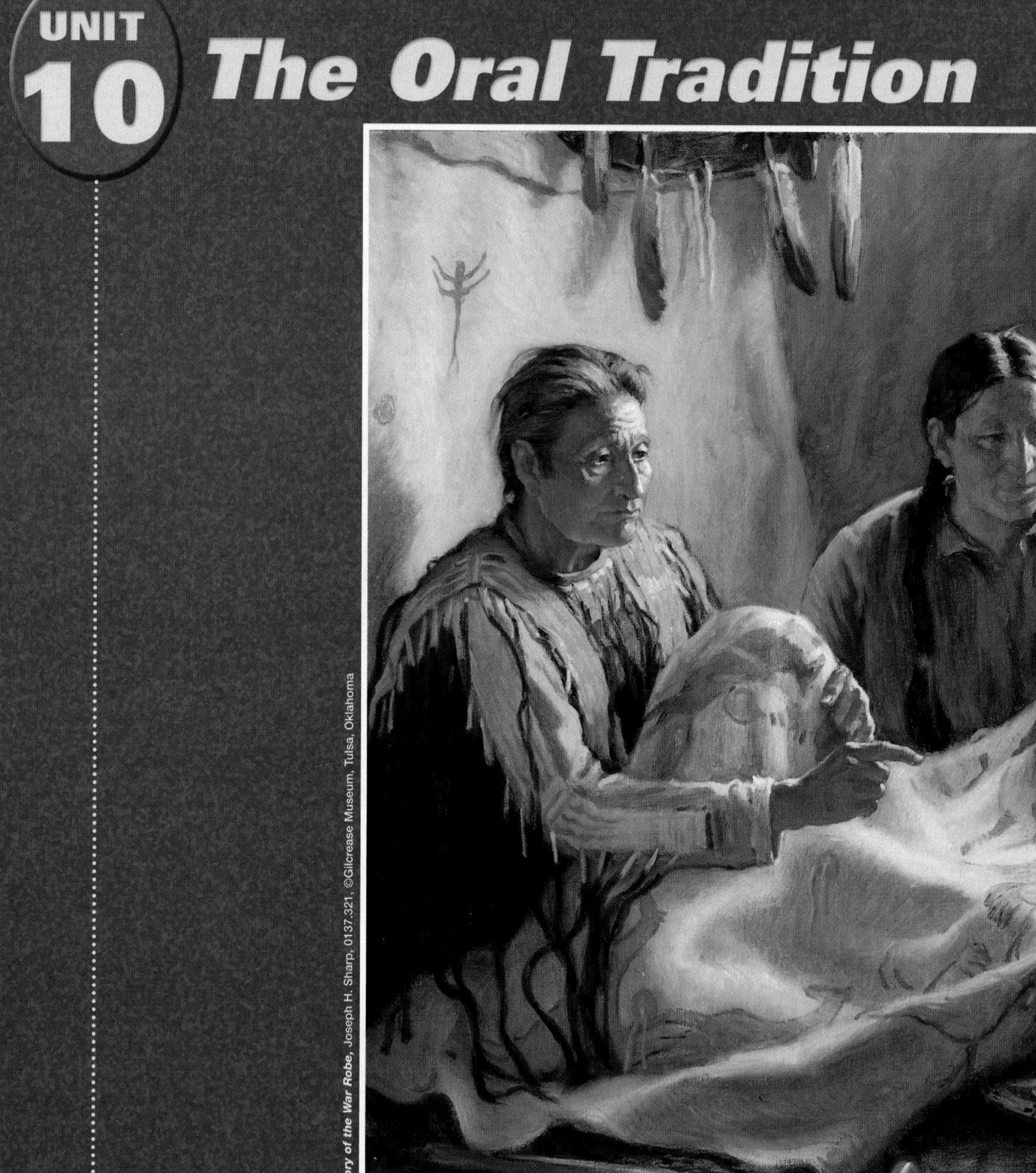

The Story of the War Robe, Joseph H. Sharp, 0137.321, ©Gilcrease Museum, Tulsa, Oklahoma

UNIT FEATURES

Connections	Reading Informational Material
Every unit contains a feature that connects literature to a related topic, such as art, science, or history. In this unit, the selection "Pericles' Funeral Oration" on p. 797 provides a connection to "Arachne." Use the information and questions on the Connections page to enrich students' understanding of the selections presented within the unit.	These selections will help students learn to analyze and evaluate informational texts, such as workplace documents, technical directions, and consumer materials. They will expose students to the organization and features unique to nonnarrative texts. In this unit, students learn the meaning and purpose of the various parts of a comparison-and-contrast article and a Web site.

Exploring the Genre

Long before there were books, there were stories—stories that were passed along from one generation to the next by storytellers. These word-of-mouth tales make up what is called an oral tradition. The oral tradition includes folk tales, myths, and fables. An oral tradition is found in every culture. Stories are told to teach important lessons and to explain the way the world works, as well as to entertain.

◀ **Critical Viewing** Who do you think is telling the story of the war robe in this picture? Why? **[Analyze]**

ASSESSMENT RESOURCES

- Selection Support: Skills Development Workbook
- Formal Assessment
- Open Book Tests
- Performance Assessment and Portfolio Management
- Extension Activities

Assessing Student Progress

Listed below are the tools that are available to measure the degree to which students meet the unit objectives.

Informal Assessment

The questions in the Review and Assess sections are a first level of response to the concepts and skills presented within the selections. Students' responses are a brief, informal measure of their grasp of the material. These responses can indicate where further instruction and practice are needed. Follow up with the practice pages in the **Selection Support: Skills Development Workbook.**

Formal Assessment

The **Formal Assessment** booklet contains Selection Tests and Unit Tests.

- Selection Tests measure comprehension and skills acquisition for each selection or group of selections.
- Each Unit Test provides students with thirty multiple-choice questions and five essay questions designed to assess students' knowledge of the literature and skills taught in the unit.

The **Open Book Tests** ask students to demonstrate their ability to synthesize and communicate information from selections or groups of selections.

To assess student writing, you will find rubrics and scoring models in the **Performance Assessment and Portfolio Management** booklet. In this booklet you will also find scoring rubrics for listening and speaking activities.

Alternative Assessment

The **Extension Activities** booklet contains writing activities, listening and speaking activities, and research and technology activities that are appropriate for students with different ability levels. You may also use these activities as an alternative measurement of students' growth.

▶Critical Viewing

Answer: The man on the left is telling the story. He is old and probably knows more about the tribe's history, and he is gesturing as if describing the robe.

Why Read Literature?

The "Why Read Literature?" page in each unit presents a list of possible purposes for reading. Each purpose for reading is connected to one or more of the selections in the unit. Good readers set a purpose before reading in order to help them read actively and focus on meaningful details.

Unit 10 introduces three purposes for reading. "Read for the Love of Literature" encourages students to read to discover valuable lessons and to enjoy entertaining tales from African American folklore. "Read to Appreciate Connections Between Past and Present" encourages students to make connections between literary works and the concept of citizenship. "Read for Information" invites students to investigate scientific discoveries about reaching the South Pole and technology used in studying elephants.

How to Use This Page

- Tell students that before reading each selection in this unit, they should set a purpose for reading. This will help them read in an active and focused manner.
- Explain that reading stories that teach valuable lessons, such as those found in "The Ant and the Dove" (p. 764), "He Lion, Bruh Bear, and Bruh Rabbit" (p. 765), and "Señor Coyote and the Tricked Trickster" (p. 770), will help them remember and appreciate literary works.
- Explain to students that they can learn about values in other cultures and times as they read the stories "Why Monkeys Live in Trees" (p. 780), "Arachne" (p. 784), "The Three Wishes" (p. 789), and "A Crippled Boy" (p. 791).
- Point out that readers can get more from what they read by reading informational texts like "Race to the End of the Earth" (p. 799) and taking note of specific facts or details as they read.

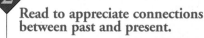

Why Read Literature?

Whenever you read a folk tale, you have a purpose, or reason. You might read a folk tale for enjoyment or to learn something new about a different culture. Preview the following specific purposes you might choose for reading the works in this unit.

1 Read for the love of literature.

Lions roar for a variety of reasons, but the main reason is to announce "Here I am." That announcement can be heard by a lot of animals, because the sound of a lion's roar can be heard from five miles away! Read an entertaining tale in which a rabbit teaches a lion to tone down his roar, **"He Lion, Bruh Bear, and Bruh Rabbit,"** page 765.

The "heroes" of folk literature are usually—but not always—strong and powerful. Read a folk tale with two unlikely heroes, **"The Ant and the Dove,"** page 764.

2 Read to appreciate connections between past and present.

Comparatively speaking, a spider's "silk" is five times as strong as steel and twice as elastic as nylon. Scientists study spiders and their webs in hopes of learning how to make synthetic spider silk. Read the ancient Greek explanation of spiders and their silk in **"Arachne,"** page 784.

The idea of citizenship was first explained, not at a political gathering, but at a funeral. Read **"Pericles' Funeral Oration,"** page 796, the speech that historians believe contains the first definition of citizenship.

3 Read for information.

Dogs don't sweat. Instead, they regulate their body temperature by panting. Find out why this fact helped decide the outcome of the race to the South Pole when you read **"Race to the End of the Earth,"** page 799.

Elephants can make a sound that other elephants can hear miles away. You might think that such a sound would be loud enough to hurt your ears. In fact, the sound can't be heard by human ears at all. Learn how technology has helped scientists discover this and other interesting animal facts when you read **"High-Tech Windows to the Animal Kingdom,"** page 804.

Take It to the Net

Visit the Web site for online instruction and activities related to each selection in this unit.
www.phschool.com

ENRICHMENT: Further Reading

Have students choose one or more of the works below to extend the unit theme "The Oral Tradition" or to read more by the unit authors.

The People Could Fly by Virginia Hamilton
Virginia Hamilton tells this African American folk tale about the enslaved Africans using magic to flee their oppressors.

The House of Dies Drear by Virginia Hamilton
This tale about an African American boy who investigates a haunted house, once part of the Underground Railroad, can be found in the **Prentice Hall Literature Library.**

"How Much Land Does a Man Need?" by Leo Tolstoy
One of Tolstoy's best-loved short stories, this tale-with-a-twist shows how greed leads to a man's death.

Ackamarackus: Julius Lester's Sumptuously Silly Fantastically Funny Fables by Julius Lester
This collection of hilarious fables from the Newbery Award winner provides moral tales about characters like lazy lions and eagles that are afraid to fly.

How to Read Literature

Strategies for Reading Folk Literature

Every culture in every country around the world has its own folk literature. Folk literature can take the form of a myth, a legend, a fairy tale, a folk tale, or a tall tale. In this unit, you will learn the following strategies that will help you understand and appreciate the different types of folk literature.

1. Understand oral tradition.

The oral tradition refers to songs, stories, and poems that were originally composed and passed along orally—in speech rather than in print. Every culture has an oral tradition: a body of literature passed down from ancient times. In contemporary times, writers have set down many of these traditional tales in writing. In this unit, you will read works from a variety of countries and cultures.

2. Predict.

Stories from the oral tradition are usually very predictable. Good behavior is rewarded; bad behavior has serious consequences. Predicting what will happen leads you to analyze characters' actions and think about the lesson being taught.

Clue: Arachne challenges the goddess Athene by saying: "If Athene herself were to come down and compete with me, she could do no better than I."

Prediction: Something bad will happen to Arachne, and she will be humbled.

Evidence: In other Greek myths, whenever a human is disrespectful to a god, he or she suffers negative consequences.

3. Recognize the storyteller's purpose.

As you read folk literature, look for the reason, or reasons, the storyteller is sharing the story. The notebook shows two purposes the tellers of "He Lion" may have had. As you read the tales in this unit, jot down notes like these about the storytellers' purposes.

As you read the selections in this unit, review the reading strategies and look at the notes in the side column. Use the suggestions to interact with the text.

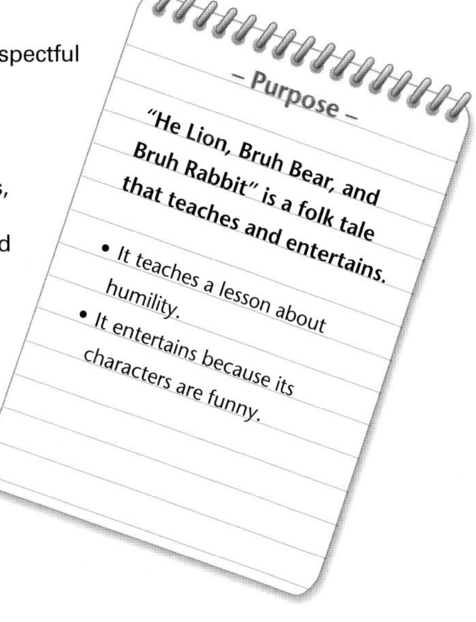

– Purpose –
"He Lion, Bruh Bear, and Bruh Rabbit" is a folk tale that teaches and entertains.
• It teaches a lesson about humility.
• It entertains because its characters are funny.

How to Read Literature

The "How to Read Literature" page in each unit presents a set of strategies to help readers understand authors' words and ideas. Each reading strategy is taught in conjunction with one or more of the selections within the unit. Good readers develop a bank of strategies from which they can draw as needed.

Unit 10 introduces two strategies for reading folk literature. Students learn to predict and to recognize the storyteller's purpose to fully understand a selection.

How to Use This Page

Introduce the strategies for constructing meaning, presenting each as a tool for developing understanding when reading the selections in this unit.

- As they read "Why Monkeys Live in Trees" (p. 780), "Arachne" (p. 784), "The Three Wishes" (p. 789), and "A Crippled Boy" (p. 791), students will learn to make predictions.
- As they read "The Ant and the Dove" (p. 764), "He Lion, Bruh Bear, and Bruh Rabbit" (p. 765), and "Señor Coyote and the Tricked Trickster" (p. 770), students will learn to recognize the storyteller's purpose.

MODEL A READING STRATEGY: Predict

Tell students that to become directly involved before, during, and after reading, they should ask themselves questions before they read, consider those questions as they read, and check their predictions when they have finished. Ask students to read this passage from "Why Monkeys Live in Trees":

"One day Leopard was looking at his reflection in a pool of water. Looking at himself was Leopard's favorite thing in the world to do. Leopard gazed, wanting to be sure that every hair was straight and that all his spots were where they were supposed to be."

Demonstrate how to use predicting to analyze and understand the passage by modeling your thinking:

I ask myself these questions: What has happened so far, and what do I think will happen next, based on what I know? The author seems to be setting Leopard up for a fall. Leopard is vain, and knowing that vanity is discouraged in folk tales, I predict that vanity will lead to problems. Then, I read to find out if my prediction is correct.

Remind students that making their prediction is the first part; they must also check predictions.

The Ant and the Dove ✦ He Lion, Bruh Bear, and Bruh Rabbit ✦ Señor Coyote and the Tricked Trickster

Lesson Objectives

1. **To analyze and respond to literary elements**
   - Literary Analysis: Folk Tales
   - Comparing Literary Works
2. **To read, comprehend, analyze, and critique three folk tales**
   - Reading Strategy: Recognizing the Storyteller's Purpose
   - Reading Check Questions
   - Review and Assess Questions
3. **To develop word analysis skills, fluency, and systematic vocabulary**
   - Vocabulary Development Lesson: Word Analysis: Forms of *dignity*
4. **To understand and apply written and oral language conventions**
   - Spelling Strategy
   - Grammar Lesson: Using Capitals for Titles of People
   - Assessment Practice (ATE)
5. **To understand and apply appropriate writing and research strategies**
   - Writing Lesson: Folk Tale
   - Extension Activity: Display
   - Extension Activity: Explanation
6. **To understand and apply listening and speaking strategies**
   - Extension Activity: Oral Presentation

STEP-BY-STEP TEACHING GUIDE	PACING GUIDE
PRETEACH	
Motivate Students and Provide Background	
Use the Motivation activity (ATE p. 762)	5 min.
Read and discuss the Preview material and Background information (SE/ATE p. 762) A	10 min.
Introduce the Concepts	
Introduce the Literary Analysis and Reading Strategy (SE/ATE p. 763) A	25 min.
Pronounce the vocabulary words and read their definitions (SE p. 763)	5 min.
TEACH	
Monitor Comprehension	
Informally monitor comprehension by circulating while students read independently or in groups A	20–25 min.
Monitor students' comprehension with the Reading Check notes (SE/ATE pp. 765, 767, 771, 773)	as students read
Develop vocabulary with Vocabulary notes (SE pp. 764, 767, 771, 772; ATE p. 772)	as students read
Develop Understanding	
Develop students' understanding of folk tales with the Literary Analysis annotations (SE/ATE pp. 768, 772, 773) A	5 min.
Develop students' ability to recognize the storyteller's purpose with the Reading Strategy annotations (SE p. 769; ATE pp. 767, 769)	5 min.
ASSESS	
Assess Mastery	
Assess students' mastery of the Reading Strategy and Literary Analysis by having them answer the Review and Assess questions (SE/ATE p. 775)	25 min.
Use one or more of the print and media Assessment Resources (ATE p. 777) A	up to 45 min.
EXTEND	
Apply Understanding	
Have students complete the Vocabulary Development Lesson and the Grammar Lesson (SE p. 776) A	20 min.
Apply students' ability to write a folk tale using the Writing Lesson (SE/ATE p. 777) A	45 min.
Apply students' understanding using one or more of the Extension Activities (SE p. 777)	20–90 min.

ACCELERATED INSTRUCTION:
Use the strategies and activities identified with an A.

UNIVERSAL ACCESS
● = Below Level Students
▲ = On-Level Students
■ = Above Level Students

Time and Resource Manager

Reading Level: Easy, Average, Average
Average Number of Instructional Days: 4

RESOURCES			
	PRINT	**TRANSPARENCIES**	**TECHNOLOGY**
	• **Beyond Literature,** Workplace Skills: Cooperation, p. 42 ▲ ■		• **Interest Grabber Videotapes,** Tape 5 ● ▲ ■
	• **Selection Support Workbook:** ● ▲ ■ Literary Analysis, p. 210 Reading Strategy, p. 209 Build Vocabulary, p. 206	• **Literary Analysis and Reading Transparencies,** pp. 83 and 84 ● ▲ ■	
	• **Adapted Reader's Companion** ● • **Reader's Companion** ● • **Authors In Depth,** Copper Level, p. 196 ■		• **Listening to Literature** ● ▲ ■ Audiocassettes, Side 27 Audio CDs, CD 13
	• **English Learner's Companion** ● ▲ • **Literatura en español** ● ▲ • **Literary Analysis for Enrichment** ■	• **Fine Art Transparencies, Volume 1,** Transparency 3 ● ▲ ■	
	• **Formal Assessment:** Selection Test, pp. 196–198 ● ▲ ■ • **Open Book Test,** pp. 124–126 ● ▲ ■ • **Performance Assessment and Portfolio Management,** pp. 13, 29 ● ▲ ■ • PRENTICE HALL ASSESSMENT SYSTEM ● ▲ ■	• PRENTICE HALL ASSESSMENT SYSTEM ● ▲ ■ Skills Practice Answers and Explanations on Transparencies	• **Test Bank Software** ● ▲ ■ • **Got It! Assessment Videotapes,** Tape 5 ● ▲
	• **Selection Support Workbook:** ● ▲ ■ Build Spelling Skills, p. 207 Build Grammar Skills, p. 208 • **Writing and Grammar,** Copper Level ● ▲ ■ • **Extension Activities,** p. 42 ● ▲ ■	• **Daily Language Practice Transparencies** ● ▲ • **Writing Models and Graphic Organizers on Transparencies** ● ▲ ■	• **Writing and Grammar iText CD-ROM** ● ▲ ■ *Take It to the Net* www.phschool.com

BLOCK SCHEDULING: Use one 90-minute class period to preteach the selection and have students read it. Use a second 90-minute class period to assess students' mastery of skills and have them complete one of the Extension Activities.

PRETEACH

Step-by-Step Teaching Guide for pp. 762–763

Motivation

Ask students to recall stories about animals that they read or heard when they were young. As each volunteer mentions a story, ask what point, if any, the tale tries to make about human behavior. Tell students that many cultures around the world use animal tales to teach lessons about human behavior. Have students speculate about why such tales are so popular.

Interest Grabber Video

As an alternative, play "Virginia Hamilton on Retelling Folk Tales" on Tape 5 to engage student interest.

1 Background

Social Studies

Two of the selections in this group of folk tales are trickster tales: "Señor Coyote and the Tricked Trickster" and "He Lion, Bruh Bear, and Bruh Rabbit." The trickster is an archetype found in many cultures—the leprechaun in Ireland, the Anansi in Africa, the rabbit in the American South, and the coyote in the American Southwest, to name a few. The trickster is usually a deceitful animal and is always sly; he or she sometimes has other negative qualities as well, such as greed or pretension. Nevertheless, the trickster is generally an underdog who cleverly outwits a more powerful or influential adversary.

Prepare to Read

1 The Ant and the Dove ◆ He Lion, Bruh Bear, and Bruh Rabbit ◆ Señor Coyote and the Tricked Trickster

Coyote at Sunset, detail from painting on wood, Maureen Mahoney-Barraclough

Take It to the Net

Visit www.phschool.com for interactive activities and instruction related to these selections, including

- background
- graphic organizers
- literary elements
- reading strategies

Preview

Connecting to the Literature

Like cartoons, "The Ant and the Dove" by Leo Tolstoy, "He Lion, Bruh Bear, and Bruh Rabbit" by Virginia Hamilton, and "Señor Coyote and the Tricked Trickster" by I. G. Edmonds use animal characters that seem like people. How do these animals and their problems remind you of real people and problems?

Background

"Señor Coyote and the Tricked Trickster" is, as the title suggests, a trickster tale. Many cultures contain trickster tales—folk stories about a clever character who outwits others through sly thinking and tricky maneuvering. Often, tricksters rely on cleverness to outsmart bigger, more powerful opponents.

TEACHING RESOURCES

The following resources can be used to enrich or extend the instruction for pp. 762–763.

Motivation

Interest Grabber Video, Tape 5 ■

Background

Beyond Literature, p. 42

Take It to the Net

Visit www.phschool.com for Background and hotlinks for the selections.

Literary Analysis

Selection Support: Literary Analysis, p. 210

Literary Analysis and Reading Transparencies, Folk Tales, p. 84

Reading

Literary Analysis and Reading Transparencies, Recognizing the Storyteller's Purpose, p. 83 ■

■ **BLOCK SCHEDULING:** Resources marked with this symbol provide varied instruction during 90-minute blocks.

❷ Literary Analysis

Folk Tales

Folk tales are stories shared by a people—the "folk." The tales usually do not originate from a single author; they are passed down from generation to generation. Often, the details of a folk tale reveal elements of the culture from which the folk tale comes. A folk tale may contain cultural details such as

- **dialect:** The characters' speech reflects the way a language is spoken in a particular region or by a particular group.
- **values:** The actions and abilities of the characters show what actions and abilities the culture admired in people.
- **geography:** The landscape, animals, and climate are ones that would have been familiar to the storytellers.

Today, many authors write down folk tales for all to enjoy. Besides entertaining, folk tales may teach a lesson or explain something in nature.

Comparing Literary Works

Folk tales often teach a lesson related to the qualities, abilities, and behavior that the people of a culture value or admire. The chart shows three general topics or subjects about which all three folk tales have something to say. Copy the chart, and complete it by explaining the specific lesson each tale teaches about one or all of the topics. Compare and contrast the lessons.

Common Topics
- consideration
- cleverness
- weak and strong

Ant — specific lesson

Lion — specific lesson

Coyote — specific lesson

❸ Reading Strategy

Recognizing the Storyteller's Purpose

You will better understand a folk tale if you recognize the **storyteller's purpose** or reason for telling the story. Many folk tales have a combination of purposes. For example, the purpose of these folk tales is to teach lessons, but they also entertain while they teach. As you read, ask yourself the following focus questions.

1. What part of each story teaches a lesson?
2. Which parts entertain?

Vocabulary Development

startled (stärt´ əld) *adj.* surprised (p. 764)

lair (lār) *n.* cave or den (p. 767)

cordial (kôr´ jəl) *adj.* warm and friendly (p. 767)

ungrateful (un grāt´ fəl) *adj.* not thankful (p. 771)

reproachfully (ri prōch´ fəl lē) *adv.* with blame (p. 771)

indignantly (in dig´ nənt lē) *adv.* angrily (p. 772)

CUSTOMIZE INSTRUCTION FOR UNIVERSAL ACCESS

For Special Needs Students	For Less Proficient Readers	For English Learners
Have students read the adapted version of "He Lion, Bruh Bear, and Bruh Rabbit" in the **Adapted Reader's Companion.** This version provides basic-level instruction in an interactive format with questions and write-on lines. Completing the adapted version will prepare students to read the selection in the Student Edition.	Have students read "He Lion, Bruh Bear, and Bruh Rabbit" in the **Reader's Companion.** This version provides basic-level instruction in an interactive format with questions and write-on lines. After students finish the selection in the Reader's Companion, have them complete the questions and activities in the Student Edition.	Have students read the adapted version of "He Lion, Bruh Bear, and Bruh Rabbit" in the **English Learner's Companion.** This version provides basic-level instruction in an interactive format with questions and write-on lines. Completing the adapted version will prepare students to read the selection in the Student Edition.

❷ Literary Analysis

Folk Tales

- Tell students that folk tales are stories shared by a people and that they are usually passed from generation to generation.
- Read aloud the instruction about folk tales. Point out that folk tales usually teach a lesson or focus on something in nature.
- Discuss the instruction for Comparing Literary Works to help students compare and contrast the human qualities that the various characters in these folk tales possess.
- Use the Folk Tales transparency on p. 84 in **Literary Analysis and Reading Transparencies** to help students comprehend the folk tales in this section.

❸ Reading Strategy

Recognizing the Storyteller's Purpose

- Tell students that every story has a purpose, whether it is to entertain, to inform, to persuade, or to teach a lesson.
- Point out that, although most folk tales do amuse and entertain, the storyteller's main purpose usually is to teach a lesson. Often these lessons involve human traits such as vanity or arrogance.
- Use the Recognizing the Storyteller's Purpose transparency on p. 83 in **Literary Analysis and Reading Transparencies** to help students focus on purpose.

Vocabulary Development

- Review the words and definitions on the vocabulary list.
- Point out the word *indignantly.* After discussing the word's definition, "angrily or stubbornly," ask students to identify several situations in which people might act indignantly.
  Possible responses: If they felt they were treated unfairly; if they strongly disagreed with an action or idea.

E-Teach

Visit E-Teach at www.phschool.com for teachers' essays on how to teach, with questions and answers.

TEACH

Step-by-Step Teaching Guide for pp. 764–774

CUSTOMIZE INSTRUCTION
For Verbal/Linguistic Learners

To help students pick out the moral lesson of "The Ant and the Dove," which is hidden in a noun clause, ask students which words in the dove's final thoughts make a general observation about human behavior.

❶ About the Selection

An ant drinking from a stream is saved from a whirlpool by a dove, who drops a twig for the ant to grab hold of. A few days later, the ant bites a hunter's foot as he is about to capture the dove, causing the hunter to drop his net. The dove flies away, thinking that you never can tell how or when a kindness may be repaid.

Answers for p. 764

Review and Assess

1. Students should be able to name at least one other story that reminds them of "The Ant and the Dove." They should support their response with an explanation.
2. **(a)** The dove drops a twig so that the ant does not drown.
   (b) Possible response: The dove helps the ant out of kindness and the desire not to see another creature suffer.
3. **(a)** The ant bites a hunter who is about to catch the dove.
   (b) Possible response: The dove is grateful to the ant and expects nothing in return.
   (c) People should behave with kindness and help others because one never knows how or when a kindness may be repaid.

❶ The Ant and the Dove

Russian Folk Tale

Leo Tolstoy

A thirsty ant went to the stream to drink. Suddenly it got caught in a whirlpool and was almost carried away.

At that moment a dove was passing by with a twig in its beak. The dove dropped the twig for the tiny insect to grab hold of. So it was that the ant was saved.

A few days later a hunter was about to catch the dove in his net. When the ant saw what was happening, it walked right up to the man and bit him on the foot. Startled, the man dropped the net. And the dove, thinking that you never can tell how or when a kindness may be repaid, flew away.

startled (stärt´ əld) *adj.* surprised

Leo Tolstoy

(1828–1910)

Leo Tolstoy was born into a wealthy family, and he inherited his family estate at the age of nineteen. Yet, by the time he was fifty and the author of some of the most famous novels in the world, *Anna Karenina* and *War and Peace*, he began to reject his life of luxury. He surrendered the rights to many of his works and gave his property to his family. This world-famous writer died alone in an obscure train station in Russia.

Review and Assess

Thinking About the Selection

1. **Respond:** What other story or stories does this tale remind you of? Explain.
2. (a) **Recall:** What does the dove do for the ant? (b) **Speculate:** Why does the dove help the ant, even when she does not think the ant can ever repay her?
3. (a) **Recall:** How does the ant repay the dove? (b) **Interpret:** What does the dove mean when she thinks, "you can never tell how or when a kindness may be repaid"? (c) **Draw Conclusions:** What lesson does this story appear to teach?

TEACHING RESOURCES

The following resources can be used to enrich or extend the instruction for pp. 764–774.

Literary Analysis
- **Literary Analysis for Enrichment**

Reading
- **Selection Support:** Reading Strategy, p. 209; Build Vocabulary, p. 206
- **Adapted Reader's Companion**
- **Reader's Companion**
- **English Learner's Companion**

- **Listening to Literature Audio CDs,** CD 13

Extension
- **Authors In Depth,** p. 196, Copper Level (The collection includes four additional selections by Virginia Hamilton for extended reading.)
- **Fine Art Transparencies,** Volume 1, Art Transparency 3 (Use the painting to generate a discussion about animals in the wild.)

BLOCK SCHEDULING: Resources marked with this symbol provide varied instruction during 90-minute blocks.

❷ He Lion, Bruh Bear, and Bruh Rabbit

African American Folk Tale

Virginia Hamilton

❸ ◀Critical Viewing Why do you think a lion might be used to represent someone who has a high opinion of himself or herself? **[Draw Conclusions]**

Say that he Lion would get up each and every mornin. Stretch and walk around. He'd roar, ME AND MYSELF, ME AND MYSELF, like that. Scare all the little animals so they were afraid to come outside in the sunshine. Afraid to go huntin or fishin or whatever the little animals wanted to do.

"What we gone do about it?" they asked one another. Squirrel leapin from branch to branch, just scared. Possum[1] playin dead, couldn't hardly move him.

He Lion just went on, stickin out his chest and roarin, "ME AND MYSELF, ME AND MYSELF."

❹ ✓Reading Check

In what way does the lion frighten the other animals?

---

1. **Possum** (päs′ əm) colloquial for "opossum," a small tree-dwelling mammal that pretends to be dead when it is trapped.
2. **Bruh** (bru) early African American dialect for "brother."

❷ About the Selection

In the forest, he Lion was scaring all the small animals with his great roar, ME AND MYSELF, ME AND MYSELF. The small animals took the problem to Bruh Bear and Bruh Rabbit, who then talked with he Lion. He Lion insisted that he was king of the forest and could roar when he pleased. Bruh Rabbit told him that the real king of the forest was Man, whom neither he Lion nor Bruh Bear had ever seen. When he Lion insisted on seeing Man, Bruh Rabbit took him all over. Finally they came upon Man. When he Lion roared at him, Man raised his gun and shot at he Lion, who ran off. The folk tale teaches a lesson about thinking too highly of one's place in the world.

❸ ▶Critical Viewing

Possible responses: Lions are among the most powerful of animals; male lions, with their manes, look regal; lions are often associated with kingship, as in "king of the jungle"; lions live in groups called "prides."

❹ ✓Reading Check

Answer: The lion scares the other animals by roaring, ME AND MYSELF, ME AND MYSELF.

CUSTOMIZE INSTRUCTION FOR UNIVERSAL ACCESS

For Special Needs Students	For English Learners
Special needs students may have difficulty with the attempt to capture the oral flavor of a storyteller speaking in African American dialect. Pair special needs students with advanced readers and have them listen to the story on **Listening to Literature Audiocassettes,** Side 27 or **Listening to Literature Audio CDs,** CD 13 pausing from time to time to discuss the nonstandard grammar and vocabulary.	Note that the dialect in which the story is told uses nonstandard grammar. Have students explain the difference between standard and nonstandard English. Ask students to rewrite the three paragraphs on p. 765 in standard, or formal, English. Provide students with the following example: "Afraid to go huntin or fishin or whatever the little animals wanted to do" is nonstandard English for "The little animals were afraid to go hunting or fishing or whatever it was they wanted to do."

5 Reinforcing Skills

Drawing Inferences

- Read aloud the bracketed paragraph on p. 766 and have students focus on how the frightened animals describe he Lion to Bruh Bear and Bruh Rabbit.
- Then, ask students the following question: What does the animals' description suggest about he Lion? **Answer:** He Lion is described as a bully who frightens the small animals with his roar. He is probably conceited and self-centered.

6 ▶ Critical Viewing

Possible response: He is big and appears to be slow-moving like Bruh Bear.

The little animals held a sit-down talk, and one by one and two by two and all by all, they decide to go see Bruh[2] Bear and Bruh Rabbit. For they know that Bruh Bear been around. And Bruh Rabbit say he has, too.

5 So they went to Bruh Bear and Bruh Rabbit. Said, "We have some trouble. Old he Lion, him scarin everybody, roarin every mornin and all day, ME AND MYSELF, ME AND MYSELF, like that.

"Why he Lion want to do that?" Bruh Bear said.

"Is that all he Lion have to say?" Bruh Rabbit asked.

"We don't know why, but that's all he Lion can tell us and we didn't ask him to tell us that," said the little animals. "And him scarin the children with it. And we wish him to stop it."

"Well, I'll go see him, talk to him. I've known he Lion a long kind of time," Bruh Bear said.

"I'll go with you," said Bruh Rabbit. "I've known he Lion most long as you."

That bear and that rabbit went off through the forest. They kept hearin somethin. Mumble, mumble. Couldn't make it out. They got farther in the forest. They heard it plain now. "ME AND MYSELF. ME AND MYSELF."

6 ▶ **Critical Viewing** How well does this bear fit the image of Bruh Bear? **[Assess]**

ENRICHMENT: Science Connection

Opossums

Explain that even though animals in folk tales often act like people, some of their qualities come from nature. In this story, squirrels leap from branch to branch, and frightened possums play dead. Both animals do, in fact, show these behaviors in real life.

The possum, short for opossum, is the only North American native in the branch of mammals called marsupials, which also includes kangaroos and other animals found in Australia. The chief characteristic of marsupials is that the female has a pouch for her young, who remain there feeding until they are mature enough to leave. The common American opossum is about the size of a domestic cat, but with its gray coloring and long tail, it more closely resembles a rat. When it is captured or frightened, its bodily functions close down in a reaction that resembles death. Have interested students research animals mentioned in the story and present their findings in a series of posters that include illustrations with informative captions.

"Well, well, well," said Bruh Bear. He wasn't scared. He'd been around the whole forest, seen a lot.

"My, my, my," said Bruh Rabbit. He'd seen enough to know not to be afraid of an old he lion. Now old he lions could be dangerous, but you had to know how to handle them.

7 The bear and the rabbit climbed up and up the cliff where he Lion had his lair. They found him. Kept their distance. He watchin them and they watchin him. Everybody actin cordial.

lair (lār) *n.* cave or den

cordial (kôr′ jəl) *adj.* warm and friendly

"Hear tell you are scarin everybody, all the little animals, with your roarin all the time," Bruh Rabbit said.

"I roars when I pleases," he Lion said.

"Well, might could you leave off the noise first thing in the mornin, so the little animals can get what they want to eat and drink?" asked Bruh Bear.

"Listen," said he Lion, and then he roared: "ME AND MYSELF. ME AND MYSELF. Nobody tell me what not to do," he said. "I'm the king of the forest, *me and myself.*"

9 **Reading Check**

What does Bruh Rabbit tell the Lion?

8 "Better had let me tell you something," Bruh Rabbit said, "for I've seen Man, and I know him the real king of the forest."

He Lion was quiet awhile. He looked straight through that scrawny lil Rabbit like he was nothin atall. He looked at Bruh Bear and figured he'd talk to him.

"You, Bear, you been around," he Lion said.

"That's true," said old Bruh Bear. "I been about everywhere. I've been around the whole forest."

"Then you must know something," he Lion said.

"I know lots," said Bruh Bear, slow and quiet-like.

"Tell me what you know about Man," he Lion said. "He think him the king of the forest?"

"Well, now, I'll tell you," said Bruh Bear, "I been around, but I haven't ever come across Man that I know of. Couldn't tell you nothin about him."

So he Lion had to turn back to Bruh Rabbit. He didn't want to but he had to. "So what?" he said to that lil scrawny hare.

"Well, you got to come down from there if you want to see Man," Bruh Rabbit said. "Come down from there and I'll show you him."

10 ▶ **Critical Viewing**

In what ways does Bruh Rabbit represent opposite qualities from Bruh Bear's? **[Compare and Contrast]**

7 Background

Science

Rabbits, bears, squirrels, and opossums are all native to the North American forest; however, lions are found not in North America but in Africa. The African Americans who first told these tales of a trickster rabbit combined details of the North American landscape with details from stories brought over from Africa.

8 Reading Strategy

Recognizing the Storyteller's Purpose

- Have a student read aloud the bracketed passage on p. 767. Point out that Bruh Rabbit is giving this advice to he Lion.
- Tell students that often the purpose of a folk tale is revealed through dialogue—the characters' words.
- Then, ask students the following question: In what way does Bruh Rabbit's statement reflect the purpose of the folk tale?
  Answer: Bruh Rabbit's warning reflects the folk tale's message that nobody should assume that he or she is the most important or most powerful.

9 Reading Check

Answer: Bruh Rabbit tells he Lion that Man is the king of the forest.

10 ▶ Critical Viewing

Answers: Unlike Bruh Bear, Bruh Rabbit is physically weak and scrawny; he is quick thinking and fast moving.

CUSTOMIZE INSTRUCTION FOR UNIVERSAL ACCESS

For Special Needs Students	For Less Proficient Readers
Have students create a word bank of colloquial expressions from the story. Remind students that although the African American dialect in the folk tale does not reflect standard English, it reveals a rich cultural version of spoken English. Students should first write the words or expressions from the story and then write the standard English word or expression for each entry in their word banks.	Have students think about people who have attitudes similar to he Lion's. Ask students to write the words they would use to name or describe someone like he Lion. For example, students might suggest *bossy, tyrant, bully,* and *selfish.* After students have written these words, ask them to consider why someone might have these attitudes. Discuss students' suggestions.

⓫ Literary Analysis

Folk Tales

- Have a volunteer read the bracketed passage aloud. Tell students to reread the passage silently, focusing on the role of Bruh Rabbit.
- Elicit a description of Bruh Rabbit based on the passage. Write some of the students' suggestions on the board.
- Ask students the first Literary Analysis question on p. 768.
  Answer: Bruh Rabbit represents leadership qualities; he is acting like a teacher. Rabbit is leading the dialogue by giving instruction to he Lion about Man and by correcting he Lion when he makes incorrect remarks.

⓬ Literary Analysis

Folk Tales

- Read the bracketed passage aloud to students, accentuating the dialogue and the sound word *PA-LOOOM.* Tell students that folk tales are often told aloud.
- Point out that in this passage and throughout the folk tale, dialogue and sound words like *PA-LOOOM* can bring the story to life for listeners.
- Then, ask students the second Literary Analysis question on p. 768: What details give this narrative the quality of being told aloud?
  Answer: The informal, conversational tone; repetition; and words like *PA-LOOOM* make the folk tale seem as if it were being told aloud.

He Lion thought a minute, an hour, and a whole day. Then, the next day, he came on down.

He roared just once, "ME AND MYSELF. ME AND MYSELF. Now," he said, "come show me Man."

So they set out. He Lion, Bruh Bear, and Bruh Rabbit. They go along and they go along, rangin the forest. Pretty soon, they come to a clearin. And playin in it is a little fellow about nine years old.

"Is that there Man?" asked he Lion.

"Why no, that one is called Will Be, but it sure is not Man," said Bruh Rabbit.

So they went along and they went along. Pretty soon, they come upon a shade tree. And sleepin under it is an old, olden fellow, about ninety years olden.

"There must lie Man," spoke he Lion. "I knew him wasn't gone be much."

"That's not Man," said Bruh Rabbit. "That fellow is Was Once. You'll know it when you see Man."

So they went on along. He Lion is gettin tired of strollin. So he roars, "ME AND MYSELF. ME AND MYSELF." Upsets Bear so that Bear doubles over and runs and climbs a tree.

"Come down from there," Bruh Rabbit tellin him. So after a while Bear comes down. He keepin his distance from he Lion, anyhow. And they set out some more. Goin along quiet and slow.

> **Literary Analysis**
> **Folk Tales** What quality or qualities does Bruh Rabbit represent?

In a little while they come to a road. And comin on way down the road, Bruh Rabbit sees Man comin. Man about twenty-one years old. Big and strong, with a big gun over his shoulder.

"There!" Bruh Rabbit says. "See there, he Lion? There's Man. You better go meet him."

"I will," says he Lion. And he sticks out his chest and he roars, "ME AND MYSELF. ME AND MYSELF." All the way to Man he's roarin proud, "ME AND MYSELF. ME AND MYSELF!"

"Come on, Bruh Bear, let's go!" Bruh Rabbit says.

"What for?" Bruh Bear wants to know.

"You better come on!" And Bruh Rabbit takes ahold of Bruh Bear and half drags him to a thicket. And there he makin the Bear hide with him.

For here comes Man. He sees old he Lion real good now. He drops to one knee and he takes aim with his big gun.

Old he Lion is roarin his head off: "ME AND MYSELF. ME AND MYSELF!"

The big gun goes off: PA-LOOOM!

He Lion falls back hard on his tail.

The gun goes off again. PA-LOOOM!

> **Literary Analysis**
> **Folk Tales** What details give this narrative the quality of being told aloud?

CUSTOMIZE INSTRUCTION FOR UNIVERSAL ACCESS

For Advanced Readers

Suggest that students read additional works by Virginia Hamilton. Provide students with the titles listed in the Enrichment box, ATE p. 775. You may also wish to use **Authors In Depth,** Copper Level, which contains the following selections:

- "Doc Rabbit, Bruh Fox, and Tar Baby" (folk tale, p. 196)
- "Carrying the Running-Aways" (nonfiction, p. 200)
- "Anthony Burns" (nonfiction, p. 203)
- "Alexander Ross, Down From Canada" (nonfiction, p. 205)

After students have read these or other works by Hamilton, have them write a paragraph in which they compare and contrast the selections they have read. Suggest criteria for comparison, such as setting, theme, and characters. Display students' completed paragraphs for others to read and enjoy.

He Lion is flyin through the air. He lands in the thicket.

"Well, did you see Man?" asked Bruh Bear.

"I seen him," said he Lion. "Man spoken to me unkind, and got a great long stick him keepin on his shoulder. Then Man taken that stick down and him speakin real mean. Thunderin at me and lightnin comin from that stick, awful bad. Made me sick. I had to turn around. And Man pointin that stick again and thunderin at me some more. So I come in here, cause it seem like him throwed some stickers at me each time it thunder, too."

"So you've met Man, and you know zactly what that kind of him is," says Bruh Rabbit.

"I surely do know that," he Lion said back.

Awhile after he Lion met Man, things were some better in the forest. Bruh Bear knew what Man looked like so he could keep out of his way. That rabbit always did know to keep out of Man's way. The little animals could go out in the mornin because he Lion was more peaceable. He didn't walk around roarin at the top of his 13 voice all the time. And when he Lion did lift that voice of his, it was like, "Me and Myself and Man. Me and Myself and Man." Like that.

Wasn't too loud at all.

Reading Strategy
Recognizing the Storyteller's Purpose
What is the purpose of showing that he Lion becomes humble?

Review and Assess

Thinking About the Selection

1. **Respond:** Which character in "He Lion, Bruh Bear, and Bruh Rabbit" do you think is most amusing? Why?
2. **(a) Recall:** In "He Lion, Bruh Bear, and Bruh Rabbit," why do the little animals seek help from Bruh Bear and Bruh Rabbit? **(b) Infer:** What do Bruh Bear and Bruh Rabbit think of he Lion? **(c) Analyze:** Why isn't Bruh Rabbit scared of he Lion?
3. **(a) Recall:** Why does he Lion want to see Man, and what happens when he sees him? **(b) Compare and Contrast:** Describe he Lion before and after he meets Man. **(c) Analyze Cause and Effect:** What causes the change in he Lion's attitude?
4. **(a) Draw Conclusions:** Based on he Lion's behavior, what lesson does this story appear to teach? **(b) Evaluate:** Is the lesson one that applies in modern life? Explain.
5. **Take a Position:** What responsibility do individuals have to other members of a community?

Virginia Hamilton

(1936–2002)

Virginia Hamilton came from Yellow Springs, Ohio, a town famous as a stop on the Underground Railroad before the Civil War. Hamilton was lucky to come from a family of storytellers who passed along tales of their family experience and heritage. Although she focused her writing mainly on African American subjects and characters, the themes in her books are meaningful to all people.

13 Reading Strategy

Recognizing the Storyteller's Purpose

- Have a student read aloud the bracketed passage on p. 769. Elicit that the change in he Lion's roar is humorous and entertaining but that it also helps teach a lesson.
- Then, ask students the Reading Strategy question.
  Answer: The purpose is to show that he Lion has changed as a result of the lesson he learned.

Answers for p. 769

Review and Assess

1. Possible responses: He Lion is amusing because of his conceit and his downfall. Bruh Rabbit is amusing because he is clever, and Bruh Bear is amusing because he thinks and moves slowly but shows common sense.
2. **(a)** He Lion is scaring them with his roar. **(b)** They think he is conceited and selfish. **(c)** Bruh Rabbit is wise and experienced; he uses his wits to interest he Lion in a situation that presents no danger to Bruh Rabbit.
3. **(a)** He Lion wants to challenge Man, who Bruh Rabbit says is the king of the forest. **(b)** Before, he Lion is self-centered and conceited; afterward, he is more humble. **(c)** He Lion's attitude changes when he discovers that Man is king of the forest.
4. Possible response: **(a)** The folk tale teaches that vanity, conceit, and pride at the expense of others will lead to one's downfall and that humility and consideration for others are admirable qualities. **(b)** The lesson would also apply in modern life because the same human characteristics can be found throughout humanity.
5. Possible response: Individuals should be responsible for their own actions and should not infringe on the rights of others.

CUSTOMIZE INSTRUCTION FOR UNIVERSAL ACCESS

For Less Proficient Readers

Point out that most folk tales were composed and recited orally for many years before they were written down. Tell students that to capture the quality of spoken English, Hamilton tells her story in dialect, a variety of language spoken in a particular region or by a particular group. Have students perform oral readings of Hamilton's story. Suggest that students use the **Listening to Literature Audiocassettes** or the **Listening to Literature Audio CDs** for clues on how to tell the story aloud and that they try out different characters' lines. Have students practice saying the dialect naturally, as if it were being spoken. When students are ready, have them make their final presentations to the class live, on audiotape, or on videotape.

⓮ About the Selection

Señor Coyote and Señor Mouse have been feuding for a long time when Mouse finds Coyote caught in a trap. He agrees to save Coyote if Coyote will promise to work for him for the rest of Coyote's life. Coyote reluctantly agrees. Then one day Mouse is caught by Señor Snake. Apparently, Snake is trapped by a rock. After Mouse helps roll it off, Snake turns on him, intent on making a meal of him. Coyote tricks Snake into letting Mouse go. When Snake does so, again pinning himself under the rock, Mouse is free to go. Mouse reluctantly agrees that Coyote's debt is paid.

⓯ Background

Humanities: Art

Coyotes,
by Maureen Mahoney-Barraclough

Maureen Mahoney-Barraclough has worked in a variety of media and artistic styles. Here, she paints in the folk style common in Mexico and the southwestern United States. Explain that the pieces of art shown here and on p. 772 are two different hand paintings that decorate a wooden desk. Folk art often decorates functional items such as furniture, pottery, or clothing. It is usually quite colorful and often depicts stories or scenes that are common in an area or culture. Connect the art to the literature by asking the following questions:

1. Which details in the two pieces reflect the setting or style of northern Mexico and the American Southwest?
   Answer: The region is reflected in the vibrant colors; the clear, starry skies; and the animals and cactus.
2. Which details from the first paragraph of the story appear in the two pieces of folk art?
   Answer: The coyote, mouse, and cactus appear in the art.

⓰ ▶Critical Viewing

Answer: Folk art, like folk tales, usually contains simple animal characters; it often depicts images from nature; and it usually reflects the culture of its creators.

⓮ Señor Coyote and the Tricked Trickster

Mexican Folk Tale **I.G. Edmonds**

⓯

Coyotes, detail from painting on wood, Maureen Mahoney-Barraclough

⓰ ▲ **Critical Viewing** What qualities does folk art share with folk tales? **[Connect]**

One day long ago in Mexico's land of sand and giant cactus *Señor* Coyote and Señor Mouse had a quarrel.

None now alive can remember why, but recalling what spirited *caballeros*[1] these two were, I suspect that it was some small thing that meant little.

Be that as it may, these two took their quarrels seriously and for a long time would not speak to each other.

Then one day Mouse found Señor Coyote caught in a trap. He howled and twisted and fought, but he could not get out. He had just about given up when he saw Señor Mouse grinning at him.

"Mouse! *Mi viejo amigo*♦—my old friend!" he cried. "Please gnaw this leather strap in two and get me out of this trap."

1. ***caballeros*** (kä bä yer´ ôs) Spanish for "gentlemen."

CUSTOMIZE INSTRUCTION FOR UNIVERSAL ACCESS

For Less Proficient Readers

Point out to students that the illustrations accompanying this tale are paintings, whereas those accompanying Hanilton's story are photographs.

Involve students in a discussion contrasting the characteristics of paintings and photographs. As students offer specific contrasts, list them on a chart on the board, making sure to cover the following contrasts: Folk Art: less realistic; subjective, personal; less detailed; more colorful. Photographs: more realistic; objective, less personal; more detailed; less colorful.

Tell students to keep the general contrast in mind as they make their own two-column charts, like the one on the board, to contrast the specific illustrations in the two stories. Their comparison-and-contrast charts should provide details about the illustrations and also evaluate their effectiveness.

"But we are no longer friends," Mouse said. "We have quarreled, remember?"

"Nonsense!" Señor Coyote cried. "Why I love you better than I do Rattlesnake, Owl, or anybody in the desert. You must gnaw me loose. And please hurry for if the *peon*[2] catches me I will wind up a fur rug on his wife's kitchen floor."

Mouse remembered how mean Señor Coyote had been to him. He was always playing tricks on Mouse and his friends. They were very funny to Señor Coyote for he was a great trickster, but often they hurt little Mouse.

"I'd like to gnaw you free," he said, "but I am old and my teeth tire easily."

"Really, Señor Mouse, you are ungrateful," said Señor Coyote reproachfully. "Remember all the nice things I have done for you."

"What were they?"

"Why—" Coyote began and stopped. He was unable to think of a single thing. There was a good reason for this. He had done nothing for Mouse but trick him.

But Señor Coyote is a sly fellow. He said quickly, "Oh, why remind you of them. You remember them all."

"I fear my memory of yesterday is too dim," Mouse said, "but I could remember very well what you could do for me tomorrow."

"Tomorrow?" Coyote asked.

"Yes, tomorrow. If I gnaw away the leather rope holding you in the trap, what will you do for me tomorrow, and the day after tomorrow and the day after the day after tomorrow and the day—"

"Stop!" Señor Coyote cried. "How long is this going on?"

"A life is worth a life. If I save your life, you should work for me for a lifetime. That is the only fair thing to do."

"But everyone would laugh at a big, brave, smart fellow like me working as a slave for a mere mouse!" Señor Coyote cried.

"Is that worse than feeling sad for you because your hide is a rug in the peon's kitchen?"

Señor Coyote groaned and cried and argued, but finally agreed when he saw that Mouse would not help him otherwise.

"Very well," he said tearfully, "I agree to work for you until either of us dies or until I have a chance to get even by saving your life." 18

Mouse said with a sly grin, "That is very fine, but I remember what a great trickster you are. So you must also promise that as

2. ***peon*** (pē´ ən) Spanish for "worker"—an unskilled laborer.

Vocabulary Connection

17 ♦ ***Spanish Words and Expressions***

Señor Coyote uses the expression *mi viejo amigo* [mē vē ā´ hō ä mē´ gō], which means *my old friend.* The word *amigo* has come to be commonly understood and used by many speakers of English. Other commonly used Spanish words and expressions include

- *Señor* Mr. (p. 770)
- *Señora* Mrs.
- *amigo* friend (p. 770)
- *mamacita* "mommy" (p. 773)
- *adiós* goodbye
- *hasta la vista* until we meet again
- *mañana* tomorrow

ungrateful (un grāt´ fəl) *adj.* not thankful

reproachfully (ri prōch´ fəl lē) *adv.* with blame

18 ✓ **Reading Check**

What does Señor Coyote want Señor Mouse to do?

17 Background Languages

Foreign words that are frequently used in English often become borrowed words over time. As foreign words are used more frequently and as people from various cultures interact, new words become assimilated into the language of each culture. Languages change and grow through word borrowing. For example, the words *taco* and *hurricane* are now common to English but were once used only in Spanish-speaking countries. Additional examples include these English words borrowed from other cultures:

India: *jungle, ginger, shampoo*

Australia and New Zealand: *boomerang, koala, kangaroo*

18  Reading Check

Answer: Señor Coyote is caught in a trap, and he wants Mouse to set him free.

CUSTOMIZE INSTRUCTION FOR UNIVERSAL ACCESS

For Less Proficient Readers	For English Learners	For Gifted/Talented Students
Have students read p. 771 for details in which the characters act like humans, such as the Coyote's wiliness or the Mouse's reluctance to help Coyote. Have students describe a situation involving human behavior similar to that of Coyote and Mouse.	Have native Spanish speakers help non-Spanish speakers with the pronunciations and meanings of the Spanish words by making a word bank together. Next to the words, students can make their own respellings to help them pronounce the words correctly.	Have students work in pairs to role-play the conflict between Mouse and Coyote presented on p. 771. After role-playing the conflict, have students write a list of rules that Coyote and Mouse should follow to avoid further conflict. Using their list of rules, students may wish to draw up a contract to which Coyote and Mouse might agree.

19 Vocabulary Development

Forms of *dignity*

- Call students' attention to the word *indignantly,* and have a volunteer read its definition.
- Tell students that *indignantly* is related to the word *dignity,* which means "being worthy of respect." Both words come from the Latin word *dignus,* which mean "worthy." Ask students how *indignantly* differs from *dignity.*
  Answer: The prefix *-in* here means "not." Coyote reacts *indignantly,* which means his angry reaction is not worthy of respect.

20 Critical Thinking

Speculate

- Read aloud the bracketed paragraph and have students think about Coyote's actions thus far in the story.
- Ask a volunteer to describe how Coyote has acted toward Mouse up to this point. Elicit from students that Coyote has not acted very honorably.
- Then, ask students the following question: What does Coyote's attitude toward a promise reveal about his character?
  Answer: Despite his trickery, Coyote has a sense of honor; he has a certain amount of integrity.

21 Literary Analysis

Folk Tales

- Have students think about where this story might take place.
- Then, after students have read the bracketed sentence, ask the Literary Analysis question.
  Answer: The original tellers of this folk tale would have been familiar with a desert landscape.

22 ▶Critical Viewing

Possible response: Among other things, Mouse may be complaining about Coyote's cruel tricks or bragging that he now has Coyote in his paws.

---

soon as I free you that you will not jump on me, threaten to kill me, and then save my life by letting me go!"

19 "Why, how can you suggest such a thing!" Coyote cried indignantly. And then to himself he added, "This mouse is getting *too* smart!"

indignantly (in dig′ nənt lē) *adv.* angrily

"Very well, promise," Mouse said.

"But I am not made for work," Señor Coyote said tearfully. "I live by being sly."

"Then be sly and get out of the trap yourself," Mouse retorted.

"Very well," Señor Coyote said sadly. "I will work for you until I can pay back the debt of my life."

And so Mouse gnawed the leather strap in two and Coyote was saved. Then for many days thereafter Señor Coyote worked for Mouse. Mouse was very proud to have the famous Señor Coyote for a servant. Señor Coyote was greatly embarrassed since he did not like being a servant and disliked working even more.

20 There was nothing he could do since he had given his promise. He worked all day and dreamed all night of how he could trick his way out of his troubles. He could think of nothing.

Then one day Baby Mouse came running to him. "My father has been caught by Señor Snake!" he cried. "Please come and save him."

"Hooray!" cried Coyote. "If I save him, I will be released from my promise to work for him."

21 He went out to the desert rocks and found Señor Rattlesnake with his coils around Señor Mouse.

"Please let him go and I will catch you two more mice," Coyote said.

Literary Analysis
Folk Tales What landscape is familiar to the original tellers of this folk tale?

22 ▼ **Critical Viewing**
What do you think Mouse is telling Owl about Coyote? **[Speculate]**

Mouse and Owl, detail from painting on wood, Maureen Mahoney-Barraclough

CUSTOMIZE INSTRUCTION FOR UNIVERSAL ACCESS

For English Learners	For Advanced Readers
Direct students' attention to the top of p. 772 to Coyote's description of himself as *sly.* Discuss with students the connotation of *sly.* Most students will agree that the word carries a negative connotation because it is associated with dishonesty, secrecy, or trickery. Some of the synonyms for *sly* listed in a thesaurus have similar connotations, but some do not. Have students decide which choices from the following words share a similar connotation: *cunning, clever, mischievous, wily.*	Point out that "A bird in the hand is worth two in the bush" is a proverb and that the lessons taught in folk tales are similar to the lessons stated in many proverbs. Have students research the meaning of this proverb. Then, encourage interested students to gather a list of proverbs with lessons similar to those taught in folk tales. Final lists might be consolidated and shared with the rest of the class.

"My wise old mother used to tell me that a bird in the hand is worth two in the bush," Snake replied. "By the same reasoning, one mouse in Snake's stomach is worth two in Coyote's mind."

"Well, I tried, Mouse," Coyote said. "I'm sorry you must be eaten."

"But you must save me, then you will be free from your promise to me," Mouse said.

"If you're eaten, I'll be free anyway," Coyote said.

"Then everyone will say that Coyote was not smart enough to trick Snake," Mouse said quickly. "And I think they will be right. It makes me very sad for I always thought Señor Coyote the greatest trickster in the world."

This made Coyote's face turn red. He was very proud that everyone thought him so clever. Now he just *had* to save Mouse.

So he said to Snake, "How did you catch Mouse anyway?"

"A rock rolled on top of him and he was trapped," Mouse said. "He asked me to help him roll it off. When I did he jumped on me before I could run away."

"That is not true," Snake said. "How could a little mouse have the strength to roll away a big rock. There is the rock. Now you tell me if you think Mouse could roll it."

It was a very big rock and Coyote admitted that Mouse could not possibly have budged it.

23 "But it is like the story *Mamacita* tells her children at bedtime," Mouse said quickly. "Once there was a poor burro who had a load of hay just as large as he could carry. His master added just one more straw and the poor burro fell in the dirt. Snake did not have quite enough strength to push the rock off himself. I came along and was like that last straw on the burro's back and together we rolled the rock away."

"Maybe that is true," Snake said, "but by Mouse's own words, he did only a very little of the work. So I owe him only a very little thanks. That is not enough to keep me from eating him."

"Hmmm," said Coyote. "Now you understand, Snake, that I do not care what happens myself. If Mouse is eaten, I will be free of my bargain anyway. I am only thinking of your own welfare, Snake."

"Thank you," said Señor Rattlesnake, "but I do enough thinking about my welfare for both of us. I don't need your thoughts."

"Nevertheless," Coyote insisted, "everyone is going to say that you ate Mouse after he was kind enough to help you."

"I don't care," Snake said. "Nobody says anything good of me anyway."

"Well," said Coyote, "I'll tell you what we should do. We should put everything back as it was. Then I will see for myself if Mouse was as much help as he said he was or as little as you claim. Then I can tell everyone that you were right, Snake."

Literary Analysis
Folk Tales What lesson is taught by the folk tale that Mouse tells?

24 

How did Snake catch Mouse?

23 Literary Analysis

Folk Tales

- Have a volunteer read the bracketed paragraph. Elicit that this is another folk tale teaching a lesson within the larger story.
- Ask students the Literary Analysis question on p. 773: What lesson is taught by the folk tale that Mouse tells?
  Answer: Every little bit of help can lead to great results even though the help might seem pointless at first.

24 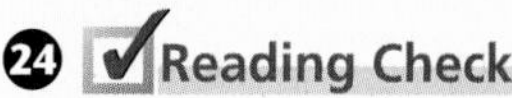

Answer: Snake caught Mouse when Mouse rolled a rock off of Snake.

ENRICHMENT: Science Connection

Desert Life

Explain that "Señor Coyote and the Tricked Trickster" is a folk tale from the part of Mexico near the United States border, where much of the land is desert. Define desert as an area of little rainfall. The lack of water means that deserts can support only certain kinds of plants and animals. List on the board the following plants and animals mentioned in the story: cactus, mouse, owl, coyote, rattlesnake.

Ask students to choose one of the plants or animals and research to learn whether it is usually found in the deserts of northern Mexico. If it is, students should find out any details about how it survives in a climate with little rainfall.

After students have completed their research, encourage them to share their findings orally or on posters as part of a special presentation about desert life.

ASSESS

25 Reading Strategy

Recognizing the Storyteller's Purpose

- Remind students that in addition to teaching a lesson, folk tales are often meant to entertain.
- Then, ask the Reading Strategy question on this page.
  Answer: Students might say that the clever tricks and arguments are entertaining.

Answers for p. 774

Review and Assess

1. **Possible responses:** Students who choose Coyote may note that he outsmarts both Mouse and Snake. Others may find Mouse's arguments especially clever.
2. **(a)** Mouse has a long-running feud with Coyote, who has often hurt his feelings by playing tricks on him. **(b)** Mouse is reluctant because he is afraid that Coyote will play more tricks on him.
3. **(a)** Mouse will save Coyote's life only if Coyote promises to devote his life to working for Mouse. **(b)** Mouse means that because Mouse saved Coyote, Coyote owes Mouse for the rest of his life.
4. **(a)** He needs Coyote to save him from Snake. **(b)** He appeals to Coyote's vanity and to his desire to maintain his reputation as a great trickster.
5. **(a)** Snake is tricked and Coyote is the trickster. **(b)** They are both self-centered.
6. **Possible response:** Most students will probably say that none of the characters owe anything to each other. They are all even.

"Very well," said Señor Snake. "I was lying like this and the rock was on me—"

"Like this?" Coyote said, quickly rolling the rock across Snake's body.

"Ouch!" said Snake. "That is right."

"Can you get out?" Coyote asked.

25 "No," said Snake.

"Then turn Mouse loose and let him push," said Coyote.

This Snake did, but before Mouse could push, Coyote said, "But on second thought if Mouse pushes, you would then grab him again and we'd be back arguing. Since you are both as you were before the argument started, let us leave it at that and all be friends again!"

Then Coyote turned to Mouse. "So, my friend, I have now saved your life. We are now even and my debt to you is paid."

"But mine is such a *little* life," Mouse protested. "And yours is so much *larger*. I don't think they balance. You should still pay me part."

"This is ridiculous!" Coyote cried. "I—"

"Wait!" Snake put in hopefully. "Let me settle the quarrel. Now you roll the rock away. I'll take Mouse in my coils just the way we were when Coyote came up. We'll be then in a position to decide if—"

"Thank you," said Mouse. "It isn't necessary to trouble everyone again. Señor Coyote, we are even."

Reading Strategy
Recognizing the Storyteller's Purpose In what ways is this folk tale entertaining?

Review and Assess

Thinking About the Selection

1. **Respond:** Which character do you think is the most clever? Why?
2. **(a) Recall:** Describe the relationship between Coyote and Mouse at the time the story begins. **(b) Infer:** Why is Mouse reluctant to help the trapped Coyote?
3. **(a) Recall:** Why does Coyote work as Mouse's servant?
   (b) Interpret: What does Mouse mean when he tells Coyote "a life is worth a life"?
4. **(a) Recall:** For what reason does Mouse need Coyote's help?
   (b) Draw Conclusions: To which of Coyote's characteristics does Mouse appeal in persuading Coyote to save him?
5. **(a) Distinguish:** In this situation, who is tricked, and who is the trickster? **(b) Compare and Contrast:** What common failing do Snake and Coyote share that makes them easy to trick?
6. **Make a Judgment:** Which character, if any, owes something to another character?

I. G. Edmonds

(b. 1917)

I. G. Edmonds is a collector of folk tales. As a soldier in the South Pacific during World War II, Edmonds decided to collect folk tales after he heard a native chief's story about how his island was created. The tales Edmonds collected are published in his book *Trickster Tales*. Other folk tales are collected in his anthology, *Ooka the Wise: Tales of Old Japan*.

Another of Edmonds's interests, communications, led to the writing of a nonfiction book, *Broadcasting for Beginners*.

ASSESSMENT PRACTICE: Writing Skills

Spelling (For more practice, see Test Preparation Workbook, p. 60.)

Some tests require students to read written passages and identify incorrectly spelled words. Write the following sentence on the board, and have students identify any errors in the sentence.

> When he was a young man growing up in Russia, Leo Tolstoy had the benefites of wealth and education.

Which of the following spelling changes would make this sentence correct?

A benefits **C** educasion
B welth **D** yung

The correct answer is *A*. The word *benefites* should be spelled *benefits*.

Review and Assess

Literary Analysis

Folk Tales

1. Record examples of the types of cultural details in "Señor Coyote and the Tricked Trickster."

2. In "He Lion, Bruh Bear, and Bruh Rabbit," how does Virginia Hamilton preserve the feeling that this is a story being told aloud?
3. Why do you think several cultures have a folk tale similar to the one taught in "The Ant and the Dove"?

Comparing Literary Works

4. Use a chart like this one to show the qualities that the different characters represent.

Character	Quality	Examples
Señor Coyote	Cleverness	He talks Snake into being trapped.

5. What is one common or shared point in the lessons of the folk tales? Explain.
6. In what ways are the lessons different from one another?

Reading Strategy

Recognizing the Storyteller's Purpose

7. What are two details in "The Ant and the Dove" that indicate that its purpose is to teach?
8. Identify one detail that entertains and one that is meant to teach in "He Lion, Bruh Bear, and Bruh Rabbit."
9. Identify three details that indicate that one purpose of "Señor Coyote and the Tricked Trickster" is to entertain.

Extending Understanding

10. **Science Connection:** Explain how prey animals (animals that are hunted) such as mice protect themselves in the wild.

Quick Review

Folk tales are stories that were composed orally and then passed down by word of mouth. They often reflect the time and place in which they were told. To review folk tales, see page 763.

The **storyteller's purpose** is his or her reason for telling the story.

Take It to the Net

www.phschool.com

Take the interactive self-test online to check your understanding of these selections.

ENRICHMENT: Further Reading

Other Works by the Authors

Works by Leo Tolstoy

Anna Karenina

Fables and Fairy Tales by Leo Tolstoy, translated by Ann Dunigan

Works by Virginia Hamilton

The People Could Fly

Her Stories: African American Folktales, Fairy Tales, and True Tales

Works by I. G. Edmonds

Ooka the Wise: Tales of Old Japan

Case of the Marble Monster and Other Stories

Take It to the Net

Visit www.phschool.com for more information on the authors.

Answers for p. 775

Review and Assess

1. Details include words from the Spanish language, a description of a setting in Mexico, the cactus, and the coyote.
2. She uses repetition, an informal tone, and a dialect that contains nonstandard grammar, pronunciation, and vocabulary.
3. Many cultures use similar stories to teach people to behave kindly toward one another even if they do not expect something in return.
4. Possible responses: **Señor Coyote:** Quality: Pride, self-interest Examples: Honors his promise; agrees to help free Mouse from Snake if he no longer has to be Mouse's servant **Señor Mouse:** Quality: Wit, cunning Examples: Uses his wit and cunning to make Coyote his servant **Señor Snake:** Quality: Self-interest Examples: More interested in eating Mouse than in helping
5. One common point in the lessons of the folk tales is the importance of helping those in need. Animals in each of the stories help others and therefore teach a valuable lesson.
6. The lessons are different in their final outcomes. The lessons the animals learn are unrelated to each other.
7. Possible responses: Students may mention the dove's kindness in saving the ant's life, and the ant's returning the kindness by saving the dove's life.
8. Entertaining details include he Lion's roar, "Me and Myself"; and the names Will Be and Was Once. Details that teach include Bruh Rabbit's teaching he Lion a lesson, and he Lion's lesson about how to treat others.
9. Details include the feud between Coyote and Mouse for no remembered reason, Mouse's seemingly logical but often outrageous bargaining, and Coyote's way of outsmarting Snake.
10. Possible response: Most animals have natural protective abilities. For example, opossums appear dead if attacked and chameleons change colors to camouflage themselves.

EXTEND

Answers for p. 776

❶ Vocabulary Development

Word Analysis

1. d
2. c
3. b
4. a

Fluency: Definitions

1. indignantly
2. startled
3. lair
4. cordial
5. reproachfully
6. ungrateful

Spelling Strategy

1. A stomachache hurts. (hurts)
2. Borrowing builds a debt. (Borrowing; builds)
3. Hold still for half an hour. (Hold; half)

❷ Grammar

1. correct
2. Mom
3. Señor
4. correct
5. Uncle

Writing Application

Sample response: Señor Coyote rolled the rock away, and Señor Snake quickly snatched up Señor Mouse and ate him for dinner.

Integrate Language Skills

❶ Vocabulary Development Lesson

Word Analysis: Forms of *Dignity*

In "Señor Coyote and the Tricked Trickster," Coyote responds *indignantly* to Mouse's accusations. He thinks that they are unfair or not respectful. The word *indignantly* is the opposite of *dignity*, which means "being worthy of respect."

Match each form of *dignity* with its definition.

1. dignity
2. dignitary
3. indignity
4. indignantly

a. angrily
b. something that insults one's worth
c. a person worthy of respect
d. the quality of being worthy

Fluency: Definitions

Write the vocabulary word that matches each definition:

1. in an insulted way
2. surprised
3. cave or den
4. friendly
5. as if blaming
6. not thankful

Spelling Strategy

Some words, such as *gnaw*, have unexpected silent letters. Practice spelling the following words.

hour stomach debt

Copy the sentences and fill in the blank with one of the words above.

1. A ________ ache hurts.
2. Borrowing builds a ________.
3. Hold still for half an ________.

Identify the words in each sentence that begin with the silent letter in the word you supplied.

❷ Grammar Lesson

Using Capitals for Titles of People

Whether or not a person's title is capitalized depends on how it is used. Most titles, whether social, professional, or family titles, are capitalized when they are used as part of a name or in place of a name. They are not capitalized when preceded by an article or a possessive pronoun.

Examples: Have you met Aunt Bridget?
Meet my aunt, Bridget Donato.
Call Dr. Cushwa.
Call the doctor.
We're meeting Dad later.
Our dad will drive us.

Practice Copy the sentences below, and add capital letters where necessary.

1. I told my grandpa about the folk tale.
2. What was your favorite part of the story, mom?
3. I liked how señor Coyote tricked Snake.
4. She saw her doctor.
5. Do you think uncle Al would like to hear a trickster story?

Writing Application Write an alternative ending for "Señor Coyote and the Tricked Trickster." Use at least three capitals in titles.

WG Prentice Hall Writing and Grammar Connection: Chapter 27

TEACHING RESOURCES

The following resources can be used to enrich or extend the instruction for pp. 776–777.

Vocabulary

- **Selection Support:** Build Vocabulary, p. 206; Build Spelling Skills, p. 207
- **Vocabulary and Spelling Practice Book** (Use this booklet for skills enrichment)

Grammar

- **Selection Support:** Build Grammar Skills, p. 208
- **Writing and Grammar,** Copper Level, p. 600

- **Daily Language Practice Transparencies** ■

Writing

- **Writing and Grammar,** Copper Level, p. 89 ■
- **Writing Models and Graphic Organizers on Transparencies,** p. 23
- **Writing and Grammar iText CD-ROM**

■ **BLOCK SCHEDULING:** Resources marked with this symbol provide varied instruction during 90-minute blocks.

❸ Writing Lesson

Folk Tale

Most folk tale characters appear in more than one folk tale in the culture from which they come. Write your own folk tale using the characters from one of the tales in this group. First, identify the point of your folk tale, such as the value of friendship or the importance of teamwork. Make a list of several problems or conflicts that will help you illustrate the point. For example, Bruh Bear and Bruh Rabbit may need to combine forces to escape from a hunter.

Prewriting Decide on a conflict, or problem, for your characters to solve. Then, review the original folk tale, and gather details about how your characters think, act, and talk.

Drafting Develop some of the action through dialogue—the conversations between characters—to show the characters' personalities.

Model: Show Action Character With Dialogue

"Quick! Follow me into this cave!" cried Bruh Rabbit.

"Hold on. I'll go first to make sure it's safe." said Bruh Bear.

The dialogue shows what they are doing and suggests how they are doing it.

Revising Be sure you have used quotation marks to show the beginning and the ending of each character's words. Each time the speaker changes, you must start a new paragraph.

WG Prentice Hall Writing and Grammar Connection: Chapter 5, Section 5

❹ Extension Activities

Research and Technology Using the Internet, prepare a **display** about folk art from various cultures. Include the following in your display:

- A caption identifying the work and where it was created
- A brief explanation of what the art shows and what is interesting and unique about the design, colors, or materials used to create it

Writing Choose one of the folk tales and write an **explanation** of the tale's message.

Listening and Speaking "Señor Coyote and the Tricked Trickster" is one of many folk tales in which a coyote appears as a trickster. In a small group, research another character that recurs in many folk tales. Then, prepare an **oral presentation** that offers the following information:

1. The qualities that the character represents
2. Summaries of two or three folk tales in which the character appears

Take It to the Net www.phschool.com

Go online for an additional research activity using the Internet.

ASSESSMENT RESOURCES

The following resources can be used to assess students' knowledge and skills.

Selection Assessment

- **Formal Assessment,** pp. 196–198
- **Open Book Test,** pp. 124–126
- **Got It! Assessment Videotapes,** Tape 5
- **Test Bank Software**

Take It to the Net

Visit www.phschool.com for self-tests and additional questions on the selections.

Writing Rubric

- **Performance Assess. and Portfolio Mgmt.,** p. 13

Listening and Speaking Rubric

- **Performance Assess. and Portfolio Mgmt.,** p. 29

PRENTICE HALL ASSESSMENT SYSTEM

- **Workbook**
- **Transparencies**
- **Skill Book**
- **CD-ROM**

Lesson Support for p. 777

❸ Writing Lesson

- Tell students that as they write their folk tales, they should carefully consider the dialogue between the characters.
- Dialogue often carries the story in folk tales by revealing character traits that lead to the actions that teach a lesson.
- Review the Writing Lesson instruction about how to use the stages in the writing process to help students write their folk tales.
- Have students use the Narration rubric on p. 13 in **Performance Assessment and Portfolio Management** to guide their writing.

❹ Listening and Speaking

- Tell students that they should find two or three other tales that contain the trickster character. Remind students that this character exists in many Spanish and African American folk tales.
- Point out that the trickster's characteristics are similar in all of the trickster folk tales. Tell students that their summaries of two or three folk tales should describe the plots and the major characters.
- Have students use the Speaking rubric on p. 29 in **Performance Assessment and Portfolio Management** as a checklist for their oral presentations.

CUSTOMIZE INSTRUCTION For Universal Access

To address different learning styles, use the activities suggested in the **Extension Activities** booklet, p. 42.

- For Visual/Spatial and Verbal/Linguistic Learners, use Activity 5.
- For Bodily/Kinesthetic and Musical Rhythmic Learners, use Activity 6.
- For Intrapersonal and Visual/Spatial Learners, use Activity 7.

Why Monkeys Live in Trees ✦ Arachne ✦ The Three Wishes ✦ The Crippled Boy

Lesson Objectives

1. **To analyze and respond to literary elements**
   - Literary Analysis: Oral Tradition
   - Comparing Literary Works
2. **To read, comprehend, analyze, and critique three folk tales and a myth**
   - Reading Strategy: Making Predictions
   - Reading Check Questions
   - Review and Assess Questions
3. **To develop word analysis skills, fluency, and systematic vocabulary**
   - Vocabulary Development Lesson: Word Analysis: Latin Root *-mort-*
4. **To understand and apply written and oral language conventions**
   - Spelling Strategy
   - Grammar Lesson: Sentence Structure and Style
   - Assessment Practice (ATE)
5. **To understand and apply appropriate writing and research strategies**
   - Writing Lesson: Ancient Theme in a Modern Setting
   - Extension Activity: Folk Tale Research
6. **To understand and apply listening and speaking strategies**
   - Extension Activity: Oral Report

STEP-BY-STEP TEACHING GUIDE	PACING GUIDE
PRETEACH	
Motivate Students and Provide Background	
Use the Motivation activity (ATE p. 778)	5 min.
Read and discuss the Preview material and Background information (SE/ATE p. 778) [A]	10 min.
Introduce the Concepts	
Introduce the Literary Analysis and Reading Strategy (SE/ATE p. 779) [A]	25 min.
Pronounce the vocabulary words and read their definitions (SE p. 779)	5 min.
TEACH	
Monitor Comprehension	
Informally monitor comprehension by circulating while students read independently or in groups [A]	20–25 min.
Monitor students' comprehension with the Reading Check notes (SE/ATE pp. 781, 785, 787, 789, 791)	as students read
Develop vocabulary with Vocabulary notes (SE pp. 785, 786, 789, 790; ATE p. 786)	as students read
Develop Understanding	
Develop students' understanding of oral tradition with the Literary Analysis annotations (SE pp. 780, 783, 787; ATE pp. 781, 782, 783, 787) [A]	5 min.
Develop students' ability to predict with the Reading Strategy annotations (SE pp. 786, 789; ATE pp. 786, 789, 791)	5 min.
ASSESS	
Assess Mastery	
Assess students' mastery of the Reading Strategy and Literary Analysis by having them answer the Review and Assess questions (SE/ATE p. 793)	25 min.
Use one or more of the print and media Assessment Resources (ATE p. 795) [A]	up to 45 min.
EXTEND	
Apply Understanding	
Have students complete the Vocabulary Development Lesson and the Grammar Lesson (SE p. 794) [A]	30 min.
Apply students' knowledge of ancient theme in a modern setting using the Writing Lesson (SE/ATE p. 795) [A]	45 min.
Apply students' understanding using one or more of the Extension Activities (SE p. 795)	20–90 min.

ACCELERATED INSTRUCTION:
Use the strategies and activities identified with an [A].

UNIVERSAL ACCESS
● = Below Level Students
▲ = On-Level Students
■ = Above Level Students

Time and Resource Manager

Reading Level: Easy, Challenging, Easy, Average
Average Number of Instructional Days: 4

RESOURCES		
PRINT	**TRANSPARENCIES**	**TECHNOLOGY**
• **Beyond Literature,** Cultural Connection: The Craft of Weaving, p. 43 ▲ ■		• **Interest Grabber Videotapes,** Tape 5 ● ▲ ■
• **Selection Support Workbook:** ● ▲ ■ Literary Analysis, p. 215 Reading Strategy, p. 214 Build Vocabulary, p. 211	• **Literary Analysis and Reading Transparencies,** pp. 85 and 86 ● ▲ ■	
• **Adapted Reader's Companion** ● • **Reader's Companion** ●		• **Listening to Literature** ● ▲ ■ Audiocassettes, Sides 27, 28 Audio CDs, CD 14
• **English Learner's Companion** ● ▲ • **Literatura en español** ● ▲ • **Literary Analysis for Enrichment** ■		
• **Formal Assessment:** Selection Test, pp. 199–201 ● ▲ ■ • **Open Book Test,** pp. 127–129 ● ▲ ■ • **Performance Assessment and Portfolio Management,** pp. 13, 29 ● ▲ ■ • PRENTICE HALL ASSESSMENT SYSTEM ● ▲ ■	• PRENTICE HALL ASSESSMENT SYSTEM ● ▲ ■ Skills Practice Answers and Explanations on Transparencies	• **Test Bank Software** ● ▲ ■ • **Got It! Assessment Videotapes,** Tape 5 ● ▲
• **Selection Support Workbook:** ● ▲ ■ Build Spelling Skills, p. 212 Build Grammar Skills, p. 213 • **Writing and Grammar,** Copper Level ● ▲ ■ • **Extension Activities,** p. 43 ● ▲ ■	• **Daily Language Practice Transparencies** ● ▲ • **Writing Models and Graphic Organizers on Transparencies** ● ▲ ■	• **Writing and Grammar iText CD-ROM** ● ▲ ■ ***Take It to the Net*** www.phschool.com

BLOCK SCHEDULING: Use one 90-minute class period to preteach the selection and have students read it. Use a second 90-minute class period to assess students' mastery of skills and have them complete one of the Extension Activities.

PRETEACH

Step-by-Step Teaching Guide for pp. 778–779

Motivation

Have students recall the stories that were told to them in childhood. What did these stories teach them? Which do they remember best, and why? After volunteers summarize several stories and state their lessons or themes, tell students that the tales and myths they are about to read were also told orally for many generations before they were ever written down.

Interest Grabber Video

As an alternative, play "Spiders" on Tape 5 to engage student interest.

❶ Background

Social Studies

Essential to understanding the role of folk tales in a culture is recognizing the importance of storytellers. They play the major role in oral traditions. In the African, Native American, Spanish, Japanese, and Russian cultures, for example, storytellers were, and remain, respected purveyors of the cultural memory. They use their eyes, voices, bodies, and even silence to bring cultural tales to life and to help others remember the tales and their lessons.

Prepare to Read

❶ Why Monkeys Live in Trees ◆ Arachne ◆ The Three Wishes ◆ A Crippled Boy

Take It to the Net

Visit www.phschool.com for interactive activities and instruction related to these selections, including

- background
- graphic organizers
- literary elements
- reading strategies

Preview

Connecting to the Literature

The characters in these stories show varying degrees of self-confidence. For some of them self-confidence becomes overconfidence. Before reading, think about what your own experience and observations have shown about the positive and negative sides of confidence.

Background

Different versions of "The Three Wishes" exist in cultures around the world. Because folk tales are passed on orally, they can "migrate" from one place to another. Each storyteller adds details based on personal experience or culture. After a number of tellings, a new version of the tale emerges.

TEACHING RESOURCES

The following resources can be used to enrich or extend the instruction for pp. 778–779.

Motivation

Interest Grabber Video, Tape 5

Background

Beyond Literature, p. 43

Take It to the Net

Visit www.phschool.com for Background and hotlinks for the selections.

Literary Analysis

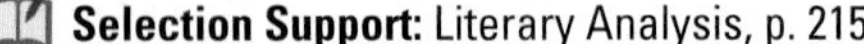

Selection Support: Literary Analysis, p. 215

Literary Analysis and Reading Transparencies, Oral Tradition, p. 86

Reading

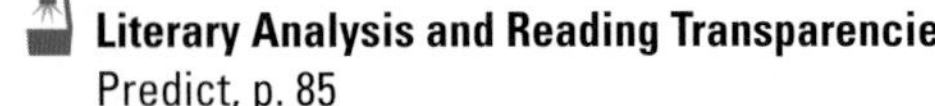

Literary Analysis and Reading Transparencies, Predict, p. 85

BLOCK SCHEDULING: Resources marked with this symbol provide varied instruction during 90-minute blocks.

❷ Literary Analysis

Oral Tradition

The **oral tradition** is the passing of songs, stories, and poems from generation to generation by word of mouth. There are several types of stories in the oral tradition.

- **Myths** tell stories of gods and goddesses. They may also explain something in nature or teach a lesson.
- **Folk tales** feature heroes, adventure, magic, and romance. They often entertain while teaching a lesson.

These works reflect the traditions, beliefs, and values of the common people. As you read, think about the following focus questions:

1. What cultural traditions are reflected in this story?
2. What beliefs and values does it reveal?

Comparing Literary Works

A story's **theme** is its central insight into life or human nature. As you read, determine the theme or message of each work by thinking about how the characters change or grow or what they learn during the course of the story. Compare the themes of these works and how they are presented.

❸ Reading Strategy

Making Predictions

A **prediction** is an educated guess about future events in a story. To make a prediction, use what you already know from your experiences in reading and in life.

Myths and folk tales are often predictable. Cleverness and bravery are usually rewarded, but undesirable qualities, such as pride, are punished.

On an organizer like this one, predict the outcome of each story as soon as you think you know what will happen. Later, record the actual outcome of the folk tale or myth.

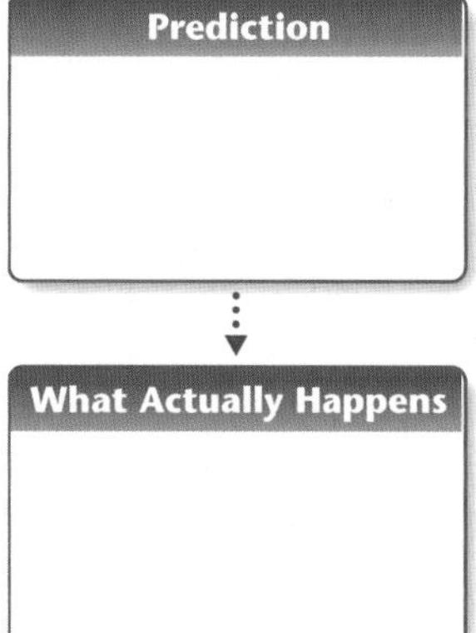

Vocabulary Development

obscure (əb skyoor′) *adj.* not well known (p. 785)

mortal (môr′ təl) *adj.* referring to humans, who must eventually die (p. 786)

obstinacy (äb′ stə nə sē) *n.* stubbornness (p. 786)

embraced (em brāsd′) *v.* clasped in the arms, usually as an expression of affection (p. 789)

covetousness (kuv′ ət əs nəs) *n.* envy; wanting what another person has (p. 790)

CUSTOMIZE INSTRUCTION FOR UNIVERSAL ACCESS

For Special Needs Students	For Less Proficient Readers	For English Learners
Have students read the adapted version of the selections in the **Adapted Reader's Companion.** This version provides basic-level instruction in an interactive format with questions and write-on lines. Completing the adapted version will prepare students to read the selection in the Student Edition.	Have students read the selections in the **Reader's Companion.** This version provides basic-level instruction in an interactive format with questions and write-on lines. After students finish the selection in the Reader's Companion, have them complete the questions and activities in the Student Edition.	Have students read the adapted version of the selections in the **English Learner's Companion.** This version provides basic-level instruction in an interactive format with questions and write-on lines. Completing the adapted version will prepare students to read the selection in the Student Edition.

❷ Literary Analysis

Oral Tradition

- Tell students that in the oral tradition, myths and tales are handed down orally from generation to generation and reflect the traditions, beliefs, and values of the common people.
- Discuss the instruction for Comparing Literary Works to compare the different themes—or insights into human nature—that the tales represent.
- Use the Oral Tradition transparency on p. 86 in **Literary Analysis and Reading Transparencies** to help students understand the tales.

❸ Reading Strategy

Making Predictions

- Remind students that a prediction is an educated guess about future events in a story.
- Help students understand that predicting can improve readers' comprehension for any type of reading, whether the material is a folk tale, a persuasive essay, or an informational report.
- Remind students that it is important not only to make predictions, but also to check their predictions for accuracy.
- Use the Predict transparency on p. 85 in **Literary Analysis and Reading Transparencies** to help students make predictions as they read the tales.

Vocabulary Development

- Review the words and definitions on the vocabulary list.
- Ask students to identify the relationship between *mortal* and *immortal*.
  Response: They are opposites.
- Ask students to suggest antonyms for other vocabulary words on the list.
  Possible responses: obscure/clear; obstinacy/flexibility; embraced/turned away; covetousness/graciousness.

E-Teach

Visit E-Teach at www.phschool.com for teachers' essays on how to teach, with questions and answers.

TEACH

Step-by-Step Teaching Guide for pp. 780–792

CUSTOMIZE INSTRUCTION
For Bodily/Kinesthetic Learners

Students might enjoy pantomiming the actions of the various characters in these four tales. Remind students that when pantomiming they use only their bodies to depict a scene or emotion; no words or sounds are used. For example, one or more students could pantomime the actions of Hippopotamus, Leopard, and/or Lion after eating the black pepper in "Why Monkeys Live in Trees."

1 About the Selection

One day when Leopard is admiring his reflection in a pool, he learns about a contest. King Gorilla has offered a pot of gold to anyone who can eat what looks like a mound of black dust in one day. When the different animals try, however, they scream, sneeze, cough, and cannot do it, for the mound is black pepper. Then Monkey says he can do it if he can lie down and rest in the tall grass between mouthfuls. Leopard, however, spies hundreds of monkeys hiding in the tall grass and realizes that each has come forward and taken a mouthful. Furious, he chases the monkeys, and others join in. The only way the monkeys can escape is to climb to the tops of tall trees—which is why they live in trees to this very day.

1 Why Monkeys Live in Trees

African Folk Tale

Julius Lester

2 One day Leopard was looking at his reflection in a pool of water. Looking at himself was Leopard's favorite thing in the world to do. Leopard gazed, wanting to be sure that every hair was straight and that all his spots were where they were supposed to be. This took many hours of looking at his reflection, which Leopard did not mind at all.

Finally he was satisfied that nothing was disturbing his handsomeness, and he turned away from the pool of water. At that exact moment, one of Leopard's children ran up to him.

"Daddy! Daddy! Are you going to be in the contest?"

3 "What contest?" Leopard wanted to know. If it was a beauty contest, of course he was going to be in it.

"I don't know. Crow the Messenger just flew by. She said that King Gorilla said there was going to be a contest."

Without another word, Leopard set off. He went north-by-northeast, made a right turn at the mulberry bush and traveled east-by-south-by-west until he came to a hole in the ground. He went around in a circle five times, and headed north-by-somersault

Literary Analysis
Oral Tradition How does the opening of the story suggest that it is a tale that has been told aloud?

TEACHING RESOURCES

The following resources can be used to enrich or extend the instruction for pp. 780–792.

Literary Analysis
- **Literary Analysis for Enrichment**

Reading
- **Selection Support:** Reading Strategy, p. 214; Build Vocabulary, p. 211
- **Adapted Reader's Companion**
- **Reader's Companion**
- **English Learner's Companion**

- **Literatura en español**
- **Listening to Literature Audiocassettes,** Sides 27, 28 ■
- **Listening to Literature Audio CDs,** CD 14 ■

■ **BLOCK SCHEDULING:** Resources marked with this symbol provide varied instruction during 90-minute blocks.

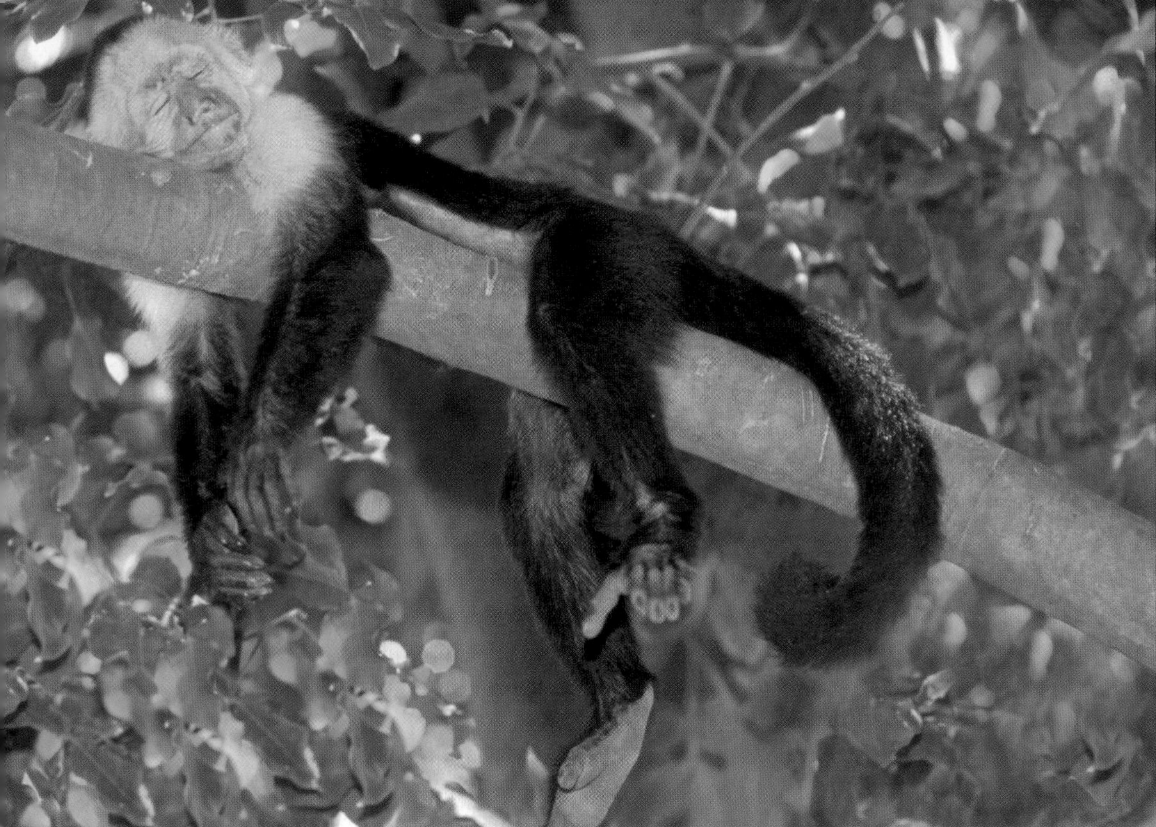

until he came to a big clearing in the middle of the jungle and that's where King Gorilla was.

King Gorilla sat at one end of the clearing on his throne. Opposite him, at the other side of the clearing, all the animals sat in a semicircle. In the middle, between King Gorilla and the animals, was a huge mound of what looked like black dust.

Leopard looked around with calm dignity. Then he strode regally over to his friend, Lion.

"What's that?" he asked, pointing to the mound of black dust.

"Don't know," Lion replied. "King Gorilla said he will give a pot of gold to whoever can eat it in one day. I can eat it in an hour."

Leopard laughed. "I'll eat it in a half hour."

It was Hippopotamus's turn to laugh. "As big as my mouth is, I'll eat that mound in one gulp."

The time came for the contest. King Gorilla had the animals pick numbers to see who would go in what order. To everybody's dismay, Hippopotamus drew Number 1.

Hippopotamus walked over to the mound of black dust. It was

4 ▲ **Critical Viewing**
Based on details in this picture, why would a storyteller choose to use monkeys as characters in a tale meant to entertain? **[Analyze]**

5 **Reading Check**
What does an animal have to do to win the contest?

2 Literary Analysis

Oral Tradition

- Discuss with students the ways in which they begin telling a story to someone they know.
- Then, elicit from students the ways in which storytellers usually begin their tales.
  Possible response: Storytellers usually begin their tales with "Once upon a time . . ."
- Ask the Literary Analysis question on p. 780.
  Answer: The conversational tone as well as the words "One day . . ." suggest that this is a tale that was once told aloud.

3 Reinforcing Skills

Drawing Inferences

- Have students consider the bracketed passage and Leopard's behavior up to this point in the story.
- Ask students the following question: What does Leopard's interest in looking at himself and in beauty contests reveal about him?
  Answer: He is vain and overly concerned with his handsome appearance

4 ▶Critical Viewing

Answer: The monkeys in this picture are incredibly humanlike. A storyteller would use monkeys in a tale meant to entertain because of their human qualities.

5 Reading Check

Answer: An animal has to eat the mound of black dust in one day to win the pot of gold.

CUSTOMIZE INSTRUCTION FOR UNIVERSAL ACCESS

For English Learners	For Gifted/Talented Students
English language learners may have difficulty with some of the animal names in the story or with connecting the animal's personality with the correct animal. Students can benefit by previewing a set of flashcards that display pictures and names of animals from this tale. After students preview the cards, have one student call out an animal name and allow others to find the matching picture.	Have students use details from the selection to draw a map of Leopard's travels. Note that the sixth paragraph on p. 780 gives details about the route Leopard takes and the landscape he crosses. Divide students into small groups. Have students use these details to create a map of Leopard's route. The map should include landmarks as well as the path he takes and should indicate relevant actions; for example, "circle five times" and "somersault."

❻ Literary Analysis

Oral Tradition

- Have a student read aloud the bracketed passage. Remind students that folk tales often explain something that occurs in nature.
- Ask students the following question: What natural occurrence is explained in this passage? Do you think this explanation is accurate?
  Answer: It explains that chickens do not have ears because Hippopotamus screamed so loudly after eating the black dust. The scream knocked the ears off of all the chickens. Students should realize that this is a fictional, humorous explanation.

❼ Literary Analysis

Oral Tradition

- Have students read the bracketed passage on p. 782. Remind students that folk tales often use repetition to help the storyteller remember the tale and to elicit listener response as the tale is being told.
- Ask students the following question: What words are repeated to describe the reactions of both Hippopotamus and Leopard to the black pepper?
  Answer: Words that are repeated include *screamed, yelled, roared, bellowed, crying, tears, ran to the river, throat,* and *tongue.*

▶ **Monitor Progress** Have students explain why storytellers in the oral tradition use repetition.
Answer: Repetition in stories that are told aloud encourage listener response and participation. It also helps storytellers and listeners alike to remember details in the story.

▶ **Reteach** If students cannot discern differences between repetition and the lack of it, reread the story without the repetitions, and discuss the differences between the two versions.

❽ ▶ Critical Viewing

Answer: Climbing ability helps them escape predators and obtain food.

bigger than he had thought. It was much too big to eat in one gulp. Nonetheless, Hippopotamus opened his mouth as wide as he could, and that was very wide indeed, and took a mouthful of the black dust.

❻ He started chewing. Suddenly he leaped straight into the air and screamed. He screamed so loudly that it knocked the ears off the chickens and that's why to this day chickens don't have ears.

Hippopotamus screamed and Hippopotamus yelled. Hippopotamus roared and Hippopotamus bellowed. Then he started sneezing and crying and tears rolled down his face like he was standing in the shower. Hippopotamus ran to the river and drank as much water as he could, and that was very much, indeed, to cool his mouth and tongue and throat.

The animals didn't understand what had happened to Hippopotamus, but they didn't care. They were happy because they still had a chance to win the pot of gold. Of course, if they had known that the mound of black dust was really a mound of black pepper, maybe they wouldn't have wanted the gold.

Nobody was more happy than Leopard because he had drawn Number 2. He walked up to the black mound and sniffed at it.

"AAAAAAAACHOOOOOOO!" Leopard didn't like that but then he remembered the pot of gold. He opened his mouth wide, took a mouthful and started chewing and swallowing.

❼ Leopard leaped straight into the air, did a back double flip and screamed. He yelled and he roared and he bellowed and, finally, he started sneezing and crying, tears rolling down his face like a waterfall. Leopard ran to the river and washed out his mouth and throat and tongue.

Lion was next, and the same thing happened to him as it did to all the animals. Finally only Monkey remained.

Monkey approached King Gorilla. "I know I can eat all of whatever that is, but after each mouthful, I'll need to lie down in the tall grasses and rest."

King Gorilla said that was okay.

Monkey went to the mound, took a tiny bit of pepper on his tongue, swallowed, and went into the tall grasses. A few minutes

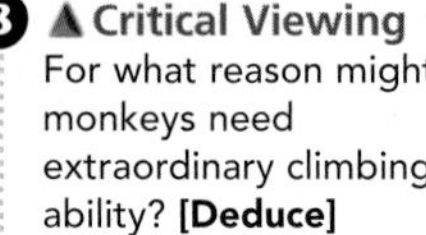

❽ ▲ **Critical Viewing** For what reason might monkeys need extraordinary climbing ability? **[Deduce]**

later, Monkey came out, took a little more, swallowed it, and went into the tall grasses.

Soon the pile was almost gone. The animals were astonished to see Monkey doing what they had not been able to do. Leopard couldn't believe it either. He climbed a tree and stretched out on a sturdy limb to get a better view. From his limb high in the tree Leopard could see into the tall grasses where Monkey went to rest. Wait a minute! Leopard thought something was suddenly wrong with his eyes because he thought he saw a hundred monkeys hiding in the tall grasses.

He rubbed his eyes and looked another look. There wasn't anything wrong with his eyes. There were a hundred monkeys in the tall grasses and they all looked alike!

Just then, there was the sound of loud applause. King Gorilla announced that Monkey had won the contest and the pot of gold.

Leopard growled a growl so scary that even King Gorilla was frightened. Leopard wasn't thinking about anybody except the monkeys. He took a long and beautiful leap from the tree right smack into the middle of the tall grasses where the monkeys were hiding.

The monkeys ran in all directions. When the other animals saw monkeys running from the grasses, they realized that the monkeys had tricked them and started chasing them. Even King Gorilla joined in the chase. He wanted his gold back.

9

The only way the monkeys could escape was to climb to the very tops of the tallest trees where no one else, not even Leopard, could climb.

And that's why monkeys live in trees to this very day.

Literary Analysis
Oral Tradition and Theme
What theme do the monkeys' actions reveal?

Review and Assess

Thinking About the Selections

1. **Respond:** Which character or characters in this story do you find most entertaining?
2. **(a) Recall:** What contest does King Gorilla hold? **(b) Infer:** Why do the animals think it will be easy to win the contest? **(c) Support:** Explain why it will not be easy for animals to win the contest.
3. **(a) Recall:** What does the monkey do between bites of pepper? **(b) Connect:** What does Leopard see in the tall grass? **(c) Deduce:** Why is the monkey able to eat all the pepper?
4. **(a) Assess:** Is the contest a fair one? **(b) Make a Judgment:** Do the monkeys deserve to win the contest?

Julius Lester

(b. 1939)

Julius Lester had a successful career in music when he turned to writing books on subjects related to his African American background. He has been a runner-up for the Newbery Medal and a finalist for the National Book Award.

CUSTOMIZE INSTRUCTION FOR UNIVERSAL ACCESS

For Less Proficient Readers

Explain to students that they will be responsible for retelling parts of the four selections in this grouping. Suggest that as they read, they jot down details about character and plot that they wish to remember. After they have read each selection, have students gather in groups of four. One student should begin to tell the story, then the others should take turns, until all four have spoken and the story is completed. To help them remember the main points of each selection, have them jot down brief summaries after they have finished reading each selection. Remind students that a summary should include only the most important events, characters, and details.

9 Literary Analysis

Oral Tradition and Theme

- After students have read the bracketed passage on p. 783, have them consider the monkeys' behavior when they are chased by other animals.
- Ask students the Literary Analysis question: What theme do the monkeys' actions reveal? Answer: Their actions give insight into the way that humans behave when they are chased and frightened: humans, like the monkeys, usually run and hide in fear.

Answers for p. 783

Review and Assess

1. Possible response: Leopard's vain actions are entertaining; the monkeys' actions are witty and humorous.
2. **(a)** The animal who can eat, in one day, the entire mound of black powder wins a pot of gold. **(b)** The Leopard is vain and thinks he can eat the mound; Hippopotamus says he could eat it in one gulp with his huge mouth. **(c)** It will be impossible for them to win because an animal cannot eat a mound of black pepper.
3. **(a)** The monkey says he needs to lie down in the grass to rest between bites. **(b)** Leopard sees hundreds of monkeys who all look alike in the grass. **(c)** Many monkeys pretend to be one monkey; after each mouthful they change places in the grass and go back to take a new mouthful.
4. **(a)** No, the contest is not fair. King Gorilla presents a challenge that the animals cannot win. **(b)** Possible responses: The monkeys deserve the gold because they are clever and they ate the mound of black pepper. Or, the monkeys do not deserve to win because the rules of the contest specified that the gold would go to "whoever" ate the mound in one day, implying that it had to be accomplished by one animal, not many.

⑩ About the Selection

Arachne is a plain young woman with great skill at weaving. She is famous throughout Greece for her lovely products. However, when people say that Athene, goddess of wisdom, must have taught Arachne, she indignantly replies that she has developed her skill with hard work and that even Athene cannot create finer cloth. One day an old woman visits and asks how Arachne can claim equality with the gods. The woman turns out to be the goddess of wisdom in disguise, and she challenges Arachne to a weaving contest. In the contest, Athene weaves scenes of humans who meet terrible fates for insulting the gods; Arachne weaves scenes in which the gods misbehave. When Athene strikes Arachne, the girl is so outraged that she tries to hang herself rather than submit. Athene, however, insists that she live on—and turns her into the spider from which all other spiders descend.

⑪ Background

Humanities: Art

Arachne by Arvis Stewart

Arvis Stewart is a contemporary illustrator based in Amarillo, Texas. Her work has appeared in many different kinds of books, from *Still Waters of the Air: Poems by Three Modern Spanish Poets* to *Sage Smoke: Tales of the Shoshoni-Bannock Indians* to the *Adventures of Wishbone* children's series. The picture of Arachne is from Stewart's award-winning illustrations in *The Macmillan Book of Greek Gods and Heroes*. Stewart is also an active artist in her local community and has collaborated with area writers on *Amarillo: The Yellow Rose of Texas*.

1. Which characters described in the story do you think are depicted in this illustration?
   Possible answer: The illustration probably shows Arachne being visited by Athene and a nymph.
2. What adjectives would you use to contrast Arachne (seated) with the other two characters?
   Answer: Arachne is simple in appearance; Athene looks tall, graceful, and elegant; the nymph looks beautiful and gentle.

Arachne (detail), Arvis Stewart, Reprinted with the permission of Macmillan Publishing Company from The Macmillan Book of Greek Gods and Heroes by Alice Low, illustrated by Arvis Stewart, Copyright © 1985 by Macmillan Publishing Company

CUSTOMIZE INSTRUCTION FOR UNIVERSAL ACCESS

For Advanced Readers

Tell students that the theme of "hubris," or excessive pride and arrogance, is found in many works of Greek literature. In this story, Arachne's "hubris" leads to her downfall. Have students research hubris in other works of Greek literature. If students do their research in the library, they should read synopses of the books. If students choose to perform their research on the Internet, suggest that it should be fairly easy to find synopses of the stories.

Students should try to answer the following questions in their research:

- In what ways is hubris demonstrated in the literature?
- Why does hubris seem such an important theme in Greek literature?

Then, ask volunteers to lead a discussion about their findings with the class.

10 

Arachne

GREEK MYTH

OLIVIA E. COOLIDGE

Arachne [ä räk′ nē] was a maiden who became famous throughout Greece, though she was neither wellborn nor beautiful and came from no great city. She lived in an obscure little village, and her father was a humble dyer of wool. In this he was very skillful, producing many varied shades, while above all he was famous for the
12 clear, bright scarlet which is made from shellfish, and which was the most glorious of all the colors used in ancient Greece. Even more skillful than her father was Arachne. It was her task to spin the fleecy wool into a fine, soft thread and to weave it into cloth on the high, standing loom within the cottage. Arachne was small and pale from much working. Her eyes were light and her hair was a dusty brown, yet she was quick and graceful, and her fingers, roughened as they were, went so fast that it was hard to follow their flickering movements. So soft and even was her thread, so fine her cloth, so gorgeous her embroidery, that soon her products were known all over Greece. No one had ever seen the like of them before.

At last Arachne's fame became so great that people used to come from far and wide to watch her working. Even the graceful nymphs[1] would steal in from stream or forest and peep shyly through the dark doorway, watching in wonder the white arms of Arachne as she stood at the loom and threw the shuttle from hand to hand between the hanging threads, or drew out the long wool,

obscure (əb skyoor′) *adj.* not well known

13 
Reading Check

What is Arachne's special skill?

1. **nymphs** (nimfz) *n.* minor nature goddesses, thought of as beautiful maidens living in rivers, trees, and so on.

14 ◀ **Critical Viewing** How can you tell that the characters in this picture are in conflict? **[Draw Conclusions]**

12 Background

Science

The famous dye described in "Arachne" was made from a type of shellfish that, when crushed and exposed to light, creates a purplish red tint. In fact, the shellfish (genus *Murex*) was called *purpura* in Latin and *porhura* in ancient Greek, and is the origin of the word *purple*. The Bible associates the dye with the ancient mideastern port city of Tyre; and so the dye's color, far redder than our purple today, is often called *Tyrian purple*.

13 Reading Check

Answer: Arachne is talented at spinning wool into fine thread and weaving it into beautiful products.

14 ▶ Critical Viewing

Answer: Arachne, seated in the chair, seems overshadowed by the tall and graceful goddess.

CUSTOMIZE INSTRUCTION FOR UNIVERSAL ACCESS

For Special Needs Students	For English Learners
Remind students to use the phonetic respellings in the footnotes to help them pronounce the names of the ancient Greek characters. Point out that in both *Arachne* and *Athene,* the final *e* is not silent. Have students pronounce the names correctly and write a transliteration of the Greek names.	Many terms having to do with the classification of animals come from the Greek language. Arachnids, or spiders, belong to a larger category of creatures called *arthropods.* Have students look up *arthropod* in a dictionary to discover that *arthro* comes from the Greek word meaning "joint," and *pod* comes from the Greek word meaning "foot." Ask students how knowing the origin of *arthropod* helps them to figure out the meaning of *arthritis, podiatrist,* and *podium.*

15 Reading Strategy

Making Predictions

- Tell students that when they make predictions, they should consider details from the story up to this point.
- Elicit that certain human faults, such as bragging, often lead to downfalls. Tell students that examples of such downfalls are often depicted in myths and folk tales. Point out that, besides teaching a lesson, this tale also explains something in nature.
- Ask students the Reading Strategy question on p. 786: What do you think will be the result of this bragging?
  Answer: Students will likely predict that Arachne will suffer a downfall in the tale as a result of her conceit and bragging.

16 Vocabulary Development

Latin Root *-mort-*

- Call students' attention to the word *mortal,* and have one student read its definition.
- Tell students that *mortal* contains the Latin root *-mort-*, which means "death."
- Have students take turns coming to the board to write sentences containing other words that contain the root *-mort-*. For example, students might use *immortal, immortality, mortician,* and *mortality*.

17 Background

Mythology

Athene was the patron goddess of the ancient Greek city-state of Athens, which bears her name, but Poseidon also took an interest in the city, since he was the god of the sea, and Athens was (and is) a major Greek port. Note that Athens is the capital of the modern nation of Greece.

fine as a hair, from the distaff[2] as she sat spinning. "Surely Athene[3] herself must have taught her," people would murmur to one another. "Who else could know the secret of such marvelous skill?"

15 Arachne was used to being wondered at, and she was immensely proud of the skill that had brought so many to look on her. Praise was all she lived for, and it displeased her greatly that people should think anyone, even a goddess, could teach her anything. Therefore when she heard them murmur, she would stop her work and turn round indignantly to say, "With my own ten fingers I gained this skill, and by hard practice from early morning till night. I never had time to stand looking as you people do while another maiden worked. Nor if I had, would I give Athene credit because the girl was more skillful than I. As for Athene's weaving, how could there be finer cloth or more beautiful embroidery than mine? If Athene herself were to come down and compete with me, she could do no better than I."

One day when Arachne turned round with such words, an old woman answered her, a gray old woman, bent and very poor, who stood leaning on a staff and peering at Arachne amid the crowd of onlookers. "Reckless girl," she said, "how dare you claim to be equal to the immortal gods themselves? I am an old woman and have seen much. Take my advice and ask pardon of Athene for your words. Rest content with your fame of being the best spinner

16 and weaver that mortal eyes have ever beheld."

17 "Stupid old woman," said Arachne indignantly, "who gave you a right to speak in this way to me? It is easy to see that you were never good for anything in your day, or you would not come here in poverty and rags to gaze at my skill. If Athene resents my words, let her answer them herself. I have challenged her to a contest, but she, of course, will not come. It is easy for the gods to avoid matching their skill with that of men."

At these words the old woman threw down her staff and stood erect. The wondering onlookers saw her grow tall and fair and stand clad in long robes of dazzling white. They were terribly afraid as they realized that they stood in the presence of Athene. Arachne herself flushed red for a moment, for she had never really believed that the goddess would hear her. Before the group that was gathered there she would not give in; so pressing her pale lips together in obstinacy and pride, she led the goddess to one of the great looms and set herself before the other. Without a word both began

Reading Strategy
Making Predictions What do you think will be the result of this bragging?

mortal (môr′ təl) *adj.* referring to humans, who must eventually die

obstinacy (äb′ stə nə sē) *n.* stubbornness

2. **distaff** (dis′ taf) *n.* a stick on which flax or wool is wound for use in spinning.
3. **Athene** (ə thē′ nə) Greek goddess of wisdom, skills, and warfare.

CUSTOMIZE INSTRUCTION FOR UNIVERSAL ACCESS

For Gifted/Talented Students

Encourage students to create illustrations of the cloth patterns described in the myth—Athene's, which includes pictures of the awful fate of those who strove with the gods, and Arachne's, which shows the gods' misbehavior. Have students investigate Greek mythology further for myths and legends to illustrate.

Encourage students to use a variety of materials, such as chalk, crayons, acrylics, markers, watercolors, and/or colored pencils to create their illustrations. Have students present their illustrations to the class and explain the myths that are depicted. Display students' completed artwork in the classroom.

to thread the long woolen strands that hang from the rollers, and between which the shuttle[4] moves back and forth. Many skeins lay heaped beside them to use, bleached white, and gold, and scarlet, and other shades, varied as the rainbow. Arachne had never thought of giving credit for her success to her father's skill in dyeing, though in actual truth the colors were as remarkable as the cloth itself.

Soon there was no sound in the room but the breathing of the onlookers, the whirring of the shuttles, and the creaking of the wooden frames as each pressed the thread up into place or tightened the pegs by which the whole was held straight. The excited crowd in the doorway began to see that the skill of both in truth was very nearly equal, but that, however the cloth might turn out, the goddess was the quicker of the two. A pattern of many pictures was growing on her loom. There was a border of twined branches of the olive, Athene's favorite tree, while in the middle, figures began to appear. As they looked at the glowing colors, the spectators realized that Athene was weaving into her pattern a last warning to Arachne. The central figure was the goddess herself competing with Poseidon[5] for possession of the city of Athens; but in the four corners were mortals who had tried to strive with gods and pictures of the awful fate that had overtaken them. The goddess ended a little before Arachne and stood back from her marvelous work to see what the maiden was doing. 18

Never before had Arachne been matched against anyone whose skill was equal, or even nearly equal to her own. As she stole glances from time to time at Athene and saw the goddess working swiftly, calmly, and always a little faster than herself, she became angry instead of frightened, and an evil thought came into her head. Thus as Athene stepped back a pace to watch Arachne

Literary Analysis
Oral Tradition and Theme What lesson is suggested here?

19 

Reading Check

Who is Athene and why is she competing with Arachne?

4. **shuttle** (shut′ əl) *n.* an instrument used in weaving to carry the thread back and forth.
5. **Poseidon** (pō sī′ dən) Greek god of the seas and of horses.

18 Literary Analysis

Oral Tradition and Theme

- Have students read the bracketed passage on p. 787. Point out that myths, like folk tales, often teach lessons about human weaknesses.
- Tell students that Athene is trying to teach Arachne a lesson through her weaving.
- Then, ask students the following question: What lesson is suggested here?
  Answer: The lesson that Athene is trying to teach Arachne is that mortals who try to fight against the gods meet an awful fate. Arachne is striving against Athene and may meet a terrible fate.

19 Reading Check

Answer: Athene is the Greek goddess of wisdom. She is competing with Arachne to see who can create the most beautiful weaving. Arachne challenged Athene in order to prove that she was justified in bragging.

CUSTOMIZE INSTRUCTION FOR UNIVERSAL ACCESS

For Gifted/Talented Students	For Advanced Readers
Challenge students to research the history of dyes and then make a chart of dye colors, including those obtained from natural products, such as shellfish, ocher, and indigo. Encourage students to find out how these dyes are processed and on which types of materials the dyes can be used. For example, the indigo plant was developed in America and is used in the dye that colors denim blue jeans. Have students share their information with the class.	Check ahead with the librarian to reserve time for students to conduct research in the library. Then, have students work in groups to use the library's catalog system to find out more about domestic arts closely tied to this myth. In advance, check on the resources under various subjects, such as weaving tapestry, textile works, cloth-making, looms, and sewing. Have each group look up a different subject heading and copy the information that they find.

Answers for p. 788

Review and Assess

1. Possible response: Students will probably say they would not challenge Athene because she is a powerful god and could harm them.
2. **(a)** She is a talented weaver who creates beautiful patterns in cloth. **(b)** She is conceited about her weaving talent and refuses to bow before anyone else. **(c)** Arachne shows her conceit when she believes that nobody, not even Athene, could teach her anything. She also shows her competitive nature when she dares Athene to compete with her at the loom.
3. **(a)** Athene weaves a scene depicting mortals coming to awful fates after attempting to fight with the gods. **(b)** Athene's first intention is to advise Arachne against claiming equality with the immortal gods. **(c)** Athene becomes angry when she sees the scene that Arachne wove into her cloth.
4. **(a)** Athene tears Arachne's work, strikes Arachne across the face, and turns her into a spider so that she and her ancestors have to spin thread forever. **(b)** The myth may have taught humility, respect for the gods, gratitude for one's talents, recognition of the talents of others, and the dangers of being too proud or competitive. **(c)** The myth demonstrates that confidence and pride in one's hard work can draw recognition and acclaim, but too much confidence and pride can lead to one's downfall. It also describes why spiders spin webs.
5. **(a)** Spiders have the same skill as Arachne: the ability to spin and weave. **(b)** It could be that spiders are called *arachnids* because they are named after Arachne.

finishing her work, she saw that the maiden had taken for her design a pattern of scenes which showed evil or unworthy actions of the gods, how they had deceived fair maidens, resorted to trickery, and appeared on earth from time to time in the form of poor and humble people. When the goddess saw this insult glowing in bright colors on Arachne's loom, she did not wait while the cloth was judged, but stepped forward, her gray eyes blazing with anger, and tore Arachne's work across. Then she struck Arachne across the face. Arachne stood there a moment, struggling with anger, fear, and pride. "I will not live under this insult," she cried, and seizing a rope from the wall, she made a noose and would have hanged herself.

The goddess touched the rope and touched the maiden. "Live on, wicked girl," she said. "Live on and spin, both you and your descendants. When men look at you they may remember that it is not wise to strive with Athene." At that the body of Arachne shriveled up, and her legs grew tiny, spindly, and distorted. There before the eyes of the spectators hung a little dusty brown spider on a slender thread.

All spiders descend from Arachne, and as the Greeks watched them spinning their thread wonderfully fine, they remembered the contest with Athene and thought that it was not right for even the best of men to claim equality with the gods.

Review and Assess

Thinking About the Selections

1. **Respond:** If you were Arachne, would you have challenged the goddess Athene? Why or why not?
2. (a) **Recall:** Describe Arachne's skills. (b) **Interpret:** Why does Arachne refuse to accept advice from the old woman? (c) **Analyze:** What character traits are revealed through her behavior?
3. **Recall:** What design does Athene weave? (b) **Infer:** What is her original intention toward Arachne? (c) **Deduce:** What makes Athene angry?
4. (a) **Recall:** What does Athene do to Arachne? (b) **Interpret:** What lesson might the Greeks have learned from this myth? (c) **Extend:** What does this show about both the benefits and the drawbacks of confidence and pride?
5. **Extend:** Explain the connection between a spider and Arachne's skill. (b) **Connect:** Why do you think spiders are also called *arachnids?*

Olivia E. Coolidge

(b. 1908)

Working as a teacher of English, Latin, and Greek, as well as a writer, Olivia E. Coolidge has lived in both the United States and Europe. She has written many stories, myths, and biographical sketches for young readers. She writes about legends because she feels that the tales express timeless values still relevant today.

In addition to writing about subjects from classical mythology, such as the Trojan War, she has also written about colonial times in American history.

CUSTOMIZE INSTRUCTION FOR UNIVERSAL ACCESS

For Less Proficient Readers

Point out that while hand weaving is a specialized craft, manufactured materials woven on factory looms have replaced most of the world's handcrafted fabrics. Ask students to imagine that they are career counselors recommending jobs or careers that might suit Arachne's talents. What careers would they suggest, and why? Tell students to work in small groups to fill out charts like the one here and then share their ideas in a class discussion.

Job or Career	How Arachne's Talents Suit It
Interior decorator	Good sense of color; knows fabrics

20 # The Three Wishes

PUERTO RICAN FOLK TALE — *Ricardo E. Alegría*

Many years ago, there lived a woodsman and his wife. They were very poor but very happy in their little house in the forest. Poor as they were, they were always ready to share what little they had with anyone who came to their door. They loved each other very much and were quite content with their life together. Each evening, before eating, they gave thanks to God for their happiness.

One day, while the husband was working far off in the woods, an old man came to the little house and said that he had lost his way in the forest and had eaten nothing for many days. The woodsman's wife had little to eat herself, but, as was her custom, she gave a large portion of it to the old man. After he had eaten everything she gave him, he told the woman that he had been sent to test her and that, as a reward for the kindness she and her husband showed to all who came to their house, they would be granted a special grace. This pleased the woman, and she asked what the special grace was.

The old man answered, "Beginning immediately, any three wishes you or your husband may wish will come true."

When she heard these words, the woman was overjoyed and
21 exclaimed, "Oh, if my husband were only here to hear what you say!"

The last word had scarcely left her lips when the woodsman appeared in the little house with the ax still in his hands. The first wish had come true.

The woodsman couldn't understand it at all. How did it happen that he, who had been cutting wood in the forest, found himself here in his house? His wife explained it all as she embraced him. The woodsman just stood there, thinking over what his wife had said. He looked at the old man who stood quietly, too, saying nothing.

Suddenly he realized that his wife, without stopping to think, had used one of the three wishes, and he became very annoyed when he remembered all of the useful things she might have asked for with the first wish. For the first time, he became angry with his wife. The desire for riches had turned his head, and he scolded his wife, shouting at her, among other things, "It doesn't seem possible that you could be so stupid! You've wasted one of our wishes, and now we have only two left! May you grow ears of a donkey!"

He had no sooner said the words than his wife's ears began to grow, and they continued to grow until they changed into the pointed, furry ears of a donkey.

Reading Strategy
Making Predictions How will the wishes turn out?

embraced (em brāsd′) *v.* clasped in the arms, usually as an expression of affection

22  **Reading Check**

What is the first wish the woman makes?

20 About the Selection

A woodsman and his wife are poor, but they are happy and generous to others. One day when the husband is away chopping wood, an old man comes to their house. The woman, though hungry herself, shares her food with him, and in exchange for her kindness, the old man grants her three wishes. As events unfold, the couple learns the lesson that greed causes unhappiness.

21 Reading Strategy

Making Predictions

- Have students summarize the story's events through the bracketed passage.
- Tell students that folk tales often contrast good with bad, or positive with negative, to make a point. For example, because the husband and wife are living happily, the result of the wishes may be negative.
- Ask students the Reading Strategy question on p. 789: How will the wishes turn out?
  Possible response: Knowing that this is a folk tale and that folk tales often teach a lesson, students will likely say that the couple will suffer a downfall; the three wishes will lead to greed, which will lead to an unhappy life.

22 Reading Check

Answer: She wishes for her husband to be in the house to hear what the old man has to say.

CUSTOMIZE INSTRUCTION FOR UNIVERSAL ACCESS

For Special Needs Students	For Advanced Readers
Remind students that folk tales such as "The Three Wishes" were part of an oral tradition long before they were written down. Then, read this tale aloud with the appropriate facial expressions, tones of voice, and gestures. Have students listen without following along in their books. Ask students which parts of the tale they found most memorable and which storytelling techniques sustained their attention.	Have students conduct a survey to find out what three wishes are most popular with their classmates. Students should develop a questionnaire and interview classmates. For example, students might ask, "If you were granted three wishes and could wish for anything, what would you wish for?" Have students compile their findings and present the three most popular wishes from the entire class in the form of a bar graph or pie chart.

Answers for p. 790

Review and Assess

1. Possible response: They made a good wish because now they are happy again.
2. **(a)** They are poor, but happy, generous, and loving. **(b)** An old man appears and rewards them with a special gift for the wife's generosity. **(c)** It reveals that the old man values generosity.
3. **(a)** They waste their first two wishes by making careless comments: The wife wishes that her husband was at home, and the husband wishes that his wife would grow donkey ears.
   (b) They change from generous and loving to greedy and angry.
   (c) It says that greed leads to unhappiness.
4. **(a)** It suggests that sometimes what you think will make you happy does not make you happy when you actually obtain or achieve it—as borne out in "The Three Wishes."
   (b) Possible response: Dreams help motivate one to accomplish specific goals; they provide a harmless escape when life is difficult. Dissatisfaction usually necessitates changing one's circumstances in order to become satisfied.

When the woman put her hand up and felt them, she knew what had happened and began to cry. Her husband was very ashamed and sorry, indeed, for what he had done in his temper, and he went to his wife to comfort her.

The old man, who had stood by silently, now came to them and said, "Until now, you have known happiness together and have never quarreled with each other. Nevertheless, the mere knowledge that you could have riches and power has changed you both. Remember, you have only one wish left. What do you want? Riches? Beautiful clothes? Servants? Power?"

The woodsman tightened his arm about his wife, looked at the old man, and said, "We want only the happiness and joy we knew before my wife grew donkey's ears."

No sooner had he said these words than the donkey ears disappeared. The woodsman and his wife fell upon their knees to ask forgiveness for having acted, if only for a moment, out of covetousness and greed. Then they gave thanks for all their happiness.

The old man left, but before going, he told them that they had undergone this test in order to learn that there can be happiness in poverty just as there can be unhappiness in riches. As a reward for their repentance, the old man said that he would bestow upon them the greatest happiness a married couple could know. Months later, a son was born to them. The family lived happily all the rest of their lives.

covetousness (kuv′ ət əs nəs) *n.* envy; wanting what another person has

Review and Assess

Thinking About the Selections

1. **Respond:** Do you think the woodsman and his wife made a good third wish? Explain your answer.
2. **(a) Recall:** Describe the life of the woodsman and his wife before they make the three wishes. **(b) Interpret:** How does the couple earn the chance to make three wishes? **(c) Interpret:** What does this reveal about the values of the old man?
3. **(a) Recall:** How does the couple use the first two wishes? **(b) Compare and Contrast:** How does the behavior of the couple change after they are given the opportunity to make wishes? **(c) Analyze:** What does this say about the consequences of greed?
4. **(a) Interpret:** How does the saying "Be careful what you wish for" apply to the woodsman and his wife? **(b) Distinguish:** What is the difference between "having a dream" and "being dissatisfied with your life"?

Ricardo E. Alegría

(b. 1921)

A native of San Juan, Ricardo Alegría has held many important positions in education, archaeology, and culture in Puerto Rico. He has served as the director of the Center for Advanced Studies of Puerto Rico and the Caribbean.

Alegría has written nonfiction books on excavations of archaeological sites in Puerto Rico and on customs and ceremonies in the West Indies. He has said, "Culture is the way mankind expresses itself to live and live collectively."

CUSTOMIZE INSTRUCTION FOR UNIVERSAL ACCESS

For Advanced Readers

Ask students to consider the common elements they detect in the myths and folk tales from different cultures. Review the characters, plots, and lessons presented in each story in Unit 10. Students might organize their ideas in a diagram like the one presented and then share them in a class discussion.

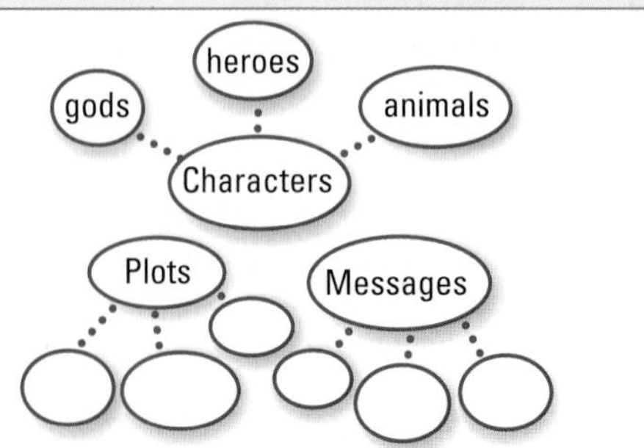

READING INFORMATIONAL MATERIALS

Web Sites

About Web Sites

A Web site is a collection of Web pages linked for posting on the World Wide Web. A Web site may be created by an organization or an individual. The type and reliability of the information supplied on a Web site depend on the provider. You can usually identify the type of provider by the last three letters of the URL, or address.

- Sites ending in .edu are maintained by educational institutions.
- Sites ending in .gov are maintained by government agencies.
- Sites ending in .org are usually maintained by nonprofit organizations and agencies.
- Sites ending in .com are commercially or personally maintained.

Just as you would evaluate the quality, bias, and validity of any other research material, judge Web site information based on the reliability and authority of the source.

Reading Strategy

Forming Questions for Investigation

The key to finding useful information efficiently is to have a focus. Whether you are searching print or electronic resources, having questions in mind will help you quickly identify information that is relevant to your investigation and skip over information that is not.

As you read the information on the Web site here, jot down questions for investigation. Circle the key words in each question. Look for these words in the alphabetically organized print listings of periodical indexes or card catalogs. Use them as the key word search terms for electronic catalogs. The notepad shows how questions and key words can be used to conduct an Internet search.

- Use a plus sign between words to retrieve documents containing all terms connected by the sign in any order.
- Use quotation marks around words to retrieve documents containing terms in specific order.

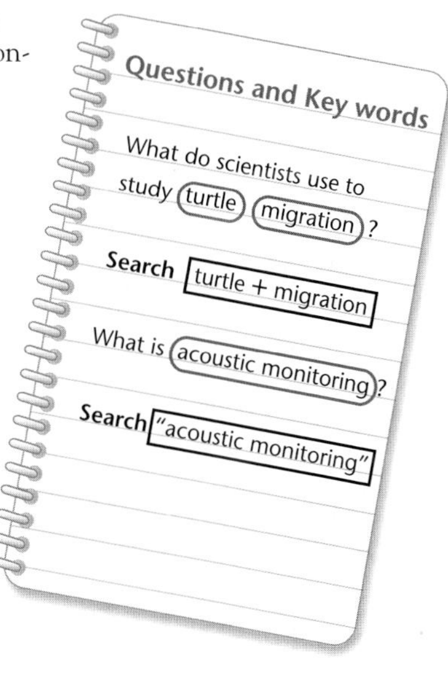

Questions and Key words
What do scientists use to study turtle migration?
Search turtle + migration
What is acoustic monitoring?
Search "acoustic monitoring"

Lesson Objectives

1. To form questions for investigation
2. To evaluate Web site information
3. To understand how to conduct an Internet search

About Web Sites

- Have students read "About Web Sites." Discuss any Web sites that students have researched recently. Challenge students to recall the types of providers of these Web sites.
- Ask students to list the different types of information they think should be included on Web sites.
  Answer: Different types of information include the title or subject of the Web site; the names of the Web site's creators; the date it was last updated; the purpose or issue presented on the Web site; any relevant images, such as photographs, charts, graphs; and text that provides information.
- Discuss how knowing the purpose and the creator of a Web site can help students in gathering research.

Reading Strategy

Forming Questions for Investigation

- Have students read the information about the Reading Strategy.
- Ask students to name some purposes for using a Web site. List the various purposes on the board. Then, have students generate the kinds of questions they would use to begin their investigations.
  Possible response: Students may use Web sites to gather information, to be entertained, or to use as a model for creating their own Web sites. Questions will vary depending on students' topics.
- Tell students that the title of the Web site on the next page is "High-Tech Windows to the Animal Kingdom." Have students discuss questions they might have about this Web site.

CUSTOMIZE INSTRUCTION FOR UNIVERSAL ACCESS

For Less Proficient Readers	For Gifted/Talented Students
After reading the Web site article on p. 804, have the class brainstorm for various key words for a search about acoustical studies with animals. Explain that if they use two words together, students should use a plus symbol between the words. For example, students might suggest these key words: *animals + acoustics, animals + monitoring, acoustics + monitoring.* Then, have students use the list to conduct actual Web searches.	Point out that scientists study animal acoustics to investigate ways in which animals communicate with each other. Assign students to work in pairs as they visit Web sites to find additional information about animal acoustics. Some Web sites will have sound bites of animal acoustics. Partners should then present their information in a multimedia presentation that includes sounds of some of the animals they studied.

High-Tech Windows to the Animal Kingdom

- Remind students that it is important to formulate research questions before searching Web sites. Once they locate Web sites, students should evaluate each site for accuracy and reliability.
- Explain to students that Web searches will reveal articles containing the key words they used for their searches as well as articles without the specific key words in the titles. These articles should be scanned for relevant information.
- Have students read through the Web site, looking for key words that might have been used to access it.
  Possible answers: Students might suggest *national geographic, animal kingdom*, or *acoustic.*
- Ask students to write two questions that could be answered with this Web site.
  Possible answers: How has technology affected our understanding of animals? How do elephants communicate with one another?

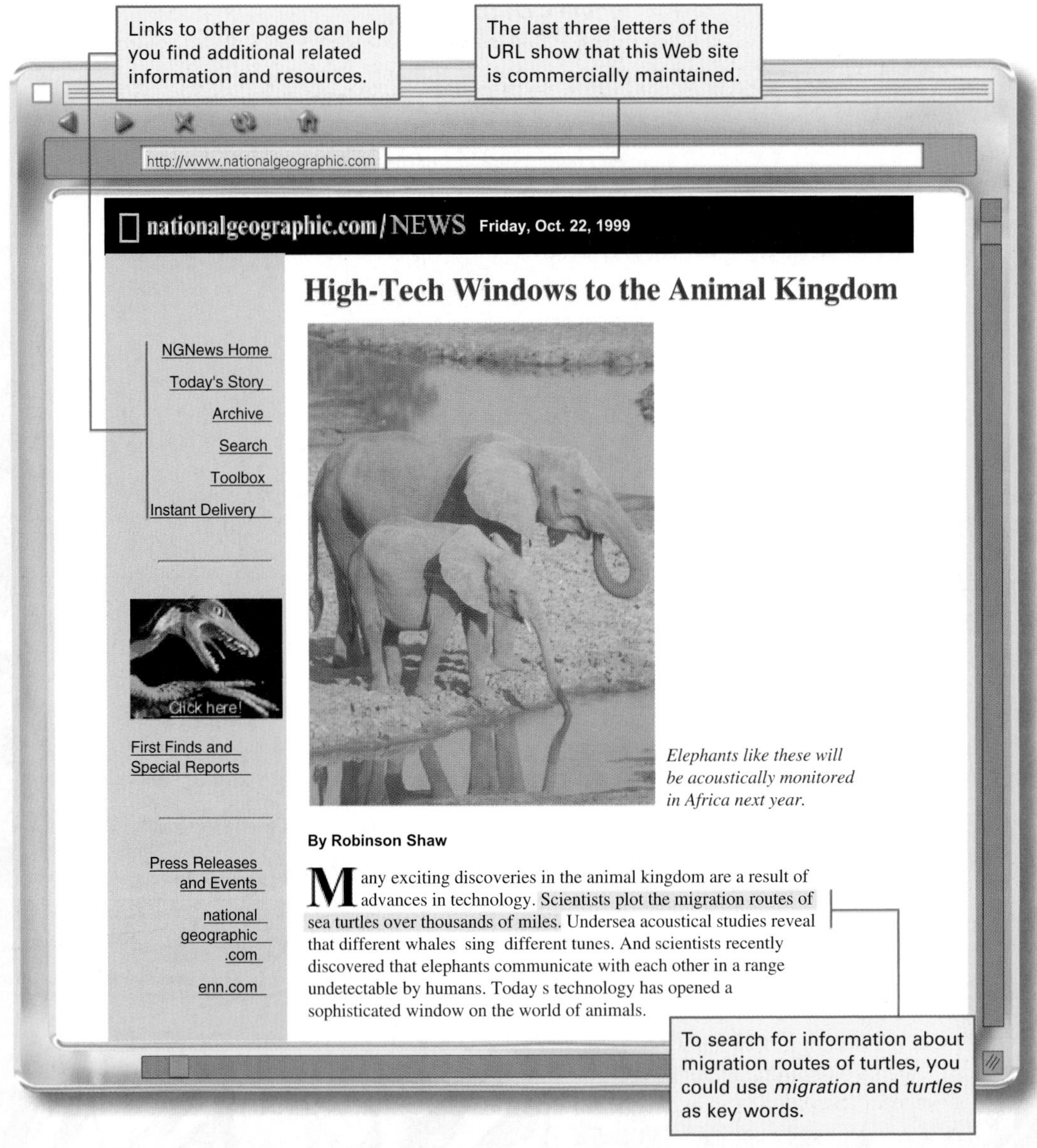
Links to other pages can help you find additional related information and resources.
The last three letters of the URL show that this Web site is commercially maintained.
http://www.nationalgeographic.com
nationalgeographic.com/NEWS Friday, Oct. 22, 1999
NGNews Home
Today's Story
Archive
Search
Toolbox
Instant Delivery
Click here!
First Finds and Special Reports
Press Releases and Events
national geographic .com
enn.com
To search for information about migration routes of turtles, you could use *migration* and *turtles* as key words.

High-Tech Windows to the Animal Kingdom

Elephants like these will be acoustically monitored in Africa next year.

By Robinson Shaw

Many exciting discoveries in the animal kingdom are a result of advances in technology. Scientists plot the migration routes of sea turtles over thousands of miles. Undersea acoustical studies reveal that different whales sing different tunes. And scientists recently discovered that elephants communicate with each other in a range undetectable by humans. Today s technology has opened a sophisticated window on the world of animals.

Check Your Comprehension

1. According to the information next to the elephant photograph, how are elephants going to be monitored?
2. In what country will the elephants be monitored?
3. What do undersea acoustical studies reveal about whales?
4. What have scientists recently learned about how elephants communicate?

Applying the Reading Strategy

Forming Questions for Investigation

5. What are two questions you will investigate about the topic?
6. What two questions might the author have investigated to write this National Geographic article?

Activity

Web Site Investigation

Find other Web sites related to the technology used to study animals. Locate at least two sites from different types of sources. With a partner evaluate the information provided on each site, based on the source.

Comparing and Contrasting Informational Materials

Web Sites and Encyclopedias

Compare and contrast a Web site and an encyclopedia article on African elephants. Make a chart like the one shown.

	Web Site	Encyclopedia
Easy/hard to find information		
Amount of information		
Suggestions for other sources		

Answers for p. 805

Check Your Comprehension

1. The elephants are going to be monitored acoustically.
2. The elephants will be monitored in Africa.
3. The undersea acoustical studies reveal that whales "sing" different tunes.
4. They have learned that elephants communicate with one another in a range undetectable by humans.

Applying the Reading Strategy

5. Possible response: Students might suggest the following questions: What kinds of animals can be studied using acoustical monitoring? How accurate is acoustical monitoring for studying animal communication?
6. Possible response: Students might say that the author of the Web site first asked these questions: How is acoustical monitoring used to investigate animal communication? How can acoustical monitoring help animals?

Activity

Before conducting their search of additional Web sites, have students make a list of criteria they will use to evaluate each Web site. For example, students might evaluate the reliability of the site's creator by considering his or her credentials. They can evaluate the information presented by considering the date on which it was last updated and by comparing the information with that provided on other Web sites and in print resources, such as textbooks and encyclopedias.

continued

Answers continued

Comparing and Contrasting Informational Materials

Web Sites and Encyclopedias: Students should use the graphic organizer to help them compare and contrast a Web site and an encyclopedia article about African elephants. Point out that students should use the criteria presented in this selection to evaluate each source. Then, students should complete the chart by comparing and contrasting the features of each source.

Lesson Objectives

1. To write a multimedia report
2. To use writing strategies to generate ideas, plan, organize, evaluate, and revise the multimedia report

Model From Literature

The language and the rhythm of the African American folk tale "He Lion, Bruh Bear, and Bruh Rabbit" provide the reader with strong images of the events in the story and the impression that the story is meant to be told aloud.

Prewriting

- Have students share with the class the topics they have chosen for their multimedia reports. Write some of the topics on the board, and point out those that are appropriate for multimedia reports.
- Point out that each student should consider the information he or she needs to include in the multimedia report to help viewers and listeners understand both the purpose of the presentation and the information that is presented.
- Discuss the Prewriting questions with students. For example, a multimedia report about the benefits infants derive from hearing classical music will be clearer and more meaningful to an audience if sound elements are incorporated into the presentation.
- Before students draft their reports, have them review the Rubric for Self-Assessment (p. 809) so they know what is expected.

Writing WORKSHOP

Research: Multimedia Report

A **multimedia report** presents information through a variety of media, including text, slides, videos, music, maps, charts, and art. In this workshop, you will learn to prepare a multimedia report that incorporates some or all of these media as appropriate.

Assignment Criteria. Your multimedia report should have the following characteristics:

- A topic that can be thoroughly covered in the time and space allotted
- Supportive facts, details, examples, and explanations
- Appropriate formatting using a word-processor and principles of design
- Appropriate and effective media elements

To see the criteria on which your multimedia research report will be assessed, see the Rubric on page 809.

Prewriting

Choose a topic. Conduct a self-interview to come up with possible topics. Ask yourself the following questions:

- What topics in other classes interest me?
- What subjects do I know a lot about?
- What topic do I want to learn more about?

Plan ahead. Once you have chosen your topic, consider how you will effectively incorporate media. If you are explaining a process, models and props will help make actions in the process clear. Ask yourself the following questions:

- What sound effects or pieces of music will enhance and support this topic?
- What visuals would dramatize my report?
- What special equipment will I need?

Conduct Research. Do research to find information on your topic and to find different ways of presenting the information. Use the ideas on the chart to get you started.

General Topic
Media Possibilities
Person
• Photos
• Audio or video of interview
Event
• Video of eyewitness account

TEACHING RESOURCES

The following resources can be used to enrich or extend the instruction for pp. 806–809.

- **Writing and Grammar,** Copper Level, Chapter 10, pp. 198–216
- **Performance Assessment and Portfolio Management,** p. 17
- **Writing Models and Graphic Organizers on Transparencies,** p. 73

 **Writing and Grammar iText CD-ROM**

Students can use the following tools as they complete their multimedia reports:

- Topic Web
- Note Cards
- Sensory Word Bin
- Homophones Revising Tool

Student Model

Before you begin drafting your multimedia report, read this portion of a student model and review the characteristics of a successful multimedia report. To see the full multimedia report, visit www.phschool.com.

David Papineau
Chris Casey
Indianapolis, Indiana

The Power of Numbers

Slide 1

Script: In this presentation, you will be shown the various uses of mathematics in a wide range of careers. You will also see some prime examples of what would happen if people did not know the fundamentals of mathematics in a real-life situation. So sit back and prepare to be amazed by . . . The Power of Numbers.

Visual: Blank screen (blues and greens). As the presentation begins, the following words appear line by line.

Sound: Typewriter

Sound: Explosion

> Math would be too broad a topic, but the writers have narrowed it to focus on how math is used in a variety of careers. Each slide will provide an example.

Slide 4

Script: A word of advice: Never go to a concert where the musicians can't add the fractions of the notes to get the correct beat count. If you do, though, you'd better have earplugs!

Visual: Violinist

Sound: Music played off tempo

> The best way to show the problems a "mathless musician" would have is to let the audience hear the results. The writers chose to include music that is played out of rhythm to support their point.

Slide 5

Script: The picture says it all. If you have a pilot who can't read graphs or make course calculations, you might find the plane way off course.

Visual: Snow-covered mountaintop with an airplane flying near it

Sound: Airplane flying

> The formatting of the text and the use of a visual emphasize the disastrous effects of a pilot's not knowing math.

Student Model

- Explain to students that the Student Model is a sample and that their own multimedia reports will differ depending on the topics they have chosen.
- Ask students to identify the topic and purpose of this multimedia report.
  Answer: The topic is the role of math in specific careers. The purpose is to demonstrate, through sound and visuals, how important math is to some careers.
- Point out that the Student Model contains specific visuals—slides—that will be used to present information. These visuals, as well as the audio information, will help the audience understand the information presented in the report.

Real-World Connection

Multimedia reports in the workplace: Explain to students that a requirement of many jobs is the ability to clearly present different types of information. Visual aids that help present information effectively include charts, graphs, and slides. For example, a medical researcher may present his or her findings in charts, graphs, and sound clips to an audience of prospective pharmaceutical investors. An editor might present a graphic display, or storyboard, to show a writer the process involved in publishing his or her writing as a bound book. Have students brainstorm for additional careers in which multimedia reports would be useful.

CUSTOMIZE INSTRUCTION FOR UNIVERSAL ACCESS

For Less Proficient Writers	For English Learners	For Advanced Writers
To help students select an appropriate topic for their multimedia reports, have them use the Topic Web from the **Writing and Grammar iText CD-ROM.** Show students how to use questioning techniques to brainstorm for ideas and select a topic for their reports.	Encourage students to use the Topic Web from the **Writing and Grammar iText CD-ROM** to help them choose topics for their multimedia reports. After students have selected topics, they should complete their multimedia reports in English.	Have students use the Topic Web to help them choose topics for their reports. Then, have them design new graphic organizers to help them and other students find topics for their reports. Students should focus on the shapes that they could add to an organizer to help them organize topics.

Drafting

- After reading the instruction on writing a script and evaluating media needs, discuss the types of scripts and media that students will use in their own multimedia reports. Remind students that these elements will vary depending on their topics and audience.
- Point out that they should write out exactly what they will say and do during their presentations. Tell students that they should place parentheses around the actions that they will perform. Read the script example together.
- Have students write their scripts and choose the media they will use in their presentations. Be sure students use the bulleted checklist on this page to prepare the media for their reports.

Revising

- After reading the Revising instruction on this page, have each student work with a partner to revise his or her presentation. Readers should note whether the report is direct, clear, and comprehensive.
- If they identify places that are unclear, students might consider adding a visual aid or a sound effect.

continued on p. 809

Drafting

Write a script. Plan every word and action in your multimedia presentation by writing a script. Include any words that you will speak and any stage directions that make actions and effects clear. Fold a paper lengthwise. In the left column, write the words of the script. In the right column, indicate sound effects, visuals, etc.

Model: Multimedia Script

Erosion—it creates amazing natural sculptures And terrible damage	**Visual:** of Bryce Canyon **Sound:** gently flowing water
Although it usually occurs over thousands or millions of years, erosion is sometimes speeded up by human activity, such as mining, farming, or developing for construction.	**Visual:** Image of creek bed washed away, barn tilting into creek **Sound:** Roaring water **Visual:** bare field with no plants, dust blowing away **Sound:** Heavy equipment like a tractor or cement truck.

Evaluate media needs. Read through your draft, making notes of media cited in the script that you need to find or prepare. Leave time during your drafting stage to do the following:

- Draw pictures, make slides, or edit video
- Edit audiotape or tape sound effects
- Make charts or graphs
- Copy or scan documents

Revising

Evaluate media. Look for places where adding media will improve the audience's understanding. Consider whether sound will emphasize an impression you want to give or whether a diagram will make a comparison clearer.

Model:

Script: A word of advice: Never go to a concert where the musicians can't add the fractions of the notes to get the correct beat count. If you do, though, you'd better have earplugs!

Sound: Music played off tempo

The writers realized that sound effects would illustrate their point about the effect of math mistakes in music better than any description could.

USING TECHNOLOGY IN WRITING

Have students use the note cards from the **Writing and Grammar iText CD-ROM** to guide them as they draft and revise their multimedia reports. The note cards will ensure that they include all the necessary information in their reports. As students revise, have partners read the note cards to make sure that the script and media choices written on the cards will lead to a clear presentation.

Fine-tune the presentation. Rehearse with any equipment used in your presentation.

- Identify the on, off, fast-forward, and rewind switches on audio or video recorders.
- Adjust volume for the size of the room and the audience.

Proofread. Mistakes in spelling, grammar, or capitalization will look twice as bad if they are projected on a screen. Proofread slides, posters, and other visuals. Check especially for homophones—words that sound the same but have different spellings and meanings (*their, they're, there*). Remember that the spell-check feature of a word-processing program will not report the misuse of a homophone as a misspelling.

Publishing and Presenting

Choose one of these ways to share your writing with classmates or a larger audience.

Report to a small audience. In a small group, take turns presenting your multimedia presentations and giving feedback.

Take it on the road. Take your report "on the road" outside your school. Contact a local library or club that might be interested in your report.

Speaking Connection

To learn more about delivering effective multimedia reports, see the **Listening and Speaking Workshops: Delivering a Research Presentation,** p. 606, and **Using Visual Aids,** p. 810.

Prentice Hall Writing and Grammar Connection: Chapter 28, Section 2

Rubric for Self-Assessment

Evaluate your multimedia research report using the following criteria and rating scale:

Criteria	Rating Scale Not very				Very
How appropriate and clear is the main idea of this report?	1	2	3	4	5
How well does the writer use supportive facts, details, examples, and explanations?	1	2	3	4	5
How appropriate is the formatting?	1	2	3	4	5
How well does the writer use visuals?	1	2	3	4	5
How well does the writer use sound?	1	2	3	4	5

Revising (continued)

- Encourage students to rehearse their entire presentations, including visual aids and sound effects, to make sure that the technology works and that they are comfortable using it.
- Have students proofread their slides, charts, and any other visuals they will use in their presentations for errors in spelling, grammar, and capitalization. Students should also check any audiotapes for clarity.

Publishing and Presenting

- Read and discuss with students the Publishing and Presenting choices on p. 809. Each student should consider the reasons that one particular method of presenting his or her report would be more appropriate than others.
- Suggest that students who need to locate audiences outside of the school contact the school librarian for help in beginning their searches.

Assessment

- Review the assessment criteria with students.
- Before students conduct a self-evaluation using this rubric, demonstrate how to use the rubric by applying it to the Student Model on p. 807. Apply each of the five questions here to the Student Model, and discuss them with students.
- The rubric on this page, and another rubric in an alternative format, can be found on p. 17 in **Performance Assessment and Portfolio Management.**

TEST-TAKING TIP

When taking a test that includes items about multimedia reports, students might be asked to list various types of media they would use to present specific information. Review the definition of *multimedia* and have students brainstorm for types of media that could be used in multimedia reports. For example, students might list charts, diagrams, tables, videotapes, audiotapes, slides, transparencies, CDs, and printouts of Web sites.

Lesson Objectives

1. To use visual aids in an oral presentation
2. To choose visual aids that support and clarify information in an oral presentation
3. To use visual aids that engage an audience

Show and Tell

- Read through the instruction about using visual aids in an oral presentation.
- Explain that displaying and defining key terms at the beginning of a presentation can prevent listeners from getting confused or distracted later.
- Tell students that some people learn best by listening and others by viewing. For this reason, they should give audience members the opportunity to do both.
- Explain to students that visual aids can provide effective evidence because pictures can be dramatic and memorable.

Listening and Speaking WORKSHOP

Using Visual Aids

Visual Aids can effectively enhance and dramatize an oral presentation. You may want to use visual aids to show detailed evidence that backs your opinions in a persuasive presentation. You might also use visual aids to reinforce statements in a research report. (To review the characteristics of a successful multimedia report, see the Writing Workshop, pp. 806–809; to review delivering a persuasive presentation, see the Writing Workshop, pp. 340–343.) Visual aids can take many forms. Use some of the strategies suggested here when choosing visual aids.

Show and Tell

You have probably heard the saying "A picture is worth a thousand words." Look for appropriate visual aids that will enhance and dramatize your statements and opinions. Try experimenting with both high-tech and low-tech displays.

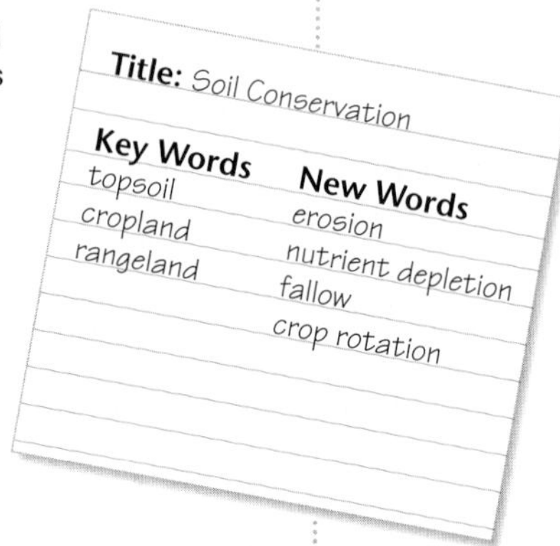

Title: Soil Conservation
Key Words
topsoil
cropland
rangeland
New Words
erosion
nutrient depletion
fallow
crop rotation

Display key terms. Keep your audience's attention focused by showing them important words and new terms. It can be as simple as writing them on a chalkboard or as high-tech as using a colorful display on a monitor or a wall.

Engage your listeners. Alternating between having your audience look at images and listen to you speak will hold their attention and keep them interested. Use visual aids that are clear, informative, and dramatic.

Provide detailed evidence. By showing your listeners a photograph, drawing, graph, or chart, you can visually represent facts and opinions. A few well-chosen images in a persuasive presentation can effectively drive home your point.

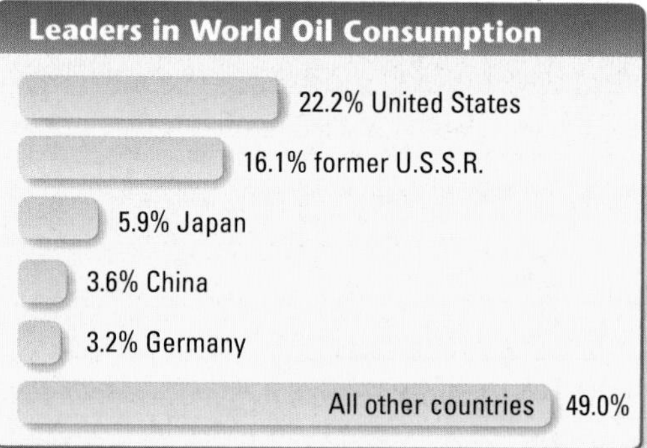

Choose a topic you are studying or have studied in science, math, or social studies. Identify three points related to the topic that are appropriately and effectively supported or illustrated with visual aids. Make the visual aids.

CUSTOMIZE INSTRUCTION FOR UNIVERSAL ACCESS

For Special Needs Students	For Less Proficient Readers
Provide students with the following list of topics: *Skateboarding, Why Cats Purr,* and *How to Make a Pizza.* Discuss the topics with students, and have them list two types of visual aids they would use for each topic. Provide students with the following example: A presentation called *Why Cats Purr* might include a transparency that lists possible reasons for purring and a diagram that shows where a cat's purr is created in its throat. Have students share their suggested visual aids for each of these topics.	Provide students with the following list of types of visual aids: charts, diagrams, photographs, actual objects, transparencies, people, maps, and Web sites. Have students think of topics with which each visual aid could be used. For example, a presentation on a World War II hero would be more effective with maps displaying the area in which the hero served in the war. Have students brainstorm for additional topics and match them with visual aids.

Assessment WORKSHOP

Spelling, Capitalization, Punctuation

The writing sections of some tests require you to read a passage and answer multiple-choice questions about spelling, capitalization, and punctuation. Use what you have learned in this unit about proofreading and punctuation to answer these types of questions.

Test-Taking Strategies

Check especially for spelling errors in

- homophones
- words with suffixes
- words with two vowels in the middle.

Sample Test Item

Directions: Read the passage and decide which type of error, if any, appears.

(1) If you think relay races are fun imagine one on horseback! (2) At United States Pony club rallies, (3) horses and there riders compete in ten different relay races.

1. **A** Spelling error
   B Capitalization error
   C Punctuation error
   D No error
2. **A** Spelling error
   B Capitalization error
   C Punctuation error
   D No error
3. **A** Spelling error
   B Capitalization error
   C Punctuation error
   D No error

Answers and Explanations

1. Use a comma after an introductory adverb clause (*fun,*). ***C*** is correct.
2. *United States Pony Club* is a compound proper noun. ***B*** is correct.
3. *There* is a homophone for *their.* ***A*** is correct.

Practice

Directions: Read the passage and decide which type of error, if any, appears.

(1) While Rick set the table, Carol strung the streamers over the dining room table (2) Suddenly, they herd a click at the door. The children quickly assembled in the dining room. (3) their parents walked in. "Happy Anniversary!" the children shouted.

1. **A** Spelling error
   B Capitalization error
   C Punctuation error
   D No error
2. **A** Spelling error
   B Capitalization error
   C Punctuation error
   D No error
3. **A** Spelling error
   B Capitalization error
   C Punctuation error
   D No error

Lesson Objective

To correctly answer test items that ask questions about spelling, capitalization, and punctuation

Applying Reading Strategies

Explain to students that test items about spelling, capitalization, and punctuation might contain choices that seem to be accurate. Often, these items *look* or *sound* correct but are actually incorrect. For example, items that test spelling might include choices that are all *homophones.* All of these choices might sound right, so students must understand each word's meaning in order to make the correct choice. On other test items, they might be asked to identify the *type* of error in a particular word, sentence, or passage.

Test-Taking Skills

- Have students read the passage in the Sample Test Item. Then, ask them to write the type of error they find in each item. Next, have them check their answers.
- Discuss the correct answers for each item, and have students explain why they are the correct choices.
- Next, have students complete the Practice test item and discuss their responses.

Answer

The correct answer for question 1 is *C*—the sentence should end in a period. The correct answer for question 2 is *A*—the homophone *heard* should be used instead of *herd.* The correct answer for question 3 is B—the sentence should begin with a capital letter.

TEACHING RESOURCES

The following resources can be used to enrich or extend the instruction for p. 811.

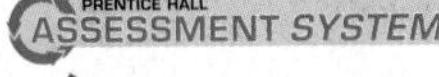

 Workbook
Transparencies
 Skill Book
CD-ROM

RESOURCES

Handbooks

Indexes

SUGGESTIONS FOR SUSTAINED READING

Following are some suggestions for longer works that will give you the opportunity to experience the fun of sustained reading. Each of the suggestions further explores one of the themes in this book. All of the titles are included in the **Prentice Hall Literature Library,** featuring the **Penguin Literature Library.**

You may want to consult your teacher before choosing one of these longer works.

Unit 1: Growing and Changing

Searching for Candlestick Park

Peg Kehret
Puffin Books, 1997

In this novel, twelve-year-old Spencer Atwood leaves his home in Seattle, Washington, to look for his father in San Francisco's Candlestick Park. This famous stadium was home to the San Francisco Giants baseball team for almost 40 years. With his cat Foxey, Spencer travels by bike about 800 miles from the state of Washington through Oregon to California. Along the way, he learns a lot about himself and about being responsible for someone else.

Going Home

Nicholasa Mohr
Puffin Books, 1986

Felita, a young girl from New York City, gets the opportunity to spend a summer with her extended family in Puerto Rico. She is excited to see the land her grandmother has so often described. She is also glad to escape the strict supervision of her family. Felita's summer, however, is not quite as she had imagined. Her Puerto Rican relatives are as strict as her parents. Her uncle, Tio Jorge, seems to spend most of his time mourning the passing of old ways. Some of the kids in Tio Jorge's small village resent her as an outsider. Felita must find a way to blend both parts of her background into her emerging identity.

Park's Quest

Katherine Paterson
Puffin Books, 1988

Eleven-year-old Parkington Waddell Broughton V is on a quest to "find" his father. His mother has told Park that his father was killed in Vietnam during a second tour of duty, but that is all she will say. After finding his father's books and reading them, Park begins his quest. In this book, the author poses important questions about war and the wreckage it leaves behind, both in lives lost and in lives that are forever changed.

Bluestem

Frances Arrington
Puffin Books, 2000

For pioneers on the American prairie in the nineteenth century, life was uncertain. They had to worry about disease and possible starvation as well as unpredictable weather—including droughts, floods, blizzards, and extreme temperatures. Many of those who arrived in the United States from Scandinavia or other parts of Europe journeyed to the wide prairies of the Midwest and the plains of the West. Most pioneers, like the families in *Bluestem,* tried to make their living by farming. In this story, two young pioneer girls, Polly and Jessie, must take care of themselves and make difficult decisions when their mother becomes seriously ill.

To the Teacher:

Because great literature reflects all of life's realities, both positive and negative, classroom discussions of literature can raise sensitive and often controversial issues. Before you recommend novels, plays, and other literature to your students, you may want to consider the values and sensitivities of the community in which you teach, as well as the age and sophistication of your students. It is also a good policy to preview any literature that you are considering recommending to your students. The notes below offer some guidance on specific titles.

Unit 1

Searching for Candlestick Park
by Peg Kehret

Students with personal experience with runaways or with homelessness may be especially sensitive to Spencer's plight. Spencer faces many real dangers and ethical questions. Spencer's father seems disinterested in his son and unwilling to offer him a home, which students may find troubling.

Going Home
by Nicholasa Mohr

Students may object to instances of swearing in the book. Young readers may be embarrassed by a passage that mentions menstruation.

Park's Quest
by Katherine Paterson

Some students may have difficulty dealing with the personal issues raised in this book, such as the death of a parent, divorce, an extramarital affair, and an illegitimate child. The issues that result from war and having a loved one involved in the military may also concern some students.

Bluestem
by Frances Arrington

Mama's abandonment of Polly and Jessie may upset some readers. Some students may also be troubled by the deaths of the babies and other children, the nighttime intruder, the threat posed by the Smith family, and the fact that Polly and Jessie run away and get lost.

Come Sing, Jimmy Jo
by Katherine Paterson

The most delicate issue raised is uncertain paternity. Students may be uncomfortable with the fact that James does not know his real father.

Unit 2

The Secret Garden
by Frances Hodgson Burnett

This novel contains an exceptionally frank portrayal of the emotional problems of two families, including parental neglect that borders on child abuse.

Destiny
by Vicki Grove

The behavior of Destiny's mother may disturb some readers. She is irresponsible in caring for her children, so the job falls on 12-year-old Destiny. The father figure is disreputable.

Letters from Rifka with Connected Readings
by Karen Hesse

This book contains incidents of extreme prejudice, persecution of Jews, humiliating experiences, family separations, death, and disease.

Come Sing, Jimmy Jo
Katherine Paterson
Puffin Books, 1985

The Johnsons are becoming country music stars. They are on television and the radio—and it is all because of James. His voice and his guitar playing bring the songs to life and make audiences beg for more. Most kids would love this life of stardom, but James does not. He has had to change his name to "Jimmy Jo," dress in clothes he hates, and pretend he is someone else. During the course of the story, James comes to terms with his gift and what it means for his own future and the future of his family.

Unit 2: Reaching Out

The Secret Garden
Frances Hodgson Burnett
Signet Classic, 1986

Orphaned Mary Lennox, lonely and sad, is sent to live at her uncle's house on the Yorkshire moors in England. Mary finds the huge house full of secrets. At night, she hears the sound of crying down one of the long corridors. Outside, she meets Dickon, a magical boy who can charm and talk to animals. Then, one day, with the help of a friendly robin, Mary discovers the most mysterious wonder of all—a secret garden, walled and locked, which has been completely forgotten for many years.

Destiny
Vicki Grove
Puffin Books, 2000

Life is complicated for twelve-year-old Destiny Louise Capperson. She has three younger siblings and a mother whose plans for the future focus solely on winning the lottery. Because she needs a job, Destiny begins reading to the mysterious Mrs. Peck, a former Latin teacher who is losing her eyesight. Through Mrs. Peck's books, Destiny discovers Greek mythology, fictional tales that tell about the causes of natural events or about the actions of gods and goddesses. Through the mythical story of a woman named Pandora, Destiny learns the importance of hope and finds the courage to solve her problems.

Letters from Rifka with Connected Readings
Karen Hesse
Pearson Prentice Hall, 2000

This novel, written in the form of letters, traces the experiences of a Russian Jewish girl named Rifka. Modeled on the author's great-aunt, Rifka overcomes one obstacle after another in this gripping story. In 1919, Rifka and her family flee Russia's brutal treatment of Jews for a new life in the United States. The path to freedom is a difficult one, but the family pushes bravely forward. At last, when it seems that Rifka's family has triumphed over every possible hardship, the doctors refuse to let Rifka board the ship to the United States—and her family must leave without her. Through her "letters," Rifka brings the immigrant experience to life for readers.

Flip-Flop Girl
Katherine Paterson
Puffin Books, 1994

After her father's death, Vinnie Matthews needs a real lifesaver—one that will let her family go home. Living with Grandma means having to be responsible for her little brother, Mason, who refuses to speak. It also means ignoring the kids who make fun of Mason. Vinnie is thrust into a new school, without friends or the right clothes and with rumors about her troubled brother wafting around her. Then, Vinnie meets Lupe, the mysterious "flip-flop girl." Lupe might just be the friend she needs, if Vinnie can only ignore the rumors about her past.

The Heart of a Chief
Joseph Bruchac
Puffin Books, 1998

Eleven-year-old Chris Nicola is a member of the Penacook nation, which is part of the Western Abaneki nation. Chris lives on the Penacook Indian Reservation and goes to school in town. At school, things are going well—he has been selected to lead a group project on using Indian names for sports teams. However, at home there is controversy. The Penacook are divided over whether or not to build a casino on a beautiful island Chris thinks of as his own. In *The Heart of a Chief,* Chris takes on two controversial subjects. One is casino gambling, and the other is the naming of sports teams. Readers of this novel will be moved by Chris's pride in his culture and his simple message of respect.

Unit 3: Proving Yourself

Amelia Earhart: Courage in the Sky
Mona Kerby, illustrated by Eileen McKeating
Puffin Books, 1990

As a child, Amelia Earhart wondered why there were no heroines in her favorite adventure stories. She resolved to change that when she grew up. This is a biography of a female adventurer, a woman who was years ahead of her time. It is also about the people who touched her life. Amelia Earhart's family background might have pointed her in a different direction, but she had the determination and purpose to achieve her goals. She also was lucky to know wealthy, powerful people who supported her during critical times and helped her achieve the goals she set for herself.

Eagle Song
Joseph Bruchac, illustrated by Dan Andreasen
Puffin Books, 1997

Danny Bigtree's family has moved to a new city, and no matter how hard he tries, Danny cannot seem to fit in. He is homesick for the Mohawk reservation where he used to live. The kids in his class call him "Chief" and tease him about being an Indian. Things finally begin to change when Danny's father visits the class to talk about the Iroquois Confederacy. However, Danny must still decide if he is up to the challenge of turning the school bully into a friend.

Flip-Flop Girl
by Katherine Paterson

Students may be upset by the death of Vinnie's father or by Lupe's status as an outcast. Other sensitive issues may include the psychological aspects of Mason's decision to be silent, Vinnie's act of vandalism, and the suggestion of the criminal behavior of Lupe's father.

The Heart of a Chief
by Joseph Bruchac

This novel contains references to gambling, alcoholism, and prejudice. Some students may be offended by the behavior of some characters toward the Native American students.

Unit 3

Amelia Earhart: Courage in the Sky
by Mona Kerby

Students may react to the alcoholism of Amelia's father.

Eagle Song
by Joseph Bruchac

Some students may be offended by those characters who make Native American students feel like outcasts and who direct negative comments toward the main character. Also, the issue of gang membership is explored briefly.

The Secret Life of Amanda K. Woods
by Ann Cameron

God and Jesus are mentioned in several instances in this book.

Brady
by Jean Fritz

This novel contains several characters who speak disparagingly of African Americans and of slaves.

Moki
by Grace Jackson Penney

Native American cultures have been severely damaged by European settlement in the Americas. Although this issue stands outside the novel's story, it may still be a sensitive one for Native American students.

Unit 4

Boy of the Painted Cave
by Justin Denzel

This novel contains few sensitive issues for young readers. Graphic scenes of hunting, though handled with restraint, may be disturbing for some readers.

Johnny Tremain
by Esther Forbes

This novel contains some violence as the Revolutionary War begins and several characters die. Johnny's accident may be distressing for some as well. There are several references to drinking alcohol.

The Secret Life of Amanda K. Woods
Ann Cameron
Puffin Books, 1998

Growing up in 1950s rural Wisconsin, Amanda Woods feels isolated and lonely. Her older sister is too smart and pretty for Amanda to feel close to her, and her parents are distant. When her best friend moves away, Amanda decides to create a new version of herself. She transforms herself from bland Amanda Woods to Amanda K. Woods—someone who is proud and strong and sure of herself. This touching coming-of-age novel was a National Book Award Finalist.

Brady
Jean Fritz, illustrated by Lynd Ward
Puffin Books, 1960

This story takes place during the period before the U.S. Civil War, when tensions were heating up about the subject of slavery. Brady Minton, the main character, has never been able to keep a secret. Then one day, he discovers an Underground Railroad Station near his family's farm. Suddenly, Brady realizes that some secrets must never be revealed—and this realization sets him on the path to manhood.

Moki
Grace Jackson Penney
Puffin Books, 1960

Moki is a young Cheyenne girl. The Cheyenne are a Native American people who once lived in the region that is now called the Great Lakes. At the time of Moki's story, however, the Cheyenne lived on the Great Plains. As the story begins, Moki is tired of merely watching while all the boys her age learn to fish and hunt and have adventures. She wants to do something important, too. Even though her friends do not understand, Moki has made up her mind to do something so important, the whole camp will take notice.

Unit 4: Seeing It Through

Boy of the Painted Cave
Justin Denzel
PaperStar Book, 1988

This novel is set in the Dordogne Valley, in what is now France, during the Paleolithic period. This period, which is sometimes called the Old Stone Age, included the earliest stages of human development as well as the greatest portion of human history. Experts date the era from about 2 million years ago to between 40,000 and 10,000 years ago. The book tells the story of a boy named Tao who longs to be a cave painter. He is forbidden from fulfilling his dream, however, because he is not a Chosen One. Instead, he is a tribal outcast with a crippled foot and no father to claim him. Forced into isolation by the superstitious leader of his tribe, Tao befriends a wolf dog, Ram, and the shaman, Greybeard, who teaches him to paint.

Johnny Tremain
Esther Forbes
Laurel-Leaf, 1971

This historical novel is set in pre-Revolutionary New England. Following a serious accident, a young apprentice silversmith, Johnny Tremain, is swept up into the colonists' rebellion against the British. Johnny participates in the Boston Tea Party and the Battle of Lexington—events that prompted the Revolutionary War. During his escapades, Johnny meets such notable figures as Paul Revere, Samuel Adams, and John Hancock.

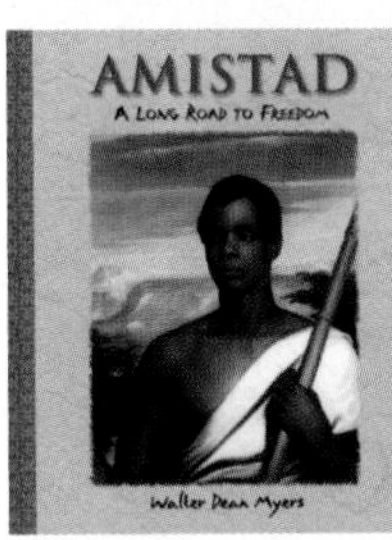

Amistad: A Long Road to Freedom

Walter Dean Myers
Puffin Books, 1998

In 1839, a young man named Sengbe Pieh led a group of illegally enslaved Africans to revolt against their captors aboard the slave ship *Amistad.* The Africans landed in the United States, where they were imprisoned and charged with murder. The *Amistad* captives faced several court battles. Some of the arguments were simply over which court had the authority to make decisions about the case. Slavery was legal in some states and illegal in others. The court battles went through the federal court system, from the Connecticut district court to the circuit court and, finally, to the Supreme Court, where the final decision was made.

My Side of the Mountain

Written and illustrated by Jean Craighead George
Puffin Books, 1988

Sam Gribley is tired of living in a crowded New York City apartment, so, with his parents' permission, he runs away to the Catskill Mountain wilderness to make a life of his own. No one takes his plans seriously—except Sam himself. With only a penknife, a ball of cord, an ax, forty dollars, and some flint and steel, he must rely on his intelligence and the resources of the land to survive. He sets up a house in a hollowed-out tree with a falcon and a weasel for companions. Sam learns about courage, danger, and independence during his year in the wilderness, a year that changes his life forever.

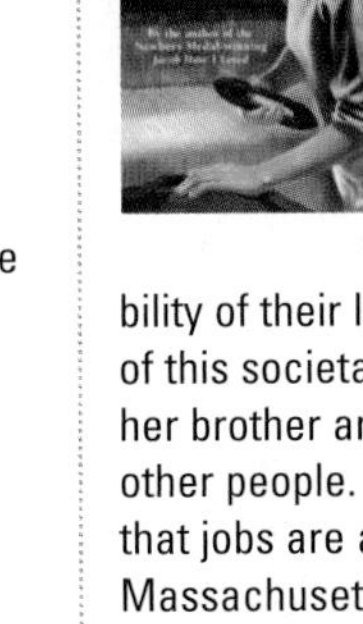

Lyddie

Katherine Paterson
Puffin Books, 1991

Lyddie is set in the mid-1800s, a time when much of American culture was undergoing tremendous change. As the nation moved from a largely agricultural society to a more industrial one, families had to make adjustments that sometimes ripped apart the stability of their lives. The character of Lyddie is a victim of this societal change. Her parents are gone, and her brother and sisters have been sent to live with other people. Lyddie is on her own. When she hears that jobs are available in the textile mills of Lowell, Massachusetts, she heads there with the goal of earning enough money to reunite her family.

Unit 5: Mysterious Worlds

Secret of the Andes

Ann Nolan Clark
Puffin Books, 1980

High up in the Andes there is a beautiful mountain valley, hidden away from the rest of the world. There, a young boy named Cusi helps an old Incan llama herder guard his precious flock. Cusi is an Incan Indian whose ancestors founded the great Incan Empire. The Incas built the capital city of Cuzco, in present-day Peru, which Cusi visits in the story. Accompanied by his pet llama, Cusi leaves the valley to go down to the "world of people" in order to search for his heart's desire. Cusi soon learns to understand the ancient Incan saying, "Grieve not if your searching circles."

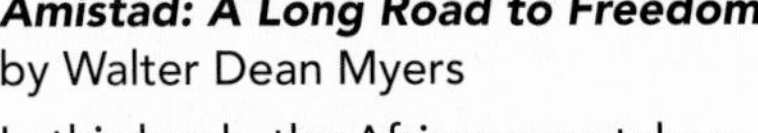

Amistad: A Long Road to Freedom
by Walter Dean Myers

In this book, the Africans are taken from their homes and enslaved against their wills. Conditions during the passage across the Atlantic Ocean are horrific, and the Africans' uprising is quite violent. Students may find these descriptions unsettling.

Lyddie
by Katherine Paterson

Students may be troubled by the hardships suffered by Lyddie's family and the girls with whom she works. Other issues are the father's abandonment of the family and the abusive sexual behavior of the overseer.

Unit 5

Secret of the Andes
by Ann Nolan Clark

This story presents Incan religious ideas, including those about creation, as well as hints of magic.

James and the Giant Peach
by Roald Dahl

Students may be troubled by the abusive treatment James receives from his aunts. In light of the attack on the World Trade Center on September 11, 2001, students may have unanticipated reactions to Chapter 33 of this book, in which the giant peach is flying over New York and people are panicked because they think the peach is a bomb.

The Little White Horse
by Elizabeth Goudge

This novel has a decidedly Christian point of view and refers to Christianity and the church as being the antidote to evil.

James and the Giant Peach

Roald Dahl, illustrated by Lane Smith
Puffin Books, 1961, 1996

After his parents are eaten by an angry rhinoceros, James Trotter is sent to live with his two horrible aunts. James is miserable until he meets an old man in the woods who gives him a bag of magic crystals. When James accidentally drops some crystals by an old peach tree, strange things begin to happen. One peach at the tip of the tree grows larger and larger until it is as big as a house. When James crawls inside, he meets a roomful of oversized insects—Grasshopper, Centipede, Earthworm, and more. With a snap of the stem, the peach starts rolling away, and the adventure begins.

Rascal

Sterling North, illustrated by John Schoenherr
Puffin Books, 1963

Having lost his mother at the age of seven, Sterling North is a very independent eleven-year-old boy. One day, he finds a baby raccoon and decides to call him Rascal. Sterling watches in amazement as this baby raccoon, barely the size of his hand, instinctively washes everything before eating it. Sterling knows that every night Rascal will sneak into the house by hooking his claws onto the back screen door and head straight for Sterling's bed! Virtually everywhere Sterling goes, Rascal is there, and life is filled with one adventure after another.

Charlie and the Chocolate Factory

Roald Dahl, illustrated by Quentin Blake
Puffin Books, 1964, 1998

Willy Wonka, the strange and solitary chocolate maker, is opening his doors to the public. Five lucky people who find a Golden Ticket in their Wonka chocolate bars will receive a private tour of the factory, given by Mr. Wonka himself. For young Charlie Bucket, this is a dream come true. When he finds a dollar bill in the street, he cannot help but buy two Wonka candy bars—even though his family could certainly use the extra money for food. As Charlie unwraps the second chocolate bar, he sees the glimmer of gold just under the wrapper! The very next day, Charlie and his fellow winners step through the factory gates to discover whether or not the rumors surrounding the Chocolate Factory and its mysterious owner are true.

The Little White Horse

Elizabeth Goudge
Puffin Books, 1974

When young orphan Maria Merryweather arrives at Moonacre Manor, she feels as if she has entered Paradise. Her new guardian, her uncle Sir Benjamin, is kind and funny. The Manor itself feels like home right away. Every person and animal she meets is like an old friend. However, there is something incredibly sad beneath all of this beauty and comfort—a tragedy that happened years ago, shadowing Moonacre Manor and the town around it. Maria is determined to learn about the tragedy, change it, and give her own life story a happy ending.

abundant (ə bun′ dənt) *adj.* plentiful

accumulations (ə kyo͞om′ yo͞o lā′ shənz) *n.* buildup occurring over a period of time

adamant (ad′ ə mənt′) *adj.* not flexible; not willing to give in; stubborn; unyielding

aggrieved (ə grēvd′) *adj.* offended; wronged

anecdotes (an′ ik dōts′) *n.* short, entertaining tales

anonymity (an′ ə nim′ ə tē) *n.* the condition of being a stranger, of not being known by name

antennae (an ten′ ē) *n.* metal rods that receive TV or radio signals

aptitude (ap′ tə to͞od′) *n.* natural ability

atone (a tōn′) *v.* make up for a wrong

becoming (bē kum′ iŋ) *adj.* suitable to the wearer

beseech (bi sēch′) *v.* beg

bough (bou) *n.* branch of a tree

bound (bound) *v.* tied

calculated (kal′ kyo͞o lāt′ id) *v.* determined by using math

catastrophic (kat′ ə sträf′ ik) *adj.* causing a complete disaster

cavernous (kav′ ər nəs′) *adj.* deep and empty

ceased (sēsd) *v.* stopped

chaotic (kā ät′ ik) *adj.* completely confused

chorus (kôr′ əs) *n.* the part of a song sung by many voices at once

clamor (klam′ ər) *n.* loud demand

coaxed (kōkst) *v.* tried to persuade

collision (kə lizh′ ən) *n.* coming together with a sudden violent force; a crash

composed (kəm pōzd′) *adj.* made up (of)

compulsory (kəm pul′ sə rē) *adj.* must be done; having specific requirements

conclusion (kən klo͞o′ zhən) *n.* belief or decision reached by reasoning

condemnation (kän′ dem nā′ shən) *n.* extreme disapproval; harsh judgment

confidence (kän′ fi dəns′) *n.* belief in one's own abilities

consequently (kän′ si kwent′ lē) *adj.* as a result

consoled (kən sōld′) *v.* comforted

consumed (kən so͞omd′) *v.* destroyed

consumption (kən sump′ shən) *n.* eating; drinking; using up

cordial (kôr′ jəl) *adj.* warm and friendly

covetousness (kuv′ ət əs nəs) *n.* envy

craned (krānd) *v.* stretched out (one's neck) for a better view

crescent (kres′ ənt) *n.* anything shaped like the moon in its first or last quarter

cudgel (kuj′ əl) *n.* short, thick stick or club

decisively (di sī′ siv lē) *adv.* with determination

declined (di klīnd′) *v.* refused

deem (dēm) *v.* judge

demise (dē mīz′) *n.* death

dense (dens) *adj.* tightly packed

detrimental (de′ trə ment′ əl) *adj.* harmful

devours (di vourz′) *v.* swallows whole

diagnosis (dī əg nō′ sis) *n.* explanation of or prediction about a person's medical condition

dilution (di lo͞o′ shən) *n.* process of weakening by mixing with something else

diminutive (də min′ yo͞o tiv) *adj.* very small

disinfect (dis′ in fekt′) *n.* dialect for disinfectant, a substance that kills germs

dispute (di spyo͞ot′) *n.* argument; debate

dissonance (dis′ ə nəns) *n.* harsh combination of sounds

distorted (di stôr′ tid) *adj.* twisted out of the normal shape

diverse (də vʉrs′) *adj.* various; with differing characteristics

documentation (däk′ yo͞o mən tā′ shən) *n.* supporting evidence

drawbacks (drô′ baks′) *n.* disadvantages

drawing (drô′ iŋ) *v.* bringing forth

drone (drōn) *n.* continuous humming sound

eased (ēzd) *v.* comforted; freed from pain

eloquent (el′ ə kwint) *adj.* persuasive and expressive

elusive (ē lo͞o′ siv) *adj.* always escaping

emaciated (ē mā′ shē āt id) *adj.* thin and bony as a result of starvation or disease

embedded (em bed′ əd) *adj.* firmly fixed in a surrounding material

embraced (em brāsd′) *v.* clasped in the arms, usually as an expression of affection

emerged (ē merjd′) *v.* came out from

emigrated (em′ i grāt′ id) *v.* left one country to settle in another

endured (en do͝ord′) *v.* suffered through

episode (ep′ ə sōd′) *n.* one in a series of related events

etiquette (et′ i ket) *n.* acceptable social manners

evaporate (i vap′ ə rāt′) *v.* disappear like vapor

evolved (ē vôlvd′) *v.* grew gradually

exact (eg zakt′) *v.* take using force or authority

executioner (ek′ si kyo͞o′ shən ər) *n.* one who carries out a death penalty

exhaust (ig zôst′) *v.* use up

exhausted (eg zôs′ tid) *adj.* tired out

expend (ek spend′) *v.* spend

exuded (eg zyo͞od′ əd) *v.* gave off; oozed

fallow (fal′ ō) *adj.* inactive; unproductive

famine (fa′ min) *n.* shortage of food

feats (fēts) *n.* remarkable deeds or acts

flaw (flô) *n.* break; crack

flee (flē) *v.* run or escape from danger

flue (flo͞o) *n.* a tube for the passage of smoke, as in a chimney

foliage (fō′ lē ij) *n.* leaves of trees and bushes

foresee (fôr sē′) *v.* know beforehand

fostering (fōs′ tər iŋ) *n.* taking care of

frenzied (fren′ zēd) *adj.* wild; frantic

fusing (fyo͞o′ ziŋ) *v.* joining permanently

gilded (gild′ id) *adj.* coated with a thin layer of gold

gnashes (nash′ iz) *v.* bites with grinding teeth

gnaw (nô) *v.* bite and wear away bit by bit with the teeth

goading (gō′ diŋ) *v.* pushing a person into acting, especially by using pain or insults

grant (grant) *v.* admit

grief (grēf) *n.* deep sadness

groveled (grä′ vəld) *v.* lay or crawled about before someone in hope of mercy

grudgingly (gruj′ iŋ lē) *adv.* in an unenthusiastic or resentful way

heathen (hē′ *th*ən) *adj.* uncivilized

hence (hens) *adv.* away

henceforth (hens fôrth′) *adv.* from now on

ignorance (ig′ nər əns) *n.* lack of knowledge, education, or experience

ignore (ig nôr′) *v.* pay no attention to

immense (i mens′) *adj.* huge

immortal (i môr′ təl) *adj.* living forever

incessantly (in ses′ ənt lē) *adj.* never ceasing

inconsistent (in′ kən sis′ tənt) *adj.* contradictory; not making sense

indignantly (in dig′ nənt lē) *adv.* angrily

inedible (in ed′ ə bəl) *adj.* not fit to be eaten

inevitably (in ev′ i tə blē) *adv.* unavoidably

initial (i nish′ əl) *adj.* original

inscribed (in skrībd′) *adj.* written on

instinctively (in stiŋk′ tiv lē) *adv.* done by instinct, without thinking

integrate (in′ tə grāt′) *v.* remove barriers and allow access to all

intimated (in′ tə māt′ id) *v.* hinted

intrigued (in trēgd′) *v.* fascinated

irrational (ir rash′ ə nəl) *adj.* unreasonable

jubilation (jo͞o′ bə lā′ shən) *n.* great joy

lair (lār) *n.* cave or den

lean (lēn) *adj.* thin

leisurely (lē′ zhər lē) *adj.* in an unhurried way

liable (lī′ ə bəl) *adj.* likely (to do something or have something happen to one)

loftily (lof′ tə lē) *adv.* in a superior way

majestically (mə jes′ tik lē) *adv.* grandly

malicious (mə lish′ əs) *adj.* showing evil intentions

mascot (mas′ kät) *n.* any person, animal, or thing adopted by a group for good luck

massive (mass′ iv) *adj.* huge; large

meanderings (mē an′ dər iŋz) *n.* aimless wanderings

meditated (med′ ə tāt id) *v.* thought deeply

melancholy (mel′ ən käl′ ē) *adj.* sad; gloomy

membranes (mem′ brānz) *n.* thin, flexible layers of tissue

menace (men′ əs) *n.* threat; a troublesome or annoying person

misapprehension (mis′ ap rē hen′ shən) *n.* misunderstanding

monotonous (mə nät′ ən əs′) *adj.* tiresome because it does not vary

monitoring (män′ i tər iŋ) *v.* watching or listening to

moot (mo͞ot) *adj.* not worthy of thought or discussion because it has been resolved

mortal (môr′ təl) *adj.* referring to humans, who must eventually die

mortified (môrt′ ə fīd′) *adj.* ashamed

nigh (nī) *adv.* near

nonchalantly (nän′ shə länt′ lē) *adv.* without concern or interest

novelty (näv′ əl tē) *n.* something new or unusual

obligatory (əb lig′ ə tôr′ ē) *adj.* required

obscure (əb skyoor′) *adj.* not well known

obstacle (äb′ stə kəl′) *n.* something that stands in the way

obstinacy (äb′ stə nə sē) *n.* stubbornness

obstructed (əb strukt′ id) *adj.* blocked

occasionally (ō kā′ zhən əl ē′) *adv.* now and then

offense (ə fens′) *n.* harmful act

opposition (äp′ ə zish′ ən) *n.* here, the other team

orator (ôr′ ə tər) *n.* speaker

peeved (pēvd) *v.* made bad-tempered or annoyed

peripheral (pə rif′ ər əl) *adj.* lying on the outside edge

piers (pirz) *n.* heavy structures supporting the sections of a bridge.

plagued (plāgd) *v.* tormented

plight (plīt) *n.* sad or dangerous situation

poising (poiz′ iŋ) *v.* balancing

precautionary (prē kô′ shən er′ ē) *adj.* taking care beforehand to prevent danger

prelude (prel′ yo͞od′) *n.* an introduction to a main event or action coming later

prey (prā) *n.* animals hunted or killed for food by other animals

prolonged (prō lôŋd′) *adj.* long and drawn out

prospectors (prä′ spekt′ erz) *n.* people who search for valuable ores, such as gold

prowled (proud) *v.* crawled quietly and secretly

pulsating (pul′ sāt′ iŋ) *v.* beating or throbbing in rhythm

quarry (kwôr′ ē) *n.* prey

querulous (kwer′ yo͞o ləs) *adj.* inclined to find mistakes; complaining

rancor (raŋ′ kər) *n.* bitter hate or ill will

rapidly (rap′ id lē) *adv.* quickly

raucous (rô′ kəs) *adj.* loud and rowdy

ravaged (rav′ ijd) *v.* violently destroyed

ravenous (rav′ ə nəs′) *adj.* greedily hungry

reckless (rek′ lis) *adj.* not careful; taking chances

reflecting (ri flekt′ iŋ) *adj.* thinking seriously

regulation (reg′ yə lā′ shən) *n.* rule

reproachfully (ri prōch′ fəl lē) *adv.* with blame

repulse (ri puls′) *v.* drive back; repel an attack

resolutions (rez′ ə lo͞o′ shənz) *n.* intentions

retaliated (ri tal′ ē at′ id) *v.* harmed or did wrong to someone in return for an injury or wrong he or she has done

rue (ro͞o) *v.* regret

savoring (sā′ ver iŋ) *v.* enjoying with appreciation; tasting; relishing

scarce (skers) *adj.* few in number or infrequent; not common

scuttled (skut′ əld) *v.* scurried; scampered

sheared (shird) *v.* cut off sharply

sibling (sib′ liŋ) *n.* brother or sister

skimming (skim′ iŋ) *v.* gliding; moving swiftly and lightly over a surface

slanderous (slan′ der əs′) *adj.* untrue and damaging

slough (sluf) *v.* cast off; get rid of

soprano (sə pran′ ō) *n.* the highest singing voice of women, girls, or young boys

startled (stärt′ əld) *adj.* surprised

stingiest (stin′ jē əst) *adj.* most unwilling to spend money; cheapest

stoic (stō′ ik) *adj.* showing no reaction to good or bad events; unaffected by hardship

sublime (sə blīm′) *adj.* majestic; causing awe

subscribed (səb skrībd′) *adj.* signed up to give money

sufficient (sə fish′ ənt) *adj.* enough

summit (sum′ it) *n.* highest part

suspended (sə spend′ id) *v.* stopped for a time

swiftest (swift′ est) *adj.* the most rapid; the fastest

tableaus (ta blōz′) *n.* dramatic scenes or pictures

tactics (tak′ tiks) *n.* methods used for a particular purpose; tricks

tempest (tem′ pist) *n.* violent storm with high winds

timidly (tim′ id lē) *adv.* in a way that shows fear or shyness

toil (toil) *n.* hard work

tolerance (täl′ ər əns) *n.* respect for something different

trace (trās) *n.* mark left behind by something

transport (trans pôrt′) *v.* carry from one place to another

treacherous (trech′ ər əs) *adj.* dangerous

trudged (trujd) *v.* walked as if tired or with effort

tyrant (tī′ rənt) *n.* cruel, unjust ruler

uncomprehending (ən cäm prē hend′ iŋ) *adj.* not understanding

undulating (un′ dyo͞o lā′ tiŋ) *adj.* moving in waves, like a snake

ungrateful (un grāt′ fəl) *adj.* not thankful

variegated (ver′ ē ə gāt′ id) *adj.* marked with different colors in spots or streaks

veranda (və ran′ də) *n.* open porch, usually with a roof, along the outside of a building

veterans (vet′ ər ənz′) *n.* those having experience

vigilance (vij′ ə ləns) *n.* watchfulness

vigorously (vig′ ər əs lē) *adv.* forcefully; powerfully

wallowed (wäl′ ōd) *v.* rolled and tilted

TIPS FOR IMPROVING READING FLUENCY

When you were younger, you learned to read. Then, you read to expand your experiences or for pure enjoyment. Now, you are expected to read to learn. As you progress in school, you are given more and more material to read. The tips on these pages will help you improve your reading fluency, or your ability to read easily, smoothly, and expressively.

Keeping Your Concentration

One common problem that readers face is the loss of concentration. When you are reading an assignment, you might find yourself rereading the same sentence several times without really understanding it. The first step in changing this behavior is to notice that you do it. Becoming an active, aware reader will help you get the most from your assignments. Practice using these strategies:

- Cover what you have already read with a note card as you go along. Then, you will not be able to reread without noticing that you are doing it.
- Set a purpose for reading beyond just completing the assignment. Then, read actively by pausing to ask yourself questions about the material as you read.
- Use the Reading Strategy instruction and notes that appear with each selection in this textbook.
- Stop reading after a specified period of time (for example, 5 minutes) and summarize what you have read. To help you with this strategy, use the Reading Check questions that appear with each selection in this textbook. Reread to find any answers you do not know.

✓ Reading Check
What common problem do many readers face?

Reading Phrases

Fluent readers read phrases rather than individual words. Reading this way will speed up your reading and improve your comprehension. Here are some useful ideas:

- Experts recommend rereading as a strategy to increase fluency. Choose a passage of text that is neither too hard nor too easy. Read the same passage aloud several times until you can read it smoothly. When you can read the passage fluently, pick another passage and keep practicing.
- Read aloud into a tape recorder. Then, listen to the recording, noting your accuracy, pacing, and expression. You can also read aloud and share feedback with a partner.
- Use the *Prentice Hall Listening to Literature* audiotapes or CDs to hear the selections read aloud. Read along silently in your textbook, noticing how the reader uses his or her voice and emphasizes certain words and phrases.

✓ Reading Check
In what ways will reading phrases rather than individual words affect your reading?

Understanding Key Vocabulary

If you do not understand some of the words in an assignment, you may miss out on important concepts. Therefore, it is helpful to keep a dictionary nearby when you are reading. Follow these steps:

- Before you begin reading, scan the text for unfamiliar words or terms. Find out what those words mean before you begin reading.
- Use context—the surrounding words, phrases, and sentences—to help you determine the meanings of unfamiliar words.
- If you are unable to understand the meaning through context, refer to the dictionary.

✓ Reading Check

Why should you look up words you do not know when reading an assignment?

Paying Attention to Punctuation

When you read, pay attention to punctuation. Commas, periods, exclamation points, semicolons, and colons tell you when to pause or stop. They also indicate relationships between groups of words. When you recognize these relationships you will read with greater understanding and expression. Look at the chart below.

Punctuation Mark	Meaning
comma	brief pause
period	pause at the end of a thought
exclamation point	pause that indicates emphasis
semicolon	pause between related but distinct thoughts
colon	pause before giving explanation or examples

Using the Reading Fluency Checklist

Use the checklist below each time you read a selection in this textbook. In your Language Arts journal or notebook, note which skills you need to work on and chart your progress each week.

Reading Fluency Checklist

- ❑ Preview the text to check for difficult or unfamiliar words.
- ❑ Practice reading aloud.
- ❑ Read according to punctuation.
- ❑ Break down long sentences into the subject and its meaning.
- ❑ Read groups of words for meaning rather than reading single words.
- ❑ Read with expression (change your tone of voice to add meaning to the word).

Reading is a skill that can be improved with practice. The key to improving your fluency is to read. The more you read, the better your reading will become.

High-Frequency Words

Approximately fifty percent of the words you read will be the same one hundred words. Learning to instantly recognize **high-frequency words**—words that are used often in print—will greatly improve your reading fluency. Learn to instantly recognize the words on this page. Practice any that give you trouble.

the
of
and
a
to
in
is
you
that
it
he
was
for
on
are
as
with
his
they
I
at
be
this
have
from
or
one
had
by
words
but
not
what
all
were
we
when
your
can

said
there
use
an
each
which
she
do
how
their
if
will
up
other
about
out
many
then
them
these
so
some
her
would
make
like
him
into
time
has
look
two
more
write
go
see
number
no
way

could
people
my
than
first
water
been
called
who
oil
sit
now
find
long
down
day
did
get
come
made
may
part
over
new
sound
take
only
little
work
know
place
years
live
me
back
give
most
very
after

things
our
just
name
good
sentence
man
think
say
great
where
help
through
much
before
line
right
too
means
old
any
same
tell
boy
following
came
want
show
also
around
form
three
small
set
put
end
does
another
well

large
must
big
even
such
because
turned
here
why
asked
went
men
read
need
land
different
home
us
move
try
kind
hand
picture
again
change
off
play
spell
air
away
animals
house
point
page
letters
mother
answer
found
study

still
learn
should
American
world
high
ever
near
add
food
between
own
below
country
plants
last
school
father
keep
trees
never
started
city
earth
eyes
light
thought
head
under
story
saw
left
don't
few
while
along
might
close
something

seemed
next
hard
open
example
beginning
life
always
those
both
paper
together
got
group
often
run
important
until
children
side
feet
car
miles
night
walked
white
sea
began
grow
took
river
four
carry
state
once
book
hear
stop
without

second
later
miss
idea
enough
eat
face
watch
far
Indians
rally
almost
let
above
girl
sometimes
mountains
cut
young
talk
soon
list
song
being
leave
family
it's

LITERARY TERMS HANDBOOK

ALLITERATION *Alliteration* is the repetition of initial consonant sounds. Writers use alliteration to draw attention to certain words or ideas, to imitate sounds, and to create musical effects.

ANALOGY An *analogy* makes a comparison between two or more things that are similar in some ways but otherwise unalike.

ANECDOTE An *anecdote* is a brief story about an interesting, amusing, or strange event. Writers tell anecdotes to entertain or to make a point.

ANTAGONIST An *antagonist* is a character or a force in conflict with a main character, or protagonist.

See *Conflict* and *Protagonist.*

ATMOSPHERE *Atmosphere,* or *mood,* is the feeling created in the reader by a literary work or passage.

AUTOBIOGRAPHY An *autobiography* is the story of the writer's own life, told by the writer. Autobiographical writing may tell about the person's whole life or only a part of it.

Because autobiographies are about real people and events, they are a form of nonfiction. Most autobiographies are written in the first person.

See *Biography, Nonfiction,* and *Point of View.*

BIOGRAPHY A *biography* is a form of nonfiction in which a writer tells the life story of another person. Most biographies are written about famous or admirable people. Although biographies are nonfiction, the most effective ones share the qualities of good narrative writing.

See *Autobiography* and *Nonfiction.*

CHARACTER A *character* is a person or an animal that takes part in the action of a literary work. The main, or *major,* character is the most important character in a story, poem, or play. A *minor* character is one who takes part in the action but is not the focus of attention.

Characters are sometimes classified as flat or round. A *flat character* is one-sided and often stereotypical. A *round character,* on the other hand, is fully developed and exhibits many traits—often both faults and virtues. Characters can also be classified as dynamic or static. A *dynamic character* is one who changes or grows during the course of the work. A *static character* is one who does not change.

See *Characterization, Hero/Heroine,* and *Motive.*

CHARACTERIZATION *Characterization* is the act of creating and developing a character. Authors use two major methods of characterization—*direct* and *indirect.* When using *direct* characterization, a writer states the *characters' traits,* or characteristics.

When describing a character indirectly, a writer depends on the reader to draw conclusions about the character's traits. Sometimes the writer tells what other participants in the story say and think about the character.

See *Character* and *Motive.*

CLIMAX The climax, also called the turning point, is the high point in the action of the plot. It is the moment of greatest tension, when the outcome of the plot hangs in the balance.

See *Plot.*

COMEDY A *comedy* is a literary work, especially a play, which is light, often humorous or satirical, and ends happily. Comedies frequently depict ordinary characters faced with temporary difficulties and conflicts. Types of comedy include *romantic comedy,* which involves problems among lovers, and the *comedy of manners,* which satirically challenges social customs of a society.

CONCRETE POEM A *concrete poem* is one with a shape that suggests its subject. The poet arranges the letters, punctuation, and lines to create an image, or picture, on the page.

CONFLICT A *conflict* is a struggle between opposing forces. Conflict is one of the most important elements of stories, novels, and plays because it causes the action. There are two kinds of conflict: external and internal. An *external conflict* is one in which a character struggles against some outside force, such as another person. Another kind of external conflict may occur between a character and some force in nature.

An *internal conflict* takes place within the mind of a character. The character struggles to make a decision, take an action, or overcome a feeling.

See *Plot.*

CONNOTATIONS The *connotation* of a word is the set of ideas associated with it in addition to its explicit meaning. The connotation of a word can be personal, based on individual experiences. More often, cultural connotations—those recognizable by most people in a group—determine a writer's word choices.

See also *Denotation.*

DENOTATION The *denotation* of a word is its dictionary meaning, independent of other associations that the word may have. The denotation of the word *lake,* for example, is "an inland body of water." "Vacation spot" and "place where the fishing is good" are connotations of the word *lake.*

See also *Connotation.*

DESCRIPTION A *description* is a portrait, in words, of a person, place, or object. Descriptive writing uses images that appeal to the five senses—sight, hearing, touch, taste, and smell.

See *Image.*

DEVELOPMENT See *Plot.*

DIALECT *Dialect* is the form of a language spoken by people in a particular region or group. Dialects differ in pronunciation, grammar, and word choice. The English language is divided into many dialects. British English differs from American English.

DIALOGUE A *dialogue* is a conversation between characters. In poems, novels, and short stories, dialogue is usually set off by quotation marks to indicate a speaker's exact words.

In a play, dialogue follows the names of the characters, and no quotation marks are used.

DRAMA A *drama* is a story written to be performed by actors. Although a drama is meant to be performed, one can also read the script, or written version, and imagine the action. The *script* of a drama is made up of dialogue and stage directions. The *dialogue* is the words spoken by the actors. The *stage directions,* usually printed in italics, tell how the actors should look, move, and speak. They also describe the setting, sound effects, and lighting.

Dramas are often divided into parts called *acts.* The acts are often divided into smaller parts called *scenes.*

DYNAMIC CHARACTER See *Character.*

ESSAY An *essay* is a short nonfiction work about a particular subject. Most essays have a single major focus and a clear introduction, body, and conclusion.

There are many types of essays. An *informal essay* uses casual, conversational language. A *historical essay* gives facts, explanations, and insights about historical events. An *expository essay* explains an idea by breaking it down. A *narrative essay* tells a story about a real-life experience. An *informational essay* explains a process. A *persuasive essay* offers an opinion and supports it.

See *Exposition, Narration,* and *Persuasion.*

EXPOSITION In the plot of a story or a drama, the *exposition,* or introduction, is the part of the work that introduces the characters, setting, and basic situation.

See *Plot.*

EXPOSITORY WRITING *Expository writing* is writing that explains or informs.

EXTENDED METAPHOR In an *extended metaphor,* as in a regular metaphor, a subject is spoken or written of as though it were something else. However, extended metaphor differs from regular metaphor in that several connected comparisons are made.

See *Metaphor.*

EXTERNAL CONFLICT See *Conflict.*

FABLE A *fable* is a brief story or poem, usually with animal characters, that teaches a lesson, or moral. The moral is usually stated at the end of the fable.

See *Irony* and *Moral.*

FANTASY A *fantasy* is highly imaginative writing that contains elements not found in real life. Examples of fantasy include stories that involve supernatural elements, stories that resemble fairy tales, stories that deal with imaginary places and creatures, and science-fiction stories.

See *Science Fiction.*

FICTION *Fiction* is prose writing that tells about imaginary characters and events. Short stories and novels are works of fiction. Some writers base their fiction on actual events and people, adding invented characters, dialogue, settings, and plots. Other writers rely on imagination alone.

See *Narration, Nonfiction,* and *Prose.*

FIGURATIVE LANGUAGE *Figurative language* is writing or speech that is not meant to be taken literally. The many types of figurative language are known as *figures of speech.* Common figures of speech include metaphor, personification, and simile. Writers use figurative language to state ideas in vivid and imaginative ways.

See *Metaphor, Personification, Simile,* and *Symbol.*

FIGURE OF SPEECH See *Figurative Language.*

FLASHBACK A *flashback* is a scene within a story that interrupts the sequence of events to relate events that occurred in the past.

FLAT CHARACTER See *Character.*

FOLK TALE A *folk tale* is a story composed orally and then passed from person to person by word of mouth. Folk tales originated among people who could neither read nor write. These people entertained one another by telling stories aloud—often dealing with heroes, adventure, magic, or romance. Eventually, modern scholars collected these stories and wrote them down.

Folk tales reflect the cultural beliefs and environments from which they come.

See *Fable, Legend, Myth,* and *Oral Tradition.*

FOOT See *Meter.*

FORESHADOWING *Foreshadowing* is the author's use of clues to hint at what might happen later in the story. Writers use foreshadowing to build their readers' expectations and to create suspense.

FREE VERSE *Free verse* is poetry not written in a regular, rhythmical pattern, or meter. The poet is free to write lines of any length or with any number of stresses, or beats. Free verse is therefore less constraining than *metrical verse,* in which every line must have a certain length and a certain number of stresses.

See *Meter.*

GENRE A *genre* is a division or type of literature. Literature is commonly divided into three major genres: poetry, prose, and drama. Each major genre is, in turn, divided into lesser genres, as follows:

1. *Poetry:* lyric poetry, concrete poetry, dramatic poetry, narrative poetry, epic poetry
2. *Prose:* fiction (novels and short stories) and nonfiction (biography, autobiography, letters, essays, and reports)
3. *Drama:* serious drama and tragedy, comic drama, melodrama, and farce

See *Drama, Poetry,* and *Prose.*

HAIKU The *haiku* is a three-line Japanese verse form. The first and third lines of a haiku each have five syllables. The second line has seven syllables. A writer of haiku uses images to create a single, vivid picture, generally of a scene from nature.

HERO/HEROINE A *hero* or *heroine* is a character whose actions are inspiring, or noble. Often heroes and heroines struggle to overcome the obstacles and problems that stand in their way. Note that the term *hero* was originally used only for male characters, while heroic female characters were always called *heroines.* However, it is now acceptable to use *hero* to refer to females as well as to males.

HISTORICAL FICTION In *historical fiction* real events, places, or people are incorporated into a fictional or made-up story.

IMAGES *Images* are words or phrases that appeal to one or more of the five senses. Writers use images to describe how their subjects look, sound, feel, taste, and smell. Poets often paint images, or word pictures, that appeal to your senses. These pictures help you to experience the poem fully.

IMAGERY See *Image.*

INTERNAL CONFLICT See *Conflict.*

IRONY *Irony* is the general name given to literary techniques that involve surprising, interesting, or amusing contradictions.

JOURNAL A *journal* is a daily, or periodic, account of events and the writer's thoughts and feelings about those events. Personal journals are not normally written for publication, but sometimes they do get published later with permission from the author or the author's family.

LEGEND A *legend* is a widely told story about the past—one that may or may not have a foundation in fact. Every culture has its own legends—its familiar, traditional stories.

See *Folk Tale, Myth,* and *Oral Tradition.*

LETTERS A *letter* is a written communication from one person to another. In personal letters, the writer shares information and his or her thoughts and feelings with one other person or group. Although letters are not normally written for publication, they sometimes do get published later with the permission of the author or the author's family.

LIMERICK A *limerick* is a humorous, rhyming, five-line poem with a specific meter and rhyme scheme. Most limericks have three strong stresses in lines 1, 2, and 5 and two strong stresses in lines 3 and 4. Most follow the rhyme scheme *aabba.*

LYRIC POEM A *lyric poem* is a highly musical verse that expresses the observations and feelings of a single speaker. It creates a single, unified impression.

MAIN CHARACTER See *Character.*

MEDIA ACCOUNTS *Media Accounts* are reports, explanations, opinions, or descriptions written for television, radio, newspapers, and magazines. While some media accounts report only facts, others include the writer's thoughts and reflections.

METAPHOR A *metaphor* is a figure of speech in which something is described as though it were something else. A metaphor, like a simile, works by pointing out a similarity between two unlike things.

See *Extended Metaphor* and *Simile.*

METER The *meter* of a poem is its rhythmical pattern. This pattern is determined by the number of *stresses,* or beats, in each line. To describe the meter of a poem, read it emphasizing the beats in each line. Then, mark the stressed and unstressed syllables, as follows:

˘ ´ ˘ ´ ˘ ´ ˘ ´
My fath | er was | the first | to hear |

As you can see, each strong stress is marked with a slanted line (´) and each unstressed syllable with a horseshoe symbol (˘). The weak and strong stresses are then divided by vertical lines (|) into groups called *feet.*

MINOR CHARACTER See *Character.*

MOOD See *Atmosphere.*

MORAL A *moral* is a lesson taught by a literary work. A fable usually ends with a moral that is directly stated. A poem, novel, short story, or essay often suggests a moral that is not directly stated. The moral must be drawn by the reader, based on other elements in the work.

See *Fable.*

MOTIVATION See *Motive.*

MOTIVE A *motive* is a reason that explains or partially explains a character's thoughts, feelings, actions, or speech. Writers try to make their characters' motives, or motivations, as clear as possible. If the motives of a main character are not clear, then the character will not be believable.

Characters are often motivated by needs, such as food and shelter. They are also motivated by feelings, such as fear, love, and pride. Motives may be obvious or hidden.

MYTH A *myth* is a fictional tale that explains the actions of gods or heroes or the origins of elements of nature. Myths are part of the oral tradition. They are composed orally and then passed from generation to generation by word of mouth. Every ancient culture has its own mythology, or collection of myths. Greek and Roman myths are known collectively as *classical mythology.*

See *Oral Tradition.*

NARRATION *Narration* is writing that tells a story. The act of telling a story is also called narration. Each piece is a *narrative.* A story told in fiction, nonfiction, poetry, or even in drama is called a narrative.

See *Narrative, Narrative Poem,* and *Narrator.*

NARRATIVE A *narrative* is a story. A narrative can be either fiction or nonfiction. Novels and short stories are types of fictional narratives. Biographies and autobiographies are nonfiction narratives. Poems that tell stories are also narratives.

See *Narration* and *Narrative Poem.*

NARRATIVE POEM A *narrative poem* is a story told in verse. Narrative poems often have all the elements of short stories, including characters, conflict, and plot.

NARRATOR A *narrator* is a speaker or a character who tells a story. The narrator's perspective is the way he or she sees things. A *third-person narrator* is one who stands outside the action and speaks about it. A *first-person narrator* is one who tells a story and participates in its action.

See *Point of View.*

NONFICTION *Nonfiction* is prose writing that presents and explains ideas or that tells about real people, places, objects, or events. Autobiographies, biographies, essays, reports, letters, memos, and newspaper articles are all types of nonfiction.

See *Fiction.*

NOVEL A *novel* is a long work of fiction. Novels contain such elements as characters, plot, conflict, and setting. The writer of novels, or novelist, develops these elements. In addition to its main plot, a novel may contain one or more subplots, or independent, related stories. A novel may also have several themes. See *Fiction* and *Short Story.*

NOVELLA A fiction work that is longer than a short story but shorter than a novel.

ONOMATOPOEIA *Onomatopoeia* is the use of words that imitate sounds. *Crash, buzz, screech, hiss, neigh, jingle,* and *cluck* are examples of onomatopoeia. *Chickadee, towhee,* and *whippoorwill* are onomatopoeic names of birds.

Onomatopoeia can help put the reader in the activity of a poem.

ORAL TRADITION *Oral tradition* is the passing of songs, stories, and poems from generation to generation by word of mouth. Folk songs, folk tales, legends, and myths all come from the oral tradition. No one knows who first created these stories and poems.

See *Folk Tale, Legend,* and *Myth.*

PERSONIFICATION *Personification* is a type of figurative language in which a nonhuman subject is given human characteristics.

PERSPECTIVE See *Narrator* and *Point of View.*

PERSUASION *Persuasion* is used in writing or speech that attempts to convince the reader or listener to adopt a particular opinion or course of action. Newspaper editorials and letters to the editor use persuasion. So do advertisements and campaign speeches given by political candidates.

See *Essay.*

PLAYWRIGHT A *playwright* is a person who writes plays. William Shakespeare is regarded as the greatest playwright in English literature.

PLOT *Plot* is the sequence of events in which each event results from a previous one and causes the next. In most novels, dramas, short stories, and narrative poems, the plot involves both characters and a central conflict. The plot usually begins with an *exposition* that introduces the setting, the characters, and the basic situation. This is followed by the *inciting incident,* which introduces the central conflict. The conflict then increases during the *development* until it reaches a high point of interest or suspense, the *climax.* The climax is followed by the *falling action,* or end, of the central conflict. Any events that occur during the falling action make up the *resolution* or *denouement.*

Some plots do not have all of these parts. Some stories begin with the inciting incident and end with the resolution.

See *Conflict.*

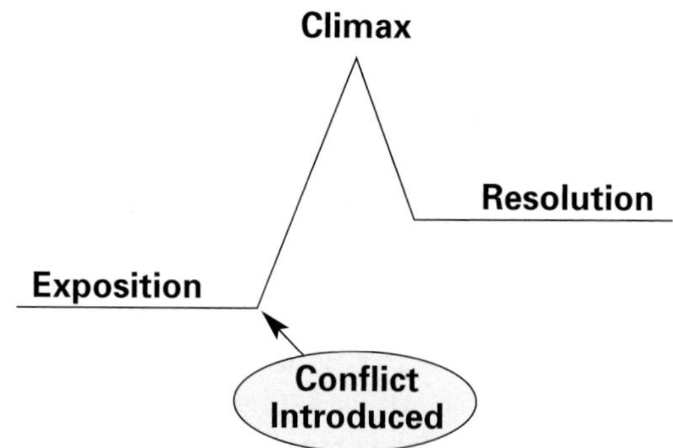

POETRY *Poetry* is one of the three major types of literature, the others being prose and drama. Most poems make use of highly concise, musical, and emotionally charged language. Many also make use of imagery, figurative language, and special devices of sound such as rhyme. Major types of poetry include *lyric poetry, narrative poetry,* and *concrete poetry.*

See *Concrete Poem, Genre, Lyric Poem,* and *Narrative Poem.*

POINT OF VIEW Point of view is the perspective, or vantage point, from which a story is told. It is either a narrator outside the story or a character in the story. *First-person point of view* is told by a character who uses the first-person pronoun "I."

The two kinds of *third-person point of view,* limited and omniscient, are called "third person" because the narrator uses third-person pronouns such as *he* and *she* to refer to the characters. There is no "I" telling the story.

In stories told from the *omniscient third-person point of view,* the narrator knows and tells about what each character feels and thinks.

In stories told from the *limited third-person point of view,* the narrator relates the inner thoughts and feelings of only one character, and everything is viewed from this character's perspective.

See *Narrator.*

PROBLEM See *Conflict.*

PROSE *Prose* is the ordinary form of written language. Most writing that is not poetry, drama, or song is considered prose. Prose is one of the major genres of literature and occurs in two forms—fiction and nonfiction.

See *Fiction, Genre,* and *Nonfiction.*

PROTAGONIST The *protagonist* is the main character in a literary work. Often, the protagonist is a person, but sometimes it can be an animal.

See *Antagonist* and *Character.*

REFRAIN A *refrain* is a regularly repeated line or group of lines in a poem or a song.

REPETITION *Repetition* is the use, more than once, of any element of language—a sound, word, phrase, clause, or sentence. Repetition is used in both prose and poetry.

See *Alliteration, Meter, Plot, Rhyme,* and *Rhyme Scheme.*

RESOLUTION The *resolution* is the outcome of the conflict in a plot.

See *Plot.*

RHYME *Rhyme* is the repetition of sounds at the ends of words. Poets use rhyme to lend a songlike quality to their verses and to emphasize certain words and ideas. Many traditional poems contain *end rhymes,* or rhyming words at the ends of lines.

Another common device is the use of *internal rhymes,* or rhyming words within lines. Internal rhyme also emphasizes the flowing nature of a poem.

See *Rhyme Scheme.*

RHYME SCHEME A *rhyme scheme* is a regular pattern of rhyming words in a poem. To indicate the rhyme scheme of a poem, one uses lowercase letters. Each rhyme is assigned a different letter, as follows in the first stanza of "Dust of Snow," by Robert Frost:

The way a crow *a*
Shook down on me *b*
The dust of snow *a*
From a hemlock tree *b*

Thus, the stanza has the rhyme scheme *abab.*

RHYTHM *Rhythm* is the pattern of stressed and unstressed syllables in spoken or written language.

See *Meter.*

ROUND CHARACTER See *Character.*

SCENE A *scene* is a section of uninterrupted action in the act of a drama.

See *Drama.*

SCIENCE FICTION *Science fiction* combines elements of fiction and fantasy with scientific fact. Many science-fiction stories are set in the future.

SENSORY LANGUAGE *Sensory language* is writing or speech that appeals to one or more of the five senses.

See *Image.*

SETTING The *setting* of a literary work is the time and place of the action. The setting includes all the details of a place and time—the year, the time of day, even the weather. The place may be a specific country, state, region, community, neighborhood, building, institution, or home. Details such as dialects, clothing, customs, and modes of transportation are often used to establish setting. In most stories, the setting serves as a backdrop—a context in which the characters interact. Setting can also help to create a feeling, or atmosphere.

See *Atmosphere.*

SHORT STORY A *short story* is a brief work of fiction. Like a novel, a short story presents a sequence of events, or plot. The plot usually deals with a central conflict faced by a main character, or protagonist. The events in a short story usually communicate a message about life or human nature. This message, or central idea, is the story's theme.

See *Conflict, Plot,* and *Theme.*

SIMILE A *simile* is a figure of speech that uses *like* or *as* to make a direct comparison between two unlike ideas. Everyday speech often contains similes, such as "pale as a ghost," "good as gold," "spread like wildfire," and "clever as a fox."

SPEAKER The *speaker* is the imaginary voice a poet uses when writing a poem. The speaker is the character who tells the poem. This character, or voice, often is not identified by name. There can be important differences between the poet and the poem's speaker.

See *Narrator.*

STAGE DIRECTIONS *Stage directions* are notes included in a drama to describe how the work is to be performed or staged. Stage directions are usually printed in italics and enclosed within parentheses or brackets. Some stage directions describe the movements, costumes, emotional states, and ways of speaking of the characters.

STAGING *Staging* includes the setting, the lighting, the costumes, special effects, music, dance, and so on that go into putting on a stage performance of a drama.

See *Drama.*

STANZA A *stanza* is a group of lines of poetry that are usually similar in length and pattern and are separated by spaces. A stanza is like a paragraph of poetry—it states and develops a single main idea.

STATIC CHARACTER See *Character.*

SURPRISE ENDING A *surprise ending* is a conclusion that is unexpected. The reader has certain expectations about the ending based on details in the story. Often, a surprise ending is *foreshadowed,* or subtly hinted at, in the course of the work.

See *Foreshadowing* and *Plot.*

SUSPENSE *Suspense* is a feeling of anxious uncertainty about the outcome of events in a literary work. Writers create suspense by raising questions in the minds of their readers.

SYMBOL A *symbol* is anything that stands for or represents something else. Symbols are common in everyday life. A dove with an olive branch in its beak is a symbol of peace. A blindfolded woman holding a balanced scale is a symbol of justice. A crown is a symbol of a king's status and authority.

THEME The *theme* is a central message, concern, or purpose in a literary work. A theme can usually be expressed as a generalization, or a general statement, about human beings or about life. The theme of a work is not a summary of its plot. The theme is the writer's central idea.

Although a theme may be stated directly in the text, it is more often presented indirectly. When the theme is stated indirectly, or implied, the reader must figure out what the theme is by looking carefully at what the work reveals about people or about life.

TONE The *tone* of a literary work is the writer's attitude toward his or her audience and subject. The tone can often be described by a single adjective, such as *formal* or *informal, serious* or *playful, bitter,* or *ironic.* Factors that contribute to the tone are word choice, sentence structure, line length, rhyme, rhythm, and repetition.

TRAGEDY A *tragedy* is a work of literature, especially a play, that results in a catastrophe for the main character. In ancient Greek drama, the main character is always a significant person—a king or a hero—and the cause of the tragedy is a tragic flaw, or weakness, in his or her character. In modern drama, the main character can be an ordinary person, and the cause of the tragedy can be some evil in society itself. The purpose of tragedy is not only to arouse fear and pity in the audience, but also, in some cases, to convey a sense of the grandeur and nobility of the human spirit.

TURNING POINT See *Climax.*

RUBRICS

What is a rubric?

A rubric is a tool, often in the form of a chart or a grid, that helps you assess your work. Rubrics are particularly helpful for writing and speaking assignments.

To help you or others assess, or evaluate, your work, a rubric offers several specific criteria to be applied to your work. Then the rubric helps you or an evaluator indicate your range of success or failure according to those specific criteria. Rubrics are often used to evaluate writing for standardized tests.

Using a rubric will save you time, focus your learning, and improve the work you do. When you know what the rubric will be before you begin writing a persuasive essay, for example, as you write you will be aware of specific criteria that are important in that kind of an essay. As you evaluate the essay before giving it to your teacher, you will focus on the specific areas that your teacher wants you to master—or on areas that you know present challenges for you. Instead of searching through your work randomly for any way to improve it or correct its errors, you will have a clear and helpful focus on specific criteria.

How are rubrics constructed?

Rubrics can be constructed in several different ways.

- Your teacher may assign a rubric for a specific assignment.
- Your teacher may direct you to a rubric in your textbook.
- Your teacher and your class may construct a rubric for a particular assignment together.
- You and your classmates may construct a rubric together.
- You may create your own rubric with criteria you want to evaluate in your work.

How will a rubric help me?

A rubric will help you assess your work on a scale. Scales vary from rubric to rubric but usually range from 6 to 1, 5 to 1, or 4 to 1, with 6, 5, or 4 being the highest score and 1 being the lowest. If someone else is using the rubric to assess your work, the rubric will give your evaluator a clear range within which to place your work. If you are using the rubric yourself, it will help you make improvements to your work.

What are the types of rubrics?

- A **holistic rubric** has general criteria that can apply to a variety of assignments. See p. R20 for an example of a holistic rubric.
- An **analytic rubric** is specific to a particular assignment. The criteria for evaluation address the specific issues important in that assignment. See p. R19 for examples of analytic rubrics.

Sample Analytic Rubrics

Rubric With a 4-point Scale

The following analytic rubric is an example of a rubric to assess a persuasive essay. It will help you evaluate audience and purpose, organization, elaboration, and use of language.

	Audience/Purpose	Organization	Elaboration	Use of Language
4	Demonstrates highly effective word choice; clearly focused on task.	Uses clear, consistent organizational strategy.	Provides convincing, well-elaborated reasons to support the position.	Incorporates transitions; includes very few mechanical errors.
3	Demonstrates good word choice; states focus on persuasive task.	Uses clear organizational strategy with occasional inconsistencies.	Provides two or more moderately elaborated reasons to support the position.	Incorporates some transitions; includes few mechanical errors.
2	Shows some good word choices; minimally states focus on persuasive task.	Uses inconsistent organizational strategy; presentation is not logical.	Provides several reasons but few are elaborated; only one elaborated reason.	Incorporates few transitions; includes many mechanical errors.
1	Shows lack of attention to persuasive task.	Demonstrates lack of organizational strategy.	Provides no specific reasons or does not elaborate.	Does not connect ideas; includes many mechanical errors.

Rubric With a 6-point Scale

The following analytic rubric is an example of a rubric to assess a persuasive essay. It will help you evaluate presentation, position, evidence, and arguments.

	Presentation	Position	Evidence	Arguments
6	Essay clearly and effectively addresses an issue with more than one side.	Essay clearly states a supportable position on the issue.	All evidence is logically organized, well presented, and supports the position.	All reader concerns and counterarguments are presented effectively.
5	Most of essay addresses an issue that has more than one side.	Essay clearly states a position on the issue.	Most evidence is logically organized, well presented, and supports the position.	Most reader concerns and counterarguments are presented effectively.
4	Essay adequately addresses issue that has more than one side.	Essay adequately states a position on the issue.	Many parts of evidence support the position; some evidence is out of order.	Many reader concerns and counterarguments are presented adequately.
3	Essay addresses issue with two sides but does not present second side clearly.	Essay states a position on the issue, but the position is difficult to support.	Some evidence supports the position, but some evidence is out of order.	Some reader concerns and counterarguments are presented.
2	Essay addresses issue with two sides but does not present second side.	Essay states a position on the issue, but the position is not supportable.	Not much evidence supports the position, and what is included is out of order.	A few reader concerns and counterarguments are presented.
1	Essay does not address issue with more than one side.	Essay does not state a position on the issue.	No evidence supports the position.	No reader concerns or counterarguments are presented.

Sample Holistic Rubric

Holistic rubrics such as this one are sometimes used to assess writing assignments on standardized tests. Notice that the criteria for evaluation are focus, organization, support, and use of conventions.

Points	Criteria
6 Points	• The writing is strongly focused and shows fresh insight into the writing task. • The writing is marked by a sense of completeness and coherence and is organized with a logical progression of ideas. • A main idea is fully developed, and support is specific and substantial. • A mature command of the language is in evidence, and the writing may employ characteristic creative writing strategies. • Sentence structure is varied, and writing is free of all but purposefully used fragments. • Virtually no errors in writing conventions appear.
5 Points	• The writing is clearly focused on the task. • The writing is well organized and has a logical progression of ideas, though there may be occasional lapses. • A main idea is well developed and supported with relevant details. • Command of the language is mature. • Sentence structure is varied, and the writing is free of fragments, except when used purposefully. • Writing conventions are followed correctly.
4 Points	• The writing is clearly focused on the task, but extraneous material may intrude at times. • A clear organizational pattern is present, though lapses may occur. • A main idea is adequately supported, but development may be uneven. • Sentence structure is generally free of fragments but shows little variation. • Writing conventions are generally followed correctly.
3 Points	• Writing is generally focused on the task, but extraneous material may intrude at times. • An organizational pattern is evident, but writing may lack a logical progression of ideas. • Support for the main idea is generally present but is sometimes illogical. • Sentence structure is generally free of fragments, but there is almost no variation. • The work generally demonstrates a knowledge of writing conventions, with occasional misspellings.
2 Points	• The writing is related to the task but generally lacks focus. • There is little evidence of organizational pattern, and there is little sense of cohesion. • Support for the main idea is generally inadequate, illogical, or absent. • Sentence structure is unvaried, and serious errors may occur. • Errors in writing conventions and spelling are frequent.
1 Point	• The writing may have little connection to the task and is generally unfocused. • There has been little attempt at organization or development. • The paper seems fragmented, with no clear main idea. • Sentence structure is unvaried, and serious errors appear. • Poor word choice and poor command of the language obscure meaning. • Errors in writing conventions and spelling are frequent.
Unscorable	The paper is considered unscorable if: • The response is unrelated to the task or is simply a rewording of the prompt. • The response has been copied from a published work. • The student did not write a response. • The response is illegible. • The words in the response are arranged with no meaning. • There is an insufficient amount of writing to score.

STUDENT MODEL

Persuasive Writing

This persuasive essay, which would receive a top score according to a persuasive rubric, is a response to the following writing prompt, or assignment:

Most young people today spend more than 5 hours a day watching television. Many adults worry about the effects on youth of seeing too much television violence. Write a persuasive piece in which you argue against or defend the effects of television watching on young people. Be sure to include examples to support your views.

Until the television was invented, families spent their time doing different activities. Now most families stay home and watch TV. Watching TV risks the family's health, reduces the children's study time, and is a bad influence on young minds. Watching television can be harmful.

> The writer clearly states a position in the first paragraph.

The most important reason why watching TV is bad is that the viewers get less exercise. For example, instead of watching their favorite show, people could exercise for 30 minutes. If people spent less time watching TV and more time exercising, then they could have healthier bodies. My mother told me a story about a man who died of a heart attack because he was out of shape from watching television all the time. Obviously, watching TV can put a person's health in danger.

> Each paragraph provides details that support the writer's main points.

Furthermore, watching television reduces children's study time. For example, children would spend more time studying if they didn't watch television. If students spent more time studying at home, then they would make better grades at school. Last week I had a major test in science, but I didn't study because I started watching a movie. I was not prepared for the test and my grade reflected my lack of studying. Indeed, watching television is bad because it can hurt a student's grades.

Finally, watching TV can be a bad influence on children. For example, some TV shows have inappropriate language and too much violence. If children watch programs that use bad language and show violence, then they may start repeating these actions because they think the behavior is "cool." In fact, it has been proven that children copy what they see on TV. Clearly, watching TV is bad for children and it affects children's behavior.

In conclusion, watching television is a bad influence for these reasons: It reduces people's exercise time and students' study time and it shows children inappropriate behavior. Therefore, people should take control of their lives and stop allowing television to harm them.

> The conclusion restates the writer's position.

Types of Writing

NARRATION

Whenever writers tell any type of story, they are using **narration.** While there are many kinds of narration, most narratives share certain elements, such as characters, a setting, a sequence of events, and, often, a theme.

Autobiographical writing tells the story of an event or person in the writer's life.

Biographical writing is a writer's account of another person's life.

Short story A short story is a brief, creative narrative—a retelling of events arranged to hold a reader's attention.

A few types of short stories are realistic stories, fantasy, science-fiction stories, and adventure stories.

DESCRIPTION

Descriptive writing is writing that creates a vivid picture of a person, place, thing, or event. Descriptive writing can stand on its own or be part of a longer work, such as a short story.

Descriptive writing includes descriptions of people or places, remembrances, observations, vignettes, and character profiles.

PERSUASION

Persuasion is writing or speaking that attempts to convince people to accept a position or take a desired action. When used effectively, persuasive writing has the power to change people's lives. As a reader and a writer, you will find yourself engaged in many forms of persuasion.

Forms of persuasive writing include persuasive essays, advertisements, persuasive letters, editorials, persuasive speeches, and public-service announcements.

EXPOSITORY WRITING

Expository writing is writing that informs or explains. The information you include in expository writing is factual or based on fact. Effective expository writing reflects a well-thought-out organization—one that includes a clear introduction, body, and conclusion. The organization should be appropriate for the type of exposition you are writing. Here are some types of exposition.

Comparison-and-Contrast essay A comparison-and-contrast essay analyzes the similarities and differences between two or more things.

Cause-and-Effect essay A cause-and-effect essay is expository writing that explains the reasons why something happened or the results an event or situation will probably produce. You may examine several causes of a single effect or several effects of a single cause.

Problem-and-Solution essay The purpose of a problem-and-solution essay is to describe a problem and offer one or more solutions to it. It describes a clear set of steps to achieve a result.

How-to essay A how-to essay explains how to do or make something. You break the process down into a series of logical steps and explain the steps in order.

Summary A summary is a brief statement of the main ideas and significant supporting details presented in a piece of writing. A summary should include

- main events, ideas, or images.
- connections among significant details.
- your own words.
- underlying meaning rather than superficial details.
- background information, such as setting or characters.

RESEARCH WRITING

Writers often use outside research to gather information and explore subjects of interest. The product of that research is called **research writing.** Good research writing does not simply repeat information. It guides readers through a topic, showing them why each fact matters and creating an overall picture of the subject. Here are some types of research writing.

Research report A research report presents information gathered from reference books, observations, interviews, or other sources.

Biographical report A biographical report examines the high points and achievements in the life of a notable person. It includes dates, details, and main events in the person's life as well as background on the period in which the person lived. The writer may also make educated guesses about the reasons behind events in the person's life.

Multimedia report A multimedia report presents information gathered from a variety of reliable sources, both print and nonprint. A wide range of materials are available, such as tape recorders, videocameras, slides, photographs, overhead projectors, prerecorded music and sound effects, digital imaging, graphics software, computers, spreadsheets, data bases, electronic resources, and Web sites.

I-Search report An I-Search report begins with a topic of immediate concern to you and provides well-researched information on that topic. Unlike a research report, it tells the story of your exploration of the topic, using the pronoun *I*. It explains

- your purpose in learning about the topic.
- the story of how you researched it.
- an account of what you learned.

RESPONSE TO LITERATURE

A **response to literature** is an essay or other type of writing that discusses and interprets what is of value in a book, short story, essay, article, or poem. You take a careful, critical look at various important elements in the work.

In addition to the standard literary essay, here are some other types of responses to literature.

Literary criticism Literary criticism is the result of literary analysis—the examination of a literary work or a body of literature. In literary criticism, you make a judgment or evaluation by looking carefully and critically at various important elements in the work. You then attempt to explain how the author has used those elements and how effectively they work together to convey the author's message.

Book or movie reviews A book review gives readers an impression of a book, encouraging them either to read it or to avoid reading it. A movie review begins with a basic response to whether or not you enjoyed the movie, and then explains the reasons why or why not.

Letter to an author People sometimes respond to a work of literature by writing a letter to the writer. It lets the writer know what a reader found enjoyable or disappointing in a work. You can praise the work, ask questions, or offer constructive criticism.

Comparisons of works A comparison of works highlights specific features of two or more works by comparing them.

CREATIVE WRITING

Creative writing blends imagination, ideas, and emotions, and allows you to present your own unique view of the world. Poems, plays, short stories, dramas, and even some cartoons are examples of creative writing. Here are some types of creative writing.

Lyric poem A lyric poem uses sensory images, figurative language, and sound devices to express deep thoughts and feelings about a subject. Writers give lyric poems a musical quality by employing sound devices, such as rhyme, rhythm, alliteration, and onomatopoeia.

Narrative poem A narrative poem is similar to a short story in that it has a plot, characters, and a theme. However, a writer divides a narrative poem into stanzas, usually composed of rhyming lines that have a definite rhythm, or beat.

Song lyrics Song lyrics, or words to accompany a song contain many elements of poetry—rhyme, rhythm, repetition, and imagery. In addition, song lyrics convey emotions, as well as interesting ideas.

Drama A drama or a dramatic scene is a story that is intended to be performed. The story is told mostly through what the actors say (dialogue) and what they do (action).

PRACTICAL AND TECHNICAL DOCUMENTS

Practical writing is fact-based writing that people do in the workplace or in their day-to-day lives. A business letter, memorandum, school form, job application, and a letter of inquiry are a few examples of practical writing.

Technical documents are fact-based documents that identify the sequence of activities needed to design a system, operate a tool, follow a procedure, or explain the bylaws of an organization. You encounter technical writing every time you read a manual or a set of instructions.

In the following descriptions, you'll find tips for tackling several types of practical and technical writing.

Business letter A formal letter that follows one of several specific formats. (See page R26.)

News release A news release, also called a press release, announces factual information about upcoming events. A writer might send a news release to a local newspaper, local radio station, TV station, or other media that will publicize the information.

Guidelines Guidelines give information about how people should act or provide tips on how to do something.

Process explanation A process explanation is a step-by-step explanation of how to do something. The explanation should be clear and specific and might include diagrams or other illustrations to further clarify the process.

Proofreading and Preparing Manuscript

Before preparing a final copy, proofread your manuscript. The chart shows the standard symbols for marking corrections to be made.

Proofreading Symbols	
insert	∧
delete	[delete mark]
close space	⁐
new paragraph	¶
add comma	^
add period	⊙
transpose (switch)	∿
change to cap	a (triple underline)
change to lowercase	A (slash)

- Choose a standard, easy-to-read font.
- Type or print on one side of unlined 8 1/2" x 11" paper.
- Set the margins for the side, top, and bottom of your paper at approximately one inch. Most word-processing programs have a default setting that is appropriate.
- Double-space the document.
- Indent the first line of each paragraph.
- Number the pages in the upper right corner.

Follow your teacher's directions for formatting formal research papers. Most papers will have the following features:

- Title page
- Table of Contents or Outline
- Works-Cited List

Avoiding Plagiarism

Whether you are presenting a formal research paper or an opinion paper on a current event, you must be careful to give credit for any ideas or opinions that are not your own. Presenting someone else's ideas, research, or opinion as your own—even if you have phrased it in different words—is *plagiarism*, the equivalent of academic stealing, or fraud.

Do not use the ideas or research of others in place of your own. Read from several sources to draw your own conclusions and form your own opinions. Incorporate the ideas and research of others to support your points. Credit the source of the following types of support:

- Statistics
- Direct quotations
- Indirectly quoted statements of opinions
- Conclusions presented by an expert
- Facts available in only one or two sources

Crediting Sources

When you credit a source, you acknowledge where you found your information and you give your readers the details necessary for locating the source themselves. Within the body of the paper, you provide a short citation, a footnote number linked to a footnote, or an endnote number linked to an endnote reference. These brief references show the page numbers on which you found the information. Prepare a reference list at the end of the paper to provide full bibliographic information on your sources. These are two common types of reference lists:

- A **bibliography** provides a listing of all the resources you consulted during your research.
- A **works-cited list** indicates the works you have referenced in your paper.

The chart on the next page shows the Modern Language Association format for crediting sources. This is the most common format for papers written in the content areas in middle school and high school. Unless instructed otherwise by your teacher, use this format for crediting sources.

Phrases, Clauses, and Sentences

Exercise A Recognizing Basic Sentence Parts Copy the following sentences, underlining each simple subject once and each simple predicate twice. Circle the complements, and label each one *direct object, indirect object, predicate nominative,* or *predicate adjective.* Then, identify each sentence as *declarative, imperative, interrogative,* or *exclamatory.*

1. Does Matt or Jeremy enjoy figure skating or speed skating?
2. Speed skating is good exercise.
3. There are races against the clock and against other skaters.
4. Speed skaters use skates with long straight edges.
5. Wow! The blades are so long and look so sharp!
6. Try that pair of skates.
7. I gave Danielle figure-skating lessons.
8. She and Hannah were eager and attentive.
9. We practiced cross-overs and snowplow stops.
10. Can you do any jumps?

Exercise B Using Basic Sentence Parts Rewrite the following sentences according to the directions in parentheses. In your new sentences, underline each simple subject once and each simple predicate twice. Circle each complement.

1. Ice hockey is a winter sport. It is a rough game. (Combine by creating a compound predicate nominative.)
2. Hockey-playing countries include Canada. Hockey is a big sport in Russia. (Combine by creating a compound direct object.)
3. Defense is an important part of the game, and so is offense. (Rewrite by creating a compound subject.)
4. The players use hockey sticks. They wear protective pads. (Rewrite by creating a compound predicate.)
5. Goaltenders wear face masks. They wear other protective equipment. (Combine by creating a compound direct object.)
6. One area on the ice is the neutral zone. Another is the attacking zone. (Combine by creating a compound predicate nominative.)
7. Substitution of players is frequent. It occurs during the game. (Combine by creating a compound predicate.)
8. Hockey skate blades are thin. They are also short. (Combine by creating a compound predicate adjective.)
9. Teams pass the puck, shooting it with their sticks. (Rewrite by creating a compound predicate.)
10. Ancient Egyptians played games similar to hockey, and so did the Persians. (Rewrite by creating a compound subject.)

Exercise C Identifying Phrases and Clauses Label each phrase in the following sentences as an *adjective prepositional phrase,* an *adverb prepositional phrase,* or an *appositive phrase.* Identify and label each clause.

1. Skiing is a popular winter sport in many countries.
2. Boots, flexible or rigid, are important pieces of equipment.
3. Ski poles that vary in length are used for balance.
4. There are three kinds of skiing that have been developed.
5. One type, Alpine skiing, involves racing down steep, snow-covered slopes.
6. Skiers descend in the fastest time possible.
7. A course is defined by a series of gates, which are made of poles and flag markers.
8. The racer passes through these gates.
9. This downhill racing includes the slalom, in which the course is made of many turns.
10. The super giant slalom, a combination of downhill and slalom, is decided after one run.

Cumulative Review

Answers for p. R41

Exercise A

1. Does Matt or Jeremy enjoy figure (skating) or speed (skating)? (direct object, interrogative)
2. Speed skating is good (exercise). (predicate nominative, declarative)
3. There are races against the clock and against other skaters. (declarative)
4. Speed skaters use (skates) with long straight edges. (direct object, declarative)
5. Wow! The blades are so (long) and look so (sharp)! (predicate adjectives, exclamatory)
6. (You) Try that (pair) of skates. (direct object, imperative)
7. I gave (Danielle) figure-skating (lessons). (indirect object, direct object, declarative)
8. She and Hannah were (eager) and (attentive). (predicate adjectives, declarative)
9. We practiced (cross-overs) and snowplow (stops). (direct object, declarative)
10. Can you do any (jumps)? (direct object, interrogative)

Exercise B

1. Ice hockey is a winter (sport) and a rough (game).
2. Hockey-playing countries include (Russia), where it is a big sport, and (Canada).
3. Defense and offense are important (parts) of the game.
4. The players use hockey (sticks) and wear protective (pads).
5. Goaltenders wear face (masks) and other protective (equipment).
6. Two areas on the ice are the (neutral zone) and the (attacking zone).
7. Substitution of players is (frequent) and occurs during the game.
8. Hockey skate blades are (thin) and (short).
9. Teams pass the (puck) and shoot (it) with their sticks.
10. Ancient Egyptians and Persians played (games) similar to hockey.

continued

Answers continued

Exercise C

1. in many countries—adverb phrase; whole sentence is an independent clause
2. flexible or rigid—appositive phrase; of equipment—adjective phrase; whole sentence is an independent clause
3. in length—adverb phrase; for balance—adverb phrase; that vary in length—subordinate clause; Ski poles . . . are used for balance—independent clause
4. of skiing—adjective phrase; that have been developed—subordinate clause; There are three kinds of skiing—independent clause
5. Alpine skiing—appositive phrase; down steep, snow-covered slopes—adverb phrase; whole sentence is an independent clause
6. in the fastest time possible—adverb phrase; whole sentence is an independent clause
7. by a series—adverb phrase; of gates—adjective phrase; of poles and flag markers—adverb phrase; which are made of poles and flag markers—subordinate clause; A course is defined by a series of gates—independent clause

Cumulative Review

Answers continued from p. R41

8. through these gates—adverb phrase; whole sentence is an independent clause
9. of many turns—adverb phrase; in which the course is made of many turns—subordinate clause; This downhill racing includes the slalom—independent clause
10. a combination of downhill and slalom—appositive phrase; of downhill and slalom—adjective phrase; after one run—adverb phrase; The super giant slalom . . . is decided after one run—independent clause

Exercise D

1. Nordic skiing, a name for cross-country skiing, is practiced in many parts of the world.
2. It is performed on courses which are longer and flatter than downhill courses.
3. Nordic skiing emphasizes two things, which are endurance and strength.
4. Cross-country skiers move in a side-to-side motion.
5. Cross-country skiing developed to fill a need for transportation.

Exercise E

1. Bobsledding was first developed in Saint Moritz, Switzerland, where the first competition was held.
2. In bobsledding, teams of two or four people descend an icy run.
3. The most critical part of a bobsled run is its start.
4. The captain, also called the driver, occupies the front position in the sled.
5. Accelerating the speed of the sled, the crew members lean backward and forward in unison.
6. Bobsledding is different from the luge.
7. Luge competitors lie on their backs with their feet at the front of the luge sled.
8. Luge courses aren't constructed for anything other than this sport.
9. These courses feature turns and straight stretches.
10. The reason it looks dangerous is that luges travel at high speeds.

continued

Exercise D Using Phrases and Clauses

Rewrite the following sentences according to the instructions in parentheses.

1. Cross-country skiing is called Nordic skiing and is practiced in many parts of the world. (Rewrite by creating an appositive phrase.)
2. It is performed on longer courses. These courses are also flatter than downhill courses. (Combine by creating a clause.)
3. Nordic skiing emphasizes two things. Those are endurance and strength. (Combine by creating a clause.)
4. A side-to-side motion is the way cross-country skiers move. (Rewrite by creating an adverb prepositional phrase.)
5. Cross-country skiing developed to fill a need. That need was for transportation. (Combine by creating an adjective prepositional phrase.)

Exercise E Revising Sentences to Eliminate Errors and Create Variety

Rewrite the following sentences according to the instructions in parentheses.

1. Bobsledding was first developed in Saint Moritz, Switzerland, the first competition was held there. (Correct the run-on sentence.)
2. Teams of two or four people descend an icy run in bobsledding. (Vary the sentence by beginning with a prepositional phrase.)
3. The part of a bobsled run most critical is its start. (Correct the misplaced modifier.)
4. The captain occupies the front position in the sled. This person is also called the driver. (Combine the sentences by creating a phrase.)
5. The crew members lean backward and forward in unison and accelerate the speed of the sled. (Vary the sentence by beginning with a participial phrase.)
6. Bobsledding is different than the luge. (Correct the common usage problem.)
7. Lie on their backs with their feet at the front of the luge sled. (Correct the sentence fragment.)
8. Luge courses are not constructed for nothing other than this sport. (Correct the double negative.)
9. These courses feature turns. Courses also feature straight stretches. (Combine by creating a compound direct object.)
10. The reason it looks dangerous is because luges travel at high speeds. (Correct the common usage problem.)

Exercise F Revision Practice: Sentence Combining

Rewrite the following passage, combining sentences where appropriate.

Most children are delighted when it snows. They wake up early. They listen for school cancellations on the radio. If school is cancelled, the children are excited. The parents say "Oh, no!" It means the schedule is off. The day has to be rearranged. They get out the boots and warm clothes. They get out the sleds. An unexpected vacation day.

Exercise G Writing Application

Write a description of a winter activity that you enjoy. Vary the lengths and beginnings of your sentences. Underline each simple subject once and each simple verb twice. Then, circle at least three phrases and three clauses. Avoid fragments, run-ons, double negatives, misplaced modifiers, and common usage problems.

Answers continued

Exercise F

Most children are delighted when it snows. They wake up early to listen for school cancellations on the radio. If school is cancelled, the children are excited, but the parents say, "Oh, no!" It means the schedule is off and the day has to be rearranged. They get out the boots, warm clothes, and sleds for an unexpected vacation day.

Exercise G

Descriptions will vary.

Usage

Exercise A Using Verbs Choose the correct verb or verb phrase in parentheses to complete each sentence below. Identify its principal part and tense.

1. Several Native American groups (brung, brought) their culture to what is now Texas.
2. The foundations of early dwellings were found where they were (lain, laid).
3. The Karankawa (did, done) a great deal of fishing in the Gulf of Mexico.
4. The Apache and the Comanche (caught, catched) and (eat, ate) the buffalo.
5. Alonzo Álvarez de Piñeda (set, sat) foot in Texas in 1519.
6. He was (leading, led) a group around the mouth of the Rio Grande.
7. Cabeza de Vaca (began, begun) to explore more of inland Texas.
8. In 1682, the Spanish (built, builded) the first mission in Texas.
9. That was near the site where present-day El Paso (is, was).
10. Spain (knew, known) that France was claiming the area.

Exercise B Identifying the Case of Pronouns Identify the case of each pronoun in the following sentences as *nominative*, *objective*, or *possessive*.

1. One French explorer was La Salle. He built a fort near Matagorda Bay.
2. La Salle named it Fort Saint Louis.
3. France claimed the Mississippi River and its tributaries.
4. In 1716, the Spanish established missions, founding them throughout the territory.
5. They include the city of San Antonio.
6. However, the Spanish found that their hold on the province of Texas was weak.
7. Expeditions of adventurers from the United States had been traveling through it.
8. Philip Nolan led one invasion, but the Spanish captured him.
9. In 1820, Moses Austin, a United States citizen, made his request to settle in Texas.
10. His son, Stephen F. Austin, carried out the plan.

Exercise C Using Agreement Fill in each blank below with a pronoun that agrees with its antecedent.

1. In our social studies class, __?__ are studying Texas and __?__ fight for independence.
2. Texans decided that they wanted to make __?__ own laws.
3. The Mexican government wanted settlers in Texas to obey __?__ laws.
4. General Santa Anna gathered __?__ troops together to crush the rebellious Texans.
5. Texans declared __?__ independence from Mexico on March 2, 1836, in the town of Washington-on-the-Brazos.
6. Either Oleg or Sam will give __?__ report on the Alamo today.
7. Fewer than 200 Texans tried to defend __?__ territory against Santa Anna's army there.
8. Jim Bowie, Davey Crockett, and William B. Travis lost __?__ lives at the Alamo.
9. I hope that I will do well on __?__ test about the Alamo.
10. Texans captured Santa Anna and forced __?__ to sign a treaty.

Exercise D Using Verb Agreement Write the form of the verb in parentheses that agrees with the subject of each sentence below.

1. All of our reports (be) about the settling of the West.
2. Many students (want) to write about California.
3. No one (know) more about the early days in California than Rudy.
4. Everybody in our class (love) to look at the maps of the trails heading west.
5. Each of the students (have) to pick a trail to report on.

Cumulative Review

Answer Key

Exercise A

1. brought, past, past
2. laid, past participle, past (passive voice)
3. did, past, past
4. caught, ate, past, past
5. set, present, present
6. leading, present participle, past progressive
7. began, past, past
8. built, past, past
9. is, present, present
10. knew, past, past

Exercise B

1. nom.
2. obj.
3. poss.
4. obj.
5. nom.
6. poss.
7. obj.
8. obj.
9. poss.
10. poss.

Exercise C

1. we, its
2. their
3. its
4. his
5. their
6. his
7. their
8. their
9. my
10. him

continued

Answers continued from p. R43

Exercise D

1. are
2. want
3. knows
4. loves
5. has
6. ask
7. has
8. hope
9. is
10. appears

Exercise E

1. more quickly
2. most
3. late
4. larger
5. smallest
6. Braver
7. Most
8. more cautiously
9. most probably
10. soon

Exercise F

1. its
2. most
3. were
4. them
5. was
6. won, became
7. their
8. they
9. was
10. resisted

Exercise G

Writing Application

Have students exchange descriptions with partners and check for correct usage and identification.

6. Julie and Thomas (ask) to read about the Oregon Trail.
7. Neither Sam nor Randy (have) picked a topic yet.
8. Tanya and I (hope) to do our report on the Santa Fe Trail.
9. Either the Santa Fe Trail or the Oregon Trail (be) interesting.
10. According to the map, each of the trails (appear) to begin in Independence, Missouri.

Exercise E Using Modifiers In the sentences below, write the form of the adjective or adverb indicated in parentheses.

1. A Texan army gathered (quickly—comparative) than expected.
2. After taking San Antonio, (many—superlative) soldiers left the city.
3. They believed that Santa Anna, the Mexican dictator, would wait until (late—positive) spring.
4. Santa Anna's army was (large—comparative) than that of the settlers.
5. The (small—superlative) of all Texan forces withdrew to the Alamo.
6. (Brave—comparative) than expected, the Texans fought for thirteen days.
7. (Many—superlative) of the Texan forces were defeated in other battles.
8. Then, a group of Texans declared independence (cautiously—comparative) than they had earlier.
9. They attacked, (probably—superlative) surprising the Mexican Army.
10. Santa Anna (soon—positive) recognized Texas's independence.

Exercise F Correcting Usage Mistakes Rewrite the following sentences, correcting any errors in usage.

1. The Republic of Texas continued their existence for almost ten years.
2. The more prominent of all Texas's problems was finances.
3. There was disputes about the new country's boundaries.
4. More immigrants came to Texas, and the troubles did not prevent they from settling.
5. Sam Houston will be one who wanted the United States to annex the republic.
6. After Sam Houston wins in the battle of San Jacinto, Texas had become independent.
7. These two groups, the Cherokee and the Mexicans, brought its concerns into battle.
8. However, the Cherokee and them were arrested by the Texas army.
9. A new president of Texas, Mirabeau Lamar, were elected in 1838.
10. The Cherokee resist his orders, but they were defeated and moved to what is now Oklahoma.

Exercise G Writing Application Write a short description of the state in which you live or one that you have visited. Be sure that the words in your sentences follow the rules of agreement and that your modifiers are used correctly. Then, list the verbs and verb phrases, identifying their tenses. Make a list of pronouns, and identify their case.

Mechanics

Exercise A Using End Marks Copy the following sentences, inserting the appropriate end marks.

1. What was your favorite toy when you were young
2. My little brother has a rattle and a teething ring
3. Hey, I *really* miss my baby toys
4. Do you still sleep with a favorite stuffed animal
5. Maybe they will be collectible items one day

Exercise B Using Commas, Semicolons, and Colons Copy the following sentences, inserting the appropriate commas, semicolons, and colons.

1. Every summer at the beach we make sand castles using sand seashells and water.
2. I play catch with my cousins who visit us for several weeks each year.
3. Last summer I learned a new sport volleyball.
4. When we first started playing the net seemed so high.
5. Then I learned how to hit the ball it was not very difficult.
6. I enjoyed volleyball in fact we played from noon until about 530 p.m.
7. Some people do not play sports at the beach They read listen to music or just lie in the sun.
8. After a full enjoyable day we like to have a barbecue.
9. We cook many of my favorite foods hamburgers hot dogs and corn on the cob.
10. When the sun sets the temperature drops but we still stay outside.

Exercise C Using All the Rules of Punctuation Copy the following sentences, inserting the appropriate end marks, commas, semicolons, colons, quotation marks, underlining, hyphens, and apostrophes.

1. Did you know that there are three types of kites
2. The most well known type is the diamond shaped kite
3. There are also box kites delta kites and bowed kites
4. Paper or cloth is used for the kite however the frame can be wood or metal
5. During the 1800s kites served an important purpose weather forecasting
6. When Benjamin Franklin flew a kite he proved his theory about electricity
7. Alexander Graham Bell the inventor of the telephone also created kites
8. Let's Go Fly a Kite is a great song
9. Remember the line Lets go fly a kite up to the highest height
10. It is from a famous movie Mary Poppins

Exercise D Using All the Rules of Capitalization Copy the following sentences, inserting the appropriate capital letters.

1. people throughout north america, south america, and europe ride bicycles.
2. around 1790, count divrac of france invented a wooden scooter.
3. a german inventor, baron drais, improved upon that model.
4. his version had a steering bar attached to the front wheel.
5. then, a scottish blacksmith, kirkpatrick macmillan, added foot pedals.
6. in 1866, pierre lallement, a french carriage maker, took out the first u.s. patent on a pedal bicycle.
7. mr. j. k. starley of england produced the first commercially successful bicycle.
8. by 1897, more than four million americans were riding bikes.
9. there are many road races like the tour de france.
10. other races, called bmx, are held on bumpy dirt tracks.

Cumulative Review

Answer Key

Exercise A

1. What was your favorite toy when you were young?
2. My little brother has a rattle and a teething ring.
3. Hey, I *really* miss my baby toys!
4. Do you still sleep with a favorite stuffed animal?
5. Maybe they will be collectible items one day.

Exercise B

1. Every summer at the beach, we make sand castles using sand, seashells, and water.
2. I play catch with my cousins, who visit us for several weeks each year.
3. Last summer, I learned a new sport: volleyball.
4. When we first started playing, the net seemed so high.
5. Then I learned how to hit the ball; it wasn't very difficult.
6. I enjoyed volleyball; in fact, we played from noon until about 5:30 p.m.
7. Some people don't play sports at the beach. They read, listen to music, or just lie in the sun.
8. After a full, enjoyable day, we like to have a barbecue.
9. We cook many of my favorite foods: hamburgers, hot dogs, and corn on the cob.
10. When the sun sets, the temperature drops, but we still stay outside.

Exercise C

1. Did you know that there are three types of kites?
2. The most well-known type is the diamond-shaped kite.
3. There are also box kites, delta kites, and bowed kites.
4. Paper or cloth is used for the kite; however, the frame can be wood or metal.
5. During the 1800's, kites served an important purpose: weather forecasting.
6. When Benjamin Franklin flew a kite, he proved his theory about electricity.
7. Alexander Graham Bell, the inventor of the telephone, also created kites.
8. "Let's Go Fly a Kite" is a great song.
9. Remember the line: "Let's go fly a kite up to the highest height"
10. It's from a famous movie: Mary Poppins.

continued

Answers continued

Exercise D

1. People throughout North America, South America, and Europe ride bicycles.
2. Around 1790, Count Divrac of France invented a wooden scooter.
3. A German inventor, Baron Drais, improved upon that model.
4. His version had a steering bar attached to the front wheel.
5. Then, a Scottish blacksmith, Kirkpatrick MacMillan, added foot pedals.
6. In 1866, Pierre Lallement, a French carriage maker, took out the first U.S. patent on a pedal bicycle.
7. Mr. J. K. Starley of England produced the first commercially successful bicycle.
8. By 1897, more than four million Americans were riding bikes.
9. There are many road races like the Tour de France.
10. Other races, called BMX, are held on bumpy dirt tracks.

Exercise E

1. "Is that a new yo-yo?" asked Pam. "I have never seen it before."
2. "No, I have had it awhile," replied Joe. "I found it underneath my bed."
3. "I bet you do not know how yo-yos were invented."
4. Joe answered, "Sure I do. They are toys for children."
5. "No," Pam said. "They originated in the Philippines."
6. "Right. As toys," Joe insisted.
7. "They were weapons *and* toys," Pam corrected.
8. "OK. Well, I know what the word *yo-yo* means."
9. Pam said, "So do I. Tell me and I will see if you are correct."
10. "Well," Joe said, "I am pretty sure it means 'come back.'"
11. "That is right,"Pam said.
12. "It is a toy that has been around for more than 3,000 years," Joe continued.
13. "It was not until the 1920s," Pam added, "that they were developed in the United States."
14. "Who was Donald Duncan?" asked Joe.
15. "He was the man who improved upon the design of the yo-yo and made it a popular toy in the United States."

Exercise F

Answers will vary. Encourage students to exchange papers and check for correct capitalization and punctuation.

Exercise G

Do children still play board games, I wonder? Perhaps TV and video games have begun to replace checkers and chess.

There was a time, you know, when I excitedly hoped for board games as gifts on certain special occasions: birthdays and holidays. One birthday when my twin sister, Lily, and I received our first checkers set, we were thrilled. We couldn't wait to begin playing. I think we played for hours. When Aunt Dotti and Uncle Larry came over with our cousins Joanie and Mark, we all took turns playing. Wow, what a great time we had!

continued

Exercise E **Proofreading Dialogue for Punctuation and Capitalization** Copy the following dialogue, adding the proper punctuation and capitalization.

1. is that a new yo-yo asked pam i have never seen it before
2. no i have had it awhile replied joe i found it underneath my bed
3. i bet you do not know how yo-yos were invented
4. joe answered sure i do they are toys for children
5. no pam said they originated in the philippines
6. right as toys joe insisted
7. they were weapons and toys pam corrected
8. ok well i know what the word yo-yo means
9. pam said so do i tell me and i will see if you are correct
10. well joe said i am pretty sure it means come back
11. that is right pam said
12. it is a toy that has been around for more than 3,000 years joe continued
13. it was not until the 1920s pam added that they were developed in the united states
14. who was donald duncan asked joe
15. he was the man who improved upon the design of the yo-yo and made it a popular toy in the united states

Exercise F **Writing Sentences With Correct Punctuation and Capitalization** Write five sentences following the instructions given below. Be sure to punctuate and capitalize correctly.

1. Write a sentence about your favorite board game or video game.
2. Describe what you like about it.
3. Write a sentence about a favorite outdoor game.
4. Tell what time of year you play it, and name some of the friends who join in.
5. Write an exclamatory sentence about a great play in a game.

Exercise G **Proofreading Paragraphs for Punctuation and Capitalization** Proofread the following paragraphs, copying them into your notebook and adding punctuation and capitalization as needed.

Do children still play board games I wonder. perhaps tv and video games have begun to replace checkers and chess.

There was a time you know when i excitedly hoped for board games as gifts on certain special occasions birthdays and holidays. one birthday when my twin sister, lily, and i received our first checkers set we were thrilled we could not wait to begin playing i think we played for hours. when aunt dotti and uncle larry came over with our cousins joanie and mark we all took turns playing. wow what a great time we had.

Exercise H **Writing Application** Write a brief dialogue between you and a friend about your favorite toy from childhood. Be sure to include proper punctuation, capitalization, and indentation.

Answers continued

Exercise H

Answers will vary. Briefly review the rules for using commas and semicolons on p. 732 and for proper capitalization of names on p. 776.

You use communication every day in writing, speaking, listening, and viewing. Having strong communication skills will benefit you both in and out of school. Many of the assignments accompanying the literature in this textbook involve speaking, listening, and viewing. This handbook identifies some of the terminology related to the oral and visual communication you experience every day and the assignments you may do in conjunction with the literature in this book.

Communication

You use speaking and listening skills everyday. When you talk with your friends, teachers, or parents, or when you interact with store clerks, you are communicating orally. In addition to everyday conversation, oral communication includes class discussions, speeches, interviews, presentations, debates, and performances. When you communicate, you usually use more than your voice to get your message across. For example, you use one set of skills in face-to-face communication and another set of skills in a telephone conversation.

The following terms will give you a better understanding of the many elements that are part of communication:

BODY LANGUAGE refers to the use of facial expressions, eye contact, gestures, posture, and movement to communicate a feeling or an idea.

CONNOTATION is the set of associations a word calls to mind. The connotations of the words you choose influence the message you send. For example, most people respond more favorably to being described as "slim" rather than as "skinny." The connotation of *slim* is more appealing than that of *skinny.*

EYE CONTACT is direct visual contact with another person's eyes.

FEEDBACK is the set of verbal and nonverbal reactions that indicate to a speaker that a message has been received and understood.

GESTURES are the movements made with arms, hands, face, and fingers to communicate.

LISTENING is understanding and interpreting sound in a meaningful way. You listen differently for different purposes.

Listening for key information: For example, when a teacher gives an assignment, or when someone gives you directions to a place, you listen for key information.

Listening for main points: In a classroom exchange of ideas or information, or while watching a television documentary, you listen for main points.

Listening critically: When you evaluate a performance, song, or a persuasive or political speech, you listen critically, questioning and judging the speaker's message.

MEDIUM is the material or technique used to present a visual image. Common media include paint, clay, and film.

NONVERBAL COMMUNICATION is communication without the use of words. People communicate nonverbally through gestures, facial expressions, posture, and body movements. Sign language is an entire language based on nonverbal communication.

PROJECTION is speaking in such a way that the voice carries clearly to an audience. It's important to project your voice when speaking in a large space like a classroom or an auditorium.

VIEWING is observing, understanding, analyzing, and evaluating information presented through visual means. You might use the following questions to help you interpret what you view:

- What subject is presented?
- What is communicated about the subject?
- Which parts are factual? Which are opinion?
- What mood, attitude, or opinion is conveyed?
- What is your emotional response?

VOCAL DELIVERY is the way in which you present a message. Your vocal delivery involves all of the following elements:

Volume: the loudness or quietness of your voice

Pitch: the high or low quality of your voice

Rate: the speed at which you speak; also called pace

Stress: the amount of emphasis placed on different syllables in a word or on different words in a sentence

All of these elements individually, and the way in which they are combined, contribute to the meaning of a spoken message.

Speaking, Listening, and Viewing Situations

Here are some of the many types of situations in which you apply speaking, listening, and viewing skills:

AUDIENCE Your audience in any situation refers to the person or people to whom you direct your message. An audience can be a group of people observing a performance or just one person. When preparing for any speaking situation, it's useful to analyze your audience, so that you can tailor your message to them.

CHARTS AND GRAPHS are visual representations of statistical information. For example, a pie chart might indicate how the average dollar is spent by government, and a bar graph might compare populations in cities over time.

DEBATE A debate is a formal public-speaking situation in which participants prepare and present arguments on opposing sides of a question, stated as a **proposition.**

The two sides in a debate are the *affirmative* (pro) and the *negative* (con). The affirmative side argues in favor of the proposition, while the negative side argues against it. Each side has an opportunity for *rebuttal,* in which they may challenge or question the other side's argument.

DOCUMENTARIES are nonfiction films that analyze news events or other focused subjects. You can watch a documentary for the information on its subject.

GRAPHIC ORGANIZERS summarize and present information in ways that can help you understand the information. Graphic organizers include charts, outlines, webs, maps, lists, and diagrams. For example, a graphic organizer for a history chapter might be an outline. A Venn diagram is intersecting circles that display information showing how concepts are alike and different.

GROUP DISCUSSION results when three or more people meet to solve a common problem, arrive at a decision, or answer a question of mutual interest. Group discussion is one of the most widely used forms of interpersonal communication in modern society.

INTERVIEW An interview is a form of interaction in which one person, the interviewer, asks questions of another person, the interviewee. Interviews may take place for many purposes: to obtain information, to discover a person's suitability for a job or a college, or to inform the public of a notable person's opinions.

MAPS are visual representations of Earth's surface. Maps may show political boundaries and physical features and provide information on a variety of other topics. A map's title and its key identify the content of the map.

ORAL INTERPRETATION is the reading or speaking of a work of literature aloud for an audience. Oral interpretation involves giving expression to the ideas, meaning, or even the structure of a work of literature. The speaker interprets the work through his or her vocal delivery. **Storytelling,** in which a speaker reads or tells a story expressively, is a form of oral interpretation.

PANEL DISCUSSION is a group discussion on a topic of interest common to all members of a panel and to a listening audience. A panel is usually composed of four to six experts on a particular topic who are brought together to share information and opinions.

PANTOMIME is a form of nonverbal communication in which an idea or a story is communicated completely through the use of gesture, body language, and facial expressions, without any words at all.

POLITICAL CARTOONS are drawings that comment on important political or social issues. Often, these cartoons use humor to convey a message about their subject. Viewers use their own knowledge of events to evaluate the cartoonist's opinion.

READERS THEATRE is a dramatic reading of a work of literature in which participants take parts from a story or play and read them aloud in expressive voices. Unlike a play, however, sets and costumes are not part of the performance, and the participants remain seated as they deliver their lines.

ROLE PLAY To role-play is to take the role of a person or character and act out a given situation, speaking, acting, and responding in the manner of the character.

SPEECH A speech is a talk or address given to an audience. A speech may be **impromptu**—delivered on the spur of the moment with no preparation—or formally prepared and delivered for a specific purpose or occasion.

- ***Purposes:*** The most common purposes of speeches are to persuade, to entertain, to explain, and to inform.
- ***Occasions:*** Different occasions call for different types of speeches. Speeches given on these occasions could be persuasive, entertaining, or informative, as appropriate.

VISUAL REPRESENTATION refers to informative texts, such as newspapers and advertisements, and entertaining texts, such as magazines. Visual representations use elements of design—such as texture and color, shapes, drawings, and photographs—to convey the meaning, message, or theme.

Index of Authors and Titles

Page numbers in *italics* refer to biographical information.

Index of Skills

LITERARY ANALYSIS

READING STRATEGIES

GRAMMAR, USAGE, AND MECHANICS

VOCABULARY

CRITICAL THINKING AND VIEWING

WRITING

Writing Applications

Writing Strategies

LISTENING AND SPEAKING

RESEARCH AND TECHNOLOGY

Index of Features

HOW TO READ LITERATURE

ACKNOWLEDGMENTS (continued)

Cleveland.com "An Astronaut's Answers" by John Glenn, from *Snappy,* published online on Cleveland Live. Copyright © 1998 by Cleveland Live. Reprint permission given by Cleveland.com, formerly Cleveland Live. All rights reserved.

Ruth Cohen Literary Agency, Inc. "The All-American Slurp," by Lensey Namioka, copyright © 1987, from *Visions,* ed. by Donald R. Gallo. Reprinted by permission of Lensey Namioka. All rights reserved by the author.

Don Congdon Associates, Inc. "The Sound of Summer Running" by Ray Bradbury. Published in *The Saturday Evening Post,* 2/18/56. Copyright © 1956 by the Curtis Publishing Co., renewed 1984 by Ray Bradbury. "Hard As Nails" from *The Good Times* by Russell Baker. Copyright © 1989 by Russell Baker. Used by permission.

Curtis Brown, Ltd. From "Adventures of Isabel" by Ogden Nash. Copyright © 1951 by Ogden Nash. First appeared in *Parents Keep Out,* published by Little, Brown & Co. Reprinted by permission.

Dell Publishing, a division of Random House, Inc., and Sheldon Fogelman Agency, Inc. "The Geese" by Richard Peck, from *Sounds and Silences: Poetry for Now* by Richard Peck, Editor, copyright © 1970, 1990 by Richard Peck. Used by permission.

Dell Publishing, a division of Random House, Inc., and Walter Dean Myers "Jeremiah's Song" by Walter Dean Myers, copyright © 1987 by Donald R. Gallo from *Visions* by Donald R. Gallo, Editor.

Doubleday, a division of Random House, Inc. "The Fun They Had" from *Earth Is Room Enough* by Isaac Asimov, copyright © 1957 by Isaac Asimov. Used by permission of Doubleday, a division of Random House, Inc.

Paul Eriksson "My Papa Mark Twain" by Susy Clemens from *Small Voices* by Josef and Dorothy Berger. © Copyright 1966 by Josef and Dorothy Berger. Reproduced by permission of Paul S. Eriksson, Publisher.

Everyman Publishers PLC From "Funeral Oration of Pericles" by Thucydides, from *The History of the Peloponnesian War.* New Introduction, copyright © 1950, by E. P. Dutton & Co., Inc. The new American edition published 1950 by E. P. Dutton & Co., Inc. All rights reserved. Reprinted by permission of Everyman Publishers PLC, Glouster Mansions, 140A Shaftesbury Avenue, London WC2H 8HD.

The Field Museum "Life and Times of Sue," from *www.fieldmuseum.org.* Copyright © 1999 by The Field Museum. Used by permission.

Fodors Travel Publications, a division of Random House, Inc. "Snorkeling Tips" from *Compass American Guides: Underwater Wonders of the National Parks* by Daniel J. Lenihan and John D. Brooks, Copyright © 1998 by Fodors LLC. Used by permission of Fodors Travel Publications, a division of Random House, Inc.

Samuel French, Inc. "The Phantom Tollbooth" by Susan Nanus from *The Phantom Tollbooth: A Children's Play in Two Acts* by Susan Nanus and Norton Juster. Copyright © 1977 by Susan Nanus and Norton Juster. Reprinted by permission of Samuel French, Inc. All rights reserved. *Caution*: Professionals and amateurs are hereby warned that "The Phantom Tollbooth," being fully protected under the copyright laws of the United States of America, the British Commonwealth countries, including Canada, and the other countries of the Copyright Union, is subject to royalty. All rights, including professional, amateur, motion picture, recitation, lecturing, public reading, radio, television and cable broadcasting, and the rights of translation into foreign languages, are strictly reserved. In its present form the play is dedicated to the reading public only. The amateur live performance rights are controlled exclusively by Samuel French, Inc. Any inquiry regarding the availability of performance rights, or the purchase of individual copies of the authorized acting edition, must be directed to Samuel French, Inc., 45 West 25th Street, NY, NY 10010 with other locations in Hollywood and Toronto, Canada.

Jean Grasso Fitzpatrick c/o Sandford J. Greenberger Associates "The Ant and the Dove" by Leo Tolstoy from *Fables and Folktales Adapted from Tolstoy,* translation by Jean Grasso Fitzpatrick. Published in 1986. Copyright © 1985 by Barrons. Used by permission.

Greenwillow Books, an imprint of HarperCollins Publishers, Inc. "Ankylosaurus" from *Tyrannosaurus Was a Beast* by Jack Prelutsky. Text copyright © 1988 by Jack Prelutsky. Used by permission.

Grolier Incorporated "How the Internet Works" from *The Internet* by Kerry Cochrane. Copyright © 1995 by Kerry Cochrane. All rights reserved. Used by permission.

Harcourt, Inc. "The Fairies' Lullaby" from *A Midsummer Night's Dream* from *Shakespeare: Major Plays and the Sonnets,* by G. B. Harrison. Published by Harcourt, Inc.

HarperCollins Publishers, Inc. "Zlateh the Goat" by Isaac Bashevis Singer from *Zlateh the Goat and Other Stories.* Text copyright © 1966 by Isaac Bashevis Singer, copyright renewed 1994 by Alma Singer. Illustrations copyright © 1966 by Maurice Sendak, copyright renewed by Maurice Sendak. Printed with permission from HarperCollins Publishers. "Aaron's Gift" from *The Witch of Fourth Street and Other Stories* by Myron Levoy. Text copyright © 1972 by Myron Levoy. "Jimmy Jet and His TV Set" from *Where the Sidewalk Ends* by Shel Silverstein. Copyright © 1974 by Evil Eye Music, Inc. "Breaker's Bridge" from *The Rainbow People* by Laurence Yep. Text copyright © 1989 by Laurence Yep. "Señor Coyote and the Tricked Trickster" from *Trickster Tales* by I. G. Edmonds. Copyright © 1966 by I. G. Edmonds. "Limerick" (Originally titled "A flea and a fly in a flue") by Anonymous, from *Laughable Limericks.* Copyright © by Sara and John E. Brewton.

HarperCollins Publishers, Inc., and Curtis Brown Ltd. From *The Wounded Wolf* by Jean Craighead George. Text copyright © 1978 by Jean Craighead George. Reprinted by permission of HarperCollins Publishers, Inc. From *The Pigman and Me* (pp. 97–100) by Paul Zindel. Copyright © 1991 by Paul Zindel. "Alone in the Nets" from *Sports Pages* by Arnold Adoff. Text copyright © 1986 by Arnold Adoff.

Harper's Magazine "Preserving the Great American Symbol" (originally titled "Desecrating America") by Richard Durbin from *Harper's Magazine,* October 1989, p. 32. Copyright © 1989 by Harper's Magazine. All rights reserved. Used by permission.

William Harwood "Space Shuttle *Challenger*" (Challenger Remembered) by William Harwood from AOL News, online service (Vienna, VA: American Online, 1996). Reprinted by permission of the author.

Harvard University Press "Fame Is a Bee" (#1763) is reprinted by permission of the publishers and the Trustees of Amherst College from *The Poems of Emily Dickinson,* Thomas H. Johnson, editor, Cambridge, Mass.: The Belknap Press of Harvard University Press, Copyright © 1951, 1955, 1979 by the President and Fellows of Harvard College. Used by permission.

Heinemann Educational Publishers "Why the Tortoise's Shell Is Not Smooth" from *Things Fall Apart* by Chinua Achebe. Copyright © 1959 by Chinua Achebe. Reprinted by permission of Heinemann Educational Publishers.

Henry Holt and Company, Inc. "Dust of Snow" by Robert Frost from *The Poetry of Robert Frost* edited by Edward Connery Lathem. Copyright 1923, © 1969 by Henry Holt & Co., copyright © 1951 by Robert Frost. Reprinted by permission of Henry Holt and Company, LLC. From *The Walrus and the Carpenter,* by Lewis Carroll (108 lines), Illustrations by Jane Breskin Zalben, with annotations by Tweedledee and Tweedledum. Published by Henry Holt and Company.

Henry Holt and Company, Inc., and Brandt and Hochman Literary Agents, Inc. "The Stone" from *The Foundling and Other Stories of Prydain* by Lloyd Alexander, © 1973 by Lloyd Alexander. Used by permission.

Houghton Mifflin Company "Arachne," from *Greek Myths.* Copyright © 1949 by Olivia E. Coolidge; copyright renewed © 1977 by Olivia E. Coolidge. Reprinted by permission of Houghton Mifflin Company. All rights reserved.

International Creative Management, Inc. *Grandpa and the Statue* by Arthur Miller. Copyright © 1945 by Arthur Miller. Reprinted by permission.

IpswichBank Corp. "Ipswich Bank Savings Account Application" from *www.ipswichbank.com* by IpswichBank Corp., Ipswich, MA. Ipswich Bank is a publicly traded company symbol IPSQ on NASDAQ. Used by permission.

Dr. Francisco Jiménez "The Circuit" by Francisco Jiménez from *America Street: A Multicultural Anthology of Stories.* Copyright © 1993 by Anne Mazer. Reprinted with permission of the author Francisco Jiménez.

Alfred A. Knopf, a division of Random House, Inc. "Dream Dust" from *The Collected Poems of Langston Hughes* by Langston Hughes. Copyright © 1994 by The Estate of Langston Hughes. "April Rain Song" from *The Collected Poems of Langston Hughes* by Langston Hughes. Copyright © 1994 by The Estate of Langston Hughes. Used by permission of Alfred A. Knopf, a division of Random House, Inc.

Alfred A. Knopf Children's Books, a division of Random House, Inc. From "Stargirl" by Jerry Spinelli, copyright © 2000 by Jerry Spinelli. "Jackie Robinson: Justice at Last" from *25 Great Moments* by Geoffrey C. Ward and Ken Burns with Jim O'Connor, copyright © 1994 by Baseball Licensing International, Inc. "He Lion, Bruh Bear, and Bruh Rabbit" from *The People Could Fly: American Black Folktales* by Virginia Hamilton, and Leo and Diane Dillon. Copyright © 1985 by Virginia Hamilton. From "Jerry Spinelli" from *The Borzoi Young Reader,* 1998, copyright © 1998 by Alfred A. Knopf, a division of Random House, Inc. Used by permission of Alfred A. Knopf Children's Books, a division of Random House, Inc.

George Laycock "The Loch Ness Monster" from *Mysteries, Monsters and Untold Secrets* by George Laycock. Copyright © 1978 by George Laycock. All rights reserved. Used by permission.

The Lazear Literary Agency "Turkeys" from *Mama Makes Up Her Mind* (Addison-Wesley, 1993), reprinted by permission of the author.

Lescher & Lescher Ltd. "The Southpaw" by Judith Viorst. Copyright © 1974 by Judith Viorst. From *Free to Be...You and Me.* This usage granted by permission of Lescher & Lescher, Ltd. All rights reserved.

Ellen Levine Literary Agency, Inc. "How to Write A Letter" by Garrison Keillor. Copyright © 1987 by International Paper Company. From *We Are Still Married,* published by Viking Penguin Inc. Reprinted by permission International Paper Company. (Originally titled "How to Write a Personal Letter")

Liveright Publishing Corporation, an imprint of W. W. Norton & Company "who knows if the moon's," copyright 1923, 1925, 1951, 1953, © 1991 by the Trustees for the E. E. Cummings Trust. Copyright © 1976 by George James Firmage, from *Complete Poems: 1904–1962* by E. E. Cummings, edited by George J. Firmage. Used by permission of Liveright Publishing Corporation.

Los Angeles Times Syndicate "TV's Top Dogs" by Deborah Starr Seibel, published in *TV Guide,* June 18, 1994. Used by permission of the Los Angeles Times Syndicate.

Madison Press Books and Penguin Canada Text © 1988 Odyssey Corporation from *Exploring the* Titanic by Robert D. Ballard, a Scholastic Inc./Madison Press Book. Used by permission.

McIntosh and Otis, Inc. "Overdoing It" from *Shadows and Light: Nine Stories* by Anton Chekhov, edited and translated by Miriam Morton, originally published by Doubleday & Company. Reprinted with the permission of McIntosh and Otis, Inc.

William Morrow & Company, Inc., a division of HarperCollins Publishers, Inc. "The World Is Not a Pleasant Place to Be" from *My House* by Nikki Giovanni. Copyright © 1972 by Nikki Giovanni. Reprinted by permission of William Morrow, a division of HarperCollins Publishers, Inc.

National Geographic World From "Race to the End of the Earth" by William G. Scheller from *National Geographic World,* Number 294, February 2000. Copyright © 2000 by National Geographic Society. "Sharks" by Susan McGrath from *National Geographic World,* Number 222, February 1994. Copyright © 1994 by National Geographic Society. All rights reserved. "National Geographic Website" (featuring "High Tech Windows to the Animal Kingdom" by Robinson Shaw) from *www.nationalgeographic.com.* "Gentle Giants in Trouble" (originally titled "Gentle Giants in Trouble: Manatees") by Ross Bankson, from *National Geographic World,* Number 199, March 1992. Used by permission.

National Wildlife Federation From "Can Oiled Seabirds Be Rescued, or Are We Just Fooling Ourselves?" by Sharon Levy from *National Wildlife,* February/March 1999. Copyright © 1999 by National Wildlife Federation. From "California's Much-Maligned Salton Sea Is a Desert Oasis for Wildlife" by Joby Warrick, from *National Wildlife,* August/September 2000. Copyright © 2000 by National Wildlife Federation. Used by permission.

New Directions Publishing Corp. "Wind and water and stone" by Octavio Paz, translation by Mark Strand, from *Collected Poems 1957–1987.* Copyright © 1979 by The New Yorker Magazine. Reprinted by permission of New Directions Publishing.

Orchard Books, an imprint of Scholastic, Inc. "Becky and the Wheels-and-Brake Boys" from *A Thief in the Village and Other Stories* by James Berry. Published by Orchard Books, an imprint of Scholastic, Inc. Copyright © 1987 by James Berry. Reprinted by permission.

Richard Orlikoff for The Estate of Gwendolyn Brooks "Cynthia in the Snow" from *Bronzeville Boys and Girls* by Gwendolyn Brooks. Copyright © 1956 by Gwendolyn Brooks Blakely.

Pasadena Youth Roller Hockey League "Pasadena Youth Roller Hockey Registration Form" from the Pasadena Youth Roller Hockey League, Pasadena, TX.

Penguin Putnam, Inc. "La leña buena" from *Places Left Unfinished at the Time of Creation* by John Phillip Santos. Copyright © John Phillip Santos, 1999. Used by permission.

Penguin Putnam, Inc. and Curtis Brown Ltd. "Greyling" from *Greyling: A Picture Story from the Islands* by Jane Yolen. Text copyright © 1968 by Jane Yolen. Used by permission. All rights reserved.

People Weekly "Throw and Tell" from *People Weekly,* October 11, 1999, VOLUME 52. Copyright © 1999 Time, Inc. Used by permission.

Philomel Books From *Greyling* by Jane Yolen, published by Philomel Books. Text copyright © 1968 and 1991, renewed 1996 by Jane Yolen. Used by permission of Philomel Books, an imprint of Penguin Putnam Books for Young Readers, a division of Penguin Putnam, Inc.

Charlotte Pomerantz c/o Writers House LLC "Door Number Four" from *If I Had a Paka* by Charlotte Pomerantz. Copyright © 1982 by Charlotte Pomerantz. Reprinted by arrangement with the author, c/o Writers House as agent to the author.

Prentice-Hall, Inc., a division of Pearson Education. "Restoring the Circle" by Joseph Bruchac, from *The Writer's Solution Sourcebook,* Bronze, copyright © 1996 by Prentice Hall, Inc. Used by permission of the publisher.

PRIMEDIA Special Interest Publications (History Group) "As Close As We Can Get" by Carl Zebrowski. This article is reprinted from the Volume XXXVIII, Number 5 issue of *Civil War Times Illustrated* with the permission of *Primedia* Special Interest Publications (History Group), copyright Civil War Times Illustrated. Used by permission.

Random House, Inc. "Life Doesn't Frighten Me," copyright © 1978 by Maya Angelou, from *And Still I Rise* by Maya Angelou. Used by permission of Random House, Inc.

Random House Children's Books, a division of Random House, Inc. "Lob's Girl," from *A Whisper in the Night* by Joan Aiken, copyright © 1984 by Joan Aiken. "Bud, Not Buddy" from *Bud, Not Buddy* by Christopher Paul Curtis, copyright © 1999 by Christopher Paul Curtis. Used by permission of Random House Children's Books, a division of Random House, Inc.

The Reader's Digest Association Limited, London "More Than a Pinch" (originally titled "More Than A Pinch of Salt") from *Did You Know?* Copyright © 1990 by The Reader's Digest Association Limited. Used by permission of The Reader's Digest Association Limited.

Marian Reiner, Literary Agent "Haiku" by Bashō from *Cricket Songs: Japanese Haiku*, translated by Harry Behn, © 1964 by Harry Behn; © Renewed 1992 Prescott Behn, Pamela Behn Adam and Peter Behn. Reprinted by permission of Marian Reiner. All rights reserved.

Marian Reiner, Literary Agent for Eve Merriam "Simile: Willow and Ginkgo" by Eve Merriam, from *A Sky Full of Poems*. Copyright © 1964, 1970, 1973 by Eve Merriam; © renewed 1992 Eve Merriam. Reprinted by permission of Marian Reiner, Literary Agent for the author. All rights reserved.

Marian Reiner, Literary Agent for Lillian Morrison "The Sidewalk Racer or On the Skateboard" by Lillian Morrison, from *The Sidewalk Racer and Other Poems of Sports and Motion* by Lillian Morrison. Copyright © 1968, 1977 by Lillian Morrison. Reprinted by permission of Marian Reiner for the author.

Marian Reiner, Literary Agent for The Jesse Stuart Foundation "Old Ben" from *Dawn of Remembered Spring* by Jesse Stuart. Copyright © 1955, 1972 Jesse Stuart. © Renewed 1983 Jesse Stuart Foundation. Reprinted by permission of Marian Reiner for The Jesse Stuart Foundation.

Scholastic, Inc. "Why Monkeys Live in Trees" from *How Many Spots Does a Leopard Have? and Other Tales* by Julius Lester. Copyright © 1989 by Julius Lester. "The Shutout" from *Black Diamond: The Story of the Negro Baseball Leagues* by Patricia C. McKissack and Fredrick McKissack, Jr. Copyright © 1994 by Patricia C. McKissack and Fredrick McKissack, Jr. Reproduced by permission of Scholastic Inc. From *Exploring the* Titanic by Robert D. Ballard. Copyright © 1988 by Ballard & Family; Copyright © 1988 by The Madison Press Ltd.

Scholastic Press, a division of Scholastic, Inc. From *Esperanza Rising* by Pam Muñoz Ryan. Published by Scholastic Press, a division of Scholastic, Inc. Copyright © 2000 by Pam Muñoz Ryan. Reprinted by permission.

Scovil Chichak Galen Literary Agency, Inc. "Feathered Friend" from *The Other Side of the Sky* by Arthur C. Clarke. Copyright © 1958 by Arthur C. Clarke. Used by permission of the author and the author's agents, Scovil Chichak Galen Literary Agency, Inc.

Scribner, a division of Simon & Schuster, Inc., and Harold Ober Associates, Inc. "Letter to Scottie" reprinted with permission of Scribner, a division of Simon & Schuster, Inc., and Harold Ober Associates, Inc., from F. Scott Fitzgerald: *A Life in Letters*, edited by Matthew J. Bruccoli. Copyright © 1994 by The Trustees Under Agreement Dated July 3, 1975, Created by Frances Scott Fitzgerald Smith.

Simon & Schuster, Inc. "February Twilight" from *The Collected Poems of Sara Teasdale*. Copyright © 1926 by Macmillan Publishing Company, renewed 1954 by Mamie T. Wheless. Used by permission.

Simon & Schuster Books for Young Readers, an imprint of Simon & Schuster Children's Publishing Division "Stray" from *Every Living Thing* by Cynthia Rylant. Copyright © 1985 by Cynthia Rylant. "Parade" from *Branches Green* by Rachel Field. Copyright © 1934 Macmillan Publishing Company; copyright renewed © 1962 by Arthur S. Pederson. Reprinted with the permission of Simon & Schuster Books for Young Readers, an imprint of Simon & Schuster Children's Publishing Division.

Virginia Driving Hawk Sneve "Thunder Butte" by Virginia Driving Hawk Sneve, from *When Thunders Spoke*. Copyright © 1974 by Virginia Driving Hawk Sneve. Reprinted by permission of the author.

St. Paul Pioneer Press "Summer Hats" by Amy Lindgren from *Saint Paul Pioneer*, Sunday 6/13/99. St. Paul, Minn.: Northwest Publications, Inc., 1990. Used by permission.

Rosemary A. Thurber and the Barbara Hogenson Agency "The Tiger Who Would Be King" by James Thurber, from *Further Fables for Our Time*, published by Simon & Schuster. Copyright © 1956 by James Thurber. Copyright © 1984 by Helen Thurber and Rosemary A. Thurber. Used by permission of Rosemary Thurber and the Barbara Hogenson Agency.

Edna St. Vincent Millay Society c/o Elizabeth Barnett "The Spring and the Fall" by Edna St. Vincent Millay. From *Collected Poems*, HarperCollins. Copyright 1923, 1951 by Edna St. Vincent Millay and Norma Millay Ellis. All rights reserved. Reprinted by permission of Elizabeth Barnett, literary executor.

Third Woman Press and Susan Bergholz Literary Services "Abuelito Who" from *My Wicked Wicked Ways* by Sandra Cisneros. Copyright © 1987 by Sandra Cisneros, published by Third Woman Press and in hardcover by Alfred A. Knopf. Used by permission of Susan Bergholz Literary Services, New York, and Third Woman Press. All rights reserved.

Dr. My-Van Tran "A Crippled Boy" from *Folk Tales from Indochina* by My-Van Tran. First published in 1987. Copyright © Vietnamese Language and Culture Publications and My-Van Tran. Used by permission.

University Press of New England and Gary Soto Gary Soto, "The Drive-In Movies," from *A Summer Life* © 1990 by University Press of New England. Used by permission.

Usborne Publishing Ltd. "Shakespeare's London" from *The World of Shakespeare* (originally titled "London Life") by Anna Claybourne and Rebecca Treays. Copyright © Usborne Publishing Ltd 1996. Used by permission.

Villa Park Public Library "Villa Park Public Library Card Application" from the Villa Park Public Library, 305 South Ardmore Avenue, Villa Park, Illinois 60181. Used by permission.

K. Wayne Wincey "Twist and Shout" by K. Wayne Wincey, from *Boys Life*, August 1999. By permission of K. Wayne Wincey and *Boys Life*, August 1999, published by the Boy Scouts of America.

The Wylie Agency, Inc. "How to Write a Poem About the Sky" from *Storyteller* by Leslie Marmon Silko. Copyright © 1981 by Leslie Marmon Silko, reprinted by permission of the Wylie Agency, Inc.

Note: Every effort has been made to locate the copyright owner of material reprinted in this book. Omissions brought to our attention will be corrected in subsequent printings.

Art Credits

Cover and Title Page *The Haystacks*, oil on canvas, Vincent van Gogh/ Nationalmuseum, Stockholm, Sweden/Bridgeman Art Library, London/New York **vii** (b.) © Dorling Kindersley/Tim Ridley **vii** (t.) David Macias/Photo Researchers, Inc. **viii** M.P. Kahl/Photo Researchers, Inc. **ix** AP/Wide World Photos **x** *Ezra Davenport*, 1929, Clarence Holbrook Carter, Oil on canvas, Courtesy of the artist **xi** (t.) *The Immortal*, 1990, Chi-Fong Lei, Courtesy of the artist; **xi** (b.) Frans Lanting/Photo Researchers, Inc. **xii** (t.) ©Stone **xii** (b.) Animals Animals/©James Watt **xiii** AP/Wide World Photos **xiv** Grace Davies/Omni-Photo Communications, Inc. **xv** © Mike & Elvan Habicht/Animals Animals **xvi** (t.) Steve Satushek/The Image Bank **xvi** (m.) Bettmann/ CORBIS **xvi–xvii** (b.) ©Richard Hamilton Smith/CORBIS **xvii** (t.) Courtesy of the Library of Congress **xviii–xix** Corel Professional Photos CD-ROM™ **xx** Philip van den Berg/HPH Photography **xxi** David Stover, Stock South/PictureQuest **1** *In the Garden*, Joseph Raphael, The Redfern Gallery **2** (t.) The Granger Collection, New York **2** (b.), **4, 6** Silverstre Machado/Tony Stone Images **9** *New Shoes for H*, 1973–1974, Don Eddy, The Cleveland Museum of Art, Acrylic on canvas, 111.7 x 121.9 cm ©The Cleveland Museum of Art, 1998, Purchase with a grant from the National Endowment for the Arts and matched by gifts from members of The Cleveland Society for Contemporary Art, 1974.53 **12** Thomas Victor **16, 18–19** ©Zig Leszczynski/Animals Animals **21** ©Margot Conte/Animals Animals **26** Everett Collection **27** ©1996 Paramount Pictures. All Rights Reserved. **28** University of Washington Press, Photo by Gordon Robotham **30** (t.) David Macias/Photo Researchers, Inc. **30** (b.) Dimitri Kessel/Life Magazine; **31** Courtesy of the Library of Congress **32** (b.) Rollie McKenna **32** (t.) University of Washington Press, Photo by Gordon Robotham **36** Frank Orel/Tony Stone Images **38** Pictor International/PictureQuest **40** Corel Professional Photos CD-ROM™ **43** *Harmonizing*, 1979, Robert Gwathmey, Courtesy Terry Dintenfass Gallery, © Estate of Robert Gwathmey/Licensed by VAGA, New York, NY **44** *Springtime Rain*, 1975, Ogden M. Pleissner, Ogden M. Pleissner Estate Marion G. Pleissner Trust, Bankers Trust Company. Photo by Grace Davies/Omni-Photo Communications, Inc. **46** John Craig Photo **50** Special Collections Division, University of Washington Libraries, E.A. Hegg, 181 **52** The Granger Collection, New York **53** ©Colin Hawkins /Stone **56** *After Dinner Music*, 1988, Scott Kennedy, © 1988, Greenwich Workshop Inc. Courtesy of the Greenwich Workshop Inc. **58** Digital Imagery ©Copyright 2001 PhotoDisc, Inc. **60** CORBIS-Bettmann **64** Marc Solomon/The Image Bank **66** *My Brother*, 1942, Guayasamin (Oswaldo Guayasamin Calero), Oil on wood, 15 7/8 x 12 3/4", Collection, The Museum of Modern Art, New York, Inter-American Fund **69** Walter Choroszewski/Stock Connection/PictureQuest **71** Charles G. Barry **72** ©Anthony Potter Collections/Archive Photos **75** ©Levick/Archive Photos **77** AP/Wide World Photos **78** CORBIS-Bettmann **83** ©Mary Kay Denny/PhotoEdit **87** AP/Wide World Photos **90** David Young-Wolff/PhotoEdit **96–97** Gogh, Vincent van (1853– 1890). *First Steps, after Millet.* Oil on canvas, 72.4 x 91.2 cm. The Metropolitan Museum of Art, Gift of George N. and Helen M. Richard. (64.165.2) **98** (b.) M.P. Kahl/Photo Researchers, Inc. **98** (m.) *The Calm After the Storm*, Edward Moran, Private Collection/SuperStock **98** (t.) © William J. Jahoda/Photo Researchers, Inc. **100** *The Calm After the Storm*, Edward Moran, Private Collection/SuperStock **102** Richard Hutchings/Photo Researchers, Inc. **104** ©Jim Cummings/FPG International Corp. **105** Minnesota Public Radio, photo by Carmen Quesada **106** (b.) Thomas Victor **106** (t.) Silver Burdett Ginn **110** ©The Stock Market/Marco Cristofori **112** Jane Burton/Bruce Coleman, Inc. **114** *Pigeons*, John Sloan, Oil on canvas, 26 x 32", The Hayden Collection, Courtesy, Museum of Fine Arts, Boston, Massachusetts **116** Steve Raymer/CORBIS **120** Photofest **122** American Foundation for the Blind **126** ©The Stock Market/Frank P. Rossotto **128, 130, 132** from "Zlateh the Goat and Other Stories" by Isaac Bashevis Singer, illustrations by Maurice Sendak © 1966, HarperCollins Publishers, Inc. **134** Thomas Victor **138** Michelle Bridwell/PhotoEdit **140** (t.) *One Child Between Doors* (Seorang Anak di Antara Pintu Ruang), 1984, Dede Eri Supria, Courtesy of Joseph Fischer **140** (b.) Hearst Books, Photo by Daniel Pomerantz. **141** Hulton Getty Images/Tony Stone Images **142** (b.) Courtesy of the author **142** (t.) NASA **146** Jacket Illustration copyright ©2000 by Alfred A. Knopf **152** © William J. Jahoda/Photo Researchers, Inc. **154** M.P. Kahl/Photo Researchers, Inc. **157** Corel Professional Photos CD-ROM™ **158** Jesse Stuart Foundation **159** © William J. Jahoda/Photo Researchers, Inc. **161** NASA **162** CORBIS-Bettmann **167, 168** *The Banjo Lesson*, 1893, Henry Ossawa Tanner, Hampton University Museum, Hampton, Virginia **170** David Young-Wolff/PhotoEdit **176– 177** ©Paul Schulenburg/Stock Illustration Source, Inc. **178** (t.) ©Tom McHugh/Photo Researchers, Inc. **178** (b.) Lou Jones/The Image Bank **182** Mary Kate Denny/PhotoEdit **185** *Elephant Tree*, ©1996 Robert Vickrey/ Licensed by VAGA, New York NY **188** Harper Collins **192, 194–195** Corel Professional Photos CD-ROM™ **196** ©The Stock Market/Bob Shaw **200** ©British Museum **203** Corel Professional Photos CD-ROM™ **204** Courtesy of the author **208** ©Tom McHugh/Photo Researchers, Inc. **210** Renne Lynn/Tony Stone Images **214** ©Tom McHugh/Photo Researchers, Inc. **216** Corel Professional Photos CD-ROM™ **218** By Courtesy of the National Portrait Gallery, London **222** Rhoda Sidney/Stock, Boston **224** © Pete Seaward/Stone **226** *Collage* (detail), 1992, Juan Sanchez, Courtesy of Juan Sanchez and Guarighen, Inc., NYC **228** Prentice Hall **229, 230** Lou Jones/The Image Bank **231** Atheneum Books, photo by Didi Cutler **232** (t.) David Young-Wolff/PhotoEdit **232** (b.) Digital Imagery ©Copyright 2001 PhotoDisc, Inc. **234** Virginia Hamilton **238** (l., r.) AP/Wide World Photos **244** The Granger Collection, New York **246** UPI/CORBIS-Bettmann **247** CORBIS-Bettmann **248** The Granger Collection, New York **249** Courtesy of Thomas Benét **250** (b.) New York Public Library **250** (t.) Jon Sanford/Photo Network/PictureQuest **255** ©The Stock Market/Kennan Ward **258** Bill Bachmann/Stock, Boston Inc. /PictureQuest **264–265** *Emigrants Crossing the Plains, 1867*, Albert Bierstadt, oil on canvas, 60 x 96 in., A.011.1T, National Cowboy Hall of Fame, Oklahoma City **266** (l.) National Baseball Library and Archive, Cooperstown, N.Y. **266** (t.) David Stover, Stock South/PictureQuest **266** (b.) National Baseball Library and Archive, Cooperstown, N.Y. **268** Renee Lynn/Photo Researchers, Inc. **270** Corel Professional Photos CD-ROM™ **272** *That's My Dog* (German Shepherd), Jim Killen, Voyageur Art **276** Brian Yarvin/Photo Researchers, Inc. **282** Renee Lynn/Photo Researchers, Inc. **283** CORBIS-Bettmann **284** The Granger Collection, New York **288** *One*, 1986, April Gornik, Edward Thorp Gallery **290** Jeremy Walker/Tony Stone Images **291, 292** Corel Professional Photos CD-ROM™ **294** Prentice Hall **298** Corel Professional Photos CD-ROM™ **300** *Ezra Davenport*, 1929, Clarence Holbrook Carter, Oil on canvas, Courtesy of the artist **301** AP/Wide World Photos **302–303** David Stover, Stock South/PictureQuest **303** Courtesy of the Library of Congress **305** (t.) ©Jeffery A. Salter **305** (b.) Henry McGee/Globe Photos **306** (t.) Digital Imagery ©Copyright 2001 PhotoDisc, Inc. **306** (b.) *Self-Portrait* (detail), 1958, E. E. Cummings, The National Portrait Gallery, Smithsonian Institution, Washington, D.C./Art Resource, New York; **310** Cover illustration ©1999 by Ernie Norcia. Cover design by Vikki Sheatsley **312, 313** AP/Wide World Photos **314** UPI/CORBIS-Bettmann **316** Courtesy of the Illinois State Historical Library **320** Lincoln Boyhood National Memorial, Photo by John Lei/Omni-Photo Communications, Inc. **324** Russell Freedman, Photograph by Charles Osgood, Copyrighted 5/23/88, Chicago Tribune Company, All rights reserved, Used with permission **325, 326** UPI/CORBIS-Bettmann **328** (t.) Villard Books, photo © John Isaac **328** (b.) Florentine Films. Photo by Pam Tubridy Baucom **333, 337** AP/Wide World Photos **340** Myrleen/PhotoEdit **346–347** *This, That, There*, 1993, Pat Adams, Courtesy of the Eleanor Munro Collection/Zabriskie Gallery **348** (b.) Corel Professional Photos CD-ROM™ **348** (t.) Frans Lanting/Photo Researchers, Inc. **350** David Crosier/Tony Stone Images **352** ©1997, Michael Simpson/FPG International Corp. **354** Benelux Press/H. Armstrong Roberts **356** Thomas Victor **360** Jacket Art ©2000 by Joe Cepeda. Jacket Design by Marijka Kostiw **362** Laurie Platt Winfrey, Inc. **363** Scholastic Art and Writing Awards **364** Maurice Huser/Tony Stone Images **366** Digital Imagery ©Copyright 2001 PhotoDisc, Inc. **367** CORBIS-Bettmann **368** Digital Imagery ©Copyright 2001 PhotoDisc, Inc. **369** Nationwide News Service **378, 380–381** Corel Professional Photos CD-ROM™ **382** (l.) Courtesy of the Library of Congress **382** (r.) Courtesy of Ken Marschall **383** (l.) Photo by Brown Bros./Ken Marschall **383** (r.) Courtesy Madison Press, Illustrated by Pronk and Associates **384** Courtesy Madison Press, Illustrated by Pronk and Associates **386** Woods Hole Oceanographic Institution **390** *The Kintai Bridge in Springtime* (detail), Kawase Hasui, Private Collection/Bridgeman Art Library, London/New York **392** *The Immortal*, 1990, Chi-Fong Lei, Courtesy of the artist; **394–395, 396** Corel Professional Photos CD-ROM™ **399** *The Eight Immortals Crossing the Sea*, illustration from "Myths and Legends of China" by Edward T.C. Werner, pub. by George G. Harrap & Co., 1922, Private Collection/Bridgeman Art Library, London/New York **400** Permission granted by Troll Communications, LLC

404 ©Popperfoto/Archive Photos **406** (b.) ©Susan Greenspan/Archive Photos **406** (t.), **409** ©Popperfoto/Archive Photos **410** Photo by Darr Bass **411** Frans Lanting/Photo Researchers, Inc. **412** M & E Bernheim/Woodfin Camp & Associates **414** AP/Wide World Photos **419** Peter H. Buckley/Pearson Education/PH College **420** Ministère de la Culture et des Communications, Paris, France **422** J. Nouvok/PhotoEdit **428–429** *The Storyteller*, Adolphe Tidemand, Christie's, London/SuperStock **430** (t.) Hulton Getty/Tony Stone Images **430** (b.) Tom and Pat Leeson/Photo Researchers, Inc. **432** ©Stone **434** Courtesy of J. Alimena **436** Reprinted with the permission of Atheneum Books for Young Readers, an imprint of Simon & Schuster Children's Publishing Division, from THE BOY'S KING ARTHUR by Sidney Lanier, illustrated by N.C. Wyeth. Copyright © 1917 Charles Scribner's Sons; copyrights renewed 1945 N.C. Wyeth and 1952 John Lanier, David Lanier and Sterling Lanier. **439** *Dick Whittington on his way to London* from "My Nursery Story Book", published by Blackie and Son (book illustration) by Frank Adams, Private Collection/ The Bridgeman Art Library, London **442** ©1979 R.E. Potter III **446** *Biking for Fun*, 1992, Carlton Murrell, Courtesy of the artist, photo by John Lei/Omni-Photo Communications, Inc.; **448** *Daddy's Girl*, 1992, Carlton Murrell, Courtesy of the artist, photo by John Lei/Omni-Photo Communications, Inc.; **451** *Mother, I Love to Ride*, 1992, Carlton Murrell, Courtesy of the artist, photo by John Lei/Omni-Photo Communications, Inc.; **454** Camera Press/Globe Photos **458** ©Elizabeth Simpson/FPG International Corp. **460** Corel Professional Photos CD-ROM™ **460** (inset) *Old Man's Head, Study*, 1955, Yuri Alexeevich Dryakhlov, Courtesy of Overland Gallery of Fine Art, Scottsdale, AZ **464** CORBIS-Bettmann **465** *Orange Sweater*, 1955, Elmer Bischoff, San Francisco Museum of Modern Art, Gift of Mr. and Mrs. Mark Schorer **466** *Portrait, From the Estate of Eloy Blanco*, Collection of El Museo del Barrio, New York, NY **468** AP/Wide World Photos **473** Jacket illustration copyright ©1991 by Elsie Lennox **474** CORBIS **476** UPI/CORBIS-Bettmann **478** Hulton Getty/Tony Stone Images **480** UPI/CORBIS-Bettmann **481** CORBIS-Bettmann **482** ©Stephen J. Krasemann/Peter Arnold, Inc. **484** Tom and Pat Leeson/Photo Researchers, Inc. **486** Prentice Hall **491** Ron Levy/Liaison Agency **494** © Stone **497** Corel Professional Photos CD-ROM™ **498, 500** Digital Imagery ©Copyright 2001 PhotoDisc, Inc. **503** David Young-Wolff/Tony Stone Images **504** Courtesy of the author. Photo by Don Perkins. **505** *Walk in the Country*, Javran, Superstock; **509** *Harvesting the Fruit Crop*, Javran, Superstock **511** Digital Imagery ©Copyright 2001 PhotoDisc, Inc. **512** Alexander Limont **517** ©Stone **520** David Young-Wolff/PhotoEdit **526–527** *Desk Set*, 1972, Wayne Thiebaud, Courtesy of the artist, Collection of The Southland Corporation **528** (t.) Culver Pictures, Inc. **528** (b.) Ebbets Field Flannels **528** (m.) Bettmann/CORBIS **530, 532–533, 535** National Baseball Library and Archive, Cooperstown, N.Y. **536** Scholastic, Inc **540** Steven E. Sutton/Duomo Photography, Inc. **542** Culver Pictures, Inc. **544** *F. Scott Fitzgerald*, David Silvette, The National Portrait Gallery, Smithsonian Institution, Washington, DC/Art Resource, New York; **545** Steven E. Sutton/Duomo Photography, Inc. **546** Jan Butchofsky-Houser/CORBIS **548** William Sallaz/Duomo Photography, Inc. **552** *El Auto Cinema*, 1985, Roberto Gil de Montes, Oil on wood, Courtesy of Jan Baum Gallery, Collection of Patricia Storace; **554, 556, 557** The Mark Twain House, Hartford, CT **558** Bettmann/CORBIS **561** Dianne Trejo **562** AP/Wide World Photos **570** *Paradise #1*, Suzanne Duranceau, Illustratrice **573** Jerry Jacka Photography **574, 575** Prentice Hall **579** Digital Imagery ©Copyright 2001 PhotoDisc, Inc. **580–581** Leonard Le Rue III/Tony Stone Images **583** Animals Animals **584** Spencer **588** Richard Cummins/CORBIS **597** Animals Animals/ ©James Watt **600** Esbin/Anderson/Omni-Photo Communications, Inc. **601** U.S. Department of the Interior, U.S. Geological Survey **608–609** *Theatre Scene*, Edgar Degas/Private Collection/Bridgeman Art Library, London/New York **610** Grace Davies/Omni-Photo Communications, Inc. **612** Illustration by Norton Juster **616** ©Robert Holmes/CORBIS **646** Digital Imagery ©Copyright 2001 PhotoDisc, Inc. **660** Photo, John Martin **664** Jon Ortner/Tony Stone Images **666** Grace Davies/Omni-Photo Communications, Inc. **670** Courtesy of the Library of Congress **674** Musée Bartholdi, Colmar, France **678** Ron Watts/Black Star **680** Garcia/Stills/ Retna, LTD **684** Penguin **685** Prentice Hall **687** David Ryan/Photo 20-20/PictureQuest **691** Wolfgang Kaehler/CORBIS **700–701** *Waves of Matsushima*, Edo period, early 18th century, six-panel folding screen, Korin Ogata, Courtesy, Museum of Fine Arts, Boston, Fenollosa-Weld Collection **702** (b.) Dave G. Houser/CORBIS **702** (m.) © Mike & Elvan Habicht/Animals Animals **702** (t.) Illustration from *Alice Through the Looking Glass* by Lewis Carroll, John Tenniel, Photography by John Lei/Omni-Photo Communications, Inc. **704, 706** (t.) Corel Professional Photos CD-ROM™ **706** (b.) Don Lewis Photography **707** AP/Wide World Photos **708, 709, 710, 711** Illustration from *Alice Through the Looking Glass* by Lewis Carroll, John Tenniel, Photography by John Lei/Omni-Photo Communications, Inc. **712** New York Public Library Picture Collection **716, 718** © Mike & Elvan Habicht/Animals Animals **719** Photo by Isidro Rodriguez **720** The Granger Collection, New York **724** Vicki Silbert/PhotoEdit **726–727** ©Richard Hamilton Smith/CORBIS **726** (b.) AP/Wide World Photos **727** (b.) CORBIS-Bettmann **728** (b.) William Shakespeare (detail), Artist unknown, by courtesy of the National Portrait Gallery, London **728–729** © Ron Dahlquist/Stone **729** (b.) CORBIS-Bettmann **730** (t.) Corel Professional Photos CD-ROM™ **730** (b.) Courtesy of Simon & Schuster, Children's Publishing Division **735** Bettmann/CORBIS **738** Debra P. Hershkowitz/Bruce Coleman, Inc. **740–741** ©Richard Hamilton Smith/CORBIS **740** (b.) Photo by Bachrach **741** (b.) The Granger Collection, New York **742** (b.) New York Public Library **742** (t.) Steve Satushek/The Image Bank **746** Digital Imagery ©Copyright 2001 PhotoDisc, Inc. **747** Courtesy of Dana Gluckstein **749** ©Carl Purcell/Photo Researchers, Inc. **760** (t.l.) ©John Gerlach/Animals Animals **760** (t.r.) Myrleen Ferguson/PhotoEdit **760** (b.) Courtesy of the Library of Congress **762** *Coyote at Sunset*: detail from hand-painted wood bird house, Maureen Mahoney-Barraclough **764** L. N. Tolstoi, I. E. Repin, Sovfoto/Eastfoto; **765, 766** Corel Professional Photos CD-ROM™ **767** ©John Gerlach/Animals Animals **769** Prentice Hall **770** *Coyotes*: detail from hand-painted wood desk, Maureen Mahoney Barraclough **772** *Mouse and Owl*: detail from hand-painted wood desk, Maureen Mahoney Barraclough **778** Nigel Dennis/Photo Researchers, Inc. **780** Wolfgang Kaehler/Liaison Agency **781** JC Carton/Bruce Coleman, Inc./PictureQuest **782** Philip van den Berg/HPH Photography **783** Scholastic Art and Writing Awards **784** *Arachne* (detail), Arvis Stewart, Reprinted with the permission of Macmillan Publishing Company from *The Macmillan Book of Greek Gods and Heroes* by Alice Low, illustrated by Arvis Stewart, Copyright © 1985 by Macmillan Publishing Company; **787** Myrleen Ferguson/PhotoEdit **788** (b.) Courtesy, Houghton Mifflin Company **788** (t.) Digital Imagery ©Copyright 2001 PhotoDisc, Inc. **791** Michael Freeman/CORBIS **796** Courtesy of the Library of Congress **799, 800** ©Bettmann/CORBIS **804** Corel Professional Photos CD-ROM™ **806** David Young-Wolff/PhotoEdit **812** Brand X Pictures/Media Bakery

Staff Credits

The people who made up the ***Prentice Hall Literature: Timeless Voices, Timeless Themes*** team—representing design services, editorial, editorial services, market research, marketing services, media resources, online services & multimedia development, production services, project office, and publishing processes—are listed below. Bold type denotes the core team members.

Susan Andariese, Rosalyn Arcilla, Laura Jane Bird, Betsy Bostwick, **Anne M. Bray,** Evonne Burgess, **Louise B. Capuano, Pam Cardiff,** Megan Chill, Ed Cordero, Laura Dershewitz, Philip Fried, **Elaine Goldman,** Barbara Goodchild, Barbara Grant, **Rebecca Z. Graziano, Doreen Graizzaro,** Dennis Higbee, **Leanne Korszoloski,** Ellen Lees, David Liston, **Mary Luthi, George Lychock,** Gregory Lynch, Sue Lyons, **William McAllister,** Frances Medico, Gail Meyer, Jessica S. Paladini, Wendy Perri, Carolyn Carty Sapontzis, **Melissa Shustyk, Annette Simmons, Alicia Solis,** Robin Sullivan, Cynthia Sosland Summers, Lois Teesdale, **Elizabeth Torjussen, Doug Utigard,** Bernadette Walsh, Helen Young

The following persons provided invaluable assistance and support during the production of this program.

Gregory Abrom, Robert Aleman, Diane Alimena, Michele Angelucci, Gabriella Apolito, Penny Baker, Sharyn Banks, Anthony Barone, Barbara Blecher, Helen Byers, Rui Camarinha, Lorelee J. Campbell, John Carle, Cynthia Clampitt, Jaime L. Cohen, Martha Conway, Dina Curro, Nancy Dredge, Johanna Ehrmann, Josie K. Fixler, Steve Frankel, Kathy Gavilanes, Allen Gold, Michael E. Goodman, Diana Hahn, Kerry L. Harrigan, Jacki Hasko, Evan Holstrom, Beth Hyslip, Helen Issackedes, Cathy Johnson, Susan Karpin, Raegan Keida, Stephanie Kota, Mary Sue Langan, Elizabeth Letizia, Christine Mann, Vickie Menanteaux, Kathleen Mercandetti, Art Mkrtchyan, Karyl Murray, Kenneth Myett, Stefano Nese, Kim Ortell, Lissette Quiñones, Erin Rehill-Seker, Patricia Rodriguez, Mildred Schulte, Adam Sherman, Mary Siener, Jan K. Singh, Diane Smith, Barbara Stufflebeem, Louis Suffredini, Lois Tatarian, Tom Thompkins, Lisa Valente, Ryan Vaarsi, Linda Westerhoff, Jeff Zoda

Prentice Hall gratefully acknowledges the following teachers who provided student models for consideration in the program.

Barbara Abel, Dawn Akuna, Kathy Allen, Joan Anderson, Amy Bales, Lisa Cobb, Ann Collier-Buchanan, Janice Crews, Denise Donahue, Becky Dressler, Nicci Durban, Nancy Fahner, Margo Graf, Jan Graham, Carleen Hemric, Karen Hurley, Max Hutto, Lenore Hynes, Kim Johnson, Gail Kidd, Ashley MacDonald, Maureen Macdonald, Akiko Morimoto, Judy Plouff, Charlene Revels, Lynn Richter, Kathleen Riley, Sandy Shannon, Marilyn Shaw, Cheryl Spivak, Lynn Striepe, John Tierney, Vanna Turner, Pam Walden, Holly Ward, Jennifer Watson, Joan West, Virginia Wong